# MARKETING
# COMMUNICATIONS

SIXTH EDITION

# MARKETING COMMUNICATIONS

Brands, experiences and participation

## CHRIS FILL

**PEARSON**

Harlow, England • London • New York • Boston • San Francisco • Toronto • Sydney • Auckland • Singapore • Hong Kong
Tokyo • Seoul • Taipei • New Delhi • Cape Town • São Paulo • Mexico City • Madrid • Amsterdam • Munich • Paris • Milan

**PEARSON EDUCATION LIMITED**
Edinburgh Gate
Harlow CM20 2JE
United Kingdom
Tel: +44 (0)1279 623623
Web: www.pearson.com/uk

First published under the Prentice Hall Europe imprint 1995 (print)
Fourth edition 2005 (print)
Fifth edition 2009 (print)
**Sixth edition published 2013 (print and electronic)**

ISBN: 978-0-273-77054-1 (print)
      978-0-273-77067-1 (PDF)
      978-0-273-78110-3 (eText)

**British Library Cataloguing-in-Publication Data**
A catalogue record for the print edition is available from the British Library

**Library of Congress Cataloging-in-Publication Data**
A catalog record for the print edition is available from the Library of Congress

10 9 8 7 6 5 4 3 2
17 16 15 14 13

Print edition typeset in 10/12pt Minion by 35
Print edition printed and bound by L.E.G.O. S.p.A., Italy

For Karen, Johnny, Mike and B

# Brief contents

# Contents

## Companion Website

For open-access **student resources** specifically written to complement this textbook and support your learning, please visit **www.pearsoned.co.uk/fill**

## Lecturer Resources

For password-protected online resources tailored to support the use of this textbook in teaching, please visit **www.pearsoned.co.uk/fill**

# Guided tour

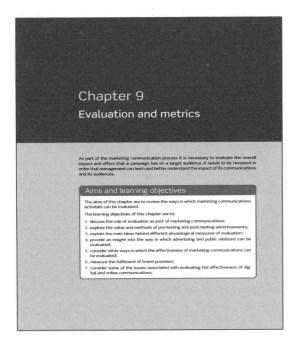

## Chapter 9
### Evaluation and metrics

As part of the marketing communication process it is necessary to evaluate the overall impact and effect that a campaign has on a target audience. It needs to be reviewed in order that management can learn and better understand the impact of its communications and its audiences.

#### Aims and learning objectives

The aims of this chapter are to review the ways in which marketing communications activities can be evaluated.

The learning objectives of this chapter are to:

1. discuss the role of evaluation as part of marketing communications;
2. explore the value and methods of pre-testing and post-testing advertisements;
3. explain the main ideas behind different physiological measures of evaluation;
4. provide an insight into the way in which advertising and public relations can be evaluated;
5. consider other ways in which the effectiveness of marketing communications can be evaluated;
6. measure the fulfilment of brand promises;
7. consider some of the issues associated with evaluating the effectiveness of digital and online communications.

**Aims and learning objectives** at the beginning of each chapter enable you to focus on what you should get out of each section of the book.

Each chapter opens with a **Minicase** that provides a real-world situation to which that chapter's topic applies.

---

Each of these dimensions is regarded as separate yet integral elements of IMC. Lee and Park developed an 18-item scale, derived from the literature, to measure these dimensions. The use of this approach may advance our understanding of IMC and provide a substantial basis on which IMC activities can be measured. It is interesting to note that Lee and Park see IMC as a customer-only communication activity and choose to exclude other critical stakeholders from their measurement model.

#### Scholars' paper 9.1    Measuring up for IMC

Ewing, M.T. (2009) Integrated marketing communications measurement and evaluation, *Journal of Marketing Communications*, 15(2–3), April–July, 103–117.

This paper marks out the difficulties and challenges involved in measuring integrated marketing communications. Working from the base that it is consumers that determine when marketing communications is integrated, Ewing identifies and considers five areas of integrated marketing communications (IMC) measurement worthy of future research.

#### Advertising

There are numerous ways in which advertising effectiveness can be measured. Chang et al. (2010: 63) refer to 'awareness (Hansen, Olsen, and Lundsteen, 2006), brand choice (Cobb-Walgren, Ruble, and Donthu 1995), purchase likelihood (Aaker, Stayman and Hagerty 1986), viewing time (Olney, Holbrook, and Batra 1991), brand perceptions (MacKenzie and Lutz 1989), purchase intentions (Bellman, Schweda, and Varan 2009), memory-based tests (Brennan, Dubas, and Babin 1999) and so on'.

The techniques used to evaluate advertising are by far the most documented and, in view of the relative sizes of the communication tools, it is not surprising that slightly more time is devoted to this tool. This is not to disregard or disrespect the contribution each of the communication tools can make to an integrated campaign. Indeed, it is the collective measure of success against the goals set at the outset that is the overriding imperative for measurement, as will be seen later.

#### Pre-testing

Advertisements can be researched prior to their release (pre-test) or after they have been released (post-test). Pre-tests, sometimes referred to as *copy tests*, have traditionally attracted more attention, stimulated a greater variety of methods and generated much controversy, in comparison with post-tests.

The effectiveness of *pre-testing*, the practice of showing unfinished commercials to selected groups of the target audience with a view to refining the commercial to improve effectiveness, is still subject to debate. Reid (2000) argues that pre-testing can be used positively to support campaign development, predictively to gauge likely audience response and generally to improve advertising performance.

The methods used to pre-test advertisements are based upon either qualitative or quantitative criteria. The most common methods used to pre-test advertisements are concept testing, focus groups, consumer juries, dummy vehicles, readability, theatre and physiological tests. Focus groups are the main qualitative method used and theatre or hall tests the main quantitative test. Each of these methods will be discussed later.

The primary purpose of testing advertisements during the developmental process is to ensure that the final creative work will meet the advertising objectives. It is better to help

---

## Minicase
### Still killing Jill?

The UK Transplant (UKT) Organ Donor Register is a central database of people who have opted to offer their organs for transplantation in the event of their death. As in many countries, it is entirely voluntary. Around 8,000 people in the UK, and 700 in Scotland, are in need of a transplant; their lives depend upon it. Without donors, it won't happen.

Unfortunately, to become a donor, you have to die, and it is this touch with their own mortality which may explain why people have a mental block when it comes to signing up. Research tells us that although 91 per cent of people claim to be 'in favour' of organ donation, only c.23 per cent actually sign up. Despite all their good intentions, something stops people from putting their name on the list. People do not like thinking about the organ donation issue.

The demand for transplants far exceeds the available organs. This is because not enough people are on the Organ Donor Register. When people die, either naturally or in accidents, many of their organs are suitable for transplants and could save lives. Transplant

Co-ordinators have the sensitive task of talking to next of kin to see if they will agree to the use of the deceased's organs. For understandable reasons, over 40 per cent of people refuse permission, which is required by law. This is primarily because they don't know their loved one's wishes. However, Transplant Co-ordinators and medical staff know anecdotally that in c.90 per cent of cases where the deceased has registered, permission is given willingly.

The cost to the NHS of a single person on kidney dialysis for a year is c.£35,023 and around 500 people in Scotland start kidney dialysis each year. The cost of a shortage of organs is not just the suffering of 8,000 people, but the large financial cost to the state, running into £ millions.

In 2005/2006 the Scottish Government ran a series of very successful campaigns to increase the number of people registering on the UKT Register. The campaign came to life most effectively in the 'Kill Jill' execution and was communicated across a wide range of media, primarily field marketing, PR and print/outdoor.

| Exhibit 9.1 | 'Kill Jill' as a 96-sheet outdoor poster |
|---|---|

Source: The Scottish Government

**Scholars' papers** point you towards academic articles that will deepen your knowledge of each subject.

Snappy **Viewpoint** boxes offer different perspectives to help improve your understanding.

| Table 9.2 | Projective techniques |
|---|---|

| Projective technique | Explanation |
|---|---|
| Association | Free word association tests require respondents to respond with the first word that comes to mind in response to a stimulus word. Often used when naming brands. |
| Completion | Spontaneous sentence or story-telling completion are the most used methods. Responses can be graded as approval, neutral or disapproval, enabling attitudes towards brands to be determined. |
| Transformation | These are also known as 'expressible' techniques and involve techniques such as psychodrawing. This requires respondents to express graphically their inner feelings about a brand or event (e.g. a shopping trip, holiday or purchase process). |
| Construction | This approach can involve role playing where respondents are asked to act out their feelings towards a purchase, a brand, event or organisation. |

Source: Based on Robson (2002).

### Projective techniques

Projective techniques are used to probe the subconscious and have close associations with Freudian thinking and the motivation school advocated by Dichter (1966). Individuals or groups can be encouraged through projective techniques to express their inner thoughts and feelings about brands, products, services and organisations, among others. Four main projective techniques can be identified (see Table 9.2).

Projective techniques have been used by many leading brands to understand how their brands are perceived, to test advertising and creative ideas and to segment their markets. For example, Guinness used projective techniques to understand how to position their brand and how advertising should be used to develop the ideal position.

| Viewpoint 9.1 | Projective engagement with Sony Bravia |
|---|---|

Projective testing techniques were used to measure the positioning success and the impact of the Sony Bravia 'Paint' ads. Sony wanted to use a creative that symbolised the technical colour development represented by the Bravia television.

Based on exploding colours around a council housing estate, Paint represented a radically different and unexpected creative, if only because there was no voice-over, no mention of attributes, features or benefits, in either copy or voice, and there were no visuals depicting the product or people consuming (watching) the television.

Paint was designed to communicate the point that the Bravia and SXRD range provide the 'colour that you'll see on these screens will be like no other' (www.Sony.com).

Part of the testing undertaken by TNS, using their AdEval™ methodology, included the use of people photosets. These are pictures of groups of personality types, used and validated internationally. Respondents were shown various different ads and asked which group of people they thought each would appeal to most. Many people have reported finding the Paint ads confusing and difficult to relate to. However, all the respondents were able to assign a personality type and the majority categorised the ads to people who were carefree, lively and bold. In terms of brand images the respondents reported vibrant colour, lively, outgoing, dynamic and cool/trendy as the key attributes (see Figure 9.1).

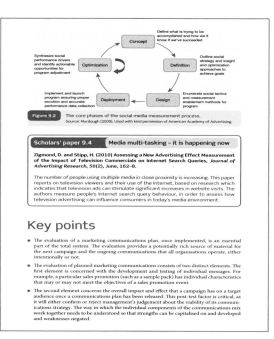

| Figure 9.2 | The core phases of the social media measurement process. |
|---|---|

Source: Murdough (2009). Used with kind permission of American Academy of Advertising.

| Scholars' paper 9.4 | Media multi-tasking – it is happening now |
|---|---|

**Zigmond, D. and Stipp, H. (2010) Assessing a New Advertising Effect Measurement of the Impact of Television Commercials on Internet Search Queries,** *Journal of Advertising Research,* **50(2), June, 162–8.**

The number of people using multiple media in close proximity is increasing. This paper reports on television viewers and their use of the Internet, based on research which indicates that television ads can stimulate significant increases in website visits. The authors measure people's Internet search query behaviour, in order to assess how television advertising can influence consumers in today's media environment.

## Key points

- The evaluation of a marketing communications plan, once implemented, is an essential part of the total system. The evaluation provides a potentially rich source of material for the next campaign and the ongoing communications that all organisations operate, either intentionally or not.
- The evaluation of planned marketing communications consists of two distinct elements. The first element is concerned with the development and testing of individual messages. For example, a particular sales promotion (such as a sample pack) has individual characteristics that may or may not meet the objectives of a sales promotion event.
- The second element concerns the overall impact and effect that a campaign has on a target audience once a communications plan has been released. This post-test factor is critical, as it will either confirm or reject management's judgement about the viability of its communications strategy. The way in which the individual components of the communications mix work together needs to be understood so that strengths can be capitalised on and developed and weaknesses negated.

The **Key points** are clearly summarised at the end of each chapter so you can check you understand everything you need to know.

- It is not helpful to just rely on measuring the numbers of clicks, dwell time, fans and followers, and to use these as surrogate measures of social media activity. What is more relevant is measuring what these fans and followers do, how they behave as a result of engaging in social media activities.
- Traditional measurement techniques of reach, frequency and target audience impressions are not easily applicable to online communications.

## Review questions

1. Why should the 'Still Killing Jill?' campaign, presented at the start of this chapter, have tried to measure attitude change to organ donation?
2. What are pre- and post-testing?
3. Write a brief report comparing recall and recognition tests.
4. What are the principal dimensions of likeability as a measure of advertising effectiveness?
5. Write brief notes explaining why media comparison techniques are inadequate measures of public relations.
6. Explain in note form the core characteristics of the Promise Index and the Net Promoter Score.
7. What are the techniques used to measure website effectiveness? Are they any good?
8. What is the core activity of online communications? Sketch out the social media measurement process.
9. Many organisations fail to undertake suitable research to measure the success of their campaigns. Why is this and what can be done to change this situation?
10. Comment on the view that, if a method of evaluation and testing lacks objectivity and measurability, then the method should not be used.

**Review questions** let you try out your knowledge and practice for tests by going over the material presented in the chapter.

**References** at the end of each chapter provide ideal information for students looking for further reading or sources for research papers.

## References

Aaker, D.A., Stayman, D.M. and Hagerty, M.R. (1986) Warmth in Advertising: Measurement, Impact, and Sequence Effects, *Journal of Consumer Research,* 12(4), 365–81.

Beeston, J. (2011) Special Report: Display, *Revolution,* September, p. 37.

Bellman, S., Schweda, A. and Varan, D. (2009) A Comparison of Three Interactive Television Ad Formats, *Journal of Interactive Advertising,* 10(1), 14–34.

Berthon, P., Pitt, L. and Watson, R. (1996) The world wide web as an advertising medium: toward an understanding of conversion efficiency, *Journal of Advertising Research,* 6(1) (January/February), 43–53.

Biel, A.L. (1993) Ad research in the US., *Admap* (May), 27–9.

Brennan, I., Dubas, K.M. and Babin, L.A. (1999) The Influence of Product-Placement Type and Exposure Time on Product-Placement Recognition, *International Journal of Advertising,* 18(3), 323–38.

Burden, S. (2007) Case study: pre-testing mould-breaking ads, *Admap,* July/August, 48–9.

Campbell, R.H. (1965) A Managerial Approach to Advertising Measurement, *Journal of Marketing,* 29(4), October, 1–6.

Chang, Y., Yan, J., Zhang, J. and Luo, J. (2010) Online in-game advertising effect: examining the influence of a match between games and advertising, *Journal of Interactive Advertising,* 11(1), (Fall), 63–73.

Cobb-Walgren, C.J., Ruble, C.A. and Donthu, N. (1995) Brand Equity, Brand Preference, and Purchase Intent, *Journal of Advertising,* 24(3), 25–40.

# Foreword

Chris Fill's exciting new edition of *Marketing Communications* reaffirms this as the UK's leading textbook in the subject. Restructured and updated, this book provides a balanced insight into the multi-faceted and fast-changing world of the industry.

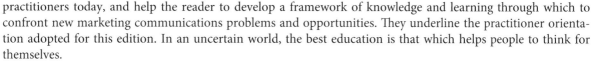

The comprehensive coverage is presented in four parts, providing readers with an expert blend of academic material and marketing communications practice. The straightforward, no-nonsense writing style makes the book accessible to those new to the subject, to those studying whose English is their second language, and to seasoned professionals.

As might be expected from a book by Chris, a range of relevant academic theories and concepts are considered. These are then brought to life through examples of marketing communications for brands from around the world, and challenging review questions. New to this edition is the highlighting of four seminal research papers in each chapter.

Each chapter opens with a real-world case study, many of which have been developed by the Institute of Practioners in Advertising agencies and their clients. These provide authentic insights into some of the problems and issues facing practitioners today, and help the reader to develop a framework of knowledge and learning through which to confront new marketing communications problems and opportunities. They underline the practitioner orientation adopted for this edition. In an uncertain world, the best education is that which helps people to think for themselves.

I like the way in which readers are encouraged to consider not just one interpretation of a topic, concept or issue, but several. I have not seen this before in a textbook but this approach, which is adopted within four important chapters, is both refreshing and great for teaching. It helps avoid dogma and enables the many and varied views of researchers and practitioners in marketing communications to be embraced and discussed.

This new edition builds on the strengths of the previous one. It is accessible yet authoritative; enjoyable and interesting; informative and revealing. It is the only marketing communications textbook that the IPA endorses, and we do so enthusiastically.

*Janet Hull*

Janet Hull
Director of Marketing and Reputation Management, IPA

IPA

# Preface

This is the sixth edition of my book *Marketing Communications*. I have made many changes to this edition, which I believe improve the text significantly. These changes are explained here in the Preface but you will be the judge of the impact of these amendments. So, thank you for reading my book and if you have any comments, observations, suggestions or opinions, please feel free to contact me through chris@fillassociates.co.uk.

This text has been written to help you in three ways:

1. To understand and appreciate the variety of ways in which organisations use marketing communications.
2. To identify and understand some of the key theories and concepts associated with marketing communications.
3. To develop insights into the reasoning behind the marketing communications activities used by organisations.

Marketing communications is a complex subject and draws on a variety of disciplines. This book has been written in the hope of disentangling some of the complexity so that you can enjoy the subject, be stimulated to want to know more and wish to engage further with the exciting and fast-changing world of marketing communications.

# A world of marketing communications

All organisations, large and small, commercial, government, charities, educational and other not-for-profit and third sector organisations need to communicate with a range of stakeholders. This may be in order to get materials and services and so undertake their business activities, or to collaborate and coordinate with others to secure suitable distribution of their goods and services. In addition, there are consumers, you and me, people who are free to choose among the many hundreds and thousands of product offerings. Marketing communications provides a core activity so that all interested parties can understand the intentions of others and appreciate the value of the goods and services offered.

The world of marketing communications is changing, and some of it is changing at an incredible speed. Technology, buyer behaviour, economic cycles, industry and organisational performance have all evolved and all impact on the way we communicate, when we communicate and how we communicate.

Many of these changes and their impact are explored in this text. It is not possible to cover them all in depth but the key academic and practitioner reactions to these developments are examined.

Following research, several goals were established for this edition. One of the primary goals was to include a stronger practitioner focus, to give more examples of the way marketing communications is used by organisations. A second goal was to continue the academic orientation and the use of conceptual underpinnings in order to understand how organisations use marketing communications and so demonstrate the application of theory in practice. A third goal was to present different perspectives and approaches, rather than present the conventional wisdom or a single approach as if it was used by everyone. The fourth goal might be regarded as a contradiction in view of the other three goals, but there was a need to reduce the overall physical size of the book.

I believe these goals have been achieved, but you are the judge of these matters. I sincerely hope you enjoy reading this book and gain a different insight into the evolving use of marketing communications.

# Overview of the book

The cover image is that of the New Zealand 'designer ice cream' brand, Kapiti. Apart from being an intriguing image, it draws on, or conjures links with, many aspects of marketing communications. These include awareness, engagement and perception; the image refers to branding and associations; it relates to advertising, symbolism, and of course suggests positioning, integration and strategy. This text, just as the Kapiti symbol, reflects the complexity of marketing communications. It considers the strategic, tactical and operational aspects, and attempts to consider the subject from an integrative perspective. Above all else, this text considers marketing communications from a contextual standpoint. This means that no one single theory is used to explain all marketing communications activities. Indeed, several theories are presented and readers are encouraged to consider multiple interpretations of marketing communications behaviour.

This text has been written from an academic perspective and seeks to provide a consistent appraisal of the ever-changing world of marketing communications. The intention is to stimulate thought, a ripple of consideration about a wide range of interrelated issues, and to help achieve this aim a number of theories and models are advanced. Some of these theories reflect marketing practice, while others are offered as suggestions for moving the subject forward. Many of the theories are abstractions of actual practice, some are based on empirical research and others are pure conceptualisation. All seek to enrich the subject, but not all need carry the same weight of contribution. Readers should form their own opinions based upon their reading, experience and judgement. Just as the shoe blends into an ice cream melt, so brand communication needs to convey clear positioning and values.

Now let's consider how the goals for this edition, mentioned earlier, have been met.

## Goal 1: To include a stronger practitioner focus, to give more examples of the way marketing communications is used by organisations

In past editions many of my academic colleagues have kindly given their time and energies to write case studies. These have been invaluable in helping readers learn about marketing communications. In this edition I have moved away from this approach and have included case studies based around marketing communication campaigns or brand communications. These are located at the front end of each chapter and serve to introduce a topic and enable readers to get a feel for the material that is to follow. At the end of each chapter the Review Questions challenge readers to reflect on the material and to use it to consider the minicase.

Several of these cases have been written and supplied by several communication agencies, many of whom are associated with the Institute of Practitioners in Advertising (IPA). Indeed, the IPA has provided important support for this edition, as noted through their Foreword and jacket comments.

## Goal 2: To use academic materials in order that readers can interpret how marketing communications is used

This is not a new goal as this book has always been founded on the use of academic materials to interpret the use of marketing communications. However, it is important to recognise this principle and to continue its use so that readers can interpret how and why organisations use marketing communications in so many different ways.

New to this edition is the inclusion of Scholars' Papers. In each chapter a brief summary of four different papers is highlighted. These papers have been selected on the basis of their prominence, their relevance, and the contribution they have made to the subject. Some are old, some new. In addition, several new theories and ideas have been included to enrich many of the chapters.

## Goal 3: Wherever possible, present alternative theories, perspectives and methods as potential explanations for the ways organisations use marketing communications

This text has always incorporated a variety of theories and conceptual ideas. However, when considering topics such as strategy and integration, it is clear that both academics and practitioners have different views and approaches, with the result that there is no one clearly defined and agreed perspective. This can make it challenging, even confusing, for readers new to the subject, especially if only one view is presented.

In this edition I present a number of different interpretations and approaches to explain how a subject or topic might work. For example, there are four interpretations about how marketing communications works, five exploring marketing communications strategy, and another five ideas about integrated marketing communications. This approach should clarify issues, strip out some confusion and promote thought and discussion. All of this is in addition to the different theories and models concerning the way advertising works, how brands can be positioned, and different ideas about consumer behaviour and decision making.

## Goal 4: To reduce the overall physical size of the book and make it appear less intimidating

This has been achieved by reorganising the material and presenting it in 26 rather than 30 chapters. Two brand-new chapters on 'Creativity', and 'Audiences: how they process information and behave' have been written and there are new chapters on 'Social media and search marketing,' and 'Multichannel campaigns', plus many new topics such as licensing, tribal consumption, behavioural economics, and consumer-generated advertising. All chapters have been updated, with fresh academic and practitioner materials.

The reduction in the number of chapters, and the restructuring of the text into four rather than six parts, has served to focus on core materials. Some topics have been merged into new chapters, or in some limited cases, removed so that they can be accessed online at the companion website.

For readers familiar with previous edition, the chapters concerning:

- Ethics in marketing communications
- Marketing: relationships and communications
- Marketing communications across borders
- Business-to-business marketing communications, plus
- Stakeholders: supply chains and interorganisational relationships

from the fourth edition, have been moved online.

Wherever appropriate, material from these chapters has been incorporated into chapters in the current edition. All of these are now available online at the companion website used for this text.

# Structure of the text

There are four main parts to the text:

**Part 1 Introduction to marketing communications.** This part introduces readers to the subject from a general perspective and then seeks to establish some of the key issues that are necessary in order to provide a foundation for the subject. These include communication theory, the ways in which audiences process information and make purchase decisions, and the final chapter in this part, ideas about how marketing communications might work.

**Part 2 Managing marketing communications.** This part explores some of the managerial aspects associated with marketing communications. The core content concerns the various aspects of *strategy* and how organisations should develop their marketing communications in the light of their contextual positions. This part then considers the role and nature of objectives and positioning, before exploring some of the issues associated with the communication industry, the financial implications associated with managing marketing communications, and the issues associated with the evaluation and measurement of marketing communications. The chapter concludes with the important topic of integrated marketing communications.

**Part 3 Branding.** The Branding part contains three chapters and serves to demonstrate the importance of marketing communications to the development of product/service, corporate and employee brands. It is located deliberately after the management part.

**Part 4 The marketing communications mix.** The marketing communications mix material constitutes by far the largest part of the book, covering half of the text's chapters. This content is of course crucial to all courses on marketing communications. Unlike other texts, the approach here emphasises the use of three components of the mix: namely, the tools, media and content. New to this edition is a chapter on 'Social media and search marketing' and another on 'Creativity'. There are six chapters on the tools, five on media and two on messages.

# Part 1: Introduction to marketing communications

This opening part serves to establish the scope of the text and provides a brief overview of the content and style adopted throughout the rest of the text. Chapter 1 provides an introductory perspective to marketing communications and sets out some important, key concepts, such as engagement, tasks and the marketing communication mix. It provides an insight into how the configuration of the marketing communication mix has effectively changed over the past 10 years. Chapter 2 addresses issues concerning communication theory and in particular moves on from the simple linear interpretation of how communication works to one that recognises the influence of people, behaviour and interactional elements on the communication process. Chapter 3 is concerned with aspects of buyer behaviour, upon which marketing communications should be developed. Only by understanding the market and the target audience can appropriate objectives, strategies, promotional methods, applications and resources be determined, allocated and implemented.

The final chapter in this part introduces ideas about how marketing communications might work. Rather than suggest a single approach, five separate approaches are presented. These are the sequential buying processes, attitude change, shaping relationships, significant value, and cognitive processing.

# Part 2: Managing marketing communications

Part 2 is concerned with a variety of managerial issues related to marketing communications. These embrace strategy, goals, industry, financial, measurement and integration issues. Chapter 5 is concerned with the nature of communication strategy and considers the interrelationship between strategy and planning. The first section of this chapter considers ideas about strategy and considers four distinct approaches to marketing communications strategy. The second section of the chapter introduces the marketing communications planning framework and works through the model, highlighting issues and linkages and ending with an operational approach to devising, formulating and implementing a strategic marketing communications plan.

Chapter 6 examines the nature of objectives and positioning in marketing communications and considers both academic and practitioner (IPA) approaches to the nature of communication-based objectives.

The nature and characteristics of the UK marketing communications industry are the focus of Chapter 7. This material can be useful as it specifically examines the strategic and operational issues of communication agencies and their interaction with client organisations.

Chapter 8 considers various budgeting approaches and issues concerning brand equity, and Chapter 9 examines the ways in which the performance of marketing communication activities can be evaluated. In effect these two chapters consider how much should be invested in the engagement process and how the engagement process should be measured.

The final chapter in this part is about integrated marketing communications. This chapter challenges ideas about the nature and validity of the 'integrated' view. Five separate interpretations about what integrated marketing communications might be are presented. This is a core chapter because it bridges the contextual elements and the application of the various disciplines. The notion that integrated marketing communications (IMC) is a valid and realistic concept is explored and readers are encouraged to consider the arguments for and against this approach. Its position at the end of the management part of the text is designed to encourage readers to reflect on what should be integrated and what integration might incorporate.

# Part 3: Branding

This part is new and is designed to focus attention not only on the nature and role of different types of brand, but also on the way communication can be used to develop brands. Chapter 11 is significant because it focuses on the role marketing communications can play in the development and maintenance of product/service brands. Chapter 12 develops the branding theme and considers corporate branding and reputational issues. The focus is again on the role of corporate communication in the identity and branding process rather than pure identity work alone. These elements are interrelated but it is intended to help readers recognise how communications can be a pivotal aspect of brand and corporate development.

The final chapter in this part considers the role of marketing communications within organisations where employees are the target audience. Increasingly recognised as a key part of a brand, the importance of engaging with employees and using them as a means of engaging with external audiences is actively considered.

# Part 4: The marketing communication mix

As mentioned earlier, this is the biggest part in the text, and looks at the various elements that constitute the marketing communication mix. There are 13 chapters in this section, configured as three sections. The first examines the tools or disciplines, the second the media and the third, message content.

Chapter 14 is about advertising and contains three elements. The first considers the role and use of advertising, and how ideas about selling propositions and emotion can be used in advertising. Prominence is also given to the different types or forms of advertising. Time is spent exploring the way advertising might work. Here consideration is given to some of the principal models and frameworks that have been published to best explain the process by which advertising might influence audiences. The third element concerns the way in which advertising can be used strategically as part of a brand's development, and to review the significance of consumer-generated advertising.

Chapter 15 examines the role and characteristics of public relations, including a review of the various methods used in public relations, and crisis communications. The following chapter leads on naturally to explore sponsorship, while Chapter 17 examines both direct marketing and personal selling.

Chapters 18 and 19 both consider a range of disciplines. The first considers the principles and techniques of sales promotion, field marketing and brand experiences. The second explores brand placement, exhibitions, packaging and the rapidly developing area of brand licensing.

This second section brings together various chapters about the media and includes a new chapter on social media and search marketing, and another on multichannel campaigns.

Chapter 20 considers traditional media, an important foundation upon which to consider the attributes of digital media, the subject of Chapter 21. This chapter commences with a consideration of the features of digitalisation and then explores the application and benefits that digital media offer marketing communications, including a section on website design from a marketing perspective.

Chapter 22 'Social, search and interactivity' is a new chapter and reflects the contemporary nature of these important and emerging topics. Chapter 23 is concerned with multichannel marketing and the ways in which digital media influence each of the communication tools online, and shape multichannel campaigns. The final media chapter considers ideas and theories associated with media planning and the way in which people use media.

The final section in this fourth part of the text, and the third element of the marketing communications mix is the content, or the messages conveyed to, with and between audiences. There are two chapters, with the first of these, 'Creativity', new to the book. This innovation, rarely found in other marketing and managerial texts, explores the nature, role, and processes organisations use to manage the creative process and the ways in which the creative process can be harnessed. Here message framing and storytelling are developed before concluding with a review of a more contemporary perspective of content generation and creativity – namely, user-generated content.

The final chapter examines message appeals through four broad elements. First, attention is given to the source of a message and issues relating to source credibility. Second, the role and issues associated with using spokespersons, to either be the face of a brand or to endorse it, is explored. Third, the need to balance the use of information and emotion in messages and the way messages are constructed is reviewed before finally exploring the various appeals and ways in which messages can be presented.

# Minicases

This edition includes 26 new minicases. These have been written by a variety of people, including client organisations, communication agencies, academics and independent authors.

| | |
|---|---|
| **Chapter 1** | **Introducing marketing communications** |
| Case | LV= • Miriam Boote of Designate and John O'Sullivan of 24-7 ideas |
| **Chapter 2** | **Communication: forms and conversations** |
| Case | MTV – Up Your Viva • Jon Howard of Quiet Storm |
| **Chapter 3** | **Audiences: how they process information and behave** |
| Case | Recruiting new teachers • Chris Fill |
| **Chapter 4** | **How marketing communications might work** |
| Case | Rolex • Chris Fill |
| **Chapter 5** | **Marketing communications: strategy and planning** |
| Case | Cravendale Milk Matters • Chris Fill |
| **Chapter 6** | **Marketing communications: objectives and positioning** |
| Case | Juan Valdez: the face of Columbian coffee • Chris Fill |
| **Chapter 7** | **The communication industry: structure, operations and issues** |
| Case | Diageo • Chris Fill |
| **Chapter 8** | **Financial resources for marketing communciations** |
| Case | Honda • Chris Fill |
| **Chapter 9** | **Evaluation and metrics** |
| Case | Organ donation • Mark Raine of the Scottish Government and Ian McAteer/Louise Campbell of The Union |

These cases either refer to broad issues concerning a particular topic, or focus on a specific issue that is included in the chapter to which the case is assigned. Some are written in the first person, others in the third person. Some refer to several campaigns undertaken for a specific brand or company, while others consider a specific campaign and associated activities. All provide an interesting introduction to the chapter's core issues and enable readers to contextualise their learning.

# Design features and presentation

In addition to the four-part structure of the text, there are a number of features that are intended to help readers navigate the material.

## Chapter objectives

Each chapter opens with both the aims of what is to be covered and a list of learning objectives. This helps to signal the primary topics that are covered in the chapter and so guide the learning experience.

## Minicases

Each chapter opens with a campaign-based minicase. These are drawn from a variety of sources, brands, sectors and countries, and are used either to introduce the broad flow of the chapter's material or to focus on a particular topic.

These short cases can be used in class for discussion purposes and to explore some of the salient issues raised in the chapter. Students working alone can use the minicases to test their own understanding.

## Visual supports

This book is produced in four colours and throughout the text there are numerous colour and black and white exhibits; figures (diagrams) and tables of information throughout the text serve to highlight, illustrate and bring life to the written word. The pictures used serve either to illustrate particular points by demonstrating theory in practice or they are used to complement individual examples. The examples are normally highlighted in the text as ViewPoints. These examples are easily distinguishable through the colour contrasts and serve to demonstrate how a particular aspect of marketing communications has been used by an organisation in a particular context. I hope you enjoy these ViewPoints of organisational practice.

## Scholars' papers

Each chapter includes bibliographic details and a short summary about four academic papers, each relevant to a topic within the orbit of the chapter as a whole. These papers may be old or new, seminal or contemporary but all provide insight into the relevant research or conceptual issues.

## Key points and Review questions

At the end of each chapter is a section headed 'Key points,' and another called 'Review questions'. The Key Points from the chapter are presented in order of appearance, and normally relate to the learning objectives listed at the beginning of each chapter.

Readers are advised to test their own understanding of the content of each chapter by considering some or all of the review questions. In this sense the questions support self-study but tutors might wish to use some of these as part of a seminar or workshop programme. The lead question always refers to the minicase at the start of each chapter.

## Web support

Students and lecturers who adopt this text have a range of support materials and facilities to help them. Readers are invited to use the website designed for *Marketing Communications* at www.pearsoned.co.uk/fill, not only as a source of additional material but also as an interactive forum to explore and discuss marketing communications issues, academic and practitioner developments and to improve learning. The site accommodates the needs of student readers and lecturers.

### Student resources

- Additional chapters
- Annotated web links
- Multiple-choice questions

### Lecturer resources

- Instructor's manual
- PowerPoint slides for each chapter

A test bank of multiple-choice questions has been developed for use by students and lecturers. In addition, there are links to a range of related sites and chapters from previous editions.

For lecturers and tutors, there is an Instructor's manual containing a range of teaching schemes and exercises in downloadable format, as well as PowerPoint slides that can be downloaded for use in lectures.

# Acknowledgements

This book could not have been written without the support of a wide range of brilliant people. Contributions range from those who provided information and permissions, those who wrote minicases, answered questions and those who tolerated my persistent nagging, sending through photographs, answering phone calls and emails and those who simply liaised with others. Finally, there are those who have read, reviewed drafts, made constructive comments and provided moral support and encouragement.

Many people have given their time and energies to either writing or to cajoling others to write a minicase. The fruits of their labours are on show here and may I express my gratitude for the time and energy you all gave to write your material.

The list of individuals and organisations involved with this book is extensive. My thanks are offered to all of you. I have tried to list everyone but if anyone has been omitted then I offer my apologies.

| | |
|---|---|
| Claire Barrow | Torbay Council |
| Sam Billet | Edelman |
| Louise Campbell | The Union |
| Mike Colling | Mike Colling and Company |
| Oliver Doerle | Office for National Statistics |
| Emma Gibbons | Institute of Advertising Practitioners |
| Jacqui Haver | Formerly of Bray Leino |
| Beverley Hill | University of the West of England |
| Jon Howard | Quiet Storm |
| Graham Hughes | Formerly of the Leeds Metropolitan University |
| Janet Hull | Institute of Practitioners in Advertising |
| Cathy Lawler | Mike Colling and Company |
| Vanessa Lee | Outdoor Media Centre |
| Gail Lyall | The Scottish Government |
| Miriam Mainwood | Designate |
| Caroline Marchant | University of Edinburgh |
| Ian McAteer | The Union |
| Neil Morris | WIRSPA |
| Jane Neill | Tangible |
| John O'Sullivan | 24/7 Ideas |
| Mark Raine | Scottish Government |
| James Robertson | Bray Leino |
| Ray Sylvester | Buckinghamshire New University |
| Emma Taylor | Credos |

Above all perhaps are the various individuals at Pearson and their associates who have taken my manuscript, managed it and published it in this form. In particular I should like to thank Rachel Gear, Amanda McPartlin and Rufus Curnow as the three editors involved in the development, evolution and production of this book. In support, Chris Kingston has both demonstrated a positive approach and helped whenever asked. Finally, my biggest thank you is for my wife Karen, who has valiantly endured the writing process once again. I should like to take this opportunity to express my love and thanks for the past 38 plus years that we have been together, and to say 'cheers' to the next 'n' years that we have.

# Publisher's acknowledgements

We are grateful to the following for permission to reproduce copyright material:

## Figures

Figure 1.2 from Redefining the nature and format of the marketing communications mix, *The Marketing Review*, 7(1), 45–57 (Hughes, G. and Fill, C., 2007), reproduced by permission of Westburn Publishers Ltd; Figures 1.3, 2.2, 2.3, 2.4, 3.9, 3.10, 3.11, 5.3, 5.4, 5.5, 6.2, 7.1 and 17.2 from *Essentials of Marketing Communications* (Fill, C., 2011), reproduced by permission of Pearson Education Ltd; Figure 2.6 from *Consumer Behaviour: Implications for Marketing Strategy*, 4th ed., Richard D. Irwin (Hawkins, D. et al., 1989), The McGraw-Hill Companies, Inc.; Figure 3.5 from *Understanding Attitudes and Predicting Social Behavior*, Prentice Hall (Ajzen, I. and Fishbein, M., 1980), © 1980. Electronically reproduced by permission of Pearson Education, Inc., Upper Saddle River, New Jersey; Figure 4.3 adapted from Managing market relationships, *Journal of the Academy of Marketing Science*, 28(1), pp. 24–30 (Day, G., 2000), with kind permission from Springer Science + Business Media; Figure 4.5 from *How Advertising Affects the Sales of Packaged Goods Brands*, Millward Brown (Brown, G., 1991); Figure 4.6 from *Attitude toward the ad as a mediator of advertising effectiveness, in Advances in Consumer Research*, Association for Consumer Research (Lutz, J., Mackensie, S.B. and Belch, G.E. (Bagozzi, R.P. and Tybout, A.M., eds) 1983), republished with permission of Association for Consumer Research, permission conveyed through Copyright Clearance Center, Inc.; Figure 5.2 adapted from Work towards an 'Ideal Self', *Marketing*, 02/02/2011 (Edwards, H.), reproduced from *Marketing* magazine with the permission of the copyright owner, Haymarket Business Publications Limited; Figure 6.4 from How El Al Airlines transformed its service strategy with employee participation, *Strategy & Leadership*, 36(3), pp. 21–25 (Herstein, R. and Mitki, Y., 2008), © Emerald Group Publishing Limited, all rights reserved; Figure 7.3 from Five approaches to organise an integrated marketing communications agency, *Journal of Advertising Research* March/April, pp. 48–58 (Gronstedt, A. and Thorsen, E., 1996); Figures 8.2 and 8.3 from Ad spending: growing market share, *Harvard Business Review* January/February, pp. 44–48 (Schroer, J., 1990); Figure 8.4 from Ad spending: maintaining market share, *Harvard Business Review* January/February, pp. 38–42 (Jones, J.P., 1990); Figures 8.5 and 8.6 from Managing advertising as an investment, *Admap*, 39(7), pp. 29–31 (Farr, A,. 2004); Figure 9.1 from Case study: pre-testing mould-breaking ads, *Admap*, July/August, pp. 28–29 (Burden, S., 2007); Figure 9.2 from Social media measurement: it's not impossible, *Journal of Interactive Advertising*, 10(1), pp. 94–9 (Murdough, C., 2009), ISSN 1525-2019, American Academy of Advertising; Figure 10.4 from Revisiting the IMC construct: a revised definition and four pillars, *International Journal of Advertising*, 27(1), pp. 133–60 (Kliatchko, J., 2008); Figure 11.2 from *The New Strategic Brand* (Kapferer, J.-N., 2012), Kogan Page; Figure 11.4 after *Brand Management: A Theoretical and Practical Approach* (Riezebos, R., 2003), reproduced by permission of Pearson Education Ltd; Figure 11.7 adapted from Branding the business marketing offer: exploring brand attributes in business markets, *Journal of Business and Industrial Marketing*, 22(6), pp. 394–9 (Beverland, M., Napoli, J. and Yakimova, R., 2007); Figure 13.1 from Rethinking internal communication: a stakeholder approach, *Corporate Communications: An International Journal*, 12(2), pp. 177–98 (Welch, M. and Jackson, P.R., 2007), © Emerald Group Publishing Limited, all rights reserved; Figure 13.3 adapted from Advertising's internal audience, *Journal of Marketing*, 62 (January), pp. 69–88 (Gilly, M.C. and Wolfinbarger, M., 1998); Figure 13.4 from The brand inside: the factors of failure and success in internal branding, *Irish Marketing Review*, 19(1/2), pp. 54–63 (Mahnert, K.F. and Torres, A.M., 2007); Figure 13.5 from *The Corporate Image: Strategies for Effective Identity Programmes*, revised edition, Kogan Page (Ind, N., 1992); Figure 14.1 after *Marketing Communications: A European Perspective*, 4th ed. (Pelsmaker de, P., Guens, M. and Bergh, van den, J., 2010), reproduced by permission of Pearson Education Ltd; Figure 14.4 from How advertising works: a planning model, *Journal of Advertising*

*Research*, October, pp. 27–33 (Vaughn, R., 1980); Figure 14.5 adapted from *Advertising, Communications and Promotion Management*, 2nd ed., McGraw-Hill (Rossiter, J.R. and Percy, L., 1997); Figure 15.1 from *Managing Public Relations*, Holt, Rineholt & Winston (Grunig, J. and Hunt, T., 1984), reprinted by permission of James E. Grunig; Figure 16.1 after Match game: linking sponsorship congruence with communication outcomes, *Journal of Advertising Research*, June, pp. 214–26 (Poon, D.T.Y., Prendergast, G. and West, D., 2010); Figure 17.3 from Proactive and reactive: drivers for key account management programmes, *European Journal of Marketing*, 43(7/8), pp. 961–84 (Brehmer, P.-O. and Rehme, J., 2009), © Emerald Group Publishing Limited, all rights reserved; Figures 19.1 and 19.2 from The transformation of the music industry supply chain, *International Journal of Operations & Production Management*, 24(11), pp. 1087–1103 (Graham, G., Burnes, B., Lewis, J.G. and Langer, J., 2004), © Emerald Group Publishing Limited, all rights reserved; Figure 19.3 from Branded entertainment: a new advertising technique or product placement in disguise?, *Journal of Marketing Management*, 22(5–6), pp. 489–504 (Hudson, S. and Hudson, D., 2006), reprinted by permission of Taylor & Francis Ltd, www.tandf.co.uk/journals; Figure 19.4 from Understanding B2C brand alliances between manufacturers and suppliers, *Marketing Management Journal*, 18(2), pp. 32–46 (Ervelles, S., Horton, V. and Fukawa, N., 2008); Figure 23.3 after Evaluating multiple channel strategies, *Journal of Business and Industrial Marketing*, 6(3/4), pp. 37–48 (Cravens, D.W., Ingram, T.N. and LaForge, R.W., 1991), © Emerald Group Publishing Limited, all rights reserved; Figure 26.2 from Does it pay to shock? Reactions to shocking and nonshocking advertising content among university students, *Journal of Advertising Research*, 43(3), pp. 268–81 (Dahl, D.W., Frankenberger, K.D. and Manchanda, R.V., 2003); Figures 26.3, 26.4, 26.5 and 26.6 after *Advertising and Promotion Management*, 2nd ed., McGraw-Hill (Rossiter, J.R. and Percy, L., 1997).

## Tables

Table 2.3 after Word of mouth effects on short-term and long-term product judgments, *Journal of Business Research*, 32(3), pp. 213–23 (Bone, P.F., 1995), copyright 1995, with permission from Elsevier; Table 2.5 from *Interpersonal Processes: New Directions in Communication Research* Sage Publications Inc. (Taylor, D. and Altman, I., 1987), republished with permission of Sage Publications, Inc., permission conveyed through Copyright Clearance Center, Inc.; Table 3.6 from Tribal mattering spaces: social-networking sites, celebrity affiliations, and tribal innovations, *Journal of Marketing Management*, 26 (3/4), March, pp. 271–89 (Hamilton, K. and Hewer, P 2010), reprinted by permission of Taylor & Francis Ltd, www.tandf.co.uk/journals; Table 4.3 from *Essentials of Marketing Communications* (Fill, C. 2011), reproduced by permission of Pearson Education Ltd; Table 4.5 from Toward a dialogic theory of public relations, *Public Relations Review*, 28(1), pp. 21–37 (Kent, M.L. and Taylor, M., 2002), copyright 2002, with permission from Elsevier; Table 7.1 after Expenditure Report, The Advertising Association/WARC, http://expenditurereport.warc.com/; Table 7.2 from Marriage material, *The Marketer*, September, pp. 22–23 (Sclater, I., 2006); Table 7.3 from *Agency Remuneration: A Best Practice Guide to Agency Search and Selection*, IPA (2006); Table 8.1 from Marketing's top 100 advertisers, http://www.rankingthebrands.com/The-Brand-Rankings.aspx?rankingID=39&nav=category, The Nielsen Company; Table 8.3 from How to set digital media budgets, *WARC Exclusive* (Renshaw, M., 2008), www.warc.com; Table 9.1 from Conceptualization and measurement of multidimensionality of integrated marketing communications, *Journal of Advertising Research*, September, pp. 222–36 (Lee, D.H. and Park, C.W., 2007); Table 9.5 adapted from The world wide web as an advertising medium: toward an understanding of conversion efficiency, *Journal of Advertising Research*, 6(1), pp. 43–53 (Berthon, P., Pitt, L. and Watson, R., 1996); Table 10.4 adapted from Jenkinson, A. and Sain, B. (2004) Open planning: media neutral planning made simple, www.openplanning.org/cases/openplanning/whitepaper.pdf; Tables 10.5 and 10.6 from *New Models of Marketing Effectiveness From Integration to Orchestration*, WARC (IPA 2011); Table 11.2 from The New Strategic Brand (Kapferer, J.-N., 2012), Kogan Page; Table 11.5 from A practical framework for developing brand portfolios, *Admap*, July/August, pp. 33–5 (Walton, P., 2007); Table 11.6 after *Brand Management: A Theoretical and Practical Approach* (Riezebos, R., 2003), reproduced by permission of Pearson Education Ltd; Table 12.2 adapted from Corporate brands: what are they? What of them? *European Journal of Marketing*, 37(7/8), pp. 972–97 (Balmer, J.M.T. and Gray, E.R., 2003), © Emerald Group Publishing Limited, all rights reserved; Table 13.2 from Rethinking internal communication: a stakeholder approach, *Corporate Communications: An International Journal*, 12(2), pp. 177–98 (Welch, M. and Jackson, P.R., 2007), © Emerald Group Publishing Limited, all rights reserved; Table 13.3 after *Organisational identity. In Research in Organizational Behavior*, JAI Press (Albert, S. and Whetten, D.A. (L.L. Cummings and B.M. Staw, eds) 1985) pp. 263–95; Table 15.3 after Toward public relations theory-based study of public diplomacy: testing the applicability of the excellence study, *Journal of Public Relations Research*, 18(4), pp. 287–312 (Yun, S.-H., 2006), reprinted by permission of Taylor & Francis Ltd, www.tandf.co.uk/journals; Table 15.7 from Image repair discourse and crisis communication, *Public Relations Review*, 23(2), pp. 177–86 (Benoit, W. L., 1997), copyright 1997, with permission from Elsevier; Table 16.3 from Changes in sponsorship value: competencies and capabilities of successful sponsorship relationships, *Industrial Marketing Management*, 35(8), pp. 1016–26 (Farrelly, F. Quester, P. and Burton, R., 2006), copyright 2006, with permission from Elsevier; Table 17.4 from From key account selling to key account management, *Journal of Marketing Practice: Applied Marketing Science*, 1(1), pp. 9–21 (Millman, T. and Wilson, K., 1995), © Emerald Group Publishing Limited, all rights reserved; Table 18.1 from *Sales promotion. In The Marketing Book*, 3rd ed., Butterworth-Heinemann (Peattie, S. and Peattie, K.J. (M.J. Baker, ed.) 1994), copyright Elsevier 1994; Table 18.4 adapted from Loyalty trends for the 21st century, *Journal of Targeting Measurement and Analysis for Marketing*, 12(3), pp. 199–212 (Capizzi, M., Ferguson, R. and Cuthbertson, R., 2004); Table 18.7 adapted from Fighting for a new view of field work, *Marketing*, 9 March, pp. 29–30 (McLuhan, R., 2000), reproduced from *Marketing* magazine with the permission of the copyright owner, Haymarket Business Publications Limited; Table 18.8 from Which way forward? *Marketing*, 13, December, p. 12 (Bashford, S., 2007), reproduced from *Marketing* magazine with the permission of the copyright owner, Haymarket Business Publications Limited; Table 19.1 © Ray Sylvester, Buckinghamshire New University; Table 19.3 from An exploratory study of attendee activities at a business trade show, *Journal of Business & Industrial Marketing*, 25(4), pp. 241–48 (Gopalakrishna, S., Roster, C.A. and Sridhar, S., 2010), © Emerald Group Publishing Limited, all rights reserved; Table 20.3 from *Advertising Statistics Yearbook*, Advertising Association (2003) World Advertising Research Centre; Table 21.1 after What is personalization? A conceptual framework, *European Journal of Marketing*, 41(5/6), pp. 409–18 (Vesanen, J., 2007), © Emerald Group Publishing Limited, all rights reserved; Table 21.3 from Web site characteristics and business performance: some evidence from international business-to-business organizations, *Marketing Intelligence and Planning*, 21(2), pp. 105–114 (Karayanni, D.A. and Baltas, G.A., 2003), © Emerald Group Publishing Limited, all rights reserved; Table 21.4 from *Introduction to E-Commerce*, McGraw-Hill/Irwin (Rayport, J.F. and Jaworski, B.J., 2004), The McGraw-Hill Companies, Inc.; Table 23.2 after Advertising on the web: is there response before click-through?, *Journal of Advertising Research*, March/April, pp. 33–45 (Briggs, R. and Hollis, N., 1997); Table 24.5 adapted from Recency planning, *Admap*, February, pp. 32–34 (Ephron, E., 1997), WARC; Table 24.6 adapted from Study reveals negativity towards ads, *Campaign*, 28 November, p. 8 (Beale, C., 1997), reproduced with the permission of the copyright owner, Haymarket Business Publications Limited; Table 24.7 from Media consumption and consumer purchasing, *Worldwide Multimedia Measurement (WM3)* (Shultz, D.E., Pilotta, J.P. and Block, M.P., 2006), ESOMAR; Table 24.8 adapted from Setting frequency levels: an art or a science? *Marketing and Media Decisions*, 24(4), pp. 9–11 (Ostrow, J.W., 1984), The Nielsen Company.

## Text

Box on page 636 from NFC Forum: NFC in Action, http://www.nfc-forum.org/aboutnfc/nfc_in_action, courtesy NFC Forum, nfc-forum.org.

## Exhibits

Exhibits 1.1 and 1.2 LV= and Designate; Exhibit 1.3 Blue Rubicon Ltd; Exhibits 2.1, 2.2 and 2.3 MTV and Quiet Storm; Exhibits 2.4, 9.4, 10.1, 10.2, 17.1, 17.2, 17.3, 18.4, 20.1, 20.2, 20.3, 20.5 and 21.4 Bray Leino Ltd; Exhibit 2.5 Premier Foods; Exhibit 2.6 Buyenlarge/Getty Images; Exhibit 3.1 Teaching Agency; Exhibit 3.2 DeBeers UK Ltd; Exhibit 3.3 Freud Communications; Exhibit 3.4 National Trust Photo Library; Exhibit 4.1 Rolex UK; Exhibit 4.2 Yorkshire Water; Exhibit 4.3 Unilever PLC and group companies; Exhibit 5.1 Arla Foods; Exhibit 5.2 Goodman Fielder Limited; Exhibit 5.3 SKV Communications; Exhibit 5.4 Kraft Foods UK; Exhibits 5.5 and 23.4 ImagineChina; Exhibit 5.6 Alliance Boots; Exhibit 6.1 Dario Cantatore/Getty Images; Exhibit 6.4 PRNewsFoto/Elizabeth Arden/Press Association Images; Exhibit 7.1 Ace Stock Limited/Alamy Images; Exhibit 7.2 Carolyn Jenkins/Alamy Images; Exhibit 8.1 Honda (UK); Exhibit 8.2 Art Directors & TRIP/Alamy Images; Exhibit 8.3 Steven May/Alamy Images; Exhibits 9.1 and 9.2 The Scottish Government; Exhibit 9.3 Guy Bell/Alamy Images; Exhibit 10.3 Wm Morrison Supermarkets PLC; Exhibit 10.4 Fabergé; Exhibit 10.5 United Biscuits; Exhibit 10.6 Nissan; Exhibit 11.1 ffotocymru/Alamy Images; Exhibit 11.2 Dong Jinlin/ColorChinaPhoto/Press Association

Images; Exhibit 11.3 whyeyephotography/Alamy Images; Exhibit 11.4 David White/Alamy Images; Exhibit 12.1 Claire Greenway/Stringer/Getty Images; Exhibit 12.2 Oleg Goloynev/Shutterstock.com; Exhibit 12.3 Charles Polidano/Touch The Skies/Alamy Images; Exhibit 13.1 Torbay Council; Exhibit 13.2 WPA Pool/Getty Images; Exhibit 13.3 Thomas Samson/Gamma-Rapho/Getty Images; Exhibit 14.1 Boston Globe/Getty Images; Exhibit 14.2 Tourism Philippines; Exhibit 14.3 BETC London; Exhibits 15.1, 15.2 and 18.1 Press Association Images; Exhibit 15.4 Eric Vandeville/ABACA/Press Association Images; Exhibit 16.1 Nick Savage/Alamy Images; Exhibit 16.2 Matthew Stockman/Getty Images; Exhibit 16.3 Tim Mosenfelder/Corbis; Exhibit 16.4 Catlin; Exhibit 16.5 Action Images; Exhibit 17.4 Direct Wines Ltd; Exhibit 17.5 The Campaign Company; Exhibit 17.6 Keith Dannemiller/Corbis; Exhibit 17.7 © ABB; Exhibit 19.1 Rune Hellestad/Corbis; Exhibit 19.2 PRNewsFoto/Press Association Images; Exhibit 19.3 Feng Li/Getty Images; Exhibit 19.4 Paddy Power; Exhibit 19.5 Christopher Furlong/Getty Images; Exhibit 20.4 Bertrand Guay/AFP/Getty Images; Exhibit 20.6 Clipper Ventures; Exhibit 20.7 St John Ambulance; Exhibit 21.1 Hiscox Insurance Company Ltd; Exhibit 21.2 Colin Underhill/Alamy Images; Exhibit 21.3 www.prshots.com and ASOS; Exhibit 22.1 Brynjar Ágústsson, brynjar.photoshelter.com/ Promote Iceland; Exhibit 22.2 Mick Tsikas/AAP/Press Association Images and Twitter, Inc.; Exhibit 22.3 Tony French/Alamy Images; Exhibit 22.4 Geoff Caddick/PA Wire/Press Association Images; Exhibits 23.1 and 23.2 Salvation Army; Exhibits 23.2 and 24.2 Mike Colling and Company Ltd; Exhibit 23.3 Transport Accident Commission; Exhibits 24.1 and 24.2 Which?; Exhibit 24.3 Peter Winterbottom/JCDecaux Airport; Exhibits 25.1 and 25.2 Johnnie Walker/Bartle Bogle Hegarty; Exhibits 26.1 and 26.2 Unilever Australia; Exhibit 26.3 Virgin Media/Tom Oldham.

In some instances we have been unable to trace the owners of copyright material, and we would appreciate any information that would enable us to do so.

# Part 1

## Introduction to Marketing Communications

This opening part serves to establish the scope of marketing communications and provides a brief overview of the content and style adopted throughout the rest of the text. In essence, this part of the book is concerned with exploring contextual aspects of marketing communications.

Chapter 1 provides an introductory perspective on marketing communications and sets out some important, key concepts. It provides an insight into how the configuration of the marketing communication mix has effectively changed over the last 10 years.

Chapter 2 addresses issues concerning communication theory and, in particular, moves on from the simple linear interpretation of how communication works to one that recognises the influence of people, behaviour and interactional elements on the communication process.

Chapter 3 is concerned with aspects of buyer behaviour, upon which marketing communications should be developed. Only by understanding the market and the target audience can appropriate objectives, strategies, promotional methods, applications and resources be determined, allocated and implemented.

The final chapter in this part introduces ideas about how marketing communications might work. Rather than suggest a single approach, five separate approaches are presented. These are the sequential buying processes, attitude change, shaping relationships, significant value, and cognitive processing.

For readers with access to the companion website that accompanies this book, there are supplementary chapters, drawn from previous editions, available in PDF format.

Understanding how customers process information

Customer decision-making

Ethics in marketing communications

Marketing: relationships and communications

# Chapter 1
## Introducing marketing communications

Marketing communications is concerned with the methods, processes, meanings, perceptions, and actions associated with the different ways in which products, services and brands are presented, considered, and developed with audiences.

## Aims and learning objectives

The primary aim of this introductory chapter is to explore some of the key concepts associated with marketing communications. In addition, readers are encouraged to consider the scope and purpose of marketing communications and to develop an appreciation of the key characteristics of the communications mix.

The learning objectives of this chapter are to:

1. appreciate the concept of exchange and how it impacts marketing communications;
2. explain the scope, role and tasks of marketing communications;
3. describe how marketing communications can be used to engage audiences;
4. define marketing communications;
5. explore ways in which the environment can influence the use of marketing communications;
6. consider the nature and characteristics of the marketing communications mix;
7. compare the use of marketing communications in consumer and business markets.

# Minicase

## LV= a spectacular revival

In 2006 Liverpool Victoria was a dying brand. It was losing customers at a terrifying rate and it was losing a dramatic number of car insurance policies each month. After decades of a lack of clear strategic direction, the company had lost sight of responding to consumer and market needs and consumers were voting with their feet at a frightening speed.

At the time the car insurance industry was a fragmented market with many providers, with many using 'quick win' price-based offers to buy market share. The market was dominated by the top three competitors who commanded 58.7 per cent market share.

Liverpool Victoria had a £2.6m marketing budget, tiny compared to their competitors. This was invested in lacklustre direct mail campaigns and TV advertising that was sporadic, dull, uninspired and totally ineffective. As a consequence the insurance business was in serious and terminal decline.

Research showed that consumers saw little difference between the numerous insurance products that were available, and key decision factors were usually a combination of price together with brand likeability and trust. This became even more important following the explosion of price-comparison sites in 2006. This development dramatically altered consumer purchasing behaviour, with many consumers prepared to invest time in finding the most suitable deal. This channel shift often resulted in lower levels of loyalty and increased brand switching, adding to the challenges of customer retention. Even so, only 20 per cent of consumers chose on price alone.

A new strategy was required, and in 2007 a five-year plan to more than quadruple the size of the business and become a top five insurer, whilst increasing profits year on year, was set out. The following core goals were agreed:

- To take on the big boys – become a top 5 insurer within the car insurance industry by 2011, achieving a market share of 5 per cent.
- To achieve ambitious sales and enforce policy targets set out year on year.
- To balance growing the brand with keeping the cost per sale below £100. Liverpool Victoria needed to grow customer numbers without simply buying market share. The cost of acquisition was to stay below £100 at all times.

- To launch a dynamic brand with emotional appeal to cut through market place apathy toward financial service brands, particularly car insurance.
- To build a well-liked and respected household name using a multichannel media strategy within a budget of £43 million over 5 years – less than half the budget of the market leader.
- To increase profits for Liverpool Victoria's general insurance division, despite the difficult market conditions.

To achieve these goals a new brand was required as the Liverpool Victoria brand had little equity. The company was rebranded to LV=, and a relaunch campaign was developed, one that would punch above its weight in a noisy market place.

The new brand needed to build likeability and trust, and to represent 'good value'. This is because LV= could not offer the lowest prices, yet their level of customer satisfaction and quality products offered excellent value for money. Previous attempts at price cutting at Liverpool Victoria had failed miserably, as consumers had limited trust in a company with little brand equity.

Car insurance is boring therefore LV= would have to earn the consumers' interest. However, to do this by outspending competitors was not an option. There were no sustainable USPs, and a strategy based on price alone, or introductory offers, or new product benefits would be doomed to fail.

In order to reach, engage, convert and build relationships with the target market of 35+ ABC1 adults, it was necessary to focus on the emotional benefits and value offered, and to develop ESPs or emotional selling propositions. The goal was to ignite interest and engage on an emotional level, if only because emotion-driven communications are proven to be more effective.

A new logo was developed with an equals sign to represent mutual status. In research, while consumers failed to grasp this reference, they did see the equals sign in combination with LV as representing the word 'love' in a hieroglyphic sense. This fortuitous outcome perfectly matched the territory of love in a natural, credible, and branded way that LV= were seeking. So, the emotional fit with the real world was strong. LV= also acquired the LV.com URL for

$1.6m in a ferocious bidding war against the obvious (non-insurance) competitors – a big improvement on the somewhat bulky liverpoolvictoria.co.uk.

And with this they developed a brand proposition:

*We look after what you love*

This positioning provided them with a fertile territory to develop a brand idea, encapsulated within the brand icon, a glossy, lime-green heart. The heart had a big role – acting as a glue across all LV= products with broad emotive associations (see Exhibit 1.1).

To accompany the heart and all it represented, they developed sonic branding by the consistent use of a love song, 'Have Love Will Travel' – a toe-tapping old R&B track made famous by the Blues Brothers. Again, like the heart, the music track was designed to be intrusive without being irritating. After all, they wanted people to love the brand, not be driven mad by it.

A decision was made to incorporate high production values throughout every execution in all media to convey substance, scale and quality. And throughout every execution in every media channel, they ensured that LV= would be recognised by existing Liverpool Victoria customers as the new iteration of a brand to which they still had considerable feelings of loyalty. The brand icon was also a vital branding and shorthand device across all media. It even works when you Sky + through the ad breaks at 30x speed, and stands out amazingly well on comparison websites and other online media.

**Exhibit 1.1**    **The LV= brand identity**
*Source*: LV=

Rational messages are better at driving short-term sales responses, but without a longer-term strategy of growing emotional equity it doesn't get easier to increase sales over time. Car insurance is a rational product, but in order to achieve the ambitious growth LV= sought, they had to balance a sales-responsive message within the territory of love, to balance short-term sales with long-term brand growth in a bid to make the LV= brand both famous and profitable. See Exhibit 1.2 for stills from the television work.

Historically, Liverpool Victoria had focused heavily on direct mail, but to deliver the new strategy, a multi-media approach was required. Media choices focused on a hybrid of brand response and direct-response advertising and media, and effective media planning was essential to deliver this to engage the target market. Media planning was an interrelated, complementary process combining 'drivers' (driving consumer interest primarily through highly branded activity – e.g. TV, outdoor, press) and 'harvesters' (capturing consumer interest through below-the-line, one-to-one methods – e.g. direct mail, door drops, directories).

Segmenting the target audience, 35+ ABC1 adults, was essential for effective targeting of marketing communications. Due to tight budgets, especially at the start of the project, national bursts of TV wouldn't provide a competitive share of voice. So, they built the brand presence through carefully selected and monitored driver activity, including a big daytime TV presence, followed by powerful Harvester communications to create a one-to-one dialogue with their future customers. Once LV= started to feel the cumulative effect of this activity and increased awareness, they were able to build peak-time TV into the schedule to unleash LV= car insurance to a much wider audience and really make the brand famous.

This positioning has been built upon and reinforced consistently throughout the five years. By establishing a campaign DNA, they aimed to be memorable and liked, and to ensure that every pound spent worked as hard as possible.

The results of the Liverpool Victoria re-launch have been spectacular and far reaching. Every target has been achieved and many substantially exceeded:

● LV= reached number three in the market by 2010 – a year ahead of plan.

● Market share increased from 2.5 per cent share in 2006 to 9.8 per cent.

● Between 2006 and 2011 annual sales grew by a staggering 696 per cent.

The Power of Love: How LV= increased car insurance sales by 696%

VO: Over the last year, half a million Britons suddenly just "upped sticks" and decided to move to somewhere new, LV.

VO: And they all probably moved their car insurance for the same reason. Price, right? Fact is, our no claims discount can reach a whopping 75% off.

VO: Over a thousand people a day are joining LV. Join them and you could enjoy cheaper car insurance too. Call 0800 723 723 or go to LV.com

| Exhibit 1.2 | **LV= television advertising** |
|---|---|
| | *Source*: LV= |

- Current customers increased by 476 per cent.
- Marketing efficiencies improved dramatically with acquisition costs falling by 77 per cent.
- LV= employed an additional 1,300 people to handle the growth.
- Profits for the General Insurance division rose in the same period from −£39.5m to £72.2m.

This demonstrates the importance of building a powerful brand through advertising in a low-interest, low-engagement market such as insurance. It is a remarkable success story of how consistent advertising with a consistent and strong idea at its core can deliver amazing results.

*This minicase was written by Miriam Boote at Designate and John O'Sullivan 24–7ideas.*

# Introduction

Have you ever considered how organisations use communications to reach and engage with their various audiences? Organisations such as LV=, whose rebranding campaign has been presented above, and others as diverse as Kraft and the Wei-Chuan Food Corporation, Google and Samsung, Delta Airlines and Air China, Oxfam and Médecins Sans Frontières, and the Swedish and Singapore governments, all use marketing communications in different ways, to achieve different goals, and to pursue their marketing and business objectives. The aim of this book is to help people just like you to explore the various academic and practitioner views of marketing communications.

The opening sentence contained the word 'engage'. 'Engagement' refers to the nature of the communication that can occur between people and between people and technology. Engagement refers to a range of communication events used to first expose, then capture the attention, captivate and then enable interaction with an audience. It is often achieved through a blend of intellectual and emotional content. Engagement may last seconds, such as the impact of a stunning ad, the sight of a beautiful person or the emotion brought on by a panoramic view, or what a piece of music might bring to an individual. Alternatively, engagement may be protracted and last hours, days, weeks, months or years, depending on the context and the level of enjoyment or loyalty felt towards the event, object or person.

There is no universally agreed definition of the term 'engagement', but there can be no doubt that organisations seek to be seen as relevant to their audiences as this helps to achieve their marketing and communication objectives.

Organisations such as Microsoft and Apple, Waitrose and Tesco, HSBC and Santander, Haier and LG, Nokia and Motorola, Ryanair and easyJet, Chanel and L'Oréal, Boeing and Airbus, Oxfam and Shelter and Merlin and Disney all operate across a number of sectors, markets and countries and use a variety of marketing communications activities to engage with their various audiences. These audiences consist not only of people who buy their products and services but also of people and organisations who might be able to influence them, who might help and support them by providing, for example, labour, finance, manufacturing facilities, distribution outlets and legal advice or who are interested because of their impact on parts of society or the business sector in particular.

The organisations mentioned earlier are all well-known brand names, but there are hundreds of thousands of smaller organisations that also need and use marketing communications to convey the essence of their products and services and to engage their audiences. Each of these organisations, large and small, is part of a network of companies, suppliers, retailers, wholesalers, value-added resellers, distributors and other retailers, which join together, often freely, so that each can achieve its own goals.

The structure of this chapter is as follows. First there is a consideration of the ideas associated with exchange, that underpin marketing principles and of course, marketing communications. We then consider the scope, role and tasks of marketing communications, which includes defining what marketing communications is. This is followed by an introduction to the elements that make up the marketing communications mix, before concluding with a view of the key differences between marketing communications used in consumer and business markets.

# The concept of marketing as an exchange

The concept of exchange, according to most marketing academics and practitioners, is central to our understanding of marketing. For an exchange to take place there must be two or more parties, each of whom can offer something of value to the other and who are prepared to enter freely into the exchange process, a transaction. It is generally accepted that there are two main forms of exchange: transactional and relational (or collaborative) exchanges.

*Transactional* (or market) exchanges (Bagozzi, 1978; Houston and Gassenheimer, 1987) occur independently of any previous or subsequent exchanges. They have a short-term orientation and are primarily motivated by self-interest. When a consumer buys a 'meal' from a burger van they have not used before, then a market exchange can be identified. Burger and chips in exchange for money. In contrast to this, *collaborative* exchanges have a longer-term orientation and develop between parties who wish to build and maintain long-term supportive relationships (Dwyer et al., 1987). So, when someone frequents the same burger van on a regular basis, perhaps on their way home after lectures, or an evening's entertainment, increasingly relational or collaborative exchanges can be considered to be taking place.

These two types of exchange represent the extremes in a spectrum of exchange transactions. This spectrum of exchanges, as depicted at Figure 1.1, is underpinned by relational theory. This means that elements of a relationship can be observed in all exchanges (Macneil, 1983). Relationships become stronger as the frequency of exchanges increases. As exchanges become more frequent so the intensity of the relationship strengthens, so that the focus is no longer on the product or price within the exchange but on the relationship itself.

In industrial societies transactional exchanges have tended to dominate commercial transactions, although recently there has been a substantial movement towards establishing collaborative exchanges. In other words, a variety of exchanges occurs, and each organisation has a portfolio of differing types of exchange that it maintains with different customers, suppliers and other stakeholders. Communication can be considered in terms of an oil in that it lubricates these exchanges and enables them to function. However, just as different types of oil are necessary to lubricate different types of equipment, so different types of communication are necessary to engage with different audiences.

Collaborative exchanges form the basis of the ideas represented in relationship marketing. Many organisations use the principles of relationship marketing manifest in the form of customer relationship marketing or loyalty marketing programmes. However, it is important to note that short-term relationships are also quite common and a necessary dimension of

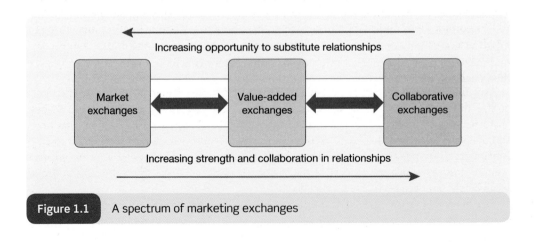

**Figure 1.1**   A spectrum of marketing exchanges

organisational exchange. This book is developed on the broad spectrum of relationships that organisations develop directly with other organisations and consumers, and indirectly on a consumer-to-consumer and interorganisational basis.

# Marketing communications and the process of exchange

The exchange process is developed and managed by:

- researching customer/stakeholder needs;
- identifying, selecting and targeting particular groups of customers/stakeholders who share similar discriminatory characteristics, including needs and wants;
- developing an offering that satisfies the identified needs at an acceptable price, which is available through particular sets of distribution channels;
- making the target audience aware of the existence of the offering. Where competition or other impediments to positive consumer action exist, such as lack of motivation or conviction, a promotional programme is developed and used to communicate with the targeted group.

Collectively, these activities constitute the marketing mix (the '4Ps' as the originator of the term McCarthy (1960) referred to them), and the basic task of marketing is to combine these 4Ps into a marketing programme to facilitate the exchange process. The use of the 4Ps approach has been criticised as limiting the scope of the marketing manager. The assumption by McCarthy was that the tools of the marketing mix allow adaptation to the uncontrollable external environment. It is now seen that the external environment can be influenced and managed strategically, and the rise and influence of the service sector is not easily accommodated within the original 4Ps. To do this, additional Ps such as Processes, Political Power and People have been suggested. A marketing mix of 20Ps has even been proposed, but the essence of the mix remains the same: namely, that it is product-focused and reflects an inside/out mentality – that is, inside the organisation looking out on the world (or customer). This deterministic approach has raised concerns about its usefulness in a marketing environment that is so different from that which existed when the 4Ps concept was conceived.

Promotion is one of the elements of the marketing mix and is responsible for the communication of the marketing offer to the target market. While recognising that there is implicit and important communication through the other elements of the marketing mix (through a high price, for example, symbolic of high quality), it is the task of a planned and integrated set of communication activities to communicate effectively with each of an organisation's stakeholder groups.

At a fundamental level it is possible to interpret the use of marketing communications in two different ways. One of these ways concerns the attempt to develop brand values. Historically, advertising has been used to focus on establishing a set of feelings, emotions and beliefs about a brand or organisation. In this way brand communication is used to help consumers think positively about a brand, helping them to remember and develop positive brand attitudes in the hope that, when they are ready to buy that type of product again, Brand *x* will be chosen because of the positive feelings.

The other and perhaps more contemporary use of marketing communications is to help shape behaviour, rather than feelings. In an age where short-term results and managerial accountability are increasingly critical, investment in brands is geared to achieve a fast return on investment (ROI). This does not allow space and money to build positive attitudes towards brands. Now the urgency is to encourage people to behave differently. This might be by driving them to a website, buying the product or making a telephone call. This behaviour change can be driven by using messages that provide audiences with a reason to act – or what is referred to as a 'call-to-action'.

So, on the one hand communications can be used to develop brand feelings and on the other to change or manage the behaviour of the target audience. These are not mutually exclusive: for example, many television advertisements are referred to as *direct-response ads* because, not only do they attempt to create brand values, but they also carry a website address, telephone number or details of a special offer (sales promotion). In other words, the two goals can be mixed into one – a hybrid approach.

At this point it is worth pointing out that marketing communications should not be used just to reach audiences external to the organisation. Good communications with internal stakeholders, such as employees, are also vital if, in the long term, successful favourable images, perceptions and attitudes are to be established. This book considers the increasing importance of suitable internal communications (Chapter 13) and their vital role in helping to form a strong and consistent brand and corporate identities (Chapters 11 and 12).

# The scope of marketing communications

At a basic level marketing communications, or 'promotion' as it was originally known, is used to communicate elements of an organisation's offering to a target audience. This offer might refer to a product, a service or the organisation itself as it tries to build its reputation. However, this represents a broad view of marketing communication and fails to incorporate the various issues, dimensions and elements that make up this important communication activity. Duncan and Moriarty (1997) and Gronroos (2004) suggest that in addition to these 'planned' events there are marketing communications experienced by audiences relating to both their experience from using products (how tasty is this smoothie?) or the consumption of services (just how good was the service in that hotel, restaurant or at the airport?). In addition to these there are communications arising from unplanned or unintended brand-related experiences (empty stock shelves or accidents). These dimensions of marketing communications are all represented at Figure 1.2 (Hughes and Fill, 2007).

Figure 1.2 helps demonstrate the breadth of the subject and the inherent complexity associated with managing communication with audiences and the way they engage with a brand. Although useful in terms of providing an overview, this framework requires elaboration in order to appreciate the detail associated with each of the elements, especially planned marketing communications. This book builds on this framework and in particular considers issues associated with both planned and unplanned aspects of marketing communications.

Planned marketing communications incorporates three key elements: tools, media and messages. The main communication tools are advertising, sales promotion, public relations, direct marketing, personal selling and added-value approaches such as sponsorship. Messages can be primarily informative or emotional but are usually a subtle blend of both dimensions, reflecting the preferences and needs of the target audience. To help get these messages through to their audiences, organisations either pay for the use of particular media that they know their target audiences will use – for example, magazines, websites or television programmes – or they use their own assets to convey messages, such as their buildings, vehicles and websites, which they do not have to pay to use.

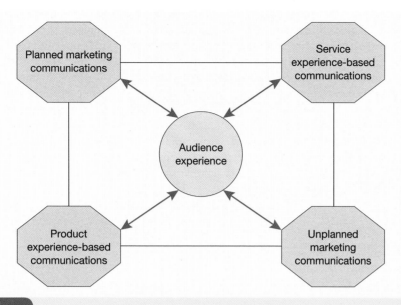

| Figure 1.2 | The scope of marketing communications |

*Source*: Hughes and Fill (2007). Adapted from ideas by Duncan and Moriarty (1997). Used with permission.

## Viewpoint 1.1    Planned and unplanned scent of a man

Old Spice was perceived as an old-fashioned brand, way past its sell-by date. Through the use of planned communications using paid-for media and then unplanned communications and earned media the brand was rebranded and revived in spectacular style, winning numerous prizes and awards.

The planned part was the launch of the campaign with a 30-sec. television ad. Fronted by a former American football player, Isaiah Mustafa, standing in a shower and wearing just a towel, he addresses his female audience with the remark: 'Hello ladies. Look at your man, now back to me, now back at your man, now back to me. Sadly, he isn't me, but if he stopped using lady-scented body wash and switched to Old Spice he could smell like me.'

The backdrop then switched to a yacht, and a striped scarf dropped from the sky to rest around his neck, as he transformed two tickets into 'that thing you really love'. . . . diamonds.

'Anything is possible when your man smells like Old Spice and not a lady,' he comments, sitting on a white horse. 'I'm on a horse,' he observes. The video has had over 13 million views on YouTube.

The ad was then taken online, with Mustafa speaking from the shower responding to questions and comments received through Twitter, Facebook and YouTube. These questions were tracked and selected according to interest, humour and PR potential. Senders of the selected questions were sent personalised videos and the respondents then started conversations and left comments on YouTube, Twitter and social networks. Over 187 video responses were made over a short period of intensive activity. All of this activity generated huge earned media commentary and attention, across multiple media channels.

*Source*:   Based on Bates (2010); Maymann (2010); Shearman (2010); Malvern (2010); UtalkMarketing (2010).

Question:   How should the Old Spice brand be developed now that it is reestablished?

Task:   Find another male fragrance brand and compare their approach to marketing communications with that of Old Spice.

Unplanned marketing communications involve communications that have not been anticipated. These may be both positive and negative, but here the emphasis is more on how the organisation reacts to and manages the meaning attributed by audiences. So, comments by third-party experts, changes in legislation or regulations by government, the actions of competitors, failures in the production or distribution processes or – perhaps the most potent of all communications – word-of-mouth comments between customers, all impact on the way in which organisations and brands are perceived and the images and reputations that are developed. Many leading organisations recognise the influence of word-of-mouth communication and are actively seeking to shape the nature, timing and speed with which it occurs. This topic is discussed in more detail in Chapter 2 and again in Chapter 25. Increasingly, digital media, the Internet in particular, are used to 'talk' with customers, potential and lapsed customers and other stakeholders.

# The role of marketing communications

Organisations communicate with a variety of audiences in order to pursue their marketing and business objectives. Marketing communications can be used to engage with a variety of audiences and in such a way that meet the needs of the audience. Messages should encourage individuals to respond to the focus organisation (or product/brand). This response can be immediate through, for example, purchase behaviour or the use of customer-care lines, or it can be deferred as information is assimilated and considered for future use. Even if the information is discarded at a later date, the communication will have attracted attention and consideration of the message.

The reason to use marketing communications will vary according to the prevailing situation or context but the essential goal is to provoke an audience response. This response might be geared to developing brand values and the positive thoughts an individual might have about a brand. This is grounded in a 'thinking and feeling orientation', a combination of both cognitive thoughts and emotional feelings about a brand. Another type of response might be one that stimulates the audience to act in particular ways. Referred to as a 'behavioural' or sometimes 'brand response', the goal is to 'encourage particular behaviours'. For example, these might include sampling a piece of cheese in a supermarket, encouraging visits to a website, placing orders and paying for goods and services, sharing information with a friend, registering on a network, opening letters, signing a petition or telephoning a number. See Figure 1.3 for a list of the factors that can drive engagement opportunities.

Apart from generating cash flows, the underlying purpose of these responses can be considered to be a strategic function of developing relationships with particular audiences and/or

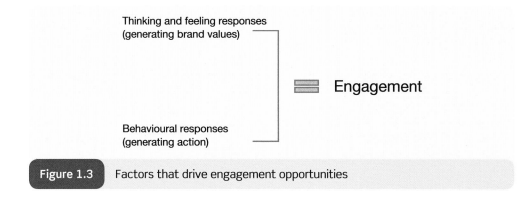

| Figure 1.3 | Factors that drive engagement opportunities |

for (re)positioning brands. For example, LV=, an insurance brand, moved from a behavioural strategy based on daytime, direct-response, TV advertising, to one based on developing brand values. The goal was to boost awareness of its mutual status (and not a plc) and so reposition the brand as a premium insurer (Brownsell, 2010a).

Engagement, therefore, can be considered to be a function of two forms of response. The quality of engagement cannot be determined, but it can be argued that marketing communications should be based on driving a particular type of response that captivates an individual. For example, Sarah Copley, former Sales and Marketing Director for Virgin Trains, explained that for several years the company spent time developing and building the brand values particularly at a time when the product was not complete. However, now Virgin Trains have a focus on growing passenger numbers (Brownsell, 2010b), a behavioural strategy that requires a complementary communications approach.

From this it can be concluded that the primary role of marketing communications is to engage audiences. Where engagement occurs, an individual might be said to have been positively captivated and, as a result, opportunities for activity should increase. Engagement acts as a bridge, the mechanism through which brands and organisations link with target audiences and through which the goals of both parties can be achieved: mutual value.

Engagement suggests that understanding and meaning have been conveyed effectively. At one level, engagement through one-way communication enables target audiences to understand product and service offers, to the extent that the audience is sufficiently engaged to want to enter into further communication activity. At another level, engagement through two-way or interactive communication enables information that is relationship-specific (Ballantyne, 2004) to be exchanged. The greater the frequency of information exchange, the more likely collaborative relationships will develop. So, the role of marketing communications is to engage audiences.

## Scholars' paper 1.1    Beware, Engaging confusion

**Verhoef, P.C., Reinartz, W.J. and Krafft, M. (2010) Customer Engagement as a New Perspective in Customer Management,** *Journal of Service Research*, **13(3), 247–52.**

As already mentioned in the text, the use of the term 'engagement' has become increasingly widespread in the marketing literature. The term is used in different ways to mean different things and this paper is a good example of the different interpretations that are available. This paper considers engagement as a behavioural manifestation toward the brand or firm, one that goes beyond transactions. The authors propose a conceptual model of the antecedents, impediments, and firm consequences of customer engagement. Readers might be interested to know that this journal published a special edition on customer engagement.

# The tasks of marketing communication

Bowersox and Morash made a significant contribution in their 1989 paper when they demonstrated how marketing flows, including the information flow, can be represented as a network that has the sole purpose of satisfying customer needs and wants. Communication is important in these exchange networks as it can help achieve one of four key tasks:

- It can *inform* and make potential customers aware of an organisation's offering.

- Communication may attempt to *persuade* current and potential customers of the desirability of entering into an exchange relationship.

- Communications can also be used to *reinforce* experiences. This may take the form of *reminding* people of a need they might have or reminding them of the benefits of past transactions with a view to convincing them that they should enter into a similar exchange. In addition, it is possible to provide *reassurance* or comfort either immediately prior to an exchange or, more commonly, post-purchase. This is important, as it helps to retain current customers and improve profitability, an approach to business that is much more cost-effective than constantly striving to lure new customers.

- Finally, marketing communications can act as a *differentiator*, particularly in markets where there is little to separate competing products and brands. Mineral water products, such as Perrier and Highland Spring, are largely similar: it is the communications surrounding the products that have created various brand images, enabling consumers to make purchasing decisions. In these cases it is the images created by marketing communications that enable people to differentiate one brand from another and position them so that consumers' purchasing confidence and positive attitudes are developed. Therefore, communication can inform, persuade, reinforce and build images to differentiate a product or service, or to put it another way, DRIP (Fill, 2002) (see Table 1.1).

At a higher level, the communication process not only supports the transaction, by informing, persuading, reinforcing or differentiating, but also offers a means of exchange itself, for example communication for entertainment, for potential solutions and concepts for education and self-esteem. Communications involve intangible benefits, such as the psychological satisfactions

| Table 1.1 | DRIP Elements of marketing communications |
|---|---|

| Task | Sub-task | Explanation |
|---|---|---|
| Differentiate | Position | To make a product or service stand out in the category |
| Reinforce | Remind or reassure | To consolidate and strengthen previous messages and experiences |
| Inform | Make aware, educate | To make known and advise of availability and features |
| Persuade | Purchase or make further enquiry | To encourage further positive purchase-related behaviour |

associated with, for example, the entertainment value of television advertisements or the experiences within a sponsored part of a social network. Communications can also be seen as a means of perpetuating and transferring values and culture to different parts of society or networks. For example, it is argued that the way women are portrayed in the media and stereotypical images of very thin or 'size zero' women are dysfunctional in that they set up inappropriate role models. The form and characteristics of the communication process adopted by some organisations (both the deliberate and the unintentional use of signs and symbols used to convey meaning) help to provide stability and continuity.

## Viewpoint 1.2    Holiday tasks

Two particular companies which operate in the holiday market serve to illustrate how important it is to understand the tasks that marketing communications are required to undertake. These companies are TUI, which owns the Thomson and First Choice brands, and Thomas Cook. The trading results show two different situations, with TUI reporting a 25 per cent rise in pre-tax profits, to £360 million, and Thomas Cook making a £398 million pre-tax loss.

At times some consumers confuse Thomson with Thomas Cook, if only because of the similarities of the first four letters of the brands' names. So, marketing communications are used to differentiate the brands, as TUI did in 2011 when it released a national press ad with the line 'Another holiday company may be experiencing turbulence, but we're in really great shape'. This sent a message that TUI Travel results were on course, yet Thomas Cook and others in the market had experienced a fall of 14 per cent. It also said TUI are different from Thomas Cook.

Branding in the holiday market usually takes second place to price-based promotional activities. However, there are signs that TUI have been trying to communicate some of the brand values associated with Thomson and First Choice. For example, Thomson invested £5 million communicating its 'exclusive' and 'tailored' offering using the strapline 'Uniquely designed holidays'. £3 million was used to relaunch and reposition First Choice, as 'the home of all-inclusive'.

Thomas Cook has had to cope with an entirely different set of circumstances. Not only did it delay the announcement of its full-year results, it was also forced to issue a third profits warning in a year. This was followed by a £100 million emergency refinancing operation and changes in senior management. These results and activities led to considerable negative publicity, all of which required their marketing communications to take a very different approach.

The response from Thomas Cook to TUI's advertising was a press ad designed to inform consumers that its business had delivered 'great value for 170 years', and that 2012 would be no different.

*Source*:   Based on Eleftheriou-Smith (2012).

| | |
|---|---|
| **Question:** | Which of the DRIP tasks do you believe the Thomas Cook marketing communication was designed to accomplish? |
| **Task:** | Make brief notes explaining how would you develop the marketing communications designed to support the TUI brand. |

Other examples of intangible satisfactions can be seen in the social and psychological transactions involved increasingly with the work of the National Health Service (NHS), charities, educational institutions and other not-for-profit organisations, such as housing associations. Not only do these organisations recognise the need to communicate with various audiences, but they also perceive value in being seen to be 'of value' to their customers. There is also evidence that some brands are trying to meet the emerging needs of some consumers who want to know the track record of manufacturers with respect to their environmental policies and actions. For example, the growth in 'Fairtrade' products, designed to provide fairer and more balanced trading arrangements with producers and growers in emerging parts of the world, has persuaded Kraft that they should engage with this form of commercial activity. Typhoo claims on its packaging, 'care for tea and our tea pickers'.

The notion of value can be addressed in a different way. All organisations have the opportunity to develop their communications to a point where the value of their messages represents a competitive advantage. This value can be seen in the consistency, timing, volume or expression of the message. Heinonen and Strandvik (2005) argue that there are four elements that constitute communication value. These are the message content, how the information is presented, where the communication occurs and its timing: in other words, the all-important context within which a communication event occurs. These elements are embedded within marketing communications and are referred to throughout this book.

### Scholars' paper 1.2    Early days of marketing communications

**Ray, M.L. (1973) A Decision Sequence Analysis of Developments in Marketing Communication,** *Journal of Marketing*, **37 (January), 29–38.**

This older paper has been included because it provides perspective. Much of contemporary marketing communications has a digital orientation. This paper reminds us of the evolution of marketing communications, way before digitisation. This paper could also be listed in Chapter 5, about Strategy and Planning, because Ray introduces a planning model in the paper, and Chapter 10 as there are embryonic ideas about integrated marketing communications as well. It may not be Da Vinci but it is certainly forward thinking.

Communication can be used for additional reasons. The tasks of informing, persuading and reinforcing and differentiating are primarily activities targeted at consumers or end-users. Organisations do not exist in isolation from each other, as each one is a part of a wider system of corporate entities, where each enters into a series of exchanges to secure raw material inputs or resources and to discharge them as value-added outputs to other organisations in the network.

The exchanges that organisations enter into require the formation of relationships, however tenuous or strong. Andersson (1992) looks at the strength of the relationship between organisations in a network and refers to them as 'loose or tight couplings'. These couplings, or partnerships, are influenced by the communications that are transmitted and received. The role that organisations assume in a network and the manner in which they undertake and complete their tasks are, in part, shaped by the variety and complexity of the communications in transmission throughout the network. Issues of channel or even network control, leadership, subservience and conflict are implanted in the form and nature of the communications exchanged in any network.

Within market exchanges, communications are characterised by formality and planning. Collaborative exchanges are supported by more frequent communication activity. As Mohr and Nevin (1990) state, there is a bi-directional flow to communications and an informality to the nature and timing of the information flows.

# Defining marketing communications

Having considered the scope, role and tasks of marketing communications, it is now appropriate to define marketing communications. There is no universal definition of marketing communications and there are many interpretations of the subject. Table 1.2 depicts some of the main orientations through which marketing communications has evolved. The origin of many definitions rests with a promotional outlook where the purpose was to use communications to persuade people to buy products and services. The focus was on products, one-way communications, and the perspective was short-term. The expression 'marketing communications' emerged as a wider range of tools and media evolved and as the scope of the tasks these communications activities were expected to accomplish expanded.

In addition to awareness and persuasion, new goals such as developing understanding and preference, reminding and reassuring customers became accepted as important aspects of the

| Table 1.2 | The developing orientation of marketing communications |
| --- | --- |
| **Orientation** | **Explanation** |
| Information and promotion | Communications are used to persuade people into product purchase, using mass-media communications. Emphasis on rational, product-based information. |
| Process and imagery | Communications are used to influence the different stages of the purchase process that customers experience. A range of tools is used. Emphasis on product imagery and emotional messages. |
| Integration | Communication resources are used in an efficient and effective way to enable customers to have a clear view of the brand proposition. Emphasis on strategy, media neutrality and a balance between rational and emotional communication. |
| Relational | Communication is used as an integral part of the different relationships that organisations share with customers. Emphasis on mutual value and meaning plus recognition of the different communication needs and processing styles of different stakeholder groups. |

communications effort. Direct marketing activities heralded a new approach as one-to-one, two-way communications began to shift the focus from mass to personal communications efforts. Now a number of definitions refer to an integrated perspective. This view has gathered momentum since the mid 1990s and is even an integral part of the marketing communications vocabulary. This topic is discussed in greater depth in Chapter 10. However, this transition to an integrated perspective raises questions about the purpose of marketing communications. For example, should the focus extend beyond products and services, should corporate communications be integrated into the organisation's marketing communications, should the range of stakeholders move beyond customers, what does integration mean and is it achievable? With the integrative perspective, a stronger strategic and long-term orientation has developed, although the basis for many marketing communication strategies appears still to rest with a promotional mix orientation.

Some of these interpretations fail to draw out the key issue that marketing communications provides added value, through enhanced product and organisational symbolism. They also fail to recognise that it is the context within which marketing communications flows that impacts upon the meaning and interpretation given to such messages. Its ability to frame and associate offerings with different environments is powerful. Today, in an age where the word 'integration' is used to express a variety of marketing and communication-related activities, where corporate marketing is emerging as the next important development within the subject (Balmer and Gray, 2003) and where interaction is the preferred mode of communication and relationship marketing is the preferred paradigm (Gronroos, 2004) marketing communications now embraces a wider remit, one that has moved beyond the product information model and now forms an integral part of an organisation's overall communications and relationship management strategy. This perspective embraces communications as a one-way, two-way, interactive and dialogic approach necessary to meet the varying needs of different audiences. The integration stage focuses on the organisation, whereas the next development may have its focus on the relationships that an organisation has with its various audiences. Above all else, marketing communications should be an audience-centred activity.

> *Marketing communications is a process through which organisations and audiences engage with one another. Through an understanding of an audience's preferred communication environments, participants seek to develop and present messages, before evaluating and acting upon any responses. By conveying messages that are of significant value, participants are encouraged to offer attitudinal, emotional and behavioural responses.*

This definition has three main themes. The first concerns the word *engages*. By recognising the different transactional and collaborative needs of the target audience, marketing communications can be used to engage with a variety of audiences in such a way that one-way, two-way, interactive and dialogic communications are used (Chapters 2 and 10) that meet the needs of the audience. It is unrealistic to believe that all audiences always want a relationship with your organisation/brand, and for some, one-way communication is fine. However, messages should encourage individual members of target audiences to respond to the focus organisation (or product/brand). This response can be immediate through, for example, purchase behaviour or use of customer carelines, or it can be deferred as information is assimilated and considered for future use. Even if the information is discarded at a later date, the communication will have attracted attention and consideration of the message.

The second theme concerns the *audiences* for, or participants in, marketing communications. Traditionally, marketing communications has been used to convey product-related information to customer-based audiences. Today, a range of stakeholders have connections and relationships of varying dimensions, and marketing communications needs to incorporate this breadth and variety. Stakeholder audiences, including customers, are all interested in a range of corporate issues, sometimes product-related and sometimes related to the policies, procedures and values of the organisation itself. Marketing communications should be an audience-centred activity and in that sense it is important that messages be based on a firm understanding of both the needs and environment of the audience. To be successful, marketing communications should be grounded in the behaviour and information-processing needs and style of the target audience. This is referred to as 'understanding the context in which the communications event is to occur' (Chapters 5, 6 and 12). From this base it is easier to present and position brands in order that they are perceived to be different and of value to the target audience.

The third theme from the definition concerns the *response*. This refers to the outcomes of the communication process, and can be used as a measure of whether a communication event has been successful. There are essentially two key responses, cognitive and emotional. Cognitive responses assume an audience to be active problem-solvers and that they use marketing communications to help them in their lives, in purchasing products and services and in managing organisation-related activities. For example, brands are developed partly to help consumers and partly to assist the marketing effort of the host organisation. A brand can inform consumers quickly that, among other things, 'this brand means *x* quality' so, through experience of similar brand purchases, consumers are assured that their risk is minimised. If the problem facing a consumer is 'which new soup to select for lunch', by choosing one from a familiar family brand the consumer is able to solve it with minimal risk and great speed. Cognitive responses assume audiences undertake rational information processing.

Emotional responses, on the other hand, assume decision-making is not made through active thought processing but as a result of emotional reaction to a communication stimulus. Hedonic consumption concerns the purchase and use of products and services to fulfil fantasies and to satisfy emotional needs. Satisfaction is based on the overall experience of consuming a product. For example, sports cars and motorbikes are not always bought because of the functionality and performance of the vehicle, but more due to the thrill of independence, power and a feeling of being both carefree and in danger. Marketing communications and content, in particular, should be developed in anticipation of an audience's cognitive or emotional response.

Marketing communications, therefore, can be considered from a number of perspectives. It is a complex activity and is used by organisations with varying degrees of sophistication and success. However, it is now possible to clarify both the roles and the tasks of marketing communications. The role of marketing communications is to engage audiences and the tasks are to differentiate, reinforce, inform or persuade audiences to think, feel or behave in particular ways.

---

## Scholars' paper 1.3    Consumerism and ethics in IMC

**Kliatchko, J.G. (2009) The primacy of the consumer in IMC: Espousing a personalist view and ethical implications, *Journal of Marketing Communications*, 15(2–3), April–July, 157–77.**

Having established that marketing communications should be audience-centred, this paper by Kliatchko provides an interesting view of some of the issues about the portrayal of consumers in marketing communications, as reflected in previous studies. His focus is integrated marketing communications (Chapter 10) and concludes that consumers have invariably been treated as 'mere subjects for financial gain at any cost above all other considerations'. This paper should be read in conjunction with Richard Christy's chapter on Ethics in Marketing Communications, which can be found on the website supporting this book.

# Environmental influences

The management of marketing communications is a complex and highly uncertain activity. This is due in part to the nature of the marketing communication variables, including the influence of the environment. The environment can be considered in many different ways, but for the purposes of this opening chapter, three categories are considered: the internal, external and market environments. The constituents of each of these are set out in Figure 1.4.

## Internal influences

The internal environment refers primarily to the organisation and the way it works, what its values are and how it wants to develop. Here various forces seek to influence an organisation's marketing communications. The overall strategy that an organisation adopts should have a huge impact. For example, how the organisation wishes to differentiate itself within its target markets will influence the messages and media used and, of course, the overarching positioning and reputation of the company. Brand strategies will influence such things as the way in which brands are named, the extent to which sales promotions are an integral part of the communication mix and how they are positioned. The prevailing organisational culture can also be extremely influential. For a long time the hierarchical management structure and power culture at Procter and Gamble led to the establishment of a pattern of behaviour whereby the marketing communication messages were largely product-benefit-orientated rather than emotionally driven, as at their arch rivals Unilever.

The amount of money available to the marketing communication budget will influence the media mix or the size of the sales force used to deliver messages. Apart from the quality and motivation of the people employed, the level of preferences and marketing skills deployed can impact on the form of the messages, the choice of media, and the use of agencies and support services. Finally, the socio-political climate of the firm shapes not only who climbs the career ladder fastest, but how and to which brands scarce marketing resources are distributed.

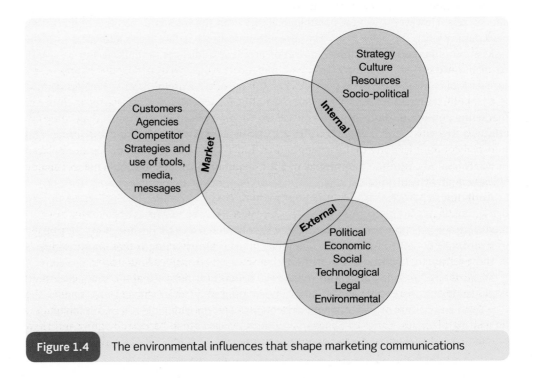

**Figure 1.4**    The environmental influences that shape marketing communications

Marketing communications is regarded as one of the elements of the marketing mix and is primarily responsible for the communication of the marketing offer and the brand promise, sometimes referred to as the *brand proposition*. Although recognising that there is implicit and important communication through the other elements of the marketing mix (through a high price, for example, symbolic of high quality), it is the task of a planned and integrated set of communication activities to communicate effectively with each of an organisation's stakeholder groups.

Marketing communications is sometimes perceived as only dealing with communications that are external to the organisation. It should be recognised that good communications with internal stakeholders, such as employees, are also vital if, in the long term, favourable images, perceptions and attitudes are to be established successfully. Influences through the workforce and the marketing plan can be both positive and effective. For example, staff used in B&Q and Halifax advertising are intended to project internal values that should reflect positively upon the respective brands.

## Market influences

Market influences are characterised by partial levels of control and typified by the impact of competitors. Competitors occupy particular positions in the market and this shapes what others claim about their own products, the media they use, the geographic coverage of the sales force and their own positioning. Intermediaries influence the nature of business-to-business marketing communications. The frequency, intensity, quality and overall willingness to share information with one another are significant forces. Of course, the various agencies an organisation uses can also be very influential. Marketing research agencies (inform about market perception, attitudes, and behaviour, communication agencies (determine what is said and then design how it is said, what is communicated) and media houses (recommend media mixes and when it is said) all have considerable potential to influence marketing communications.

However, perhaps the biggest single market group consists of the organisation's customers and network of stakeholders. Their attitudes, perceptions and buying preferences and behaviours, although not directly controllable, (should) have a far-reaching influence on the marketing communications used by an organisation.

## External influences

As mentioned earlier, the external group of influencers are characterised by the organisation's near-lack of control. The well known PESTLE framework is a useful way of considering these forces. Political forces, which can encompass both legal and ethical issues, shape their use of marketing communication through legislation, voluntary controls and individual company attitudes towards issues of right and wrong, consequences and duties and the formal and informal communications an organisation uses. Indeed, increasing attention has been placed upon ethics and corporate responsibility to the extent that in some cases a name and shame culture might be identified.

Economic forces, which include demographics, geographics and geodemographics, can determine the positioning of brands in terms of perceived value. For example, if the government raises interest rates, then consumers are more inclined not to spend money, especially on non-staple products and services. This may mean that marketing communications needs to convey stronger messages about value and to send out strident calls-to-action.

Social forces are concerned with the values, beliefs and norms that a society enshrines. Issues to do with core values within a society are often difficult to change. For example, the American gun culture or the once-prevalent me-orientation with respect to self-fulfilment set up a string of values that marketing communications can use to harness, magnify and align brands. The current social pressures with regard to obesity and healthier eating habits have forced fast-food companies such as McDonald's to introduce new menus and healthier food options. As a result, marketing communications not only has to inform and make audiences aware of the new menus but also convey messages about differentiation and positioning plus provide a reason to visit the restaurant.

Technological forces have had an immense impact on marketing communications. New technology has revolutionised traditional forms of marketing communications and led to more personalised, targeted, customised and responsive forms of communication. What was once predominantly one-way communications based upon a model of information provision and persuasion, has given way to a two-way model in which integration with audiences and where sharing and reasoning behaviours are enabled by digital technology, is now used frequently with appropriate target audiences.

Legal forces may prevail in terms of trademarks and copyrights, while environmental forces might impact in terms of what can be claimed and associated credibility and social responsibility issues.

New forms of marketing communications have been developed in response to changing environmental conditions. For example, public relations are now seen by some to have both a marketing and corporate dimension. Direct marketing is now recognised as an important way of developing relationships with buyers, both consumer and organisational, while new and innovative forms of communication through sponsorship, floor advertising, video screens on supermarket trolleys and checkout coupon dispensers, plus Internet and associated technologies, mean that effective communication requires the selection and integration of an increasing variety of communication tools and media.

# The marketing communications mix

In the past decade there have been some major changes in the communications environment and in the way organisations communicate with their target audiences. Digital technology has given rise to a raft of different media at the same time as people have developed a variety of ways to spend their leisure time. These phenomena are referred to as *media* and *audience fragmentation* respectively, and organisations have developed fresh combinations of the communications mix in order to reach their audiences effectively. For example, there has been a dramatic rise in the use of direct-response media as direct marketing has become a key part of many campaigns. The Internet and digital technologies have enabled new interactive forms of communication, where the receiver has greater responsibility for their part in the communication process. An increasing number of organisations are using public relations to communicate messages about the organisation (corporate public relations) and also messages about their brands (marketing public relations).

Successful marketing communications involves managing various elements according to the needs of the target audience and the goals the campaign seeks to achieve. The elements that made up the traditional marketing communication mix were tools (or disciplines), advertising, sales promotions, public relations, direct marketing and personal selling. These were mixed together in various combinations and different degrees of intensity in order to attempt to communicate meaningfully with a target audience.

This mix was used at a time when brands were developed through the use of advertising to generate 'above-the-line' mass communication campaigns. The strategy was based around buying space in newspapers and magazines, or advertising time (called spots) in major television programmes that were watched by huge audiences (20+ million people). This strategy required media owners to create programmes (content) that would attract brand owners because

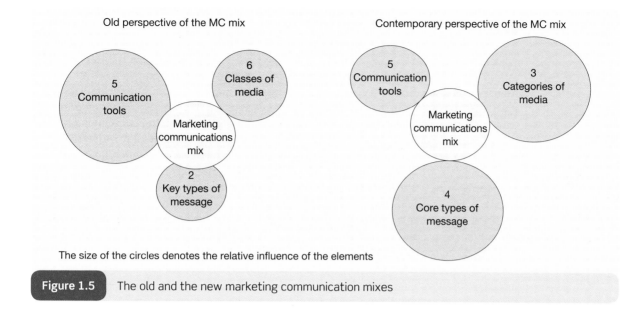

The size of the circles denotes the relative influence of the elements

**Figure 1.5**    The old and the new marketing communication mixes

of the huge, relatively passive, audiences. By interrupting the audience's entertainment, brand owners could talk to (or at) their markets in order to sell their brands.

However, since the days of just two commercial television stations there has been a proliferation of media. Although the use of television is actually increasing, audiences no longer use the television as their main form of information or entertainment. When considered together with falling newspaper and magazine readership, it is clear that consumers are using media for a variety of purposes. These include a need to explore and discover new activities, people, experiences and brands, to participate in events and communities, to share experiences and information, and to express themselves as individuals.

This reveals that people require active engagement with media. We now have a huge choice of media and leisure activities, and we decide how and when to consume information and entertainment. Consumers are now motivated and able to develop their own content, be it through text, music or video, and consider topics that they can share with friends on virtual networks. Thus, media and messages are the key to reaching consumers today, not the tools. More direct and highly targeted, personalised communication activities using direct marketing and the other tools of the mix now predominate. This evidence indicates that, in order to reach audiences successfully, it is necessary to combine not just the tools, but also the media and the content and messages. A new marketing communication mix emerges, as depicted at Figure 1.5.

So, in addition to the five principal marketing communications tools, it is necessary to add the media, or the means by which advertising and other marketing communications messages are conveyed. Tools and media should not be confused as they have different characteristics and seek to achieve different goals. Also, just in case you were thinking something is missing, the Internet is a medium, not a tool.

To complete the trilogy, messages need to be conveyed to the target audience. Four forms of content can be identified: informational messages, emotional messages, user-generated content and branded content. Once organisations were primarily responsible for the content of messages, whereas today an increasing number of messages are developed by consumers, and shared with other consumers.

The new mix represents a shift in approach. The old or conventional format represents an *intervention*-based approach to marketing communications, one based on seeking the attention of a customer who might not necessarily be interested, by interrupting their activities. The shift is towards *conversation*-based marketing communications, where the focus is on communications with and between members of an audience who may have contributed content to the campaign. This has a particular impact on direct marketing, interactive communications and, to some extent, personal selling.

## Advertising

Advertising is largely a non-personal form of paid-for mass communication that offers a high degree of control for those responsible for the design and delivery of advertising messages. However, the ability of advertising to persuade the target audience to behave in a particular way is suspect. Furthermore, the effect on sales is extremely hard to measure. Advertising also suffers from low credibility in that audiences are less likely to believe messages delivered through advertising than they are messages received through some other tools and word-of-mouth communication.

The flexibility of this tool is good because it can be used to communicate with a national audience or a particular specialised segment. Although the costs can be extremely high, a vast number of people can be reached with a message, so the cost per contact can be the lowest of all the tools in the mix. Advertising is explored in Chapter 14.

## Sales promotion

Sales promotion comprises various marketing techniques, which are often used tactically to provide added value to an offering. The aim is to accelerate sales and gather marketing information. Like advertising, sales promotion is a non-personal form of communication but has a greater capacity to target smaller audiences. It is controllable and, although it has to be paid for, the associated costs can be much lower than those of advertising. As a generalisation, credibility is not very high, as the sponsor's goals are easily identifiable. However, the ability to add value and to bring forward future sales is strong and complements a macroeconomic need, which focuses on short-term financial performance. Sales promotion techniques and approaches are the subject of Chapter 18.

## Personal selling

Personal selling is traditionally perceived as an interpersonal communication tool that involves face-to-face activities undertaken by individuals, often representing an organisation, in order to inform, persuade or remind an individual or group to take appropriate action, as required by the sponsor's representative. A salesperson engages in communication on a one-to-one basis where instantaneous feedback is possible. The costs associated with interpersonal communication are normally very high.

This discipline, considered in Chapter 17, differs from the previous two in that, while still lacking in relative credibility and control, the degree of control is potentially lower, because the salesperson is free at the point of contact to deliver a message other than that intended (Lloyd, 1997). Indeed, many different messages can be delivered by a single salesperson. Some of these messages may enhance the prospect of the salesperson's objectives being reached (making the sale), or they may retard the process and so incur more time and hence costs. Whichever way it is viewed, control is lower than with advertising.

## Public relations

Public relations is concerned with establishing and maintaining relationships with various stakeholders and with enhancing the reputation of the organisation. This indicates that public relations should be a part of the wider perspective of corporate strategy. The increasing use of public relations, and in particular publicity, is a reflection of the high credibility attached to messages conveyed through this form of communication.

Publicity involves the dissemination of messages through third-party media, such as magazines, newspapers or news programmes. There is no charge for the media space or time but there are costs incurred in the production of the material. There is a wide range of other tools used by public relations, such as event management, public affairs, sponsorship and lobbying. It is difficult to control a message once it is placed in the media channels, but the endorsement offered by a third party can be very influential and have a far greater impact on the target audience than any of the other tools in the marketing communications mix.

This non-personal form of communication offers organisations a different way to communicate, not only with consumers but also with many other stakeholders.

## Direct marketing

The four elements of the communications mix discussed so far have a number of strengths and weaknesses. As a response to some of the weaknesses that revolve around costs and effectiveness, direct marketing emerged in the 1990s as a new and effective way of building relationships with customers over the long term.

Direct marketing represents a shift in focus from mass to personalised communications. In particular, the use of direct mail, telemarketing and the fast-developing area of interactive marketing communications, represents 'through-the-line' communications. By removing the face-to-face aspect of personal selling and replacing it with an email communication, a telephone conversation or a direct mail letter, many facets of the traditional salespersons' tasks can be removed, freeing them to concentrate on their key skill areas.

Direct marketing seeks to target individual customers with the intention of delivering personalised messages and building a relationship with them based on their responses to the direct communications. In contrast to conventional approaches, direct marketing attempts to build a one-to-one relationship, a partnership with each customer, by communicating with the customers on a direct and personal basis. If an organisation chooses to use direct marketing, it has to incorporate the approach within a marketing plan. This is because distribution is different and changes in the competitive environment may mean that prices need to change. For example, charges for packing and delivery need to be incorporated. The product may also need to be altered or adapted to the market. For example, some electrical products are marketed through different countries on home shopping channels and websites. The electrical requirements of each country or region need to be incorporated within the product specification of each country's offering. In addition to these changes, the promotion component is also different, simply because communication is required directly with each targeted individual. To do this, direct-response media must be used.

In many cases, direct-response media are a derivative of advertising, such as direct mail, magazine inserts and television and print advertisements that use telephone numbers and Web addresses to encourage a direct response. However, direct response can also be incorporated within personal selling through telemarketing and sales promotions with competitions to build market knowledge and develop the database, which is the key to the direct marketing approach.

This text regards direct marketing as a management process associated with building mutually satisfying customer relationships through personal and intermediary-free interaction and dialogue. Direct-response media are the primary communication tools when direct marketing is an integral part of the marketing plan.

The Internet is both a distribution channel and communication medium, one that enables consumers and organisations to communicate in radically different ways. It allows for interactivity and is possibly the best medium to enable dialogue. Communication is two-way, often interactive, and very fast, allowing businesses and individuals to find information and enter exchange transactions in such a way that some traditional communication practices and shopping patterns are being reconfigured.

## Viewpoint 1.3    Brand builders in the home

Paint brands such as Crown and Dulux are not newcomers to a marketing communications strategy based on emotional benefits. Since 77 per cent of consumers say they feel better when they decorate, Dulux try to connect with this, using an emotional approach to their communications.

However, for a large proportion of brands in the home improvement sector this approach is unusual. The primary approach has been to place undue emphasis on advertising, direct marketing and sales promotion to offer low prices, discounts and 'buy me now' offers. This behavioural approach is now giving way to advertising designed to build a brand through emotionally led messages.

For example, the furniture retailer DFS has used a formulaic approach of functionally driven advertising, conveyed through the use of minor celebrities sitting on sofas, urging viewers to get to the sale to take advantage of the low prices and extended credit facilities. However, this has changed as a more emotionally led campaign has evolved. Now, instead of prices, comfort is stressed, as children are seen playing on sofas and a slogan that says 'Making everyday more comfortable', using an updated, heart-shaped logo, appeals to the mind rather than the wallet or credit card.

In a similar way, bedroom-furniture retailers Dreams and Harvey's have released more emotional campaigns. Harvey's used to use their communications to push several – as many as ten – products in an ad. This is now seen as too masculine, since the decision-makers are more often than not women, who are getting more involved in home improvements anyway. One of their changes has been to develop a mobile app that lets users 'test-drive' sofas in their own homes. Dreams show people switching off their lights to go to sleep, accompanied by soothing music.

Why the change, especially in times of recession when typically price-based brands lead the way? There are several reasons put forward. First, research by Mintel reveals that over 40 per cent of consumers express more trust in retailers such as John Lewis and IKEA, who use an emotional approach. Unfortunately, less than 20 per cent of consumers trust price-focused brands. More women are getting involved in home improvements and the success of the pre-Christmas 2011 John Lewis campaigns is felt to have prompted a review of brand development . . . in home and in marketing communications.

*Source*:   Based on Brownsell (2012).

> **Question:**   To what extent have informational messages a role to play in the DIY market communications?
>
> **Task:**      List the different types of key message a furniture retailer might use.

(a)

(b)

**Exhibit 1.3**    **(a) is a traditional DFS ad where price, functionality and style are predominant**
**(b) represents a more emotional approach to advertising. Gone are the prices, in are the fun, the comfort and the joy of living with DFS furniture**
*Source*: Blue Rubicon Ltd

# The key characteristics of the communication tools

Each of the tools of the communication mix performs a different role and can accomplish different tasks. This reflects their different capabilities, their various attributes and key characteristics. These are the extent to which each of the tools is controllable, whether it is paid for by the sponsor and whether communication is through mass media or undertaken personally. One additional characteristic concerns the receiver's perception of the credibility of the source of the message. If the credibility factor is high, then there is a greater likelihood that a message from that source will be accepted by receivers.

The 4Cs framework set out in Table 1.3 depicts the key characteristics and shows the relative effectiveness of the communication tools across a number of different characteristics. These are the ability of each to communicate, the credibility they bestow on messages, the costs involved and the control that each tool can maintain.

**Table 1.3**  The 4Cs framework – a summary of the key characteristics of the tools of marketing communications

|  | Advertising | Sales promotion | Public relations | Personal selling | Direct marketing |
|---|---|---|---|---|---|
| **Communications** | | | | | |
| Ability to deliver a personal message | Low | Low | Low | High | High |
| Ability to reach a large audience | High | Medium | Medium | Low | Medium |
| Level of interaction | Low | Medium | Low | High | High |
| **Credibility** | | | | | |
| Given by the target audience | Low | Medium | High | Medium | Medium |
| **Costs** | | | | | |
| Absolute costs | High | Medium | Low | High | Medium |
| Cost per contact | Low | Medium | Low | High | High |
| Wastage | High | Medium | High | Low | Low |
| Size of investment | High | Medium | Low | High | Medium |
| **Control** | | | | | |
| Ability to target particular audiences | Medium | High | Low | Medium | High |
| Management's ability to adjust the deployment of the tool as circumstances change | Medium | High | Low | Medium | High |

# Media and the MCs mix

There is a huge and expanding variety of media used to convey messages to target audiences. For ease of understanding it is helpful to categorise these into six main classes. These consist of broadcast, print, outdoor, digital, in-store and other media classes. Of these the digital class is growing the most and is the most influential. These classes can be broken down into types and vehicles, all of which are explored in greater detail later (in Chapter 20).

An alternative way of classifying the media from a usage perspective is known as POEM. The P stands for paid for media: that is, time or space that has to be rented in a media vehicle, the traditional view. O stands for owned media. These are represented by the use of an organisation's own assets to convey messages to audiences – for example, a name or product display on a building, a sign on a vehicle or use of the website. E stands for earned: that is, comments and conversations in social media, in the news or through face-to-face communications. The POEM approach is considered in more detail later in the text (Chapters 20 and 24).

# Key differences between conventional and digital media

There is a trend to move communication-related resources from conventional media to digital media. Each of these classes has particular characteristics that make the decision to use particular combinations of media, referred to as the 'media mix', a complex and challenging marketing decision.

A comparison of conventional and digital media provides an interesting insight into the capabilities of the two main forms of media. These are set out in Table 1.4. Space (or time) within conventional media is limited and costs rise as demand for the limited space/time increases. Internet space is unlimited, so absolute costs remain very low and static, while relative costs plummet as more visitors are recorded as having been to a site. Another aspect concerns the focus of the advertising message. Traditionally, advertisers tend to emphasise the emotional rather than information aspect, particularly within low-involvement categories. Digital media allow focus on the provision of information, so that the emotional aspect of advertising messages tends to have a lower significance. As branding becomes a more important aspect of Internet activity, it is probable that there will be a greater use of emotions, especially when the goal is to keep people at a website, rather than driving them to it.

Apart from the obvious factor that digital media, and the Internet in particular, provide interactive opportunities that traditional media cannot provide, it is important to remember that opportunities-to-see are generally driven by customers rather than by the advertiser

| Table 1.4 | Comparison of conventional and digital media |
| --- | --- |
| **Conventional media** | **Digital media** |
| One-to-many | One-to-one and many-to-many |
| Greater monologue | Greater dialogue |
| Active provision | Passive provision |
| Mass marketing | Individualised marketing |
| General need | Personalised |
| Branding | Information |
| Segmentation | Communities |

who interrupts viewing or reading activities. People drive the interaction at a speed that is convenient to them; they are not driven by others.

Management control over some Internet-based marketing communications is relatively high, as not only are there greater opportunities to control the position and placement of advertisements, promotions and press releases, but it is also possible to change the content of these activities much more quickly than is possible with traditional media. The goals outlined above indicate the framework within which advertising needs to be managed.

# Messages and the MCs mix

Brand-related messages have two main sources. One is the organisation itself in terms of how it chooses to present its organisation or brand, a planned aspect of marketing communications. What organisations say and how they say it needs careful consideration. The other source involves audiences and the brand messages that customers create and communicate, both positive and negative. These messages may be directed to the brand or shared with one another. In an age of interaction, individual consumers can create and share content with others, and these are largely unstructured and unplanned communications.

What is common to both the planned and unplanned messages is that they both contain two elements, information and emotion. Ensuring that the right balance of information and emotions is achieved and that the presentation of the message is appropriate for the target audience represents a critical part of the planned communication process for agencies, clients and individuals.

Messages should reflect a balance between the need for information and the need for pleasure or enjoyment in consuming the message. Messages can be product-oriented and rational or customer-oriented and based on feelings and emotions. All messages contain information and emotional content; it is the balance between the two that needs to be managed according to the task and context.

Messages where there is high involvement require an emphasis on the information content, in particular the key attributes and the associated benefits. This style is often factual and product-oriented. Where there is low involvement, the message should contain a high proportion of emotional content and seek to develop brand values through imagery and associations. These issues are discussed in Chapter 26.

Messages should be developed that not only enable recipients to respond to the source but also encourage them to talk to others through conversation, offline or online. For example, when Toyota launched the up-rated Prius, social media was an important element of the campaign. Woods (2009) reports that use was made of organic search in order to increase visibility of information about the Prius, but in addition model previews, news stories, videos and other influential content was seeded across relevant websites, all in an attempt to provoke conversation about the brand.

In addition to considering the attributes of both traditional and digital media, it is also worth considering the content of the information that each is capable of delivering. These are set out in Table 1.5.

As mentioned earlier, digital media are superior at providing rational, product-based information, whereas traditional media are much better at conveying emotional brand values. The former have a dominant cognition orientation and the latter an emotional one. There are other differences, but the predominant message is that these types of media are, to a large extent, complementary, suggesting that they should be used together, not one independently of the other.

**Table 1.5** Comparison of content

| Websites/internet | Conventional media |
|---|---|
| Good at providing rational, product-based information | Better at conveying emotional brand values |
| More efficient as costs do not increase in proportion to the size of the target audience | Costs are related to usage |
| Better at prompting customer action | Less effective for calling to action except point-of-purchase and telemarketing |
| Effective for short-term, product-oriented brand action goals and long-term corporate identity objectives | Normally associated with building long-term values |
| Average at generating awareness and attention | Strong builders of awareness |
| Measures of effectiveness weak and/or in the process of development | Established methodologies, some misleading or superficial (mass media); direct marketing techniques are superior |
| Dominant orientation – cognition | Dominant orientation – emotion |

## Viewpoint 1.4    Coca-Cola seeks engagement

This chapter has introduced a range of topics and issues associated with marketing and communications. Now consider this news item about Coca-Cola and see how many of the topics introduced so far can be seen within this brand's intentions.

The soft drinks giant announced in 2010, through its Chief Marketing and Commercial Officer, Joseph Tripodi, that the company had established a 'philosophy of consumer engagement'.

Coca-Cola operates in 206 markets, and serves 1.6 billion (yes that is billion) servings each day. To deliver this and meet customer expectations, the company cannot operate as if there were 206 independent markets, each operating in its own discrete silo. Coca-Cola needs to be managed, considered and perceived to be an integrated business system, designed to connect people with brands.

Marketing communications needs to engage customers, from a prime time ad, right through to the store and beyond into consumption. The 'spray and pray' model of communication, Tripodi said, was gone and Coca-Cola now needs a precision marketing approach based on aligning content effectiveness with impact. This involves using 'emotionally driven consumer engagement points' . . . the Olympics, World Cup or even a film.

He said that Coca-Cola will continue to use paid media but acknowledges the need to increase its presence in owned and earned media. The role of digital media will increase significantly, and the 5.5 million Facebook fans are a testimony to the importance of earned comments and conversations around the brand. The company intends to use mobile much more and to combine this with a drive towards increased experience-based activities. Through sponsorship it brings these elements together to engage with teenagers, retain them in their twenties and build 'brand love.'

*Source*: Warc (2010); Matherne (2010).

**Question:** If Coca-Cola is concerned about its business system and networks, why restrict engagement to a consumer-only perspective?

**Task:** Make list of the main topics listed in this chapter and see how many are referred to in this short example.

# Criteria when selecting the tools for the mix

Using the key characteristics it is possible to determine the significant criteria organisations should consider when selecting communication tools. These are as follows:

- the degree of control required over the delivery of the message;
- the financial resources available to pay a third party to transmit messages;
- the level of credibility that each tool bestows on the organisation;
- the size and geographic dispersion of the target audiences;
- the communication tasks each tool is best at satisfying.

## Control

Control over the message, particularly in traditional mass media communication, is necessary to ensure that the intended message is transmitted to and received by the target audience. Furthermore, this message must be capable of being understood in order that the receiver can act appropriately. Message control is complicated by interference or negative 'noise' that can corrupt and distort messages. For example, the media spotlight shone brightly on Eurostar when a number of trains broke down in the Channel tunnel during the 2009 Christmas period. The disruption for thousands of passengers, many stranded for hours in the tunnel, generated negative media comments about the company. All advertising and campaign work was stopped immediately by Eurostar and only resumed six months later (Clark, 2010).

Advertising and sales promotions can allow for a high level of control over the message, from design to transmission. Interestingly, they afford only partial control or influence over the feedback associated with the original message.

Control can also be an important factor when considering online and digital-based communications. For example, the ability to place banner ads, to bid for sponsored links and determine keyword rankings in search engines requires control and deliberation. However, it should be noted that message control is an ambiguous term. Brand owners desire control over message placement and seeding but they also want people to talk about their brands. Here owners sacrifice control over what is said about a brand, who says it and in which context. Engagement is about provoking conversations and that implies that there is virtually no control over this aspect. Planned marketing communications carries a high level of control, while unplanned word-of-mouth conversations carry little control.

## Financial resources

Control is also a function of financial power. In other words, if an organisation is prepared to pay a third party to transmit the message, then long-term control will rest with the sponsor for as long as the financial leverage continues. However, short-term message corruption can exist if management control over the process is less than vigilant. For example, if the design of the message differs from that originally agreed, then partial control has already been lost. This can happen when the working relationship between an advertising agency and the client is less than efficient and the process for signing off work in progress fails to prevent the design and release of inappropriate creative work.

Advertising and sales promotion are tools that allow for a high level of control by the sponsor, whereas public relations, and publicity in particular, is weak in this aspect because the voluntary services of a third party are normally required for the message to be transmitted.

There is a great variety of media available to advertisers. Each media type (for example television, radio, newspapers, magazines, posters and the Internet) carries a particular cost, and the financial resources of the organisation may not be available to use particular types of media, even if such use would be appropriate on other grounds.

## Credibility

Public relations is highly credible because receivers perceive the third party as unbiased and endorsing the offering. They view the third party's comments as objective and trustworthy in the context of the media in which the comments appear.

At a broad level, advertising, sales promotion and, to a slightly lesser extent, personal selling are tools that can lack credibility, as perceived by a target audience. Because of this, organisations often use celebrities and 'experts' to endorse their offerings. The credibility of the spokesperson is intended to distract the receiver from the sponsor's prime objective, which is to sell the offering. Credibility, as we see shall later, is an important aspect of the communication process and of marketing communications.

## Dispersion – size and geography

The size and geographic dispersion of the target audience can be a significant influence on the choice of tools. A national consumer audience can only be reached effectively if tools of mass communication are used, such as advertising and sales promotion. Similarly, various specialist businesses require personal attention to explain, design, demonstrate, install and service complex equipment. In these circumstances personal selling – one-to-one contact – is of greater significance. The tools of marketing communications can enable an organisation to speak to vast national and international audiences through advertising and satellite technology, or to single persons or small groups through personal selling and the assistance of word-of-mouth recommendation.

## Communication tasks

Each communication tool has particular strengths, therefore the selected mix of tools should be based on a combination of tools designed to accomplish particular DRIP tasks. One of the reasons direct marketing has become so successful is that it delivers a call-to-action and is therefore a very good persuasive tool as well as being good at reinforcing messages. Advertising, on the other hand, is much better at differentiating offerings and informing audiences about key features and benefits.

| Table 1.6 | | Key selection criteria for the tools of the marketing communications mix | | | | |
|---|---|---|---|---|---|---|
| | | Advertising | Sales promotion | Public relations | Direct marketing | Personal selling |
| Level of control | | Medium | High | Low | High | Medium |
| Level of cost | | High | Medium | Low | Medium | High |
| Level of credibility | | Low | Medium | High | Medium | Medium |
| Level of dispersion | *High* | Low | Medium | High | High | Medium |
| | *Low* | Medium | High | High | Medium | High |
| Primary tasks | | Differentiating Informing | Persuading | Differentiating Informing | Persuading Reinforcing | Persuading |

*Source*: Baines et al. (2011) By permission of Oxford University Press.

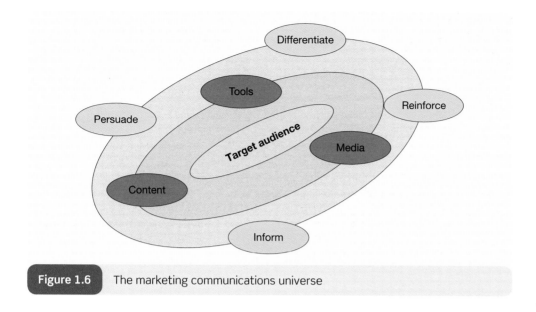

| Figure 1.6 | The marketing communications universe |

At this point it is worth consolidating our understanding about the role, the tasks and the marketing communications mix. The role is to engage audiences, the tasks are to DRIP and through the selection and deployment of the elements of the mix, organisations seek to engage audiences and achieve their goals (DRIP). Figure 1.6 portrays this visually.

# Communication differences

Having identified the need to communicate with a number of different audiences, it seems appropriate to conclude this opening chapter by examining the differences between communications used by and targeted at two very different and specific audiences. These are organisations (commonly referred to as 'business-to-business' markets) and consumer markets. Some writers (Brougaletta, 1985; Gilliland and Johnston, 1997) have documented a variety of differences between consumer and business-to-business markets. The following is intended to set out some of the more salient differences (see also Table 1.7).

## Message reception

The contextual conditions in which messages are received and ascribed meanings are very different. In the organisational setting the context is much more formal, and as the funding for the purchase is to be derived from company sources (as opposed to personal sources for consumer market purchases) there may be a lower orientation to the price as a significant variable in the purchase decision. The item is intended for company usage, whereas products bought in a consumer context are normally intended for personal consumption.

## Number of decision-makers

In consumer markets a single person very often makes the decision. In organisational markets decisions are made by many people within a buying centre. This means that the interactions of the participants should be considered. In addition, a variety of different individuals need

| **Table 1.7** | Differences between consumer and business-to-business marketing communications | |
| --- | --- | --- |
| | **Consumer-oriented markets** | **Business-to-business markets** |
| **Message reception** | Informal | Formal |
| **Number of decision-makers** | Single or few | Many |
| **Balance of the promotional mix** | Advertising and sales promotions dominate | Personal selling dominates |
| **Specificity and integration** | Broad use of communications mix with a move towards integrated mixes | Specificity use of below-the-line tools but with a high level of integration |
| **Message content** | Greater use of emotions and imagery | Greater use of rational, logic and information-based messages although there is evidence of a move towards the use of imagery |
| **Message origin** | Increasing use of user-generated-content | Limited use of user-generated materials |
| **Length of decision time** | Normally short | Longer and more involved |
| **Negative communications** | Limited to people close to the purchaser/user | Potentially an array of people in the organisation and beyond |
| **Target marketing and research** | Great use of sophisticated targeting and communication approaches | Limited but increasing use of targeting and segmentation approaches |
| **Budget allocation** | Majority of budget allocated to brand management | Majority of budget allocated to sales management |
| **Evaluation and measurement** | Great variety of techniques and approaches used | Limited number of techniques and approaches used |

to be reached and influenced and this may involve the use of different media and message strategies.

## The balance of the communications mix

The role of advertising and sales promotions in business-to-business communications is primarily to support the personal selling effort. This contrasts with the mix that predominates in consumer markets. Personal selling plays a relatively minor role and is only significant at the point of purchase in some product categories where involvement is high (cars, white goods and financial services), reflecting high levels of perceived risk. However, the increasing use of direct marketing in consumer markets suggests that personal communications are becoming more prevalent and in some ways increasingly similar to the overall direction of business-to-business communications.

## The constituent tools of the marketing communications mix

Business-to-business markets have traditionally been quite specific in terms of the tools and media used to target audiences. While the use of advertising literature is very important, there has been a tendency to use a greater proportion of 'below-the-line' activities. This compares with consumer markets, where a greater proportion of funds have been allocated to 'above-the-line' activities. It is interesting that the communications in the consumer market are moving towards a more integrated format, more similar in form to the business-to-business model than was previously considered appropriate.

## Message content

Generally, there is high involvement in many business-to-business purchase decisions, so communications tend to be much more rational and information-based than in consumer markets. However, there are signs that businesses are making increased use of imagery and emotions in the messages.

## Message origin

Increasingly, consumers are taking a more active role in the creation of content. Blogging for example, is important in both consumer and business markets, but the development of user-generated-content and word-of-mouth communication is becoming a significant part of consumer-based marketing communications activities.

## Length of purchase decision time

The length of time taken to reach a decision is much greater in the organisation market. This means that the intensity of any media plan can be dissipated more easily in the organisational market.

## Negative communications

The number of people affected by a dissatisfied consumer, and hence negative marketing communication messages, is limited. The implications of a poor purchase decision in an organisational environment may be far-reaching, including those associated with the use of the product, the career of participants close to the locus of the decision and, depending on the size and spread, perhaps the whole organisation.

## Target marketing and research

The use of target marketing processes in the consumer market is more advanced and sophisticated than in the organisational market. This impacts on the quality of the marketing communications used to reach the target audience. However, there is much evidence that the business-to-business market organisations are becoming increasingly aware and sophisticated in their approach to segmentation techniques and processes.

## Budget allocation

The sales department receives the bulk of the marketing budget in the organisation market and little is spent on research in comparison with the consumer market.

## Measurement and evaluation

The consumer market employs a variety of techniques to evaluate the effectiveness of communications. In the organisation market, sales volume, value, number of enquiries and market share are the predominant measures of effectiveness.

> ## Scholars' paper 1.4    Abandon island thinking
>
> **Gummesson, E. and Polese, F. (2009) B2B is not an island!** *Journal of Business & Industrial Marketing*, 24(5/6), 337–50.
>
> The reason for encouraging readers to see this paper is because it suggests that marketing should be considered not as just B2B or B2C, but as a joined-up part of the same marketing context and service system, one in which there is a coherent network of relationships. The authors stress the interdependency between B2B and B2C. The implications are that marketing planning should incorporate the relational patterns within a company's network and that systematic attention should be given to the customers' role in value creation and treating them as a resource and co-creator.

There can be no doubt that there are a number of major differences between consumer and organisational communications. These reflect the nature of the environments, the tasks involved and the overall need of the recipients for particular types of information. Information need, therefore, can be seen as a primary reason for the differences in the way communication mixes are configured. Advertising in organisational markets has to provide a greater level of information and is geared to generating leads that can be followed up with personal selling, which is traditionally the primary tool in the promotional mix. In consumer markets, advertising used to play the primary role with support from the other tools of the promotional mix. This is not always true today as organisations use other tools such as public relations, combined with digital media, to reach particular audiences. Interestingly, digital media are helping to reconfigure the marketing communications mix and perhaps reduce the gulf and distinction between the mix used in business-to-business and consumer markets. Throughout this book, reference will be made to the characteristics, concepts and processes associated with marketing communications in each of these two main sectors.

# Key points

- There are two broad types of exchange and they can be considered to sit at either end of a spectrum of exchange transactions. At one end are discrete or market exchanges which are characterised as one-off exchanges in which price and product are central elements. At the other end are relational or collaborative exchanges where there has been a stream of transactions and the relationship is the central element.

- Relationships become stronger as the frequency of exchanges increases. As exchanges become more frequent, the intensity of the relationship strengthens so that the focus is no longer on the product or price within the exchange but on the relationship itself.

- The scope of marketing communications embraces an audience-centred perspective of planned, unplanned, product and service experiences. The role of marketing communications is to engage audiences with a view to provoking relevant conversations. The tasks of marketing communications are based within a need to differentiate, reinforce, inform and persuade audiences to think and behave in particular ways.

- Engagement is a function of two elements. The first is the degree to which a message encourages thinking and feeling about a brand: the development of brand values. The second is about the degree to which a message stimulates behaviour or action. Engagement may last a second, a minute, an hour, a day or even longer.

● Definitions have evolved as communications have developed. Here marketing communications is defined as:

> *a process through which organisations and audiences engage with one another. Through an understanding of an audience's preferred communication environments, participants seek to develop and present messages, before evaluating and acting upon any responses. By conveying messages that are of significant value, participants are encouraged to offer attitudinal, emotional and behavioural responses.*

● The internal, market and external environments all influence the use of marketing communications. The internal environment refers to employees, the culture, the financial resources and the marketing skills available to organisations. The market environment refers principally to the actions of competitors and the perceptions and attitudes held by customers towards an organisation or its brands.

● The external environment can be considered in terms of the PEST framework. The influence of any one of these elements on marketing communications can be significant, although the impact is usually generic and affects all organisations rather than any single brand or organisation.

● The marketing communication mix consists of various tools, media and messages that are used to reach, engage and provoke audience-centred conversations. The five tools, six classes of media and two broad types of message can be configured in different ways to meet the needs of the target audience.

● The way in which the marketing communication mix is configured for consumer markets is very different from the mix used for business markets. The tools, media and messages used are all different as the general contexts in which they operate require different approaches. Business markets favour personal selling – consumer markets, advertising. Both make increasing use of digital media, and while rational messages are predominant in business markets, emotion-based messages tend to prevail in consumer markets.

# Review questions

1. Briefly compare and contrast the two main types of exchange transaction. How does communication assist the exchange process?

2. What is the role of marketing communications? Identify the key tasks that it is required to undertake. What is the role of marketing communications at LV=?

3. Define marketing communications. What are the key elements in the definition?

4. Name the three main elements that make up the marketing communications mix.

5. How does the external environment influence an organisation's marketing communications?

6. How might public relations contribute to a marketing communications programme?

7. How do each of the tools compare across the following criteria: control, communication effectiveness and cost?

8. What does POEM stands for?

9. How does the content delivered through traditional media differ from that delivered through digital media?

10. Explain how marketing communications supports the marketing and business strategies of the organisation.

# References

Andersson, P. (1992) Analysing distribution channel dynamics, *European Journal of Marketing*, 26(2), 47–68.

Bagozzi, R. (1978) Marketing as exchange: a theory of transactions in the market place, *American Behavioral Science*, 21(4), 257–61.

Baines, P., Fill, C. and Page, K. (2011) *Marketing*, 2e, Oxford: Oxford University Press.

Ballantyne, D. (2004) Dialogue and its role in the development of relationship specific knowledge, *Journal of Business and Industrial Marketing*, 19, 2, 114–23.

Balmer, J.M.T. and Gray, E.R. (2003) Corporate brands: what are they? What of them? *European Journal of Marketing*, 37(7/8), 972–97.

Bates, D. (2010) Hello, ladies: He's back! Old Spice man's latest ad becomes new internet sensation . . . and he's more manly than ever, 16 July 2010, retrieved 16 September 2011 from http://anewkindofmarketing.utalkmarketing.com/why-old-spice%E2%80%99s-viral-campaign-is-utter-brilliance/.

Bowersox, D. and Morash, E. (1989) The integration of marketing flows in channels of distribution. *European Journal of Marketing*, 23(2), 58–67.

Brougaletta, Y. (1985) What business-to-business advertisers can learn from consumer advertisers, *Journal of Advertising Research*, 25(3), 8–9.

Brownsell, A. (2110a) LV= flags mutual status with primetime activity, *Marketing*, 31 March, p. 9.

Brownsell, A. (2010b) Keeping Virgin firmly on track, *Marketing*, 10 February, 22–3.

Brownsell, A. (2012) Brand-building comes home, *Marketing*, 21 March, 14–15.

Clark, N. (2010) Eurostar plots mag to boost customer loyalty, *Marketing*, 17 February, p. 4.

Duncan T.R. and Moriarty, S. (1997) *Driving Brand Value*, New York: McGraw Hill.

Dwyer, R., Schurr, P. and Oh, S. (1987) Developing buyer–seller relationships, *Journal of Marketing*, 51 (April), 11–27.

Eleftheriou-Smith, L.-M. (2012) TUI Travel marketing director Jeremy Ellis on keeping clear of troubled rivals, *Marketing*, 23 February, retrieved 27 March from: http://www.brandrepublic.com/features/1118064/TUI-Travel-marketing-director-Jeremy-Ellis-keeping-clear-troubled-rivals/?DCMP=ILC-SEARCH.

Fill, C. (2002) *Marketing Communications*, 3rd edn, Harlow: Financial Times Prentice Hall.

Gilliland, D.I. and Johnston, W.J. (1997) Toward a model of business-to-business marketing communications effects, *Industrial Marketing Management*, 26, 15–29.

Gronroos, C. (2004) The relationship marketing process: communication, interaction, dialogue, value, *Journal of Business and Industrial Marketing*, 19(2), 99–113.

Gummesson, E. and Polese, F. (2009) B2B is not an island! *Journal of Business & Industrial Marketing*, 24(5/6), 337–50.

Heinonen, K. and Strandvik, T. (2005) Communication as a element of service value, *International Journal of Service Industry Management*, 16(2), 186–98.

Houston, F. and Gassenheimer, J. (1987) Marketing and exchange, *Journal of Marketing*, 51 (October), 13–18.

Hughes, G. and Fill, C. (2007) Redefining the nature and format of the marketing communications mix, *The Marketing Review*, 7(1), 45–57.

Kliatchko, J.G. (2009) The primacy of the consumer in IMC: Espousing a personalist view and ethical implications, *Journal of Marketing Communications*, 15(2–3), April–July, 157–77.

Lloyd, J. (1997) Cut your rep free, *Pharmaceutical Marketing* (September), 30–2.

McCarthy, E.J. (1960) *Basic Marketing: A Managerial Approach*, Homewood, IL: Irwin.

Macneil, I.R. (1983) Values in Contract: internal and external, *Northwestern Law Review*, 78(2), 340–418.

Malvern, J. (2010) Web ads rescue Old Spice from the old man, *The Times*, Saturday 31 July, p. 33.

Matherne, R. (2010) Coca-Cola Wants You to Get Emotional, *Social Media News, Trends & Tips*, 25 May 2010, retrieved 5 April 2012 from http://sixestate.com/coca-cola-wants-you-to-get-emotional/.

Maymann, J. (2010) Viral View: Old Spice campaign smells great, *Campaign*, Friday, 16 July, retrieved 16 September 2011 from www.campaignlive.co.uk/news/1016750/Viral-View-Old-Spice-campaign-smells-great/?DCMP=ILC-SEARCH.

Mohr, J. and Nevin, J. (1990) Communication strategies in marketing channels, *Journal of Marketing*, 54 (October), 36–51.

Philips, R. and Cooper, J. (2008) PR Essays: Conversation with content, *Marketing*, 26 November, p. 15.

Ray, M.L. (1973) A Decision Sequence Analysis of Developments in Marketing Communication, *Journal of Marketing*, 37 (January), 29–38.

Shearman, S. (2010) FMCG brands increase online ad expenditure, *Marketing*, 46 October, p. 4.

UTalkMarketing (2010) Why Old Spice's viral campaign is utter brilliance, retrieved 25 April 2012 from http://anewkindofmarketing.utalkmarketing.com/why-old-spice%E2%80%99s-viral-campaign-is-utter-brilliance/.

Verhoef, P.C., Reinartz, W.J. and Krafft, M. (2010) Customer Engagement as a New Perspective in Customer Management, *Journal of Service Research*, 13(3), 247–52.

WARC (2010) Coca-Cola takes new approach to engagement, retrieved 17 May 2010 from http://www.warc.com/LatestNews/News/ArchiveNews.news?ID=26705.

Woods, A. (2009) Searching in social circles, *Marketing*, 2 December, pp. 39–41.

# Chapter 2
# Communication: forms and conversations

Communication is concerned with interpreting messages and sharing meaning. Only by using messages that reduce levels of ambiguity and which share meaning with audiences, can it be hoped to stimulate meaningful interaction and dialogue. To create and sustain valued conversations the support of significant others is often required. These may be people who are experts, those who share common interests, those who have relevant knowledge or people who have access to appropriate media channels.

## Aims and learning objectives

The aims of this chapter are to introduce communication theory and to set it in the context of marketing communications.

The learning objectives of this chapter are to:

1. understand the linear model of communication and appreciate how the various elements link together and contribute to successful communication;

2. examine the impact of the media and personal influences on the communication process;

3. demonstrate the characteristics of the influencer and interactional forms of communication;

4. explain the characteristics associated with opinion leaders, formers and followers;

5. examine the nature and characteristics associated with word-of-mouth communication;

6. appreciate ideas associated with relational and network forms of communication;

7. describe the processes of adoption and diffusion as related to marketing communications.

# Minicase

## Up your Viva

The TV station, MTV, is well known and reasonably well understood even by those who have never tuned in. Unfortunately, the same could not be said of The Music Factory (or TMF as it was abbreviated to), even amongst its core 16–24 demographic. TMF was MTV's free-to-air offering, and as such vital to its broader business success. Being on Freeview meant TMF dwarfed its more famous parent some tenfold in terms of sheer audience numbers, and therefore potential advertising revenue.

All of this represented a challenge to MTV. TMF was a brand viewers had no real affection for, or engagement with. The station lacked a clear personality, with no attitude or buzz in the way it talked to its youth audience. Compounding this, its programming offer was seen as confused (music videos during the day; US reality TV and sitcoms in the evening). As a result, TMF fell between two stools: pure-play music channels on the one hand and speciality youth stations, such as E4, BBC3 and ITV2, on the other. Moreover, the fact that much of TMF's non-music content was also available elsewhere, even on these direct competitor stations, stations that viewers did engage with, dramatised the significance of the challenge.

The issue was that TMF had become wallpaper for its viewers, and so was a station easy to defect from (as was increasingly happening). And these defections, combined with disengaged viewing amongst those still tuning in, was undermining the station's media value: big numbers alone have little appeal to advertisers if the people they are paying to reach aren't actively engaged.

To overcome this, Quiet Storm, MTV's appointed agency, decided that a clean break with the past was required. So the decision was taken to rename the station as Viva (borrowed from an MTV channel in Germany) and, in launching this 'new' property, to attempt to imbue it with a dynamic, more youthful visual identity and personality. There was also a desire to shift the station's perceptual centre of gravity from daytime and music to evening and entertainment.

The relaunch and repositioning would have to be achieved with a limited budget and few meaningful changes to the programming schedule itself. The danger was that the youth audience might see the relaunch simply as an exercise in smoke and mirrors, the kind of empty marketing spin that alienates them from brands. It was entirely possible, therefore, that in (re)launching Viva, we might actually exacerbate the negative situation and accelerate the business decline.

The solution lay in changing the viewing experience of that programming for our audience. Creatively, then, as well as cutting through the media clutter on a limited budget, we would need to engage our audience in a way that spoke their language and demonstrated an understanding of their lives. Or, to put it another way: our challenge was to establish Viva as 'their' station, a place they would actively chose to hang out: even if the same programmes were available elsewhere, watching on Viva should just feel 'right'.

This meant establishing 'Viva-ness' as something appealing in and of itself; an attitude, personality and visual identity lived out not just in advertising but on-air as well, with station idents, continuity and trailers having as much value and meaning to viewers as the programmes themselves.

One of the elements that unified the audience was an attitude to life. These were people who lived for the weekend, for the chance to kick back, chill out, get down, and basically escape the boring, mundane conformity of school, college or work, where their lives were constrained by the rules of others.

We wanted to celebrate the attitude of these sofa rebels and their two-fingers to the world, embracing with them the mindless and the dumb . . . and saying it's OK. As a term, 'viva' has always been a celebratory call to arms – 'viva la revolution', 'viva la vida' – and in tone we wanted to capture this same sense of 'long live . . .'. This was the 'Viva-ness' we needed to live out: *'long live doing what I want, when I want, how I want . . . and to have the most fun doing it'*. One of our touchstones for this was the toga party scene in *National Lampoon's Animal House*: the sense of *'let's just have a good time . . . and damn the consequences'*.

The cornerstone of the idea we developed was our own 'call to arms': taking up the cry of rebels and revolutionaries everywhere, we wanted to do the same for our brand . . . to shout 'Viva Viva!' Or in more colloquial terms . . . 'Up your Viva'.

The advertising had to engage a notoriously cynical, hard-to-please audience spoilt for content choice in the social media space that was their second home. Two goals emerged: one to make a big noise, and second, to generate conversations about the brand through earned media.

In the lead TV medium there was to be a celebration of the *spirit* of Viva, not its shows. Much as

| Exhibit 2.1 | **MTV's call to arms for the relaunched Viva brand** |
|---|---|
| | *Source*: MTV |

'toga toga' had been the rallying cry for the disenfranchised Delta Frat in *Animal House*, our idea would be brutally simple in execution and easily mimicable in its dramatisation of 'Up your Viva'

as something to shout out loud, and with pride. Reflecting the warts and all reality of the station, and the characters in its shows, Viva would celebrate hyper-normality. And taking inspiration from films like *Napoleon Dynamite*, normality at its strangest and most memorable . . . particularly when it came to our facially distinctive hero. See Exhibit 2.2.

With close to a million views on Youtube, and many 100s of remakes and mashups, a trending phrase on Twitter, and rapid, completely organic growth of a fanbase on Facebook, 'Up Your Viva' began to take on a life of its own in social media, within two months. All of which would have been meaningless, if not for the 33 per cent increase in viewers Viva enjoyed over the same period (compared to TMF), propelling it into the Freeview top 10, and making it the most watched music-related station (with a 25 per cent share).

*This case was written by Jon Howard of Quiet Storm. Permission to use the material was kindly given by MTV. A longer version can be found at the website supporting this book at www.pearson.com/ and at www.Fillassociates.co.uk/*

| Exhibit 2.2 | **The New Face of MTV** |
|---|---|
| | *Source*: MTV |

| Exhibit 2.3 | **Quiet Storm logo and MTV logo** |
|---|---|
| | *Source*: Quiet Storm and MTV |

# An introduction to the process of communication

It was established in the previous chapter that marketing communications is partly an attempt by an organisation/brand to create and sustain a dialogue with its various audiences. It is also important to encourage members of these audiences to talk amongst themselves about a brand. As communication is the process by which individuals share meaning, each participant in the communication process needs to be able to interpret the meaning embedded in the messages, and be able to respond in an appropriate way.

For MTV, presented in the mini case, understanding the nature and characteristics of the target audience was an important element of their successful campaign. Their campaign required that information was transmitted to, from and among key participants. It is important, therefore, that those involved with marketing communications understand the complexity of the process. Through knowledge and understanding of the communications process, participants are more likely to achieve their objective of sharing meaning with each member of their target audiences and so have an opportunity to enter into a dialogue.

In the previous chapter the point was established that there are a variety of reasons why organisations need to communicate with various groups. Of these, one of the more prominent is the need to influence or persuade. As an initial observation, persuasive communications can be seen in three different contexts. These are set out in Table 2.1.

These three perspectives focus upon the use of persuasion, but there is a strong need for organisations also to inform and remind. Furthermore, these approaches are too specific for general marketing purposes and fail to provide assistance to those who wish to plan and manage particular communication activities.

This chapter examines several models of forms of the communication process. It considers the characteristics associated with word-of-mouth communications and looks at the way products and ideas are adopted by individuals and markets.

**Table 2.1**   Forms of persuasion

| Form of persuasion | Explanation |
| --- | --- |
| Negotiation | Individuals use a variety of overt and subtle rewards and punishments to persuade the other of the superiority of their point of view. |
| Propaganda | Organisations seek to influence their target audiences through the use of symbols, training and cultural indoctrination. |
| Use of speakers | When a speaker addresses a large group, influence is achieved through the structure of the material presented, the manner in which the presentation is delivered and the form of evidence used. |

# A linear model of communication

Wilbur Schramm (1955) developed what is now accepted as the basic model of mass communications (Figure 2.1). The components of the linear model of communication are:

1. Source:      the individual or organisation sending the message.
2. Encoding:   transferring the intended message into a symbolic style that can be transmitted.

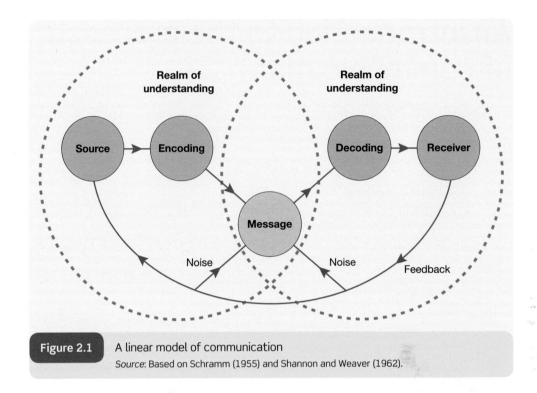

| Figure 2.1 | A linear model of communication |
|---|---|

*Source*: Based on Schramm (1955) and Shannon and Weaver (1962).

**3.** Signal:     the transmission of the message using particular media.

**4.** Decoding:   understanding the symbolic style of the message in order to understand the message.

**5.** Receiver:   the individual or organisation receiving the message.

**6.** Feedback:   the receiver's communication back to the source on receipt of the message.

**7.** Noise:      distortion of the communication process, making it difficult for the receiver to interpret the message as intended by the source.

This is a linear model that emphasises the 'transmission of information, ideas, attitudes, or emotion from one person or group to another (or others), primarily through symbols' (Theodorson and Theodorson, 1969). The model and its components are straightforward, but it is the quality of the linkages between the various elements in the process that determine whether a communication event will be successful.

## Source/encoding

The source, an individual or organisation, identifies a need to transmit a message and then selects a combination of appropriate words, pictures, symbols and music to represent the message to be transmitted. This is called 'encoding'. The purpose is to create a message that is capable of being understood by the receiver. Look at the 'Up your Viva' mini case at the beginning of this chapter to see how Viva encoded a message that would be understood by their audience.

There are a number of reasons why the source/encoding link might break down. For example, the source may fail to diagnose a particular situation accurately. By not fully understanding a stakeholder's problem or level of knowledge, inappropriate information may be included in the message, which, when transmitted, may lead to misunderstanding and misinterpretation by the receiver. By failing to appreciate the level of education of the target receiver, a message might be encoded in words and symbols that are beyond the comprehension of the receiver.

Some organisations spend a great deal of time and expense on marketing research, trying to develop their understanding of their target audience. The source of a message is an important factor in the communication process. A receiver who perceives a source lacking conviction, authority, trust or expertise is likely to discount any message received from that source, until such time as credibility is established.

Most organisations spend a great deal of time and expense recruiting sales representatives. The risk involved in selecting the wrong people can be extremely large. Many high-tech organisations require their new sales staff to spend over a year receiving both product and sales training before allowing them to meet customers. From a customer's perspective, salespersons who display strong product knowledge skills and who are also able to empathise with the individual members of the decision-making unit are more likely to be perceived as credible. Therefore, an organisation that prepares its sales staff and presents them as knowledgeable and trustworthy is more likely to be successful in the communication process than one that does not take the same level of care.

The source is a part of the communication process, not just the generator of detached messages. Patzer (1983) determined that the physical attractiveness of the communicator, particularly if they are the source, contributes significantly to the effectiveness of persuasive communications.

This observation can be related to the use, by organisations, of spokespersons and celebrities to endorse products. Spokespersons can be better facilitators of the communication process if they are able to convey conviction, if they are easily associated with the object of the message, if they have credible expertise and if they are attractive to the receiver, in the wider sense of the word.

This legitimate authority is developed in many television advertisements by the use of the 'white coat', or product-specific clothing, as a symbol of expertise. Dressing the spokesperson in a white coat means that they are immediately perceived as a credible source of information ('they know what they are talking about'), and so are much more likely to be believed.

## Signal

Once encoded, the message must be put into a form that is capable of transmission. It may be oral or written, verbal or non-verbal, in a symbolic form or in a sign. Whatever the format chosen, the source must be sure that what is being put into the message is what is required to be decoded by the receiver.

The channel is the means by which the message is transmitted from the source to the receiver. These channels may be personal or non-personal. The former involves face-to-face contact and word-of-mouth communications, which can be extremely influential. Non-personal channels are characterised by mass media advertising, which can reach large audiences.

Information received directly from personal influence channels is generally more persuasive than information received through mass media. This may be a statement of the obvious, but the reasons for this need to be understood. First, the individual approach permits greater flexibility in the delivery of the message. The timing and power with which a message is delivered can be adjusted to suit the immediate 'selling' environment. Second, a message can be adapted to meet the needs of the customer as the sales call progresses. This flexibility is not possible with mass media messages, as these have to be designed and produced well in advance of transmission and often without direct customer input.

| Viewpoint 2.1 | Encoding, spread the tasty way |
| --- | --- |

Marmite is a sticky, dark brown, yeast extract paste. It is used to spread on bread and toast, and is made from the by-products of brewing, the brewer's yeast that's been used to ferment sugars into alcohol. Not surprising then that Marmite has a strong, distinctive taste. The manufacturers believe the word Marmite is derived from the French word for casserole dish, a marmite (pronounced MAR-MEET). The original Marmite dish is still pictured on the front of the pot.

The nutritional and healthy qualities of Marmite were used in early campaigns positioning it as 'The growing up spread you never grow out of'. In the 1980s the brand was repositioned with television ads showing an army platoon chanting the slogan 'My mate, Marmite'. However, it was the 1990s when it was realised, or accepted, that Marmite attracts a lot of people who like the taste, but there are many who dislike it intensely, with very few in the middle. Out of this came the slogan, 'Marmite . . . love it or hate it'. This has formed a platform from which numerous 'love it' and 'hate it' campaigns have been developed. For example, a campaign in 2010 featured a mock election contested by The Love Party and The Hate Party, which encouraged people to vote on Facebook.

The Marmite website has two addresses – 'I Love Marmite' and 'I Hate Marmite' – which not only help people share their experiences of Marmite but also encourage conversations around the brand, even to the point that an 'I Hate Marmite' registration form was generated. It is from this insight into consumer behaviour and preferences that the Marmite message has been encoded and this in turn facilitates accurate decoding. Even the phrase 'Marmite effect' or 'Marmite reaction' has entered popular language to mean anything which provokes such strong and polarised feelings. http://en.wikipedia.org/wiki/Marmite – cite_note-23

*Source*: Edwards (2011); Farey-Jones (2010), Anon (2010); www.marmite.com.

**Question:** Is there any benefit to having a section of an audience who 'hate' your brand?

**Task:** Find two other brands where audiences are polarised around a love / hate attitude.

## Decoding/receiver

Decoding is the process of transforming and interpreting a message into thought. This process is influenced by the receiver's realm of understanding, which encompasses the experiences, perceptions, attitudes and values of both the source and the receiver. The more the receiver understands about the source and the greater their experience in decoding the source's messages, the more able the receiver will be to decode the message successfully.

## Feedback/response

The set of reactions a receiver has after seeing, hearing or reading the message is known as the *response*. These reactions may vary from the extreme of calling an enquiry telephone number, returning or downloading a coupon or even buying the product, to storing information in long-term memory for future use. Feedback is that part of the response that is sent back to the sender, and it is essential for successful communication. The need to understand not just whether the message has been received but also which message has been received is vital. For example, the receiver may have decoded the message incorrectly and a completely different set of responses may have been elicited. If a suitable feedback system is not in place then the source will be unaware that the communication has been unsuccessful and is liable to continue wasting resources. This represents inefficient and ineffective marketing communications.

---

### Scholars' paper 2.1        Mass communication – uncut

**Schramm, W. (1962) Mass Communication, *Annual Review of Psychology*, 1962, 13(1), 25–84.**

This is a seminal paper. Schramm explores mass communication and the various elements that influence or constitute the mass communication process. This paper provides an excellent insight into the theoretical development of the topic, at which point the linear model of communication was possibly at its highest point of popularity. You will be surprised at the range of elements considered by Schramm.

---

The evaluation of feedback is vital if effective communications are to be developed. Only through evaluation can the success of any communication be judged. Feedback through personal selling can be instantaneous, through overt means such as questioning, raising objections or signing an order form. Other means, such as the use of gestures and body language, are less overt, and the decoding of the feedback needs to be accurate if an appropriate response is to be given. For the advertiser, the process is much more vague and prone to misinterpretation and error.

Feedback through mass media channels is generally much more difficult to obtain, mainly because of the inherent time delay involved in the feedback process. There are some exceptions: namely, the overnight ratings provided by the Broadcasters' Audience Research Board to the television contractors, but as a rule feedback is normally delayed and not as fast. Some commentators argue that the only meaningful indicator of communication success is sales. However, there are many other influences that affect the level of sales, such as price, the effect of previous communications, the recommendations of opinion leaders or friends, poor competitor actions or any number of government or regulatory developments. Except in circumstances such as direct marketing, where immediate and direct feedback can be determined, organisations should use other methods to gauge the success of their communications activities – for example, the level and quality of customer inquiries, the number and frequency of store visits, the degree of attitude change and the ability to recognise or recall an advertisement. All of these represent feedback, but, as a rough distinction, the evaluation of feedback for mass communications is much more difficult than the evaluation of interpersonal communications.

## Noise

A complicating factor, which may influence the quality of the reception and the feedback, is noise. Noise, according to Mallen (1977), is 'the omission and distortion of information', and there will always be some noise present in all communications. Management's role is to ensure that levels of noise are kept to a minimum, wherever it is able to exert influence.

Noise occurs when a receiver is prevented from receiving all or part of a message in full. This may be because of either cognitive or physical factors. For example, a cognitive factor may be that the encoding of the message was inappropriate, thereby making it difficult for the receiver to decode the message. In this circumstance it is said that the realms of understanding of the source and the receiver were not matched. Another reason noise may enter the system is that the receiver may have been physically prevented from decoding the message accurately because the receiver was distracted. Examples of distraction are that the telephone rang, or someone in the room asked a question or coughed. A further reason could be that competing messages screened out the targeted message.

Some sales promotion practitioners are using the word 'noise' to refer to the ambience and publicity surrounding a particular sales promotion event. In other words, the word is being used as a positive, advantageous element in the communication process. This approach is not adopted in this text.

## Realms of understanding

The concept of the 'realm of understanding' was introduced earlier. It is an important element in the communication process because it is a recognition that successful communications are more likely to be achieved if the source and the receiver understand each other. This understanding concerns attitudes, perceptions, behaviour and experience: the values of both parties to the communication process. Therefore, effective communication is more likely when there is some common ground – a realm of understanding between the source and receiver.

Some organisations, especially those in the private sector, spend a huge amount of money researching their target markets and testing their advertisements to ensure that their messages can be decoded and understood. The more organisations understand their receivers, the more confident they become in constructing and transmitting messages to them. Repetition and learning are important elements in marketing communications. Learning is a function of knowledge and the more we know, the more likely we are to understand.

# Factors that influence the communication process

The linear, sequential interpretation of the communication process fails to accurately represent all forms of communication. It was developed at a time when broadcast media dominated commercial communication and can be argued to no longer provide an accurate representation of contemporary communication processes. Issues concerning media and audience fragmentation, the need to consider social and relational dimensions of communication and the impact of interactive communication have reduced the overall applicability of the linear model.

However, there are two particular influences on the communication process that need to be considered. First, the media used to convey information, and second, the influence of people on the communication process. These are considered in turn.

## The influence of the media

The dialogue that marketing communications seeks to generate with audiences is partially constrained by an inherent time delay based on the speed at which responses are generated by the participants in the communication process. Technological advances now allow participants to conduct marketing communication-based 'conversations' at electronic speeds. The essence of this speed attribute is that it allows for real-time interactively based communications, where enquiries are responded to more or less instantly.

New, digital-based technologies, and the Internet in particular, provide an opportunity for interaction and dialogue with customers. With traditional media the tendency is for monologue or at best delayed and inferred dialogue. One of the first points to be made about these new, media-based communications is that the context within which marketing communications occurs is redefined. Traditionally, dialogue occurs in a (relatively) familiar context, which is driven by providers who deliberately present their messages through a variety of communication devices into the environments that they expect their audiences may well pass or recognise. Providers implant their messages into the various environments of their targets. Yuan et al. (1998) refer to advertising messages being 'unbundled', such as direct marketing, which has no other content, or 'bundled' and embedded with other news content such as television, radio and Web pages with banner ads. Perhaps more pertinently, they refer to direct and indirect online advertising. Direct advertising is concerned with advertising messages delivered to the customer (email) while indirect advertising is concerned with messages that are made available for a customer to access at their leisure (websites).

Digital media-based communications tend to make providers relatively passive. Their messages are presented in an environment that requires targets to use specific equipment to actively search them out. The roles are reversed, so that the drivers in the new context are active information seekers, represented by a target audience (members of the public and other information providers such as organisations), not just the information-providing organisations.

## The influence of people

The traditional view of communication holds that the process consists essentially of one step. Information is directed and shot at prospective audiences, rather like a bullet is propelled from a gun. The decision of each member of the audience to act on the message or not is the result of a passive role or participation in the process. Organisations can communicate with different target audiences simply by varying the message and the type and frequency of channels used.

The linear model has been criticised for its oversimplification, and it certainly ignores the effect of personal influences on the communication process and potential for information deviance. To accommodate these influences two further models are introduced, the influencer model and the interactional model of communication.

# The influencer model of communication

The influencer model depicts information flowing via media channels to particular types of people (opinion leaders and opinion formers; see p. 56) to whom other members of the audience refer for information and guidance. Through interpersonal networks, opinion leaders not only reach members of the target audience who may not have been exposed to the message, but may reinforce the impact of the message for those members who did receive the message (Figure 2.2). For example, feedback and comments from travellers on Tripadvisor.com assist others when making travel plans, and constitute opinion leadership. However, editors of travel sections in the Sunday press, television presenters of travel programmes, and professional travel bloggers fulfil the role of opinion former and can influence the decision of prospective travellers through their formalised knowledge.

Originally referred to as the 'two-step model', this approach indicates that the mass media do not have a direct and all-powerful effect over their audiences. If the primary function of the mass media is to provide information, then personal influences are necessary to be persuasive and to exert direct influence on members of the target audience.

The influencer approach can be developed into a multi-step model. This proposes that communication involves interaction among all parties to the communication process (see Figure 2.3). This interpretation closely resembles the network of participants who are often involved in the communication process.

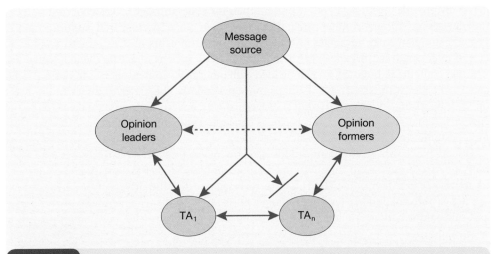

**Figure 2.2**    The influencer model of communication

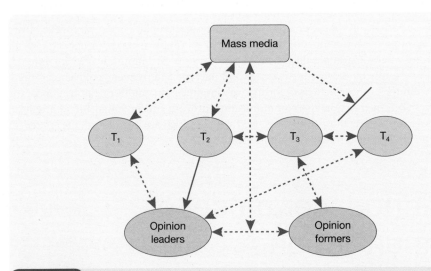

**Figure 2.3**    Multi-step variation of the influencer model of communication

**Exhibit 2.4**    **Influencer communications to promote Authentic Caribbean Rum (see Chapter 10)**
*Source*: Bray Leino Ltd

# Interactional model of communication

The models and frameworks used to explain the communication process so far should be considered as a simplification of reality and not a true reflection of communication in practice. The linear model is unidirectional, and it suggests that the receiver plays a passive role in the process. The influencer model attempts to account for an individual's participation in the communication process. These models emphasise individual behaviour but exclude any social behaviour implicit in the process.

The interactional model of communication attempts to assimilate the variety of influences acting upon the communication process. This includes the responses people give to communications received from people and machines. Increasingly communication is characterised by attributing meaning to messages that are shared, updated and a response to other messages. These 'conversations' can be termed interactional and are an integral part of society. Figure 2.4 depicts the complexity associated with this form of communication.

Interaction is about actions that lead to a response. The development of direct marketing helped make a significant contribution to the transition from what is essentially one-way to two-way and then interactive-based communication. Digital technology has further enabled this interaction process. However, interaction alone is not a sufficient goal, simply because the content of the interaction could be about a radical disagreement of views, an exchange of opinion or a social encounter.

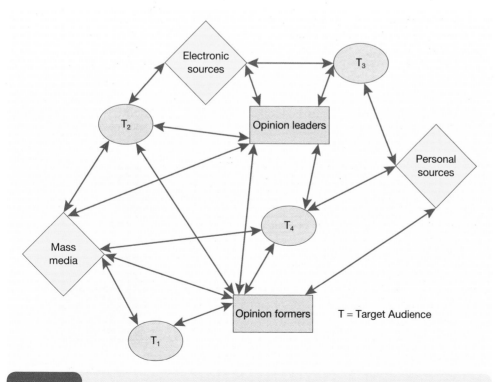

**Figure 2.4**   The interactional model of communication

| Table 2.2 | Communication matrix | | |
|---|---|---|---|
| **Direction** | **Mass markets** | **Portfolio/ mass-customised** | **Networks** |
| One-way. Planned communications designed to inform and persuade. Medium to high wastage. | Communication 'to'. Planned persuasive messages aimed at securing brand awareness and loyalty; e.g. communication of USPs and ESPs. | Communication 'for'. Planned persuasive messages with augmented offerings for target markets; e.g. communicating targeted lifecycle products, guarantees, loyalty programmes. | |
| Two-way. Formal and informal with a view to listening and learning. Minimal wastage. | | Communication 'with'. Integrated mix of planned and interactively shared knowledge; e.g. face to face, direct (database), contact centres, interactive b2b Internet portals. | Communication 'between'. Dialogue between participants based on trust, learning and adaptation with co-created outcomes; e.g. key account liaison, expansion of communities, staff teamwork. |

*Source*: Ballantyne (2004)

Ballantyne refers to two-way communication with audiences in two ways. First, as a 'with' experience, as manifest in face-to-face encounters and contact centres. He also distinguishes a higher order of two-way communication based on communication 'between' parties. It is this latter stage that embodies true dialogue where trust, listening and adaptive behaviour are typical. These are represented diagrammatically in Table 2.2. L'Oréal have gradually been adapting their strapline, 'Because I'm worth it'. In the mid 2000s this changed to 'Because you are worth it' and then in 2009 there was a further move to 'Because we're worth it' (Clark, 2012), a recognition perhaps of the word 'we' as a key to building customer relationships.

A key question emerges, what is interaction and what are its key characteristics? If we can understand the dynamics and dimensions of interactivity then it should be possible to develop more effective marketing communications. In the context of marketing communications, inter-activity can be considered from one of two perspectives. One is the technology, tools and features (e.g. multimedia, www, online gaming) that provide for interaction. The second, according to Johnson et al. (2006), is the added value that interactivity is perceived to bring to the communication process.

Arising out of interaction is dialogue. This occurs through mutual understanding and a reasoning approach to interactions, one based on listening and adaptive behaviour. Dialogue is concerned with the development of knowledge that is specific to the relationship of the parties involved. Ballantyne refers to this as 'learning together' (Ballantyne, 2004: 119).

The adoption of dialogue as the basis for communication changes an organisation's per-spective on its audiences. Being willing and able to enter into a dialogue indicates that there is a new emphasis on the relationships organisations hold with their stakeholders. Dialogue requires interaction as a precursor. In other words, for dialogue to occur there must first be interaction and it is the development and depth of the interaction that leads to meaningful dialogue.

The influencer model is important because it demonstrates the importance of people in the communication process. However, successful communication is often determined by the level of interactivity the communication encourages.

# Word-of-mouth communication

Consumer-to-consumer conversations about products, services and brand-related marketing messages and meanings are naturally occurring events. Buyers, potential buyers and non-buyers exchange information without influence or being prompted by the brand owner.

However, many organisations use word of mouth as an integral part of their marketing communications and deliberately encourage people to have positive conversations about their particular brand. They do this because word-of-mouth communication is considered to be the primary driver behind 20 to 50 per cent of all purchasing decisions (Bughin et al. 2010).

Word-of-mouth (WoM) communications are characterised as informal, unplanned and unsolicited conversations. These recommendations provide information and purchasing support and serve to reinforce an individual's purchasing decisions. At the heart of this approach is the source credibility that is assigned to people whose opinions are sought after and used in the purchase decision process. Those who provide information in WoM communications can be characterised as informal experts who are unbiased, trustworthy and who can be considered to be objective. Personal influence is important and can enrich the communication process. Unlike advertising, where messages are primarily linear and unidirectional, WoM communication is interactive and bidirectional.

---

**Scholars' paper 2.2**    **So, why am I talking about this brand?**

**Berger J. and Schwartz, E.M. (2011) What drives immediate and ongoing word of mouth?** *Journal of Marketing Research*, vol. XLVIII (October), 869–80.

These researchers consider the psychological drivers of WoM and how companies can design more effective WoM marketing campaigns. Whereas most of the research in this area looks at the consequences of WoM, the focus here is on what causes WoM, how the product itself can shape what is discussed, and how WoM may vary over different time horizons. They distinguish between immediate and ongoing WoM. This paper should be considered in terms of updating Dichter's 1966 paper.

---

## Definition and motives

Arndt (1967: 66) sets out word of mouth as 'an oral, person-to-person communication between a receiver and a communicator whom the receiver perceives as non-commercial, regarding a brand, product, or service'. Put in more simple terms, word of mouth concerns the sharing of an opinion among people independent from the company or its agents (Santo, 2006: 29).

Stokes and Lomax (2002) define word-of-mouth communication as 'interpersonal communication regarding products or services where the receiver regards the communicator as impartial'. This simple definition was developed from some of the more established interpretations that failed to accommodate contemporary media and the restrictions concerning the perceived independence of the communicator.

People like to talk about their product (service) experiences for a variety of reasons that are explored in the next section. However, by talking with a neighbour or colleague about the good experiences associated with a holiday – for example, the first-hand 'this has actually happened to someone I know' effect will be instrumental in the same views being passed on to other colleagues, irrespective of their validity or the general impression people have of other holidays and destinations. Mazzarol et al. (2007) identify the 'richness of the message' and the 'strength of the implied or explicit advocacy' as important triggers for WoM. Palmer (2009) brings these together and refers to WoM as information people can trust as it comes from people just like them and it helps them make better decisions.

Helm and Schlei (1998: 42) refer to WoM as 'verbal communications (either positive or negative) between groups such as the product provider, independent experts, family, friends and the actual or personal consumer'. However, as discussed later, organisations now use electronic WoM techniques in a commercial context in order to generate brand-based conversations around a point of differentiation. Indeed, an important point is that WoM is transmitted person-to-person through a variety of media (Lam et al. 2009). Where WoM used to be a one-to-one conversation, the digital influence makes this a one-to-many communication when product reviews are posted online or when blogs or films go viral.

One important question that arises is, why do people want to discuss products or advertising messages? Bone (1995) cited by Stokes and Lomax (2002) refers to three elements of WoM (see Table 2.3).

Dichter (1966) determined that there were four main categories of output WoM.

1. *Product involvement*

   People, he found, have a high propensity to discuss matters that are either distinctly pleasurable or unpleasurable. Such discussion serves to provide an opportunity for the experience to be relived, whether it be the 'looking for' or the 'use' experience, or both. This reflects the product and service experience elements of marketing communications, identified as part of the scope of the topic, in Chapter 1.

2. *Self-involvement*

   Discussion offers a means for ownership to be established and signals aspects of prestige and levels of status to the receiver. More importantly, perhaps, dissonance can be reduced as the purchaser seeks reassurance about the decision.

3. *Other involvement*

   Products can assist motivations to help others and to express feelings of love, friendship and caring. These feelings can be released through a sense of sharing the variety of benefits that products can bestow.

4. *Message involvement*

   The final motivation to discuss products is derived, according to Dichter, from the messages that surround the product itself, in particular the advertising messages and, in the business-to-business market, seminars, exhibitions and the trade press, which provide the means to provoke conversation and so stimulate word-of-mouth recommendation.

Marketing communications can be used to stimulate conversations, by using these motivations as the anchor for the messages.

People who identify very closely with a brand and who might be termed 'brand advocates' often engage in word-of-mouth communications. Advocacy can be demonstrated not only through word-of-mouth communications but also through behaviour – for example, by wearing branded clothing or using tools and equipment. The issue of advocacy is explored further in Chapter 8 in the section on loyalty and retention schemes.

**Table 2.3**    Elements of word-of-mouth communication

| Element of WoM | | Explanation |
|---|---|---|
| Direction | Input WoM | Customers seeking recommendation prior to purchase |
| | Output WoM | Expression of feelings as a result of the purchase experience |
| Valence | | The positive or negative feelings resulting from the experience |
| Volume | | The number of people to which the message is conveyed |

*Source*: After Bone (1995).

## Viewpoint 2.2     Spreading the word about Hovis

Founded in 1888, Hovis has become an established household name in the UK bread market. Hovis uses WoM in its attempt to regain the market leadership, both deliberately, and perhaps as a secondary aspect of its branded communications. The planned approach seeks to drive awareness by recruiting 800 advocates to help support the launch of their Hearty Oats brand. In what was referred to as a 'marketing advocacy campaign', women over 35 were identified as the best opinion leaders (advocates), partly because of their interest in health issues, social networking and a tendency to be early adopters of emerging trends. Selected advocates, as Hovis refers to them, were sent samples and they were encouraged to feed back comments and exchange recipes. The expectation is that they will talk amongst their friends and acquaintances, both off and online, about their positive feelings towards the Hearty Oats (and Hovis) brand.

The secondary approach borrows on Dichter's ideas about why people talk about products and services. When Hovis recognised the difficulties their brand was facing, research was undertaken amongst typical consumers. This revealed that the consumers differentiated between good bread and bad bread, and an increasing proportion aligned Hovis with bad bread. The relaunch campaign revived a famous Hovis ad that featured a small lad on a bike. This time the lad travelled through time, featuring significant world events. The 122-second ad was voted campaign of the year by the BBC and awarded the best marketing communications prize by the Marketing Society. The point of this story is that the ad was so well made, so memorable and so good that people like to talk about these quality communications. In Dichter's terms, this is message involvement, and is a potent source of word-of-mouth communication.

*Source*: Reynolds (2010); Smith (2010).

**Question:** If WoM communication is so important, why is it not a core activity within marketing communications for all brands?

**Task:** When you next visit a leisure or entertainment complex, make a mental note of the ways in which the brand owner encourages visitors to talk about the complex.

| Exhibit 2.5 | **The famous bread delivery lad from the original award–winning Hovis TV ad** |
| --- | --- |
| | *Source*: Premier Foods Group Ltd |

These motivations to discuss products and their associative experiences vary between individuals and with the intensity of the motivation at any one particular moment. There are two main persons involved in this process of word-of-mouth communications: a sender and receiver. Research indicates that the receiver's evaluation of a message is far from stable over time and accuracy of recall decays (expectedly) through time. What this means for marketing communications is that those people who have a positive product experience, especially in the service sector, should be encouraged to talk as soon as possible after the event (Christiansen and Tax, 2000). For example, Pepsi Raw was launched in pubs and bars in order to reach young affluent consumers. The goal was to encourage this target audience to talk about the brand and in doing so imbue the brand with social group associations, and then roll the brand out across supermarkets (Simms, 2007). Goldsmith and Horowitz (2006) found that risk reduction, popularity, reduced costs, access to easy information, and even inspiration from offline sources such as cinema, TV and radio were some of the primary reasons why people seek the opinions of others online.

According to Reichheld (2003), cited by Mazur (2004), organisations should measure word-of-mouth communication, because those who speak up about a brand are risking their own reputation when they recommend a brand. Looking at the financial services sector, Reichheld argues that measures based on customer satisfaction or retention rates can mask real growth potential because they are measures of defection, and switching barriers may induce inertia. He found three particular groups based on their type of word-of-mouth endorsement: promoters, passively satisfied and detractors. In particular, he identified a strong correlation between an organisation's growth rate and the percentage of customers who are active promoters.

## Opinion leaders

Katz and Lazarsfeld (1955) first identified individuals who were predisposed to receiving information and then reprocessing it to influence others. Their studies of American voting and purchase behaviour led to their conclusion that those individuals who could exert such influence were more persuasive than information received directly from the mass media. These opinion leaders, according to Rogers (1962), tend 'to be of the same social class as non-leaders, but may enjoy a higher social status within the group'. Williams (1990) uses the work of Reynolds and Darden (1971) to suggest that they are more gregarious and more self-confident than non-leaders. In addition, they have a greater exposure to relevant mass media (print) and, as a result, have more knowledge/familiarity and involvement with the product class, are more innovative and more confident of their role as influencer (leader) and appear to be less dogmatic than non-leaders (Chan and Misra, 1990).

Opinion leadership can be simulated in advertising by the use of product testimonials. Using ordinary people to express positive comments about a product to each other is a very well-used advertising technique.

The importance of opinion leaders in the design and implementation of communication plans should not be underestimated. Midgley and Dowling (1993) refer to *innovator communicators*: those who are receptive to new ideas and who make innovation-based purchase decisions without reference to or from other people. However, while the importance of these individuals is not doubted, a major difficulty exists in trying to identify just who these opinion leaders and innovator communicators are. While they sometimes display some distinctive characteristics, such as reading specialist media vehicles, often being first to return coupons, enjoying attending exhibitions or just involving themselves with new, innovative techniques or products, they are by their very nature invisible outside their work, family and social groups.

Nisbet (2005) provides a useful insight into the background of opinion leadership. He observes that opinion leadership has been previously defined as exhibiting three primary dimensions: social embeddedness (Weimann, 1994), information-giving (Rogers, 2003), and information-seeking (Keller and Berry, 2003) behaviours. Table 2.4 sets out some of the main characteristics associated with opinion leaders.

## Viewpoint 2.3    Bladeless influencers

Most fans are inefficient, noisy, difficult to clean and prone to children experimenting with their fingers to see if the blades are really going round. The response from James Dyson, innovator and entrepreneur, was to invent The Dyson Air Multiplier fan, one which has no blades. In its place it uses Air Multiplier technology to amplify air 15 times, expelling 405 litres of cool and uninterrupted air every second.

Apart from the technology, what is interesting about this development is the campaign used to launch the product. Dyson started the launch with a video which they uploaded to their website. The film was shot at a series of focus groups held by the brand, in order to show how people reacted to an unseen gadget. Their bewilderment, astonishment and amazement were etched all over their faces and comments such as 'Oh my gosh! Wow! How does it work? That's awesome!' were typical. This acted as a teaser campaign and served to prompt excitement, buzz, speculation and debate amongst technology fans.

Dyson then announced: 'Now we've turned our attention to another familiar device – and made it work better by removing something you might have thought was essential.' This only inflamed people's curiosity even more and sparked off a heated discussion on Twitter as these technological influencers became obsessed with trying to guess what the new appliance might be.

The answer, a bladeless fan, was announced at the formal launch of the product.

*Source*:   Smithers (2009).

**Question:**   To what extent are influencers an integral part of contemporary marketing communications?

**Task:**   Find another example where technology influencers were used in a campaign, and determine any similarities or differences in their role.

---

| Table 2.4 | Characteristics associated with opinion leaders |
| --- | --- |

| OL characteristic | Explanation |
| --- | --- |
| **Social gregariousness** | Refers to an opinion leader's level of social embeddedness because they tend to have more social ties, more friends, and more social contacts than non-leaders. |
| **Efficacy and trust** | Opinion leaders have a higher of self-confidence and self-reliance than non-leaders, although it is noted that they generally have lower confidence in political systems. |
| **Values and satisfaction** | Opinion leaders are less concerned with material gain and financial success than non-leaders. They tend to exhibit higher levels of social responsibility, political tolerance, civic-mindedness, and environmental concern. |

## Opinion formers

Opinion formers are individuals who are able to exert personal influence because of their authority, education or status associated with the object of the communication process. Like opinion leaders, they are acknowledged and sought out by others to provide information and advice, but this is because of the formal expertise that opinion formers are adjudged to have. For example, community pharmacists are often consulted about symptoms and medicines, and film critics carry such conviction in their reviews that they can make or break a new production.

Popular television programmes, such as *Eastenders*, *Casualty* and *Coronation Street*, all of which attract huge audiences, have been used as vehicles to draw attention to and open up debates about many controversial social issues, such as contraception, abortion, drug use and abuse, and serious illness and mental health concerns.

The influence of opinion formers can be great. For example, the editor of a journal or newspaper may be a recognised source of expertise, and any offering referred to by the editor in the media vehicle is endowed with great credibility. In this sense the editor acts as a gatekeeper, and it is the task of the marketing communicator to ensure that all relevant opinion formers are identified and sent appropriate messages.

However, the credibility of opinion formers is vital for communication effectiveness. If there is a suspicion or doubt about the impartiality of the opinion former, then the objectivity of their views and comments is likely to be perceived as tainted and not believed so that damage may be caused to the reputation of the brand and those involved.

Many organisations constantly lobby key members of parliament in an effort to persuade them to pursue 'favourable' policies. Opinion formers are relatively easy to identify, as they need to be seen shaping the opinion of others, usually opinion followers.

## Opinion followers

The vast majority of consumers can be said to be opinion followers. The messages they receive via the mass media are tempered by the opinions of the two groups of personal influencers just discussed. Some people actively seek information from those they believe are well informed, while others prefer to use the mass media for information and guidance (Robinson, 1976). However, this should not detract from the point that, although followers, they still process information independently and use a variety of inputs when sifting information and responding to marketing stimuli.

Ethical drug manufacturers normally launch new drugs by enlisting the support of particular doctors who have specialised in the therapy area and who are recognised by other doctors as experts. These opinion formers are invited to lead symposia and associated events to build credibility and activity around the new product. At the same time, public relations agencies prepare press releases with the aim that the information will be used by the mass media (opinion formers) for editorial purposes and create exposure for the product across the target audience, which, depending upon the product and/or the media vehicle, may be GPs, hospital doctors, patients or the general public. All these people, whether they be opinion leaders or formers, are active influencers or talkers (Kingdom, 1970).

## Developing brands with word-of-mouth communication

So far in this section word-of-mouth communication (WoM) has been examined as naturally occurring, unplanned conversations. This is not necessarily correct, as many organisations deliberately attempt to reach their audiences using WoM principles. The term 'word-of-mouth marketing' (WoMM) refers to the electronic version of the spoken endorsement of a product or service, where messages are targeted at key individuals who then voluntarily pass the message to friends and colleagues. In doing so they endorse the message and provide it with a measure of credibility. WoMM is a planned, intentional attempt to influence consumer-to-consumer communications using professional marketing methods and technologies (Kozinets et al., 2010) to prompt WoM conversations.

From this it can be assumed that there are a variety of methods that organisations use to influence their audiences, all in the name of WoM. Of these, three main forms of WoM can be identified; voluntary, prompted and managed.

1. *Voluntary* – WoM can be considered to be the most natural form of interpersonal conversation, free from any external influence, coercion or intent. This still occurs among genuine opinion leaders, formers and followers for reasons considered earlier.

2. *Prompted* – WoM occurs when organisations convey information to opinion leaders and formers, with a view to deliberately encouraging them to forward and share the information with their followers. The goal is to prompt conversations among followers based around the credibility bestowed on the opinion leader. This outward perspective can be counterbalanced by an inward view. For example, some organisations use various elements of social media – e.g. blogs, online communities and forums – to prompt consumer-to-consumer conversations and to then listen, observe and revise their approaches to the market.

3. *Managed* – WoM occurs when organisations target, incentivise and reward opinion leaders for recommending their offerings to their networks of followers. In these situations opinion leaders lose their independence and objectivity within the communication process, and become paid representatives of a brand. As a result, the credibility normally attached to these influencers diminishes and the essence of freely expressed opinions about products and brands is removed.

There is evidence that organisational use of contemporary marketing communications seeks to drive voluntary conversations, stimulated by positive product and service experiences. The prompted approach is used extensively and enables organisations to retain credibility and a sense of responsibility. PQ Media reported in 2010 that the managed approach is increasing as clients seek to move their communication budgets closer to where target audiences spend their time online. They expect this sector to grow very quickly. The organisations that exploit their audiences through managed WoM conversations are not acting illegally, but may be guilty of transgressing ethical boundaries and demonstrating disrespect for their audiences: not a position for long-term strength.

Traditionally brands were built partly through offline communications directed to opinion leaders, when they could be identified, and through opinion formers. Sporting and entertainment celebrities have been used as brand ambassadors for a long time. They are used to enable audiences to develop positive associations between the personality of the ambassador and a brand. McCracken (1989) believes that celebrity endorsement works through the theory of meaning transfer. Consumers make an overall assessment of what a celebrity 'represents' to them, based on their perception and interpretation of the celebrity's identity cues. These cues relate to their behaviour, comments, ability, and attributes that are of particular interest to the consumer. McCracken (1989: 315) refers to their public image as demonstrated in 'television, movies, military, athletics, and other careers'.

The meaning assigned to a celebrity is transferred from the celebrity endorser to the product when the two are paired in a commercial message. Gwinner and Eaton (1999) argue that, when a consumer acquires/consumes the product, the meaning is transferred to the user and the process is complete.

---

### Scholars' paper 2.3     Effective WoM through bloggers

**Kozinets, R.V., de Valck, K., Wojnicki, A.C., and Wilner, S.J.S. (2010) Networked Narratives: Understanding Word-of-Mouth Marketing in Online Communities,** *Journal of Marketing*, **74 (March), 71–89.**

This paper considers the use and effectiveness of word-of-mouth communications through online influencers, bloggers. The authors reveal four distinct blogger communication strategies. These are evaluation, embracing, endorsement, and explanation. Each of them is influenced by character narrative, communications forum, communal norms, and the nature of the marketing promotion. The implications for online and offline and word-of-mouth campaigns are presented.

Contemporary brand development now incorporates the use of social media, and bloggers in particular, who play an increasingly critical role in the dissemination of brand-related information. More detailed information about these elements can be found in Chapter 22, but here it is important to establish the way in which brands can be developed through word-of-mouth marketing/communication.

Opinion formers such as journalists find or receive information about brands through press releases. They then relay the information, after editing and reformatting, to their readers and viewers through their particular media. Accordingly, brand-related information is targeted at journalists, with the intention that their messages will be forwarded to their end-user audience through media channels.

Bloggers are now an important and influential channel of communication. However, they do not share the same characteristics as journalists. For example, the number of bloggers in any one market can be counted in terms of tens of thousands of people (Clark, 2010), in contrast to the relatively small, select number of opinion formers. The majority of bloggers have an informal interest in a subject, whereas opinion formers are deemed to have formal expertise. Bloggers however, are not tied to formal processes or indeed an editor. As a result, bloggers do not have to be objective in their comments and are not constrained by any advertising messages. Most importantly, bloggers conduct conversations among themselves and their followers, whereas journalists receive little feedback. More information about blogging can be found in Chapter 22.

---

## Viewpoint 2.4   Fashionable bloggers

In January 2010 fashion blogger Tavi Gevinson, aged 14, sat in the front row at the Christian Dior couture show in Paris, and in front of the Grazia journalist. Clark (2010) observes this as a reflection of the way key influencers are changing the branding process. No longer are glossy magazines the primary vehicle to reach consumers. Now it is word of mouth through social media, and blogging in particular, that is shaping the way the fashion industry operates. This change in emphasis is even recognised by many of the leading fashion magazines, who have run features about fashion blogs. For example, Clark reports that WhatKatieWore.com has been featured in *The Sunday Times Style magazine*, *Marie Claire* and *Grazia*.

In an attempt to promote the island and reduce the average age of visitors, the Barbados Tourism Authority harnessed the power of bloggers and their propensity to communicate their experiences through social media and their networks. The initiative was supported by airlines and hotels who service the island.

Eight entrepreneurs were taken on a three-week tour to experience not only the holiday dimension but also both the business activities and opportunities.

There was no formal requirement to inform others, but it was inevitable that the trip would trigger conversations. In addition to email and general comments, the entrepreneurs blogged regularly, made videos and posted these and their comments on various sites, including Facebook. The reach of these influencers and the credibility of their messages meant that the trip was deemed to more cost-effective than a single ad in a national newspaper.

*Source:*   Clark (2010); Roberts (2010).

**Question:**   Is blogging a means of self-expression or is it something else?

**Task:**   Find three different blogs in fashion, travel and sport. Make a list of their similarities and differences.

To conclude this section on word-of-mouth communication, three elements concerning the potential of any one word-of-mouth recommendation to change behaviour or dissuasion from doing so can be identified. According to Bughin et al. (2010) these are what is said, who says it and where it is communicated.

The primary driver is the content of a message, what is said. The message must address important product or service features. For example, in skin care, functional aspects such as packaging and ingredients create more powerful word-of-mouth communications than emotional messages about how a product makes people feel.

The second driver concerns the person sending the message. Opinion leaders or influentials embody trust and competence. As a result, they generate three times more word-of-mouth messages than non-influentials. Each leader-based message has four times more impact on a recipient's purchasing decision.

The third driver is about the environment and power with which word-of-mouth messages circulate. Compact, trust-based networks enable low reach, but messages in this type of environment have great impact, relative to those circulated through dispersed communities. This is because there is often a high correlation between people whose opinions we trust and the members of networks we most value.

# Relational approaches to communications

The previous model accounts for social behaviour but does not account for the context within which the behaviour occurs. Communication events always occur within a context (Littlejohn, 1992) or particular set of circumstances, which not only influence the form of the communication but also the nature and the way the communication is received, interpreted and acted upon. There are a huge number of variables that can influence the context, including the disposition of the people involved, the physical environment, the nature of the issue, the history and associated culture, the goals of the participants and the expected repercussions of the dialogue itself.

Littlejohn identifies four main contextual levels: interpersonal, group, organisational and mass communication. These levels form part of a hierarchy whereby higher levels incorporate the lower levels but 'add something new of their own'.

The relational approach means that communication events are linked together in an organised manner, one where the events are 'punctuated' by interventions from one or more of the participants. These interventions occur whenever the participants attempt cooperation or if conflict arises.

Soldow and Thomas (1984), referring to a sales negotiation, state that a relationship develops through the form of negotiations rather than the content. An agreement is necessary about who is to control the relationship or whether there will be equality. Rothschild (1987) reports that 'sparring will continue' until agreement is reached or the negotiations are terminated. In other words, without mutual agreement over the roles of the participants, the true purpose of the interaction, to achieve an exchange, cannot be resolved.

An interesting aspect of relational communication theory is social penetration (Taylor and Altman, 1987). Through the disclosure of increasing amounts of information about themselves, partners in a relationship (personal or organisational) develop levels of intimacy, which serve to build interpersonal (interorganisational?) relationships. The relationship moves forward as partners reveal successive layers of information about each other and, as a greater amount or breadth of information is shared, confidence grows. These levels can be seen to consist of orientation, exploratory affective exchange, affective exchange and stable exchange

| Table 2.5 | Layers of social penetration |
|---|---|
| Orientation | The disclosure of public information only. |
| Exploratory affective exchange | Expansion and development of public information. |
| Affective exchange | Disclosure, based upon anticipated relationship rewards, of deeper feelings, values and beliefs. |
| Stable exchange | High level of intimacy where partners are able to predict each other's reactions with a good level of accuracy. |

*Source*: Taylor and Altman (1987).

(see Table 2.5). These layers are not uncovered in a logical, orderly sequence. It is likely that partners will return to previous levels, test the outcomes and rewards and reconsider their positions as the relationships unfold through time. This suggests that social penetration theory may lie at the foundation of the development of trust, commitment and relational exchanges between organisations.

Relationships need not be just dyadic, as the interactional approach suggests, but could be triadic or even encompass a much wider network or array of participants. Through this perspective a 'communication network' can be observed, through which information can flow. Participants engage in communication based upon their perception of the environment in which the communication occurs and the way in which each participant relates to the others.

Rogers (1986) identifies a communication network as 'consisting of interconnected individuals who are linked by patterned communication flows'. This is important, as it views communication as transcending organisational boundaries. In other words, it is not only individuals within an organisation that develop patterned communication flows but also individuals across different organisations. These individuals participate with one another (possibly through exchanges) and use communication networks to achieve their agenda items.

The extent to which individuals are linked to the network is referred to as *connectedness*. The more a network is connected, the greater the likelihood that a message will be disseminated, as there are few isolated individuals. Similarly, the level of integration in a network refers to the degree to which members of the network are linked to one another. The greater the integration, the more potential channels there are for a message to be routed through.

Systems theory, as discussed in the previous chapter, recognises that organisations are made of interacting units. The relational approach to communications is similar to systems theory. The various 'criss-crossing' flows of information between reciprocating units allow individuals and groups to modify the actions of others in the 'net', and this permits the establishment of a pattern of communication (Tichy, 1979).

## Scholars' paper 2.4    Let's get relational

**Soldow, G.F. and Thomas, G.P. (1984) Relational Communication: Form Versus Content in the Sales Interaction,** *Journal of Marketing*, **48, (Winter), 84–93.**

This was the first paper that attempted to develop ideas about face-to-face communications, which until that point had been well established. Soldow and Thomas introduced the concept of relational communication, which refers to that part of a message beyond the actual content which enables participants to negotiate their relative positions. Thus, the message sender can either bid for dominance, deference, or equality. The message receiver, in turn, can accept the bid or deny it.

# Network approaches to communications

The regular use of these patterned flows leads to the development of communication networks, which have been categorised as *prescribed* and *emergent* (Weick, 1987). Prescribed networks are formalised patterns of communication, very often established by senior management within an organisation or by organisational representatives when interorganisational communications are considered. It follows that emergent networks are informal and emerge as a response to the social and task-oriented needs of the participants.

The linear or one-way model of communication fails to accommodate the various complexities associated with communication. As discussed earlier, the model is too simplistic and fails to represent many aspects of communication events. Although the linear model is essentially a sequential rather than an interactional approach, it is still used and practised by many organisations. Varey (2002) refers to this as the 'Informational model' of communication and, as both Grunig (1992) and Ballantyne (2004) suggest, it is just one of a number of ways in which communication can work. Communication is an integral part of relationship marketing, and within this collaborative context, interaction and dialogue are essential factors. Varey refers to this as 'Transformational communication'.

# Process of adoption

An interesting extension to the concept of opinion followers and the discussion on WoM communications is the process by which individuals become committed to the use of a new product. Rogers (1983) has identified this as the process of adoption and the stages of his innovation decision process are represented in Figure 2.5. These stages in the adoption process

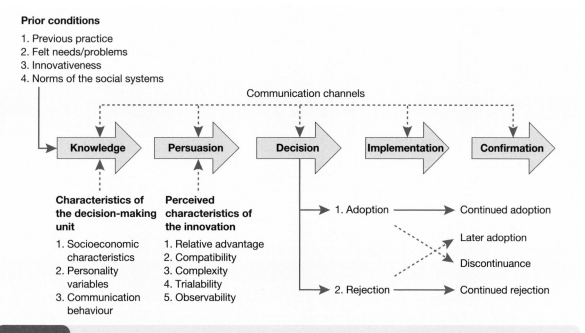

| Figure 2.5 | Stages in the innovation decision process of adoption |

*Source*: Reprinted with the permission of The Free Press, a division of Simon & Schuster, Inc., from *Diffusion of Innovations*, Third Edition by Everett M. Rogers. Copyright © 1962, 1971, 1983 by The Free Press. All rights reserved.

are sequential and are characterised by the different factors that are involved at each stage (e.g. the media used by each individual).

1. *Knowledge*

   The innovation becomes known to consumers, but they have little information and no well-founded attitudes. Information must be provided through mass media to institutions and people whom active seekers of information are likely to contact. Information for passive seekers should be supplied through the media and channels that this group habitually uses to look for other kinds of information (Windahl et al., 1992).

   *Bill washes his hair regularly, but he is beginning to notice tufts of hair on his comb. He becomes aware of an advertisement for Mane in a magazine.*

2. *Persuasion*

   The consumer becomes aware that the innovation may be of use in solving known and potential problems. Information from those who have experience of the product becomes very important.

   *Bill notices that the makers of Mane claim that, not only does their brand reduce the amount of hair loss, but also aids hair gain. Mane has also been recommended to him by someone he met in the pub last week. Modelling behaviour predominates.*

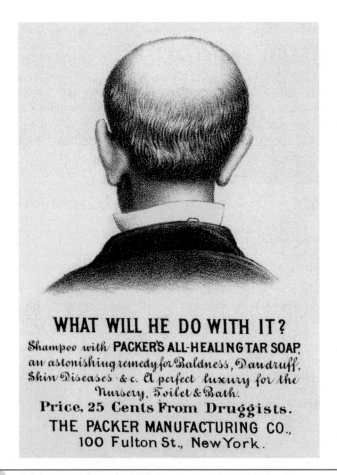

| Exhibit 2.6 | **A Victorian trade card for Packer's All-Healing Tar Soap, a hair restorative from 1890.** |
| --- | --- |

*Source*: Getty Images/Buyenlarge

3. *Decision*

An attitude may develop and may be either favourable or unfavourable, but as a result a decision is reached whether to trial the offering or not. Communications need to assist this part of the process by continual prompting.

*Bill is prepared to believe (or not to believe) the messages and the claims made on behalf of Mane. He thinks that Mane is potentially a very good brand (or not). He intends trying Mane because he was given a free sample (or because it was on a special price deal).*

4. *Implementation*

For the adoption to proceed in the absence of a sales promotion, buyers must know where to get it and how to use it. The product is then tested in a limited way. Communications must provide this information in order that the trial experience be developed.

*Bill tries the Mane treatment.*

5. *Confirmation*

The innovation is accepted or rejected on the basis of the experience during trial. Planned communications play an important role in maintaining the new behaviour by dispelling negative thoughts and positively reaffirming the original 'correct' decision. McGuire, as reported in Windahl et al. (1992), refers to this as *post-behavioural consolidation*.

*It works. Bill's hair stops falling out as it used to before he tried the Mane treatment. He reads an article that reports that large numbers of people are using these types of products satisfactorily. Bill resolves to buy use Mane in the future.*

This process can be terminated at any stage and, of course, a number of competing brands may vie for consumers' attention simultaneously, so adding to the complexity and levels of noise in the process. Generally, mass communications are seen to be more effective in the earlier phases of the adoption process for products that buyers are actively interested in, while more interpersonal forms are more appropriate at the later stages, especially trial and adoption. This model assumes that the stages occur in a predictable sequence, but this clearly does not happen in all purchase activity, as some information that is to be used later in the trial stage may be omitted, which often happens when loyalty to a brand is high or where the buyer has experience in the marketplace.

# Process of diffusion

The process of adoption in aggregate form, over time, is diffusion. According to Rogers (1983), diffusion is the process by which an innovation is communicated through certain channels over a period of time among the members of a social system. This is a group process and Rogers again identified five categories of adopters. Figure 2.6 shows how diffusion may be fast or slow and that there is no set speed at which the process occurs. The five categories are as follows:

1. *Innovators*

These groups like new ideas and have a large disposable income. This means they are more likely to take risks associated with new products.

2. *Early adopters*

Research has established that this group contains a large proportion of opinion leaders and they are, therefore, important in speeding the diffusion process. Early adopters tend to be younger than any other group and above average in education. Internet activity and use of publications is probably high as they actively seek information. A high proportion of early adopters are active bloggers. This group is important to the marketing communications process because they can determine the speed at which diffusion occurs.

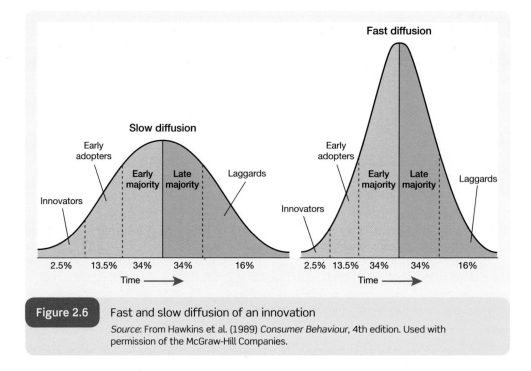

**Figure 2.6** Fast and slow diffusion of an innovation

*Source*: From Hawkins et al. (1989) *Consumer Behaviour*, 4th edition. Used with permission of the McGraw-Hill Companies.

3. *Early majority*

The early majority are usually composed of opinion followers who are a little above average in age, education, social status and income. Although not capable of substantiation, it is probable that Web usage is high and they rely on informal sources of information and take fewer publications than the previous two groups.

4. *Late majority*

This group of people is sceptical of new ideas and only adopts new products because of social or economic factors. They take few publications and are below average in education, social status and income. Their Web usage may be below average.

5. *Laggards*

This group of people is suspicious of all new ideas and is set in their opinions. Lowest of all the groups in terms of income, social status and education, this group takes a long time to adopt an innovation.

This framework suggests that, at the innovation stage, messages should be targeted at relatively young people in the target group, with a high level of income, education and social status. This will speed word-of-mouth recommendation and the diffusion process. Mahajan et al. (1990) observe that the personal influence of word-of-mouth communications does not work in isolation from the other communication tools and media. Early adopters are more likely to adopt an innovation in response to 'external influences' and only through time will the effect of 'internal influences' become significant. In other words, mass-media communications need time to work before word-of-mouth communications can begin to build effectiveness. However, digital developments circumvent the need to use mass media, which means that viral communications and social networks alone can lead to substantial WoM penetration.

Gatignon and Robertson (1985) suggest that there are three elements to the diffusion process, which need to be taken into account, particularly for the fast-moving consumer goods sector:

1. The rate of diffusion or speed at which sales occur.

2. The pattern of diffusion or shape of the curve.

3. The potential penetration level or size of the market.

Care should be taken to ensure that all three of these elements are considered when attempting to understand the diffusion process. It can be concluded that if a campaign is targeted at innovators and the early majority, and is geared to stimulating word-of-mouth communications, then the diffusion process is more likely to be successful than if these elements are ignored.

# Key points

- The linear or one-way communication process suggests that messages are developed by a source, encoded, transmitted, decoded and meaning applied to the message by a receiver. Noise in the system may prevent the true meaning of the messages from being conveyed, while feedback to the source is limited. The effectiveness of this communication process is determined by the strengths of the linkages between the different components.

- There are two particular influences on the communication process that need to be considered. First, the media used to convey information have fragmented drastically as a raft of new media have emerged. Second, people influence the communication process considerably, either as opinion leaders or formers or as participants in the word-of-mouth process.

- The influencer model depicts information flowing via media channels to particular types of people (opinion leaders and opinion formers; see p. 56) to whom other members of the audience refer for information and guidance. Through interpersonal networks, opinion leaders not only reach members of the target audience who may not have been exposed to the message, but may reinforce the impact of the message for those members who did receive the message.

- Increasingly communication is characterised by attributing meaning to messages that are shared, updated and a response to other messages. These 'conversations' can be termed 'interactional' and are an integral part of society. The interactional model of communication attempts to assimilate the variety of influences acting upon the communication process and account for the responses (interactions) people give to messages received from people and machines.

- Opinion leaders are members of a peer group who have informal expertise and knowledge about a specific topic. Opinion formers have formal expertise bestowed upon them by virtue of their qualifications, experience and careers. Opinion followers value and use information from these sources in their decision-making processes. Marketing communications should, therefore, target leaders and formers as they can speed the overall communication process.

- Word-of-mouth communication (WoM) is 'interpersonal communication regarding products or services where the receiver regards the communicator as impartial'. WoM is an increasingly important form of effective communication. It is relatively cost-free yet very credible, and embodies the increasingly conversational nature of marketing communications.

- The process of adoption in aggregate form, over time, is diffusion. It is a group process by which an innovation is communicated through certain channels over a period of time among the members of a social system. Five particular groups, each with distinct characteristics, can be identified.

# Review questions

1. Name the elements of the linear model of communication and briefly describe the role of each element.

2. Make brief notes explaining why the linear interpretation of the communication process is not entirely satisfactory.

3. Draw the Influencer model of communication.

4. Discuss the differences between linear, influencer and interactional models of communications. Which of these best illustrates how communication worked for MTV, as presented in the mini case?

5. How do opinion leaders differ from opinion formers and opinion followers?

6. Why is word-of-mouth communication so important to marketing communications?

7. What are the three elements of word-of-mouth communication identified by Bone?

8. If voluntary is one form of WoM, what are the other two and how do they differ?

9. Using a product of your choice, show how the stages in the process of adoption can be depicted.

10. Draw a graph to show the difference between fast and slow diffusion.

# References

Anon (2010) Case Study – Marmite, *The Marketer* (May), p. 35.

Arndt, J. (1967) Role of Product-Related Conversations in the Diffusion of a New Product,' *Journal of Marketing Research*, 4 (August), 291–95.

Ballantyne, D. (2004) Dialogue and its role in the development of relationship specific knowledge, *Journal of Business and Industrial Marketing*, 19, 2, 114–23.

Berger J. and Schwartz, E.M. (2011) What drives immediate and ongoing word of mouth? *Journal of Marketing Research*, Vol XLVIII (October), 869–80.

Bone, P.F. (1995) Word of mouth effects on short-term and long term product judgments, *Journal of Business Research*, 32, 3, 213–23.

Bughin, J., Doogan, J., and Vetvik, O.J. (2010) A new way to measure word-of-mouth marketing, *McKinsey Quarterly*, Issue 2.

Chan, K.K. and Misra, S. (1990) Characteristics of the opinion leader: a new dimension, *Journal of Advertising*, 19, 3, 53–60.

Christiansen, T. and Tax, S.S. (2000) Measuring word of mouth: the questions of who and when, *Journal of Marketing Communications*, 6, 185–99.

Clark, N. (2010) How brands can reach bloggers, *Marketing*, 3 March, 24–6.

Clark, N. (2012) Meet the new Type A, *Marketing*, 29 February, 28–30.

Dichter, E. (1966) How word-of-mouth advertising works, *Harvard Business Review*, 44 (November/December), 147–66.

Edwards, H. (2011) Helen Edwards on Branding: Blurred visionaries, *Marketing*, 7 December, retrieved 21 March 2012 from www.brandrepublic.com/opinion/1107725/Helen-Edwards-Branding-Blurred-visionaries/?DCMP=ILC-SEARCH.

Farey-Jones, D. (2010) Marmite election ads make debut appearance, *campaignlive.co.uk*, 31 March 2010, retrieved 21 March 2012 from http://www.brandrepublic.com/news/994073/Marmite-election-ads-debut-appearance/?DCMP=ILC-SEARCH.

Gatignon, H. and Robertson, T. (1985) A propositional inventory for new diffusion research, *Journal of Consumer Research*, 11, 849–67.

Goldsmith, R.E. and Horowitz, D. (2006) Measuring motivations for online opinion seeking, *Journal of Interactive Advertising*, 6, 2, (Spring) 3–14. Retrieved 5 April 2010 from http://www.jiad.org/article76.

Grunig, J. (1992) Models of public relations and communication, in *Excellence in Public Relations and*

*Communications Management* (eds J.E. Grunig, D.M. Dozier, P. Ehling, L.A. Grunig, F.C. Repper and J. Whits), Hillsdale, NJ: Lawrence Erlbaum, 285–325.

Gwinner, K.P. and Eaton, J. (1999) Building Brand Image Through Event Sponsorship: The Role of Image Transfer, *Journal of Advertising*, 28, 4 (Winter), 47–57.

Hawkins, D.I., Best, R.J. and Coney, K.A. (1989) *Consumer Behaviour: Implications for Marketing Strategy*, Homewood, IL: Richard D. Irwin.

Helm, S. and Schlei, J. (1998) Referral potential – potential referrals: An investigation into customers' communication in service markets, Proceedings from 27th EMAC Conference, *Marketing Research and Practice*, 41–56.

Johnson, G.J., Bruner II, G.C. and Kumar, A. (2006) Interactivity and its facets revisited, *Journal of Advertising*, 35, 4 (Winter), 35–52.

Katz, E. and Lazarsfeld, P.F. (1955) *Personal Influence*. Glencoe, IL: Free Press.

Keller, J.A. and Berry, J.L. (2003) *The influential: One American in ten tells the other nine how to vote, where to eat, and what to buy*, New York : Simon & Schuster.

Kingdom, J.W. (1970) Opinion leaders in the electorate, *Public Opinion Quarterly*, 34, 256–6.

Kozinets, R.V., de Valck, K., Wojnicki, A.C. and Wilner, S.J.S. (2010) Networked Narratives: understanding word-of-mouth marketing in online communities, *Journal of Marketing*, 74 (March), 71–89.

Lam, D., Lee, A. and Mizerski, R. (2009) The Effects of Cultural Values in Word-of-Mouth Communication, *Journal of International Marketing*, 17, 3, 55–70.

Littlejohn, S.W. (1992) *Theories of Human Communication*, 4th edn., Belmont, CA: Wadsworth.

Mahajan, V., Muller, E. and Bass, F.M. (1990) New product diffusion models in marketing, *Journal of Marketing*, 54 (January), 1–26.

Mallen, B. (1977) *Principles of Marketing Channel Management*, Lexington, MA: Lexington Books.

Mazur, L. (2004) Keep it simple, *Marketing Business*, (March), 17.

Mazzarol, T., Sweeney, J.C. and Soutar, G.N. (2007) Conceptualising word-of-mouth activity, triggers and conditions: an exploratory study, *European Journal of Marketing*, 41, 11/12, 1475–94.

McCracken, G. (1989) Who is the Celebrity Endorser? Cultural Foundations of the Endorsement Process, *Journal of Consumer Research*, 16 (December), 310–21.

Midgley, D. and Dowling, G. (1993) Longitudinal study of product form innovation: the interaction between predispositions and social messages, *Journal of Consumer Research*, 19 (March), 611–25.

Nisbet, E.C. (2005) The engagement model of opinion leadership: Testing validity within a European context, *International Journal of Public Opinion Research*, 18(1), 1–27.

Palmer, I. (2009) WoM is about empowering consumers in shaping your brand, *Admap*, 504, (April) retrieved 2 June 2010 from www.warc.com/admap.

Patzer, G.L. (1983) Source credibility as a function of communicator physical attractiveness, *Journal of Business Research*, 11, 229–41.

PQ Media (2010) More brands start paid conversations online, *Warc News*, retrieved 17 May 2010 from www.warc.com/news/.

Reichheld, F.F. (2003) The one number you need to grow, *Harvard Business Review*, (December), 47–54.

Reynolds, J. (2010) Hovis embarks on first 'buzz marketing' drive, *Marketing*, 2 June, p. 3.

Reynolds, F.D. and Darden, W.R. (1971) Mutually adaptive effects of interpersonal communication, *Journal of Marketing Research*, 8 (November), 449–54.

Roberts, J. (2010) Mobilise the people to shape your brand, *Marketing Week*, 4 February, retrieved 23 June 2010 from www.marketingweek.co.uk/in-depth-analysis/cover-stories/mobilise-the-people-to-shape-your-brand/3009483.article.

Robinson, J.P. (1976) Interpersonal influence in election campaigns: two step flow hypothesis, *Public Opinion Quarterly*, 40, 304–19.

Rogers, E.M. (1962) *Diffusion of Innovations*, 1st edn, New York: Free Press.

Rogers, E.M. (1983) *Diffusion of Innovations*, 3rd edn, New York: Free Press.

Rogers, E.M. (1986) *Communication Technology: The New Media in Society*, New York: Free Press.

Rogers, E.M. (2003) *Diffusion of Innovations*, 5th edn, New York: Free Press.

Rothschild, M. (1987) *Marketing Communications*, Lexington, MA: D.C. Heath.

Schramm, W. (1955) How communication works, in *The Process and Effects of Mass Communications* (ed. W. Schramm), Urbana, IL: University of Illinois Press, 3–26.

Shannon, C. and Weaver, W. (1962) *The Mathematical Theory of Communication*, Urbana, IL: University of Illinois Press.

Simms, J. (2007) Bridging the gap, *Marketing*, 12 December, 26–8.

Smith, N. (2010) Hovis: Marketing Society Award for Excellence, *Marketing*, 9 June, p. 15.

Smithers, R. (2009) Dyson teaser campaign has fans all a Twitter, *Guardian*, Tuesday 13 October, retrieved http://www.guardian.co.uk/technology/2009/oct/13/dyson-fan-green-airblade.

Soldow, G.F. and Thomas, G.P. (1984) Relational Communication: Form Versus Content in the Sales Interaction, *Journal of Marketing*, 48 (Winter), 84–93.

Stokes, D. and Lomax, W. (2002) Taking control of word of mouth marketing: the case of an entrepreneurial hotelier, *Journal of Small Business and Enterprise Development*, 9, 4, 349–57.

Taylor, D. and Altman, I. (1987) Communication in interpersonal relationships: social penetration theory, in *Interpersonal Processes: New Directions in Communication Research* (eds M.E. Roloff and G.R. Miller), Newbury Park, CA: Sage, 257–77.

Theodorson, S.A. and Theodorson, G.R. (1969) *A Modern Dictionary of Sociology*, New York: Cromwell.

Tichy, N. (1979) Social network analysis for organisations, *Academy of Management Review*, 4, 507–19.

Varey, R. (2002), Requisite communication for positive involvement and participation: A critical communication theory perspective, *International Journal of Applied Human Resource Management*, 3(2), 20–35.

Weick, K. (1987) Prescribed and emergent networks, in *Handbook of Organisational Communication* (ed. F. Jablin). London: Sage.

Weimann, G. (1994) *The influentials: People who influence people*, Albany: State University of New York Press.

Williams, K. (1990) *Behavioural Aspects of Marketing*, Oxford: Heinemann.

Windahl, S., Signitzer, B. and Olson, J.T. (1992) *Using Communication Theory*, London: Sage.

Yuan, Y., Caulkins, J.P. and Roehrig, S. (1998) The relationship between advertising and content provision on the Internet, *European Journal of Marketing*, 32, 7/8, 667–87.

# Chapter 3

# Audiences: how they process information and behave

Understanding the way in which customers perceive their world, the way they learn, develop attitudes and respond to marketing communication stimuli is fundamental if effective communications are to be developed. In the same way, understanding the ways in which people make decisions and the factors that impact upon the decision process can influence the effectiveness of marketing communications.

## Aims and learning objectives

The aims of this chapter are first to consider some of the ways information is processed by people and second to examine the key issues associated with purchase decision making and their impact on marketing communications.

The learning objectives are to enable readers to:

1. examine the primary elements associated with information processing: perception, learning, attitudes;

2. explain how information is used by both consumers and organisations when making purchase decisions;

3. appreciate the significance of stages and phases when explaining the decision-making processes;

4. describe ways in which involvement influences the form and type of marketing communications;

5. understand how marketing communications can be used to manage customer perceived risk;

6. explore the principles of both hedonic and tribal consumption;

7. suggest ways in which marketing communications should be influenced by an understanding of behavioural economics.

# Minicase

## Recruiting teachers – nudging the journey

The path to becoming a teacher can be fraught, involving many stages and numerous high-risk decisions. Two main markets for teachers can be identified. First, there are final year undergraduates about to enter the job market and, second, there are career switchers. These are graduates aged 25–45, looking for a change in their career.

Responsibility for the recruitment of up to 40,000 new school teachers every year, in England and Wales, rests with The Training and Development Agency for Schools (TDA). For the period 1998 to 2005 advertising had been used to help recruit record numbers of additional teachers, mainly through the use of advertising to counteract the negative perceptions of the profession.

However, by 2007 the number of eligible enquiries and applications was starting to decline and the percentage of people applying in the same year as they first enquired had dropped from 50 to 37 per cent. In other words, the campaign was still generating the right positive attitudes, but it was failing to generate the right behaviour. Research indicated that the cause of the decline rested with career switchers. They regarded this career change as a huge life decision with some equating it to emigrating, and others to leaping out of a plane. They saw risks associated with paying mortgages and supporting families, earning lower salaries and having to start their careers all over again. They also wondered if they would be any good at it, so there was the fear of failure. The result was decision paralysis, as career switchers felt they could not move forward, let alone complete the long application process.

The realisation that an individual's progress towards becoming a teacher was far from linear and consisted of various steps forward, sideways and then even some backward, all laced with a lack of decisiveness and uncertainty, indicated that advertising needed to be present at all times in this process. By helping to keep people moving towards another positive TDA experience, and ultimately to application, the use of advertising, and media in particular, was equated to that of a pinball machine helping to keep potential teachers 'in-play'. This meant cutting the big bursts of media usage and spreading activity. Now media was to be used to prompt people into action and to be present at all parts of the journey to making an application.

Reaching people when they are more likely to feel glum became an important media planning approach. So, ads were placed in newspapers popular with commuters, on Monday mornings. Poster sites on the underground and rail platforms were used as this is where people stand in the same place every day. Press was used to highlight priority subjects such as ICT and physics, and digital posters were used to inspire readers. This material even appeared in Facebook.

Media activity was integrated with the other disciplines involved with the campaign, such as public relations, event management, direct marketing and telemarketing. The PR strategy used real life stories in national and local media to bring to life how switching careers to teaching could be rewarding. Articles about how teaching is really fulfilling were available on the TDA website. Train-To-Teach events were held across the country, and advertising, email and outbound telemarketing was used to encourage people to pre-register.

Most of the ad content featured real teachers. Their role was to reassure career switchers that 'people like them' had made the switch, survived and were happy. Real teachers were also used at events, on social networking profiles, and in films and articles made for press and online publishers.

Several behavioural studies have demonstrated that people with sub goals are more likely to attain their final goal. This campaign was based on understanding the audience, understanding their thoughts, perceptions, and fears. Through this insight a series of behavioural triggers were developed designed to 'nudge' potential career switchers into and along the application journey, by turning a big decision into a series of small steps. In effect, this campaign reframed the communication task as a behavioural problem. This led to a radically different media strategy: from selling 'teaching' (an outcome) to encouraging people to take the necessary steps to make a career change and retrain and qualify as teachers.

The campaign achieved a minimum payback of £101 for every £1 spent, and increased the number of enquiries and applications to become teachers to record-breaking levels.

*This minicase, written by Chris Fill, is based largely on Boyd et al. (2010) and Hollingworth and Davies (2011).*

| Exhibit 3.1 | **Teacher recruitment ad** |
| | *Source*: Teaching Agency |

# Introduction

People consume products and services not only because of the utilitarian value but also because of what the products represent, their meaning and symbolic value. In other words, people make purchase decisions, either knowingly or subconsciously, about their identity and how they might want to be seen. The teacher recruitment campaign outlined in the minicase worked partly because it understood the mental journey and issues involved when people make decisions about changing careers and becoming a teacher.

Marketing communications is about making promises, and it makes sense, therefore, to understand buyer behaviour, in order that these promises remain realistic and effective. Understanding the ways in which buyers make decisions, the factors that impact upon the decision process and their preferred identities, can influence the effectiveness of marketing communications. In particular, it can affect message structure, content and scheduling. In this chapter, and indeed the book, reference is made both to buyers and audiences. This is because, although all buyers constitute an audience, not all audiences are buyers.

This chapter has three main sections. The first considers issues relating to the way people are thought to process information, the second embraces ideas about decision making and the third looks at some alternative, less orthodox, approaches to understanding consumer behaviour.

# Information processing

Marketing communications is an audience-centred activity, so it is vitally important to understand the way in which audiences process information prior to, during and after making product/service purchase decisions. Traditionally, awareness has been considered an integral part of information processing. However, this important topic is considered (see Chapter 6) as part of an organisation's objectives and positioning activities. Here three main information-processing issues are considered: perception, learning and attitudes.

## Perception

Perception is concerned with how individuals see and make sense of their environment. It is about how individuals select, organise and interpret stimuli, so that they can understand their world.

### Perceptual selection

The vast number of messages mentioned earlier need to be filtered, as individuals cannot process them all. The stimuli that are selected result from the interaction of the nature of the stimulus with the expectations and the motives of the individual. Attention is an important factor in determining the outcome of this interaction: 'Attention occurs when the stimulus activates one or more sensory receptor nerves and the resulting sensations go to the brain for processing' (Hawkins et al., 1989).

The nature of the stimuli, or external factors such as the intensity and size, position, contrast, novelty, repetition and movement, are factors that have been developed and refined by marketing communicators to attract attention. Animation is used to attract attention when the product class is perceived as bland and uninteresting, such as margarine or teabags. Unexpected camera angles and the use of music can be strong methods of gaining the attention of the target audience, as used successfully in the 'Still Red Hot' Virgin Atlantic campaign. Sexual attraction can be a powerful means of capturing the attention of audiences and, when associated with a brand's values, can be a very effective method of getting attention.

---

### Viewpoint 3.1    Silhouetting personality

Some brands are deliberately stripped of personality, as this enables them to appeal to a wider audience and avoid being labelled or stereotyped. For example, BMW's long-running advertising campaign is based on the functional excellence of their cars. BMW's advertising is characterised by the absence of people. For many years the driver was never seen and there are no passengers or children, so viewers cannot categorise certain types of drivers as typically BMW.

DeBeers have used the strapline 'a diamond is forever' because they feel it has universal appeal. One of their more successful campaigns 'Shadows', presented couples in silhouette form progressing through various stages in their lives. The ad was designed to reach and appeal to a wide range of people, signifying that a diamond was for everyone.

In much the same way, Apple used a silhouette of a person wearing/using an iPod. Although the visual suggested male, female and age-group characteristics, the silhouette focused attention on the product, not the type of person who should use it. This representation of a new product, without showing what it even looked like up close, gave it currency and made it instantly recognisable, across languages and cultures.

In all of these cases the absence of clearly defined users, or the use of a silhouette devoid of personality, invited viewers to superimpose themselves and their own personalities into the car, relationship and music environment respectively. By not presenting a particular type of person and their distinguishing personality traits, these brands have been able to reach and appeal to diverse audiences.

*Sources*:   Based on Parpis (2009); Anon (2004); Cobau (2000).

---

**Question:**   To what extent do you think potential purchasers might find it difficult to associate with these brands, when there is nobody to identify with?

**Task:**   Get copies of these three ads. Apart from the silhouette, is there anything else that they have in common?

| Exhibit 3.2 | **DeBeers shadows** |
| --- | --- |
| | Source: DeBeers UK Ltd |

The expectations, needs and motives of an individual, or internal factors, are equally important. Individuals see what they expect to see, and their expectations are normally based on past experience and preconditioning. From a communications perspective, the presentation of stimuli that conflict with an individual's expectations will invariably receive more attention. The attention-getting power of erotic and sexually driven advertising messages is understood and exploited. For example, jeans manufacturers such as Levis, Wranglers and Diesel often use this type of stimulus to promote their brands. However, advertising research based on recall testing often reveals that the attention-getting stimulus (e.g. the male or female) generates high recall scores, but the product or brand is very often forgotten. Looked at in terms of Schramm's model of communication (Chapter 2), the process of encoding was inaccurate, hence the inappropriate decoding.

Of particular interest is the tendency of individuals to select certain information from the environment. This process is referred to as *selective attention*. Through attention, individuals avoid contact with information that is felt to be disagreeable in that it opposes strongly held beliefs and attitudes.

Individuals see what they want or need to see. If they are considering the purchase of a new car, there will be heightened awareness of car advertisements and a correspondingly lower level of awareness of unrelated stimuli. Selective attention allows individuals to expose themselves to messages that are comforting and rewarding. For example, reassurance is often required for people who have bought new cars or expensive technical equipment and who have spent a great deal of time debating and considering the purchase and its associated risk. Communications congratulating the new owner on their wise decision often accompany post-purchase literature such as warranties and service contracts. If potentially harmful messages do get through this filter system, perceptual defence mechanisms help to screen them out after exposure.

## Perceptual organisation

For perception to be effective and meaningful, the vast array of selected stimuli needs to be organised. The four main ways in which sensory stimuli can be organised are figure–ground, grouping, closure and contour.

### Figure–ground

Each individual's perception of an environment tends to consist of articles on a general background, against which certain objects are illuminated and stand proud. Williams (1981) gives the examples of trees standing out against the sky and words on a page. This has obvious implications for advertisers and the design and form of communications, especially advertisements, to draw attention to important parts of the message, most noticeably the price, logo or company/brand name.

### Grouping

Objects that are close to one another tend to be grouped together and a pattern develops. Grouping can be used to encourage associations between a product and specific attributes. For example, food products that are positioned for a health market are often displayed with pictures that represent fitness and exercise, the association being that consumption of the food will lead to a lifestyle that incorporates fitness and exercise, as these are important to the target market.

### Closure

When information is incomplete, individuals make sense of the data by filling in the gaps. This is often used to involve consumers in the message and so enhance selective attention. Advertisements for American Express charge cards or GM credit cards ('if invited to apply'), for example, suggest that ownership denotes membership, which represents exclusiveness and privilege.

Television advertisements that are run for 60 seconds when first launched are often cut to 30 or even 15 seconds later in the burst. The purpose is two-fold: to cut costs and to keep reminding the target audience. This process of reminding is undertaken with the assistance of the audience, who recognise the commercial and mentally close the message even though the advertiser only presents the first part.

### Contour

Contours give objects shape and are normally formed when there is a marked change in colour or brightness. This is an important element in package design and, as the battle for shelf space in retail outlets becomes more intense, so package design has become an increasingly important aspect of attracting attention. The Coca-Cola bottle and the packaging of the Toblerone bar are two classic examples of packaging that conveys the brand.

These methods are used by individuals in an attempt to organise stimuli and simplify their meanings. They combine in an attempt to determine a pattern to the stimuli, so that they are perceived as part of a whole or larger unit. This is referred to as *gestalt psychology*.

## Perceptual interpretation

Interpretation is the process by which individuals give meaning to the stimuli once they have been organised. As Cohen and Basu (1987) state, by using existing categories, meanings can be given to stimuli. These categories are determined from the individual's past experiences and they shape what the individual expects to see. These expectations, when combined with the strength and clarity of the stimulus and the motives at the time perception occurs, mould the pattern of the perceived stimuli.

The degree to which each individual's ascribed meaning, resulting from the interpretation process, is realistic is dependent upon the levels of distortion that may be present. Distortion may occur because of stereotyping: the predetermined set of images which we use to guide our expectations of events, people and situations. Another distortion factor is the halo effect that occurs when a stimulus with many attributes or dimensions is evaluated on just a single attribute or dimension. Brand extensions and family branding strategies are based on the understanding that if previous experiences with a different offering are satisfactory, then risk is reduced and an individual is more likely to buy a new offering from the same 'family'.

## Marketing and perception

Individuals, therefore, select and interpret particular stimuli in the context of the expectations arising from the way they classify the overall situation. The way in which individuals perceive, organise and interpret stimuli is a reflection of their past experiences and the classifications used to understand the different situations each individual frames every day. Individuals seek to frame or provide a context within which their role becomes clearer. Shoppers expect to find products in particular situations, such as rows, shelves or display bins of similar goods. They also develop meanings and associations with some grocery products because of the utility and trust/emotional satisfaction certain pack types evoke. The likelihood that a sale will be made is improved, if the context in which a purchase transaction is undertaken does not contradict a shopper's expectations.

| Exhibit 3.3 | KFC – Gender-driven advertisement |

When KFC introduced their BBQ Rancher, a range launched in response to market needs for a healthy non-fired burger, the 400-calorie, chicken-based product was communicated through two ad themes. One was aimed at men using a 'fun-loving' approach. The other was designed to appeal to women (see Exhibit 3.3) and was based on etiquette (Reynolds, 2012).

*Source*: Freud Communications

Marketing communications should attempt to present products (objects) in a frame or 'mental presence' (Moran, 1990) that is recognised by a buyer, such as a consumption or purchase situation. A product has a much greater chance of entering an evoked set if the situation in which it is presented is one that is expected and relevant. However, a new pack design can provide differentiation and provoke people into reassessing their expectations of what constitutes appropriate packaging in a product category.

Javalgi et al. (1992) point out that perception is important to product evaluation and product selection. Consumers try to evaluate a product's attributes using the physical cues of taste, smell, size and shape. Sometimes no difference can be distinguished, so the consumer has to make a judgement on factors other than the physical characteristics of the product. This is the basis of branding activity, where a personality is developed for the product which enables it to be perceived differently from its competitors. The individual may also set up a separate category or evoked set in order to make sense of new stimuli or satisfactory experiences.

---

### Scholars' paper 3.1 | Simply a cosmetic perception

**Guthrie, M.F. and Kim, H-S. (2009) The relationship between consumer involvement and brand perceptions of female cosmetic consumers, *Journal of Brand Management*, 17(2), 114–133.**

Although this may not be ranked as a seminal or great paper, it is interesting because it provides an application of Kapferer and Laurent's consumer-involvement profile. It shows how segmentation can be undertaken based on consumer perceptions and from this brand communications used to develop suitable images.

---

Goodrich (1978) discusses the importance of perception, which can be seen in terms of the choices tourists make when deciding which destination to visit. The decision is influenced by levels of general familiarity, levels of specific knowledge and perception. It follows that the more favourable the perception of a particular destination, the more likely it is to be selected from its competitors.

Finally, individuals carry a set of enduring perceptions or images. These relate to themselves, to products and to organisations. For example, many consumers perceive the financial services industry negatively. This is simply because of the inherent complexity associated with the product offerings and the rumble of negative publicity caused by the debate over account-charges and the Northern Rock issue (Nottage, 2007). The concept of positioning the product in the mind of the consumer is fundamental to marketing strategy and is a topic that will be examined in greater depth (see Chapter 6).

Organisations develop multiple images to meet the positioning requirements of their end-user markets and stakeholders. They need to monitor and adjust their identities constantly in respect of the perceptions and expectations held by the other organisations in their various networks. For example, the level of channel coordination and control can be a function of the different perceptions of channel members. These concern the perception of the channel depth, processes of control and the roles each member is expected to fulfil. Furthermore, the perception of an organisation's product quality and its associated image (reputation) are becoming increasingly important. Both end-user buyers and channel members are attempting to ensure that the intrinsic and extrinsic cues associated with their products are appropriate signals of product quality (Moran, 1990).

**Viewpoint 3.2**    **Time Spent . . . changing perceptions**

Many campaigns are designed to change the way people see or perceive a brand. For example, the National Trust used marketing communications to change away from an image based on formality, a demographic rooted in middle/older age, and a brand that was way out of date. The strategy was to broaden the range of products and experiences people could have with the National Trust.

The campaign has now been running for several years and uses the strapline, 'Time well Spent'. The principle was that people should be encouraged to perceive the National Trust as an opportunity for 'simple pleasures and quality, memorable experiences at affordable rates'. This was translated into a series of outdoor ads that showed various types of people enjoying different experiences. A couple might be attempting a topiary maze, or a family might be shown sitting near a beautiful river. Radio ads featured chirping birds and the delight of children playing. Online ads included an interactive facility helping people identify their nearest National Trust property. All the ads began with the message, 'Time to . . .' which was followed by a message, such as, be together . . . see something . . . unwind . . . explore.

Since then the Trust has launched an iPhone app designed to help gardeners and day-trippers to find and explore and browse any of the 150 National Trust gardens whenever they want. In 2010 visitor numbers increased 16 per cent and membership increased by nearly 18 per cent.

*Source*:   McMeeken (2012); Eleftheriou-Smith (2011); Anon (2011).

**Question:**   How might the National Trust use social media?

**Task:**   Find a campaign where the core task appears to be to change perceptions about health issues.

**Exhibit 3.4**    **National Trust campaign ad**
*Source*: National Trust Images

# Learning

There are two mainstream approaches to learning: behavioural and cognitive.

| Table 3.1 | | Types of learning |
| --- | --- | --- |
| **Type of learning** | | **Explanation** |
| Behavioural | Classical | Individuals learn to make associations or connections between a stimulus and their responses. Through repetition of the response (the behaviour) to the stimulus, learning occurs. |
| | Operant | Learning occurs as a result of an individual operating or interacting with the environment. The response of the individual is instrumental in getting a positive reinforcement (reward) or negative reinforcement (punishment). Behaviour that is rewarded or reinforced will be continued, whereas behaviour that is not rewarded will cease. |
| Cognitive | | Assumes that individuals attempt to actively influence their immediate environment rather than be subject to it. They try to resolve problems by processing information from past experiences (memory) in order to make reasoned decisions based on judgements. |

## Behavioural learning

The behavourist approach to learning views the process as a function of an individual's acquisition of responses. There are three factors important to behavioural learning: association, reinforcement and motivation. However, it is the basic concept of the stimulus–response orientation that will be looked at in more detail.

It is accepted that for learning to occur all that is needed is a 'time–space proximity' between a stimulus and a response. Learning takes place through the establishment of a connection between a stimulus and a response. Marketing communications are thought to work by the simple process of people observing messages and being stimulated/motivated to respond by requesting more information or purchasing the advertised product in search of a reward. Behaviour is learned through the conditioning experience of a stimulus and response. There are two forms of conditioning: classical and operant.

### Classical conditioning

Classical conditioning assumes that learning is an associative process that occurs with an existing relationship between a stimulus and a response. By far the best-known example of this type of learning are the experiments undertaken by the Russian psychologist Pavlov. He noticed that dogs began to salivate at the sight of food. He stated that this was not taught, but was a reflex reaction. This relationship exists prior to any experimentation or learning. The food represents an unconditioned stimulus and the response (salivation) from the dogs is an unconditioned response.

Pavlov then paired the ringing of a bell with the presentation of food. Shortly the dogs began to salivate at the ringing of the bell. The bell became the conditioned stimulus and the salivation became the conditioned response (which was the same as the unconditioned response).

From an understanding of this work it can be determined that two factors are important for learning to occur:

● To build the association between the unconditioned and conditioned stimulus, there must be a relatively short period of time.

● The conditioning process requires that there be a relatively high frequency/repetition of the association. The more often the unconditioned and conditioned stimuli occur together, the stronger will be the association.

Classical conditioning can be observed operating in each individual's everyday life. An individual who purchases a new product because of a sales promotion may continue to buy the product even when the promotion has terminated. An association has been established between the sales promotion activity (unconditioned stimulus) and the product (conditioned stimulus). If product quality and satisfaction levels allow, long-run behaviour may develop despite the absence of the promotion. In other words, promotion need not act as a key purchase factor in the long run.

Advertisers attempt to associate their products/services with certain perceptions, images and emotions that are known to evoke positive reactions from consumers. Image advertising seeks to develop the associations that individuals have when they think of a brand or an organisation, hence its reputation. Messages of this type show the object with an unconditioned stimulus that is known to evoke pleasant and favourable feelings. So, the puppet 'Aleksandr Orlov' is the face for comparethemarket.com, Gary Lineker is associated with Walker's crisps, and Nicole Kidman and Penelope Cruz are the brand ambassadors for Chanel No. 5. and L'Oréal Paris respectively. The product becomes a conditioned stimulus eliciting the same favourable response. The advertisements for Bounty Bars use images of desert islands to evoke feelings of enjoyment and pleasure and associations with coconuts.

### Operant conditioning

In this form of conditioning, sometimes known as *instrumental conditioning*, learning occurs as a result of an individual operating or acting on some part of the environment. The response of the individual is instrumental in getting a positive reinforcement (reward) or negative reinforcement (punishment). Behaviour that is rewarded or reinforced will be continued, whereas behaviour that is not rewarded will cease.

B.F. Skinner was a pioneer researcher in the field of operant conditioning. His work, with rats who learned to press levers in order to receive food and who later only pressed the lever when a light was on (discriminative stimulus), highlights the essential feature of this form of conditioning: that reinforcement follows a specific response.

Many organisations use reinforcement in their communications by stressing the benefits or rewards that a consumer can anticipate receiving as a result of using a product or brand. For example, Tesco offer 'reward points' and Nectar offer a reward of money savings which 'makes the difference'. Reinforcement theories emphasise the role of external factors and exclude the individual's ability to process information internally. Learning takes place either through direct reinforcement of a particular response or through an associative conditioning process.

However, operant conditioning is a mechanistic process that is not realistic, as it serves only to simplify an extremely complex process.

## Cognitive learning

This approach to our understanding of learning assumes that individuals attempt to control their immediate environments. They are seen as active participants in that they try to resolve problems by processing information that is pertinent to each situation. Central to this process is memory. Just as money can be invested in short-, medium-, and long-term investment accounts, so information is memorised for different periods of time. These memories are sensory, short-term and long-term, set out at Figure 3.1.

*Sensory storage* refers to the period in which information is sensed for a split second, and if an impression has been made the information will be transferred to short-term memory where it is rehearsed before transfer to long-term memory. *Short-term* memory lasts no longer than approximately eight seconds and a maximum of four or five items can be stored in short-term memory at any one time. Readers will probably have experienced being introduced to someone at a social event only to forget the name of the guest when they next meet them at the same event. This occurs because the name was not entered into *long-term* memory. Information can be stored for extended periods in long-term memory. This information is not lying dormant, however, it is constantly being reorganised and recategorised as new information is received.

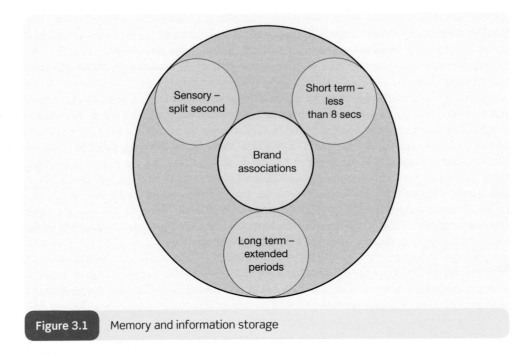

**Figure 3.1**    Memory and information storage

There are four basic functions by which memory operates. These are, first, *rehearsal*, where information is repeated or related to an established category. This is necessary so that the second function, *encoding*, can take place. This involves the selection of an image to represent the perceived object. Once in long-term memory it is *categorised and stored*, the third function. *Retrieval* is the final function, a process by which information is recovered from storage.

Cognitive learning is about processing information in order that problems can be resolved. These information-handling processes can range from the simple to the complex. There are three main processes: iconic, modelling and reasoning.

*Iconic rote learning* involves understanding the association between two or more concepts when there is an absence of a stimulus. Learning occurs at a weak level through repetition of simple messages. Beliefs are formed about the attributes of an offering without any real understanding of the source of the information. Advertisers of certain products (low value, frequently purchased) will try to remind their target audiences repeatedly of the brand name in an attempt to help consumers learn. Through such repetition, an association with the main benefits of the product may be built, if only via the constant reminders by the spokesperson.

Learning through the *modelling* approach involves the observation and imitation of others and the associated outcomes of their behaviour. In essence, a great deal of children's early learn- ing is developed in this way. Likewise, marketing communicators use the promise of rewards to persuade audiences to act in a particular way. By using positive images of probable rewards, buyers are encouraged to believe that they can receive the same outcome if they use the particular product. For example, clothing advertisements often depict the model receiving admiring glances from passers-by. The same admiration is the reward 'promised' to those who wear the same clothing. A similar approach was used by Kellogg's to promote their Special K breakfast cereal. The commercial depicted a (slim) mother and child playing on a beach. The message was that it is important to look after yourself and to raise your family through healthy eating, an outdoor life and exercise.

*Reasoning* is perhaps the most complex form of cognitive learning. Through this process, individuals need to restructure and reorganise information held in long-term memory and combine it with fresh inputs in order to generate new outputs. Financial services providers have to convey complex information, strictly bounded by the Financial Services legislation and the Financial Services Authority. So, brands such as Nationwide and Hiscox convey key points about simplicity and specialist services respectively, to differentiate their brands. This enables current and potential customers to process detailed information about these brands and to make judgements or reason that these brands reach acceptable (threshold) standards.

Of all the approaches to understanding how we learn, cognitive learning is the most flexible interpretation. The rational, more restricted approach of behavioural learning, where the focus is external to the individual, is without doubt a major contribution to knowledge. However, it fails to accommodate the complex internal thought processes that individuals utilise when presented with various stimuli.

It is useful to appreciate the way in which people are believed to learn and forget as there are several issues which are useful to media planners in particular.

## Decay

The rate at which individuals forget material assumes a pattern, as shown in Figure 3.2. Many researchers have found that information decays at a negatively decelerating rate. As much as 60 per cent of the initial yield of information from an advertisement has normally decayed within six weeks. This decay, or wear-out, can be likened to the half-life of radioactive material. It is always working, although it cannot be seen, and the impact of the advertising reduces through time. Like McGuire's (1978) retention stage in his hierarchy of effects model (see Chapter 14), the storage of information for future use is important, but with time, how powerful will the information be and what triggers are required to promote recall?

Advertising wear-out is thought to occur because of two factors. First, individuals use selective perception and mentally switch off after a critical number of exposures. Second, the monotony and irritation caused by continued exposure lead to counter-argument to both the message and the advertisement (Petty and Cacioppo, 1979). Advertisements for alcoholic drinks such as Carlsberg and Stella Artois attempt to prevent wear-out by using variations on a central theme to provide consistency yet engage audiences through interest and entertainment.

## Cognitive response

Learning can be visualised as following either of the curves set out in Figure 3.3. The amount learnt 'wears out' after a certain repetition level has been reached. Grass and Wallace (1969) suggest that this process of wear-out commences once a satiation point has been reached. A number of researchers (Zielske, 1959; Strong, 1977) have found that recall is improved when messages are transmitted on a regular weekly basis, rather than daily, monthly or in a concentrated or dispersed format.

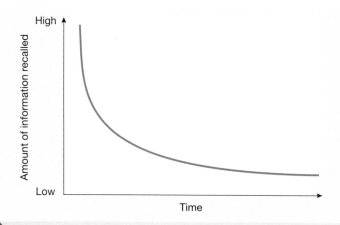

| **Figure 3.2** | A standard decay curve |

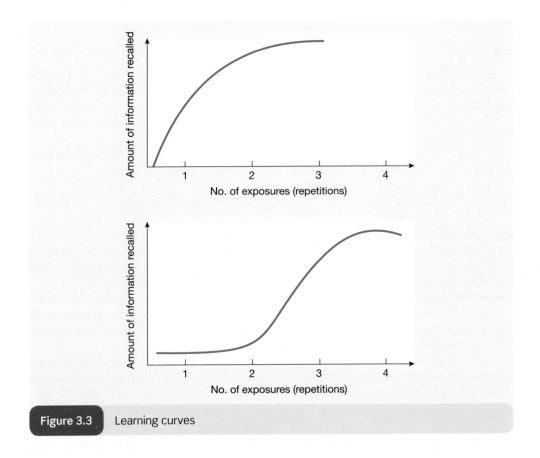

**Figure 3.3**    Learning curves

An individual's ability to develop and retain awareness or knowledge of a product will, therefore, be partly dependent not only on the quality of the message but also on the number and quality of exposures to a planned message. To assist the media planner, there are a number of concepts that need to be appreciated and used within the decisions about what, where and when a message should be transmitted. There are a number of other concepts that are of use to media planners: these are reach and coverage, frequency, gross rating points, effective frequency, efficiency and media source effects.

---

**Scholars' paper 3.2**    **Learning about brands**

**Heath, R. (2001) Low involvement processing – a new model of brand communication, *Journal of Marketing Communications*, 7, 27–33.**

At the beginning of the noughties, Heath began publishing papers about low-involvement processing and how we learn about brands through communications. He subsequently changed the terminology to low- and high-attention theory. Since then he has published a stream of papers on this topic, one which contradicts the traditional rational view of brand choice. Heath offers a new and different perspective on how consumers are influenced by advertising. This paper provides an insight into the literature and his thinking. It also serves to link various concepts, many of which are covered in this chapter.

# Attitudes

The perceptual and learning processes usually lead to the formation of attitudes. These are predispositions, shaped through experience, to respond in an anticipated way to an object or situation. Attitudes are learned through past experiences and serve as a link between thoughts and behaviour. These experiences may relate to the product itself, to the messages transmitted by the different members of the channel network (normally mass media communications) and to the information supplied by opinion leaders, formers and followers.

Attitudes tend to be consistent within each individual: they are clustered and very often interrelated. This categorisation leads to the formation of stereotypes, which is extremely useful for the design of messages as stereotyping allows for the transmission of a lot of information in a short time period (30 seconds) without impeding learning or the focal part of the message.

## Attitude components

Attitudes are hypothetical constructs, and classical psychological theory considers attitudes to consist of three components:

1. *Cognitive component (learn)*
   This component refers to the level of knowledge and beliefs held by individuals about a product and/or the beliefs about specific attributes of the offering. This represents the learning aspect of attitude formation.

   Marketing communications are used to create attention and awareness, to provide information and to help audiences learn and understand the features and benefits a particular product/service offers.

2. *Affective component (feel)*
   By referring to the feelings held about a product – good, bad, pleasant or unpleasant – an evaluation is made of the object. This is the component that is concerned with feelings, sentiments, moods and emotions about an object.

   Marketing communications are used to induce feelings about the product/service such that it becomes a preferred brand. This preference may be based on emotional attachment to a brand, conferred status through ownership, past experiences and longevity of brand usage or any one of a number of ways in which people can become emotionally involved with a brand.

3. *Conative component (do)*
   This is the action component of the attitude construct and refers to the individual's disposition or intention to behave in a certain way. Some researchers go so far as to suggest that this component refers to observable behaviour. Marketing communications therefore, should be used to encourage audiences to do something. For example, visit a website, phone a telephone number, take a coupon, book a visit, press red (on a remote control unit) for interactivity though digital television.

This three-component approach to attitudes, set out at Figure 3.4, is based upon attitudes towards an object, person or organisation. The sequence of attitude formation is generally considered to be learn, feel and do. However, this approach to attitude formation is limited in that the components are seen to be of equal strength. A single-component model has been developed where the attitude only consists of the individual's overall feeling towards an object. In other words, the affective component is the only significant component.

## Intentions

Of the many advances in this area, those made by Ajzen and Fishbein (1980) have made a significant contribution. They reasoned that the best way of predicting behaviour was to measure an individual's intention to purchase (the conative component). Underlying intentions

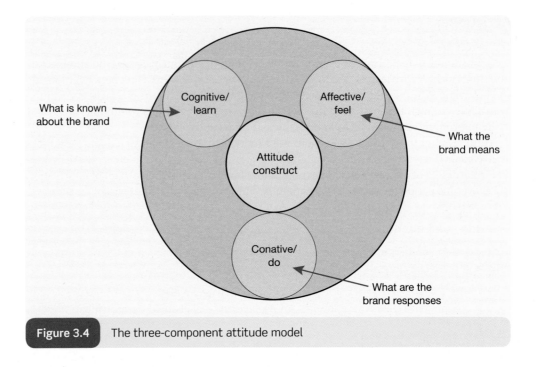

What is known
about the brand

Cognitive/
learn

Affective/
feel

What the
brand means

Attitude
construct

Conative/
do

What are the
brand responses

**Figure 3.4**    The three-component attitude model

are the individual's attitude towards the act of behaviour and the subjective norm. In other words, the context within which a proposed purchase is to occur is seen as important to the attitude that is developed towards the object.

The subjective norm is the relevant feelings others are believed to hold about the proposed purchase, or intention to purchase. Underpinning the subjective norm are the beliefs held about the people who are perceived to 'judge' the actions an individual might take. Would they approve or disapprove, or look favourably or unfavourably upon the intended action?

Underpinning the attitude towards the intention to act in a particular way are the strengths of the beliefs that a particular action will lead to an outcome. Ajzen and Fishbein argue that it is the individual's attitude to the act of purchasing, not the object of the purchase, that is important. For example, a manager may have a positive attitude towards a particular type of expensive office furniture, but a negative attitude towards the act of securing agreement for him to purchase it.

The theory of reasoned action (Ajzen and Fishbein, 1980; Figure 3.5) shows that intentions are composed of interrelated components: subjective norms, which in turn are composed of beliefs and motivations about relevant others, towards a particular intention, and attitudes, which in turn are made up of beliefs about the probable outcomes that a behaviour will lead to.

This approach recognises the interrelationship of the three components of attitudes and that it is not attitude but the intention to act or behave that precedes observable behaviour that should be the focus of attention. It should be understood that attitudes do not precede behaviour and cannot be used to predict behaviour, despite the attempts of a number of researchers. Attitudes are important, but they are not the sole determinant of behaviour, and intentions may be a better indicator of behaviour.

Attitudes impact on consumer decision-making, and the objective of marketing communications is often to create a positive attitude towards a product and/or to reinforce or change existing attitudes. An individual may perceive and develop a belief that British Airways has a friendly and informal in-flight service and that the service provided by Lufthansa is cold and formal. However, both airlines are perceived to hold a number of different attributes, and each individual needs to evaluate these attributes in order that an attitude can be developed. It is necessary, therefore, to measure the strength of the beliefs held about the key attributes

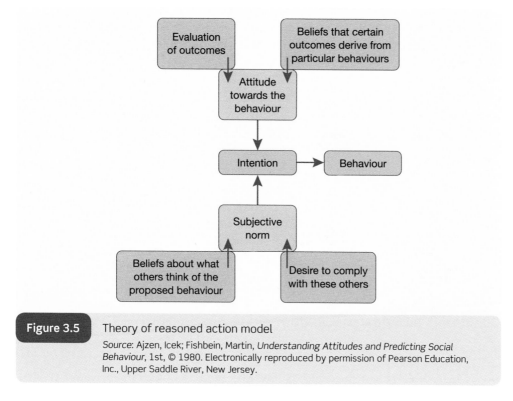

| Figure 3.5 | Theory of reasoned action model |
|---|---|

*Source*: Ajzen, Icek; Fishbein, Martin, *Understanding Attitudes and Predicting Social Behaviour*, 1st, © 1980. Electronically reproduced by permission of Pearson Education, Inc., Upper Saddle River, New Jersey.

of different products. There are two main processes whereby beliefs can be processed and measured: compensatory and non-compensatory models.

## Compensatory models

Through this approach, attributes that are perceived to be weak can be offset by attributes that are perceived to be strong. As a result, positive attitudes are determined in the sense that the evaluation of all the attributes is satisfactory. For example, Table 3.2 sets out a possible evaluation of three package holidays. Despite the weakness on hotel cleanliness, the strength of the other attributes in package 2 scores this one the highest, so the strongest attitude is formed towards this product. Some individuals make decisions about products on the basis that their attributes must not contain any weaknesses. Therefore, package 2 would not be considered, as it fails to reach a minimum level of expected satisfaction on cleanliness. Thus, despite its strengths, it is relegated from the decision alternatives.

| Table 3.2 | Compensatory and non-compensatory models |
|---|---|

| Attribute | Weighting | Package 1 Rating | Package 1 Score | Package 2 Rating | Package 2 Score | Package 3 Rating | Package 3 Score |
|---|---|---|---|---|---|---|---|
| Price | 5 | 5 | 25 | 6 | 30 | 5 | 25 |
| Hotel cleanliness | 3 | 3 | 9 | 2 | 6 | 4 | 12 |
| Travel times | 2 | 7 | 14 | 9 | 18 | 4 | 8 |
| Attitude rating | | | 48 | | 54 | | 45 |
| Possible decisions | | | | | | | |
|   Compensatory model | | Not considered | | *Winner* | | Not considered | |
|   Non-compensatory model | | *Winner* | | Not considered | | Considered | |

An understanding of attitude components and the way in which particular attributes can be measured not only enables organisations to determine the attitudes held towards them and their competitors but also empowers them to change the attitudes held by different stakeholders, if it is thought necessary.

# Decision making

Much of marketing communication activity has been orientated towards a customer's decision-making processes. This is to identify the right type of information, to be conveyed at the right time, in the appropriate format, in order to engage the target audience. There are two broad types of buyer, consumers and organisational buyers, and each is considered to follow particular rational, sequential and logical pathways when making purchase decisions. The consumer decision making process is depicted at Figure 3.6 and the organisational process at Figure 3.7. The consumer pathway consists of five stages, and marketing communications can impact upon any or all of these stages with varying levels of potential effectiveness.

## Consumer purchase decision-making process

In reality buyers do not follow these decision steps. There are too many factors that impact on decision making and the procedure adopted may vary depending upon the time available, levels of perceived risk and the degree of involvement a buyer has with the type of product, past experience and a host of other factors. Perceived risk and involvement are issues that will be explored later. At this point three types of problem-solving behaviour (extended problem solving, limited problem solving and routinised response) will be considered.

### Extended problem solving (EPS)

Consumers considering the purchase of a car or house undertake a great deal of external search activity and spend a lot of time reaching a solution that satisfies, as closely as possible, the evaluative criteria previously set. This activity is usually associated with products that are unfamiliar, where direct experience and hence knowledge are weak, and where there is considerable financial risk.

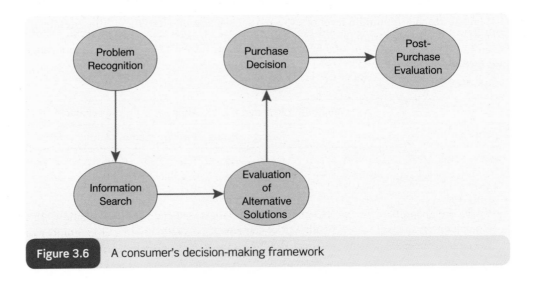

**Figure 3.6**    A consumer's decision-making framework

Marketing communications should aim to provide a lot of information to assist the decision process. The provision of information through sales literature, such as brochures and leaflets, websites for determining product and purchase criteria in product categories where there is little experience, access to salespersons and demonstrations and advertisements, are just some of the ways in which information can be provided.

### Limited problem solving (LPS)

Having experience of a product means that greater use can be made of internal, memory-based search routines and the external search can be limited to obtaining up-to-date information or to ensuring that the finer points of the decision have been investigated.

Marketing communications should attempt to provide information about any product modification or new attributes and convey messages that highlight those key attributes known to be important to buyers. By differentiating the product, marketing communications provides the buyer with a reason to select that particular product.

### Routinised response behaviour (RRB)

For a great number of products the decision process will consist only of an internal search. This is primarily because the buyer has made a number of purchases and has accumulated a great deal of experience. Therefore, only an internal search is necessary, so little time or effort will be spent on external search activities. Low-value items that are frequently purchased fall into this category – for example, toothpaste, soap, tinned foods and confectionery.

Some outlets are perceived as suitable for what are regarded as distress purchases. Tesco Express and many petrol stations position themselves as convenience stores for distress purchases (for example a pint of milk at 10 o'clock at night). Many garages have positioned themselves as convenience stores suitable for meeting the needs of RRB purchases. In doing so, they are moving themselves away from the perception of being only a distress-purchase outlet.

Communicators should focus upon keeping the product within the evoked set or getting it into the set. Learning can be enhanced through repetition of messages, but repetition can also be used to maintain attention and awareness.

## Organisational decision-making process

Now we need to turn to the equivalent processes associated with organisational buying decisions. In order to function, organisations need to buy materials, parts, general supplies and services from a range of other organisations. Some texts refer to this as *industrial marketing* or, in the more current terminology, *business-to-business marketing*, reflecting the growth and importance of the public sector and the increasing use of the services sector within mature economies. However, the term 'organisational marketing' is used here to reflect the wide range of organisations involved with such activities.

The term 'buyphases' was given by Robinson et al. (1967) to the several stages of the organisational buying decisions, as depicted in Figure 3.7. However, considering the buying process in terms of these neat steps is also misleading, again owing to the various forces acting on organisations.

Just like consumers, organisational buyers make decisions that vary with each buying situation and buyclass. Buyclasses, according to Robinson et al. (1967), comprise three types or contexts: new task, modified rebuy and straight rebuy (see Table 3.3).

1. *New buy*

    As the name implies, the organisation is faced with a first-time buying situation. Risk is inevitably large at this point, and partly as a consequence there are a large number of decision participants. Each participant requires a lot of information and a relatively long period of time is required for the information to be assimilated and a decision to be made.

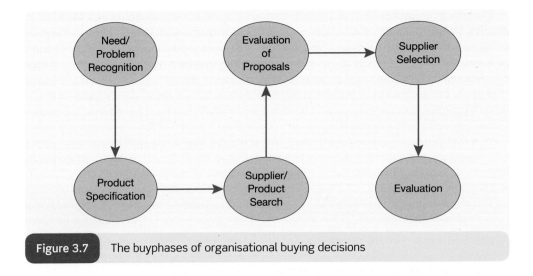

**Figure 3.7** The buyphases of organisational buying decisions

**Table 3.3** The main characteristics of the buyclasses

| Buyclass | Degree of familiarity with the problem | Information requirements | Alternative solutions |
|---|---|---|---|
| New buy | The problem is fresh to the decision-makers | A great deal of information is required | Alternative solutions are unknown, all are considered new |
| Modified rebuy | The requirement is not new but is different from previous situations | More information is required but past experience is of use | Buying decision needs new solutions |
| Rebuy | The problem is identical to previous experiences | Little or no information is required | Alternative solutions not sought or required |

2. *Modified rebuy*

   Having purchased a product, the organisation may request through its buyer that certain modifications be made to future purchases: for example, adjustments to the specification of the product, further negotiation on price levels or perhaps the arrangement for alternative delivery patterns. Fewer people are involved in the decision process than in the new task situation.

3. *Straight rebuy*

   In this situation, the purchasing department reorders on a routine basis, very often working from an approved list of suppliers. No other people are involved with the exercise until different suppliers attempt to change the environment in which the decision is made. For example, they may interrupt the procedure with a potentially better offer.

Some readers may have noticed how these phases bear a strong resemblance to the extended, limited and routinised responses identified earlier with respect to the consumer market.

Organisational buying, according to Webster and Wind (1972), is 'the decision making process by which formal organisations establish the need for purchased products and services and identify, evaluate and choose among alternative brands and suppliers'. Of particular significance is the relationship that develops between organisations that enter market exchange transactions. As mentioned previously, the various networks that organisations belong to will influence the purchase decisions that other organisations in the network make. However, before exploring these issues, it is necessary to review the context in which organisational decisions are made.

One way of examining the context is to compare organisational decisions with those made in consumer markets. There are far fewer buyers in the organisational context than in the consumer market, although there can be a number of people associated with a buying decision in an organisation. Orders are invariably larger and the frequency with which they are placed is much lower. It is quite common for agreements to be made between organisations for the supply of materials over a number of years. Similarly, depending upon the complexity of the product (photocopying paper or a one-off satellite), the negotiation process may also take a long time.

Many of the characteristics associated with consumer decision-making processes can be observed in the organisational context. However, organisational buyers make decisions which ultimately contribute to the achievement of corporate objectives. To make the necessary decisions, a high volume of pertinent information is often required. This information needs to be relatively detailed and is normally presented in a rational and logical style. The needs of the buyers are many and complex and some may be personal. Goals, such as promotion and career advancement within the organisation, coupled with ego and employee satisfaction combine to make organisational buying an important task, one that requires professional training and the development of expertise if the role is to be performed optimally.

Reference has been made on a number of occasions to organisational buyers, as if these people are the only representatives of an organisation to be involved with the purchase decision process. This is not the case, as very often a large number of people are involved in the purchase decision. This group is referred to as either the decision-making unit (DMU) or the buying centre.

Buying centres vary in size and composition in accordance with the nature of each individual task. Webster and Wind (1972) identified a number of people who make up the buying centre.

*Users* are people who not only initiate the purchase process but also use the product, once it has been acquired, and evaluate its performance. *Influencers* very often help set the technical specifications for the proposed purchase and assist the evaluation of alternative offerings by potential suppliers. *Deciders* are those who make purchasing decisions. In repeat buying activities the buyer may well also be the decider. However, it is normal practice to require that expenditure decisions involving sums over a certain financial limit be authorised by other, often senior, managers. *Buyers* (purchasing managers) select suppliers and manage the process whereby the required products are procured. As identified previously, buyers may not decide which product is to be purchased but they influence the framework within which the decision is made.

*Gatekeepers* have the potential to control the type and flow of information to the organisation and the members of the buying centre. These gatekeepers may be technical personnel, secretaries or telephone switchboard operators.

The size and form of the buying centre is not static. It can vary according to the complexity of the product being considered and the degree of risk each decision is perceived to carry for the organisation. Different roles are required and adopted as the nature of the buying task changes with each new purchase situation (Bonoma, 1982). It is vital for seller organisations to identify members of the buying centre and to target and refine their messages to meet the needs of each member of the centre.

The task of the communications manager and the corresponding sales team is to decide which key participants have to be reached, with which type of message, with what frequency, and to what depth should contact be made. Just like individual consumers, each member of the buying centre is an active problem solver and processes information so that personal and organisational goals are achieved.

## Influences on the buying centre

Three major influences on organisational buyer behaviour can be identified as stakeholders, the organisational environment and those aspects which the individual brings to the situation, as set out in Table 3.4.

| Table 3.4 | Major influences on organisational buying behaviour | |
| --- | --- | --- |
| **Stakeholder influences** | **Organisational influences** | **Individual influences** |
| Economic conditions | Corporate strategy | Personality |
| Legislation | Organisational culture and values | Age |
| Competitor strategies | Resources and costs | Status |
| Industry regulations | Purchasing policies and procedures | Reward structure and systems |
| Technological developments | Interpersonal relationships | |
| Social and cultural values | | |
| Interorganisational relationships | | |

*Source*: Based on Webster and Wind (1972).

Stakeholders develop relationships between the focus organisation and other stakeholders in the network. The nature of the exchange relationship and the style of communications will influence buying decisions. If the relationship between organisations is trusting, mutually supportive and based on a longer-term perspective (a relational structure) then the behaviour of the buying centre may be seen to be cooperative and constructive. If the relationship is formal, regular, unsupportive and based on short-term convenience (a market, structure-based relationship) then the purchase behaviour may be observed as courteous yet distant.

Without doubt the major determinant of the organisational environment is the cost associated with switching from one supplier to another (Bowersox and Cooper, 1992). When one organisation chooses to enter into a buying relationship with another organisation, an investment is made in time, people, assets and systems. Should the relationship with the new supplier fail to work satisfactorily, then a cost is incurred in switching to another supplier. It is these switching costs that heavily influence buying decisions. The higher the potential switching costs, the greater the loss in flexibility, and the greater the need to make the relationship appropriate at the outset.

Behaviour within the buying centre is also largely determined by the interpersonal relationships of the members of the centre. Participation in the buying centre has been shown to be highly influenced by individuals' perceptions of the personal consequences of their contribution to each stage in the process. The more that individuals think they will be blamed for a bad decision or praised for a good one, the greater their participation, influence and visible DMU-related activity (McQuiston and Dickson, 1991). The nature and dispersal of power within the unit can influence the decisions that are made. Power is increasingly viewed from the perspective of an individual's ability to control the flow of information and the deployment of resources (Stone and Gronhaug, 1986). This approach reflects a network approach to, in this case, intra-organisational communications.

From a communications perspective there is strong evidence that the provision/collection of information is a major contributor to risk reduction (Mitchell, 1995). Figure 3.8 depicts some of the more common approaches used by organisations to reduce risk.

Organisational buying has shifted from a one-to-one dyadic encounter, salesperson to buyer, to a position where a buying team meets a selling team. The skills associated with this process are different and are becoming much more sophisticated, and the demands on both buyers and sellers are more pronounced. The processes of buying and selling are complex and interactive.

Developments in the environment can impact on a consumer or organisation buyer and change both the way decisions are made and their nature. For example, the decision to purchase new plant and machinery requires consideration of the future cash flows generated by the capital item. Many people will be involved in the decision, and the time necessary for consultation may mean that other parts of the decision-making process are completed simultaneously.

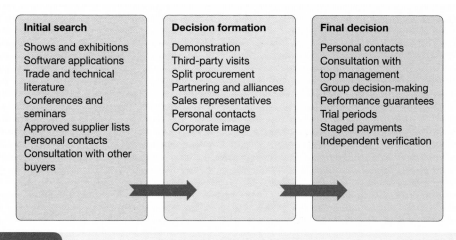

| **Initial search** | **Decision formation** | **Final decision** |
| --- | --- | --- |
| Shows and exhibitions<br>Software applications<br>Trade and technical<br>literature<br>Conferences and<br>seminars<br>Approved supplier lists<br>Personal contacts<br>Consultation with other<br>buyers | Demonstration<br>Third-party visits<br>Split procurement<br>Partnering and alliances<br>Sales representatives<br>Personal contacts<br>Corporate image | Personal contacts<br>Consultation with<br>top management<br>Group decision-making<br>Performance guarantees<br>Trial periods<br>Staged payments<br>Independent verification |

**Figure 3.8**    Risk reduction approach for organisational purchase decisions

There are a number of other issues concerned with the manner in which the members of a buying centre interact and make choices. An interesting new approach to strategic management considers the subjective, cognitive thoughts of the strategist to be more important than has been considered previously. Porter (1980), Ansoff and McDonnell (1990) and others in what is referred to as the design school of thought, assume that strategic decisions result from rational, logical analysis and interpretation of the environment. An alternative view is that, as environments are too complex and dynamic for objective analysis to be any practical use (Simon, 1976), then strategy or choices are fashioned from individuals' interpretations of their environment. Projections of historical data in uncertain, highly unpredictable environments mean that strategists, or members of the buying centre in this case, will rely more on knowledge and experience as the main platform for decision-making.

The rest of this chapter deals with consumer-related purchase decisions.

## Perceived risk

An important factor associated with the purchase decision process is the level of risk perceived by buyers. The concept of perceived risk was first proposed by Bauer (1960) and concerns the uncertainty of the consequences arising from a decision to purchase a particular brand.

Risk is perceived because the buyer has little or no experience of the performance of the product or the decision process associated with the purchase. As Chang and Hsiao (2008) state, perceived risk includes two factors. The first can occur prior to a purchase and the second subsequent to a purchase when an individual experiences the unfavourable consequences of a purchase (Cox and Rich, 1967).

Risk is related not only to brand-based decisions but also to product categories, an especially important aspect when launching new technology products, for example. The level of risk an individual experiences varies through time, across products, and is often a reflection of an individual's propensity to manage risk. Settle and Alreck (1989) suggest that there are five main forms of risk that can be identified; the purchase of a laptop demonstrates each element. These are set out in Table 3.5 with respect to the purchase of a laptop.

A sixth element, time, is also considered to be a risk factor (Stone and Gronhaug, 1993):

*Using the laptop example, will purchase of the computer lead to an inefficient use of my time? Or can I afford the time to search for a good laptop so that I will not waste my money?*

What constitutes risk is a function of the contextual characteristics of each situation, the individuals involved and the product under consideration.

| Table 3.5 | Types of perceived risk |
|---|---|
| **Type of perceived risk** | **Explanation** |
| Performance | Will the laptop perform all the functions properly? |
| Financial | Can I afford that much or should I buy a less expensive version? |
| Physical | Is the laptop built to the required safety standards . . . will it catch fire? |
| Social | Will my friends and colleagues approve? |
| Ego | Will I feel cool about using this equipment? |

A major task of marketing communications is to reduce levels of perceived risk. By providing extensive and relevant information a buyer's risks can be reduced substantially. Mass media, word-of-mouth, websites and sales representatives, for example, are popular ways to set out the likely outcomes from purchase and so reduce the levels of risk. Brand loyalty can also be instrumental in reducing risk when launching new products. The use of guarantees, third-party endorsements, money-back offers (some car manufacturers offer the opportunity to return a car within 30 days or exchange it for a different model) and trial samples (as used by many haircare products) are also well-used devices to reduce risk.

---

## Viewpoint 3.3    Back page risk reducers

Many print-based direct response advertisements use a variety of ways to reduce the risk inherent in buying 'off the back page'. Holiday companies, direct wine and book clubs use a variety of sales channels but Web-based companies and direct response magazine advertisements provide a rich source of business.

Magazine advertisements, often to be found on or near the back of magazines and Sunday newspaper supplements, allow for a large amount of text as well as the eye-catching visual work. The text is often used to reduce functional risk by explaining the features and extolling the benefits of the product or service. Social and ego risks are reduced by setting the right visual scene and depicting people using the product who may either be seen as aspirational or represent the target market.

Financial risk is reduced through opportunities to buy now at a reduced or discounted price (credit card) and promises of warranties and money-back guarantees further reduce the uncertainty of this form of exchange. Finally, time risk is reduced through buy-now opportunities and delivery to the door, negating the need to travel, park, browse, compare, decide and carry home the purchase.

| | |
|---|---|
| **Question:** | With so many different forms of risk, can advertising be used to eliminate them all? |
| **Task:** | Get a copy of a magazine that accompanies many weekend newspapers, look at the direct response ads and identify the ways in which perceived risk is reduced. |

---

Many direct-response magazine ads seek to reduce a number of different types of risk. Companies offering wine for direct home delivery, for example, try to reduce performance risk by providing information about each wine being offered. Financial risk is reduced by comparing their 'special' prices with those in the high street, social risk is approached by developing the brand name associations trying to improve credibility and time risk is reduced through the convenience of home delivery.

> **Scholars' paper 3.3**    **Well, it must be risky**
>
> **Stone, R.N. and Gronhaug, K. (1993) Perceived risk: further considerations for the marketing discipline,** *European Journal of Marketing*, 27, 3, 39–50.
>
> Readers interested in consumer behaviour and marketing communications should understand the basic principles associated with perceived risk. This is the seminal paper in this area, although the concept was introduced much earlier by Bauer. This paper provides an insight into the literature and issues associated with perceived risk and references the uncertainty experienced by consumers when making purchasing decisions.

## Involvement theory

Purchase decisions made by consumers vary considerably, and one of the factors thought to be key to brand choice decisions is the level of involvement (in terms of individual importance and relevance) a consumer has with either the product or the purchase process.

Involvement is about the degree of personal relevance and risk perceived by consumers when making a particular purchase decision (Rossiter et al., 1991). This implies that the level of involvement may vary through time as each member of the target market becomes more (or less) familiar with the purchase and associated communications. At the point of decision-making, involvement is high or low, not somewhere on a sliding scale or on a continuum between two extremes.

### High involvement

*High involvement* occurs when a consumer perceives an expected purchase that is not only of high personal relevance but also represents a high level of perceived risk. Cars, washing machines, houses and insurance policies are seen as 'big ticket' items, infrequent purchases that promote a great deal of involvement. The risk described is financial but, as we saw earlier, risk can take other forms. Therefore, the choice of perfume, suit, dress or jewellery may also represent high involvement, with social risk dominating the purchase decision. The consumer, therefore, devotes a great deal of time to researching the intended purchase and collecting as much information as possible in order to reduce, as far as possible, levels of perceived risk.

### Low involvement

A *low-involvement* state of mind regarding a purchase suggests little threat or risk to the consumer. Low-priced items such as washing powder, baked beans and breakfast cereals are bought frequently, and past experience of the product class and the brand cues the consumer into a purchase that requires little information or support. Items such as alcoholic and soft drinks, cigarettes and chocolate are also normally seen as low-involvement, but they induce a strong sense of ego risk associated with the self-gratification that is attached to the consumption of these products.

## Two approaches to decision-making

From this understanding of general decision-making processes, perceived risk and involvement theory, it is possible to identify two main approaches to consumer decision-making.

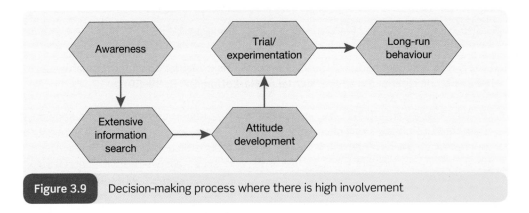

**Figure 3.9**    Decision-making process where there is high involvement

### High-involvement decision-making

If an individual is highly involved with the initial purchase of a product, EPS is the appropriate decision sequence, as information is considered to be processed in a rational, logical order. Individuals who are highly involved in a purchase are thought to move through the process shown in Figure 3.9. When high-involvement decision-making is present, individuals perceive a high level of risk and are concerned about the intended purchase. The essential element in this sequence is that a great deal of information is sought initially and an attitude is developed before a commitment or intention to trial is determined.

Information search is an important part of the high-involvement decision-making process. Because individuals are highly motivated, information is actively sought, processed and evaluated. Many media sources are explored, including the mass media, word-of-mouth communications, websites, and point-of-sale communications. As individuals require a lot of information, print media used to be the primary media where high involvement was identified. Today, websites are the primary source of large volumes of detailed information. Unlike print, these sites can also be updated quickly but both types enable visitors to search and process information at a speed they can control.

### Low-involvement decision-making

If an individual has little involvement with an initial purchase of a product, LPS is the appropriate decision process. Information is processed cognitively but in a passive, involuntary way. Processing occurs using right-brain thinking so information is stored as it is received, in sections, and this means that information is stored as a brand association (Heath, 2000). An advertisement for Andrex toilet tissue featuring the puppy is stored as the 'Andrex Puppy' without any overt thinking or reasoning. Because of the low personal relevance and perceived risk associated with this type of processing, message repetition is necessary to define brands and create meaningful brand associations. Individuals who have a low involvement with a purchase decision choose not to search for information and are thought to move through the process shown in Figure 3.10.

Communications can assist the development of awareness in the low-involvement decision-making process. However, as individuals assume a passive problem-solving role, messages need to be shorter than in the high-involvement process and should contain less information. Broadcast media are preferred as they complement the passive learning posture adopted by individuals. Repetition is important because the receiver has little or no motivation to retain information, and his or her perceptual selection processes filter out unimportant information. Learning develops through exposure to repeated messages, but attitudes do not develop at this part of the process (Harris, 1987).

Where low involvement is present, each individual relies upon internal, rather than external, search mechanisms, often prompted by point-of-purchase displays.

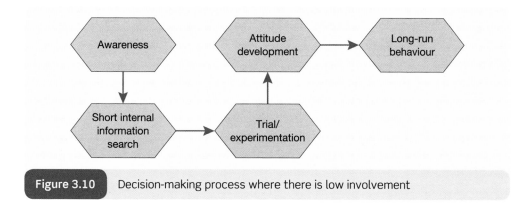

**Figure 3.10**    Decision-making process where there is low involvement

## Impact on communications

Involvement theory is central to our understanding of the way in which information is processed and the way in which people make decisions about product purchases. We have established in the preceding section that there are two main types of involvement, high and low. These two types lead directly to two different uses of marketing communications. In decisions where there is high involvement, attitude precedes trial behaviour. In low-involvement cases this position is reversed.

Where there is high involvement, consumers seek out information because they are concerned about the decision processes and outcomes. This can be because of the levels of uncertainty associated with the high costs of purchase and usage, inexperience of the product (category) – often due to the infrequency of purchases – the complexity of product and doubts about its operational usefulness. Because they have these concerns, people develop an attitude prior to behaviour. Informational ads that require cognitive processing are recommended.

Where there is low involvement, consumers are content to select any one of a number of acceptable products and often rely on those that are in the individual's evoked set. Low involvement is thought to be a comfortable state, because there are too many other decisions in life to have to make decisions about each one of them, so an opportunity not to have to seek information and make other decisions is welcome. See Figure 3.11, which indicates the marketing communication strategies best suited for each level within both involvement sequences. Emotional or transformational ads are recommended.

Planning communications based on involvement is not as straightforward as the preceding material might suggest. There are various factors that might influence the outcomes. For example, some individuals who are cognitively capable of processing information may not always be able to process information in information-based ads because they are overloaded. In these circumstances they are more likely to develop positive attitudes towards affective or transformational ads. Ranjbariyan and Mahmoodi (2009) also found that people under time pressure are more prone to use transformational ads as they will pick up visual cues to help their decision making.

The material presented so far in this section is based on classical research, theoretical development and is supported by empirical research. However, much of the knowledge has been developed in a non-digital era, and that raises questions about the depth of its validity in the contemporary world. Foley et al. (2009) undertook research that showed that people organise product categories according to the level of risk associated with brand-choice decisions and the level of reward, together with the enjoyment people derive from the decisions they make. They also found that the types of categories people organise lead to different patterns of decision making. Four main product categories were identified:

1. *Routine*

   In this category people perceive low risk and low reward. Brand choice decision making is therefore characterised by inertia and decision making is robotic.

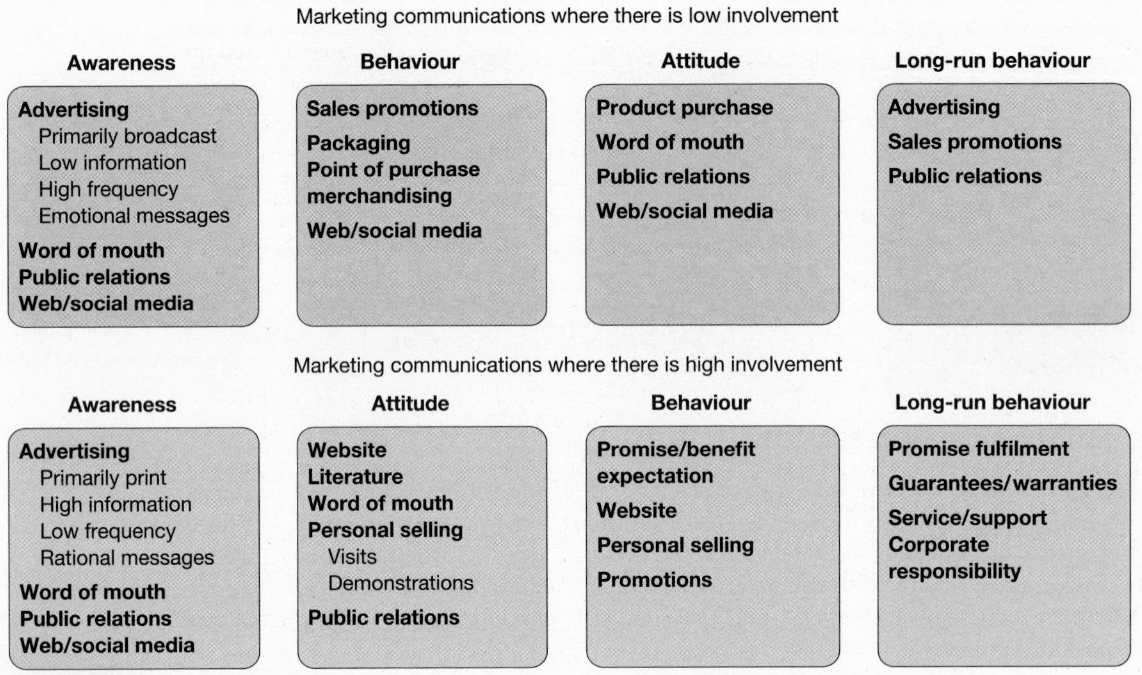

Marketing communications where there is low involvement

| Awareness | Behaviour | Attitude | Long-run behaviour |
|---|---|---|---|
| **Advertising**<br>　Primarily broadcast<br>　Low information<br>　High frequency<br>　Emotional messages<br>**Word of mouth**<br>**Public relations**<br>**Web/social media** | **Sales promotions**<br>**Packaging**<br>**Point of purchase merchandising**<br>**Web/social media** | **Product purchase**<br>**Word of mouth**<br>**Public relations**<br>**Web/social media** | **Advertising**<br>**Sales promotions**<br>**Public relations** |

Marketing communications where there is high involvement

| Awareness | Attitude | Behaviour | Long-run behaviour |
|---|---|---|---|
| **Advertising**<br>　Primarily print<br>　High information<br>　Low frequency<br>　Rational messages<br>**Word of mouth**<br>**Public relations**<br>**Web/social media** | **Website**<br>**Literature**<br>**Word of mouth**<br>**Personal selling**<br>　Visits<br>　Demonstrations<br>**Public relations** | **Promise/benefit expectation**<br>**Website**<br>**Personal selling**<br>**Promotions** | **Promise fulfilment**<br>**Guarantees/warranties**<br>**Service/support**<br>**Corporate responsibility** |

**Figure 3.11**　Marketing communication approaches for the two levels of involvement

2. *Burden*

　　People perceive high risk and low reward. Search is extensive and decision making improved if someone can assist.

3. *Passion*

　　Risk is high and reward is high because people are emotionally engaged with these types of products and services. The symbolism and meaning attached to brands in the category is high, reflected in high ego and social risks.

4. *Entertainment*

　　People use this category where risk is low but reward can be high. This means that decision making can be a pleasant, if brief, experience.

Each of these categories has implications for the communications strategies necessary to reach people and be effective. For example, consideration of the type of website that best suits each of these categories provides immediate insight into how having an understanding or insight into the target audience can shape marketing communications.

# Alternative approaches

Consideration so far has been given to what might be called 'the rational and cognitive approach' to both information processing and decision making. These are informative and enable us to build our understanding in an organised way. Indeed, organisations often install logical buying procedures as a means of controlling and managing the procurement process. However, there are alternative ways of looking at these issues. The first to be considered is called *hedonic consumption*, the second is *tribal consumption* and the third is *behavioural economics*, which although not new, has received increased attention in the few years.

## Hedonic consumption

There is a range of products and services that can evoke high levels of involvement based on the emotional impact that consumption provides to the buyer. This is referred to as 'hedonic consumption', and Hirschmann and Holbrook (1982) describe this approach as 'those facets of consumer behaviour that relate to the multi sensory, fantasy and emotive aspects of one's experience with products'. With its roots partly in the motivation research and partly in the cognitive processing schools, this interpretation of consumer behaviour seeks to explain how and why buyers experience emotional responses to the act of purchase and consumption of particular products.

*Historical imagery* occurs when, for example, the colour of a dress, the scent of a perfume or cologne, or the aroma of a restaurant or food can trigger an individual's memory to replay an event. In contrast, *fantasy imagery* occurs when a buyer constructs an event, drawing together various colours, sounds and shapes to compose a mental experience of an event that has not occurred previously. Consumers imagine a reality in which they derive sensory pleasure. Some smokers were encouraged to imagine themselves as 'Marlboro Men': not just masculine, but as idealised cowboys (Hirschmann and Holbrook, 1982).

The advertising of fragrances and luxury brands is often based on images that encourage individuals to project themselves into a desirable or pleasurable environment or situation: for example, those which foster romantic associations. Some people form strong associations with particular fragrances and use this to develop and maintain specific images. Advertising is used to create and support these images and, in doing so, enhance the emotional benefits derived from fragrance brand associations. As Retiveau (2007) indicates, hedonics are closely related and influence the simultaneous perception of fragrances.

There are a number of challenges with this approach – namely, measurement factors of reliability and validity – nevertheless, appreciating the dreams, ideals and desires of the target audience can be an important contribution to the creation of promotional messages.

## Tribal consumption

Another approach to understanding consumption concerns the concept of individualism and tribes. Cova (1997) identifies two schools of thought about consumption and identity. The Northern school believe that consumption enables individuals to reveal their self-identity in society. People consume as an end in itself as this allows them to *take* meaning for their lives through what they consume. Here consumption is a means of individual differentiation.

The Southern school believe that it is important to maintain a culture's social fabric. As society reconfigures itself into groups of people that, according to Maffesoli (1996), reflect primitive tribes, so the role of consumption evolves into a means of linking people to multiple communities, or tribes. Here consumption is a means of offering value to a tribe (Cooper et al., 2005).

In the work of Maffesoli (1996), contemporary culture is considered not to be one of individualism, but one defined by 'fluidity, occasional gatherings and dispersal'. This might be likened to a fragmentation of social groupings (Hamilton and Hewer, 2010) many of which are transient. According to Jenkins (2006), tribes represent a participatory culture where business and social interests and affiliations come together.

The term 'tribe' refers to communities characterised by people who share emotions, experiences, lifestyles and patterns of consumption. In order that these tribes are able to effect tribal communion (Cova et al., 2007) so that members can reaffirm their identity, various emblems, sites, recognition or support are used. Products and services are not consumed for their utility value, or for the sense of individual identification. Their consumption is considered to be important for the 'linking value' they provide within a tribal network. Tribes serve to link people who share passions and interests, examples of which, according to Hamilton and Hewer (2010), include brands such as Harley-Davidson, Saab, Star Trek and the X-Files, adrenalin activities

| Table 3.6 | Eight E's of eTribes |
| --- | --- |

| E reference | Explanation |
| --- | --- |
| Electronic | e-tribes communicate via the medium of the Internet |
| Enculturating | e-tribe members learn and adopt the language, practices, rituals, and values of the community |
| Emotive | e-tribes generate a high level of emotional involvement from members |
| Expressive | e-tribe members engage in creative, product work |
| Empowered | e-tribe members gain great satisfaction from the agentic potential of their practices |
| Evangelical | e-tribe membership can be compared with a quasi-religious or spiritual experience |
| Emergent | e-tribes are self-generated, emerging on their own rather than under the control of a company |
| Entangled | Network boundaries overlap and merge |

*Source*: Hamilton and Hewer (2010) adaption of Kozinets (2008).

such as skydiving, dancing, river rafting, or a variety of sports or even sports stars and celebrities. Tribes are loosely interconnected communities (Cova and Cova, 2001) where bonding and linking represent key activities designed to retain tribal membership.

Tribes proliferate on the Internet, thanks mainly to its power to aggregate communities who share similar interests. These eTribes have the same characteristics as traditional communities: namely, shared rituals and traditions, a similar consciousness of kind, and an obligation, or sense of duty to the community and to its individual members (Kozinets, 2001; Muniz and O'Guinn, 2001). Kozinets (2008) established that there were eight E's that can be associated with e-tribes. These are set out at Table 3.6.

According to Hamilton and Hewer, this listing indicates the breadth and complexity of the virtual tribal environment and the openness and opportunities that people have to explore, work, play and become immersed and passionate about interests, which Kozinets et al. (2008) relate to the intimate feelings people experience in childhood.

The recognition and acceptance of eTribes and tribal consumption for marketing communications practitioners is not clear cut. Indeed some commentators warn against outright tribal intrusion and recommend activities that encourage a tribe's social and linking behaviours, simply because these are critical for members. Organisations should aim to become listeners and to work 'with' tribes by fostering conversations and enabling them to function through the provision of 'play rich mattering spaces' (Hamilton and Hewer, 2010: 285).

---

### Scholars' paper 3.4     How tribal are we?

**Cova, B. and Cova, V. (2001) Tribal aspects of postmodern consumption research,** *Journal of Consumer Behaviour*, **1(1), June, 67–76.**

This paper considers some of the characteristics, issues and research methods associated with understanding neo-tribes. The word 'tribe' is used to represent the 're-emergence of quasi-archaic values' whereby the community serves to root a local sense of identification, whether that be in religiosity, syncretism, or group narcissism, for example. These tribes tend to be transient and lacking stability. They are held together through shared emotions, lifestyles, new moral beliefs, and consumption practices and patterns.

# Behavioural economics

Just as ideas about tribal consumption are a rejection of 'rational man' perspectives, so behavioural economics is grounded in the belief that people are 'fundamentally irrational in their decision making and motivated by unconscious cognitive biases' (Ariely, 2009). The third issue to be considered under the banner of alternative approaches to understanding consumer behaviour, therefore, concerns the emerging popularity of the concept called 'behavioural economics'. One of the interesting points about behavioural economics is that it challenges established thinking, and another is that it is not a million miles from the idea of low-attention processing, as discussed above.

Behavioural economics has emerged following decades of frustration with classical economic theory. Conventional economic theory suggests that people make rational choices in their decision making and even seek to maximise their opportunities and minimise expenditure. The 'rational man' makes the best possible decisions, on the basis of maximising benefits and minimising costs, in order to obtain the most advantageous economic outcome. This approach has been doubted by most economists, if privately, and by most students of economics when they are introduced to their first macro- and micro-economic lectures. Despite these doubts, various arguments have been offered over the years to perpetuate the use of classical theory.

Classical economics assumes rational decision making and that, in general, markets and institutions are self-regulating, yet the collapse of the banks and much of the financial sector in 2008, casts serious doubt on the efficacy of this view. Behavioural economics, therefore, challenges the conventional view about the way people and organisations behave. Indeed, the central platform on which behavioural economics is constructed is behaviour. This moves advertising and marketing communications forward because the focus is no longer on attitudes, beliefs and opinions, or even on what people intend to do, but on how they behave, what they actually do.

In order to change existing behaviours, or encourage new ones, people need to be presented with a choice that makes decision making feel effortless, even automatic, or as Gordon (2011) puts it, 'a no-brainer'. Thaler and Sunstein (2008) refer to this as 'choice architecture'. This posits that there is no neutral way to present a choice. People choose according to what is available, not what they absolutely want. What is also important is that they do not expend much energy or thought when they make a choice, and they use *heuristics*, or rules of thumb to assist them. The idea that people follow a sequential decision-making process is a long way from the truth. Both Kooreman and Prast (2010) and Grapentine and Altman Weaver (2009) agree that people's behaviour is often not congruent with their intentions, that they are sensitive to the way choices are presented to them, and that they have limited cognitive abilities. However, not everyone agrees that BE is a good step forward. For example, Mitchell (2010) puts forward a number of doubts about the validity of the concept.

---

| **Viewpoint 3.4** | **Getting into action with BE** |

Various organisations have adopted behavioural economics, partly as a result of the IPA championing it by providing visibility, information and insight. Here are a few examples:

**Hyundai** – Consumer fear at the huge depreciation incurred when buying a new car prompted Hyundai into reframing the choice car buyers are faced with. Instead of shying away from the issue, Hyundai offered new car buyers a guaranteed price for their car, valid for four years after purchase. Television advertising was used to communicate the deal and so reduce the perceived risk.

**Transport for London** (TfL) had been telling people about the advantages of cycling to work for many years, but the communication had not been very successful. So, rather than keep telling people, TfL installed a bicycle hire scheme, sponsored by Barclays, which enabled two things. First, people could hire a bike and leave it at a designated point in London, and avoid capital outlay, maintenance, and storage costs. Second, the scheme encouraged a change in behaviour because the bikes were made available, and their distinctive Barclays logo and bike stands are visible across the capital.

**Domino's Pizza** used the principles of BE to develop a new set of incentives. One of these was to credit a customer's account which could be spent on future orders. This can increase purchase intentions.

**Cadbury's** reintroduced the Wispa bar in 2007 following its axing in 2003, and the subsequent campaigns on various social network sites Bebo, Myspace and Facebook, and a stage rush by Wispa fans at Glastonbury. Instead of simply announcing its return, Cadbury's announced that Wispa would be back with a special-edition limited run. Sales went through the roof, and the Wispa bar was available on a regular basis. However, by announcing a limited run of the brand it encouraged people to think that they needed to buy a Wispa, otherwise it would be removed once again. In other words, loss aversion was used to stimulate demand.

*Source*:   McCormick (2011a); McCormick (2011b); Panlogic (2011).

**Question:**   Choose a brand and consider ways in which the principles of behavioural economics might be utilised.

**Task:**   Choose three product categories and make notes about the way BE might be applied to enhance communications

| Table 3.7 | Elements of behavioural economics |
| --- | --- |

| BE element | Explanation |
| --- | --- |
| **Who** | People observe the behaviour of others and use this to make their decisions. Behaviour is supported by unconsciously held identity issues. |
| **How** | Helping people to make a decision by presenting easy methods can encourage action now, rather than in the future. For example, paying for tickets for a festival online is easier than being in a queue on the telephone. Schemes that require people to opt out are more likely to generate the desired behaviour, than requiring people to make the choice to opt in. |
| **When** | When required to do something disagreeable, people are more likely to delay making a decision or taking action – for example, to stop smoking, to complete an income tax return form, or start an essay. |
| **Where** | Although price and perceived value can be important, it can be location and convenience that shape a decision. Questions such as 'Do I have to go there to do this or should I do it here where it is convenient?' can often influence behaviour. |
| **Availability** | Items that appear to be scarce have a higher value than those items that are plentiful. For example, recorded music is abundant and virtually free, yet live music is relatively expensive, as it is scarce. |
| **Price** | The price of an item leads people to give it a value. So, people who pay more for a product/service often perceive increased benefit or gain. However, price needs to be contextualised and supported by other indicators of value. |
| **Task duration** | People prefer to complete parts of a task rather than try to finish in a single attempt. Therefore, the way a task is presented can influence the behaviour and the number of people completing the task. Filling in forms seems less daunting with the opportunity to save and return. Colour coding antibiotic pills might ensure more people complete the treatment and avoid repeat visits, further illness and lost days from work. |

Based on Gordon (2011); IPA (2010).

So, decisions are not made deliberatively and consciously by evaluating all permutations and outcomes. Decisions are made around choices that are based on comparison, rather than absolutely. These decisions are based on what is available rather than scanning the whole market or options and, as Gordon says, in terms of 'how this makes me feel' both emotionally, and instinctively, but not rationally.

One of the main areas in which behavioural economics impacts advertising and brand communications is choice architecture. Indeed, the Institute of Practitioners in Advertising (IPA, 2010) have embraced behavioural economics and observe its relevance to campaign planning, purchase decisions, brand experiences, how behaviour can be changed, and the way that choice works in complex situations. All of these can be reflected in the advertising and brand communications.

# Key points

- Awareness of the existence and availability of a product/service or an organisation is necessary before information can be processed and purchase behaviour expected. Much of marketing communications activity is directed towards getting the attention of the target audience,

- Awareness needs to be created, developed, refined or sustained, according to the characteristics of the market and the particular situation facing an organisation at any one point in time.

- Perception is concerned with how individuals see and make sense of their environment. The way in which individuals perceive, organise and interpret stimuli is a reflection of their past experiences and the classifications used to understand the different situations each individual frames every day.

- Marketing communications are used to position brands using a variety of stimuli so that consumers understand and recognise them.

- There are three factors important to the behavourist approach to learning: association, reinforcement and motivation. Behaviour is learned through the conditioning experience of a stimulus and response.

- Cognitive learning considers learning to be a function of an individual's attempt to control their immediate environment. Cognitive learning is about processing information in order that problems can be resolved. Central to this process is memory.

- Information-handling processes can range from the simple to the complex. There are three main processes: iconic, modelling and reasoning.

- Attitudes are predispositions, shaped through experience, to respond in an anticipated way to an object or situation. Attitudes are learned through past experiences and serve as a link between thoughts and behaviour. Attitudes tend to be consistent within each individual: they are clustered and very often interrelated. Attitudes consist of three interrelated elements: the cognitive, affective and conative, otherwise referred to as learn, feel, do.

- Marketing communications can be used to influence the attitudes held by a target market. When developing campaigns, consideration needs to be given to the current and desired attitudes to be held by the target audience. The focus of communications activities can be on whether the audience requires information (learning), an emotional disposition (feeling) or whether the audience needs to be encouraged to behave in a particular way (doing).

- Classical theory suggests that there are five stages to the general process whereby buyers make purchase decisions and implement them. These are problem recognition, information search, alternative evaluation, purchase decision and post-purchase evaluation. Organisations use marketing communications in different ways in order to influence these different stages.

- Buyers do not follow the general purchase decision sequence at all times and three types of problem-solving behaviour are experienced by consumers. These are extended problem solving, limited problem solving and routinised response. The procedure may vary depending upon the time available, levels of perceived risk and the degree of involvement a buyer has with the type of product.

- The organisational buying decision process consists of six main stages or buyphases. These are need/problem recognition, product specification, supplier and product search, the evaluation of proposals, supplier selection and evaluation.

- There are a wide variety of individuals involved in organisational purchase decisions. There are *Users*, *Influencers*, *Deciders*, *Buyers* and *Gatekeepers*. All fulfil different functions, all have varying degrees of impact on purchase decisions and all require different marketing communications in order to influence their decision-making.

- Consumers and organisational buyers experience risk when making purchasing decisions. This risk is perceived and concerns the uncertainty of the proposed purchase and the outcomes that will result from a decision to purchase a product. The level of risk an individual experiences varies through time, across products and is often a reflection of an individual's propensity to manage risk. Individual risk is related to involvement, trust and other buyer behaviour concepts. Five types of perceived risk can be identified. These are ego, social, physical, financial and performance risks.

- Individuals and groups make purchasing decisions on behalf of organisations. Different types of risk can be experienced, relating to a range of organisational and contextual issues. Marketing communications has an important task to reduce risk for consumers and organisational buyers.

- Involvement is about the degree of personal relevance and risk perceived by individuals in a particular purchase situation. Individuals experience involvement with products or services to be purchased.

- The level of involvement may vary through time as each member of the target market becomes more (or less) familiar with the purchase and associated communications. At the point of decision-making, involvement is either high or low.

- Some products and services can evoke high levels of involvement based on the emotional impact that consumption provides the buyer. This is referred to as *hedonic consumption*, and refers to behaviour that relates to the multi-sensory, fantasy and emotive aspects of an individual's experience with products. *Historical imagery* and *fantasy imagery* are two aspects of hedonic consumption.

- Tribes are loosely interconnected communities where bonding and linking represent key activities designed to retain tribal membership. Tribes serve to link people who share passions and interests and 'tribal consumption' refers to consumption of products and services, not for their utility value, or for the sense of individual identification. Their consumption is considered to be important for the 'linking value' they provide within a tribal network.

- Tribes proliferate on the Internet, thanks mainly to its power to aggregate communities who share similar interests. These eTribes have the same characteristics as traditional communities: namely, shared rituals and traditions, a similar consciousness of kind, and an obligation, or sense of duty, to the community and to its individual members.

- Behavioural economics is grounded in the belief that people make irrational rather than rational decisions and the central platform is about actual behaviour, not attitudes or opinions. People choose according to what is available, not what they absolutely want.

# Review questions

1. What are the three elements of perception used for processing stimuli?

2. How might an understanding of perception assist marketing communications?

3. Find two examples to illustrate behavioural, iconic and rote learning when applied to marketing communications. Which of these might best be used to interpret the teacher recruitment campaign set out in the minicase?

4. Make brief notes about the characteristics of each of the attitude components and explain how marketing communications can be used to change attitudes.

5. Make brief notes explaining each of the following: buyclasses, buying centre, EPS, LPS and RRB.

6. Describe the elements that constitute perceived risk and explain how marketing communications can be used to reduce these types of uncertainty.

7. Describe the high- and low-involvement decision-making processes.

8. Explain how marketing communications works with regard to attitude development in low- and high-involvement situations.

9. Find examples of tribal consumption or hedonic consumption.

10. What is behavioural economics and what does it mean for marketing communications?

# References

Ajzen, I. and Fishbein, M. (1980) *Understanding Attitudes and Predicting Social Behavior*, Englewood Cliffs, NJ: Prentice-Hall.

Anon (2004) Apple Computer: iPod Silhouettes, *New York American Marketing Association*, Effie Awards, retrieved 12 February 2006 from www.nyama.org.

Anon (2010) North America Effies: Hyundai – Assurance, *Effie Worldwide*, retrieved 10 July 2010 from www.effie.org.

Anon (2011) Voluntary Sector: The Week in Charities, *PR Week UK*, 4 November, retrieved 21 March 2012 from http://www.brandrepublic.com/features/1102013/Voluntary-Sector-Week-Charities/?DCMP=ILC-SEARCH.

Ansoff, H.I. and McDonnell, E.J. (1990) *Implanting Strategic Management*, 2nd edn. Hemel Hempstead: Prentice-Hall.

Ariely, D. (2009) The End of Rational Economics, *Harvard Business Review*, July–August, 78–84.

Bauer, R.A. (1960) Consumer behavior as risk taking, in R.S. Hancock (ed.) *Dynamic marketing in the changing world*, Chicago: American Marketing Association, pp. 389–98.

Bonoma, T.V. (1982) Major sales: who really does the buying? *Harvard Business Review* (May/June), p. 113.

Bowersox, D. and Cooper, M. (1992) *Strategic Marketing Channel Management*, New York: McGraw-Hill.

Boyd, D., Vaas, A., Smith, A. and Caig, J. (2010) TDA Teacher Recruitment: best in class, *IPA Effectiveness Awards*, London: IPA.

Chang, H.-S. and Hsiao, H.-L. (2008) Examining the casual relationship among service recovery, perceived justice, perceived risk, and customer value in the hotel industry, *The Service Industries Journal*, 28, 4 (May), 513–28.

Cobau, S. (2000) DeBeers Consolidated Mines Ltd: a diamond is forever campaign, *Encyclopedia of Major Marketing Campaigns*, 1. Retrieved 10 August 2007 from: http://www.warc.com/ArticleCenter/Default.asp?CType=A&AID=WORDSEARCH84137&Tab=A.

Cohen, J. and Basu, K. (1987) Alternative models of categorisation, *Journal of Consumer Research* (March), 455–72.

Cooper, S., McLoughlin, D. and Keating, A. (2005) Individual and neo-tribal consumption: Tales from the Simpsons of Springfield, *Journal of Consumer Behaviour*, 4, 5, 330–44.

Cova, B. (1997) Community and consumption: Towards a definition of the 'linking value' of product or services, *European Journal of Marketing*, 31 (May), 297–316.

Cova, B. and Cova, V. (2001) Tribal aspects of postmodern consumption research: The case of French in-line roller skaters, *Journal of Consumer Behaviour*, 1(1), 61–76.

Cova, B., Kozinets, R.V. and Shankar C.A. (2007) *Consumer tribes*, Oxford, England: Butterworth-Heinemann.

Cox, D.F. and Rich, S.U. (1967) Perceived risk and consumer decision making – the case of telephone shopping, in D.F. Cox (ed.) *Consumer behavior*, Boston: Harvard University Press.

Eleftheriou-Smith, L.-M. (2011) Clare Mullin on cleaning out the cobwebs at the National Trust, *Marketing*, 24 August, retrieved 21 March from http://www.brandrepublic.com/features/1085979/Clare-Mullin-cleaning-cobwebs-National-Trust/?DCMP=ILC-SEARCH.

Foley, C., Greene, J. and Cultra, M. (2009) Effective ads in a digital age, *Admap*, 503, (March), retrieved 2 June 2010 from www.warc.com/article centre.

Goodrich, J.N. (1978) The relationship between preferences for and perceptions of vacation destinations: application of a choice model, *Journal of Travel Research*, 17(2), 8–13.

Gordon, W. (2011) Behavioural economics and qualitative research – a marriage made in heaven? *International Journal of Market Research*, 53(2), 171–85.

Grapentine, T.H. and Altman Weaver, D. (2009) What Really Affects Behavior? *Marketing Research*, 21(4), Winter, 12–17.

Grass, R.C. and Wallace, H.W. (1969) Satiation effects of TV commercials, *Journal of Advertising Research*, 9(3), 3–9.

Guthrie, M.F. and Kim, H.-S. (2009) The relationship between consumer involvement and brand perceptions of female cosmetic consumers, *Journal of Brand Management*, 17(2), 114–33.

Hamilton, K. and Hewer, P. (2010) Tribal mattering spaces: Social-networking sites, celebrity affiliations, and tribal innovations, *Journal of Marketing Management*, 26, 3–4 (March), 271–89.

Harris, G. (1987) The implications of low involvement theory for advertising effectiveness, *International Journal of Advertising*, 6, 207–21.

Hawkins, D., Best, R. and Coney, K. (1989) *Consumer Behavior*, Homewood, IL: Richard D. Irwin.

Heath, R. (2000) Low-involvement processing, *Admap* (March), 14–16.

Heath, R. (2001) Low involvement processing – a new model of brand communication, *Journal of Marketing Communications*, 7, 27–33.

Hirschmann, E.C. and Holbrook, M.B. (1982) Hedonic consumption: emerging concepts, methods and propositions, *Journal of Marketing*, 46 (Summer), 92–101.

Hollingworth, C. and Davies, S. (2011) Behavioural Economics: a perfect storm, retrieved 21 May 2012 from http://www.aqr.org.uk/indepth/autumn2011/paper1.shtml.

IPA (2010) *Behaviour economics: red hot or red herring?*, London: IPA.

IPA (2011) *New Models of Marketing Effectiveness: From Integration to Orchestration*, WARC.

Javalgi, R., Thomas, E. and Rao, S. (1992) US travellers' perception of selected European destinations, *European Journal of Marketing*, 26, 7, 45–64.

Jenkins, H. (2006) *Fans, bloggers and gamers: Essays on participatory culture*, New York: New York University Press.

Jukes, M. (2009) Creative review: Comparethemarket.com *revolutionmagazine.com*, 26 February 2009, retrieved 3 November 2010 from www.brandrepublic.com/features/888761/Creative-review-Comparethemarketcom/?DCMP=ILC-SEARCH.

Kooreman, P. and Prast, H. (2010) What Does Behavioral Economics Mean for Policy? Challenges to Savings and Health Policies in the Netherlands, *De Economist*, 158(2), June, 101–22.

Kozinets, R.V. (2001) Utopian enterprise: Articulating the meanings of Star Trek's culture of consumption, *Journal of Consumer Research*, 28(1), 67–88.

Kozinets, R.V., Hemetsberger, A. and Schau, H.J. (2008) The wisdom of crowds: Collective innovation in the age of networked marketing, *Journal of Macromarketing*, 28(4), 339–54.

Kozinets, R.V. (2008) e-Tribes and marketing: The revolutionary implications of online communities, Seminar presented at Edinburgh University Business School, 24/11/2008.

Maffesoli, M. (1996) *The Time of Tribes*, London: Sage Publications.

McCormick, A. (2011a) Behavioural economics: When push comes to nudge, *Marketing*, 19 May 2011, retrieved 27 April 2012 from http://www.brandrepublic.com/features/1070184/Behavioural-economics-When-push-comes-nudge/?DCMP=ILC-SEARCH.

McCormick, A. (2011b) Domino's to integrate behavioural economics, *Marketing*, 5 May 2011, retrieved 27 April 2012 from www.brandrepublic.com/news/1068007/Dominos-integrate-behavioural-economics/?DCMP=ILC-SEARCH.

McGuire, W. (1978) An information processing model of advertising effectiveness, in *Behavioral and Management Science in Marketing* (eds H.J. Davis and A.J. Silk), New York: Ronald Press, 156–80.

McMeeken, R. (2012) A Fresh Start, *The Marketer*, March/April, 22–4.

McQuiston, D.H. and Dickson, P.R. (1991) The effect of perceived personal consequences on participation and influence in organisational buying, *Journal of Business*, 23, 159–77.

Mitchell, V.-M. (1995) Organisational risk perception and reduction: a literature review, *British Journal of Management*, 6, 115–33.

Mitchell, A. (2010) Behavioural economics has yet to deliver on its promise, *Marketing*, 15 September, 28–9.

Moran, W. (1990) Brand preference and the perceptual frame, *Journal of Advertising Research* (October/November), 9–16.

Muniz, A.M. and O'Guinn, T.C. (2001) Brand community, *Journal of Consumer Research*, 27(4), 412–23.

Nottage, A. (2007) Clarity will boost consumer trust, *Marketing*, 10 October, 21.

Panlogic (2011) Getting people to do what you want, retrieved 4 September 2011 from http://www.panlogic.co.uk/downloads/Behavioural-Economics-Getting-people-to-do-what-you-want.pdf.

Parpis, E. (2009) Out-of-Home Ad of the Decade, *Brandweek*, 50, 44, 14 December, retrieved 23 November 2011 from web.ebscohost.com/ehost/detail?vid=15&hid=7&sid=99dec141-7f13-4dc6-85d9-c1e6bbc68885%40sessionmgr13&bdata=JnNpdGU9ZWhvc3QtbGl2ZQ%3d%3d#db=bch&AN=47062432.

Petty, R.E. and Cacioppo, J.T. (1979) Effects of message repetition and position on cognitive responses, recall and persuasion, *Journal of Personality and Social Psychology*, 37 (January), 97–109.

Porter, M.E. (1980) *Competitive Strategy: Techniques for Analysing Industries and Competitors*, New York: Free Press.

Ranjbariyan, B. and Mahmoodi, S. (2009) The Influencing Factors in Ad Processing: Cognitive vs. Affective Appeals, *Journal of International Marketing and Marketing Research*, 34, 3, 129–40.

Retiveau, A. (2007) The Role of Fragrance in Personal Care Products, retrieved 26 October 2008 from www.sensoryspectrum.com/presentations/Fragrances.

Reynolds, J. (2012) KFC rolls out 'his and hers' ads, *Marketing*, 15 February, p. 4.

Robinson, P.J., Faris, C.W. and Wind, Y. (1967) *Industrial Buying and Creative Marketing*, Boston, MA: Allyn & Bacon.

Rossiter, J.R., Percy, L. and Donovan, R.J. (1991) A better advertising planning grid, *Journal of Advertising Research* (October/November), 11–21.

Settle, R.B. and Alreck, P. (1989) Reducing buyers' sense of risk, *Marketing Communications* (January), 34–40.

Simon, H.A. (1976) *Administrative Behavior: A Study of Decision Making Processes in Administrative Organizations*, New York: Free Press.

Spekman, R.E. and Gronhaug, K. (1986) Conceptual and methodological issues in buying centre research, *European Journal of Marketing*, 20(7), 50–63.

Stone, R.N. and Gronhaug, K. (1993) Perceived risk: further considerations for the marketing discipline, *European Journal of Marketing*, 27, 3, 39–50.

Strong, E.C. (1977) The spacing and timing of advertising, *Journal of Advertising Research*, 17 (December), 25–31.

Thaler, R. and Sunstein, C. (2008) *Nudge: Improving Decisions About Health, Wealth and Happiness*, Yale University Press.

Webster, F.E. and Wind, Y. (1972) *Organizational Buying Behavior*, Englewood Cliffs, NJ: Prentice-Hall.

Williams, K.C. (1981) *Behavioural Aspects of Marketing*, London: Heinemann.

Zielske, H.A. (1959) The remembering and forgetting of advertising, *Journal of Marketing*, 23 (January), 239–43.

# Chapter 4

# How marketing communications might work

Understanding how marketing communications might work with its rich mosaic of perceptions, emotions, attitudes, information and patterns of behaviour is challenging in itself. Any attempt to understand how marketing communications might work must be cautioned by an appreciation of the complexity and contradictions inherent in this complicated commercial activity.

## Aims and learning objectives

The aims of this chapter are to explore some of the theoretical concepts associated with ideas about how marketing communications might work and to consider the complexities associated with understanding how clients can best use marketing communications.

The learning objectives of this chapter are to:

1. explore ideas concerning the strategic context of marketing communications;
2. explore engagement and the role of marketing communications;
3. explain how marketing communications works through sequential processing;
4. understand how managing attitudes through marketing communications is important;
5. appraise the way relationships can be shaped through the use of marketing communications;
6. consider ways in which marketing communications might develop significant value;
7. examine the role marketing communications might play in helping people process information.

# Minicase

## Rolex: a range of quality communications

Rolex is a Swiss manufacturer of luxury watches. The company is grounded in innovation, demonstrated by their list of 'firsts'. Rolex made the first watches to be dustproof, waterproof and airtight. They were the first to market a wristwatch with an automatic date changing facility on the dial, the first with automatic date and day changing with waterproof technology, the first to show two time zones simultaneously, and the first to achieve chronometer certification. The reputation of Rolex is extremely high, evidenced by its first position in the Consumer Superbrands 2012 index. Coca-Cola and Google were second and third, respectively.

It has been this innovation and devotion to precision engineering that has helped inform their positioning and communications, which in turn have helped propel the company to superbrand status. Rolex is associated with high prices, with very high quality, and a brand synonymous with prestige and affluence. Rolex is perceived to be a status item and symbolic of an individual's wealth and achievements. Rolex targets affluent people aged 35 to 60, where the household income is $100,000+. A Rolex purchase can be complex and often protracted, mainly because a watch of this type is central to an individual's self-concept. Many customers have aspired to own a Rolex and when they achieve this they stick with the brand for life. The timeless, classic appeal of Rolex therefore engenders its own sense of loyalty.

Rolex watches cannot be bought from the company website, but only through appointed, authorised retailers, or through Rolex's own branded retail outlet in Geneva. Part of the reasoning for this is to provide individual attention and support through the purchasing process, and so enable Rolex to control and enhance the shopping experience.

In order to sustain this luxury brand reputation, Rolex embrace a wide range of marketing communications activities. Their primary tools are advertising, sponsorship, product placement, public relations and personal selling (through their retail outlets). The media mix comprises paid media such as print, cinema, television, online and mobile, owned media through their website and video advertising, plus earned media through word of mouth, user-generated content and consumer-generated ads. Where possible, these are carefully controlled and synthesised to reinforce their positioning.

A substantial part of Rolex's communications strategy is structured around arts, culture, event sponsorship and the use of brand ambassadors. Perhaps the most notable of the events they are involved with is their role as official timekeeper for the prestigious Wimbledon tennis tournament. Other events include 'The Masters' (golf), the 'Maxi Yacht Rolex Cup', the 'Rolex Grand Slam of Eventing' and the 'Hahnenkamm Race' (skiing).

People who become Rolex brand ambassadors are clear winners in their chosen field. Leaders such as Roger Federer in tennis, skiers Carlo Janka and Lindsey Vonn, Zara Phillips in equestrian, and Phil Mickelson and Luke Donald from the world of golf, are just a few who represent the Rolex brand.

In a similar, and consistent approach, the Rolex Awards for Enterprise support pioneering individuals whose projects benefit communities and the world. Work undertaken in science, health, applied technology, exploration and discovery, the environment and cultural heritage have been supported through this scheme for over 35 years. Just as in sport, Rolex seek to associate themselves with extraordinary individuals who possess the courage and conviction to take on major challenges. People acknowledged in this way are referred to as Rolex Laureates.

Rolex advertising can be considered to be either factually product-orientated, or associative through the use of brand ambassadors and the events they sponsor. Brand ambassadors such as Ed Visteurs, a mountain climber who has conquered 14 of the world's highest peaks without the use of supplemental oxygen, provide a rich form of source credibility.

Ambassadors demonstrate qualities such as endurance and individual achievement, that Rolex hope others will value and associate with the brand. The individual performance of a brand ambassador is associated with the functional performance of a Rolex watch. This can be observed through an ad which depicts Mercedes Gleitze, who wore a Rolex during her 10-hour swim of the English Channel in 1926 (see Exhibit 4.1). This demonstrated the world's first waterproof watch and the ad associates the functionality of resilience and durability.

The amount of copy used these days in most Rolex ads, regardless of type, is minimal. For example, the copy for an ad featuring Roger Federer ran as

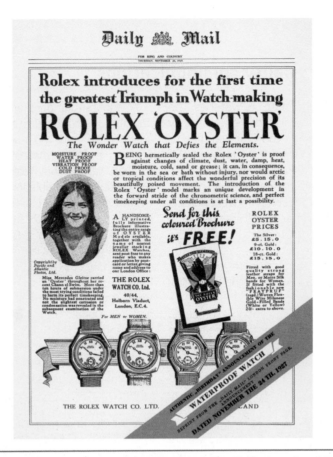

| Exhibit 4.1 | A Rolex ad published in 1927 celebrating Mercedes Gleitze's swim of the English Channel |
|---|---|
| | *Source*: Rolex UK |

'Master of the Court, Grand Slam Conductor. Longest consecutive streak as world's number one . . .' All of these are qualities upon which Rolex have positioned themselves and which serve to reinforce their reputation.

Rolex have not ignored digital media and have again undertaken some innovative and cutting-edge communications. It might be expected that Rolex would wish to maintain control over their communications, yet they have been involved with consumer-generated advertising. Readers of the magazine *Wallpaper* were offered the chance to design their own Rolex ad, which was featured in a personalised copy of the August 2011 issue of the magazine. The ad appeared on the back cover of the magazine and could be tailored by readers using an online application. Readers chose a watch to appear in the ad from a choice of two, and then selected a date that would appear on the face of their chosen watch, next to the line 'Some days

are made for greatness'. Readers accessed a palette of graphics, shapes, colours, photography and animations to personalise the front page and again received a copy of the magazine with their own cover.

*W Magazine* is a luxury and fashion lifestyle magazine. In one particular issue every ad had a mobile component powered by Pongr. The Rolex ad featured its Oyster Perpetual watch from its DateJust collection. Readers took a picture of the ad with their smartphone and sent it to w@pongr.com. Consumers were then given two site links from Rolex. In the first link they saw a mobile video from Rolex, and the second link directed the user to Rolex's website. As a result they were entered for a chance to win $1,000 from *W Magazine*.

*This minicase was written by Chris Fill using a range of sources, including Kats (2011); Eleftheriou-Smith (2012); Lufft (2011); www.rolex.com.*

# Introduction

The Rolex minicase describes aspects of the marketing communications used by a luxury brand. A range of tools, media and messages are used within a common theme to reinforce predetermined brand messages. What may not be clear is just how these elements work together and how marketing communications might actually work. This chapter explores this topic, how marketing communications might work, and introduces a number of concepts and frameworks that have contributed to our understanding. This chapter should be read in conjunction with those parts of the text in which various models are used to explain how advertising works (Chapter 14), and, in addition, those which complement this chapter in considering the content of advertising messages (Chapters 25 and 26).

Ideas about how advertising works dominate the literature, whereas ideas about how marketing communications are thought to work are often regarded as of secondary importance. Although it is recognised that both these approaches are important, it is necessary to change this priority, if only in recognition of the principles of integrated marketing communications. This chapter, therefore, deals with ideas concerning explanations and interpretations about how marketing communications might work.

# The strategic context

For a long time many considered marketing communications to be a purely operational issue, one which worked by delivering messages about products, to audiences who then, if the communication was effective, purchased the product. No real consideration was given to combining and synchronising the tools, reinforcing messages, understanding the target audience or keying the communications into an overall organisational strategy.

This silo approach has changed. Propelled by the emerging focus on a wider range of stakeholders, the excitement about relationship marketing, surging developments in digital technology and media applications (Chapters 21 and 22) and the emerging questions about integrated marketing communications (Chapter 10), have raised the profile and importance of a strategic orientation for marketing communications.

The corporate strategy that organisations pursue should be supported by business, operational and functional level strategies. Therefore, to be effective, marketing communications should be used to complement the marketing, business and corporate strategies. Such harmonisation serves to reinforce core messages, reflect the mission and provide a means of using resources efficiently yet at the same time provide reinforcement for the whole business strategy.

It could be argued that marketing communications works when it reflects the corporate-level strategy and supports the marketing plan and other related activities. It does not work simply because it complements strategy, but it certainly will not work unless it does reflect the marketing and business imperatives.

# Engagement and the role of marketing communications

Earlier in the text (Chapter 1) the term 'engagement' was introduced and offered to explain the role of marketing communications. 'Engagement', rather like 'integrated marketing communications', is a term that is used regularly and inconsistently by commentators, journalists and academics. Originally engagement was used in the context of media and media usage. Subsequently it has been used as means of explaining the relationship people have with brands (Rappaport, 2007). These are both object-orientated interpretations and we know that engagement can be a transient, as well as a long-term experience and has a contextual element, which is why the term 'engagement' is used here as a form of communication.

For engagement to occur there must first be some attention or awareness, be that overt or at a low level of processing. Engagement can be considered to consist of two main elements: intellectual and emotional (Thomson and Hecker, 2000). The intellectual element is concerned with audiences engaging with a brand on the basis of processing rational, functional information. The emotional element is concerned with audiences engaging and aligning themselves with a brand's values on the basis of emotional and expressive information.

It follows that communication strategies should be based on the information-processing styles and needs of audiences and their access to preferred media. Communications should reflect a suitable balance between the need for rational information to meet intellectual needs and expressive types of communication to meet emotional needs in an organisation's different audiences. These ideas are important foundations and will be returned to later.

Organisations communicate with a variety of audiences in order to pursue their marketing and business objectives. Advertising can be used to engage with a variety of audiences and in such a way as to meet the needs of the audience. In this case it is not just the choice of media that is influential, but also the content. Messages should encourage individual members of target audiences to respond to the focus organisation (or product/brand). This response can be immediate through, for example, purchase behaviour or use of customer care lines, or it can be deferred as information is assimilated and considered for future use. Even if the information is discarded at a later date, the communication will have attracted attention and consideration of the message.

The primary role of marketing communications therefore is to engage audiences in one of two ways:

- To drive a response to the message itself, often reflected in building awareness, and brand associations, cultivating brand values or helping to position brands in markets, or the minds of people in target audiences.

- To drive a response to the brand itself. This might be to encourage calls to a particular number, visits to a website, shop, or showroom, or participation in a game, discount scheme or other form of entertainment. These requests within a message are referred to as a *call-to-action*.

When engagement occurs an individual might be said to have been positively captivated, and as a result opportunities for further communication activity should increase. Engagement involves attention getting and awareness but it also encompasses the decoding and processing of information at a conscious or subconscious level, so that meaning can be attributed to a message, at the appropriate time.

### Viewpoint 4.1    Successful engagement

The marketing communications used to support Comfort fabric conditioner in SE Asia up until 2006 was based largely on a behavioural strategy. This used direct response advertising and sales promotions to compete in a price-based market. However, sales were declining steadily, so Unilever turned to a strategy that was designed to develop the perceived value of the brand by provoking a brand-value response. The 'Andy and Lily in Clothworld' campaign transformed the brand in three years, with 40 per cent growth in year one and incremental sales worth $157 million across three years.

For example, the UK supermarket Waitrose has positioned itself for many years as an upmarket food store providing high-quality food. The recession in 2008 threatened their performance targets as people started to shop at alternative, value-orientated stores. The strategy was to introduce a new brand, 'Essential Waitrose'. In 2009 Waitrose experienced the fastest growth of all the supermarkets, with the essential range contributing 16 per cent of total revenue, up from 5 per cent in 2008. This move from a brand value (ad response) to a behavioural (brand response) use of advertising reflects the growing preference of many advertisers, especially post-recession, to drive people into action rather than simply using advertising to manage perception, attitudes and brand values.

*Source*:   Based on Wiesser et al. (2010); Nairn and Wyatt (2010).

**Question:**    Having introduced and established a value-orientated range, to what extent might Waitrose struggle to reassert their premium positioning when markets and economies recover?

**Task:**    Compare the advertising for two brands, one from the service sector and the other from a food manufacturer. What might be the core differences in their approach?

Successful engagement suggests that understanding and meaning have been conveyed effectively. At one level, engagement through one-way communication enables target audiences to understand product and service offers, to the extent that the audience is sufficiently engaged to want further communication activity. This is what advertising does well. At another level, engagement through two-way, or interactive, communication enables information that is relationship-specific (Ballantyne, 2004) to be exchanged. Advertising is not always able to generate or sustain this frequency or type of information exchange so other communication tools are often used to support these relationship needs.

The communication mix has expanded and become more complex managerially, but essentially it is capable of developing brand values, and changing behaviour through the delivery of calls to action. From a strategic perspective, the former is oriented to the long term and the latter to the short term. It is also apparent that the significant rise of the below-the-line tools within the mix is partly a reflection of the demise of the USP, but it is also a reflection of the increasing financial pressures experienced by organisations to improve performance and improve returns on investment.

# How does marketing communications work?

The main thrust of this chapter is to consider how marketing communications works in order to achieve successful engagement. Unfortunately, there is no single model, despite years of research and speculation by a great many people that can be presented as the definitive way marketing communications works. However, from all the work undertaken in this area, mainly with regard to advertising, a number of views have been expressed, and the following sections attempt to present some of the more influential perspectives. (For an interpretation of how advertising might work, this chapter should be read in conjunction with Chapter 14.) Here are five different interpretations of how marketing communications are considered to work, as presented in Figure 4.1. These are

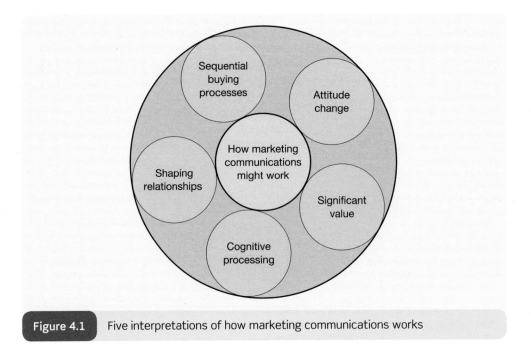

**Figure 4.1**    Five interpretations of how marketing communications works

- Approach 1 = Sequential buying processes
- Approach 2 = Attitude change
- Approach 3 = Shaping relationships
- Approach 4 = Significant value
- Approach 5 = Cognitive processing.

For a message to be communicated successfully, it should be meaningful to the participants in the communication process. Messages need to be targeted at the right audience, be capable of gaining attention, be understandable, relevant and acceptable. For effective communication to occur, messages should be designed that fit the context in which the messages are 'processed'. In the sections that follow, a number of different approaches to how marketing communications works are considered, each in a different context.

## Interpretation 1: Sequential models

Various models have been developed to assist our understanding of how communication tasks are segregated and organised effectively. Table 4.1 shows some of the better-known models. These models were developed primarily to explain how advertising worked. However, the principle of these hierarchical models also applies to marketing communications. The context for all of these sequential models is the general purchase process.

### AIDA

Developed by Strong (1925), the AIDA model was designed to represent the stages that a salesperson must take a prospect through in the personal selling process. This model shows the prospect passing through successive stages of attention, interest, desire and action. This expression of the process was later adopted, very loosely, as the basic framework to explain how persuasive communication, and advertising in particular, was thought to work.

| Table 4.1 | Sequential models of marketing communications | | |
|---|---|---|---|
| **Stage** | **AIDA**[a] | **Hierarchy of effects**[b] | **Information processing**[c] |
| | | Awareness | Presentation |
| | | | ↓ |
| Cognitive | | | Attention |
| | | ↓ | ↓ |
| | Attention | Knowledge | Comprehension |
| | ↓ | ↓ | ↓ |
| | Interest | Liking | Yielding |
| | | ↓ | |
| Affective | | Preference | |
| | ↓ | ↓ | ↓ |
| | Desire | Conviction | Retention |
| Conative | ↓ | ↓ | ↓ |
| | Action | Purchase | Behaviour |

*Source*: [a] Strong (1925); [b] Lavidge and Steiner (1961); [c] McGuire (1978).

## Hierarchy of effects models

An extension of the progressive, staged approach advocated by Strong emerged in the early 1960s. Developed most notably by Lavidge and Steiner (1961), the hierarchy of effects models represent the process by which advertising was thought to work and assume that there is a series of steps a prospect must pass through, in succession, from unawareness to actual purchase. Advertising, it is assumed, cannot induce immediate behavioural responses; rather, a series of mental effects must occur, with fulfilment at each stage necessary before progress to the next stage is possible.

## The information-processing model

McGuire (1978) contends that the appropriate view of the receiver of persuasive advertising is as an information processor or cognitive problem solver. This cognitive perspective becomes subsumed as the stages presented reflect similarities with the other hierarchical models, except that McGuire includes a retention stage. This refers to the ability of the receiver to retain and understand information that is valid and relevant. This is important, because it recognises that marketing communication messages are designed to provide information for use by a prospective buyer when a purchase decision is to be made at some time in the future.

## Difficulties with the sequential approach

For a long time the sequential approach was accepted as the model upon which advertising was to be developed. However, questions arose about what actually constitute adequate levels of awareness, comprehension and conviction and how it can be determined which stage the majority of the target audience has reached at any one point in time.

The model is based on the logical sequential movement of consumers towards a purchase via specified stages. The major criticism is that it assumes that the consumer moves through the stages in a logical, rational manner: learn, then feel and then do. This is obviously not the case, as anyone who has taken a child into a sweet shop can confirm. There has been a lot of research that attempts to offer an empirical validation for some of the hierarchy propositions, the results of which are inconclusive and at times ambiguous (Barry and Howard, 1990). Among these researchers is Palda (1966), who found that the learn–feel–do sequence cannot be upheld as a reflection of general buying behaviour and provided empirical data to reject the notion of sequential models as an interpretation of the way advertising works.

The sequential approach sees attitude towards the product as a prerequisite to purchase, but, as discussed earlier (Chapter 3), there is evidence that a positive attitude is not necessarily a good predictor of purchase behaviour. What is important, or more relevant, is the relationship between attitude change and an individual's intention to act in a particular way (Ajzen and Fishbein, 1980). Therefore, it seems reasonable to suggest that what is of potentially greater benefit is a specific measure of attitude *towards* purchasing or *intentions* to buy a specific product. Despite measurement difficulties, attitude change is considered a valid objective, particularly in high-involvement situations.

A great deal of time and money must be spent on research, determining what needs to be measured. As a result, only large organisations can utilise the model properly: those with the resources and the expertise to generate the data necessary to exploit this approach fully.

All of these models share the similar view that the purchase decision process is one in which individuals move through a series of sequential stages. Each of the stages from the different models can be grouped in such a way that they are a representation of the three attitude components, these being cognitive (learn), affective (feel) and conative (do) orientations. This could be seen to reflect the various stages in the buying process, especially those that induce high involvement in the decision process but do not reflect the reality of low-involvement decisions.

---

### Scholars' paper 4.1      Doing it sequentially

**Lavidge, R.J. and Steiner, G.A. (1961) A model for predictive measurements of advertising effectiveness, *Journal of Marketing* (October), 61.**

Published in the *Journal of Marketing* in 1961, this paper was pivotal in changing the way we considered advertising. Up until then advertising research and measurement was very much orientated to techniques and methods. This paper asked the question: what is advertising supposed to do and what function should it have?

The answer was broadly that advertising should help consumers move through the various steps in the purchasing process. Lavidge and Steiner then made the link to the attitude construct, upon which so much work has been done and from which so many ideas have subsequently emerged.

---

## Interpretation 2: Changing attitudes with marketing communications

Attitude change has been regarded by many practitioners as the main way to influence audiences through marketing communications. Although it is recognised that product and service elements, pricing and channel decisions all play an important part in shaping the attitudes held, marketing communications has a pivotal role in conveying each of these aspects to the target audience and in listening to responses. Branding (Chapter 11) is a means by which attitudes can be established and maintained in a consistent way, and it is through the use of the tools of the communications mix that brand positions can be sustained. The final point that needs to be made is that there is a common thread between attributes, attitudes and positioning. Attributes provide a means of differentiation, and positions are shaped as a consequence of the attitudes that result from the way people interpret the associated marketing communications.

Environmental influences on the attitudes people hold towards particular products and services are a consequence of many factors. First, they are a reflection of the way different people interpret the marketing communications surrounding them. Second, they are an expression of their direct experience of using them and, third, they are the result of the informal messages and indirect messages received from family, friends and other highly credible sources of information. These all contribute to the way people perceive (and position) products and services and the feelings they have towards them and towards competing products. Managing brand attitudes is considered to be very important, and marketing communications can play an important part in changing or maintaining the attitudes held by a target audience. There are a number of ways in which attitudinal change can be implemented:

## Change the physical product or service element

At a fundamental level, attitudes might be so ingrained that it is necessary to change the product or service. This may involve a radical redesign or the introduction of a significant new attribute. Only when these changes have been made should marketing communications be used to communicate the new or revised object.

## Change misunderstanding

In some circumstances people might misunderstand the benefits of a particularly important attribute, and marketing communications is required to correct the beliefs held. This can be achieved through product demonstration of functionally based communications. Packaging and even the name of the product may need to be revised.

## Build credibility

Attitudes towards a brand might be superficial and lack sufficient conviction to prompt behaviour. This can be corrected through the use of an informative strategy, designed to build credibility. Product demonstration, hands-on experience (e.g. through sampling) and testimonials from leading experts or opinion leaders and formers can be effective strategies.

## Change performance beliefs

Beliefs held about the object and the performance qualities of a brand can be adjusted through appropriate marketing communications. For example, by changing the perceptions held about the attributes, it is possible to change the attitudes about the object.

## Change attribute priorities

By changing the relative importance of the different attributes and ratings it is possible to change attitudes. Therefore, a strategy to emphasise a different attribute or one not featured by competitors can change the attitude not only towards a brand but also to a product category. By stressing the importance of travel times, the importance of this attribute might be emphasised in the minds of potential holiday-makers. Dyson changed attitudes to carpet cleaning equipment by stressing the efficiency of its new cyclone technology rather than the ease of use, aesthetic design or generic name (Hoover) associations used previously.

## Introduce a new attribute

Opportunities might exist to introduce a radically different, perhaps new or previously unused attribute. This provides a means for clear differentiation and positioning until competitors imitate and catch up. For example, use communications to make prominent new service levels, which are coupled with guaranteed refunds in the event of performance failure.

### Change perception of competitor products

By changing the way competitor products are perceived, it is possible to differentiate your own brand. This could be achieved by using messages that distance a competitor's brand from your own. For example, an airline could highlight a key competitor's punctuality record, and this might help change the way its own performance level is perceived. In much the same way, Ryanair always seek to highlight their low prices and compare them to their competitors'.

### Change or introduce new brand associations

By using celebrities or spokespersons with whom the target audience can identify, it might be possible to change the way in which a brand is perceived. For example, a bread producer might use a well-known athlete to represent their brand as a healthy food. Alternatively, it may use children in its marketing communications to suggest that it is fun to eat and that all children love the brand.

### Use corporate branding

By altering the significance of the parent brand relative to the product brand, it is possible to alter beliefs about brands and their overall value. In some situations there is little to differentiate competitive brands and little credible scope to develop attribute-based attitudes. By using the stature of the parent company, it is possible to develop a level of credibility and brand values that other brands cannot copy, although they can imitate by using their parent brand. Procter & Gamble has introduced its name to the packs of many of its brands.

### Change the number of attributes used

Many brands still rely on a single attribute as a means of providing a point of differentiation. As explored later (Chapter 14), this was popularly referred to as a *unique selling proposition* at a time when attribute and information-based communications reflected a feature-dominated understanding of branding. Today, two or even three attributes are often combined with strong emotional associations in order to provide a point of differentiation and a set of benefit-oriented brand values.

## Using marketing communications to influence attitudes

As outlined previously (Chapter 3), attitudes are made up of three components; cognitive, affective and conative. Marketing communications can be used to influence each of these elements: namely, the way people either think, feel or behave towards a brand.

### Cognitive component

When audiences lack information, misunderstand a brand's attributes or when their perception of a brand is inappropriate, the essential task of marketing communications is to give the audience the correct or up-to-date information. This enables perception, learning and attitude development based on clear truths. This is a rational, informational approach, one that appeals to a person's ability to rationalise and process information in a logical manner. It is, therefore, important that the level and quality of the information provided is appropriate to the intellectual capabilities of the target audience. Other tasks include showing the target audience how a brand differs from those of competitors, establishing what the added value is and suggesting who the target audience is by depicting them in the message.

Both advertising and public relations are key tools, and television, print and the Internet are key media for delivering information and influencing the way people perceive a brand.

Rather than provide information about a central or popular attribute or aspect of an offering, it is possible to direct the attention of an audience to different aspects of the object and so shape their beliefs about the brand in ways different from competitors'. So, some crisp and snack food manufacturers used to communicate the importance of taste. Now in an age of chronic social obesity, many of these manufacturers have changed the salt and fat content and appeal to audiences on the basis of nutrition and health. They have changed the focus of attention from one attribute to another.

Although emotion can be used to provide information, the overriding approach is informational.

---

### Scholars' paper 4.2    Do I really need to get your attention?

**Heath, R. and Feldwick, P. (2008) 50 years using the wrong model of TV advertising,** *International Journal of Market Research,* **50, 1, 29–59.**

For several years Heath (and Feldwick) have challenged the dominance and pervasiveness of the information-processing approach and believe that attention is not necessary for ads to be effective. Students will find this paper helpful because it sets out the arguments and history associated with information processing. The authors argue that people can be influenced by advertising, even when they cannot recall ads. Decision making is founded on emotions triggered through associations made at subconscious levels.

---

### Affective component

Rational, logical information may not be enough to stimulate behaviour, in which case marketing communications can be used to convey a set of emotional values that will appeal to and, hopefully, engage the target audience.

When attitudes to a brand or product category are discovered to be either neutral or negative, it is common for brands to use an emotional rather than rational or information-based approach. This can be achieved by using messages that are unusual in style, colour and tone and, because they stand out and get noticed, they can change the way people feel and their desire to be associated with that object, brand or product category. There is great use of visual images and the appeal is often to an individual's senses, feelings and emotional disposition. The goal is to help people feel, 'I (we) like, I (we) desire (aspire to), I (we) want or I (we) belong to' whatever is being communicated. Establishing and maintaining positive feelings towards a brand can be achieved through reinforcement and to do this it is necessary to repeat the message at suitable intervals.

Creating positive attitudes used to be the sole preserve of advertising, but today a range of tools and media can be used. For example, product placement within films and music videos helps to show how a brand fits in with a desirable set of values and lifestyles. The use of music, characters that reflect the values of either the current target audience or an aspirational group, a tone of voice, colours and images all help to create a particular emotional disposition and understanding about what the brand represents or stands for.

Perhaps above all else, the use of celebrity endorsers to create desire through association is one of the main ways attitudes are developed, based on an emotional disposition. This approach focuses on changing attitudes to the communication (attitudes to the ad) rather than the offering. Fashion brands are often presented using a celebrity model and little or no text. The impact is visual, inviting the reader to make positive attitudes and associations with the brand and the endorser.

Marmite use an emotional approach based on challenging audiences to decide whether they love or hate the unique taste. The government have used a variety of approaches to change people's attitude to drink/driving, smoking, vaccinations, tax, pensions and the use of rear seat belts, to name but a few of their activities. They will often use an information approach, but in some cases use an affective approach based on dramatising the consequences of a particular behaviour to encourage the audience to change their attitudes and behaviour. The overriding strategy is therefore emotional.

### Conative element

In some product categories people are said to be inert because they are comfortable with a current brand, have little reason to buy into a category, do not buy any brand or are just reluctant to change their brand. In these situations attitude change should be based on provoking behaviour. As explained later in this book, the growth and development of direct marketing and Web-based communications is based partly on the desire to encourage people to do something rather than undertake passive attitude change that does not necessarily result in action or a sale. Accordingly, a conative approach stimulates people to try, test, trial, visit (a showroom or website) a brand, usually free and often without overt commitment.

Sales promotion, personal selling and direct marketing are the key tools used to drive behavioural change. For example, sales promotions are geared to driving behaviour by getting people to try a brand, direct marketing seeks to encourage a response and hence engage in interaction, and salespeople will try to close a customer to get a sale. Advertising can be used to raise awareness and direct people to a store or website.

In addition to these approaches, experiential marketing has become very popular, as it is believed that direct experience of touching, feeling or using a product helps establish positive values and develop commitment. For example, many car manufacturers offer opportunities to test drive a car not only for a few hours but several days. They have test circuits where drivers can spend time driving several different cars in the range across different terrain.

The overriding strategy in this context is to provoke customers into action.

---

### Viewpoint 4.2    What a load of waste

The UK's sewers and drains have become a problem, simply because people have been throwing away the wrong type of waste. Cooking oil, grease, fat and baby wipes have been disposed of down sinks and toilets, and the result of this misuse has been a series of gigantic blockages causing widespread flooding in homes and costing millions of pounds every year just to clear them. It was estimated that there was over 1,000 tonnes of putrid fat lining sewer walls under London's Leicester Square.

In a single year Yorkshire Water recorded 352 floods caused by blocked drains, and dealt with 18,000 blockages, 37 per cent of which were preventable. They set themselves a target of reducing this to 313 incidents in 2011.

One way to reduce the problem is to invest in the sewer infrastructure, but a complementary approach is to educate customers through marketing communications. Yorkshire Water developed a campaign called 'Are you doing the dirty?' One part of this was targeted at consumers, and another at businesses, especially take-away restaurants who are prone to pour grease and fat into the drains.

To reach consumers an e-newsletter was sent to 200,000 customers, hospitals, health care professionals, surgeries, social housing authorities and councils. Through collaboration with UK parenting club Bounty, e-newsletters were sent to 28,217 new parents in Yorkshire. The core message was that nappies and baby wipes were causing problems and the solution was free nappy bags, available on request at the website. Messages were pushed through Facebook and Twitter at Yorkshire Water's online forums.

The media launch featured the star of the television programme *Help! My house is falling down*, Sarah Beany. This was set in a flooded kitchen and provided credibility and background information. In addition to the provision of information, the scheme used solutions to change behaviour. For example, the 'fat cakes' scheme was launched, where people can create fat balls for birds, using fat mixed with bird seed.

*Source:*   Bolger (2011).

**Question:**   How does this campaign demonstrate how marketing communications can be used to change attitudes?

**Task:**   Make brief notes outlining other ways in which attitudes towards waste disposal might be changed.

| Exhibit 4.2 | **Yorkshire Water communication** |
|---|---|
| | *Source*: Yorkshire Water |

## Interpretation 3: Shaping relationships

So far in this chapter the way marketing communications might work has been considered in terms of progressing the buying process, and by changing or influencing attitudes. Here we explore ideas that marketing communications works by influencing relationships. To do this, we shall look first at ideas about the relationship lifecycle, and then close by considering how marketing communications can support an audience's preferred mode of exchange. The context for this approach is the buyer–seller relationship.

### The customer relationship lifecycle

Customer relationships can be considered in terms of a series of relationship-development phases; customer acquisition, development, retention and decline. Collectively these are referred to as the *customer lifecycle*. The duration and intensity of each relationship phase in the life-cycle will inevitably vary and it should be remembered that this representation is essentially idealistic. A customer relationship cycle is represented at Figure 4.2.

Marketing communications can play an important role throughout all stages of the customer lifecycle. Indeed, marketing communications should be used to engage with audiences according to each audience's relational needs, whether transactional and remote or collaborative and close.

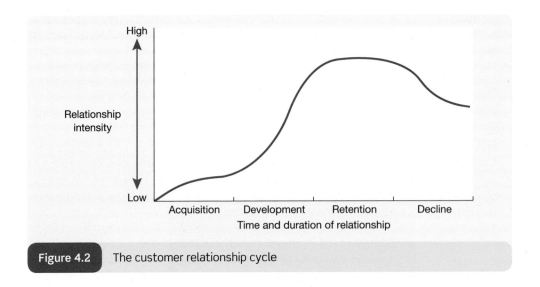

**Figure 4.2**   The customer relationship cycle

## Customer acquisition

The acquisition phase is characterised by three main events: search, initiation and familiarisation (see Table 4.2).

The logical sequence of acquisition activities moves from search and verification through the establishment of credentials. The length of this initiation period will depend partly on the importance of the buying decision and the complexity of the products, and partly upon the nature of the introduction. If the parties are introduced by an established and trusted source, certain initiation rites can be shortened.

Once a transaction occurs, the buyers and sellers start to become more familiar with each other and gradually begin to reveal more information about themselves. The seller receives payment, delivery and handling information about the buyer, and as a result is able to prepare customised outputs. The buyer is able to review the seller's products and experience the service quality of the seller.

During the acquisition phase, marketing communications needs to be geared towards creating awareness and providing access to the brand. Included within this period will be the need to help potential customers become familiar with the brand and to help them increase their understanding of the key attributes, possible benefits from use and to know how the brand is different from and represents value that is superior to the competition. Indeed, marketing communications has to work during this phase because it needs to fulfil a number of different roles and it needs to be targeted at precise audiences. Perhaps the main overriding task is to create a set of brand values that are relevant and which represent significant value for the

**Table 4.2**   Customer acquisition events

| Acquisition event | Explanation |
|---|---|
| Search | Buyers and sellers search for a suitable pairing |
| Initiation | Both parties seek out information about the other before any transaction occurs |
| Familiarisation | The successful completion of the first transaction enables both parties to start revealing more information about themselves |

target audience. In DRIP terms, differentiation and information will be important and, in terms of the communications mix, advertising and direct marking in the b2c market and personal selling and direct marketing in the b2b market.

## Customer development

The development phase is characterised by the seller attempting to reduce buyer risk and enhancing credibility. This is achieved by encouraging cross-selling whereby the buyer consumes other products, by improving the volume of purchases, by engaging the buyer with other added-value services and by varying delivery times and quantities. The buyer's acquiescence is dependent upon their specific needs and the degree to which the buyer wishes to become more involved with the supplier. Indeed, it is during this phase that the buyer is able to determine whether or not it is worth developing deeper relationships with the seller.

The main goals during the development phase are for the seller to reduce buyer-perceived risk and to simultaneously enhance their own credibility. In order to reduce risk, a number of messages will need to be presented though marketing communications. The selection of these elements will depend upon the forms of risk that are present either in the market sector or within individual customers. Marketing communications needs to engage by communicating messages concerning warranties and guarantees, finance schemes, third-party endorsements and satisfied customers, independent testing and favourable product performance reports, awards and the attainment of quality standards, membership of trade associations, delighted customers, growth and market share, new products and alliances and partnerships, all of which seek to reduce risk and improve credibility.

In DRIP terms, information and persuasion will be important, and in terms of the communications mix, public relations, sales promotion and direct marking in the b2c market and personal selling, public relations and direct marketing in the b2b market.

## Customer retention

The retention phase is the most profitable, where the greatest level of relationship value is experienced. The retention phase will generally last as long as both the buyer and seller are able to meet their individual and joint goals. If the relationship becomes more involved, greater levels of trust and commitment between the partners will allow for increased cross-buying and product experimentation and, for b2b relationships, joint projects and product development. However, the very essence of relationship marketing is for organisations to identify a portfolio of customers with whom they wish to develop a range of relationships. This requires the ability to measure levels of retention and also to determine when resources are to be moved from acquisition to retention and back to acquisition.

The length of the retention phase will reflect the degree to which the marketing communications is truly interactional and based on dialogue. Messages need to be relational and reinforcing. Incentive schemes are used extensively in consumer markets as a way of retaining customers and minimising customer loss (or churn, defection or attrition). They are also used to cross-sell products and services and increase a customer's commitment and involvement with the brand. Through the use of an integrated programme of communications, value can be enhanced for both parties and relational exchanges are more likely to be maintained. In business markets, personal contact and key account management are crucial to maintaining interaction, understanding and mutual support. Electronic communications have the potential to automate many routine transactions and allow for increased focus on one-to-one communications.

In DRIP terms, reinforcement and information will be important and, in terms of the communications mix, sales promotion and direct marking in the b2c market and personal selling (and key accounts), public relations and direct marketing in the b2b market.

| Viewpoint 4.3 | Lynx seek customer retention |
| --- | --- |

Many brands have moved an increasing proportion of their marketing activities into social media. One of these is Lynx, the Unilever-owned brand, which focuses much of its communications on Facebook, seeking to build on its customer loyalty and increate sales.

Lynx, a range of male grooming products, is designed for 16–24-year-old males. It uses the communication platform 'the Lynx effect', which is about how young men can attract more girls through the use of Lynx. The site uses videos, some previously presented as TV ads, as a means of driving conversations about the brand. Some of these ads have a cult status, to the point of being mimicked by other brands – for example, Specsavers. A more recent development has been the Lynx Attract, a variant for women. This has been supported through sponsorship of the panda mating programme at Edinburgh Zoo. The brand hopes that, should the pandas mate – a rare occurrence as females will only mate for three days a year – the public will make positive associations with the 'Lynx effect', if humorously.

Lynx initiates brand-based discussions by asking questions such as 'Which Lynx is best for you?' and 'What Lynx are you wearing tonight?' No doubt the panda sponsorship will provide discussion and engagement opportunities as well. The Facebook page has become the brand's core online presence, relegating the global website to a supporting role. An interesting view of being audience-centred can be seen in the creation of a conversation calendar. This enables content to be planned around what is happening in the lives of the brand's active audience, rather than simply product-driven.

Unilever recruited a tracking panel of 400 people from their Facebook page and then matched this with a control group. By monitoring sales of both groups, Lynx claims that the brand fans bought 31 per cent more Lynx products than non-fans.

*Source*:   Baker (2012); Eleftheriou-Smith (2012).

**Question:** How might Lynx develop other animal-related sponsorships and would it be stretching the theme too far?

**Task:** Find two press releases about the Lynx panda sponsorship. To what extent is Lynx or the panda the central story?

| Exhibit 4.3 | **A Lynx effect ad** |
| --- | --- |

*Source*: Sykes et al. (2011)

## Customer decline

Customer decline is concerned with the closure of a relationship. Termination may occur suddenly as a result of a serious problem or episode between the parties. The more likely process is that the buying organisation decides to reduce its reliance on the seller because its needs have changed, or an alternative supplier who offers superior value has been found. The buyer either formally notifies the established supplier or begins to reduce the frequency and duration of contact and moves business to other, competitive organisations.

The termination process therefore may be sharp and sudden or slow and protracted. Marketing communications plays a minor role in the former but is more significant in the latter. During an extended termination, marketing communications, especially direct marketing in the form of telemarketing and email, can be used to deliver orders and profits. These forms of communication are beneficial, because they allow for continued personal messages but do not incur the heavy costs associated with field selling (b2b) or advertising (b2c).

In DRIP terms, reinforcement and persuasion will be important and, in terms of the communications mix, direct marketing in both markets and sales promotion in the b2c market will be significant.

This cycle of customer attraction (acquisition), development, retention and decline provides a customer- rather than a product-orientated approach to explaining how marketing communications might work. The car manufacturer Audi developed the Audi Customer Journey. This is used to chart the ownership cycle and then to superimpose optimised brand communications for each owner. This approach is reflected in Audi's loyalty rate, which has grown consistently since the 'Journey' was introduced.

---

**Scholars' paper 4.3**    **Relationship-based communication**

**Gronroos, C. (2004) The relationship marketing process: communication, interaction, dialogue, value, *Journal of Business and Industrial Marketing*, 19(2), 99–113.**

This is a classic paper and one that all students of marketing communications should experience first-hand. Gronroos considers relationship marketing as a process and then explores ideas about planned and integrated marketing communications. He observes that, if the interaction and planned communication processes are successfully integrated and geared towards customers' value processes, a relationship dialogue may emerge. There are a large number of interesting issues in this paper.

---

## Influencing value exchanges

Earlier in the text (Chapter 1) the notion of transactional and collaborative exchanges was established. It is within this framework that ideas about how engagement might be established through a relationship marketing perspective are now considered.

A useful way of considering these types of exchanges is to see them at either end of a continuum, as set out in Figure 4.3. At one end of the continuum are transactional exchanges. These are characterised by short-term, commodity- or price-oriented exchanges, between buyers and sellers coming together for one-off exchanges independent of any other or subsequent exchanges. Both parties are motivated mainly by self-interest. Movement along the continuum represents increasingly valued relationships. Interactions between parties are closer, more frequent and stronger. The focus moves from initial attraction, to retention and to mutual understanding of each other's needs.

At the other end of the continuum is what Day (2000) refers to as *collaborative exchanges*. These are characterised by a long-term orientation, where there is complete integration of

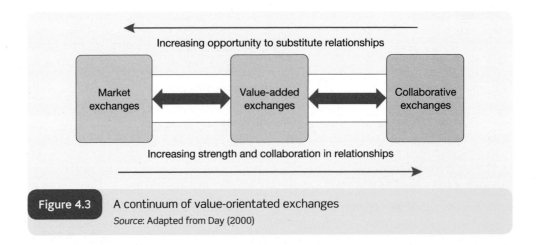

**Figure 4.3** A continuum of value-orientated exchanges
*Source*: Adapted from Day (2000)

systems and processes and the relationship is motivated by partnership and mutual support. Trust and commitment underpin these relationships, and these variables become increasingly important as collaborative exchanges become established.

These two positions represent extremes. In the middle there are a range of exchanges where the interaction between customers and sellers is based around the provision and consumption of perceived value. The quality, duration and level of interdependence between buyers and sellers can vary considerably. The reasons for this variance are many and wide-ranging, but at the core are perceptions of shared values and the strength and permanence of any relationship that might exist.

Perceived value may take many forms and be rooted in a variety of attributes, combined in different ways to meet segment needs. However, the context in which an exchange occurs between a buyer and a seller provides a strong reflection of the nature of their relationship. If the exchange is focused on the product (and the price) then the exchange is considered to be essentially transactional. If the exchange is focused around the needs of customers and sellers, the exchange is considered to be collaborative. The differences between transactional and collaborative exchanges are set out in Table 4.3 and provide an important starting point in understanding the nature of relationship marketing.

Relationship marketing can be characterised by the frequency and intensity of the exchanges between buyers and sellers. As these exchanges become more frequent and more intense, so

**Table 4.3** The characteristics of transactional and collaborative exchanges

| Attribute | Market exchange | Collaborative exchange |
|---|---|---|
| Length of relationship | Short-term<br>Abrupt end | Long-term<br>A continuous process |
| Relational expectations | Conflicts of goals<br>Immediate payment<br>No future problems (there is no future) | Conflicts of interest<br>Deferred payment<br>Future problems expected to be overcome by joint commitment |
| Communication | Low frequency of communication<br>Formal, mass-media communication predominates | Frequent communication<br>Informal, personal, interactive communication predominates |
| Cooperation | No joint cooperation | Joint cooperative projects |
| Responsibilities | Distinct responsibilities<br>Defined obligations | Shared responsibilities<br>Shared obligations |

the strength of the relationship between buyer and seller improves. It is this that provided the infrastructure for a new perspective on marketing, one based on relationships (Spekman, 1988; Rowe and Barnes, 1998), rather than the objects of a transaction: namely products and services. Using this relationship framework, it is possible to superimpose ways in which marketing communications might be considered to work.

Transactional exchanges where the relationship has little value for the buyer, and possibly the seller, are best supported with communications that do not seek to build the relationship but are generally orientated towards engaging through the provision of product and price (attribute-based) information. The communication is essentially a monologue as the buyer does not wish to respond, so the one-way or linear model of communication is predominant. The communications might coincide with purchase cycles but are generally infrequent and regularised. These communications are one-sided, so an asymmetric pattern of communication emerges as they are driven by the seller. In many cases the identity of the buyers is unknown, so it is not possible to personalise messages and media channels and the largely informational messages are delivered through mass-communication media. These communications are formal and direct.

Collaborative exchanges, on the other hand, reflect the strong bond that exists between buyer and seller. Marketing communications, therefore, should seek to engage buyers by maintaining or strengthening the relationship. This means that communication patterns are irregular, informal, frequent and indirect. This is because buyers and sellers working collaboratively seek to provide mutual value. It means there are frequent interactions, often through dialogue, as one party responds to the other when discussing and resolving issues and challenges. The communication flow is symmetrical, messages are indirect and personalised as the identities are known. See Figure 4.4 for a visual interpretation of this spectrum and Table 4.4 for an explanation of the terms used.

Key to these ideas is the notion of dialogue. The adoption of dialogue as the basis for communication changes an organisation's perspective of its audiences and signals a transition from transactional relationships. Being willing and able to enter into a dialogue indicates that there is a new emphasis on the relationships organisations hold with their stakeholders. Kent and Taylor (2002) argue that there are five main features of a dialogical orientation. These are presented in Table 4.5.

It can be seen in Table 4.5 that many aspects of dialogue require interaction as a precursor. In other words, for dialogue to occur there must first be interaction and it is the development and depth of the interaction that leads to meaningful dialogue.

However, a word of caution is necessary as not everyone believes relationship marketing is an outright success. For example, Rapacz et al. (2008: 22) suggest that the current view of

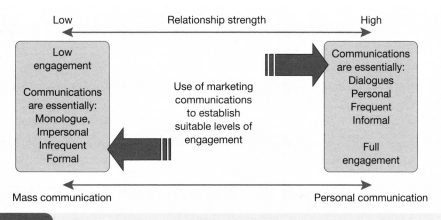

**Figure 4.4**    Achieving engagement through relationships

| Table 4.4 | Elements of relational marketing communications | | | |
|---|---|---|---|---|
| **Elements** | **Explanation** | **Transactional exchanges** | **Collaborative exchanges** | |
| Content | The extent to which the content of the message is intended to change behaviour (direct) or attitudes and beliefs (indirect) | Direct | Indirect | |
| Formality | The extent to which communication is structured and routinised (formal) or spontaneous and irregular (informal) | Formal | Informal | |
| Individuality | The extent to which recipients are identified by name | Impersonal | Personal | |
| Frequency | How often do communication events occur? | Infrequent | Frequent | |
| Audience | The size of the target audience for a communication event | Mass | Personal | |
| Interaction | The level of feedback allowed or expected | Monologue | Dialogue | |

Based on Mohr and Nevin (1990).

| Table 4.5 | The five features of a dialogical orientation |
|---|---|
| **Role** | **Explanation** |
| Mutuality | The recognition of the presence of organisational stakeholder relationships |
| Propinquity | The temporality and spontaneity of organisation–stakeholder interactions |
| Empathy | Support for stakeholder interests and their goals |
| Risk | Willingness to interact with others on their terms |
| Commitment | The extent to which an organisation actually interprets, listens to and practises dialogical communications |

*Source*: Kent and Taylor (2002). Used with permission.

relationship marketing has become 'stuck in a rut'. They argue that audits of the relationship marketing practices used to support many leading brands indicate that relationship marketing is not working. The goal, Rapacz et al. suggest, should be commitment to the brand rather than the relationship itself. They refer to the over-promise of one-to-one marketing, the difficulties and inefficiencies associated with databases and CRM technology and issues concerning loyalty programmes. The result of their critique is that they advocate the greater use of a variety of marketing communications techniques to generate increased brand commitment. They use the Jack Daniels brand to make their point about good practice, highlighting communications that, if disciplined, entertaining, benefit-oriented and multifaceted, serve to bring greater commitment to a brand.

### Viewpoint 4.4    Storytelling to build relationships

Building customer loyalty and commitment has been key to the success of many brands. An example of how this was achieved, way before the term 'relationship marketing' became part of the marketing lexicon, can be seen in the strategies used by Jack Daniel's, the iconic Tennessee whiskey brand.

In 1954 a brand discipline was established, one that sought to provide a strong point of differentiation for the brand. The purpose of Jack Daniel's advertising was to deliver the differentiation though a series of stories.

The stories told about its distilling process, its bottle, barrels, Jack Daniel himself and the people who worked there. The stories were presented within a set format of black and white photo vignettes with the accompanying text. The copy was designed to be intriguing, multifaceted, as well as fun to read so that each ad became a form of entertainment it its own right. Not only print ads, but stores and all sorts of other points where consumers touched the brand were used to convey the Jack Daniel's story. Everyone was invited to join the relationship. It was not exclusive to just brand advocates.

The brand promise, conveyed through the advertising, enveloped the crafted, unhurried, yet caring approach that was brought to the Jack Daniel's distilling process. Each ad and each story featured the people at Jack Daniel's. They were presented as gentle and caring, 'folk' who perpetuated the processes that had been handed down to them, working steadily in a hollow in Tennessee. The result was that readers had access to a very different, handcrafted, consistent, exceptional quality 'sippin' whiskey'.

Ideas about brand experiences and customer relationships are far from new. Back in the 1950s for example, Jack Daniel's readers and customers were invited to visit 'The Hollow', and see and feel for themselves the processes, the people and experiences the ads depicted. Today consumers are invited to email, text, like/dislike, phone, rank or vote for brands. Before all of these facilities became available Jack Daniel's invited people to 'drop-them-a-line' (write in), all of which served to demonstrate that customers were valued by Jack Daniel's.

*Source*:   Rapacz, Reilly, and Schultz (2008).

**Question:**   To what extent is a brand's heritage a useful form of communication? Is it only suitable for a certain type of brand?

**Task:**   Find another whiskey brand and compare its approach to marketing communications with that of Jack Daniel's.

The notion that relationships will improve as they evolve across a continuum is not accepted by all. The expectation that relationships can be enhanced through the application of marketing programmes is not one that is always experienced in practice. For example, Palmer (2007) believes that the continuum perspective is too simplistic and unrealistic. Better to consider the prevailing contextual conditions as the key dynamics that shape relationships, which inevitably wax and wane over time.

Rao and Perry (2002), cited by Palmer, suggest that relationship development can be considered in terms of stages theory or states theory. Stages theory reflects the notion of incremental development (along the continuum), while stages theory suggests that relationship development does not conform to the processional interpretation, because of the complexity and sheer unpredictability of relationship dynamics.

Palmer offers a compromise, namely a 'stages-within-a-state' interpretation. He draws on the work of Anderson and Narus (1999) and Canning and Hammer-Lloyd (2002) to make his point. There may be some validity in this view but the notion that all exchanges reflect a degree of relational commitment (Macneil, 1983) should not be ignored.

Ideas about how marketing communication works must be founded, in part, on the notion and significance of the level of interaction and dialogue that the organisation and their stakeholders desire. One-way communication, as reflected in traditional, planned, mass-media-based communication, still plays a significant role, especially for audiences who prefer transactional exchanges. Two-way communication based on interaction with audiences who desire continuing contact, or dialogue for those who desire a deeper more meaningful relationship, will form an increasingly important aspect of marketing communications strategy in the future.

## Interpretation 4: Developing significant value

Marketing communications consists of a set of tools and media that are used in varying ways to convey messages to and with audiences. Depending upon the context in which the message is created, delivered and interpreted, the brand and the individual have an opportunity to interact. Marketing communication messages normally pass individuals unobserved. Those that are remembered contain particular characteristics (Brown, 1991; Fletcher, 1994). These would appear to be that the product must be different or new, that the way the message is executed is different or interesting and that it proclaims something that is personally significant to the individual in their current context. The term 'significance' means that the message is meaningful, relevant (e.g. the individual is actually looking to buy a new car or breakfast cereals tomorrow or is planning to gather information on a new project), and is perceived to be suitably credible. These three characteristics can be tracked from the concept of ad likeability (Chapter 14), which many researchers believe is the only meaningful indicator of the effectiveness of an advertisement.

To be successful therefore, it is necessary for marketing communication messages to:

- present an offering that is new to the receiver;
- be interesting and stimulating;
- be personally significant.

The object referred to in the first element refers to both products and services (or an offering that is substantially different from others in the category) and to organisations as brands. The net effect of all these characteristics might be that any one message may be *significantly valuable* to an individual.

Messages announcing new brands or new attributes may convey information that is perceived to be significantly different. As a result, individuals may be intrigued and interested enough to want to try the brand at the next purchase opportunity. For these people there is a high level of personal relevance derived from the message, and attitude change can be induced to convince them that it is right to make a purchase. For them the message is significantly valuable and as a result may well generate a purchase decision, which will, from a market perspective, drive a discernible sales increase.

However, the vast majority of marketing communications are about products that are not new or that are unable to proclaim or offer anything substantially different. These messages are either ignored or, if interest is aroused, certain parts of the message are filed away in memory for use at a later date. The question is, if parts are filed away, which parts are filed and why and how are they retrieved?

Marketing communications can provide a rationale or explanation for why individuals (cognitive processors) have bought a brand and why they should continue buying it. Normally, advertising alone does not persuade – it simply reminds and reassures individuals. Or, to put it another way, individuals use advertising and public relations to remind themselves of preferred brands or to reassure themselves of their previous (and hence correct) purchase behaviour. Sales promotions, personal selling and direct marketing are then used by organisations to help consumers behave in particular ways.

Consumers, particularly in fast-moving consumer goods (FMCG) markets, practise repertoire buying based on habit, security, speed of decision-making and, to some extent, self-expression. The brands present in any single individual repertoire normally provide interest and satisfaction. Indeed, advertising needs to ensure that the brand remains in the repertoire or is sufficiently interesting to the individual that it is included in a future repertoire. Just consider the variety of messages used by mobile phone operators. These are continually updated and refreshed using particular themes, all of which are intended to be visually and cognitively engaging.

Messages, in particular advertising messages that are interesting, immediately relevant or interpreted as possessing a deep set of personal meanings (all subsequently referred to as 'likeable' (see Chapter 16), will be stored in long-term memory.

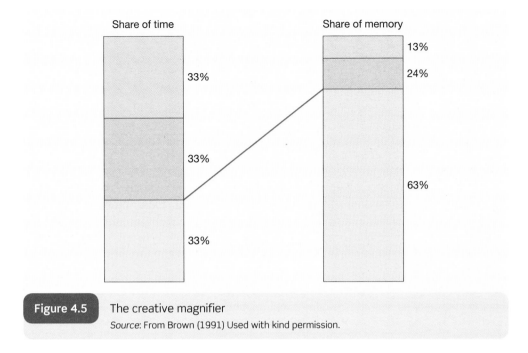

**Figure 4.5**   The creative magnifier
*Source*: From Brown (1991) Used with kind permission.

Research shows repeatedly that only parts of an advertisement are ever remembered – those parts that are of intrinsic value to the recipient and are sometimes referred to as 'the take-out'. Brown (1991) refers to this selectivity as the *creative magnifier* effect. Figure 4.5 illustrates the effect that parts of a message might have on the way a message is remembered.

The implication of this is that messages work best through the creation of interest and likeable moments, from which extracts are taken by individuals and stored away in memory. However, it might also be reasonable to suggest that the other tools of the mix are also capable of enabling individuals to take extracts. For example, the size of a sales promotion offer, or the tone of a sales presentation, the professionalism of a direct mail piece or the immediacy of an online promotion might all give due reason for an individual to generate a take-out. Interest is generated through fresh, relevant ideas where the brand and the messages are linked together in a meaningful and relevant way. This in turn allows for future associations to be made, linking brands and marketing communication messages in a positive and experiential way.

Marketing communications is used to trigger brand associations and experiences for people, not only when seated in front of a television or laptop, when reading a magazine or reading text or mobile messages, but also when faced with product purchase decisions. Of all low-value FMCG purchase decisions 70 per cent are said to be made at the point of purchase. All forms of marketing communication, but principally advertising, can be used to generate brand associations, which in turn are used to trigger advertising messages or, rather, 'likeable' extracts. The other tools of the mix can benefit from the prior use of advertising to create awareness so that the call-to-action brought about through below-the-line communications can occur naturally, unhindered by brand confusion or uncertainty.

This last point is of particular importance, because advertising alone may not be sufficient or appropriate to trigger complete recall of brand and communication experiences. The brand, its packaging, sales promotion, digital media, POP and outdoor media all have an important role to play in providing consistency and interest and prompting recall and recognition. Integrated marketing communications is important, not just for message take-out or likeable extracts, but also for triggering recall and recognition and stimulating relevant brand associations.

Messages that customers perceive as being of significant value to them as individuals, are key to developing effective marketing communications. In order to create such messages, a complex array of disciplines, media, people, technology and intuition need to be coordinated and deployed. These principles apply equally to consumer and business markets, it is just that the mix of marketing communication elements changes with each context.

## Interpretation 5: Cognitive processing

Reference has already been made to whether buyers actively or passively process information. In an attempt to understand how information is used, cognitive processing tries to determine 'how external information is transformed into meanings or patterns of thought and how these meanings are combined to form judgments' (Olsen and Peter, 1987).

By assessing the thoughts (cognitive processes) that occur to people as they read, view or hear a message, an understanding of their interpretation of a message can be gained, which is useful in campaign development and evaluation (Greenwald, 1968; Wright, 1973). These thoughts are usually measured by asking consumers to write down or verbally report the thoughts they have in response to such a message. Thoughts are believed to be a reflection of the cognitive processes or responses that receivers experience and they help shape or reject a communication.

Researchers have identified three types of cognitive response and have determined how these relate to attitudes and intentions. Figure 4.6 shows these three types of response, but

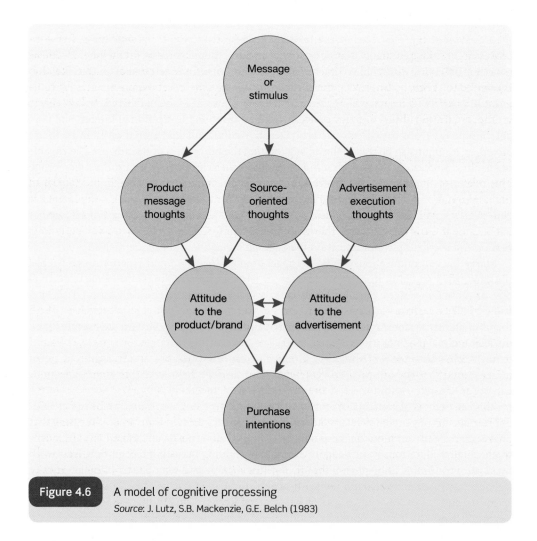

| Figure 4.6 | A model of cognitive processing |

*Source*: J. Lutz, S.B. Mackenzie, G.E. Belch (1983)

readers should appreciate that these types are not discrete; they overlap each other and blend together, often invisibly.

## Product/message thoughts

These are thoughts that are directed to the product or communication itself. Much attention has been focused on the thoughts that are related to the message content. Two particular types of response have been considered: counter-arguments and support arguments.

A counter-argument occurs when the receiver disagrees with the content of a message. According to Belch and Belch (2004):

> The likelihood of counter-argument is greater when the message makes claims that oppose the beliefs or perceptions held by the receiver. Not surprisingly, the greater the degree of counter-argument, the less likely the message will be accepted. Conversely, support-arguments reflect acceptance and concurrence with a message. Support-arguments, therefore, are positively related to message acceptance.

Advertisements and general communications should encourage the generation of support arguments.

## Source-oriented thoughts

A further set of cognitive responses is aimed at the source of the communication. This concept is closely allied to that of source credibility, where, if the source of the message is seen as annoying or untrustworthy, there is a lower probability of message acceptance. Such a situation is referred to as *source derogation*; the converse as a *source bolster*. Those responsible for communications should ensure, during the context analysis, that receivers experience bolster effects to improve the likelihood of message acceptance.

## Message-execution thoughts

This relates to the thoughts an individual may have about the overall design and impact of the message. Many of the thoughts that receivers have are not always product-related but are emotionally related to the message itself. Understanding these feelings and emotions is important because of their impact upon attitudes towards the message, most often an advertisement, and the offering.

## Attitudes towards the message

It is clear that people make judgements about the quality of commercial communications. These include advertisements, their creativity, the tone and style in which they or the website, promotion or direct mail piece, has been executed. As a result of their experiences, perceptions and the degree to which they like a message, they form an attitude towards the message itself. From this base an important stream of thought has developed about cognitive processing. Lutz's work led to the attitude-toward-the-ad concept which has become an important foundation for much of the related marketing communications literature. As Goldsmith and Lafferty (2002: 319) argue, there is a substantial amount of research that clearly indicates that advertising that promotes a 'positive emotional response of liking an ad is positively related to subsequent brand-related cognitions (knowledge), brand attitudes and purchase intentions'. Similar work by Chen and Wells (1999) shows that this attitude-towards-the-ad concept applies equally well with new media, and e-commerce in particular. They refer to an attitude-toward-the-site concept and similar ideas developed by Bruner and Kumar (2000) conclude that the more a website is liked, the more attitudes improve to the brand and purchase intentions.

It seems highly reasonable therefore, to conclude that attitudes-towards-the-message (and delivery mechanism) impact on brand attitudes, which in turn influence consumers' propensity to purchase. It is also known that an increasing proportion of advertisements attempt to appeal to feelings and emotions, simply because many researchers believe that attitudes towards both the advertisement and the product should be encouraged and are positively correlated with purchase intention. Similarly, time and effort are invested in the design of sales promotion instruments, increasing attention is given to the design of packaging in terms of a pack's communication effectiveness and care is taken about the wording in advertorials and press releases. Perhaps above all else, more and more effort is being made to research and develop websites with the goal of designing them so that they are strategically compatible, user-friendly and functional, or to put it another way – liked.

Just as a word of caution was offered with regard to the continuum of marketing relationships, so an alternative view needs to be mentioned with regard to cognitive processing. The cognitive processing model assumes that people attend to and process information in a logical rational way. Sometimes referred to as the 'Information Processing (IP)' model, the approach assumes that messages are processed and stored in memory, and later retrieved and updated (see Chapter 3 for more information on this topic). This processing approach is related to both informational and emotional messages. The latter were considered to be a consequence of people's thoughts and that by understanding what we think then we can understand everything (Heath and Hyder, 2005). Unfortunately psychologists such as Zajonc (1980) and Damasio (2000) upset this thinking, because their research showed that this was the wrong way round and that it was feelings and emotions (affect) that shaped our thoughts, at all times. This meant that advertising might be effective through mere exposure, rather than having to attend to, and cognitively process, the message.

In 2001 Heath published his 'Low Attention Processing Model', previously referred to as the Low *Involvement* Processing Model. The core characteristics of the Low Attention Processing (LAP) model are summarised by Heath and Hyder in Table 4.6.

The prevailing view is that messages need only be seen, that is, attended to, just once or twice. This is known as *high-attention processing* (HAP). What the LAP model says is that advertising can exploit low-attention processing when an individual is able to see the ad several times. The argument, based around empirical research, is that advertising messages can be processed with low attention levels. Typically people watch television passively (Krugman, 1965) and today many multitask with other media, so their attention to ads can be extremely low. As a result, people may not have any conscious recall of 'receiving' the message yet make decisions based on the emotions and the associations made at a low level of consciousness. According

| Table 4.6 | Core characteristics of the Low Attention Processing Model |

| Characteristic | Explanation |
| --- | --- |
| Intuitive choice | Intuitive decision making is more common than considered choice, so emotions will be more influential |
| Information acquisition | Intuitive decision making dampens information seeking and minimises the need to attend to ads |
| Passive and implicit learning | Brand information is acquired through low level of attention by passive learning and implicit learning. |
| Enduring associations | Associations are developed and reinforced through time and linked to the brand through passive learning. These associations can activate emotional markers, which in turn influence decision making. |
| Semi-automatic | Learning occurs semi-automatically, regardless of the level of attention paid. |

to Heath and Feldwick (2008) ad messages do not necessarily need to create impact and they do not need to deliver a proposition or functional benefit. What is important is a creative 'that influences emotions and brand relationships' (p. 45).

If this view is accepted then cognitive processing does not explain how marketing communications works, or at least dismisses the conventional view that advertising works through information processing.

# Conclusion

In this chapter five different approaches or interpretations about how marketing communications might work have been considered. None of them is completely wrong or completely right. Indeed, it is safe to conclude that marketing communications works in different ways in different contexts and that traces of several of these interpretations can be found in most campaigns.

For example, the sequential interpretation includes the principle of attitude change, while some would argue that cognitive processing underpins all of these approaches.

Some of these approaches evolved in the pre-digital era and, therefore, it might be unsafe to suggest that they are equally applicable or relevant today. For example, it could be argued that marketing communications needs to include more emphasis on listening to audiences, customers and tribes in social networks, yet this aspect is not explicit in any of the models presented here.

---

**Scholars' paper 4.4**    **Modelling b2b communications**

**Gilliland, D.I. and Johnston, W.J. (1997) Towards a model of marketing communications effects, *Industrial Marketing Management*, 26, 15–29.**

This paper provides a useful counterbalance to the wealth of consumer-orientated papers about marketing communications. As the title describes, the authors develop a well-respected model that explains how marketing communications works in a business-to-business context.

---

# Key points

- Corporate strategy should be supported by business-, operational- and functional-level strategies. To be effective, marketing communications should be used to complement the marketing, business and corporate strategies. Such harmonisation serves to reinforce core messages, reflect the mission and provide a means of using resources efficiently yet at the same time to provide reinforcement for the whole business strategy.

- The primary role of marketing communications is to engage audiences by either driving a response to the message itself, or encouraging a response to the brand itself, referred to as a *call-to-action*.

- There are five main ways in which marketing communications can be considered to work. These are the sequential buying process, attitude change, shaping relationships, developing significant value, and cognitive processing.

- The sequential approach assumes that marketing communications needs to take consumers through the decision making process in a series of logical steps.

- Attitude change has been regarded by many as the main way to influence audiences through marketing communications. Marketing communications can be used to focus one of the three elements of the attitudinal construct: that is, either the cognitive, affective or conative component.

- Relationship marketing can be characterised by the frequency and intensity of the exchanges between buyers and sellers. As these exchanges become more frequent and more intense, so the strength of the relationship between a consumer and a brand improves.

- These customer relationships can be considered in terms of a series of relationship development phases; customer acquisition, development, retention and decline. Collectively these are referred to as the *customer lifecycle*. The duration and intensity of each relationship phase in the lifecycle varies. Marketing communications works by influencing customers according to the stage they have reached in the lifecycle.

- Marketing communications is used to trigger brand associations and experiences for people.

- Those messages that are remembered contain particular characteristics. These are that the product must be different or new, that the way the message is executed is different or interesting, and that the message proclaims something that is personally significant to the individual in their current context.

- The term 'significance' means that the message is meaningful, relevant, and is perceived to be suitably credible. This is based on the concept of ad likeability, which many researchers believe is the only meaningful indicator of ad effectiveness. The net effect of all these characteristics might be that any one message may be *significantly valuable* to an individual.

- The cognitive processing model assumes that people attend to and process information in a logical rational way. Three types of cognitive response and how these relate to attitudes and intentions have been determined. These are attitudes towards the product, attitudes towards the message and attitudes towards the ad and its execution.

- There is a substantial amount of research that indicates that marketing communications (advertising) which promotes a 'positive emotional response of liking an ad is positively related to subsequent brand-related cognitions (knowledge), brand attitudes and purchase intentions'.

- Marketing communications works because liking an ad is positively related to subsequent brand-related cognitions (knowledge), brand attitudes, and purchase intentions. Attitude-towards-the-ad concept applies equally well with interactive media, ecommerce (attitude-toward-the-site), sales promotion and personal selling.

# Review questions

1. Explain the role that marketing communications plays within relationship marketing.
2. Write brief notes outlining the difference between three sequential models and evaluate the ways in which they are considered to work.
3. Which element in McGuire's model separates it from other similar models?
4. How do Rolex, as set out in the minicase, use marketing communications to change attitudes?

5. Set out how marketing communications can work by influencing transactional and collaborative exchange-based relationships.

6. Sketch the customer relationship lifecycle and show how marketing communications can be used to influence each of the stages.

7. Describe the creative magnifier effect. Why is it important?

8. Evaluate the concept of significant value.

9. Cognitive processing consists of three main elements. Name them.

10. Why might cognitive processing not be an entirely acceptable approach?

# References

Ajzen, I. and Fishbein, M. (1980) *Understanding Attitudes and Predicting Social Behavior*, Englewood Cliffs, NJ: Prentice Hall.

Anderson, J.C. and Narus, J.A. (1998) Business marketing: understand what customers value, *Harvard Business Review*, 76 (June) 53–65.

Anderson, J.C. and Narus, J.A. (1999) *Business Market Management*, Upper Saddle River, NJ: Prentice Hall.

Baker, R. (2012) Pandas get the 'Lynx Effect', *Marketing Week*, 16 March 2012, retrieved 25 March 2012 from http://www.marketingweek.co.uk/news/pandas-get-the-lynx-effect/4000697.article.

Ballantyne, D. (2004) Dialogue and its role in the development of relationship specific knowledge, *Journal of Business and Industrial Marketing*, 19(2), 114–23.

Barry, T. and Howard, D.J. (1990) A review and critique of the hierarchy of effects in advertising, *International Journal of Advertising*, 9, 121–35.

Belch, G.E. and Belch, M.A. (2004) *Advertising and Promotion: An Integrated Marketing Communications Perspective*, 6th edn, Homewood, IL: Richard D. Irwin.

Bolger, M. (2011) Marketing behaviour change: money down the drain?, *The Marketer,* November.

Brown, G. (1991) *How Advertising Affects the Sales of Packaged Goods Brands*, Warwick: Millward Brown.

Bruner, G.C. and Kumar, A. (2000) Web commercials and advertising hierarchy of effects, *Journal of Advertising Research*, January/April, 35–42.

Canning, L. and Hammer-Lloyd, S. (2002) Modelling the adaptation process in interactive business relationships, *Journal of Business & Industrial Marketing*, 17(7), 615–36.

Chen, Q. and Wells, W.D. (1999) Attitude toward the site, *Journal of Advertising Research*, September/October, 27–37.

Damasio, A.A. (2000) *The Feeling of What Happens*, London: Heinemann.

Day, G. (2000) Managing market relationships, *Journal of the Academy of Marketing Science*, 28, 1, Winter, 24–30.

Eleftheriou-Smith, L.-M. (2012) Rolex, Coca-Cola and Google top Consumer Superbrands of 2012, *Marketing*, 27 February 2012, retrieved 25 May 2012 from http://www.brandrepublic.com/news/1119186.

Eleftheriou-Smith, L.-M. (2012) Lynx sponsors panda mating programme at Edinburgh 200, *Marketing*, 19 March 2012, retrieved 9 September 2012 from http://marketingmagazine.co.uk/bulletin/daily news/article/1122828/?OCMP=EMC-BreakingnewsfromMarketing.

Fletcher, W. (1994) The advertising high ground, *Admap* (November), 31–4.

Gilliland, D.I. and Johnston, W.J. (1997) Towards a model of marketing communications effects, *Industrial Marketing Management*, 26, 15–29.

Goldsmith, R.E. and Lafferty, B.A. (2002) Consumer response to websites and their influence on advertising effectiveness, *Internet Research: Electronic Networking Applications and Policy*, 12(4), 318–28.

Greenwald, A. (1968) Cognitive learning, cognitive response to persuasion and attitude change, in *Psychological Foundations of Attitudes* (eds A. Greenwald, T.C. Brook and T.W. Ostrom), New York: Academic Press, 197–215.

Gronroos, C. (2004) The relationship marketing process: communication, interaction, dialogue, value, *Journal of Business and Industrial Marketing*, 19(2), 99–113.

Heath, R. and Feldwick, P. (2008) 50 years using the wrong model of TV advertising, *International Journal of Market Research*, 50, 1, 29–59.

Heath, R. and Hyder, P. (2005) Measuring the hidden power of emotive advertising, *International Journal of Market Research*, 47, 5, 467–86.

Kats, R. (2011) Rolex taps mobile to make print ad more interactive, retrieved 25 May 2012 from http://www.mobilemarketer.com/cms/news/advertising/6063.html.

Kent, M.L. and Taylor, M. (2002) Toward a dialogic theory of public relations, *Public Relations Review*, 28(1) (February), 21–37.

Krugman, H.E. (1965) The impact of television advertising: learning without involvement, *Public Opinion Quarterly*, 29 (Fall), 349–56.

Lavidge, R.J. and Steiner, G.A. (1961) A model for predictive measurements of advertising effectiveness, *Journal of Marketing* (October), 61.

Lufft, O. (2011) Wallpaper magazine allows readers to personalise Rolex ad, Campaignlive, 18 May, retrieved 25 May 2012 from http://www.brandrepublic.com/news/1070630/Wallpaper-magazine-allows-readers-personalise-Rolex-ad/?DCMP=ILC-SEARCH.

Lutz, J., Mackenzie, S.B. and Belch, G.E. (1983) Attitude toward the ad as a mediator of advertising effectiveness, *Advances in Consumer Research*, X. Ann Arbor, MI: Association for Consumer Research.

McGuire, W.J. (1978) An information processing model of advertising effectiveness, in *Behavioral and Management Science in Marketing* (eds H.L. Davis and A.J. Silk), New York: Ronald/Wiley, 156–80.

Macneil, I.R. (1983) Values in contract: internal and external, *Northwestern Law Review*, 78(2), 340–418.

Nairn, A. and Wyatt, M. (2010) *Essential Waitrose*, IPA Effectiveness Awards, 2010, London: IPA.

Olsen, J.C. and Peter, J.P. (1987) *Consumer Behavior*, Homewood, IL: Irwin.

Palda, K.S. (1966) The hypothesis of a hierarchy of effects: a partial evaluation, *Journal of Marketing Research*, 3, 13–24.

Palmer, R. (2007) The transaction–relational continuum: conceptually elegant but empirically denied, *Journal of Business and Industrial Marketing*, 22(7), 439–51.

Rao, S. and Perry, C. (2002) Thinking about relationship marketing: where are we now? *Journal of Business and Industrial Marketing*, 17(7), 598–614.

Rapacz, D., Reilly, M., and Schultz, D.E. (2008) Better Branding Beyond Advertising, *Marketing Management*, 17(1), January/February, 25–9.

Rappaport, S. (2007) Lessons from Online Practice: New Advertising Models, *Journal of Advertising Research*, (June) 135–41.

Rowe, W.G. and Barnes, J.G. (1998) Relationship marketing and sustained competitive advantage, *Journal of Market-Focused Management*, 2, 3, 281–9.

Spekman, R. (1988) Perceptions of strategic vulnerability among industrial buyers and its effect on information search and supplier evaluation, *Journal of Business Research*, 17, 313–26.

Strong, E.K. (1925) *The Psychology of Selling*, New York: McGraw-Hill.

Sykes, S., Harrison, M., and Clark, S. (2011) Lynx: Using social media to drive brand loyalty – Facebook campaign, *Institute of Practitioners in Advertising*, Bronze, IPA Effectiveness Awards, retrieved from www.warc.com.

Thomson, K. and Hecker, L.A. (2000) The business value of buy-in, in *Internal Marketing: Directions for Management* (eds R.J. Varey and B.R. Lewis), London: Routledge, 160–72.

Wiesser, B. Soliman, A., and Brenikov, D. (2010) *IPA Effectiveness Awards – Comfort Fabric Conditioner*, campaignlive.co.uk, 5 November, retrieved 25 April 2012 from http://www.brandrepublic.com/features/1040715/IPA-Effectiveness-Awards-2010-Silver-Award---Comfort-Fabric-Conditioner/?DCMP=ILC-SEARCH.

Wright, P.L. (1973) The cognitive processes mediating the acceptance of advertising, *Journal of Marketing Research*, 10 (February), 53–62.

Zajonc, R.B. (1980) Feeling and thinking: Preferences need no inferences, *American Psychologist*, 39, 151–75.

# Part 2
# Managing marketing communications

Part 2 is concerned with a variety of issues related to the management of marketing communications. These embrace strategy, goals, industry, financial, measurement and integration.

Chapter 5 is concerned with the nature of communication strategy and considers the interrelationship between strategy and planning. The first section of this chapter considers ideas about strategy and contains four distinct approaches to marketing communications strategy. The second section of the chapter introduces the marketing communications planning framework and works through the model, highlighting issues and linkages; it ends with an operational approach to devising, formulating and implementing a strategic marketing communications plan.

Chapter 6 examines the nature of objectives and positioning in marketing communications and considers both academic and practitioner (IPA) approaches to the nature of communication-based objectives.

The nature and characteristics of the UK marketing communications industry is the focus of Chapter 7. This material can be useful as it specifically examines the strategic and operational issues of communication agencies and their interaction with client organisations.

Chapter 8 considers various budgeting approaches and issues concerning brand equity, while Chapter 9 examines the ways in which the performance of marketing communication activities can be evaluated. In effect, these two chapters consider how much should be invested in the engagement process and how the engagement process should be measured.

The final chapter in this part is about integrated marketing communications. This chapter challenges ideas about the nature and validity of the 'integrated' view of marketing communications. Five separate interpretations about what integrated marketing communications might be are presented. This is a core chapter because it bridges the contextual elements and the application of the various disciplines. The notion that integrated marketing communications (IMC) is a valid and realistic concept is explored and readers are encouraged to consider the arguments for and against this approach. Its position at the end of the management part of the book is designed to encourage readers to reflect on what should be integrated and what integration incorporates.

For readers with access to the companion website that accompanies this book, there are supplementary chapters, drawn from previous editions, available in PDF format:

Marketing communications across borders

Business-to-business marketing communications

Stakeholders: supply chains and interorganisational relationships

# Chapter 5
# Marketing communications: strategies and planning

Marketing communications strategies should be aligned with the business and marketing strategies an organisation is pursuing. Marketing communications strategy refers to a brand's overall positioning orientation and their preferred approach to communicating with customers and other stakeholders. Tactics are concerned with the communication mix developed to deliver the positioning strategy.

Marketing communication plans are concerned with ongoing programmes and campaigns designed to articulate a brand's marketing communication tactics and strategy.

## Aims and learning objectives

The aims of this chapter are to develop understanding about the elements and concepts associated with marketing communications strategy and planning, and a planning framework within which to implement these strategies.

The learning objectives of this chapter are to:

1. appreciate the essence of strategy;
2. evaluate positioning as an approach to marketing communications strategy;
3. appraise the audience approach to marketing communications strategy;
4. consider the use of various platforms as an approach to marketing communications strategy;
5. explain the configuration approach to marketing communications strategy;
6. present a planning framework and consider the different elements involved in the development of marketing communication plans;
7. highlight the importance of the linkages and interaction between the different elements of the plan.

# Minicase

## Cravendale – Milk Matters

For a long time milk had become a commoditised market, one in which the majority of consumers are triggered into purchase by need, the colour of the plastic cap, and price. It is also a market subject to both environmental and health concerns. For a long time parents have been aware of the importance of milk to children and the role calcium plays in strengthening bones and teeth. In addition, however, research reveals that drinking milk can guard against several conditions experienced later in life such as high blood pressure, cancer, and Alzheimer's disease. This represents significant communication opportunities for those wishing to invest. Against this background and an increased focus on obesity and the need for healthy eating, sales of skimmed and 1 per cent fat milk have grown in recent years, in line with the desire for healthier products.

Milk production and the associated supply chain have also received considerable media attention. The alleged low prices paid by supermarkets to dairy farmers have been well publicised and the delivery of milk to the doorstep with easily recycled glass bottles has been slashed. Milk is now available from a number of different types of retail outlets, but in plastic cartons, which are recyclable but not as effectively so as glass bottles.

Own-label brands now dominate the milk market with more than two-thirds of the share. Mintel predicted the market would grow by 6 per cent in volume and 10 per cent in value over the five years ending 2012, when it was forecast to reach £3.7 billion. However, this represents an overall drop of 16 per cent when inflation is taken into account.

Apart from flavoured milks, such as FRijj, the leading flavoured-milk brand, there has been little innovation in the fresh milk market. One brand that has attempted to differentiate itself has been Arla Foods who have invested heavily in their Cravendale brand.

Arla Foods, originally a Scandinavian company, developed its UK operations by buying various UK dairies. However, as with most merger and acquisition programmes, each of the purchased dairies had its own conditions and practices. Arla realised the need to craft a single culture and this was achieved through the 'Arla Advantage' programme. The values-driven culture that evolved seeks to enable all employees to contribute to the company's growth. The emerging company culture was framed around new-product development, and it was from this context that an opportunity to create growth in the market and develop a milk brand was identified.

Arla have a strong supply of milk and, following the development in the Canadian market of a pure filtered milk, one that has lower bacteria levels than regular milk, Arla could produce and offer the UK market pure filtered milk.

This enabled Cravendale to establish three strong and sustainable selling propositions.

- Cravendale can be distinguished by its creamier and pure taste which consumers prefer.
- Cravendale stays fresher for longer, up to 20 days unopened and 7 days opened.
- Cravendale is perceived to provide the consumer with more value.

Before investing in the new production facilities Arla undertook extensive market research. This included identifying consumer requirements for a new milk brand, and then determining how best to satisfy them. A new milk segment, socio-economic groups ranging across ABC1 families with children, was identified as a result of this work.

From this point it was necessary to develop a brand strategy that would make consumers feel differently about milk and help them to be passionate about their choice of milk. As Cravendale doesn't just pasteurise milk, it filters it finely so that it has a purer, fresher taste and, because more bacteria are removed, it lasts longer. From this a campaign was developed around the theme, 'Milk Matters'. A premium price was required not only to reflect the quality positioning and the value of a quality milk brand, but also to incorporate the complexity of the production processes. The packaging had to also reflect the values and benefits of the brand and this meant that it had to be strongly differentiated. The distinctive plastic packaging was opaque – this helps to prolong the length of time the milk can be used, as it prevents UV rays penetrating the product.

The next consideration was how to bring the campaign to life and engage consumers. As the brand offers several advantages, so positioning and

| Exhibit 5.1 | **Cravendale's 'Cats with Thumbs' campaign** |
| | *Source*: Arla Foods |

messaging were critical. For example, it was emphasised that 'the brand can do what fresh milk cannot' as well as that 'it contains milk so good the cows want it back!'

In 2007 an animated ad was developed featuring plastic cow, cyclist and chicken figurines. Following testing in the Meridian TV region in the South of England, the brand was rolled out nationally. This was a very different experience whereby the tangible product benefits, supported by a branding process, led to rapid growth for the brand.

In 2009 a new creative approach featuring 'The Milk Bar', a pub for milk drinkers, was introduced. Using three different executions, Bad Bull, Slurp, and Toe Tapping, the ads conveyed the essential purity of Cravendale and the different usage occasions. The ads also conveyed fun and passion whilst the different executions reinforced the impact frequency.

In 2011 Cravendale launched a new TV campaign called 'Cats with Thumbs'. This was launched after the concept was first seeded through a YouTube video of a cat apparently giving a thumbs up and thumbs down in response to his owner. The TV ad features a man imagining what might happen if cats were to grow opposable thumbs. The lead cat in the film, Bertrum, also features on Cravendale's revamped website www.themilkmatters.co.uk, which allows fans to interact with the adventures of Bertrum, who is also on Facebook and Twitter. The ad was voted as the number 1 funniest commercial on the TV in 'Funniest Commercials of the Year 2011'.

In 2012 Cravendale ran a TV and cinema campaign featuring The Muppets, as part of its first brand partnership. At the same time a campaign featuring a 'Kermit the Frog' backpack began, with people having to get codes to order the backpack.

Arla Foods built a brand in a commodity market by taking a strategic orientation and using marketing communications to reflect both brand and company values. Cravendale's brand value has grown continuously, sometimes by as much as 18.2 per cent year on year, and at the retail level volume sales increases of 7 per cent have been recorded. This is at a time when overall volume sales of milk have declined by 1.8 per cent.

*This minicase was written by Chris Fill using a variety of sources, including Bainbridge (2010); Anon (2011, 2010); www.milkmatters.co.uk/; www. arlafoods.co.uk/; www.thinkbox.tv/server/show/ ConCaseStudy.1563; www.figarodigital.co.uk/case-study/cravendale.aspx.*

# Introduction

For a long time it has been assumed by many that a marketing communication strategy is simply the combination of tools of the communications mix. In other words, strategy is about the degree of direct marketing, personal selling, advertising, sales promotion and public relations that is incorporated within a planned sequence of communication activities.

This is important, but it is not the full picture since it represents a tactical rather than a strategic approach to marketing communications. As the Cravendale minicase highlights, a strategic perspective involves key decisions about the overall direction of the programme and target audiences, the fit with marketing and corporate strategy, the key message and desired positioning the brand is to occupy in the market, plus the resources necessary to deliver the position and accomplish the goals.

Communications strategy can also be considered in terms of the form of the communication. For example, message flows can be either simultaneous or serial. Where *simultaneous* flows occur, messages are received by all participants in a communication network at approximately the same time. Email messages, social network updates, webinars, direct mail, business seminars and dealer meetings, promotional activities and the use of integrated IT systems between levels (overnight ordering procedures) are examples of this type of flow. *Serial* flows involve the transmission of messages so that they are received first by a preselected number of people who then transmit the message to others at lower levels within the network. So there is a strategic implication in terms whether a serial or simultaneous approach is best.

The degree of permanence that a message has is determined by the technology used in the communication process. Essentially, the more a message can be recalled without physical distortion of the content, the more permanent the flow. So what role does the website play in a proposed communication activity? Information can be made available on a permanent basis, if necessary.

This chapter begins with a consideration of some fundamental ideas concerning the nature of strategy. A contextual and customer perspective on which to build marketing communications strategy is advocated. This is used in preference to a production orientation, which is founded purely on a resource base. From this, four different approaches to the development of marketing communications strategy are considered. The chapter closes with an exploration of a framework within which to plan, develop, and implement marketing communications strategies.

# Understanding strategy

In order to appreciate the role and nature of communication strategy it is useful to appreciate the dimensions of the strategy concept. The management literature on strategy is extensive, yet there seems to be little agreement or consensus about what it is, what it means or how it should be developed. A full discussion of this topic is beyond the scope of this book but what follows is a brief overview of some of the more general views about management strategy.

Hambrick (1983) suggested that the disparity of views about strategy is the result of the multidimensional nature of the strategy concept, that strategy is situational and that it varies according to industry and the environment in which it operates. In other words, contextual issues determine the nature of strategy. This may be true but it does not help us understand what strategy is.

The one main area wherein most authors find agreement concerns the hierarchical nature of strategy within organisations (Johnson et al., 2008; Mintzberg and Ghoshal, 2003; Kay, 1993). This refers to the notion that there are three main levels of organisational strategy;

corporate, competitive and functional. Corporate strategy is considered to be directional and sets out the broad, overarching parameters and means through which the organisation operates in order to realise its objectives. Strategies at the functional level – for example, marketing, finance and production – should be integrated in such a way that they contribute to the satisfaction of the higher-level competitive strategies, which in turn should satisfy the overall corporate goals. Competitive-level strategies are important because, not only do they set out the way in which the organisation will compete and use resources, but they should also provide clear messages about the way in which the organisation seeks to manage its environment.

Chaffee (1985) identifies several themes associated with the various strategic interpretations. The first is that strategy is used by organisations as a means of adjusting to changing environmental conditions, and the second is that strategy is often referred to in terms of decision making, actions and implementation. Apart from the hierarchical element mentioned previously, one of her other significant observations concerned the point that strategy could take various forms, most notably, deliberate, emergent and realised formats.

Two main strategy schools of thought can be identified: namely, the planning and the emergent approaches. The planning school is the pre-eminent paradigm and is based on strategy development and implementation, which is explicit, rational and planned as a sequence of logical steps. Andrews (1987) comments that strategy is concerned with a company's objectives, purpose and policies and its plans to satisfy the goals using particular resources with respect to a range of internal and external stakeholders. The organisation interacts with, and attempts to shape, its environment in pursuit of its goals. This perspective of strategy was first formulated in the 1950s and 1960s when the operating environments of most organisations were simple, stable and, thus, predictable. However, these conditions rarely exist in the twenty-first century and the validity of the rational model of strategy has been questioned.

The emergent school of thought considers strategy to develop incrementally, step-by-step, as organisations learn, sometimes through simple actions of trial and error. The core belief is that strategy comprises a stream of organisational activities that are continuously being formulated, implemented, tested, evaluated and updated. Chaffee suggests that strategy should be considered in terms of a linear, adaptive or interpretive approach, each one reflecting a progressively sophisticated perspective. While the linear approach reflects the more traditional and deliberate approach to strategy (Ansoff, 1965; Andrews, 1987), the adaptive strategy is important because it reflects the view that organisations flex and adjust to changing environments, while the interpretive or higher-order point of view considers strategy to be a reflection of the influence of social order on strategic decision making.

Two other strategic authors to be mentioned are Mintzberg (1994) and Whittington (1993). Mintzberg argues that strategy can be regarded as one or more of 5Ps of strategy. These are strategy as a Plan, Position, Perspective, Ploy and Pattern. Whittington (1993) offers four generic strategies: Classical, Evolutionary, Processual and Systemic. See Table 5.1.

There are a number of common points shared within these various views and perspectives of strategy. Chaffee, Mintzberg and Whittington all agree that strategy can be considered to be deliberate in nature, as reflected in their respective linear, planned and classical approaches. They also agree that strategy can be emergent and can evolve from the actions of the organisation. This can be seen in their adaptive, pattern and processual approaches. They also develop views on the extent to which an organisation interacts with its environment or seeks to directly influence it. Chaffee refers to *interpretive strategies*, Mintzberg to *strategy as a perspective* and Whittington to *systemic interpretations*.

Views on strategy have evolved as our understanding has developed. Strategy is not just about a deliberate, planned approach to business development, although it can be at the functional and competitive levels. Strategy is about the means, speed and methods by which organisations adapt to and influence their environments in order that they can achieve their goals. What is also clear is that the demarcation between an organisation and its environment

| Table 5.1 | Views of strategy | |
|---|---|---|
| **Author** | **Type of strategy** | **Explanation** |
| Mintzberg | Plan | A predetermined, deliberate course of action, implementation and evaluation. |
| | Position | An attempt to locate an organisation within a market. |
| | Perspective | A collective view of the world, one that is ingrained within the organisation and its position within it. |
| | Ploy | A scheme or manoeuvre to sidestep or outwit competitors. |
| | Pattern | A stream of actions in which there are consistent patterns of behaviour. |
| Whittington | Classical | Planned, rational and deliberate. |
| | Evolutionary | Darwinian in outlook, this strategy perceives a manager's task as trying to survive by fitting as closely as possible to the prevailing environmental conditions. |
| | Processual | An essentially incremental perspective whereby strategy is concerned with learning from past actions and experience. Little emphasis is given to long-term planning and horizons. |
| | Systemic | Strategy is a reflection of the social systems in which strategists participate. |

*Sources*: Whittington (1993); Mintzberg (1994).

is less clear than it used to be. An imaginary line was once used to refer to a border between an organisation and its environment. This line is no longer deemed valid as organisations are now viewed as boundary-free. The implications of this borderless concept for marketing communications are potentially enormous. Not only do contemporary views of strategy amplify the significance of the interaction between strategy and an organisation's environment, but they also stress the importance for strategy, at whatever level, to be contextually oriented and determined.

---

**Scholars' paper 5.1    How to realise strategy**

**Mintzberg, H. and Waters, J.A. (1985) Of strategies, deliberate and emergent,** *Strategic Management Journal*, **6(3), 257–72.**

This is a classic paper, one used on most postgraduate strategy programmes. The authors explore the complexity and variety of the strategy formation processes and they do this by investigating the concepts of deliberate and emergent strategy. Several forms of strategy are explored, all of which are useful for thinking about the way marketing communications strategy might develop.

# Marketing communications strategy

As indicated, the prevailing approach to marketing communications strategy has traditionally been founded upon the configuration of the 'promotional' mix. Strategy was an interpretation of the tools in the mix and, hence, the resources an organisation deployed. Unfortunately this represents a production rather than a market orientation to marketing communications and is intrinsically misplaced. This inside-out form of strategy is essentially resource-driven. However, a market orientation to strategy requires a consideration of the needs of the audience first and then a determination of the various messages, media and disciplines necessary to accomplish the strategy: an outside-in approach.

Many organisations do not develop and implement a communication strategy. They may develop brand strategies, advertising strategies, message strategies, and indeed some form of integrated marketing communication strategy, but there is little evidence of organisations developing corporate-led communication strategies. Steyn (2003) believes that this might be because practitioners do not fully understand the word *strategy*, while Moss and Warnaby (1998) suggest that academics have neglected the role of corporate communication in the strategy process. Holm (2006) reported that the programmes at two leading Swedish communication schools contained 90 per cent communication-related material and just 10 per cent on leadership matters. In contrast, the programme at Sweden's leading management school designed to deliver strategic education, devotes just 3 per cent of the time to communication issues. The general conclusion Holm draws is that those responsible for organisation, strategic leadership and decision-making appear to lack insight, awareness and communication-related skills.

Undoubtedly ideas concerning communication and strategy have not always been well articulated or taught together; they are often tactical and there is certainly little agreement on what constitutes corporate communication and marketing communication strategies.

Just as general strategy has been interpreted in different ways, so there are various explanations regarding what is marketing communications strategy. Here, four main explanations are considered. These are marketing communications as a position, as an audience, as a platform and as a configuration or pattern. These should not be considered to be discrete or exclusive approaches, as aspects of each can be observed within the others. See Figure 5.1 and note that these strategic forms are loosely aligned with Mintzberg's interpretation of strategy.

## Strategy approach 1 – Positioning

The process of market analysis and evaluation leading to planned strategies designed to meet prescribed and measurable goals is well established. It is argued that this enables finite resources to be used more efficiently as they can be directed towards markets that hold, potentially, greater value than other markets. This approach involves three main activities: market segmentation, target market selection, and positioning (otherwise referred to as STP).

Market segmentation is the means by which organisations define the broad context within which their strategic business units (SBUs) and products are offered.

Market segmentation is the division of a mass market into identifiable and distinct groups or segments, each of which has common characteristics and needs and displays similar responses to marketing actions. Through this process specific target segments can be selected and marketing plans developed to satisfy the individual needs of the potential buyers in these chosen segments. The development, or rather identification, of segments can be perceived as opportunities, and, as Beane and Ennis (1987) suggest, 'a company with limited resources needs to pick only the best opportunities to pursue'.

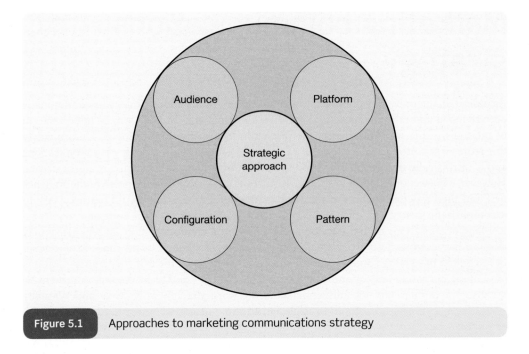

| Figure 5.1 | Approaches to marketing communications strategy |

## Viewpoint 5.1    Segments to meet customer needs

United Airlines segments its global markets using psychographic data about its customers. Among its categories are:

- *Schedule optimisers*: must reach their destination by a certain time and select their flights accordingly.
- *Mile accumulators*: go out of their way to take flights that will build up their air miles entitlement.
- *Quality vacationers*: treat the travel as part of the holiday experience and so fly with carriers that provide superior services.
- *Frugal flyers*: seek out the lowest-cost carriers, but still expect their flight experience to be a good one.

*Source*: http://www.thetimes100.co.uk/case_study.

According to T-Mobile's website it targets four key market segments: *personal, small businesses, medium businesses, corporates*.

The segments identified for a women's portal include the following groups:

- *Pillars*: characterised by their family orientation, high income and broad range of interests.
- *Explorers*: notable for being single, thirty-something, outgoing and more social than career-oriented.
- *Free spirits*: the youngest segment, typically unmarried, Internet savvy, and not yet committed to careers or raising a family.

*Source*: www.debmcdonald.com/.

| Question: | How might these segment characteristics inform the marketing communications to be used by United and T-Mobile? |
| Task: | Choose an industry and find out how it has been segmented by the principal brands. |

This process of segmentation is necessary because a single product is unlikely to meet the needs of all customers in a mass market. If it were, then a single type of toothpaste, chocolate bar or car would meet all of our needs. This is not so, and there are a host of products and brands seeking to satisfy particular buyer needs.

Having identified a market's various segments, the next step is to select particular target markets. These represent the best marketing potential and, once selected, require that resources are concentrated on these and no others. Targeted segments, therefore, constitute the environment and the context for a marketing communications strategy and activities. It is the characteristics of the target segment and their perception that should shape an audience-centred marketing communication strategy. Edwards (2011) suggests that rather than refer to a *target* audience, a static interpretation of people, better to consider them on an emotional journey, and that we all fluctuate between four different emotional states.

The *actual* self represents who we really are on a day-to-day basis, and perhaps this is the static person that the term 'target audience' refers to. However, there are times when we move into a *worry* state, and times when we daydream and move into a *fantasy* self. Closest to our actual self is the *idealised* self, that person we would like to be, the person we strive to become. Marketing communications, as well as other elements of the marketing strategy, could be shaped to engage people according to their perceptions of themselves and their emotional states (see Figure 5.2).

The final element in this process is *positioning*. As noted in the earlier discussion about strategy, positioning is an integral concept, and for some the essence of strategy. Wind (1990) stated quite clearly that positioning is the key strategic framework for an organisation's brand-based communications, as cited by Jewell (2007). All products and all organisations have a position in the minds of audiences. The task, therefore, is to actively manage the way in which audiences perceive brands. This means that marketing communications strategy should be concerned with achieving effective and viable positions so that the target audience understands what the brand does, what it means (to them) and can ascribe value to it. This is particularly important in markets that are very competitive and where mobility barriers (ease of entry into and exit from a market – e.g. plant and production costs) are relatively low.

Positioning is about visibility and recognition of what a product/service/organisation represents to a buyer. In markets where the intensity of rivalry and competition are increasing and buyers have greater choice, the fast identification and understanding of a product's intrinsic values become critical. Channel members have limited capacities, whether this is the level or range of stock they can carry or, for retailers, the amount of available shelf space that can be allocated. An offering with a clear identity and orientation to a particular target segment's needs will not only be stocked and purchased, but can warrant a larger margin through increased added value.

It is generally accepted that positioning is the natural conclusion to the sequence of activities that constitute a core part of strategy. Market segmentation and target marketing are

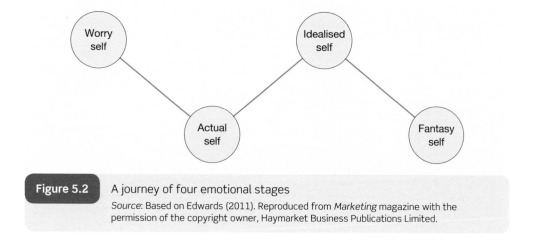

| **Figure 5.2** | A journey of four emotional stages |
| --- | --- |

*Source*: Based on Edwards (2011). Reproduced from *Marketing* magazine with the permission of the copyright owner, Haymarket Business Publications Limited.

prerequisites to successful positioning. Having established that marketing communications should be an audience-centred rather than product-centred activity, it can be concluded with some confidence that marketing communications strategy is essentially about positioning. For new products and services, marketing communications needs to engage target audiences so that they can understand what the brand means, how it differs from similar offerings and, as a result, position it in their minds. For the vast majority of products and services that are already established, marketing communications strategy should be concerned either with developing a strong position or repositioning it in the minds of the target audiences. The following chapter explores the positioning concept and the different strategies used by organisations to position their brands.

---

### Viewpoint 5.2    Positioning traditional bread, Aussie style

The falling consumption of bread in Australia can be attributed to a number of factors. Apart from the adverse economic conditions, some of the main reasons include more people avoiding eating breakfast, the substitution of cereals for toast, and the use of rice as an alternative to bread. In addition, however, it has been health issues that have had most effect, as Australians seek to limit their intake of carbohydrates such as bread, rice and pasta, to help them to lose or control their weight.

As a result of this there has been a growing interest in nutrition as Australians have become focused on consuming the 'right type' of carbohydrates. Foods that are free of artificial ingredients, that are unprocessed, and most of all, are seen to be fresh have become popular. Unsurprisingly, supermarkets began to develop their own in-store bakeries.

In 2008 Lawson's Traditional Bread was launched. Based on health, convenience and pleasure as the key consumer drivers, Lawson's was targeted at a niche market – namely, Australian tradition with modern-day convenience. Lawson's positioned the brand with the proposition: 'bread as it used to be'. They claimed that their bread was 'baked in the spirit and traditions of country Australia, where bread was handmade, took time, was generous in size and full of abundant goodness'. The brand soon held 5 per cent of the premium bread market.

The unique and unrivalled wide-pan loaf shape, which is 20 per cent wider than conventional loaves, is designed to make the loaf look homemade. The bread itself has a dense texture and a full-bodied flavour and lasts longer than bread produced in hot bread shops. Lawson's replication of traditional, fresh bread was reinforced through the distinct yet humble packaging of a basic brown paper, and simple branded label. This serves to emphasise the brand's understated authenticity, while still containing and preserving the product.

The launch was based around the simple pleasure of a good sandwich, consumed with good company. This was achieved by sending packs of bread, plus vouchers for fillings, to consumers at home and work. Recipients were encouraged to get friends, family and colleagues together to generate recipe ideas using the traditional-style loaf. This approach not only encouraged trial, but the word-of-mouth component helped evoke the discovery and recommendation elements that provided credibility and brand ownership.

In 2010 Lawson's launched a nationwide promotion, 'Lunch on Lawson's', in association with prominent restaurants and cafes. Using a 'Signature Sandwich' based on one of the four varieties of Lawson's bread, consumers had a complimentary gourmet sandwich. For a limited number of days in each participating state, Lawson's gave away sandwiches to the first 2,000 people who registered online and who printed out an invitation to collect their 'Signature Sandwich'. In addition, the company offered the Lunch on Lawson's Good Sandwich Guide at various venues, so that consumers could recreate their favourite restaurant's signature recipe at home. By collaborating with celebrity chefs and restaurants, the 'Lunch on Lawson's' promotion extended the idea of the sandwich as a gourmet dining option and not just a convenience food, while also keeping the Lawson's brand name synonymous with the concept.

*Source*: Based on YouTube (2011): Datamonitor (2010); Katulka (2010).

**Question:**    To what extent is positioning contingent on sound segmentation?

**Task:**    Find two bread manufacturers and compare their positioning statements.

| Exhibit 5.2 | **Lawson's traditional bread** |
|---|---|
| | *Source*: Goodman Fielder Limited |

## Strategy approach 2 – Audience

Consumer purchase decisions can be characterised, very generally, by a single-person buying centre, whereas organisational buying decisions can involve a large number of different people fulfilling different roles and all requiring different marketing communication messages. In addition to this there are other stakeholders who have an interest in a brand's development – for example, suppliers and the media. It follows from this that communications with these three very different audiences should be radically different, especially in terms of what, where, when and how a message is communicated. Three audience-focused marketing communication strategies emerge:

- *Pull strategies* – these are intended to influence end-user customers (consumers and b2b);
- *Push strategies* – these are intended to influence marketing (trade) channel buyers;
- *Profile strategies* – these are intended to influence a wide range of stakeholders, not just customers and intermediaries.

These are referred to as the '3Ps' of marketing communications strategy and can be considered to be generic strategies thanks to their breadth. *Push and pull* relate to the direction of the communication in a marketing channel: pushing communications down through a marketing channel or pulling consumers/buyers into a channel via retailers, as a result of receiving the communications. They do not relate to the intensity of communication and only refer to the overall approach. *Profile* refers to the presentation of the organisation as a whole and the reputation that it bestows on its brands. The identity is said to be 'profiled' to various other target stakeholder audiences, which may well include consumers, trade buyers, business-to-business customers and a range of other influential stakeholders. Normally, profile strategies do not contain or make reference to the specific products or services that the organisation offers. See Table 5.2 for a further explanation of each of these three dimensions.

| Table 5.2 | An audience approach to marketing communications strategy | | |
|---|---|---|---|
| **Strategy** | **Target audience** | **Message focus** | **Communication goal** |
| Pull | Consumers | Product/service | Purchase |
| | End-user b2b customers | Product/service | Purchase |
| Push | Channel intermediaries | Product/service | Developing relationships and distribution network |
| Profile | All relevant stakeholders | The organisation | Building reputation |

## A pull strategy

If messages designed to position a brand are to be directed at targeted, end-user customers, then the intention is invariably to generate increased levels of awareness, change and/or reinforce attitudes, reduce risk, encourage involvement and ultimately provoke a motivation within the target group. This motivation is to stimulate action so that the target audience expects the offering to be available to them when they decide to enquire, experiment or make a repeat purchase. This approach is a *pull (positioning)* strategy and is aimed at encouraging customers to 'pull' products through the channel network (see Figure 5.3). This usually means that consumers go into retail outlets (shops) to enquire about a particular product and/or buy it, or to enter a similar transaction direct with the manufacturer or intermediary through direct mail or the Internet. B2B customers are encouraged to buy from dealers and distributors while both groups of consumers and b2b customers have opportunities to buy through direct marketing channels where there is no intermediary.

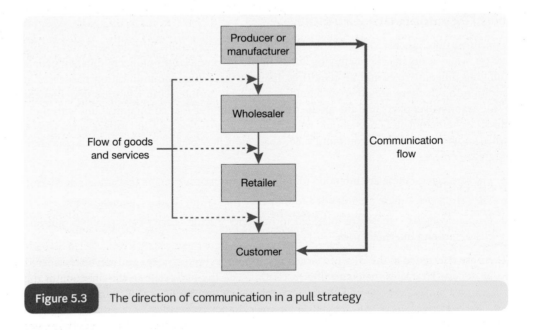

| Figure 5.3 | The direction of communication in a pull strategy |

## A push strategy

A second group or type of target audience can be identified on the basis, first, of their contribution to the marketing channel and, second, because these organisations do not consume the products and services they buy, but add value before selling the product on to others in the demand chain. The previous strategy was targeted at customers who make purchase decisions

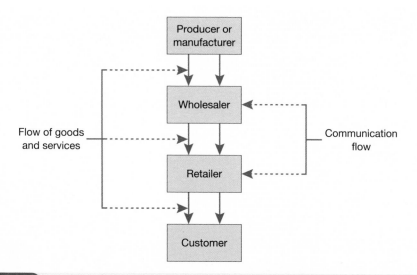

**Figure 5.4**    The direction of communication in a push strategy

related largely to their personal (or organisational) consumption of products and services. This second group buys products and services, performs some added-value activity and moves the product through the marketing channel network.

The 'trade' channel has received increased attention in recent years as the strategic value of intermediaries has become both more visible and questioned in the light of the Internet. As the channel networks have developed, so has their complexity, which impacts upon the marketing communications strategies and tools used to help reach marketing goals.

A *push* communication strategy concerns an attempt to influence other trade channel organisations and, as a result, encourage them to take stock, to allocate resources (e.g. shelf space) and to help them to become fully aware of the key attributes and benefits associated with each product with a view to adding value prior to further channel transactions. This strategy is designed to encourage resale to other members of the network and contribute to the achievement of their own objectives. This approach is known as a *push* strategy, as it is aimed at pushing the product down through the channel towards the end-users for consumption (see Figure 5.4).

## A profile strategy

The strategies considered so far concern the need for dialogue with customers (pull) and trade channel intermediaries (push). However, there is a whole range of other stakeholders, many of whom need to know about and understand the organisation rather than actually purchase its products and services (see Figure 5.5). This group of stakeholders may include financial analysts, trade unions, government bodies, employees or the local community. It should be easy to understand that these different stakeholder groups can influence the organisation in different ways and, because of this, need to receive (and respond to) different types of messages. Thus, the financial analysts need to know about financial and trading performance and expectations, and the local community may be interested in employment and the impact of the organisation on the local environment, whereas the government may be interested in the way the organisation applies health and safety regulations and pays corporation, VAT and other taxes. It should also be remembered that consumers and business-to-business customers may also be more interested in the organisation itself and so help initiate an umbrella branding strategy.

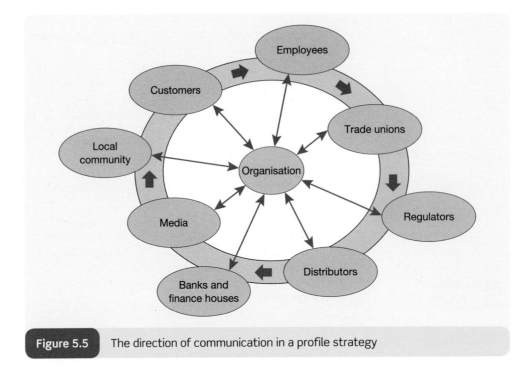

**Figure 5.5**    The direction of communication in a profile strategy

Traditionally these organisation-oriented activities have been referred to as *corporate communication*, as they deal more or less exclusively with the corporate entity or organisation. Products, services and other offerings are not normally the focus of these communications. It is the organisation and its role in the context of the particular stakeholders' activities that are important. Communications used to satisfy this array of stakeholder needs and the organisation's corporate promotional goals are developed through what is referred to as a *profile strategy*, a major element of which is corporate branding (see Chapter 12).

A *profile* strategy focuses an organisation's communications upon the development of stakeholder relationships, corporate image and reputation, whether that be just internally, just externally or both. To accomplish and deliver a profile strategy, public relations, including media relations, sponsorship and corporate advertising, become the pivotal tools of the marketing communications mix.

Within each of these overall strategies, individual approaches should be formulated to reflect the needs of each particular case. So, for example, the launch of a new shampoo product will involve a push strategy to get the product on the shelves of the appropriate retailers. The strategy would be to gain retailer acceptance of the new brand and to position it as a profitable new brand to gain consumer interest. Personal selling supported by trade promotions will be the main marketing communications tool. A pull strategy to develop awareness about the brand will need to be created, accompanied by appropriate public relations work. The next step will be to create particular brand associations and thereby position the brand in the minds of the target audience. Messages may be primarily functional or expressive, but they will endeavour to convey a brand promise. This may be accompanied or followed by the use of incentives to encourage consumers to trial the product. To support the brand, care lines and a website will need to be put in place to provide credibility as well as a buyer reference point and an opportunity to interact with the brand.

The 3Ps provide a generic approach to marketing communications strategy. To provide more precision and utility it is possible to combine the positioning approach considered previously with each of these 3Ps.

---

### Scholars' paper 5.2      The benefits of keeping the ivories clean

**Haley, R. I. (1968) Benefit segmentation: a decision-oriented research tool, *Journal of Marketing*, 32 (July), 30–5.**

Russell Haley's paper is a classic as it demonstrates some pioneering research through which he identifies four distinct types of customer. Those who bought toothpaste for white teeth (sociables); those who wished to prevent decay (worriers); those who liked the taste and refreshment properties (sensors); and, finally, those who bought on a price basis (independents). Each of these groups has particular demographic, behaviouristic and psychographic characteristics from which different brands have developed, all of which require audience-focused brand communications.

---

## Strategy approach 3 – Platform

A brand's communications should express its promise, and much of this is achieved through the brand's values and differential claims. In order to maintain brand authority and legitimacy, it is critical to maintain consistency in these communications. This requires a brand to be anchored, to have a set of grounded principles through which the brand is presented at all times. This anchoring has a central role in developing the core images stakeholders have of a brand.

Many organisations, in conjunction with their agencies, determine a strategic theme or platform to anchor their brands. These platforms concern the essence of the promise a brand makes to its customers. For example, this promise may be that the brand delivers happiness (Coca-Cola), safety (Volvo – cars), whiteness (Persil – washing powder), winning mentality (Nike), extra long life (Duracell – batteries), value (ASDA and Tesco – supermarkets), reliability (Kia – cars), adrenalin rush (Red Bull), or any number of things.

Marketing communications strategy should be developed thematically and consistently around an agreed core theme, or a platform. If stakeholders do not discern any core messages then the brand will not be positioned clearly and the resultant diffused or confused messages might lead to underperformance.

### Strategy and the Institute of Practitioners in Advertising

Utilising some of the findings of the IPA's research into successful campaigns, three main platforms can be identified. These are based on an advertising-led creative platform, a brand concept or need-state platform, and platforms based on conversation and participation.

*Creative platforms* are strategies based on a big, core advertising-led idea that enables audiences to recognise the idea across different media and touch points. These campaigns might share the same 'look and feel', response mechanic, competition, brand icon across channels, or central idea that is disseminated through the most appropriate media. P&O Ferries uses a flag as its visual identity across all channels, including on-board communications, advertising and customer communications. The Hovis (bread) revival campaign, the Still Red Hot campaign by Virgin Atlantic, and the 118 118 directory service all serve to illustrate the advertising-led platform. See also Viewpoint 5.3.

## Viewpoint 5.3    Advertising-led strategies

**Swinton Insurance**

The advertising-led idea with the Swinton Insurance campaign which targeted taxi drivers, was promotional, and centred on a competition. The creative solution was based around the Swinton Mystery Tipper, characterised as a cartoon character.

When taxi drivers called Swinton for an insurance quote they were offered a sticker that had to be displayed in the window of their taxi. A Mystery Tipper then offered a £1,000 tip every month to taxi drivers throughout the UK who were displaying the sticker. The communications channels used included direct mail to lapsed and current taxi drivers, taxi trade press, flyers, a campaign micro-site, social media and local radio.

**Iceland**

Real people, as well as animated characters and symbols can be icons. The supermarket, Iceland, used Kerry Katona, a former minor pop star and entertainment celebrity, as its brand ambassador to integrate the brand with its sponsorship of the TV programme *I'm a Celebrity Get Me Out of Here*. As she was a former contestant on the show, she had a strong association with the programme, and for some she represented a credible source of information, relative to the show.

The campaign ran in the period up to Christmas to promote Christmas party food, using the slogan, 'Party like a celebrity'. Katona was used as a brand spokesperson across TV spots, TV sponsorship credits, and TV editorial. She was also a commentator on the *I'm a Celebrity* show. In addition to this she wrote a blog which was hosted on Iceland's website, while logos from the TV programme were used as part of the in-store signage. Field marketing activity within the stores supported a linked scratch-card sales promotion.

*Source*:  IPA (2011).

**Question:**   Why might an advertising-led platform be considered to be an insufficient communications approach?

**Task:**   Find a third example of an advertising-led communications programme from 2012 or later. How do you know it is advertising-led?

| Exhibit 5.3 | **The Swinton mystery tipper** |
| --- | --- |
| | *Source*: SKV Communications |

*Brand concept platforms* are characterised by their root within the brand. This means they can be communicated using a variety of different creative expressions, over time: something an advertising-led idea cannot accomplish.

These types of campaigns can be disaggregated into those based on tangible product attributes and those founded on more intangible conceptual ideas. Tangible campaigns identify a specific occasion (e.g. a birthday celebration), a tightly defined target audience (e.g. first-time mothers) or a specific 'point of market entry' (e.g. a new product).

Intangible campaigns are developed from emotional concepts which allow them a high degree of creative inconsistency, are used across a range of tools and, unlike the advertising-led platforms, last a long time. Honda's 'The Power of Dreams' (2004) and Johnnie Walker's global campaign in 2009 are cited by the IPA as great examples of the use of this type of strategic platform.

---

## Viewpoint 5.4 — Food brands provide a participatory feast

### Walkers (2010)

The Walkers 'Do us a Flavour' campaign was based on the public's participation in finding a new flavoured crisp. First the public were asked to submit new crisp flavour, and six were short-listed and produced. The finalists were encouraged to develop their own support, while the public were invited to vote for their favourite flavour. A full range of publicity angles were developed and implemented.

### Cadbury Wispa (2010)

Following several decades of decline in the UK, the Wispa chocolate bar was discontinued in 2003 due to poor sales. Soon after the closure, however, fans started to demand that the brand be restored and used a support group on Facebook as the initial vehicle. When Wispa was relaunched, with a view to turning existing Wispa fans into advocates, social media played an important role. First, through the use of social media, Cadbury's generated content which was then presented to mainstream audiences, using paid media, with a view to recruiting more Wispa fans.

*Source*: IPA (2011).

**Question:** If participatory programmes are dependent on fanaticism and extreme loyalty, then to what extent are a brand's long-term prospects limited?

**Task:** Make a list of any conditions that might need to be present for a participatory approach to work.

| Exhibit 5.4 | **A poster from the 'Bring Back Wispa' campaign, 2008** |
|---|---|
| | *Source*: Kraft Foods UK |

*Participation platforms* represent a more recent strategic approach, thanks mainly to the interactive properties of digital media. This enables brands and audiences to interact, engage in dialogue, conversations and participation in a range of events, actions and communities.

The platform aims to integrate a brand into people's life patterns in a way that is significant and relevant to them. Audiences are invited to participate in a centrally driven brand idea, which is then played back through public media in order to involve others. BT (telecoms) invited audiences to suggest storylines for the relationship that was developing, and later sagging, between their ad-brand couple.

## Strategy approach 4 – Configuration

The configuration approach to marketing communications strategy gives emphasis to the structural aspects associated with a message's design, and the way it is conveyed and received. This approach seeks to maximise the effectiveness of a communication activity by matching goals and resources with an audience's needs. This might involve varying the frequency with which a message is received by the target audience, continuity issues; others involve managing the formality, permanence or direction of a message. Communication strategies designed to get the attention of the audiences are commonplace, while others seek to be immersed or provide continual presence. This approach to communication strategy involves the configuration of the four facets of communication: the frequency, direction, modality and content of communications (Mohr and Nevin, 1990).

### Frequency

The amount of contact between members of a communication network can impact effectiveness. Too much information (too frequent, aggregate volume or pure repetition) can overload people and have a dysfunctional effect. Too little information can undermine the opportunities for favourable performance outcomes by failing to provide the necessary operational information, motivation and support. As a consequence, it is important to identify the current volume of information being provided and to make a judgement about the desired levels of communication.

### Direction

This refers to the horizontal and vertical movement of communication within a network. Each network consists of people who are dependent on others, but the level of dependence will vary, so that the distribution of power and influence is unequal.

Communications can be unidirectional in that they flow in one direction only. For example, information from a major food retailer, such as Aeon in Japan, Pão de Acucar in Brazil, or Metro in Canada, to small food manufacturers might be considered to be unidirectional because the small food manufacturers perceive little reason to respond, as these supermarkets represent a source of power. Communications can also be bidirectional: that is, to and from organisations and influential opinion leaders and formers.

### Modality

Modality refers to the method used to transmit information and there is a wide variety of interpretations of the methods used to convey information. Modality can be seen as communications that are formal, planned and regulated, or informal, unplanned and spontaneous, such as word-of-mouth communications and water-cooler conversations.

## Content

This refers to what is said. Frazier and Summers (1984) distinguish between direct and indirect influence strategies. Direct strategies are designed to change behaviour by specific request (recommendations, promises and appeals to legal obligations). Indirect strategies attempt to change another person's beliefs and attitudes about the desirability of the intended behaviour. This may take the form of an information exchange, where the source uses discussions about general business issues to influence the attitudes of the receiver. Social networks and online communities serve to influence consumer attitudes and change behaviour.

Communication strategies work within particular contexts, often characterised by the nature of the prevailing level of relationships and associated exchanges, the level of trust and support experienced by those in the communication network, and aspects of power as perceived by organisations in a b2b environment.

## Exchange relationship

According to Stern and El-Ansary (1988), the nature of the exchange relationship structures the way communications should be used. Collaborative exchanges have a long-term perspective and high interdependence and involve joint decision-making. By contrast, market exchanges are ad hoc and hence have a short-term orientation where interdependence is low.

## Climate

Climate refers to the degree of mutual supportiveness that exists between participants. Anderson et al. (1987) used measures of trust and goal compatibility in defining communication climate.

## Power

Dwyer and Walker (1981) showed that power conditions within a marketing channel can be symmetrical (with power balanced between members) or asymmetrical (with a power imbalance).

Two specific forms of communication strategy can be identified. The first is a combination referred to as a 'collaborative communication strategy' and includes higher-frequency, more bidirectional flows, informal modes and indirect content. This combination is likely to occur where there are collaborative structures, supportive climates or symmetrical power. The second combination is referred to as an 'autonomous communication strategy' and includes lower-frequency, more unidirectional communication, formal modes and direct content. This combination is likely to occur in channel conditions of market structures, unsupportive climates and asymmetrical power.

Communication strategy should, therefore, be built upon the characteristics of the situation facing each communication episode. Not all audiences share the same conditions, nor do they all possess the same degree of closeness or collaborative expectations. By considering the nature of the channel conditions and then developing communication strategies that complement them, the performance of the focus organisation and other members can be considerably improved, and conflict and tension substantially reduced.

Although the configuration approach is often associated with marketing-channel-based communications, the principles can be observed in consumer markets. Stern and El-Ansary (1992) stress consideration of information flows and movement, and, in particular, the timing and permanence of the communication flows. In addition, work by Mohr and Nevin (1990) takes into account the various facets of communication and the particular channel structures through which communications are intended to move.

| Scholars' paper 5.3 | Configuration and communications |
| --- | --- |

**Mohr, J. and Nevin, J.R. (1990) Communication strategies in marketing channels,** *Journal of Marketing* **(October), 36–51.**

Written at a time when there was little published material on marketing communication strategy, this paper shed new light on strategy within marketing channels. Now the contingency principles presented by Mohr and Nevin have relevance in terms of the configuration approach to marketing communications strategy. All marketing communication students should read this paper.

# Planning marketing communications

The context in which a communication event occurs shapes not only what and how messages are developed and conveyed, but also influences the interpretation and meaning ascribed to the communication. In other words, the goals can be missed if the marketing communication is not entirely effective. The development of marketing communication plans helps to minimise errors and provide for efficiency and effectiveness.

There are a number of contexts that influence or shape marketing communications. All marketing managers (and others) should understand these contextual elements and appreciate how they contribute and influence the development of marketing communication programmes. In addition, there are a number of other elements and activities that need to be built into a programme in order that it can be implemented. These elements concern the goals, the resources, the communication tools to be used and measures of control and evaluation. Just like the cogs in a clock, these elements need to be linked together if the plan is to work. Planning frameworks aim to bring together the various elements into a logical sequence of activities. The rationale for decisions is built on information generated at previous levels in the framework. It also provides a checklist of activities that need to be considered.

However, there needs to be a word of caution as sometimes unforeseen events can lead to serious disruption of marketing communications plans. For example, companies working in the holiday industry set out detailed marketing communications plans accounting for economic conditions and forecasts. Unfortunately these plans can be disrupted by a number of different crises, such as volcanic ash clouds, the Arab Spring, heavy snow or terrorist alarms (Eleftheriou-Smith, 2012).

To help students and managers comprehend the linkages between the elements and to understand how these different components complement each other, the rest of this chapter deals with the development of marketing communication plans. To that extent it will be of direct benefit to managers seeking to build plans for the first time or for those familiar with the activity to reconsider current practices. Second, the material should also be of direct benefit to students who are required to understand and perhaps prepare such plans as part-fulfilment of an assessment or examination in this subject area.

# The marketing communications planning framework

It has been established (see Chapter 1) that the principal tasks facing those managing marketing communications are to decide:

- Who should receive the brand's messages.
- What is to be achieved.
- What the messages should say.
- How the messages are to be delivered.
- What actions the receivers should take.
- What image of the organisation/brand receivers are expected to retain.
- How much is to be spent establishing this new image.
- How to control the whole process once it has been implemented.
- What was achieved.

Note that more than one message is transmitted and that there is more than one target audience. This is important, as recognition of the need to communicate with multiple audiences and their different information requirements, often simultaneously, lies at the heart of marketing communications. The aim is to generate and transmit messages which present the organisation and their offerings to their various target audiences, encouraging them to enter into a dialogue. These messages must be presented consistently and they must address the points stated above. It is the skill and responsibility of the marketing communications planner to blend the communication tools and to create a mix that satisfies these elements.

The marketing communications planning framework (MCPF), presented at Figure 5.6, represents a sequence of decisions that marketing managers undertake when preparing, implementing and evaluating communication strategies and plans. It does not mean that this sequence reflects reality; indeed, many marketing decisions are made outside any recognisable framework. However, as a means of understanding the different components, appreciating the way in which they relate to one another and bringing together various aspects for work or for

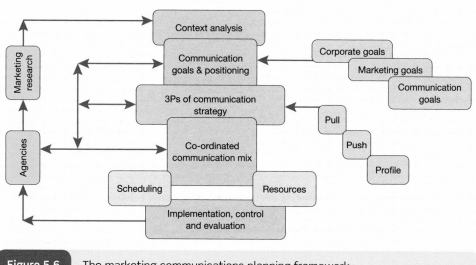

**Figure 5.6**   The marketing communications planning framework

answering examination questions leading to a qualification, both academic and professional, this approach has many advantages and has been used by a number of local, national and international organisations.

Marketing communications activities should seek to satisfy particular objectives through the explicit and deliberate development of a communication strategy. The MCPF will be used to show first, the key elements, second, some of the linkages and third, the integrated approach that is considered good practice.

This framework reflects the deliberate or planned approach to strategic marketing communications. The processes associated with marketing communications, however, are not linear, as depicted in this framework, but integrative and interdependent. To that extent, this approach recognises the value of stakeholder theory and the requirement to build partnerships with buyers and other organisations networked with an organisation.

Other 'decision sequences' have been advanced, in particular one by Rothschild (1987) and another by Engel et al. (1994). One of the difficulties associated with these frameworks is that they fail to bring strategy into the development of the promotional mix. These frameworks rely on the objective and task approach, whereby plans are developed for each of the individual communication tools, and then aggregated to form strategy.

---

### Viewpoint 5.5    Pringles plan a Chinese crunch

The snack brand Pringles had a small share of the highly competitive market in China. Additionally, their 50 per cent price premium made life even more challenging. In 2009 the product was made 'crunchier' than earlier offerings. An integrated campaign was launched aimed at promoting the functional product benefit – 'crunchiness' – fun and engaging. Following the Hughes and Fill model, the campaign consisted of the following stages:

1. Campaign responsibilities
   Agency, Grey Advertising in Hong Kong, was appointed to develop the campaign for Pringles.

2. Target audience
   This was termed Generation (G) Y – single males and females 18–24 years old. In most other markets, the target audience is primarily mothers with children.

3. Campaign objectives
   - Engage target audience.
   - Strengthen brand equity attributes (crunchiness).
   - Drive sales and profit.

4. Budget
   Media budget was less than $1 million.

5. Media selection and planning
   - Online videos.
   - Application game and social networking site.
   - Bulleting Board System (BBS) programme – Internet forum.
   - Flash mobbing video in Beijing – used top video-sharing sites.
   - Online press releases.
   - Instore activity.

6. Advertising development and testing
   Consumer insights were gained via visits to Gen Y homes, accompanied store visits and social interaction. This identified that Gen Y spend little time watching TV compared to online sources of entertainment. Other information was gathered from published market research, magazines, blogs and websites. Qualitative product research was carried out on the crunchiness – 'KaCha' – concept. Positive results were followed up using quantitative techniques.

7. Implementation and scheduling

Three branded online videos were launched at the end of July 2009. Two weeks later, three unbranded videos with a twist were released.

- Game and brand zone went live in mid August 2009.
- End of August – BBS programme launched.
- Flash mobbing, one month after online videos.
- August–September in-store activities, point of sale and tastings.

8. Campaign evaluation

- Sales outperformed category average annualised growth.
- Online videos achieved excellent impact on brand metrics and significantly increased all Pringles brand equity attributes (Millward Brown). Over 10 million hits in eight weeks.
- Brand zone and application game performed much better than most site campaigns (Millward Brown).
- Flash mobbing video generated over 1.1 million views.

*Source*:  Based on www.warc.com/prize.

**Question:**  Why were the media chosen by Pringles effective in this case?

**Task:**  Prepare an outline advertising campaign plan for a consumer brand in a market of your choice.

| Exhibit 5.5 | **Chinese Pringles** |
| --- | --- |
| | *Source*: ImagineChina |

Another more recent framework is the SOSTAC® (situation, objectives, strategy, tactics, action, control) approach developed by Smith (2003). This is essentially a sound system, and moves closer than most of the others to helping formulate suitable marketing communication plans. However, as the framework is multi-purpose and is intended for application to a variety of planning situations, there is a danger that the communication focus is lost at the situation analysis phase. This can lead to a reiteration of a SWOT (strengths, weaknesses, opportunities, threats) and/or a general marketing plan, with subsequent problems further down the line in terms of the justification and understanding of the communications strategy and mixes that need to be deployed. In addition, the SOSTAC model does not give sufficient emphasis to the need to identify and understand the characteristics of the target audience, which is so important for the development of coherent marketing communications plans.

The MCPF approach presented here is not intended to solve all the problems associated with the formulation of such plans, but it is sufficiently robust to meet the needs of employers and examiners, and is recommended.

# Elements of the plan

Marketing communications plans should consist of the following elements. These elements are now considered in turn.

- Context analysis
- Communication objectives
- Marketing communications strategy
- Coordinated communication mix (tools, media and content)
- Resources (human and financial)
- Scheduling and implementation
- Evaluation and control
- Feedback.

## Context analysis

Analysing the context in which marketing communication events occur is a necessary, indeed vital, first step in the planning process. The purpose is to understand the key market and communication drivers that are likely to influence (or already are influencing) a brand (or organisation) and either help or hinder its progress towards meeting its long-term objectives. This is different from a situation analysis, because the situation analysis considers a range of wider organisational factors, most of which are normally considered in the development of marketing plans (while the communication focus is lost). Duplication is to be avoided, as it is both inefficient and confusing.

The compilation of a context analysis (CA) is very important, as it presents information and clues about what the promotional plan needs to achieve. Information and market research data about target audiences (their needs, perception, motivation, attitudes and decision-making characteristics), the media and the people they use for information about offerings, the marketing objectives and time-scales, the overall level of financial and other resources that are available, the quality and suitability of agency and other outsourced activities, and the environment in terms of societal, technological, political and economic conditions, both now and at some point in the future, all need to be considered.

At the root of the CA is the marketing plan. This will already have been prepared and contains important information about the target segment, the business and marketing goals, competitors and the time-scales in which the goals are to be achieved. The rest of the CA seeks to elaborate and build upon this information so as to provide the detail in order that the plan can be developed and justified.

## Viewpoint 5.6    Boots UK understand the changing context

Understanding the context in which a brand operates is a crucial first step when developing a marketing communications strategy and plan. Very often the marketing strategy will reflect changes in the internal and/or external environments. Therefore, it is the task of marketing communications to communicate the strategy by understanding the communications issues within the context.

For example, Boots UK, the pharmacy-led high street retailer, appraised its business and marketing approach following changes to NHS service provision in the UK. The NHS formerly used national commissioned services, but these have now been replaced by clinical commissioning groups. These have more autonomy to decide which healthcare services and advice are provided within particular geographic areas. For example, some retail stores might emphasise services associated with diabetes or sexual health, and other stores in a different region might focus on eye care, travel vaccinations and asthma.

Boots UK responded with a business and marketing strategy designed to expand its pharmacy services into hospitals, to introduce GP and dentist surgeries in its larger stores and to provide different services in different stores that reflected the priorities of the local commissioning group. As a result of these decisions, marketing communications were required to inform customers of these changes and, in particular, the different store services. The campaign 'let's feel good together' used press and television advertising to build awareness of the new services and also to inform of some of the specialist services offered by Boots UK, such as eye health. In-store communications needed to communicate the new look and feel associated with the service and to make it more accessible to customers.

*Source*:    Based on Chapman (2012); www.boots.com

Question:    To what extent is communications strategy based on changes in the environment?

Task:        Find another retailer-based communications campaign and assess the impact of the environment on the strategy.

## Exhibit 5.6    New instore signage at Boots UK
*Source*: Alliance Boots

| Table 5.3 | The main elements of the context analysis |
|---|---|

| Context element | Dimensions |
|---|---|
| The customer context | Segment characteristics |
| | Levels of awareness, perception and attitudes towards the brand/organisation |
| | Levels of involvement and types of perceived risk |
| | DMU characteristics and issues |
| | Media usage |
| The business context | Corporate and marketing strategy and plans |
| | Brand/organisation analysis |
| | Competitor analysis |
| The internal context | Financial constraints |
| | Organisation identity |
| | Culture, values and beliefs |
| | Marketing expertise |
| | Agency availability and suitability |
| The external context | Who are the key stakeholders and why are they important? |
| | What are their communication needs? |
| | Social, political, economic and technological restraints and opportunities. |

The CA provides the rationale for the communications plan. It is from the CA that the marketing objectives (from the marketing plan) and the marketing communications objectives are derived. The type, form and style of the message are rooted in the characteristics of the target audience, and the media selected to convey messages will be based on the nature of the tasks, the media habits of the audience and the resources available. The main components of the context analysis are set out in Table 5.3.

## Communication objectives

The role of promotional objectives in the planning process is important for a number of reasons. First, they provide a balance to the plan and take away the sole emphasis on sales that inevitably arises. Second, they indicate positioning issues, third, they highlight the required balance of the promotional mix, fourth, they provide time parameters for campaigns and, finally, they provide a crucial means by which particular marketing communication activities are evaluated.

Ideally, communication objectives should consist of three main elements:

### Corporate objectives

These are derived from the business or marketing plan. They refer to the mission and the business area that the organisation believes it should be in.

### Marketing objectives

These are derived from the marketing plan and are output-oriented. Normally these can be considered as sales-related objectives, such as market share, sales revenues, volumes, ROI and profitability indicators.

## Marketing communication objectives

These are derived from an understanding of the current context in which a brand exists and the future context in the form of where the brand is expected to be at some point in the future. These will be presented as awareness levels, perception, comprehension/knowledge, attitudes towards and overall degree of preference for the brand. The choice of communication goal depends on the tasks that need to be accomplished. In addition, most brands need either to maintain their current brand position or reposition themselves in the light of changing contextual conditions.

These three elements constitute the promotional objectives and they all need to be set out in SMART terminology (see Chapter 6). What also emerges is a refinement to the positioning that managers see as important for success. Obviously, not all plans require express attention to positioning (e.g. government information campaigns) but most commercial and brand-oriented communication programmes need to communicate a clear position in their market. Thus, at this point the positioning intentions are developed and these will be related to the market, the customers or some other dimension. The justification for this will arise from the CA.

## Marketing communications strategy

As noted earlier, the communication strategy can take many different forms, but should always be customer-, not method/media-oriented. Therefore, the strategy depends on whether the target audience is a customer segment, a distributor or dealer network or whether other stakeholders need to be reached. In addition, it is imperative that the strategy be geared to the communication needs of the target audience that is revealed during the customer and business context analyses. This will show what the task is that marketing communications needs to fulfil. Having established who the audience is, push-, pull- or profile-dominated strategies can be identified. The next step is to determine the task that needs to be accomplished. This will have been articulated previously in the marketing communications objectives, but the approach at this stage is less quantitative and softer.

The DRIP tasks of marketing communications can be used to suggest the strategy being pursued. For example, if a new brand is being launched, the first task will be to inform and differentiate the brand for members of the trade before using a pull strategy to inform and differentiate the brand for the target, end-user customers. An organisation wishing to signal a change of strategy and/or a change of name following a merger or acquisition may choose to use a profile strategy and the primary task will be to inform of the name change. An organisation experiencing declining sales may choose to remind customers of a need or it may choose to improve sales through persuasion.

## Coordinated communication mix

Having formulated, stated and justified the required position, the next step is to present the basic form and style of the key message that is to be conveyed. Is there to be a lot of copy or just a little? Is there to be a rational or emotional approach or some weighting between the two? What should be the tone of the visual messages? Is there to be a media blitz? It is at this point that those responsible for the development of these plans can be imaginative and try some new ideas. Trying to tie in the message to the strategic orientation is the important part, as the advertising agency will refine and redefine the message and the positioning.

From this the communication mixes need to be considered *for each* of the strategies proposed: that is, a mix for the consumer strategy, a mix for the trade strategy and a distinct mix for the communications to reach the wider array of stakeholders.

The choice of methods should clearly state the tools and the media to be used. A short paragraph justifying the selection is very important, as the use of media in particular is to a large extent dependent upon the nature of the goals, the target audience and the resources. The key is to provide message consistency and a measure of integration.

## Resources

This is a vitally important part of the plan, one that is often avoided or forgotten about. The resources necessary to support the plan need to be determined and these refer not only to the financial issues but to the quality of available marketing expertise and the time that is available to achieve the required outcomes.

Project management software such as Prince2, and Gantt charts and other planning aids are best used to support this part of the plan. Preferably, actual costs should be assigned, although percentages can be allocated if being written for examination purposes. What is important is the relative weighting of the costs, and a recognition and understanding of the general costs associated with the proposed communication activities.

It must be understood that the overall cost of the strategy should be in proportion to the size of the client organisation, its (probable) level of profitability and the size and dynamics of the market in which it operates.

## Scheduling and implementation

The next step is to schedule the deployment of the methods and the media. Events should be scheduled according to the goals and the strategic thrust. So, if it is necessary to communicate with the trade prior to a public launch, those activities tied into the push-positioning strategy should be scheduled prior to those calculated to support the pull strategy.

Similarly, if awareness is a goal then, if funds permit, it may be best to use television and posters first before sales promotions (unless sampling is used), direct marketing, point of purchase and personal selling.

## Evaluation and control

Unless there is some form of evaluation, there will be no dialogue and no true marketing communications. There are numerous methods to evaluate the individual performance of the tools and the media used, and for examination purposes these should be stated. In addition, and perhaps more meaningfully, the most important measures are the communication objectives set in the first place. The success of a promotional strategy and the associated plan is the degree to which the objectives set are achieved.

## Feedback

The planning process is completed when feedback is provided. Not only should information regarding the overall outcome of a campaign be considered but so should individual aspects of the activity. For example, the performance of the individual tools used within the campaign, whether sufficient resources were invested, the appropriateness of the strategy in the first place, any problems encountered during implementation and the relative ease with which the objectives were accomplished are all aspects that need to be fed back to all internal and external parties associated with the planning process.

This feedback is vitally important because it provides information for the context analysis that anchors the next campaign. Information fed back in a formal and systematic manner constitutes an opportunity for organisations to learn from their previous campaign activities, a point often overlooked and neglected.

# Links and essential points

It was mentioned earlier that there are a number of linkages associated with different parts of the marketing communications plan. It is important to understand the nature of these links as

| Table 5.4 | Linkages within the MCPF |
|---|---|
| Objectives | From the marketing plan, from the customer, stakeholder network and competitor analysis and from an internal marketing review |
| Strategic balance between push, pull and profile | From an understanding of the brand, the needs of the target audiences, including employees and all other stakeholders, and the marketing goals |
| Brand positioning | From users' and non-users' perceptions, motivations, attitudes and understanding about the brand and its direct and indirect competitors |
| Message content and style | From an understanding about the level of involvement, perceived risk, DMU analysis, information-processing styles and the positioning intentions |
| Promotional tools and media | From the target audience analysis of media habits, involvement and preferences, from knowledge about product suitability and media compatibility, from a competitor analysis and from the resource analysis |

they represent the interconnections between different parts of the plan and the rationale for undertaking the contextual analysis in particular. The contextual analysis (CA) feeds the items shown in Table 5.4. For example, research undertaken by Interbrand for Intercontinental Hotels to find out what influenced the brand experience of hotel guests, discovered that one of the key factors was the hotel concierge. As a result, the role of the concierge became a central element in the communication strategy, influencing the campaign goals, positioning and message strategy (Gustafson, 2007). The objectives derived from the CA feed decisions concerning strategy, tools and media, content, scheduling and evaluation.

The marketing communications strategy is derived from an overall appreciation of the needs of the target audience (and stakeholders) regarding the brand and its competitive position in the market. The communication mix is influenced by the previous elements and the budget that follows. However, the nature of the tools and the capacity and characteristics of the media influence scheduling, implementation and evaluation activities.

---

### Scholars' paper 5.4    Planning Renault's expansion

**Caemmerer, B. (2009) The planning and implementation of integrated marketing communications, *Marketing Intelligence & Planning*, 27(4), 524–38.**

Students of marketing communications should read this paper, simply because it illustrates the tasks involved in the planning and implementation of integrated marketing communications. Using a case study approach based on Renault's attempt to expand their market share in Germany, the paper considers the range of tasks involved in planning an integrated marketing communications campaign. These include the context analysis and the identification of marketing communications opportunities; choosing the right marketing communications agency; campaign development and implementation, including the selection of the marketing communications mix, creative execution and media planning; campaign evaluation; planning of follow-up campaigns; and managerial coordination between all tasks and parties involved to ensure integration of marketing communications initiatives throughout the campaign.

# Key points

- There are many different views of what constitutes strategy. The planning and emergent perspectives have gained most agreement.

- Marketing communications strategy is not just about the mix, and should start with an audience-centred orientation.

- Marketing communications strategy should be concerned with the overall direction of the programme and target audiences, the fit with marketing and corporate strategy, the key message and desired positioning the brand is to occupy in the market, plus the resources necessary to deliver the position and accomplish the goals.

- There are four core interpretations of marketing communications strategy. These are the positioning, audience, platform and configuration approaches. Each of these emphasises particular elements and issues but they are not mutually discrete. Aspects of each can be found in the others.

- The positioning approach is derived from the STP process.

- The audience approach is referred to as the '3Ps' of marketing communications strategy

- The platform approach can be advertising-led (around a creative idea), brand-led (around a core brand characteristic) or take the form of a participatory platform.

- The configuration approach requires managing the structural elements of an intended communication event, within the prevailing relationship, climate and power context, where appropriate.

- To manage efficiently and perhaps more effectively, marketing communications should be implemented through the use of a planning framework.

- The framework consists of a number of elements which are presented sequentially, but in reality often happen simultaneously. Key to understanding the planning framework are the linkages between the various elements.

# Review questions

1. Write brief notes explaining some of the key approaches to understanding strategy.

2. Explain the role strategy plays in marketing communications, using the Cravendale minicase to illustrate your points.

3. Compare strategy with planning. In what ways might planning be the same as strategy?

4. Which of the four interpretations of strategy presented in this chapter might best be used to explain the success of the Cravendale brand, described at the beginning of this chapter?

5. What are the 3Ps of marketing communications strategy? Explain the differences between each of them and use the marketing communications eclipse to support your answer.

5. Explain the key characteristics associated with a pull strategy.

6. Draw two diagrams depicting the direction of communications in both the push and the pull strategies.

7. Make notes for your friend in which you explain the differences between an advertising-led and a brand-led platform for marketing communications strategy.

8. Explain the configuration approach to marketing communications strategy.

9. Sketch the marketing communications planning framework – from memory.

10. Following on from the previous question, check your version of the MCPF with the original and then prepare some bullet-point notes, highlighting the critical linkages between the main parts of the framework.

# References

Anderson, E., Lodish, L. and Weitz, B. (1987) Resource allocation behaviour in conventional channels, *Journal of Marketing Research* (February), 85–97.

Andrews, K. (1987) *The Concept of Corporate Strategy*, Homewood, IL: Richard D. Irwin.

Anon (2010) The Natural 1st Choice Dairy Company, *The Times 100 Business Case Studies*, retrieved 2 July 2012 from http://businesscasestudies.co.uk/arla-foods/the-natural-1st-choice-dairy-company/values-in-action.html.

Anon (2011) The Work: Cravendale 'cats with thumbs', *Campaign*, 24 February, retrieved 2 July 2012 from http://www.campaignlive.co.uk/thework/1056544/Cravendale-cats-thumbs-Wieden-+-Kennedy/?DCMP=ILC-SEARCH.

Ansoff, H.I. (1965) *Corporate Strategy*, New York: McGraw-Hill.

Bainbridge, J. (2010) Sector Insight: Sour side to growth, *Marketing*, Wednesday 25 August, retrieved 30 June 2012 from http://www.campaignlive.co.uk/news/1023620/Sector-Insight-Sour-side-growth/?DCMP=ILC-SEARCH.

Beane, T.P. and D.M. Ennis (1987) Market segmentation: a review, *European Journal of Marketing*, 21(5), 20–42.

Caemmerer, B. (2009) The planning and implementation of integrated marketing communications, *Marketing Intelligence & Planning*, 27(4), 524–38.

Chaffee, E. (1985) 'Three models of strategy', *Academy of Management Review*, 10(1), 89–98.

Chapman, M. (2012) Boots revamps pharmacies to reflect specialities, *Marketing*, 4 May.

Datamonitor (2010) Lawson's Traditional Bread Case Study, June, retrieved 28 December 2011 from http://web.ebscohost.com/ehost/pdfviewer/pdfviewer?vid=4&hid=122&sid=4f5cd539-89d4-475c-bcc6-41b2a2c83dce%40sessionmgr112.

Dwyer, R. and Walker, O.C. (1981) Bargaining in an asymmetrical power structure, *Journal of Marketing*, 45 (Winter), 104–15.

Edwards, H. (2011) Work towards an 'Ideal Self', *Marketing*, 2 February, p. 21.

Eleftheriou-Smith, L.-M. (2012) TUI Travel marketing director Jeremy Ellis on keeping clear of troubled rivals, *Marketing*, 23 February, retrieved 27 March from: http://www.brandrepublic.com/features/1118064/TUI-Travel-marketing-director-Jeremy-Ellis-keeping-clear-troubled-rivals/?DCMP=ILC-SEARCH.

Engel, J.F., Warshaw, M.R. and Kinnear, T.C. (1994) *Promotional Strategy*, 8th edn., Homewood, IL: Richard D. Irwin.

Frazier, G.L. and Summers, J.O. (1984) Interfirm influence strategies and their application within distribution channels, *Journal of Marketing*, 48 (Summer), 43–55.

Gustafson, R. (2007) Best of all worlds, *Marketing: Brands by Design*, 14 November, 11.

Haley, Russell I. (1968) Benefit segmentation: a decision-oriented research tool, *Journal of Marketing*, 32 (July), 30–5.

Hambrick, D.C. (1983) High profit strategies in mature capital goods industries: a contingency approach, *Academy of Management Journal*, 26, 687–707.

Holm, O. (2006) Integrated marketing communication: from tactics to strategy, *Corporate Communications: An International Journal*, 11(1), 23–33.

IPA (2011) *New Models of Marketing Effectiveness: From Integration to Orchestration*, WARC.

Jewell, R.D. (2007) Establishing effective repositioning communications in a competitive marketplace, *Journal of Marketing Communications*, 13(4), 231–41.

Johnson, G., Scholes, K. and Whittingham, R. (2008) *Exploring Corporate Strategy*, 8th edn., Harlow: Pearson Education.

Katulka, L. (2010) Free Lunch at Selected Sydney Restaurants with Lawson's Bread, *iStopover Magazine*, 26 May, retrieved 28 December 2011 from http://www.planeteyetraveler.com/2010/05/26/free-lunch-at-selected-sydney-restaurants-with-lawsons-bread/.

Kay, J. (1993) The structure of strategy, *Business Strategy Review*, 4(2) (Summer), 17–37.

Mintzberg, H. and Waters, J.A. (1985) Of strategies, deliberate and emergent, *Strategic Management Journal*, 6(3), 257–72.

Mintzberg, H. (1994) *The Rise and Fall of Strategic Planning*, Englewood Cliffs, NJ: Prentice-Hall.

Mintzberg, H. and Ghoshal, S. (2003) *Strategy Process: Concepts, Context and Cases*, Global edn., Englewood Cliffs, NJ: Financial Times/Prentice-Hall.

Mohr, J. and Nevin, J.R. (1990) Communication strategies in marketing channels, *Journal of Marketing* (October), 36–51.

Moss, D. and Warnaby, G. (1998) Communications strategy? Strategy communication? Integrating different perspectives, *Journal of Marketing Communications*, 4(3), 131–40.

Rothschild, M. (1987) *Marketing Communications*, Lexington, MA: DC Heath.

Smith, P.R. (2003) *Great Answers to Tough Marketing Questions*, 2e, London: Kogan Page.

Stern, L. and El-Ansary, A.I. (1988) *Marketing Channels*, Englewood Cliffs, NJ: Prentice-Hall.

Stern, L. and El-Ansary, A.I. (1992) *Marketing Channels*, 4th edn., Englewood Cliffs, NJ: Prentice-Hall.

Steyn, B. (2003) From strategy to corporate communication strategy; a conceptualisation, *Journal of Communication Management*, 8(2), 168–83.

YouTube (2011) Lunch On Lawson's – Case Study, retrieved 28 December 2011 from http://www.youtube.com/watch?v=rb5aNVfAvtQ.

Whittington, R. (1993) *What is Strategy and Does it Matter?* London: Routledge.

Wind, Y.J. (1990) Positioning analysis and strategy, in *The Interface of Marketing and Strategy* (eds G. Day, B. Weitz and R. Wensley), Greenwich, CT: JAI Press, 387–412.

# Chapter 6
# Marketing communications: objectives and positioning

The formal setting of marketing communications objectives is important because they provide guidance about what is to be achieved and when. These objectives form a pivotal role between the business/marketing plans and the marketing communications strategy. The way in which a product or service is perceived by buyers is the only positioning that really matters.

## Aims and learning objectives

The aims of this chapter are to establish the role and characteristics of marketing communication objectives and to explore the concept of positioning.

The learning objectives of this chapter are to:

1. examine the need for organisational objectives;
2. specify the different types of organisational goals;
3. examine the relationship between corporate strategy and promotional objectives;
4. determine the components of SMART-determined promotional objectives;
5. examine the differences between sales- and communication-based objectives;
6. evaluate the concept of positioning;
7. understand the importance of perceptual mapping;
8. explain the main types of positioning strategies.

# Minicase

## Juan Valdez: the face of Colombian Coffee

Commercial coffee growing in Colombia dates back to the 1870s and the country has a long tradition of producing and exporting coffee. So important is coffee to the Colombian economy, it is said to have under-pinned the country's economic growth and development. This is because the production and marketing of coffee activates other important human and financial resources and fuels an entire interlinked set of economic processes. However, the path to establishing a stable efficient industry has not been clear and there have been many hurdles to overcome.

The National Federation of Coffee Growers of Colombia (Federacafe) is a not-for-profit business association. Formed in 1927, the cooperative, mainly made up of small family businesses, is designed to develop the production and exports of Colombian coffee growers. Federacafe operates a minimum price for growers, it develops agronomic and technical research and extension, it monitors quality standards, processes coffee, and invests in rural infrastructure of the coffee-growing regions. This institution also pro-tects farmers' incomes through a stabilisation fund.

For several decades Federacafe had worked hard to build the infrastructure and processes necessary for the international development of Colombian coffee. Much of the Colombian coffee production is high-quality beans but is used by roasters primarily as part of a blended coffee formula. In addition, two environmental issues struck in the late 1950s, major hurdles that were out of the country's immediate or direct control. First, the demand for coffee from the USA began to wane, and research showed that con-sumers in the USA clearly preferred Brazilian coffee. The second issue concerned international prices for coffee, which were falling.

It was clear that if Colombian coffee was to be successful in this new context, a revised strategy was required. It was important to develop new markets as well as penetrate existing ones. However, this strategy alone would not be successful as it was necessary to change the perceptions international markets had of Colombian coffee. To change perceptions requires a repositioning, a communication strategy that would provide a strong, clear point of differentiation for the brand. The goal was to reposition Colombian coffee as a high-quality product, something that would warrant consumers and coffee roasters paying premium prices. In turn, these higher prices would enable the Colombian coffee growers to receive higher incomes.

Federacafe approached Doyle Dane Bernback, the New York advertising agency, to help achieve the repositioning. They developed a character called Juan Valdez. He was depicted with a sombrero, leather bag, poncho and his faithful mule 'Conchita'. The character was designed to represent the thousands of coffee farmers that constitute the Colombian coffee industry, and be a means by which consumers could recognise and identify with the Colombian coffee brand. Juan Valdez was not just the face of Colombian coffee, he embodied the values of the coffee growers them-selves; their pride, simplicity, dedication and knowledge. See Exhibit 6.1.

Juan Valdez was first presented to American con-sumers in January 1960 through a full-page ad in the *New York Times*. His picture was accompanied by the strapline 'Colombian Coffee is drinking New York'. How-ever, it was television that established the character, as his task was to educate consumers about what it was that made Colombian coffee such high quality. This was achieved through a creative that showed him on his own farm, hand-picking coffee beans, with family and donkey, talking to camera and explaining how the various ingredients, such as soil components, altitude, varieties and harvesting methods, all combine to create rich flavour, contributing to the high quality of Colombian coffee. This informational message was conveyed using the Juan Valdez character in order to drive an emotional response and bond consumers with the brand. This proved highly effective to the point that consumer demand for Colombian coffee encouraged coffee roasters to included increasing amounts of Colombian coffee in their blends, before offering 100 per cent Colombian coffee.

Federacafe soon incorporated the character into the Federation's logo. This was important because the symbol became the logo and a means of certify-ing that the coffee was 100 per cent Colombian. The Federation insists that all packages of coffee using the logo consist of 100 per cent Colombian coffee. As if to emphasise the point, the words 'No blending allowed!' have to be visible.

Other campaigns followed the success of these early educational ads. Subsequent ads showed Juan Valdez demonstrating how to make coffee, and with his donkey he showed consumers where to find Colombian coffee in supermarkets. More recent campaigns have been targeted at younger adult audi-ences as a response to the surge in coffee houses,

| Exhibit 6.1 | **Juan Valdez – the face of Colombian Coffee** |
| --- | --- |
| | *Source*: Getty Images/Dario Cantatore |

espresso bars, and out-of-home coffee consumption, all of which attracted a new generation of younger coffee drinkers. These campaigns featured Juan Valdez experiencing various diverse extreme sports, such as surfing, snowboarding and hang-gliding. The campaign was called 'Grab Life by the Beans'.

The strapline 'The Richest Coffee in the World' was introduced and when launched was supported by a campaign which used humour and various sophisticated settings. Cars, trains and planes were shown making 180 degree turns in order to retrieve Colombian coffee.

In September 2002 Federacafe established Juan Valdez Cafe as their official coffeehouse brand. Locations in Bogotá, Medellín and Cal were followed by others domestically and internationally in the USA, Spain, Ecuador and plans for Peru, Argentina, Mexico and Panama.

Federacafe enters into various promotional agreements with various well-known multinational corporations. One of these involves Federacafe contributing to the multinational's advertising campaigns, and in return the company agrees, on an exclusive basis, to use '100% Colombian Coffee' products. In addition to joint advertising campaigns, roasters are allowed to use the Juan Valdez logo on their packages. This informs customers and reinforces the message that they are purchasing pure Colombian coffee.

Federacafe signs annual supply agreements with the majority of international coffee roasters. These agreements stipulate the minimum amount of Colombian coffee roasters are to take annually. These agreements also require roasters to report to Federacafe all purchases of coffee from Colombian suppliers, as they occur. This not only allows Federacafe to ensure that roasters are purchasing the coffee they are committed to buy, but also verifies that exporters are shipping the product as agreed with the roaster. Over 90 per cent of total Colombian coffee exports are governed by supply agreements.

The Juan Valdez campaign has now been running for over 50 years. During that time only two actors have been used to depict Juan Valdez, the second retiring from the role after 40 years. The campaigns have won numerous awards – Clios, Effies – and in September 2005 Juan Valdez was named *Advertising Week*'s 'Advertising icon of the year'. This was significant in that it beat some very well-known US brands, including Ronald McDonald, Geico Gecko, the Energizer Bunny and the Doublemint Twins from Wrigley.

In 1959 less than 4 per cent of Americans were aware of Colombian coffee. In 2010 this figure was 80 per cent, with 85 per cent able to identify the logo.

*This minicase was written by Chris Fill using a variety of sources including: Kurata (2008); Paajanen (2012); Ramirez-Vallejo (2003).*

# Introduction

There are many different opinions about what it is that marketing communications seeks to achieve. The conflicting views have led some practitioners and academics to polarise their thoughts about what constitutes an appropriate set of objectives. First, much effort has been spent trying to determine what 'promotion' and marketing communication activities are supposed to achieve; second, how should the success of a campaign be evaluated, and finally, how is it best to determine the degree of investment that should be made in each of the areas of the communication mix? The Juan Valdez campaign shows that marketing communications worked to elevate Colombian coffee, and this was partly accomplished through the utilisation of a clear set of objectives, which involved a clear re-positioning of the brand in the mind of buyers.

The process of resolving these different demands that are placed on organisations has made the setting of 'promotional' objectives very complex and difficult. It has been termed 'a job of creating order out of chaos' (Kriegel, 1986). This perceived complexity has led a large number of managers to fail to set promotional objectives or to set the wrong ones. Many of those who do set them do so in such a way that they are inappropriate, inadequate or merely restate the marketing objectives. The most common marketing communications objectives set by managers are sales-related. These include increases in market share, return on investment, sales volume increases and improvements in the value of sales made after accounting for the rate of inflation.

Such a general perspective ignores the influence of the other elements of the marketing mix and implicitly places the entire responsibility for sales performance with the promotional mix. This is not an accurate reflection of the way in which businesses and organisations work. In addition, because sales tests are too general, they would be an insufficiently rigorous test of promotional activity and there would be no real evaluation of promotional activities. Sales volumes vary for a wide variety of reasons:

- competitors change their prices;
- buyers' needs change;
- changes in legislation may favour the strategies of particular organisations;
- favourable third-party communications become known to significant buyers;
- general economic conditions change;
- technological advances facilitate improved production processes;
- economies of scale, experience effects and, for some organisations, the opportunity to reduce costs;
- the entry and exit of different competitors.

These are a few of the many reasons why sales might increase and conversely why sales might decrease. Therefore, the notion that marketing communications is entirely responsible for the sales of an offering is clearly unacceptable, unrealistic and incorrect.

# The role of objectives in corporate strategy

Objectives play an important role in the activities of individuals, social groups and organisations because:

1. They provide direction and an action focus for all those participating in the activity.
2. They provide a means by which the variety of decisions relating to an activity can be made in a consistent way.
3. They set out the time period in which the activity is to be completed.
4. They communicate the values and scope of the activity to all participants.
5. They provide a means by which the success of the activity can be evaluated.

It is generally accepted that the process of developing corporate strategy demands that a series of objectives be set at different levels within an organisation (Johnson et al. (2011) and Quinn et al. 2003). This hierarchy of objectives consists of mission, strategic business unit (SBU) or business objectives and functional objectives, such as production, finance or marketing goals.

The first level in the hierarchy (mission) requires that an overall direction be set for the organisation. If strategic decisions are made to achieve corporate objectives, both objectives and strategy are themselves constrained by an organisation's mission. Mission statements should be a vision that management has of what the organisation is trying to achieve in the long term. A mission statement outlines who the organisation is, what it does and where it is headed. A clearly developed, articulated and communicated mission statement enables an organisation to define whose needs are to be satisfied, what needs require satisfying and which products and technologies will be used to provide the desired levels of satisfaction. The mission should clearly identify the following:

- the customers/buyers to be served;
- the needs to be satisfied;
- the products and/or technologies by which these will be achieved.

In some organisations these points are explicitly documented in a mission statement. These statements often include references to the organisation's philosophy, culture, commitment to the community and employees, growth, profitability and so on, but these should not blur or distract attention from the organisation's basic mission. The words 'mission' and 'vision' are often used interchangeably, but they have separate meanings. Vision refers to the expected or desired outcome of carrying out the mission over the agreed period of time.

The mission provides a framework for the organisation's objectives, and the objectives that follow should promote and be consistent with the mission. While the word 'mission' implies a singularity of purpose, organisations have multiple objectives because of the many aspects of the organisation's performance and behaviour that contribute to the mission, and should, therefore, be explicitly identified. However, many of these objectives will conflict with each other. In retailing, for example, if an organisation chooses to open larger stores, then total annual profit should rise, but average profit per square metre will probably fall. Short-term profitability can be improved by reducing investment, but this could adversely affect long-term profitability. Organisations therefore have long-term and short-term objectives.

At the SBU level, objectives represent the translation of the mission into a form that can be understood by relevant stakeholders. These objectives are the performance requirements for the organisation or unit, which in turn are broken down into objectives or targets that each functional area must achieve, as their contribution to the unit objectives. Marketing strategies are functional strategies, as are the strategies for the finance, human resource management, production and other departments. Combine or aggregate them and the SBU's overall target will, in reductionist theory, be achieved.

The various organisational objectives are of little use if they are not communicated to those who need to know what they are. Traditionally, such communication has focused on employees, but there is increasing recognition that the other members of the stakeholder network need to understand an organisation's purpose and objectives. The marketing objectives developed for the marketing strategy provide important information for the communications strategy. Is the objective to increase market share or to defend or maintain the current situation? Is the product new or established? Is it being modified or slowly withdrawn? The corporate image is shaped partly by the organisation's objectives and the manner in which they are communicated. All these impact on the objectives of the communications plan.

Marketing communication objectives consist of three main components. The first component concerns issues relating to the buyers of the product or service offered by the organisation. The second concerns issues relating to sales volume, market share, profitability and revenue. The third relates to the image, reputation and preferences that other stakeholders have towards the organisation. Each of these three streams is developed later in this chapter.

# The role of brand communication objectives and plans

Many organisations, including some advertising agencies, fail to set realistic (if any) communication or campaign objectives. There are several explanations for this behaviour, but one of the common factors is that managers are unable to differentiate between the value of promotion as an expense, and as an investment. This issue is addressed later (Chapter 9), but for now the value of these objectives can be seen in terms of the role they play in communications planning, evaluation and brand development.

The databank created by the Institute of Practitioners in Advertising consists of data concerning over 850 successful campaigns, recorded since 1980. This clearly shows that those campaigns that set clear objectives are more successful than those that do not (Binet and Field, 2007).

The setting of marketing communication objectives is important for three main reasons. The first is that they provide *a means of communication and coordination* between groups (e.g. client and agency) working on different parts of a campaign. Performance is improved if there is common understanding about the tasks the promotional tools have to accomplish. Second, objectives constrain the number of options available to an organisation. Campaign objectives act as *a guide for decision-making* and provide a focus for decisions that follow in the process of developing communication plans. The third reason is that objectives provide *a benchmark* so that the relative success or failure of a programme can be evaluated.

There is no doubt that organisations need to be flexible, to be able to anticipate and adjust to changes in their environments. This principle applies to the setting of campaign objectives. To set one all-encompassing objective and expect it to last the year (or whatever period is allocated) is both hopeful and naïve; multiple objectives are necessary.

---

**Viewpoint 6.1**     **Goals galore**

Different brands encounter different situations, and arising from this are a rich variety of goals.

The Shangri-La Hotels and Resorts campaign, 'It's in our nature', set a goal of achieving an extra US $90 million in room revenues, and this meant that it had to sell 10 more rooms per hotel per night.

VisitScotland attempted to inspire tourists to visit the country during winter. The campaign was designed to appeal to all of the senses, reversing preconceptions of dreariness and presenting Scotland as a romantic and exciting destination, with an emphasis on luxury.

Country Life's campaign goals were to correct the misperception that their main rival 'Anchor' was a British brand, and to enable consumers to make an informed butter choice.

China's shower gel market segment has 11 brands and 93 variants. Unilever's Dove was had been dormant for five years. Its campaign aim was to challenge market leader Olay and grow market share from 2 per cent to 3.4 per cent. This meant persuading 4 million Chinese women to buy Dove Bodywash.

Minute Maid Pulpy is the biggest juice brand in China, but the challenge was to convert brand 'triers' into brand 'lovers', and to grow sales.

The campaign goal for Leeds Castle was to encourage repeat visits, particularly during the winter period, by emphasising the different events that take place at the castle all year round.

When the b2b market in Singapore started to recover, HP and Intel joined forces to accomplish two main goals. The first was to generate new business leads by an incremental positive 30 per cent over the previous year. The second was to change their image from being perceived as cold and corporate to a more personable and approachable profile. A target of a 1:3 return on investment was set.

*Source*:   Various including *The Marketer* and www.ame.asia/winnerCategory/2011/.

**Question:**   If goals are designed to focus activities, are they the most important element of marketing communications or is something else more important?

**Task:**   Make a list of the different types of goal that might be used for marketing communications.

The academic literature suggests a combination of sales and communication objectives. Practitioners appear to use a variety of approaches and demonstrate inconsistency in their use and format. Consideration is given first to the academic interpretations before turning to the practitioner views. The content of campaign objectives has also been the subject of considerable debate. Academics refer to two distinct schools of thought: those that advocate sales-related measures as the main factors and those that advocate communication-related measures as the main orientation.

## The sales school

As stated earlier, many managers see sales as the only meaningful objective for campaigns. Their view is that the only reason an organisation spends money on communication is to sell its product or service. Therefore, the only meaningful measure of the effectiveness of the spend is in the sales results.

These results can be measured in a number of different ways. Sales turnover is the first and most obvious factor, particularly in business-to-business markets. In consumer markets and the fast-moving consumer goods sector, market share movement is measured regularly and is used as a more sensitive barometer of performance. Over the longer term, return-on-investment measures are used to calculate success and failure. In some sectors the number of products sold, or volume of product shifted, relative to other periods of activity, is a common measure. There are a number of difficulties with this view. One of these has been considered earlier, that *sales result from a variety of influences*, such as the other elements in the marketing mix, competitor actions and wider environmental effects, such as the strength of a currency, changing social preferences or the level of interest rates.

A second difficulty rests with the concept of *adstock or carryover*. The impact of 'promotional' expenditure may not be immediately apparent, as the receiver may not enter the market until some later date, but the effects of the promotional programme may influence the eventual purchase decision. This means that, when measuring the effectiveness of a campaign, sales results will not always reflect its full impact.

Sales objectives *do little to assist the media planner, copywriters and creative team* associated with the development of the communications programme, despite their inclusion in campaign documents such as media briefs.

Sales-oriented objectives are, however, applicable in particular situations. For example, where direct action is required by the receiver in response to exposure to a message, measurement of sales is justifiable. Such an action, a behavioural response, can be solicited in direct-response advertising. This occurs where the sole communication is through a particular medium, such as television or print.

The retail sector can also use sales measures, and it has been suggested that packaged goods organisations, operating in mature markets with established pricing and distribution structures, can build a databank from which it is possible to isolate the advertising effect through sales. For example, supermarkets that have used celebrity chefs such as Jamie Oliver, Delia Smith and Nigella Lawson can monitor the stock movements of particular ingredients used in 'celebrity recipe' commercials. Not only does this enable supermarkets to evaluate the success of particular campaigns, recipes and particular celebrities, but they can also learn to anticipate demand and stock ingredients in anticipation of particular advertisements being screened. However, despite this cause-and-effect relationship, it can be argued that this may ignore the impact of changes in competitor actions and changes in the overall environment. Furthermore, the effects of the organisation's own corporate advertising, adstock effects and other family brand promotions need to be accounted for if a meaningful sales effect is to be generated.

The sales school advocates the measure on the grounds of simplicity. Any manager can utilise the tool, and senior management does not wish to be concerned with information which is complex or unfamiliar, especially when working to short lead times and accounting periods. It is a self-consistent theory, but one that may misrepresent consumer behaviour and the purchase process (perhaps unintentionally), and to that extent may result in less than optimal expenditure on marketing communications.

## The communications school

There are many situations, however, where the aim of a communications campaign is to enhance the image or reputation of an organisation or product. Sales are not regarded as the only goal. Consequently, promotional efforts are seen as communication tasks, such as the creation of awareness or positive attitudes towards the organisation or product. To facilitate this process, receivers have to be given relevant information before the appropriate decision processes can develop and purchase activities become established as a long-run behaviour.

Various models have been developed to assist our understanding about how these promotional tasks are segregated and organised effectively. AIDA and other hierarchy of effects models were considered earlier (Chapter 4) at some length and need not be repeated here. However, one particular model was developed deliberately to introduce clear objectives into the advertising development process: Dagmar.

### Dagmar

Russell Colley (1961) developed a model for setting advertising objectives and measuring the results. This model was entitled 'Defining Advertising Goals for Measured Advertising Results – Dagmar'. Colley's rationale for what is effectively a means of setting communications-oriented objectives was that advertising's job, purely and simply, is to communicate to a defined audience information and a frame of mind that stimulates action. Advertising succeeds or fails depending on how well it communicates the desired information and attitudes to the right people at the right time and at the right cost.

Colley proposed that the communications task be based on a hierarchical model of the communications process: awareness – comprehension – conviction – action.

| Table 6.1 | Hierarchy of communications |
| --- | --- |

| Stage | Explanation |
| --- | --- |
| Awareness | Awareness of the existence of a product or brand is necessary before any purchase will be made. |
| Comprehension | Audiences need information and knowledge about the product and its specific attributes. Often the audience needs to be educated and shown either how to use the product or how changes (in attributes) might affect their use of the product. |
| Conviction | By encouraging beliefs that a product is superior to others in a category or can confer particular rewards through use, audiences can be convinced to trial the product at the next purchase opportunity. |
| Action | Potential buyers need help and encouragement to transfer thoughts into behaviour. Providing call-free numbers, website addresses, reply cards, coupons and sales people helps people act upon their convictions. |

*Source*: Based on Colley (1961).

---

**Scholars' paper 6.1**   **First time to set advertising goals**

**Colley, R. (1961) *Defining Advertising Goals for Measured Advertising Results*, New York: Association of National Advertisers.**

Colley is credited with introducing the idea that good advertising practice requires setting precise advertising goals. Defining Advertising Goals for Measured Advertising Results, or DAGMAR as it inevitably became, was first published in this book. In tune with the then current practice, Colley recommended a hierarchical model of communications – one which parallelled the purchase decision process. Colley's model is significant in its focus on the setting and measurement of objectives and is not purely an examination of the communications process itself. It has also been used widely in the context of setting advertising budgets (see Chapter 8).

---

### Awareness

Awareness of the existence of a product or an organisation is necessary before purchase behaviour can be expected. Once awareness has been created in the target audience, it should not be neglected. If there is neglect, an audience may become distracted by competing messages and the level of awareness of the focus product or organisation may decline. Awareness, therefore, needs to be created, developed, refined or sustained, according to the characteristics of the market and the particular situation facing an organisation at any one point in time (see Figure 6.1).

In situations where the buyer experiences high involvement and is fully aware of a product's existence, attention and awareness levels need only be sustained, and efforts need to be applied to other communication tasks, which may be best left to the other elements of the communications mix. For example, sales promotion and personal selling are more effective at informing, persuading and provoking purchase of a new car once advertising has created the necessary levels of awareness.

Where low levels of awareness are found, getting attention needs to be a prime objective so that awareness can be developed in the target audience. Where low involvement exists, the decision-making process is relatively straightforward. With levels of risk minimised, buyers with sufficient levels of awareness may be prompted into purchase with little assistance from

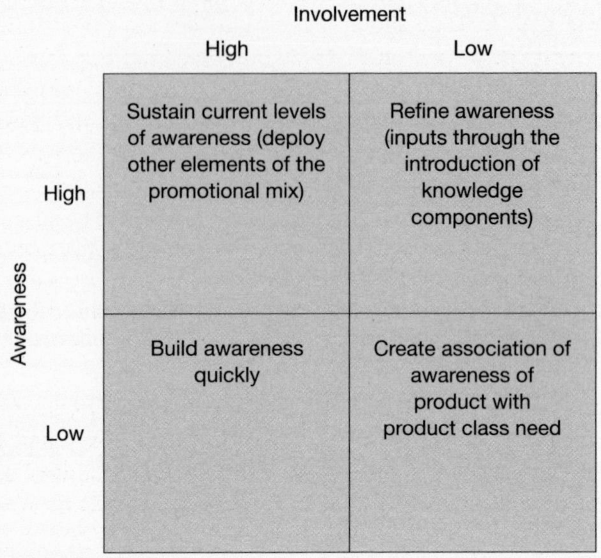

**Figure 6.1** An awareness grid

the other elements of the mix. Recognition and recall of brand names and corporate images are felt by some (Rossiter and Percy, 1987) to be sufficient triggers to stimulate a behavioural response. The requirement in this situation would be to refine and strengthen the level of awareness in order to provoke interest and stimulate a higher level of involvement during recall or recognition.

Where low levels of awareness are matched by low involvement, the prime objective has to be to create awareness of the focus product in association with the product class. It is not surprising that organisations use awareness campaigns and invest a large proportion of their resources in establishing their brand or corporate name. Many brands seek to establish 'top of mind awareness' as one of their primary objectives for their advertising spend.

It is interesting to observe that most advertising programmes still include awareness as an objective. The logic is clear: if the ad is not seen, it is not going to be effective. However, in the light of the low attention processing theory, are high awareness goals necessary and, more important, are they a waste of financial resources? Heath (2009) and colleagues would argue that they are, but convincing a client, or agency even, that driving high levels of awareness is not necessary is going to be problematic.

### Comprehension

Awareness on its own is, invariably, not enough to stimulate purchase activity. Knowledge about the product (or what the organisation does) is necessary, and this can be achieved by providing specific information about key brand attributes. These attributes and their associated benefits may be key to the buyers in the target audience or may be key because the product has been adapted or modified in some way. This means that the audience needs to be educated about the change and shown how their use of the product may be affected. For example, in attempting to persuade people to try a different brand of mineral water, it may be necessary to compare the product with other mineral water products and provide an additional usage benefit, such as environmental claims.

### Conviction

Having established that a product has particular attributes that lead to benefits perceived by the target audience as important, it is then necessary to establish a sense of conviction. By creating interest and preference, buyers are moved to a position where they are convinced that one particular product in the class should be tried at the next opportunity. To do this, the audience's beliefs about the product need to be moulded, and this can be accomplished by using messages that demonstrate a product's superiority over its main rival or by emphasising the rewards conferred as a result of using the product – for example, the reward of social acceptance associated with many fragrance, fashion clothing and accessory advertisements, and the reward of self-gratification associated with many confectionery messages, such as 'Cadbury's Flake' and Terry's 'Chocolate Orange'.

High-involvement decisions are best supported with personal selling and sales promotion activities, in an attempt to gain conviction. Low-involvement decisions rely on the strength of advertising messages, packaging and sales promotion to secure conviction.

### Action

A communications programme is used to encourage buyers to engage in purchase activity. Advertising can be directive and guide buyers into certain behavioural outcomes: for example, to the use of free phone numbers (0800 in the United Kingdom), direct mail activities and reply cards and coupons. However, for high-involvement decisions the most effective tool in the communications mix at this stage in the hierarchy is personal selling. Through the use of interpersonal skills, buyers are more likely to want to buy a product than if the personal prompting is absent. The use of direct marketing activities by Avon Cosmetics, Tupperware, Betterware and suppliers of life assurance and double-glazing services has been instrumental in the sales growth experienced by organisations in these markets.

Colley's dissatisfaction with the way in which advertising agencies operated led him to specify the components of a good advertising objective: 'A specific communications task to be accomplished among a defined audience to a given degree in a given period of time' (Dutka, 1995). An analysis of this statement shows that it is made up of four distinct elements:

- a need to specify the communications task;
- a need to define the audience;
- a need to state the required degree of change;
- a need to establish the time period in which the activity is to occur.

Colley's statement is very clear – it is measurable and of assistance to copywriters. Indeed, Dagmar revolutionised the approach taken by advertisers to the setting of objectives. It helped to move attention from the sales effect to the communication effect school and has led to improved planning processes, as a result partly of a better understanding of advertising and promotional goals.

Many of the difficulties associated with sequential models (as presented in Chapter 4) are also applicable to Dagmar. Additional to problems of hierarchical progression, measurement and costs are issues concerning the sales orientation, restrictions upon creativity and short-term accountability.

### Sales orientation

This criticism is levelled by those who see sales as the only valid measure of effectiveness. The sole purpose of communication activities, and advertising in particular, is to generate sales. So, as the completion of communications tasks may not result in purchases, the only measure that need be undertaken is that of sales. This point has been discussed earlier and need not be reproduced here.

### Restrictions upon creativity

Dagmar is criticised on the grounds that creative flair can be lost as attention passes from looking for the big idea to concentration on the numbers game, of focusing on measures of recall, attitude change and awareness. It is agreed that the creative personnel are held to be more accountable under Dagmar and this may well inhibit some of their work. Perhaps the benefits of providing direction and purpose offset the negative aspects of a slight loss in creativity.

### Short-term accountability

To the above should be added the time period during which management and associated agencies are required to account for their performance. With accounting periods being reduced to as little as 12 weeks, the communications approach is impractical, for two reasons. The first is that the period is not long enough for all of the communication tasks to be progressed or completed. Sales measures present a much more readily digestible benchmark of performance.

The second concerns the unit of performance itself. With the drive to be efficient and to be able to account for every communication pound spent, managers themselves need to use measures that they can understand and that they can interpret from published data. Sales data and communications spend data are consistent measures and make no further demands on managers. Managers do not have enough time to spend analysing levels of comprehension or preference and to convert them into formats that are going to be of direct benefit to them and their organisations. Having said that, organisations that invest in a more advanced management information system will be able to take a more sophisticated view.

The approach adopted by the communication school is not universally accepted. Those who disagree argue that it is too difficult and impractical to translate a sales objective into a series of specific communications objectives. Furthermore, what actually constitutes adequate levels of awareness and comprehension and how can it be determined which stage the majority of the target audience has reached at any one point in time? Details of measurement, therefore, throw a veil over the simplicity and precision of the approach taken by the communication-orientation school.

From a practical perspective, it should be appreciated that most successful marketing organisations do not see the sales and communications schools as mutually exclusive. They incorporate both views and weight them according to the needs of the current task, their overall experience, the culture and style of the organisation and the agencies with whom they operate.

# Derivation of campaign objectives

It has been established that specific campaign objectives need to be set up if a suitable foundation is to be laid for the many communications-orientated decisions that follow. Campaign objectives are derived from understanding the overall context in which the communications will work. Comprehending the contexts of the buyer and the organisation allows the objectives of the planned communications to be identified: the *what* that is to be achieved. For example, objectives concerning the perception that different target customers have of a brand, the perception that members of a performance network have of the organisation's offerings, the reactions of key stakeholders to previous communications and the requirements of the current marketing plan all impact upon the objectives of the communication plan. Therefore, campaign objectives evolve principally from a systematic audit and analysis of the key communication contexts, and specifically from the marketing plan and stakeholder analysis.

It was established earlier that there are three main streams of objectives. These are set out in Figure 6.2. The first concerns issues relating to the buyers of the product or service offered by the organisation. The second concerns issues relating to market share/sales volume, profitability and revenue. The third stream relates to the image, reputation and preferences that other stakeholders have towards the organisation.

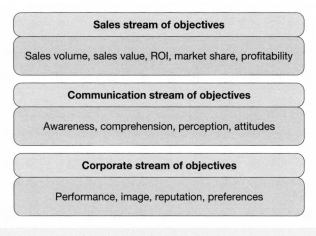

**Figure 6.2**    The three streams of objectives

All these objectives are derived from an analysis of the current situation. The marketing communication brief that flows from this analysis should specify the sales-related objectives to be achieved, as these can be determined from the marketing plan. Sales-related objectives might concern issues such as market share and sales volume.

Customer-related objectives concern issues such as awareness, perception, attitude, feelings and intentions towards a brand or product. The exact issue to be addressed in the plan is calculated by analysing the contextual information driven by the audit.

Issues related to the perception of the organisation are often left unattended or, worse, ignored. Research may indicate that the perception of particular stakeholders, in either the performance or the support network, does not complement the current level of corporate performance or may be misplaced or confused. Objectives will need to be established to correct or reinforce the perception held of the organisation. The degree of urgency may be directly related to the level of confusion or misunderstanding or be related to competitive or strategic actions initiated by competitors and other members of the network. Corporate strategy may have changed and, as identified earlier, any new strategy will need to be communicated to all stakeholders.

# Setting realistic marketing communication objectives

Hierarchy of effects models which specify stages of development were first proposed as far back as 1898 by E. St Elmo Lewis (Barry and Howard, 1990) and similar views were expressed by Colley (Dagmar) in 1961. Yet, despite the passage of time since their publication, a large number of organisations still either fail to set any promotional objectives or confuse objectives with strategy. Organisations seeking to coordinate their communications need to recognise the necessity of setting multiple objectives at different times in the campaign period and of being prepared to adjust them in the light of environmental changes. These changes may be due to ever-decreasing product lifecycles or technological developments that may give a competitor comparative advantage, and perhaps legislative developments (or the timing of management's interpretation and implementation of certain legislation) may bring about a need to reconfigure the promotional mix.

Management's failure to set objectives is often the result of a lack of awareness of the current position, or a lack of understanding of how and why appropriate objectives need to be established. With increasingly competitive and turbulent environments, a greater number of organisations are turning their attention to ways in which they can communicate more effectively with their stakeholders. Furthermore, as more executives undertake management education programmes, so a higher level of skill is being transferred to organisations, and this in turn will bring a higher incidence of better practice.

The overall objective of any promotional programme is to increase the level of sales. While it seems unreasonable to expect the communication mix to bear total responsibility for this, it is also unreasonable and impractical to expect the communications approach to bear total responsibility. It is imperative that organisations are willing and prepared to set promotional objectives that utilise basic communications tasks, such as awareness and intentions, and that they utilise sales benchmarks as means of determining what has been achieved and how. Campaign objectives are a derivative of both marketing and corporate strategies. Just as revenue and income targets are part of marketing strategy, so they should form part of the promotional objectives. They cannot be separated and they cannot be neglected.

The choice depends on the situation facing each manager and, in particular, whether the product or organisation is new. Establishing and maintaining levels of awareness is, however, paramount to any communications programme, and must be considered one of the primary communication objectives.

Campaign objectives need to be set that reflect the communication and sales tasks that the product or organisation needs to accomplish. It should be appreciated that objectives are vitally important, as they provide the basis for a string of decisions that are to be taken at subsequent stages in the development of the communication plan.

Management's next task is to make decisions regarding which of these different campaign objectives will receive attention first. In order that decisions can be made regarding communication strategy, the communications mix and the level of resources allocated to each discipline and media, it is necessary to rank and weight the objectives at this stage in the management process. The criteria used to weight the different objectives will inevitably be subjective, because they reflect each manager's perception, experience and interpretation of their environment. However, it is also their skill and judgement that are the important elements, and as long as the criteria are used and applied in a consistent manner, the outcome of the communication plan is more likely to be successful.

# The practitioners' view

Analysis of the IPA databank mentioned earlier shows that successful campaigns are characterised not only by the use of objectives but also by the use of tiered or a hierarchy of objectives. These are set out in Figure 6.3.

## Business objectives

At the top of this hierarchy are objectives that concern the business and these include profit, market share and pricing goals. Campaigns that clearly make increasing profit the ultimate objective outperform others (Binet and Field, 2007). However, only 7 per cent of the cases in the IPA databank use profit as an objective. One of the reasons for this may be the difficulties associated with defining and using suitable measures of payback, and isolating the other factors that impact profitability. This is where the use of econometric modelling is important. One of the other business objectives recommended as a result of the analysis of the IPA databank is market share. Although sales are used as a primary goal by 62 per cent of cases, these campaigns underperform. It is market share (by value), used with profitability, that leads to the

**Figure 6.3**    A hierarchy of campaign goals (IPA)

best performance outcomes. Linking market share with profitability is crucial, otherwise it is likely that share will be gained at the expense of profitability. One highly successful way of achieving this is to develop campaigns that seek to reduce price sensitivity.

## Behavioural objectives

The business objectives are the primary goals. In order that these are achieved, relevant behavioural objectives need to be established. Although various required behaviours can be identified, Binet and Field (2007) reduce these to two: the acquisition of new customers (penetration) and the retention of customers (loyalty). It is interesting that loyalty features in twice as many campaigns as an objective than penetration, yet it is those with the latter objective that are the most successful, in all categories, not just grocery and fmcg. This objective should be used when market share is the main business objective.

## Intermediate objectives

At the third level in the hierarchy the IPA identify factors that will influence future business performance. They refer to these as *intermediate objectives*, such as awareness, beliefs, attitudes. These correspond to the communication goals considered earlier and contain many of the elements used in Dagmar. Awareness, perception, attitude and brand image goals are the more common factors to be accommodated in this part of the hierarchy. These goals are regarded as secondary as they can lead to the achievement of the behavioural goals in the future.

A large number of campaigns set awareness as the main objective, yet analysis shows that these are the least effective from a business perspective. It is suggested that their heavy usage is due to their relative ease of achievement and accountability. When there is more than one intermediate objective, such as building brand awareness and improving perceptions, then success rates improve. Also, setting out to achieve brand fame achieves very strong results. Fame is concerned with being perceived as an authority in a category, as opposed to knowledge which characterises awareness. This is best considered as a strategy and was examined earlier (Chapter 5).

However, one interesting point emerges. The measures used to test for most communication effects are geared to reflect high-attention processing. As noted previously, the development of ideas about low-attention processing and the long-term effects of advertising suggest that further insight is required, as the impact of these objectives may be underestimated.

The issue therefore is to encourage brands not only to ensure that they use objectives, but that they also use them in a tiered format, and make profit or market share the primary, clear and overriding goal.

## Viewpoint 6.2    Driving customised demand

Thunderhead is a leading provider of customised communications software. Used by large companies to personalise the way they engage with customers, they can deliver the right message, through the right channel at the right time.

The campaign 'I am' was developed to generate demand among leading retail banks and insurers, by engaging senior executives operating in Europe's largest banks and insurers. It was important that the campaign should demonstrate the highly personalised, multi-channel communications functionality that their product provided.

The 'I am' campaign had three core objectives:

- Generate leads to drive Thunderhead's revenue growth in EMEA.
- Build a strategic dialogue with board-level executives in target companies.
- Extend engagement beyond the IT department.

The first step required the identification of the target markets and all the key people in each target account, across a number of functions. From here the message was built around the issues faced by different contacts, based on their role, the function they operate in, the type of organisation and even their company's strategic goals. This was established from reports and accounts and news releases. From this data a messaging matrix was developed and tested with external and independent consultants.

The creative theme needed to accommodate different messages, different regional languages and nuances, and to work across different media. The 'I am' title delivered that theme and a method for showing the many ways Thunderhead helps each target address their issues and the benefits it brings.

At a strategic level, gatekeepers were sent a personalised postcard giving them advance warning that a box was being delivered to the named executive they were responsible for. There was a request that they pass it on.

TIER 1 board-level executives received a direct mail pack containing an iPod Shuffle which was pre-loaded with a tailored 60-second message from Thunderhead. The accompanying booklet was personalised according to their role. For a select number of targets, these booklets were 'hyper-personalised': that is tailored to address their organisation's stated business priorities. Each booklet featured a personalised URL.

TIER 2 board-level executives also received a DM pack but this contained a coffee pot, cup, saucer and Arabic ground coffee. The accompanying booklet was personalised according to their role. Each booklet featured a personalised URL.

At a functional level TIER 1 and 2 operational level executives received a series of three personalised postcards and emails, delivered weekly, with the content tailored according to their role within the organisation.

The personalised URLs enabled the delivery of a tailored online experience for each recipient. The site aggregated content that was relevant to their businesses – for example, white papers, podcasts and case studies. A sharing function enabled them to readily share content with their colleagues.

The site was integrated with SalesForce.com, which meant that any interaction with the site could be captured and used to trigger key events. This included automated emails sent to all site visitors thanking them for their visit, providing them with the contact details of their sales rep and encouraging them to follow Thunderhead via social media.

Concurrent activity included a research video called the 'Disconnected Customer'. This showed the customer communication issues faced by banks and insurers today. The video was promoted through targeted Google and LinkedIn keyword campaigns, along with active promotion via Twitter, YouTube, and blog comment.

In order to ensure the volumes were manageable for follow-up by the sales force, the campaign was implemented in sequential waves, starting with the UK, and then rolled out to Germany, Austria and Switzerland before the US and Asia-Pacific regions.

The initial results indicated that a £4.4 million pipeline had been generated, representing a return on investment of 110:1.

*Source*:    Earnest (2011); www.thunderhead.com; www.b2bmarketing.net/awards.

**Question:**    Why might utilising multiple objectives casue problems for campaign management?

**Task:**    Find a campaign for the not-for-profit sector and compare the objectives with those for a profit-based brand.

# SMART objectives

To assist managers in their need to develop suitable objectives, regardless of source, a set of guidelines has been developed, commonly referred to as SMART objectives. This acronym stands for specific, measurable, achievable, relevant, targeted and timed.

The process of making objectives SMART requires management to consider exactly what is to be achieved, when, where and with which audience. This clarifies thinking, sorts out the logic of the proposed activities and provides a clear measure for evaluation at the end of the campaign:

● *Specific*
   What is the actual variable that is to be influenced in the campaign? Is it awareness, perception, attitudes or some other element that is to be influenced? Whatever the variable, it must be clearly defined and must enable precise outcomes to be determined.

● *Measurable*
   Set a measure of activity against which performance can be assessed. For example, this may be a percentage level of desired prompted awareness in the target audience.

● *Achievable*
   Objectives need to be attainable, otherwise those responsible for their achievement will lack motivation and a desire to succeed.

● *Realistic*
   The actions must be founded in reality and be relevant to the brand and the context in which they are set.

● *Targeted and timed*
   Which target audience is the campaign targeted at, how precisely is the audience defined and over what period are the results to be generated?

Multiple objectives rather than a single objective should be set. The primary objectives should be business-orientated, preferably around profit. Next, the appropriate behavioural objectives need to be established. From this point communication goals should be determined. Whatever the level, the objectives should be written in SMART format.

# Positioning

As discovered in Chapter 4, the final act in the target marketing process of segmentation and targeting is positioning. Following on from the identification of potential markets, determining the size and potential of market segments and selecting specific target markets, positioning is the process whereby the brand is perceived by the consumer/stakeholder to be differentiated from the competition, to occupy a particular space in the market, and will achieve the business goals. According to Kotler (2003), 'Positioning is the act of designing the company's offering and image so that they occupy a meaningful and distinct competitive position in the target customers' minds'.

---

### Scholars' paper 6.2    Positioning is key

**Ries, A. and Trout, J. (1972) The positioning era cometh, *Advertising Age*, 24 April, 35–8.**

This is a classic paper that should be read by everyone associated with this subject. It was the first paper to outline the positioning concept. Ries and Trout argue that it is not what marketers do to a product itself, but how they influence the mind of a prospective customer. As the level of competition has extended so much, there is often little to choose between the actual products themselves. It should, therefore, be the role of marketing to differentiate on the basis of what customers think about them. Such differences might be real or merely perception.

---

This is an important aspect of the positioning concept. Positioning is not about the product but what the buyer thinks about the product or organisation. It is not the physical nature of the product that is important for positioning, but how the product is perceived that matters. This is why part of the context analysis (Chapter 5) requires a consideration of perception and attitudes and the way stakeholders see and regard brands and organisations. Of course, this may not be the same as the way brand managers intend their brands to be seen or how they believe the brand is perceived.

This audience orientation is emphasised by Blankstson and Kalafatis (2007). They considered the positioning strategies of several leading credit card providers from three perspectives. These were the banks' executives, the positioning strategies that were implemented, and finally, but most important, the perception of the target audiences of the positioning strategies. In the words of the researchers: presumed practice, actual practice and perceived practice. One of the outcomes of their work was the need to manage the potential gulf that may occur when the presumed and actual positioning strategies drift away from the way audiences actually perceive the brand.

In the consumer market established brands from washing powders (Ariel, Daz, Persil) and hair shampoos (such as Wash & Go, Timotei), to cars (Peugeot, GM, Nissan) and grocery multiples (Sainsbury's, Tesco and Maxi ICA Stormarknad) each carry communications that enable audiences to position them in their respective markets.

The positioning concept is not the sole preserve of branded or consumer-oriented offerings or indeed those of the business-to-business market. Organisations are also positioned relative to one another, mainly as a consequence of their corporate identities, whether they are deliberately managed or not. The position an organisation takes in the mind of consumers may be the only means of differentiating one product from another. King (1991) argues that, given the advancement in technology and the high level of physical and functional similarity of products in the same class, consumers' choices will be more focused on their assessment of the company they are dealing with. Therefore, it is important to position organisations as brands in the minds of actual and potential customers.

One of the crucial differences between the product and the corporate brand is that the corporate brand needs to be communicated to a large array of stakeholders, whereas the product-based brand requires a focus on a smaller range of stakeholders: in particular, the consumers and buyers in the performance network.

Whatever the position chosen, either deliberately or accidentally, it is the means by which customers understand the brand's market position, and it often provides signals to determine a brand's main competitors, or whether (as is often the case) customers fail to understand the brand or are confused about what the brand stands for.

# The development of the positioning concept

This perspective was originally proposed by Ries and Trout (1972). They claimed that it is not what you do to a product that matters; it is what you do to the mind of the prospect that is important. They set out three stages of development: the product era, the image era and the positioning era.

The product era occurred in the late 1950s and early 1960s and existed when each product was promoted in an environment where there was little competition. Each product was regarded as an innovation and was readily accepted and adopted as a natural development. In the pharmaceutical market, drugs such as Navidex, Valium and Lasix became established partly because of the lack of competition and partly because of the ability of the product to fulfil its claims. This was a period when the features and benefits of products were used in communications – the unique selling proposition was of paramount importance.

The image era that followed was spawned by companies with established images, which introduced new me-too products against the original brands. It was the strength of the perceived company image that underpinned the communications surrounding these new brands that was so important to their success. Products such as Amoxil, Tagamet and Tenormin were launched on an image platform.

The positioning era has developed mainly because of the increasingly competitive market conditions, where there is now little compositional, material or even structural difference between products within each class. Consequently, most products are now perceived relative to each other. In most markets the level and intensity of 'noise' drives organisations to establish themselves and their offerings in particular parts of the overall market. It is now the ability of an offering to command the attention of buyers and to communicate information about how it is differentiated from the other competitive offerings that helps to signal the relative position the offering occupies in the market.

---

**Scholars' paper 6.3**    **The benefit of positioning**

**Fuchs, C. and Diamantopoulos, A. (2010) Evaluating the effectiveness of brand-positioning strategies from a consumer perspective, *European Journal of Marketing*, 44(11/12), 1763–86.**

This paper considers the overall effectiveness of positioning strategies. The paper provides an interesting and readable review of the positioning literature. The results of the authors' research show that the success of a brand is influenced by the type of positioning strategy used. They also find that benefit-based positioning and surrogate (user) positioning generally outperform feature-based positioning strategies along the three effectiveness dimensions.

# The positioning concept

From the research data and the marketing strategy, it is necessary to formulate a positioning statement that is in tune with the promotional objectives.

One of the roles of marketing communications is to convey information so that the target audience can understand what a brand stands for and differentiate it from other competing brands. Clear, consistent positioning is an important aspect of integrated marketing communications. So, the way in which a brand is presented to its audience influences the way it is going to be perceived. Therefore, accepting that there are extraneous reasons why the perception of a brand might not be the same as that intended, it seems important that managers approach the positioning task in an attentive and considered manner.

Generally there are two main ways in which a brand can be positioned: *functional* and *expressive* (or *symbolic*) positioning. Functionally positioned brands stress the features and benefits, while expressive brands emphasise the ego, social and hedonic satisfactions that a brand can bring.

Both approaches make a promise, a promise to deliver a whiter, cleaner and brighter soap powder (functional) or clothes that we are confident to hang on the washing line (for all to see), dress our children in and send to school and not feel guilty, or dress ourselves in and complete a major business deal (symbolic).

---

## Viewpoint 6.3    Sticky, yet functional positioning

Marketing communications in the adhesives market place heavy reliance on demonstrating the performance of each of the individual brands. Solvite, for example, presents a man glued to a board and suspended in dangerous situations (above sharks, towed into the sky and at a theme park on a 'vertical drop ride').

Another brand, 'No More Nails', uses a similar functional approach. One execution shows a man sitting on a chair that has been glued halfway up a wall inside a house.

Adhesives provoke low-involvement decision-making and there is generally little consumer interest in the properties of each brand. The essential information that consumers require is that the brand has strong performance characteristics. This sets up umbrella brand credibility so that sub-brands for different types of glue are perceived to have the same properties as the umbrella brand and will do the 'job'.

Advertising needs to have dramatic qualities in order to attract attention and to build up a store of images that enable people to recall a brand of adhesives which do actually stick.

**Question:**  To what extent is the success of a functional position dependent on the quality of the attribute rather than the communications used to convey it?

**Task:**  Determine the key functions associated with a product category and then find communications that reflect those key functions.

## Viewpoint 6.4   Sit tight it's expressive positioning

The range of expressive positioning opportunities can vary from the subtle suggestion that a brand of hair colourant can change not only a person's ego and the way they feel they are perceived, to a more extreme, sometimes bizarre and remote expression of a brand's identity.

For example, much of Toshiba's communications have been product-led, partly a result of the dominant Japanese culture. Recent management changes in the UK operation have seen a move towards advertising and a position that hardly features the company's products. The award-winning 'Space Chair' ad takes viewers, seated on an ordinary living room chair, on a breathtaking journey to the edge of space. The goal was to communicate the amazing quality of the Toshiba viewing experience, delivered through sharper, smoother images that crisply define every cloud and every star. This form of ad not only helped Toshiba break away from its past, but also symbolised Toshiba's brand philosophy and positioning as a leader in innovation.

Filmed in the Nevada desert, a helium balloon was used to take the purpose-made, lightweight chair and Toshiba cameras, to 98,268 feet above the earth. After 83 minutes, the rig broke up and the chair took 24 minutes to crash back to earth.

*Source*:   Tylee (2010); Ball (2009).

**Question:**   What the advantages and disadvantages of using this type of expressive form of communication to position a brand?

**Task:**   Go to page 454 to see the press release relating to this piece.

**Exhibit 6.2**   **The 'Space Chair' falling towards Earth in Toshiba's ad**
*Source*: Toshiba

# Managing positions

The development and establishment of a position is a core strategic marketing communications activity. Positioning is one of two dynamics considered within communications strategy considered previously (Chapter 5). The first dynamic is concerned with who, in broad terms, is the target audience. End-user customers need to derive particular benefits based on perceived value from the exchange process. These benefits are very different from those that intermediaries expect to derive, or indeed any other stakeholder who does not consume the product or service. The second dynamic concerns the way in which an audience understands the offering they are experiencing either through use or through communications. The way in which people interpret messages and frame objects in their mind is concerned with positioning. Therefore, positioning is an integral part of marketing communications strategy.

In order that suitable positions be set, managers wishing to develop a position can be guided by the following process:

1. Determine the positions held by competitors. This will almost certainly require research to determine attitudes and perceptions and, possibly, the key attributes that consumers perceive as important. Use perceptual mapping.

2. From the above, it will be possible to determine which position, if any, is already held by the focus brand.

3. From the information gathered so far, will it be possible to determine a positioning strategy – that is, what is the desired position for the brand?

4. Is the strategy feasible in view of the competitors and any budgetary constraints? A long-term perspective is required, as the selected position has to be sustained.

5. Implement a programme to establish the desired position.

6. Monitor the perception held by consumers of the brand, and of their changing tastes and requirements, on a regular basis.

## Perceptual mapping

In order to determine how the various offerings are perceived in a market, the key attributes that stakeholders use to perceive products in the market need to be established. A great deal of this work will have been completed as part of the research and review process prior to developing a communications plan. The next task is to determine perceptions and preferences in respect of the key attributes as perceived by buyers.

The objective of the exercise is to produce a perceptual map (brand and multidimensional maps) where the dimensions used on the two axes are the key attributes, as seen by buyers. This map represents a geometric comparison of how competing products are perceived (Sinclair and Stalling, 1990). Figure 6.4 shows that consumers considered national/international and popular/exclusive as key dimensions in the airline market. Each airline is positioned on the

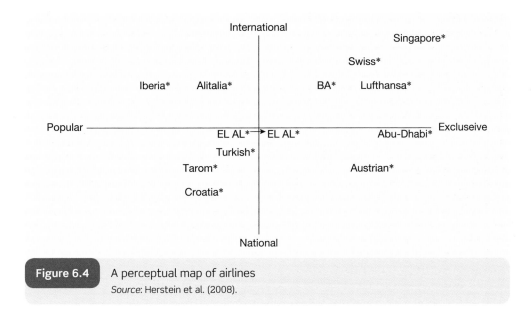

**Figure 6.4**    A perceptual map of airlines
*Source*: Herstein et al. (2008).

map according to the perception that buyers have of the strength of each attribute of each airline. By plotting the perceived positions of each brand on the map, an overall perspective of the market can be developed.

The closer airlines are clustered together, the greater the competition. The further apart the positions, the greater the opportunity to enter the market, as competition is less intense. From the map it can be seen that Croatia Airlines is perceived to be a strong national airline, whereas Swiss Air and Singapore Airlines are seen to be very international and exclusive. El Al was repositioned from being reasonably popular to one that was more exclusive, yet retained the same level of nationality. It may be that both Turkish and Tarom might find it less competitive if they attempted to become more popular and so provide a strong point of differentiation. However, such a move would only be endorsed if research showed that it would be acceptable to consumers, and profitable.

Substitute products are often uncovered by their closeness to each other (Day et al., 1979). It is also possible to ask buyers and other stakeholders what an ideal brand would consist of. This perfect brand can then be positioned on the map, and the closer an offering is to the ideal point, the greater its market share should be, as it is preferred over its rivals. These maps are known as *preference maps*.

By superimposing the position of an ideal brand on the map, it is possible to extend the usefulness of the tool. Perceptions of what constitutes the right amount of each key attribute can assist management in the positioning exercise. Marketing communications can, therefore, be designed to convey the required information about each attribute, thus adjusting buyers' perceptions so that they are closer to the ideal position, or to the position on the map that management wants the brand to occupy. For example, Austrian airlines may wish to reposition by changing the perception that users have of their exclusivity and relative unpopularity. Following any necessary adjustments to the routes followed and services provided, marketing communications would emphasise the popularity and accessibility attributes and hope to move it away from its association with exclusivity.

Neal (1980) offered the following reasons why perceptual mapping is such a powerful tool for examining the position of products:

1. It develops understanding of how the relative strengths and weaknesses of different products are perceived by buyers.

2. It builds knowledge about the similarities and dissimilarities between competing products.

3. It assists the process of repositioning existing products and the positioning of new products.

4. The technique helps to track the perception that buyers have of a particular product, and assists the measurement of the effectiveness of communication programmes and marketing actions intended to change buyers' perceptions.

Perceptual mapping is an important tool in the development and tracking of marketing communications strategy. It enables brand managers to identify gaps and opportunities in the market and allows organisations to monitor the effects of past marketing communications. For example, in the early 1980s none of the available brands in the newly emerging lager market was seen as refreshing. All brands were perceived as virtually the same. Heineken saw the opportunity and seized the position for refreshment, and has been able to occupy and sustain the position ever since.

# Positioning strategies

The development of positions that buyers can relate to and understand is an important and vital part of the marketing communications plan. In essence, the position adopted is a statement about what the brand is, what it stands for and the values and beliefs that customers (hopefully) will come to associate with the particular brand. The visual images or the position statement represented in the strapline may be a significant trigger that buyers use to recall images and associations of the brand.

There are a number of overall approaches to developing a position. These can be based on factors such as the market, the customer or redefining the appeal of the brand itself.

To implement these three broad approaches, various strategies have been developed. The list that follows is not intended to be comprehensive or to convey the opinion that these strategies are discrete. They are presented here as means of conveying the strategic style, but in reality a number of hybrid strategies are often used.

## Product features

This is one of the easier concepts and one that is more commonly adopted. The brand is set apart from the competition on the basis of the attributes, features or benefits that the brand has relative to the competition. For example, Red Bull gives you energy; Weetabix contains all the vitamins needed each day; and the Royal Bank of Scotland promotes its credit card by extolling the benefits of its interest rate compared with those of its competitors.

## Price/quality

This strategy is more effectively managed than others because price itself can be a strong communicator of quality. A high price denotes high quality, just as a low price can deceive buyers into thinking a product to be of low quality and poor value. Retail outlets such as Harrods and Aspreys use high prices to signal high quality and exclusivity. At the other end of the retail spectrum, Matalan, BHS and Primark position themselves to attract those with less disposable income and to whom convenience is of greater importance. The price/quality appeal used to be best observed in Sainsbury's, 'where good food costs less' before it was changed, and with the alcoholic lager Stella Artois, which was positioned as 'refreshingly expensive'.

## Use

By informing markets of when or how a product can be used, a position can be created in the minds of the buyers. For example, Kellogg's, the breakfast cereal manufacturer, repositioned itself as a snack food provider. Its marketing strategy of moving into new markets was founded on its over-dependence on breakfast consumption. By becoming associated with snacks, not only is usage increased, but the opportunity to develop new products becomes feasible. The launch of Pop Tarts is a testimony to this strategy. Milky Way, 'the sweet you can eat between meals', informs just when it is permissible to eat chocolate, and After Eight chocolate mints clearly indicate when they should be eaten. The hair shampoo Wash & Go positions the brand as a quick and easy-to-use (convenience) product, for those whose lifestyles are full and demanding.

## Product class dissociation

Some markets are essentially uninteresting, and most other positions have been adopted by competitors. A strategy used by margarine manufacturers is to disassociate themselves from other margarines and associate themselves with what was commonly regarded as a superior product, butter. The moisturising bar Dove is positioned as 'not a soap'. The UK-based bank, NatWest, position themselves with the strapline, 'Another way', which suggests that their approach is different from their competitors. The foundation for their claim is based on their prominent use of local branches and of UK-based call centres. This is to counter the perception that other banks provide poor-quality international support for their Internet banking operations. The position, therefore, sets out to promise customers that NatWest are different from other banks and offer better services and customer care.

## User

A sensible extension of the target marketing process is to position openly so that target users can be clearly identified. Flora margarine was for men, and then it became 'for all the family'. Perfumes are not only endorsed by celebrities but some celebrities launch their own perfume brands, such as Katie Price, Christina Aguilera, Kate Moss, David Beckham, Donald Trump, Cliff Richard and of course, Beyoncé, Britney Spears and Paul Smith. Some hotels position themselves as places for weekend breaks, as leisure centres or as conference centres. The cookware brand Le Creuset repositioned itself to appeal to a younger customer segment.

## Competitor

For a long time, positioning oneself against a main competitor was regarded as dangerous and was avoided. Avis, however, performed very successfully 'trying even harder' against Hertz, the industry number one. Saab contested the 'safest car' position with Volvo and Qualcast took on its new rival, the hover mower, by informing everyone that 'it is a lot less bovver than a hover', because its product collected the grass cuttings and produced the manicured lawn finish that roller-less mowers cannot reproduce.

| Exhibit 6.3 | **Britney Spears perfume** |
| --- | --- |
| | *Source*: Elizabeth Arden, Inc. |

## Benefit

Positions can also be established by proclaiming the benefits that usage confers on those who consume. Sensodyne toothpaste appeals to all those who suffer from sensitive teeth, and a vast number of pain relief formulations claim to smooth away headaches or relieve aching limbs, sore throats or some offending part of the anatomy. Daewoo entered the UK market offering car buyers convenience by removing dealerships and the inherent difficulties associated with buying and maintaining cars.

## Heritage or cultural symbol

An appeal to cultural heritage and tradition, symbolised by age, particular heraldic devices or visual cues, has been used by many organisations to convey quality, experience and knowledge. Kronenbourg 1664, 'Established since 1803', and the use of coats of arms by many universities to represent depth of experience and a sense of permanence are just some of the historical themes used to position organisations.

Whatever the position adopted by a brand or organisation, both the marketing and communication mixes must endorse and support the position so that there is consistency throughout all communications. For example, if a high-quality position is taken, such as that of the Ritz Carlton Hotel Group, then the product quality must be relatively high compared with competitors, the price must be correspondingly excessive and distribution synonymous with quality and exclusivity. Sales promotion activity will be minimal in order not to convey a touch of inexpensiveness, and advertising messages should be visually affluent and rich in tone and copy, with public relations and personal selling approaches transmitting high-quality, complementary cues.

The dimensions used to position brands must be relevant and important to the target audience and in the image cues used must be believable and consistently credible. Positioning strategies should be developed over the long term if they are to prove effective, although minor adaptions to the position can be carried out in order to reflect changing environmental conditions.

# Repositioning

Technology continues to develop rapidly, consumer tastes and behaviours are evolving and new and substitute offerings enter the market. This dynamic perspective of markets means that the relative positions occupied by offerings in the minds of consumers will be challenged and shifted on a frequent basis. If the position adopted by an offering is strong, if it was the first to claim the position and the position is being continually reinforced with clear simple messages, then there may be little need to alter the position originally adopted.

However, there are occasions when offerings need to be repositioned in the minds of consumers/stakeholders. This may be due to market opportunities and development, mergers and acquisitions or changing buyer preferences, which may be manifested in declining sales. Research may reveal that the current position is either inappropriate or superseded by a competitor, or that attitudes have changed or preferences been surpassed; whatever the reason, repositioning is required if past success is to be maintained. However, repositioning is difficult to accomplish, often because of the entrenched perceptions and attitudes held by buyers towards brands and the vast (media) resources required to make the changes. Google began to reposition itself as a collaborative, technology brand, rather than a media company focused on aggregating and distributing content (Boyd, 2010).

Jewell (2007) draws attention to the need to consider repositioning from a customer's perspective, something neglected in the literature. He also shows that two key tasks need to be accomplished during a repositioning exercise. First, the old positioning needs to be suppressed so that customers no longer relate to it and second, consumers need to learn the new position. These twin tasks are complementary, as interference or rather the deliberate weakening of the old position will help strengthen acceptance of the new position.

---

**Scholar's paper 6.4**    **Repositioning through interference**

**Jewell, R.D. (2007) Establishing effective repositioning communications in a competitive marketplace, *Journal of Marketing Communications*, 13(4), 231–41.**

This paper considers positioning from a consumer's perspective, rather than through the traditional manufacturer's lens. Product positioning is important to marketers because it can influence consumers. The author proposes that successful repositioning should be based not only on the audience learning the new positioning but also on interfering with competitors' communications in order to inhibit messages about the previous positioning.

---

# Key points

- Objectives play an important role in the activities of individuals, social groups and organisations for a variety of reasons. These include providing direction and an action focus for all those participating in the activity, a means by which the variety of decisions relating to an activity can be made in a consistent way, and they set out the time period in which the activity is to be completed. In addition, they communicate the values and scope of the activity to all participants and finally, they provide a means by which the success of the activity can be evaluated.

- The use of objectives in the management process is vital if an organisation's desired outcomes are to be achieved. Each of the objectives, at corporate, unit and functional levels, contributes to the formulation of the communication objectives. They are all interlinked, interdependent, multiple and often conflicting.

- The various organisational objectives are of little use if they are not communicated to those who need to know what they are. Traditionally, such communication has focused on employees, but there is increasing recognition that the other members of the stakeholder network need to understand an organisation's purpose and objectives.

- The major task for communication objectives is twofold: first, to contribute to the overall direction of the organisation by fulfilling the communication requirements of the marketing mix; second, to communicate the corporate thrust and values to various stakeholders so that they understand the organisation, can respond to its intentions and help develop appropriate relationships.

- Communication objectives are derived from an initial review of the current situation and the marketing plan requirements. They are not a replication of the marketing objectives but a distillation of the research activities that have been undertaken subsequently.

- There are three main streams of objectives. The first concerns issues relating to the buyers of the product or service offered by the organisation. The second concerns issues relating to market share/sales volume, profitability and revenue. The third stream relates to the image, reputation and preferences that other stakeholders have towards the organisation.

- The IPA has identified a hierarchy of brand communication objectives following their analysis of effective campaigns. These are business, behavioural, and intermediate goals.

- Communication objectives consist of two main elements: sales-oriented and communication-oriented. A balance between the two will be determined by the situation facing the organisation, but can be a mixture of both product and corporate tasks. These objectives, once quantified, need to be ranked and weighted in order that other components of the plan can be developed.

- To assist managers in their need to develop suitable objectives, a set of guidelines has been developed, commonly referred to as SMART objectives. This acronym stands for specific, measurable, achievable, relevant, targeted and timed.

- The position adopted is a statement about what the brand is, what it stands for and the values and beliefs that customers (hopefully) will come to associate with the particular brand. Visual and text/copy images or the position statement represented in a strapline may be a significant trigger that buyers use to recall images and associations of the brand.

- There are two main ways in which a brand can be positioned; these are functional and expressive (or symbolic) positioning. Functionally positioned brands stress the features and benefits, and expressive brands emphasise the ego, social and hedonic satisfactions that a brand can bring.

- A perceptual map represents a geometric comparison of how competing products are perceived by customers, based on important attributes. Each product is positioned on the map according to the perception that buyers have of the strength of each attribute of each product. By plotting the perceived positions of each brand on the map, an overall perspective of the market can be developed and strategies formed to develop clearer, more rewarding positions.

- There are a number of overall approaches that can be used to develop a position. These can be based on factors such as the market, the customer or redefining the appeal of the brand itself. To implement these three broad approaches, various strategies have been developed. These include product features, price/quality, use, product class dissociation, user, competitor, benefit and heritage or use of cultural symbols.

# Review questions

1. Why do organisations use objectives as part of their planning processes?

2. What should a mission statement clearly identify?

3. Suggest three reasons why the setting of promotional objectives is important.

4. Write a brief report arguing the case both for and against the use of an increase in sales as the major objective of all promotional activities.

5. Repeat the exercise as for the previous question, but this time focus on communication-based objectives.

6. How and from where are promotional objectives derived?

7. Why is positioning an important part of marketing communications? Use the Juan Valdez mini case to illustrate your response.

8. What is perceptual mapping?

9. Select four print advertisements for the same product category and comment on the positions they have adopted.

10. What are the main positioning strategies?

# References

Ball, K. (2009) Toshiba premieres new 'Space Chair' ad campaign – Campaign to support Toshiba's SV REGZA LCD TV and Satellite T series laptops, *Toshiba Social Media News Release*, 16 November, retrieved 21 July 2010 from http://socialnews.toshiba.co.uk/?ReleaseID=14262.

Barry, T. and Howard, D.J. (1990) A review and critique of the hierarchy of effects in advertising, *International Journal of Advertising*, 9, 121–35.

Binet, L. and Field, P. (2007) *Marketing in an era of accountability*, Henley: IPA-WARC.

Blankson, C. and Kalafatis, S.P. (2007) Positioning strategies of international and multicultural-orientated service brands, *Journal of Services Marketing*, 21(6), 435–450.

Boyd, M. (2010) Google shows adland the new tools of its trade, *Campaign*, 25 June, p. 11.

Colley, R. (1961) *Defining Advertising Goals for Measured Advertising Results*, New York: Association of National Advertisers.

Day, G., Shocker, A.D. and Srivastava, R.K. (1979) Customer orientated approaches to identifying product markets, *Journal of Marketing*, 43(4), 8–19.

Dutka, S. (1995) *Defining Advertising Goals for Measured Advertising Results*, 2nd edn., New York: Association of National Advertisers.

Earnest (2011) B2B Marketing Awards 2011; Grand Prix Winner: Thunderhead, *B2B Marketing Awards – The Winners*, 20 October, p. 42.

Fuchs, C. and Diamantopoulos, A. (2010) Evaluating the effectiveness of brand-positioning strategies from a consumer perspective, *European Journal of Marketing*, 44(11/12), 1763–86.

Heath, R. (2009) Emotional Engagement: How Television Builds Big Brands At Low Attention, *Journal of Advertising Research*, March, 62–73.

Herstein, R. and Mitki, Y. (2008) How El Al Airlines transformed its service strategy with employee participation, *Strategy & Leadership*, 36(3), 21–5.

Jewell, R.D. (2007) Establishing effective repositioning communications in a competitive marketplace, *Journal of Marketing Communications*, 13(4), 231–41.

Johnson, G., Whittington, R. and Scholes, K. (2011) *Exploring Strategy: Text and Cases*, 9th edn., Harlow: Prentice-Hall.

King, S. (1991) Brand building in the 1990s, *Journal of Marketing Management*, 7, 3–13.

Kotler, P. (2003) *Marketing Management – Analysis, Planning, Implementation and Control*, 11th edn., Englewood Cliffs, NJ: Prentice-Hall.

Kriegel, R.A. (1986) How to choose the right communications objectives, *Business Marketing* (April), 94–106.

Kurata, P. (2008) Juan Valdez Travels the World, Sends Profits Home to Colombia, America.gov, 9 April, retrieved 24 May 2012 from http://www.america.gov/st/business-english/2008/April/20080409101828cpataruk0.7881891.html.

Neal, W.D. (1980) Strategic product positioning: a step by step guide, *Business (USA)* (May/June), 34–40.

Paajanen, S. (2012) Who is Juan Valdez? This face has been selling Colombian coffee for over 40 years, retrieved 24 May 2012 from http://coffeetea.about.com/cs/culture/a/juanvaldez.htm.

Quinn, J.B., Mintzberg, H., James, R.M., Lampel, J.B. and Ghosal, S. (2003) *The Strategy Process*, 4th edn., New York: Prentice-Hall.

Ramirez-Vallejo, J. (2003) Colombian Coffee, *ReVista: Harvard Review of Latin America*, retrieved 24 May 2012 from http://www.drclas.harvard.edu/revista/articles/view/273.

Ries, A. and Trout, J. (1972) The positioning era cometh, *Advertising Age*, 24 April, 35–8.

Rossiter, J.R. and Percy, L. (1987) *Advertising and Promotion Management*, Lexington, MA: McGraw-Hill.

Sinclair, S.A. and Stalling, E.C. (1990) Perceptual mapping: a tool for industrial marketing: a case study, *Journal of Business and Industrial Marketing*, 5(1), 55–65.

Tylee, J. (2010) The man who revealed Toshiba's emotional side, *Campaign*, 14 May, p. 16.

# Chapter 7

## The communication industry: structure, operations and issues

The communication industry, in all parts of the world, has been subject to a variety of influences and pressures. These range from the severe economic trading conditions, and changing consumer behaviours, to the restructuring undertaken by agencies and clients, the rapid developments in digital technologies, and the changing legislation and regulations governing the sector.

### Aims and learning objectives

The aim of this chapter is to explore issues relating to the communications industry, including the structure, the types of organisations involved and the operations and processes used to develop marketing communications for clients.

The learning objectives of this chapter are to:

1. provide an introductory understanding of the nature of the communications industry;

2. consider the nature and role of the main types of organisations involved in the industry;

3. consider the principal methods and operations used within agencies to meet their clients' needs;

4. explore relationships and methods of remuneration used within the industry;

5. examine industry issues in the light of the development of integrated marketing communications;

6. anticipate some of the future trends that might affect the industry.

# Minicase

## Diageo: reaching underage drinkers

For a long time beer and wine were the dominant forms of alcohol consumed by young people in the USA. Distilled spirits were perceived to be the choice of older people. This was partly the legacy of prohibition when distilled spirits were considered to be dangerous drinks because of their high alcohol content. They were also linked to organised crime and moonshining. Beer and wine were seen as moderate drinks. As if to reinforce this, regulators had established three key policies:

1. Distilled spirits were taxed at much higher rates per unit of alcohol, than beer and wine.

2. The types of retail outlets where distilled spirits could be sold were strictly limited and controlled, thereby restricting the availability of distilled brands.

3. Both beer and wine were allowed to be advertised on electronic media (television and radio). Distilled spirits were not allowed to advertise through these media, by voluntary agreement.

These policies helped secure and make the market for brewers increasingly attractive. For example, Philip Morris, at the time the world's largest tobacco company, bought Miller Beer. This enabled them to use and adapt their tobacco marketing strategies to the beer industry, and in so doing transform the beer market. The result was a sharp upward investment in television advertising, youth-oriented advertising copy became commonplace, and the two brands that dominated the beer market, Miller and Anheuser Busch, became fierce competitors.

In addition, there were some significant contextual elements that impacted the marketing strategies of both brewers and distillers. One of these was the population shift into the suburbs, thereby generating a proliferation of convenience stores. Beer and tobacco became key staples of these new retail outlets. As a general rule convenience stores did not sell distilled spirits, so the gap between the number of beer and distilled spirits retailers grew.

Brewers also started to centralise their brewing processes, establishing high-tech breweries which produced huge volumes that generated economies of scale. This led to significant reductions in the cost per unit and enabled brewers to reduce beer prices, relative to the cost of living and inflation. In addition

to this, tax differentials meant that distilled spirit prices were higher than were those of beer.

The key long-term advantage of this situation for brewers lay in the role underage drinking generally plays in the alcohol market. In the USA alcohol consumption is not permitted before the age of 21. However, US statistics show significant underage drinking, and of these those who begin drinking before they are 15 are much more likely to become heavy consumers. Incidentally, they are also more likely to experience a wider range of alcohol problems than those who wait until age 21 years.

According to a National Research Council/Institute of Medicine report, underage drinking generates between $10 and $20 billion in annual revenues. If beer was the choice of the young, distillers were not only losing revenues to beer in the short term but they were also faced with a declining market in the long term, as underage drinkers became adults.

Market predictions indicated that the increasing numbers of young consumers would further the decline of distilled spirits. However, at the end of the 1990s the growth in beer consumption started to flatten out, while that of distilled spirits grew rapidly. In particular brands of 'white spirits' such as vodka, rum, and tequila became increasingly popular, whereas 'brown spirits' such as whiskeys and bourbons, were perceived to have a harsh taste. Some argue that the reason for this revolution is youth-marketing innovation, as demonstrated by Diageo's entry into the market.

In 1997 Grand Metropolitan and Guinness merged to form Diageo, a British-based multinational corporation, and the largest distilled spirits producer in the world. Diageo realised they had to stop and reverse the downward sales trend of their core brands in the United States.

Their response was to develop a marketing strategy designed around their white distilled spirits brands that could be mixed with fruit flavours and sugar to create a drink similar to traditional soft drinks, which were the most popular commercial drink in the US market, particularly among young people. Public health groups were to refer to these as 'alcopops'.

Diageo's strategy was to reposition their Smirnoff Vodka brand. This involved three key components:

1. Develop new products that tasted like soft drinks.
2. Market the Smirnoff Vodka brand name as a malt-based drink. This enabled it to compete with beer on price, availability, and advertising.
3. Reposition Smirnoff Vodka as a young person's brand by adding new fruit flavours and using other youth marketing practices and innovative practices.

In 1999 both the federal and state regulators accepted Diageo's claim that Smirnoff Ice was a 'flavoured malt drink' and that it should be regulated as a beer because the production process started with beer.

Following this decision, Diageo were free to adopt marketing strategies associated with the beer industry, and this involved heavy advertising investment. In 2002 only the four most popular beer brands (Bud Light, Miller Lite, Budweiser, and Coors Light) had higher electronic media advertisement spending than Smirnoff Ice.

Smirnoff Ice advertising shot up from 2 to 50 per cent of all alcopop advertising between 2000 and 2001, and Diageo invested nearly $50 million in 2002.

They used a range of media, including television, radio, magazines, newspapers, and outdoor platforms. Unsurprisingly Smirnoff Ice quickly became the dominant drink in the alcopop category. Between 2000 and 2002 Diageo increased their market share in the alcopop market from 0.6 to 29.0 per cent.

It is alleged that Diageo placed their Smirnoff Ice advertising in media vehicles with relatively large youth audiences. The Center for Alcohol Marketing and Youth (CAMY) reported that Smirnoff Ice had the highest number of television advertisements placed on programmes that overexposed this younger generation.

Diageo coordinated the marketing strategies for Smirnoff Vodka and Smirnoff Ice in an attempt to encourage consumer associations between the two products. They created numerous fruit-flavoured Smirnoff Vodka Twist flavours that had similar tastes, containers, advertising, and flavourings as the Smirnoff Twisted V alcopop brands.

In addition to heavy television advertising, Diageo started to use digital marketing. Through the use of

**Exhibit 7.1**    **Not only is underage drinking an issue for drinks companies and society, but binge drinking is also a major concern**
*Source*: Ace Stock Limited/Alamy

interactive websites, positioning on social network sites such as Facebook, Internet games, YouTube videos, and viral marketing, Diageo were able to reach a high proportion of underage youths. This medium is largely unregulated and in 2010 Diageo allocated 21 per cent of their marketing budget to digital advertising.

Diageo's public relations strategy also played a significant role in reversing the trends. Its purpose was to convince stakeholders, most notably, regulators, public health and medical groups, plus of course the public, that the company was committed to deterring underage drinking and other social harms associated with its products. They used broadcast 'responsibility' ads, instituted fund prevention programmes designed to educate, raise public awareness, and communicate responsible retail practices. They also built partnerships with medical and public health organisations and government agencies, and established industry-based 'social aspects' organisations.

Although beer remains the dominant beverage of choice among all drinkers, distilled spirits have experienced a 16 per cent increase in per capita alcohol consumption since 1999, whereas beer has shown a 2 per cent decline. However, underage drinking is said to constitute a public health crisis in the USA. The extent to which the marketing practices of companies such as Diageo have contributed to this situation is debatable, not confined to the USA, nor this category of drinks.

*This case was written by Chris Fill and is based on a number of resources including a paper by Mosher (2012).*

# Introduction

The marketing communications industry consists of four principal actors or types of stakeholders. These are the media, clients, who fund the whole process, agencies, historically the most notable of which are advertising agencies, and finally the thousands of support organisations, such as production companies and fulfilment houses, that enable the whole communication process to function. At the centre of this theatre are consumers, audiences who engage with the output with varying levels of intensity and involvement.

It is the operations and relationships between these organisations and, increasingly, audiences that not only drive the industry but also form an important context within which marketing communications can be understood. Figure 7.1 sets out the main actor organisations in the industry.

There is an argument that organisations should manage and develop their marketing communications 'in-house' – that is, do it themselves. This could enable better control and lower costs. However, this argument is now very weak due to the increasing complexity and diversity of communication activities and the restructuring of organisations aimed at de-layering and hollowing out their organisations. It can only be through outsourcing that organisations experience increased levels of flexibility and gain access to the special skills and expertise necessary to engage audiences in competitive environments.

One of the many decisions an organisation has to make is whether to employ people on a permanent basis, recruit temporary workers as demand requires or use specialists on a continuous or ad hoc basis. Most organisations use a mixture of these different types and adjust the balance between them according to trading and other environmental factors.

With regard to marketing communications, organisations can do it themselves and develop what is called an 'in-house facility'. This provides a good level of control over the tools, messages and media used, and can improve on the speed of decision making, compared to using an outside agency. On the other hand, it increases fixed costs, reduces flexibility and introduces political dimensions, often around budgets, which tend to deflect from objectivity

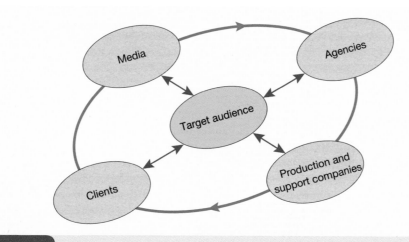

| Figure 7.1 | The key stakeholders in the marketing communications industry |

and creativity. Perhaps the most critical dimension concerns the lack of access to expertise. In an age where integration is a popular concept, it is important to have access to experts in the various communication disciplines. It is extremely unlikely that such experts can be readily found in-house. Having said this, many retail and business-to-business organisations choose to use in-house facilities, if only because of a lack of resources.

An alternative route is to use freelancers or self-employed consultants. Although each individual's skills may have been developed within a particular discipline, such as public relations or advertising, freelancers can provide flexibility and access to some experts through their network of personal contacts. However, it should be remembered that the use of freelancers and in-house facilities requires use of the client organisation's resources, if only to manage the freelancers. Crowd-sourcing, the use of the public to generate creative advertising content, is an attempt by clients to circumnavigate the agency sector in order to find new material and cut costs. This form of user-generated content is explored in more detail later in the text (Chapter 25).

The use of agencies is popular because they can provide objectivity, access to expertise and specialist technologies while at the same time allowing the client to concentrate on their core business activities. Indeed, this is the route taken by the vast majority of organisations who regard the use of communication agencies in the same way as they do accountants, consultants, lawyers and other professionals. By outsourcing these activities, organisations buy experts whose specialist services can be used as and when required. This flexibility has proved to be both efficient and effective for both client and agency. However, the decision to use an agency leads to further questions to be resolved: which type of agency and what do we want them to do, how many agencies should we use and what role should the client play in the relationship with the agency?

These may sound strange questions, but consider the question of strategy. Should the client decide on the marketing communications, branding and positioning strategies or is this a part of the agency's tasks? Different client organisations will adopt different positions depending upon their experience, size and the nature of the task that needs to be undertaken. Another question concerns whether a single agency is required to deliver integrated marketing communication activities, whether a single agency should manage the integration process and sub-contract tasks to other specialist or group-based agencies (and in doing so act as lead agency) or whether a series of specialist agencies should be appointed, each reporting to the client.

# Dimensions of the UK marketing communications industry

It is useful to consider the size and value of the industry by considering the sums of money spent by clients on marketing communications. Some of these figures are acknowledged to be estimates, and there is some evidence of 'double counting' (one or more sectors claiming part of the overall spend for itself), so any figures produced cannot be seen as being totally accurate. That said, however, the total spend for advertising, as can be seen from Table 7.1, was £16.2 billion in 2011.

The Institute of Promotional Marketing claims that the growth of sales promotion has been 'explosive'. However, measuring the growth is problematic because there are no rate cards (price lists) and the breadth of activities that are attributable to sales promotion are many and varied. As a broad estimate, the annual investment in sales promotion can be considered to be approximately £11–13 billion. Although not yet formally exceeding the spend on advertising, it is widely believed inside the industry that sales promotion may have overtaken advertising in terms of the proportion of client spend, in particular sectors.

Estimates vary, mainly because of problems of definition, but of the other areas in the industry sponsorship has grown significantly. The European Sponsorship Association (ESA) estimates the size of the European sponsorship industry at €23.33bn (£19 billion) (www.sponsorship-awards.co.uk).

Accounting for the huge breadth in what can be classified as direct marketing activities can lead to double counting. There is no doubt that the direct marketing industry contributes enormously to the economy, but activity levels are normally referred to in terms of direct mail, as this can be measured more precisely. Since a peak of £2.3 billion in 2006, investment and growth in direct mail has fallen to £1.7 billion in 2011 (http://expenditurereport.warc.com/).

Publicly available figures regarding the size of the public relations, exhibitions and indeed direct marketing industries are based on value and contribution to the economy. These are not the same as what has been invested in each activity by clients. However, in terms of providing some comparison, public relations can be considered in terms of £8 billion and exhibitions £800 million per year. Expenditure patterns do change, albeit at different rates, but, given the domination of advertising and sales promotion, the overall balance is unlikely to change dramatically in the short term. However, it is clearly important for those responsible for the future and current planning of marketing communications activities to monitor trends,

| Table 7.1 | Total UK advertising expenditure (including direct mail) £ million | | |
|---|---|---|---|
| | **2011 (£m)\*** | **2006 (£m)** | **2000 (£m)** |
| Press | 3,945 | 8,346 | 8,604 |
| Television (excl. sponsorship) | 4,159 | 4,594 | 4,646 |
| Direct mail | 1,729 | 2,322 | 2,049 |
| Outdoor and transit | 886 | 1,084 | 810 |
| Radio | 427 | 534 | 595 |
| Cinema | 182 | 188 | 128 |
| Internet | 4,784 | 2,016 | 155 |
| **Total** | **16,182** | **19,084** | **16,988** |

*Source*: http://expenditurereport.warc.com/. Used with permission from WARC.

particularly those in the fastest growing sectors of the industry, in order to identify and target creative opportunities.

Having painted a picture of the size and dynamics of the industry, a word needs to be said about the consumer view of the industry. Here issues about ethics and morality surface, accompanied by a suggestion that the public view the industry with cynicism and distrust. Mitchell (2012) reports that the chief executive of the Advertising Association said that: 'Advertising is facing a problem, favourability has evaporated, the public's trust and confidence in (it) has fallen through the floor and the industry has missed a trick by failing to renegotiate its deal with society in which it operates.' He continued by commenting on the increasing media criticism and the number of people calling for more regulation.

Some of the problems faced by the advertising/communications industry have been revealed by Gordon cited by Mitchell (2012) as bombardment, intrusiveness, poor creativity, irrelevance and condescension. Much of this is seen to be a function of the increasing power, often afforded by technology, that consumers have experienced in recent years. It can be argued that consumers today are not so reliant on ads as they can now search, compare, contrast, ask friends and peers and use ads. According to Research Director Karen Fraser at Credos, this means that ads are not so critical in the decision-making process as they used to be (Bain, 2012).

# Structure and development of the marketing communications industry

As with any industry, growth and development spawn new types and structures. Adaptation to the environment is important for survival. The same applies to the marketing communications industry, where, to take the advertising industry as an example, many organisational configurations have evolved. Before considering some of the structural issues, it is useful to understand the main types of organisation that populate the industry. These are set out at Figure 7.1.

Clients can decide to undertake the communications functions in-house. However, this is both costly and inefficient, and most outsource their requirements. Of the four main groups, the production and media houses require that the clients and agencies agree and specify campaigns in order that they are able to contribute. So, to some extent therefore, agencies and clients are the lead players in this industry.

## Agency types and structures

The marketing communications industry consists of a number of different types of organisations whose purpose is to enable clients to communicate effectively and efficiently with their target audiences. Essentially, clients appoint agents to develop and implement campaigns on their behalf. To accomplish this, advertising agencies buy media time and space from media owners, public relations agencies place stories with the media for their clients' representation, and other agencies undertake a range of other communications activities on behalf of their clients.

Originally, advertising agents undertook two main roles, creative message design and media planning and buying. The media component has subsequently been spun off to specialist agencies. However, the interest in and drive towards integrated marketing communications, have helped agents assume new, more independent roles in the communications industry.

The development of digital media has had a profound impact on the public relations industry and the development of integrated marketing communications. For example, agencies that can form teams of specialists who can work across different audiences, yet provide an integrated approach, are much sought after by clients (Wilson, 2009). Ideally these teams should consist of 12 members. Too many, and ineffectiveness becomes an issue; too few and creativity is sacrificed. The real difficulty that Wilson identifies is how to ensure all 12 are client-focused.

In addition to this, White (2007) identifies several pressures working on agencies. These are the growth in importance of direct marketing, the increasing range of media and the need among large organisations for quasi-global ad networks. The result of this development is that a number of different types of agencies have emerged, all of which seek to fulfil particular roles.

### Full-service agencies

The full-service agency offers the full range of services that a client requires in order to advertise its products and services. Agencies such as J. Walter Thompson and Leo Burnett offer a full service consisting of strategic planning, research, creative development, production, media planning and buying, and evaluation services. Very often these are offered on a global basis, but this does not mean a full-service agency needs to be large, employing thousands of people. Some mid-size agencies employing a couple of dozen people can offer a full service. Whatever the size, some of these activities may be subcontracted, but overall responsibility rests with the full-service agency. Further discussion of some of the issues concerning full-service agencies follows later.

### Boutiques

A derivative of this type of agency is the boutique or creative shop, which often forms when creative personnel (teams) leave full-service agencies to set up their own business. Boutiques provide specialist or niche services for clients such as copyrighting, developing creative content and other artistic services. These agencies provide clients with an alternative source of ideas, new ways of thinking about a problem, issue or product. Clients choose to use them because they either wish to use particular styles and approaches for their creative work or they want to generate a raft of creative ideas.

---

### Viewpoint 7.1    Agencies cluster into groups

The larger agencies are normally part of a global communication group. WPP is one of the world's leading communications services groups with 2011 revenues of some £10 billion, and profits of £1 billion. Formed in 1985 by Sir Martin Sorrell as a small holding company for marketing services companies, the WPP Group now provides services across communications disciplines, media and information. Advertising agencies include J. Walter Thompson, and Young & Rubicam, direct marketing agency OgilvyOne, and media planning agency Mindshare.

Clients include over 350 companies from the Fortune Global 500, operating in over 100 countries. WPP represents at least three communications disciplines for over 700 clients and for almost 350 clients in six or more countries. Major clients include HSBC, Unilever, Vodafone, Procter & Gamble, Ford and Shell.

In terms of coordination, over 300 clients work with three or more WPP companies, 150 clients work with four or more and over 100 clients are served in six or more countries. North America accounts for 35 per cent of WPP's revenues and the UK 12 per cent. Latin America is identified as WPP's strongest growth region and accounts for 12 per cent of revenues.

Other major groups competing alongside WPP on a global scale include Omnicom, Interpublic, Publicis, Havas and Dentsu. Dentsu has its origins in Japan, being formed in 1901 as the Japan Advertising Service and Telegraphic Service Co. The Dentsu Group now operates via a global network although, unlike WPP, which is a conglomerate of individual agencies, acquired over a period of time and retaining their individual identities, Dentsu is a single-branded agency with all parts of the network operating under the Dentsu name. Major clients include Canon, Hitachi, Tetley and Omega. In July 2012 Dentsu announced that it had bought the London-based Aegis Group in a cash deal worth $4.9 billion. This makes Dentsu the number 1 agency is Asia Pacific, and the second largest agency in Western Europe.

*Sources*:   Based on Sweney (2011); Beattie (2012); www.wpp.com, www.dentsu.com.

**Question:**   Why is Latin America considered to be a growth area for WPP?

**Task:**   List the advantages and disadvantages of WPP'S individual approach to agency identity compared to Dentsu's single brand identity.

## Media specialists

Similarly, media specialists provide clients with media services expertise. These organisations deliver media strategy and consulting services for both client advertisers and agencies. Their core business, however, is focused on the planning, scheduling, buying and monitoring of a client's media schedule. Child (2007) reports that advertisers believe the role of strategic media planning is 50 per cent more important today than it was seven years ago. The key advantage of using a media specialist is that they have the capacity to buy media time and space at rates far lower than a client or advertising agency can procure them. This is because of the sheer volume of business that media specialists buy. Child also believes that there are some indications that clients believe it is more important to have a global media network rather than a global advertising agency.

Two main forms of media specialist have emerged: media independents, where the organisation is owned and run free of the direction and policy requirements of a full-service agency, and media dependents, where the organisation is a subsidiary of a creative or full-service organisation. The largest dependent in Britain is ZenithOptimedia, owned originally by Saatchi & Saatchi, and the largest independent is Carat.

## Digital media

The development of digital media agencies is the inevitable consequence of the huge and rapid growth of the digital media industry. The growth has come from two main areas. The first concerns the surge of online brands that hit the market full of expectation of transforming the way business is conducted. The second concerns established offline brands seeking to reach customers by adding interactive capabilities to their marketing channels.

The market can be considered in terms of a spectrum of activities. At one end are those agencies that are marketing-oriented and at the other are technology-based organisations. Real growth is likely to develop in the middle with organisations referred to as 'interactive architects' who can offer a blend of skills and consultancy services. Merger and acquisition activity has been intense, mainly a reaction to rapid industry growth, which was not capable of being sustained. The move towards what is referred to as 'integrated marketing communications' (see Chapter 10) has been accelerated by the greater efficiency and harmonisation that digital technology can bring. However, one trend emerging from this changing environment is a polarisation around either traditional or digital work. There is a general absence of agencies that can work in both arenas (Grosso et al., 2006) and one of the outcomes of this skill shortage is that spending on online ads might slow.

## A la carte

Partly in response to the changing needs of clients and consumers, many organisations require greater flexibility in the way their advertising is managed. Consequently, these clients prefer to use the services of a range of organisations. So, the planning skills of a full-service agency, the creative talent of a particular boutique and the critical mass of a media-buying independent provide an *à la carte* approach. This approach requires the client advertiser to manage the entire marketing communication process, an 'in-house' arrangement. This process enables improved flexibility yet demands strong management coordination and control as the process is more complex and problematic.

## Other communication agencies

The agencies and organisations set out so far in this chapter have their roots and core business firmly set within the advertising part of the communications industry. In addition to these there is a raft of other agencies, each specialising in a particular aspect of the marketing communications industry. So, there are agencies that provide sales promotion, public relations, sponsorship, field marketing and direct marketing. Their structure and operations reflect the needs of their market specialism, and many are based on the principles through which the advertising agencies operate.

## Direct marketing agencies

Direct marketing has become a significant and influential part of the marketing communications industry. Direct marketing and direct response agencies create and deliver campaigns through direct mail, telemarketing or through a variety of offline and online media, which is referred to as direct response media.

One of the distinguishing elements of a direct marketing agency is the database. These agencies maintain large databases that contain mailing lists. These data can be merged and reconstructed to reflect a client's target market. The agency helps to develop promotional materials and then implements the campaign through the data list. Direct agencies will either own or have access to a fulfilment house. These organisations fulfil customer orders – that is, process the order and take payment resulting from the direct marketing campaign, send out the ordered products and deal with after-sales services as necessary.

---

### Scholars' paper 7.1    Grandstanding Amsterdam

**Röling, R.W. (2010) Small Town, Big Campaigns: The Rise and Growth of an International Advertising Industry in Amsterdam, *Regional Studies*, 44(7), August, 829–843.**

For those interested in international advertising this paper provides an interesting analysis through the use of 'four waves of advertising' from early twentieth-century Western capitalism. This analysis considers the structure of the industry and provides reasoning for the development of small, flexible, and independent international advertising agencies, especially those that use Amsterdam as a hub to create advertisements for the international market.

# Industry structure

The structure of the industry has inevitably changed through time. Some may argue that it has not changed enough, but the shape and size of the industry have developed. Over the last 20 years the size of the industry has increased in response to changes in technology, the growth in the number of marketing communications activities and with it the real value of advertising, sales promotion, public relations and direct marketing. The rate of growth among these tools has been variable with only direct marketing showing consistent levels of real growth.

The configuration of the agency services industry partly reflects the moves made by the larger agencies to consolidate their positions. They have attempted to buy either smaller, often medium-sized competitors, in an attempt to protect their market shares or provide an improved range of services for their clients. (See the section below on one-stop shopping.) This has led to an industry characterised by a large number of very large agencies and an even larger number of very small agencies. These smaller agencies have formed as the result of people formerly employed in large agencies becoming frustrated with having to work within tight margins and increased administration leaving and setting up their own fledgling businesses.

Broadly speaking, the industry consists of a few very large groups of agencies, some big agencies, a large number of very small agencies and relatively few medium-sized agencies. Although ownership has been an important factor driving industry development, the current preference for loose, independent networks has enabled some large organisations to offer clients an improved range of services (IMC) and the small agencies a chance to work with some of the bigger accounts. Miln (2004) speculated that structural changes to the way in which clients and agencies work together would give rise to what he referred to as 'new agencies', who would provide a limited range of specific communication services, most commonly involved with thinking around the creative or media elements, but would outsource or delegate the implementation to a third-party organisation. These organisations possess the core skills associated with project management and are better placed to fulfil this specialist role. The agency will remain responsible to the client for the implementation, but would be in a better position to continue advising about the overall communication strategy and media imperatives. The extent to which this has happened is questionable, but the principles behind this thinking remain interesting, even if they require a change of cultural awareness and strategic reorientation.

The recession in 2008 heralded a major restructuring within most agencies. The goal was to lower costs and their vulnerability as billings shrank. For many it was an opportunity to reshape their businesses at a time of great uncertainty and differing economic predictions. Some agencies attempted to broaden their services into new areas away from their traditional billings-based business (Beale, 2012).

# A short history of one-stop shopping

As with most industries, the structure of the communications industry has evolved in response to changes in the environment. However, if there is a holy grail of communications, it is an agency's ability to offer clients a single point from which all of their communication needs can be met, and be integrated. In search of this goal, WPP and Saatchi & Saatchi set about building the largest marketing communications empires in the world. According to Green (1991), Saatchi & Saatchi attempted to become the largest marketing services company in the world. The strategy adopted in the early 1980s was to acquire companies outside its current area of core competence, media advertising. Organisations in direct marketing, market research, sales promotion and public relations were brought under the Saatchi banner.

By offering a range of services under a single roof, rather like a 'supermarket', the one-stop shopping approach made intrinsic sense. Clients could put a package together, rather like eating from a buffet table, and solve a number of their marketing requirements, without the expense and effort of searching through each sector to find a company with which to work.

Green also refers to the WPP experience in the late 1980s. J. Walter Thompson and Ogilvy and Mather were grouped together under the umbrella of WPP and it was felt that synergies were to be achieved by bringing together their various services. Six areas were identified: strategic marketing services, media advertising, public relations, market research, non-media advertising and specialist communications. A one-stop shopping approach was advocated once again.

The recession of the early 1990s brought problems to both of these organisations, as well as others. The growth had been built on acquisition, which was partly funded from debt. This required considerable interest payments, but the recession brought a sharp decline in the revenues of the operating companies, and cash flow problems forced WPP and Saatchi & Saatchi to restructure their debt and their respective organisations. As Phillips (1991) points out, the financial strain and the complex task of managing operations on such a scale began to tell.

However, underpinning the strategy was the mistaken idea that clients actually wanted a one-stop shopping facility. It was unlikely that the best value for money was going to be achieved through this, so it came as no surprise when clients began to question the quality of the services for which they were paying. There was no guarantee that they could obtain from one large organisation the best creative, production, media and marketing solutions to their problems. Many began to shop around and engage specialists in different organisations (*à la carte*) in an attempt to receive not only the best quality of service but also the best value for money. Evidence for this might be seen in the resurgence of the media specialists whose very existence depends on their success in media planning and buying. By 1990 it was estimated that in Britain 30 per cent of market share in media buying was handled by media specialist companies.

It is no wonder then that clients, and indeed many media people working in agencies who felt constrained, decided to leave and set up on their own account, feeling that full-service agencies were asking too much of their staff, not only in terms of providing a wide range of integrated marketing services generally, but also in giving full attention and bringing sufficient expertise to bear in each of the specific services they had to offer (account management, creative, production, media research, etc.).

The debate about whether or not to use a full-service agency becomes even more crucial, perhaps, for those in specialist areas. For example, a large number of business-to-business communication agencies have been set up by people leaving full-service agencies. They spotted opportunities to provide specialist services in a market area that at the time was under-resourced, often marginalised or even ignored. In many ways it comes back to the quality of relationships. Arguments for the specialist agency were based on the point that, while there may be some convergence of approaches between consumer goods marketing and business-to-business advertising, it can be easier for a business-to-business advertising agency to do consumer advertising than it is to do the reverse.

As a general view, business-to-business shops survive on their ability to execute some very fundamental techniques for clients, such as direct mail or sales promotion. In contrast, the large, consumer goods-oriented shops, whose traditional skills are market research, planning and media advertising, often lack the core skills, initiative or expertise to deliver business-to-business marketing services.

The same has been said of direct marketing, where there appears to be the same sort of disenchantment with the full-service agency. Criticisms include the exclusion of direct marketing experts from presentations to clients, a lack of education among mainstream agency types as to what direct marketing actually does or the complaint that clients do not want to be force-fed a direct marketing subsidiary that may be incompetent or inappropriate. The experience of those involved in direct marketing has been further destabilised by the growth in the Internet. Direct mail has gained rather than lost, because many online brands have used direct mail as offline promotion to drive website traffic. Telemarketing has flourished because call centres have repositioned themselves as multimedia contact centres and have extended their range of services.

There is a spectrum of approaches for clients. They can find an agency that can provide all of the required marketing communication services under one roof, or find a different agency for each of the services, or mix and match. Clearly, the first solution can only be used if the budget holder is convinced that the best level of service is being provided in *all* areas, and the second only if there are sufficient gains in efficiency (and savings in expenditure) to warrant the amount of additional time they would need to devote to the task of managing marketing communications.

One area that has experienced significant change has been in media. Industry concentration and the development of global networks have shifted the structure and composition of the industry. Clients have responded by centralising their business into a single media network agency in search of higher discounts and improved efficiency. As a general rule, the stronger the competitive forces, the lower the profitability in the market. An organisation needs to determine a competitive approach that will allow it to influence the industry's competitive rules, protect it from competitive forces as much as possible and give it a strong position from which to compete. At the turn of the century, media networks had yet to find a competitive form of differentiation although some were beginning to offer additional services as a way of trying to enhance brand identities (Griffiths, 2000). At the time, the power of the media agencies, the low switching costs of buyers and the large threat of substitute products made this a relatively unattractive industry in its current form. This has changed. Media are now perceived to be much more important, much more significant than they used to be and as a result have developed increased market value.

Finer segmentation to determine markets that permit higher margins and a move to provide greater differentiation among agencies, together with a policy to reduce the threats from substitute products, perhaps through more visible alliances and partnerships, has helped to enable the industry to recover its position and provide greater stability. It is interesting to note that many leading agencies have moved into strategic consultancy, away from the reliance on mass media, where a substantially higher margin can be generated.

# Selecting an agency

In the areas that have traditionally dominated marketing communications, advertising and sales promotion, there has never been a shortage of advice on how to select an agency. Articles informing readers how to select an agency (Young and Steilen, 1996; Woolgar, 1998; Finch, 2000; McKee, 2004; Bruce, 2006; Constable, 2010) appear regularly, and there are a large number of publications and organisations to assist in the process.

The process of selecting an agency that is set out below appears to be rational and relatively straightforward. Readers should be aware that the reality is that the process is infused with political and personal issues, some of which can be contradictory. Logically the process commences with a *search*, undertaken to develop a list of potential candidates. This is accomplished by referring to publications such as *Campaign Portfolio* and the *Advertising Agency Roster*, Internet searches, together with personal recommendations. The latter are perhaps the most potent and influential of these sources. As many as 10 agencies could be included at this stage although six or seven are to be expected.

## Viewpoint 7.2    Social networks, relationships and influence

Agencies and clients have formed varying forms of relationships over the years. However, in the digital era we are witnessing new collaborations and partnerships as organisations from all sides of the communications industry reconfigure their strategies and operations.

One such alliance concerns the initiative taken by Facebook to tie into various leading brands. Facebook want those brands that use their platform to get the very best return, so their strategy is to help their customers achieve optimum outcomes. Procter & Gamble, Heineken, American Express, Wal-mart and Diageo, the latter signing a $10 million deal, have all aligned themselves with Facebook, with a view to getting strategic and tactical assistance, plus early access and some influence over the development of new products and services.

The alignment is regarded as a way of keeping in close contact with a major media platform. Facebook is evolving so these brands wish to be in at an early stage. For example, Heineken pass all their campaigns by Facebook just to check that they are social through and through. Diageo have sent 950 marketers to what is known as the Facebook 'boot camp'. Here they learn about communicating through the social network, what works, what doesn't and how campaigns need to be structurally aligned for Facebook, rather than creatively justified. It is reported that US sales increased 20 per cent following Diageo's involvement with Facebook.

*Source*:   Woods (2012).

Question:   Should it be mandatory that all agency appointments be made as a result of a fair and equal pitching process?

Task:   Pick two brands of your choice, go to their websites and find out how long their current agency has been with the brand.

---

Next, the client will visit each of the short-listed candidates in what is referred to as a *credentials presentation*. This is a crucial stage in the process, as it is now that the agency is evaluated for its degree of fit with the client's expectations and requirements. Agencies could develop their websites to fulfil this role, which would save time and costs. The agency's track record, resources, areas of expertise and experience can all be made available on the Internet from which it should be possible to short-list three or possibly four agencies for the next stage in the process: the pitch.

In the PR industry agencies are selected to pitch on the basis of the quality and experience of the agency people, its image and reputation and relationships with existing clients. In addition, Pawinska (2000) reports that the track record of the agency and the extent of its geographical coverage are also regarded as important. The same is true for other disciplines in the industry.

To be able to make a suitable bid the agencies are given a brief and then required to make a formal presentation (the *pitch*) to the client some 6–8 weeks later. This presentation is about how the agency would approach the strategic and creative issues and the account is awarded to whichever produces the most suitable proposal. Suitability is a relative term, and a range of factors need to be considered when selecting an organisation to be responsible for a large part of a brand's visibility. A strategic alliance is being formed and, therefore, a strong understanding of the strategic objectives of both parties is necessary, as is an appreciation of the structure and culture of the two organisations.

The selection process is a bringing together of two organisations whose expectations may be different but whose cooperative behaviour is essential for these expectations to have any chance of materialising. For example, agencies must have access to comprehensive and often commercially confidential data about products and markets if they are to operate efficiently. Otherwise, they cannot provide the service that is expected. However, it should be noted that pitches are not mandatory, and as Jones (2004) reports, nearly one-third of clients move their accounts without involving pitches. One of the reasons for this is the increasing cost involved in running the whole process, as much as £50,000 according to Jones. Indeed Wethey (2006) questions the whole validity and efficacy of the pitching process. He argues that many pitches are a waste of resources (time and money), that too many agencies devote too much of their resources to chasing new business, that pitches do not solve client problems and that the whole process is often unrealistic. In 2011 McCormick reports that the industry bodies, ISBA and the IPA, launched a website called 'The Good Pitch'. This was designed to help brands adhere to six core principles and improve the manner in which pitches are undertaken, as some commentators refer to the events as 'war zones'.

---

### Scholars' paper 7.2    Creative codes provide creative insight

**Stuhlfaut, M. (2011) The creative code: An organisational influence on the creative process in advertising, *International Journal of Advertising*, 30(2), 283–304.**

The creative code refers to the idea that each creative department in an advertising agency has a preferred way of working, that creative products are generated in particular ways of working. The author tests the idea and concludes that a creative code could be considered as an antecedent or moderator of the creative process: an interesting and thought-provoking idea, one which is explored later (Chapter 25) on creativity.

---

The immediate selection process is finalised when terms and conditions are agreed and the winner is announced to the contestants and made public, often through press releases and the use of trade journals such as *Campaign*, *Marketing* and *Marketing Week*.

This formalised process is now being questioned as to its suitability. The arrival of new media firms and their need to find communication solutions in one rather than eight weeks has meant that new methods have had to be found. In addition, agencies felt that they had to invest a great deal in a pitch with little or no reward if the pitch failed. Their response has been to ask for payment to pitch, which has not been received well by many clients. The tension that arises is that each agency is required to generate creative ideas over which they have little control once a pitch has been lost. The pitching process also fails to give much insight into the probable working relationships and is very often led by senior managers who will not be involved in the day-to-day operations. One solution has been to invite agencies to discuss mini-briefs. These are essentially discussion topics about related issues rather than the traditional challenge about how to improve a brand's performance. Issuing the mini-brief on the day eliminates weeks of preparation and associated staff costs, and enables the client to see agency teams working together. Another approach promoted by the IPA is the use of workshops and trial projects. However, it should be noted that it is the IPA's experience that 'many successful appointments are founded on reputation, personal chemistry, credentials and references from other clients, as opposed to pitches' (2009: 3).

# Agency operations

Many communications agencies are generally organised on a functional basis. There have been moves to develop matrix structures utilising a customer orientation, but this is very inefficient and the low margins prohibit such luxuries. There are departments for planning, creative and media functions coordinated on behalf of the client by an account handler or executive.

The account executive fulfils a very important role, in that these people are responsible for the flow of communications between the client and the agency. The quality of the communications between the two main parties can be critical to the success of the overall campaign and to the length of the relationship between the two organisations. Acting at the boundary of the agency's operations, the account executive needs to perform several roles, from internal coordinator and negotiator to presenter (of the agency's work), conflict manager and information gatherer. Very often account executives will experience tension as they seek to achieve their clients' needs while trying to balance them with the needs of their employer and colleagues. These tensions are similar to those experienced by salespersons and need to be managed in a sensitive manner by management.

Once an account has been signed, a client brief is prepared that provides information about the client organisation (Figure 7.2). It sets out the nature of the industry it operates in, together with data about trends, market shares, customers, competitors and the problem that the agency is required to address. This is used to inform agency personnel. In particular, the account planner will undertake research to determine market, media and audience characteristics and make proposals to the rest of the account team concerning how the client problem is to be resolved.

---

## Viewpoint 7.3    Google tools assist agencies

Google's strategy is very different to that pursued by others in or related to the media industry. For many, innovation is about closed, payment-based systems. In contrast, Facebook and Google follow an open, collaborative systems approach. This means that developers can develop innovative applications using the Google platform, without having to pay for the access to the underpinning technology. This helps ensure that the innovations and applications are compatible and based on a common platform.

In another dimension, communications agencies can benefit from the stream of ideas and applications from Google. Boyd (2010) considers the Google Wonder Wheel, a tool which simplifies and arranges search results, similar to a mind map. Sketchup, a new 3D modelling facility, and Google Insight, a tool that enables keyword research, provides trend data on keyword searches and permits the data to be filtered by location. All of these have high potential usage by agencies. Edge (2010) refers to the range of free tools that can be used to track campaign performance, ad development and testing, using YouTube (which is owned by Google). In the same article Rebelo (2010) refers to the power of the Google tools to assist the creativity process and to move the way agencies operate, forward.

*Source*:  Rebelo (2010); Edge (2010); Boyd (2010).

---

**Question:**   To what extent do these advances assist marketing communications?

**Task:**   Find out two other recent innovations by Google and make notes about how they might help agencies do a better job for their clients.

**Project management** – Provide basic project details, e.g. timescales, contacts and people, project numbers

**Where are we now?** – Describe current brand details, e.g. background, position, competitors, key issues

**Where do we want to be?** – What needs to be achieved in terms of goals, e.g. sales, market share, ROI, shareholder value, awareness, perception, etc?

**What are we doing to get there?** – What is the context in terms of the marketing strategy, overall communication strategy and campaign strategy?

**Who do we need to talk to?** – What is understood about the audiences the communications are intended to influence?

**How will we know if we have arrived?** – What will be measured, by whom, how and when to determine whether the activity has been successful?

**Practicalities** – Budgets, timings and schedules, creative and media imperatives

**Approvals** – Who has the authority to sign off the brief and the agency work?

**Figure 7.2**    A new briefing structure

Briefing is a process that is common across all client–agency relationships in the communication industry. Regardless of whether working in direct marketing, sales promotion, advertising, public relations, media planning and buying or other specialist area, the brief has a special importance in making the process work and the outcomes significant. However, the importance of preparing a brief of suitable quality has for some been underestimated. With agencies having to brief themselves and some briefs insufficiently detailed, a recent joint industry initiative sought to establish common working practices. The outcome of the process was a briefing template intended to be used by all across the communications agencies in the industry. Eight key headings emerged from the report and these can be seen at Figure 7.2.

In addition to the role of account handler, which might be regarded as one of traffic management, is the role undertaken by account planners (or creative planners). The role of the account planner has been the subject of debate (Collin, 2003; Zambarino and Goodfellow, 2003; Grant and McLeod, 2007; Mackert and Munoz, 2011). The general conclusion of these papers is that the role of account planner, which has been evolving since the beginning of the 1960s, has changed as the communications industry has fragmented and that a new role is emerging in response to integrated marketing communication and media-neutral planning initiatives (see Chapter 10 for details about these concepts).

The traditional role of the account planner, which began in full-service agencies, was to understand the client's target consumers and develop strategies for the creative and media departments. As media broke away from full-service agencies, so the role of the account planner shifted to the creative aspect of the agency work. Media planners assumed the same type of work in media companies, although their work focused on planning the right media mix to reach the target audience. With the development of integrated perspectives and the move towards a broader view of a client's communication needs comes an expectation that the planning role will evolve into a strategic role. The role will be to work with a broad range of marketing disciplines (tools) and media, but not to brief creatives or media planners directly (Collin, 2003). As media broke away from full-service agencies, so the role of the account planner shifted to the creative aspect of the agency work. Account planning is a strategically important activity in agencies, and a major source of power and conflict (Grant et al., 2012).

---

### Scholars' paper 7.3    Indian account planning

**Patwardhan, P., Patwardhan, H. and Vasavada-Oza, F. (2012) Diffusion of account planning in Indian ad agencies: An organisational perspective, *International Journal of Advertising*, 30(4), pp. 665–92.**

This paper reports on account planning in India, a region which is rapidly becoming important to international advertisers and advertising agencies. The authors refer to a two-stage organisational innovation diffusion framework, used to examine planning initiation and assimilation in the Indian ad industry. Similarities with and differences from account planning use in UK and US agencies are discussed, but it is the orientation of the paper that makes this an interesting paper.

---

Creative teams comprise a copywriter and an art director, supported by a service team. This team is responsible for translating the proposal into an advertisement. In a full-service agency, a media brief will also be generated, informing the media planning and buying department of the media and the type of media vehicles required. However, the vast majority of media planning work is now undertaken by specialist media agencies, media independents, and these will be briefed by the client, with some support from those responsible for the creatives.

In recent years, partly as a response to the growth of new media, a raft of small entrepreneurial agencies has emerged, to exploit the new opportunities arising from the digital revolution. Many of these are run without the control and structures evident in large, centralised agencies. While dedicated teams might theoretically be the best way to manage a client's project, the reality in many cases is the use of project teams comprising expert individuals working on a number of projects simultaneously. This is not a new phenomenon, but as a result many people are multi-tasking and they assume many roles with new titles. For example, the title *Head of Content* has arisen to reflect the significance of content issues in the new media market. Project managers assume responsibility for the implementation phase and the coordination of all aspects of a client's technological facilities. In addition, there are positions such as head of marketing, mobile (increasing focus on WAP technology), production and technology. The result is no hierarchies, flat structures and flexible working practices and similar expectations.

# Relationships

The relationships inevitably shape and influence the strategies and operations that are pursued. There are a vast number of relationships that form between various clients and agencies, disciplines and within individual organisations.

## Client/agency relationships

If the briefing process provides the mechanism for the agency operations, it is the relationship between the agency and the client that very often determines the length of the contract and the strength of the solutions advanced for the client.

| Table 7.2 | Longer-lasting agency/client relationships |
|---|---|

| Agency | Clients since |
|---|---|
| Abbott Mead Vickers BBDO | Volvo (1985), Sainsbury's (1981), *The Economist* (1986), Homebase (1991) BT (1994) |
| Grey Advertising | GlaxoSmithKline (1955, 21 brands), Procter & Gamble (1956, 31 brands) |
| Lowe Worldwide | Unilever/Lever Faberge (1963) Unilever/Best Foods (1964) Stella Artois (1981), Vauxhall (1983), Johnson & Johnson (1986) |
| Ogilvy & Mather | Unilever (1952), Mattel (1954) Kraft Foods (1954), Nestlé (1959) American Express (1963), Ford (1975) |
| Saatchi & Saatchi | Carlsberg (1973), Pepsi, (1981), Procter & Gamble (1983), NSPCC (1984) Toyota (1992) |

*Source*: Adapted from Sclater (2006).

There are a number of agency/client relationships that have flourished over a very long period of time, and some for several decades. Sclater (2006) refers to the agency BBH, which was established in 1982. The agency started with three key clients, Audi, Levi's and Whitbread (now InBev UK) and in all three cases they are still working together over two decades later. Similarly WCRS has had a long-term relationship with BMW, since 1979. Spanier (2010) also reports on examples of agencies that have retained clients over long periods of time. These include DDB who have held the Volkswagen car account for more than 25 years, JWT has had Shell as a client for approaching 50 years, Rolex for over 60 and Unilever for over 100. There are a huge number of other accounts who have excellent relationships that have lasted a long time (see Table 7.2 for a snapshot of some of the longer public agency/client relationships). However, these appear to be in the minority, as many relationships appear to founder as clients abandon agencies and search for better, fresher solutions, because a contract expires, the client needs change or owing to takeovers and mergers between agencies, which require that they forfeit accounts that cause a conflict of interest.

From a contextual perspective these buyer/seller relationships can be seen to follow a pattern of formation, maintenance and severance, or pre-contract, contracting process and post-contract stages (Davidson and Kapelianis, 1996). Clients and agencies enter into a series of interactions (West and Paliwoda, 1996) or exchanges through which levels of trust and commitment develop. Hakansson (1982) identified several contexts, or atmospheres, within which relationships develop. These contexts had numerous dimensions: closeness/distance, cooperation/conflict, power/dependence, trustworthiness and expectations. Therefore, the client/agency relationship should be seen in the context of the network of organisations and the exchanges or interactions that occur in that network. It is through these interactions that the tasks that need to be accomplished are agreed, resources made available, strategies determined and goals achieved. The quality of the agency/client relationship is a function of trust, which is developed through the exchanges and which fosters confidence. Commitment is derived from a belief that the relationship is worth continuing and that maximum effort is warranted to maintain the relationship (Morgan and Hunt, 1994). The development of new forms of remuneration (see p. 89) based around payment by results, also signifies a new client focus and a willingness to engage with clients and to be paid according to the success and contribution the agency can provide (Lace and Brocklehurst, 2000).

The way in which clients use multiple agencies to fulfil the whole range of communication tasks does not encourage the establishment of strong relationships nor does it help the cause of integrated marketing communications. The use of roster agencies means that marketing teams have to manage more agencies, often with reduced resources. This means that agencies get a smaller share of the available budget, which in turn does not help agencies feel comfortable (Child, 2007).

Poor relationships between agencies and clients are likely to result from a lack of trust and falling commitment. As it appears that communication is a primary element in the formation and substance of relational exchanges, clients might be advised to consider the agencies in their roster as an extended department of the core organisation and use internal marketing communication procedures to assist the development of identity and belonging.

One last point to be made is the increasing age gap between those in the industry, both agency and client, and their audiences. Those people that produce marketing communications tend to be under 35 and the average age of those targeted to receive the communications is rising. Curtis (1999) reports that Reg Starkey, a creative partner of Prime Advertising, Marketing and Research, claims that this may increase the chance of misunderstanding older consumers and that this error of interpretation can become a self-fulfilling prophecy.

---

### Scholars' paper 7.4 — Cooperative advertisers and agencies

**Duhan, D.F. and Sandvik, K. (2009) Outcomes of advertiser–agency relationships: The form and the role of cooperation, *International Journal of Advertising*, 28(5), 881–919.**

Duhan and Sandvik examine the theoretical basis for developing and comparing two models of the role of cooperation between agencies and their clients. The first is a shared-influence model and the second a sole-mediator model. The two models have the same form of advertiser–agency relationship, including trust, commitment, cooperation, agency performance, advertisers' willingness to pay more, but differ in the nature of the influence of the relationship and outcome components. They discuss why some relationships are more successful than others. The paper provides a comprehensive review of the academic literature underpinning relationships and the models developed give both parties a basis for performance assessment.

---

# Agency remuneration

One factor that has a significant impact on the quality of the relationship between the parties is the remuneration or reward for the effort (added value) the agency makes in attempting to meet and satisfy the needs of its client. One major cause for concern and complaint among marketing managers is the uncertainty over how much their marketing communications programmes will finally cost and the complexity surrounding the remuneration system itself.

According to the IPA there are 10 different ways in which agencies can be remunerated. These are explained in Table 7.3. Of these *payment by results* (PBR) and *value based* approaches are considered to be leading edge and the most appropriate forms of remuneration. Each of these approaches is discussed below and it should be noted that it is very rare for a single method to be used within a single contract.

Traditionally, advertising agencies were paid a commission by media owners for selling space in their publications. This commission was soon referred to as 'the line' and a figure of 15 per cent above the line emerged as the norm and was adjudged to be a fair reward for the efforts of the agency. However, as relationships between agencies and clients strengthened, it seemed only reasonable that the clients should feel that agencies should act for them (and in their best interests), and not for the media owners. A number of questions were raised about whether the agency was actually being rewarded for the work it did and whether it was being

| Table 7.3 | The IPA's ten forms of agency remuneration |
|---|---|

| Method | Explanation |
|---|---|
| Payment by results | PBR is based on the attainment of predetermined KPIs. Here both parties can win and results are transparent and measurable. |
| Value-based | Value-based approaches consider the agency's results in terms of outputs and outcomes. This can incorporate a base fee to cover the agency's cost of producing the outputs, with a mark-up, rather than discretionary bonus, based on actual performance metrics. |
| Retainers | A negotiated activity fee for a defined period (e.g. one year) is paid monthly in advance for agreed workloads and activities. |
| Project fees | Rather than an annual fee, fees are based on an individual project. |
| Variable fees | Fees are based on actual time spent on a client's account, paid after the activity has been incurred. |
| Scale fees + win bonus | Client pays a 'salary' based on sales (bonus included) or marketing budget plus a bonus if based on a marketing budget. |
| Consultancy and Concept fees | This is a one-off fee designed to reward an agency for developing a creative concept. |
| Licensing fees | The client pays for concept development but at a reduced rate before paying a Licence fee for the finished concept, once approved. |
| Output or 'off-the-shelf' rate fee | Used where the output can be readily measured and costed. Here a fixed price per unit of output is agreed, typically suited to the 'pay-per-click' approach. |
| Commission | A percentage (originally 15 per cent of the gross media cost within a full service arrangement) is paid by media owners for the work placed with them by agencies on behalf of their client |

*Source*: IPA/ISBA/CIPS (2012).

objective when recommending media expenditure. As media independents emerged, questions started to be asked about why media agencies received 3 per cent and the creative agency received 12 per cent.

Client discontent is not the only reason why agency remuneration by commission has been called into question, and alternatives are being considered. In times of recession marketing budgets are inevitably cut, which means less revenue for agencies. Increasing competition means lower profit margins if an agency is to retain the business, and if costs are increasing at the same time, the very survival of the agency is in question. As Snowden stated as long ago as 1993, 'Clients are demanding more for less.' She went on to say, 'It is clear to me that the agency business needs to address a number of issues; most important amongst them, how agencies get paid. It is the key to the industry's survival.' Well, changes have been made since then, but there are still various combinations of methods used to suit particular agencies, clients and projects.

During the early 1990s there was a great deal of discussion and energy directed towards non-commission payment systems. This was a direct result of the recession, in which clients cut budgets, and there was a consequent reduction in the quantity of media purchased and hence less revenue for the agencies. Fees became more popular, and some experimented with payment by results. Interestingly, as that recession died and the economy lifted, more revenue resulted in larger commission possibilities, and the death throes of the commission system were quickly replaced by its resuscitation and revival. It is likely that there will continue to be a move away from a reliance on the payment of commission as the only form of remuneration to the agency.

For many, payment by results seems a good solution. In 2009 Coca-Cola introduced a new way by which their agencies were to be remunerated. It is referred to as a *value-based compensation model*, and Tylee (2010) argues that it extends the PBR model. Agencies are promised profit mark-ups of 30 per cent if specific targets are met. If they are not, then only their costs are covered. At the time of writing it is uncertain whether this model will be adopted by other clients. Procter & Gamble have also adopted a similar value-based reward programme, and as Williams (2010) indicates, value-based systems can involve a variety of factors, as long as they are not timesheets and hours and costs.

However, agencies have no control over the other marketing activities of the client, which might determine the degree of success of the campaign. Indeed, this raises the very thorny question of what 'success' is and how it might be measured. Despite these considerations, it appears that PBR is starting to become an established form of remuneration with over 30 per cent of agency–client contracts containing an element of PBR.

The use of bonuses is widespread but, whereas the intention is to reward excellent work, some agencies see bonuses as a means by which fees are reduced and, as some clients refuse to pay, the impact on relationships can be far from positive (Child, 2007). It is likely that there will continue to be a move away from a reliance on the payment of commission as the only form of remuneration to the agency. Fees have been around for a long time, either in the form of retainers or on a project-by-project basis. Indeed, many agencies charge a fee for services over and above any commission earned from media owners. The big question concerns the basis for calculation of fees (and this extends to all areas of marketing communications, not just advertising), and protracted, complicated negotiations can damage client/agency relationships.

A different way of looking at this is to consider what the client thinks the agency does, and from this evaluate the outcomes from the relationship. Jensen (1995) proposed that advertising agencies should be regarded as an *ideas business* that seeks to build brands for clients. An alternative view is that agencies are *advertising factories*, where the majority of the work is associated with administration, communication, coordination and general running around to ensure that the advertisement appears on the page or screen as desired.

If the 'ideas business' view is accepted, the ideas generated add value for the client, so the use the client makes of the idea should be rewarded by way of a royalty-type payment. If the 'factory concept' is adopted, then it is the resources involved in the process that need to be considered and a fee-based system is more appropriate. Both parties will actively seek to reduce costs that do not contribute to the desired outcomes. These are different approaches to remuneration and avoid the volume of media purchased as a critical and controversial area.

# Agency structures and IMC

The development of integrated marketing communications has been mentioned earlier and, although the concept is subject to considerable debate and uncertainty, the underlying good sense inherent in the concept resonates with clients and agencies. As a result the influence of IMC on agencies and clients should not be underestimated.

In order for messages to be developed and conveyed through an integrated approach, the underlying structure supporting this strategy needs to be reconsidered. Just as the structure of the industry had a major impact on the way in which messages were developed and communicated as the industry developed, so the structural underpinning needs to adapt to the new and preferred approaches of clients. Kitchen et al. (2007) report that a survey incorporating well-established PR and advertising agencies found resistance towards the integration of certain working practices. These, the authors conclude, need to be refashioned in order that the agencies' working practices enable all the promotional disciplines to be incorporated in an integrated manner.

## Viewpoint 7.4 | Procter & Gamble's BAL agency model

For an organisation with 400 brands, operating in 80 countries and employing 135,000 people, it is important for Procter & Gamble (P&G) to manage its agencies effectively and efficiently. A Brand Agency Leader (BAL) model was introduced in 2006 in an attempt to streamline agency management. P&G's Financial Director, Rich Delcore, is reported to claim that the BAL programme now accounts for over 40 per cent of new sales and is soon to reach 60 per cent as the programme develops.

BAL is centred around a 'one-agency mentality', very different to what Delcore calls the 'spaghetti chart' of an organisation with internal and external silos across different communications platforms, advertising agencies, PR, digital, strategy, and media management. At brand level, there is now one global creative director and a global planner. For each brand BAL has the following main components:

- a lead P&G person and a lead agency;
- BAL leads an integrated agency team;
- responsibility for managing work of each member agency;
- BAL is accountable for team performance;
- members of BAL team agree a single global fee;
- BAL owns partner-agency compensation over and above the fee.

Further benefits of the BAL system include improved integrated communications, increased flexibility and faster executions, and added value derived from stronger agency partnerships and collaborations.

For the Oral-B toothbrush brand available in 180 different markets, adoption of the BAL model led to significant changes in approaches to creative development. P&G used seven agencies in advertising, planning, shopper marketing, digital, PR and design, each with their different ideas as to how the brand should be presented. BAL responsibilities were placed with the Publicis agency in New York. All other agencies involved in the account report through Publicis. The agency created a 'team manifesto' for sharing ownership so that all work would be seamlessly integrated. The BAL programme was supported with the setting-up of a Creative Agency Leader (CAL). The CAL has responsibility for breaking down different team briefs into a shared document and sharing knowledge, integrating ideas and engaging appropriate technological expertise.

*Source*:   Based on Precourt (2010).

**Question:**   Is the BAL model suitable for either a standardised or adapted approach to advertising?

**Task:**   Assess whether the integrated agency structures in Table 7.4 offer beneficial alternatives to the BAL model.

| Exhibit 7.2 | **A Procter and Gamble brand used within the BAL system** |
| --- | --- |
| | *Source*: Carolyn Jenkins/Alamy |

| Table 7.4 | Integrated agency options |
| --- | --- |
| **Type of agency** | **Explanation** |
| Integrated agency | A single agency that provides the full range of communication disciplines. |
| Complementary agencies | The client selects a range of different agencies; each from a different discipline and self-manages or appoints a lead agency. |
| Networked agencies | A single group agency is appointed (e.g. WPP or Interpublic) who then appoint agencies within their own profit-oriented network. |
| Mini-group agencies | Clusters of small independent specialist agencies who work on a non-competitive basis for a client. |

The use of outside agencies that possess skills, expertise and purchasing advantages that are valued by clients is not new and is unlikely to change. However, the way in which these outsourced skills are used and how they are structured has been changing. Aspects of client–agency relationships are important and are considered later. What is important at this stage is a consideration of the way in which those organisations who provide outsourcing facilities and contribute to a client's IMC can be configured to provide optimal servicing and support.

Clients who seek a marketing communications campaign which draws on more than one marketing communications discipline have a basic choice of four main options. These are set out in Table 7.4.

None of these four approaches can provide a perfect solution, and the variety of integrated possibilities reflects the different client structures and cultures and consequently the different needs and relationships that need to be satisfied (Murphy, 2004). The mini-group option is a relatively recent development and can include the use of product development, research, design and interactive services. This means that this approach serves a broad range of needs, typical of smaller client organisations whose budgets do not match those of mainstream firms.

The IPA recognise that there are four primary ways in which clients and agencies can be organised.

- The *client-led model* requires the client to formulate the strategy and agencies to implement it.

- The *lead-agency model* acknowledges agency expertise to create the communication strategy. One agency is appointed to formulate strategy and to provide leadership. Other agencies then implement the strategy according to their channel or discipline speciality.

- The *all-agency model* recognises the importance of collective expertise and brings together agencies from different disciplines (DM, PR, advertising and different media). The client manages the process as a ringmaster and perhaps this interpretation might be the closest to an integrated approach.

- The *one-stop shop model* combines the lead-agency and all-agency approaches with leadership provided by a one-agency group (WPP, Publicis) with the individual agencies collaborating to develop the communication strategy.

For more information on these models, visit the IPA website (www.IPA.co.uk).

Gronstedt and Thorsen (1996) suggest five ways in which agencies could be configured to provide integrated marketing communications. The research is centred upon US-based advertising agencies, so, while not immediately transferable to the European, Asian or other regional markets, their proposals provide a base from which other agencies might evolve in other geographic markets.

The models are presented in Figure 7.3 (overleaf) and, although the authors acknowledge that a mix of forms could be identified, one particular form tended to dominate each agency. The forms denote a continuum, at one end of which is a highly centralised organisation that can provide a high level of integration for a variety of communication disciplines. Staffed by generalists with no particular media bias, these organisations are structured according to client needs, not functional specialisms. Total integration is offered at the expense of in-depth and leading-edge knowledge in new and developing areas.

At the other end of the continuum are those providers who group themselves in the form of a network. Often led by a main advertising agency that has divested itself of expensive over-heads, the independent yet interdependent network players each provide specialist skills under the leadership of the main contractor agency. One of the two main weaknesses associated with this model concerns the deficiency associated with communications across the players in the network. This horizontal aspect means that individual members of the network tend to identify with their own area of expertise and advance their specialism, possibly at the expense of the client's overriding requirements. The other main weakness concerns the transitory or temporary nature of a member organisation's involvement within such networks. Therefore, the level of potential integration is possibly weakest in this model, although the level of expertise available to clients is highest at this end of the continuum.

One of the essential points emerging from this research is that there seems to be a trade-off between levels of integration and the expertise provided by different agencies. Clients who want to retain control over their brands and to find an integrated agency where all the required services are of the exact level and quality demanded may be expecting too much. The inevitability of this position is that clients may choose to select marketing communication expertise from a variety of sources, and the integrated agency may well lose out.

Furthermore, environmental factors should not be ignored, and it may be that clients in the future will state their preferred structural requirements at the pitching or client briefing stage of the agency–client relationship. Increasingly, agencies may well be required to mix and match their structures and provide structural flexibility to meet the varying needs of their clients.

A further point concerns global branding and the standardisation/adaptation debate when considered in the light of IMC. One argument is that standardisation is the only way in which IMC can be achieved. However, as it is generally accepted that there are few examples of truly standardised global brands, does that suggest that IMC is not possible for global brands? A strong counter-view is that globalisation encourages integration where it matters, at the point of implementation. Furthermore, to have adaptation, there must be strong internal integration between head office (and business/marketing strategies) and those responsible for local adaptation and implementation. For example, Fielding (2000) shows that many Japanese and Korean advertising messages emphasise the inclusion of product-related information. However, many Western brands require an emphasis on the development of brand personality and character. If such a difference is to be overcome and IMC is to succeed, a consistent core message and local or regional flavour need to be delivered.

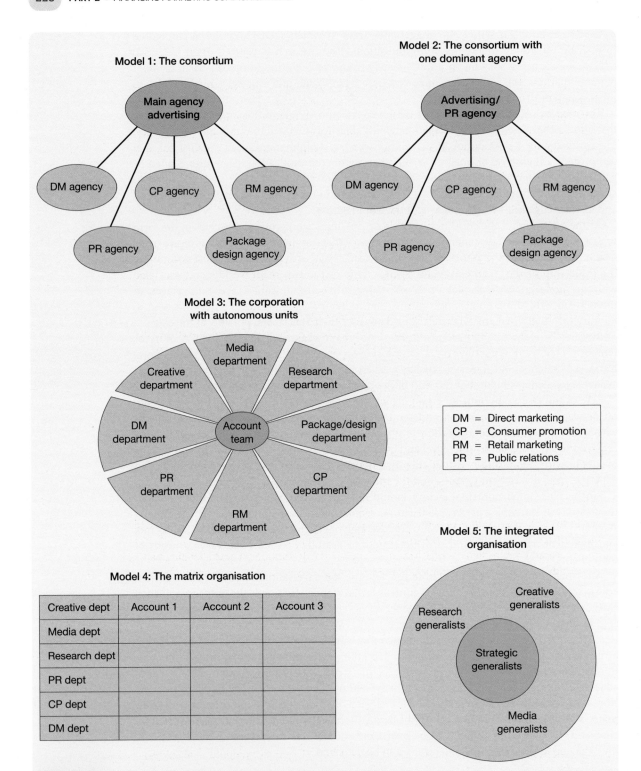

**Figure 7.3**   An overview of the five agency structures

*Source*: Gronstedt and Thorson (1996). Used with kind permission from WARC.

# Key points

- The structure of the communications industry is similar in most countries but the relationships and operations will inevitably vary. However, the marketing communication industry in Britain has evolved slowly, with the large agencies seeking to bring a range of communication skills and facilities together within a single group. Mid-size and small agencies still maintain a functional orientation (e.g. advertising, promotion, digital, or public relations).

- Agencies broker or facilitate the communication needs of clients, while media houses plan, buy and monitor media purchases for their clients. Production facilitators ensure the processes work by making videos, providing fulfilment or staging events. All deliver specific value to the industry and have different roles to play.

- Relationships between clients and agencies are of critical importance and part of their trust and commitment is reflected in the remuneration agencies receive for their contribution. There are three keys methods: commission, payment by results and fees. These are normally combined within a contract.

- The processes used to select agencies are fairly standardised and are based on search, filtering, pitching, selecting and contracting. Once established, the operational procedures are based on briefings, and there are three main ones: the client, creative and media briefs.

- Various agency solutions have been developed to meet client needs for integrated marketing communications. These range on a continuum where at one end is a highly centralised organisation that can provide a high level of integration for a variety of communication disciplines. Total integration is offered at the expense of in-depth and leading-edge knowledge in new and developing areas. At the other end of the continuum are providers who group themselves in the form of a loose network. Often led by a main advertising agency that has divested itself of expensive overheads, the independent yet interdependent players in the network each provide specialist skills under the leadership of the main contractor agency.

- The industry is changing, with some areas changing faster than others. Technology has had a big impact and it is likely that further consolidation among the large groups will attempt to cut costs and retain clients. Legislation and regulation will continue to be challenging issues as the industry seeks to ward off consumer and government attacks on their activities.

# Review questions

1. What are the main types of organisation that make up the marketing communication industry?

2. Identify some of the issues that prevail in the industry. What are the key issues at stake in the Diageo mini case?

3. Write notes for a presentation explaining the different types of agency available to clients.

4. Outline the arguments for and against using an agency.

5. What factors should be taken into consideration and what procedures might be followed when selecting an agency?

6. What problems might be encountered in agency/client relationships?

7. What are the basic dimensions for the development of good agency/client relationships?

8. Write brief notes about the briefing system.

9. Explain the commission payment system, and outline alternative approaches.

10. How can an organisation best acquaint itself with the relevant controls in a chosen area of marketing communications?

# References

Bain, R. (2012) Do you want the good news or the bad news? *Research*, retrieved 9 September 2012 from http://www.research-live.com/features/do-you-want-its-good-news-or-the-bad-news?/4006957.article.

Beale, C. (2012) School Reports 2012: A-Z of agencies, Introduction, *Campaign*, 2 April, retrieved 3 April 2012 from http://www.brandrepublic.com/news/1122211/School-Reports-2012-A-Z-agencies/?DCMP=ILC-SEARCH.

Beattie, A.C. (2012) Japan's Dentsu to Acquire Aegis Group for $4.9 Billion, Adage, 12 July, retrieved 13 July from http://adage.com/article/agency-news/japan-s-dentsu-acquire-aegis-group-4-9-billion/235996/.

Billings, C. (2004) DM's new wave, *Campaign*, 7 September. Retrieved from http://www.brandrepublic.com/news/newsArticle.cfm.

Boyd, M. (2010) Google shows adland the new tools of its trade, *Campaign*, 25 June, p. 11.

Bruce, L. (2006) Decision time, *The Marketer*, September, 11–13.

Charles, G. (2008) The buddy system, *Marketing*, 6 February, p. 16.

Child, L. (2007) How to manage your relationship, *Marketing Agency*, (December), 4–7.

Collin, W. (2003) The interface between account planning and media planning – a practitioner perspective, *Marketing Intelligence and Planning*, 21(7), 440–5.

Constable, J. (2010) The right questions will find you the right retail agency, *Marketing Week*, 31 March, from www.marketingweek.co.uk/the-right-questions-will-find-you-the-right-retail-agency/3011737.article, accessed 26 December 2012.

Curtis, J. (1999) Why grey is golden, *Marketing*, 15 July, 25–8.

Davidson, S. and Kapelianis, D. (1996) Towards an organisational theory of advertising: agency–client relationships in South Africa. *International Journal of Advertising*, 15, 48–60.

Edge, M. (2010) Google shows adland the new tools of its trade, *Campaign*, 25 June, p. 11.

Fielding, S. (2000) Developing global brands in Asia, *Admap* (June), 26–29.

Finch, M. (2000) How to choose the right marketing agency, *Admap* (October), 46–7.

Grant, I. and McLeod, C. (2007) Advertising agency planning: conceptualising network relationships, *Journal of Marketing Management*, 23(5/6), July, 425–42.

Grant, I. McLeod, C. and Shaw, E. (2012) Conflict and advertising planning: consequences of networking for advertising planning, *European Journal of Marketing*, 46(1/2), 73–91.

Green, A. (1991) Death of the full-service ad agency? *Admap* (January), 21–4.

Griffiths, A. (2000) More than a media network. *Campaign Report*, 20 October, 3–4.

Gronstedt, A. and Thorsen, E. (1996) Five approaches to organise an integrated marketing communications agency, *Journal of Advertising Research* (March/April), 48–58.

Grosso, C., Guggenheim Shenkan, A. and Sichel, H.P. (2006) A reality check for online advertising, *McKinsey Quarterly*, 3.

Hakansson, H. (1982) *International Marketing and Purchasing of Industrial Goods: An Interaction Approach*, Chichester: John Wiley.

IPA (2006) *Agency remuneration: a best practice guide to agency search and selection*, London.

IPA (2009) *Finding an agency: a best practice guide to agency search and selection*, London.

IPA/ISBA/CIPS (2012) *Agency remuneration: a best practice guide to agency search and selection*, London: IPA/ISBA/CIPS.

Jensen, B. (1995) Using agency remuneration as a strategic tool, *Admap* (January), 20–2.

Jones, M. (2004) 10 things agencies need to know about clients, *Admap*, 39(5), (May), 21–3.

Kitchen, P.J., Spickett-Jones, G. and Grimes, T. (2007) Inhibition of brand integration amid changing agency structures, *Journal of Marketing Communications*, 13(2), (June), 149–68.

Lace, J.M. and Brocklehurst, D. (2000) You both win when you play the same game. *Admap* (October), 40–42.

Mackert, M. and Munoz, I.I. (2011) Graduate Account Planning Education: insights from the classroom, *Journal of Advertising Education*, 15(2), September, 35–9.

McCormick, A. (2011) ISBA and IPA initiative aims to clarify pitching, *Marketing*, p. 12, October, p. 5.

McKee, S. (2004) Pick an agency . . . any agency, *Admap*, 39(5), (May), 24–5.

Miln, D. (2004) New marketing, new agency? *Admap*, 39(7), (July/August), 47–8.

Mitchell, A. (2012) Face it, your consumers hate you, *Marketing*, 28 March 2012, 30–32.

Morgan, R.M. and Hunt, S.D. (1994) The commitment–trust theory of relationship marketing, *Journal of Marketing*, 58 (July), 20–38.

Mosher, J.F. (2012) Joe Camel in a Bottle: Diageo, the Smirnoff Brand, and the Transformation of the Youth Alcohol Market, *American Journal of Public Health*, 102(1), January, 56–63.

Murphy, C. (2004) Small but perfectly formed? *Marketing*, 15 December, p. 12.

Murphy, D. (2002) Automation assists business efficiency, *Marketing*, 30 May, p. 23.

Pawinska, M. (2000) The passive pitch, *PR Week*, 12 May, 14–15.

Phillips, W. (1991) From bubble to rubble, *Admap* (April), 14–19.

Precourt, G. (2010) Procter & Gamble's BAL Compensation Moves Beyond Experimentation. WARC (March), retrieved 15 March 2011 from www.warc.com.

Rebelo, M. (2010) Google shows adland the new tools of its trade, *Campaign*, 25 June, p. 11.

Sclater, I. (2006) Marriage material, *The Marketer*, September, 22–3.

Snowden, S. (1993) The remuneration squeeze, *Admap* (January), 26–8.

Spanier, G. (2010) What's the secret of a long-term relationship in advertising? *London Evening Standard*, 19 July, retrieved 8 August, 2011 from www.thisislondon.co.uk.

Tylee, J. (2010) Will others follow Coke's remuneration model? *Campaign*, 19 February, p. 17.

West, D.C. and Paliwoda, S.J. (1996) Advertising client–agency relationships, *European Journal of Marketing*, 30(8), 22–39.

Wethey, D. (2006) The shocking truth about the pitch, *The Marketer*, September, 7–8.

White, R. (2007) Structuring the (ad) agency, *Admap*, March, 14–15.

Williams, T. (2010) Why agencies should call time on selling time, *Campaign*, 16 July, p. 12.

Wilson, S. (2009) The purpose of integration, *PRWeek-Thought Leader*, (December) p. 15.

Woods, A. (2012) The Real Deal, *Revolution*, March, 3–5.

Woolgar, T. (1998) Choosing an agency, *Campaign Report*, 9 October, 6–7.

Young, M. and Steilen, C. (1996) Strategy-based advertising agency selection: an alternative to 'spec' presentation, *Business Horizons*, 39 (November/December), 77–80.

Zambarino, A. and Goodfellow, J. (2003) Account planning in the new marketing and communications environment (has the Stephen King challenge been met?), *Marketing Intelligence and Planning*, 21(7), 424–34.

# Chapter 8
# Financial resources for marketing communications

Organisations need to ensure that they achieve the greatest possible efficiency with each unit of resource (e.g. pounds sterling, dollars, yuan, euros, rubles, Swedish kronor) they allocate to marketing communications activities. They cannot afford to be profligate with scarce resources and managers are accountable to the owners of the organisation for the decisions they make, including those associated with the investments they make in their marketing communications.

## Aims and learning objectives

The aim of this chapter is to examine the financial context within which organisations undertake marketing communications activities and campaigns.

The learning objectives of this chapter are to:

1. determine current trends in advertising and promotional expenditure;
2. explain the role of the communication budget;
3. clarify the benefits of using budgets for communication activities;
4. examine various budgeting techniques, both practical and theoretical;
5. introduce the advertising-to-sales (A/S) ratio;
6. explain the principles concerning the strategic use of the share of voice (SOV) concept;
7. appreciate how budgets might be set for the other elements of the communication mix.

# Minicase

## Honda

Honda is the world's largest motorcycle manufacturer and the second largest Japanese car manufacturer. Its core product range can be divided into three categories: cars, including hybrid electric vehicles, motorcycles and power division products, including lawn mowers and all-terrain vehicles. Other products include aircraft, solar panels, and robotics. Honda admits that it is obsessed with making highly engineered and, hence, reliable products. On the plus side of this global product strategy, customer satisfaction and company reputation are strong; on the downside, the cost base is expensive.

Understanding the prevailing Honda context is important as the company has been hit not only by the recession and a slump in global demand, but also by the earthquake and tsunami in Japan which wrecked the company's supply chain. In addition to this, environmentalists are pressuring governments over carbon emissions and pollution, fuel prices and insurance premiums are rising, while a raft of product recalls from various car manufacturers has generated negative publicity, changing the way car ownership is perceived.

Because of a shortage of parts from Japan, Honda was forced to close its Swindon factory for two months, and cut production by 50 per cent, so profits fell. In 2010 Honda sold 63,652 new cars in the UK, giving it a 3.13 per cent share of the UK market. The target is now to sell at least of 90,000 cars by 2015.

The average age of people buying Honda's best-selling car, the Civic, is 53, so it is not surprising that Honda aims to be regarded by this age group as an organisation that is trustworthy and accessible, not cold or remote. It also realises that it has a need to engage with a younger audience and lower the average age of a typical Honda customer.

In the UK Honda has a marketing department of 19 people, responsible for marketing communications, events, B2B marketing, and sales and digital marketing.

Of the many marketing challenges facing Honda some of the key ones concern the type of brand message to be communicated, which media are to be used, and how much should be invested in delivering these messages. Should the marketing team aim to increase sales immediately and so ease pressures on production? If it did not relieve the pressure on production, the need to introduce discounts and sales promotion offers would increase. However, discounting erodes margins and works against the development of Honda's long-term brand values.

Honda recognises that its communications should not be about generating short-term sales; it is more fruitful to develop brand values. The communications strategy and plan should accommodate potential customers, people who are not yet in the market. So, unlike many organisations, Honda has been increasing its marketing spend year on year. The strategy focuses on the experiences of customers and potential customers, from their first visit to its website through to purchase, servicing and onwards. Corporately, it is recognised and accepted that the return on Honda's marketing investment is not expected to be realised for 2 to 3 years.

A great example of this was Honda's award-winning brand campaign, 'The Power of Dreams', which utilised themes of technological progress, and the aspirations of those who use its cars, motorcycles and other products. There was no brand response mechanism, offers or deals, just an emotional message designed to stimulate prolonged engagement with the brand, until an individual's purchase needs are activated.

However, although the level of spend has increased, the balance of its deployment has changed. Like many companies, Honda has scaled back its TV advertising spend by 25 per cent. New technology allows people to skim through TV adverts, so Honda now prefers to use idents on documentaries, including Channel 4's *My Big Fat Gypsy Wedding*, which can attract an audience of over 8 million. Idents are posted just before a programme break and immediately prior to it starting again. This creates opportunities to capture an audience before they start their own break.

Honda spends £2 million on idents for a Channel 4 programme schedule of 80 hours. With repeats on sister channels, this exposure can reach up to 300 hours, and so compares very favourably with a traditional TV advertising campaign, with a similar budget that runs in 30-second spots over six weeks. It is argued that the indent strategy allows Honda greater control over the type of audience it targets, as it can segment on the basis of the demographic/people who are likely to watch those programmes and target the people it wants aligned to Honda.

However, Honda has shifted its media focus away from the passivity of television to the interactivity of digital channels. For example, it launched an online campaign to find 'Britain's most talented makers'. This was partly an employee-branding campaign as it aimed to promote the skills of its car-building engineers. The launch of Honda's TV channel online aimed to encourage viewers to generate their own content.

The company also incorporated digital media into its £2.5 million campaign 'This Unpredictable Life', which promotes the new model Jazz. It was designed to engage a younger audience and viewers were prompted to download a free iPhone app, using audio recognition software. The characters in the ad appear to 'jump' from the TV to the handset. 35,000 people downloaded the app and, although experimental, the ad successfully created brand noise and conversations.

Honda seeks an emotional response from its engagement strategy. Its approach is to generate positive brand values, to use communications to get the brand talked about. By generating consumer interest, desire, and trust, demand for the brand increases. Creating sufficient demand generates the revenues necessary to offset the cost of the investment. In other words, Honda wants to elicit emotional responses from consumers through its various activities, rather than drive an immediate sales boost. The expectation is that these increasing revenues will be sufficient to repay the investment in communications and more than cover the company's substantial engineering cost base.

*This minicase was written by Chris Fill using a variety of sources, including Barnett (2011), Bolger (2011) and www.Honda.com.*

| Exhibit 8.1 | **A scene from Honda's digital campaign, 'This Unpredictable Life'** |
| --- | --- |
| | *Source*: Honda U/C |

# Introduction

As the Honda mini case suggests, one of the key questions associated with investing in marketing communications is – what is the right amount an organisation should spend on marketing communications? In addition, how should organisations divide this sum across their brands, regions, territories and various activities? These two questions underpin the setting of communication budgets and the allocation of the budget once it is agreed (Corstjens et al. 2011). According to White (2007) the answers to these questions can lead directly to operational success or failure.

The rate at which advertising and associated media costs have outstripped the retail price index in developed economies was regarded as both alarming and troublesome. This disproportionate increase in the costs of advertising served to make it less and less attractive to some clients. Larger clients became more discerning and introduced procurement specialists to overview media purchasing. Unsurprisingly, this has spurred the increased use of other tools such as brand placement, sponsorship, event marketing, direct marketing, and new media formats, especially online and interactive-based marketing communications media, and more recently, mobile communications.

---

### Scholars' paper 8.1    Allocating the budget

**Abratt, R. and van der Westhuizen, B. (1985) A new promotion mix appropriation model,** *International Journal of Advertising,* **4, 209–21.**

One of the earlier papers to consider the budgeting and appropriation mix allocation issue. The authors look at some of the fundamental issues concerning which of the promotional tools should be used in different contexts but then develop these outcomes to suggest a new promotion mix appropriation model.

---

Some advertising agencies have argued that this disproportionately high increase was necessary because of the increasing number of new products and the length of time it takes to build a brand. Levels of advertising spend have continued to grow, although the growth has not been distributed evenly across all media. Between 2003 and 2006 UK cinema advertising expenditure grew 20 per cent, yet by 2011 had fallen to £182 million. Outdoor has grown significantly, fuelled largely by demand for six-sheet posters. The biggest advertiser was Procter & Gamble who spent £203 million in the UK across their product portfolio, while Kellogg spent £77 million, $O_2$ £49 million and Sony invested £17 million in their brands respectively. See Table 8.1 which specifies the top 10 brands (The Nielsen Company).

Large investment and commitment are required over a period of years if long-term, high-yield performance is to be achieved. Many accountants and procurement managers, however, view communications from a different perspective. For a long time their attitude has been to consider these activities, and advertising in particular, as an expense, to be set against the profits of the organisation. Many see planned marketing communications as a variable, one that can be discarded in times of recession (Whitehead, 2008).

These two broad views of advertising and of all marketing communications activities, one as an investment to be shown on the balance sheet and the other as a cost to be revealed in the profit and loss account, run consistently through discussions of how much should be allocated to advertising and other brand communications spend. For management, the four tools of the communication mix are often divided into two groups. The first contains advertising, sales promotion and public relations, while the second group contains the financial aspects that relate to personal selling.

| Table 8.1 | Top ten UK advertisers in 2011 |
| --- | --- |

| Organisation | £million total (2011) |
| --- | --- |
| Procter & Gamble | 204 |
| BSkyB | 145 |
| Unilever | 126 |
| Tesco | 115 |
| ASDA | 113 |
| Central Office of Information | 105 |
| DFS Furniture | 94 |
| Reckitt Benckiser | 81 |
| BT | 79 |
| Kellogg | 77 |

*Source*: The Nielsen Company.

This division reflects not only a functional approach to marketing but also the way in which, historically, the selling and marketing departments have developed. This is often observed in older, more established organisations, those that find innovation and change seriously difficult and challenging. Accountability and responsibility for communications expenditure in the first group often fall to the brand or product manager. In the second group, this aspect is managed by sales managers who often, at national level, report to a sales director.

The communication costs that need to be budgeted include the following. First, there is the airtime on broadcast media or space in print media that has to be bought to carry the message to the target audience. Then there are the production costs associated with generating the message and the staff costs of all those who contribute to the design and administration of the campaign. There are agency and professional fees, marketing research and contributions to general overheads and to expenses such as cars, entertainment costs and telephones that can be directly related to particular profit centres. In addition to all of these are any direct marketing costs, for which some organisations have still to find a suitable method of cost allocation. In some cases a particular department has been created to manage all direct marketing activities, and in these cases the costs can be easily apportioned.

The budget for the sales force is not one that can be switched on and off like an electric light. Advertising budgets can be massaged and campaigns pulled at the last minute, but communication through personal selling requires the establishment of a relatively high level of fixed costs. In addition to these expenses are the opportunity costs associated with the lengthy period taken to recruit, train and release suitably trained sales personnel into the competitive environment. This process can take over 15 months in some industries, especially in the fast-changing, demanding and complex information technology markets.

Strategic investment to achieve the right sales force, in terms of its size, training and maintenance, is paramount. It should be remembered, however, that managing a sales force can be rather like turning an ocean liner: any move or change in direction has to be anticipated and actioned long before the desired outcome can be accomplished. Funds need to be allocated strategically, but for most organisations a fast return on an investment should not be expected.

This chapter concentrates on the techniques associated with determining the correct allocation of funds to the first group of communication tools and, in particular, emphasis will be placed upon advertising. Attention will then be given to the other measures used to determine the correct level of investment in sales promotion, public relations and the field sales force. Finally, in an era in which shareholder value is becoming increasingly prominent and a means of distinguishing between alternative strategic options, the question of how a brand's value might influence the budget setting is considered.

# Trends in communication expenditure

It was stated earlier that advertising expenditure in the United Kingdom rose faster for a while than consumer expenditure. While this is true, the rapid increases in advertising spend in the 1980s slowed at the beginning of the 1990s, then speeded up again as the economy recovered only to waver again in 2001 after a buoyant previous year fuelled by the dot-com excitement. After a few years during which the advertising spend levels stabilised, only online advertising has grown substantially, in percentage terms. There has been considerable speculation that offline advertising revenues were about to plummet as organisations moved their spend online. Although many organisations have increased their online investment by some considerable amount and have reduced their offline, especially television, spend, the impact has not been as great as some commentators had feared. In 2005 there were signs that real growth was emerging once again, especially in the United Kingdom, but this was not continued and stabilisation of the top-line figures has been the norm.

The cutback in offline advertising expenditure when trading conditions tighten reflects the short-term orientation that some organisations have towards brand development or advertising. The IPA warn that budget reductions can lead to a 'loss of market share, a decline in brand image and long term sales damage', as reported by Donnelly (2008: 4). The report suggests that if a company cuts its advertising to zero it could take five years to recover, whereas a budget slashed by 50 per cent will take three years to recover.

What is also of interest is the way in which the communication mix has been changing over the past 20 years. For a long time spend on media advertising dominated the marketing budget of consumer brands. Sales promotion became a strong influence but spend on this tool stagnated, although revived as the recession took hold. Now sponsorship, direct marketing and digital activities attract the most investment. The reasons for this shift are indicative of the increasing attention and accountability that management is attaching to marketing communications. Increasingly, marketing managers are being asked to justify the amounts they invest/spend on their entire budgets, including advertising and sales promotion. Senior managers want to know the return they are getting for their communication investments, in order that they meet their business objectives and that scarce resources can be used more efficiently and effectively in the future.

It is not uncommon to find companies that are experiencing trading difficulties deciding to slash their adspend, if only on a temporary basis. Exceptions to this have been companies such as Marks & Spencer and Sainsbury's who, although experiencing difficulties, either increased or maintained their above-the-line spend and improved brand and share value. Research by Profit Impact on Market Strategy (PIMS) (Tomkins, 1999; Tylee, 1999) found that companies that maintain or even increase their adspend during a recession are likely to grow three times faster when the economy turns round than those companies that cut the adspend.

A report undertaken for the Advertising Association (2004) found that the majority of brand leaders that use advertising as a substantial proportion of the communication mix continue to dominate their markets, just as they did 30 years ago. In doing so, the report concludes, they have thwarted the challenge of own brands. In other words, advertising can protect brands, as long as the adspend is substantial.

In anticipation of the recent recession the Institute of Practitioners in Advertising (IPA) launched a book of case studies. This was sent to the CEOs of 350 FTSE companies and opinion formers such as journalists in the financial sector, fund managers and analysts. The 38 cases demonstrated how the use of advertising can improve brand value (Whitehead, 2008).

## Viewpoint 8.1    Bundling to save costs

As the recession bit into revenues and profits, brands started to look for new ways to make their communications budgets stretch further. One new approach is called *brand bundling*, or *collective marketing*, which involves marketing multiple items at the same time, or different companies bundling selected products together. Presenting a variety of products in one advert not only reduces costs but it can also encourage cross-selling. Procter and Gamble (P&G), the UK's biggest advertiser, has used the approach because it believes bundling brands makes sense since it provides a strong return on investment.

An example of this is its purchase of all the advertising spots in a particular programme and showing 'makeover breaks', where a woman is made over using multiple P&G products such as Max Factor make-up, Aussie hair products and Olay face cream. These work in TV programmes where viewers are highly involved and tend to watch the show from beginning to end. Another collective marketing example is P&G's use of Science Behind the Beauty spots. Typically an entire ad break is booked, and white-coated technicians explain how Head & Shoulders, Oral B toothbrushes and Olay all work.

Chevrolet, the car manufacturer, has been using both its brand name and multiple models within one ad to change perceptions of the brand in Europe. One campaign featured all of Chevrolet's car range driving together, but there were two distinct conclusions (end frames). One promoted the Spark city car, while the other focused on the five-door Cruze hatchback.

In France Kraft and Unilever worked together on a brand bundling project, where they produced an ezine to bundle together 25 product categories. Without the bundling approach these products these products would probably not have been advertised together. It is reported that over 2 million people visited the site, when it was first launched.

*Source*:   Based on Handley (2011).

**Question:**   How much of an impact might brand bundling have on brand visibility and long-term strength?

**Task:**   Choose a product category, select a manufacturer and compose a brand bundle for a target audience of your choice.

### Exhibit 8.2    A bundle of P&G products
*Source*: Art Directors & TRIP/Alamy Images

# The role of the communication budget

The role of the communication budget is the same whether the organisation is a multinational, trading from numerous international locations, or a small manufacturing unit on an industrial estate outside a semi-rural community. Both types of organisation want to ensure that they achieve the greatest efficiency with each euro they allocate to promotional activities. Neither can afford to be profligate with scarce resources, and each is accountable to the owners of the organisation for the decisions it makes.

There are two broad decisions that need to be addressed. The first concerns how much of the organisation's available financial resources (or relevant part) should be allocated to marketing communications over the next period. The second concerns how much of the total amount should be allocated to each of the individual disciplines of the communication mix.

## Benefits of budgeting

The benefits of engaging in budgeting activities are many and varied, but in the context of marketing communication planning they can be considered as follows:

1. The process serves to focus people's attention on the costs and benefits of undertaking the planned communication activities.

2. The act of quantifying the means by which the marketing plan will be communicated to target audiences instils a management discipline necessary to ensure that the objectives of the plan are capable of being achieved. Achievement must be at a level that is acceptable and will not overstretch or embarrass the organisation.

3. The process facilitates cross-function coordination and forces managers to ensure that the planned communications are integrated and mutually supportive. The process provides a means by which campaigns can be monitored and management control asserted. This is particularly important in environments that are subject to sudden change or competitive hostility.

4. At the end of the campaign, a financial review enables management to learn from the experiences of the promotional activity in order that future communications can be made more efficient and the return on the investment improved.

The process of planning the communications budget is an important one. Certain elements of the process will have been determined during the setting of the campaign objectives. Managers will check the financial feasibility of a project prior to committing larger resources. Managers will also discuss the financial implications of the communication strategy (that is, the push/pull positioning dimension) and those managers responsible for each of the individual tools will have estimated the costs that their contribution will involve. Senior management will have some general ideas about the level of the overall appropriation, which will inevitably be based partly upon precedent, market and competitive conditions and partly as a response to the pressures of different stakeholders, among them key members of the distribution network. Decisions now have to be made about the viability of the total plan, whether the appropriation is too large or too small and how the funds are to be allocated across the promotional tools.

Communication budgets are not formulated at a particular moment in a sequence of management activities. The financial resources of an organisation should be constantly referred to, if only to monitor current campaigns. Therefore, budgeting and the availability of financial resources are matters that managers are constantly aware of and able to tap into at all stages in the development and implementation of planned communications.

# Difficulties associated with budgeting for communications

There are a number of problems associated with the establishment of a marketing communications budget. Of them all, the following appear to be the most problematic. First, it is difficult to quantify the precise amount that is necessary to complete all the required tasks. Second, communication budgets do not fit neatly with standard accounting practices. The concept of brand value is accepted increasingly as a balance sheet item, but the concept of investment in communication to create value has only recently begun to be accepted, for example by Jaguar and Nestlé. Third, the diversity of the tools and the means by which their success can be measured renders like-for-like comparisons null and void. Finally, the budget-setting process is not as clear-cut as it might at first appear.

There are four main stakeholder groups that contribute to the budget decision. These are the organisation itself, any communication agencies, the media and production or fulfilment houses whose resources will be used to carry designated messages and the target audience. It is the ability of these four main stakeholders to interact, to communicate effectively with each other and to collaborate that will impact most upon the communications budget. However, determining the 'appropriate appropriation' is a frustrating exercise for marketing managers. The allocation of scarce resources across a communication budget presents financial and political difficulties, especially where the returns are not easily identifiable. The development and significance of technology within marketing can lead to disputes concerning ownership and control of resources. For example, in many companies management and responsibility for the website rests with the IT department, which understandably takes a technological view of issues. Those in marketing, however, see the use of the website from a marketing perspective and need a budget to manage it. Tension between the two can result in different types of website design and effectiveness and this leads to different levels of customer support.

Smallbone (1972) suggested a long time ago that the allocation of funds for promotion is one of the primary problems facing marketers, if not one of the major strategic problems. Audience and media fragmentation, changed management expectations and a more global orientation have helped ensure that budgeting remains problematic.

# Techniques and approaches

At a broad level there are a number of models proposed by different authors concerning the appropriation of the communication mix. In particular, Abratt and van der Westhuizen (1985) who refer, among others, to Smallbone's (1972) and Gaedeke and Tootelian's (1983) models of promotional appropriation. Abratt and van der Westhuizen have determined, among other things, that personal selling dominated the mix of all their respondents in a particular study of business-to-business markets and that the models themselves were too simplistic to be of any direct benefit.

These broad approaches to budget allocation are not therefore appropriate, and it is necessary to investigate the value of using particular techniques. It is useful to start this section by establishing the theoretical approach associated with the determination of communication and, in particular, advertising budgets.

### Marginal analysis: the advertising response function

This method is normally depicted as a tool for understanding advertising expenditures but, as Burnett (1993) points out, it has been used for all elements of the communication mix,

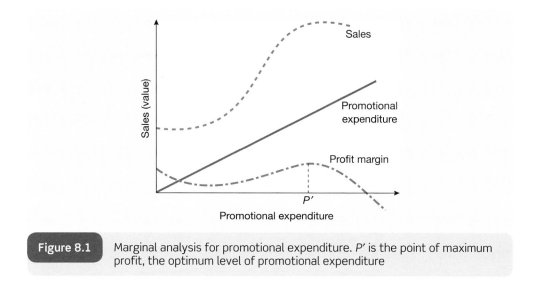

| **Figure 8.1** | Marginal analysis for promotional expenditure. *P'* is the point of maximum profit, the optimum level of promotional expenditure |
|---|---|

including personal selling, so it is included here for understanding the overall promotional allocation.

Marginal analysis, or the advertising response function enables managers to determine how many extra sales are generated from an extra unit of communication spend. A point will be reached when an extra pound/euro/dollar spent on communication will generate an equal amount (a single pound/euro/dollar's-worth) of revenue. At this point marginal revenue is equal to marginal costs, the point of maximum communication expenditure has been reached and maximum profit is generated. In other words, this approach helps advertisers identify the point at which they can achieve the highest advertising efficiency and maximise their return on investment (Kim and Cheong, 2009).

Another way of looking at this approach is to track the path of sales and communication expenditure. Even with zero promotional effort some sales will still be generated. In other words, sales are not totally dependent upon formal communication activity, a point that will be returned to later. When there is a small amount of promotion effort, the impact is minimal, as the majority of potential customers are either unaware of the messages or they do not think the messages are sufficiently credible for them to change their current behaviour. After a certain point, however, successive increments in communication expenditure will produce more than proportionate increments in sales. The sales curve in Figure 8.1 can now be seen to rise steeply and the organisation moves into a position where it can begin to take advantage of the economies of scale in communication. Eventually the sales curve starts to flatten out as diminishing returns to promotion begin to set in. This is because the majority of the target market has become aware of the offering, and has decided whether or not to become customers.

This model suffers from a number of disadvantages, as set out at Table 8.2. First, it assumes that communications can be varied smoothly and continuously. This is not the case. Second, it assumes that communications are the only influence upon sales. As discussed previously, sales are influenced by a variety of factors, of which planned communication is but one. Controllable and uncontrollable elements in the environment influence sales. Next, no account is taken of the other costs associated indirectly with the presentation of the offering, such as those allied to distribution. Each communication thrust will often be matched, or even bettered, by the competition. Furthermore, the actions of rivals may even affect the sales performance of all products in the same category.

It is fair to say, therefore, that the marginal approach fails to account for competitor reactions. The model assumes that sales are the result of current communication campaigns. No attempt is made to account for the effects of previous campaigns and that adstock (or carryover) may

| **Table 8.2** | Difficulties with the marginal analysis as a way of setting communication budgets |
|---|---|

Assumes communication activities can be varied in a smooth and uniform manner.

Requires perfect data that in reality are very difficult to obtain.

Assumes only communication activities impact upon sales.

Does not consider all the costs associated with communication activities.

No account is made of the actions of direct and indirect competitors.

Adstock effects are ignored.

All messages are regarded as having equal impact. No consideration is given to the quality of messages.

well be a prime reason for a sale occurring. The time parameters used to compute the marginal analysis could be totally inaccurate.

One of the most important shortcomings of the theory is its failure to account for the qualitative effects of the messages that are transmitted. It is assumed that all messages are of a particular standard and that relative quality is unimportant. Clearly this cannot be the case.

The marginal approach is suspect in that it operates outside the real world, and it requires data and skill in its implementation that are difficult and expensive to acquire. Theoretically, this approach is sound, but the practical problems of obtaining the necessary information and the absence of qualitative inputs render the technique difficult for most organisations to implement.

However, before moving to some of the more pragmatic approaches, it should be noted that marginal analysis is not entirely without practical foundation. For example, Weaver and Merrick (2004) consider ways in which response-curve approaches can be combined with econometrics and management judgement and through the merged processes a more accurate and meaningful budget can be determined.

---

### Scholars' paper 8.2    How to allocate resources

**Corstjens, M., Umblijs, A. and Wang, C. (2011) The Power of Inertia: Conservatism in Marketing Resource Allocation, *Journal of Advertising Research*, (June), 356–72.**

In some ways this is a contemporary version of the Abratt and van der Westhuizen (1985) paper. The range of tools/instruments incorporated is much broader than the previous paper, and the aim is to provide management with directional guidance regarding the allocation decisions, based on market response functions. For example, is there overspend, or is there underspend on particular drivers?

---

## Practical approaches

If the marginal approach is not workable because it is impracticable, then a consideration of the alternative approaches is necessary. Practitioners have developed a range of other methods that tend to reflect simplicity of deduction and operation but raise doubts over their overall contribution and effectiveness.

The following represent some of the more common approaches. It should be noted, at this point, that none of the techniques should be seen in isolation. Organisations use a variety of approaches to reduce any dependence, and hence risk, on any one method. The main methods are arbitrary, inertia, media multiplier, percentage of sales, affordable, quantitative, objective and task, and share of voice (SOV).

## Arbitrary

This is sometimes referred to as 'chairperson's rules', but the arbitrary method is the simplest and most inappropriate of all the available techniques. Under chairperson's rules, what the boss says or guesses at, is what is implemented. The fact that the boss may not have a clue what the optimal figure should be is totally irrelevant. Very often the budget is decided 'on the hoof', and as each demand for communication resources arrives so decisions are made in isolation from any overall strategy.

Apart from the merit of flexibility, this method has numerous deficiencies. It fails to consider customer needs, the demands of the environment or marketing strategy, and there is an absence of any critical analysis. Unfortunately this approach is often used by many small organisations.

## Inertia

An alternative to guesswork is the 'let's keep it the same' approach. Here all elements of the environment and the costs associated with the tasks facing the organisation are ignored. This too is not recommended.

## Media multiplier

One step more advanced is the method that recognises that media rate card costs may have increased. So, in order to maintain the same impact, the media multiplier rule requires last year's spend to be increased by the rate at which media costs have increased. This assumes all previous decisions to be ok and that marketing strategies and the environment remain unchanged. This is unlikely.

## Percentage of sales

One of the more common and thoughtful approaches is to set the budget at a level equal to some predetermined percentage of past or expected sales. Invariably, organisations select a percentage that is traditional to the organisation, such as 'We always aim to spend 5.0 per cent of our sales on advertising.' The rationale put forward is that it is the norm for the sector to spend about 4.5–5.5 per cent or that 5.0 per cent is acceptable to the needs of the most powerful stakeholders or is set in recognition of overall corporate responsibilities. For example, a local authority will be mindful of the needs of its council taxpayers, whose finances contribute to the funding and maintenance of local tourism activities, for example a museum or park facilities.

There are a number of flaws with this technique. It is focused upon the sales base on which the budget rests. Planned communications and advertising in particular, are intended to create demand, not to be the result of past sales. If the demand generators of the communication mix are to be based on the last period's performance, then it is likely that the next period's results will be similar, all things being equal. This must be the logical implication when the percentage is based on past performance.

Another way of looking at this method is to base the spend on a percentage of the next period's sales. This overcomes some of the problems, but still constrains the scope and the realistic expectations of a budget. No consideration is given to the sales potential that may exist, so this technique may actually limit performance.

## Affordable

This approach is still regarded by many organisations as sophisticated and relatively free of risk. It requires each unit of output to be allocated a proportion of all the input costs and all the costs associated with the value-adding activities in production and manufacturing, together with all the other costs in distributing the output. After making an allowance for profit, what is left is to be spent on advertising and communication. In other words, what is left is what we can afford to spend.

## Viewpoint 8.2    Roll-over payments

Following Procter & Gamble's initial attempt to introduce a cost-per-engagement (CPE) model, Universal Music's Polydor Records introduced a similar scheme in an attempt to get better value from its communications investments. Polydor Records launched a model to assist the measurement of their ad campaigns, in a bid to support artists such as La Roux, Danish pop group Alphabeat and Manchester band Delphic.

The model works on the basis that, if a visitor/fan rolls over an MPU ad and watches the video, then Polydor pays the publisher an agreed fee. This, it is thought is an appropriate approach as it is cost-effective and suitable to promote niche artists. The model is not so appropriate for high-profile artists, as the key here is to generate mass awareness.

*Source*:    Based on Faber (2009).

**Question:**    How much do you agree with the view that as payment systems become more complex so a focus on sales performance might fall?

**Task:**    If you were a recording artist, think of the different factors you would want incorporated into a remuneration programme.

**Exhibit 8.3**    **The Polydor record label introducing new digital methods of measurement**
*Source*: Steven May/Alamy Images

The affordable technique is not in the least analytical, nor does it have any market or task orientation. It is a technique used by organisations of differing sizes (Hooley and Lynch, 1985) that are product- rather than customer-oriented. Their view of advertising is that it is a cost and that the quality of their product will ensure that it will sell itself. Organisations using this technique will be prone to missing opportunities that require advertising investment. This is because a ceiling on advertising expenditure is set and borrowings are avoided. As sales fluctuate in variable markets, the vagueness of this approach is unlikely to lead to an optimal budget.

## Quantitative approaches

Various quantitative approaches have been offered in an attempt to determine a precise, all-encompassing model to derive a budget. Weaver and Merrick (2004) refer to Dyson (1999), who published a mathematical model to help apportion a budget within a brand portfolio. They also mention Harper and Bridges (2003), whose scoring system approach was offered as a contrast to the algorithms of Dyson. Neither is entirely satisfactory, if only for their lack of flexibility and interpretation of the competitive environment.

### Objective and task

The methods presented so far seek to determine an overall budget and leave the actual allocation to products and regions to some arbitrary method. This is unlikely to be a realistic, fair or optimal use of a critical resource.

The objective and task approach is different from the others in that it attempts to determine the resources required to achieve each objective. It then aggregates these separate costs into an overall budget. For example, the costs associated with achieving a certain level of awareness can be determined from various media owners who are seeking to sell time and space in their media vehicles. The costs of sales promotions and sales literature can be determined and the production costs of these activities and those of direct marketing (e.g. telemarketing) and PR events and sponsorships can be brought together. The total of all these costs represents the level of investment necessary to accomplish the communication objectives that have been established earlier in the marketing communications plan. This approach is sometimes referred to as zero-based budgeting.

The attractions of this technique are that it focuses management attention on the goals to be accomplished and that the monitoring and feedback systems that have to be put in place allow for the development of knowledge and expertise. On the downside, the objective and task approach does not generate realistic budgets, in the sense that the required level of resources may not be available and the opportunity costs of the resources are not usually determined. More important, it is difficult to determine the best way to accomplish a task and to know exactly what costs will be necessary to complete a particular activity. Very often the actual costs are not known until the task has been completed, which rather reduces the impact of the budget-setting process. What is also missing is a strategic focus. The objective and task method deals very well with individual campaigns, but is not capable of providing the overall strategic focus of the organisation's annual (period) spend. The case of Procter & Gamble illustrates this point.

The use of this approach leads to the determination of a sum of money. This sum is to be invested, in this case in promoting the offerings of the organisation, but it could equally be a new machine or a building. To help discover whether such a sum should be invested and whether it is in the best interests of the organisation, a 'payout plan' can be undertaken.

#### Payout plans

These are used to determine the investment value of the advertising plan. This process involves determining the future revenues and costs to be incurred over a two- or three-year period. The essential question answered by such an exercise is 'How long will it take to recover the expenditure?'

*Sensitivity analysis*

Many organisations use this adjusting approach to peg back the advertising expenditure because the payout plan revealed costs as too large or sales developing too slowly. Adjustments are made to the objectives or to the strategies, with the aim of reducing the payback period.

# Competitive parity

In certain markets, such as the relatively stable FMCG market, many organisations use investment in communication as a competitive tool. The underlying assumption is that advertising is the only direct variable that influences sales. The argument is based on the point that, while there are many factors that impact on sales, these factors are all self-cancelling. Each factor impacts on all the players in the market. The only effective factor is the amount that is spent on planned communications. As a result, some organisations deliberately spend the same amount on advertising as their competitors spend: competitive parity.

Competitive parity has a major benefit for the participants. As each organisation knows what the others are spending and while there is no attempt to destabilise the market through excessive or minimal communication spend, the market avoids self-generated turbulence and hostile competitive activity.

There are, however, a number of disadvantages with this simple technique. The first is that, while information is available, there is a problem of comparing like with like. For example, a carpet manufacturer selling a greater proportion of output into the trade will require different levels and styles of advertising and promotion from another manufacturer selling predominantly to the retail market. Furthermore, the first organisation may be diversified, perhaps importing floor tiles. The second may be operating in a totally unrelated market. Such activities make comparisons difficult to establish, and financial decisions based on such analyses are highly dubious.

The competitive parity approach fails to consider the qualitative aspects of the advertising undertaken by the different players. Each attempts to differentiate itself, and very often the communication messages are one of the more important means of successfully positioning an organisation. It would not be surprising, therefore, to note that there is probably a great range in the quality of the planned communications. Associated with this is the notion that, when attempting to adopt different positions, the tasks and costs will be different and so seeking relative competitive parity may be an inefficient use of resources. The final point concerns the data used in such a strategy. The data are historical and based on strategies relevant at the time. Competitors may well have embarked upon a new strategy since the data were released. This means that parity would not only be inappropriate for all the reasons previously listed, but also because the strategies are incompatible.

The competitive parity approach fails to consider the qualitative aspects of the advertising undertaken by the different players.

# Advertising-to-sales ratio

An interesting extension of the competitive parity principle is the notion of advertising-to-sales (A/S) ratios. Instead of simply seeking to spend a relatively similar amount on communication to one's main competitors, this approach attempts to account for the market shares held by the different players and to adjust communication spend accordingly.

If it is accepted that there is a direct relationship between the volume of advertising (referred to as *weight*) and sales, then it is not unreasonable to conclude that if an organisation spends more on advertising then it will see a proportionate improvement in sales. The underlying principle of the A/S ratio is that, in each industry, it is possible to determine the average advertising spend of all the players and compare it with the value of the market. Therefore, it is possible for each organisation to determine its own A/S ratio and compare it with the industry average. Those organisations with an A/S ratio below the average may conclude either that they have advertising economies of scale working in their favour or that their advertising is working much harder, pound for pound, than some of their competitors. Organisations can also use A/S ratios as a means of controlling expenditure across multiple product areas. Budgets can be set based upon the industry benchmark – and variances spotted quickly – and further information requested to determine shifts in competitor spend levels or reasons leading to any atypical performance.

Each business sector has its own characteristics, which in turn influence the size of the advertising expenditure. In 2011 the A/S ratio for perfumes was 19.8 per cent, soap and detergent, 10.3, sports and athletic goods, 7.1, household appliances, 1.9, restaurants, 2.2 and engineering services, 0.3 (AdAge, 2011). It can be seen that the size of the A/S ratio can vary widely. It appears to be higher (that is, a greater proportion of revenue is used to invest in advertising) when the following are present:

- the offering is standardised, not customised;
- there are many end-users;
- the financial risk for the end-user customer is small;
- the marketing channels are short;
- a premium price is charged;
- there is a high gross margin;
- the industry is characterised by surplus capacity;
- competition is characterised by a high number of new product launches.

A/S ratios provide a useful benchmark for organisations when they are trying to determine the adspend level. These ratios do not set out what the communication budget should be, but they do provide a valuable indicator around which broad commercial decisions can be developed.

# Share of voice

Brand strategy in the FMCG market has traditionally been based on an approach that uses mass media advertising to drive brand awareness, which in turn allows premium pricing to fund the advertising investment (cost). The alternative approach has been to use price-based promotions to drive market share. The latter approach has often been regarded as a short-term approach that is incapable of sustaining a brand over the longer term.

The concept underlying the A/S ratio can be seen in the context of rival supporters chanting at a football match. If they chant at the same time, at the same decibel rating, then it is difficult to distinguish the two sets of supporters, particularly if they are chanting the same song. Should one set of supporters shout at a lower decibel rating, then the collective voice of the other supporters would be the one that the rest of the crowd, and perhaps any television audience, actually hears and distinguishes.

This principle applies to the concept of share of voice (SOV). Within any market the total of all advertising expenditure (adspend) – that is, all the advertising by all of the players – can be analysed in the context of the proportions each player has made to the total. Should one advertiser spend more than any other, it will be *its* messages that are received and stand a better chance of being heard and acted upon. In other words, its SOV is the greater. This implies, of course, that the quality of the message transmitted is not important and that it is the sheer relative weight of adspend that is the critical factor.

This concept can be taken further and combined with another: share of market (SOM). The relationship between SOV and SOM is recognised by a number of authors, including Broadbent (1989), Schroer (1990), Jones (1990) and Buck (2001). When a brand's market share is equal to its share of advertising spend, equilibrium is said to have been reached (SOV = SOM). Increasing the SOV above the point of equilibrium generally raises SOM, whilst lowering SOV reduces SOM and reaches a new point of stability.

## Strategic implications of the SOV concept

These concepts of SOV and SOM frame an interesting perspective of competitive strategy based upon the relative weight of advertising expenditure. Schroer (1990) reports that, following extensive research on the US packaged goods market (FMCG), it is noticeable that organisations can use advertising spend to maintain equilibrium and to create disequilibrium in a market. The former is established by major brand players maintaining their market shares with little annual change to their advertising budgets. Unless a competitor is prepared to inject a considerable increase in advertising spend and so create disequilibrium, the relatively stable high spend deters new entrants and preserves the status quo. Schroer claims that, if the two market leaders maintain SOV within 10 per cent of each other, then competitive equilibrium will exist. This situation is depicted in Figure 8.2. If a market challenger launches an aggressive assault upon the leader by raising advertising spend to a point where SOV is 20–30 per cent higher than the current leader, market share will shift in favour of the challenger.

In Figure 8.2 brands 1, 3, 4 and 6 have an SOM that is greater than their SOV. This suggests that their advertising is working well for them and that the larger organisations have some economies of scale in their advertising. Brands 2 and 5, however, have an SOM that is less than their SOV. This is because brand 2 is challenging for the larger market (with brand 1) and is likely to be less profitable than brand 1 because of the increased costs. Brand 5 is competing in a niche market and, as a new brand, may be spending heavily (relative to its market share) to gain acceptance in the new market environment.

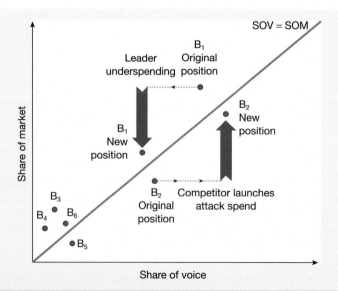

| Figure 8.2 | Strategy to gain market share by an increase in adspend |

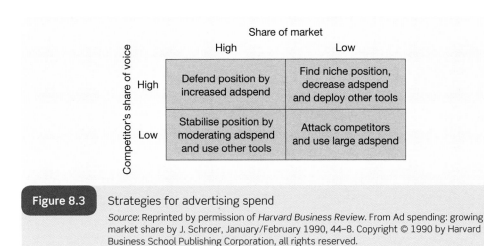

**Figure 8.3** Strategies for advertising spend

Source: Reprinted by permission of *Harvard Business Review*. From Ad spending: growing market share by J. Schroer, January/February 1990, 44–8. Copyright © 1990 by Harvard Business School Publishing Corporation, all rights reserved.

This perspective brings implications for advertising spend at a strategic level. This is shown in the matrix, Figure 8.3, which shows that advertising spend should be varied according to the adspend of the company's competitors in different markets. The implications are that advertising budget decisions should be geared to the level of adspend undertaken by competitors in particular markets at particular times. Decisions to attack or to defend are also set out. For example, communication investments should be placed in markets where competitors are underspending. Furthermore, if information is available about competitors' costs, then decisions to launch and sustain an advertising spend attack can be made in the knowledge that a prolonged period of premium spending can be carried through with or without a counter-attack.

This traditional perspective of static markets being led by the top two brands using heavy above-the-line strategies and the rest basing their competitive thrusts on price-based promotions was challenged by Buck (1995) through reference to a study of Superpanel data by Hamilton. It was found that the brand leaders in many FMCG markets spent nearly 50 per cent more than the industry average on advertising, while the number two brand spent about 8 per cent less than the industry average. In addition, the gap with the other actors was not as significant as Schroer reported. This is, of course, a comparison of European and US markets, and there is no reason why they should be identical or at least very similar. However, the data are interesting in that the challenge of brand 2, postulated by Schroer, is virtually impossible in many of the UK, if not also in continental European, markets.

The concepts of SOV and SOM have also been used by Jones (1990) to develop a new method of budget setting. He suggests that those brands that have an SOV greater than their SOM are 'investment brands', and those that have a SOV less than or equal to their SOM are 'profit-taking brands'.

There are three points to notice. First, the high advertising spend of new brands is an established strategy and represents a trade-off between the need for profit and the need to become established through advertising spend. The result, invariably, is that smaller brands have lower profitability because they have to invest a disproportionate amount in advertising. Second, large brands are often 'milked' to produce increased earnings, especially in environments that emphasise short-termism. The third point is that advertising economies of scale allow large brands to develop with an SOV consistently below the SOM.

Using data collected from an extensive survey of 1,096 brands across 23 different countries, Jones 'calculated the difference between share of voice and share of market and averaged these differences within each family of brands' (p. 40). By representing the data diagrammatically (Figure 8.4), Jones shows how it becomes a relatively simple task to work out the adspend that is required to achieve a particular share of market. The first task is to plot the expected (desired) market share from the horizontal axis; then move vertically to the intersect with the curve and read off the SOV figure from the vertical axis.

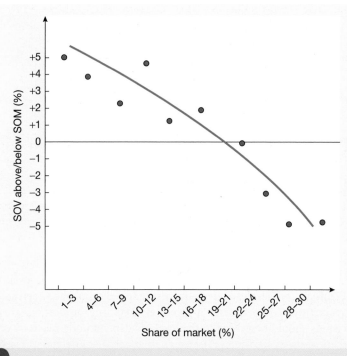

## Scholars' paper 8.3        Shouting louder than the rest

**Schroer, J. (1990) Ad spending: growing market share, *Harvard Business Review* (January/February), 44–8.**

This article is based on research amongst US FMCG firms that shows how varying ad spends can be used to maintain equilibrium or create disequilibrium in a market. Schroer identifies that if two market leaders maintain SOV within 10 per cent of each other, competitive equilibrium in terms of share of market (SOM) will be maintained. Further, if a challenger raises SOV by 20–30 per cent more than the current market leader, they will increase SOM.

See also:

Jones, J.P. (1990) Ad spending: maintaining market share, *Harvard Business Review* (January/February), 38–42.

Field, P. (2009) Account planners need to care more about share of voice, *Admap* (September), 28–30.

This study utilises data from the IPA databank of effectiveness case studies for the past 20 years. This shows evidence of the relationship between SOV and SOM. The author encourages account planners to engage with the principle alongside media planners, in the context of shifts in agency remuneration based on payment by results.

As Binet and Field (2007) point out, marketing success is predicated on share of voice rather than size of budget. In addition, the vast proportion of budget is invested in order to maintain or slow the decline of market share, rather than grow it.

# Appropriation brand types

Using this approach it is possible to determine three main types of brands, based upon the amount of advertising investment. In each market there are brands that are promoted without the support of any advertising. These small niche players can be regarded as zero-based brands.

Where brands are supported by token advertising, represented by a small SOV, the brand is probably being milked and the resources are being channelled into developing other brands. New launches are typified by the heavy advertising investment, which is necessary to get them off the ground. Here the SOV will be larger than the SOM and these can be referred to as investment brands.

In situations where the SOM is very large and the SOV much smaller, these profit-taking brands run a risk of losing market share if a competitor spots the opportunity to invest a large sum in a prolonged attack. Finally, there is a group of brands that maintain stability by respecting each other's positions and by not initiating warfare. These brands can be referred to as equilibrium brands.

- *Investment brands* – SOV > SOM; heavy advertising to drive growth.
- *Milking brands* – SOV < SOM; low-level advertising to take profits out of the brand.
- *Equilibrium brands* – SOM = SOV; steady advertising to maintain position and avoid confrontation.

Assessing brands in the context of the advertising resources they attract is a slightly different way of reflecting their power and importance to their owners. If the SOV approach is limited by its applicability to stable, mature market conditions then at least it enables the communication spend to be seen and used as a competitive weapon.

It is interesting to note that the SOV concept commanded a reasonable profile in the early to mid 1990s but then subsided from view. Its revival by Binet and Field (2007) when communicating with advertising practitioners is helpful and commensurate with the emerging emphasis on accountability and the use of metrics.

# The value of brand communications

The ideas and principles associated with the SOV concept provide a foundation upon which to consider the value of marketing communications as an aid to brand development. The importance of brands cannot be understated. Indeed, many organisations have attempted (and succeeded) in valuing the worth of their brands and have had them listed as an asset on their balance sheets. While this has stimulated the accountancy profession into some debate, the concept of a brand's worth to an organisation cannot be refuted. Among other things, when companies buy other companies or brands, they are purchasing the potential income streams that these target brands offer, not just the physical assets of plant, capital and machinery. However, communications are a vital element used to develop these assets and so it is important to understand the relationship between the required level of investment in communications and the asset value that results from this activity.

Butterfield (1999) argued that marketers are required to account for their activities in terms of the contribution they make to the financial performance of an organisation. This means that markets and customers will be viewed as assets, which in turn will become subject to development, cultivation and leverage. Marketers will also be required to use different measures of performance. Market share, margin and revenues will give way to terms such as return on investment, net present value of future cash flows or just shareholder value. He commented that it will not be just a question of how much your adspend is, but how much you spend relative to your main competitors' market share. Although some of his views have yet to become reality, there are signs that this longer-term, strategic-value-oriented approach is beginning to become part of the overall marketing communications vocabulary, if not yet part of everyday practice. Ideas concerning shareholder value as a means of developing marketing strategy have become quite common and articulated by many authors since Butterfield first speculated about future techniques.

Although there are exceptional cases, it is generally accepted that stronger brands are more likely to maintain market share in the following year than weaker brands. This means that the revenue streams from stronger brands are more secure and attract lower risk than weaker brands. Farr (2004) refers to the use of brand-related communications as media pressure. He defines media pressure 'as the brand's share of communications spending minus its prior-year market share' (p. 30). A brand's strength is in (major) part due to the accumulated investments and activities in the past. It follows, therefore, that these investments in communications should be continued rather than truncated. Figure 8.5 shows the relationship between risk (of share loss) and media pressure.

Farr uses data from 350 brands, across a range of categories that have been divided into 20 groups based on media pressure. As media pressure grows so the risk (per cent) of losing share declines. This approach can be used to determine media budgets. Using discounted cash flows (DCFs) Farr shows that it is possible to estimate changes in the net present value (NPV) of the cash flows arising from different levels of media pressure. In the example depicted in Figure 8.6, investments up to around £40 million provide a positive impact on NPV but further investments fail to increase the value of future earnings, and should therefore not be utilised. He acknowledges that the assumption that investments in stronger brands will be more profitable may be misleading and other approaches to budget setting may need to be used when weaker (smaller) brands launch new variants or extensions.

At the end of the communication process one of the benefits that management hopes will emerge is an overall increase in the valuation of the brand. This net value arises as a result

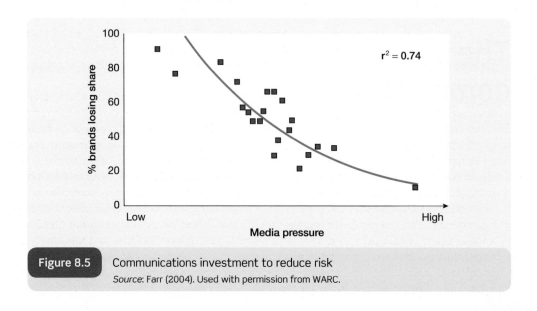

| Figure 8.5 | Communications investment to reduce risk |

*Source*: Farr (2004). Used with permission from WARC.

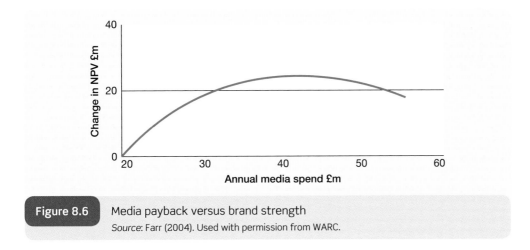

**Figure 8.6**  Media payback versus brand strength
*Source*: Farr (2004). Used with permission from WARC.

of the investment (for example, communication expenditures) generating a return to reward those who risked the capital invested in the brand. Some believe that this value arises from these activities and that the brand itself is worth £x; this should therefore be regarded as an asset and be placed on the balance sheet.

# Which methods are most used?

From this review and commentary it is necessary to draw out the degree to which these particular tools are used in practice. Mitchell's (1993) study to determine the methods and criteria used by companies to determine their advertising budgets found that 40 per cent of respondents claimed to use the objective and task approach, 27 per cent used percentage of future sales (8 per cent used past sales) and 19 per cent used a variety of company-specific methods that do not fit neatly within any one item from the list presented above.

---

**Viewpoint 8.3    Just how much do companies spend?**

UK industry invested £16.2 billion on advertising in 2011. Add together an approximate £14 billion for sales promotion, £7 billion for public relations, and £14 billion for direct marketing and we have a grand total of £50 billion invested in marketing communications each year. Companies have to allocate their resources carefully in order to generate the best possible return.

The advertising budgets allocated by companies differ widely, and of course it is only the big blue chip brands that invest heavily in advertising and marketing communications. Table 8.1 presents the amounts spent by the leading advertisers. Here the huge difference between competitors Procter & Gamble (P&G) and Unilever and very close figures of supermarket retail groups Tesco and Asda are visible. There is significant difference between the two fast-moving consumer goods brands but little difference between the retailers. P&G and Unilever are, of course, advertising individual brands within their respective portfolios. This includes supporting new brand launches as well as promoting existing brands. In any one period differences in marketing activity could have a significant effect on the amount of budget required.

Although Tesco have a larger market share than Asda in the UK, these figures identify similar levels of advertising expenditure. As market leader, it could be argued that there is a need for Tesco to outspend their rivals. As the second largest supermarket group in the UK, Asda are clearly targeting the use of advertising to challenge their rivals, with other competitors in this sector spending considerably less.

The government's communications body, the Central Office of Information has reduced its advertising expenditure substantially since 2010, by over 50 per cent. Budget pressures resulting from the UK's economic situation led to these dramatic reductions in spending.

*Source*:   Based on O'Reilly (2011); www.adassoc.org.uk;
Nielsen Media Research – www.rankingthebrands.com;
www.brandrepublic.com/league_tables/1059790/Biggest-Brands-Top-100- advertisers-2011/.

**Question:**   Does spending more than competitors guarantee advertising success?

**Task:**   Use information from trade magazines such as *Marketing, Marketing Week* and *Campaign* and compile a list of recent advertising campaigns and how much they cost.

Although the figures resulting from the study can only be used to indicate trends of overall preferences, another set of important factors also emerged from this study. These are the range of organisational influences that impact on individual organisations. Over half the respondents reported that the method used to set these budgets actually varied, internally, across product categories. Different methods were used for new and established products.

The criteria used by organisations to set their communication budgets are many and varied. Mitchell suggests that the criteria used could be grouped as *controllables* (41 per cent), such as financial, product, production and goals; *uncontrollables* (41 per cent), such as sales, competition, market, media and distribution and *signals* (18 per cent), such as national activities, experience, effectiveness of expenditures and awareness. He reported that the processes used to determine the budgets were found as either essentially centralised or top down (52 per cent), decentralised or bottom up (13.5 per cent) or bargaining (top down and bottom up) (21 per cent). Gullen (2003) suggests ways in which all of the techniques can be grouped, but concludes that management judgement based on weighting key criteria is required to determine the optimal budget.

West and Prendergast (2009) found that approximately 28 per cent of their respondents claimed that their firms used judgmental budgeting methods, with a similar number claiming use of the objective and task processes. Measurement-based budgeting methods were reported by 20 per cent, sales 15 per cent and competitive with roughly 8 per cent. However, their key finding was that budgeting is not about methods, measurement or analysis. The real factors that influence budgets are 'personalities, organization, timing, planning, the nature of the market and access to data'. They identify a 'cultural code' which permeates and shapes the budgeting strategy within organisations.

## Scholars' paper 8.4    So, What do practitioners use?

**West, D. and Prendergast, G.P. (2009) Advertising and promotions budgeting and the role of risk, *European Journal of Marketing*, 43(11/12), 1457–76.**

The authors provide a useful insight into the budgetary methods used by industry. They find that judgmental methods tend to dominate, especially the 'what is affordable' method. They also uncover methods such as 'objective and task', and measurement techniques such as 'return on investment' are used by a good percentage of respondents. It appears that on average, two methods are used by managers to determine the most efficient budget.

Indeed, organisational culture was found to be the most important budgetary factor. Culture serves as an 'interpretive frame' through which managers act and may even influence individuals who authorise and sanction budgets. Culture, therefore, provides the decision-making frame within which budgets are developed, balanced, influenced, and agreed.

The main factors associated with the determination of marketing communications (advertising) budgets are:

- organisational culture, plus strategy, direction, and values;
- the relative amount of financial resources that are available;
- competitive activities and market conditions;
- the overall level of economic confidence felt by buyers and sellers;
- the level of product/brand development and the marketing objectives.

It appears that over time a number of models and methods have been developed. A selected number, usually two, are then utilised within an organisation and its cultural framework, to reinforce the expected outcomes, rather than develop purposeful and market-orientated budgets.

Kim and Cheong (2009) have developed an approach to budgeting that is intended to improve the efficiency with which advertising budgets are determined. Referred to as Data Envelopment Analysis or DEA, the approach is based on setting advertising budgets across different media, relative to other firms in the market. This idea was first advanced by Farrell (1957), and is based on the principle that efficiency is a function of the relationship between input and output variables. Advertising effectiveness is considered in terms of the 'spend' on six specific media (television, radio, magazines, newspapers, outdoor, and the Internet) as input variables, and revenue and brand value as two output variables. DEA complements competitive parity, and leads to benchmarking activities within the advertising budget decision process. From this these researchers believe managers can develop performance ratios such as revenue per advertising spend for each medium.

# Budgeting for the other elements of the communication mix

The methods presented so far have concentrated on the FMCG sector. The assumption has been that only one product has been considered. In reality, a range of products will need investment for communication and the allocation decision needs to reflect the requirements of an organisation's portfolio of brands. Broadbent (1989) suggests that this situation and others (e.g. direct marketing, corporate advertising) require particular combinations of the approaches presented so far. The recommendation again is that no single method will help organisations to determine the optimal investment sum.

*Sales promotion* activities can be more easily costed than advertising in advance of a campaign. Judgements can be made about the expected outcomes, based upon experience, competitive conditions and the use of predictive software tools. The important variable with sales promotion concerns the redemption rate. How many of the extra pack, price deals and samples will customers demand? How much extra of a brand needs to be sold if all the costs associated with a campaign are to be covered? The production and fulfilment costs can also be determined, so in general terms a return can be calculated in advance of a sales promotion event. However, there are a large number of sales promotion activities and these will often overlap. From a management perspective the brand management system is better, since a single person is responsible for the budget, one who is able to take a wider view of the range of activities. While the objective and task approach appears to be more easily applied to this element of the mix, other methods, such as competitive parity and fixed ratios, are often used.

The costs of *public relations* activities can also be predicted with a reasonable degree of accuracy. The staffing and/or agency costs are relatively fixed and, as there are no media costs involved, the only other major factor is the associated production costs. These are the costs of the materials used to provide third parties with the opportunity to 'speak' on the organisation's behalf. As with sales promotion, if a number of public relations events have been calculated as a necessary part of the overall communication activities of the organisation, then the costs of the different tasks need to be anticipated and aggregated and a judgement made about the impact the events will make. The relative costs of achieving a similar level of impact through advertising or other elements of the mix can often be made, and a decision taken based on relative values.

It has already been stated that the costs associated with the *sales force* can be the highest of all the elements of the mix, especially in business-to-business situations. This would indicate that the greatest degree of care needs to be taken when formulating the size and deployment of the sales force. The costs associated with each activity of personal selling and the support facilities (e.g. car, expenses, training) can be calculated easily, but what is more difficult to predict is the return on the investment.

These approaches to calculating the amount that should be invested in communication activities vary in their degree of sophistication and usefulness. Of all these methods, none is the ideal answer to the question of how much should be allocated to marketing communications or, more specifically, the advertising spend. Some of the methods are too simplistic, while others are too specific to particular market conditions. For example, formulating strategy to gain market share through increasing SOV seems to ignore the dynamic nature of the markets and the fact that organisations need to satisfy a range of stakeholders and not concentrate solely on winning the greatest market share.

Setting budgets specifically across digital media has not yet been well researched. Renshaw (2008) offers advice for those with and without digital budgets. Where there is a digital budget, he advocates 70 per cent allocated to 'emerged' digital media, 20 per cent to media 'going mainstream' and the remaining 10 per cent going to emerging digital media (see Table 8.3).

| Table 8.3 | Leo Burnett's recommended allocations for digital media budgets |
|---|---|
| **Status of digital media** | **Explanation** |
| Emerged digital media 70% | These media can be optimised and will provide results. Key media include: broadband video, rich media/video-based ads and search marketing. |
| Going mainstream 20% | These are media that are not as well proven as emerged media but which are increasingly prominent and likely to be emerged media at some point in the future. These include: mobile marketing, online social networks and specific types of gaming. |
| Emerging digital media 10% | These media are just appearing and are not well known either by large audiences or by researchers in terms of their commercial potential and performance. |

*Source*: Renshaw (2008). Used with permission from WARC.

Organisations that do have a digital marketing budget are advised to consider a step process.

- *Audiences* – what do they do, when do they do it, when and what media/content do they consume?
- *Media* – which media type has worked in the past?
- *Competitors* – use media that deliver results, but are there media which present opportunities for advantage?
- *Be bold* – consider all digital opportunities, not just the Internet.

Readers may well have reached the conclusion that the most appropriate way forward for management is to consider several approaches in order to gather a ball-park figure. Such a composite approach negates some of the main drawbacks associated with particular methods. It also helps to build a picture of what is really necessary if the organisation is to communicate effectively and efficiently. West and Prendergast (2009) found that the mean number of methods used by organisations in their sample was two, indicating that organisations are not relying on a single method.

Of all the methods and different approaches, the one constant factor that applies to them all concerns the objectives that have been set for the campaign. Each element of the communication mix has particular tasks to accomplish and it is these objectives that drive the costs of the promotional investment. If the ultimate estimate of the communication spend is too high, then the objectives, not the methods used, need to be revised.

# Key points

- The decision to invest in marketing communications is relatively easy. The real difficulty lies in determining just how much to invest and in which tools and media. This is because the direct outcomes are intangible and often distant, as the advertising effects may be digested by potential buyers immediately but not acted upon until some point in the future.

- Current trends in communication are a general move away from offline advertising and sales promotion and an increase in direct marketing and online investments, particularly advertising.

- The role of the communication budget is to ensure that the organisation achieves the greatest efficiency with each euro allocated to communication activities. Managers cannot be profligate with scarce resources, and they are accountable to the owners of the organisation for the decisions made. The budgeting process provides for internal coordination and helps ensure that communications support the marketing strategy.

- There are many benefits associated with marketing communication budgets, among which the following are significant. The process serves to focus people's attention on the costs and benefits of undertaking planned communication activities. The act of quantifying the means by which the marketing plan will be communicated to target audiences instils a management discipline necessary to ensure that the objectives of the plan are achievable. The process facilitates cross-function coordination and forces managers to ensure that the planned communications are integrated and mutually supportive. The process provides a means by which campaigns can be monitored and management control asserted. This is particularly important in environments that are subject to sudden change or competitive hostility.

- Marginal analysis provides a theoretical basis to determine the 'right' budget. However, this approach is impractical so organisations use a variety of practical approaches. These range from guesswork, a percentage of sales, what is affordable, inertia and objective and task. The last is considered to be the most appropriate.

- If it is accepted that there is a direct relationship between the weight of advertising and sales, then as an organisation spends more on advertising it will see a proportionate improvement in sales. The underlying principle of the A/S ratio is that, in each industry, it is possible to determine the average advertising spend of all the players and compare it with the value of the market. Therefore, it is possible for each organisation to determine its own A/S ratio and compare it with the industry average.

- Within any market the total of all advertising expenditure (adspend), that is, all the advertising by all of the players, can be analysed in the context of the proportions each player has made to the total. Should one advertiser spend more than any other then it will be its messages that are received and stand a better chance of being heard and acted upon. In other words, its SOV is the greater. This implies, of course, that the quality of the message transmitted is not important and that it is the sheer relative weight of adspend that is the critical factor.

- This concept can be taken further and combined with another, share of market (SOM). When a brand's market share is equal to its share of advertising spend, equilibrium is said to have been reached (SOV = SOM).

- In reality, a range of products will need investment and the allocation decision needs to reflect the requirements of an organisation's portfolio of brands. The recommendation is that no single method will help organisations to determine the optimal investment sum and that a combination of approaches is necessary. Each of the remaining tools requires different approaches. There are specific techniques available to determine the optimum sales force size and costs. The size of the public relations effort depends on usage, but the financial investment can be reduced to a judgement. Sales promotions and direct marketing are project-oriented and can be costed accordingly.

# Review questions

1. How might Honda, as set out in the mini case at the beginning of this chapter, divide their annual budget across the media? What issues might arise in this process?

2. What problems might be encountered when setting communications budgets?

3. Write a brief paper outlining the essence of marginal analysis. What are the main drawbacks associated with this approach?

4. Why is the objective and task method gaining popularity?

5. What is a payout plan?

6. Discuss the view that if the A/S ratio only measures average levels of spend across an industry then its relevance may be lost as individual organisations have to adjust levels of promotional spend to match particular niche market conditions.

7. How might the notion of SOV assist the appropriation-setting process?

8. What are 'profit-taking' and 'investment' brands?

9. Determining the level of spend for sales promotion is potentially difficult. Why?

10. How might understanding brand value assist in developing a communications budget?

# References

Abratt, R. and van der Westhuizen, B. (1985) A new promotion mix appropriation model, *International Journal of Advertising*, 4, 209–21.

AdAge (2011) Advertising to sales ratios by industry, retrieved 28 April 2012 from http://adage.com/article/datacenter-advertising-spending/advertising-sales-ratios-industry/106575/.

Advertising Association (2004) *Advertising Statistics Year Book*, Henley: World Advertising Research Centre.

Barnett, M. (2011) Engagement strategy aims to take long-term interest rates higher, *Marketing Week*, 26 June, retrieved 26 June from www.marketingweek.co.uk/engagement-strategy-aims-to-take-long-term-interest-rates-higher/3023291.article.

Binet, L. and Field, P. (2007) Marketing in the era of accountability, *IPA dataMine*, Henley-on-Thames: WARC.

Bolger, M. (2011) Profile: Martin Moll, Honda UK – Fasten your seatbelts, *The Marketer*, 27 June, retrieved 26 June 2012 from www.themarketer.co.uk/articles/interviews/profiles/martin-moll-honda-uk/.

Broadbent, S. (1989) *The Advertising Budget*, Henley: NTC Publications.

Buck, S. (2001) Advertising and the long-term success of the premium brand, *Advertising Association*, Henley-on-Thames: WARC.

Burnett, J. (1993) *Promotion Management*, New York: Houghton Mifflin.

Butterfield, L. (1999) *Excellence in Advertising: The IPA Guide to Best Practice*, Oxford: Butterworth Heinemann.

Corstjens, M., Umblijs, A. and Wang, C. (2011) The Power of Inertia: Conservatism in Marketing Resource Allocation, *Journal of Advertising Research*, (June), 356–72.

Donnelly, A. (2008) Cut spend, damage the brand, *Marketing*, 19 March, 4.

Dyson, P. (1999) How to manage the budget across a brand portfolio, *Admap*, 37(10) (December), 39–42.

Faber, A. (2009) Polydor takes up engagement model for band campaigns, *New Media Age*, Wednesday, 14 October, retrieved 16 December 2011 from www.nma.co.uk/news/polydor-takes-up-engagement-model-for-band-campaigns/3005445.article?nl=WN.

Farr, A. (2004) Managing advertising as an investment, *Admap*, 39(7) (July/August), 29–31.

Farrell, M.J. (1957), The Measurement of Productive Efficiency, *Journal of the Royal Statistical Society*, Series A CXX, Part 3, 253–90.

Field, P. (2009) Account planners need to care more about share of voice, *Admap* (September), 28–30.

Gaedeke, R.M. and Tootelian, D.H. (1983) *Marketing: Principles and Application*, St Paul, MN: West.

Gullen, P. (2003) 5 steps to effective budget setting, *Admap* (July/August), 22–4.

Hall, E. (1999) When advertising becomes an expensive luxury, *Campaign*, 10 December, 18.

Handley, L. (2011) Roll up for brand bundling, *Marketing Week*, 25 August, retrieved 26 March 2012 from http://www.marketingweek.co.uk/roll-up-for-brand-bundling/3029515.article.

Harper, G. and Bridges, D. (2003) Budgeting for healthier ROI, *Admap*, 38(7) (July/August), 25–7.

Hooley, G.J. and Lynch, J.E. (1985) How UK advertisers set budgets, *International Journal of Advertising*, 3, 223–31.

Jones, J.P. (1990) Ad spending: maintaining market share, *Harvard Business Review* (January/February), 38–42.

Kim, K. and Cheong, Y. (2009) A Frontier Analysis for Advertising Budgeting: Benchmarking Efficient Advertisers, *Journal of Current Issues and Research in Advertising*, 31, 2 (Fall), 91–104.

Mitchell, L.A. (1993) An examination of methods of setting advertising budgets: practice and literature, *European Journal of Advertising*, 27(5), 5–21.

O'Reilly, L. (2011) P&G biggest spending advertiser in 2010, *Marketing Week*, retrieved 24/10/2011 from www.marketingweek.com.

Renshaw, M. (2008) How to set digital media budgets, *WARC Exclusive*, retrieved 20 March 2008 from www.warc.com.

Schroer, J. (1990) Ad spending: growing market share, *Harvard Business Review* (January/February), 44–8.

Smallbone, D.W. (1972) *The Practice of Marketing*, London: Staple Press.

Tomkins, R. (1999) If the return is right, keep spending, *Financial Times*, 19 March, 8.

Tylee, J. (1999) Survey warns against adspend cuts, *Campaign*, 12 March, 10.

Weaver, K. and Merrick, D. (2004) Budget allocation revisited, *Admap*, 39(7) (July/August), 26–8.

West, D. and Prendergast, G.P. (2009) Advertising and promotions budgeting and the role of risk, *European Journal of Marketing*, 43, 11/12, 1457–76.

White, R. (2007) How to use the budget better, *Admap*, July/August, 14–15.

Whitehead, J. (2008) IPA backs ads in face of downturn, *Marketing*, 9 January, 4.

# Chapter 9
# Evaluation and metrics

As part of the marketing communication process it is necessary to evaluate the overall impact and effect that a campaign has on a target audience. It needs to be reviewed in order that management can learn and better understand the impact of its communications and its audiences.

## Aims and learning objectives

The aims of this chapter are to review the ways in which marketing communications activities can be evaluated.

The learning objectives of this chapter are to:

1. discuss the role of evaluation as part of marketing communications;
2. explore the value and methods of pre-testing and post-testing advertisements;
3. explain the main ideas behind different physiological measures of evaluation;
4. provide an insight into the way in which advertising and public relations can be evaluated;
5. consider other ways in which the effectiveness of marketing communications can be evaluated;
6. measure the fulfilment of brand promises;
7. consider some of the issues associated with evaluating the effectiveness of digital and online communications.

# Minicase

## Still killing Jill?

The UK Transplant (UKT) Organ Donor Register is a central database of people who have opted to offer their organs for transplantation in the event of their death. As in many countries, it is entirely voluntary. Around 8,000 people in the UK, and 700 in Scotland, are in need of a transplant; their lives depend upon it. Without donors, it won't happen.

Unfortunately, to become a donor, you have to die, and it is this touch with their own mortality which may explain why people have a mental block when it comes to signing up. Research tells us that although 91 per cent of people claim to be 'in favour' of organ donation, only c.23 per cent actually sign up. Despite all their good intentions, something stops people from putting their name on the list. People do not like thinking about the organ donation issue.

The demand for transplants far exceeds the available organs. This is because not enough people are on the Organ Donor Register. When people die, either naturally or in accidents, many of their organs are suitable for transplants and could save lives. Transplant Co-ordinators have the sensitive task of talking to next of kin to see if they will agree to the use of the deceased's organs. For understandable reasons, over 40 per cent of people refuse permission, which is required by law. This is primarily because they don't know their loved one's wishes. However, Transplant Co-ordinators and medical staff know anecdotally that in c.90 per cent of cases where the deceased has registered, permission is given willingly.

The cost to the NHS of a single person on kidney dialysis for a year is c.£35,023 and around 500 people in Scotland start kidney dialysis each year. The cost of a shortage of organs is not just the suffering of 8,000 people, but the large financial cost to the state, running into £ millions.

In 2005/2006 the Scottish Government ran a series of very successful campaigns to increase the number of people registering on the UKT Register. The campaign came to life most effectively in the 'Kill Jill' execution and was communicated across a wide range of media, primarily field marketing, PR and print/outdoor.

| Exhibit 9.1 | **A poster used to communicate the need for organ donors in the 'Still Kill Jill?' campaign** |
| --- | --- |
| | *Source*: The Scottish Government |

This success saw the number of registered organ donors in Scotland rise from 25.5 to 28.6 per cent of the population – a rise of 12.15 per cent. Over 108,000 people were signed up thanks to the campaign, a +32 per cent increase on the previous year, when there was no activity. This success even made front page news: the first time a successful Scottish Government ad campaign has been a lead story.

The next campaign worked on the idea of 'short-circuiting' the donating decision process by offering people an *immediate choice*, and almost 'demanding' a call to action.

The previous campaign had worked well so we decided to stick with the same insight and the same creative concept. But we needed to improve results. This was achieved by adding TV and online to the media mix. TV had the benefit of huge coverage and impact. We also knew from experience on retail and financial services that TV could work as a direct response medium. Online was especially attractive to us since the National UK Transplant website has the facility to sign up immediately; with no fuss. Thus, online had the potential to drive response in a measurable and direct way.

With £354,121 budgeted, the final plan thus included:

- TV
- outdoor
- online
- field marketing
- PR.

Thus our next task was to develop the 'Kill Jill' concept into a 40-second TV commercial. This was based around the following principles:

- Don't provoke too much thought about organ donation, provoke action.
- Link registration with an immediate outcome – people like to know their actions have consequences.
- Emphasise the ease of registration or participation.
- Provide a specific 'call to action'.

Our creative solution was wonderfully simple; present the 'Kill Jill? Yes? No?' dilemma directly to the viewer in real time; with no fuss and no drama; and let the viewer choose how to respond.

We knew from the 2005/2006 campaigns that PR had worked exceptionally well in conjunction with the advertising, apparently providing an accelerator to the response. How could we use this learning? In negotiations for the TV airtime, STV offered a new medium which was effectively a broadcast form of PR. They offered the Scottish Government a series of one-minute, advertiser-funded programmes, broadcast in key early peak airtime.

Thus, we converted the editorial equivalent of a newspaper story into a series of five one-minute programmes, which focused on real organ donation stories. These ran as features within *The Five-thirty Show* over the launch week of the TV, with 40-second ads immediately following the sponsored programmes to provide the call to action.

We knew from previous activity that field marketing, face-to-face contact with people in shopping malls or supermarkets, was very effective, with up to 1 out of every 2 people signing up to the Register. Field marketing was therefore a core activity, so we planned three field marketing teams touring 43 venues throughout Scotland from Inverness to Dumfries. Across 15 days the teams were to visit a combination of larger shopping centres and local supermarkets.

| Exhibit 9.2 | **The Scottish Government logo** |
| --- | --- |
| | *Source*: The Scottish Government |

The campaign ran during National Transplant Week, and maximised the PR during this period for awareness. The campaign was designed to generate direct response – registrations to the Organ Donor Register, so this had to be the key measurement dimension.

Over the two campaign periods in 2008 the total number of Scots who signed up to the Organ Donation Register was 120,722. The same periods the previous year (when there was no activity) recorded 35,695 registrations. Thus the campaign generated an extra 85,027 Scottish registrations or a massive uplift: 242 per cent.

Field marketing generated 4,534 sign-ups. This was on target and in line with expectations. The online campaign delivered 641 sign-ups. This was a disappointment – and the results were analysed for future use. Thus, the balance of 79,852 registrations can be attributed either to the TV or to PR activity. Registrations came either via the UKT call centre or the website.

*This case was written by Mark Raine of the Scottish Government and Ian McAteer/Louise Campbell of The Union. Permission to use the material was kindly given by the Scottish Government.*

*A longer version can be found at the website supporting this book at www.pearsoned.co.uk/fill and at www.Fillassociates.co.uk/.*

# Introduction

All organisations should review and evaluate the performance of their various activities. In the Still Killing Jill? mini case the key measure was said to be the number of registrations driven by the campaigns. This is an example of a campaign that had objectives and where measurement was seen to be important. Many organisations do use formal mechanisms to evaluate their campaigns, but there are many others who do not review and if they do it is informal, and ad hoc.

The process of evaluation or reflection is a well-established management process. The objective is to monitor the often diverse activities of the organisation so that management can exercise control. It is through the process of review and evaluation that an organisation has the opportunity to learn and develop. In turn, this enables management to refine its competitive position and to provide for higher levels of customer satisfaction.

The evaluation of planned marketing communications consists of two distinct elements. The first element is concerned with the development and testing of individual messages. For example, a particular sales promotion (such as a sample pack) has individual characteristics that may or may not meet the objectives of a sales promotion event.

An advertising message has to achieve, among other things, a balance of emotion and information in order that the communication objectives and message strategy be achieved. To accomplish this, testing is required to ensure that the intended messages are encoded correctly and are capable of being decoded accurately by the target audience and the intended meaning ascribed to the message. The second element concerns the overall impact and effect that a campaign has on a target audience once a communications plan has been released. This post-test factor is critical, as it will either confirm or reject management's judgement about the viability of its communications strategy. The way in which the individual components of the communications mix work together needs to be understood so that strengths can be capitalised on and developed and weaknesses negated.

Prediction and evaluation require information about options and alternatives. For example, did sales presentation approach A prove to be more effective than B and, if so, what would happen if A was used nationally? Predictably, the use of quantitative techniques is more prevalent with this set of reasons.

So, should measurement in the 'Still Killing Jill?' campaign be based solely on registrations or should there be some measurement of attitudes to organ donation? Should there be a measure other than of registrations, of the contributions of the individual tools and media? And why did the online element fail to secure a reasonable level of registrations? This chapter should read with these questions in mind. It starts with a review of the principles and need for measurement and evaluation. It then examines the traditional methods used to test and evaluate marketing communications activities. It also reviews some of the more contemporary approaches and the issues associated with the measurement and evaluation of online communications.

# The role of evaluation in planned communications

The evaluation process is a key part of marketing communications. The findings and results of the evaluative process feed back into the next campaign and provide indicators and benchmarks for further campaign decisions. The primary role of evaluating the performance of a communications strategy is to ensure that the communications objectives have been met and that the strategy has been effective. The secondary role is to ensure that the strategy has been executed efficiently, and that the full potential of the individual tools and media has been extracted and that resources have been used economically.

The prevalence and acceptance of the integrated marketing communications concept (Chapter 10) suggests that its measurement should be a central aspect when evaluating marketing communications activities. One of the predominant issues surrounding the development of IMC is the challenges and lack of empirical evidence concerning the measurement of this concept. In an attempt to resolve this, Lee and Park (2007) provide one of the first multidimensional-scaled measures of IMC. Their model is based on four key dimensions drawn from the literature. These are set out in Table 9.1.

| Table 9.1 | Four dimensions of IMC |

| Dimension of IMC | Explanation |
| --- | --- |
| Unified communications for consistent messages and images | Activities designed to create a clear, single position, in the target market, delivering a consistent message through multiple channels. |
| Differentiated communications to multiple customer groups | The need to create different marketing communications campaigns (and positions) targeted at different groups (in the target market) who are at different stages of the buying process. Sequential communication models based on the hierarchy of effects or attitude construct apply. |
| Database-centred communications | This dimension emphasises the need to generate behavioural responses through direct marketing activities created through information collected and stored in databases. |
| Relationship fostering communications for existing customers | The importance of retaining customers and developing long-term relationships is a critical element of marketing communications. |

*Source*: Lee and Park (2007). Used with permission from WARC.

Each of these dimensions is regarded as separate yet integral elements of IMC. Lee and Park developed an 18-item scale, derived from the literature, to measure these dimensions. The use of this approach may advance our understanding of IMC and provide a substantial basis on which IMC activities can be measured. It is interesting to note that Lee and Park see IMC as a customer-only communication activity and choose to exclude other critical stakeholders from their measurement model.

---

**Scholars' paper 9.1**    **Measuring up for IMC**

**Ewing, M.T. (2009) Integrated marketing communications measurement and evaluation,** *Journal of Marketing Communications,* **15(2–3), April–July, 103–117.**

This paper marks out the difficulties and challenges involved in measuring integrated marketing communications. Working from the base that it is consumers that determine when marketing communications is integrated, Ewing identifies and considers five areas of integrated marketing communications (IMC) measurement worthy of future research.

---

## Advertising

There are numerous ways in which advertising effectiveness can be measured. Chang et al. (2010: 63) refer to 'awareness (Hansen, Olsen, and Lundsteen, 2006), brand choice (Cobb-Walgren, Ruble, and Donthu 1995), purchase likelihood (Aaker, Stayman and Hagerty 1986), viewing time (Olney, Holbrook, and Batra 1991), brand perceptions (MacKenzie and Lutz 1989), purchase intentions (Bellman, Schweda, and Varan 2009), memory-based tests (Brennan, Dubas, and Babin 1999) and so on'.

The techniques used to evaluate advertising are by far the most documented and, in view of the relative sizes of the communication tools, it is not surprising that slightly more time is devoted to this tool. This is not to disregard or disrespect the contribution each of the communication tools can make to an integrated campaign. Indeed, it is the collective measure of success against the goals set at the outset that is the overriding imperative for measurement, as will be seen later.

## Pre-testing

Advertisements can be researched prior to their release (pre-test) or after they have been released (post-test). Pre-tests, sometimes referred to as *copy tests*, have traditionally attracted more attention, stimulated a greater variety of methods and generated much controversy, in comparison with post-tests.

The effectiveness of *pre-testing*, the practice of showing unfinished commercials to selected groups of the target audience with a view to refining the commercial to improve effectiveness, is still subject to debate. Reid (2000) argues that pre-testing can be used positively to support campaign development, predictively to gauge likely audience response and generally to improve advertising performance.

The methods used to pre-test advertisements are based upon either qualitative or quantitative criteria. The most common methods used to pre-test advertisements are concept testing, focus groups, consumer juries, dummy vehicles, readability, theatre and physiological tests. Focus groups are the main qualitative method used and theatre or hall tests the main quantitative test. Each of these methods will be discussed later.

The primary purpose of testing advertisements during the developmental process is to ensure that the final creative work will meet the advertising objectives. It is better to help shape the way an advertising message is formed, rather like potters continuously review their progress as they craft their vases, than make a pot and then decide that it is not big enough or that the handle is the wrong shape. The practical objectives of pre-testing creative work are to provide opportunities to optimise ads before publication and second, and if necessary, to terminate an advertisement before costs become so large and commitment too final. Changes to an advertisement that are made too late may be resisted partly because of the sunk costs and partly because of the political consequences that 'pulling' an advertisement might have. The Newspaper Marketing Agency (NMA) in conjunction with Millward Brown has pre-tested a large number of newspaper ads and has found that pre-testing newspaper ads can more than double ad recognition levels. See www.nmauk.co.uk.

Once a series of advertisements has been roughed or developed, advertisers seek reassurance and guidance regarding which of the alternatives should be developed further. Concept tests, in-depth interviews, focus groups and consumer juries can be used to determine the better of the proposed ads, by using ranking and prioritisation procedures. Of those selected, further testing can be used to reveal the extent to which the intended message is accurately decoded. These comprehension and reaction tests are designed to prevent inappropriate advertisements reaching the finished stage.

## Pre-testing unfinished advertisements

### Concept testing

The concept test is an integral part of the developmental stage of advertising strategy. The purpose is to reduce the number of alternative advertising ideas, to identify and build upon the good ideas, and to reject those that are judged by the target audience not to be suitable.

Concept testing can occur very early on in the development process, but is usually undertaken when the target audience can be presented with a rough outline or storyboard that represents the intended artwork and the messages to be used. There are varying degrees of sophistication associated with concept testing, from the use of simple cards with no illustrations to photomatics, which are films of individual photographs shot in sequence, and livematics, which are films very close to the intended finished message. Their use reflects the size of the advertiser's budget, the completion date of the campaign and the needs of the creative team.

Concept testing, by definition, has to be undertaken in artificial surroundings, but the main way of eliciting the target's views is essentially qualitatively oriented, based on group discussion. This group discussion is referred to as a focus group and is a technique used by most agencies.

Once a client has approved the agency's plans, ad production can begin. Very often the creative team or an independent artist will produce roughs or drawings for the agency and advertiser to see before the final artwork is finished. This is seen as necessary as the costs of producing finished work and going live without any pre-testing can be critical, and expensive.

Storyboards are a way in which it is possible to inexpensively simulate a 'rough' version of the advertisement. Pen-and-ink line drawings, animatics or cartoons and photoboards are some of the more common approaches. Some storyboards will consist of as many as 20 sketches, depicting key scenes, camera and product shots, close-ups, along with background scenery and essential props.

### Focus groups

When a small number (8–10) of target consumers are brought together and invited to discuss a particular topic a focus group is formed. By using in-depth interviewing skills a professional moderator can probe the thoughts and feelings held by the members of the group towards a product, media vehicles or advertising messages. One-way viewing rooms allow clients to observe the interaction without the focus group's behaviour being modified by external influences.

The advantage of focus groups is that they are relatively inexpensive to set up and run and they use members of the target audience. In this sense they are representative and allow true feelings and emotions to be uncovered in a way that other methods deny. They do not attempt to be quantitative and, in that sense, they lack objectivity. It is also suggested that the group dynamics may affect the responses in the 'artificial' environment. This means that there may be in-built bias to the responses and the interaction of the group members. Focus groups are very popular, but they should not be used on their own.

## Consumer juries

A 'jury' of consumers, representative of the target market, is asked to judge which of a series of paste-ups and rough ideas would be their choice of a final advertisement. They are asked to rank in order of merit and provide reasons for their selections.

There are difficulties associated with ranking and prioritisation tests. First, the consumers, realising the reason for their participation, may appoint themselves as 'experts', so they lose the objectivity that this process is intended to bring. Second, the halo effect can occur, whereby an advertisement is rated excellent overall simply because one or two elements are good and the respondent overlooks the weaknesses. Finally, emotional advertisements tend to receive higher scores than informational messages, even though the latter might do better in the marketplace.

# Pre-testing finished advertisements

When an ad is finished it can be subjected to a number of other tests before being released.

## Dummy vehicles

Many of the pre-testing methods occur in an artificial environment such as a theatre, laboratory or meeting room. One way of testing so that the reader's natural environment is used is to produce a dummy or pretend magazine that can be consumed at home, work or wherever participants normally read magazines. Dummy magazines contain regular editorial matter with test advertisements inserted next to control advertisements. These 'pretend' magazines are distributed to a random sample of households, which are asked to consume the magazine in their normal way. Readers are encouraged to observe the editorial and at a later date they are asked questions about both the editorial and the advertisements.

The main advantage of using dummy vehicles is that the setting is natural but, as with the focus group, the main disadvantage is that respondents are aware that they are part of a test and may respond unnaturally. Research also suggests that recall may not be the best measure for low-involvement decisions or where motivation occurs through the peripheral route of the elaboration likelihood model (ELM). If awareness is required at the point of sale, then recognition may be a more reliable indicator of effectiveness than recall.

## Readability tests

Rudolph Flesch (1974) developed a formula to assess the ease with which print copy could be read. The test involves, among other things, determining the average number of syllables per 100 words of copy, the average length of sentence and the percentage of personal words and sentences. By accounting for the educational level of the target audience and by comparing results with established norms, the tests suggest that comprehension is best when sentences are short, words are concrete and familiar, and personal references are used frequently.

| Table 9.2 | Projective techniques |
|---|---|

| Projective technique | Explanation |
|---|---|
| Association | Free word association tests require respondents to respond with the first word that comes to mind in response to a stimulus word. Often used when naming brands. |
| Completion | Spontaneous sentence or story-telling completion are the most used methods. Responses can be graded as approval, neutral or disapproval, enabling attitudes towards brands to be determined. |
| Transformation | These are also known as 'expressible' techniques and involve techniques such as psychodrawing. This requires respondents to express graphically their inner feelings about a brand or event (e.g. a shopping trip, holiday or purchase process). |
| Construction | This approach can involve role playing where respondents are asked to act out their feelings towards a purchase, a brand, event or organisation. |

*Source*: Based on Robson (2002).

## Projective techniques

Projective techniques are used to probe the subconscious and have close associations with Freudian thinking and the motivation school advocated by Dichter (1966). Individuals or groups can be encouraged through projective techniques to express their inner thoughts and feelings about brands, products, services and organisations, among others. Four main projective techniques can be identified (see Table 9.2).

Projective techniques have been used by many leading brands to understand how their brands are perceived, to test advertising and creative ideas and to segment their markets. For example, Guinness used projective techniques to understand how to position their brand and how advertising should be used to develop the ideal position.

---

**Viewpoint 9.1** | **Projective engagement with Sony Bravia**

Projective testing techniques were used to measure the positioning success and the impact of the Sony Bravia 'Paint' ads. Sony wanted to use a creative that symbolised the technical colour development represented by the Bravia television.

Based on exploding colours around a council housing estate, Paint represented a radically different and unexpected creative, if only because there was no voice-over, no mention of attributes, features or benefits, in either copy or voice, and there were no visuals depicting the product or people consuming (watching) the television.

Paint was designed to communicate the point that the Bravia and SXRD range provide the 'colour that you'll see on these screens will be like no other' (www.Sony.com).

Part of the testing undertaken by TNS, using their AdEval™ methodology, included the use of people photosets. These are pictures of groups of personality types, used and validated internationally. Respondents were shown various different ads and asked which group of people they thought each would appeal to most. Many people have reported finding the Paint ads confusing and difficult to relate to. However, all the respondents were able to assign a personality type and the majority categorised the ads to people who were carefree, lively and bold. In terms of brand images the respondents reported vibrant colour, lively, outgoing, dynamic and cool/trendy as the key attributes (see Figure 9.1).

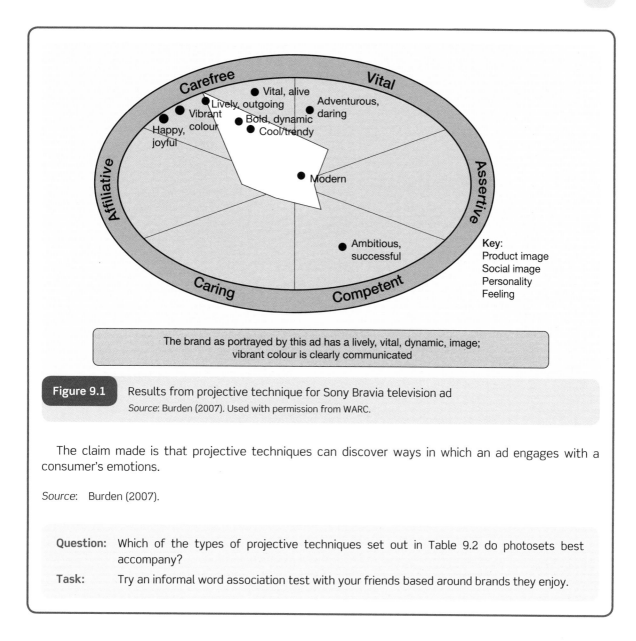

The brand as portrayed by this ad has a lively, vital, dynamic, image; vibrant colour is clearly communicated

**Figure 9.1** Results from projective technique for Sony Bravia television ad

*Source*: Burden (2007). Used with permission from WARC.

The claim made is that projective techniques can discover ways in which an ad engages with a consumer's emotions.

*Source*: Burden (2007).

**Question:** Which of the types of projective techniques set out in Table 9.2 do photosets best accompany?

**Task:** Try an informal word association test with your friends based around brands they enjoy.

## Theatre tests

As a way of testing finished broadcast advertisements, target consumers are invited to a theatre (laboratory or hall) to pre-view television programmes. Before the programme commences, details regarding the respondents' demographic and attitudinal details are recorded and they are asked to nominate their product preferences from a list. At the end of the viewing their evaluation of the programme is sought and they are also requested to complete their product preferences a second time.

There are a number of variations on this theme: one is to telephone the respondents a few days after the viewing to measure recall and another is to provide joysticks, push buttons and pressure pads to measure reactions throughout the viewing. The main outcome of this process is a measure of the degree to which product preferences change as a result of exposure to the controlled viewing. This change is referred to as the persuasion shift. This approach provides for a quantitative dimension to be added to the testing process, as the scores recorded by respondents can be used to measure the effectiveness of advertisements and provide benchmarks for future testing.

It is argued that this form of testing is too artificial and that the measure of persuasion shift is too simple and unrealistic. Furthermore, some believe that many respondents know what is happening and make changes because it is expected of them in their role of respondent. Those in favour of theatre testing state that the control is sound, that the value of established norms negates any 'role play' by respondents and that the actual sales data support the findings of the brand persuasion changes in the theatre.

A major evaluation of 400 individual advertising tests in the United States found, among many other things, that there is no clear relationship between measures of persuasion shift and eventual sales performance. This questions the use of an organisation's scarce resources and the viability of using these techniques (Lodish and Lubetkin, 1992).

This technique is used a great deal in the United States, but has had limited use in Britain. Agencies are concerned that the simplistic nature of recording scores as a means of testing advertisements ignores the complex imagery and emotional aspects of many messages. If likeability is an important aspect of eventual brand success then it is unlikely that the quantitative approach to pre-testing will contribute any worthwhile information.

The increasing use of, or at least interest in, theatre tests and the movement towards greater utilisation of quantitative techniques in pre-testing procedures runs concurrently with the increasing requirements of accountability, short-termism and periods of economic downturn. As no one method will ever be sufficient, a mix of qualitative and quantitative pre-test measures will, inevitably, always be required.

# Physiological measures

A bank of physiological tests has been developed, partly as a response to advertisers' increasing interest in the emotional impact of advertising messages and partly because many other tests rely on the respondents' ability to interpret their reactions. Physiological tests are designed to measure the involuntary responses to stimuli that avoid the bias inherent in other tests. There are substantial costs involved with the use of these techniques, and the validity of the results is questionable. Consequently they are not used a great deal in practice, but, of them all, eye tracking is the most used and most reliable (see Table 9.3).

On the surface, pupil dilation has a number of attractions, but it is not used very much as research has shown little evidence of success. The costs are high and the low number of respondents that can be processed limits the overall effectiveness. Eye tracking can be a useful means of reviewing and amending the layout of an advertisement. Galvanic skin response is flawed because the range of reactions and emotions, the degree of learning and recall, and aspects of preference and motivation are all ignored. When these deficiencies are combined with the high costs and low numbers of respondents that can be processed, it is not surprising that this method of pre-testing has little value. The hemispheric lateralisation theory has been rejected by many researchers. Although the right side of the brain is best for recognition, and the left better for recall, only Vaughn (1980) has developed this approach in terms of advertising theory (Chapter 14).

Although now superseded, his grid was regarded as an important breakthrough in our understanding of how advertising works. However, while the grid has been used extensively, there is little evidence of any commercial application of electro-encephalographs. Advertisements should be designed to appeal to each hemisphere, but recent research now appears to reject this once-popular notion.

| Table 9.3 | Physiological tests |
|---|---|

### Pupil dilation

Pupil dilation is associated with action and interest and is used to measure a respondent's reaction to a stimulus. If the pupil is constricted then interest levels are low and energy is conserved. The level of arousal is used to determine the degree of interest and preference in a particular advertisement or package design.

### Eye tracking

This technique requires the use of eye movement cameras that fire an infrared beam to track the movement of the eye as it scans an advertisement. The sequence in which the advertisement is read can be determined and particular areas that do or do not attract attention can be located.

### Galvanic skin response

This measures the resistance the skin offers to a small amount of current passed between two electrodes. Response to a stimulus will activate the sweat glands, which in turn will increase the resistance. Therefore the greater the level of tension induced by an advertisement, the more effective it is as a form of communication.

### Tachistoscopes

These measure the ability of an advertisement to attract attention. The speed at which an advertisement is flashed in front of a respondent is gradually slowed down until a point (about 1/100 second) is reached at which the respondent is able to identify components of the message. This can be used to identify those elements that respondents see first as a picture is exposed, and so facilitates the creation of impact-based messages.

### Electro-encephalographs

This involves the use of a scanner that monitors the electrical frequencies of the brain. Hemispheric lateralisation concerns the ability of the left-hand side of the brain to process rational, logical information and the right-hand side handles visual stimuli and responds more to emotional inputs.

Brain activation measures the level of alpha-wave activity, which indicates the degree to which the respondent is aroused by and interested in a stimulus. Therefore, the lower the level of alpha activity, the greater the level of attention and cognitive processing. It would follow that, by measuring the alpha waves while a respondent is exposed to different advertisements, different levels of attention can be determined.

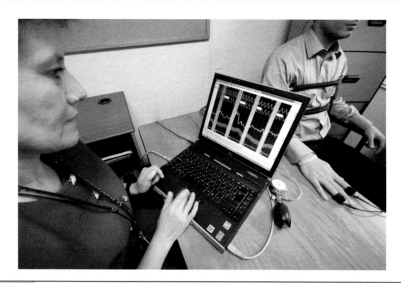

| Exhibit 9.3 | **The Galvanic skin response process being used** |
|---|---|
| | *Source*: Guy Bell/Alamy Images |

**Scholars' paper 9.2**      **The medium does matter**

Treutler, T., Levine, B. and Marci, C.D. (2010) Biometrics and Multi-Platform Messaging; The Medium Matters, *Journal of Advertising Research*, 50(3), September, 243–9.

This short paper provides an insight into the future of advertising and the effectiveness of various advertising platforms. The study uses biometrics and eye-tracking systems to study the effectiveness of media platforms in relation to emotional response. The central outcome is that television ads deliver the greatest advertising impact, as measured by unconscious attention and emotional response, compared with other channels of communication.

# Post-testing

Testing advertisements that have been released is generally more time-consuming and involves greater expense than pre-testing. However, the big advantage with post-testing is that advertisements are evaluated in their proper environment, or at least the environment in which they are intended to be successful.

There are a number of methods used to evaluate the effectiveness of such advertisements, and of these inquiry, recall, recognition and sales-based tests predominate.

## Inquiry tests

These tests are designed to measure the number of inquiries or direct responses stimulated by advertisements. Inquiries can take the form of returned coupons and response cards, requests for further literature or actual orders. They were originally used to test print messages, but some television advertisements now carry 0800 (free) telephone numbers. An increase in the use of direct-response media will lead to an increase in the sales and leads generated by inquiry-stimulating messages, so this type of testing will become more prevalent.

Inquiry tests can be used to test single advertisements or a campaign in which responses are accumulated. Using a split run, an advertiser can use two different advertisements and run them in the same print vehicle. This allows measurement of the attention-getting properties of alternative messages. If identical messages are run in different media then the effect of the media vehicles can be tested.

Care needs to be given to the interpretation of inquiry-based tests, as they may be misleading. An advertisement may not be effective simply because of the responses received. For example, people may respond because they have a strong need for the offering rather than the response being a reflection of the qualities of the advertisement. Likewise, other people may not respond despite the strong qualities of the advertisement, simply because they lack time, resources or need at that particular moment.

## Recall tests

Recall tests are designed to assess the impression that particular advertisements have made on the memory of the target audience. Interviewers, therefore, do not use a copy of the advertisement as a stimulus, as the tests are intended to measure impressions and perception, not behaviour, opinions, attitudes or the advertising effect.

Normally, recall tests require the cooperation of several hundred respondents, all of whom were exposed to the advertisement. They are interviewed the day after an advertisement is screened, hence the reference to day-after-recall (DAR) tests. Once qualified by the interviewer, respondents are first asked if they remember a commercial for, say, air travel. If the respondent replies 'Yes, Virgin', then this is recorded as unaided recall and is regarded as a strong measure of memory. If the respondent says 'No', the interviewer might ask the question 'Did you see an advertisement for British Airways?' A positive answer to this prompt is recorded as aided recall.

These answers are then followed by questions such as, 'What did the advertisement say about British Airways?', 'What did the commercial look like?' and 'What did it remind you of?' All the answers provided to this third group of questions are written down word for word and recorded as verbatim responses.

The reliability of recall scores is generally high. This means that each time the advertisement is tested, the same score is generated. Validity refers to the relationship or correlation between recall and the sales that ultimately result from an audience exposed to a particular advertisement. The validity of recall tests is generally regarded by researchers as low.

Recall tests have a number of other difficulties associated with them. First, they can be expensive, as a lot of resources can be consumed by looking for and qualifying respondents. Second, not only is interviewing time expensive, but the score may be rejected if, on examination of the verbatim responses, it appears that the respondent was guessing.

It has been suggested by Zielske (1982) that thinking/rational messages appear to be easier to recall than emotional/feeling ones. Therefore, it seems reasonable to assume that recall scores for emotional/feeling advertisements may be lower. It is possible that programme content may influence the memory and lead to different recall scores for the same offering. The use of a preselected group of respondents may reduce the costs associated with finding a qualified group, but they may increase their attention towards the commercials in the knowledge that they will be tested the following day. This will inevitably lead to higher levels of recall than actually exist.

On-the-air tests are a derivative of recall and theatre tests. By using advertisements that are run live in a test area, it is possible to measure the impact of these test advertisements with DAR. As recall tests reflect the degree of attention and interest in the advertisement, this is a way of controlling and predicting the outcome of a campaign when it is rolled out nationally.

Recall tests are used a great deal, even though their validity is low and their costs are high. It is argued that this is because recall scores provide an acceptable means by which decisions to invest heavily in advertising programmes can be made. Agencies accumulate vast amounts of recall data that can be used as benchmarks to judge whether an advertisement generated a score that was better or less than the average for the product class or brand. Having said that, and despite their popularity, they are adjudged to be poor predictors of sales (Lodish and Lubetkin, 1992).

---

### Viewpoint 9.2    Total recall

The techniques available to measure the ability of most media to deliver on core attributes such as reach and frequency are well rehearsed and understood. However, what is more problematic is measuring whether any particular variation or format within a type of media can impact on a viewer's/reader's attention or as some would have it, engagement with a medium and message.

Research has shown that people standing on London Underground stations and travelling in tube trains accumulate considerable dwell time with respect to the ads they are exposed to. However, it was not known how dwell time might affect recall or the extent to which dwell time might impact on brand perceptions.

A research project, called Total Recall, was created. This exercise sought to measure the extent to which recall improves with length of exposure and whether positive perception (brand empathy) improves.

Various poster ads were used, some complex with extensive copy and some using simple visual branding techniques. Respondents were exposed to these ads and to the control ads within a managed testing environment. The results were quite clear. Respondents who were exposed to the ads for longer periods of time were more likely to remember what they had seen and were more likely to develop more positive feelings towards the brands.

*Source*:   Cox (2007).

**Question:**   Are the results of this research exercise surprising or could they have been confidently anticipated?

**Task:**   Make a list of the ways in which people might be exposed to billboard and magazine ads more frequently.

| Exhibit 9.4 | **Underground advertising for the WIRSPA campaign (see Chapter 10)** |
|---|---|
| | *Source*: Bray Leino Ltd |

# Recognition tests

Recall tests are based upon the memory and the ability of respondents to reprocess information about an advertisement. A different way of determining advertising effectiveness is to ask respondents if they recognise an advertisement. This is the most common of the post-testing procedures for print advertisements. One of the main methods used to measure the readership of magazines is based on the frequency-of-reading and generally there are three main approaches:

- *recency*: reading any issue during the last publishing interval (e.g. within the last seven days for a weekly magazine);
- *specific issue*: reading of a specific issue of a publication;
- *frequency-of-reading*: how many issues a reader has read in a stated period (such as a month in respect of a weekly magazine).

Worldwide, the recency approach is the most widely used method in national readership surveys (www.roymorgan.com). Of the many services available, perhaps the Starch Readership Report is the best known. These recognition tests are normally conducted in the homes of approximately 200 respondents. Once it has been agreed that the respondent has previously seen a copy of the magazine, it is opened at a predetermined page and the respondent is asked, for each advertisement, 'Did you see or read any part of the advertisement?' If the answer is yes, the respondent is asked to indicate exactly which parts of the copy or layout were seen or read.

Four principal readership scores are reported: noted, seen-associated, read most and signature (see Table 9.4).

The reliability of recognition tests is very high, higher than recall scores. Costs are lower, mainly because the questioning procedure is simpler and quicker. It is also possible to deconstruct an advertisement into its component parts and assess their individual effects on the reader. As with all interviewer-based research, bias is inevitable. Bias can also be introduced by the respondent or the research organisation through the instructions given or through fatigue of the interviewer.

The validity of recognition test scores is said to be high, especially after a number of insertions. However, there can be a problem of false claiming, where readers claim to have seen an advertisement but, in fact, have not. This, it is suggested, is because when readers confirm they have seen an advertisement the underlying message is that they approve of and like that sort of advertisement. If they say that they have not seen an advertisement, the underlying message is that they do not usually look at that sort of advertisement. Krugman (1988) believes that readers are effectively voting on whether an advertisement is worth spending a moment of their time to look at. It might be that readers' memories are a reliable indicator of what the reader finds attractive in an advertisement and this could be a surrogate indicator for a level of likeability. This proposition has yet to be fully investigated, but it may be that the popularity of the recognition test is based on the validity rating and the approval that high scores give to advertisers.

| Table 9.4 | Principal readership scores |
| --- | --- |

| Readership scores | Explanation |
| --- | --- |
| Noted | The percentage of readers who remember seeing the advertisement. |
| Seen-associated | The percentage of readers who recall seeing or reading any part of the advertisement identifying the offering. |
| Read most | The percentage of readers who report reading at least 50 per cent of the advertisement. |
| Signature | The percentage of readers who remember seeing the brand name or logo. |

## Sales tests

If the effectiveness of advertisements could be measured by the level of sales that occurs during and after a campaign, then the usefulness of measuring sales as a testing procedure would not be in doubt. However, the practical difficulties associated with market tests are so large that these tests have little purpose. Counting the number of direct response returns and the number of enquiries received are the only sales-based tests that have any validity.

Practitioners have been reluctant to use market-based tests because they are not only expensive to conduct but they are also historical by definition. Sales occur partly as a consequence of past actions, including past communication strategies, and the costs (production, agency and media) have already been sunk. There may be occasions where it makes little political and career sense to investigate an event unless it has been a success, or at the very least reached minimal acceptable expectations.

---

### Viewpoint 9.3     Ford measure their media

Measuring the return on their investment in marketing communications is really important to Ford. In addition to specific sponsorships Ford use a wide range of media, such as press, television, radio and online. It is critical that they understand what works and what does not work for them.

When Ford buy media space it is important that they achieve leverage. For example, when they launched the S-Max they took space in the *Observer* on- and offline as the readership profile matched that of the car.

Ford measure two key elements. The first concerns performance outputs or market measures such as market share at the retail level, profitability and ROI. They also measure the ROI on their direct mail and data-rich online activities. The second element concerns softer measures such as brand likeability, directly associated with some of their more emotionally oriented marketing goals.

However, the interesting aspect of Ford's media measurement activities concerns not what they measure but who actually does the measurement. All media buying and associated purchases are undertaken by MindShare, but Ford then use the consulting company Accenture to measure the efficiency with which Mindshare buy media on Ford's behalf.

*Source*: Ovenden (2007).

**Question:**    Why do Ford use Accenture to measure their own supplier's media buying effectiveness?

**Task:**       Visit the Accenture website www.accenture.com. How else do they contribute to the world of marketing communications?

---

For these reasons and others, advertisers have used test markets to gauge the impact their campaigns have on representative samples of the national market.

### Simulated market tests

By using control groups of matched consumers in particular geographic areas, the use of simulated test markets permits the effect of advertising on sales to be observed under controlled market conditions. These conditions are more realistic than for tests conducted within a theatre setting and are more representative of the national market than the limited in-house tests. This market representation is thought by some to provide an adequate measure of advertising effect. Other commentators, as discussed before, believe that unless advertising is the dominant element in the marketing mix, there are usually too many other factors that can affect sales. It is therefore unfair and unrealistic to place the sole responsibility for sales with advertising.

### Single-source data

With the advances in technology it is now possible to correlate consumer purchases with the advertisements they have been exposed to. This is known as *single-source data* and involves the controlled transmission of advertisements to particular households whose every purchase is monitored through a scanner at supermarket checkouts. In other words, all the research data are derived from the same households.

The advent of cable television has facilitated this process. Consumers along one side of a street receive one set of control advertisements, while the others on the other side receive test advertisements. Single-source data provide exceptionally dependable results, but the technique is expensive, is inappropriate for testing single advertisements and tends to focus on the short-term effect, failing, for example, to cope with the concept of adstock.

In the United Kingdom facilities such as Adlab, then ScatScan and Homescan have helped advertisers assess their advertising effectiveness in terms of copy testing, weight testing and even the use of mixed media. The use of split regions can be very important, allowing comparisons to made of different strategies.

---

**Scholars' paper 9.3    Oldie but interesting**

**Campbell, R.H. (1965) A Managerial Approach to Advertising Measurement,** *Journal of Marketing*, 29(4), October, 1–6.

This paper provides an interesting insight into the way advertising effectiveness was considered in the 1960s. Although the advancements since then have been tremendous, some things do not change.

---

# Other tests

There is a range of other measures that have been developed in an attempt to understand the effect of advertisements. Among these are tracking studies and financial analyses.

## Tracking studies

A tracking study involves interviewing a large number of people on a regular basis, weekly or monthly, with the purpose of collecting data about buyers' perceptions of marketing communication messages – not just advertisements – and how these messages might be affecting buyers' perceptions of the brand. By measuring and evaluating the impact of a campaign when it is running, adjustments can be made quickly. The most common elements that are monitored, or tracked, are the awareness levels of an advertisement and the brand, image ratings of the brand and the focus organisation, and attributes and preferences.

Tracking studies can be undertaken on a periodic or continuous basis. The latter is more expensive, but the information generated is more complete and absorbs the effect of competitors' actions, even if the effects are difficult to disaggregate. Sherwood et al. (1989) report that in a general sense, continuous tracking appears to be more appropriate for new products, and periodic tracking to be more appropriate for established products.

A further form of tracking study involves monitoring the stock held by retailers. Counts are usually undertaken each month, on a pre- and post-exposure basis. This method of measuring sales is used frequently. Audited sales data, market share figures and return on investment provide other measures of advertising effectiveness.

Tracking studies are also used to measure the impact and effectiveness of online activities. These may be applied to banner ads, email campaigns and paid-for search engine placements and have for a long time been geared to measuring site visitors, clicks through or pages visited. Increasingly these studies are attending to the volume and value of traffic with regard to the behaviour undertaken by site visitors. Behaviour, or the more common term, *call-to-action*, can be considered in terms of the engagement through exchanges or transactions, the number of site or subscription registrations, the volume of downloads requested or the number of offline triggers such as 'call me buttons' that are activated.

## Financial analysis

The vast amount of resources that are directed at planned communications and, in particular, advertising requires that the organisation reviews, on a periodic basis, the amount and the manner in which its financial resources have been used. For some organisations the media spend alone constitutes one of the major items of expenditure. For example, many grocery products incur ingredient, packaging and distribution plus media as the primary costing elements to be managed.

Variance analysis enables a continuous picture of the spend to be developed and acts as an early warning system should unexpected levels of expenditure be incurred. In addition to this and other standard financial controls, the size of the discount obtained from media buying is becoming an important and vital part of the evaluation process.

Increasing levels of accountability and rapidly rising media costs have contributed to the development of centralised media buying. Under this arrangement, the promotion of an organisation's entire portfolio of brands, across all divisions, is contracted to a single media-buying organisation. Part of the reasoning is that the larger the account, the greater the buying power an agency has, and this in turn should lead to greater discounts and value of advertising spend.

The point is that advertising economies of scale can be obtained by those organisations that spend a large amount of their resources on the media. To accommodate this, centralised buying has developed, which in turn creates higher entry and exit barriers, not only to and from the market but also from individual agencies.

## Likeability

A major study by the American Research Foundation investigated a range of different pretesting methods with the objective of determining which were best at predicting sales success. The unexpected outcome was that, of all the measures and tests, the most powerful predictor was likeability: 'how much I liked the advertisement'.

From a research perspective, much work has been undertaken to clarify the term 'likeability', but it certainly cannot be measured in terms of a simple Likert scale of 'I liked the advertisement a lot', 'I liked the advertisement a little', etc. The term has a much deeper meaning and is concerned with the following issues (Gordon, 1992):

● personally meaningful, relevant, informative, true to life, believable, convincing;

● relevant, credible, clear product advantages, product usefulness, importance to 'me';

● stimulates interest or curiosity about the brand; creates warm feelings through enjoyment of the advertisement.

The implication of these results is that post-testing should include a strong measure of how well an advertisement was liked at its deepest level of meaning.

Research by Smit et al. (2006) determined that there are four main elements associated with likeability. These are entertainment, relevance, clearness (or clarity) and pleasantness. Of these they found relevance to be the most important for changing viewers' opinions and entertainment for explaining how people process ads.

There are two main approaches to measuring likeability. One seeks to isolate what it is that viewers think and feel after seeing particular ads: i.e. how they feel. The other measures attitudes toward the ad itself. Essentially likeability is concerned with the affective element of the attitude construct. Indeed, some researchers argue that likeability is a suitable response to the cognitive processing school of thought where individuals are considered to be rational problem-solvers.

Cognitive response analysis is an attempt to understand the internal dynamics of how an individual selects and processes messages, of how counter-arguing and message bolstering, for example, might be used to retain or reject an advertisement (see Chapter 17). Back in 1993 Biel reported a growing body of research evidence linking behaviour, attitude change and cognitive processing. He went on to predict, correctly, that this approach, unlike many of the others, was not restricted to FMCG markets and would be deployed across service markets, durables and retailers.

One of the important points to be made from this understanding of likeability is the linkage with the concept of 'significant value' (considered in Chapter 8). The degree to which advertising works is a function of the level of engagement a message creates. This engagement is mediated by the context in which messages are sent, received and personally managed. The main factors are that the product in question should be new or substantially different, interesting, stimulating and personally significant. For advertising to be successful, it must be effective, and to be effective it should be of personally significant value to members of the target audience (those in the market to buy a product from the category in the near future).

The future use of technology will help the measurement and evaluation of advertising. The technology is now in place to meter what people are watching, by appending meters not to sets, but to people. Strapped-on mobile people meters can pick up signals indicating which poster site, television or radio programme is being walked past, seen or heard respectively.

# Public relations

The objectives that are established at the beginning of a campaign must form the basis of any evaluation and testing activity. However, much of the work of public relations (PR) is continuous, and therefore measurement should not be campaign-oriented or time-restricted but undertaken on a regular, ongoing basis. PR is mainly responsible for the identity cues that are presented to the organisation's various stakeholders as part of a planned programme of communications. These cues signal the visibility and profile of the organisation and are used by stakeholders to shape the image that each has of the focus organisation.

PR is, therefore, focused on communication activities, such as awareness, but there are others such as preference, interest and conviction. Evaluation should, in the first instance, measure levels of awareness of the organisation. Attention should then focus on the levels of interest, goodwill and attitudes held towards the organisation as a result of all the planned and unplanned cues used by the organisation.

Traditionally these levels were assumed to have been generated by public relations activities. The main method of measuring their contribution to the communication programme was to collect press cuttings and to record the number of mentions the organisation received in the electronic media. These were then collated in a cuttings book that would be presented to the client. This would be similar to an explorer presenting an electric toaster to a tribe of warriors hitherto undisturbed by other civilisations. It looks nice, but what do you do with it and is it of any real use? Despite this slightly cynical interpretation, the cuttings book does provide a rough and ready way of appreciating the level of opportunities to see created by public relations activities.

The content of the cuttings book and the recorded media mentions can be converted into a different currency. The exchange rate used is the cost of the media that would have been incurred had this volume of communication or awareness been generated by advertising activity. For example, a 30-second news item about an organisation's contribution to a charity event may be exchanged for a 30-second advertisement at rate card cost. The temptation is clear, but the validity of the equation is not acceptable. By translating public relations into advertising currency, the client is expected not only to understand, but also to approve of the enhanced credibility that advertising possesses. It is not surprising that the widely held notion that public relations is free advertising, has grown so substantially when practitioners use this approach.

A further refinement of the cuttings book is to analyse the material covered. The coverage may be positive or negative, approving or disapproving, so the quality of the cuttings needs to be reviewed in order that the client organisation can make an informed judgement about its next set of decisions. This survey of the material in the cuttings book is referred to as a content analysis. Traditionally, content analyses have had to be undertaken qualitatively and were therefore subject to poor interpretation and reviewer bias, however well they approached their task. Today, increasingly sophisticated software is being used to produce a wealth of quantitative data reflecting the key variables that clients want evaluated.

## Corporate image

The approaches discussed so far are intended to evaluate specific media activity and comment on the focus organisation. Press releases are fed into the media and there is a response that is measured in terms of positive or negative, for or against. This quality of information, while useful, does not assist the management of the corporate identity. To do this requires an evaluation of the position that an organisation has in the eyes of key members of the performance network. In addition, the information is not specific enough to influence the strategic direction that an organisation has or the speed at which the organisation is changing. Indeed, most organisations now experience perpetual change; stability and continuity are terms related to an environment that is unlikely to be repeated.

The evaluation of the corporate image should be a regular exercise, supported by management. There are three main aspects. First, key stakeholders (including employees, as they are an important source of communications for external stakeholders), together with members of the performance network and customers, should be questioned regarding their perceptions of the important attributes of the focus organisation and the business they are in (Chapter 12). Second, how does the organisation perform against each of the attributes? Third, how does the organisation perform relative to its main competitors across these attributes?

The results of these perceptions can be evaluated so that corrective action can be directed at particular parts of the organisation and adjustments made to the strategies pursued at business and functional levels. For example, in the computer retailing business, prompt home delivery is a very important attribute. If company A had a rating of 90 per cent on this attribute, but company B was believed to be so good that it was rated at 95 per cent, regardless of actual performance levels, then although A was doing a superb job it would have to improve its delivery service and inform its stakeholders that it was particularly good at this part of the business.

# Recruitment

Recruitment for some organisations can be a problem. In some sectors, where skills are in short supply, the best staff gravitate towards those organisations that are perceived to be better employers and provide better rewards and opportunities. Part of the task of corporate public relations (CPR) is to provide the necessary communications so that a target pool of employees is aware of the benefits of working with the focus organisation and develops a desire to work there.

Measurement of this aspect of CPR can be seductive. It is tempting just to measure the attitudes of the pool of talent prior to a campaign and then to measure it again at the end. This fails to account for the uncontrollable elements in CPR – for example, the actions of others in the market, but, even if this approach is simplistic and slightly erroneous, it does focus attention on an issue. A major chemical-processing company found that it was failing to attract the necessary number of talented undergraduates, partly because the organisation was perceived as unexciting, bureaucratic and lacking career opportunities. A coordinated marketing communications campaign was targeted at university students, partly at repositioning the organisation in such a way that the students would want to work for them when they finished their degrees. The results indicated that students' approval of the company as a future employer rose substantially in the period following the campaign.

# Crisis management

During periods of high environmental turbulence and instability, organisations tend to centralise their decision-making processes and their communications (Quinn and Mintzberg, 1992). When a crisis occurs, communications with stakeholders should increase to keep them informed and aware of developments. It can be observed that crises normally follow a number of phases, during which different types of information must be communicated (Chapter 15). When the crisis is over, the organisation enters a period of feedback and development for the organisation. 'What did we do?', 'How did it happen?', 'Why did we do that?' and 'What do we need to do in the future?' are typical questions that socially aware and mature organisations, which are concerned with quality and the needs of their stakeholders, should always ask themselves.

Pearson and Mitroff (1993) report that many organisations do not expose themselves to this learning process in the fear of 'opening up old wounds'. Those organisations that do take action should communicate their actions to reassure all stakeholders that the organisation has done all it can to prevent a recurrence, or at least to minimise the impact should the origin of the crisis be outside the control of management. A further question that needs to be addressed concerns the way the organisation was perceived during the different crisis phases. Was the image consistent? Did it change, and if so why? Management may believe that it did an excellent job in crisis containment, but what really matters is what stakeholders think – it is their attitudes and opinions that matter above all else.

The objective of crisis management is to limit the effect that a crisis might have on an organisation and its stakeholders, assuming the crisis cannot be prevented. The social system in which an organisation operates means that the image held of the organisation may well change as a result of the crisis event. The image does not necessarily become negative. On the contrary, it may be that the strategic credibility of the organisation could be considerably enhanced if the crisis were managed in an open and positive way. However, it is necessary that the image that stakeholders have of an organisation should be tracked on a regular basis. This means that the image and impact of the crisis can be monitored through each of the crisis phases. Sturges et al. (1991) argue that the objective of crisis management is to influence public opinion to the point that 'post-crisis opinions of any stakeholder group are at least positive, or more positive, or not more negative than before the crisis event'. This ties in with the need to monitor corporate image on a regular basis. The management process of scanning the environment for signals of change, along with change in the attitudes and the perception held by stakeholders towards the organisation, make up a joint process that public relations activities play a major role in executing.

## Other PR measuring techniques

Of all the tools available to practitioners, Goften (1999) reports the following as the most common approaches to measuring public relations:

- *set objectives* and agree the criteria in advance of a campaign;
- *press cuttings*, radio and television tapes, but this is a measure of volume and not quality of impact. A media equivalent value is then applied;
- *media evaluation* through commercial systems such as CAMMA, impact, precis. Under this approach, panels of readers judge whether a mention is positive or negative and whether the client's key message has been communicated. Computer programmes then cut through the data;
- *tracking studies* are expensive but important when changing a perception of a brand, etc.

Practitioners use a variety of methods, but few provide the objectivity and validity that is necessary. For example, Comic Relief monitor the impact of media coverage on the organisation in the run-up to Red Nose Day. It was able to track which initiatives were failing to attract attention and which issues were attracting negative coverage. It evaluated coverage over six key areas: television initiatives, education, grants (Africa and the United Kingdom), special projects, public fundraising and corporate fundraising.

Issues concerning the measurement of sales promotion, sponsorship, and personal selling can be found on the website supporting this text.

# Measuring the fulfilment of brand promises

Brands make promises and communicate them in one of two main ways. One is to make loud claims about the brand's attributes and the benefits these deliver to customers. This approach tends to rely on advertising and the strength of the brand to deliver the promise. The alternative is not to shout, but to whisper, and then surprise customers by exceeding their expectations when they experience the brand. This is an under promise/over deliver strategy, one which reduces risk and places a far greater emphasis on word-of-mouth communication, and brand advocacy. This in turn can reduce an organisation's investment in advertising and lead to a redirection of communication effort and resources in order to improve the customer experience.

It follows therefore that there are measurable gaps between the image and perceptions customers have of brands and their actual experiences. Where expectations are exceeded the promise gap is said to be positive. Where customers feel disappointed through experience of a brand, a negative promise gap can be identified. These gaps are reflected in the financial performance of brands.

The Promise Index reported by Simms (2007) found that, although 66 per cent of the brands surveyed had positive promise gaps, only 15 per cent had gaps that impacted significantly on business performance. Other research by Weber Shandwick found that the main factor for creating brand advocacy was the ability to 'surprise and delight customers'. This survey of 4,000 European consumers, reported by Simms, found that brand advocacy is five times more likely to prompt purchase than advertising.

A related metric, the Net Promoter Score (NPS), seeks to identify how likely an individual is to recommend a brand. Again, a key outcome is that brand growth is driven principally by surprising and delighting customers.

On the basis that brand advocacy is of major importance, two key marketing communication issues emerge. The first concerns how the marketing communications mix should be reformulated in order to encourage brand advocacy. It appears that advertising and mass media have an important role to play in engaging audiences to create awareness and interest. However, more emphasis needs to be given to the other tools and media in order to enhance each customer's experience of a brand beyond their expectations.

The second issue concerns identifying and communicating with passive rather than active advocates. Encouraging customers to talk about a brand means developing content that gives passive advocates a reason to talk about a brand. This means that the message component of the mix needs to be designed away from product attributes and towards stories and memorable events that can be passed on through all customer contact points. This in turn points to a greater use of public relations, viral and the use of user-generated-content, networks and communities and the use of staff in creating brand experiences.

# Online communications

Online research has grown as the Internet population has soared and the measures used have developed through trial and experience. However, the notion that measurement of online communications is easy simply because all that is necessary is 'counting clicks' is misleading. Indeed, when speaking about marketing communications, Roisin Donnelly, UK & Ireland Corporate Marketing Director and Head of Marketing for Procter & Gamble, states that measurement is 'their biggest difficulty'. It is not an issue to measure the overall impact of a campaign but, when measuring the return generated by integrated campaigns, the contribution that word-of-mouth, blogging, online and public relations make, for example, is extremely difficult to isolate (Lannon, 2007).

---

### Viewpoint 9.4    Measuring engagement – it's Intel inside

Intel are an ingredient brand, and only sell to OEMs such as Dell and HP. Intel's online advertising and media mix are complex due to the nature of their highly technical products and the length of time it takes to sell into clients. Intel use advertising to increase brand awareness and preference, and to improve category relevance. Unfortunately the attitudinal data necessary to measure performance were infrequent and invariably late. This made performance measurement a challenge and delayed the chance to make real-time changes to current activities. All of this meant that it was difficult to measure engagement and to judge the value of their online advertising and user behaviour.

To correct this situation, OMD and Intel developed the Value Point System (VPS). This is a weighted digital engagement measurement system which measures the success of Intel's online consumer engagement, reaching across ads, Intel.com, and off-domain sponsorships.

The VPS measures engagement in terms of a user's interaction with Intel's ads or their behaviour on the Intel site to learn more about the company and its products. The system recognises that not all interactions or behaviour are of the same value, so each interaction is weighted according to its value of engagement. Low values are assigned to shallow levels of engagement and the consumption of low-value propositions. So, landing on an Intel page that directs users to a variety of possible Web pages and links, has a very low engagement value. Conversely, considering a page which explains the benefits of using Intel processor(s) has a much higher value. As a result of the metrics generated, Intel can make a range of informed decisions across digital paid media, social, and creative message performance.

Intel's messaging has become more product- than branding-focused and its ads are now optimised on a continuous basis. The media planning teams are more effective and efficient as they can now move media budgets from lower-engagement/value to higher-engagement/value sites in real time. By analysing data at placement level, media planners can identify high performance areas within sites.

There have been many other benefits, including the identification of just how effective video advertising is worldwide, detecting highly active Intel-focused social media audiences, particularly in Russia, India, and Brazil, and discovering new brand advocates in each country, as these people can lead to higher levels of engagement.

The cost efficiency of Intel's campaigns rose by 74 per cent in 2010 and brand engagement increased 172 per cent.

*Source*:   Intel (2011); www.Intel.com.

**Question:**   Identify the criteria you would specify to measure engagement with a brand of your choice.

**Task:**   Find another campaign for a B2B brand and make list of the ways in which success was measured.

Ideas and approaches towards measuring the effectiveness of banner ads and websites, in whatever shape or form, have always been a cause of controversy. The notion that click-through or dwell time represents engagement or a sign of an embryonic relationship has now been dismissed by the majority. The reasons organisations have for setting up a website are many and varied. These might be to establish a Web presence, to move to new methods of commercial activity, to enter new markets, to adhere to parent company demands or to supplement current distribution channels. Consequently, it is not practicable to set up a definitive checklist to use as a measure of website effectiveness, although certain principles need to be followed. See Table 9.5.

However, a core activity still persists. This is the need to develop insights and understanding about the nature and characteristics of website visitors. From this it is necessary to develop visitor profiles so that media planners can optimise banner ad placement.

**Table 9.5**   Criteria to assess website effectiveness

| Type of visitor | Cognitive state | Management action |
|---|---|---|
| All surfers | Level of awareness that a site exists: aware or not aware | Provide offline and online information and directions |
| Those aware | Level of interest in the site: interested or not interested | Create interest and curiosity |
| Those interested | Known route to the site: determined or accidental | Enable greater opportunities for site hit |
| Determined visitors | Was the visit completed successfully? Transaction or no transaction | Encourage bookmarking and post-purchase communication to permit legitimate dialogue |
| Those who transacted | Will these visitors return to the site? Retained or not retained | Maintain and enhance top-of-mind site recall |

*Source*: Adapted from Berthon et al. (1996). Used with kind permission from WARC.

Changes to the transactional aspects associated with online display ads, the emergence of demand-side platforms that aggregate data for from multiple sources, and the development of real-time bidding (see Chapter 24) have all advanced the processes and means by which this core activity is undertaken and through which online advertising is measured and interpreted. Attention is not given to the detail associated with these developments, as these are changing rapidly, and information about current practices can be found elsewhere. However, it is useful to consider ways in which social media can be measured, especially as social networks serve around 30 per cent of the online display ads in the UK (Beeston, 2011).

# Social media

Ideas and approaches to measuring social media activities are in their infancy (Murdough, 2009), and as such many of the tools, techniques and our understanding are evolving. An example of this development is the misplaced reliance on measuring the numbers of clicks, fans and followers and using these as surrogate measures of social media activity (Owyang, 2011). What is more relevant is measuring what these fans and followers do, the outcomes of the social media activities.

For example, rather than measure the number or volume of blogs and tweets, it is thought that a measure of the level of social influence exacted is more appropriate. This is because online influence can help attract and develop brand ambassadors, and also convey an intention to interact with consumers (McCormick, 2011). Klout and PeerIndex are typical services which aim to interpret influence in terms of the number of followers, the frequency of activity, and the quality of interaction. However, influence is dependent on a number of elements and so these services can only be considered to be indicative of performance rather than anything else.

From this we should conclude that measurement should focus on the associated business outcomes arising from the deliberate use of social media. This might be related to the level of influence, leads or conversions, generating conversations and word of mouth, improving customer service and support, or stimulating ideas for brand development.

In order to be able to measure these business outcomes, it is necessary to develop a digital marketing strategy. The strategy and plan should contain the social media goals that are to be achieved (the objectives) and the ways in which performance is to be measured (the metrics), and how the data is to be collected and analysed (the tools or analytics).

The goals can vary from selling more products, and getting more traffic through the website, to increasing a fan base, reaching a specific audience, or getting established as a thought leader. Benchmarks are the quantified goals against which all metrics are measured. These might include current sales volumes or values, the number of hits in Google, various website stats or whatever is relevant to a particular type of business (Hay, 2012).

Another key part of the social media strategy is the channel mix that is to be utilised to reach and engage audiences. Where the engagement takes place is the location for the information to be collected. So, if Facebook, Twitter and a blog are the core channels, then the tools and technologies associated with these channels are going to be the most appropriate: for example, Google Analytics and Hootsuite Analytics (Reid, 2012). At the end of the process the goal is to determine the return on investment. However, as several commentators observe, it can be difficult to derive an accurate ROI in social media.

Murdough (2009) suggests that certain core phases associated with the social media measurement process can be isolated. These are set out in Figure 9.2.

Each of the phases requires a consideration of the goals and both the quantitative and qualitative measures that reveal insight and performance. As Murdough (2009: 95) states: 'Social media is unique in bringing both types of insight together to characterize performance and the value derived from social media efforts.'

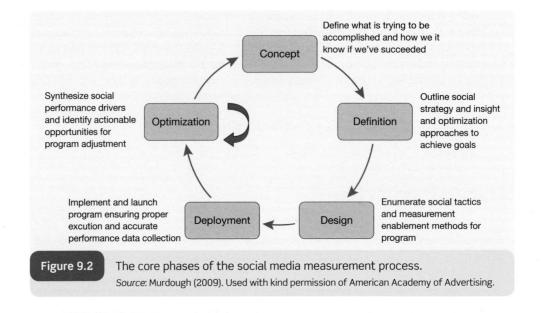

**Figure 9.2**    The core phases of the social media measurement process.
*Source*: Murdough (2009). Used with kind permission of American Academy of Advertising.

---

**Scholars' paper 9.4**    **Media multi-tasking – it is happening now**

**Zigmond, D. and Stipp, H. (2010) Assessing a New Advertising Effect Measurement of the Impact of Television Commercials on Internet Search Queries, *Journal of Advertising Research*, 50(2), June, 162–8.**

The number of people using multiple media in close proximity is increasing. This paper reports on television viewers and their use of the Internet, based on research which indicates that television ads can stimulate significant increases in website visits. The authors measure people's Internet search query behaviour, in order to assess how television advertising can influence consumers in today's media environment.

# Key points

- The evaluation of a marketing communications plan, once implemented, is an essential part of the total system. The evaluation provides a potentially rich source of material for the next campaign and the ongoing communications that all organisations operate, either intentionally or not.

- The evaluation of planned marketing communications consists of two distinct elements. The first element is concerned with the development and testing of individual messages. For example, a particular sales promotion (such as a sample pack) has individual characteristics that may or may not meet the objectives of a sales promotion event.

- The second element concerns the overall impact and effect that a campaign has on a target audience once a communications plan has been released. This post-test factor is critical, as it will either confirm or reject management's judgement about the viability of its communications strategy. The way in which the individual components of the communications mix work together needs to be understood so that strengths can be capitalised on and developed and weaknesses negated.

- Pre-testing is the practice of showing unfinished commercials to selected groups of the target audience with a view to refining the commercial to improve effectiveness; it is still subject to debate about its effectiveness. Many practitioners feel that pre-testing limits creativity. The most common methods used to pre-test advertisements are concept testing, focus groups, consumer juries, dummy vehicles, projective assessments, readability, theatre and physiological tests.

- Post-testing is the practice of evaluating ads that have been released. The main advantage with post-testing is that advertisements are evaluated in their proper environment. There are a number of methods used to evaluate the effectiveness of such advertisements, and of these inquiry, recall, recognition and sales-based tests predominate.

- A bank of physiological tests has been developed, partly as a response to advertisers' increasing interest in the emotional impact of advertising messages and partly because many other tests rely on the respondents' ability to interpret their reactions. Physiological tests have been designed to measure the involuntary responses to stimuli and so avoid the bias inherent in the other tests. There are substantial costs involved with the use of these techniques, and the validity of the results is questionable. Consequently, they are not used a great deal in practice, but, of them all, eye tracking is the most used and most reliable.

- The tools of the mix require different forms of evaluation or testing, simply because of the way they work. Advertising and public relations both have a number of established forms of measurement and evaluation based on quantitative and qualitative methods. Of the two, public relations is far more subjective and measurement is much more problematic.

- Tracking studies involve interviewing a large number of people on a regular basis, weekly or monthly, with the purpose of collecting data about buyers' perceptions of marketing communication messages. Perceptions, attitudes and meanings attributed to campaigns can be tracked and adjustments made to campaigns as necessary.

- Considering the vast amount of resources that are directed at planned communications, and in particular advertising, it is important to review, on a periodic basis, the amount and the manner in which its financial resources have been used. For some organisations the media spend alone constitutes one of the major items of expenditure.

- Likeability refers to the deep-seated set of meanings and associations an individual makes with particular ads and its measurement has proven to be a good indicator of an ad's performance.

- There are measurable gaps between the image and perceptions customers have of brands and their actual experiences. Where expectations are exceeded, the promise gap is said to be positive. Where customers feel disappointed through experience of a brand, a negative promise gap can be identified. These gaps are reflected in the financial performance of brands.

- The Promise Index and the Net Promoter Score (NPS) are two approaches to measuring the success of delivering brand promises.

- Online communications are perhaps the easiest to measure as web servers can indicate which and how many pages have been requested, the time spent on each page and even the type of computers that were used to request the page.

- However, this type of information is largely superficial and fails to provide insight into the user, their motivation to visit the site or the behavioural or attitudinal outcomes as a result of the interaction.

- A core activity is to develop insights and understanding about the nature and characteristics of website visitors. From this it is necessary to develop visitor profiles so that media planners can optimise banner ad placement.

- It is not helpful to just rely on measuring the numbers of clicks, dwell time, fans and followers, and to use these as surrogate measures of social media activity. What is more relevant is measuring what these fans and followers do, how they behave as a result of engaging in social media activities.

- Traditional measurement techniques of reach, frequency and target audience impressions are not easily applicable to online communications.

# Review questions

1. Why should the 'Still Killing Jill?' campaign, presented at the start of this chapter, have tried to measure attitude change to organ donation?

2. What are pre- and post-testing?

3. Write a brief report comparing recall and recognition tests.

4. What are the principal dimensions of likeability as a measure of advertising effectiveness?

5. Write brief notes explaining why media comparison techniques are inadequate measures of public relations.

6. Explain in note form the core characteristics of the Promise Index and the Net Promoter Score.

7. What are the techniques used to measure website effectiveness? Are they any good?

8. What is the core activity of online communications? Sketch out the social media measurement process.

9. Many organisations fail to undertake suitable research to measure the success of their campaigns. Why is this and what can be done to change this situation?

10. Comment on the view that, if a method of evaluation and testing lacks objectivity and measurability, then the method should not be used.

# References

Aaker, D.A., Stayman, D.M. and Hagerty, M.R. (1986) Warmth in Advertising: Measurement, Impact, and Sequence Effects, *Journal of Consumer Research*, 12(4), 365–81.

Beeston, J. (2011) Special Report: Display, *Revolution*, September, p. 37.

Bellman, S., Schweda, A. and Varan, D. (2009) A Comparison of Three Interactive Television Ad Formats, *Journal of Interactive Advertising*, 10(1), 14–34.

Berthon, P., Pitt, L. and Watson, R. (1996) The world wide web as an advertising medium: toward an understanding of conversion efficiency, *Journal of Advertising Research*, 6(1) (January/February), 43–53.

Biel, A.L. (1993) Ad research in the US., *Admap* (May), 27–9.

Brennan, I., Dubas, K.M. and Babin, L.A. (1999) The Influence of Product-Placement Type and Exposure Time on Product-Placement Recognition, *International Journal of Advertising*, 18(3), 323–38.

Burden, S. (2007) Case study: pre-testing mould-breaking ads, *Admap*, July/August, 48–9.

Campbell, R.H. (1965) A Managerial Approach to Advertising Measurement, *Journal of Marketing*, 29(4), October, 1–6.

Chang, Y., Yan, J., Zhang, J. and Luo, J. (2010) Online in-game advertising effect: examining the influence of a match between games and advertising, *Journal of Interactive Advertising*, 11(1), (Fall), 63–73.

Cobb-Walgren, C.J., Ruble, C.A. and Donthu, N. (1995) Brand Equity, Brand Preference, and Purchase Intent, *Journal of Advertising*, 24(3), 25–40.

Cox, S. (2007) Total recall: advertising exposure and engagement, *Admap*, 480 (February), 44–6.

Dichter, E. (1966) How word-of-mouth advertising works, *Harvard Business Review*, 44 (November/December), 147–66.

Ewing, M.T. (2009) Integrated marketing communications measurement and evaluation, *Journal of Marketing Communications*, 15(2–3), April–July, 103–117.

Flesch, R. (1974) *The Art of Readable Writing*, New York: Harper & Row.

Goften, K. (1999) The measure of PR, *Campaign Report*, 2 April, 13.

Gordon, W. (1992) Ad pre-testing's hidden maps, *Admap* (June), 23–7.

Hansen, F., Olsen, J.K. and Lundsteen, S. (2006) The Effects of Print vs. TV Advertising, Documented Using Short-Term Advertising Strength (STAS) Measures, *International Journal of Advertising*, 25(4), 431–46.

Hay, D. (2012) 4 simple steps to measuring social media success, *Socialmedia.biz*, retrieved 9 May 2012 from http://www.socialmedia.biz/2012/03/19/4-steps-to-measuring-social-media-success/.

Intel (2011) Intel: Measuring Online Global Advertising Based on Business Value and Engagement, *ARF Ogilvy Awards*, WARC Cases, retrieved 14 September 2011 from www.WARC.com.

Krugman, H.E. (1988) Point of view: limits of attention to advertising, *Journal of Advertising Research*, 38, 47–50.

Lannon, J. (2007) Marketing is the Boss, *Market Leader*, 39 (Winter), retrieved 27 February 2008 from www.warc.com.

Lee, D.H. and Park, C.W. (2007) Conceptualization and measurement of multidimensionality of integrated marketing communications, *Journal of Advertising Research* (September), 222–36.

Lodish, L.M. and Lubetkin, B. (1992) General truths? *Admap* (February), 9–15.

MacKenzie, S.B. and Lutz, R.J. (1989) An Empirical Examination of the Structural Antecedents of Attitude Toward the Ad in an Advertising Pretesting Context, *Journal of Marketing*, 53(2), 48–65.

Mazur, L. (1993) Qualified for success? *Marketing*, 23 January, 20–2.

McCormick, A. (2011) Online Influence, *Revolution*, September, 32–33.

Murdough, C. (2009) Social media measurement: it's not impossible, *Journal of Interactive Advertising*, 10(1), Fall, 94–9.

Olney, T.J., Holbrook, M.B. and Batra, R. (1991) Consumer Responses to Advertising: The Effects of Ad Content, Emotions, and Attitude toward the Ad onViewing Time, *Journal of Consumer Research*, 17(4), 440–53.

Ovenden, M. (2007) 21st century media: right on target, *Marketing*, 5 December, 6–7.

Owyang, J. (2011) Number of Fans and Followers is NOT a Business Metric – What You Do With Them Is, retrieved 9 May 2012 from http://www.webstrategist.com/blog/category/social-media-measurement/.

Pearson, C.M. and Mitroff, I. (1993) From crisis prone to crisis prepared: a framework for crisis management, *Academy of Management Executive*, 7(1), 48–59.

Quinn, J.B. and Mintzberg, H. (1992) *The Strategy Process*, 2nd edn., Englewood Cliffs, NJ: Prentice-Hall.

Reid, A. (2000) Testing Times, *Campaign*, 22 September, 40.

Reid, A. (2012) Measuring Social Media: A Step-by-Step Guide for Newbies, retrieved 9 May 2012 from http://www.business2community.com/social-media/measuring-social-media-a-step-by-step-guide-for-newbies-0163705.

Robson, S. (2002) Group discussions, in *The International Handbook of Market Research Techniques* (ed. Robin Birn), London: Kogan Page.

Sherwood, P.K., Stevens, R.E. and Warren, W.E. (1989) Periodic or continuous tracking studies: matching methodology with objectives, *Market Intelligence and Planning*, 7, 11–13.

Simms, J. (2007) Bridging the gap, *Marketing*, 12 December, 26–8.

Smit, E.G., van Meurs, L. and Neijens, P.C. (2006) Effects of advertising likeability: a 10-year perspective, *Journal of Advertising Research*, 46(1) (March), 73–83.

Sturges, D.L., Carrell, B.J., Newsom, D.A. and Barrera, M. (1991) Crisis communication management: the public opinion node and its relationship to environmental nimbus, *SAM Advanced Management Journal*, (Summer), 22–7.

Treutler, T., Levine, B. and Marci, C.D. (2010) Biometrics and Multi-Platform Messaging; The Medium Matters, *Journal of Advertising Research*, 50(3), September, 243–9.

Vaughn, R. (1980) How advertising works: a planning model, *Journal of Advertising Research* (October), 27–33.

Zielske, H.A. (1982) Does day-after recall penalise 'feeling' ads? *Journal of Advertising Research*, 22(1), 19–22.

Zigmond, D. and Stipp, H. (2010) Assessing a New Advertising Effect Measurement of the Impact of Television Commercials on Internet Search Queries, *Journal of Advertising Research*, 50(2), June, 162–8.

# Chapter 10
## Integrated marketing communications

The value and potential of integrated marketing communications appear to be universally supported by academics and practitioners. However, the subject remains theoretically under-developed, empirically unproven and rutted with controversy and disagreement. Is IMC just a matter of rhetoric or does it deliver enhanced engagement opportunities and cut through?

## Aims and learning objectives

The aims of this chapter are to explore the nature and characteristics of integrated marketing communications and to understand the complexities associated with developing and implementing this form of marketing communications.

The learning objectives of this chapter are to:

1. introduce the concept of integrated marketing communications (IMC);
2. explain the background and reasons for the development of and interest in IMC;
3. explore the elements that need to be integrated;
4. examine definitions of IMC through time;
5. analyse five different interpretations of IMC;
6. consider how structure influences IMC.

# Minicase

## Authentic Caribbean Rum

The West Indies Rum and Spirits Producers' Association (WIRSPA) is a trade association based in Barbados, whose aim is to represent and promote over 30 Caribbean rum brands located in 15 country locations throughout the Caribbean.

WIRSPA aimed to enhance the long-term competitiveness of Caribbean rum producers through exporting branded and value-added rums. A coordinated marketing communications campaign was developed to raise consumer and trade awareness of the provenance of Caribbean rum through the launch of the Authentic Caribbean Rum (ACR) marque, in the UK, Spain and Italy.

The ACR marque was developed to serve as a visual symbol of origin and quality, designed to help trade and consumers identify ACR brands and to be used to promote the development of Authentic Caribbean Rum.

The objectives were to develop and implement a category campaign specifically for the emerging golden rum category which would:

1. Create recognition, value and meaning for the ACR marque as a symbol of origin and quality for Caribbean rums.

2. Influence attitudes within the drinks distribution trade – creating a positive environment for brand owners to market their products.

3. Create awareness of Caribbean rum among consumers so that they include ACR brands in their regular drinks repertoire.

| Exhibit 10.1 | **The ACR marque** |
|---|---|
| | *Source*: Bray Leino Ltd |

### Market research

Extensive market research and audience analysis was used to identify the primary target audience for golden rum in all three country markets. The core audience were defined more by their lifestyles and attitudes than by traditional demographics and labelled 'New Authentics' – a combination of the traditional 'Adventurer: 18–44 years, urban, well-off, male bias' and 'Sophisticate: 25–45 years, suburban, affluent, male bias' – with the addition of demanding personal growth and authentic experiences.

These 'New Authentics' were united by their 'spirit of discovery' and a desire for products steeped in heritage and authenticity, a perfect audience for the ACR proposition.

### Strategic planning

The core creative campaign was, like all good marketing campaigns, based on an inherent truth from the product. The creative idea reflects the depth of history, honesty and passion behind the production of Caribbean rum and strongly implies that if you're not drinking Authentic Caribbean Rum, then you're not drinking the real thing. To bring the idea of 'True Rum' to life, the campaign captured the faces of real people and the wonderfully emotive stories that can be told about Caribbean rum.

Using the creative theme of 'True Rum', the campaign was based around powerful portrait photography of real individuals with a true connection to Authentic Caribbean Rum. From master blenders to bartenders, each of the subjects featured had an authentic and longstanding association with the spirit. Every element of the campaign related the story of the subject's relationship with rum, to evoke a personal engagement with the ACR brands.

Designed to reflect the heritage, integrity and passion behind the diverse range of rums originating from the Caribbean, the words 'Authentic Caribbean Rum – True Rum' were used in tandem with the ACR marque throughout.

Neil Morris, Head of Marketing for the West Indies Rum and Spirits Producers' Association (WIRSPA), explains: 'The aim of the True Rum campaign was to bring real Caribbean heritage to life in an emotive

**Exhibit 10.2**    **A long-copy ad**
*Source*: Bray Leino Ltd

and aspirational way. The images and style that have been developed incorporate a character and integrity that is unmistakeably Caribbean. We wanted to link rum's past to its present, representing both its rich heritage and its place in contemporary life. It is a simple, distinctive and memorable concept . . . with a really powerful impact across all media and marketing applications.'

## A truly integrated campaign

An integrated multichannel communications campaign was created, built around the core campaign idea of 'True Rum' to support the awareness of the ACR marque; the more sophisticated re-positioning of the Caribbean rum category; and to motivate trade distribution and consumer trial of ACR brands.

This integrated campaign, which included: trade and consumer advertising, trade and consumer relations, online, retailer promotions, experiential and events, as well as extensive bartender training and consumer sampling activity, was rolled out across the UK, Spain and Italy.

## Advertising

Trade and consumer advertising campaigns were developed including key trade titles, consumer lifestyle magazines, national Sunday supplements, Caribbean magazines, outdoor cross-track posters and radio advertising.

The initial advertising was designed to launch and build awareness of the ACR marque specifically for the trade and then for consumer audiences. A series of long-copy advertising executions were used to tell the story of True Rum and educate both the trade and consumer audiences. These were followed by a series of testimonial/portrait advertising executions, to deliver the emotive element of the campaign.

## Public relations

A full media relations campaign was implemented (national and regional print, online and broadcast), with news, features, recipe development and support photography as well as ambassador and advocate endorsement, to maximise advocate support and stakeholder relations through ongoing reporting and presentations to all stakeholders, including an online bulletin.

## Influencer engagement

A programme of influencer engagement was rolled out in the form of a bartender training programme, key venue communication, retailer engagement (meetings/briefings/presentations) and retailer support presentations. This engagement activity was important to secure trade and bar tender advocate endorsement in all three country markets.

## Digital and social media

A website for both consumers and the trade www.truerum.com was created, including profiles of the rum brands and cocktail recipes, for all three country markets. Further online activity also included an SEO campaign, online advertising, True Rum TV, a creative viral campaign and social media activity.

## Events and experiential

As the showpiece of the experiential strategy, a permanent, interactive and educational 'True Rum Experience' was created at Vinopolis in London. A UK-wide campaign of events and sampling activity was rolled out for both the trade and consumers, to trial and experience rum cocktails and mixers. The equivalent experiential activity was also rolled out in Spain and Italy.

## A golden success

Over a five-year period up to 2009, sales of ACR brands as measured by IWSR had grown by just 5 per cent internationally, but by 69 per cent within Italy, Spain and the UK, demonstrating the clear effects of the True Rum campaign in promoted markets. Within the UK trade, ACR marque rum producers obtained new distribution for 10 new brands and 18 SKUs (Stock Keeping Units).

Tracking research showed ad recognition of over 10 per cent, with the creative well appreciated and delivering the desired brand and strategic messages. The campaign obtained advertising media coverage in the UK at 63 per cent of target audience @ 7 OTS versus a target of 47 per cent and 5 OTS. The PR coverage resulted in over 200 pieces of editorial at AVE of €4.5 million.

*This case was written by Neil Morris, Head of Marketing at WIRSPA and James Robertson, Strategy Director at Bray Leino. Permission to use the material was kindly given by WIRSPA.*

# Introduction

The WIRSPA minicase describes an integrated marketing communications campaign. It illustrates the many facets and issues associated with driving a contemporary campaign. This chapter explores the essence of integrated marketing communications (IMC), its origins and the key factors that have helped shape its development.

For many years agencies and clients believed that to deliver messages to particular audiences it was necessary to use specific tools of the communications mix. At the time it was a common belief that to achieve specific communication effects *on* buyers it was necessary to use particular tools. So, for example, clients were recommended to use advertising to create awareness, sales promotions to generate immediate sales uplifts and public relations to create interest and goodwill towards a brand. This view held that each tool has specific characteristics and particular communication abilities. As a result, clients were required to deal with a variety of functionally different and independent agencies in order to complete their communication requirements with their various audiences.

This 'specialisation' resulted in a proliferation of advertising agencies, the development of sales promotion houses and the emergence of direct marketing agencies. Public relations specialists stood off from any direct association with marketing. Personal selling had already evolved as a discrete function within organisations. This approach was also legitimised by the development of trade associations and professional management groups (for example, the Institute of Practitioners in Advertising (UK) and the Institute of Promotional Marketing, that seek to endorse, advance, protect and legitimise the actions of their professions and members. One of the outcomes of this silo perspective and functional development of the marketing communications industry has been entrenchment and the inevitable opposition to change.

Now that clients have begun to re-orient their communications away from mass-media approaches to increased levels of interaction with customers, the structural inadequacies of the marketing communication industry have served to constrain them. IMC has emerged partially as a reaction to this structural inadequacy and the realisation by clients that their communication needs can (and should) be achieved more efficiently and effectively than previously. In other words, just as power has moved from brand manufacturers to multiple retailers and now to consumers, so power is moving from agencies to clients.

This trend away from traditional communication strategies based on mass communications, directing generalised messages to huge segmented audiences has played a part in the development of IMC. Contemporary strategies are based more on personalised, customer-oriented and technology-driven approaches, and are often referred to as integrated marketing communications (IMC). Duncan and Everett (1993) recall that this new, largely media-oriented approach, has been referred to variously as *orchestration*, *whole egg* and *seamless communication*. More recent notions involve the explicit incorporation of corporate communication, reflected in titles such as integrated marketing and integrated communications.

It is interesting that the rapid development of direct marketing initiatives since the second half of the 1980s and the impact the Internet has made, have coincided with a move towards what has become regarded as integrated marketing communications. A further significant development has been the shift in marketing philosophies, from transaction to relationship marketing (introduced in Chapter 1 and considered in more detail in Chapter 4).

# The development of IMC

The word 'integration' has been used in various ways and it is the interpretation of the word that determines whether integrated marketing communications is real, achievable or even practised. In many ways, reality suggests that the claims many organisations and the communications industry make in the name of IMC are simply a reflection of improved management and coordination of the communication tools. The recent interest in media-neutral planning (MNP) may be a good thing for the cause of improved communications and relationship development, but MNP does not address the wider strategic issues, the importance of internal communications or the structural issues of IMC on both the client and agency sides.

As established above, early interpretations of IMC were constructed around the idea that what was to be integrated were the promotional tools and media. Scholars such as Shultz et al. (1993) and Duncan and Everett (1993) led much of the IMC activity and many organisations were enthusiastic about the new ideas, driven by the desire to restructure internally, reduce costs and deliver consistent messages. Kitchen et al. (2004) refer to this as the *inside-out IMC approach*.

The next phase was characterised by an exploration of the nature, direction and content typified by definitions that introduced management, strategy and brand development into the IMC process. Shimp (2000), among others, supported the explicit introduction of these aspects to IMC.

The current interpretation has moved the IMC concept forward, this time as an audience- or customer-driven process, one that incorporates ideas concerning relationship marketing. Duncan and Mulhern (2004), cited by Reid (2005), Gronroos (2004) and Duncan (2002), have provided valuable insights into this dimension of IMC, one which Kitchen et al. (2004) refer to as the *outside-in IMC approach*.

It should be noted that while many writers, such as Kitchen and Shultz (1997 and 1998) and Duncan (2002), have written positively and consistently promoting ideas about IMC, other authors such as Cornelissen and Lock (2000), Percy et al. (2001) and Spotts et al. (1998), to name but a few, have been critical of the concept and have doubted the merits inherent in the concept. This dichotomy of views reveals the inherent instability of the IMC concept. Readers interested in a fuller appraisal of IMC are referred to Kitchen et al. (2004) and Cornelissen (2003).

As part of his critique Cornelissen (2003) distinguishes two different themes running through the IMC literature. The first is that IMC is regarded as a predominantly *process*-oriented concept and the second is that it is a *content*-oriented concept. These are examined in the following section.

Unsurprisingly, therefore, there is no agreement about what IMC is, what it encompasses or how it should be measured. Indeed, there is no universally agreed definition and, apart from some anecdotal comment, there is little practical evidence of the application of a strategic, customer-oriented IMC programme. There are numerous claims of IMC practice but these are little more than coordinated promotional mix activities using themed messages (inside-out). Liodice (2008), cited by Smith (2012), reports that only 25 per cent of companies give a positive rating to their IMC programmes.

IMC is a not a proven marketing theory (Cornelissen, 2003). There is no empirical evidence to support the concept, yet the ideas inherent in the overall approach hold value. Although Cornelissen refers to the IMC concept as only worthy of symbolic value, a view later refuted by Kitchen, it does appear that what is integration to one person (or agency) may be coordination or simply good professional practice to another.

# Reasons for the developing interest in IMC

The interest in IMC has resulted from a variety of drivers. Generally they can be grouped into three main categories: those drivers (or opportunities) that are market-based, those that arise

| Table 10.1 | Drivers of IMC |
| --- | --- |

**Organisational drivers for IMC**
- Increasing profits through improved efficiency
- Increasing need for greater levels of accountability
- Rapid move towards cross-border marketing and the need for changing structures and communications
- Coordinated brand development and competitive advantage
- Opportunities to utilise management time more productively
- Provide direction and purpose for employees

**Market-based drivers for IMC**
- Greater levels of audience communications literacy
- Media cost inflation
- Media and audience fragmentation
- Stakeholders' need for increasing amounts and diversity of information
- Greater amounts of message clutter
- Competitor activity and low levels of brand differentiation
- Move towards relationship marketing from transaction-based marketing
- Development of networks, collaboration and alliances

**Communication-based drivers for IMC**
- Technological advances (Internet, databases, segmentation techniques)
- Increased message effectiveness through consistency and reinforcement of core messages
- More effective triggers for brand and message recall
- More consistent and less confusing brand images
- Need to build brand reputations and to provide clear identity cues

from changing communications, and those that are driven by opportunities arising from within the organisation itself. These are set out in Table 10.1.

The opportunities offered to organisations that contemplate moving to IMC are considerable and it is somewhat surprising that so few organisations have been either willing or able to embrace the approach. One of the main organisational drivers for IMC is the need to become increasingly efficient. Driving down the cost base enables managers to improve profits and levels of productivity. By seeking synergistic advantages through its communications and associated activities and by expecting managers to be able to account for the way in which they consume marketing communication resources, so integrated marketing communications becomes increasingly attractive. At the same time, organisation structures are changing more frequently and the need to integrate across functional areas reflects the efficiency drive.

From a market perspective, the predominant driver is the reorientation from transaction-based marketing to relationship marketing. The extension of the brand personality concept into brand relationships (Hutton, 1996) requires a customer consideration in terms of asking not only 'What do our customers want?', but also 'What are their values, do they trust us, and are we loyal to them?' By adopting a position designed to enhance trust and commitment, an organisation's external communications need to be consistent and coordinated, if only to avoid information overload and misunderstanding.

From a communication perspective, the key driver is to provide a series of triggers by which buyers can form brand associations, understand a brand's values and consider the extent to which the brand might become or continue to be a part of their lives, however peripherally. By differentiating the marketing communications, often by providing clarity and simplicity, advantages can be attained.

An integrated approach should attempt to provide a uniform or consistent set of messages. These should be relatively easy to interpret and to assign meaning. This enables audiences to think about and perceive brands within a relational context, and so encourage behaviour as expected by the source. Those organisations that try to practise IMC understand that buyers refer to and receive messages about brands and companies from a wide range of information sources. Harnessing this knowledge is a fundamental step towards enhancing marketing communications.

---

### Scholars' paper 10.1     Integrated meaning

**Finne, A. and Gronroos, C. (2009)** *Journal of Marketing Communications*, **15(2–3) (April–July), 179–195.**

Although this paper does not focus on advertising, these authors present a new way of considering integrated communication. In that sense it is important to appreciate the consumer-centric perspective on IMC as the principle applies equally to advertising. Much of the integration literature considers outgoing messages, whereas the authors switch the focus to consumers and the way they integrate messages.

---

It is useful to itemise the advantages and disadvantages associated with IMC. These are set out in Table 10.2. General opinion suggests that the advantages far outweigh the disadvantages and that increasing numbers of organisations are seeking to improve their IMC resource. As stated earlier, database technology and the Internet have provided great impetus for organisations to review their communications and to implement moves to instal a more integrated communication strategy.

---

**Table 10.2**     Advantages and disadvantages of IMC

**Advantages of IMC**
Provides opportunities to cut communication costs and/or reassign budgets
Has the potential to produce synergistic and more effective communications
Can deliver competitive advantage through clearer positioning
Encourages coordinated brand development with internal and external participants
Provides for increased employee participation and motivation
Has the potential to cause management to review its communication strategy
Requires a change in culture and fosters a customer focus
Provides a benchmark for the development of communication activities
Can lead to a cut in the number of agencies supporting a brand

**Disadvantages of IMC**
Encourages centralisation and formal/bureaucratic procedures
Can require increased management time seeking agreement from all involved parties
Suggests uniformity and single message
Tendency to standardisation might negate or dilute creative opportunities
Global brands restricted in terms of local adaptation
Normally requires cultural change from employees and encourages resistance
Has the potential to severely damage a brand's reputation if incorrectly managed
Can lead to mediocrity as no single agency network has access to all sources of communications

## Viewpoint 10.1　Integrated growth for Morrisons

With the economy becoming increasingly harsh in 2008, Morrisons wanted a campaign that would help avoid the looming price wars and communicate their brand values in order to strengthen relationships with customers and young families.

The growing interest in food – whether it be the source, freshness, or quality – is associated with societal concern about obesity. Morrison's brand values are rooted in fresh food, and so it was natural to develop a programme anchored around schools and schoolchildren. This was the seed for the 'Let's grow' community engagement programme. For each £10 spent in Morrisons, customers earned a voucher. This was redeemable as gardening tools, equipment and seeds for schools. The goal was to help children to learn about and of course grow their own fruit and vegetables.

Following consultation with agencies, partner organisations and charities such as Farming and Countryside Education and the Federation of City Farms and Gardens, a carefully crafted set of learning resources was produced, designed to support Key Stage 1 teachers. This also enabled Morrisons to specify the gardening equipment so that it matched the lesson plans.

The campaign had to be managed in many ways. In addition to the 'Let's grow' creative, there were communications with schools, third-party gardening equipment suppliers and the media planning and public relations activities. Most of this was assigned to the Billington Cartmell agency appointed to run the campaign.

In-store posters and leaflets were distributed throughout all the Morrisons stores, and staff briefings were held to inform about the campaign mechanics, prior to launch.

Direct mail was used to inform schools of the 'Let's Grow' campaign and to tell them how they could get involved. This was supported by a TV advert featuring celebrity gardener Diarmuid Gavin, and coverage in local and national press. Online activity on parenting websites provided links to the 'Let's Grow' pages on Morrisons' website. Each school was provided with banners for the school gates and visits and lessons from local gardening experts.

With a target of 8,000 schools, the campaign resulted in over 18,000 signing up, 39 million vouchers were collected, and £3.2 million's worth of gardening equipment was distributed by Morrisons. Using econometric modelling to measure performance, it was found that an additional 1.733 million shopping visits were made as a direct result of the campaign, and incremental turnover was £52 million. With a campaign budget of £2.5 million, the return on investment was £21.57 for every £1. And if that was not enough, perceptions of Morrisons being linked to food sources, and that they were involved in the local community rose substantially.

*Source*: Barda (2010); Anon (2010); Heyworth and Djurdjevic (2009).

### Exhibit 10.3

**Although the 'Let's Grow' campaign has finished, the ideas and strapline have since been revived by Morrisons. Here it can be seen in their in-house magazine.**

*Source*: Wm Morrison Supermarkets PLC

**Question:**　To what extent is this campaign integrated? What else could have been included?

**Task:**　Identify the elements that have been integrated in this campaign and comment on the extent to which advertising has played an integral role.

# What is to be integrated?

The notion that some aspects of marketing communications should be integrated begs the question, what is it that needs to be integrated? While the origins of IMC might be found in the prevailing structural conditions and the needs of particular industry participants, an understanding of what elements should be integrated in order to achieve IMC needs to be established.

The problem with answering this question is that unless there is an agreement about what IMC is then identifying appropriate elements is far from easy, practical or in any one's best interests. Figure 10.1 shows some of the elements that need integrating.

The following represents some of the fundamental elements, but readers are advised to consider some of the other issues that have been raised in this chapter before confirming their views about this stimulating yet relatively young concept.

## Communication tools

One of the early and more popular views of IMC was that the messages conveyed by each of the 'promotional' tools should be harmonised in order that audiences perceive a consistent set of meanings within the messages they receive. One interpretation of this perspective is that the key visual triggers (design, colours, form and tag line) used in advertising should be replicated across the range of promotional tools used, including POP and the sales force. At another level, integration is about bringing together the communication tools (Pitta et al. 2006). One such combination is the closer alliance of advertising with public relations. Increasing audience fragmentation means that it is more difficult to locate target audiences and communicate with them in a meaningful way. By utilising the power of public relations to get advertisements talked about, what the trade refers to as media equivalents, a form of communications consistency, or integration to some, becomes possible.

The rapid development of direct marketing approaches has helped some organisations bring together the different tools such that they undertake more precise roles and reinforce each other. For example, the use of direct mail and telemarketing to follow through on an ad campaign is commonplace, but now Web-enabled communications, customer care centres and sales promotions can be linked together through database applications, and all are designed to communicate the same core message.

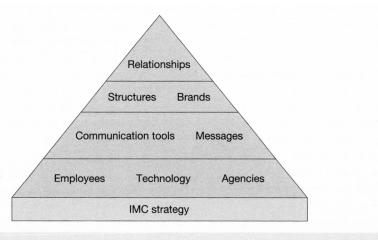

**Figure 10.1**   Elements to be integrated

## Messages

A further interpretation, at a deeper level, is that the theme and set of core messages used in any campaign should first be determined and then deployed as an integrated whole across the communication mix (sometimes referred to as *synergy*). One of the differences is the recognition that mass-media advertising is not always the only way to launch consumer or business-to-business promotional activities, and that a consideration of the most appropriate mix of communication tools and media might be a better starting point when formulating campaigns.

Another perspective of IMC, provided by Duncan and Moriarty (1998), is that stakeholders (including customers) automatically integrate brand messages. This suggests that as long as the gaps between the different messages (in content and meaning) are acceptable, then management's task is to manage the process and seek to narrow these gaps that may be perceived.

What runs through both these approaches is the belief that above-the-line and below-the-line communications need to be moulded into one cohesive bundle, from which tools can be selected and deployed as conditions require.

## Marketing mix

The elements of the marketing mix, however configured, also need to be integrated because they too communicate (Smith, 1996). The price and associated values, the product, in terms of the quality, design and tangible attributes, the manner and efficiency of the service delivery people and where and how it is made available, for example the location, website, customer contact centres, retailer/dealer reputation and overall service quality need to be perceived by customers as a coordinated and consistent whole. These touch points with brands are aspects of a consumer's brand experience and are used to develop images that through time may shape brand reputations. Traditionally the marketing mix was expected to deliver the brand proposition. Now it is expected that all these elements will be coordinated to maximise impact and enable customers to experience the brand through pre-, actual and post-product use.

## Branding

Brands are themselves a form of integration. This means that internally organisations need to be sufficiently coordinated so that the brand is perceived externally as consistent and uniform. However, this proposition is based on the view that a brand is prepared and delivered for a single target audience but audience and media fragmentation make this task more challenging. Audience sizes are shrinking, which means that in many situations a single audience is no longer economically viable. Brands therefore, need to appeal to a number of different audiences (White, 2000) and, to do this, it is necessary to develop brands that appeal to diverse consumer groups. White refers to these new brands as 'chameleon' brands. They are characterised by their ability to adapt to different situations (audiences and media) yet retain a core proposition that provides a form of continuity and recognition. For example, a top-of-the-range music system may be seen by the owner as prestigious and technically superb, by a guest at a party as ostentatiously outrageous and overpriced and by a friend as a product of clever design and marketing. All three might have developed their attitudes through different sources (e.g. different print media, exhibitions, the Internet, retail stores, word-of-mouth) but all agree that the brand has a common set of values and associations that are important to each of them.

The presentation of chameleon brands requires high levels of integration, a need to develop a series of innovative messages based around a core proposition. The use of a single ad execution needs to be replaced by multiple executions delivered through a variety of media, each complementing and reinforcing the core brand proposition. This means that the audience is more likely to be surprised or reminded of the brand (and its essence) through a series of refreshingly interesting messages, thereby raising the probability that the likeability factor (see Chapter 14) will be strengthened, along with the brand and all relevant associations.

A further dimension of the branding factor concerns the role of corporate brands and issues of corporate communications. Should these be integrated with product brand communications, and if so what are the branding strategies that should be followed?

## Strategy

IMC is regarded by some as a means of using the tools of the communication mix in a more efficient and synergistic manner. At some level this can be true but IMC requires a deeper understanding of how and where messages are created. At a strategic level, IMC has its roots in the overall business strategy of an organisation. Using Porter's (1980) generic strategies, if a low-cost strategy (e.g. Asda) is being pursued, it makes sense to complement the strategy by using messages that either stress any price advantage that customers might benefit from or at least do not suggest extravagance or luxury. If using a differentiation focus strategy (e.g. Waitrose), price should not figure in any of the messages and greater emphasis should be placed on particular attributes that convey the added value and enable clear positioning. There is no right way (or formula) to establish IMC but there is a need to recognise that it is a developmental exercise and that it should have a strategic orientation as well as strategic outputs.

## Employees

The next element that should be integrated concerns the recognition that IMC cannot be sustained unless it is supported by all customer-facing employees. It is generally agreed that all employees should adopt a customer focus and 'live' the brand. While this can be achieved partially through the use of training courses and in-house documentation (including electronic forms), this usually requires a change of culture and that means a longer-term period of readjustment and the adoption of new techniques, procedures and ways of thinking and behaving.

Once the internal reorientation has begun (not been completed), it is possible to take the message to external audiences. As long as they can see that employees are starting to act in different ways and do care about them as customers and do know what they are talking about in support of the products and services offered, then it is likely that customers (and other stakeholders) will be supportive. IMC should be concerned with blending internal and external messages so that there is clarity, consistency and reinforcement of the organisation's (or brand's) core proposition.

## Technology

The interest and debate about IMC has been accelerated by developments in technology. The use of technology, and in particular database technologies, has enabled marketing managers to have a vastly improved view of customer behaviour, attitudes and feelings towards brands. This has allowed more precise and insightful communications to be generated and the subsequent feedback and measurement facilities have further developed the overall quality of customer communications. However, the mere presence of technology does not result in effective marketing communications. Technology needs to be integrated into not just the overall information systems strategy but also the marketing strategies of organisations. Technology is an enabler and to use it effectively requires integration. The effective use of technology can touch a number of areas within the IMC orbit. For example, technology can be used to develop effective websites, extranets and intranets, customer contact centres, databases, advertising campaigns, fulfilment processes, CRM and salesforce automation. If each of these applications is deployed independently of the others their impact will be limited. Developed within an integrated framework, the potential for marketing and customer service can be tremendous.

Associated with the use of technology are issues concerning the measurement and evaluation of IMC activities. One of the criticisms of IMC is that no evaluation system has yet been proposed or implemented so that the claims made about IMC delivering superior returns can be validated (Swain, 2004). This is part of the planning process and so integration of all aspects of the campaign planning process is necessary.

## Agencies

Reference has been made earlier to some of the structural issues involving agencies in the marketing communications industry and with the development of IMC. Agencies play a critical role in marketing communications and if IMC is to be established it cannot be accomplished without the explicit involvement of all those working on the supply side.

Questions arise concerning the level of expertise that a single agency might have access to in order to deliver IMC. For example, in 2011 Virgin Media called an ad review for their £36 million budget. Their then agency was DDB, who had only been in position for 15 months. It is suggested that the review was called because the agency had struggled to provide 'best-in-class' across the disciplines for Virgin Media's entire business. This meant that integration had not been achieved as the direct marketing aspect was maintained. It was only the creative advertising element that failed to live up to expectations (Williams, 2011).

Apart from questions concerning the range of promotional services offered by individual agencies and whether these are all delivered by a single agency or through a network of interacting agencies, two particular issues arise. The first concerns leadership and the other remuneration.

With regard to leadership, should the agency or the client lead the process of developing IMC? The consensus appears to be that this is the client's role (Swain, 2004), mainly because clients are better positioned to make integration happen across their own organisation. However, Swain then points out that there is no agreement about who in the client organisation should be responsible for implementing IMC. Indeed, Kitchen et al. (2007) confirm the reluctance of both advertising and public relations agencies to provide for integrative working practices.

A similar question concerns the implementation of integrated campaigns. Most major brands operate with several agencies, each providing different skills. These are known as 'roster agencies' simply because different agencies can be brought into different campaigns to provide support when necessary. Herein lies the problem for clients implementing an integrative programme: how best to manage an integrative approach? One way is to appoint a lead agency that assumes responsibility for integration. Another way is for the client to drive the programme forward and to involve the roster agencies. However, many client organisations, such as Shell, prefer to appoint a lead agency and very often it is the generalist ad agency that is appointed.

The second issue, remuneration, should be regarded as related to the measurement factor (Swain, 2004). This is because clients see reward as a derivative of performance. The traditional remuneration system is based on activities (Spake et al. (1999) cited by Swain). Commission earned from the use of media to gain awareness or change attitudes is not measured against revenue or profit performance, and is referred to as 'an activity'. Results- or 'outcome'-based systems are considered a performance measure. A move to IMC requires a change in agency performance measures and consequently, a change in their method of remuneration. Closer integration of agencies within the IMC process will, among other things, bring changes in structure, operations, performance measures, remuneration and new responsibilities within the client relationship.

This list of elements that need to be integrated is not exclusive. There are other influences that are particular to individual organisations that could have been included. However, consideration of these various elements suggests strongly that what is being integrated is far more than just the communication tools. Indeed, viewed holistically, integration is a strategic concept that strikes at the heart of an organisation's marketing and business orientation.

## Viewpoint 10.2    Integrated, luxurious and simply Fabergé

Fabergé's re-entry to the luxury jewellery market is remarkable for many reasons, but of these one stands out: the brand's use of marketing communications to build relationships.

The average price of a piece of Fabergé jewellery is over £100,000 so issues concerning security, access, positioning, and service and support are critical. The traditional channel strategy is to establish a small number of prestigious retail stores where all of these factors can be managed. Indeed, Fabergé has developed an integrated network of worldwide retail stores, retail concessions and wholesalers, including boutiques in Geneva, London and New York and counters in Harrods and Lane Crawford. However, the downside is that this product-orientated strategy fails to maximise customer convenience.

Fabergé's solution was to develop customer relationships based on an integrated online/offline strategy. Customers can visit the website at Faberge.com and inspect jewellery in their own time, from any part of the world. Using high-quality photography, it is possible for customers to see jewellery in greater depth than they can physically in store. Help is provided by online sales assistants. Using voice, video, and text according to the customer's choice, customers are able to refine their preferences. However, purchasing is not carried out online. Once an item is selected, a sales assistant flies out to meet the customer to allow them to see, touch and try on the product, as necessary. Experience suggests that a purchase is made on most occasions once the product is seen physically.

*Source*:    Murphy (2009); www.faberge.com.

**Question:**    List the ways the elements of the marketing communications mix have been used to build customer relationships at Fabergé.

**Task:**        Visit the Fabergé website (www.faberge.com/) and find the bell!

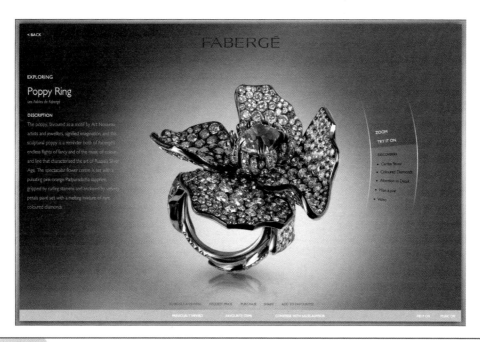

| Exhibit 10.4 | **The Poppy Ring epitomises Fabergé's positioning in the luxury jewellery market** |
| --- | --- |
| | *Source*: Fabergé |

# Definitions of IMC

| Table 10.3 | The development of IMC definitions |
|---|---|
| **Author** | **Definition** |
| Shultz, Tannenbaum and Lauterborn (1993) | A concept of marketing communications planning that recognises the added value of a comprehensive plan that evaluates the strategic role of a variety of communication disciplines (such as advertising, direct response, sales promotion, etc.) and combines them to provide clarity, consistency and maximum communication impact. |
| Duncan and Moriarty (1997) | A cross-functional process for creating and nourishing profitable relationships with customers and other stakeholders by strategically controlling or influencing all messages sent to these groups and encouraging purposeful dialogue with them. |
| Keller (2001) | Involves the development, implementation, and evaluation of marketing communication programmes using multiple communication options where the design and execution of any communication option reflects the nature and content of other communication options that also make up the communication programme. |
| Kliatchko (2008) | An audience-driven business process of strategically managing stakeholders, content, channels, and results of brand communication programmes. |

These definitions, from Shultz et al.'s (1993) original to those used today, reveal how the term has evolved. In much the same way, the very diversity of the term 'integration' has been highlighted by The Institute of Practitioners in Advertising (IPA). Their research into what is meant by integration, as practised by clients and agencies, reveals several different interpretations, leading them to the conclusion that the term is ambiguous in practice.

For example, the IPA observe that integration can be just about channel (tools) planning, the integration of communications with brand values, the integration of data, the merging of data sources and customer understanding, the integration of offline and online media channels to achieve maximum click-throughs and sales, the facilitation of seamless working practices across internal client departments and agencies, and finding ideas that integrate into the target audience's lives.

In order to provide clarity and insight into the way integration is considered and practised, the IPA analysed over 250 cases submitted to the IPA Effectiveness Awards in the period 2000–9. They searched for a common definition of integration, but it became clear that just as the academic definitions had evolved, so had working practices developed over this period.

From this review and bearing in mind that no single form of IMC can be identified, the following general definition of IMC is offered:

> *IMC can represent both a strategic and tactical approach to the planned management of an organisation's communications. IMC requires that organisations coordinate their various strategies, resources and messages in order that they enable meaningful engagement with audiences. The main purposes are to develop a clear positioning and encourage stakeholder relationships that are of mutual value.*

This definition serves to link IMC with business-level strategies and relationships. The importance of coherence within the organisation is made explicit, whether this be through systems or structural change. Implicit is the underpinning notion that IMC is necessary for the development of effective relationships and that not all relationships need be collaborative and fully relational, as so often assumed to be the case in many contemporary interpretations.

---

**Scholars' paper 10.2** | **Four pillars of IMC strength**

**Kliatchko, J. (2008) Revisiting the IMC construct: a revised definition and four pillars,** *International Journal of Advertising,* **27(1), 133–60.**

Kliatchko published this paper as an update to his 2005 paper on IMC. Here he re-examines and revises his definition of integrated marketing communications (IMC). His goal is to advance the theoretical foundations and definitional issues of IMC and to that end he introduces and examines his four pillars of IMC before exploring the interconnection between the pillars and levels of IMC.

---

# Interpretations of IMC

The relative failure of both academics and practitioners to agree on a definition for IMC is indicative of the debate, contradiction and perhaps vagueness of the concept. It is also reflective of an emerging concept, one that has had little chance to stabilise in the context of a rapidly changing media landscape and new forms of communications. Consideration is now given to some of the different views of IMC. There are some common threads but also some points of divergence.

Five interpretations are offered here, in no particular order. Harmonisation, which was an early view and still practised, is considered first. We then review planning, perspective, portfolio, and relational interpretations. See Figure 10.2.

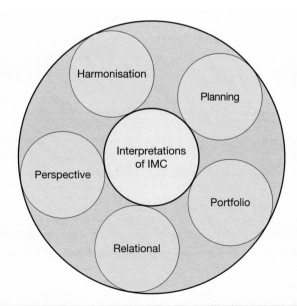

**Figure 10.2**    Five interpretations of IMC

## Interpretation 1: Harmonisation-based IMC

One of the early interpretations of IMC, indeed the leading view at the time, was that integration was a function of the harmonisation of the elements of communication. This involved communicating consistent messages through all forms of relevant media to target audiences. In this view, sometimes referred to rather dismissively as 'matching luggage', harmonisation represented a largely visual interpretation of IMC.

Typically brand colours, logos and straplines had to be placed and presented in a consistent manner across all media where the target audience encountered the brand. This content view aimed to achieve a 'one voice, one look' position. Despite being perceived as an advertising-led communication programme at this stage, other disciplines were incorporated into the process, so that sales promotion, public relations, and increasingly direct marketing, all became part of the harmonised approach to integrated marketing communications. Through harmonisation of all the elements of the marketing communications mix, the channels, as practitioners refer to them, represented the key integration factors. Schultz (1993, p. 17) refers to IMC as 'the process of developing and implementing various forms of persuasive communication programs with customers and prospects over time'. This customer-only perspective merely served to limit the scope, not only of IMC but of marketing communications as a whole.

Interestingly, this view is still prevalent today, as evidenced by some of the journalistic accounts of current campaigns. For example, TUI Travel announced that they had 'launched integrated marketing campaigns for Thomson and First Choice in the past five months (of 2012) in an effort to clarify their propositions. The £5m Thomson push promoted its "exclusive" and "tailored" offering using the strapline "Uniquely designed holidays". This was followed by a £3m relaunch campaign for First Choice, repositioning it as "the home of all-inclusive"' (Eleftheriou-Smith, 2012).

One of the issues however, is that harmonisation represents a resource-driven view of IMC, an inside-out approach, which by definition is not audience-centred and lacks any strategic, structural, or market view. Furthermore, harmonisation fails to consider the context in which communications are to occur and remains a predominantly advertising-led activity. These issues were to be reconsidered as IMC research and practice evolved.

## Interpretation 2: Planning-based IMC

The media-neutral planning (MNP) approach emerged partly as a response to criticism of IMC and partly as an attempt to articulate the potential practice of IMC. For many MNP is

---

| Exhibit 10.5 | **Integrated Quirks** |

When McVitie's launched its new biscuit range, *Quirks*, it was reported in the trade press that they had used an advertising campaign which integrated a 30-second TV spot, aired throughout February, alongside cinema, in-store and digital activity (Joseph 2012).

In other words this report suggests that integration is something that is done to advertising, and not the other disciplines. However, it can be safely assumed that field marketing, sales promotion, public relations, online and other digital activities were also being used to support the new brand, but they do not get mentioned.

*Source*: United Biscuits

integration under a different guise, but one of the strengths of the concept is that it focuses openly on the needs of clients and agencies. It attempts to stimulate the use of a communication mix that is driven by the needs of a target audience and not those of the communication industry. This means that, rather than keep recommending that clients use mass-media communications, which have traditionally rewarded agencies through a more than generous commission system, a more balanced mix of tools and media should be adopted in order to be more effective and efficient.

One of the main reasons for the interest in IMC is the potential to reduce costs. The rise in some media costs, most notably television through the 1990s, the specialised and independent nature of the agency side of the industry, the proliferation of media opportunities and the splintering of audiences, the increasing clamour for measures of return on investment in communications have led to a reappraisal of the role and nature of marketing communications and the emergence of MNP ideas. As clients have tried to reduce costs they have made greater use of both through and below-the-line tools.

Agencies interested in preserving margins have attempted to maintain the prominence of advertising in their media plans, but have reduced the emphasis on television advertising or have sought better deals through use of multiple television channel mixes, improved negotiation and more alliances. Some client organisations (e.g. Kraft, Kellogg's, Unilever and Procter & Gamble) have moved, if unintentionally, towards a form of coordinated marketing communication activity. These organisations have reduced their reliance on above-the-line media and have attempted to move towards the use of below-the-line tools in order to reduce costs and deliver consistent messages in an attempt to cut through the increasing clutter. Ray (2002) refers to organisations such as Nike, Reebok and Alliance & Leicester who have practised MNP. However, he also refers to some of the problems, such as structures, areas of expertise and attitudes, faced by agencies attempting to offer a more neutral media approach for their clients.

The drive behind the development of MNP appears to be concerned more with reducing the emphasis on television advertising in media plans, rather than the formulation of distinct media plans that deliver advertising messages in the most effective way, regardless of media selection. Many of those that support media-neutral approaches are often quoted using examples that involve a mix of tools and media.

MNP recognises that mass media advertising is not always the most appropriate way to launch or develop consumer or business-to-business promotional activities, and that a consideration of the most suitable mix of communication tools might be a better starting point when formulating campaigns. Advertising alone cannot carry the weight of a brand adequately to build and sustain the desired associations. Public relations, sales promotions and field marketing (merchandising), for example, have increasingly important roles to play in establishing and sustaining a brand. However, where advertising is used, the changing media landscape and the increasing penetration of new technology mean that a greater use of cross-media planning approaches is likely to enhance the effectiveness of a campaign and reduce costs, especially if previous campaigns used television as the primary medium. The traditional model of media planning, whereby a primary medium and perhaps two or three secondary media are scheduled over a five-week campaign has now to be surpassed by a more contemporary mix that uses a cross-media plan combining new and old media and that is appropriate to target audience preferences and the context of the marketing communications activities.

Therefore, it might be interpreted that media-neutral mixes represent the response of the agency side of the marketing communications industry while IMC represents the client side approach to managing their marketing communications in a more effective and strategic manner. MNP should not be about mixing tools and media but should be regarded as an integral part of IMC. However, IMC is not the same as MNP.

The development and delivery of a marketing communications programme that repeatedly delivers significant value cannot be based solely on media-neutral planning or loose notions of IMC. What is necessary is the development of a strategic marketing communications approach that delivers a total brand experience (Tobaccowala and Kugel, 2001). This requires a coordinated approach to the selection and implementation of the right promotional tools and media that will deliver messages that are of significant value to the target audience. However, it also requires the integration of a cross-functional, multi-audience strategic approach to marketing communications – one that delivers a brand experience for the target audience.

## Open planning

In many ways media-neutral planning is an approach to planning where all media have equal probability of selection and those that are chosen are deemed the best vehicles to achieve the media plan's objectives. Although there are many benefits, such as changing attitudes and perhaps reducing some costs, the neutrality perspective seeks to address industry issues about the planning process and the thinking the planners undertake, rather than demonstrating direct concern with audience issues.

In an attempt to move thinking a step forward, the open-planning concept was developed by Jenkinson, who in 2002/03 coordinated a panel of leading marketers who shared a goal to simplify the media-neutral planning concept. The main goal was to reappraise the way organisations consider their processes and thinking about marketing communication activities with a view to optimising their communication potential. The MNP group argues that this requires rethinking the way communication disciplines (tools) and media are used, to develop new methods of evaluating communication activity and to accelerate the speed at which organisations are able to integrate their communications with their business and marketing strategies.

The MNP group has proposed a series of new approaches based mainly on ideas concerning open planning. Open planning is concerned with eight action areas, each of which contributes to the process of MNP. These action areas are set out in Table 10.4. Readers wishing to know more should visit www.openplanning.org.uk.

| Table 10.4 | Action areas within the open planning approach |
|---|---|
| **Action area** | **Explanation** |
| Disciplines | Any promotional tool (i.e. discipline) can be used with any medium to achieve stated business and marketing objectives. |
| Media | Any medium can be used, by any tool (i.e. discipline), in almost all mixes. This means redefining media to mean anything that conveys a message to an audience. A salesperson becomes a medium. |
| Channels | Any mix of disciplines within a single medium becomes an open channel. |
| Process | All agencies (and others) should be involved with the thinking and planning process at the outset, to determine the message and goals before any resources are allocated (i.e. budgets). |
| Structure | The communication process should be driven by the communication preferences of a target audience (or community) rather than the silo structure-based functional specialisation present in much of the industry today. |
| Relationships | The relationship between client and agency should be open and functional. Agency remuneration should be based on the achievement of brand goals and not commission based on media choice. |
| Results | Defining more precise communication goals that enable a level playing field for all disciplines, media and agencies to maximise their contribution. |
| Tools | Use of media planning tools that embrace all touch points with customers. |

*Source*: Adapted from Jenkinson and Sain (2004).

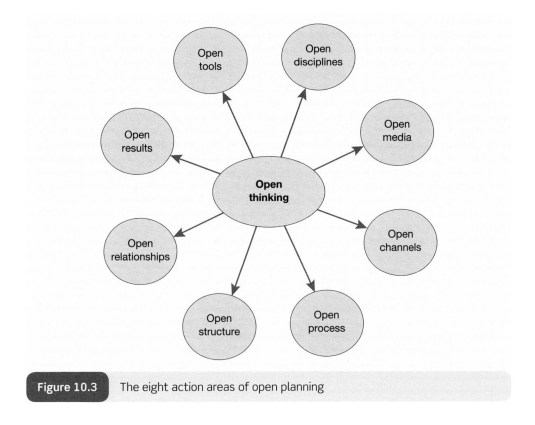

**Figure 10.3**   The eight action areas of open planning

Thinking in terms of these action areas should promote marketing communications that are audience-centred rather than promulgate the previous model that focused on the needs of the communication industry (see Figure 10.3).

## Interpretation 3: Perspective-based IMC

Cornelissen argues that the literature indicates that there are two main interpretations of IMC: a 'content' and a 'process' perspective respectively.

The *content* perspective assumes that message consistency is the major goal in order to achieve the 'one voice, one look' position. IMC works when there is consistency throughout the various materials and messages. Interestingly, Delgado-Ballester et al. (2012) find that high levels of consistency are important when building new or unfamiliar brands, whereas moderate levels of consistency are suitable for established or familiar brands.

However, this is not a new practice, as Cornelissen points out that practitioners have been doing this long before the term 'IMC' surfaced. This view is also associated with the zero-based planning approach that holds that the choice of tools and media should be based on effectiveness criteria rather than the specialist functions for which the planners and managers are responsible. This means that the various agencies and personnel responsible for campaign design and deployment do so without prejudice or bias towards a preferred tool or media. This approach is discussed later in this chapter.

## Viewpoint 10.3    Nissan gets integrated

Nissan recently created a Marcoms Group and in doing so insisted that each of the individual disciplines kept their integrity. However, for each project, announcement, product launch and event, all the functions contribute and help to align strategy and tactics.

Nissan's view is that an integrated marcoms team helps make sure that messages can be delivered through an optimised channel network, regardless of which function 'manages' which channel. Apart from increasing effectiveness, and lowering costs, integration is seen in terms of ensuring message consistency and accurate timing of initiatives and announcements. It is about different functions using communications channels in a coordinated way. This helps to build collective awareness and understanding through multiple touchpoints.

The 'Urbanproof' campaign designed by Nissan showcased the Qashqai and Murano models in a variety of urban settings. These included 'Play with the city', 'Skateboard', and 'Gangs'. In March 2010 Nissan launched a new campaign under this framework, called 'Artistic Paintball'. This was designed to support the unveiling of the updates to the new Qashqai model. The work started with a teaser campaign designed to encourage the audience to follow the Qashqai's journey to Urbanproof, online.

The next step was a TV commercial which displayed the new shape and the changes made. A print campaign, based on an international competition about urban parking, was used to back the programme, while 3D videos were posted online to increase the product experience.

The campaign also featured user-generated content. Users designed their own Nissan ads and the winners had their ads shown in cinemas and online, and used as support for the launch of 'Juke', Qashqai's baby brother.

*Source*:   Benjamin (2012); Fernandez (2010).

**Question:**   Has Nissan adopted a process or content perspective on IMC?

**Task:**   Visit the Nissan website and comment on whether you believe the Urbanproof element is a genuine part of an integrated approach.

| Exhibit 10.6 | **Nissan Qashqai – an integrated campaign** |
| --- | --- |
| | *Source*: Nissan |

The second interpretation offered by Cornelissen is referred to as a *process* perspective. Here the emphasis is on a structural realignment of the communication disciplines within organisations, even to the point of collapsing all communications into a single department. Even if this extreme interpretation is not a valid goal for an organisation, cross-functional systems and processes are regarded as necessary to enable integrated marketing communications.

The process perspective of IMC is rooted in the belief that real IMC can only be generated through an organisational structure that brings the various communication disciplines together in a single body or unit. By creating a single department out of which advertising, public relations and the other disciplines operate, cross-functional coordination between the disciplines is enabled. Some argue that the process view needs to incorporate a series of intervening stages as systems, processes and procedures are brought together incrementally to enable the cross-functionality to work.

Research suggests that organisations have made little attempt to restructure their marketing communications disciplines and that public relations and marketing remain as a clear divide. What has happened, however, is that there are much closer cross-functional relationships and systems and processes to support them. Some organisations are moving incrementally towards a process perspective on IMC.

---

### Scholars' paper 10.3    Advancing the view of IMC

**Cornelissen, J.P. (2003) Change, continuity and progress: the concept of integrated marketing communications and marketing communications practice,** *Journal of Strategic Marketing*, **11 (December), 217–34.**

This paper should be read because it challenges the orthodox view of IMC. Cornelissen takes an objective view of the literature and forms the conclusion that IMC should be considered from a content or process perspective.

---

In an attempt to develop our understanding of IMC, Lee and Park (2007) proposed a multidimensional model of IMC, based on four key dimensions. These have been drawn from the literature and, unlike Cornelissen's work, represent an attempt to measure IMC. Their four dimensions are concerned with a single message, multiple customer groups, database marketing and the need to use IMC to build customer relationships. (A fuller account of these dimensions can be seen in Chapter 9.)

Kliatchko (2008) suggests that IMC has several distinctive attributes and he refers to them as the 'four pillars of IMC'. These are stakeholders, content, channels and results. Figure 10.4 sets out the constituent elements within each of the pillars.

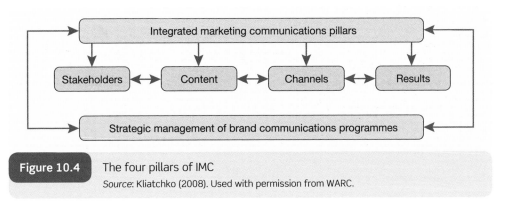

| **Figure 10.4** | The four pillars of IMC |
|---|---|

*Source*: Kliatchko (2008). Used with permission from WARC.

---

### Viewpoint 10.4    Integrated savings

Ideas about IMC should not be restricted to private sector organisations. The UK government's National Savings and Investments agency, known as NS&I, is a 150-year-old organisation which serves 26 million customers and provides various types of savings and investment programmes through the postal facilities, online and by telephone, generating more than £100 billion in investments, which help to keep the Treasury financially liquid. According to Shultz, NS&I is the perfect example of IMC in practice, for three main reasons.

First, the people responsible for income generation are not part of a marketing group but are responsible for 'demand generation'. Their role is to create attractive investment products, promote them and implement them in the marketplace so that the public will invest. They have to achieve this at a cost that generates sufficient returns to meet the government funding requirements. In other words, they are responsible for both sales and 'profits'.

Second, the main focus is on forecasting, not on measuring ROI. That means that the NS&I team has to understand the marketplace, the competition and the potential returns on their efforts, and match that to the government needs in such a way that the balance of incoming and outgoing funds meets the needs of the government. In other words, they are fully accountable as an income centre for NS&I, and not, like so many marketing groups, a cost centre.

Third, unlike so many private practice organisations, the communications are not rooted in discrete, functional silos. The focus is on matching customers with products to generate returns. That means that they use a variety of tools and any resource, including people, that are available to them. There are media and promotional specialists in NS&I, but they are nomadic and are free to move around the organisation as needed. Demand generators have to build products and promote them to generate the levels of return that they have forecast. So, they use mass media, digital, promotions, public relations, direct response media, and other tools and media, in various combinations, to generate the returns they have forecast. If that means mass media, fine.

The focus on accountability and the generation of returns is a contrast to the norm of creating and sending out numerous communications through predetermined, advertising-led channels. As Shultz comments, at NS&I they build promotional programmes with returns, not awards, in mind.

*Source*:    Shultz (2012).

**Question:**    Why should public service organisations attempt to develop integrated marketing communications?

**Task:**    Find two other public service or third sector campaigns and make notes about how they might be more integrated.

---

His argument is that these four elements can be observed at different levels of IMC and that at each level one of the elements tends to dominate.

It may be that a suitable theoretical basis upon which to develop IMC is emerging through the relationship marketing literature. We know that a relationship orientation requires a multidisciplinary approach to trigger interaction and dialogue (Gronroos, 2004). So, it may be that a deeper understanding of relational theory will help to advance the IMC concept and provide researchers with a surer footing upon which to explore the topic.

However, whether a content or process perspective is adopted, the position remains that, until there is empirical evidence to support a theoretical base upon which to build IMC strategy and operations, the phrase will probably continue to be misused, misunderstood and used in a haphazard and inconsistent way.

## Interpretation 4: Portfolio-based IMC

Reference was made to the IPA's research and analysis of their *Effectiveness Awards* programmes. From an investigation of the various submissions for the best integrated campaign they uncovered four distinct forms of integrated programmes. See Table 10.5.

| Table 10.5 | Four ways for integration |
| --- | --- |

| Form of integration | Explanation |
| --- | --- |
| No integration | No attempt is made to unify the tools in a consistent way. |
| Advertising-led integration | Based around a common creative platform. |
| Brand idea-led orchestration | Unification occurs around a shared brand concept or platform. |
| Participation-led orchestration | Characterised by a common dialogue, co-creation, experience or 'conversation' between brand and audience. |

*Source*: IPA, 2011. Used with permission from WARC.

Within each of these four forms of integration, the IPA observe various sub-categories. These are outlined in Table 10.6.

| Table 10.6 | Sub-categories of integration |
| --- | --- |

| Form of Integration | Sub-category | Explanation |
| --- | --- | --- |
| No integration | Single tool | Campaigns where there is no specific requirement to integrate other tools, media or marketing activity (such as packaging, on-pack promotions, in-store or website), into the advertising or marketing campaign. |
| | Pragmatically non-integrated | These campaigns use a wide variety of communication tools but there is no message integration. These campaigns tend to have no unifying concept, message or idea across any of the activities, and do not share a unifying strapline. |
| Advertising-led integration | Visual | These campaigns are only united by 'look and feel'. This is the so-called 'matching luggage' concept. These share the same visual identity but do not seek to integrate all campaign messages across channels. |
| | Promotion | Unification is achieved both visually and through a single promotional platform, competition or response mechanic. |
| | Icon | This refers to the use of the same brand icon across all tools and media – for example, by using the same celebrity in the store promotion, PR photo calls and events (e.g. Kerry Katona for Iceland) or by developing a specific brand persona for use in all channels (e.g. Felix for Felix Catfood). |
| | Idea | Here integration is achieved through one big advertising idea, which is disseminated through the most appropriate media. |
| Brand idea-led orchestration | Tangible | These campaigns are built on the more tangible foundations associated with a specific need-state, occasion, tightly defined target audience or a specific 'point of market entry' upon which to focus the activity and the channel orchestration. |
| | Intangible | Developed for higher-order, emotional engagement, these campaigns exhibit a high degree of creative inconsistency across time, while still retaining their orchestrating elements. |
| Participation-led orchestration | | Here digital media are used to engage audiences in conversation and so improve brand and audience interaction. The goal is to *integrate brands into people's lives* in a way that is both relevant and valuable for the audience, rather than aiming a message out towards a target audience and hoping they will be receptive. |

*Source*: Based on IPA (2011). Used with permission from WARC.

In many ways the revelation that there are different forms of integration should not be surprising, especially in the light of the multitude of definitions. What is interesting is the terminology used to identify the different forms. In particular attention is drawn to the use of the word 'orchestration'. This is a term identified in the very early days by academics to explain the integration concept. Here we are, roughly 20 years later, and it is practitioners who are reviving the term. Perhaps of greater interest is what the term 'orchestration' represents. In a musical context 'to orchestrate' means to arrange or compose music to be played by an orchestra in a predetermined order. The conductor then interprets the score in order to reproduce the composer's original idea. This suggests a planned way of operating, one where there is some, but limited, flexibility. Another interpretation of the word 'orchestration' involves the organisation of an event to achieve a desired, again predetermined, effect or outcome. What is common to both of these ideas about orchestration is that there is a planned outcome. To what extent however, is integration more concerned with flexibility than planning, and what part of the difficulties associated with IMC are to be found rooted in planning and linear thinking?

## Viewpoint 10.5 Participative yet integrated crisps

A campaign launched in July 2008 by Walkers sought to forge stronger bonds with their customers. By actively integrating them with the campaign not only did the brand win extensive product exposure but also the relationship between consumers and the brand was developed. The campaign, called 'Do Us a Flavour' challenged the public to think up a unique flavour of crisp.

The campaign involved all of Walkers' agencies working together, as different stages required different contributions. The first stage began with a TV push created by AMV, with the goal of stimulating members of the public to come up with flavour ideas. Simultaneously, a PR drive, led by Freud, had the goal of creating excitement among TV hosts and radio presenters. This was achieved partly by Freud devising bespoke flavours for different presenters. For example, the flavour for Chris Moyles was 'meat and two veg'.

*The Sun* newspaper generated a great deal of PR as did a substantial cross-section of the media. Underpinning it all was the drive to encourage people to visit a dedicated website. At the end of this first stage, customers sent in over 1.2 million entries.

Stage 2 was about a judging panel, led by chef Heston Blumenthal, picking the top six entries. These were Cajun Squirrel, Crispy Duck and Hoisin, Fish & Chips, Builder's Breakfast, Chilli and Chocolate, and Onion Bhaji.

Stage 3 was the period ending May 2009 during which the flavours could be bought individually or in a special multipack containing all six flavours. Votes could be cast on the Walkers website, through Facebook, and through Yahoo!, which hosted a 'do us a flavour' channel. In addition to all the multi-channel activity it was the well-established technique of the on-pack promotion that worked well for many contestants, including one of the six finalists.

Builders Breakfast won the most votes, and the person behind it won £50,000, in addition to the £10,000 that each finalist was awarded. Better still, the winner was set to receive 1 per cent of profits from all future sales of their flavour, an estimated £50,000+ a year.

One of the points this campaign illustrates is the way the brand and its customers worked together to create value that both parties enjoyed consuming, either physically or emotionally. Here real performance value emerged through the parties to the relationship working together.

*Source*: Nettleton (2009); Anon (2009); Angear and Sambles (2009); White et al. (2010).

**Question:** Identify the key elements that support the relationship between Walkers and their customers. Is this form of the relationship sustainable?

**Task:** Write notes explaining how this example demonstrates trust and commitment in a relationship.

## Interpretation 5: Relational-based IMC

This interpretation has emerged naturally as marketing has become more relationship-aware and as a result, more orientated towards relational issues. Relationships are dynamic and vary in strength and intensity through time. Some are referred to as *transactional exchanges*, characterised by short-term, product- or price-oriented exchanges between buyers and sellers coming together for one-off exchanges independent of any other or subsequent exchanges. Both parties are motivated mainly by self-interest.

Other relationships are characterised by relational exchanges or what Day (2000) refers to as *collaborative exchanges*. These are characterised by a long-term orientation, where ultimately there is complete integration of systems and processes and where the relationship is motivated by partnership and mutual support. Trust and commitment underpin these relationships, and these variables become increasingly important as relational exchanges become established. IMC therefore needs to consider and adapt to these very different relational contexts. Each is considered in turn.

### IMC and transactional marketing

The discussion so far has been based largely on the assumption that exchanges are (or should be) essentially collaborative in character and that customers are willing and eager to enter into a wide range of relationships. However, it appears that some, if not the majority of exchanges, are essentially transactional in character. Buyers do not always wish to enter into a deep, complex relationship with all suppliers, nor do some consumers wish to enter into a relationship with the supplier of their favourite chocolate bar, dishwasher tablets or frozen peas. As a result these convenience-based exchanges are oriented towards a value based on the product, its price and overall availability and convenience. Depending upon the product category, after-sales and service support will be important but, by definition, customers in transactional mode do not wish to enter into any serious interaction, let alone dialogue.

The target-marketing process requires the development and implementation of a distinct marketing mix to meet the requirements of selected target markets. The elements are mixed together in such a way that they should meet the needs of the target segment. Each element of the marketing mix has a variable capacity to communicate (see Figure 10.5).

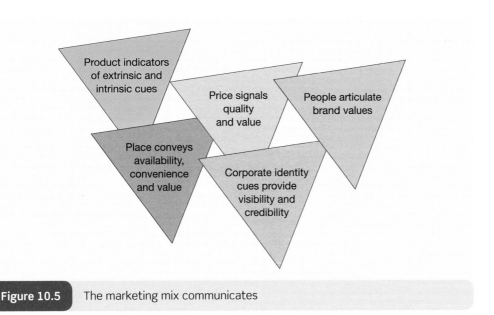

**Figure 10.5**    The marketing mix communicates

Therefore, it may be that traditional forms of marketing communications are sufficient to reach transactional customers. Messages that focus mainly on attributes, features and benefits, emotional values, price and availability will continue to be valid and improved if delivered though a coordinated mix of tools and media that are customer-oriented. Using communications that contain a coordinated communications mix, which makes greater use of a range of tools and media that are neutral and seek to cut waste and improve efficiency, will be advantageous.

## IMC and relationship marketing

As stated already, there is no universally agreed definition of IMC, and the development of this relatively new, embryonic concept is strewn with attempts to pin it down and label it. What can be observed, however, is that the relationship-marketing paradigm has developed at the same time as IMC and that there are areas where the two concepts intertwine and reinforce each other.

One of the difficulties associated with the IMC view, and with its half-sister, media-neutral planning, is that successful marketing communications results from an entirely planned approach. Planning is an essential aspect of managing marketing communications, but customers interact with products and services in different ways. They experience brands through their observation of others consuming them, through their own use, as well as through planned, unplanned and word-of-mouth communications. It is the totality of this communication experience that impacts on relationship development. IMC therefore has a critical role in the development of relationship marketing. This is because it is an important process, one that seeks to generate a response from customers, provoke interaction and then dialogue, which is a key characteristic of relationship marketing (Gronroos, 2004).

The Duncan and Moriarty IMC mini-audit has been designed to help assess an organisation's IMC relationship-building practices. It recognises the influence of organisational structure and marketing communication strategies and objectives and attempts to measure the strategic consistency of the brand messages. Many of the elements considered earlier in the section 'what is to be integrated' can be identified in the nine drivers identified by Duncan and Moriarty. These can be grouped into three categories, as presented in Table 10.7.

IMC therefore has a potentially greater role to play within collaborative transactions and with customers who wish to become involved within mutually rewarding relationships.

To date, IMC has been regarded as a concept that needs to be applied across an organisation's entire marketing communications and customer base. The suggestion is that aspects of IMC should be applied to both transactional and collaborative customers, but greater emphasis on interaction and dialogue should be given to communication with current and potential relationship-driven customers and other stakeholders.

**Table 10.7**    Duncan–Moriarty categories of relationship drivers

| Relationship drivers | Explanation |
| --- | --- |
| Relationship development | Everything an organisation does and says is seen, heard and interpreted by stakeholders. The need is to provide a consistent relational focus through all messages |
| Processes | The need for a process and system to provide consistent strategic positioning and in doing so help support the identity and reputation of the organisation |
| Organisational | Structural and cross-functional cohesion is necessary to support internal marketing and an unbiased use of all communication resources |

*Source*: Derived from Reid (2005).

# Structuring for IMC

Any discussion of IMC should at least acknowledge the higher-order background issue concerning integration between corporate communication and brand-based communications. It might be expected that, as responsibility for communication does, or should, rest with a single person, integration would be a natural outcome. This inevitably is not the case, often due to structural requirements. The result is that IMC becomes even harder to achieve. Separate marketing, advertising, promotion and PR budgets, combined with internal politics and personality clashes that bounce back on strategy, internal structures, which include siloed teams often accompanied by self-reinforcing functional budgets, almost inevitably lead to independent planning and action by different teams. Integration is not going to happen when the right hand may not know what the left one is doing (Benjamin 2012).

Clients have also embraced IMC and its influence on their structures. The hierarchical structures common in many organisations in the period up to the 1970s have been subject to attack. In search of survival in recession and increasing profits and dividends in times of plenty, organisations have sought to restructure and realign themselves with their environment. Hierarchies delivered a management structure that delegated authority in compartmentalised units. The brand management system that accompanied this structural approach provided a straitjacket and gave only partial authority to incumbents. At the same time, responsibility for pricing, channel management, personal selling and public relations activities was split off and allocated to a number of others. It follows from this that the likelihood of internal integration has been hampered by the structure of the organisation and the way in which structural units have been assembled.

The restructuring process has resulted in organisations that have delayered and are leaner. This means that the gap between senior management and those within the operating core (Mintzberg et al. 2003) is both smaller and now capable of sustaining viable internal communications that are truly two-way and supportive.

---

**Scholars' paper 10.4     Small but still needs to be integrated**

Gabrielli, V. and Balboni, B. (2010) SME practice towards integrated marketing communications, *Marketing Intelligence & Planning*, 28(3), 275–90.

Unlike the majority of papers about IMC, this empirical publication considers the ways in which SMEs approach marketing communication management and planning in particular. Their weakness for managing the internal processes associated with planned communications is exposed.

---

Increasingly, organisations are operating in overseas or cross-border markets. However, as organisations develop structurally, from international to multinational to global and transnational status, so the need to coordinate internally and to integrate internal communications becomes ever more vital to sustain integrated marketing communications (Grein and Gould, 1996). Internal communications (Chapter 13) are becoming more popular with clients (and agencies) as it is realised that employees are important contributors to corporate identity programmes and invaluable spokespersons for the products they market. Internal communications can help not only to inform and remind/reassure but also to differentiate employees in the sense that they understand the organisation's direction and purpose, appreciate what the brand values are and so identify closely with the organisation as a whole. This is a form of integration from which marketing communications can benefit.

# Key points

- Integrated marketing communications (IMC) is concerned with the development, coordination and implementation of an organisation's various strategies, resources and messages.

- The role of IMC is to enable coherent and meaningful engagement with target audiences. In an age when consumers can touch brands across a range of channels it is important that each contact reinforces previous messages and facilitates the development of valued relationships.

- While the concept of IMC is attractive, to date the development of the approach in practical terms has not been very encouraging. There has been a great deal of debate about the meaning and value of an integrated approach and some attempt to coordinate the content and delivery of marketing communication messages. Most organisations have yet to achieve totally integrated marketing communications; only partial or coordinated levels of activity have so far been achieved.

- The interest in IMC has resulted from three main drivers. These include market-based drivers, those that arise from changing communications, and those that are driven from opportunities arising from within the organisation itself.

- A wide range of elements needs to be integrated. These include the communication tools, media and messages, plus the elements of the marketing mix, brands, strategy, employees, agencies and technology.

- Definitions of IMC have evolved from a simple coordination of the disciplines and messages perspective, to one that incorporates the development of relationships and mutual value.

- There is no single agreed definition or view of IMC. The IPA observe that it is an ambiguous concept. Five interpretations of IMC can be identified. These are harmonisation, planning, perspective, portfolio, and relational interpretations. Each has its own origins and theoretical grounding.

- The move away from hierarchical and highly bureaucratic organisational structures has resulted in leaner, flatter organisations. This facilitates improved internal communications which assist employee support for the brand. Horizontal reporting lines are reorganised and silo-based functions removed, along with budget processes that only serve to encourage independent behaviour and repel IMC initiatives and progression.

# Review questions

1. Discuss the main reasons for the development of IMC.

2. Prepare brief notes explaining four different elements that should be part of the integration process.

3. Explain how various definitions of IMC have evolved.

4. What are the reasons for interest in IMC and is it a valid concept?

5. Appraise the main reasons offered for the failure of organisations to develop IMC.

6. Identify three different interpretations of IMC and make brief notes explaining the principles which underpin each of them. Which of these is best at interpreting the WIRSPA campaign?

7. Explain the ideas concerning media-neutral planning. What is open planning?

8. Discuss the view that IMC is essentially the same as relationship marketing.

9. What are the structural issues that can accelerate or hinder the development of IMC?

10. Prepare the outline for an essay exploring whether IMC is a strategic approach or just a means to correct internal operational difficulties and reduce media costs.

# References

Angear, B. and Sambles, M. (2009) How Walkers used co-creation to get the UK to do it a flavour, *Admap*, 508 (September), retrieved 6 November, 2010 from www.warc.com/ArticleCenter/Default.asp?CType=A&AID=WORDSEARCH89872&Tab=A.

Anon (2009) Cajun squirrel among crisp flavours tested by Walkers, *The Telegraph*, retrieved 1 March 2010 from www.telegraph.co.uk/foodanddrink/4206310/Cajun-squirrel-among-crisp-flavours-tested-by-Walkers.html.

Anon (2010) Morissons – Let's grow: 'getting your hands dirty with Morissons', ARF Ogilvy Awards, retrieved 7 July 2010 from www.warc.com/article centre.

Barda, T. (2010) Growing Up, *The Marketer*, March, 20–23.

Benjamin, K. (2012); Insight: Public Relations – In-house alignment – Brands find strength by uniting divisions, *Campaign Asia-Pacific*, January, retrieved 28 March 2012 from http://web.ebscohost.com/ehost/detail?vid=6&hid=11&sid=315cc079-6217-4fd6-9f0b-2d63997952bf%40sessionmgr11&bdata=JnNpdGU9ZWhvc3QtbGl2ZQ%3d%3d#db=bch&AN=70287902.

Cornelissen, J.P. (2003) Change, continuity and progress: the concept of integrated marketing communications and marketing communications practice, *Journal of Strategic Marketing*, 11 (December), 217–34.

Cornelissen, J.P. and Lock, A.R. (2000) Theoretical concept or management fashion? Examining the significance of IMC, *Journal of Advertising Research*, 50(5), 7–15.

Day, G. (2000) Managing market relationships, *Journal of the Academy of Marketing Science*, 28, 1, Winter, 24–30.

Delgado-Ballester, E., Navarro, A. and Sicilia, M. (2012) Revitalising brands through communication messages: the role of brand familiarity, *European Journal of Marketing* 46(1/2), 31–51.

Duncan (2002) *IMC: using advertising and promotion to build brand* (International edition), New York: McGraw-Hill.

Duncan, T. and Everett, S. (1993) Client perceptions of integrated marketing communications, *Journal of Advertising Research*, 3(3), 30–39.

Duncan, T. and Moriarty, S. (1998) A communication-based marketing model for managing relationships, *Journal of Marketing*, 62 (April), 1–13.

Duncan, T. and Mulhern, F. (2004) *A white paper on the status, scope and future of IMC programs* (from the IMC symposium by the IMC programs at Northwestern University and University of Denver), New York: McGraw-Hill.

Eleftheriou-Smith, L.-M. (2012) TUI Travel marketing director Jeremy Ellis on keeping clear of troubled rivals, *Marketing*, 23 February, retrieved 27 March from: http://www.brandrepublic.com/features/1118064/TUI-Travel-marketing-director-Jeremy-Ellis-keeping-clear-troubled-rivals/?DCMP=ILC-SEARCH.

Fernandez, J. (2010) Nissan plots integrated campaign for the new Qashqai push, *Marketing Week*, retrieved 30 March 2010 from www.marketing.co.uk/news/.

Fill, C. (2011) *Essentials of Marketing Communications*, Harlow: FT/Prentice Hall.

Finne, A. and Gronroos, C. (2009) Rethinking marketing communication: from integrated marketing communication to relationship communication, *Journal of Marketing Communications*, 15, 2–3 (April–July), 179–95.

Gabrielli, V. and Balboni, B. (2010) SME practice towards integrated marketing communications, *Marketing Intelligence & Planning*, 28(3), 275–90.

Grein, A.F. and Gould, S.J. (1996) Globally integrated communications, *Journal of Marketing Communications*, 2, 141–58.

Gronroos, C. (2004) The relationship marketing process: communication, interaction, dialogue, value, *Journal of Business and Industrial Marketing*, 19(2), 99–113.

Heyworth, S. and Djurdjevic, V. (2009) Getting your hands dirty with Morrisons, IPA Effectiveness Awards, *IPA*, 13 November, p. 7.

Hutton, J.G. (1996) Integrated relationship-marketing communications: a key opportunity for IMC, *Journal of Marketing Communications*, 2, 191–9.

IPA (2011) *New Models of Marketing Effectiveness From Integration to Orchestration*, WARC.

Jenkinson, A. and Sain, B. (2004) Open planning: media neutral planning made simple. Retrieved 14 November 2004 from www.openplanning.org/cases/openplanning/whitepaper.pdf.

Joseph, S. (2012) McVitie's unveils debut ad campaign for new biscuit range, *Marketing Week*, Thursday 26 January, retrieved 27 March 2012 from http://www.marketingweek.co.uk/ mcvities-unveils-debut-ad-campaign-for-new-biscuit-range/ 3033613.article.

Keller, K.L. (2001) Mastering the Marketing Communications Mix: Micro and Macro Perspectives on Integrated Marketing Communication Programs, *Journal of Marketing Management*, 17, 819–47.

Kitchen, P.J. and Shultz, D.E. (1997) Integrated marketing communications in US advertising agencies: an exploratory study, *Journal of Advertising Research*, 37(5), 7–18.

Kitchen, P.J. and Shultz, D.E. (1998) IMC – a UK ads agency perspective, *Journal of Marketing Management*, 14(2), 465–85.

Kitchen, P., Brignell, J., Li, T. and Spickett-Jones, G. (2004) The emergence of IMC: a theoretical perspective, *Journal of Advertising Research*, 44 (March), 19–30.

Kitchen, P.J., Spickett-Jones, G. and Grimes, T. (2007) Inhibition of brand integration amid changing agency structures, *Journal of Marketing Communications*, 13(2), 149–68.

Kliatchko, J. (2008) Revisiting the IMC construct: a revised definition and four pillars, *International Journal of Advertising*, 27(1), 133–60.

Lee, D.H. and Park, C.W. (2007) Conceptualization and measurement of multidimensionality of integrated marketing communications, *Journal of Advertising Research*, 47(3) (September), 222–36.

Liodice, B. (2008), Essentials for integrated marketing, *Advertising Age*, 72(23).

Mintzberg, H., Lampel, J.B., Quinn, J.B. and Ghoshal, S. (2003) *The Strategy Process*, 4th edn, Englewood Cliffs, NJ: Pearson Education.

Murphy, D. (2009) Structural Change, *Revolution*, December, 38–9.

Nettleton, K. (2009) Close-Up: Walkers' 'do us a flavour' is engaging the nation, *Campaign*, 23 January, retrieved 1 March 2010 from www.campaignlive.co.uk/news/ features/875884/close-up-walkers-do-us-flavour-engagi.

Perey, L., Rossitev, J.R. and Elliot, R. (2001) *Strategic Advertising Management*, New York: Oxford University Press.

Pitta, D.A., Weisgal, M. and Lynagh, P. (2006) Integrating exhibit marketing into integrated marketing communications, *Journal of Consumer Marketing*, 23(3), 156–66.

Porter, M.E. (1980) *Competitive Strategy: Techniques for Analyzing Industries and Competitors*, New York: Free Press.

Ray, A. (2002) How to adopt a neutral stance, *Marketing*, 27 June, 27.

Reed, D. (2006) Media rivalry barring integrated path, *Precision Marketing*, 25 August, 6.

Reid, M. (2005) Performance auditing of integrated marketing communication (IMC) actions and outcomes, *Journal of Advertising*, 34(4) (Winter), 41–54.

Shultz, D.E., Tannenbaum S.L. and Lauterborn R. (1993) *Integrated Marketing Communications: Putting It Together and Making It Work*, Lincolnwood, IL: NTC Business Books.

Shultz, D.E. (2012) IMC: Who's Doing it Right? *Marketing News*, 29 February, p. 14.

Shimp, T.A. (2000) *Advertising Promotion: Supplemental Aspects of Integrated Marketing Communications*, 5th edn, Fort Worth, TX: Dryden Press, Harcourt College Publishers.

Smith, P. (1996) Benefits and barriers to integrated communications, *Admap* (February), 19–22.

Smith, B.G. (2012) Organic integration: the natural process underlying communication integration, *Journal of Communication Management*, 16(1), 4–19.

Spake, D.F., D'Souza, G., Crutchfield, T.N. and Morgan, R.M. (1999) Advertising agency compensation: an agency theory explanation, *Journal of Advertising*, 28(3), 53–72.

Spotts, H.E., Lambert, D.R. and Joyce, M.L. (1998) Marketing déjà vu: the discovery of integrated marketing communications, *Journal of Marketing Education*, 20(3), 210–18.

Swain, W.N. (2004) Perceptions of IMC after a decade of development: who's at the wheel, and how can we measure success? *Journal of Advertising Research*, 44(1) (March), 46–65.

Tobaccowala, R. and Kugel, C. (2001) Planning and evaluating cross-media programs, *Admap*, February, 33–6.

White, R. (2000) Chameleon brands: tailoring brand messages to consumers, *Admap*, (July/August), 8–40.

White, T., Wassef, S. and Angear, B. (2010) Walkers – Embracing the unfamiliar: Walkers do us a flavour, *IPA Effectiveness Awards 2010*, retrieved 6 November from www.warc.com/ArticleCenter/Default.asp?CType= A&AID=WORDSEARCH92547&Tab=A.

Williams, M. (2011) How can agencies crack the puzzle of ad integration? *campaignlive.co.uk*, 8 September, retrieved 298 March 2012 from http://www.brandrepublic.com/ analysis/1089822/agencies-crack-puzzle-ad-integration/ ?DCMP=ILC-SEARCH.

# Part 3
# Branding

This part is designed to focus attention not only on the nature and role of different types of brand, but also on the way communication can be used to develop brands. For readers new to branding some of the core concepts and issues relating to branding are explored. However, the main thrust is to build on this knowledge and to consider the ways in which marketing communications can be used to develop and establish brands.

Chapter 11 is significant because it focuses on the role marketing communications can play in the development and maintenance of product/service brands. Chapter 12 develops the branding theme and considers corporate branding and reputational issues. The focus is again on the role of corporate communication in the identity and branding process rather than pure identity work alone. These elements are interrelated, but central is the recognition of how communications can be a pivotal aspect of brand and corporate development.

The final chapter in this part considers the role of marketing communications within organisations where employees are the target audience. Increasingly recognised as a key part of a brand, the importance of engaging with employees and enabling them to communicate a brand's or organisational values to external audiences is explored.

# Chapter 11

# Brand communications

The images, associations and experiences that customers have with brands, and the brand identities that managers seek to create, need to be closely related if long-run brand purchasing behaviour is to be achieved. Marketing communications can play an important and integral part in the development of positive brand associations that have meaning and purpose for customers.

## Aims and learning objectives

The aims of this chapter are to explore the nature and characteristics of branding and to identify the way in which marketing communications can be used to develop and maintain brands that engage their respective target audiences.

The learning objectives of this chapter are to:

1. introduce and explore the brand concept through definitions;
2. examine the characteristics and benefits of branding;
3. consider the issues associated with brand portfolios;
4. explore the strategic role of branding;
5. appraise the significance of associations and personalities in branding;
6. understand the way in which marketing communications can be used to build and support brands;
7. consider issues associated with online branding and in virtual brand communities;
8. appraise the nature and characteristics of brand equity.

# Minicase

## The Domino effect – honesty's the best policy

What is more important to you when ordering a take-away pizza: speed of delivery or a tasty, high-quality pizza? This is the question that the Domino's pizza marketing team had to ask itself in 2008. For all their 50 years in operation, Domino's had consistently focused their communications message on the speed of delivery of the pizza. However, by 2008, research showed that delivery speed was becoming an expectation or assumption for customers ordering a takeaway and the main driver for purchase choice was the quality and taste of the pizza. Unfortunately, the youthful core target audience for Domino's thought their pizzas were like 'cardboard' and below standard, a deadly perception for any food product to have.

Domino's, although still a key player in the pizza takeaway sector, had seen sales flatten and then fall for four years in a row, while competition, such as Pizza Hut, were showing modest growth. Other factors were against Domino's, such as the worldwide recession affecting spending habits, an increased emphasis on healthy eating and strong competition in a squeezed market from the likes of Papa John's, Pizza Hut and Perfect Pizza. It was clear things had to change for Domino's to survive.

After extensive research amongst customers, by autumn 2009 the quality of the pizzas and the choice offered on menus had improved dramatically and, most important, prices were kept broadly the same. The marketing communications team were now ready to launch, not just a new message, but a new brand story. Domino's openly admitted in its advertising that their pizzas had been of poor quality and promised that this had now changed. The senior managers and local staff all held themselves accountable for the quality of their food and encouraged a dialogue with customers, offering money back guarantees if standards were not met and using a consistent and integrated marketing communications plan to spread the 'brutally honest' positioning they had created.

Domino's utilised traditional marketing communications methods to promote their proud new pizzas. TV advertising slots were booked on prime time TV such as *American Idol* in the USA and *X Factor* in the UK, as well as TV sponsorship of popular Saturday night shows like *Britain's Got Talent*. This exploited the developing 'Saturday Night Effect' where families, no longer able to afford to go out, would stay in and share TV viewing as well as a takeaway. As with the rest of the pizza sector, sales promotion was used, with discount vouchers to encourage repeat purchase and door drop leaflets with discounts to encourage trial. The local appeal of Domino's was extended further, with local radio ads and outdoor posters near outlets. All traditional media carried the message of honesty and new quality pizzas, all with a consistent corporate identity. Crucially, to link in with the honesty theme, it was agreed that no ads would be 'touched up'. The pizza which customers saw on the ad was like the pizza which customers would get!

Instead of reacting to the economic downturn by spending less, Domino's announced it was boosting worldwide advertising budgets. In the UK alone spend went from £15 million in 2008 to £20 million in 2009, and, given the weak media industry, this meant better advertising deals could be struck, this at a time when other pizza companies were spending less.

Domino's capitalised on the trends of its younger target audience, launching a mobile unit to offer pizza at outdoor events, such as music festivals. However, it was the combination of traditional and new media usage which created the greatest turnaround for Domino's. The company was the first in its sector to entirely adopt digital media in a consistent and open way. All traditional advertising had a response mechanism directing interest to 'Pizzaturnaround.com', which became a social media hub with information, videos, chat and comments (negative and positive) about Domino's. Similar sites were set up on Facebook, Twitter and YouTube. Social media helped generate a two-way conversation between the brand and the customer and, critically, all content was treated fairly; Domino's did not shy away from negative comments. It set up online data monitoring, tracking up to 150 million blogs, user groups and social networking sites worldwide, to scrutinise conversations, track issues and compliments and ensure they were responding to what customers want.

New media were used in other innovative ways too. Customers could order online and, via a simple but very popular tracking device, follow the progress of their pizza from the oven to the door. Mobile phone apps were introduced to locate the nearest Domino's and/or order, as well as to play online games, where points can be won and reclaimed against a pizza. This strategy paid off, with online sales increasing by 74 per cent between 2008 and 2009, and a further 24 per cent between 2009 and 2010 in the UK, with an average order value 20 per cent higher than phone orders. Also online orders can now be analysed by Domino's, so special offers can be tailored to individual's tastes.

In the meantime Domino's main rival, Pizza Hut, was slow to adopt digital marketing and, although some developments did occur such as online table booking and eventually ordering online, the real focus of Pizza Hut promotions remained on TV advertising backed up by extensive price promotions. Price promotions, although good for creating increased purchase, can become an expectation for customers if used too often and can also cheapen a brand image. Some of the TV advertising had a negative effect. In order to promote their pasta range, Pizza Hut changed its name to 'Pasta Hut' in all marketing communications for three months, and Pizza Hut increasingly referred to the brand as 'The Hut' which confused many customers. Second, Pizza Hut in the UK has been slow to promote its takeaway service despite the trend towards eating at home. In 11 countries worldwide the parent company has successfully launched PHD, a takeaway sub-brand appealing to younger clientele. However, by 2011 PHD was still being trialled and had not launched in Britain. Other competitors such as Perfect Pizza and Pizza Go-Go were suffering too. As healthy food became a more important issue, these brands were thought to have lower-quality ingredients as they were markedly cheaper than their rivals.

By 2010 Domino's sales had increased by over 15 per cent on its 2008 figures, while Pizza Hut sales fell for three consecutive years. Domino's notion that 'We won't stop until every pizza is great' not only became known but, what is more important, trusted by customers. In 2011 Domino's continued to be innovative and honest about its pizzas, posting a 125-foot electronic billboard in New York's Times Square which included good, bad and neutral feedback. In the same year it was the first company in any sector to launch a new product solely on YouTube. It also began to expand its retail outlets aggressively. Customers have come back to Domino's. The improved quality of its pizzas, the transparency of its message, consistent and innovative communications campaigns and more open approach to dealing with customers have created a brand story which is bigger than the product itself and have enabled customers to trust the brand. Maybe this proves that honesty is the best policy?

*This minicase was written by Caroline Marchant at the University of Edinburgh. It is based on a variety of sources including Liddle (2009); Goodman (2011); Handley (2011); Jackson and Feld (2011) and various Keynote and Mintel reports.*

**Exhibit 11.1**    **Using sandwich boards to promote Domino's Pizza**
*Source*: ffotocymru/Alamy Images

# Introduction

Brands are promises which frame the way they are positioned in the minds of stakeholders, and which structure their expectations. Ideally these expectations match the promises, which are realised or experienced through brand performance. Brand performance can be experienced directly, perhaps through consumption, sampling, or first-hand interpretation, or indirectly through observations and comments made by other people and the media. Successful brands deliver consistently on their promises, by meeting or exceeding expectations, and in doing so reinforce the positioning and the credibility of the promise.

Therefore, successful brands might be considered to encapsulate three core brand elements; promises, positioning and performance. These are depicted at Figure 11.1, as the Three Brand Ps (3BPs).

Central to the interaction of these three BPs is communication. Communication is used to make the promise known, to position a brand correctly and to encourage and realise brand performance. Unsurprisingly, advertising has a critical role to play in building and sustaining this interaction of branding elements.

As the Domino's minicase indicates, consistent brand performance, fulfilled brand promises and strong levels of customer satisfaction through time can help consumers to trust a brand. Trust, over time, leads to commitment (Morgan and Hunt, 1994) and is reflected in customers prioritising a brand within their buying repertoire for a product category. Accepting that consumers are active problem-solvers means that brands can be regarded as a way in which the amount of decision-making time and associated perceived risk can be reduced for buyers. This is because brand names provide information about content, taste, durability, quality, price and performance, without requiring a buyer to undertake time-consuming comparison tests with similar offerings or other risk-reduction approaches to purchase decisions.

In much of the literature, brands assume a myopic perspective: namely, one centred just on customers. In reality, brands encompass a range of stakeholders (de Lencastre, and Côrte-Real, 2010) and branding should be considered not only from a managerial but also from service, relational and social perspectives (Brodie, and de Chernatony, 2009).

Successful brands such as Domino's create strong, positive and lasting impressions, all of which are perceived by audiences to be of value to them personally. Individuals perceive brands without having to purchase or have direct experience of them. The elements that make up this impression are numerous, and research by de Chernatony and Dall'Omo Riley (1998a) suggests

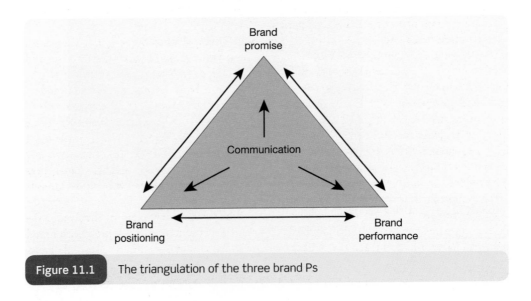

**Figure 11.1**  The triangulation of the three brand Ps

| Table 11.1 | Brand definitions |
| --- | --- |

| Author | Brand definition |
| --- | --- |
| **Alexander (1960)** American Marketing Association | 'a name, term, sign, symbol, or design, or a combination of them, intended to identify the goods or services of one seller or group of sellers and to differentiate them from those of competitors'. |
| **Assael (1990)** | '. . . name, symbol, packaging and service reputation'. |
| **Schmitt (1999)** | 'a rich source of sensory, affective, and cognitive associations that result in memorable and rewarding brand experiences'. |
| **Riezebos (2003)** | '. . . every sign that is capable of distinguishing the goods or services of a company and that can have a certain meaning for consumers both in material and in immaterial terms'. |
| **Keller (2008)** | '. . . something that has actually created a certain amount of awareness, reputation, prominence . . . in the marketplace'. |

that there is little close agreement on the definition of a brand. They identified 12 types of definition; among them is the visual approach adopted by Assael (1990) that a brand is the name, symbol, packaging and service reputation. The differentiation approach is typified by Kotler (2000), who argues that a brand is a name, term, sign, symbol or design or a combination of these intended to identify the goods or services of one seller or group of sellers, and to differentiate them from those of competitors. Some of the more commonly quoted definitions are presented in Table 11.1.

Since 2008 there have been few significant developments in how a brand is defined. There has been increasing recognition of brand co-creation (see later), and this has evolved into ideas about brand types and typologies. For example, Muzellec et al. (2012) consider how the brand as a concept may now be detached from being merely a physical embodiment. They explore the application of the branding to the fictional and computer-synthesised worlds, using examples of virtual brands from books, films, video games and other multi-user virtual environments.

In 2009 de Chernatony suggested that, from a managerial perspective, there is a 'plethora of interpretations', which can lead to brand management inefficiencies. To support his argument, he identifies a spectrum of brand interpretations, ranging from differentiation through to added value. He suggests a brand might be defined 'as a cluster of values that enables a promise to be made about a unique and welcomed experience'.

What these researchers have identified is that brands are a product of the work of managers who attempt to augment their products with values and associations that are recognised by, and are meaningful to, their customers. In other words, brands are a composite of two main logics: the first is an identity that managers wish to portray, while the second is images, construed by audiences, of the identities they perceive. The development of Web 2.0 and user-generated-content in the form of blogs, wikis and social networks have added a new dimension to the managerial-driven perspective of brands. Consumers are assuming a greater role in defining what a brand means to them, and now they are prone to sharing this with their friends, family and contacts rather than with the organisation itself. What this means is that brand managers have reduced levels of influence over the way their brands are perceived and this in turn impacts on the influence they have in managing brand reputation.

It is important, therefore, to recognise that both managers and customers are involved in the branding process. In the past, the emphasis and control of brands rested squarely with brand owners. Today, this influence has shifted to consumers as they redefine what brands mean to them and how they differentiate among similar offerings and associate certain attributes or feelings and emotions with particular brands. Indeed, there is now a discussion about whether brands should be considered outside the narrow marketing perspective, since they are a construct of a wider realm of influences. For those interested in these issues see Brodie and de Chernatony (2009), and for developments in managerial aspects, see de Chernatony (2009) and de Lencastre and Côrte-Real (2010).

Branding is a task that requires a significant contribution from marketing communications and is a long-term exercise. Organisations that cut their brand advertising in times of recession reduce the significance and power of their brands. The Association of Media Independents claims, not surprisingly, that the weaker brands are those that reduce or cut their advertising when trading conditions deteriorate.

In line with moves towards integrated marketing communications (see Chapter 10), many organisations are moving the balance of their communication mix away from an emphasis on advertising (especially offline) towards other tools and media. For example, mobile phone companies have used advertising to develop brand awareness and positioning and have then used sales promotion and direct marketing activities to provide a greater focus on loyalty and reward programmes. These companies operate in a market where customer retention is a problem. Customer loss (or churn rate) used to exceed 30 per cent, and there was a strong need to develop marketing and communications strategies to reduce this figure and provide for higher customer satisfaction levels and, from that, improved profitability. One solution is to use experiential-based communications – for example, sponsorship of events and festivals – to get closer to customers and drive associations that are of value.

# Brand characteristics

The essence of a strong brand is that it is sufficiently differentiated to the extent that it cannot be easily replicated by its competitors. This level of differentiation requires that a brand possess many distinctive characteristics and, to achieve this, it is important to understand how brands are constructed.

Brands consist of two main types of attributes: intrinsic and extrinsic. Intrinsic attributes refer to the functional characteristics of the product, such as its shape, performance and physical capacity. If any of these intrinsic attributes were changed, it would directly alter the product. Extrinsic attributes refer to those elements that are not intrinsic and, if changed, do not alter the material functioning and performance of the product itself: devices such as the brand name, marketing communications, packaging, price and mechanisms that enable consumers to form associations that give meaning to the brand. Buyers often use the extrinsic attributes to help them distinguish one brand from another, because in certain categories it is virtually impossible for them to make decisions based on the intrinsic attributes alone.

Biel (1997) refers to brands being composed of a number of elements. The first refers to the functional abilities a brand claims and can deliver. The particular attributes that distinguish a brand are referred to as *brand skills*. He cites cold remedies and their skill to relieve cold symptoms, for six hours, 12 hours or all day.

The second element is the personality of a brand and its fundamental traits concerning lifestyle and perceived values, such as being bland, adventurous, exciting, boring or caring. The idea of brand personification is not new, but it is an important part of understanding how a brand might be imagined as a person and how the brand is different from other brands (people). The comedian Peter Kay endorses the John Smith's brand (beer) through humour and, in doing so, makes a strong measure of association between the John Smith's brand (and its values) and the popular, witty character of the well-liked celebrity.

The third branding element is about building a relationship with individual buyers. People are said to interact with brands. A two-way relationship can be realistically developed when it is recognised that the brand must interact with the consumer just as much as the consumer must interact with the brand. Blackston (1993) argues that successful branding depends on consumers' perceptions of the attitudes held by the brand towards them as individuals. He illustrates the point with research into the credit card market, where different cards share the same demographic profile of users and the same conventional brand images. Some cards provide recognition or visibility of status, which by association are bestowed upon the owner in the form of power and authority. In this sense the card enhances the user. This contrasts with other cards, where the user may feel intimidated and excluded from the card because as a person the attitudes of the card are perceived to be remote, aloof, condescending and hard to approach. For example, respondents felt the cards were saying, 'If you don't like the conditions, go and get a different card', and 'I'm so well known and established that I can do as I want.'

The implications for brand development and associated message strategies become clearer. In line with this thinking, Biel cites Fournier (1995), who considers brand/consumer relationships in terms of levels of intimacy, partner quality, attachment, interdependence, commitment and love.

Therefore, Biel sees brands as being made up of three elements: brand personality, brand skills and brand relationships. These combine to form what he regards as 'brand magic', which underpins added value.

A more recent approach to brand development work involves creating a brand experience. Tango was an early pioneer of this approach. They used roadshows to create indirect brand-related experiences, such as bungee jumping, trampolining and other out-of-the-norm activities. FujiFilm underpin a great deal of their UK marketing communications with events, if only because they provide opportunities to provide direct experiences, in this case of the features and benefits of Fujifilm's brand values. Their events are grouped under three main headings: exhibitions, product launches and sponsorship. The first two of these enable contact with trade customers and consumers, who can handle the products and become immersed in the brand. They can also provide direct feedback.

Kapferer (2012) refers to a brand identity prism and its six facets (see Figure 11.2). The facets to the left represent a brand's outward expression, while Kapferer argues that those to the right are incorporated within the brand, an *inner expression* or *spirit* as he refers to it. These facets represent the key dimensions associated with building and maintaining brand identities and are set out in Table 11.2; they are interrelated and define a brand's identity, while also representing the means by which brands can be managed, developed and even extended.

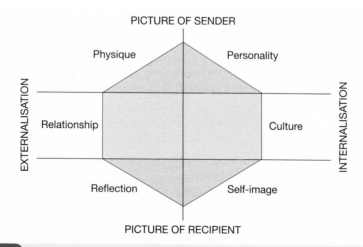

**Figure 11.2**    Brand identity prism
*Source*: Kapferer (2012). Used with permission.

| Table 11.2 | Brand facets |
| --- | --- |

| Brand facet | Explanation |
| --- | --- |
| Physique | Refers to the main physical strength of the brand and its core added value. What does the brand do and what does it look like (e.g. the Coca-Cola bottle)? |
| Personality | Those human characteristics that best represent the identity, best understood by the use of celebrity spokespersons who provide an instant personality. |
| Culture | A set of values that are central to a brand's aspirational power and essential for communication and differentiation. |
| Relationship | A brand's relationship defines the way it behaves and acts towards others. Apple exudes friendliness, IBM orderliness and Nike provocation. Important in the service sector. |
| Customer reflection | Refers to the way customers see the brand . . . for old people, for sporty people, clever people, people who want to look younger. This is an outward reflection. |
| Self-image | Refers to how an individual feels about themselves, relative to the brand. This is an inner reflection. |

*Source*: Adapted from Kapferer (2012). Used with permission.

All brands consist of a mixture of intrinsic and extrinsic attributes and management's task is to decide on the balance between them. Indeed, this decision lies at the heart of branding in the sense that it is the strategy and positioning that lead to strong brands.

---

**Scholars' paper 11.1    Brand worlds united**

Berthon, P., Pitt, L., Chakrabarti, R., Berthon J.-P. and Simon, M. (2011) Brand Worlds: From Articulation to Integration, *Journal of Advertising Research (Supplement)*, 51 (March), 182–8.

There are many papers on branding, but this one looks back over the past 50 years of branding research, and provides an interesting view of how brands have evolved. The authors move from the origins of branding through mimesis, expression, and symptom to a self-organising phenomenon. They use Popper's 'Three Worlds' hypothesis, (We, I and It) to show how the different streams of branding research can be integrated.

---

# Benefits of branding

As a brand becomes established with a buyer, so the psychological benefits of ownership are preferred to competing offerings, and a form of relationship emerges. Brands are said to develop personalities and encapsulate the core values of a product. They are a strong means by which a product can be identified, understood and appreciated. Marketing communications plays an

| Table 11.3 | Benefits of branding |
| --- | --- |

| Customer benefits | Supplier benefits |
| --- | --- |
| Assists the identification of preferred products | Permits premium pricing |
| Can reduce levels of perceived risk and so improve the quality of the shopping experience | Helps differentiate the product from competitors |
| Easier to gauge the level of product quality | Enhances cross-product promotion and brand |
| Can reduce the time spent making product-based decisions and in turn reduce the time spent shopping | Encourages customer loyalty/retention and repeat-purchase buyer behaviour |
| Can provide psychological reassurance or reward | Assists the development and use of integrated marketing communications |
| Provides cues about the nature of the source of the product and any associated values | Contributes to corporate identity programmes |
| | Provides for some legal protection |
| | Provides for greater thematic consistency and uniform messages and communications |

important role in communicating the essence of the personality of the brand and in providing the continuity for any relationship – a necessity for a brand to be built through time. This can be achieved through the development of emotional links and through support for any product symbolism that might be present.

Just as brands provide benefits for buyers, so there are important direct benefits for manufacturers and resellers. Brands provide a means by which a manufacturer can augment its product in such a way that buyers can differentiate the product, recognise it quickly and make purchase decisions that exclude competitive products in the consideration set. Premium pricing is permissible, as perceived risk is reduced and high quality is conveyed through trust and experience formed through an association with the brand. This in turn allows for loyalty to be developed, which in turn allows for cross-product promotions and brand extensions. Integrated marketing communications becomes more feasible as buyers perceive thematic ideas and messages, which in turn can reinforce positioning and values associated with the brand. For a summary of the benefits of branding, see Table 11.3.

# Brand portfolios: architecture and forms

The way in which an organisation structures and manages its brands not only affects its overall success but also influences the marketing communications used to support them. The development of brand portfolios is a means of gaining and protecting brand advantage. The fundamental structure of a brand portfolio consists of three main levels: the architecture, the form and the individual brand (see Figure 11.3).

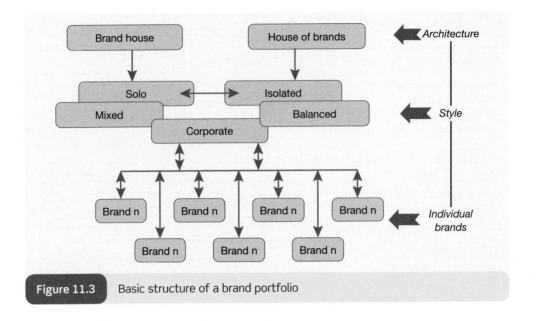

**Figure 11.3**   Basic structure of a brand portfolio

# Brand architecture

An organisation's brand architecture represents the overall marketing interface with the community of stakeholders. Petromilli et al. (2002) identify the two most common types of brand architecture as branded house and the house of brands. These were formerly known as *family brands* and *multi-brand structures*.

*Branded house* architecture uses a single (master) brand to cover a series of offerings that may operate within descriptive sub-brand names. This approach is used by companies such as Boeing, IBM, Virgin and Disney. Each seeks to dominate entire markets and categories through their single, highly relevant and highly leveraged master corporate brand, typical of the branded house structure. Tesco use the classic branded house architecture. All of its brands are tied into the Tesco name. However, when it entered the US market it broke away from this strategy and used the name 'Fresh and Easy'. US consumers have a different set of needs compared with the UK market and what Ritson (2007) refers to as their parochial nature led Tesco to break away from their established brand approach.

The *house of brands* architecture is characterised by a group or collection of brands that have no outward connections and operate independently of each other. These are brands that stand alone. General Motors and Procter & Gamble use this brand architecture. These two approaches represent the two extremes of a spectrum. Many organisations operate a mix of these two architectures, and their brand architecture lies somewhere between the two, indicating that neither strategy is inherently superior.

Pierce and Moukanas (2002) claim that most large companies organise their portfolio of brands as a disparate collection of individual brands. This strategy becomes more effective when these brands are integrated.

This spectrum of brand architectures is a reflection of an organisation's corporate strategy, culture and inter-product, or brand relationships. The approach each organisation adopts not only influences the deployment of resources to support the brands but also shapes the messages and media used within the marketing communications. Five main relationships can be identified: solo, isolated, mixed, balanced and corporate styles (see Table 11.4).

| Table 11.4 | Organisation/product brand relationships |
| --- | --- |

| Relationship | Explanation |
| --- | --- |
| Solo style | Organisations whose brand offer is a single product type. Images of the organisation and the product tend to be the same; for example: Kwik-Fit, Pirelli, Coca-Cola. |
| Isolated style | Essentially a multi-product branding approach that requires promotional expenditure to support each individual brand. Should a particular brand be damaged, the other brands in the portfolio and the corporate name are protected. |
| Balanced style | The identity of each individual product is related to the parent organisation: for example, Ford UK, where each car brand is prefixed by Ford. The Ford Fiesta 1.3L, Ford Focus and Ford Transit all convey the balance between the corporate name and the individual brands. |
| Mixed style | There is no pattern of relationship between the products and the parent organisation. For example, the German organisation Bosch GmbH identifies its spark plugs and power tools range under the Bosch name, but uses the name Blaupunkt for its radios. |
| Corporate style | Although an organisation may operate in a number of different strategic business areas, this approach requires all communications to be targeted at reinforcing the corporate image. IBM, Mars, Hewlett-Packard and Black & Decker are examples of this form. |

*Source*: Based on Gray and Smeltzer (1985).

The way in which an organisation structures its portfolio of brands influences the strategic development and leverage of the assets it owns. One primary source of motivation to manage the portfolio is the desire to protect the most profitable brands from competitive attack. Riezebos (2003) identifies a range of different types of brand based on the role they each play within an overall portfolio. Bastion brands are of major importance to an organisation, usually because they are the most valuable in terms of profit, revenue and market share and, consequently, they are prone to attack. One major form of strategic response is to develop other brands in order to protect the premier brand (see Figure 11.4).

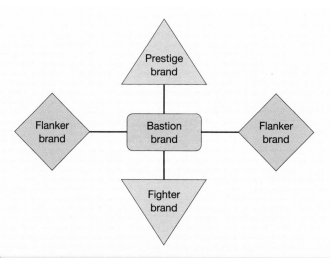

| Figure 11.4 | Portfolio of brands |
| --- | --- |

*Source*: After Riezebos (2003). Used with permission from Pearson Education Ltd.

The role of flanker brands is to protect the bastion brand by warding off competitors. By charging a slightly lower price and by offering a different set of attributes, these brands make it more difficult for competitor brands to enter the market. Rather than lose sales to competitors, it is better to lose sales to an internal brand, even if the retained profits are not as high as those generated by the bastion brand.

Fighter brands are used to fend off competitors who compete on discounted prices. Prices of fighter brands are set between the bastion brand and the competitor's low-cost offering, while the quality is adjusted to be perceived as lower than that of the bastion brand. Marketing communications should focus on name awareness, not price (see Viewpoint 11.1). However, according to Ritson (2009), the majority of fighter brands do not work as planned, and can even inflict significant damage on the brands and companies that they seek to protect. Examples of failed fighter brands include Saturn (General Motors), Ted (United Airlines) and Song (Delta Air Lines).

Prestige brands can also be aimed at niche markets, but this time the focus is on high quality and luxury. Prices are set high but marketing communications needs to focus on the high quality and status associated with ownership.

---

### Viewpoint 11.1    Brands fight back

There are several examples of airlines using fighter brands as a strategic approach to brand attack. For example, Qantas successfully launched Jetstar as a budget airline to counter the entrance of Virgin Blue. Jetstar was launched with 14 planes flying to 14 destinations and took over the tourist routes that Qantas had lost money on. Because Jetstar proved profitable on those routes, it cannibalised only revenues, not profits. This enabled Qantas to refocus on its more profitable business routes, boost its profits and redevelop Qantas's business lounges and business-class cabins. This helped to strengthen the Qantas brand and the differentiation with its Jetstar brand.

British Airways launched GO, in response to the rise of easyJet and Ryanair. However, GO operated on many of BA's routes and, with a substantial cost advantage, started to cannibalise BA's revenues and profits. So, despite GO's success, BA sold the airline and concentrated on its premium markets and operations.

Malaysian Airlines, with over 250 aircraft in its fleet, faced competition from a low-cost start-up called Air Asia. Operating with just two types of plane to generate economies of scale, Air Asia's business model started to hurt the larger brand. The response was to launch Fire-Fly, a fighter brand designed to fend off the pricing attack from Air Asia.

The use of fighter brands can be observed in other markets. In the soft drinks market East African Breweries launched Alvaro in Kenya, only for Coca-Cola respond with Novida, a rival, low-priced, non-alcoholic drink. In the UK retailing market Waitrose, part of John Lewis, introduced an 'Essentials' fighter brand which was 'benchmarked' against Tesco's own-brand products.

*Source*:   Opati (2009); Tutton (2009); Ritson (2009).

**Question:**   To what extent are fighter brands loss leaders in a company's portfolio of brands?

**Task:**       Chose an industry and find the fighter brands

---

## Brand forms

There are many forms of branding but primarily there are four key types: manufacturer, distributor, price and generic brands.

*Manufacturers' brands* help to identify the producer of a brand at the point of purchase. For example, Cadbury's chocolate, Ford cars and Coca-Cola are all strong manufacturers' brands. This type of brand usually requires the assistance of channel intermediaries for wide distribution. Marketing communications are driven by the manufacturer in an attempt to persuade end-users to adopt the brand, which in turn stimulates channel members to stock and distribute the brand.

*Distributor (or own-label) brands* do not associate the manufacturer with the offering in any way. Distributor brands are owned by channel members, typically a wholesaler, such as Nurdin & Peacock, or a retailer, such as Tesco, Boots and WHSmith. This brand form offers many advantages both to the manufacturer, who can use excess capacity, and to the retailer, who can earn a higher margin than they can with manufacturers' branded goods and at the same time develop organisational (e.g. store) images. Channel members have the additional cost of promotional initiatives, necessary in the absence of a manufacturer's support. Some manufacturers, in an attempt to restrict availability and number of brands from which consumers can choose, refuse to make distributor products. There have been occasions where multiple grocers have launched products that are alleged to be too similar to key manufacturer brands. Often this leads to channel conflict as the name and/or packaging of the distributor brand is alleged to resemble too closely that of the brand leader.

The growth of distributor brands at the expense of manufacturer brands need not be expected to continue unchecked. Consumers value or expect a certain level of brand choice in stores and, as some store traffic and spend per visit rates have declined, some grocery multiples have taken steps to stem the volume of their distributor brand provision and increased the volume of manufacturer brands on their shelves.

*Price brands* are produced by manufacturers in an attempt to compete with private brands. Tesco has used this approach to respond to the arrival of a number of low-cost retailers such as KwikSave and Aldi. The product is low-priced and is further characterised by an absence of any substantial promotional support. The effect on the other brands in the manufacturer's portfolio may be to stimulate promotional support to prevent the less loyal buyers from trading over to the low-priced offering.

The fourth and final form is the *generic brand*. This is sold without any promotional materials and the packaging displays only that information required by law. Manufacturers are even less inclined to produce these 'white carton' products than price brands. They are often sold at prices 40 per cent below the price of normal brands. They consume very few promotional resources, for obvious reasons, but their popularity, after a burst in the 1970s, has waned considerably, particularly in the supermarket sector where they gained their greatest success. However, generics are significant in some markets. In the early 1990s the pharmaceuticals industry experienced growth in the use of generic products, spurred by the government's NHS reforms (Blackett, 1992), but outside the pharmaceuticals industry generic brands have had minimal influence.

# The strategic role of branding

Walton (2007) suggests that there three dimensions to brand strategy: meaning, space and expression (see Table 11.5).

From a strategic perspective, brands play one of three significant roles. In broad terms, they can be used to defend market share or a group of brands by protecting established positions. They can be used to attack competitor brands and win market share or they can provide a way of deterring potential competitors from entering the market. In other words, they act either as a market entry barrier or as an aid to customer retention. To enable these strategic roles to be accomplished, there are three elements that need to be attended to. These are integration,

| Table 11.5 | Brand dimensions |
| --- | --- |

| Brand dimension | Explanation |
| --- | --- |
| Meaning | Refers to how consumers perceive a brand. This may be functional, emotional or symbolic. |
| Space | This concerns the actual product and the category in which it operates. |
| Expression | How the brand projects its identity through marketing communications in order that it relates to the target market in terms of its 'look and feel'. |

*Source*: Walton (2007). Used with kind permission from WARC.

which in turn can lead to differentiation and deliver added value (see Figure 11.5 and the following discussion).

## Integration

For a brand to be maintained and to work, it is important that the communications used to develop and maintain the brand are consistent and meaningful. Part of the essence of integrated marketing communications is that the mix used to support a brand, including the messages that are used to convey brand values, must be consistent, uniform and reinforcing. Therefore, successful branding is partly the result of effective integrated marketing communications.

When Levi Strauss attempted to prevent Asda from selling its clothing, it was attempting to protect the way it wanted to be perceived: that is, its positioning. If Asda had continued to sell Levi Strauss products, market forces would ultimately have determined whether the positioning determined by Levi Strauss was of value to customers.

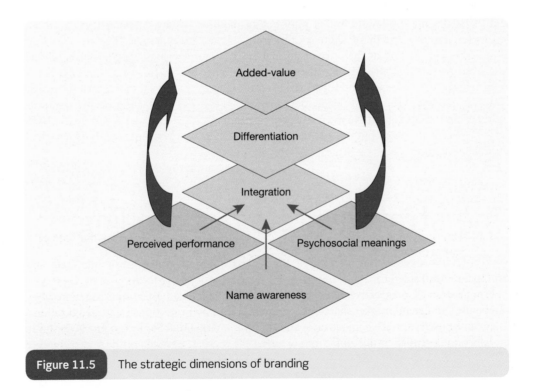

| Figure 11.5 | The strategic dimensions of branding |
| --- | --- |

## Differentiation

Brands that are integrated provide opportunities to be perceived as different, relative to a competitor's product. Branding is a method of separation and positioning so that customers can recognise and understand what a brand stands for, relative to other brands. However, not all brands choose to be different as there is some strategic advantage for smaller, new-entry brands to associate themselves closely with the market leader. This is witnessed by the disagreements between distributors and manufacturers over the packaging, names and type faces used for some products (e.g. Coca-Cola and Sainsbury's Cola, Penguin and Asda's Puffin bars).

## Added value

The final key element is added value. Brands enable customers to derive extra benefits as one brand can provide different advantages from another. These advantages might be in the form of rational, attribute-based advantages (e.g. whiter, stronger or longer) or they may be more emotionally based advantages derived through the augmented aspects of the products (e.g. the way you feel about a brand). This issue is evidenced by the vigour with which Levi Strauss resisted the distribution of its jeans through price-oriented distributors such as Asda. One of the arguments proposed by the company was that the inherent brand value was effectively removed through this form of distribution.

Value is added to brands through three main components: perceived performance, psychosocial meaning and the extent of brand-name awareness (Riezebos, 2003) (see Table 11.6). Added value is developed using different combinations of these three components.

Marketing communications is required to build these components so that consumers deduce particular meanings, perceive and value certain performance characteristics and build awareness and name familiarity.

**Table 11.6**   Brand added value

| Added value component | Explanation |
|---|---|
| Perceived performance | Derived from consumer perceptions of relative quality and perceived associations concerning key attributes. |
| Psychosocial meanings | Refers to the immaterial associations consumers make about brands from which they deduce meanings about personality and expressions of individuality. |
| Brand-name awareness | The level of name awareness can provoke feelings of familiarity and reduced risk or uncertainty. |

*Source*: After Riezebos (2003). Used with permission from Pearson Education Ltd.

**Scholars' paper 11.2**   **Brand relationships for everyone**

**Fournier, S. (1998) 'Consumers and their Brands: Developing Relationship Theory in Consumer Research', *Journal of Consumer Research*, 24 (4), 343–73.**

Fournier argues that it is important to understand people's life experiences as this frames the assortment of brands and the relationships they develop with brands. She argues that meaningful consumer brand relationships are shaped not by symbolism/functional category measures, or by involvement, but through the ego significance a brand offers an individual. This much-cited paper should be read by all involved in both academic and practitioner brand management.

# The task of marketing communications in branding

Marketing communications plays a vital role in the development of brands and is the means by which products become brands. The way in which marketing communications is used to build brands is determined strategically by the role that the brand is expected to play in achieving an organisation's goals. de Chernatony and Dall'Olmo Riley (1998b) argue that there are several tasks that marketing communications can play in relation to brand development. For example, they suggest the task during brand extensions is to show buyers how the benefits from the established brand have been transferred or extended to the new brand.

Another task, based on the work of Ehrenberg (1974), is to remind buyers and reinforce their perceptions and in doing so defend the market. However, above all of these, marketing communications has a primary task: namely, to build associations through which consumers identify, recognise, understand, assign affection, become attached, and develop relationships with a brand. These associations can be many and varied but they are crucial to brand strength and equity.

# Associations and personalities

Successful brands trigger associations in the minds of consumers, and these are not necessarily based on a function or utility. These associations enable consumers to construe an emotional connection with a particular brand. McCraken (1986) found that consumers might search for brands with a personality that complements their self-concept. Belk (1988) suggested that brands offer a means of self-expression, whether this be in terms of who they want to be (a desired self), who they strive to be (an ideal self) or who they think they should be (an ought self). Brands, therefore, provide a means for individuals to indicate to others their preferred personality, as they relate to these 'self' concepts.

This emotional and symbolic approach is intended to provide consumers with additional reasons to engage with a brand, beyond the normal functional characteristics a brand offers (Keller, 1998), and which are so easily copied by competitors. Aaker (1997) refers to brand personality as the set of human characteristics that consumers associate with a brand. She developed the Brand Personality Scale, which consists of five main dimensions of psychosocial meaning, which subsume 42 personality traits. The dimensions are sincerity (wholesome, honest, down-to-earth), excitement (exciting, imaginative, daring), competence (intelligent, confident), sophistication (charming, glamorous, smooth), and ruggedness (strong, masculine).

| Viewpoint 11.2 | Structural luxury |
| --- | --- |

The focus of luxury brand communications is not on the intrinsic but on the extrinsic attributes. Strategies are often based on developing brand-name associations that appeal to the aspirational needs and social and psychological motivations of the target audiences.

Luxury brands such as Dior, Rolex, Gucci, Cartier and Donna Karan have been developed mainly through a combination of advertising, public relations, craftsmanship, word-of-mouth and a touch of mythology. For example, 'I found this material in a Scandinavian shop in Bath', claimed shoe designer Manolo Blahnik. Much of L'Oréal's recent success in the luxury sector has been attributed to its use of social media.

In order to grow and to reach new target markets, luxury brands are faced with a dilemma. They can lower their prices to attract new customers, but this threatens to impact the perception of the main brand by undermining its values and reputation, the one important point of differentiation that has made the brand successful. L'Oréal has created a raft of new luxury products following research that revealed that affluent consumers were looking for brands that are innovative, provide bespoke product features, are authentic, and which provide a unique brand experience. This is in contrast to the previous purchase drive based on conspicuous consumption.

For some brands the route forward is to introduce sub-brands that cannot be seen to be part of the main brand. Thus, Klein Cosmetics splits its business into two, classic brands and the CK franchise line that includes CkOne and CkB fragrances. Tudor is a sub-brand of Rolex and Donna Karan uses Signature and DKNY as associate labels.

*Sources*:   Based on Datamonitor (2010); Brooke and Nottage (2008); Lovett (2008).

**Question:**   To what extent can luxury brands be personified?

**Task:**   Choose a luxury brand and try to collect as many communication artefacts relating to that brand as you can. Now, perform a mini content analysis to isolate core approaches and branding approaches.

**Exhibit 11.2**    **A giant billboard used to position and convey the sophistication of a Dior watch**

*Source*: Dong Jinlin/ColorChinaPhoto/Press Association Images

**Exhibit 11.3**    **Claimed to be the most valuable perfume in the world, Amouage perfume originates in the Sultanate of Oman**

*Source*: whyeyephotography/Alamy Images

Aaker's initial research was conducted in the mid-1990s and revealed that in the USA, MTV was perceived to be best on excitement, CNN on competence, Levi's on ruggedness, Revlon on sophistication, and Campbell's on sincerity.

These psychosocial dimensions have subsequently become established as dimensions of brand personality. Aaker developed a five-point framework around these dimensions in order to provide a consistent means of measurement. The framework has been used frequently and cited many times by both academics and marketing practitioners. For example, Arora and Stoner (2009) report that various studies have found that consumers choose offerings which they feel possess personalities similar to their own personalities (Linville and Carlston, 1994; Phau and Lau, 2001). They prefer brands that project a personality that is consistent with their self-concepts. As Arora and Stoner (2009: 273) indicate, 'brand personality provides a form of identity for consumers that expresses symbolic meaning for themselves and for others'. Brand personality, therefore, can be construed as a means of creating and maintaining consumer loyalty, if only because this aspect is difficult for competitors to copy. Readers are encouraged to reconsider the ideas about tribal consumption considered previously (Chapter 3).

Customers assign a level of trust to the brands they encounter. Preferred brands signify a high level of trust and indicate that the brand promise is delivered. Marketing managers, therefore, need to ensure that they do not harm or reduce the perceived levels of trust in their brands. Indeed, actions should be taken to enhance trust. One way of achieving this is to use labels and logos to represent a brand's values, associations, and source. For example, all Apple products are signified, and identified by, the fruit with a bite removed; UK meat products carry a red tractor symbol. According to the National Farmers Union, the red tractor logo indicates that the meat was produced to exacting standards of food safety, kindness to animals, and environmental protection. This is intended to reassure customers about the origin and quality of the meat. A more recent symbol is that of a footprint. This refers to the carbon dioxide associated with the production and transportation of a brand. This emerged because some brands wanted a means of demonstrating the carbon savings they had made in their supply chains. Walkers Crisps and then Tesco were the first brands to use the symbol. However, as Charles (2009) points out, one of the issues arising from the use of the carbon footprint symbol is that consumers do not understand what the figures mean. This will take time, just as the Fairtrade brand was not established overnight.

There are various ways in which these associations can be developed to shape brands. However, the initial decision to pursue one brand association strategy rather than another is partly a function of the size of the financial resources that are available. They are also partly a function of the context in which the communications are intended to work. As a result, brand associations can be developed in one of four main ways, as presented at Figure 11.6

- *Above-the-line*: Should the budget be high, advertising will often be the main way through which brand name associations are shaped. The brand name itself will not need to be related to the function or use experience of the brand as the advertising will be used to create and maintain brand associations. Expressive propositions predominate.

- *Through-the-line*: Sometimes the brand strategy requires a direct marketing approach. Here some advertising is necessary but in combination with sales promotion, public relations, merchandising and online activity. A mix of functional and expressive associations can be observed.

- *Below-the-line*: Where resources are restricted and advertising is not an option, the brand name needs to be closely related to the function and use experience of the product. In the FMCG sector packaging should also play a significant role in building brand associations. Functional associations tend to predominate.

- *Around-the-line*: Whether resources are tight or available, there are circumstances when the sole use of a formal mix of brand building tools and media is inappropriate. Here word of mouth communication and brand experience are sufficient to propel a brand's visibility. Expressive propositions predominate, although both approaches are possible.

Each of these is now considered in turn.

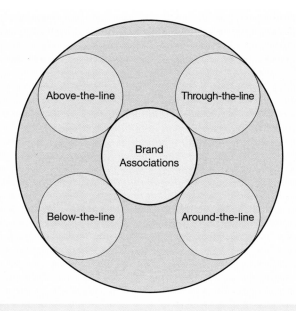

**Figure 11.6**    Four generic ways to build brand associations

# Brand building

## Brand building: above-the-line

When there are sufficient resources, and competitive conditions are intense and margins small, advertising is used to help consumers to make brand associations. Two main approaches can be used: a rational or an emotional approach. When a rational approach is used, the functional aspects of a brand are emphasised and the benefit to the consumer is stressed. Very often product performance is the focus of the message and a key attribute is identified and used to position the brand. Typically, unique selling propositions (USPs) were often used to draw attention to a single superior functional advantage that consumers found attractive – for example, a washing powder that washes clothes whiter, drinks that have the highest percentage of fruit juice content and paint that covers more square metres than any other paint.

Many brands now try to present two or even three brand features as the USP has lost ground. For example, when Britvic launched *Juice Up* into the chilled fruit juice sector to compete with *Sunny Delight*, it used the higher fruit juice and lower sugar attributes as the main focus of the communication strategy. The rational approach is sometimes referred to as an *informative approach* (and complements functional positioning).

When an emotional approach is used, advertising should provide emotional selling points (ESPs). These can enable consumers to make positive brand associations based on both psychological and socially acceptable meanings, a psychosocial interpretation. Product performance characteristics are dormant while consumers are encouraged to develop positive feelings towards and associations with the brand. A further goal can be to create positive attitudes towards the advertising itself, which in turn can be used to make associations with the brand. In other words, the role of likeability, discussed later in this chapter, becomes paramount when using an emotional advertising approach. Therefore, these types of advertisements should be relevant and meaningful, credible, and of significant value to the consumer. In essence, therefore, emotional advertising is about people enjoying the advertisement (and complements expressive positioning).

## Viewpoint 11.3 · Coca-Cola – built above-the-line

Coca-Cola has used advertising consistently since its launch in 1886. The goal is invariably brand aware-ness, to help audiences make brand associations, and to position the brand as an accompaniment to or a catalyst for a joyous life. This joyous life has for a long time, in Coca-Cola's terms, been associated with the American way of life and values. This has often been depicted through the 'Coca-Cola girl', to represent images of American beauty.

Early Coca-Cola print ads were derived from their first calendar. Magazines, newspapers, and advertis-ing cards were popular before playing cards, posters, serving trays, uniquely shaped bottles, jewellery, sports programmes, bookmarks, sheet music, signage, delivery trucks, Santa icons and even the sides of buildings, became legitimate media vehicles.

Coca-Cola ads have reflected prevailing cultural and political contexts. In the 1980s the Watergate scandal and the Vietnam war resulted in Coke trying to protect the world with a hillside of singers want-ing 'to teach the world to sing and . . . furnish it with love'.

In the 1980s the brand worked with the Bobby Brown band, New Edition, in an attempt to align itself with popular culture and to reach the MTV generation. Michael Jackson's huge success with Pepsi may have been a catalyst. The next decade brought ads where Coke was to be a part of a fun-filled life, immortalised as 'Always Coca-Cola'.

Since then ads have drawn associations with happiness, lifestyle and health, the most recent being a gang of insects relieving a man sleeping under tree, of his bottle of Coke, and using it to replenish nature.

The target for these ads has been consumers, pulling them into the brand and touchpoints where the brand is available.

*Source*:   Barda (2010); Parsons (2011); www.topdesignmag.com/vintage-coca-cola-girl-ads/ www.prnewswire.com/news-releases/worlds-largest-private-collection-of-coca-cola-advertising-art-and-memorabilia-to-become-available-to-public-80000-pieces-in-collection-worth-10-million-120769309.html.

**Question:**   Other than advertising, how else could brands like Coca-Cola help audiences make brand associations?

**Task:**   Choose another manufacturers' brand and track the way advertising has been used to help consumers make brand associations.

**Exhibit 11.4**   **An outdoor poster for Coca-Cola in Luxor, Egypt**
*Source*: David White/Alamy Images

Above-the-line incorporates online advertising and both display and search are used to develop strong positive brand associations.

## Brand building: through-the-line

As the name suggests, through-the-line offers a blend of above and below the line approaches, with direct marketing playing a strong role in the communication mix. As many brand owners have moved away from using marketing communications for brand-building purposes and then used communications to change or motivate buyer behaviour, so the development of direct marketing emerged.

Through-the-line communications involve the use of advertising to deliver a call-to-action. Often this is associated with sales promotions, events and merchandising, all of which reinforce behaviour. A variety of tools and media can be used in the name of direct marketing, usually configured to complement the business and marketing strategies (Chapter 17). In consumer markets advertising is used to drive awareness as well as behaviour but in business markets advertising has a relatively minor role to play, as greater emphasis is placed on email, trade shows and website facilities.

Brand associations in consumer markets are therefore driven by advertising, direct mail and a functional brand name, all reinforced through brand experience and word-of-mouth communication. In business markets brand associations are developed through direct mail, telemarketing, personal selling, trade shows as well as the quality of the website and relationship potential. The name is not always important in terms of providing a functional association. A mix of functional and expressive associations can be observed.

## Brand building: below-the-line

When the marketing communications budget is limited or where the target audience cannot be reached reasonably or effectively through advertising, then it is necessary to use various other communication tools to develop brand associations.

Direct marketing and public relations are important methods used to build brand values, especially when consumers experience high involvement. The Internet offers opportunities to build new dot.com brands and the financial services sector has tried to harness this method as part of a multichannel distribution policy. What appears to be overridingly important for the development of brands operating with limited resources is the brand name and the merchandising activities, of which packaging, labelling and POP are crucial. In addition, as differentiation between brands becomes more difficult in terms of content and distinct symbolism, the nature of the service encounter is now recognised to have considerable impact on brand association. The development of loyalty schemes and carelines for FMCG, durable and service-based brands is a testimony to the importance of developing and maintaining positive brand associations.

---

### Viewpoint 11.4    Stanley Tools do it below-the-line

Although the name 'Stanley' says little about the functionality of the business brand, the word 'Tools' helps customers to develop the right associations. The company creates, manufactures and distributes tools and equipment for professional tradesmen.

Following various environmental developments and changes in the market place, it soon became clear that Stanley needed to re-establish their position as the number 1 supplier for professional tradesmen.

To achieve this, a three-stage programme was developed. The first of these required Stanley to create a new range of tools and equipment called Stanley 'FatMax XL'. This was only available through professional trade channels. Research found that advocacy was really important in the market and that key influencers or opinion formers (onsite tradesmen whose opinion is sought by others) were critical to the flow of communication in the industry.

The third stage was the design and implementation of a communication strategy. The research indicated that an engagement strategy that emphasised behaviour rather than the brand-values approach, one that was previously employed by Stanley through conventional media such as TV, print and online, would be more effective.

The campaign was called 'Judgement Day', echoing the judgement a key influencer could make. The aim was to demonstrate through individual experience the quality of the FatMax XL range. This was achieved by visiting major building sites and professional trades events (e.g. InterBuild) and inviting the key influencers to trial the FatMax XL range against competitor products. Using a boxing ring to stage the event, 'contestants' had to take on challenges such as how long it would take to hammer a 6-inch nail into a piece of wood, using a Stanley hammer. Winners received tool belts of Stanley products and were encouraged to talk about their experiences and become advocates.

In addition to the onsite events, trade buyers were invited to meetings and open discussions at Stanley's head office. Public relations was used to reach journalists. This was important, as it provided credibility and reassured advocates of their role.

The overall impact of the programme exceeded expectations and enabled Stanley to achieve the majority of their objectives, including an ROI of 69 per cent and a return to growth after a period of decline. What is clear is that advertising did not feature in the campaign and that the necessary brand associations were built through experience, competitions, events, word of mouth, and public relations. All of these are below-the-line activities.

*Source*:    Turland et al. (2009), Reiter (2009).

---

**Question:**    Why do you think Stanley used a behavioural rather than a brand value approach to engagement?

**Task:**    Make a list of any other methods or forms of marketing communications that Stanley might have used.

---

The below-the-line route needs to achieve a transfer of image. Apart from the clarity of the brand name, which needs to describe the product functions, it is the packaging and associated labelling that shapes the way a brand is perceived.

## Brand building: around-the-line

Although not an entirely contemporary strategy, a further approach involves the development of brands without the use of formal communication tools or conventional media. The key to success is to seed the brand through word-of-mouth communication. Two of the most notable examples are Google and Hotmail. Both are global brands and both have been developed without any advertising, sales promotion or direct marketing. They have used some public relations, but their market dominance has been developed through word-of-mouth communication (often viral) and experience through usage strategies.

Digital communications, in particular social networks, email, viral marketing, blogging and in some cases Twitter, have enabled people to pass on news and views about brands. When opinion leaders and formers are targeted with relevant and interesting brand-related material, they pass on information and views, usually with an exponential impact. Brand-based conversations among consumers enable the development of brand associations.

Brand experience has become an important factor both in marketing practice and in the marketing literature. These experiences are considered to be the 'internal responses (sensations, feelings and thoughts) and behavioural responses evoked by brand-related stimuli that are part of a brand's design and identity, packaging, communications and environments' (Brakus et al. 2009: 53).

Consumers experience brands in a number of ways, but perhaps the most common experiences occur at one of three distinct points. According to Arnould et al. (2002), cited by Brakus et al. (2009), these are when searching for brands, when they buy brands and when they consume them. Brakus et al. (2009) go on to demonstrate that brand experiences consist of four dimensions, all of which vary according to brand type and category. These are sensory, affective, intellectual and behavioural. Therefore, the sound management of these elements and dimensions can have a positive impact on developing the right brand associations.

---

### Viewpoint 11.5   Spreading it around the line

Marmite, the yeast extract which is loved or hated, launched an extra-strong version called XO. This was achieved without any paid-for media. Consumers were simply asked to prove their dedication to the brand and were then offered the opportunity to sample the XO version. The creative was based on 'The Marmarati', a community of devoted lovers of Marmite, and through a variety of social media, achieved sales of £600,000 in six months and reached 2.4 million Web users.

Waterstone's, the high street book retailer, embarked on a social media and brand experiences campaign, seeking to drive website traffic and boost the Waterstone's brand name. Activities undertaken include use of Twitter to promote Ant and Dec's book, a Flickr activity to find an unpublished illustrator to work with a best-selling book author and several blogger promotions.

Consider the role of The $O_2$. Originally known as the 'Millennium Dome', the structure was scorned by the population, but $O_2$ have transformed the structure into a major music venue and branded entertainment experience. The $O_2$ offers opportunities for brand extensions and added-value opportunities for $O_2$ customers over non-$O_2$ customer visitors. For example, the Priority Ticket Offer enables $O_2$ customers to book tickets 48 hours before others. Over 1 million $O_2$ customers have signed up, and over 180,000 priority sales have been made.

*Source*:   Revolution (2011); Woods (2009); Anon (2009).

| | |
|---|---|
| **Question:** | Why do you think Marmite, Waterstone's and $O_2$ avoided using advertising in their campaigns? |
| **Task:** | Identify three other brands who have used the around-the-line approach, and write brief notes explaining why they have been successful. |

---

In addition to these three forms of brand development, there are several additional mechanisms through which brand associations can be developed. These include: co-branding, geographical identifiers, the use of ingredient brands, support services and award symbols.

Marketing communications is the means through which products can evolve into brands. People make associations immediately they become aware of a brand name. It is the brand manager's task to ensure that the associations made are appropriate and provide a means of differentiation. By communicating the key strengths and differences of a brand, by explaining how a brand enables a customer to create value for themselves, and by reinforcing and providing consistency in the messages transmitted, a level of integration can be brought to the way a brand is perceived by the target market.

Finally in this section, the importance of branding as a part of integrated marketing communications should not be forgotten and, for this, internal brand education is crucial. The way a brand relates internally to departments and individuals and the way the brand is articulated by senior management are important parts of brand education. Brands are not just external elements – they should form part of the way in which an organisation operates, be part of its internal, cultural configuration (Marquardt et al. 2011).

# Business-to-business branding

Branding has been used by a number of manufacturers (e.g. Intel, Caterpillar, Cisco, DuPont, FedEx, Teflon, Nutrasweet) to achieve two particular goals. Rich (1996) reports that the first goal is to develop an identity which final end-users perceive as valuable. For example, Intel has developed its microprocessors such that PCs with the Intel brand are seen to be of high quality and credibility. This provides PC manufacturers with an added competitive advantage. The second goal is to establish a stronger relationship with the manufacturer. Nutrasweet works with food manufacturers, advising on recipes, simply because the final product is the context within which Nutrasweet will be evaluated by end-users.

A B2B brand is often tied closely to the company itself, as opposed to B2C brands, which often distance themselves from the manufacturer or company name. For example, a Rolls-Royce power turbine is branded Rolls-Royce because of the perception of tradition, high quality, performance and global reach that are associated with the Rolls-Royce name. Marketing communications should be developed so that they incorporate and perpetuate the personality of the brand. Thus, all the Rolls-Royce advertising materials should be in corporate colours and contain the logo. All copy should be in the house style and reinforce brand perceptions.

Beverland et al. (2007) offer an alternative model to Kapferer's (2012) prism (above) in order to address the needs of the business market. Their approach, depicted at Figure 11.7 uses five main dimensions upon which business brands are built: product, service, adaptation, logistics and advice.

The researchers argue that the tangible elements (product benefits) are normally more prominent at the beginning of a business relationship. However, as the relationship develops

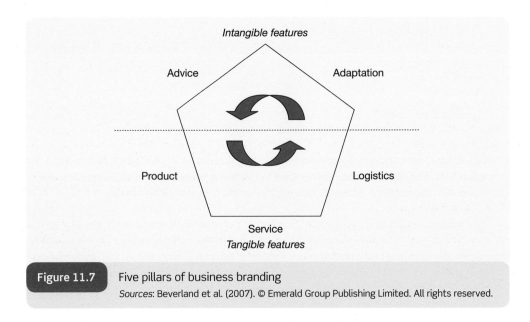

| Figure 11.7 | Five pillars of business branding |

*Sources:* Beverland et al. (2007). © Emerald Group Publishing Limited. All rights reserved.

and as the decision-making becomes increasingly complex, so there is a shift away from the tangible to the intangible aspects and abstract associations.

The use of event sponsorship, whereby an organisation provides financial support for a conference or exhibition, has become increasingly popular (Miller, 1997). Mainly because of the costs involved, event organisers have sought sponsorship aid. For sponsors, events provide a means of promoting visibility within a narrowly focused target market. In addition, they provide a means of highlighting their own particular contribution within the conference or on their exhibition stand.

The use of joint promotional activities between manufacturers and resellers will continue to be an important form of communication behaviour. The desire to build networks that provide cooperative strength and protection for participants is likely to continue. Manufacturers will use joint promotional activities as a means of forging close relationships with retailers and as a means of strengthening exit barriers (routes away from relationships).

Mudambi et al. (1997) agree that risk and performance are critical aspects in the buying decision, and that both of these are signalled by a firm's brand. In their investigation of the buying process for industrial precision bearings, they conclude that the development of relationships with individuals within supplier organisations is critical, simply because the final decision can often be a matter of 'personal preference' (Mudambi et al., 1997: 442).

---

### Scholars' paper 11.3    Business brands

**Beverland, M., Napoli, J. and Yakimova, R. (2007) Branding the business marketing offer: exploring brand attributes in business markets, *Journal of Business and Industrial Marketing*, 22(6), 394–9.**

This conceptual paper is used to develop five potential strategies for building brands in business markets. The authors refer to the business-market offer which consists of five components that can be imitated by competitors (products, services, and logistics), while two less tangible and difficult-to-imitate components (adaptation and advice) reflect the intangible capabilities of the firm.

---

# Online branding

The major difference between online and offline branding is the context in which the brand associations are developed and sustained. Both forms of branding are about developing and sustaining valuable relationships with consumers, but online branding occurs in a virtual context. This context deprives consumers of many of the normal cues used to sense and interpret brands. Opportunities to touch and feel, to try on and physically feel and compare products are largely removed and a new set of criteria has to be used to convey and interpret brand associations.

One of the strengths of the Internet is its ability to provide copious amounts of regularly updated information, available '24/7'. As a result, online brands tend towards the use of rational messages, using product attributes, quality and performance measures, third-party endorsements, comparisons and price as a means of brand differentiation and advantage. However, it should be remembered that online branding strategies are influenced by the nature of the brand itself. If the brand has a strong offline presence, then the amount of online branding work will be smaller than if it is a pure-play brand. Branding should be a part of an overall communications strategy, where online and offline work is coordinated.

In 2007/08 the online reliance on rational, informational approaches started to give way as brands became more interactive and capable of emotional engagement. Brand building, once the preserve of offline communications, is now an online expectation.

Each website provides a focus for the brand identity and it is the experience consumers have with a site that determines whether the site will be revisited. The website acts as a prime means of differentiating online brands and those that fail to develop differential advantage will probably learn that visitors are only one click away from leaving a site (Oxley and Miller, 2000). These commentators refer to a site's 'stickiness' and ability to retain visitors, which in turn can increase advertising rate card costs. However, as they point out, a long visit does not necessarily mean that the experience was beneficial as the site may try to facilitate customer transactions quickly, or enable them to find the information they need without difficulty; in other words, reduced levels of stickiness may be appropriate in some circumstances.

All online branding activities need to extend across all key consumer contact points, in both offline and online environments. Internet users generally exhibit goal-directed behaviour and experiential motivations. Goal-directed behaviour that is satisfied is more likely to make people want to return to a site. Therefore, it can be concluded (broadly) that satisfying experiential motivations makes people stay, and in doing so boosts the potency of an online brand.

# Virtual brand communities

Virtual brand communities (VBC) have emerged in recent years as a result of the positive inter-action generated through the use of several online tools, most notably chat rooms, forums and discussion areas. Firms such as Procter & Gamble have developed VBCs not only to engage with target audiences but to also enable interaction among their audiences. The two main benefits are that VBCs enable increased brand exposure in a semi-clean environment and also provide rich opportunities to learn about the motivations, feelings and issues related to buyer behaviour and market trends (Pitta and Fowler, 2005).

A VBC is a group of individuals who interact online in order to share their interest in a brand or product. Muniz and O'Guinn (2001) suggest that there are three core components within a community:

- a consciousness of kind (a feeling or passion that binds participants);
- rituals and traditions (shared codes of behaviour and values plus memories of significant events);
- a sense of moral responsibility (moral commitment among members to enable survival of the community).

Casaló et al. (2008) undertook one of the first empirical research exercises to determine the effectiveness of community participation. They found that trust in the community itself may increase participation levels, with satisfaction with previous interactions and perceived levels of communication as key factors driving trust. They also discovered that involvement in these communities also had a positive effect on the participants' commitment to the brand. In other words, VBCs can increase the strength of the ties felt towards the brand, which in turn can improve loyalty and drive higher levels of retention.

| Scholars' paper 11.4 | Customer branding |
|---|---|

**Pennington, J.R. and Ball, A.D. (2009) Customer branding of commodity products: The customer-developed brand, *Brand Management*, 16(7), 455–67.**

In an age when co-creation and crowd-sourcing are increasingly prevalent, this topical paper considers issues related to the role customers have in brand creation. The focus is on the transition from commodities into brands. The paper starts with a review of the branding activities undertaken by marketers, and then suggests ways in which these activities can be performed by customers, makes several propositions on customer branding and finally examines the managerial implications for customer branding.

# Brand equity

The concept of brand equity has arisen from the increasing recognition that brands represent a value both to organisations and shareholders. Brands as assets can impact heavily on the financial well-being of a company. Indeed, Pirrie (2006: 40) refers to the evidence that organisations with strong brands 'consistently outperform their markets'.

According to Ehrenberg (1993), market share is the only appropriate measure of a brand's equity or value and, as a result, all other measures taken individually are of less significance, and collectively they come together as market share. However, this view excludes the composition of brands, the values that consumers place in them and the financial opportunities that arise with brand development and strength.

Lasser et al. (1995) identify two main perspectives of brand equity: namely a financial and a marketing perspective. The financial view is based on a consideration of a brand's value as a definable asset, based on the net present values of discounted future cash flows (Farquahar, 1989). The marketing perspective is grounded in the beliefs, images and core associations consumers have about particular brands. Richards (1997) argues that there are both behavioural and attitudinal elements associated with brands and recognises that these vary between groups and represent fresh segmentation and targeting opportunities. A further component of the marketing view is the degree of loyalty or retention a brand is able to sustain. Measures of market penetration, involvement, attitudes and purchase intervals (frequency) are typical. Feldwick (1996) used a three-part definition to bring these two approaches together. He suggests brand equity is a composite of:

- *brand value*, based on a financial and accounting base;
- *brand strength*, measuring the strength of a consumer's attachment to a brand;
- *brand description*, represented by the specific attitudes customers have towards a brand.

In addition to these, Cooper and Simmons (1997) offer *brand future* as a further dimension. This is a reflection of a brand's ability to grow and remain unhindered by environmental challenges such as changing retail patterns, alterations in consumer buying methods and developments in technological and regulative fields. As if to reduce the increasing complexity of these measures, Pirrie (2006) argues that brand value needs to be based on the relationship between customer and brand owner and this has to be grounded in the value experienced by the customer, which is subsequently reflected on the company. For consumers the brand value is about 'reduction'; reducing search time and costs, reducing perceived quality assurance risks, and making brand associations by reducing social and ego risks (see Chapter 6 for

| Table 11.7 | Approaches to measuring brand equity |
| --- | --- |

| Source | Factors measured |
| --- | --- |
| David Aaker | Awareness, brand associations, perceived quality and market leadership, loyalty, market performance measures. |
| BrandDynamics (Millward Brown) | Brand – earnings, contribution, multiple. |
| Brand asset valuator (Young and Rubicam) | Strength (differentiation and relevance), stature (esteem and knowledge). |
| Interbrand (Omnicom) | Economic profit, the role of the brand, brand strength. |
| Christodoulides et al. (online brands) | Emotional connection, online experience, responsive service nature, trust and fulfilment. |

*Sources:* Adapted from Mirzaei, Gray and Baumann (2011); Pirrie (2006); Christodoulides et al. (2006); Cooper and Simmons (1997); Haigh (1997).

more information about perceived risks). For brand owners, the benefits are concerned with 'enablement'. She refers to enabling brand extensions, premium pricing and loyalty.

Attempts to measure brand equity have to date been varied and have lacked a high level of consensus, although the spirit and ideals behind the concept are virtually the same. Table 11.7 sets out some of the approaches adopted. As a means of synthesising these approaches the following are considered the principal dimensions through which brand equity should be measured:

- *brand dominance*: a measure of its market strength and financial performance;
- *brand associations*: a measure of the beliefs held by buyers about what the brand represents;
- *brand prospects*: a measure of its capacity to grow and extend into new areas.

Brand equity is considered important because of the increasing interest in trying to measure the return on promotional investments. This in turn aids the valuation of brands for balance sheet purposes. A brand with a strong equity is more likely to be able to preserve its customer franchise and so fend off competitor attacks. From the BrandZ Top 100 model Farr (2006) determined that the top brands are characterised by four factors. They are all strong in terms of innovation, great customer experience, clear values and strong sector leadership.

Developing brand equity is a strategy-related issue and whether a financial, marketing or twin approach is adopted, the measurement activity can help focus management activity on brand development. However, there is little agreement about what is measured and how and when it is measured. Ambler and Vakratsas (1998) argue that organisations should not seek a single set of measures simply because of the varying circumstances and contextual factors that impinge on brand performance. In reality, the measures used by most firms share many common elements.

# Key points

- Branding is a strong means by which a product can be identified, understood and appreciated. Brands are a composite of two main constructs: **1**) an identity that managers wish to portray, and **2**) images, construed by audiences, of the identities they perceive. The development of Web 2.0 and user-generated-content in the form of blogs, wikis and social networks have added a new dimension to the manager-driven perspective of brands. It is important therefore to recognise that both managers and customers are involved in the branding process.

- Brands consist of two main types of attributes: intrinsic and extrinsic. Intrinsic attributes refer to the functional characteristics of the product such as its shape, performance and physical capacity. If any of these intrinsic attributes were changed, it would directly alter the product. Extrinsic attributes refer to those elements that are not intrinsic and if changed do not alter the material functioning and performance of the product itself: devices such as the brand name, marketing communications, packaging, price and mechanisms which enable consumers to form associations that give meaning to the brand.

- Branding provides customers with a quick and easy way of understanding what a product is, what value it represents and can also represent a measure of psychosocial reassurance.

- Branding provides manufacturers and distributors with a means of differentiating their products in order to gain competitive advantage in such a way that customers perceive added value. This allows for premium pricing and the improved margin can be used to invest in new opportunities for commercial initiatives through, for example, innovation or improved levels of customer service.

- An organisation's brand architecture represents the overall marketing interface with the community of stakeholders. The way in which an organisation structures and manages its brands not only affects its overall success but also influences the marketing communications used to support them. The two most common types of brand architecture are branded house and the house of brands.

- The development of brand portfolios is a means of gaining and protecting brand advantage. The fundamental structure of a brand portfolio consists of three main levels: the architecture, the form and the individual brand.

- Branding is a key strategic communication issue and not only affects FMCG products but is increasingly used by B2B organisations as a means of differentiation, added value and increasingly, integration.

- Marketing communications has an important role to play in building brand associations. To help customers make associations with brands either a rational, information-based approach might be adopted or alternatively a more emotional relationship might be forged, one based more on imagery and feelings. Brand associations can be developed in one of four main ways; above, through, below and around-the-line.

- The major difference between online and offline branding is the context in which the brand associations are developed and sustained. Both forms of branding are about developing and sustaining valuable relationships with consumers, but online branding occurs in a virtual context. This context deprives consumers of many of the normal cues used to sense and interpret brands. Opportunities to touch and feel, to try on and physically feel and compare products are largely removed and a new set of criteria has to be used to convey and interpret brand associations.

- All online branding activities need to extend across all key consumer contact points, in both offline and online environments. A VBC is a group of individuals who interact online in order to share their interest in a brand or product. VBCs can increase the strength of the ties felt towards the brand, which in turn can improve loyalty and drive higher levels of retention.

- Brands as assets can impact heavily on the financial well-being of a company. Indeed, Pirrie (2006: 40) refers to the evidence that organisations with strong brands 'consistently outperform their markets'. There are two main ways of considering brand equity: namely financial perspective and marketing perspective.

# Review questions

1. Write brief notes explaining what branding is.

2. How do brands assist customers and brand owners?

3. Summarise Biel's concept of 'brand magic'.

4. Select five consumer brands and evaluate their characteristics.

5. Explain the concept of a brand portfolio and set out what you understand by the terms 'architecture', 'bastion' and 'fighter brands'.

6. Discuss the relative importance of the three elements that determine the strategic aspect of branding. Which of these was used by Domino's?

7. Explain four different ways in which marketing communications can be used to develop brand associations.

8. Find three non-FMCG brands and evaluate how their brand strength has been developed without the aid of advertising. How might you improve the strength of these brands?

9. How might online branding complement offline branding activities?

10. Discuss two approaches to brand equity.

# References

Aaker, J. (1997) Dimensions of Brand Personality, *Journal of Marketing Research*, 34 (August), 347–56.

Alexander, R.S. (1948) Report of the Definitions Committee – American Marketing Association, *Journal of Marketing*, 13 (October), 202–10.

Ambler, T. and Vakratsas, D. (1998) Why not let the agency decide the advertising? *Market Leader*, 1 (Spring), 32–7.

Anon (2009) O₂ – Marketing Society Leading-edge category winner, *Marketing*, 10 June, p. 7.

Arnould, E.J., Price, L.L. and Zinkhan, G.L. (2002) *Consumers*, 2nd edn, New York: McGraw-Hill.

Arora, R. and Stoner, C. (2009) A mixed method approach to understanding brand personality, *Journal of Product & Brand Management*, 18, 4, 272–83.

Assael, H. (1990) *Marketing: Principles and Strategy*, Orlando, FL: Dryden Press.

Barda, T. (2010) Pop culture, *The Marketer*, (May) 24–7.

Belk, Russell (1988), Possessions and the Extended Self, *Journal of Consumer Research*, 15, 2 (September), 139–68.

Berthon, P., Pitt, L., Chakrabarti, R., Berthon, J.-P. and Simon, M. (2011) Brand Worlds: From Articulation to Integration, *Journal of Advertising Research (Supplement)*, 51 (March), 182–8.

Beverland, M., Napoli, J. and Yakimova, R. (2007) Branding the business marketing offer: exploring brand attributes in business markets, *Journal of Business and Industrial Marketing*, 22(6), 394–9.

Biel, A. (1997) Discovering brand magic: the hardness of the softer side of branding, *International Journal of Advertising*, 16, 199–210.

Blackett, T. (1992) Branding and the rise of the generic drug, *Marketing Intelligence and Planning*, 10(9), 21–4.

Blackston, M. (1993) A brand with an attitude: a suitable case for treatment, *Journal of Market Research Society*, 34(3), 231–41.

Boehringer, C. (1996) How can you build a better brand? *Pharmaceutical Marketing* (July), 35–6.

Brakus, J.J., Scmitt, B.H. and Zarantonello, L. (2009) Brand experience: what is it? How is it measured? Does it affect loyalty? *Journal of Marketing*, 73 (May) 52–68.

Brodie, R.J. and Chernatony de, L. (2009) Towards new conceptualizations of branding: theories of the middle range, *Marketing Theory*, 9, 1, 95–100.

Brooke, S. and Nottage, A. (2008) Luxe in flux, *Marketing*, 13 February, 30–1.

Casaló, V., Flavián, C. and Guinalíu, M. (2008) Promoting consumers' participation in virtual brand communities: a new paradigm in branding strategy, *Journal of Marketing Communications*, 14(1) (February), 19–36.

Charles, G. (2009) Get to grips with the carbon agenda, *Marketing*, 30 September, 26–7.

Chernatony de, L. (2009) Towards the holy grail of defining 'brand', *Marketing Theory*, 9, 1, 101–105.

Chernatony de, L. and Dall'omo Riley, F. (1998a) Defining a brand: beyond the literature with experts' interpretations, *Journal of Marketing Management*, 14, 417–43.

Chernatony de, L. and Dall'omo Riley, F. (1998b) Expert practitioners' views on roles of brands: implications for marketing communications, *Journal of Marketing Communications*, 4, 87–100.

Christodoulides, G., de Chernatony, L., Furrer, O., Shiu, E., and Abimbola, T. (2006) Conceptualising and Measuring the Equity of Online Brands, *Journal of Marketing Management*, 22, 799–825.

Cooper, A. and Simmons, P. (1997) Brand equity lifestage: an entrepreneurial revolution, TBWA Simmons Palmer. Unpublished working paper.

Datamonitor (2010) L'Oreal Luxury Brand Case Study: Serving the post-recessionary affluent market, December, pp. 1–19, retrieved 12 December 2011 from http://web.ebscohost.com/ehost/pdfviewer/pdfviewer?vid=10&hid=18&sid=95842928-a199-47ac-a233-d32f241214b9%40sessionmgr15.

Ehrenberg, A.S.C. (1974) Repetitive advertising and the consumer, *Journal of Advertising Research*, 14 (April), 25–34.

Ehrenberg, A.S.C. (1993) If you are so strong why aren't you bigger? *Admap* (October), 13–14.

Farquahar, P. (1989) Managing brand equity, *Marketing Research*, 1(9) (September), 24–33.

Farr, A. (2006) Soft measure, hard cash, *Admap*, November, 39–42.

Feldwick, P. (1996) What is brand equity anyway, and how do you measure it? *Journal of Market Research*, 38(2), 85–104.

Fournier, S. (1995) A consumer–brand relationship perspective on brand equity, presentation to Marketing Science Conference on Brand Equity and the Marketing Mix, Tucson, Arizona, 2–3 March, Working paper 111, 13–16.

Fournier, S. (1998) 'Consumers and their Brands: Developing Relationship Theory in Consumer Research', *Journal of Consumer Research*, 24, 4, 343–73.

Goodman, M. (2011) We can still find room for many more pizzas, *Sunday Times*, 18 December 2011.

Gray, E.R. and Smeltzer, L.R. (1985) SMR Forum: corporate image – an integral part of strategy, *Sloan Management Review* (Summer), 73–8.

Haigh, D. (1997) Brand valuation: the best thing to ever happen to market research. *Admap* (June), 32–5.

Handley, L. (2011) Culture of openness gets the thumbs up, *Marketing Week*, 4 August, retrieved from http://www.marketingweek.co.uk/culture-of-openness-gets-the-thumbs-up/3028969.article, accessed 21 January 2013.

Jackson, A. and Feld, A. (2011) Domino's 'Brutally Honest' ads offset slow consumer spending, retrieved 17 October 2011 from www.Businessweek.com/news/2011-10-17.

Kapferer, J.-N. (2012) *The New Strategic Brand Management*, London: Kogan Page.

Keller, K.L. (1998) *Strategic Brand Management: Building, Measuring, and Managing Brand Equity*, Upper Saddle River, NJ: Prentice-Hall.

Keller, K.L. (2008) *Strategic Brand Management: Building, Measuring and Managing Brand Equity*, Pearson Education: NY/Englewood Cliffs.

Keynote (2011) Market Report Plus 'Restaurants'.

Kotler, P. (2000) *Marketing Management: The Millennium Edition*, Upper Saddle River, NJ: Prentice-Hall.

Lasser, W., Mittal, B. and Sharma, A. (1995) Measuring customer based brand equity, *Journal of Consumer Marketing*, 12(4), 11–19.

Lencastre de, P. and Côrte-Real, A. (2010) One, two, three: A practical brand anatomy, *Brand Management*, 17, 6, 399–412.

Liddle, A. (2009) Pizza Hut franchise urges Yum to strengthen brand, add value, *Restaurant News*, 23 November 2011, p. 43.

Linville, P. and Carlston, D.E. (1994) Social cognition of the self, in P.G. Devine, D.L. Hamilton and T.M. Ostrom (eds), *Social Cognition: Impact on Social Psychology*, San Diego: Academic Press, pp. 143–93.

Lovett, L. (2008) Why the shoe fits, *The Times Luxx Magazine*, p. 22.

Marquardt, A.J., Golicic, S.L. and Davis, D.F. (2011) B2B services branding in the logistics services industry, *Journal of Services Marketing*, 25(1), 47–57.

McCraken, G. (1986) Culture and Consumption: A Theoretical Account of the Structure and Movement of the Cultural Meaning of Consumer Goods, *Journal of Consumer Research*, 13 (June), 71–84.

Miller, R. (1997) Make an event of it, *Marketing*, 5 June, 28.

Mintel (2010) Report: Pizza and Pasta Restaurants (and takeaway), *Leisure Intelligence*, January.

Mintel (2011) Report: Pizza and Pasta Restaurants, *Leisure Intelligence*, January.

Mirzaei, A., Gray, D., and Baumann, C. (2011) Developing a new model for tracking brand equity as a measure of marketing effectiveness, *The Marketing Review*, 11(4), 323–36.

Morgan, R.M., and Hunt, S.D. (1994), 'The commitment–trust theory of relationship marketing', *Journal of Marketing*, 58 (July), 20–38.

Mudambi, S.M., Doyle, P. and Wong, V. (1997) An exploration of branding in industrial markets, *Industrial Marketing Management*, 26, September, 433–46.

Muniz, A. and O'Guinn, T.C. (2001) Brand communities, *Journal of Consumer Research*, 27 (March), 412–32.

Muzellec, L., Lynn, T. and Lambkin, M. (2012) Branding in fictional and virtual environments: introducing a new conceptual domain and research agenda, *European Journal of Marketing*, 46(6), 811–26.

Opati, Z.T. (2009) Fighter Brands: Knee-Jerk Reactions? *African Executive*, 26 May, retrieved 13 December 2011 from www.africanexecutive.com/modules/magazine/articles.php?article=4322.

Oxley, M. and Miller, J. (2000) Capturing the consumer: ensuring website stickiness, *Admap* (July/August), 21–4.

Parsons, R. (2011) Coca-Cola: A history in ads, *Marketing Week*, Friday 6 May, retrieved 9 August 2011 from www.marketingweek.co.uk/sectors/food-and-drink/soft-drinks/coca-cola-a-history-in-ads/3026155.article.

Pennington, J.R. and Ball, A.D. (2009) Customer branding of commodity products: The customer-developed brand, *Brand Management*, 16(7), 455–67.

Petromilli, M., Morrison, D. and Million, M. (2002) Brand architecture: building brand portfolio value, *Strategy and Leadership*, 30(5), 22–8.

Phau, I. and Lau, K.C. (2001) Brand personality and consumer self-expression: Single or dual carriageway?, *Journal of Brand Management*, 8, 6, 428–44.

Pierce, A. and Moukanas, H. (2002) Portfolio power: harnessing a group of brands to drive profitable growth, *Strategy and Leadership*, 30(5), 15–21.

Pirrie, A. (2006) What value brands? *Admap* (October), 40–2.

Pitta, D.A. and Fowler, D. (2005) Online communities and their value to new product developers, *Journal of Product and Brand Management*, 14(5), 283–91.

Reiter, (2009) Profile David Osbourne – Head of Marketing, Stanley Tools, retrieved 10 March 2011 from www.b2bm.base01.co.uk/features.

Revolution (2011) Social Media: The Marmarati, *Revolution Awards*, p. 41.

Rich, M. (1996) Stamp of approval, *Financial Times*, 29 February, p. 9.

Richards, T. (1997) Measuring the true value of brands, *Admap* (March), 32–6.

Riezebos, R. (2003) *Brand Management: A Theoretical and Practical Approach*, Harlow: Pearson.

Ritson, M. (2007) Welcome to the house of brands, *Marketing*, 12 December 2007, 21.

Ritson, M. (2009) Should You Launch a Fighter Brand? *Harvard Business Review*, October, 65–81.

Turland, C., Power, J., Holmes, T., Aston, A., Nealon, D. and Sutton, N. (2009) Stanley Tools – Stanley 'Judgement Day': The Case for Turning Communications Inside-Out, *Institute of Practitioners in Advertising, IPA Effectiveness Awards*. Retrieved 10 March 201, from www.warc.com.

Tutton, M. (2009) Businesses hit back with 'fighter brands', *CNN*, retrieved 13 December 2011 from http://edition.cnn.com/2009/BUSINESS/10/01/fighter.brands.recession/index.html.

Walton, P. (2007) A practical framework for developing brand portfolios, *Admap*, (July/August), 33–5.

Woods, A. (2009) Searching in social circles, *Marketing*, 2 December, 39–41.

# Chapter 12

## Corporate branding and communication

During a period when the reputation and trust held in business and organisations is exceedingly low, it is critical that organisations actively manage their company brands, not just their product- and service-based brands.

Raising and maintaining the profile of an organisation is an integral part of reputation management. This demands continuous attention from all of those in an organisation, not just senior managers, but all employees, and not just those who are customer facing.

Corporate branding and the attendant communications seek dialogue continual with stakeholders which can lead to the development of trust-based relationships. This is necessary in order that stakeholders think and act favourably towards an organisation, and enable the organisation to develop strategies that are compatible with the environment and its own objectives.

### Aims and learning objectives

The aim of this chapter is to consider corporate branding issues and associated communications that are designed to encourage a dialogue with stakeholders, with a view to influencing the image and reputation of the organisation.

The learning objectives of this chapter are to:

1. understand the meaning of the terms 'corporate identity' and 'corporate brand identity';
2. describe the characteristics of each of the building blocks of corporate reputation;
3. explain the meaning and importance of corporate reputation;
4. consider how managing corporate reputation is concerned with minimising the gaps that can appear between the various building blocks;
5. explore some of the ideas and issues associated with the nature of corporate communication;
6. analyse the elements that constitute the corporate communication mix;
7. draw the corporate identity management process framework and appraise ways in which communication can be used to link the various elements.

# Minicase

## The BBC's 'Sachsgate'

Apologising in public has become common practice in recent years, with institutions such as the church, governments and public figures offering apologies for current and past transgressions. Communications scholars advise that an apology, as a crisis response strategy, can maintain an organisation's reputation and restore its image (Benoit 1997). Yet, many corporate apologies are criticised for being insincere (Brown 2000), offered only as a means of avoiding negative media coverage. The public apology therefore carries a high risk, as a weak, late or insincere apology causes further harm to the organisation. This creates something of a reputational dilemma: there is an expectation (often a demand), that an apology will be given, and it can bolster the organisation's reputation to do so. However, once given, that apology is criticised for being an impression management technique (L'Etang, 2008) rather than a sincere attempt to rebuild relationships with stakeholders. This mini case explores the development of a crisis at the BBC and the apologies offered by the corporation as it tried to navigate its way through a crisis that subsequently became known as 'Sachsgate'.

On the evening of 18 October 2008 the BBC aired Russell Brand's Radio 2 programme, co-hosted that night by Brand's friend and fellow TV presenter, Jonathan Ross. At the time they were two of the BBC's highest paid stars. During the programme, Brand and Ross made a series of 'lewd' phone calls to *Fawlty Towers* actor Andrew Sachs, leaving answerphone messages about Brand's relationship with the actor's grand-daughter, Georgina Baillie. With 'strong' language and 'crude' content, these messages were broadcast to 2 million listeners, and were available to listen to again on the BBC iPlayer website. It was subsequently revealed that the programme had been pre-recorded and approved for broadcast by senior BBC executives.

So began a reputational crisis for the BBC. In the immediate period following the broadcast, the BBC received three complaints. One was a complaint on behalf of Sachs (from his agent) and two further complaints objected to Ross's on-air swearing.

The turning point in the crisis came eight days later, when, on 26 October, the *Mail on Sunday* covered the story of the 'prank calls', suggesting that the BBC could face prosecution (it is a criminal offence in the UK to make abusive phone calls). The media coverage focused on the fact that this was not a 'live' broadcast of Brand's programme but was pre-recorded two days prior to airing, and was cleared for broadcast by the BBC, with the warning, 'The next programme contains some strong language which some listeners may find offensive.'

As a consequence of the *Mail's* coverage, the BBC reported a deluge of complaints: 1,585 by 9 a.m. on 27 October; 4,772, the next morning, rising to over 10,000 by the end of that day. By 30 October, the BBC had received 37,500 complaints about the programme (BBC figures). This delayed public response, over a week after the broadcast, prompted Oasis guitarist Noel Gallagher, a frequent guest on Brand's programme, to comment on Radio Ulster, 'It's so typical of the English – 10,000 people get outraged, but only five days after it happened.'

The BBC issued its first apology on 27 October, stating: 'We recognise that some of the content broadcast was unacceptable and offensive', and that they 'would like to sincerely apologise to Mr. Sachs for the offence caused'. In addition, they stated: 'We also apologise to listeners for any offence caused' (bbc.co.uk).

The BBC did not, in this statement, apologise for the act itself (i.e. the approval and broadcasting of the programme) but for the offence caused, shifting the emphasis on to the listeners (for being offended) rather than the BBC (for making a mistake). There is no acceptance of responsibility or blame, which is a compulsory component of an apology (Harris, Grainger and Mullany 2006) and the lateness of the statement suggested a reluctance to apologise. A more personal apology was issued by the BBC Director General, Mark Thompson, on 29 October, during which he also announced the suspension of Brand and Ross pending an investigation:

> 'I would like to add my own personal and unreserved apology to Andrew Sachs, his family and to licence fee payers for the completely unacceptable broadcast on BBC Radio 2. BBC audiences accept that, in comedy, performers attempt to push the line of taste. However, this is not a marginal case. It is clear from the views expressed by the public that this broadcast has caused severe offence and I share that view.' (bbc.co.uk)

In this statement some attempt was made to explain or justify the decision to broadcast, corrective action was taken in suspending both stars and a promise was given that 'any lessons will be learnt and appropriate action taken'. By claiming shared views, Thompson signalled inclusiveness with the audience, but there was no direct admission that the BBC had made a mistake. A third apology was issued on 7 November by the BBC Trust's Editorial Standards Committee which included the following admission:

> '. . . It was a serious breach of editorial standards, and should never have been recorded or broadcast. The BBC would like to apologise unreservedly to Mr. Sachs, Ms. Baillie and to our audiences as licence fee payers.' (bbc.co.uk)

For the first time the statement included an explicit reference to the error that caused the crisis, described as a 'breach of editorial standards'. There was also an admission of the BBC's responsibility in recording and broadcasting the programme. The use of the passive voice, however ('it should never have been broadcast'), rather than the active ('we should never have broadcast it') diluted the force of the apology, and the use of 'would like to apologise'

rather than the more direct 'we apologise' appeared tentative and further weakened the apology.

Following the crisis, action was taken by the BBC Trust to avoid a recurrence of events. A list of high-risk radio programmes was compiled, and tougher penalties were introduced for staff not complying with the BBC's editorial guidelines. The crisis had brought the BBC and its two popular presenters into disrepute, attracting condemnation from the public, politicians and the media and resulting in the resignation of two senior BBC managers and the suspension of Brand and Ross. In April 2009 Ofcom, the media regulator, fined the BBC £150,000 for what it considered to be serious failures within the corporation and a breach of the broadcasting code.

*This minicase was written by Beverley Hill, at the Bristol Business School at the University of the West of England.*

*The author wishes to acknowledge the contribution of Kathryn Wilson for collecting case material under the University of Winchester Research Apprentice Scheme.*

| Exhibit 12.1 | **Russell Brand and Jonathan Ross** |
| --- | --- |

*Source*: Claire Greenway/Stringer/Getty Images

# Introduction

Just as the BBC is concerned about the way it presents itself, and justifies its actions when required, most organisations take care to present the company, rather their products, in a way that is acceptable and which reflects their aims, values, and objectives. This chapter is concerned with the way in which organisations like the BBC are presented and perceived, and how they interact with their various stakeholder audiences. It is also concerned with the images that people form as a result of interpreting the various identity signals that organisations convey, and any interaction that may ensue. Melewar (2003) derived the following definition from a consideration of the literature. For him, corporate identity is concerned with 'the set of meanings by which an organisation allows itself to be known and through which it enables people to describe, remember and relate to it'.

All organisations use corporate communication to help deliver their corporate identity and brand. It is through the identity that stakeholders form images of the organisation and, through time, corporate reputations are built. People form images of an organisation based on the cues or signals that organisations transmit. These cues may be sent deliberately or they may be accidental or unintended. Whatever the source, these cues can be critical, because the way they are interpreted shapes the way organisations are regarded and even whether transactions occur. It should be noted that Blombäck and Ramirez-Pasillas (2012) report that there is limited empirical research about how organisations actually determine their corporate brand identity.

Hatch and Schultz (2000) refer to two schools of thought about strategic identity management. The first is the 'visual' school, which is concerned with operational aspects. The second is a 'strategic' school, which is concerned with an organisation's aims and how it positions and distinguishes itself. This demarcation is useful because, not only does it help identify the scope of the topic, but it also shows how identity management, indeed reputation management, has evolved.

Organisations are said to have a personality, a persona that reflects their inner spirit and heart. From this cultural core, identities are developed and presented to the outside world. The management of the corporate identity is vital if the image held of the organisation, by all stakeholders, is to be consistent and accurately represent the organisation's personality (Dowling, 1993).

Gorb (1992) refers to a continuum of differentiation where at one end there is a total loss of personality and at the other end a schizoid position is achieved. The trick is to change with the environment and maintain a differentiated position by providing continuity in the way the identity is represented and perceived. He quotes Shell, whose logo, established over a century ago, appears to have been preserved unchanged. In reality, however, the Shell logo has undergone many changes and what we see today is nothing like the original. This has occurred through careful continuity of the idea of the seashell and adaptation of it to the various contexts through time.

There are a number of identity-related topics, including visual identity, strategic corporate identity, social identity and organisational identity (He and Balmer, 2007). These are set out at Table 12.1.

Although He and Balmer separate the visual and strategic forms of corporate identity, these are often considered to be part of the same area of study. The social and organisational forms of identity are part of the organisational behaviour school of thought, and assume a different, organisational behaviour perspective. However, although there is evidence to suggest that the organisational and corporate identity schools are beginning to overlap (Cornelissen et al., 2007; Anisimova, 2007), this chapter concentrates on corporate identity that encapsulates a marketing orientation and both the visual and strategic perspectives.

| Table 12.1 | Perspectives on identity schools of thought | |
| --- | --- | --- |

| Form of identity | | Explanation |
| --- | --- | --- |
| Corporate identity | Visual | Using visual expression for organisational self-presentation. |
| | Strategic | Using an organisation's characteristics, traits and attributes as cues to express how an organisation wants to be seen. |
| Social identity | | How members see themselves as a social part of the organisation. |
| Organisational identity | | The identity of an organisation as perceived by the members. |

# Corporate identity or corporate branding?

Before proceeding it is worth establishing the differences between product and corporate branding. Although some argue that the two are intrinsically the same and it is only the implementation and context that differ, there is a generally held view that corporate and product brands are different. Anisimova (2007) suggests that corporate branding represents a blend of the perspectives held by the corporate identity and the organisational theorists. Balmer and Gray (2003) set out several differences and these are presented in Table 12.2.

Some researchers, authors and marketing practitioners prefer the term 'corporate branding' and are using it to replace the expression 'corporate identity'. Balmer (1998) suggested that corporate identity was the accepted terminology in the 1980s and early 1990s, and that this gave way to corporate branding at the turn of the century. However, it can be argued that there are some intrinsic differences in this terminology. Balmer and Gray (2003) claim that there are strong and fundamental differences between these two concepts. Bernstein (1984) makes an important point when he observes that all organisations have an identity, whether they like it or not. Some organisations choose deliberately to manage their identities, just as individuals

| Table 12.2 | Differences between product and corporate brands | |
| --- | --- | --- |

| | Product brand | Organisation brand |
| --- | --- | --- |
| Focus of attention on . . . | The product | The organisation |
| Managed by . . . | Middle management | CEO/top management |
| Attract attention and gain support of . . . | Customers | Multiple stakeholders |
| Delivered by . . . | Marketing | Whole organisation |
| Communicated by . . . | Marketing communications | Multiple communications, activities, and contacts |
| Time horizon . . . | Short (product life) | Long (organisation life) |
| Importance to organisation . . . | Tactical for function | Strategic for organisation |

*Source*: Adapted from Balmer and Gray (2003). Used with permission.

| Table 12.3 | Corporate brand criteria |
| --- | --- |

| Corporate brand criteria | Explanation |
| --- | --- |
| Rarity | Corporate brand values (functional and emotional) developed over time that cannot be easily imitated. |
| Durability | The value of the brand depreciates slowly, relative to product brands. |
| Inappropriability | Only the owning organisation can derive performance-related outcomes. |
| Imperfect imitability | It is very difficult for a competitor to copy or replicate the brand. |
| Imperfect substitutability | Strong corporate brands maintain their position through continuous improvement and protect themselves from competitors and from being overtaken. |

*Source*: Based on Balmer and Gray (2003).

choose to frequent particular shops or restaurants, drive certain cars or wear specific fabrics or colours. Other organisations take less care over their identities and the way in which they transmit their identity cues, and as a result confuse and mislead members of their networks and underperform in the markets in which they operate. Corporate identity is the way an organisation presents itself to all of its stakeholders. Some organisations actively seek answers and readjust to changing circumstances. Others do not.

If corporate identity is a necessity for all organisations, corporate branding is not. Corporate brands are developed from their identity and, unlike traditional approaches to corporate messages, are primarily concerned with the delivery of specific corporate brand promises. These promises are often conveyed through a short strapline or 'mantra' (Keller, 1999). Balmer and Gray (2003) use Disney and Nike as examples: 'fun, family entertainment' and 'authentic athletic performance' respectively. These straplines might be linked to reputation platforms, or common themes, used by organisations to anchor their communications strategy. These brands are seen to consist of certain criteria, which are set out in Table 12.3.

Balmer and Gray developed these criteria based on the 'resource-based view of the firm', which is grounded in the brand, having considerable resources and capabilities that can be used as a major source of sustainable value. The basis therefore, of a strong corporate brand and its ability to deliver its promise is the organisation's ability to continually leverage its resources to deliver superior value. Not all organisations need a corporate brand, if, for example, they are a public utility, monopoly or work in commodities. Even though this area is of increasing interest to academics and organisations, issues concerning the development and criticality of corporate reputation appear to be of greater importance to organisations.

So should we be concerned with corporate identity or corporate branding? The answer is both. There are many forms of identity but corporate identity involves how an organisation chooses to define its core characteristics (Cornelissen et al., 2007): that is, communicate answers to questions such as 'what are we?' and 'what do we do?' This requires a multidisciplinary perspective involving legal, economic and stakeholder viewpoints of contemporary organisations (Balmer, 2008).

Corporate branding is concerned with how an organisation chooses to deliberately emphasise specific features and values that are to be associated with a corporate brand, and to represent the company and its market offering. The goal is to foster a specific corporate 'brand' image. Balmer and Greyser (2002) refer to this as 'corporate brand identity', a term that is used frequently by many academics, and is used throughout the rest of this chapter. In answer to the question therefore, corporate brands are a complex, and extended form of corporate identity.

# The building blocks of corporate reputation

Abratt and Shee (1989) have identified three main elements that are central to the development of corporate image. These are corporate personality, corporate identity/brand and corporate image. Individuals and organisations project their personalities through their identity. The identity is communicated through corporate communication that includes symbolism, behaviour and marketing communications.

An audience's perception of the identity/brand becomes the image they have of the object, in this case, the corporate body. Through time and accumulated contacts with an organisation, these images coalesce into a reputation, a disposition which individuals attribute to an organisation.

An organisation's reputation has twin perspectives. The first is the more obvious external view, the view held by stakeholders, customers, shareholders, communities, regulators, among others. The second, and more recent perspective, incorporates employees, an internal view. As explored later in the text (Chapter 13), employee attitudes ultimately impact upon the external perspective of a brand. Associations can be made between the two perspectives and any gaps between the two can be identified.

So, the terms 'corporate personality', 'identity/brand', 'image', and 'communication' are interlinked and are to some degree, mutually interdependent. Together these elements can be considered to constitute the building blocks of corporate reputation. Figure 12.1 sets out a visual interpretation of these building blocks, although the linear depiction should not be taken at face value.

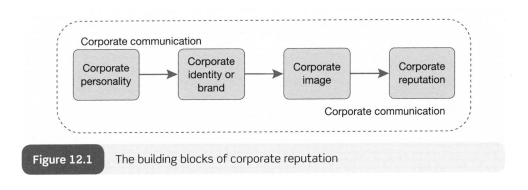

**Figure 12.1**    The building blocks of corporate reputation

# Corporate personality

Sometimes referred to as the *corporate character*, corporate personality is concerned with the core nature of an organisation, its natural poise. Corporate personalities are derived partly from the cultural characteristics of the organisation: the core values and beliefs that in turn are part of a corporate philosophy. Essential to corporate personality is the strategy process adopted by the organisation. The degree to which the strategic process is either formalised and planned, or informal and emergent, and whether a strategy is well communicated, play major roles in shaping the personality of the organisation.

So, although there are many facets that make up the corporate personality, two key ones can be identified: the dominant corporate culture and the processes through which strategy is developed (Markwick and Fill, 1997). These facets are interrelated.

Organisational culture is a composite of the various sectional interests and drives held by various key members. The blend of product offering, facilities, values and beliefs, staff, structure, skills and systems leads to the formation of particular characteristics or traits. Traits are rarely uniform in their dispersal throughout an organisation, so the way in which these interests are bound together impacts upon the form of the primary culture.

The powerful influence that an organisation's corporate objectives have in informing and guiding the operations of each of the functional departments is now understood. The formulation of the mission statement requires management and employees to understand what the organisation seeks to achieve. To understand what the organisation wants to achieve requires understanding what the organisation values and believes in, which in turn involves and reflects the involvement of all members of the organisation, either deliberately or involuntarily. Indeed, the stated philosophy and values that are articulated through the mission statement (and other devices) are important in establishing the preferred relationship it has with its various constituencies (Leuthesser and Kohli, 1997).

---

### Viewpoint 12.1    Changing personality: growing corporate culture

IKEA is a distinctly Swedish company and has three distinct features; function, quality, and low price. These are used to develop product ranges that are said to reflect its Swedish heritage and which inform of IKEA values and the IKEA culture. Part of its culture is grounded in doing things differently. For example, it started as a catalogue marketing company which was combined with a showroom so that customers could see and touch IKEA products. A huge retail store was opened in Stockholm in the 1960s so that customers could pick the products they wanted, directly from the shelves themselves. In doing so IKEA switched a problem of capacity into a new way of delivering products to their customers – the warehouse principle.

IKEA has an informal, unassuming culture, where cost-consciousness and responsibility are paramount. IKEA's corporate strategy is influenced by its culture.

Samsung's rise from a low-cost original equipment manufacturer to world leader and a brand worth more than Pepsi, American Express or Nike has required a change in corporate culture. So, in order to embark on a growth strategy in the 1990s the company needed to become agile, innovative, and creative. To do this, it needed to break with its then inward-facing culture and cautious business strategy. Accordingly, Samsung utilised some Western best practices concerning strategy formulation, financing, market dynamics (pricing) and compensation. These were integrated into Samsung's existing business model. For example, rather than perpetuate the current compensation system where the more senior staff got paid the most, differential pay was introduced, dependent on performance, as used on schemes run at Hewlett Packard and General Electric

Global growth required Samsung to break away from the status quo and start to use non-Koreans in non-Korean contexts. Selected South Korean staff were sent abroad to learn a language, become immersed in the country and to learn about its practices and culture. This has led to longstanding relationships and networks upon which business was later established. Non-Koreans were also recruited, bringing with them new styles and methods of working.

*Source:*    Based on Khanna et al. (2011); Nayar (2010); Kling and Goteman (2003).

---

**Question:**    To what extent should a country culture, or any other regional culture, be successfully 'copied and pasted' into organisations in different countries?

**Task:**    Choose a multinational organisation and determine the dominant culture.

| Exhibit 12.2 | **IKEA culture** |
| --- | --- |
| | *Source*: Oleg Goloynev/Shutterstock.com |

The second main element within corporate personality concerns the strategic processes adopted by an organisation. Note that this is about the processes by which strategy develops, not the strategy itself. Processes are relatively constant because the roots of a process are embedded within the spectrum of organisational activities. Changing the strategic process is very different from changing the content of a strategy. Stuart (1999a) refers specifically to the contribution the organisational structure can make to an organisation's corporate identity. Interestingly, she considers Mintzberg and Quinn's (1988) typology of organisational structures, and from this states that structure impacts on strategy, which in turn informs the identity process.

### Scholars' paper 12.1    The stars are a vision, culture, and image

**Hatch, M.J. and Schultz, M. (2001) Are the Strategic Stars Aligned for Your Corporate Brand?** *Harvard Business Review*, **79(2), February, 128–34.**

One of many significant papers on corporate branding, this one is based on empirical research that determines the importance of vision, culture and image when building strong corporate brands.

Corporate personality is the totality of the characteristics that identify an organisation. Consider the values held by organisations such as Carrefour, Apple, UBS, the NHS, the Red Cross, M&S and Samsung. Not only are the images different but so are the values and the personalities.

The BBC and Channel 5 are interesting organisations to consider from a personality perspective. The BBC is a mature organisation where stability, security and reliability have long been regarded as important characteristics. However, these are now regarded by some as impediments to progress and innovation, not helped by the events surrounding the Savile affair and the Hutton inquiry. Channel 5 is young and vibrant, where programme quality is measured differently from the BBC and where innovation is seen as an important part of challenging the rules of standard broadcasting.

Corporate personality is what an organisation actually is.

# Corporate identity

As considered earlier, corporate brand identity is about the cues an organisation uses, deliberately or by default, to shape the way it wants to be perceived. Identity is about how it presents itself to both internal and external stakeholders. As Otubanjo et al. (2010: 157) phrase it, 'Corporate identity is the planned presentation of a firm's internal personality, corporate culture, business behaviour, structure and strategy to stakeholders . . . and can be communicated formally and informally.'

According to Olins (1989), management of corporate identity can communicate three key ideas to its audiences. These are what the organisation is, what it does and how it does it. Identity therefore provides a mechanism by which an organisation can differentiate and position itself with regard to other organisations, and impact on the achievement of its performance goals. As noted earlier, organisations that actively manage their identities might extend their identity into the development of a corporate brand. Brands are promises that serve to differentiate an organisation and provide stakeholders with associations that represent added value and competitive advantage.

When considering the development of a corporate brand, the stewardship dimension also needs to be considered. This refers to the degree of importance that a company places on the development and maintenance of a corporate brand. The steward of a corporate brand identity is responsible for the consistency of the brand, in terms of the way it is presented, and for the way in which external members develop their images of the organisation. Consider the way Michael O'Leary stewards the Ryanair brand and compare his approach to that of Mark Zuckerberg at Facebook, or Meg Witman at HP.

Much of this is an external perspective on identity, whereas much of the organisational behaviour literature sees identity as embedded within the organisation, an internal view. This therefore refers to the organisational identity school of thought, not corporate identity, which belongs to the marketing school. With organisational identity it is employees who are considered to have a sense of identity and who are responsible for projecting their group identity, to non-members, those outside the organisation. Organisational identity theorists believe identity develops through feelings about what is central, distinctive and enduring (Albert and Whetten, 1985) about the character of the organisation, and is drawn from the personality (see Chapter 13 for greater detail).

# Corporate image

Bernstein (1984) observes that 'the image does not exist in the organisation but in those that perceive the organisation'. Corporate image is concerned with the perception that different audiences have of an organisation and results from the audience's interpretation and meaning that they ascribe to the identity cues presented by an organisation.

The images stakeholders hold of an organisation are a result of a combination of different elements, but are essentially a distillation of the values, beliefs and attitudes that an individual or organisation has of an organisation. The images held by members of a marketing channel, a regulatory body, or employees, for example, may vary according to their individual experiences, and will almost certainly be different from those that management thinks exist. This means that an organisation does not have a single image, but may have multiple images.

This suggests that an organisation cannot change its image in a directly managed way, but it can change its identity. It is through the management of its identity that an organisation can influence the image held of it.

Corporate images are shaped by stakeholder interpretations of the identity cues they perceive at an individual level. These cues are the identity signals transmitted by an organisation, either planned and timed or accidental, often unknown to the organisation and very often unwelcome. Planned corporate communication reflected through symbolism, various types of planned communication and behaviour, are accompanied by unplanned communications such as those generated by competitors, through word-of-mouth and the personal experiences and memories held by an individual (Cornelissen, 2000).

For an image to be sustainable, the identity cues around which the image is fashioned must be based on reality and reflect the values and beliefs of the organisation. Images can be consistent, but are often based on a limited amount of information. Images are prone to the halo effect, whereby stakeholders shape images based on a small amount of information. The strategic credibility of Ryanair may be based largely on the image of Michael O'Leary rather than the current financial performance of the low-cost airline's actual strategies. Stakeholders extrapolate that Michael O'Leary has a high reputation for business success, so anything to do with Michael O'Leary is positive and likely to be successful.

## Dimensions of corporate image

The images that stakeholders have of organisations are important for many reasons. The main ones are listed in Table 12.4, where it can be observed that the dimensions of corporate image are quite diverse.

The relational dimension refers to the exchange of attitudes and perceptions with stakeholders of the organisation itself. As will be seen later, organisations consider who they are and what they would like to be, and then project identity cues to those stakeholders who it is believed need to be informed. A more advanced understanding then allows for the adaptation of the organisation based on the feedback or the dialogue thus created.

Management also benefits from corporate identity programmes as they encourage senior staff to reflect on the organisation's sense of purpose and then provide a decision framework for the decisions that management and others, perhaps functional managers, follow.

The final dimension refers to the advantages that a strong positive identity can give products and services. It is possible to develop more effective and efficient promotional programmes by focusing on an organisation's distinctiveness and then allowing for the ripple to wash over the variety of offerings. Banks have traditionally used this approach, and car manufacturers have also partially attempted this strategy. Although the car marque (brand) is a very important decision determinant (e.g. BMW, Audi, Honda, VW, Toyota), it is common for particular models within the marque to be featured heavily.

| Table 12.4 | Dimensions of corporate image |
| --- | --- |

| Image dimension | Elements of perception |
| --- | --- |
| Relational | Government, local community, employees, network members. |
| Management | Corporate goals, decision-making, knowledge, understanding. |
| Product | Product endorsement and support, promotional distinctiveness, competitive advantages. |

Apart from a positive relationship between reputation and corporate performance, the principal reasons for managing corporate identity are to make clear to all stakeholders what the values and beliefs of the organisation are and how it is striving to achieve its objectives. In addition, a strong reputation provides better opportunities to develop lasting relationships with key stakeholder groups and improved access to resources. There are a number of secondary benefits, but these distil down to creating a supportive environment for the offerings, employees and external stakeholders associated with the organisation. Finally, a strong reputation can provide some protection should an organisation encounter environmental turbulence or crisis.

Corporate image is how internal and external stakeholders perceive the organisation.

---

**Scholars' paper 12.2**    **Well, is it employers' or internal branding?**

Foster, C., Punjaisri, K. and Cheng, R. (2010) Exploring the relationship between corporate, internal and employer branding, *Journal of Product & Brand Management*, 19(6), 401–9.

In addition to providing helpful information and background insight, this paper provides an interesting and useful perspective on the characteristics, and issues associated with three different forms of branding. These are corporate, employer and internal branding, and the authors seek to synthesise all three through a single framework.

---

# Corporate reputation

Corporate reputation is a collective term referring to all stakeholders' views of corporate reputation, including identity and image (see Fombrun, 1996; Hatch and Schultz, 1997; Balmer, 1998; Davies and Miles, 1998).

A deeper set of images constitute what is termed 'corporate reputation'. This concept refers to an individual's reflection of the historical and accumulated impacts of previous identity cues fashioned in some cases by near or actual transactional experiences. It is much harder and takes a lot longer to change reputation, whereas images may be influenced quite quickly. The latter are more transient and the former more embedded (Markwick and Fill, 1997).

This view of reputation, that image is different from reputation, is regarded as part of the 'differentiated' school of thought, but is a view not held by all writers. Gotsi and Wilson (2001) argue that, although in the minority, authors such as Kennedy (1977) see the two terms as having the same meaning, while authors such as Alvesson (1998), Dichter (1985) and Dutton et al. (1994) regard the terms as interchangeable. The view held here is that they are not interchangeable but interrelated, if only because reputations are developed through time, whereas images can be instantaneous and relatively superficial.

A strong reputation is considered strategically important for four main reasons:

- it is a primary means of differentiation when there is little difference at product level;
- it is a support facility during times of turbulence and as a measure of corporate value (Greyser, 1999);
- the effect on a company's share price, perhaps as much as 15 per cent (Cooper, 1999);
- the higher the quality of customer relationships, the higher the reputation afforded the organisation (Broon, 2007).

In a survey reported by Gray (2000) the importance of a company's reputation was regarded by 1,005 CEOs consulted to be either important or very important. Fombrun (1996) claims that, in order to build a favourable reputation, four attributes need to be developed. These are credibility, trustworthiness, reliability and responsibility. Using these criteria it may be possible to speculate about the reputation developed by a company such as Samsung, the largest mobile phone manufacturer. Credibility is established through its range of products, which are perceived to be of high quality and branded. Trustworthiness has been developed through attention to customer service and support. Reliability and consistency have been achieved by setting and adhering to particular standards of quality, and responsibility is verified through a strong orientation to service and values manifested through the company's strong product development and innovation policy.

Reputation itself is developed through a number of variables. Greyser (1999) suggests that the key drivers are competitive effectiveness, market leadership, customer focus, familiarity/favourability, corporate culture and communications. It is the combination of these elements that drives corporate reputation. However, he states that the most important dimension impacting on reputation is the relationship between expectation and action. Whether this be at corporate level or at product/brand level, the brand promise must be delivered if reputation is to be enhanced, otherwise damage to the corporate reputation is most likely.

The recent recession and subsequent debates about CEO remuneration rates demonstrates that the reputation of many corporate brands, particularly but not exclusively related to the financial services sector, can be damaged quite quickly. However, the strength of a brand, and management's flexibility and willingness to be open and transparent with inquisitive stakeholders, appears to determine the extent to which a reputation can be defended.

# Mind the gaps

Gaps can occur at many points between the building blocks and within the reputation management process. For example, there may be differences between what employees think the brand is (identity) and what the external stakeholders such as customers think the brand is (image). There may be a gap between the brand promise and the behaviour of employees, or between management communication and image.

Managing corporate reputation and corporate brands is partly about identifying and continually attempting to minimise the gaps that can emerge between the different building blocks, as expressed through corporate communication. As an example: the image and identity of the Harley-Davidson brand are closely intertwined, giving it an overall strength and reputation that is the envy of many other organisations. This brand showcases the co-creation of value in the development of a formidable brand equity, which signifies that consumers themselves are simultaneously constructing and developing the corporation's reputation.

The gap between organisational image and identity, often uncovered during research, determines the nature of the communications task. A communications strategy is required to address all matters of structure and internal communications and the conflicting needs of different stakeholders so as to produce a set of consistent messages, all within the context of a coherent corporate identity programme. The British Broadcasting Corporation (BBC) changed its identity partly as a means of enabling it to compete more effectively in an environment that was changing quickly. With the, then, emergence of digital television, the developing international competitive arena and the impending launch of a range of new services it was important that the BBC logo became distinctive and reflected the BBC core values of quality, fairness, accuracy and artistic integrity. The previous visual identity was expensive (four-colour), not suitable for the increasing volumes and range of applications, had become fragmented and was reproduced in an inconsistent manner. In addition, it did not work on digital formats and was technically difficult to integrate with other graphics. The new visual identity signalled changes about the BBC and the culture, attitudes and behaviour of the people who work there.

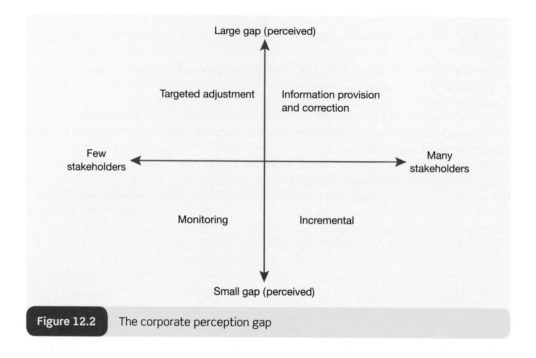

**Figure 12.2**   The corporate perception gap

Analysis of the perceptions and attitudes of stakeholders towards an organisation will often reveal the size of the gap between actual and desired perception. The nature and size of the gap will determine the task and objectives necessary to close the gap. This corporate perception gap may be large or small, depending upon who the stakeholder is. Organisations have multiple images and must develop strategies that attempt to stabilise, and if possible equalise, the images held.

Using a four-cell matrix, as set out at Figure 12.2, where the vertical axis scales the size of the perceived gap and the horizontal axis the number of stakeholders who share the same perception, a series of strategies can be identified. Should a large number of stakeholders be perceived to hold an image of an organisation that is a long way from reality, then a correction strategy is required to communicate the desired position and performance of the focus organisation. Most common of these is the gap between perceived corporate performance and the real performance of the organisation when put in the context of the actual trading conditions.

If a small number of stakeholders perceive a large gap, then a targeted adjustment strategy would be required, aimed at particular stakeholder groups and taking care to protect the correct image held by the majority of stakeholders. For example, some students perceive some financial institutions (e.g. banks) as not particularly attractive for career progression or compatible with their own desired lifestyles. A targeted adjustment strategy would be necessary by the banks to alter this perception in order that they attract the necessary number of high-calibre graduates.

Should research uncover a small number of stakeholders holding a relatively small disparity between reality and image, a monitoring strategy would be appropriate and resources would be better deployed elsewhere. The best position would be if the majority of stakeholders perceived a small difference, in which case a maintenance strategy would be advisable and the good communications continued. The natural extension of this approach is to use it as a base tool in the determination of the communication budget. Funds could be allocated according to the size of the perceived perception gap.

The reasons for the gap do not necessarily rest solely with stakeholders. If the image they hold is incorrect and the organisation's performance is good, then it is poor communications that are to blame, which are the fault of the organisation. If the image is correct and accurately reflects performance, then management must take the credit or the criticism for their performance as managers (Bernstein, 1984).

> ### Scholars' paper 12.3    Reputation: what is it?
>
> **Chun, R. (2005) Corporate reputation: Meaning and measurement, *International Journal of Management Reviews*, 7(2), 91–109.**
>
> Chun reviews terms and issues associated with corporate reputation and the allied constructs of image and identity. She considers some of the confusing terminology and how reputation has and can be measured. Written in an accessible manner, the paper complements the building blocks of reputation approach and covers a wide array of topics. Not to be missed.

# Corporate communication

So far reference has been made to, but no exploration has been made of, the final element of these building blocks – namely, corporate communication. This enables important linkages, integration and coherence between the various activities. It provides for a corporate reputation or branding process to be developed and sustained and is a key instrument through which identities become brands. Corporate communication cues enable stakeholders to form images about the organisation. The rest of this chapter is concerned with corporate communication and its role in developing corporate brands.

According to Ind (1992) corporate communication refers to the process that translates corporate identity/brand into corporate image. As mentioned earlier, increasingly organisations are taking an active interest in corporate branding (Dowling and Moran, 2012; Cowlett, 2000) mainly because of the benefits that can be achieved across the organisation. By attempting to control the messages that it transmits, an organisation can inform and motivate stakeholders concerning what it is, what it does and how it does it in a credible and consistent way.

Organisations convey signals, through the use of a variety of cues, about who they are, what they stand for and their value to stakeholders. The cues can be considered collectively as a corporate communication mix. This is composed of five communication elements. These are symbolic, management, marketing, organisational and behavioural communications. This formulation, presented in Table 12.5, acknowledges the work of both Birkigt and Stadler (1986) and van Riel and Fombrun (2007).

| Table 12.5 | The corporate communication mix |
| --- | --- |

| Form of corporate communication | Explanation |
| --- | --- |
| Symbolic | Communications concerning the visual aspects of an organisation. These encompass names, letterheads, logos, signage, emblems, colour schemes, architecture and the overall appearance of all the design aspects associated with the company. |
| Management | Communications by managers who have a responsibility for the deployment of resources. These communications may be directed to internal or external audiences. |
| Marketing | Communications designed to engage customer-orientated audiences with regard to the promotion of an organisation's products and services. |
| Organisational | Communications aimed at a range of stakeholders, not just customers, that are designed to build identification, commitment and relationships with an organisation, and are not sales-orientated. |
| Behavioural | Communications that that emanate from the interactions, decisions, tone of voice and overall empathy between employees and with others outside the organisation. |

(Based on Birkigt and Stadler (1986); van Riel and Fombrun, 2007).

## Viewpoint 12.2    Communications signal change at MDA

The Magen David Adom (MDA) Society is the Israeli equivalent of the Red Cross.

The organisation supplies instruction in first-aid, pre-hospital emergency medicine, maintains a volunteer infrastructure and trains them in the provision of first-aid and basic and advanced life support, transports patients and women in labour, evacuates people injured in accidents and transports doctors, nurses and medical auxiliary forces.

For a long time communications aimed to present the organisation as a 'hero'. The emphasis was on the organisation as an important life saver. The MDA attempted to build an image that would help it to recruit volunteers, mainly from among high-school students, and in raising blood donations and funds. However, the rise in terrorism activities changed the context in which the MDA operated. Whereas peace and relative calm prevailed previously, the new terrorism context served to disconnect the organisation from the community and show it to be unreliable. This was because the organisation was forced to decrease its ongoing community-related activities, reducing its contact with volunteers, and potential blood donors in order to attend to terrorist incidents. The high frequency of terrorist attacks and the difficulty in adapting to new work routines led the organisation to operate under difficult and unfamiliar conditions. This led to operational difficulties and the provision of some inaccurate reports. When this was exposed, some perceived the MDA to be unprofessional and not doing its job properly.

The MDA needed to communicate more effectively with its stakeholders and management made a strategic decision to change and strengthen the organisation's identity. Management realised people identify more easily with the service providers and their personal stories than with the organisation as a whole. It was, therefore, decided to shift the focus from 'the organisation as a hero' to 'service providers as heroes'. Management decided to adopt an integrated communication strategy to deliver its new 'service profiles as heroes' corporate identity to its internal audiences (workers and volunteers) and to its external audiences (the general public, health funds, governmental agencies and the media) basing this on the characteristics of terrorist events.

New procedures, workshops and newsletters constituted the formal internal communications used to inform all personnel of the organisation's conceptual change and new values. Informal internal communications were encouraged as well. Private employee parties and the celebration of birthdays, marriages, birth of children enhance employees' pride as members of a team and enable its employees to relax, connecting to the personal life stories of other employees, which bond the employees and impart a sense of family. The informal information communicated at these events has helped the MDA build its reputation as a fair and sensitive employer.

Formal external communications are used in two main ways. The Internet allows the organisation to present to the general public its values and mainly the uniqueness of the service provided by each of the organisation's personnel. A television campaign focuses on the importance of contributing funds/money to the organisation. This increases awareness of both present and potential donors and focuses on the organisation's personnel as heroes. It depicts personal stories of employees and volunteers in several areas throughout the country, in order to form a connection between local citizens and the organisation.

PR activities are crucial for MDA's attempts to communicate its values and image. For example, press conferences are held at which the Director General and the spokesperson present journalists with the main findings of the investigations they have conducted and information on actions that were taken in order to better prepare for future terrorist attacks. In addition, immediately after each terrorist event, managers meet representatives of the army, police, fire brigade and heads of local government to share their experience to improve communication and cooperation between the various authorities.

The main form of informal external communications concerns feedback and word-of-mouth communications from citizens. In addition an Israeli TV drama series based on the personal stories of MDA employees before, during and after a terrorist event, with an emphasis on the life of the organisation's employees and volunteers and on their experiences, became popular. This conveys the essence of the organisation to the general public better than extensive communication campaigns have done in the past.

*Source*:  Based on Herstein, Mitki, and Jaffe (2008).

**Question:**   To what extent should television dramas feature as an integral part of an organisation's brand identity?

**Task:**   Select a similar organisation to MDA and consider the effectiveness of their communications using the elements of the corporate communications mix to structure your thoughts.

# Corporate communication mix

## Symbolic communication

Symbolism refers to the visual aspect of identity and was once regarded as the sole aspect of corporate identity management. Salame and Salame (1975) were some of the first researchers to consider visual identity in this way. Indeed, there are many today who regard visual identity as the only real element of corporate identity, mentioned earlier as the visual school of corporate identity. Schein (1985), in his hierarchy of corporate culture, determines 'visible artefacts' as the first level. These are the more immediately observable aspects of the culture, such as the letterheads, logos, signage, emblems, colour schemes, architecture and the overall appearance of all the design aspects associated with the company. Dowling (1994) refers to visual identity and its composition consisting of four key elements: corporate names, logos and symbols, typefaces and colour. It is thought that, through the use of symbolism, a level of harmonisation can be achieved by bringing all of these identity cues together. To these elements should be added architecture and physical location (Melewar et al. (2006)).

### Names

The name of an organisation is a strong corporate cue as it is often people's first contact with an organisation. Company names can be derived through a range of techniques. Employees created the name *Accenture*, which connotes ascent or an emphasis on the future. Computers can be used to generate lists of names, or the use of Latin and Greek words can add a feeling of permanence and distinction. For example, *Altria* expresses 'high performance and constant improvement' and may have been a name chosen to disguise the Philip Morris tobacco business that was at the root of the group's interests in 1985 when the restructuring and renaming occurred. *Novartis* is Latin for 'new skills' and was the name adopted for the healthcare company, following the merger of the Swiss-based life sciences companies, Ciba-Geigy and Sandoz.

Another approach is to shorten the name of the existing organisation into its initials. For example, the Royal and Sun Alliance shrank its name to *RSA* when it embarked on a rebranding exercise.

Names used in the telecommunications sector were for a long time dominated by purely descriptive, functionally oriented titles. In 1994 this started to change when Wolff Olins created the Orange brand for Hutchinson Telecom. Orange offered instant differentiation that also reflected the 'different' service being offered for the first time. Owning a 'colour' offered a sense of exclusivity and allowed for a number of creative advertising opportunities (Murphy, 1999).

Some names need to change as a result of a strategic development, such as when Group 4 merged with Securicor. The new name G4S needed to reflect the dimensions of the new global company and its activities in all markets. Some new company names, such as Accenture, have to be developed quickly. Sims (2008) reports that the Andersen Consulting rebrand into Accenture was achieved in just 147 days. Some new names just do not work, such as the new name for the Post Office 'Consignia', which was rejected by many stakeholder groups for many reasons. Some names just fade if not looked after and refreshed. For example, P&O was found to mean slow, had not moved with the times, lacked investment in people and infrastructure and had strong links to the colonial past. Not surprising then that their new owners, DPWorld, concluded that the P&O name lacked brand equity (Sims, 2008).

## Slogans

One of the strongest mechanisms used to position brands is the slogan. Slogans should complement the strategy and the other visual cues used to position the organisation. For example, 'Blue Ocean' refers to the creation of new markets where previously there was nothing. Nintendo adopted the term internally as it complemented its business strategy. Rather than follow competitors and add faster processors and more violent games, its strategy was to attract new users in different demographic groups, people who hadn't played games before. By using innovative touch-screens, voice activation and motion-sensing technology, the games were less gimmicky, more accessible, easier to play yet equally addictive and resulted in increased numbers of women and middle-age people becoming regular gamers. Nintendo now outsells Microsoft and Sony, and in 2008 its market capitalisation outstripped Sony's.

However, the use of a slogan that fails to reinforce or, worse, contradicts the other messages conveyed by the organisation can lead to either confusion or under-positioning. For example, Stuart and Muzellec (2004) refer to Griffith University in Australia who used the slogan 'Get Smarter' in an advertising campaign. However, they used celebrities such as Bob Geldof and Ray Charles to associate themselves with core values based around social justice and equity. The slogan and the values did not complement each other and this can lead to brand obscurity or unknown positioning.

Slogans are contentious issues and perhaps the only guideline to developing effective slogans is to make them memorable. *Forbes Magazine* (2008) reports an issue of the Strategy & Innovation newsletter which made the point that, in their opinion, the most effective *corporate* catchphrases are sticky. To put it another way, slogans should 'be understandable, memorable and effective in changing thought or behaviour'.

## Logos

The use of logos to encapsulate the values and personality of an organisation and to promote recognition and recall among stakeholders, is both common and well practised. One of the more common problems arises when the designer has a crystal clear understanding of what the logo represents but the meaning is obscure to stakeholders. The use of abstract logos in particular can frequently exacerbate this problem.

The logo is an important brand identifier. In 2011, when energy prices started to soar and energy companies were being criticised for abuse of power, profiteering, and customer neglect, BGas saw the need to change the way their brand was perceived. This they attempted with a new identity, featuring a green leaf-shaped gas flame or ribbon, to reflect the brand's values and range of energy-based products and services. The identity was introduced on a needs basis, no fanfare and no press release . . . all to keep criticism down (Chapman, 2011).

When Peugeot and Citroen merged in 1976, the change was not marked by a new logo, or one of the two being dropped. Both organisations retained their marques and their identities for several years. Melewar et al. (2006) also cite the takeover of Midland Bank by HSBC. The Midland's Griffin logo was retained for several years, enabling stakeholders to transfer their trust to the new company gradually.

Many universities have dropped their official heraldic logos and have developed modern abstract identities in an attempt to be perceived as modern, commercially orientated organisations. This realignment might be said to reflect the changing financial structures as these institutions are required by government to seek a higher proportion of their income from private rather than public sources. Once again the personality of the organisation is reflected in the visual identity.

Some universities adopt dual logos. The abstract, often contemporary logo is used for everyday use on letterheads, Web pages and signage. However, the original, heraldic devices are still used for public events such as graduation ceremonies and the installation of chancellors and vice chancellors. On the one hand, this might be seen as a clever way of meeting the needs of their students without throwing away the credibility, heritage and intellectual associations attached to heraldic devices. On the other hand, however, this might be interpreted as uncertainty about how an organisation wants to be seen or, worse, neglect or poor strategic management on behalf of the owners – namely, the government.

Visual identity is also an important element in an organisation's international strategy and the way in which it wishes to be perceived in different countries and regions. In particular, multinational organisations need to find new ways of identifying themselves as a result of merger, acquisition, technological developments, restructuring and other changes in their various marketplaces (Melewar, 2001).

---

**Viewpoint 12.3**    **Continental and United merge identities**

Continental and United, two of the world's largest airlines merged into one that dwarfed Europe's top carrier, Air France-KLM, and overtook its US rival, the recently merged combination of Delta Air Lines and Northwest. Although both had transatlantic routes, one of the main attractions of this merger was the complementary nature of the two route networks. United was strong across the Pacific to Asia, while Continental had a big presence in southern and eastern USA and Latin America.

In a mature market where competition was tough, price competition severe and costs often too heavy for the revenue streams, many airlines were merging and forming alliances. It was, therefore, not surprising that both sets of shareholders were enthusiastic and supportive of the move, but unions expressed concern about job losses. Some stakeholders were reluctant to abandon United's signature 'tulip' logo. One Boston-based frequent flier, Timothy Jasionowski, even started a campaign to save United's red and blue tulip logo. This was to no avail as the merged airline adopted United's name and Continental's logo of a yellow globe on a blue background, plus much of its senior management team.

United claimed that their new logo represented more than just a visual change. They say the combination of United's name and Continental's globe logo symbolises a bringing-together of the best of each airline to create the world's leading airline. The globe symbolises the combined worldwide network spanning six continents and serving more than 370 global destinations. It also signals United and Continental coming together to form the world's leading airline.

*Source*:   Clark (2010); http://hub.united.com/Videos/Pages/emerging.aspx.

**Question:** In the absence of a clear business strategy, why do you think these symbolic elements were selected in the first place? Was it just to pacify the different shareholders and to get the merger ratified?

**Task:** Identify another airline merger and consider how the symbolic elements of both airlines were managed.

| Exhibit 12.3 | **A United aircraft featuring the Continental logo** |
|---|---|

*Source:* Charles Polidano/Touch the Skies/Alamy Images

## Management communications

Management communicate externally and internally. Their role with external stakeholders is one of representation and negotiation and in doing so they seek to communicate the vision and values of the organisation. In addition to this the CEO has a specific role, one of symbolic leadership. Their views, actions and comments are often regarded by the media and financial markets as particularly significant. For example, Justin King, the CEO of Sainsbury's, a leading supermarket brand, regularly appears in the media for one of two main reasons. The first of these is to answer questions and provide contextual information about his company's performance, and in doing so fulfil the role of strategic leader. The second reason to appear in the media is either to provide expert comment on events in the industry or to make an executive speech. In both these circumstances it is intended that the CEO is perceived as an expert, so providing objectivity and credibility, and enhancing the company's status. These attributes may enhance the perception stakeholders have of Justin King in terms of how trustworthy and reliable he is, which in turn may be transferred to the company.

External management communication is not confined to senior managers as all managers who have external-facing elements to their job communicate with stakeholders, who form images of the organisation as a result of what is said, how it is said and the impact it has on others.

Perhaps the greatest impact of management communications is with employees, internal stakeholders. One of management's key tasks is to enable employees to accomplish the corporate objectives. To do this, management need to agree and then use communications to reinforce corporate values in such a way that they have meaning for employees, who in turn are prepared to work to satisfy them. Communication is an instrumental skill for managers, not only to develop a shared vision but to also strengthen the level of engagement employees have with the organisation. Internal communication (employee branding) issues are explored in more detail later (Chapter 13).

## Marketing communications

The range of activities, tools, media, and messages referred to in this book constitute marketing communications. As indicated in the opening chapter, marketing communications is an audience-centred activity whose role is to engage an organisation's customers with its products, services and brands, and to provoke conversations (Fill, 2009).

The way in which each mix is configured varies according to the nature of the prevailing customer relationship, the task to be achieved and other contextual issues.

## Organisational communications

Organisational communications is the term given by van Riel and Fombrun (2007) to embrace a range of public relations activities. These activities concern public affairs, investor relations, corporate advertising, environmental and sustainability communications and media relations. What is common to these communication activities is that they are targeted at corporate audiences rather than individual consumers. They centre on corporate issues, not products and services, and they are generally focused on seeking agreement, acceptance and the development of relationships.

Chapter 15 explores public relations and the methods and approaches used on behalf of organisational communication.

---

### Viewpoint 12.4    Communicating responsible drinking

The largest distilled spirits producer in the world is Diageo, a British-based multinational corporation which was formed in 1997 through the merger of Grand Metropolitan and Guinness.

One of its immediate tasks was to reverse the downward sales trend of its core brands in the United States.

Readers are referred to the minicase that leads Chapter 7. Here Diageo's marketing strategy designed to re-energise its Smirnoff Vodka brand is documented. This needs to be understood in the context of an environment in which there were increasing regulations designed to control underage drinking.

In parallel to the marketing strategy Diageo used corporate communication – in particular, organisational communication – to influence various external stakeholders that Diageo was committed to deterring underage drinking and other social harms associated with its products. Key stakeholders included policymakers, public health and medical groups, and the public.

Diageo appointed a new head for its marketing public relations division. The appointee was a former advisor to President Clinton, and perhaps more significantly, a former vice president of Philip Morris, who had overseen what were known as the 'tobacco wars'.

Five core strategies were established:

1. *Responsible marketing code*: Diageo established its own responsible marketing code, a self-regulatory structure designed to monitor the company's alcohol advertising. Among other things, this states that the company's advertising must be aimed only at adults and never targeted, placed, or designed to appeal to those younger than the legal purchase age for alcohol.

2. *Responsibility advertising*: Diageo invests nearly 20 per cent of its communications budget each year on 'responsibility' advertisements. These are designed primarily to educate viewers about how to prevent underage drinking and drunk driving. This spend is far greater than any other alcoholic beverage producer.

3. *Responsible drinking fund*: Diageo supports prevention programmes that focus on education, public awareness, and responsible retail practices. The Diageo responsible drinking fund, which has had annual resources of £400,000, provides financial support, and expert advice.

4. *Partnerships*: Diageo builds partnerships with government agencies and medical and public health organisations. The company developed a cooperative approach with governmental agencies and medical groups, a policy which complemented the organisation's extensive political lobbying activities.

5. *'Social aspects' organisations*: Diageo has helped to organise and fund 14 social aspects organisations worldwide. These industry-member organisations sponsor programmes similar to those funded by the Diageo responsible drinking fund and seek to further the goals of the Diageo public relations campaign. For example, organisations such as the Century Council and the International Centre on Alcohol Policy in the United States have been established through this strategy.

*Source*:   Mosher (2012); www.diageo.com/en-row/csr/alcoholinsociety/Pages/programmes.aspx.

**Question:**    To what extent is the responsibility approach a genuine, authentic approach to driving demand?

**Task:**    Read the paper by Mosher and make notes on the techniques he asserts have been used to limit the influence these strategies might have.

### Behavioural communications

The behavioural element is largely concerned with the way in which employees and managers interact with one another and, more importantly, with external members of the organisation. The tone of voice used, the actions and consideration of customer needs by employees, are often represented within a customer service policy, which is an important part of an organisation's interface with various stakeholder groups.

Communication is used to inform stakeholders quickly of episodes concerning products and the organisation. This is normally achieved through the use of visual and verbal messages. However, a broad use can be seen in communicating not only values but also the direction the organisation is taking and notable traits of which the organisation wishes to inform its audiences.

The behaviour exhibited by an organisation has a strong influence on the way it is perceived by stakeholders. Behaviour is manifested in various ways. At one level, the behaviour of employees provides cues about the extent to which individuals support and understand the organisation. Their interactions with stakeholders reveal levels of endorsement, engagement and empathy with audience needs plus their depth of support and association with their company. At another level, behaviour is expressed through the way managers act and the decisions they make.

At a third level, behaviour can be considered in terms of the way CEOs communicate. CEOs represent the public face of an organisation, and their deeds, words and actions can provide insight into its true values. Finally, there are behaviours exhibited by the organisation as a whole, not attributable to particular individuals. These may concern the its level of disclosure concerning financial issues, or its position regarding environmental and sustainability issues.

# A framework for managing corporate brands

Various models have been developed to provide a visual interpretation of the elements involved in corporate identity (Kennedy, 1977; Dowling, 1986; Abratt and Shee, 1989; Stuart, 1999b). These models reflect the development of the subject and the growing integrative nature of

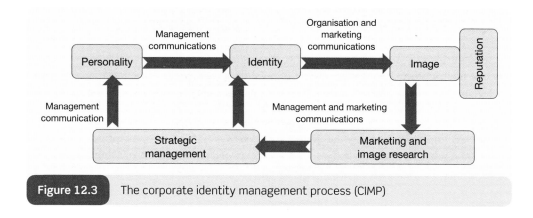

**Figure 12.3** The corporate identity management process (CIMP)

corporate identity within an organisation's overall strategy. One such framework, presented by Markwick and Fill (1997), is entitled the corporate identity management process (CIMP). See Figure 12.3 which incorporates the main elements of the process as identified by Abratt and Shee (1989): corporate personality, corporate identity and corporate image. In order for management to be able to use such a model, there must be understanding of the linkages between the components. Just as the linkages in the value chain determine the extent of competitive advantage that may exist, so the linkages within the corporate identity process need to be understood in order to narrow the gap between reality and perception.

To assist with the linking process, van Riel's (1995) composition of corporate communication is used. These are marketing, management and organisational communications. The first linkage is to interpret, through self-analysis, the corporate personality. This will help those responsible for the management of the corporate identity to have a realistic perception of the corporate personality. This can be assumed to be what management thinks the personality is and the principal method is through management communication.

The second linkage is between corporate identity and the corporate image. In order that stakeholders are able to perceive and understand the organisation, the corporate identity is projected to them. The identity can be projected with orchestrated cues, planned and delivered to a timed schedule, or it can be projected as a series of random, uncoordinated events and observations. In virtually all cases, corporate identity cues are a mixture of the planned (e.g. literature, telephone style and ways of conducting business) and the unplanned (e.g. employees' comments, media views and product failures). The principal linkages are through organisation and marketing communications.

---

**Scholars' paper 12.4**    **Reputation and strategy**

**Dowling, G. and Moran, K. (2012) Corporate Reputations: Built in or bolted on?** *California Management Review,* **54(2), Winter, 25–42.**

Dowling has written a large number of papers and books on corporate reputation, identity and related topics. He and Moran acknowledge the notion that, with better reputations, organisations outperform their rivals. Their review here is about the best way to create a reputation, and they examine the need for reputation to be founded on the company strategy, not just loosely attached.

All organisations communicate all the time; everything they make, do, say or do not say is a form of communication. The totality of the way the organisation presents itself, and is visible, can be called its identity (Olins, 1989). Corporate image is how stakeholders actually perceive the identity. It is, of course, unlikely that all stakeholders will hold the same image at any one point in time. Owing to the level of noise and the different experiences stakeholders have of an organisation, multiple images of an organisation are inevitable (Dowling, 1986). It is important that organisations monitor these images to ensure that the (corporate) position is maintained.

The third linkage is between the image that stakeholders have of an organisation and the corporate strategy formulation and implementation processes that an organisation adopts. This research-based linkage provides feedback and enables the organisation to adjust its personality and its identity, thus affecting the cues presented to stakeholders. Image research is an important method of linking back into the strategy process.

The cues used to project the corporate identity are many and varied; some are controllable and others beyond the reach of management. These cues include the logo and letterheads, the way employees speak of the organisation, the buildings and architecture, the perception of the ability of the organisation to fulfill its obligations, its technical skills, prices, dress code, competitor communications, word-of-mouth and the way the telephone is answered. Of all these and the many others, however, research needs to determine those attributes that key stakeholders perceive as important.

Having determined the important attributes, stakeholders should be asked to evaluate how well the organisation rates on each of them and how well it performs on each attribute in comparison with competitors. Through analysis this provides opportunities to isolate attributes where competitors perform under- or overperform. Effort should then be concentrated on developing either corporate identity or personality in areas where the customer rating is poor and competitor rating is high on a factor that is important.

By understanding the strength of images held by key stakeholders across attributes that are important to them, corrective action can be applied to the personality and cues presented to stakeholders as part of the identity process. Strategic development therefore can result from an understanding of the images held about an organisation by its stakeholders.

For the CIMP framework to be complete, management is required to analyse and interpret the research data and then use corporate communications either to develop the personality or to provide adjusted corporate identity cues for positioning and goal-setting purposes. This is not the only corporate identity framework to have been developed. For example, Stuart (1999b) developed the CIMP idea and offered a composite framework drawing on a variety of models and Balmer and Gray (1999) formulated a new model of the corporate identity–corporate communications process. Each of these has developed our understanding of this subject and extended the breadth and depth of corporate identity, branding and reputation management.

It may be concluded that corporate identity is not a peripheral tool to be used ad hoc, but is a component that is central to the strategic management process. It should be used regularly by managers to understand how the organisation is being interpreted and understood by different stakeholders and to understand the essence of the organisation and whether the symbolic, behavioural and communication cues are contextually appropriate. Managing an organisation's identity and reputation is a complex, variable and necessary aspect of developing stakeholder relationships in the twenty-first century.

# Key points

- Corporate identity is concerned with the set of meanings by which an organisation allows itself to be known and through which it enables others to describe, remember and relate to it. There are various forms of identity, one of which is a corporate brand.

- Corporate brands are developed from their identity and, unlike traditional approaches to corporate messages, are primarily concerned with the delivery of specific corporate promises. The term 'corporate brand identity' is used here to refer to the brand variant of identity.

- Corporate brands are a complex form of identity but not all organisations need a corporate brand, if, for example, they are a public utility, monopoly or work in commodities.

- The terms 'corporate personality', 'identity/brand', 'image', and 'communication' together constitute the building blocks of corporate reputation. Each of these elements has particular characteristics but to function they need to be considered as interlinked elements and are mutually interdependent.

- Corporate personality is concerned with the core nature of an organisation, its natural poise. Corporate personalities are derived partly from the cultural characteristics of the organisation.

- Corporate brand identity refers to the cues an organisation uses, deliberately or by default, to shape the way it wants to be perceived. Branding is about how an organisation presents itself to both internal and external stakeholders in order to differentiate itself and add value.

- Corporate image is concerned with the perception that different audiences have of an organisation and results from the audience's interpretation and meaning they ascribe to the identity cues presented by that organisation.

- 'Corporate reputation' refers to an individual's reflection of the historical and accumulated impacts of previous brand identity cues fashioned in some cases by near or actual transactional experiences. It is much harder and takes a lot longer to change reputation, whereas images may be influenced quite quickly.

- A strong reputation is considered strategically important, for three main reasons: as a primary means of differentiation when there is little difference at product level, as a support facility during times of turbulence and as a measure of corporate value.

- 'Corporate communication' refers to the processes that not only translate corporate identity/brand into corporate image, but also link together the building blocks.

- Managing corporate reputation and corporate brands is partly about identifying and continually attempting to minimise the gaps that can emerge between the different building blocks.

- The corporate communication mix is composed of five communication elements. These are symbolic, management, marketing, organisational and behavioural communications.

- The corporate identity management process (CIMP) depicts the way management use different forms of corporate communication to interlink the building blocks of reputation.

- In order for management to be able to use such a model there must be understanding of the linkages between the components. Just as the linkages in the value chain determine the extent of competitive advantage that may exist, so the linkages within the corporate identity management process need to be understood in order to narrow the gap between reality and perception.

# Review questions

1. Explain what a corporate brand is. How does it differ from a product brand?

2. Discuss the characteristics of corporate branding and corporate identity. How are they related?

3. What are the building blocks of corporate reputation? What might be the building blocks of the BBC?

4. What are the main facets of the BBC's corporate personality?

5. Describe the personality or defining characteristics of five organisations. What are their distinctive differences?

6. What is the role of corporate communication?

7. Suggest ways in which planned and unplanned corporate identity cues are presented to stakeholders. Use an organisation with which you are familiar to illustrate your answer.

8. What are the elements that make up the corporate communication mix?

9. What is corporate image and how does it differ from corporate identity and corporate reputation?

10. Draw the CIMP model, paying particular attention to the linkages between the components

# References

Abratt, R. and Shee, P.S.B. (1989) A new approach to the corporate image management, process, *Journal of Marketing Management*, 5(1), 63–76.

Albert, S. and Whetten, D.A. (1985) Organisational identity, in *Research in Organizational Behavior* (eds L.L. Cummings and B.M. Straw), Greenwich, CT: JT Press, 239–95.

Alvesson, M. (1998) The business concept as a symbol, *International Studies of Management and Organisation*, 28(3), 86–108.

Anisimova, T.A. (2007) The effects of corporate brand attributes on attitudinal and behavioral consumer loyalty, *Journal of Consumer Marketing*, 24(7), 395–405.

Balmer, J.M.T. (1998) Corporate identity and the advent of corporate marketing, *Journal of Marketing Management*, 14(8), 963–96.

Balmer, J.M.T. (2008) Identity based views of the corporation: insights from corporate identity, organisational identity, social identity, visual identity and corporate image, *European Journal of Marketing*, 42(9–10), 879–906.

Balmer, J.M.T. and Gray, E.R. (1999) Corporate identity and corporate communications: creating a competitive advantage, *Corporate Communications; An International Journal*, 4(4), 171–6.

Balmer, J.M.T. and Gray, E.R. (2003) Corporate brands: what are they? What of them? *European Journal of Marketing*, 37(7/8), 972–97.

Balmer, J.M.T. and Greyser, S.A. (2002) Managing the multiple identities of the corporation, *California Management Review*, 44(3), 72–86.

BBC news coverage available from http://news.bbc.co.uk/1/hi/entertainment/7694989.stm (Accessed 14.06.2011).

Benoit, W.L. (1997) 'Image Repair Discourse and Crisis Communication', *Public Relations Review*, 23, 2, pp. 177–86.

Bernstein, D. (1984) *Company Image and Reality: A Critique of Corporate Communications*, London: Holt, Rinehart and Winston.

Birkigt, K. and Stadler, M.M. (1986) *Corporate Identity, Grundlagen, Funktionen, Fallspielen*, Landsberg am Lech, Verlag Moderne Industrie.

Blombäck, A. and Ramýrez-Pasillas, M. (2012) Exploring the logics of corporate brand identity formation, *Corporate Communications: An International Journal*, 17(1), 7–28.

Broon, P.S. (2007) Relationship outcomes as determinants of reputation, *Corporate Communications: An International Journal*, 12(4), 376–93.

Brown, R. (2000) 'Contrition Chic', *Public Relations Review*, 26, 4, 517–20.

Chapman, M. (2011) British Gas set to launch modern brand identity, *Marketing*, 5 October, pp. 1 and 13.

Chun, R. (2005) Corporate reputation: Meaning and measurement, *International Journal of Management Reviews*, 7(2), 91–109.

Clark, A. (2010) United and Continental merge to create world's biggest airline, the *Guardian*, Friday 17 September, retrieved Tuesday 1 February 2012 from http://www.guardian.co.uk/business/2010/sep/17/united-continental-merger-agreement?INTCMP=SRCH.

Cooper, A. (1999) What's in a name? *Admap*, 34(6), 30–2.

Cornelissen, J. (2000) Corporate image: an audience centred model, *Corporate Communications: An International Journal*, 5(2), 119–25.

Cornelissen, J., Haslam, S.A. and Balmer, J.M.T. (2007) Social identity, organisational identity and corporate identity: towards an integrated understanding of processes, patternings and products, *British Journal of Management*, 18(1) (March), 1–16.

Cowlett, M. (2000) Buying into brands, *PR Week*, 24 November, p. 13.

Davies, G. and Miles, L. (1998) Reputation management: theory versus practice, *Corporate Reputation Review*, 2, 1, 16–27.

Dichter, E. (1985) What's in an image? *Journal of Consumer Marketing*, 2, 75–81.

Dowling, G.R. (1986) Measuring your corporate images, *Industrial Marketing Management*, 15, 109–15.

Dowling, G.R. (1993) Developing your company image into a corporate asset, *Long Range Planning*, 26(2), 101–9.

Dowling, G.R. (1994) *Corporate Reputations: Strategies for Developing the Corporate Brand*, London: Kogan Page.

Dowling, G. and Moran, K. (2012) Corporate Reputations: Built in or bolted on? *California Management Review*, 54(2), Winter, 25–42.

Dutton, J.E., Dukerich, J.M. and Harquail, C.V. (1994) Organisational images and member identification, *Administrative Science Quarterly*, 39, 239–63.

Fill, C. (2009) *Marketing Communications: interactivity, communities and content*, Harlow: FT/Prentice Hall.

Fombrun, C. (1996) *Reputation: Realising Value from the Corporate Image*, Cambridge, MA: Harvard Business School Press.

Forbes Staff (2008) Slogans That Work, *Forbes Magazine*, 7 January, retrieved 23 March 2011 from http://www.forbes.com/forbes/2008/0107/099.html.

Foster, C., Punjaisri, K. and Cheng, R. (2010) Exploring the relationship between corporate, internal and employer branding, *Journal of Product & Brand Management*, 19(6), 401–9.

Gorb, P. (1992) The psychology of corporate identity, *European Management Journal*, 10(3) (September), 310–13.

Gotsi, M. and Wilson, A.M. (2001) Corporate reputation: seeking a definition, *Corporate Communications: an International Journal*, 6(1), 24–30.

Gray, R. (2000) The chief encounter, *PR Week*, 8 September, 13–16.

Greyser, S.A. (1999) Advancing and enhancing corporate reputation, *Corporate Communications: An International Journal*, 4(4), 177–81.

Harris, S., Grainger, K. and Mullany, L. (2006) 'The pragmatics of political apologies', *Discourse & Society*, 17(6), 715–37.

Hatch, M.J. and Schultz, M. (1997) Relations between organizational culture, identity and image, *European Journal of Marketing*, 31(5), 356–65.

Hatch, M.J. and Schultz, M. (2000) Scaling the Tower of Babel: relational differences between identity, image and culture in organisations, in *The Expressive Organisation: Linking Identity, Reputation and the Corporate Brand* (eds M. Schultz, M.J. Hatch and M.H. Larsen), Oxford: Oxford University Press.

Hatch, M.J. and Schultz, M. (2001) Are the Strategic Stars Aligned for Your Corporate Brand? *Harvard Business Review*, February, 128–34.

He, H.-W., and Balmer, J.M.T. (2007) Identity studies: multiple perspectives and implications for corporate level marketing, *European Journal of Marketing*, 41(7/8), 765–85.

Herstein, R., Mitki, Y. and Jaffe, E.D. (2008) Corporate Image Reinforcement in an Era of Terrorism through Integrated Marketing Communication, *Corporate Reputation Review*, 11, 4, 360–370.

Ind, N. (1992) *The Corporate Image: Strategies for Effective Identity Programmes*, London: Kogan Page.

Keller, K.L. (1999) Brand mantra: rationale, criteria and examples, *Journal of Marketing Management*, 15(1–3) (January–April), 43–51.

Kennedy, S. (1977) Nurturing corporate images, *European Journal of Marketing*, 11(3), 120–64.

Khanna, T., Song, J. and Lee, K. (2011) The Paradox of Samsung's Rise, *Harvard Business Review*, July–August, 142–7.

Kling, K. and Goteman, I. (2003) IKEA CEO Anders Dahlvig on international growth and IKEA's unique corporate culture and brand identity, *Academy of Management Executive*, 17, 1 (February), 31–7.

L'Etang, J. (2008) *Public Relations, Concepts, Practice and Critique*, London, Sage.

Leuthesser, L. and Kohli, C. (1997) Corporate identity: the role of mission statements, *Business Horizons*, 40(3) (May–June), 59–67.

Markwick, N. and Fill, C. (1997) Towards a framework for managing corporate identity, *European Journal of Marketing*, 31(5/6), 396–409.

Melewar, T.C. (2001) Measuring visual identity: a multi-construct study, *Corporate Communications: An International Journal*, 6(1), 36–42.

Melewar, T.C. (2003) Determinants of the corporate identity construct: a review of the literature, *Journal of Marketing Communications*, 9, 195–220.

Melewar, T.C., Bassett, K. and Simões, C. (2006) The role of communication and visual identity in modern organisations, *Corporate Communications: An International Journal*, 11(2), 138–47.

Mintzberg, H. and Quinn, J. (1988) *The Strategy Process: Concepts, Contexts and Cases*, 3rd edn, Englewood Cliffs, NJ: Prentice-Hall.

Mosher, J.F. (2012) Joe Camel in a Bottle: Diageo, the Smirnoff Brand, and the Transformation of the Youth Alcohol Market, *American Journal of Public Health*, 102(1), 56–63.

Murphy, C. (1999) The real meaning behind the name, *Marketing*, 14 October, p. 31.

Nayar, V. (2010) A Maverick CEO Explains How He Persuaded His Team to Leap into the Future, *Harvard Business Review*, 88(6), June, 110–13.

Olins, W. (1989) *Corporate Identity: Making Business Strategy Visible Through Design*. London: Thames & Hudson.

Otubanjo, O., Amujo, O.C. and Cornelius, N. (2010) The Informal Corporate Identity Communication Process, *Corporate Reputation Review*, 13(3), 157–171.

Riel van, C.B.M. (1995) *Principles of Corporate Communication*, Hemel Hempstead: Prentice-Hall.

Riel van, C.B.M. and Fombrun, C.J. (2007) *Essentials of Corporate Communication*, London: Routledge.

Salame, E. and Salame, J. (1975) *Developing a Corporate Identity: How to Stand out in the Crowd*, New York: Wiley.

Schein, E.H. (1985) *Organizational Culture and Leadership*, San Francisco, CA: Jossey-Bass.

Sims, J. (2008) Ditch the name, not the customers, *Marketing*, 8 August, 24–6.

Stuart, H. (1999a) The effect of organisational structure on corporate identity management, *Corporate Reputation Review*, 2(2), 151–64.

Stuart, H. (1999b) Towards a definitive model of the corporate identity management process, *Corporate Communications: an International Journal*, 4(4), 200–7.

Stuart, H. and Muzellec, L. (2004) Corporate Makeovers: can a hyena be rebranded? *Brand Management*, 11, 6, 472–82.

# Chapter 13
## Employee branding

The concept of 'internal marketing' recognises the importance of organisational members, principally employees, as important markets in their own right. These markets can be regarded as segments (and can be segmented), each of which has particular needs and wants that require satisfaction in order that an organisation's overall goals be accomplished. An alternative approach is to consider employees as a community, one which can have a critical impact on the way the brand is perceived.

Internal (marketing) communications not only serve to convey managerial intentions and members' feelings, but in many circumstances represent the development of an employee brand, an integral aspect of communications with external stakeholder groups.

## Aims and learning objectives

The aim of this chapter is to examine the context of internal marketing and how such issues might impact on an organisation's overall marketing communications and brand development.

The learning objectives of this chapter are to:

1. introduce the concept of employee branding;
2. consider the purpose of internal marketing and communication;
3. explore issues associated with organisational identity;
4. examine the impact of corporate culture on planned communications;
5. explain the intellectual and emotional dimensions of brand engagement;
6. develop an insight into the notion of strategic credibility and stakeholder perception of organisations;
7. explain how the use of communication audits can assist the development of effective marketing communications.

# Minicase

## Torbay Council

Torbay has a unique natural coastal location in the South-West of England. It is an east-facing bay and natural harbour, at the westernmost end of Lyme Bay. It consists of the towns of Torquay, Paignton and Brixham, and is roughly equidistant from the cities of Exeter and Plymouth. Tourism is a major part of the local economy, in part due to the beaches and mild climate, which attract holiday makers. Tourist authorities refer to the area as the 'English Riviera' with its award-winning beaches, and exotic palm trees.

Torbay Council, a unitary authority, is responsible for providing a range of public services for approximately 134,000 people. Its income budget for 2010/11 was £134 million. The council employs 1,300 people.

In an internal staff survey Torbay Council found that only 11 per cent of staff felt that staff morale was good. Only 37 per cent of staff surveyed agreed that they knew what is going on within the council as a whole. It was clear that Torbay Council employees were not as involved with the council's overriding mission and values as would be hoped and that work was required to change this situation. The information also served to crystallise the campaign goals. The first was to ensure that staff had an understanding of how their work contributes to the overall priorities of the council. The second was to keep staff up to date on key issues, and third, create an environment so that staff feel they are involved in the life of the council. This meant making sure they had access to the right information.

The first action was to form an Internal Communications Working Group, with staff representation from all levels, to help give advice on and develop a new strategy. The strategy was based directly on the principal comments and feelings that had been fed back through the internal communications staff survey.

One of the issues that had been uncovered was the huge volume of emails that staff had to work with. So, rather than flood staff with 'all-staff' emails that were largely irrelevant, a 'daily news', all-staff email was introduced detailing 'need to know' information that is relevant to all staff. Any other news is placed on the news page of the intranet 'inSIGHT'.

In order to help understanding about what it is others do in the organisation, 'shadowing days' were introduced, designed to allow staff to spend time in other departments and so become more familiar with the work undertaken in different parts of the organisation.

To counter the complaint that team meetings are not very informative, and that some did not happen at all, 'monthly team talks' were made compulsory. Team talk briefing packs are sent to all managers each month, containing corporate information. This helps ensure that not only do staff get briefed, but that they also all receive the same message. Each team is now encouraged to feed back on any recent successes, comments or questions.

Staff had reported that the notice boards were consistently messy and contained information that was invariably out of date. These boards were revamped with a new banner 'Keeping staff informed'. Designated 'key communicators' were then assigned to each board. They were sent regular emails containing consistent and relevant information for use on the boards. Staff can also post questions and comments for the board, anonymously.

The staff newsletter was modernised and now contains a mix of need-to-know and nice-to-know features including 'Meet the Team', staff announcements, shared successes, updates from the senior management team and a guest editor. It is sent electronically to all staff and a hard copy is available on notice boards for those people who do not have access to a PC.

To engage staff in the new strategy a film was produced internally by the communications team as an alternative to a corporate strategy document and circulated to all staff. The film showed council staff going about their daily work quoting 'It's good to talk' and provided an overview of the new strategy and the changes that were being introduced as a result of staff feedback.

A 'you said, we did'-style document was also produced for staff, which detailed the feedback from the 2009 internal communications survey and what has been done as a result. In January 2011 an internal communications survey was implemented. Staff morale had shot up from 11 to 68 per cent, despite the economic conditions, and government-funding cutbacks. The percentage of staff who feel they know what is going on in the council as a whole increased from 37 to 78 per cent.

*This minicase was written by Chris Fill using information from the Torbay Council Winning Submission to the CIPR 2011 Excellence Awards. Additional material was obtained from various sources including www.torbay.gov.uk/index/yourcouncil/.*

| Exhibit 13.1 | **Torbay Council offices** |
| --- | --- |
| | *Source*: Torbay Council |

# Introduction

It was established earlier that marketing communications is concerned with the way in which various stakeholders interact with one another and with an organisation. Traditionally, external stakeholders – for example, customers, intermediaries and financiers – are the prime focus of marketing communications. However, recognition of the importance of internal stake-holders as a group who should receive marketing attention has increased, and the concept of *internal marketing* emerged in the 1980s. This developed with greater impetus in the 1990s and is now a major focus of attention for both academics and managers, with 'employee branding' a hot topic.

Berry (1980) is widely credited as the first to recognise the term 'internal marketing', in a paper that sought to distinguish between product- and service-based marketing activities. The notion that the delivery of a service-based offering is bound to the quality of the personnel delivering it has formed the foundation of a number of research activities and journal papers.

The popular view is that employees constitute an internal market in which paid labour is exchanged for designated outputs. An extension to this view is that employees are a discrete group of customers with whom management interacts (Piercy and Morgan, 1991), in order that relational exchanges can be developed and maintained with external stakeholders. Although care needs to be taken to ensure that different groups of employees are recognised, employees are, as Christensen and Askegaard (2001) state, the most central audience for organisational communication.

Both employees and managers impose their own constraints upon the range and nature of the activities an organisation pursues, including its external 'promotional' activities. Employees, for example, are important to external stakeholders not only because of the tangible aspects of service and production that they provide, but also because of the intangible aspects, such as attitude and the way in which the service is provided: 'How much do they really care?' Images are often based more on the intangible than the tangible aspects of employee communications. Punjaisri et al. (2009) find that employee branding influences the extent to which employees identify with, and are committed to the brand. They also provide empirical evidence concerning the positive impact of internal communications on the alignment of employee behaviour and their consistent delivery of the brand promise.

Management, on the other hand, is responsible for the allocation of resources and the process and procedures used to create value. Its actions effectively constrain the activities of the organisation and, either consciously or unconsciously, shape the nature and form of the communications the organisation adopts. It is important, therefore, to understand how organisations can influence and affect the communication process.

Therefore, as a legitimate type of 'customer', they should be subject to similar marketing practices. Each organisation is a major influence on its own marketing communications. Indeed, the perception of others is influenced by the character and personality of the organisation.

It can be argued that the role of the employee has been changing. Once they could be just part of the company, but this role has been extended so that they are now recognised as, and need to adopt the role of, brand ambassadors (Freeman and Liedtka, 1997; Hemsley, 1998). This is particularly important in service environments where employees represent the interface between an organisation's internal and external environments and where their actions can have a powerful effect in creating images among customers (Schneider and Bowen, 1985; Balmer and Wilkinson, 1991). It is evident that many people now recognise the increasing importance of employee branding and the instrumental role internal communications plays in this process (Punjaisri et al. 2009; Storey, 2001).

# Member/non-member boundaries

The demarcation of internal and external stakeholders is not as clear as many writers suppose. The boundaries that exist between members and non-members of an organisation are becoming increasingly indistinct as a new, more flexible workforce emerges. For example, part-time workers, consultants, outsourced workers and temporary workforces spread themselves across organisational borders (Hatch and Schultz, 1997) and in many instances assume multiple roles of employee, consumer (product) and financial stakeholder (e.g. Royal Bank of Scotland or Direct Line employees, who may be borrowers or savers and are now also shareholders).

According to Morgan (1997), many organisations have a problem, as they do not recognise that they are themselves part of their environment. The context in which they see themselves and other organisations is too sharp. They see themselves as discrete entities faced with the problem of surviving against the vagaries of the outside world, which is often constructed as a domain of threat and opportunity. He refers to these as *egocentric* organisations. They are characterised by a fixed notion of who they are or what they can be, and are determined to impose or sustain that identity at all times. This can lead to an overplay of their own importance and an underplay of the significance of the wider system of relationships of which they are a part. In attempting to sustain unrealistic identities, they produce identities that end up destroying important elements of the context of which they are part. The example provided by Morgan is of typewriter manufacturers who failed to see technological developments leading to electronic typewriters and then word processors.

It would appear that by redrawing or even collapsing boundaries with customers, competitors and suppliers, organisations are better able to create new identities and use internal marketing communications to better effect.

# Internal communication

Employees are an integral and crucial part of a corporate brand. Their behaviour can help to minimise any gap that may appear between the way external stakeholders perceive an organisation (image) and the perception hoped for by the organisation (the identity) (Vallaster and de Chernatony, 2006). To achieve this outcome, internal brand building is necessary. This involves using internal communications with the goal of aligning employee behaviour with a corporate brand's values and identity. There are many approaches to achieving this. However, corporate brand structures, leadership and change management (Vallaster and de Chernatony, 2006) through strategic communication are key.

---

**Scholars' papers 13.1**   **Community-based internal comms**

White, C., Vanc, A. and Stafford, G. (2010) Internal Communication, Information Satisfaction, and Sense of Community: The Effect of Personal Influence, *Journal of Public Relations Research*, 22(1), 65–84.

This easy-to-read paper addresses some interesting and relevant issues concerning internal communications. The research is set within a university which provides contextual relevance for students, and the literature review is broad and helpful.

---

There are several terms and phrases that can be used interchangeably. For example, internal marketing or communication means the same as employee branding. Part of the public relations vocabulary refers to employee relations, which effectively means the same as employee branding. However, it should be recognised that not all employee-relations-based communications are aimed at employee branding, although all employee branding will encompass employee relations.

---

**Viewpoint 13.1**   **Using internal comms strategically**

Some organisations recognise the strategic importance of internal communications – for example, management spent over a year consulting with Norwich Union staff before the relaunch as Aviva.

One of the main reasons Lloyds Banking Group became a sponsor of the London Olympics was that the investment enabled the bank to engage staff with the brand and its values. When the bank took over HBOS, the sponsorship provided a point of interest for staff spanning two cultures and two sets of values. Lloyds used the Games as a way of recognising staff performance and rewarding them with incentives such as the chance to be a torchbearer and to attend the opening ceremony.

Using internal branding as a means of integration is considered a worthwhile activity although the practice is not as common as might be expected. A recent campaign by BUPA, Called 'Helping you find healthy', enabled the health care brand to integrate internal communications with PR, advertising and social media. BUPA involved their staff three months before the campaign was released externally, and they even made their staff a focal part of the campaign. This was achieved by incorporating staff stories about how they go the extra mile to help customers. B&Q have used a similar approach, involving real staff in their television and print ads.

British Airways was also a sponsor of the Olympics but they faced a different set of problems. With 32,000 staff spread out across the globe, undertaking a range of jobs, and some in open conflict with management, the timing of any internal communications programme had to be carefully considered, lest it appear cynical and disrespectful.

All of these internal branding campaigns can use a rich variety of media. These include conventional approaches such as print, road-shows, radio, forums and intranets, but also more contemporary media such as social media, apps and video.

*Source*:   Based on Bashford (2011); Gray (2010).

| | |
|---|---|
| **Question:** | What should be the balance of conventional media, social media and video, and face-to-face communications when communicating with employees? |
| **Task:** | Select an organisation with which you are familiar and briefly analyse their internal communications. Do they work, and if so, why? |

Research by Foreman and Money (1995) indicates that managers see the main components of internal communication falling into three broad areas: development, reward and vision for employees. These will inevitably vary in intensity on a situational basis.

All three of these components have communication as a common linkage. Employees and management (members) need to communicate with one another and with a variety of non-members, and do so through an assortment of methods. Communication with members, wherever they are located geographically, needs to be undertaken for a number of reasons. These include the DRIP factors (Chapter 1), but these communications also serve the additional purposes of providing transaction efficiencies and affiliation needs. See Table 13.1.

Aggerholm et al. (2010) refer to managerial interaction with employees that embraces issues related to planning, organising, commanding, coordinating, controlling and persuading employees about the desirability of striving towards corporate goals. In essence, this approach to internal communication is about 'control and information management'. However, they

| **Table 13.1** | The roles of internal marketing communications |
|---|---|
| DRIP factors | To provide information |
| | To be persuasive |
| | To reinforce – reassure/remind |
| | To differentiate employees/groups |
| Transactional | To coordinate actions |
| | To promote the efficient use of resources |
| | To direct developments |
| Affiliation | To provide identification |
| | To motivate personnel |
| | To promote and coordinate activities with non-members |

extend this perspective by exploring the nature and potential for managerial conversations to communicate corporate strategies and values.

They identify four types of conversation that can be considered from a corporate communication perspective. These are recruitment conversations, job appraisal interviews, sickness leave and dismissal-focused conversations. Their research found that, in recruitment and job appraisal conversations, a wide range of issues are often explored. In the latter two – sickness and dismissal conversations – the focus was invariably on the role of the employee.

What this indicates is that the communication of corporate values is very evident in the sickness and dismissal conversations. However, it is often absent in the recruitment and appraisal conversations, which is primarily due to the breadth of issues considered. The researchers conclude that there is considerable potential for organisations to develop the communication of corporate strategies and values through management conversations. They also recognise the challenges associated with integrating values into these conversations and ensuring consistency.

The values transmitted to customers, suppliers and distributors through external communications need to be reinforced by the values expressed by employees, especially those who interact with these external groups. Internal marketing communications are necessary in order that internal members should be motivated and involved with the brand in such a way that they are able to present a consistent and uniform message to non-members. This is an aspect of integrated marketing communications and involves product- and organisation-centred messages. If there is a set of shared values, internal communications are said to blend and balance the external communications. This process whereby employees are encouraged to communicate with non-members so that organisations ensure that what is promised is realised by customers is referred to as 'living the brand', or 'employee branding'. Hiscock (2002) claims that employees can be segmented according to the degree and type of support they give a brand. He claims that, in the United Kingdom, 30 per cent of employees are brand neutral, 22 per cent are brand saboteurs and 48 per cent are brand champions, of whom 33 per cent would talk about the brand positively if asked, and 15 per cent do so spontaneously.

In a large number of both b2b and b2c organisations new products and services are often developed through the use of project teams. According to Lievens and Moenart (2000), project communication is characterised by both flows of communication among project members (intra-project communication) and flows across boundaries with external members (extra-project communication). Boundary spanners act as mediators facilitating communications flows internally (for resources) and externally to customers, suppliers, competitors and technologies. Project teams perceive differing levels of uncertainty associated with their task and these are related to external (user needs, technologies and the competition) and internal (human and financial resources) factors.

Uncertainty about the resources needs to be reduced in order to lower doubt associated with external stakeholders, improve communication effectiveness and achieve project tasks. As will be seen later, the integration of internal and external communications is a key factor in the development of integrated marketing communications. Project teams have an important role to play in enhancing corporate reputation, particularly in the B2B sector.

---

### Scholars' paper 13.2    Internal Communication Matrix

**Welch, M. and Jackson, P.R. (2007) Rethinking internal communication: a stakeholder approach, *Corporate Communications: An International Journal*, 12(2), 177–98.**

The internal corporate communication concept offers a lens through which communicators can consider communication strategy and tactics. Following an interesting review of the literature and its gaps, the authors present an Internal Communication Matrix as a new or fresh orientation towards internal communication.

Welch and Jackson (2007) provide an interesting and helpful insight into some of the issues associated with understanding internal communication. Although they assume a stakeholder approach and refrain from considering any related marketing issues, they suggest that internal communication should be considered in terms of four dimensions: internal line management communication; internal peer communication; internal project communication and internal corporate communication. These are intended to provide a typology of internal communication and are set out in Table 13.2.

Attention is given to the fourth dimension, internal corporate communication. Welch and Jackson believe that this refers to communication between an organisation's strategic managers and its internal stakeholders, with the purpose of promoting *commitment* to the organisation, a sense of *belonging* (to the organisation), *awareness* of its changing environment and *understanding* of its evolving goals (2007: 186). These four goals are depicted in Figure 13.1.

| Table 13.2 | Internal communication matrix | | | |
|---|---|---|---|---|
| **Dimension** | **Level** | **Direction** | **Participants** | **Content** |
| Internal line management communication | Line managers/ supervisors | Predominantly two-way | Line managers– employees | Employees' roles; personal impact, e.g. appraisal discussions, team briefings |
| Internal team peer communication | Team colleagues | Two-way | Employee– employee | Team information, e.g. team task discussions |
| Internal project peer communication | Project group colleagues | Two-way | Employee– employee | Project information, e.g. Project issues |
| Internal corporate communication | Strategic managers/top management | Predominantly one-way | Strategic managers– all employees | Organisational/corporate issues, e.g. goals, objectives, new developments, activities and achievements |

*Source*: Welch and Jackson (2007). © Emerald Group Publishing Limited. All rights reserved.

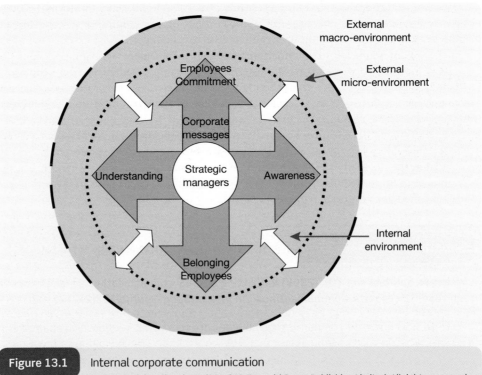

| Figure 13.1 | Internal corporate communication |
|---|---|

*Source*: Welch and Jackson (2007). © Emerald Group Publishing Limited. All rights reserved.

These four goals serve to engage employees not only with their roles, tasks and jobs but also with the organisation. It is recognised that the internal environment incorporates the organisation's structure, culture, sub-cultures, processes, behaviour and leadership style and that this interacts with the external environment and provides context for the internal communication. Employees, especially 'the disgruntled within' (Grossman, 2005, p. 3) represent a real threat to organisations that do not make sure that external and internal messages are consistent and congruent. Just as Cubbage (2005) found, employees with sufficient information about their organisation are more likely to defend it and much less likely to spread malicious content and rumours. Some of these ideas about commitment, belonging and identity with an organisation are explored later in this chapter.

Very often employees perceive the value of internal communication in terms of the richness of information and the media used to convey it. In other words, to quote McLuhan (1964), 'the medium is the message'. White et al. (2010) interpret media richness theory in terms of the different media used to communicate with employees. Email is invariably used for short and fast updates, important information is released through printed paper, while websites are used to alert staff to fresh information but also to archive it for retrieval as necessary. Above all else, interpersonal communication is the richest and most important form of communication to employees, as this strongly influences attitudes and behaviours. This is maximised through personal contact with the CEO and other members of the dominant coalition.

---

## Viewpoint 13.2    High employee satisfaction at McDonald's

The fast food chain McDonald's understands the importance and contribution that their employees bring to the brand. As a result they have employed positive strategies towards their employees over several years, and have been recognised for their work by various awards. For example, in 2009 McDonald's were presented with an Investors in People (IIP) Gold award. This level of award is hard to attain and organisations who achieve IIP Bronze, Silver and Gold status represent the top 1 per cent of recognised IIP organisations.

McDonald's were recognised for their investment in 'talent' management and their use of people metrics to identify the impact of development strategies. McDonald's employees were enabled to identify inspirational leaders at all levels and their view about how they were managed had improved remarkably. A survey of McDonald's staff found an unusual statistic: namely, that 100 per cent of employees felt that any feedback they gave was listened to and used to make improvements within the company, regardless of position. In addition, over 80 per cent believed that whilst their training helped them to progress in their job, it was directly linked to business objectives.

In 2010 McDonald's UK served an additional 72 million customers. Coincidentally, research also showed that at McDonald's, 84.5 per cent of staff feel valued, 83.8 per cent feel proud to work at the restaurant chain, and 83.5 per cent feel motivated.

In 2012 the Marketing Society awarded McDonald's an Excellence Award for Employee Engagement. The engagement strategy was designed to enhance employee pride in the business, improve brand perception, contribute to improving business performance and develop people.

Negative brand publicity and hostile customers can place employees in difficult situations, often demeaning the job and demotivating staff. So the challenge was to transform the public's view of working life at McDonald's. A campaign called 'Meet our People' was developed. This involved showcasing and celebrating a selection of McDonald's staff, and also trying to provide a human side to those working in uniform. The campaign featured McDonald's employees who became the stars of the campaign. They were presented as 'talented individuals from all walks of life'. A competition was held to find the face of the campaign, and staff best-suited to deliver messages were identified. This resulted in an online film which featured Elisha, a crew member. The film was supported by a four-week broadsheet press campaign showcasing McDonald's support for its employees, a four-week digital display campaign, and the redesign of the McDonald's 'people' website.

In addition to this campaign, McDonald's sponsorship of the London 2012 Olympic games also helped develop employee pride. 2,000 employees volunteered to be directly involved.

*Source*:   Anon (2012); HR Editorial (2011); Kornacki, M. (2009).

**Question:**   Under what circumstances might these types of engagement strategies be seen to be employee/brand exploitation?

**Task:**   Find another example of an employee relations programme. Was it successful and if so, why?

| Exhibit 13.2 | **McDonald's employees are an integral part of the engagement strategy** |
| --- | --- |
| | *Source*: WPA Pool/Getty Images |

# Organisational identity

Organisational identity is concerned with what individual members think and feel about the organisation to which they belong. When their perception of the organisation's characteristics accords with their own self-concept, then the strength of organisational identity is strong (Dutton et al., 1994). Organisational identity also refers to the degree to which feelings and thoughts about the distinctive characteristics are shared among the members (Dutton and Dukerich, 1991). There are, therefore, both individual and collective aspects to organisational identity.

Mention was made earlier of brand ambassadors, people who identify closely with a brand and speak openly and positively about it. Albert and Whetten (1985) stated that organisations must make three main decisions: who they are, what business they are in and what they want to be. In order that these decisions can be made, they claim that consideration must be given to what is central, what is distinctive and what is enduring about the character of the organisation.

Non-members of an organisation also develop feelings and thoughts about what are the organisation's central, enduring and distinctive characteristics. It is highly probable that there will be variances between the perceptions and beliefs of members and non-members, and this may be a cause of confusion, misunderstanding or even conflict.

| Table 13.3 | When organisational identity is important |
|---|---|

During the formation of the organisation

At the loss of an identity-sustaining element

On the accomplishment of an organisation's *raison d'être*

Through extremely rapid growth

If there is a change in the collective status

Retrenchment

*Source*: After Albert and Whetten (1985). Emerald Group Publishing Limited.

This discrepancy between what Goodman and Pennings (1977) termed 'private' and 'public' identities can impair the 'health' of the organisation. The 'unhealthier' or greater the discrepancy, the more will be the difficulty in generating the resources required to guarantee corporate survival. In other words, the closer the member/non-member identification, the better placed the organisation will be to achieve its objectives.

Organisational identity is deemed to be important at a collective level, when an organisation is formed or when there is a major change to the continuity of the goals of the organisation or when the means of accomplishment are hindered or broken (see Table 13.3). According to Dutton and Penner (1993), what an individual sees as important, distinctive and unique about an organisation will affect the individual's assessment of the importance of an issue facing the organisation and also the degree to which it is of personal importance.

For members, organisational identity may be conceptualised as their perception of their organisation's central and distinctive attributes, including its positional status and relevant compositional group. Consequently, external events that refute or call into question these defining characteristics may threaten the perception that organisational members have of their organisational identity (Dutton and Dukerich, 1991). Research by Elsbach and Kramer (1996) found that members of a high-ranking organisation (MBA school) perceived a threat because the ranking devalued their central and cherished identity dimensions and so refuted their prior claims of positional status.

Members used selective categorisations to re-emphasise positive perceptions of their organisational identities both for themselves and their non-member audiences by highlighting identity dimensions or alternative groups with which they should be compared and that were not previously identified, the intention being to deflect attention.

Dutton and Dukerich state that there is a significant interdependence between individuals' social identities and their perceptions of their organisational identities. Thus, as they care about how their organisations are described and how they are compared with other organisations, so they experience cognitive distress (identity dissonance) when they think that their organisation's identity is being threatened by what they perceive as inaccurate descriptions or misleading (unfair) comparisons with other organisations.

In response to this distress, members restore positive self-perceptions by highlighting their organisation's membership in alternative comparison groups. It is normal to assume that identity is relatively static. However, just as organisations can experience strategic drift when the corporate strategy and performance move further away, each period, from the intended or expected pattern, so organisations can suffer from identity drift away from the expected lifecycle. Kimberley (1980) argues that this can occur for three main reasons: environmental complexity; identity divestiture; and organisational success.

This indicates that care must be given to understanding and managing the organisational identity to ensure that any discrepancy between members' and non-members' perceptions of what is central, enduring and distinctive is minimised and to be aware of identity dissonance should the organisation be threatened and the values upheld by its members challenged.

# Organisational culture

According to Beyer (1981), organisational identity is a subset of the collective beliefs that constitute an organisation's culture. Indeed, employee branding is shaped by the prevailing culture, as it is the culture that provides the context within which internal marketing practices are accomplished.

Corporate culture encompasses the basic assumptions and beliefs that members of an organisation take for granted, share and use to shape their view of it (Schein, 2004). A more common view of organisational culture is 'the way we do things around here'. It is the result of a number of factors, ranging through the type and form of business the organisation is in, its customers and other stakeholders, its geographical position, and its size, age and facilities. These represent the more tangible aspects of corporate culture. There are a host of intangible elements as well, including the assumptions, values and beliefs that are held and shared by members of the organisation. These factors combine to create a unique environment, one where norms or guides to expected behaviour influence all members, whatever their role or position.

## Levels of organisational culture

Corporate culture, according to Schein (1985), consists of a number of levels. The first of these is the most visible level. This includes physical aspects of the organisation, such as the way in which the telephone is answered, the look and style of the reception area, the navigability and style of the website and the general care afforded to visitors. Other manifestations of these visible aspects are the advertisements, logos, letterheads and other written communications that an organisation generates.

The second level consists of the values held by key personnel. For example, should particular sales teams who regularly exceed their targets have their targets increased or should certain members of the sales team be redeployed to less successful teams or new markets? If the decision is made to increase the target, and the outcome is successful, then the decision is more likely to be repeated when the same conditions arise again.

The third level in Schein's approach is achieved when the decision to increase the target becomes an automatic response to particular conditions. A belief is formed and becomes an assumption about behaviour in the organisation. This automatic approach can lead to complementary behaviour by members of the sales team. The placing of orders can become manipulated, to the extent that orders placed in month 4 may be 'delayed' or stuck in the top drawer of the sales representative's desk, until some point in month 5, when it is appropriate to release them.

The belief that the targets will be increased can lead to a behaviour that was referred to earlier as 'the way we do things around here'. This behaviour leads to relative stability for all concerned and need not be disturbed unless a change is introduced, whose source is elsewhere in the system – i.e. outside the team.

## Culture and communication

Corporate culture is not a static phenomenon; the stronger the culture, the more likely it is to be transmitted from one generation of organisational members to another, and it is also probable that the culture will be more difficult to change if it is firmly embedded in the organisation. Most writers acknowledge that effective cultural change is difficult and a long-term task. Achieving a cultural fit is necessary if an organisation wishes to embrace a strategy that is compatible with the current mindset of the organisation.

Mitchell (1998) considers the strong corporate culture that exists at Procter & Gamble. Depending upon one's perspective, this once rigid formal hierarchical culture could be considered an advantage or a disadvantage. On the plus side it allowed for strong identity, consistency and people development opportunities, as the company has a 'promote from within' policy. On the downside, the strength and penetration of the culture and need to toe the party line could restrict innovation, entrepreneurship and the use of initiative.

This strength of culture and the cautious approach to risk taking may have been responsible for the company's consistent emphasis on product attributes, performance and pack shots in its advertising and communications, unlike its close rival Unilever, which makes greater use of emotions in its advertising. Procter & Gamble appears to have recognised this as a limitation and embarked on a change of emphasis, incorporating a more emotional approach in its communications. Changing the culture will be a challenge, but to be successful senior management will, among other things, need to be 'obsessive' about communicating the following to all members of the organisation (Gordon, 1985):

1. the current performance and position of the organisation in comparison with its competition and the outlook for the future;

2. the vision of what the organisation is to become and how it will achieve it;

3. the progress the organisation has made in achieving those elements identified previously as important.

The focus of this communication is internal, usually through training and development programmes. Certain complex offerings, such as information-technology-based products, require channel members to provide high levels of training and support. It is also important to communicate the objectives of the network and to share responsibility for the performance of the channel as a whole. This is partly achieved by members fulfilling their roles as successful dealers, retailers or manufacturers, but there is still a strong requirement for the channel leader to set out what is required from each member of its different networks and to report on what has been achieved to date.

---

### Viewpoint 13.3    Communicating El Al's UPE

For over 50 years El Al was a popular, yet underperforming, government-owned airline. El Al management operated through a production orientation, manifest in average service quality, standardised aircraft and with crews that worked without a real service vision. There was minimal management–employee collaboration, which resulted in many strikes and damage to the airline's reputation.

After years of successive losses and a growing image problem, the airline was privatised. El Al's new management adopted a marketing approach and actively embraced employees as the company's true 'ambassadors'. One of the first tasks undertaken by the incoming CEO was to enable a transition from providing a standard service to one that offered a unique personal experience (UPE) for all clients, a premium service. The idea for the UPE originated from the company's employees, following a request for ideas about how each division could deliver a premium service.

A new identity was developed but the company had to communicate the positioning and values to its employees and customers, in that order. Formal internal communications were used to ensure that all employees were aware of the company's new values and understood the idea behind the new strategy. A new handbook was developed which set out the new procedures, regulations, and expectations at both a department and individual level. The introduction of weekly, departmental meetings and annual tests concerning the norms and work practices, were designed to reinforce employees' knowledge about norms of behaviour and work procedures.

The selection process for the recruitment of new staff was changed to screen for attitudes and personal values that were consistent and congruent with those of the company. Only service-orientated people were accepted into the company's training programme. New employees are helped to internalise the company's mission and values, through exposure to positive examples of exemplary customer service or behaviours that are consistent with the company's new values. An internal newsletter is used to report company successes, tasks achieved, actual or planned structural changes, dates of special departmental courses and to announce the names of the company's outstanding employees, accompanied by photos taken with the chairman of the company and the CEO.

In addition El Al used a range of informal internal communications to reinforce the company's new culture and values. One of these is an annual company day so that employees can meet each other and share their knowledge and experiences in a free and open atmosphere. The company also encourages employees to share and celebrate special events such as birthdays, marriages and the birth of children with their co-workers. These events reinforce pride as members of a departmental team, within a special company.

In order to underline that the relationship between management and staff is real, an open-door policy is in force and each new employee is assigned a personal supervisor and has a contact person from management. All employees are free to approach senior personnel about any question, suggestion or complaint without fear.

*Source*:   Based on Herstein, et al. (2008); www.elal.co.il/.

| | |
|---|---|
| **Question:** | To what extent should reducing fear and uncertainty be the primary goals of internal communication strategies? |
| **Task:** | Visit the websites of two different airlines and attempt to consider the tone and quality of the internal communications. Are employees a central part of the overall communications? |

Management of the communication finances, through time, will show the degree to which an organisation values such investments. Brands need time, the long term, to build and develop strength. Cutting back on investment in communications, especially advertising, in times of recession and difficulty, reveals management to view such activities as an expense, a cost against short-run needs. Furthermore, the expectation of channel members may be that a certain volume of marketing communications is necessary, not only to sustain particular levels of business, but also because competitors are providing established levels of communication activity. What is important is that managers understand the culture of the organisation and the primary networks, values, styles, motivations and norms so that the communications work with, rather than against, the corporate will.

---

**Scholars' paper 13.3**     **Top managers look into their identity**

**Hatch, M.J. and Schultz, M. (1997) Relations between organisational culture, identity and image, *European Journal of Marketing*, 31(5/6), 356–65.**

At a time when there were several papers being published on corporate reputation and related topics, this paper made a significant contribution to our knowledge of these topics. The authors consider the actions and statements of top managers that affect organisational identity and image. This they claim is due to increasing levels of interaction between organisational members and suppliers, customers, regulators and other environmental actors, and the multiple roles of organisational members who often act both as 'insiders' (i.e. as employees) and as 'outsiders' (e.g. as consumers, community members and/or members of special interest groups).

# Brand engagement

The relationship between corporate strategy and communications is important. Traditionally, these communications are perceived as those that make the network between an organisation's employees and its managers. This internal perspective of communications is important, particularly when organisations are in transition. This is only one part of the communication process. Employees are just one of the many stakeholders each organisation must seek to satisfy. Communications regarding strategic issues should also be targeted at internal and external stakeholders in order to gain their goodwill, involvement and understanding.

It is clear that long-term relationships cannot be sustained if the brand delivery is unsatisfactory and where the people behind the brand do not match the expectation generated by the promise. Apart from computer-mediated communication, employees provide the main points of contact between organisations or with customers. These interactions or 'moments of truth' as Gummesson (1999) refers to them, need to be consistent and of high quality.

The effectiveness of internal communication is shaped by several characteristics. These are the structure, flow, content and climate (van Riel and Fombrun, 2007) which together provide the context in which employee relations operates. The key dimensions of these characteristics are set out in Table 13.4.

## Intellectual and emotional aspects

Employees are required to deliver both the functional aspects of an organisation's offering and the emotional dimensions, particularly in service environments. By attending to these twin elements it is possible that long-term relationships between sellers and buyers can develop effectively. Hardaker and Fill (2005) explore ideas concerning the notion that employees need

| Table 13.4 | The characteristics of internal communications |
|---|---|
| **Dimension** | **Explanation** |
| **Structure** | Information can be disseminated and shared in three main ways.<br>1 through a formal organisational structure (eg hierarchical),<br>2 through supporting media endorsed by the organisation (newsletters, internal magazines, intranets, etc.)<br>3 through informal networks, word-of-mouth and what some might refer to as 'water cooler' chats or the grapevine, as van Riel and Fombrun (2007) refer to it. |
| **Flow** | This refers to the direction of the communication. Typically communications flow vertically and downward, especially through formalised organisational channels. These refer to decisions, assignments and requests. Flows from employees upwards towards senior management often concern reports and information. |
| **Content** | Employees prefer content that is easily understood, timely, sufficient and readable. Interestingly, information that serves to clarify the role of an employee and the relative standing is often well received and has been shown to improve levels of self-confidence. |
| **Climate** | Sometimes referred to as the 'communication atmosphere', the climate reflects how conducive or receptive the culture is to positive and negative information. A positive climate has been shown to improve productivity and in doing so improve employee identification with the organisation through a sense of participation. |

*Source*: Based on van Riel and Fombrun, 2007.

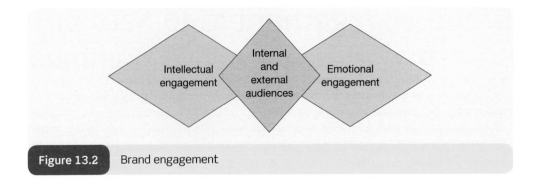

**Figure 13.2**    Brand engagement

to buy in to organisational vision, goals and strategy and, as White et al. (2010: 67) confirm, 'employees want to know where their organization is headed and how they contribute to achieving the vision'.

This buy-in, or engagement, consists of two main components: intellectual and emotional (see Figure 13.2). The intellectual element is concerned with employees buying in and aligning themselves with the organisation's strategy, issues and overall direction. The emotional element is concerned with employees taking ownership of their contribution and becoming committed to the achievement of stated goals. Communication strategies should be based on the information-processing styles of employees and access to preferred media. Communications should reflect a suitable balance between the need for rational information to meet intellectual needs and expressive types of communication to meet the emotional needs of the workforce. It follows that the better the communication, the higher the level of engagement.

The development of internal brands based around employees can be accomplished effectively and quickly by simply considering the preferred information-processing style of an internal audience. By developing messages that reflect the natural processing style and using a diversity of media that best complements the type of message and the needs of each substantial internal target audience, the communication strategy is more likely to be successful.

The key to successful employee branding hinges upon an organisation's ability to communicate desirable values and goals, as this helps employees to identify with the organisation. This in turn prompts employees to speak positively about the organisation and, so influence external stakeholders.

# Advertising and the impact on employees

Gilly and Wolfinbarger (1998) concluded that an organisation's advertising can have both a positive and a negative effect on its employees. Such advertising can serve to clarify roles, make promises that can be realistically delivered and demonstrate that the organisation values its employees. These positive outcomes can be seen in terms of improved morale and commitment.

Conversely, negative effects ensue when the advertising promises are unrealistic and cannot be delivered, messages are not true or the roles portrayed are far from flattering. For example, Boots used a campaign to inform consumers about its 'mix-and-match' offer. The ads depicted a member of staff explaining the deal to a confused customer, and then apologising, announcing that it is her first day. Staff, according to Witt (2001), complained that they were made to look stupid and incompetent. The outcome is low morale, distrust and unfavourable attitudes

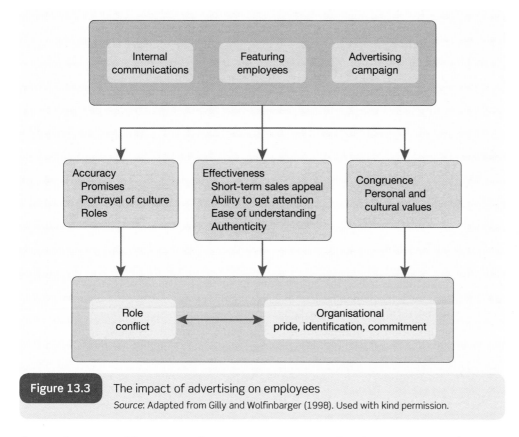

**Figure 13.3**    The impact of advertising on employees
*Source*: Adapted from Gilly and Wolfinbarger (1998). Used with kind permission.

that can be perceived by non-members. It seems important, therefore, to generate advertising messages that are perceived by employees to be transparently achievable and consistent, and this may involve the participation of a few staff in the development of advertising strategy.

Gilly and Wolfinbarger developed a framework that presents the impact of advertising on employees (see Figure 13.3). This shows that employees use three main criteria when evaluating the advertising used by their employers: namely, accuracy of the message, value congruence and effectiveness. In order to reduce any gap that might emerge as a result of an advertising campaign (and consequent deterioration in morale and commitment), increased vertical and horizontal communications are deemed necessary. This might require staff to be involved in both advertising development and, in some cases, actual participation in the advertisement, the pretesting of ideas and the dissemination of the advertising and the supporting rationale.

All stakeholders need to know what the objectives of the organisation are, particularly the organisation's mission and overriding vision, as this will impact on the other organisations in the performance network. For example, if Heinz or Pedigree Petfoods were to announce that, in the future, all their products were to be presented in recyclable containers, then current suppliers might need to reformulate their offerings and any future suppliers would be aware of the constraint this might place on them. The information is provided in order that others may work with them and continue supplying offerings to end-users with a minimum of interruption.

Barich and Kotler (1991) suggest that the concept of positioning (the process whereby offerings are perceived by consumers relative to the competition) applies at the brand and corporate levels. If an organisation is pursuing a generic strategy of differentiation, the positioning statements of the organisation need to reflect this. The image that stakeholders have of an organisation and its offerings affects their disposition towards it, their intentions to undertake market transactions and the nature of the relationships between members.

Good external communications are important because, among other benefits, they can provide a source of competitive advantage. Perrier has built its share of the mineral water market on the volume and style of its planned communications. It has dominated communications in the market and has effectively set a mobility barrier that demands that any major challenger must be prepared to replicate the size of Perrier's investment in communications. The quality of the Perrier communications has also led distributors and other network members to support and want to be involved with the organisation, as evidenced by the swift recovery in market share after all world stocks had to be withdrawn because a small number of bottles had been identified as 'contaminated'. Morden (1993) refers to these positive external perceptions as intangible benefits that help to differentiate the organisation from its competitors.

All marketing strategies, such as those to harvest, build, hold and divest, require different communication strategies and messages. Similarly, market penetration, product development, market development and product penetration strategies all require varying forms of support that must be reflected in the communications undertaken by the organisation.

Marketing research may indicate that different stakeholders do not perceive the corporate and marketing strategies of an organisation in the same way as that intended by management. Some stakeholders may perceive the performance of an organisation inaccurately. This means that the organisation is failing to communicate in an effective and consistent way, and any such mismatch will, inevitably, lead to message confusion and relative disadvantage in the markets in which the organisation operates.

The communication of strategic intent and corporate performance must be harmonised. Understating, or even misleading different stakeholders may influence performance, and if claims are made for an organisation that suggest a level of performance or intent beyond reality, then credibility may be severely jeopardised.

# Strategic credibility

According to Higgins and Bannister (1992), strategic credibility refers to 'how favourably key stakeholders view the company's overall corporate strategy and its strategic planning processes'.

If stakeholders perceive the focus organisation as strategically capable, it is suggested that it will accrue a number of benefits. The benefits vary from industry to industry and according to each situation, but it appears from the early research that those organisations experiencing transition and that are not regulated in any way have potentially the most to gain from open corporate communication with their stakeholders. The benefits from this open attitude include improved stock market valuations and price/earnings multiples, better employee motivation and closer relationships with all members of the performance and support networks, particularly those within the financial community. There are four main determinants of strategic credibility:

- an organisation's strategic capability;
- past performance;
- communication of corporate strategy to key stakeholders;
- the credibility of the CEO.

## Strategic capability

Capability is a prerequisite for credibility. The perception that stakeholders have of the strategic processes within an organisation will influence their belief that the focus organisation can or cannot achieve its objectives. This is important in networks that are characterised by close working arrangements and high levels of interdependence. Should one organisation indicate that it lacks the necessary capability to perform strategically, then other members of the network are likely to be affected. The sharing of a strategic vision, one that may be common to all members of the stakeholder network, is a positive indicator of the acceptance that the focus organisation is strategically capable.

## Past performance

The maintenance of a sustained strategic capability profile depends partly on corporate performance. Poor performance does not sustain confidence, but even the existence of a strong performance is only worthwhile if it is communicated properly. The communication should inform the target audiences that the performance was planned and that there was sound reasoning and management judgement behind the performance.

## Corporate communications

Organisations should inform members of the network of their strategic intentions as well as their past performance. This requires the accurate targeting and timing of the messages at a pace suitable and appropriate to the target's requirements. Higgins and Bannister refer to financial analysts, in particular, as stakeholders in need of good information. They argue that trying to evaluate the performance of a diversified organisation operating in a number of different markets, of which many of the analysts lack knowledge and expertise, is frustrating and difficult. Good information delivered through appropriate media and at particular times can be beneficial in the development of the realm of understanding between parties.

By keeping financial analysts aware of the strategic developments and the strategic thinking of the organisation and the industries in which it operates, the value of the organisation is more likely to reflect corporate performance.

## The credibility of the CEO

The fourth element proposed by Higgins and Bannister concerns the ability of the CEO to communicate effectively with a variety of audiences. By projecting strong, balanced and positive communications, it is thought that a visible CEO can improve the overall reputation of the organisation. Coupled with the improvement will be a perception of the strategic capability of the organisation. The CEO, can therefore, be regarded as a major determinant of the organisation's perceived strategic credibility. As White et al. (2010) believe, the CEO sets the tone for internal branding and communication, partly because employees want to be able to see and talk to their leaders.

---

**Scholars' paper 13.4     CEOs and employee engagement**

**Men, L.R. (2012) CEO credibility, perceived organizational reputation, and employee engagement, *Public Relations Review*, 38(1), (March), 171-3.**

This paper should be read because it considers the link between credible leadership and employee engagement. Through empirical research the author shows that perceived organisational reputation significantly and positively affects employee engagement.

---

Haji-Ioannou, Alan Sugar, James Dyson and Richard Branson are some of the major CEOs to promote themselves on behalf of their organisations, but there are many others who have tried and failed. However, research by Newell and Shemwell (1995) suggests that care should be taken when using CEOs as endorsers. They argue that the impact of source credibility may be reduced because of beliefs about product attributes, and this in turn may affect behavioural intentions. Therefore, CEOs might be best used as endorsers when informational-, rather than emotional- or transformational-based messages predominate.

For example, Richard Branson has been used as CEO endorser of the Virgin Group. As chairman, he has been a focal point in the promotion of Virgin financial products (mainly informational messages), but has not played such a central role in the planned communications concerning the airline Virgin Atlantic, where emotionally based messages have been used to influence brand choice decisions.

---

## Viewpoint 13.4    CEOs critical to company reputation

A Weber Shandwick report in 2012 indicated that 60 per cent of a company's market value is attributed to its reputation. Their research also revealed that 66 per cent of consumers attribute their perceptions of CEOs to their opinion of a company's reputation. Executives attribute nearly 50 per cent of a company's overall reputation to the CEO's reputation.

There can be no doubt that a CEO's influence on an organisation's performance can be critical, and it is clear that consumer trust in CEOs and multinational organisations has fallen in recent years. CEO and company reputation are inextricably linked, as together, company and CEO reputation make a solid contribution to a company's market value.

One way for CEOs to create positive links with consumers that will impact reputation, is to be seen to be contributing at an organisation's sharp end. For example, easyJet's CEO Carolyn McCall walks up and down the aisle with a bin bag collecting passengers' rubbish, every time she takes one of its flights. Michael O'Leary, Ryanair's outspoken chief executive, has helped to load baggage on to planes, something he likes to do when launching routes. Edwards (2012) speculates that it was this first-hand experience that may have led him to propose that Ryanair passengers may in future carry their own bags to the aircraft hold, cutting fares by reducing the number of luggage handlers from five per plane to just one.

*Source*: Weber Shandwick (2012); Edwards (2012); PRNewswire (2012).

**Question:** If CEOs are to get involved at the customer interface, does this send out signals of interference or involvement?

**Task:** Choose a major company and find out the extent to which the CEO has customer contact.

| Exhibit 13.3 | **Michael O'Leary of Ryanair** |
| --- | --- |
| | *Source*: Thomas Samson/Gamma-Rapho/Getty Images |

In addition to advertising, some CEOs are using personal blogs as a means of communications and standout. For example, Mark Price, Managing Director of Waitrose, launched a blog through the company's website. His theme is healthy eating and the blog monitors his attempt to lose weight.

As Bokaie (2008) argues, this approach has difficulties because blogging requires answers and interaction. So, when Charles Dunstone, CEO of Carphone Warehouse, started his blog, he promised to keep everyone up to date. Unfortunately he began just as the company had launched TalkTalk, a free broadband offer. The demand was so heavy that the company could not keep up. Thousands of customers became extremely frustrated and the media leveraged the story in their inimitable way. The result was that even though the connections were eventually made, the blog stopped immediately.

# Internal communications: auditing and planning

Increasingly, organisations understand the need to adopt a planned approach to the deployment of their employees in order to support the external brand. One such approach has been identified by Mahnert and Torres (2007) who offer a framework to the process of developing an internal brand. They identify seven key factors that influence the success or failure of internal branding. These are set out in Table 13.5.

Mahnert and Torres develop a consolidated internal branding framework, drawn from the key, salient and confirmed elements in the literature. These they group into the planning, execution and evaluation phases. Their framework is replicated at Figure 13.4.

Research is an important element in the design of communication plans. Associated with this should be an evaluation of the most recent attempts at communicating with target audiences. The accumulation of this type of short-run information is useful because it builds into a database

| Table 13.5 | Seven factors for internal branding |
| --- | --- |

| Internal factors | Explanation |
| --- | --- |
| Organisation | Cultural change is difficult but may be necessary where there is no match with the objectives. Use cross-functional coordination and cooperation to reduce departmentalised thinking and internal competition. |
| Information | Important to provide in-depth knowledge of the external and internal environments. Changes to current programmes may emerge as a result. |
| Management | Senior management must not only support and actively endorse the internal programme, they must be *seen* to do so as well. Visibility is key. |
| Communication | Critical to keep everyone informed but without overloading them. |
| Strategy | Need to align strategies and programmes in order to reduce the potential for conflict where there is a poor fit between the brand and the objectives of the organisation. |
| Staff | Support at all levels internally is an antecedent for success. Therefore, recruiting, motivating and rewarding staff is important for internal branding. |
| Education | It is necessary to understand and monitor employee beliefs, attitudes and perceptions in order that an internal programme be kept on track. |

*Source*: Based on Mahnert and Torres (2007).

| STAGE | STEP | ELEMENTS | |
|-------|------|----------|--|
| Stage 1: Planning | I Preparation | 1 | Decide on timing |
| | | 2 | Establish quantifiable short- and long-term targets |
| | | 3 | Gain managerial support and generate awareness |
| | | 4 | Secure a suitable budget |
| | II Investigation | 5 | Constituency assessment |
| | | 6 | Internal market research |
| | | 7 | Cultural fit analysis |
| | III Configuration | 8 | Align business objectives and brand values |
| | | 9 | Link external and internal messages |
| | | 10 | Segment where appropriate |
| | | 11 | Ensure appropriate frequency |
| | | 12 | Decide on language and message design |
| Stage 2: Executing | IV Facilitation | 13 | Decide on degree of staff empowerment |
| | | 14 | Obtain and sustain staff involvement |
| | V Implementation | 15 | Utilise multiple channels in multiple directions |
| | | 16 | Reduce hierarchical communicative and executive boundaries to ensure organisational permeation |
| | VI Remuneration | 17 | Develop a fair bonus system |
| | | 18 | Offer brand-oriented education and training |
| | | 19 | Link measurable effective brand commitment and team spirit to promotional prospects |
| Stage 3: Evaluating | VII Quantification | 20 | Establish a coherent balanced scorecard measurement system |
| | | 21 | Regularly assess internal brand commitment and external orientation |
| | VIII Reaction | 22 | Facilitate constant, multi-directional feedback |
| | IX Alteration | 23 | Conduct regular review of programme and alter where necessary |

**Figure 13.4**   The consolidated internal branding framework

*Source*: Mahnert and Torres (2007).

that can be used to identify key factors over the long run. Regression analysis can eventually be used to identify key variables in the marketing communications and marketing plans.

The communications strategies of competitors should also be measured and evaluated. Organisations and offerings do not exist in isolation from each other and competitor activities; messages, styles and levels of spend should also be taken into account. If a differentiation strategy is being pursued, it would appear pointless and wasteful to position an offering in the same way as a main competitor.

The process by which an organisation communicates with its target audiences is, as we have seen, extremely important. To assist the process of evaluating the effectiveness of past communication strategies, strategic credibility and the corporate image held by different members of all networks, a communications audit should be undertaken. Financial audits examine the processes by which organisations organise and systematically manage their financial affairs. Some of the underlying agenda items may be to prevent fraud and malpractice, but the positive aspects of the financial audit are to understand what is happening, to develop new ways of performing certain tasks and to promote efficiency and effectiveness. The same principle holds for the communications audit. How is the organisation communicating and are there better ways of achieving the communication objectives?

A communications audit is a process that can help assess whether an organisation is communicating with its consumers and other stakeholders in an effective and meaningful way. A further important goal of such an exercise is to determine whether the communications perceived and understood by the target audiences are the messages that were intended in the first place. Are the messages being decoded in the manner in which they were designed when they were encoded? This exercise helps organisations to develop their realm of understanding with their respective network members and includes all internal and external communications, whether overt or covert.

## Procedures associated with a communications audit

All forms of printed and visual communications (brochures, leaflets, annual reports, letter-heads, advertisements, etc.) need to be collected and assembled in a particular location. Examples of main competitors' materials should also be brought together, as this will provide benchmarks for market evaluation. Once collated, the task is to identify consistent themes and the logic of the organisation's communications.

Ind (1992) suggests that one way of accomplishing this is to develop a communications matrix (see Figure 13.5). Information needs to be grouped by type of offering (vertically) and then by each type of medium (horizontally). The vertical grouping helps determine the variety of messages that customers receive if they are exposed to all the communications relating to a single offering. Are the messages consistent? Are the messages logically related? Is the related logic one that is intended and what is the total impact of these communications? The horizontal grouping helps determine message consistency across a number of different offerings, perhaps from different divisions. If a single dealer or end-user receives the communications relating to a product line or even a particular product mix, is the perception likely to be confusing?

Internal communications should be included in the audit. An analysis of official publications, such as in-house magazines, is obvious, but materials posted on notice boards and the way in which the telephone is answered affect the perception that stakeholders have of the organisation.

The audit needs to incorporate research into the attitudes of employees to the organisation and the perceptions held by various stakeholders. This will involve both qualitative and quantitative research. The objective is to determine whether the image of the organisation reflects reality. If corporate performance exceeds the overall image, then corporate communications are not working effectively. If the image is superior to performance, then the operations of the organisation need to be improved.

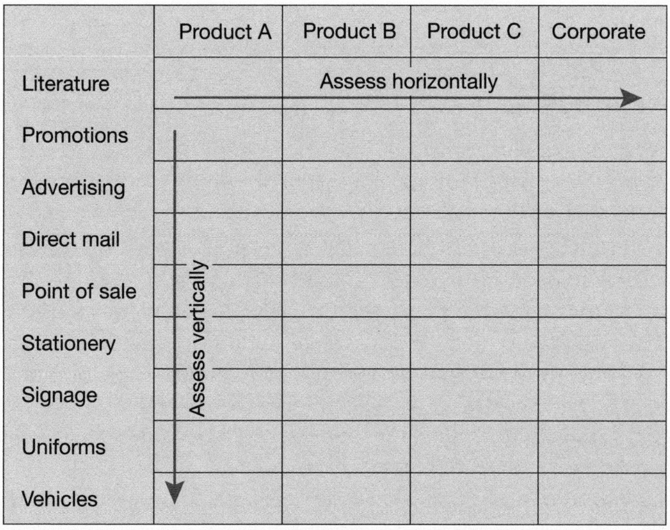

| | Product A | Product B | Product C | Corporate |
|---|---|---|---|---|
| Literature | | Assess horizontally → | | |
| Promotions | | | | |
| Advertising | | | | |
| Direct mail | | | | |
| Point of sale | Assess vertically ↓ | | | |
| Stationery | | | | |
| Signage | | | | |
| Uniforms | | | | |
| Vehicles | | | | |

**Figure 13.5**   A communications audit matrix
*Source*: Ind (1992). Used with kind permission.

Organisations should understand how they are perceived by their stakeholders. A communications audit focuses attention on the totality of messages transmitted and provides a framework for corporate identity programmes.

## Functional capability

The final elements to be reviewed as part of the internal marketing context are those relating to the individual functional areas within an organisation. A firm's overall core competence may be the result of a number of competences held at functional level. Internal marketing can be regarded as a key to providing strong external marketing performance (Greene et al., 1994). This is achieved by releasing high levels of internal service provision within the functional areas. As Varey (1995: 42) confirms, 'Internal service quality is necessary for superior external service quality'.

## Financial capability

Before any communications plan can be devised in any detail, it is necessary to have a broad understanding of the financial capability of the organisation; in other words, how much money is available for communications? This is important, as it affects the objectives that are to be set later and the choice of media necessary to carry the organisation's messages. For example, it is pointless asking dealers to undertake training programmes with end-users if the manufacturer does not have the sales representatives and training staff to instruct the dealers in the first place. Most medium-sized tour operators do not have the capital to fund television-based campaigns, even though some of the major national tour operators regularly use television.

## Manufacturing capablility

One of the main aims of the communications plan is to stimulate and maintain demand. If production resources are limited, the capacity needs to be aligned with the potential demand of a region or local area rather than nationally. Equally, the communications programme should be geared to the same area. All demand must be satisfied and likewise much of the communications programme will be ineffective in the short term if full production capacity has been reached.

## Marketing capability

Discussion so far has assumed that the available corporate and marketing expertise is of sufficient calibre not only to formulate, but also to implement, a marketing strategy and its associated communications requirements. This raises questions about the customer orientation of the organisation, its attitude towards marketing and its general disposition towards the provision of a sustained level of customer service and satisfaction.

In a Research International study reported by Simms (2004) it was found that 47 per cent of respondents had little or no idea of what marketing does, while 54 per cent believe that if marketing was abolished it would have little or no manageable impact on the company. This type of information is fairly typical of a number of studies in this area. Marketing appears to have difficulty establishing itself within many organisations, although its prominence in FMCG companies is high.

Many CEOs still have a poor understanding of what marketing is: to a number of them marketing is about selling and promotion. Such a shallow perspective is unlikely to lead to an organisational culture that will support a marketing orientation (Lings and Greenley, 2009), especially when so few marketing directors have a main board position. The ability of an organisation to deliver consistently effective marketing communications is dependent upon many things, but among them are the presence of a customer-oriented organisational culture and leadership with a broad mix of marketing skills.

It seems reasonable to extend these conclusions by surmising that the same values and beliefs are necessary for the successful adoption of a planned approach to marketing communications, if only because it is a subsystem of marketing planning.

# Key points

- Employees constitute a major stakeholder group, and an internal market based on the exchange of wages for labour. However, they have many other roles of varying complexity and they make a major contribution to the success and performance of the organisation. Their role in providing service and support for a brand has become increasingly recognised. The boundaries that exist between members and non-members of an organisation are becoming increasingly indistinct as a new, more flexible workforce emerges.

- Managers see the main components of internal marketing as falling into three broad areas: development; reward; and vision for employees. These will inevitably vary in intensity on a situational basis. Internal communication can be considered in terms of four dimensions: internal line management communication; internal peer communication; internal project communication; and internal corporate communication.

- The values transmitted to customers, suppliers and distributors through external communications need to be reinforced by the values expressed by employees, especially those who interact with these external groups. Internal marketing communications are necessary in order that internal members are motivated and aligned with the brand strategy such that they are able to present a consistent and uniform message to non-members.

- Organisational identity is concerned with what individual members think and feel about the organisation to which they belong. When their perception of an organisation's characteristics concurs with those held by most employees, the strength of organisational identity will be strong. Organisational identity also refers to the degree to which feelings and thoughts about the distinctive characteristics are shared among the members. There are, therefore, both individual and collective aspects to organisational identity.

- Corporate culture is concerned with the basic assumptions and beliefs that are shared by members of an organisation, that operate unconsciously and define an organisation's view of itself and its environment. A more common view of organisational culture is 'the way we do things around here'.

- Both internal and external communications often reflect the prevailing and dominant culture, whether this be adventurous or cautious, innovative or solid, pessimistic or optimistic, the theme and tone of the communications is often mirrored.

- Employees are required to deliver both the functional aspects of an organisation's offering and the emotional dimensions, particularly in service environments. By attending to these twin elements, it is possible that long-term relationships between sellers and buyers can develop effectively.

- Employee engagement consists of two main components – an intellectual and an emotional element. The intellectual element is concerned with employees buying into and aligning themselves with the organisation's strategy, issues and overall direction. The emotional element is concerned with employees taking ownership of their contribution and becoming committed to the achievement of stated goals.

- Strategic credibility refers to the extent to which key stakeholders favour the company's overall corporate strategy and its strategic planning processes.

- If stakeholders perceive the focus organisation as strategically capable, it is suggested that the benefits include improved stock market valuations and price/earnings multiples, better employee motivation and closer relationships with all members of the performance and support networks, particularly those within the financial community. There are four main determinants of strategic credibility: an organisation's strategic capability; past performance; communication of corporate strategy to key stakeholders; and the credibility of the CEO.

- A communications audit is a process that can assist marketing communications managers to assess whether an organisation is communicating with its consumers and other stakeholders in an effective and meaningful way. A further important goal is to determine whether the communications perceived and understood by the target audiences are the messages that were intended in the first place. Are the messages being decoded in the manner in which they were designed when they were encoded?

# Review questions

1. Write a short definition of internal marketing and explain how marketing communications needs to assume both internal and external perspectives.

2. What is the role of internal marketing communications?

3. Write short notes explaining why organisational boundaries appear to be less clear than was once thought.

4. What is organisational identity and what do Albert and Whetten (1985) consider to be the three important aspects of identity?

5. Write a brief paper explaining why an understanding of corporate culture is important for successful marketing communications.

6. Why should marketing communications accommodate corporate strategy?

7. What are the elements of strategic credibility?

8. Select three different CEOs from a variety of organisations and evaluate their strategic credibility. What is your justification for selecting these individuals?

9. Prepare a communications matrix for an organisation (or brand/product) with which you are familiar.

10. Why might the functional capabilities of an organisation affect an organisation's marketing communications?

# References

Aggerholm, H.K., Andersen, M.A., Asmuß, B. and Thomsen, C. (2010) Management conversations in Danish companies, *Corporate Communication: an International Journal*, 14, 3, 264–79.

Albert, S. and Whetten, D.A. (1985) Organisational identity, in *Research in Organizational Behavior* (eds L.L. Cummings and B.M. Staw), Greenwich, CT: Jai Press, 263–95.

Anon (2012) Marketing Society Awards for Excellence 2012: Employee engagement, *Marketing*, 13 June, retrieved 23 June 2012 from http://www.brandrepublic.com/features/1135809/MARKETING-SOCIETY-AWARDS-EXCELLENCE-2012-Employee-engagement/?DCMP=ILC-SEARCH.

Balmer, J.M.T. and Wilkinson, A. (1991) Building societies: change, strategy and corporate identity, *Journal of General Management*, 17(2), 22–33.

Barich, H. and Kotler, P. (1991) A framework for marketing image management, *Sloan Management Review*, 94 (Winter), 94–104.

Bashford, S. (2011) British Airways: building a brand, from the inside out, *Marketing*, 27 July, 15–15.

Berry, L.L. (1980) Services marketing is different, *Business*, (May/June), 24–9.

Beyer, J.M. (1981) Ideologies, values and decision making in organisations, in *Handbook of Organisational Design* (eds P. Nystrom and W. Swarbruck), London: Oxford University Press.

Bokaie, J. (2008) Corporations get personal, *Marketing*, 6 February, p. 17.

Christensen, L.T. and Askegaard, S. (2001) Corporate identity and corporate image revisited, *European Journal of Marketing*, 35(3/4), 292–315.

Cubbage, A.K. (2005) Inside voices, *Currents*, 31, 14–19.

Dutton, J.E. and Dukerich, J.M. (1991) Keeping an eye on the mirror: image and identity in organisational adaptation, *Academy of Management Review*, 34, 517–54.

Dutton, J.E. and Penner, W.J. (1993) The importance of organisational identity for strategic agenda building, in *Strategic Thinking: Leadership and the Management of Change* (eds J. Hendry, G. Johnson and J. Newton), Chichester: Wiley, 89–113.

Dutton, J.E., Dukerich, J.M. and Harquail, C.V. (1994) Organisational images and member identification, *Administrative Science Quarterly*, 39, 239–63.

Edwards, H. (2012) Helen Edwards: Get personal with your brand, *Marketing*, 16 May, retrieved 24 June 2012 from www.brandrepublic.com/opinion/1131682/Helen-Edwards-personal-brand/?DCMP=ILC-SEARCH.

Elsbach, K.D. and Kramer, R.M. (1996) Members' responses to organisational identity threats: encountering and countering the *Business Week* rankings, *Administrative Science Quarterly*, 41, 442–76.

Foreman, S.K. and Money, A.H. (1995) Internal marketing: concepts, measurements and application, *Journal of Marketing Management*, 11, 755–68.

Freeman, E. and Liedtka, J. (1997) Stakeholder capitalism and the value chain, *European Management Journal*, 15(3), 286–96.

Gilly, M.C. and Wolfinbarger, M. (1998) Advertising's internal audience, *Journal of Marketing*, 62 (January), 69–88.

Goodman, P.S. and Pennings, J.M. (1977) *New Perspectives on Organisational Effectiveness*, San Francisco, CA: Jossey-Bass.

Gordon, G. (1985) The relationship of corporate culture to industry sector and corporate performance, in *Gaining Control of the Corporate Culture* (eds R.H. Kilman, M.J. Saxton, R. Serpa and associates), San Francisco, CA: Jossey-Bass, 103–25.

Gray, L. (2010) Rallying the workforce around Aviva's new brand, *Strategic Communication Management*, 14(2), Feb/Mar, 24–27.

Greene, W.E., Walls, G.D. and Schrest, L.J. (1994) Internal marketing: the key to external marketing success, *Journal of Services Marketing*, 8(4), 5–13.

Grossman, R. (2005). Sometimes it pays to play the fool, *Business Communicator*, 6, 3.

Gummesson, E. (1999) *Total Relationship Marketing: Rethinking Marketing Management: From 4Ps to 30Rs*, Oxford: Butterworth-Heinemann.

Hardaker, S. and Fill, C. (2005) Corporate service brands: the intellectual and emotional engagement of employees, *Corporate Reputation Review: an International Journal*, 8(1), 365–76.

Hatch, M.J. and Schultz, M. (1997) Relations between organisational culture, identity and image, *European Journal of Marketing*, 31(5/6), 356–65.

Hemsley, S. (1998) Internal affairs. *Marketing Week*, 2 April, 49–53.

Herstein, R., Mitki, Y. and Jaffe, E.D. (2008) Communicating a new corporate image during privatization: the case of El Al airlines, *Corporate Communications: An International Journal*, 13(4), 380–93.

Higgins, R.B. and Bannister, B.D. (1992) How corporate communication of strategy affects share price, *Long Range Planning*, 25(3), 27–35.

Hiscock, J. (2002) The brand insiders, *Marketing*, 23 May, 24–5.

HR Editorial (2011) HR Excellence Awards 2011 – Outstanding Employee Engagement Strategy: McDonald's, *HRMagazine.co.uk*, 28 June, retrieved 23 June 2012 from www.hrmagazine.co.uk/hro/news/1019676/hr-excellence-awards-2011-outstanding-employee-engagement-strategy-mcdonalds.

Ind, N. (1992) *The Corporate Image: Strategies for Effective Identity Programmes*, rev. edn., London: Kogan Page.

Kimberley, J. (1980) Initiation, innovation and institutionalisation in the creation process, in *The Organizational Lifecycle* (eds J. Kimberley and R. Miles), San Francisco, CA: Jossey-Bass, 18–43.

Kornacki, M. (2009) Exceptional staff engagement scoops McDonalds an Investors in People Gold Award, *Training Journal*, 25 September, retrieved 23 June 2012 from www.trainingjournal.com/news/2009-09-25-exceptional-staff-engagement-scoops-mcdonalds-an-investors-in-people-gold-award/.

Lievens, A. and Moenart, R.K. (2000) Communication flows during financial service innovation, *European Journal of Marketing*, 34(9/10), 1078–110.

Lings, I.N. and Greenley, G.E. (2009) The impact of internal and external market orientations on firm performance, *Journal of Strategic Marketing*, 17(1), (February), 41–53.

Mahnert, K.F. and Torres, A.M. (2007) The brand inside: the factors of failure and success in internal branding, *Irish Marketing Review*, 19(1/2), 54–63.

McLuhan, M. (1964) *Understanding Media: the extensions of man*, New York: Mentor.

Men, L.R. (2012) CEO credibility, perceived organizational reputation, and employee engagement, *Public Relations Review*, 38(1), (March), 171–3.

Mitchell, A. (1998) P&G's new horizons, *Campaign*, 20 March, 34–5.

Morden, T. (1993) *Business Strategy and Planning*, London: McGraw-Hill.

Morgan, G. (1997) *Images of Organisation*, 2nd edn., New York: Sage.

Newell, S.J. and Shemwell, D.J. (1995) The CEO endorser and message source credibility: an empirical investigation of antecedents and consequences, *Journal of Marketing Communications*, 1, 13–23.

Piercy, N. and Morgan, R. (1991) Internal marketing: the missing half of the marketing programme, *Long Range Planning*, 24 (April), 82–93.

PRNewswire (2012) The Company behind the Brand: In Reputation We Trust – CEO Spotlight, Weber Shandwick, 2 May 2012, retrieved 5 September 2012 from http://www.webershandwick.com/resources/ws/flash/CEO_Spotlight_FINAL_links.pdf.

Punjaisri, K., Evanschitzky, H. and Wilson, A. (2009) Internal branding: an enabler of employees' brand-supporting behaviours, *Journal of Service Management*, 20(2), 209–26.

Riel van, C.B.M. and Fombrun, C.J. (2007) *Essentials of Corporate Communication*, London: Routledge.

Schein, E.H. (1985) *Organizational Culture and Leadership*, San Francisco, CA: Jossey-Bass.

Schein, E.H. (2004) *Organizational Culture and Leadership*, 3rd edn, San Francisco, CA: Jossey-Bass.

Schneider, B. and Bowen, D. (1985) Employee and customer perceptions of service in banks: replication and extension, *Journal of Applied Psychology*, 70, 423–33.

Simms, J. (2004) You're not paranoid, they do hate you, *Marketing*, 19 May, 32–4.

Storey, J. (2001) Internal marketing comes to the surface, *Marketing Week*, 19 July, p. 22.

Vallaster, C. and de Chernatony, L. (2006) Internal brand building and saturation: the role of leadership, *European Journal of Marketing*, 40, 7/8, 761–84.

Varey, R.J. (1995) Internal marketing: a review and some interdisciplinary research challenges, *International Journal of Service Industry Management*, 6(1), 40–63.

Weber Shandwick (2012) The Company behind the Brand: In Reputation We Trust – CEO Spotlight, retrieved 5 September 2012 from http://www.weberstandwick.com/resources/ws/flash/CEO_Spotlight_FINAL_links.pdf.

Welch, M. and Jackson, P.R. (2007) Rethinking internal communication: a stakeholder approach, *Corporate Communications: An International Journal*, 12(2), 177–98.

White, C., Vanc, A. and Stafford, G. (2010) Internal Communication, Information Satisfaction, and Sense of Community: The Effect of Personal Influence, *Journal of Public Relations Research*, 22(1), 65–84.

Witt, J. (2001) Are your staff and ads in tune? *Marketing*, 18 January, p. 21.

# Part 4

## The marketing communication mix

This is the biggest part in the book, configured as three sections, and looks at the various elements that constitute the marketing communication mix. The first section examines the tools or disciplines, the second the media and the third, message content.

Chapter 14 is about advertising and considers the role, use, and types of advertising. Ideas about selling propositions are explored and how emotion precedes an exploration of the way advertising might work. Here consideration is given to some of the principal models and frameworks that have been published to best explain the process by which advertising might influence audiences.

Chapter 15 examines the role and characteristics of public relations, including a review of the various methods used in public relations, and crisis communications. The following chapter leads on naturally to explore sponsorship, while Chapter 17 examines both direct marketing and personal selling.

Chapters 18 and 19 both consider a range of disciplines. The first considers the principles and techniques of sales promotion, field marketing and brand experiences. The second explores brand placement, exhibitions, packaging and the rapidly developing area of brand licensing. This second section brings together various chapters about the media and includes a new chapter on 'Social media and search marketing', and another on 'Multichannel campaigns'.

Chapter 20 considers traditional media, an important foundation upon which to consider the attributes of digital media, the subject of Chapter 21. This chapter commences with a consideration of the features of digitalisation and then explores the application and benefits that digital media offer marketing communications, including a section on website design from a marketing perspective.

Chapter 22 is entitled 'Social, search and interactivity'. This is a new chapter and reflects the contemporary nature of these important and emerging topics. Chapter 23 is concerned with multichannel marketing and the ways in which digital media influence each of the communication tools online, and how they shape multichannel campaigns. The final media chapter considers ideas and theories associated with media planning and the way in which people use media.

The final element in this fourth part of the book, and the third element of the marketing communications mix is the content, or the messages conveyed to, with and between audiences. There are two chapters, with the first of these, 'Creativity', new to the book. This explores the nature, role, and processes organisations use to manage the creative process and the ways in which the creative process can be harnessed. Here message framing and storytelling are developed before concluding with a review of a more contemporary perspective of content generation and creativity – namely, user-generated content.

The final chapter examines message appeals. Attention is first given to the message source, and issues relating to source credibility, and the use of spokespersons, either as the face of a brand or as an endorser. This is followed by a review of the need to balance the use of information and emotion in messages, and the way messages are constructed, before finally exploring the various appeals and ways in which messages can be presented.

# The tools

# The media

# Content

# Chapter 14

# Advertising: role, forms and strategy

Advertising is an integral part of society and affects people in many ways: commercially, culturally and psychologically at an individual level. Indeed, advertising is a powerful force, one that can shape perceptions, feelings, emotions, attitudes, understanding and patterns of individual and group behaviour. Advertising has been of interest to academics, researchers, authors and marketing professionals for a long time. Any attempt to understand what advertising is, how it might work and how it is developing, should be tempered with an appreciation of its complexity and inherent contradictions.

## Aims and learning objectives

The aims of this chapter are to explore different ideas about advertising and to consider the complexities associated with understanding how clients can best use advertising in the marketing communications mix.

The learning objectives of this chapter are to:

1. consider the role that advertising plays in influencing our thoughts and behaviour;
2. develop a definition of advertising as an independent discipline;
3. examine the use of selling propositions, and the role of emotion in advertising;
4. identify different types or forms of advertising;
5. explore various models, concepts and frameworks which have been used to explain how advertising is thought to influence individuals;
6. consider ways in which advertising can be used strategically;
7. review issues associated with consumer-generated advertising.

# Minicase

## Apple – 'Think Different'

Apple had launched the Macintosh during the Superbowl, with what is now regarded as a classic ad '1984'.

However, following the departure of Steve Jobs in 1985, the marketing strategy changed so that by 1996 Apple was a brand in big trouble. It had been losing millions on developing products such as the Newton, that was ahead of its time, and some which never reached the market. There were numerous articles in the media referring to Apple in a negative way, some even suggesting that the purchase of an Apple was ridiculous, to the point of calling Apple computers 'toys', that were not capable of 'real' computing. Market share was falling and the Apple share price was tumbling.

The return of Steve Jobs in 1997 heralded a revival and the transformation of the brand and the company. This was based on his strategic attention to product development and the rejuvenation of Apple's image, based primarily on the legendary 'Think Different' campaign.

The main objective of this revival campaign was to change the way people saw Apple. This required providing evidence that Apple was still alive and conveying messages about what creative people could do with their computers, rather than the traditional approach which was based on what Apple computers can do for you. This meant that the campaign had to provide a way of differentiating Apple strongly, and this had to be accomplished through a focus on brand image and values, and not just show the features and benefits of a series of products. A key principle of the campaign was that there would be no products in the ads.

As the creative team all used and understood Apple computers, there was no formal strategy, just an urgent request to start creating ideas, and they had seven days in which to do it. At the same time the account team, agency planners and new business team began researching Apple's strengths and weaknesses in the marketplace.

At the agency meeting the following week, the room was filled with ideas, photos, roughs and sketches, and taglines, most pinned to wallboards. Of the many ideas, one stood out. To quote Rob Siltanen, the creative director:

*'It was a billboard campaign that had simple black and white photographs of revolutionary people and events. One ad had a photo of Einstein. Another had a photo of Thomas Edison. Another had a photo of Gandhi. Another had the famous photo of flowers placed in gun barrels during the protest of the Vietnam War. At the top of each image was the rainbow-coloured Apple logo and the words "Think Different". Nothing else.'*

This was the work of the art director Craig Tanimoto. His thinking had been rooted in IBM, Apple's major competitor. Their campaign tagline was 'Think IBM', based on their ThinkPad. As Apple is very different from IBM, so the phrase 'Think Different' evolved. By using the rainbow-coloured logo, a stark contrast to the black and white photography was achieved, and reinforced the 'Think Different' statement.

A mood video, or rip-o-matics as Chiat/Day call it, was created for the campaign in order to help convey a tone of voice. This was embodied in the use of Seal's poignant song 'Crazy'. Here the key lyric, 'We're never going to survive unless we get a little crazy' was used to drive the video. A title card, to be played after the video, was developed. This explained that, throughout history, true visionaries have gone against the grain and thought differently, and that Apple makes tools for these types of people. With the mood video completed, and the outdoor, print and storyboarded TV concepts finished, it was time to take the ideas and pitch them to Apple.

Steve Jobs apparently liked the idea but was worried the media would rip him apart if he tried to associate Apple and himself with geniuses. He soon changed his mind and wanted to use Seal's song. However, it proved impossible to cut this to 60 seconds and an alternative poem was written by the agency. It was based on the struggles experienced by exceptional people throughout history. They all had amazing visions but at some point were given unflattering labels. For example, before Einstein became regarded as the world's greatest thinker, he was thought to be plain crazy. Martin Luther King was seen as a troublemaker before he assumed universal sainthood, and Ted Turner was ridiculed when he first tried to sell the concept of a 24-hour news channel. From this the 'Think different' poem developed.

The actual campaign incorporated black and white prints of individuals who had contributed to improving the world, yet had taken risks, defied failure, and pursued their goals doing things in a different way. These included Albert Einstein, Gandhi, Muhammed Ali, Martin Luther King Jr, the Dalai Lama, Nelson Mandela and Bob Dylan.

| Exhibit 14.1 | Apple's 'Think Different' campaign featured people who had made significant changes to the way we live. A range of people were used, such as Martin Luther King, all of whom saw the world differently and tried to make it a better place for everyone. |
| --- | --- |

*Source*: Boston Globe/Getty Images

Each was accompanied by the rainbow-coloured Apple logo and the 'Think different' slogan. See Exhibit 14.1. The TV ad featuring these celebrities was in black and white, and Richard Dreyfus narrated the poem 'Crazy ones', people who changed the world.

There was concern about appearing to exploit these people so, in lieu of payment, all of the participants (or their estates) were given money and computer equipment to be donated to the charities or non-profits of their choice.

Placement of the print and billboard ads was also different. Rather than go down the conventional route of using general computing magazines and billboards, Apple bought space in popular and fashion magazines. Outdoor it used hundreds of major spaces in New York and Los Angeles, never before used for technology-based products. After the first campaign

Apple sent complimentary posters to public schools across the nation, featuring different celebrities, to hang in classrooms.

Soon after the campaign broke people were talking about Apple once again. Market share rose, Apple became popular, not only with consumers but also the media. A year after the 'Think Different' launch, Apple introduced their multi-coloured iMacs. These computers represented revolutionary design, and became some of the best-selling computers in history. The share price tripled within twelve months, and the 'Think Different' campaign went on to win numerous awards and universal acclaim.

*This minicase was written by Chris Fill using a variety of sources including Hormby (2009) and Siltanen (2011).*

# Introduction

Advertising is considered to have been a major element in the change of fortunes at Apple. Indeed, advertising has been considered to be a significant means of communicating with target audiences, based on its potential to influence the way people think/feel, and behave. The thinking element may be concerned with the utilitarian or aspirational benefits of product ownership, or simply a matter of memorising the brand and its features for future recall. The behavioural element may be seen in terms of buying an advertised brand, visiting a website to enquire about a product's features or even sharing brand-related ideas with a friend or colleague.

Whatever the motivation, the content and delivery of advertising messages are derived from an understanding of the variety of contexts in which the messages are to be used. For example, research might reveal a poor brand image relative to the market leader, or audiences might misunderstand when or how to use a product or service. In both cases the messages are going to be different.

This chapter explores three main advertising issues. The first is about the role and use of advertising, how ideas about selling propositions and emotion can be used in advertising, and the different types or forms of advertising that can be identified.

The second concerns the way advertising might work. Here consideration is given to some of the principal models and frameworks that have been published to best explain the process by which advertising might influence audiences.

The third concerns the way in which advertising can be used strategically as part of a brand's development, and to review the significance of consumer-generated advertising.

# The role of advertising

If the role of marketing communications is to engage audiences, as it did so captivatingly for Apple, then it is not surprising that the principal role of advertising is also concerned with engagement. Whether it is on an international, national, local or direct basis, advertising can engage audiences by creating awareness, changing perceptions/attitudes and building brand values, or by influencing behaviour, often through calls-to-action.

Advertising has the capacity to reach huge audiences with simple messages. These messages are intended to enable individuals to comprehend what an offering is, appreciate what its primary benefit is and how this might be of value to an individual. Wherever these individuals are located, the prime goals are to build awareness of a product or an organisation in the mind of the audience and engage them. Engagement (as explored in Chapter 1) occurs when audiences are stimulated to either think about or take action about featured products, services, brands and organisations.

Having successfully engaged an audience, advertising can be used to achieve a number of DRIP-based outcomes, again (as set out in Chapter 1). Advertising is excellent at differentiating and positioning brands. It can be used to reinforce brand messages by reminding, reassuring or even refreshing an individual's perception of a brand. Advertising is excellent at informing audiences, mainly by creating awareness or helping them to learn about a brand or how it works. The one part of the DRIP framework where its ability is challenged is persuasion. Advertising is not so good at provoking or changing behaviour, and a different marketing communications mix is necessary to stimulate change. In this circumstance sales promotion, direct marketing and personal selling are going to be prominent tools in the mix.

Management's control over advertising messages is strong; indeed, of all the tools in the communications mix, advertising has the greatest level of control. The message, once generated and signed off by the client, can be transmitted in an agreed manner and style and at times that match management's requirements. This means that, should the environment change unexpectedly, advertising messages can be 'pulled' immediately. For example, had Research in Motion (RIM, owners of Blackberry) planned a global image campaign designed to build the reputation of the company for November 2011, it would have had to have been 'pulled' (stopped) following the Internet service failure in October. For three days millions of Blackberry Internet service users in the UK, Europe and Africa had no email, web browsing or instant messages. This was probably the result of a failed switch in its core network (Williams, 2011). The impact of this event on business users, and the consequent media comment would have prevented RIM's messages from being received and processed positively or with any credibility. It is more likely that there would have been a negative effect had the planned advertising been allowed to proceed.

Advertising costs can be considered in one of two ways. On the one hand, there are the absolute costs, which are the costs of buying the space in magazines or newspapers or the time on television, cinema or radio. These costs can be enormous, and they impact directly on cash flow. For example, the rate card cost of a full-page (colour) advertisement in the *Daily Mail* on a Thursday or Friday was £48,636 in June 2012. The national rate card cost to show an ad for five weeks with a blockbuster film in June 2012, through Pearl and Dean, was £85,982.

On the other hand, there are the relative costs, which are those costs incurred to reach a member of the target audience with the key message. So, if an audience is measured in hundreds of thousands, or even millions on television, the cost of the advertisement spread across each member of the target audience reduces the cost per contact significantly.

Advertising's main tasks are to build awareness and to (re)position brands, by enabling people to make appropriate brand-related associations. These associations may be based on the utility and functional value a brand represents, or on the imagery and psychological benefits that are conveyed. The regular use of advertising, in coordination with the other elements of the communication mix, can be important to the creation and maintenance of these associations and even build a brand personality.

Advertising can be used as a mobility barrier, deterring exit from and entry to markets. Some organisations are initially attracted to a new market by the potential profits, but a key entry decision factor will be the weight of advertising – that is, the investment or 'spend' necessary to generate demand and a sufficient return on the investment. Many people feel that some brands sustain their large market share by sheer weight of advertising: for example, the washing powder brands of Procter & Gamble and Unilever. In many product categories word-of-mouth communications and the use of digital technologies can stimulate strong levels of awareness. Google and Hotmail are prime examples of contemporary brands developed without the use of advertising. However, advertising, both offline and online, is still a key driver of both brand values and directing certain behaviour, most notably driving people to a website.

Advertising can create competitive advantage by providing the communication necessary for target audiences to frame a product or service. By providing a frame or the perceptual space within which to categorise a product, target audiences are enabled to position an offering relative to their other significant products much more easily. Therefore, advertising can provide the means for differentiation and sustainable competitive advantage. It should also be appreciated, however, that differentiation may be determined by the quality of the execution of the advertisements, rather than through the content of the messages.

There has also been a shift in focus away from mass communications, towards more personalised messages delivered through different, often interactive media. This shift has been demonstrated by the increased use of direct marketing and the Internet, by organisations over the past ten years. It can also be argued that the development of direct marketing is a response to some of the weaknesses, to do with cost and effectiveness of the other tools, most notably advertising.

The marketing communication mix has expanded and become a more complex concept, but essentially it is now capable of delivering two main solutions. On the one hand it can be used to develop and maintain brand values, and on the other it could be used to change behaviour through the delivery of calls-to-action. From a strategic perspective, the former is oriented to the long term and the latter to the short term. It is also apparent that the significant rise of the below-the-line and around-the-line approaches within the communication mix is partly a result of the demise of the unique selling proposition (USP), but it is also a reflection of the increasing financial pressures experienced by organisations to improve performance and return on investment, and at the same time demonstrate increased accountability.

Organisations, therefore, are faced with a dilemma. On the one hand they need to create brands that are perceived to be of value, but on the other they need to prompt or encourage customers into purchase behaviour. To put it another way, marketing communications should be used to encourage buyers along the purchase decision path, but how should advertising be involved, what is its contribution in creating brand values, and which and how many of an organisation's other yet scarce communication resources should be used to prompt behaviour?

---

**Scholars' paper 14.1**    **OK, so what are the ethics in advertising?**

**Drumwright, M.E. and Murphy, P.E. (2009) The Current State of Advertising Ethics: Industry and Academic Perspectives,** *Journal of Advertising*, **38(1), Spring, 83–107.**

The radically transformed communications industry raises the question: what is the current state of advertising ethics? These authors distinguish between ethics in messages and the industry as a whole and conduct interviews with practitioners, academics, review textbooks and the academic literature. The paper provides a useful review of the literature regarding ethics in advertising.

---

# Defining advertising

For many consumers everything they see, hear or log on to that attempts to influence them to consider products and services constitutes a form of advertising. For these people all the promotional methods and techniques such as public relations, sponsorship credits, promotions or direct mail are the same, and they call them all 'advertising'. This blurred vision of the commercial communication landscape is of no consequence to the public. For those practising marketing or the communication disciplines these differences are important, since there are significant differences between the elements that configure the marketing communications mix and what each can accomplish. One of these elements, and some might argue the most significant, is advertising.

Academics Richards and Curran (2002) found variances in the way advertising was defined by authors of various textbooks. They also noted that many of the definitions used the same or similar words. These core words were *paid*, *non-personal*, *identified sponsor*, *mass media*, and *persuade* or *influence*. This enabled them to propose a definition that encapsulated a general consensus around the essence of these words. They referred to this as a *current* definition.

> *Advertising is a paid, non-personal communication from an identified sponsor, using mass media to persuade or influence an audience.*

This interpretation however is debatable. The development of digital technology and the Internet in particular has led to a plethora of new communication techniques and approaches that raises questions about the validity of some of the words in the current definition. Is 'paid' still viable? Can some forms of advertising be unpaid? Surely the use of commercial text messaging indicates that advertising can be 'personal' and the 'mass media' label must therefore be an invalid restriction.

Using a Delphi research approach, Richards and Curran (2002) sought to develop a more contemporary definition of advertising. After much discussion and re-evaluation of the issues and wording, a consensus formed around the following *proposed* definition.

> *Advertising is a paid, mediated form of communication from an identifiable source, designed to persuade the receiver to take some action, now or in the future.*

These changes might be subtle, but they represent an important and methodical attempt to review and update the meaning of advertising. The word 'mediated' replaces the restriction of 'mass media'. 'Source' replaces 'an identified sponsor', and 'persuasion' replaces the duplication apparent in 'persuade' and 'influence'. Whether this proposed definition has infiltrated the textbooks and dictionaries published since 2002 should be the subject of further research. However, marketing practitioners and students are encouraged to use the proposed definition and to ignore the cry of consumers who will no doubt continue to lump all promotional activities under the advertising banner.

# Selling propositions

For a very long time in the advertising world, great emphasis was placed upon the use of unique selling propositions, or USPs. Advertising was thought to work most effectively when the message said something about a product that no competitor brand could offer. For example, Olay claim their products offer 'younger looking skin'. USPs are based on product features and are related to particular attributes that differentiate one product from another, as demonstrated by many washing powders that wash 'whiter', presumably than the competition. If this uniqueness was of value to a consumer then the USP alone was thought sufficient to persuade consumers to purchase. However, as Barwise and Meehan (2009:1) point out: customers rarely buy a product because it offers something unique. What they want are better products and services, something that delivers real value.

However, the reign of the USP was short-lived when technology enabled me-too and own-label brands to be brought to market very quickly and product lifecycles became increasingly short. The power of the USP was eroded and with it the basis of product differentiation as it was known then. In addition, the power and purpose of advertising's role to differentiate was challenged. It is interesting that many people still refer to a product and its advertising in terms of its USP. Some companies believe USP refers to a 'single' selling point. In some cases people refer to USPs, as if a product is capable of having several unique qualities. This is unlikely and is essentially a contradiction in terms.

What emerged were emotional selling propositions or ESPs. Advertising's role became more focused on developing brand values, ones that were based on emotion and imagery. This approach to communication helps build brand awareness, desire and aspirational involvement. However, it often fails to provide customers with a rationale or explicit reason to purchase, what is often referred to as a 'call-to-action'.

Other tools were required to provide customers with an impetus to act and sales promotions, event marketing, road-shows and, later, direct marketing evolved to fulfil this need. These tools are known collectively as *below-the-line communication tools* and their common characteristic is that they are all capable of driving action or creating behavioural change. For example, sales promotions can be used to accelerate customer behaviour by bringing forward sales that might otherwise have been made at some point in the future. Methods such as price deals, premiums and bonus packs are all designed to change behaviour by calling customers into action. This may be in the form of converting or switching users of competitive products, creating trial use of newly introduced products or encouraging existing customers to increase their usage of the product.

| Viewpoint 14.1 | Moving from oral healthcare USPs to ESPs |

Toothpaste, the biggest part of the oral hygiene market (including dental floss, mouthwashes, dental gum and dental cleaners and fixatives), has experienced declining sales. This is due in part to competitive price deals, bonus packs and the increasing use of electronic toothbrushes that require less toothpaste.

Toothpaste has traditionally been presented on an attribute basis, with each brand focusing on a particular USP – for example, Sensodyne for sensitive teeth and gums and Colgate for decay prevention and tartar control. In the 1990s manufacturers started to develop and position brands on whitening agents with cosmetic benefits. The use of USPs in this market was quite common as products are launched for smokers, children and for people with gum disease. This focus on USPs began to decline, if only because competitors were able to neutralise each other's USPs.

The change to emotional positioning and ESPs was evident in Crest's 'Revitalise'. Targeted at women, Revitalise used celebrities such as Ulrika Jonsson in their advertising. The focus and positioning became lifestyle-orientated with demonstrations about how teeth contribute to an individual's overall beauty, appearance and feelings about oneself. Growing interest in the cosmetic benefits of toothpaste has led Crest's owners, Procter & Gamble, to move the brand from the oral care to the beauty division. In 2009 Macleans launched a new brand, called Macleans Confidence. The brand is positioned for those for whom 'social confidence' is important and aims to be based on 'being ready' for unexpected romantic encounters, a strong emotive positioning.

*Source*:　Based on Jack (2009); Bainbridge (2004).

**Question:**　Discuss the notion that to be really effective messages should include both USPs and ESPs.

**Task:**　Find out the USPs or ESPs used in the cosmetics, fruit juice, digital cameras and PDA categories.

# The use of emotion in advertising

The role of emotion in advertising is very important. For a long time advertising was thought to work by people responding to advertising in a logical, rational and cognitive manner. This indicated that people only take out the utilitarian aspect of advertising messages (cleans better, smells fresher). This is obviously not true and there is certainly a strong case for the use of emotion in advertising in order to influence and change attitudes through the affective component of the attitudinal construct (which was considered in Chapter 3).

Most advertised brands are not normally new to consumers as they have had some experience of the brand, whether that be through use or just through communications. This experience affects their interpretation of advertising as memories have already been formed. The role of feelings in the way ads work suggests a consumerist interpretation of how advertising works rather than the rational view, which is much more a researchers' interpretation (Ambler, 1998).

Consumers view advertising in the context of their experience of the category and memories of the brand. Aligned with this approach is the concept of likeability, where the feelings evoked by advertising trigger and shape attitudes to the brand and attitudes to the advertisement (Vakratsas and Ambler, 1999). Feelings and emotions play an important role in advertising, especially when advertising is used to build awareness levels and brand strength.

Most of the models presented later in this chapter are developed on the principle that individuals are cognitive processors and that ads are understood as a result of information processing. The best examples of these are the sequential models referred to earlier (Chapter 4) where information is processed step by step. This view is not universally accepted. Researchers such as Krugman (1971), Ehrenberg (1974), Corke and Heath (2004), Heath and Feldwick (2008) and Heath et al. (2009) all dispute the importance of information processing, denying that attention is necessary for people to understand ads and that the creativity within an ad is more important in many circumstances, than the rational message the ad purports to deliver.

---

**Scholars' paper 14.2**     **LAP service will be resumed**

Grimes, A. (2008) Towards an integrated model of low attention advertising effects: a perceptual-conceptual framework, *European Journal of Marketing*, 42, 1/2, 69–86.

Although this paper may not be ranked as seminal, it provides important background information and explains reasonably coherently both low-involvement processing (LIP) and low-attention advertising. The author proposes an integrated model of advertising effects that identifies two distinct routes to the creation of advertising effects under conditions of low attention.

---

# Types of advertising

There are many ways of categorising advertising, but five perspectives encapsulate the variety of types available. These are the source, the message, the recipient, the media and place. See Figure 14.1.

**The source** or sender of a message results in different forms of advertising. Using the value chain as a frame, we can identify manufacturers, who in turn will use *manufacturing advertising* to promote their brands to end users, and retailers who use advertising to attract consumers, *retail advertising*. On some occasions manufacturers collaborate with retailers and use *cooperative advertising*.

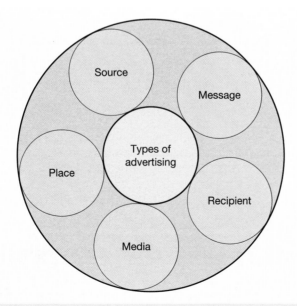

**Figure 14.1**    Types of advertising
*Source*: de Pelsmaker et al. (2010). Used with permission from Pearson Education Ltd.

Outside the commercial arena, governments use *collective advertising* to communicate with nations, regions and districts, while many not-for-profit organisations use *idea-based advertising*.

*The message* can provide a further way of categorising advertising. *Informational advertising* uses messages that predominantly provide information about product and service attributes and features. *Transformational advertising* uses messages that are essentially emotional and which have the capacity to transform the way an individual feels about a product or service. An extreme form of transformational advertising is shock advertising.

*Institutional or corporate advertising* is undertaken by organisations to express values, intentions, position, or other organisation-based issues. It can be withdrawn as Ford did in response to revelations about the *News of the World's* involvement in phone-hacking. This type can also be used to build reputation, goodwill and relationships, at either a product/service or corporate level.

*Theme advertising* is most easily represented by ads designed for employee recruitment, or to attract people to events and entertainment venues. The origins of recruitment advertising are of course rooted in hiring help and employees in order to develop an organisation. However, more recently some employers have started to use this type of advertising as a form of reputational instrument. Whether it is through broadcast, print, or online and social network media, advertising is used to influence corporate image and reputation in order to create perceptions that the organisation is a desirable place to work. This might be to sow the seeds and build relationships, in order to recruit at some point in the future, rather than now.

***Generic advertising*** is used to promote a category of products such as dog food, New Zealand lamb, or South African wine. For example, Kolsarici and Vakratsas (2010) cite Ono (1994) and Campbell's generic campaign 'Never Underestimate the Power of Soup'. This was used to promote the general qualities of soup as a meal, and the result was increased sales for the brand.

| Exhibit 14.2 | **An ad from the Philippine Tourist Authority aimed at promoting its own country to its population.** |

*Source*: Tourism Philippines

Finally in this section, *direct response advertising* is used to provoke action. Sometimes referred to as *call-to-action* advertising, this approach is often used to support sales promotion programmes.

*The recipient* of advertising messages may be *consumers (advertising)* or *businesses*. The latter can be broken down to *industrial* and *trade* advertising. The former represents advertising for products that are used within production and manufacturing processes, whereas the latter concerns products that are resold down the supply chain.

*The media* category refers to the type of media used to carry advertising messages. For example, *broadcast advertising* refers to the use of television and radio, *print advertising* to newspapers and magazines, *out-of-home* to billboards, posters, transport and terminal building, *digital* to Internet, mobile and online advertising. In addition, there is *ambient advertising* (petrol pump nozzles, golf holes, washrooms) and *cinema advertising*. Each of these media is explored in greater detail later in the text. Related to this are display ads that are placed in media for recipients to view, consider, process and form views. These might be magazine or newspaper ads, or banners and pop-ups. Digital media enables interactivity and here both search and social media advertising have become prominent types of advertising.

*Place advertising* is most commonly represented by *international advertising*. Reference is normally made to *standardised advertising*, where a single message is used in all countries and regions, and to *adapted advertising* where messages and media are altered and amended to reflect local needs and customs. (See Exhibit 14.2.)

# Advertising models and concepts

For many years a large number of researchers have attempted to determine how advertising works. Finding a real answer would bring commercial success. We know that for a message to be communicated successfully it should be meaningful to the recipient. Messages need to be targeted at the right audience, be capable of gaining attention, be understandable, relevant and acceptable.

One approach to answering this question has been to model the advertising process. From such a model it should be possible to test the linkages and deduce how advertising works. Unfortunately, despite the effort of many researchers over many years, no single model has attracted widespread agreement. However, from all the work undertaken in this area, a number of views have been prominent. The following sections seek to present some of these more influential perspectives.

## The elaboration likelihood model

What should be clear from the preceding sections is that neither the purely cognitive nor the purely emotional interpretation of how marketing communication works is realistic. In effect, it is probable that both have an important part to play in the way the various tools, and advertising in particular, works. However, the degree of emphasis should vary according to the context within which the marketing communication message is expected to work.

One approach to utilise both these elements has been developed by Petty and Cacioppo (1983). The elaboration likelihood model (ELM) has helped to explain how cognitive processing, persuasion and attitude change occur when different levels of involvement are present. Elaboration refers to the extent to which an individual needs to develop and refine information necessary for decision-making to occur. If an individual has a high level of motivation or ability to process information, elaboration is said to be high. If an individual's motivation or ability to process information is poor, then their level of elaboration is said to be low. The ELM distinguishes two main cognitive processes, as depicted in Figure 14.2.

Under the central route the receiver is viewed as very active and involved. As the level of cognitive response is high, the ability of the message (advertisement) to persuade will depend

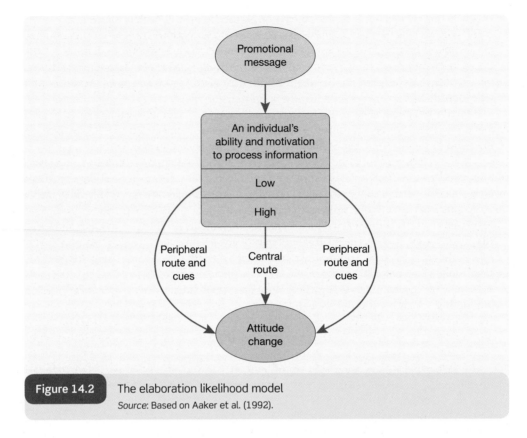

**Figure 14.2**   The elaboration likelihood model
*Source*: Based on Aaker et al. (1992).

on the quality of the argument rather than executional factors. For example, the purchase of a consumer durable such as a car or washing machine normally requires a high level of involvement. Consequently, potential customers would be expected to be highly involved and willing to read brochures and information about the proposed car or washing machine prior to demonstration or purchase. Their decision to act would depend on the arguments used to justify the model as suitable for the individual. For the car purchase these might include the quiet and environmentally friendly engine, the relatively excellent fuel consumption and other safety and performance indicators, together with the comfort of the interior and the effortless driving experience. Whether the car is shown as part of a business executive's essential 'kit' or the commercial is flamboyant and rich will be immaterial for those in the central route.

| Viewpoint 14.2 | Emotional shower power with Philips |

Philips used to be the world leader in electric shavers, but the revival of wet shaving with a blade, led principally by Gillette, saw the steady decline of electric shavers, from the 1980s. Young men didn't want to shave with electric razors any more – they were something their dads used.

To re-establish Philips, they launched the Moisturising Shaving System (MSS) which used a built-in moisturiser by Nivea for Men. Technically this was a superior product as it was waterproof, meaning it could also be used in the shower. In addition, the built-in Nivea lotion dispenser moisturised and protected the face during shaving, so nullifying the skin irritation complaints. Sales were good at the outset but started to fade, despite TV ads which proclaimed the product features and benefits.

Something needed to happen fast as sales and share were falling away. After looking at the research it was decided not to target existing electric shavers as they were older, very loyal and there was a danger of cannibalising their own sales. The marketing strategy was to target the huge opportunity offered by the blade-user segment. However, this generation had grown up shaving with blades and so their habits and rituals were established. This meant that a rational argument based around features and benefits was not likely to work. The new message needed to be about emotion and was revealed when research showed that the target segment was into feeling good, rather than merely being seen as successful.

The futuristic term 'skin technology' emerged, and this led to ideas about a robot shaving assistant. Inevitably the robot was transformed into a sexy female accomplice, one who was mysterious, mesmeric and who sensually represented fusion of MSS technology and Nivea care.

The TV ad showed a human man entering a futuristic bathroom, where a Fembot was laying out towels and preparing the shower. The Fembot then helps him to shave with the moisturising shaver. There was no product information, no message and no voice-over. The background music was slow, haunting designed to create a sensuous atmosphere. The ad represented many things, but one of them was the move by Philips away from simply telling men about shaving towards enabling them to feel things about this ritualistic aspect of their lives. The ad targeted young men and referenced sci-fi, technology and sex.

The campaign had two distinct phases. The first was to develop intrigue and interest, to introduce the Fembot and to keep hidden all information about Philips or MSS. It was totally unbranded. This was accomplished by three animated viral films that introduced the new grooming robot in a futuristic new world. These films directed people to www.robotskin.com, where men could create and email their friends with personalised films about the Fembot. Teaser snippets of the TV ad were shown on video sites. TV was used to launch the ad, featuring the new shaver in a futuristic world. Press and outdoor were used to support the main work.

The second phase was about encouraging trial. Press, a product website (www.feeldifferent.com), online banner ads and public relations were used to accompany the TV work.

The decline in MSS market share stopped immediately the campaign broke. In five months, market share had doubled, in both value and volume. Target share was achieved one year ahead of schedule. Sales results rocketed in all countries where the ad was used. 50 per cent of the new electric shavers were extremely likely to recommend a Philips shaver like MSS to a friend. From Fembots to brand advocates.

*Source*:   Based on Moellmann, Carter, and Binet (2010).

**Question:**   Apart from the underlying and superficial sexual reasoning, why should an animated, female robot empower men to buy a razor?

**Task:**   Find two other examples where animation is used to influence adults.

Under the peripheral route, the receiver is seen to lack the ability to process information and is not likely to engage cognitive processing. Rather than thinking about and evaluating the message content, the receiver tends to rely on what have been referred to as 'peripheral cues', which may be incidental to the message content. Panasonic use peripheral cues to attract attention to their brand. This is because most people have low levels of elaboration concerning picture technology and electronics.

In low-involvement situations, a celebrity may serve to influence attitudes positively. This is based upon the creation of favourable attitudes towards the source rather than engaging the viewer in the processing of the message content. For example, Gary Lineker has been the celebrity spokesperson used to endorse Walkers crisps for many years. Gary Lineker, former Tottenham and England football hero and now BBC sports presenter, was an important peripheral cue for Walkers crisps (more so than the nature of the product), in eventually persuading a consumer to try the brand or retaining current users. Think crisps, think Gary Lineker, think Walkers. Where high involvement is present, any celebrity endorsement is of minor significance to the quality of the message claims.

Communication strategy should be based upon the level of cognitive processing that the target audience is expected to engage in and the route taken to affect attitudinal change. If the processing level is low (low motivation and involvement), the peripheral route should dominate and emphasis needs to be placed on the way the messages are executed and on the emotions of the target audience (Heath, 2000). If the central route is expected, the content of the messages should be dominant and the executional aspects need only be adequate.

---

### Scholars' paper 14.3    Peripheral or central thinking

**Petty, R.E. and Cacioppo, J.T. (1984) Source factors and the elaboration likelihood model of persuasion, *Advances in Consumer Research*, 11(1), 668–72.**

This is an important paper because it introduces the elaboration likelihood model. This is based on ideas about how people process ads, relative to how motivated they are to process the information. When people lack motivation and are unable to process a message, they prefer to rely on simple cues in the persuasion context, such as the expertise or attractiveness of the message source. When people are highly motivated and able to process the arguments in a message, they are interested in reviewing all the available information.

---

## Eclectic models of advertising

A number of new frameworks and explanations have arisen, all of which claim to reflect practice. In other words these new ideas about how advertising works are a practitioner reflection of the way advertising is considered to work, or at least used, by advertising agencies. The first to be considered here are four main advertising frameworks developed by O'Malley (1991) and Hall (1992). These reflect the idea that there are four keys ways in which advertising works, depending on context and goals. This also says that different advertising works in different ways, there is no one all-embracing model. These were updated by Willie (2007) to incorporate the impact of digital media and interactivity. Figure 14.3 depicts the essence of all of these ideas. The essential point is that advertising cannot be explained by a single interpretation or model.

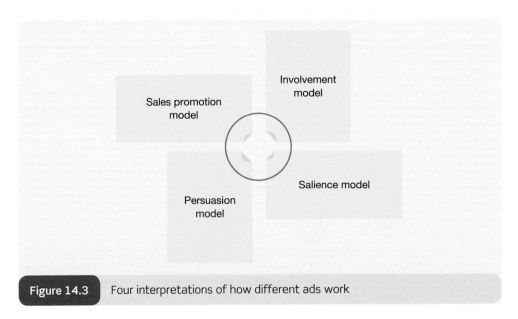

**Figure 14.3**    Four interpretations of how different ads work

Each of the following sections has two components. The first refers to the original inter-pretation, and the second to the work of Willie and the digital element.

1. **The persuasion framework**

   *Analogue* – The first framework assumes advertising works rationally, and that a 'brand works harder for you'. This is based on messages that are persuasive, because they offer a rational difference, grounded in unique selling propositions (USPs). Persuasion is effected by gradually moving buyers through a number of sequential steps, as depicted through hierarchy of effects models such as AIDA.

   *Digital* – Digitisation enables persuasion to be extended into opportunities for exploration, as individuals can now be encouraged to search, 'go to', and to find out more. Willie points out that this is still persuasion, but it occurs through guided exploration, rather than mere narration.

2. **The involvement framework**

   *Analogue* – Involvement-based advertisements work by drawing the audience into the advertisement and eliciting a largely emotional form of engagement. Involvement with the brand develops because the messages convey that the 'brand means more to you'. As Willie indicates, involvement can be developed through shared values (Dove), aspirational values (American Express) or by personifying a brand, perhaps by using celebrities (Adidas).

   *Digital* – Today digitisation develops the notion of involvement by encouraging people to play. This is about content creation and consumers controlling brands. User-generated content can be seen through ads (crowd sourcing), blogs, wikis, videos and social networking, for example.

---

## Viewpoint 14.3    Korona – involving women and chocolate

Korona is the Ukrainian word for 'crown', and it is also the name of one of the country's favourite brands of chocolate, the one which uses a crown as its logo.

Targeted at 17- to 50-year-old, middle-class women, the brand has pursued a consistent commun-ications strategy since the mid 1990s. Based on romance and fantasy, the ads use a storyline that is anchored around the 'woman meets man' scenario, with the twist that she is always shown eating Korona chocolate. Indeed, not just any woman is featured in the advertising, as the actress always has dark hair. It is thought this is an attempt to cement associations with Korona's dark chocolate.

Each video is supported by the voice of a Ukrainian female singer who, although not visible in the ad, is instantly recognisable to those who live in the Ukraine. For example, the ad in 2010 campaign depicted a woman waking up, rushing for and catching a train, and then opening and savouring a piece of Korona chocolate. At this point she meets a man who puts a ring, in the form of a crown, on her finger.

Korona make two types of video ads. A short one is used for television ads, and a longer one for use in-store, through social media such as YouTube, and other digital formats. Television advertising is supported by print and outdoor work, plus sales promotion, public relations and sponsorship, including a Miss Korona beauty contest.

The familiarity of the storyline serves to reinforce brand associations and remind audiences of Korona.

*Source*:   Based on Kharina (2012).

> **Question:**   Why might this clichéd approach to communication work?
>
> **Task:**   Find a copy of the Ferrero Rocher: 'The Ambassador's Party' series of ads on YouTube. How do they compare in principle to those used by Korona?

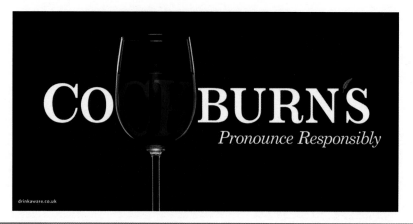

> **Exhibit 14.3**   **This salience ad enables Cockburns to stand out in the category through the use of subtle humour**
>
> This outdoor ad was part of a campaign designed to reintroduce Cockburns Port to the British public. Despite the spelling, the correct pronunciation is Co-burns.
>
> *Source*: BETC London.

**3 The salience framework**

*Analogue* – This interpretation is based upon the premise that advertising works by standing out, by being different from all other advertisements in the product class (see Exhibit 14.3). The ads used by brands such as Cillit Bang, GoCompare.com, Injurylawyers4u, and Sheila's Wheels were deemed by consumers to be irritating, partly because the messages make people think about the brand more frequently than they would prefer.

*Digital* – Contemporary interpretations of salience incorporate ideas about sharing messages about the brand either directly or virally, and getting the brand discussed, mentioned and talked about.

**4 The sales promotion framework**

*Analogue* – This view holds that advertising activities are aimed ultimately at shifting product: that is, generating sales. Messages are invitations to participate in promotions, sales, and various forms of price deals. This framework, oriented mainly to direct-response work, is based on the premise that the level of sales is the only factor that is worth considering when measuring the effectiveness of an advertising campaign.

*Digital* – Digitisation has not affected this framework, simply because sales promotion was always a 'do' or behavioural model.

The analogue-based frameworks represent communications that induce a thinking, value-based response. The digital-based frameworks represent a behavioural response that is related to the brand, not the communications. These two fundamentally different types of response can be seen in Table 14.1. Furthermore, the models bring to attention two important points about people and advertising. Advertisements are capable of generating two very clear types of response: a response to the advertisement itself and a response to the featured brand. Both have clear roles to play in advertising strategy.

## The Strong and the Weak theories of advertising

Many of the explanations offered to date are based on the premise that advertising is a potent marketing force, one that is persuasive and which is done *to* people. More recent views of advertising theory question this fundamental perspective. The second group of eclectic interpretations about how advertising works concerns ideas about advertising as a force

| Table 14.1 | Digital and analogue advertising messages | |
| --- | --- | --- |
| **Analogue-delivered messages say** | | **Digitally delivered messages encourage** |
| This is the reason why this brand is different | Persuasion | People to explore a brand such as search |
| Imagine you are associated with the brand | Involvement | People to play and create content |
| Please think about this brand | Salience | People to talk and share information about a brand |
| Act now because you will be rewarded | Promotion | People to act now because they will be rewarded |

for persuasion and as a force for reminding people about brands. Prominent among these theorists are Jones, McDonald and Ehrenberg, some of whose views will now be presented. Jones (1991) presented the new views as the Strong theory of advertising and the Weak theory of advertising.

## The Strong theory of advertising

All the models presented so far are assumed to work on the basis that they are capable of affecting a degree of change in the knowledge, attitudes, beliefs and sometimes, the behaviour of audiences. Jones refers to this as the *strong theory of advertising*, and it appears to have been universally adopted as a foundation for commercial activity.

According to Jones, exponents of this theory hold that advertising can persuade someone to buy a product that they have never previously purchased. Furthermore, continual long-run purchase behaviour can also be generated. Under the Strong theory, advertising is believed to be capable of increasing sales at the brand and class levels. These upward shifts are achieved through the use of manipulative and psychological techniques, which are deployed against consumers who are passive, possibly because of apathy, and are generally incapable of processing information intelligently. The most appropriate theory would appear to be the hierarchy of effects model, where sequential steps move buyers forward to a purchase, stimulated by timely and suitable promotional messages.

## The Weak theory of advertising

Increasing numbers of European writers argue that the Strong theory does not reflect practice. Most notable of these writers is Ehrenberg (1988, 1997), who believes that a consumer's pattern of brand purchases is driven more by habit than by exposure to promotional messages. The framework proposed by Ehrenberg is the awareness–trial–reinforcement (ATR) framework. Awareness is required before any purchase can be made, although the elapsed time between awareness and action may be very short or very long. For the few people intrigued enough to want to try a product, a trial purchase constitutes the next phase. This may be stimulated by retail availability as much as by advertising, word-of-mouth or personal selling stimuli. Reinforcement follows to maintain awareness and provide reassurance to help the customer to repeat the pattern of thinking and behaviour and to cement the brand in the repertoire for occasional purchase activity. Advertising's role is to breed brand familiarity and identification (Ehrenberg, 1997) and is considered to be a weak force.

Following on from the original ATR model (Ehrenberg, 1974), various enhancements have been suggested. However, Ehrenberg added a further stage in 1997, referred to as the nudge.

He argues that some consumers can 'be nudged into buying the brand more frequently (still as part of their split-loyalty repertoires) or to favour it more than the other brands in their consideration sets'. Advertising need not be any different from before; it just provides more reinforcement that stimulates particular habitual buyers into more frequent selections of the brand from their repertoire.

According to the Weak theory, advertising is capable of improving people's knowledge, and so is in agreement with the Strong theory. In contrast, however, consumers are regarded as selective in determining which advertisements they observe and only perceive those that promote products that they either use or have some prior knowledge of. This means that they already have some awareness of the characteristics of the advertised product. It follows that the amount of information actually communicated is limited. Advertising, Jones continues, is not potent enough to convert people who hold reasonably Strong beliefs that are counter to those portrayed in an advertisement. The time available (30 seconds in television advertising) is not enough to bring about conversion and, when combined with people's ability to switch off their cognitive involvement, means there may be no effective communication. Advertising is employed as a defence, to retain customers and to increase product or brand usage. Advertising is used to reinforce existing attitudes, not necessarily to drastically change them.

Unlike the Strong theory, this perspective accepts that, when people say that they are not influenced by advertising, they are in the main correct. It also assumes that people are not apathetic or even stupid, but capable of high levels of cognitive processing.

In summary, the Strong theory suggests that advertising can be persuasive, can generate long-run purchasing behaviour, can increase sales and regards consumers as passive. The Weak theory suggests that purchase behaviour is based on habit and that advertising can improve knowledge and reinforce existing attitudes. It views consumers as active problem-solvers.

These two perspectives serve to illustrate the dichotomy of views that has emerged about this subject. They are important because they are both right and they are both wrong. The answer to the question 'How does advertising work?' lies somewhere between the two views and is dependent upon the particular situation facing each advertiser. Where elaboration is likely to be high if advertising is to work, then it is most likely to work under the strong theory. For example, consumer durables and financial products require that advertising urges prospective customers into some form of trial behaviour. This may be a call for more information from a sales representative or perhaps a visit to a showroom. The vast majority of product purchases, however, involve low levels of elaboration, where involvement is low and where people select, often unconsciously, brands from an evoked set.

New products require people to convert or change their purchasing patterns. It is evident that the Strong theory must prevail in these circumstances. Where products become established, their markets generally mature, so that real growth is non-existent. Under these circumstances, advertising works by protecting the consumer franchise and by allowing users to have their product choices confirmed and reinforced. The other objective of this form of advertising is to increase the rate at which customers reselect and consume products. If the Strong theory were the only acceptable approach then, theoretically, advertising would be capable of continually increasing the size of each market, until everyone had been converted. There would be no 'stationary' markets.

Considering the vast sums that are allocated to advertising budgets, not only to launch new products but also to pursue market share targets aggressively, the popularity and continued implicit acceptance of the power of advertising suggest that a large proportion of resources are wasted in the pursuit of advertising-driven brand performance. Indeed, it is noticeable that organisations have been switching resources out of advertising into digital, interactive and sales promotion activities. There are many reasons for this, but one of them concerns the failure of advertising to produce the expected levels of performance: to produce market share. The Strong theory fails to deliver the expected results, and the Weak theory does not apply to all circumstances. Reality is probably a mixture of the two.

# Using advertising strategically

There are many varied and conflicting ideas about the strategic use of advertising. For a long time the management of the tools of the communication mix was considered strategic. Indeed, many practitioners still believe in this approach. However, ideas concerning integrated marketing communications and corporate identity (Chapters 10 and 12) have helped provide a fresh perspective on what constitutes advertising strategy, and issues concerning differentiation, brand values and the development of brand equity have helped establish both a strategic and a tactical or operational aspect associated with advertising.

One of the first significant attempts to formalise advertising's strategic role was developed by Vaughn when working for an advertising agency, Foote, Cone and Belding. These ideas (see below) were subsequently debated and an alternative model emerged from Rossiter and Percy. Both frameworks have been used extensively by advertising agencies, and although their influence has now subsided, the underlying variables and approach remain central to strategic advertising thought.

## The FCB matrix

Vaughn (1980) developed a matrix utilising involvement and brain specialisation theories. Brain specialisation theory suggests that the left-hand side of the brain is best for handling rational, linear and cognitive thinking, whereas the right-hand side is better able to manage spatial, visual and emotional issues (the affective or feeling functions).

Vaughn proposed that by combining involvement with elements of thinking and feeling, four primary advertising planning strategies can be distinguished. These are informative, affective, habitual and self-satisfaction (see Figure 14.4). According to Vaughn, the matrix is intended to be a thought provoker rather than a formula or model from which prescriptive solutions are to be identified. The FCB matrix is a useful guide to help analyse and appreciate consumer/product relationships and to develop appropriate communication strategies. The four quadrants of the grid identify particular types of decision-making and each requires different advertising approaches. Vaughn suggests that different orderings from the learn–feel–do sequence can be observed. By perceiving the different ways in which the process can be ordered, he proposed that the learn–feel–do sequence should be visualised as a continuum, a circular concept. Communication strategy would, therefore, be based on the point of entry that consumers make to the cycle.

Some offerings, generally regarded as 'habitual', may be moved to another quadrant, such as 'responsive', to develop differentiation and establish a new position for the product in the minds of consumers relative to the competition. This could be achieved by the selection of suitable media vehicles and visual images in the composition of the messages associated with an advertisement. There is little doubt that this model, or interpretation of the advertising process, has made a significant contribution to our understanding of the advertising process and has been used by a large number of advertising agencies (Joyce, 1991).

## The Rossiter-Percy grid

Rossiter et al. (1991), however, disagree with some of the underpinnings of the FCB grid and offer a new one in response (revised 1997) (Figure 14.5). They suggest that involvement is not a continuum because it is virtually impossible to decide when a person graduates from high to low involvement. They claim that the FCB grid fails to account for situations where a person moves from high to low involvement and then back to high, perhaps on a temporary basis, when a new variant is introduced to the market. Rossiter et al. regard involvement as the level of perceived risk present at the time of purchase. Consequently, it is the degree of familiarity buyers have at the time of purchase that is an important component.

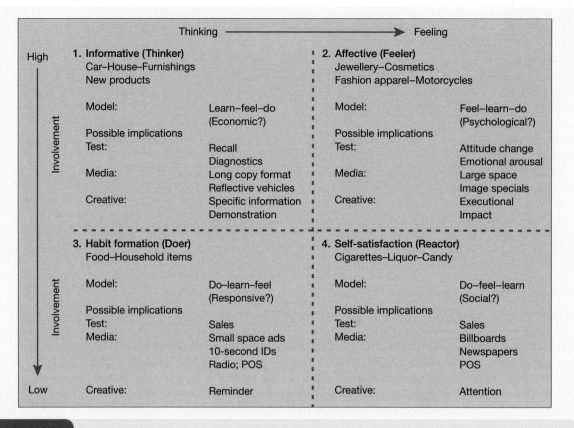

| **Figure 14.4** | The FCB grid |
| --- | --- |

*Source*: Vaughn (1980). Used with kind permission from WARC.

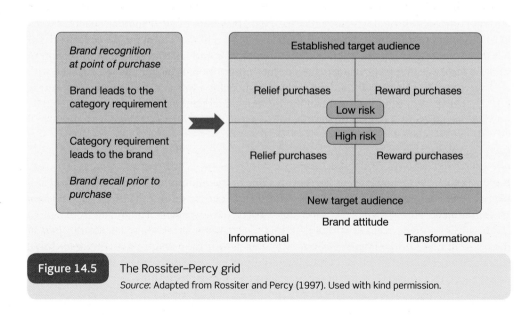

| **Figure 14.5** | The Rossiter–Percy grid |
| --- | --- |

*Source*: Adapted from Rossiter and Percy (1997). Used with kind permission.

A further criticism is that the FCB grid is an attitude-only model. Rossiter et al. identify the need for brand awareness to be built into such grids as a prerequisite for attitude development. However, they cite the need to differentiate different purchase situations. Some brands require awareness recall because the purchase decision is made prior to the act of purchasing. Other brands require awareness recognition at the point of purchase, where the buyer needs to be prompted into brand choice decisions. Each of these situations requires different message strategies (and these are explored in Chapter 26).

The other major difference between the two grids concerns the 'think–feel' dimension. Rossiter et al. believe that a wider spectrum of motives must be incorporated, as the FCB 'think–feel' interpretation fails to accommodate differences between product category and brand purchase motivations. For example, the decision to use a product category may be based on a strictly functional and utilitarian need. The need to travel to another country often requires air transport. The choice of carrier, however, particularly over the North Atlantic, is a brand choice decision, motivated by a variety of sensory and ego-related inputs and anticipated outputs. Rossiter et al. disaggregate motives into what they refer to as *informational* and *transformational*. By detailing motives into these classifications, a more precise approach to advertising tactics can be developed. Furthermore, the confusion inherent in the FCB grid, between the think and involvement elements, is overcome.

It should be understood that these 'grids' are purely hypothetical, and there is no proof or evidence to suggest that they are accurate reflections of advertising. It is true that both models have been used as the basis for advertising strategy in many agencies, but that does not mean that they are totally reliable or, more importantly, that they have been tested empirically so that they can be used in total confidence. They are interpretations of commercial and psychological activity and have been instrumental in advancing our level of knowledge. It is in this spirit of development that these models are presented in this text.

There are parts in both of these frameworks that have a number of strong elements of truth attached to them. However, for products that are purchased on a regular basis, pull strategies should be geared to defending the rationale that current buyers use to select the brand. Heavy buyers select a particular brand more often than light users do from their repertoire. By providing a variety of consistent stimuli, and by keeping the brand alive, fresh buyers are more likely to prefer and purchase a particular brand than those that allow their brands to lose purchase currency and the triggers necessary to evoke memory impressions.

For products purchased on an irregular basis, marketing communications need only touch the target audience on a relatively low number of occasions. Strategies need to be developed that inform and contextualise the purchase rationale for consumers. This means providing lasting impressions that enable consumers to understand the circumstances in which purchase of a particular product/brand should be made once a decision has been made to purchase from the product category. Here the priorities are to communicate messages that will encourage consumers to trust and bestow expertise on the product/brand that is offered.

Traditionally advertising has been used to develop brand identities by stimulating awareness and perception. Advertising had evolved to a point in the 1980s where the focus on developing brand identities and brand values alone was commercially insufficient for clients. The subsequent growth of direct marketing approaches and one-to-one, preferably interactive communications have become paramount. Marketing budgets have swung in sympathy, and are now very often allocated towards communications that drive a call-to-action; in particular, online communications have been taking a progressively larger share of advertising budgets since 2004. Consequently, the imperative today is about generating a behavioural rather than an attitudinal response to advertising and other marketing communications campaigns.

So, in this context, what is the role for advertising and what strategies should be used in the contemporary media landscape? One approach would be to maintain current advertising strategies on the grounds that awareness and perception are always going to be key factors. Another approach would be to call for advertising to be used solely for direct-response work. Neither of these two options seems appropriate or viable in the twenty-first century.

| Viewpoint 14.4 | Dreaming of sleeping with wolves? |

Each of the 57 Shangri-La hotels and resorts epitomises the very essence of Asian hospitality, and the group has grown steadily over the past 40 years. However, as part of its global expansion strategy it set itself the business goal of increasing its revenue by US$ 90 million. This equated to selling ten more rooms per hotel, each night.

Rather than use promotional pricing, it decided to develop a stronger Shangri-La brand, to drive more visitors and secure longer-term growth. The target audiences were the 66,000 employees, and the 35+, up-market, premium business travellers who account for around 70 per cent of Shangri-La's business. These travellers spend a lot of time away from home, preferring to stay at familiar 5-star hotels. However, research showed that the luxury could never compensate them for the loneliness and alienation of yet another foreign trip.

The Shangri-La delivers Asian luxury service with a smiling face and a respectful bow and treats each guest as if they are royalty. Yet, at the Shangri-La the culture expresses a deeper sense of humanity, with staff referring to and treating guests as if they were visitors to their own homes. Even the training materials emphasised 'everything should come from the heart'. Loyal guests called Shangri-La 'a part of the family'. From this the engagement strategy started to emerge – namely, that at Shangri-La the guest was not a King – but Kin, a human being.

In order to convey this proposition, communications needed to be very distinctive, unorthodox for the sector, yet emotionally engaging. Using visual and aural language to express pure luxury, stories were told, using metaphors about the benevolence of animals who embraced humans as their own. This was expressed through a striking film and three print executions. These depicted a traveller lost in the snow, who to his surprise was rescued by wolves. These were supported by the line, 'There is no greater act of hospitality than to embrace a stranger as one's own. Shangri-La. It's in our nature.'

Ahead of the campaign launch, all staff were presented with a brand manifesto which was also printed in a pocket book. This contained Shangri-La's proposition translated into principles of behaviour. All staff training was redesigned, and all 66,000 employees attended launch events at every hotel to see the creative before anyone else. With huge jigsaw puzzles to illustrate the print executions, and postcards inviting staff to feed back their views of the proposition, the goal was to convey the importance of each member of staff as an integral part of the brand promise.

The media strategy included the usual high reach media of in-flight TV and magazines and lifestyle and business press. However, it also included BBC *News24*, CNN and Starworld, and similar media, as this reflected the frequency with which business travellers attempt to re-connect with home by visiting their home news portals, business sites, TV channels and magazines.

In 2010 revenue increased by US$302.7 million year-on-year. The campaign generated an extra 937,980 more room sales, which is equivalent to 45 more rooms per hotel per night. This exceeded the objective more than four times. The media spend amounted to US$7.5 million, which meant that the campaign paid back US$40 for each US$1 media spent.

*Source*: Moustou and Tam (2011); www.shangri-la.com; Walters (2010) www.warc.com.

| | |
|---|---|
| **Question:** | What are the strategic issues associated with this ad? |
| **Task:** | Find another luxury brand hotel and evaluate their brand communications. |

In an age where values and response are both necessary ingredients for effective overall communication, advertising strategy in the future will probably need to be based on emotional engagement and an increased level of integration with a range of other forms of communication. Customers will want to engage with the values offered by a brand that are significant to them individually. However, clients will also need to engage with them at a behavioural level and to encourage individuals to want to respond to advertising. Advertising strategy should therefore reflect a brand's context and be adjusted according to the required level of engagement regarding identity development and the required level of behavioural response. Advertising will no longer be able to assume the lead role in a campaign as of right and should be used according to the engagement needs of the audience, first, the brand, second, and the communication industry, third, in that order. One of the more integrative approaches concerns the need to use advertising to drive Web traffic. This offline/online bridge is a critical aspect of many communication strategies.

# Consumer-generated advertising

To conclude this chapter and the strategic perspective on advertising, attention needs to be given to the inexorable rise in user- or consumer-generated advertising (CGA). This is a subsection of user-generated content which, according to Stoeckl et al. (2007), cited by Campbell et al. (2011), is about circumstances where 'consumers freely choose to create and share information of value'. CGA, on the other hand, refers to specific instances where consumers create brand-focused messages with the intention of influencing others. For Campbell et al. (2011: 88) CGA is 'any publicly disseminated, consumer-generated advertising messages whose subject is a collectively recognized brand'. In other words, CGA is about ads concerning recognised brands, which are made available to the public. (UGC is considered in Chapter 25 on Creativity, and that material will not be repeated here.)

Much of the advertising explored in this chapter is based on the brand-to-consumer dynamic, a unidirectional interpretation, anchored in a client/agency origin. Increasingly today consumers not only reject this passive-response-based model but are now creating and distributing their own ads, very often as videos hosted on video-sharing sites such as YouTube.

Campbell et al. (2011) claim that it is these video facilities, and the exponential growth in their utilisation, that is fuelling a revolution in advertising. The disintegration of various forms of advertising can be seen to have mutated over time as new media become available. They point to the transition from print to radio, to television, and how message themes evolved from 'hard sell' in the 1950s to 'subtle' in the 1990s. However, the critical issue associated with CGA concerns control and the ability of organisations to control in a precise way messages surrounding their brands. It is much more challenging to control brand messages today, and new approaches and formats need to be considered.

There are several ways of considering CGA but the main two are from a viewer's and a brand's perspective. Berthon, Pitt, and Campbell (2008) identify three fundamental motivations that consumers have for creating and broadcasting ads: intrinsic enjoyment, self-promotion, and perception change. These are explained in Table 14.2.

CGA is connected to WoM communications that flow as a result of the posting and viewing of ads online. Although the authenticity of WoM from GCA may be varied, viewers of CGA can, according to Campbell et al. (2011) consider it to be a reliable source of WoM.

Campbell et al. (2011) suggest that the primary responses to CG ads can be considered on two broad dimensions. The first dimension spans the *conceptual* – that is, curiosity in how or who created the ad, and *emotion* – how responses to the ad are driven essentially by emotion rather than reason.

| Table 14.2 | Three consumer motivations to create ads |
| --- | --- |
| **Dominant motivation** | **Explanation** |
| **Intrinsic enjoyment** | Here people are primarily creative and enjoy the process for the satisfaction and personal reward the activity brings. They are not so interested in what becomes of their work. |
| **Self-promotion** | In this situation people generate advertising materials as a means to an end. It may be that the activity is part of the process of attracting the attention of others, possibly a potential employer. |
| **Perception change** | Rather than achieve a tangible outcome, some advertising is generated by people in order to influence the way others think or feel, intangible outcomes. The goal is to change opinions, sentiments or attitudes but for altruistic reasons rather than personally driven, career-based goals. |

Based on Berthon, Pitt, and Campbell (2008).

The second dimension concerns how a consumer's response to the ad can either be collaborative, where the viewer supports the ad's creator, or is in opposition and is hostile toward the ad, and/or its creator. From these dimensions a classic 2x2 grid can be determined identifying four response archetypes to CG ads. These are termed inquiry, laudation, debate, and the flame. See Figure 14.6.

Inquiry refers to responses that say: 'That is interesting, tell me more.' Laudation is about how good the ad is thought to be, the praise viewers give it. Debate concerns the different voices and divergent views or opinions on the topic of interest. Finally, flame concerns the outpouring of emotions, the diatribe that occurs when the debate becomes enflamed and hostile.

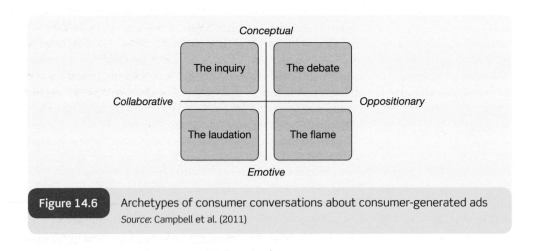

| Figure 14.6 | Archetypes of consumer conversations about consumer-generated ads |
| --- | --- |

*Source*: Campbell et al. (2011)

Research by Campbell et al. (2011) reveals that WoM conversations around brands driven by CGA indicate that the brand itself is often not very prominent. The discussion they found was on other issues: the music in the ad, the creators of the ad, 'and larger social themes such as international justice, globalization, poverty, and corporate social responsibility'. This could have an important bearing on advertising messages and appeals in the future, especially for functional brands.

> ### Scholars' paper 14.4    Mapping conversations around consumer-generated ads
>
> **Campbell, C., Pitt, L.F., Parent, M. and Berthon, P.R. (2011) Understanding Consumer Conversations Around Ads in a Web 2.0 World,** *Journal of Advertising,* **40(1) (Spring), 87–102.**
>
> The development of consumer-generated advertising has been considerable, yet research has not been able to keep pace. This paper reports on research designed to interpret the conversations consumers have about and around consumer-generated ads. This is undertaken using the comments posted to each ad's Web page. They map and interpret these conversations and then develop a typology of consumer-generated ad conversations.

# Key points

- The role of advertising in most marketing communications campaigns is to engage audiences and enable people to make brand-orientated associations. Engagement is enabled either by informing, changing perceptions and building brand values, or by encouraging a change in behaviour.

- In an age where values and response are both necessary ingredients for effective overall communication, future advertising strategy will probably need to be based on engagement. Advertising strategy should therefore reflect a brand's context and be adjusted according to the required level of engagement regarding identity development and the required level of behavioural response.

- A few of the established definitions have been perpetuated by both practitioners and by academics. These have generally failed to accommodate the changing media landscape and so a new definition is presented.

   *Advertising is a paid, mediated form of communication from an identifiable source, designed to persuade the receiver to take some action, now or in the future.*

- The idea that a product might have a unique selling proposition is in many cases totally misplaced and inaccurate. The rise of emotional selling points (ESPs) is much more realistic and practised by leading brands. This approach to communication helps build brand awareness, desire and aspirational involvement. However, it often fails to provide customers with a rationale or explicit reason to purchase, what is often referred to as a 'call-to-action'.

- The use of emotion in advertising is considered to be more important, and effective, than the use of information-based messages. Feelings and emotions play an important role in advertising, especially when advertising is used to build awareness levels and brand strength.

- There are many ways of categorising advertising, but five perspectives encapsulate the variety of types available. These are the source, the message, the recipient, the media and place.

- The elaboration likelihood model (ELM) has helped to explain how cognitive processing, persuasion and attitude change occur when different levels of involvement are present. Elaboration refers to the extent to which an individual needs to develop and refine information necessary for decision-making to occur. If an individual has a high level of motivation or ability to process information, elaboration is said to be high and central route processing is used. If an individual's motivation or ability to process information is poor, then their level of elaboration is said to be low, and peripheral processing is appropriate.

- Many of the ideas about how advertising works are a practitioner reflection of the way advertising is considered to work, or at least is used, by advertising agencies. The first to be considered here are the frameworks developed by O'Malley (1991) and Hall (1992), and later supplemented by Willie (2007). They suggest that there are four core advertising frameworks: persuasion/exploration, sales/do, salience/sharing and involvement/play.

- The Strong theory of advertising indicates that advertising is a strong influencing force and reflects the persuasion concept. The Weak theory suggests that advertising has little influence and that advertising should be regarded as a means of defending customers' purchase decisions and for protecting markets, not building them. Reality suggests that the majority of advertising cannot claim to be of significant value to most people and that the Strong and the Weak theories are equally applicable, although not at the same time nor in the same context.

- The FCB and Rossiter–Percy grids represent formalised attempts to interpret the strategic use of advertising. Intended to provide agencies with a method that might ensure consistency, meaning and value with respect to their clients' brands, these are no longer considered by agencies to be sufficiently flexible, rigorous or representative of how contemporary advertising performs.

- A more current perspective on advertising strategy suggests that advertising should become more engaged with the customer's experience of the brand and not be rooted just in the development of brand values.

- Consumer-generated advertising (CGA) is about ads developed by members of the public about recognised brands, and which are made available to the public. There are three fundamental motivations that consumers have for creating and broadcasting ads: intrinsic enjoyment, self-promotion, and perception change.

- However, the critical issue associated with CGA concerns control and the ability of organisations to control the messages surrounding their brands. It is much more challenging to control brand messages today and hence new approaches and formats need to be considered.

# Review questions

1. Write brief notes outlining the differences between a USP and an ESP.

2. Find advertisements and write notes explaining how they depict the thinking and feeling aspect of advertising, and the behavioural aspect of advertising.

3. Select an organisation of your choice and find three ads it has used recently. Are the ads predominantly trying to persuade audiences or are they designed to reinforce brand values?

4. Find four ads and write notes explaining how the elaboration likelihood model can be used to interpret how they might work.

5. What are the essential differences between the involvement and salience frameworks of advertising?

6. Find four advertisements (other than those described in this book) that are examples of these two approaches.

7. Which of the eclectic models of advertising explains how the Apple 'Think Different' ads work? These ads are presented in the minicase at the start of the chapter.

8. Write a short presentation explaining the differences between the Strong and Weak theories of advertising.

9. Draw the FCB grid and place on it the following product categories: shampoo, life assurance, sports cars, kitchen towels, a box of chocolates.

10. Write brief notes outlining the strategic role advertising plays within an organisation's overall promotional activities.

# References

Ambler, T. (1998) Myths about the mind: time to end some popular beliefs about how advertising works, *International Journal of Advertising*, 17, 501–9.

Bainbridge, J. (2004) Dental diversification, *Marketing*, 12 September, 36–7.

Barwise, P. and Meehan, S. (2009) Differentiation that Matters, *Market Leader*, Quarter 2, retrieved 4 May 2012 from www.warc.com.

Berthon, Pierre R., Pitt, Leyland F. and Campbell, Colin (2008) 'Ad Lib: When Customers Create the Ad', *California Management Review*, 50(4), 6–30.

Campbell, C., Pitt, L.F., Parent, M. and Berthon, P.R. (2011) Understanding Consumer Conversations Around Ads in a Web 2.0 World, *Journal of Advertising*, 40, 1 (Spring), 87–102.

Corke, S. and Heath, R.G. (2004) The hidden power of newspaper advertising, *Media Research Group Conference*, Madrid (November).

Ehrenberg, A.S.C. (1974) Repetitive advertising and the consumer, *Journal of Advertising Research*, 14 (April), 25–34.

Ehrenberg, A.S.C. (1988) *Repeat Buying*, 2nd edn., London: Charles Griffin.

Ehrenberg, A.S.C. (1997) How do consumers come to buy a new brand? *Admap* (March), 20–4.

Hall, M. (1992) Using advertising frameworks, *Admap* (March), 17–21.

Heath, R. (2000) Low Involvement Processing – a new model of brands and advertising, *International Journal of Advertising*, 19(3), 287–98.

Heath, R. and Feldwick, P. (2008) 50 years using the wrong model of TV advertising, *International Journal of Market Research*, 50(1), 25–59.

Heath, R.G., Nairn, A.C. and Bottomley, P.A. (2009) How Effective is Creativity? Emotive Content in TV Advertising Does Not Increase Attention, *Journal of Advertising Research* (September), 450–63.

Hormby, T. (2009) 'Think Different': The Ad Campaign that Restored Apple's Reputation, 4 September 2007, retrieved 8 June 2012 from http://lowendmac.com/orchard/07/apple-think-different.html.

Jack, L. (2009) GSK unveils raft of oral care launches to beat back Colgate, *Marketing Week*, Wednesday 4 February, retrieved 16 July 2010 from www.marketingweek.co.uk/news/.

Jones, J.P. (1991) Over-promise and under-delivery, *Marketing and Research Today* (November), 195–203.

Joyce, T. (1991) Models of the advertising process, *Marketing and Research Today* (November), 205–12.

Kharina, A. (2012) Unpublished MSc Marketing Assignment, *Grenoble Graduate School of Business*.

Kolsarici, C., and Vakratsas, D. (2010). Category versus Brand-Level Advertising Messages in a Highly Regulated Environment, *Journal of Marketing Research*, 47, 6, 1078–1089.

Krugman, M.E. (1971) Brain wave measurement of media involvement, *Journal of Advertising*, 11, 1, 3–9.

Moellmann, A., Carter, S. and Binet, L. (2010) Philips – Girl power: how a female robot grew sales for the Philips MSS sharer, IPA Effectiveness Awards, retrieved 14 September from www.warc.com.

Moustou, C. and Tam, C. (2011) *Shangri-La Hotels & Resorts: Turning a human touch into business advantage,* WARC Asia Prize Contender, retrieved 24 May from www.warc.com/Content/ContentViewer.aspx?MasterContentRef=eb33cafb-d6aa-4f7d-a29a-9379d5c07663&q=Shangri-La.

O'Malley, D. (1991) Sales without salience? *Admap* (September), 36–9.

Ono, Y. (1994), Campbell's New Ads Heat Up Soup Sales, *The Wall Street Journal*, (March 17), B3.

Pelsmaker de, P., Guens, M. and Bergh, van den, J. (2010) *Marketing Communications: A European Perspective,* 4/E, Harlow: FT/Prentice Hall.

Petty, R.E. and Cacioppo, J.T. (1983) Central and peripheral routes to persuasion: application to advertising, in *Advertising and Consumer Psychology* (eds L. Percy and A. Woodside), 3–23. Lexington, MA: Lexington Books.

Richards, J.I. and Curran, C.M. (2002) Oracles on 'Advertising': Searching for a Definition, *Journal of Advertising*, XXXI, (2) Summer, 63–77.

Rossiter, J.R., Percy, L. and Donovan, R.J. (1991) A better advertising planning grid, *Journal of Advertising Research* (October/November), 11–21.

Siltanen, R. (2011) The Real Story Behind Apple's 'Think Different' Campaign, *Forbes*, 14 December 2011, retrieved 8 June 2012 from http://www.forbes.com/sites/onmarketing/2011/12/14/the-real-story-behind-apples-think-different-campaign/.

Stoeckl, R., Rohrmeier, P. and Hess, T. (2007) Motivations to Produce User Generated Content: Differences Between Webloggers and Videobloggers, Twentieth Bled eConference on eMergence: Merging and Emerging Technologies, Processes, and Institutions, Bled, Slovenia, June 4–6.

Vakratsas, D. and Ambler, T. (1999) How advertising works: what do we really know? *Journal of Marketing*, 63 (January), 26–43.

Vaughn, R. (1980) How advertising works: a planning model, *Journal of Advertising Research* (October), 27–33.

Walters, R. (2010) *Shangri-la Hotel & Resorts embrace strangers in new global campaign created by O&M Hong Kong*, Monday, 31 May, retrieved 24 May 2011 from www.campaignbriefasia.com/2010/05/shangri-la-hotel-resorts-embra.html.

Williams, C. (2011) BlackBerry blackout: how it happened, *The Telegraph*, 14 October, retrieved 31 March 2012 from http://www.telegraph.co.uk/technology/blackberry/8825661/BlackBerry-blackout-how-it-happened.html.

Willie, T. (2007) New models of communication for the digital age, *Admap*, October, 487, retrieved 23 July 2010 from www.warc.com.

# Chapter 15
## Public relations

Public relations is a communication discipline used to help shape the attitudes and opinions held by an organisation's stakeholders. Through interaction and dialogue with these stakeholders an organisation seeks to adjust its own position and/or strategy. Therefore, there is an attempt to identify with, and adjust an organisation's policies to, the interests of its stakeholders. To do this it formulates and executes a programme of action to develop mutual goodwill and understanding. Profile communication strategies make substantial use of public relations when developing understanding about their intentions and their identity.

## Aims and learning objectives

The aim of this chapter is to explore the role and characteristics of public relations in the context of profiling organisations and their products.

The learning objectives of this chapter are to:

1. explain the nature and characteristics of public relations;
2. highlight the main audiences to which public relations activities are directed;
3. discuss the role of public relations in the communications mix;
4. appreciate ways in which public relations works;
5. provide an overview of some of the main tools used by public relations;
6. examine the nature and context of crisis management;
7. determine ways in which public relations can be integrated with the other tools of the marketing communications mix.

# Minicase

## BP – crisis response

The BP Gulf of Mexico oil spill in April 2010 was a disaster on a major scale; one that caused loss of life, had a significant environmental and economic impact, and threatened to escalate into a trans-national 'war of words' between the UK and the US. Of all crises, one that is sudden, prolonged and with wide impact is the most difficult to manage. The oil spill cost the livelihood of fishermen on the Gulf Coast, and further damaged the tourism trade of a community just recovering from Hurricane Katrina. Taking three months to stop, the oil leak caused significant environmental damage. The Gulf of Mexico spill was soon referred to as the worst oil spill in US history, with President Barak Obama claiming that this event would dominate environmental policy for years to come.

On 21 April 2010 an explosion and fire ripped through an off-shore drilling platform, the Deepwater Horizon, operated by BP off the coast of the Gulf of Mexico, sinking the rig and costing the lives of eleven men. BP's Chief Executive Tony Hayward was quick to offer expressions of regret to the families of those who lost their lives, and to promise that BP would do all it could to contain the spill. With bad weather hampering the clean-up operation and reports estimating that 42,000 gallons of oil a day were leaking into the sea (bbc.co.uk), the Gulf Coast was at risk of an environmental disaster. Attempts to block the leak failed, and by 30 April, with oil now washing ashore, Louisiana declared a state of emergency. Throughout the next month repeated attempts to block the leak were unsuccessful, with over 500,000 gallons of oil a day leaking into the sea (bbc.co.uk). The leak was eventually stopped in mid July, by which time, estimates of the amount of leaked oil had doubled.

The financial impact for BP was considerable, with a steep decline in its stock market value due to investor anxiety over the cost of US claims. In July the low share price caused speculation of a possible takeover (bbc.co.uk). By the end of September, the crisis response had cost BP approximately $11.2 billion, including actions to stop the leak and contain the damage, grants and compensation claims to shrimpers and commercial fishermen who had lost their income.

The scale of the disaster threatened to damage the political relationship between the UK and the US as communication from the US administration changed from supportive to confrontational, with President Barak Obama warning 'We will make BP pay for the damage their company has caused' (bbc.co.uk). In the UK it did not go unnoticed that the US administration had reverted to using BP's former name of British Petroleum. Mayor of London, Boris Johnson, accused the US of 'anti-British rhetoric' and Prime Minister David Cameron faced pressure to 'speak up for' BP.

BP had to respond to stakeholders about the cause of the crisis, to keep them informed about what it was doing to manage the spill and to cap the well, as well as to appease the anger expressed by those directly affected, and those concerned about the impact on the local economies, the environment and the health of people caught up in the vicinity of the disaster.

The dramatic images of oil-covered shorelines and dead fish provided clear evidence of the spill, and BP did not attempt to evade responsibility for this damage. BP did point out the involvement of other parties (Transocean, Halliburton, Cameron International) but did not shift the blame more squarely onto their shoulders. It was not until September that their role in the crisis was more fully acknowledged.

BP made a statement claiming that 'this accident was brought about by the failure of a number of processes, systems and equipment . . .'. The emphasis on inanimate objects and processes rather than human error might have been a strategy for distancing BP from direct responsibility for the crisis, but the compensation later paid to the Gulf Coast communities suggests that BP took its responsibilities seriously.

Some companies seek to bolster their reputation in these situations by highlighting their 'good record'. BP emphasised that safety was a priority and that it had a 'strong record of safe and reliable operations in the Gulf of Mexico' (bp.com). Media coverage, however, reminded readers that in 2009 BP had been fined $87 million for failing to improve safety conditions following a fatal explosion at its Texas City refinery. Tony Hayward, BP's Chief Executive Officer, tried to mitigate US anger by adopting a conciliatory tone, stressing their mutual goals and taking action, through the payment of compensation, to reduce the suffering of the shoreline communities. However, he was accused of making several inappropriate comments that were to eventually cost him his position, as he was forced to resign.

Exhibit 15.1    **The BP oil spill**
*Source*: AP/Press Association Images

BP immediately attempted to rectify the problem with expert help, noting 'it is difficult to imagine the gathering of a larger, more technically proficient team in one place in peacetime'. The response effort involved 27,000 personnel in containing the oil, and in clean-up operations and wildlife protection. Hayward claimed that BP was 'committed to a transparent response' and stressed that analysis would '. . . provide valuable lessons about how to prevent future incidents of this nature'.

In addition to the condolences offered to the families of those who lost their lives, Hayward also stressed to the US Committee on Energy and Commerce that the explosion, fire and the resulting oil spill 'never should have happened, and I am deeply sorry that they did'.

Many well-established companies often fail to respond adequately to crises. BP however demonstrated some understanding of an effective crisis response, acting immediately to limit the damage and communicated regularly with stakeholders, and the media in particular. The departure of Hayward in July, who by then was 'the most hated man in the US', symbolically marked the end of the crisis. By January 2011 CNN was calling the crisis a PR disaster, reporting that the BP brand was 'in tatters' and that the US criticism had damaged BP and Hayward 'beyond repair'. The scale of the event and its long-term implications for the Gulf Coast communities and environment suggest that BP's reputation may take some time to recover.

*This minicase was written by Beverley Hill at the Bristol Business School, University of the West of England, using a variety of resources including Benoit (1997); Cornelissen (2011); www.bp.com; www.bbc.co.uk; www.cnn.com;*

*The author wishes to acknowledge the contribution of Daniel Wakefield for collecting case material under the University of Winchester Research Apprentice Scheme.*

# Introduction

The shift in the degree of importance given by organisations to public relations over recent years is a testimony to its power and effectiveness. BP's use of public relations during and after the crisis that hit the company after the massive oil spill in the Gulf of Mexico, demonstrates some of the various public relations approaches that can be used, and some that should not. Most organisations now recognise the role that public relations can play in their external and internal communications. Therefore, all organisations in the public, hybrid, not-for-profit, third and private sectors can use this tool to raise visibility, generate interest and goodwill, and build relationships with critical stakeholder audiences.

Traditionally public relations has been perceived as a tool that dealt with the manner and style with which an organisation interacted with its major 'publics'. It sought to influence other organisations and individuals through public relations, projecting an identity that would affect the image that different publics held of the organisation. By spreading information and improving the levels of knowledge that people held about particular issues, the organisation sought ways to advance itself in the eyes of those it saw as influential. This approach is reflected in the definition of public relations provided by the Institute of Public Relations: 'Public

Relations practice is the planned and sustained effort to establish and maintain goodwill and mutual understanding between an organisation and its publics.' For many the core interpretation of public relations was provided by Grunig and Hunt (1984) who define public relations as the 'management of communication between an organization and its publics' (p. 6). Laskin (2009) refers to this work as the foundation upon which most models of public relations have been built.

Cutlip et al. (1994: 199) consider the 'essential role of public relations is to help organizations adjust and adapt to changes in their environments'. As Greenwood (2011) indicates, public relations can be seen to be about managing the interdependence of organisations and others in their environments.

A later definition from Bruning and Ledingham (2000) suggests that public relations is the management of relationships between organisations and their stakeholders (publics). This definition indicates the direction in which both public relations and marketing theory have moved.

Public relations has long been concerned with the development and communication of corporate and competitive strategies. Public relations provides visibility for an organisation, and this in turn, it is hoped, allows it to be properly identified, positioned and understood by all of its stakeholders. What some definitions do not emphasise or make apparent is that public relations should also be used by management as a means of understanding issues from a stakeholder perspective. Good relationships are developed by appreciating the views held by others and by 'putting oneself in their shoes'.

Through this sympathetic and patient approach to planned communication, a dialogue can be developed that is not frustrated by punctuated interruptions (anger, disbelief, ignorance and objections). Public relations can therefore be regarded as a management activity that attempts to shape the attitudes and opinions held by an organisation's stakeholders. It seeks to identify its policies with the interests of its stakeholders by formulating and executing a programme of action to develop mutual goodwill and understanding, and in turn develop relationships that are in the long-term interests of all parties.

---

**Scholars' paper 15.1**     **Historical views of public relations**

**Vos, T.P. (2011) Explaining the Origins of Public Relations: Logics of Historical Explanation, *Journal of Public Relations Research*, 23(2), 119–140.**

A contemporary paper that is useful for those interested in the academic roots of public relations. Vos considers the historical explanations underpinning the emergence of public relations as a social institution. He identifies three distinct logics of explanation, a functionalist logic, an institutional logic, and a cultural logic.

---

# Characteristics of public relations

Insight into the characteristics of public relations can be helped by first understanding its origins. There are many interpretations but Vos (2011) identifies three main theoretical perspectives, or 'logics of historical explanation' (p. 119). These are set out in Table 15.1. Each of these has fundamental flaws but they provide an interesting perspective on the roots of public relations.

| Logic | Explanation |
|---|---|
| Functionalism | Functionalism is concerned with the different parts of a social system striving to counter-balance and adjust in order to achieve reach equilibrium. Public relations is considered to be an institutional response to muck-raking. Bernays (1928: 41) refers to 'a result of insurance scandals coincident with the muck-raking of corporate finance in the popular magazines'. |
| Institutionalism | The institutional perspective considers public relations to be rooted in an organisation-based, systematic, rules-and-routines approach to influencing groups through communication and persuasion. For many this was first noted when the Committee on Public Information (CPI) was formed in the USA at the outset of World War One. The committee consisted of various journalists, intellectuals, novelists and others who sought to 'unite public opinion behind the war at home and to propagandize American peace aims abroad' (Cutlip, 1994, p. 106) |
| Culture | This interpretation of public relations is that it was founded on meaning systems adopted from the prevailing culture. These meaning systems include cultural values, attitudes, ideas, which provide both constraints and opportunities (Geertz, 1973) for behaviour. The then new PR practitioners saw this as a natural, right, or logical approach to communication. A dominant view within the cultural movement concerns the influence of the progressive movement. 'This ideology was concerned with reform, cooperation and participation of society' (Hallahan, 2003). They believed that public policy should not be crafted by party bosses and neither should public life be dictated by business tycoons. |

**Table 15.1**    Logics of historical explanation

*Source*: Vos (2011).

Public relations should, therefore, be a planned activity, one that encompasses a wide range of events. However, there are a number of characteristics that single out this particular tool from the others in the marketing communications mix. The use of public relations does not require the purchase of airtime or space in media vehicles, such as television or magazines. The decision about whether an organisation's public relations messages are transmitted, or not, rests with those charged with managing the media resource, not the message sponsor. Those messages that are selected are perceived to be endorsements or the views of parties other than management. The outcome is that these messages usually carry greater perceived credibility than those messages transmitted through paid media, such as advertising.

The degree of trust and confidence generated by public relations singles out this tool from others in the marketing communications mix as an important means of reducing buyers' perceived risk. However, while credibility may be high, the amount of control that manage-ment is able to bring to the transmission of a public relations message is very low. For example, a press release may have been carefully prepared in-house, but as soon as it is passed to the editor of a magazine or newspaper, a possible opinion former, all control is lost. The release may be destroyed (highly probable), printed as it stands (highly unlikely) or changed to fit the available space in the media vehicle (almost certain, if it is decided to use the material). This means that any changes will not have been agreed by management, so the context and style of the original message may be lost or corrupted.

The costs associated with public relations also make this an important tool in the marketing communications mix. The absolute costs are minimal, except for those organisations that retain an agency, but even then their costs are low compared with those of advertising. The relative costs (the costs associated with reaching each member of a target audience) are also very low. The main costs associated with public relations are the time and opportunity costs associated with the preparation of press releases and associated literature. If these types of activity are organised properly, many small organisations could develop and shape their visibility much more effectively and in a relatively inexpensive way.

A further characteristic of this tool is that it can be used to reach specific audiences in a way that paid media cannot. With increasing media fragmentation and finer segmentation (customisation) of markets, the use of public relations represents a cost-effective way of reaching such markets and audiences.

Digital technology has played a key role in the development and practice of public relations. Gregory (2004) referred to the Internet and electronic communication as 'transforming public relations', and identifies two main schools of practitioner. One refers to those who use the Internet as an extension to traditional or pre-Internet forms of communication. The second uses the Internet to develop two-way, enhanced communication. There can be little doubt that new technology has assisted communication management in terms of improving the transparency, speed and reach of public relations messages, while at the same time enabling interactive communication between an organisation and its specific audiences.

The main characteristics of public relations are that it represents a very cost-effective means of carrying messages with a high degree of credibility. However, the degree of control that management is able to exert over the transmission of messages can be limited.

---

| Viewpoint 15.1 | Strictly an X factor for public relations |
| --- | --- |

There are two big UK Saturday night television shows in the Autumn: the *X Factor (XF)* and *Strictly Come Dancing (SCD)*. These shows command audiences of approximately 8 and 10 million respectively, and they run head-to-head in the three months leading to Christmas. Public relations is used to support both of them, but in slightly different ways.

*SCD* is produced by the BBC, and all the PR relating to the show is managed in-house. PR agencies are used to create attention. However, many of the celebrity contestants, one of the judges, and the two presenters have their own personal PR support, all of which is coordinated by the BBC. The show has incurred many issues, varying from affairs between professional dancers and celebrities, the sacking of one of the judges and replacing her with a younger, former winner of the show, and those concerning the positioning of the show, as a form of entertainment or dance competition. The latter issue is often exposed through the way the public votes to keep certain celebrities in.

*XF* is produced by ITV but all the judges have their own PR support. ITV's PR is involved but does not coordinate activities in the same way as the BBC. It appears that the central figure driving the show, and various offshoots, is Simon Cowell. When the show was launched, his PR team (Max Clifford) drew attention by shaping Cowell's nasty image. Now, with the show well established, PR is used to manage the controversy and issues that emerge as the show moves forward and to cover relevant media stories concerning contestants and their backgrounds.

Interest in *SCD* is partly driven by providing exclusive information to websites and portals. This is achieved through the use of targeted niche blogs, forums and social networking groups. To increase the audience's experience of the show, a new application was used in September 2009 which let online viewers interact with the live show by commenting on the performances and engaging emotionally with electronic 'boos', 'gasps' and 'wows'.

*Source*:   Magee (2009); O'Reilly (2009); Deans (2012).

---

**Question:**   What is the main role of entertainment PR?

**Task:**   Storytelling can be powerful. Find stories that were used about SCD and X Factor.

Developments in digital media have been instrumental in assisting public relations' move from a predominantly one-way model of communication to an interactive model. In 2001 Hurme suggested that public relations practitioners could be divided into two broad groups: those that predominantly use traditional media and those that adopt online communications. Since that article was written, most practitioners have incorporated online communications, but the realisation of the potential to develop true dialogue with stakeholders remains unfilled in many cases. Therefore, opportunities for online interactivity and dialogue have increased even if websites are not being designed to fulfil this requirement completely.

## Media catching

The use of online public relations is an increasingly important part of an organisation's marketing communications. Online public relations is concerned with maximising opportunities to present an organisation, and its products and services, in a positive manner. One of the goals, as with traditional media relations work, is to create 'mentions' in a variety of targeted media, including other websites, and social media such as social networks, blogs and Twitter. This is important for establishing links and achieving higher search engine rankings.

Another goal involves creating opportunities for interaction and dialogue with stakeholders – in particular, journalists. The stronger the communication tie, the more likely the relationship will grow and provide an effective means of distributing content and client materials. It is important to build relationships, both with the target stakeholder groups and with journalists and others in the media. We know that interpersonal relationships between public relations practitioners and journalists can have a substantial influence on the effectiveness of an organisation's media relations performance (Shin and Cameron, 2003). Indeed, there is clear evidence that journalists are no longer the passive recipients of news releases and media kits from practitioners who are striving to generate publicity for their organisation. As Waters et al. (2010) indicate, journalists are using social media to get the information they need from practitioners.

As a general rule, public relations has been considered to work through the 'content throw' pattern of communication. In this approach organisations use public relations as a means of contacting journalists, broadcasters, and bloggers in the hope of gaining media comment and placements to disseminate news content. A more contemporary approach is referred to as 'media catching'. Using digital media, this pattern of communication involves reversing the content throw approach. Now practitioners are being contacted by journalists and others for specific material for inclusion in stories, articles, blogs, and websites where there are pressing deadlines. Rather than 'Here is a story/content please run it', media catching is about 'Do you have a story/content please?'

There are several issues arising from media catching. One of these is that strong relationships can emerge between a journalist and a public relations practitioner, which result in a better understanding of each other. For practitioners, this understanding manifests itself as an increased awareness of communication preferences and relevant media deadlines. For journalists, a stronger relationship provides an improved insight into what and how practitioners can contribute to their stories.

Back in 1998 Gray and Balmer suggested that public relations practitioners might be more successful if they used the contact methods preferred by journalists and the media. Subsequent research by Sallot and Johnson (2006) indicates practitioners had improved their performance because there was evidence that an increasing number of journalists were being asked to update their contact information and preferences.

# Which publics?

The first definition of public relations quoted earlier uses, as indeed does most of the public relations industry, the word *publics*. This word is used traditionally to refer to the various organisations and groups with which an organisation interacts. So far, this text has referred to these types of organisation as *stakeholders*. 'Stakeholders' is a term used in the field of strategic management, and as public relations can be concerned with strategic issues, it could be argued that the word 'stakeholders' should be used. However, the phrase 'public relations' is so well established and culturally entrenched that a change to 'stakeholder relations' would achieve little other than confusion.

The stakeholder concept recognises that various networks of stakeholders can be identified, with each network consisting of members who are oriented towards supporting the organisation either in an indirect way or directly through the added-value processes. For the purposes of this chapter it is useful to set out who the main stakeholders are likely to be. Stakeholder groups, it should be remembered, are not static and new groups can emerge in response to changes in the environment. The main core groups, however, tend to be employees, the public, financial communities, customers through the media, and other influential organisations, and are set out in Table 15.2.

These various forms of public relations are considered later in this chapter.

| Table 15.2 | Stakeholder audiences for public relations |
| --- | --- |
| **Stakeholder group** | **Explanation** |
| **Employees** | A major stakeholder group who can influence external stakeholders and influence the strength of corporate brands. This form of public relations is also referred to as *internal communications* or *employee relations*. |
| **Financial groups** | To supply analysts, shareholders and investors with current information and materials about an organisation and the markets in which it operates, organisations use investor relations. |
| **Customers** | Information is directed through the media in order to shape attitudes, perceptions and images. This form of public relations is referred to as *media relations*. |
| **Organisations and communities** | Organisations seek to inform significant other organisations of their strategic intentions and ways in which the objectives of both parties can be satisfied. A variety of public relations methods are used, including: *public affairs* directed at government and local authorities; *industry relations* targeted at suppliers, and other trade stakeholders; and *issues management* designed to influence various audiences about potentially sensitive issues. |

# A framework of public relations

Communications with such a wide variety of stakeholders need to vary to reflect different environmental conditions, organisational objectives and forms of relationship. Grunig and Hunt (1984) have attempted to capture the diversity of public relations activities through a framework. They set out four models to reflect the different ways in which public relations is, in their opinion, considered to work. These models, based on their experiences as public relations

| Characteristic | Model | | | |
|---|---|---|---|---|
| | Press agentry/publicity | Public information | Two-way asymmetric | Two-way symmetric |
| Purpose | Propaganda | Dissemination of information | Scientific persuasion | Mutual understanding |
| Nature of communication | One way; complete truth not essential | One way; truth important | Two way; imbalanced effects | Two way; balanced effects |
| Communication model | Source→Rec.* | Source→Rec.* | Source ⇄ Rec.* Feedback | Group ⇄ Group |
| Nature of research | Little; 'counting house' | Little; readability, readership | Formative; evaluative of attitudes | Formative; evaluative of understanding |
| Leading historical figures | P.T. Barnum | Ivy Lee | Edward L. Bernays | Bernays, educators, professional leaders |
| Where practised today | Sports, theatre, product promotion | Government, not-for-profit associations, business | Competitive business, agencies | Regulated business, agencies |
| Estimated percentage of organisations practising today | 15% | 50% | 20% | 15% |

\* Receiver.

| Figure 15.1 | Models of public relations |
|---|---|

*Source*: Grunig and Hunt (1984). Used with kind permission.

practitioners, constitute a useful approach to understanding the complexity of this form of communication. The four models are set out in Figure 15.1.

## The press agentry/publicity model

The essence of this approach is that communication is used as a form of propaganda. That is, the communication flow is essentially one-way, and the content is not bound to be strictly truthful as the objective is to convince the receiver of a new idea or offering. This can be observed in the growing proliferation of media events and press releases.

## The public information model

Unlike the first model, this approach seeks to disseminate truthful information. While the flow is again one-way, there is little focus on persuasion, more on the provision of information. This can best be seen through public health campaigns and government advice communications in respect of crime, education and health.

## The two-way asymmetric model

Two-way communication is a major element of this model. Feedback from receivers is important, but as power is not equally distributed between the various stakeholders and the organisation, the relationship has to be regarded as asymmetric. The purpose remains to influence attitude and behaviour through persuasion.

## The two-way symmetric model

This represents the most acceptable and mutually rewarding form of communication. Power is seen to be dispersed equally between the organisation and its stakeholders and the intent of the communication flow is considered to be reciprocal. The organisation and its respective publics are prepared to adjust their positions (attitudes and behaviours) in the light of the information flow. A true dialogue emerges through this interpretation, unlike any of the other three models, which see an unbalanced flow of information and expectations.

---

### Scholars' paper 15.2   Models of public relations

Grunig, J. (1992) Models of public relations and communication, in *Excellence in Public Relations and Communications Management* (eds J.E. Grunig, D.M. Dozier, P. Ehling, L.A. Grunig, F.C. Repper and J. Whits), Hillsdale, NJ: Lawrence Erlbaum, 285–325.

Although first announced in 1976, and then published fully in 1984, this 1992 chapter is an essential work with which all serious readers of public relations should be conversant. The four primary models of public relations developed by Grunig are considered by most scholars to be the theoretical anchor for the subject.

---

The model has attracted a great deal of attention and has been reviewed and appraised by a number of commentators (Miller, 1989; Laskin, 2009). As a result of this and a search for excellence in public relations, Grunig (1992) revised the model to reflect the dominance of the 'craft' and the 'professional' approaches to public relations practices. That is, those practitioners who utilise public relations merely as a tool to achieve media visibility can be regarded as 'craft'-oriented.

Those organisations whose managers seek to utilise public relations as a means of mediating their relationships with their various stakeholders are seen as 'professional' practitioners. They are considered to be using public relations as a longer-term and proactive form of planned communication. The former see public relations as an instrument, the latter as a means of conducting a dialogue.

These models are not intended to suggest that those responsible for communications should choose among them. Their use and interpretation depend upon the circumstances that prevail at any one time. Organisations use a number of these different approaches to manage the communication issues that exist between them and the variety of different stakeholder audiences with whom they interact. However, there is plenty of evidence to suggest that the press/agentry model is the one most used by practitioners and that the two-way symmetrical model is harder to observe in practice.

These models have been subjected to further investigation and Grunig (1997) concluded that these four models are not independent but coexist with one another. Therefore, it is better to characterise public relations as dimensions of communication behaviour (Yun, 2006). These dimensions are direction, purpose, channel and ethics, and are explained at Table 15.3.

| Table 15.3 | Dimensions of public relations |
| --- | --- |

| Dimension of public relations | Explanation |
| --- | --- |
| **Direction** | Refers to whether communication is one-way (disseminating) or two-way (exchange). |
| **Purpose** | Purpose refers to degree to which there are communication effects on both parties. Symmetry refers to communications effects on both sides, leading to collaboration, whereas asymmetry leads to one-sided effects and, in turn, advocacy. |
| **Channel** | Interpersonal communication refers to direct, face-to-face communication. Mediated communication is indirect and routed through the media. |
| **Ethics** | The degree to which public-relations-based communications are ethical. Grunig refers to three sub-dimensions: teleology (the consequences), disclosure (whose interests does the communication serve?) and social responsibility (who is affected?). |

*Source*: After Yun (2006).

# Public relations and relationship management

It is important to remember that the shift to a relationship management perspective effectively alters the way public relations is perceived and practised by organisations. Ehling (1992) suggests that, instead of trying to manipulate audience opinion so that the organisation is of primary importance, the challenge is to use symbolic visual communication messages with behaviour such that the organisation–audience relationship improves for all parties. Kent and Taylor (2002) and Bruning and Ledingham (2000) develop this theme by suggesting that it is the ability of organisations to encourage and practise dialogue that really enables truly symmetrical relationships to develop. What follows from this is a change in evaluation, from measuring the dissemination of messages to one that measures audience influence and behavioural and attitudinal change and, of course, relationship dynamics. Bruning and Ledingham describe this as a change from measuring outputs to one that measures outcomes.

In addition to this discernible shift in emphasis, there has been a change in the way public relations is used by organisations. Traditionally, public relations has been used as a means of managing communication between parties, whereas now communication is regarded as a means of managing relationships (Kent and Taylor, 2002). In order to use communication to develop the full potential within relationships many argue that dialogic interaction should be encouraged. Earlier in the text (Chapter 8) five tenets of dialogue were presented: mutuality, empathy, propinquity, risk and commitment. These have been offered by Kent and Taylor as the elements that may form a framework through which dialogue may be considered and developed. On a practical level, they argue that organisations should place email, web addresses, contact telephone numbers, Twitter and organisational addresses prominently in all forms of external communication, most notably advertisements and websites, to enable dialogue.

In consideration of the role of public relations, namely to build relationships that are of mutual value, Bruning et al. (2008) conclude that input, interaction and participation of key public members in the organisation–public dynamic are critically important. In other words, dialogue arising through interaction and the personalisation of communications is important for relationship development.

# Objectives and public relations

As established, the main reasons for using public relations are to provide visibility for the corporate body and to support the marketing agenda at the product level. The marketing communications objectives, established earlier in the plan, will have identified issues concerning the attitudes and relationships stakeholders have with an organisation and its products. Decisions will have been made to build awareness and to change perception, preferences or attitudes. The task of public relations is to deliver a series of coordinated activities that complement the overall marketing communications strategy and which develop and enhance some of the identity cues used by stakeholders. The overall goal should be to develop the relationship between the organisation and its different audiences.

Public relations can be used to develop understanding, perceptions and positive attitudes towards the organisation. Public relations can also contribute to the marketing needs of the organisation and will therefore be focused at the product level and on consumers, seeking to change attitudes, preferences and awareness levels with respect to products and services offered. Therefore, a series of programmes is necessary – one to fulfil the corporate requirements and another to support the marketing of products and services.

# Cause-related marketing

One major reason for the development of public relations and associated corporate reputation activities has been the rise in importance and use of cause-related marketing activities. This has partly been due to the increased awareness of the need to be perceived as credible, responsible and ethically sound. Developing a strong and socially oriented reputation has become a major form of differentiation for organisations operating in various markets, especially where price, quality and tangible attributes are relatively similar. Being able to present corporate brands as contributors to the wider social framework, a role beyond that of simple profit generators, has enabled many organisations to achieve stronger, more positive market positions.

Cause-related marketing is a commercial activity through which profit-oriented and not-for-profit organisations form partnerships to exploit, for mutual benefit, their association in the name of a particular cause.

The benefits from a properly planned and constructed cause-related campaign can accrue to all participants. Cause-related marketing helps improve corporate reputation, enables product differentiation and appears to contribute to improved customer retention through enhanced sales. In essence, cause-related marketing is a means by which relationships with stakeholders can be developed. As organisations outsource an increasingly large part of their business activities and as the stakeholder networks become more complex, so the need to be perceived as (and to be) socially responsible becomes a critically important dimension of an organisation's image.

A public relations programme consists of a number of planned events and activities that seek to satisfy communication objectives. Some of the broad tools and techniques associated with public relations are considered in this chapter, but it should be noted that the list is not intended to be comprehensive.

| Scholars' paper 15.3 | Relationships and public relations |

Bruning, S.D. and Ledingham, J.A. (2000) Perceptions of relationships and evaluations of satisfaction: an exploration of interaction, *Public Relations Review*, 26(1), 85–95.

This is a research paper based on work undertaken with a bank and the perceptions members of the public have of the various personal, professional and community relationships they have with the organisation. These perceptions are related to the respondents' evaluation of the satisfaction they have with the organisation. The paper puts relationships at the heart of public relations activities.

# Public relations: methods and techniques

An organisation's corporate identity consists of those activities that reflect, to a large extent, the personality of the organisation (see Chapter 12). Public relations provides some of the intentional or deliberate cues that enable stakeholders to develop images and perceptions through which they recognise, understand, select and converse with organisations.

The range of public relations cues or methods available to organisations is immense. Different organisations use different permutations in order that they can communicate effectively with their various stakeholder audiences. For the purposes of this text, a general outline is provided of the more commonly used methods. Cues are to some extent interchangeable and can be used to build credibility or to provide visibility for an organisation. It is the skill of the public relations practitioner that determines the right blend of techniques. The various types of cue are set out in Table 15.4.

While there is general agreement on a definition, there is a lower level of consensus over what constitutes public relations. This is partly because the range of activities is diverse and categorisation problematic. The approach adopted here is that public relations consists of a range of communication activities, of which media relations, publicity and event management appear to be the main ones used by practitioners.

**Table 15.4**    Cues used by PR to project corporate identity

| Cues to build credibility | Cues to signal visibility |
|---|---|
| Product quality | Sales literature and company publications |
| Customer relations | Publicity and media relations |
| Community involvement | Speeches and presentations |
| Strategic performance | Event management |
| Employee relations | Marketing communications/messages |
| Crisis management skills | Media mix |
| Third-party endorsement | Design (signage, logo, letterhead) |
| Perceived ethics and environmental awareness | Dress codes |
| Architecture and furnishing | Exhibitions/seminars; sponsorships |

# TOSHIBA
## Leading Innovation >>>

### Toshiba premieres new 'Space Chair' ad campaign
*Campaign to support Toshiba's SV REGZA LCD TV and Satellite T series laptops*

**London, UK, 16th November 2009** – Toshiba UK continues to lead innovation as it premieres its latest advertising campaign, 'Space Chair'; a piece of film which takes viewers on an awe-inspiring journey to the edge of space.

Created for Toshiba by Grey London, 'Space Chair' builds on the phenomenal success of 2008's record-breaking 'Timesculpture' ad campaign and has once again been filmed using Toshiba cameras. Shot in the wilderness of the Nevada Black Rock desert, the advertisement follows the journey of an ordinary living room chair to the extraordinary heights of the edge of space, lifted to an altitude of 98,268 feet by a simple helium balloon.

The advert is split into two executions, the first playing in 2009 for the **Toshiba REGZA SV LCD TV Series** and 2010 for the new range of **Satellite T Series** of ultra low voltage laptops. The REGZA SV is Toshiba's first-ever model to include an LED backlight with local dimming, and is set to redefine the armchair viewing experience by delivering sharper, smoother images that clearly define every cloud and every star. The ultra portable, lightweight Satellite T Series enables users to go further by offering up to eleven hours of battery life – enough to take you to space and back.

The ad was shot by Haris Zambarloukos, the acclaimed cinematographer behind films including 'Enduring Love' and 'Mamma Mia' and was directed by Andy Amadeo, Creative Director at Grey London. The shoot was made possible via the construction of a unique custom-built camera rig engineered by John Powell of JP Aerospace – experts in this field who have successfully sent over 100 balloons into the upper atmosphere. A specially created full-sized model chair made of biodegradable balsa wood; light enough to make the 83 minute journey up towards space was tied to the rig and launched by the team.

Four independent GPS systems were placed on the rig to accurately record its height at any second to within 4 metres in altitude, and within 30cm in longitude and latitude position. This information was transmitted every 15 seconds back to ground control where it was monitored via a computer satellite system to enable the team to locate the rig once it had fallen back to earth.

The film is cinematic, opening with a shot of the solitary chair silhouetted against the Nevada sunrise and taking the viewer on its journey above the desert, into the clouds and beyond.

Matt McDowell, Marketing Director at Toshiba UK comments: 'Our aim was to create a new advertising campaign that would bring to life Toshiba's brand philosophy of leading innovation. We chose to send a chair on the journey as it is central to the user's experience of Toshiba's products; whether they are watching TV or using a laptop.'

'The ad features two exciting new products. The REGZA SV Series is the first-ever Toshiba LCD TV to combine Toshiba's Resolution+ technology and an LED backlight – delivering stunning high quality images that enhance the viewers' armchair experience. Offering the performance and functionality of full-sized laptops with portability and a battery life of up to eleven hours, the Satellite T Series frees users from the shackles of their desks, empowering them to explore new environments.'

Andy Amadeo, Creative Director at Grey London comments: 'Keeping with our tactic of being as innovative as the brand, we once again created a mould-breaking commercial with Toshiba. Last year we set a new world record with "Timesculpture" and proved that their domestic camcorders could produce a breathtaking, never before seen piece of film. This time we have used Toshiba HD cameras to produce some of the most stunning footage shot at the edge of space.'

**Facts about the shoot:**
- The shots were taken at a staggering 98,268 feet above the earth using Toshiba's own cameras
- To reach the altitude required and to conform with Federal Aviation Administration regulations, the weight of the rig had to be carefully managed to a weight of no more than four pounds

# Press Release

- Tied to the rig was a specially created full-sized model chair made of biodegradable balsa wood – the chair was made by a company called Artem and cost about £2,500
- Launch coordinates of the rig were – 119 degrees, 14 minutes by 40 degrees, 48 minute (12 miles North-East of the town of Gerlach, Nevada)
- The quality of the footage from the Toshiba IK-HR1S cameras was: 1920 × 1080 pixel count; 1080i @ 50hz; 100 Mbps
- The temperature dropped to minus 90 degrees when the chair reached 52,037 feet
- The chair took 83 minutes to reach an altitude of 98,268 feet where it broke and took just 24 minutes to fall back down to earth with the rig.

**Notes to Editors**

The full 60 second advert premieres on 16 November on ITV1 and runs for three weeks. The ad will then run again in February 2010.

**Creative Credits**

| | |
|---|---|
| Creative Agency: | Grey London |
| Production Company: | Hungry Man LTD |
| Director: | Andy Amadeo |
| Editor and editing company: | The Whitehouse / Russell Ike |
| Post-production company: | The Mill |

*– Ends –*

For more information, interview requests or photography, please contact:
Katy Ball @ Nelson Bostock Communications
E: katy.ball@nelsonbostock.com
T: 020 7792 7489

**About Toshiba**

Toshiba is a world leader and innovator in pioneering high technology, a diversified manufacturer and marketer of advanced electronic and electrical products spanning information and communications systems; digital consumer products; electronic devices and components; power systems, including nuclear energy; industrial and social infrastructure systems; and home appliances. Toshiba was founded in 1875, and today operates a global network of more than 740 companies, with 199,000 employees worldwide and annual sales surpassing 6.6 trillion yen (US$73 billion). Visit Toshiba's web site at www.toshiba.co.jp/index.html

**About Grey London**

We are 200 people, drawn from different marketing and media backgrounds, working together in a wonderfully open environment in Holborn, London. We do the lot: multi-channel, integrated, online, offline, above, through and below the line for a wide range of clients including Ryvita, P&G, GlaxoSmithKline, IPC Media, the British Heart Foundation, Dairy Crest and Toshiba.

We don't believe in agency positionings. We do believe in making our clients both successful and happy. We believe we're better than most agencies at listening to what clients really want. Which means we're better at understanding the problem and getting to the most exciting and effective answer.

---

| Exhibit 15.2 | **Press release for the launch of the Toshiba Space Chair ad** |
|---|---|
| | *Source*: Toshiba |

# Media relations

Media relations consist of a range of activities designed to provide media journalists and editors with information. The intention is that they relay the information, through their media, for consumption by their audiences. Obviously, the original message may be changed and subject to information deviance as it is processed, but audiences perceive much of this information as highly credible simply because opinion formers (Chapter 2) have bestowed their judgement on the item. Of the various forms of media relations, press releases, interviews, press kits and press conferences are most used.

## Press releases

The press release is a common form of media relations activity. A written report concerning a change in the organisation is sent to various media houses for inclusion in the media vehicle as an item of news. The media house may cover a national area, but very often a local house will suffice. These written statements concern developments in the organisation, such as promotions, new products, awards, prizes, new contracts and customers. The statement is deliberately short and written in such a style that it attracts the attention of the editor. Further information can be obtained if it is to be included within the next publication or news broadcast. See Exhibit 15.2 for the press release issued by Toshiba concerning their Toshiba Space Chair ad (also mentioned in Chapter 6).

## Press conferences

Press conferences are used when a major event has occurred and where a press release cannot convey the appropriate tone or detail required by the organisation. Press conferences are mainly used by politicians, but organisations in crisis (e.g. accidents and mergers) and individuals appealing for help (e.g. police requesting assistance from the public with respect to a particular incident) can use this form of communication. Press kits containing a full reproduction of any statements, photographs and relevant background information should always be available.

## Interviews

Interviews with representatives of an organisation enable news and the organisation's view of an issue or event to be conveyed. Other forms of media relations include bylined articles (articles written by a member of an organisation about an issue related to the company and offered for publication), speeches, letters to the editor, and photographs and captions.

Media relations can be planned and controlled to the extent of what is sent to the media and when it is released. While there is no control over what is actually used, media relations allow organisations to try to convey information concerning strategic issues and to reach particular stakeholders.

The quality of the relationship between an organisation and the media will dramatically affect the impact and dissemination of news and stories released by an organisation. The relationships referred to are those between an organisation's public relations manager and the editor and journalists associated with both the press and the broadcast media.

## Publicity and events

Control over public relations events is not as strong as that for media relations. Indeed, negative publicity can be generated by other parties, which can impact badly on an organisation by raising doubts about its financial status or perhaps the quality of its products. Three main event activity areas can be distinguished: product, corporate and community events (see Chapter 18).

In addition to these key activities the following are important forms of public relations:

- lobbying (out of personal selling and publicity);
- sponsorship (out of event management and advertising) (see Chapter 26);
- corporate advertising (out of corporate public relations and advertising);
- crisis management (which has developed out of issues management, a part of corporate public relations).

---

### Viewpoint 15.2    Celebrity eclipse rescues the day

At the time when the Celebrity Cruises' new £500m ship, *Celebrity Eclipse*, was due to arrive in Southampton for a week of inaugural celebrations, a dust cloud had settled over much of Northern Europe. Iceland's Eyjafjallajokull volcano had erupted, sending millions of tons of dust into the atmosphere. This resulted in massive disruption to airline services as aircraft were grounded and travellers were stranded around the continent, unable to get home.

The travel industry was in disarray and a lavish celebration of a new cruise liner was not going to work. So, a brief designed to maximise awareness for the ship's arrival in Southampton, involving taster VIP/media sailings, the official naming ceremony and a Southampton charity event with breast cancer charity 'Walk the Walk', had to change. This was cancelled and parent company Royal Caribbean Cruises Limited (RCCL) directed that the ship be used to help rescue tourists stranded in Europe.

The repatriation mission to Bilbao was announced the evening before the ship's arrival in the UK. This enabled the news piece to be included in the early news agenda, presenting the four-day rescue mission as the ship's maiden voyage, and effectively replacing a VIP cruise.

Live filming and photography of the ship's arrival in Southampton was distributed to TV stations throughout the day, timed to hit the major news bulletins. In addition, the company president was available for interviews. A small number of the UK media were invited onboard to accompany the mission and an onboard film crew (TNR) and photographer were used to distribute press materials to TV, online and print media. A 24-hour media response hotline was enabled and cruise-specialist online media were provided with a release to make details easily available via Internet searches.

Rough-cut video was distributed to online media along with a two-minute news edit which was also uploaded to video streaming sites. An invited ITN news crew fed footage to GMTV, national and regional ITV news and NBC (US). BBC and Sky News reported from Southampton and sent crews to meet the ship in Bilbao for the return leg.

On arrival in Bilbao, the onboard film crew and photographer shot footage and images of stranded travellers and logistical information was provided to media to enable them to send their satellite trucks to greet the ship in Spain. The crews were met by the onboard PR team and provided with spokespeople.

The reactions of the 2,200 passengers 'rescued' by *Celebrity Eclipse* were filmed, and a Broll (a digital rough-cut and two-minute news piece) were edited and distributed using the ship's wifi to secure TV and online coverage. An updated news edit was uploaded to video streaming sites.

Live radio interviews took place with a range of Celebrity Cruises spokespeople and guests for news bulletins, and commissioned film crews covered the ship's return. The media were kept updated with logistical details of the ship's arrival. News crews were met at Southampton by the PR team and spokespeople were made available for interviews, including meeting live evening news slots.

The results of the campaign were impressive, including widespread branded coverage, achieved during one of the busiest news weeks of the year. There were huge increases in traffic to the Celebrity Cruises website, relationships with those in the travel business strengthened, and those rescued took away strong reputational cues, increasing word-of-mouth communication. Media coverage was extensive, including all national UK TV networks and over 640 broadcast, online and print pieces. All for a budget of £10,000.

*Source*:   Siren (2011); Palmer (2010); Batty and Haynes (2010).

| Exhibit 15.3 | *Celebrity Eclipse* **sails into Southampton** |
| --- | --- |
| | *Source*: PA/Press Association Images |

**Question:**    Is this good public relations or just exploitation of others in need?

**Task:**    Find two other PR events which had to be changed at the last minute. Were the outcomes successful?

# Lobbying

The representation of certain organisations or industries within government is an important form of public relations work. While legislation is being prepared, lobbyists provide a flow of information to their organisations to keep them informed about events (as a means of scanning the environment), but they also ensure that the views of the organisation are heard in order that legislation can be shaped appropriately, limiting any potential damage that new legislation might bring.

Moloney (1997) suggests that lobbying is inside public relations as it focuses on the members of an organisation who seek to persuade and negotiate with its stakeholders in government on matters of opportunity and or threat. He refers to in-house lobbyists (those members of the organisation who try to influence non-members) and hired lobbyists contracted to complete specific tasks.

His view of lobbying is that it is one of:

*monitoring public policy-making for a group interest; building a case in favour of that interest; and putting it privately with varying degrees of pressure to public decision makers for their acceptance and support through favourable political intervention. (p. 173)*

Where local authorities interpret legislation and frame the activities of their citizens and constituent organisations, the government determines legislation and controls the activities of people and organisations across markets.

This control may be direct or indirect, but the power and influence of government are such that large organisations and trade associations seek to influence the direction and strength of legislation, because any adverse laws or regulations may affect the profitability and the value of the organisation. Recent initiatives by the UK government to reduce the length of time that new drugs are protected by patent were severely contested by representatives from drug manufacturers and their trade association, the Association of British Pharmaceutical Industries. Despite a great deal of lobbying, the action was lost, and now manufacturers have only eight years to recover their investment before other manufacturers can replicate the drug. The pharmaceutical industry has also been actively lobbying the European Union with respect to legislation on new patent regulations and the information that must be carried in any marketing communications message. The tobacco industry is well known for its lobbying activities, as are chemical, transport and many other industries.

# Corporate advertising

In an attempt to harness the advantages of both advertising and public relations, corporate advertising has been seen by some as a means of communicating more effectively with a range of stakeholders. The credibility of messages transmitted through public relations is high, but the control that management has over the message is limited. Advertising, however, allows management virtually total control over message dispersion, but the credibility of these messages is usually low. Corporate advertising is the combination of the best of advertising and the best of public relations.

Corporate advertising, that is, advertising on behalf of an organisation rather than its products or services, has long been associated with public relations rather than the advertising department. This can be understood in terms of the origins and former use that organisations made of corporate advertising (Figure 15.2). The first major period was the 1960s, when institutional advertising became prominent. According to Stanton (1964), the primary task of institutional advertising was to create goodwill. The next period was the 1970s, when corporate image advertising became popular. During this decade, organisations used issue and advocacy advertising as a means of promoting political and social ideas in an attempt to generate public support for the position adopted by an organisation.

During the 1980s, which witnessed a large number of mergers and takeovers, there was an increase in the use of umbrella advertising. Organisations used the name of the organisation as a broad banner, under which a range of products and services was promoted. There was also a pronounced movement towards the incorporation of products and services within the use of public relations. This is reflected in the use of corporate advertising in the 1990s. Although the generation of goodwill continues to be a dominant theme, there is also a need to focus on organisations as discrete units. As many organisations de-layered and returned to core

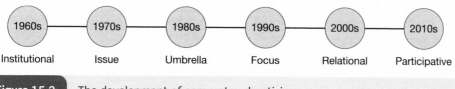

**Figure 15.2**    The development of corporate advertising

| Table 15.5 | Goals of corporate advertising |
|---|---|

Enhance corporate reputation

Improve credibility

Provide a point of differentiation

Support for products and services

Attract higher-quality employees

Underpin shareholder value

Easier access to new markets and suppliers

Advocacy of a position

Public communication of the company's social and environmental actions

business activities, so corporate advertising became an integral part of corporate rebranding. In the first decade of this century, issues around corporate behaviour became critical together with ideas about ethics and organisations' contribution to society and local communities. Here corporate advertising has been used to proclaim good works, social deeds, and apologies as necessary.

However, the main purpose of corporate advertising appears to be the provision of cues by which stakeholders can identify and understand an organisation. This is achieved by presenting the personality of the organisation to a wide range of stakeholders, rather than presenting particular functions or products that the organisation markets. Schumann et al. (1991) conclude that a number of US studies indicate that the first goal of corporate advertising is to enhance the company's reputation and the second is to provide support for the promotion of products and services. Table 15.5 sets out the most important goals that executives see corporate advertising as responsible for satisfying.

## Reasons for the use of corporate advertising

The need to improve and maintain goodwill and to establish a positive reputation among an organisation's stakeholders has already been mentioned. These are tasks that need to be undertaken consistently and continuously, with the aim of building a reputational reservoir. In addition, however, there are particular occasions when organisations need to use corporate advertising:

- during change and transition;
- when the organisation has a poor image;
- for product support;
- recruitment;
- repositioning;
- advocacy or issues.

### Change

When an organisation experiences a period of major change, perhaps the transition before, during and after a takeover or merger, corporate advertising can be used in a variety of ways. The first is defensively, to convince stakeholders, particularly shareholders, of the value of the organisation and of the need not to accept hostile offers; second, to inform and to advise of current positions; finally to position any 'new' organisation that may result from the merger activity. The defence of Marks & Spencer led by Stuart Rose, when Philip

Green attempted a takeover in 2004, was based around messages communicated to current shareholders of the superior future value of the business under the current ownership and managers. This was intended to raise credibility and hence prevent a takeover based on differing projections.

## Poor image

Corporate advertising can also be used to correct any misunderstanding that stakeholders might have of corporate reality (Reisman, 1989). For example, financial analysts may believe that an organisation is underperforming, but reality indicates that performance is good. As we have seen before, this can be a result of poor communication, and through corporate advertising the organisation can correct such misunderstandings and help establish strategic credibility with the financial community and other stakeholders.

## Product support

Corporate advertising can also assist the launch of new products. The costs normally associated with a launch can be lowered, and it is feasible to assume, although difficult to measure, that the effectiveness of a product launch can be improved when corporate advertising has been used to establish good reputational equity.

## Recruitment

Corporate advertising is used to recruit employees by creating a positive and attractive image of the organisation. The development of source credibility, in particular trust, is fundamental, and through the process of identification individuals can become attracted to the notion of working for a particular organisation and are stimulated to seek further information.

## Repositioning

Organisations periodically undergo self-review that may lead to repositioning. Hewlett-Packard launched its 'Invent' campaign as part of a process of preparing stakeholders for the future. The campaign sought to take the company back to its roots, its original ideology, 'the rules of the garage', in which the founders first developed the organisation and the values that are part of the corporate philosophy. The campaign sought to encourage invention and to legitimise exploration and risk taking, remembering, of course, that the HP way determines how employees work and that the customer defines whether the job is well done.

Organisations can be repositioned by the activities of competitor organisations. New products, new corporate messages, an improved trading performance or the arrival of a new CEO and the implementation of a new strategy can displace an organisation in the minds of its different stakeholders. This may require an adjustment by the focus organisation to re-establish itself. The Pepsi Challenge, referred to earlier, effectively dislodged Coca-Cola from its position as brand leader and led to a stream of product adjustments and messages from Coca-Cola aimed at repositioning itself.

## Advocacy

The reasons presented so far for the use of corporate advertising are strongly related to image. A further traditional reason for the use of this tool is the opportunity for the organisation to inform its stakeholders of the position or stand that it has on a particular issue. This is referred to as *advocacy advertising*. Rather than promoting the organisation in a direct way, this form of corporate advertising associates an organisation with an issue of social concern, which public relations very often cannot achieve alone.

The organisation can be seen as a brand in much the same way as products and services are branded. Just as a product-based brand can be tracked, so can the corporate entity be tracked for levels of awareness, attitudes and preferences held by stakeholders.

# Investor relations

Investor relations was previously regarded as a financial function of organisations (Petersen and Martin, 1996) and, although sometimes loosely attached to public relations, it was more often conducted by the department of financial affairs (Hong and Ki 2007). Today, the role of investor relations is seen to be of strategic importance and one which requires clarity and transparency, with communication not finance as a central tenant of investor relations (Laskin, 2009).

Partly as a result of deregulation, the number of target audiences for financial services and related communications has grown. On the one hand, there are large institutional investors such as the government, multinational organisations and agencies such as stock exchanges, all of which require financially related information. On the other hand, there are increasing numbers of individual investors who wish to invest part of their savings in various funds, equities and savings plans. In addition to these there are the financial press, shareholders, investment analysts, financial advisers and fund managers. This means that communication, and the provision of timely, transparent and accurate information should have become significant factors in the market place.

Cutlip et al. define investor relations as 'a specialized part of corporate public relations that builds and maintains mutually beneficial relationships with shareholders and others in the financial community to maximize shareholder value' (1999: 21). The UK Investor Relations Society (2009) describes investor relations as follows:

> *Investor Relations is the communication of information and insight between a company and the investment community. This process enables a full appreciation of the company's business activities, strategy and prospects and allows the market to make an informed judgement about the fair value and appropriate ownership of a company.*

Interestingly, the former stresses the maximisation of shareholder value and relationships, while the latter emphasises fair value rather than maximisation, and implicitly stresses the significance of one-way communication, which is not suitable for relationship development. In practice, the core activity of investor relations is to react to requests for information although the development and use of websites has helped to make the discipline more proactive.

If investor relations are to have an enhanced communication focus, a variety of public relations strategies are necessary to reach different target audiences. Hanrahan (1997) highlights four particular strategies; expansive, defensive, creative and adaptive.

*Expansive strategies* are followed during periods of growth, when the size of product portfolios increases. In this context competition can be aggressive, so it is critical that awareness, recognition and trust are developed. This can be achieved through serving on committees and public interest groups, publishing white papers, speaking at conferences, writing articles and other activities that serve to raise the profile and credibility or the organisation. Sponsorship can also be used to make associations with an event. This in turn can also be used as a way of establishing networks and leveraging goodwill.

*Defensive strategies* are needed in times of crisis, such as a recession, very poor trading performance, when accused of malpractice or irregular reporting or when faced by a hostile takeover bid. In these situations the timely provision of the correct information, perhaps as a separate report, is important.

*Creative strategies* involve the use of digital technologies to deliver the corporate identity in novel and interesting ways. This might be through the use of interviews which can be beamed across the television world instantly, if necessary, across the Internet and through Reuters and world services. With information and analysis instantly available, 24/7, the prime role of the press has shifted to one focused on the provision of comment and interpretation.

*Adaptive strategies* are used when an organisation experiences considerable change. Moving into new financial product and/or geographic markets, merging with another organisation or simply developing key services, all warrant strategies that are flexible and can adapt to local press and media needs. Corporate advertising, adapted for local use, has been a significant tool. Today, one of the roles of the website is to provide fast, localised information that can be targeted at particular opinion leaders and formers.

---

### Viewpoint 15.3    Personal IR at SingTel

Investor relations (IR) at Singapore Telecommunications (SingTel), is a critical activity. While the company's operations are focused on the Asian region, it has investors from around the world. It might be reasonably expected that communications over this geographically dispersed audience might be best managed through technology. Well, some of it is, but face-to-face communication is still perceived to be important. This is used in order to generate interaction with investors, so that the company can listen to what they are thinking about, and answer their questions. For example, different teams of SingTel senior managers spend over four weeks every year travelling to the United States and Europe to meet with investors.

SingTel's IR department consists of seven professionals. They manage shareholder questions, advise senior management on material disclosure and monitor the press and investment communities to make sure messages are clearly received and understood. From this information, it is possible to brief senior managers on what the market doesn't know or misunderstands.

Some of the technical aspects of the IR's operations are outsourced to service providers in the IR industry. For example, Orient Capital (London) conducts shareholder analysis for SingTel on a quarterly basis.

In addition to the international meetings, IR activities include events, conferences, presentations and business luncheons, which are organised in-house. For example, SingTel organises annual investor days that bring together investors and analysts from both the buy and sell sides. Senior management from the Singapore and Australian operations, as well as from the Regional Associates, are present to provide brief presentations on each of the different business divisions. Ample time is allocated for questions and answers, as well as informal interaction.

Although SingTel does not use social media, it does use some technology. The company sends out substantial market analysis and material information, in addition to communications mandated by the Singapore Exchange. Investor presentations, annual reports, webcasts of earnings presentations, announcements to SGX and ASX are also available on the IR website. Conference calls with investors and analysts are transcribed and posted on the IR website, as are PowerPoint presentations that explain the company's business, prospects and market overviews. The website also hosts other relevant information, including the investor calendar, shareholder meetings, shares and dividend information, factsheets and financial summaries.

*Source*:   Based on Pisik (2010) and SingTel Investor Relations.

**Question:**   How might use of social media assist investor relations at SingTel?

**Task:**      Using the Web, try to identify resources that focus on investor relations.

# Defensive or crisis communications

A growing and important part of the work associated with public relations is crisis communications. At one time, when a crisis such as a threat of takeover or workplace accident struck an organisation, the first stakeholders to be summoned by the CEOs were merchant bankers. Today the public relations consultant is first through the door. The power of corporate and marketing communications is beginning to be recognised and appreciated. Indeed, the astute CEO summons the public relations consultant in anticipation of crisis, on the basis that being prepared is a major step in weakening the energy with which some crises can affect organisations.

Organisational crises can be usefully considered in the context of chaos theory (Seeger, 2002). Chaos occurs when complex systems break down and the established order and equilibrium are broken by events that are often abrupt and discontinuous. Chaos theory considers system breakdown as a necessary event in order that the system be refreshed. Seeger phrases this process as 'disorder necessary for order, decay a precursor to renewal, decline a step in growth and collapse a prelude to rebuilding as one of the most attractive and optimistic features of chaos theory' (p. 331).

Crises can occur because of a simple or minor managerial mistake, an incorrect decision or because of a seemingly distant environmental event. All organisations face the prospect of managing a crisis, indeed, some commentators ominously suggest that all organisations have a crisis just around the corner (Fink, 2000). Crises are emerging with greater frequency as a result of a number of factors. Table 15.6 sets out some of the main factors that give rise to crises for organisations.

Figure 15.3 is used to present organisational crises in the context of two key variables. On the horizontal axis is the degree to which management has control over the origin of the crisis. Is the origin of the crisis outside management's control, such as an earthquake, or is it within its control, such as those crises associated with poor trading results? The vertical axis

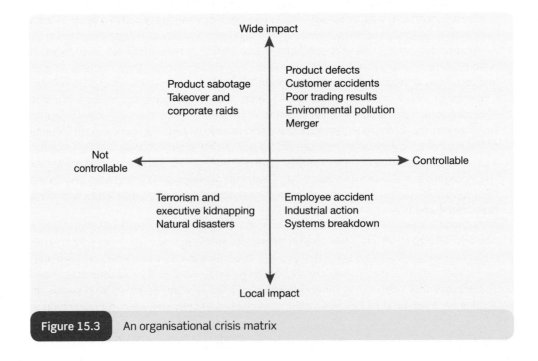

**Figure 15.3**   An organisational crisis matrix

| Table 15.6 | Common causes of disasters |
|---|---|

| Origin of crisis | Explanation |
|---|---|
| Economic | As new economies emerge (e.g. BRIC), so many established industries in developed economies decline – for example, the UK's steel and shipbuilding industries. |
| Managerial | Human error and the pursuit of financial goals by some organisations give rise to the majority of disasters. For example, cutting costs at the expense of safety and repair of systems. |
| Political | Issues concerning war and terrorism have encouraged kidnapping, as well as organisations having to change the locations of their business. |
| Climate | The climate is changing substantially in certain parts of the world, and this has brought disaster to those who lie in the wake of natural disturbances. For example, the hurricanes in 2004 that decimated the Cayman Islands and Grenada in the Caribbean; south-east Asia's December 2004 tsunami. |
| Technology | The rate at which technology is advancing has brought about crises such as those associated with transportation systems and aircraft disasters. Human error is also a significant factor, often associated with the rate of technological change. |
| New media | Digital media and instant communication means that information can be disseminated throughout the world within minutes of an event occurring. |
| Consumer groups | The rise of consumer groups (e.g. Amnesty International and Greenpeace) and their ability to investigate and publicise the operations and policies of organisations. |

reflects the potential impact that a crisis might have on an organisation. All crises, by definition, have a potential to inflict damage on an organisation. However, some can be contained, perhaps on a geographic basis, whereas others have the potential to cause tremendous damage to an organisation, such as those experienced through product tampering and environmental pollution.

The increasing occurrence of crises throughout the world has prompted many organisations to review the manner in which they anticipate managing such events, should they be implicated. It is generally assumed that those organisations that take care to plan in anticipation of disaster will experience more favourable outcomes than those that fail to plan. Quarantelli (1988) reports that there is only a partial correlation between those that plan and those that experience successful outcomes. He attributes this to the fact that only some of the organisations that take care to prepare do so in a professional way. Poor planning can only deliver poor results. Fink (2000) reports that organisations that do not plan experience crises that last over twice as long as those that do plan.

The second reason concerns the expectations of those who design and implement crisis plans. It is one thing to design a plan; it is entirely another to implement it. Crisis planning is about putting into position those elements that can affect speedy outcomes to the disaster sequence. When a crisis strikes, it is the application of contingency-based tactics by all those concerned with the event that will determine the strength of the outcome. Spillan (2003) sought to determine whether the experience of a crisis encourages concern and attention to preventing further crisis events. This was based on the evidence of Barton (2001) and Mitroff and Anagnos (2001) that most organisations only prepare crisis management plans after suffering and then recovering from a disaster. The central issue appears to revolve around the need to assess an organisation's vulnerabilities at the earliest opportunity, before a crisis occurs (Caponigro, 2000, as cited by Spillan, 2003).

## Crisis phases

The number of phases through which a crisis passes varies according to author and the management model they are proposing. For example, Penrose (2000) mentions Littlejohn's six-step model, Fink's audit, Mitroff's portfolio planning approach and Burnett's crisis classification matrix. The number of phases is also influenced by the type of crisis management an organisation uses. Essentially there are two main models, as presented at Figure 15.4: organisations that plan in order to manage crisis events and in doing so attempt to contain the impact; secondly there are organisations that fail to plan and manage by reacting to crisis events.

The differences between these two approaches are that there are fewer phases in the shorter 'reactionary' model and that the level of detail and attention given to the anticipation, management and consideration of crisis events is more deliberate in the planning model. Time is spent here considering the sequence of events within the planning model. A three-phase (and five-episode) framework is adopted: pre-impact, impact and readjustment phases. It should be remembered that the duration of each phase can vary considerably, depending upon the nature of the crisis and the manner in which management deals with the events associated with the crisis.

The first period is referred to as the *pre-impact phase* and consists of two main episodes: scanning and planning; and event identification and preparation. Good strategic management demands that the environment be scanned on a regular basis to detect the first signs of significant change. Organisations that pick up signals that are repeated are in a better

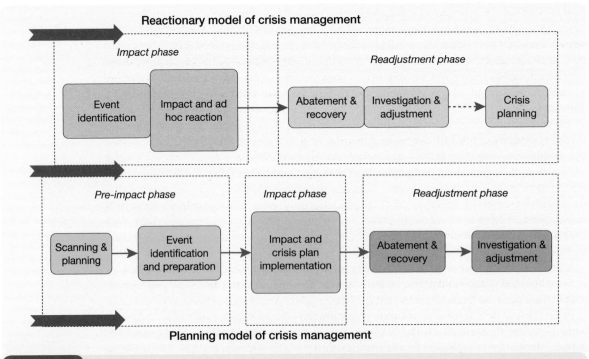

**Figure 15.4**     Twin models of crisis management

position to prepare for disaster than those that do not scan the environment. Penrose (2000) reports that those who perceive the impact of a crisis to be severe or very damaging and plan accordingly tend to achieve more successful outcomes. Those that fail to scan are often taken by surprise and have to react with less time and control to manage the events that hit them. Even if they do pick up a signal, many organisations not only ignore it but also attempt to block it out (Pearson and Mitroff, 1993). It is as if management is attempting to deny the presence of the signals in order that any stability and certainty they may have can continue.

Many of the signals detected during the pre-impact phase wither and die. Some gather strength and develop with increasing force. The next episode is characterised by the identification of events that move from possible to probable status. There is increasing activity and preparation in anticipation of the crisis, once its true nature and direction have been determined. Much of the activity should be geared to training and the preparation and deployment of crisis teams. The objective is not to prevent the crisis but to defuse it as much as possible, to inform significant stakeholders of its proximity and possible effects, and finally to manage the crisis process.

The impact phase is the period when the 'crisis breaks out' (Sturges et al., 1991). Management is tested to the limit and if a plan has been developed it is implemented with the expectation of ameliorating the damage inflicted by the crisis. One method of reducing the impact is to contain or localise the crisis. Neutralising and constraining the event can prevent it from contaminating other parts of the organisation or stakeholders. Pearson and Mitroff (1993) suggest that the containment of oil spills and the evacuation of buildings and aircraft are examples of containment and neutralisation. Through the necessity to talk to all stakeholders, management at this point will inevitably reveal its attitude towards the crisis event. Is its attitude one of genuine concern for the victims and stakeholders? Is the attitude consistent with the expectations that stakeholders have of the management team? Alternatively, is there a perception that management is making lame excuses and distancing itself from the event, and is this consistent with expectations? Readers should note that, within the reactionary model, the pre-impact and impact phases are merged into one, simply because there is little or no planning, no scanning and, by definition, no preparation in anticipation of a crisis.

The readjustment phase within the planning model consists of three main episodes. The period concerns the recovery and realignment of the organisation and its stakeholders to the new environment, once the deepest part of the crisis event has passed. The essential tasks are to ensure that the needs of key stakeholders can still be met and, if they cannot, to determine what must be done to ensure that they can be. For example, continuity of product supply is critically important. This may be achieved by servicing customers from other locations. Common characteristics of this phase are the investigations, police inquiries, public demonstrations, court cases and media probing that inevitably follow major crises and disasters. The manner in which an organisation handles this fall-out and tries to appear reasonable and consistent in its approach to such events can have a big impact on the perception that other stakeholders have of the organisation.

The rate at which organisations readjust depends partly on the strength of the image held by stakeholders prior to the crisis occurring. If the organisation had a strong reputation then the source credibility attributed to the organisation will be high. This means that messages transmitted by the organisation will be received favourably and trusted. However, if the reputation is poor, the effectiveness of any marketing communications is also going to be low. The level of source credibility held by the organisation will influence the speed with which stakeholders allow an organisation to readjust and recover after a crisis.

Benoit (1997) developed a theory concerning image restoration in the light of an organisational crisis. The theory states that there are five general approaches: denial, evade responsibility, reduce offensiveness, use corrective action and, lastly, mortification (see Table 15.7). Benoit has used these approaches to evaluate the responses given by a variety of organisations when faced by different disasters and crises (see Viewpoint 15.4).

| Table 15.7 | Image restoration approaches |
|---|---|

| Damage retrieval | Explanation |
|---|---|
| Simple denial | Outright rejection that the act was caused by them or even occurred in the first place, or shifting the blame by asserting that another organisation (person) was responsible for the act. |
| Evasion (of responsibility) | Provocation . . . a reasonable response to a prior act. |
| | Defeasibility . . . the act occurred because of a lack of time or information. |
| | Accident . . . the act was not committed purposefully. |
| | Good intentions . . . the wrongful act was caused despite trying to do well. |
| Reducing offensiveness | This involves demonstrating that the act was of minor significance or by responding so as to reduce the impact of the accusor. |
| Corrective action | This may involve putting right what was damaged and taking steps to avoid a repeat occurrence. |
| Mortification | An apology or statement of regret for causing the act that gave offence. |

*Source*: Benoit (1997).

Organisations that have not planned their management of crisis events and have survived a disaster may decide to instigate a more positive approach in order to mitigate the impact of future crisis events. This is not uncommon and crisis management planning may occur at the end of this cycle.

---

**Scholars' paper 15.4**   **Dialogue in public relations**

**Pieczka, M. (2011) Public relations as dialogic expertise?** *Journal of Communication Management*, 15(2), 108–24.

This paper provides an insight into the theory and background of a public relations cornerstone word, dialogue. The author rightly argues that, although dialogue is referred to and used extensively within public relations theory, there has been little or no research into the concept itself. The author seeks to rejuvenate and stimulate research into dialogue with this paper.

---

## Framing for crisis communication

The use of framing can serve to shape the way stakeholders perceive the organisation and the associated crisis. Crises can be categorised by type (Coombs, 2007) and the type provides the frame through which stakeholders pick up clues about how to interpret the event. Coombs identifies three main types: the extent to which the event was caused by an uncontrollable external force or agent; whether it was the result of an intentional or accidental action by the organisation; or if it was caused by human or technical error. The frame, therefore, enables stakeholders to determine the extent to which the organisation was responsible for the crisis occurring in the first place. From these three clusters of types of crisis can be identified; victim, accident and preventable clusters. See Table 15.8.

| Table 15.8 | Crisis types by crisis clusters |
|---|---|

| Crisis clusters | Explanation |
|---|---|
| Victim cluster | The organisation is seen as a victim of the crisis. Stakeholders attribute little responsibility to the organisation, so there is only a mild reputational threat. Common events include natural disasters, rumours, workplace violence and product tampering. |
| Accident cluster | The actions of the organisation leading to the crisis were minimal and the threat to reputational status is moderate. Typical events include stakeholder challenges to the operations, technical error accidents and technical errors resulting in product defect and subsequent recall. |
| Preventable cluster | The organisation deliberately placed people at risk, took inappropriate actions or violated regulations and in doing so caused a strong threat to the reputation. Typical events include human-error accidents and product harm/defects, deception, misconduct and actions that lead to injury. |

Based on Coombs (2007).

Coombs (1995) claims that, in order to repair reputation, crisis response strategies are necessary to shape perceptions of those responsible, change perceptions of the organisation and reduce the negative effects caused through the crisis event. He identifies three main forms of response based on the perceptions of those responsible for the crisis. The first are *denial strategies*, which attempt to remove connections between the organisation and the crisis. The second are *diminish strategies*, which argue that the organisation did not lack control over the crisis and that it is not as bad as is claimed by others. The third are *rebuild strategies* which involve offering compensation or an apology to victims (2006). Coombs develops a situational crisis communication theory which anticipates how stakeholders will perceive a crisis and how they will react to various response strategies. He argues that his approach bridges deficiencies in Benoit's image restoration theory which offers 'no conceptual links between the crisis response strategies and elements of the crisis situation' (p. 171).

## Viewpoint 15.4    All at sea with Costa Cruises

Costa Cruises, the Italian owners of the 950-feet-long cruise liner *Costa Concordia* which ran into trouble just two hours after its departure from the port of Civitavecchia near Rome in January 2012, faced a continuing crisis as they wrestled with the consequences of the accident, including the deaths of 32 people.

The crisis was unusual in the sense that there was no warning of the impending drama. The night-time evacuation of the ship happened when the liner grounded off the Tuscan island of Giglio, following a collision with a rocky islet.

Once the ship grounded, the impact phase was experienced. First, the guests and staff had to be evacuated, made safe and those injured or bereaved helped. More or less immediately the media had to be kept informed, and the facts made readily available, as they unfolded.

The reasons for the disaster were then sought, with speculation and rumour rife. The ship's captain, Francesco Schettino, was blamed for the incident and put under house arrest.

Then, there were issues associated with the regulators and even politicians who were concerned about any breaches of the law or procedure. This was partly a duty-of-care issue to ensure that other similar ships and passengers were not at risk. The crisis was also perpetuated by the sight of the stricken liner lying on its side off a beautiful island. The media were free to keep taking pictures, but there was the risk that tons of diesel oil would leak, contaminating the island and affecting tourist business. Worse, the liner might have slip off the rocks and sunk, making retrieval even more hazardous and expensive.

Once the ship was removed from the island and was out of sight, the crisis moved into the post-impact phase with a period of introspection, accusation and enquiry, both internally and externally. It was at this stage also that court cases and law suits were brought against the liner's owners. It was reported that Costa Cruises had offered passengers a lump sum of 11,000 euros each in compensation, provided they dropped any other litigation. However, it was understood that the deal was rejected by some passengers, including a group of six, who have filed a law suit in the US demanding £292 million as compensation. Apart from the financial issues, the continuing publicity will drag the crisis out over many years.

After all of this there is the issue associated with the cruise line's reputation, and, indeed, the notion of cruise holidays as a whole. It might have been anticipated that the crisis would damage the reputation and business performance of Costa Cruises. Initial reports indicate that business performance rose 25 per cent following the disaster. This has been attributed to the increased media coverage, which served to raise awareness of the availability of cruises in the Mediterranean, and this attracted new customers.

*Source*:    Based on various media reports.

| Question: | What evidence is there to indicate that Costa Cruises had a crisis plan in place before the disaster occurred? |
| --- | --- |
| Task: | Develop a time line of significant events concerning the *Costa Concordia* disaster. Does this inform about the management and media behaviour relating to this crisis? |

| Exhibit 15.4 | **The cause of the crisis – the stricken *Costa Concordia*** |
| --- | --- |
| | *Source*: Vandeville Eric/ABACA/Press Association Images |

# Integrating public relations in the communications mix

Public relations has three major roles to play within the communications mix: the development and maintenance of corporate goodwill; the continuity necessary for good product support; and through these, the development and maintenance of suitable relationships.

The first is the traditional role of creating goodwill and stimulating interest between the organisation and its various key stakeholders. Its task is to provide a series of cues by which the stakeholders can recognise, understand and position the organisation in such a way that it builds a strong reputation. This role is closely allied to the corporate strategy and the communication of strategic intent.

The second role of public relations is to support the marketing of the organisation's products and services, and its task is to integrate with the other elements of the marketing communications mix. Public relations and advertising have complementary roles. For example, the launch of a new product commences not with advertising to build awareness in target customers but with the use of public relations to inform editors and news broadcasters that a new product is about to be launched. This news material can be used within the trade and consumer press before advertising occurs and the target buyers become aware (when the news is no longer news). To some extent this role is tactical rather than strategic but, if planned, and if events are timed and coordinated with the other elements of the marketing communications mix, then public relations can help build competitive advantage.

The third role is to provide the means by which relationships can be developed. To do this, public relations has a responsibility to encourage interaction and dialogue to provide the means through which interaction, discourse and discussion can occur and to play a full part in the communication process and the messages that are conveyed, listened to, considered and acted upon.

# Key points

- Public relations is a communication discipline that can develop and maintain a portfolio of relationships with a range of key stakeholder audiences. The use of public relations does not require the purchase of airtime or space in media vehicles, such as television or magazines. The decision on whether an organisation's public relations messages are transmitted or not rests with those charged with managing the media resource, not the message sponsor.

- The main characteristics of public relations are that it represents a very cost-effective means of carrying messages with a high degree of credibility. However, the degree of control that management is able to exert over the transmission of messages can be limited.

- Public relations can be used to communicate with a range of publics (or stakeholders). These vary from employees (internal public relations), financial groups (financial or investor relations), customers (media relations) and *organisations and communities (corporate public relations)*.

- Public relations enables organisations to position themselves and provide stakeholders with a means of identifying and understanding them. This may be accomplished inadvertently through inaction or deliberately through a planned presentation of a variety of visual cues.

- Public relations can be seen to work at a practitioner level where it is used as a tool to achieve media visibility. At a different level public relations is seen as a means of mediating the relationships organisations develop with various stakeholders. Here, public relations is perceived as a longer-term and proactive form of planned communication. In the former view, public relations is seen as an instrument, in the latter, as a means of conducting a dialogue.

- Grunig and Hunt (1984) have attempted to capture the diversity of public relations activities through a framework. They set out four models to reflect the different ways in which public relations is, in their opinion, considered to work.

- The overall goal should be to develop the relationship between the organisation and its different audiences.

- There are four dimensions of communication behaviour. These dimensions are direction, purpose, channel and ethics. Using predetermined campaign objectives, ranging from publicity through press releases, to the manner in which customers are treated and products perform, events are managed and expectations are met.

- Public relations consists of a range of communication activities, of which media relations, publicity and event management appear to be the main ones used by practitioners. However, in addition investor relations, lobbying, corporate advertising and crisis communications form an important aspect of public relations activities.

- Public relations plays an important role in preparing for and constraining the impact of a crisis and re-establishing an organisation once a crisis has passed. Crisis planning is about putting into position those elements that can affect speedy outcomes to the disaster sequence.

- Public relations has three major roles to play within the communications programme of an organisation: the development and maintenance of corporate goodwill; the continuity necessary for good product support; and through these, the development and maintenance of suitable relationships. These roles can be accomplished more easily when public relations is integrated with the other tools and media of the communication mix.

# Review questions

1. Define public relations and set out its principal characteristics.

2. Using the BP minicase at the start of this chapter, identify the main stakeholders and comment on why it was important to communicate with each of them.

3. Highlight the main objectives of using public relations.

4. Write a brief paper describing the main methods of publicity.

5. Identify the different strategies associated with investor relations.

6. Suggest occasions when corporate advertising might be best employed.

7. Identify the main phases associated with crisis management.

8. Suggest how BP's various apologies, explained in the minicase, can be interpreted through use of Benoit's 'approaches to image restoration'.

9. What roles might stakeholders adopt when a crisis occurs?

10. Discuss the view that public relations can only ever be a support tool in the marketing communications mix.

# References

Barton, L. (2001) *Crisis Organisations II*, Cincinnati, OH: South Western Publishing.

Batty, D. and Haynes, J. (2010) Volcano continues to ground flights as ash cloud spreads over Europe, *Guardian*, Saturday 17 April, retrieved 22 June 2012 from www.guardian.co.uk/world/2010/apr/17/volcano-disruption-flights-grounded-ash.

BBC news coverage available from www.bbc.co.uk (accessed 20 June 2011).

Benoit, W. L. (1997) Image Repair Discourse and Crisis Communication, *Public Relations Review*, 23, 2, 177–86.

Berrays, E. (1928) *Propaganda*, London: Ig Publishing.

BP (2010) press releases available from www.bp.com (accessed 22 June 2011).

Bruning, S.D. and Ledingham, J.A. (2000) Perceptions of relationships and evaluations of satisfaction: an exploration of interaction, *Public Relations Review*, 26(1), 85–95.

Bruning, S.D., Dials, M. and Shirka, A. (2008) Using dialogue to build organisation–public relationships, engage publics, and positively affect organizational outcomes, *Public Relations Review*, 34, 25–31.

Caponigro, J.R. (2000) *The Crisis Counsellor: A-Step-by-Step Guide to Managing a Business Crisis*, Chicago, IL: Contemporary Books.

CNN (2010) news coverage available from www.cnn.com (accessed 24 June 2011).

Coombs, W.T. (1995) Choosing the right words: the development of guidelines for selection of 'appropriate' crisis response strategies, *Management Communication Quarterly*, 8(4), 447–76.

Coombs, W.T. (2006) The protective powers of crisis response strategies: managing reputational assets during a crisis, *Journal of Promotion Management*, 12, 241–59.

Coombs, W.T. (2007) Protecting organization reputations during a crisis: The development and application of situational crisis communication theory, *Corporate Reputation Review* 10, 3, 163–176.

Cornelissen, J. (2011) *Corporate Communication: A Guide to Theory and Practice*, London: Sage.

Cutlip, S.M., Center, A.H. and Broom, G.M. (1994) *Effective public relations*, Englewood Cliffs, NJ: Prentice-Hall.

Cutlip, S.M., Center, A.H. and Broom, G.M. (1999) *Effective Public Relations*, 8th edn, Englewood Cliffs, NJ.: Prentice-Hall.

Deans, J. (2012) Strictly Come Dancing beats X Factor to pole position yet again, *The Guardian*, 5 November, retrieved from http://www.guardian.co.uk/media/2012/nov/05/strictly-come-dancing-x-factor, accessed 29 December 2012.

Ehling, W.P. (1992) Estimating the value of public relations and communication to an organisation, in *Excellence in Public Relations and Communication Management* (eds J.E. Grunig, D.M. Dozier, P. Ehling, L.A. Grunig, F.C. Repper and J. Whits), Hillsdale, NJ: Lawrence Erlbaum, 617–38.

Fink, S. (2000) *Crisis Management Planning for the Inevitable*, New York: AMACON.

Geertz, C. (1973) The Interpretation of Cultures, New York: Basic Books.

Gray, E.R., and Balmer, J.M.T. (1998) Managing corporate image and corporate reputation, *Long Range Planning*, 31, 695–702.

Greenwood, C.A. (2011) Evolutionary Theory: The Missing Link for Conceptualizing Public Relations, *Journal of Public Relations Research*, 22(4), 456–76.

Gregory, A. (2004) Scope and structure of public relations: a technology driven view, *Public Relations Review*, 30(3) (September), 245–54.

Grunig, J. (1992) Models of public relations and communication, in *Excellence in Public Relations and Communications Management* (eds J.E. Grunig, D.M. Dozier, P. Ehling, L.A. Grunig, F.C. Repper and J. Whits), Hillsdale, NJ: Lawrence Erlbaumk, 285–325.

Grunig, J.E. (1997) A situational theory of publics: Conceptual history, recent challenges and new research, in *Public Relations Research: An International Perspective* (eds D. Moss, T. MacManus and D. Vercic), London: International Thomson Business, 3–48.

Grunig, J. and Hunt, T. (1984) *Managing Public Relations*, New York: Holt, Rineholt & Winston.

Hanrahan, G. (1997) Financial and investor relations, in P. Kitchen (ed.) *Public Relations Principles and Practice*, London: Thomson.

Hong, Y. and Ki, E.-J. (2007) How do public relations practitioners perceive investor relations? An exploratory study, *Corporate Communications: An International Journal* 12(2), 199–213.

Kent, M.L. and Taylor, M. (2002) Toward a dialogic theory of public relations, *Public Relations Review*, 28(1) (February), 21–37.

Laskin, A.V. (2009) The evolution of models of public relations: an outsider's perspective, *Journal of Communication Management*, 13(1), 37–54.

Magee, K. (2009) Prime-time TV wars: Entertainment PR, *PR Week*, 27 November, 20–25.

Miller, G. (1989) Persuasion and public relations: two 'Ps' in a pod, in *Public Relations Theory* (eds C. Botan and V. Hazelton), Hillsdale, NJ: Lawrence Erlbaum.

Mitroff, I. and Anagnos, G. (2001) *Managing Crises Before They Happen*, New York: American Management Association.

Moloney, K. (1997) Government and lobbying activities, in *Public Relations: Principles and Practice* (ed. P.J. Kitchen), London: International Thomson Press.

O'Reilly. G. (2009) BBC hires Headstream to promote latest series of *Strictly Come Dancing* online, prweek.com, Retrieved 05 January 2009 from www.prweek.com/uk/news/929883/BBC-hires-Headstream-promote-latest-series-Strictly-Dancing-online/.

Palmer, J. (2010) On Celebrity Eclipse cruise ship Bilbao rescue, *BBC News*, 21 April 2010, retrieved 22 June 2012 from http://newsbbc.co.uk/local/hampshire/hi/people_and_places/newsid_8632000/863850.stm.

Pearson, C.M. and Mitroff, I. (1993) From crisis prone to crisis prepared: a framework for crisis management, *Academy of Management Executive*, 7(1), 48–59.

Penrose, J.M. (2000) The role of perception in crisis planning, *Public Relations Review*, 26(2), 155–71.

Petersen, B.K. and Martin, H.J. (1996) CEO perception of investor relations as a public relations function: an exploratory study, *Journal of Public Relations Research*, 8(3), 173–209.

Pieczka, M. (2011) Public relations as dialogic expertise? *Journal of Communication Management*, 15(2), 108–124.

Pisik, B. (2010) How they do investor relations at SingTel, *Inside Investor Relations*, 9 September 2010 retrieved 10 December 2010 from www.insideinvestorrelations.com/articles/16368/how-they-do-investor-relations-singtel/.

Quarantelli, E.L. (1988) Disaster crisis management: a summary of research findings, *Journal of Management Studies*, 25(4), 373–85.

Reisman, J. (1989) Corporate advertising in disguise, *Public Relations Journal* (September), 21–7.

Sallot, L.M., and Johnson, E. (2006) To contact . . . or not? Investigating journalists' assessments of public relations subsidies and contact preferences, *Public Relations Review*, 32, 83–86.

Schumann, D.W., Hathcote, J.M. and West, S. (1991) Corporate advertising in America: a review of published studies on use, measurement and effectiveness, *Journal of Advertising*, 20(3), 35–56.

Seeger, M.W. (2002) Chaos and crisis: propositions for a general theory of crisis communication, *Public Relations Review*, 28(4) (October), 329–37.

Shin, J.H. and Cameron, G.T. (2003) Informal relations: A look at personal influence in media relations, *Journal of Communication Management*, 7, 239–253.

Siren (2011) Royal Caribbean Cruises, *CIPR Excellence Awards Winner*, retrieved 22 June from http://www.cipr.co.uk/sites/default/files/Lanuching%20new%20ship%20Celebrity%20Eclipse%20with%20a%20repatriation%20mission.pdf.

Spillan, J.E. (2003) An exploratory model for evaluating crisis events and managers' concerns in non-profit organisations, *Journal of Contingencies and Crisis Management*, 11(4) (December), 160–9.

Stanton, W.J. (1964) *Fundamentals of Marketing*, New York: McGraw-Hill.

Sturges, D.L., Carell, B.J., Newsom, D.A. and Barrera, M. (1991) Crisis communication management: the public opinion node and its relationship to environmental nimbus, *SAM Advanced Management Journal* (Summer), 22–7.

UK Investor Relations Society (2009) retrieved 23 March 2011 from www.ir-soc.org.uk/.

Vos, T.P. (2011) Explaining the Origins of Public Relations: Logics of Historical Explanation, *Journal of Public Relations Research*, 23(2), 119–140.

Waters, R.D., Tindall, N.T.J. and Morton, T.S. (2010) Media Catching and the Journalist-Public Relations Practitioner Relationship: How Social Media are Changing the Practice of Media Relations, *Journal of Public Relations Research*, 22(3), 241–64.

Yun, S.-H. (2006) Toward public relations theory-based study of public diplomacy: testing the applicability of the excellence study, *Journal of Public Relations Research*, 18(4), 287–312.

# Chapter 16

## Sponsorship

Sponsorship has been used by organisations for the past two decades as a means of supporting primary media activities and as a way of building effective relationships. However, the recent recession led many organisations to either curtail or even cease their sponsorship activities in an attempt to save costs. The good news is that this was short-lived as there is extensive evidence that organisations have been returning to sponsorship. Some organisations are using it in a variety of new and exciting ways to generate awareness, create lasting brand associations and to cut through the clutter of commercial messages.

## Aims and learning objectives

The aim of this chapter is to introduce and examine sponsorship as an increasingly significant form of marketing communications.

The learning objectives of this chapter are to:

1. explain how sponsorship activities have developed and provide an insight into the main characteristics of this form of communication;

2. consider reasons for the use of sponsorship and the types of objectives that might be set;

3. understand how sponsorship might work;

4. explain some of the conceptual and theoretical aspects of sponsorship;

5. appreciate the variety and different forms of sponsorship activities;

6. understand the reasons why sponsorship has become an important part of the communication mix.

# Minicase

## The London Olympics

The Olympic Games, staged every four years, are regarded as the world's number one sporting event. Each Olympiad attracts a global audience of billions and, as a result, brands are prepared to invest huge sums of marketing money in order that they can be closely associated with the Olympic brand.

The five Olympic rings are one of the most recognised brand symbols and serve as a visual ambassador for the Olympic Movement. The Games provide a unique platform upon which the Olympic Marketing Programme (OMP) is developed. The OMP plays an integral role in the financial security, stability, and promotion of the Olympic Movement. The OMP not only seeks to protect the Olympic brand equity inherent in the Olympic image and ethos, but also aims to maximise the number of people throughout the world who are able to experience the Olympic Games, either through attendance, or more realistically, via broadcast television and digital media platforms.

The IOC generates revenue in a number of ways. Of these, the sale of broadcast rights, the Olympic Partners (TOP) worldwide sponsorship programme and the IOC official supplier and licensing programme, are key. The IOC openly recognises that the various sponsorship agreements provide a substantial part of the funding to support the Olympic Movement. The official partners also provide technical services and product support to the IOC, Organising Committees of the Olympic Games and the National Olympic Committees.

The Olympic Partner Programme (TOP) is the highest level of Olympic sponsorship. The programme has 11 worldwide Olympic partners, and each receives exclusive global marketing rights within a designated product or service category. These partners are appointed on a 4-year cycle, although some have been involved with the Olympics for a long time. For example, the Coca-Cola Company has supported the Olympic Movement since 1928 and is the longest, continuous partner of the Games.

The revenues from TOP help finance the staging of the Games, and are also used to develop sport across the world. Partners also help promote the Games and the Olympic values around the world by using their Olympic association in their marketing campaigns.

In 2012 Coca-Cola supported the Olympic Torch Relay around the UK. Through music, 'The Beat of London', Coca-Cola provided a live TV show broadcast worldwide, which focused on the social side of the Olympic Games, and featured Olympic athletes, celebrities and musical performances. Coca-Cola's Olympic Park pavilion also enabled people to create their own beat for London 2012 by remixing the sounds of Olympic sports. The pavilion's shape was inspired by the iconic glass Coca-Cola bottle.

Another partner is Acer. They provided the technical infrastructure for the Olympic Park, as well as the Technology Operations Centre (TOC), Media Centres, the Olympic Villages, the LOCOG headquarters, and all the competition venues.

All the partners provide distinct services. Dow, for example, provided sustainable science and chemistry-based solutions that assisted in the design of roofs, sports floors and pitches. Visa provided the only acceptable payment card at the London event, and through all Olympic Games to 2020. Atos managed and provided the security for the IT system that relayed results, events and athlete information to spectators and media around the world. Omega provided the timekeeping devices, Panasonic the digital audio/video equipment, such as flat-screen TVs, digital video cameras, DVD recorders, and professional audio/video equipment. Procter & Gamble provided the personal care and household products, and Samsung the proprietary wireless communications platform, called WOW (Wireless Olympic Works), and mobile phones. GE provided power, lighting, water treatment and transportation, and supplied local hospitals with diagnostic imaging equipment and healthcare IT solutions.

Following these partner collaborations, there is a further level of sponsorship. These are referred to 'tier-one' brands, and they are appointed to particular Games. The following were only involved with the London event and included BMW, British Airways, BT Adidas, BP, EDF and Lloyds TSB. A further step down the Olympic sponsorship ladder there are 'London Olympic Supporters': Adecco, ArcelorMittal, Cadbury, Cisco, Deloitte, Thomas Cook and UPS. Another rung down finds a group of official 'providers and suppliers'. There were 28 of these, from Heineken and Holiday Inn, to John Lewis, Next and Ticketmaster. In total there were 52 sponsors for the London 2012 Olympic Games.

In addition to these official sponsors there are team-related sponsorships such as *Team Sky* in cycling, plus personal sponsorship deals associated with individual athletes. Jessica Ennis was sponsored by Adidas, Aviva, British Airways, BP, Jaguar, Powerade, Olay and Omega. Usain Bolt was sponsored by Virgin Media, Gatorade, Puma, Visa, and Hublot watches.

However, several Olympic sponsors, such as Coca-Cola, Cadbury and McDonald's have been criticised for their involvement. The claim is that many of their products are high in sugar, fat and salt, which is contributing to the obesity crisis. As an official partner for over 35 years, McDonald's role was to feed the athletes, coaches, officials, media and spectators on-site at the Games. Research prior to the London Games indicated that 25 per cent of consumers disagreed that McDonald's is a 'good fit' as an Olympic sponsor. Perhaps more crticially, 32 per cent said that the fast-food brand's involvement conflicts with what the Olympics stands for, and 39 per cent believed that its products and services were not relevant to the Games. Other sponsors, such as BP and Dow, have been criticised for their business practices and ethics. In their defence, LOCOG argue that these companies (fast food, soft drinks) are important in terms of making sport come alive for young people.

An interesting issue therefore concerns the reasons why brands choose to become Olympic sponsors, when the costs and resources, and fees are so enormous. Cadbury saw it as a way of moving towards global status. Lloyds Banking Group use the communication platform 'For the Journey', so involvement with London 2012 was a natural progression.

BT's research indicated that involvement and association with the Olympics would build consideration, favourability and purchase. For Cisco it was an opportunity to change corporate perceptions and also impact positively on staff.

Procter & Gamble give three reasons why they decided to become Olympic partners. First, to build the business and make additional sales of £325m, second to use the Olympics as the launch of Procter & Gamble as a corporate brand: that is, something separate from P&G's individual brands. The third reason is that it can be an effective way of developing employee relations.

The reasons are many and varied, all are supported by research and figures but the association with the values and ethos of the Olympics and the global reach of an audience of over 5 billion is a powerful driver to be an Olympic sponsor.

*This minicase was written by Chris Fill using a variety of sources, including Clark (2012); Derrick (2012); IOC (2012); Mitchell (2012); Sweney (2012); Wilson (2012).*

**Exhibit 16.1    The Olympic Rings at London 2012**
*Source*: Nick Savage/Alamy Images

# Introduction

Sponsorship has become an increasingly popular element of the communication mix. The sponsorship activities associated with the Olympic Games outlined in the preceding minicase, demonstrate not only the importance to brands of being associated with a major event, but also how important sponsorship is in funding and sustaining the Olympic movement. In other words, sponsorship can be mutually rewarding.

Before the recession, sponsorship was also one of the fastest growing forms of marketing communications (Cunningham et al., 2009). This is because of the quality and richness of the communication the sponsor generates and because of the increasing effectiveness of some traditional media. It is a mix of advertising, with its capacity for message control, and public relations with its potential for high levels of credibility and message diffusion, directed through or with a third party. So, in this sense, sponsorship lacks the harshness of advertising and the total lack of control that characterises much of the work of public relations.

There is a commonly held expectation that organisations should contribute to their local communities with a view to being seen as participative, caring and involved with local affairs. One of the drawbacks of these tie-ups is that the degree of control that can be levied is limited once a commitment has been made. By adopting a more commercial perspective, some organisations have used sponsorship, particularly of sports activities, as a means of reaching wider target audiences. Sponsorship can provide the following opportunities for the sponsoring organisation:

1. To gain exposure to particular audiences that each event attracts in order to convey simple awareness-based brand messages.

2. To suggest to the target audiences that there is an association between the sponsored and the sponsor and that, by implication, this association may be of interest and/or value.

3. To allow members of the target audiences to perceive the sponsor indirectly through a third party and so mitigate any negative effects associated with traditional mass media and direct persuasion.

4. To provide sponsors with the opportunity to blend a variety of tools in the communication mix and use resources more efficiently and, arguably, more effectively.

From this it is possible to define sponsorship as a commercial activity in which one party permits another an opportunity to exploit an association with a target audience in return for funds, services or resources.

It is necessary to clarify the distinction between sponsorship and charitable donations. The latter are intended to change attitudes and project a caring identity, with the main returns from the exercise being directed to society or the beneficiaries. The beneficiaries have almost total control over the way in which funds are used. When funds are channeled through sponsorship the recipient has to attend to the needs of the sponsor by allowing it access to the commercial associations that are to be exploited, partly because they have a legal arrangement, but also to ensure that the exchange becomes relational and longer-term; in other words, there is repeat purchase (investment) activity. The other major difference is that the benefits of the exchange are intended to accrue to the participants, not society at large.

Normally sponsorship involves two parties, the sponsor and the sponsee, although many sponsors may be assigned to a single sponsee. The degree of fit between these two parties partly determines the relative effectiveness of the relationship (Poon and Prendergast, 2006). The degree of fit, or product relevance, as proposed by McDonald (1991) cited by Poon and Prendergast, can be considered in terms of two main dimensions. *Function-based similarity*

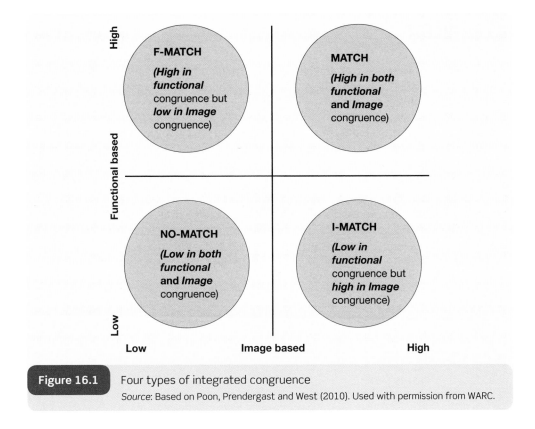

| Figure 16.1 | Four types of integrated congruence |

*Source*: Based on Poon, Prendergast and West (2010). Used with permission from WARC.

occurs when the product is used in the event being sponsored. For example, function-based similarity occurs when a piano manufacturer such as Bösendorfer sponsors a Viennese piano recital. The second dimension concerns *image-based similarities*, which reflects the image of the sponsor in the event. Here Airbus's sponsorship of a major technical or even artistic exhibition serves to bestow prestige on all parties. Poon et al. (2010) identify two levels (high and low) of functional and image-based congruence, before offering a four-quadrant classification, as set out at Figure 16.1.

To illustrate how this works, these authors give as an example an airline's sponsorship of environmental activities. This, they say, is low in both functional and image congruence and there is no clear link to the airline's function or image other than to rectify the situation. The airline has a limited travel scheme, called 'Miles for Kids in Need'. This gives assistance to children who are seriously ill and in need of emergency medical treatment. This equates to high functional congruence but low image congruence (F-MATCH). Low functional congruence with high image congruence (I-MATCH) occurs with the airline's sponsorship of a variety of cultural events. The final quadrant (MATCH) occurs through the airline's travel sponsorship of a symphony orchestra, as this generates both high functional and image congruence.

Coppetti et al. (2009) emphasise the value of congruence but also demonstrate that even when there is a lack of fit, the effectiveness of the sponsorship can be enhanced by involving the audience in what they refer to as 'attractive sponsor activities'. This suggests that by building in experiences for the audience and encouraging their participation, and by using advertising before and after the sponsorship event, such integration can serve to increase the value of the communication programme.

| Scholars' paper 16.1 | Matching sponsorship opportunities |

**Poon, D.T.Y., Prendergast, G. and West, D. (2010) Match Game: Linking Sponsorship Congruence with Communication Outcomes, *Journal of Advertising Research*, 4(80) June, 214–26.**

Building on the 2006 paper by Poon and Prendergast, these authors seek to develop the debate about the importance of congruence between a sponsor and the event being sponsored. Their research into the subject found no evidence of interaction effects between functional and image congruence. They determined that sponsorships involving low functional and low image congruence did as little to create favourable communication outcomes as if there were no sponsorship. This is an important paper for those requiring an in-depth understanding of sponsorship.

# The growth and development of sponsorship

Many researchers and authors agree that the use of sponsorship by organisations is increasing (Sneath et al., 2005; Harvey et al., 2006; Cornwell, 2008; Walraven et al., 2012) and that it is becoming a more significant part of the marketing communications mix. The development of sponsorship as a communication tool has been spectacular since the early 1990s. This is because of a variety of factors, but among the most important are the government's policies on tobacco and alcohol, the escalating costs of advertising media during the 1990s, the proven effectiveness of sponsorship, new opportunities due to increased leisure activity, greater media coverage of sponsored events and the recognition of the inefficiencies associated with the traditional media (Meenaghan, 1991). In addition to this list of drivers can be added regulations and technology. In the UK the Independent Television Commission, which is now subsumed by Ofcom, acted to restrict the nature and form of programme (or broadcast) sponsorship. However, a relaxation in the regulations has allowed for the development of this type of sponsorship.

The reference to technology concerns digital video recorders, such as TiVo and PVRs that allow users to skip over advertising breaks. These machines have now achieved strong consumer penetration and it can be argued that the sponsorship credits have become more important than advertising in achieving brand presence. See Table 16.1.

| Table 16.1 | Growth and development of sponsorship |

Increased media coverage of events

Relaxation of government and industry regulations

Increased incidence of sponsorship event supply (and demand)

Relationship orientation and association between sponsorship participants

Positive attitude change toward sponsorship by senior management

Awareness and drive towards integrated marketing communications

Increasing rate of other media costs

Need to develop softer brand associations and to reach niche audiences

## Viewpoint 16.1     Sports sponsorship gets timed-out

Many watch manufacturers have developed associations with particular sports personalities or sporting events. The main goals of these sponsorships have been to develop brand awareness, associations and favourable values. The following examples are just some of the associations that have been developed between particular events and watch manufacturers:

**Motor racing:** The TAGHeuer brand has long been associated with Grand Prix motor racing.

Certina sponsors the BMW Sauber Formula 1 team.

Chopard makes the Mille Liglia chronograph at the time of the road race and presents one to all competitors.

Seiko sponsors Honda F1 and Jenson Button.

**IndyCar** Tissot sponsors Danica Patrick (the first woman to win a race in the IndyCar Series).

**Water sports:** Omega promotes its Seamaster in association with the America's Cup.

**Polo:** Cartier sponsors many prestige polo events.

**Equestrian:** Rolex sponsors the International Equestrian Federation (FEI) properties and the Rolex Rankings.

**Golf:** Alfred Dunhill sponsors the annual Alfred Dunhill Golf Championship at St Andrews.

**Cricket:** Citizen sponsor Kevin Pietersen, the Surrey and England cricketer.

**Aviation:** Breitling has developed an association with aviation.

*Source*:   Balfour (2000); company websites.

**Question:** If timing and sporting achievement are the key associations for watch houses, what might be important for fashion designers?

**Task:** Find a watch house that associates itself with the Olympic Games.

| Exhibit 16.2 | **Roger Federer – an endorser for Rolex** |
|---|---|
| | *Source*: Matthew Stockman/Getty Images |

Sponsorship, a part of public relations, should be used as an element of an integrated approach to an organisation's communications. In other words, sponsorship needs to be harnessed strategically. For example, many companies and brands originating in South-East Asia and the Pacific regions have used sponsorship as a means of overseas market entry in order to develop name or brand awareness. Panasonic, JVC and Daihatsu have used this approach, as indeed many companies are now doing in an attempt to become established in the BRIC countries. See Viewpoint 16.4 about Catlin's entry into China later in this chapter.

In addition, many sponsorship arrangements have survived recessionary periods. This may be because of the two- to three-year period that each sponsorship contract covers and the difficulty and costs associated with terminating such agreements. It may also be because of the impact that sponsorship might have on core customers who continue to buy the brand during economic downturns. Easier targeting through sponsorship can also assist the reinforcement of brand messages. Readers are reminded of the Weak theory of advertising (Chapter 14), and it may be that sponsorship is a means of defending a market and providing additional triggers to stimulate brand recall/recognition.

# Sponsorship objectives

Any organisation developing a sponsorship strategy should always include well-defined objectives, especially where, according to Nickell et al. (2011), the sponsorship, through its various other activities, seeks to define the organisation's brand image. However, despite the large amounts invested in sponsorship activities, Kim et al. (2011) find that sponsorship objectives, in terms of marketing communications, are not always fully realised.

There are both primary and secondary objectives associated with using sponsorship. The primary reasons are to build awareness, to develop relationships, possibly through loyalty, and to improve perception (image) held of a brand or organisation. Secondary reasons are more contentious, but generally they can be seen to be to attract new users, to support dealers and other intermediaries and to act as a form of staff motivation and morale building.

Sponsorship is normally regarded as a communications tool used to reach external stakeholders. However, if chosen appropriately, sponsorship can also be used effectively to reach internal audiences. Care is required because different audiences transfer diverse values (Grimes and Meenaghan, 1998). According to Harverson (1998), one of the main reasons IT companies sponsor sports events is that this form of involvement provides opportunities to 'showcase' their products and technologies, in context. Through application in an appropriate working environment, the efficacy of a sponsor's products can be demonstrated. The relationship between sports organisers and IT companies becomes reciprocal as the organisers of sports events need technology in order for the events to run. Corporate hospitality opportunities are often taken in addition to the brand exposure that the media coverage provides. EDS claims that it uses sponsorship to reach two main audiences, customers (and potential customers) and potential future employees. The message it uses is that the EDS involvement in sport is sexy and exciting.

A further interesting point arises from a view of a company sponsor through time. Meenaghan (1998) suggests that, at first, the sponsor acts as a donor, through the pure exchange of money in order to reach an audience. The next stage sees the sponsor acting as an investor, where, although large sums of money may well be involved, the sponsor is now actively involved and is looking for a return on the investment made. The third stage is reached when the sponsor assumes the role of an impresario. Now the sponsor is vigorously involved and seeks to control activities so that they reflect corporate/brand values and thus assist the positioning process.

A further important characteristic concerns the impact of repeat attendance on brand image. Work by Lacey et al. (2007) found that a car manufacturer's image improved modestly by sponsoring a sporting event. However, through repeat attendance, positive opinion scores towards the sponsor improved. The obvious implication for marketing is that it is important to attract attendees back to sporting events.

---

### Viewpoint 16.2  Galloping sponsorship

The Cheltenham Festival is a major event in the horse racing calendar and with attendances and interest in all forms of the sport increasing, despite the recession, sponsorship remains an attractive form of marketing communications for many organisations. It was estimated that sponsorship was worth £1.68m in 2010. Thomas Pink (the quality fashion retailer), Spinal Research (a charity) and Ryanair (the low cost airline) all sponsored events at the festival for the first time in 2010.

Thomas Pink sponsored the prestigious Leading Rider and Trainer Awards and so associated themselves with a sport and some of its most talented individuals, with their own heritage.

Cenkos Securities plc funded the Spinal Research Supreme Novices' Hurdle and so gave visibility to an important and racing-related charity, as many involved in horse racing suffer spinal injury.

Sponsors can provide financial support for individual races and in return generate brand awareness and local visibility. In addition, the event provides a focus for the sponsor to provide corporate hospitality for selected customers and other stakeholders. The race will also attract media coverage and a certain level of word-of-mouth communication generated by spectators.

*Source*: Turner (2010); www.cheltenhamfestival.net/New-sponsorship-ofFestival-awards.php
www.southwestbusiness.co.uk/news/Cheltenham-Festival-win/article-1918458-detail/article.html.

**Question:** How might a brand message integrated into a racing programme through sponsorship be an effective form of marketing communication?

**Task:** Go to www.Utalkmarketing and find out why Ryanair choose to sponsor a race at the festival.

---

Following on from this is the issue of whether sponsorship is being used to support a product or the organisation. Corporate sponsorships, according to Thwaites (1994), are intended to focus on developing community involvement, public awareness, image, goodwill and staff relations. Product- or brand-based sponsorship activity is aimed at developing media coverage, sales leads, sales/market share, target market awareness and guest hospitality. What is important is that sponsorship is not a tool that can be effective in a standalone capacity. The full potential of this tool is only realised when it is integrated with some (or all) of the other tools of the communications mix. As Tripodi (2001) comments, the implementation of integrated marketing communications is further encouraged and supported when sponsorship is an integral part of the mix in order to maximise the full impact of this communication tool.

# How sponsorship might work

Interpretations of how sponsorship might work are varied, and research limited. However, assuming a cognitive orientation, sponsorship works through associations that consumers make with a brand. These associations will be an accumulation of previous advertising and other communication activities, and the event being supported. In addition, people make a judgement based on the fit between the event and sponsorship such that the greater the degree of compatibility, the more readily acceptable the sponsorship will be. Poon and Prendergast (2006) argue that sponsorship outcomes can best be understood in terms of the attitude construct and cite product quality, attitude to the brand and purchase intention as representative of the cognition, affection and conation components.

If a behavourist orientation is used to explain how sponsorship works, then sponsorship should be perceived as reinforcement of previous brand experiences. An event generates rewards by reminding individuals of pleasurable brand experiences. However, this assumes that individuals have previous brand experience, and fails to explain adequately how sponsorship works when launching new products.

For many organisations sponsorship plays a supporting or secondary role in the communications mix. This is largely because the communication impact of sponsorship is limited, as sponsorship only reinforces previously held corporate (or product) images (positive or negative) rather than changing them (Javalgi et al., 1994). It is also suggested that the only significant relationship between sponsorship and corporate image occurs where there has been direct experience of the brand. This in turn raises questions about whether sponsorship should be used to influence the image of the product category and its main brands in order to be of any worthwhile effect (Pope and Voges, 1999).

As Dolphin (2003) suggests, the range of activities, events, goals and the variety of ways in which it is used by organisations suggests that it is not entirely clear how sponsorship might best be used to help an organisation achieve its business goals. It is used to shape and assist corporate image, develop name association and awareness, drive product sales, build brands, help with recruitment, defend against hostile competitors and as a means of developing and providing opportunities for corporate hospitality. However, the primary goal for its use will generally reflect the context within which it is used. In situations where transactional exchanges are predominant within the target audience, broad-based sponsorship activities are likely to be preferred. In contexts where the target audience is relatively small or geographically discrete and where relational exchanges are preferred or sought, then relationship development sponsorship activities are more likely to be successful.

---

### Scholars' paper 16.2 　　What is it all about?

**Meenaghan, T. (1991) The role of sponsorship in the marketing communications mix, *International Journal of Advertising*, 10(1), 35–47.**

This is a classic paper written by one of the early leading researchers and authors about sponsorship. This paper sets out some of the initial perspectives on sponsorship and is recommended. Readers might also choose to read his 1998 paper which serves to update his thoughts about sponsorship.

# Theoretical aspects of sponsorship

The limited amount of theoretical research into sponsorship suggests that the role of sponsorship within the marketing communications mix has not yet been fully understood. Problems associated with goals, tools and measurement methods and approaches have hindered both academics and practitioners. However, two developments have helped resolve some of these dilemmas. First, the development of relationship marketing and an acknowledgement that there are different audiences, each with different relationship needs, has helped understanding about which types of sponsorship should be used with which type of audience. Second, our understanding of the nature and role of integrated marketing communications within relationship marketing has helped focus thinking about the way in which sponsorship might contribute to the overall communication process.

Relationship marketing is concerned with the concept of mutual value rather than the mere provision of goods and services (Gummesson, 1996) and is therefore compatible in many ways with the characteristics and range of benefits, both expected and realised, associated with sponsorship (Farrelly et al., 2003). Sponsorship represents a form of collaborative communication, in the sense that two (or more) parties work together in order that one is enabled to reach the other's audience. Issues regarding the relationship between the parties involved will impact on the success of a sponsorship arrangement and any successive arrangements. As Farrelly et al. quite rightly point out, further work concerning the key drivers of sponsorship and relationship marketing is required as sponsorship matures as an increasingly potent form of marketing communications.

Olkkonen (2001) adopted a similar approach as he considered sponsorship within interactional relationships and ultimately a network approach. The network approach considers the range of relationships that impact on organisations within markets and, therefore, considers non-buyers and other organisations – indeed, all who are indirectly related to the exchange process. This approach moves beyond the simple dyadic process adopted by the interaction interpretation. Some scholars have advanced a broad conceptual model within which to consider interorganisational networks (Hakansson and Snehota, 1995, cited by Olkkonen). These are actors, activities and resources and are set out at Table 16.2.

A relationship consists of activity links based on organisations working together. Some of the activities will use particular resources in different configurations and differing levels of intensity. These activities will impact on other organisations and affect the way they use resources.

| Table 16.2 | Basic variables underpinning interorganisational networks |
| --- | --- |

| Network variable | Explanation |
| --- | --- |
| Actors | These are organisations and individuals who are interconnected; they control the other two variables. |
| Activities | Activities are created through the use of resources, and complex activity chains arise with different organisations (actors) contributing in different ways. |
| Resources | There are many different types of resource that can be combined in different ways to create new resources. The relationships that organisations develop create resource ties and these ties become shaped and adapted as the relationship develops. |

*Source*: Based on Olkkonen (2001).

| Table 16.3 | Sponsorship relationship capabilities |
|---|---|

| Competence | Explanation |
|---|---|
| **Reciprocal commitment** | This is demonstrated by the reaction that one party makes to any additional investment in the sponsorship by the other. Sponsors expect the sponsee to reciprocate the investments (e.g. advertising) that the sponsor makes in the relationship. The greater the reciprocity, the greater the commitment. |
| **Building capabilities** | Sponsorship is increasingly perceived to be of value in terms of strategic branding rather than mere exposure. To what extent, therefore, do the parties link their sponsorship to broader marketing objectives? |
| **Collaborative capabilities** | This concerns the extent to which the sponsee is proactive within the relationship and sets out the ways in which the relationship and the sponsor's brand will be developed in the future. In effect, this is about collaboration. |

*Source*: Farrelly et al. (2006).

In addition, organisations try to develop their attractiveness to other organisations in order to access other resources and networks. This is referred to as *network identity* and is a base for determining an organisation's value as a network partner. Sponsorship, therefore, can be seen as a function of an organisation's value to others in a network. The sponsored and the sponsor are key actors in sponsorship networks but agencies, event organisers, media networks and consultancies are also players, each of whom will be connected (networked) with the sponsor and sponsored.

Sponsorship has, traditionally, lacked a strong theoretical base, relying on managerial cause-and-effect explanations and loose marketing communications mix interpretations. The network approach may not be the main answer, but it does advance our thought, knowledge and research opportunities with respect to this subject.

One concept that has been established in the literature concerns emotional intensity. This concerns the audience's attention, and associated cognitive orientation, toward the stimulus that is provoking the emotion (Bal et al., 2007). So, if the event becomes dramatic and highly engaging, it is probable that attention will be diverted from the sponsors and any information they might provide (e.g. ads). What this means is that a strongly emotional event (sport, exhibition, programme, film) is likely to reduce the awareness scores associated with the sponsor.

Research by Farrelly et al. (2006), undertaken to better understand how value is perceived by parties to sponsorship agreements, has identified three key marketing competences necessary for the maintenance of successful sponsorship relationships. These are: reciprocal commitment, building capabilities and collaborative capabilities. These are set out in Table 16.3.

# Types of sponsorship

It is possible to identify particular areas within which sponsorship has been used. These areas are sports, programme/broadcast, the arts and others that encompass activities such as wildlife/conservation and education. Of all of these, sport has attracted most attention and sponsorship money.

## Sports sponsorship

Sports activities have been very attractive to sponsors, partly because of the high media coverage they attract. Sport is the leading type of sponsorship, mainly for the following reasons:

- Sport has the propensity to attract large audiences, not only at each event but, more importantly, through the media that attach themselves to these activities.
- Sport provides a simplistic measure of segmentation, so that as audiences fragment generally, sport provides an opportunity to identify and reach often large numbers of people who share particular characteristics.
- Visibility opportunities for the sponsor are high in a number of sporting events because of the duration of each event (e.g. the Olympics or the FIFA World Cup).

In football, Barclaycard's sponsorship of the Premier League and Coca-Cola's sponsorship of the Championship have been motivated partly by the attraction of large and specific target audiences with whom a degree of fit is considered to exist. The constant media attention enables the sponsors' names to be disseminated to distant audiences, many of them overseas. Marshall and Cook (1992) found that event sponsorship (e.g. the Olympics or the Ideal Home Exhibition) is the most popular form of sponsorship activity undertaken by organisations. This was followed by team, league and individual support.

Vodafone sponsored Manchester United in order to boost global awareness. Next, the company bought Mannesman and found it then sponsored Benfica, Porto, Olympiakos and teams in La Liga in Spain and the Bundesliga in Germany. Rationalisation was necessary and, still wanting to maintain an association with football, it then became a Champions League sponsor (Murphy, 2007). AIG became United's next shirt sponsor in an attempt to fuel AIG's expansion out of North America and reach new markets, principally Asia, where a high percentage of the target market are football (and Manchester United) fans. AIG terminated their involvement when the global financial crisis struck in 2008.

Golf has attracted a great deal of sponsorship money, mainly because it has a global upmarket appeal and generates good television and press coverage. Golf clubs are also well suited for corporate entertainment and offer the chance of playing as well as watching. The World Golf Championships are seen as golf's most prestigious global competition, a series of events sanctioned by all six of the six major golf tours (the PGA TOUR, European Tour, Japan Golf Tour, PGA Tour of Australasia, Southern Africa Tour, and the Asian Tour). Collectively these form the International Federation of PGA Tours, which is supported financially by a few umbrella sponsors. At the time of writing, they were Accenture, Bridgestone and Cadillac and HSBC. The official sponsors of these events, a second level of sponsorship, are Kohler and Rolex (WGC, 2011).

Toyota used to support the World Matchplay Championship at Wentworth each year because the tournament fitted into a much wider promotion programme. Toyota dealers sponsored competitions at their local courses, with qualifiers going through to a final at Wentworth. The winner of that played in the pro-am before the World Matchplay. Toyota incorporated the tournament into a range of incentive and promotional programmes and flew in top distributors and fleet customers from around the world. In addition, the environment was used to build customer relationships. This championship is now supported by HSBC.

## Programme sponsorship

Television programme sponsorship began to receive serious attention in Britain in the late 1990s. The market has grown, as reflected in TV sponsorship revenues, from £81.2 million in 2000 to nearly £200 million in 2009. This growth has occurred partly because of a relaxation in the regulations. For example, the visibility that each sponsor was allowed was strictly controlled, being restricted to certain times: before, during the break and after each programme with the credits. This was changed so that, while sponsors are not allowed to influence the content or scheduling of a programme so as to affect the editorial independence and responsibility of the broadcaster, it is now permissible to allow the sponsor's product to be seen along with the sponsor's name in bumper credits and to allow greater flexibility in terms of the use of straplines. There is a requirement on the broadcaster to ensure that the sponsored credit is depicted in such a way that it cannot be mistaken as a spot advertisement. So, Hedburg (2000) gives the example of Nescafé sponsoring *Friends* showing a group of people sitting on a sofa and drinking coffee and of *Coronation Street* and former sponsor Cadbury's, which presented a whole chocolate street and set of chocolate characters.

Masthead programming, where the publisher of a magazine such as *Amateur Photographer* sponsors a programme in a related area, such as *Photography for Beginners*, is generally not permitted, although the regulations surrounding this type of activity are being relaxed. There are a number of reasons why programme sponsorship is appealing. First, it allows clients to avoid the clutter associated with spot advertising. In that sense it creates a space, or mini-world, in which the sponsor can create awareness and provide brand identity cues unhindered by other brands. Second, it represents a cost-effective medium when compared with spot advertising. Although the cost of programme sponsorship has increased as the value of this type of communication has appreciated, it does not command the high rates required for spot advertising. Third, the use of credits around a programme offers opportunities for the target audience to make associations between the sponsor and the programme.

Research by the Bloxam Group suggests that for a sponsorship to work there needs to be a linkage between the product and the programme. Links that are spurious, illogical or inappropriate are very often rejected by viewers. For example, a branded soft drink might work well with a youth-oriented programme, but a financial services brand supporting a sports programme or film series would not have a strong or logical linkage.

The line between product placement, brand entertainment and programme sponsorship has become increasingly blurred. However, programme sponsorship is not a replacement for advertising. The argument that sponsorship is not a part of advertising is clearly demonstrated by the point that many sponsors continue with their spot advertising when running major sponsorships.

## Arts sponsorship

Arts sponsorship, according to Thorncroft (1996), began as a philanthropic exercise, with business giving something back to the community. It was a means of developing an organisation's image and was used extensively by tobacco companies as they attempted to reach their customer base. It then began to be appreciated for its corporate hospitality opportunities: a cheaper, more civilised alternative to sports sponsorship, and one that appealed more to women.

Many organisations sponsor the arts as a means of enhancing their corporate status and of clarifying their identity. Another important reason organisations use sponsorship is to establish and maintain favourable contacts with key business people, often at board level, together with other significant public figures. Through related corporate hospitality, companies can reach substantial numbers of their targeted key people.

More recently, sponsorship has been used to reach specific groups of consumers. Orange sponsors a range of music-related events, one of them being the Glastonbury Festival. One of the key facilities is the 'chill n'charge' tent. This is a bright orange-coloured tent in which people can use the phone-charging equipment or the Internet facilities to pick up their email and over 50,000 people used the tent at the 2007 festival. Orange see their sponsorship of the festival as a way to develop their brand and purchase consideration, but not as a means of directly acquiring customers (Bartlett, 2007).

The sponsorship of the arts has moved from being a means of supporting the community to a sophisticated means of targeting and positioning brands. Sponsorship, once part of corporate public relations, is now a significant aspect of marketing public relations.

**Exhibit 16.3    Virgin's sponsorship of music festivals**

Sponsorship of music festivals is an integral part of Virgin's communication strategy.

*Source*: Tim Mosenfelder/Corbis.

## Viewpoint 16.3    Robinsons support juicy pantos

Robinsons have been involved with many sponsorship events over the years and are probably most associated with the Wimbledon tennis tournament. In 2009 Robinsons sponsored festive pantomimes in conjunction with First Family Entertainment. This is a large theatrical production company who had recruited several celebrities to star in pantomimes around the country. Robinsons wanted to raise awareness of the events and their association without using television, a costly route, one that they use for their Wimbledon work.

The result was a website to help children and parents develop and run their own pantomimes at home. The intention was to provide a way in which families could work together. The website contained information about writing scripts; costumes and promotional posters were all made available online. In order to enrich the experience an Iphone app was developed providing sound effects.

The launch was delivered through an on-pack promotion involving over 41 million bottles of Robinsons soft drinks. PR and promotional activity at pantomime events was also used to publicise the sponsorship. Ads were placed in First Family panto magazines, editorial content was seeded across 100 blog sites associated with motherhood and parenting, and a Flash game was placed on 25 children-oriented game sites.

*Source*:    Anon (2009).

**Question:**    To what extent might Robinsons be overly dependent on their relationship with Wimbledon?

**Task:**        Make a list of the other activities Robinsons could sponsor successfully.

To support their global brand HSBC run a 'Cultural Exchange programme'. This aims to improve 'understanding and interaction among cultures around the world through the exploration of culture in all its varied forms – including fine art, cuisine, music, language and literature' (HSBC, 2011). In 2008 the bank supported cultural events in China, in 2009 they backed various Indian cultural initiatives and in 2010 they supported 'Festival Brazil'. This event was focused on exhibitions and various artistic performances by Brazilian artists in London. HSBC also support events in South America, the Middle East, South-East Asia and the USA. The bank has co-partnered with the *Financial Times* and the Economist Intelligence Unit to advise companies thinking of exporting and setting up in Brazil (Brownsell, 2010). HSBC believe sponsorship to be an investment for their business growth, and an opportunity to connect and build relationships with people in the local communities that they serve.

---

### Scholars' paper 16.3     Attitudinal sponsorships

**Nickell, D., Cornwell T.B. and Johnston, W.J. (2011) Sponsorship-linked marketing: a set of research propositions, *Journal of Business & Industrial Marketing*, 26(8), 577–89.**

Following a very useful literature review and theoretical insight into the subject, this paper considers the way attitudes are formed through sponsorship. Sponsors with a moderate amount of established brand attitude are likely to experience the biggest attitude change. This paper suggests that this relationship is actually non-linear and is, in fact, an S-shaped relationship. This paper proposes that the association between awareness and congruency is a U-shaped phenomenon.

---

## Other forms of sponsorship

It has been argued that there is little opportunity to control messages delivered through sponsorship, and far less opportunity to encourage the target audiences to enter into a dialogue with sponsors. However, the awareness and image opportunities can be used by supporting either the local community or small-scale schemes. In March 2012 a Climate Week was held, with many leading companies supporting the cause. Companies such as Aviva, RBS, EDF Energy and Kellogg sought to demonstrate what actions they are taking with regard to climate change as well as assist other organisations to become involved.

Some brands use sponsorship to own particular space. For example, Benjamin (2011) points out that Orange have owned cinema Wednesdays for some time and now Thursdays, through which they can reward customers. The insurers Beazley sponsor British fencing (£1m) Sky cycling, British Gas swimming and Aegon tennis. Many get involved with the national governing associations as this then bestows important source credibility.

Samsung Electronics use sponsorship to link up with a variety of activities, one of which is football. Samsung is a partner with Chelsea FC, Inter Milan FC, Palmeiras, Suwon Bluwings, Olympiacos and Feyenoord. The company is also an official sponsor for the Olympic Games, and the Asian Games. However, they feel that the greater the number of sponsors tied to an event, the less opportunity there is to leverage the linkage. The one exception to this rule is the Olympics. This event involves all nations and Samsung signed an agreement in 2010 to be a main sponsor of the Olympics until 2016.

The majority of sponsorships, regardless of type, are not the sole promotional activity undertaken by the sponsors. They may be secondary and used to support above-the-line work or they may be used as the primary form of communication but supported by a range of off-screen activities, such as sales promotions and (in particular) competitions. For example, Sony Pictures developed a programme to encourage school pupils to be innovative and to develop their interest in science. It uses an unbranded animated film, *Cloudy with a Chance of Meatballs*, to provide a context for activities, quizzes and competitions (Thomas, 2009). More of a partnership than a straight sponsorship, the relationship furthers Sony's positioning as an innovator.

---

### Viewpoint 16.4    Strategic sponsorships at Catlin

The Catlin Group is a specialty property/casualty insurer and reinsurer, with underwriting hubs in London/UK, Bermuda, the United States, Asia Pacific, Europe, and Canada. It owns and operates the largest insurance syndicate at Lloyd's of London.

Catlin uses sponsorship in order to provide active support to people and causes that help it achieve 'our vision for our business'. It sees sponsorship as a long-term activity.

For example, Catlin sponsors scientific research into climate change because of the potential impact such changes may have on its business and those of its clients. Understanding, evaluating and helping them to minimise risk is an important part of its business, so Catlin believes that assessing the impact of climate change is a natural extension of what it does. Catlin currently sponsors the Catlin Seaview Survey, a scientific expedition that documents the composition and health of coral reefs around the world. This will allow researchers to measure the environmental impact of increasing sea temperatures and ocean acidification as a key indicator of climate change. Before this, Catlin sponsored the Catlin Arctic Survey for three years. This was an investigation into the potential impact of climate change on the Arctic region. Both surveys have enabled Catlin to reposition itself as a thought leader in the insurance business. The Catlin Seaview Survey provides a strong visual theme, which when combined with the range of stories that the programme generates enables Catlin to have a high media profile, with content that works in broadcast, print, online and social networks.

In addition, Catlin sponsors an annual art competition designed to showcase the work of recent UK art graduates. The Catlin Guide features the 40 most promising graduate artists in the UK, and works created by finalists for the Catlin Art Prize are exhibited in London each spring at a special gallery event, with the winner awarded a monetary prize plus extensive recognition and publicity within the field.

The London Phoenix Orchestra is also supported by Catlin. Originally named the Insurance Orchestra, it was formed to provide members of the insurance industry with an opportunity to play music together. Today it is a leading amateur orchestra, and gives regular concerts at top venues in London, with an aim of raising money for charity.

On the sports side, Catlin China works with the Chinese Three-Day Eventer, Alex Hua Tian. When he qualified at just 18 years old, he became the youngest Olympian to take part at the Beijing Olympics. However, he lost his best horse in a freak accident just before the Beijing Olympics. Catlin Equine Insurance has sponsored him as it wishes to be associated with a horse owner and professional rider, and someone who values Equine Insurance.

*Source*: Paley (2011); www.catlin.com/en/About/Sponsorship.

**Question:** Why do you believe Catlin develops such a variety of sponsorships?

**Task:** Go to the Catlin website (www.catlin.com/en/Insurance), pick one of the markets in which it operates and make a list of potential sponsorship opportunities.

**Exhibit 16.4** **Catlin is sponsor of the Seaview Survey**
*Source*: Catlin

This section would not be complete without mention of the phenomenon called 'ambush marketing'. This occurs when an organisation deliberately seeks an association with a particular event but does so without paying advertising or sponsorship fees. Such hijacking is undertaken to get free publicity by communicating their brand, unofficially, in places where spectators, cameras or reporters are present, will see them, and pass on the message. The purpose therefore is to influence the audience to the extent that they believe the ambusher is legitimate. According to Meenaghan (1998), this can be achieved by overstating the organisation's involvement in the event, perhaps through major communication activity using theme-based advertising or by sponsoring the media coverage of the event. See ViewPoint 16.5.

## Viewpoint 16.5    Ambush in South Africa

At the 2010 World Cup in South Africa, 36 orange-clad women were ejected from the Holland versus Denmark game. They were accused of participation in an unofficial campaign to promote the Dutch brewery, Bavaria. Anheuser Busch's Budweiser was the official beer for the tournament. There had been a similar incident at the 2006 World Cup finals in Germany. On that occasion, the football governing body FIFA ordered that a number of Dutch men take off orange lederhosen which bore the name 'Bavaria' (Anon, 2010).

Kulula is a South African budget airline, and shortly before the start of the World Cup finals they ran an online ad describing themselves as the 'Unofficial National Carrier of the You-Know-What'. It also featured pictures of stadiums, vuvuzelas and national flags.

FIFA stated that the airline was entitled to show pictures of footballs, national flags or stadia, and use the words 'South Africa', but they were not entitled to bundle them together, as this constituted ambush marketing and breached South African law. The airline admitted that their ad pushed bound-aries but argued that FIFA did not own the stadia, the flag or footballs. However, the airline, noted for its quirky approach to communication, decided to cease running it.

*Source*:   Based on BBC (2010); Anon (2010).

**Question:**   Consider the view that ambush advertising is unethical, merely a form of cheating.

**Task:**   Using different media, find examples of ambush marketing at the European Football Championships and the Olympic Games in 2012.

| Exhibit 16.5 | **Ambush marketing at the 2010 Football World Cup** |
| --- | --- |
| | *Source*: Action Images |

# The role of sponsorship in the communication mix

Whether sponsorship is a part of advertising, sales promotion or public relations, has long been a source of debate. It is perhaps more natural and comfortable to align sponsorship with advertising. Since awareness is regarded as the principal objective of using sponsorship, advert-ising is a more complementary and accommodating part of the mix. Sales promotion from the sponsor's position is harder to justify, although from the perspective of the sponsored the value-added characteristic is interesting. The more traditional home for sponsorship is public relations (Witcher et al., 1991). The sponsored, such as a football team, a racing car manufacturer or a theatre group, may be adjudged to perform the role of opinion former. Indirectly, therefore, messages are conveyed to the target audience with the support of significant participants who endorse and support the sponsor. This is akin to public relations activities.

Hastings (1984) contests that advertising messages can be manipulated and adapted to changing circumstances much more easily than those associated with sponsorship. He suggests that the audience characteristics of advertising and sponsorship are very different. For advertising there are viewers and non-viewers. For sponsorship there are three groups of people that can be identified. First, there are those who are directly involved with the sponsor or the event, the active participants. The second is a much larger group, consisting of those who attend sponsored events, and these are referred to as *personal spectators*. The third group is normally the largest, comprising all those who are involved with the event through various media channels; these are regarded as media followers.

As if to demonstrate the potential sizes of these groups, estimates suggest that in excess of 4 million people attend the Formula 1 Grand Prix championship races (active participants) and over half a billion people (media followers) watch the races on television.

Exploratory research undertaken by Hoek et al. (1997) suggests that sponsorship is better able to generate awareness and a wider set of product-related attributes than advertising when dealing with non-users of a product, rather than users. There appears to be no discernible difference between the impact that these two promotional tools have on users.

---

### Scholars' paper 16.4     Name that stadium

**Clark, J.M., Cornwell, T.B. and Pruitt, S.W. (2002) Corporate Stadium Sponsorships; Signaling Theory, Agency Conflicts, and Shareholder Wealth, *Journal of Advertising Research*, 42(6), (November/December), 16–32.**

This paper was published over a decade ago, and predates the eagerness of organisations to secure the naming rights of stadia. The authors find that that there is a large and statistically significant positive change in stock prices when the deal is announced and that overall, the average firm experiences an *increase* in share prices of 1.65 per cent having named a stadium.

---

The authors claim that sponsorship and advertising can be considered to work in approximately the same way if the ATR (attention, trial, reinforcement) model developed by Ehrenberg (1974) is adopted (Chapter 14). Through the ATR model, purchase behaviour and beliefs are considered to be reinforced by advertising rather than new behaviour patterns being established. Advertising offers a means by which buyers can meaningfully defend their purchase patterns. Hoek et al. regard this approach as reasonably analogous to sponsorship. Sponsorship can create awareness and is more likely to confirm past behaviour than prompt new purchase behaviour. The implication, they conclude, is that, while awareness levels can be improved with sponsorship, other communication tools are required to impact upon product experimentation or purchase intentions. Indeed, Smoliannov and Aiyeku (2009) make the point that integrated TV and major event sponsorship appear to work by influencing markets through TV audiences.

It was suggested earlier in this chapter that one of the opportunities that sponsorship offers is the ability to suggest that there is an association between the sponsored and the sponsor which may be of value to the message recipient. This implies that there is an indirect form of influence through sponsorship. This is supported by Crimmins and Horn (1996), who argue that the persuasive impact of sponsorship is determined in terms of the strength of links that are generated between the brand and the event that is sponsored.

These authors claim that sponsorship can have a persuasive impact and that the degree of impact that a sponsorship might bring is as follows:

$$\begin{array}{c} persuasive \\ impact \end{array} = \begin{array}{c} strength \\ of\ link \end{array} \times \begin{array}{c} duration \\ of\ the\ link \end{array} \times \left\{ \begin{array}{c} gratitude\ felt \\ due\ to\ the\ link \end{array} + \begin{array}{c} perceptual\ change \\ due\ to\ the\ link \end{array} \right\}$$

The strength of the link between the brand and the event is an outcome of the degree to which advertising is used to communicate the sponsorship itself. Sponsors that failed to invest in advertising during the Olympic Games have been shown to be far less successful in building a link with the event than those who chose to invest.

The *duration* of the link is also important. Research based on the Olympic Games shows that those sponsors who undertook integrated marketing communications long before the event itself were far more successful than those who had not. The use of mass media advertising to communicate the involvement of the sponsor, the use of event graphics and logos on packaging, and the creative use of promotional tie-ins and in-store, event-related merchandising facilitated the long-term linkage with the sponsorship and added value to the campaign.

*Gratitude* exists if consumers realise that there is a link between a brand and an event. For example, 60 per cent of US adults said that they 'try to buy a company's product if they support the Olympics'. They also stated that 'I feel I am contributing to the Olympics by buying the brands of Olympic sponsors.'

*Perceptual change* occurs as a result of consumers being able to understand the relationship (meaning) between a brand and an event. The sponsor needs to make this clear, as passive consumers may need the links laid out before them. The link between a swimwear brand and the Olympics may be obvious, but it is not always the case. Crimmins and Horn (1996) describe how Visa's 15 per cent perceived superiority advantage over MasterCard was stretched to 30 per cent during the 1992 Olympics and then settled at 20 per cent ahead one month after the Games had finished. The perceptual change was achieved through the messages that informed audiences that Visa was the one card that was accepted for the Olympic Games; American Express and MasterCard were not accepted.

This research, while based only upon a single event, indicates that sponsorship may bring advantages if care is taken to invest in communications long before and during the event to communicate the meaning between the brand and the event, which will leverage gratitude from a grateful audience. Finally, as if to confirm the point, Olson and Thjømøe (2009) find that combining television advertising increases the effectiveness of a sponsorship activity, while Nickell et al. 2011 go further by stating that leveraging sponsorships – that is, using other marketing communications activities to realise the full potential of the investment – is absolutely necessary.

# Key points

- Sponsorship permits one party an opportunity to exploit an association with a target audience of another organisation, in return for funds, services or resources.

- This form of communication has developed partly as a result of the government's policies on tobacco and alcohol, the escalating costs of advertising media during the 1990s, the proven effectiveness of sponsorship, new opportunities due to increased leisure activity, greater media coverage of sponsored events, recognition of the inefficiencies associated with the traditional media, a relaxation in the regulations and the advances in digital technology.

- Some organisations use sponsorship, particularly sports activities, as a means of reaching wider target audiences. Sponsorship can provide exposure to particular audiences that each event attracts in order to convey simple, awareness-based brand messages. It can be used to suggest to the target audiences that there is an association between the sponsored and the sponsor and that by implication this association may be of interest and/or value.

- Sponsorship works through associations that consumers make with a brand (which will be an accumulation of previous advertising and other promotional activities) and the event being supported. In addition, people make a judgement based upon the fit between the event and sponsorship in such a way that, the greater the degree of compatibility, the more readily acceptable the sponsorship will be.

- An alternative view holds that a sponsorship can be perceived as a reinforcement of previous brand experiences. An event generates rewards by reminding individuals of pleasurable brand experiences.

- Sponsorship represents a form of collaborative communication, in the sense that two (or more) parties work together in order that one is enabled to reach the other's audience. Issues regarding the relationship between the parties concerned will impact on the success of a sponsorship arrangement and any successive arrangements.

- Sponsorship can be seen as a function of an organisation's value to others in a network. The sponsored and the sponsor are key actors in sponsorship networks, but agencies, event organisers, media networks and consultancies are also actors, each of whom will be connected (networked) with the sponsor and sponsored.

- Sponsorship is used in three key areas. These are sports, programme/broadcast, and the arts. There is also growing interest in other activities such as wildlife/conservation and education. Of all of these, sport has attracted most attention and sponsorship money.

- Sponsorship has become an important part of the mix as it allows brands to be communicated without the clutter and noise associated with advertising. At the same time sponsorship enables associations and linkages to be made that add value for all the participants in the communication process.

- There seems little doubt that the introduction of new products and brands can be assisted by the use of appropriate sponsorships. Indeed, it appears that sponsorship, in certain contexts, can be used to prepare markets for the arrival and penetration of new brands.

- It is perhaps more natural and comfortable to align sponsorship with advertising but it has also been associated with sales promotion and public relations. Since awareness is regarded as the principal objective of using sponsorship, advertising is a more complementary and accommodating part of the mix.

# Review questions

1. List five reasons why organisations choose to sponsor events such as the Olympics.

2. To what extent is sponsorship more a leap of faith than a calculated marketing investment?

3. If the objective of using sponsorship is to build awareness (among other things), then there is little point in using advertising. Discuss this view.

4. Name four types of sponsorship.

5. Why is sport more heavily sponsored than the arts or television programmes?

6. Choose eight sporting events and name the main sponsors. Why do you think they have maintained their associations with the events?

7. Consider five television programmes that are sponsored and evaluate how viewers might perceive the relationship between the programme content and the sponsor.

8. How might sponsorship have a persuasive impact on its target audiences? What is the formula used to measure this impact?

9. Explain the role of sponsorship within the marketing communications mix.

10. How might sponsorship develop in the future?

# References

Anon (2009) The Work: Robinsons, *Revolution*, December, 56–7.

Anon (2010) World Cup 2010: Women arrested over 'ambush marketing' freed on bail, *Guardian*, Wednesday 16 June, retrieved 7 November 2011 from www.guardian.co.uk/football/2010/jun/16/fifa-world-cup-ambush-marketing.

Bal, C., Quester, P.G. and Boucher, S. (2007) *Admap*, 486, (September), 51–2.

Balfour, M. (2000) Precision technology delivered in record time, *Financial Times*, 25 March.

Bartlett, M. (2007) Glowing at Glastonbury, *The Marketer* (September), 20–3.

BBC (2010) Fifa orders South African airline to drop 'ambush' ad, retrieved 7 November 2011 from http://news.bbc.co.uk/1/hi/8576220.stm.

Benjamin, K. (2011) Sponsorship still a hot property, *Marketing*, 5 October, 25–7.

Brownsell, A. (2010) HSBC launches Brazilian cultural sponsorship programme, *Marketing*, 16 June.

Clark, J.M., Cornwell, T.B. and Pruitt, S.W. (2002) Corporate Stadium Sponsorships; Signaling Theory, Agency Conflicts, and Shareholder Wealth, *Journal of Advertising Research* (November/December), 16–32.

Clark, N. (2012) McDonald's a 'poor fit' for Olympics, claims survey, *Marketing*, 5 July, p. 5.

Coppetti, C., Wentzel, D., Tomczak, T. and Henke, S. (2009) Improving incongruent sponsorships through articulation of the sponsorship and audience participation, *Journal of Marketing Communications*, 15(1), February, 17–34.

Cornwell, T.B. (2008) State of the art and science in sponsorship-linked marketing, *Journal of Advertising*, 37(3), 41–55.

Crimmins, J. and Horn, M. (1996) Sponsorship: from management ego trip to marketing success, *Journal of Advertising Research* (July/August), 11–21.

Cunningham, S., Cornwell, T. and Coote, L. (2009) Expressing identity and shaping image: the relationship between corporate mission and corporate sponsorship, *Journal of Sports Management*, 23, 65–86.

Derrick, S. (2012) The Olympic marketers: why we sponsored London 2012; what we've learned; what we'd do differently, *Marketing*, 29 June, pp. 26–9.

Dolphin, R.R. (2003) Sponsorship: perspectives on its strategic role, *Corporate Communications: An International Journal*, 8(3), 173–86.

Ehrenberg, A.S.C. (1974) Repetitive advertising and the consumer, *Journal of Advertising Research*, 14 (April), 25–34.

Farrelly, F., Quester, P. and Mavondo, F. (2003) Collaborative communication in sponsor relations, *Corporate Communications: An International Journal*, 8(2), 128–38.

Farrelly, F., Quester, P. and Burton, R. (2006) Changes in sponsorship value: competencies and capabilities of successful sponsorship relationships, *Industrial Marketing Management*, 35(8) (November), 1016–26.

Grimes, E. and Meenaghan, T. (1998) Focusing commercial sponsorship on the internal corporate audience, *International Journal of Advertising*, 17(1), 51–74.

Gummesson, E. (1996) Relationship marketing and imaginary organisations: a synthesis, *European Journal of Marketing*, 30(2), 31–45.

Hakansson, H. and Snehota, I. (1995) *Developing Relationships in Business Networks*, London: Routledge.

Harverson, P. (1998) Why IT companies take the risk, *Financial Times*, 2 June, p. 12.

Harvey, B., Gray, S. and Despain, G. (2006) Measuring the effectiveness of true sponsorship, *Journal of Advertising Research*, 46(4) (December), 398–409.

Hastings, G. (1984) Sponsorship works differently from advertising, *International Journal of Advertising*, 3, 171–6.

Hedburg, A. (2000) Bumper crop, *Marketing Week*, 19 October, 28–32.

Hoek, J., Gendall, P., Jeffcoat, M. and Orsman, D. (1997) Sponsorship and advertising: a comparison of their effects, *Journal of Marketing Communications*, 3, 21–32.

HSBC (2011) Cultural sponsorship, retrieved 7 November 2011 from http://www.hsbc.com/1/2/about/sponsorship.

IOC (2012) *IOC Marketing: Media Guide London – 2012*, International Olympic Committee, retrieved 8 July from www.olympic.org/sponsors.

Javalgi, R.G., Traylor, M.B., Gross, A.C. and Lampman, E. (1994) Awareness of sponsorship and corporate image: an empirical investigation, *Journal of Advertising*, 24 (June), 1–12.

Kim, Y.K., Ko, Y.F. and James, J. (2011) The impact of relationship quality on attitude toward a sponsor, *Journal of Business & Industrial Marketing*, 26(8), 566–76.

Lacey, R., Sneath, J.Z., Finney, R.Z. and Close, A.G. (2007) The impact of repeat attendance on event sponsorship effects, *Journal of Marketing Communications*, 13(4) (December), 243–55.

Marshall, D.W. and Cook, G. (1992) The corporate (sports) sponsor, *International Journal of Advertising*, 11, 307–24.

McDonald, C. (1991) Sponsorship and the image of the sponsor, *European Journal of Marketing*, 25(11), 31–8.

Meenaghan, T. (1991) The role of sponsorship in the marketing communications mix, *International Journal of Advertising*, 10, 35–47.

Meenaghan, T. (1998) Current developments and future directions in sponsorship, *International Journal of Advertising*, 17(1), 3–28.

Mitchell, A. (2012) The marketing Olympics: which sponsors are leading the race to London 2012, *Marketing*, 4 July, pp. 24–6.

Murphy, D. (2007) Lost in the crowd, *Marketing*, 29 August, 36–7.

Nickell, D., Cornwell, T.B. and Johnston, W.J. (2011) Sponsorship-linked marketing: a set of research propositions, *Journal of Business & Industrial Marketing*, 26(8), 577–89.

Olkkonen, R. (2001) Case study: the network approach to international sport sponsorship arrangement, *Journal of Business & Industrial Marketing*, 16(4), 309–29.

Olson, E.L. and Thjømøe, H.M. (2009) Sponsorship effect metric: assessing the financial value of sponsoring by comparisons to television advertising, *Journal of the Academy of Marketing Science*, 37, 504–15.

Paley, V. (2011) Arctic Mission, *B2B Marketing Magazine*, September, p. 10.

Poon, D.T.Y. and Prendergast, G. (2006) A new framework for evaluating sponsorship opportunities, *International Journal of Advertising*, 25(4), 471–87.

Poon, D.T.Y., Prendergast, G. and West, D. (2010) Match Game: Linking Sponsorship Congruence with Communication Outcomes, *Journal of Advertising Research*, June, 214–26.

Pope, N.K.L. and Voges, K.E. (1999) Sponsorship and image: a replication and extension, *Journal of Marketing Communications*, 5, 17–28.

Smolianov, P. and Aiyeku, J.F. (2009) Corporate Marketing Objectives and Evaluation Measures of Integrated Television Advertising and Sports Event Sponsorships, *Journal of Promotion Management*, 15, 1&2 (January), 74–89.

Sneath, J.Z., Finney, R.Z. and Close, A.G. (2005) An IMC approach to event marketing: the effects of sponsorship and experience on customer attitudes, *Journal of Advertising Research*, 45(4) (December), 373–81.

Sweney, M. (2012) Lord Coe defends sponsorship of London, *Guardian*, Friday 22 June, retrieved 8 July 2012 from www.guardian.co.uk/media/2012/jun/22/lord-coe-sponsorship-london-olympics.

Thomas, J. (2009) Sony Pictures in school science tie, *Marketing*, 23 September, p. 10.

Thomas, J. (2010) Climate Week signs up key sponsors for event, *Marketing*, 20 June, p. 9.

Thorncroft, A. (1996) Business arts sponsorship: arts face a harsh set of realities, *Financial Times*, 4 July, 1.

Thwaites, D. (1994) Corporate sponsorship by the financial services industry, *Journal of Marketing Management*, 10, 743–63.

Tripodi, J.A. (2001) Sponsorship: a confirmed weapon in the promotional armoury, *International Journal of Sports Marketing and Sponsorship*, 3(1) (March/April), 1–20.

Turner, C. (2010) Why brands are lining up for the Cheltenham Horse Racing Festival, *Utalk Marketing.com*, retrieved 18 April 2012 from http://www.utalkmarketing.com/pages/article.aspx?articleid=17062&title=why_brands_are_lining_up_for_the_cheltenham_horse_racing_festival.

Walraven, M., Koning, R.H. and Bottenburg van, B. (2012) The effects of sports sponsorship: A review and research agenda, *The Marketing Review*, 12(1), 17–38.

WGC (2011) Sponsors: World Gold Championships, retrieved 7 November 2011 from www.worldgolfchampionships.com/wgc/sponsors/index.html.

Wilson, B. (2012) London 2012: Olympic sponsors seek a winning performance, *BBC*, 6 June, retrieved 8 July 2012 from www.bbc.co.uk/news/business-18101619.

Witcher, B., Craigen, G., Culligan, D. and Harvey, A. (1991) The links between objectives and functions in organisational sponsorship, *International Journal of Advertising*, 10, 13–33.

# Chapter 17
# Direct marketing and personal selling

Direct marketing is a strategy used to create a personal and intermediary-free dialogue with customers. This should be a measurable activity and it is very often media-based, with a view to creating and sustaining a mutually rewarding relationship. Personal selling involves a face-to-face dialogue between two persons or by one person and a group. Message flexibility is an important attribute, as is the immediate feedback that often flows from use of this promotional tool.

## Aims and learning objectives

The aims of this chapter are first to consider the characteristics of direct marketing and second to explore some of the principal issues and concepts associated with personal selling.

The learning objectives are to enable readers to:

1. define direct marketing and set out its key characteristics;
2. describe the different methods used to implement direct marketing;
3. explain the significance of the database in direct marketing and consider different direct response media;
4. consider the different types, roles and tasks of personal selling;
5. consider the strengths and weaknesses of personal selling as a form of marketing communication;
6. explain the concept of multiple sales channels;
7. consider how direct marketing and personal selling might best be integrated with the other tools of the marketing communications mix.

# Minicase

## Office for National Statistics – the 2011 Census

The 2011 Census campaign was totally unique: the challenge was to reach everyone, everywhere! The target audience was all 25.4 million households in England and Wales, all of whom were to be motivated to complete their census questionnaire accurately and on time.

The census is the most comprehensive population survey. It is conducted every ten years and the data provide unique information necessary to inform a variety of decisions about central and local government funding, and policy making, and over the last ten years has informed the allocation of £100 billion government public expenditure every year. This was a once-in-a-decade event; there was no second chance to get it right.

For the past 200 years, the census questionnaire had been hand-delivered to every household by field staff; and at considerable expense. The 2011 Census broke with this approach and adopted a mail-out and mail-back method; for the first time there was also an option to complete the questionnaire online.

The minimised face-to-face contact with census field staff increased the likelihood of non-response. Consequently, the 2011 Census campaign had to create awareness and at the same time motivate people to return their completed questionnaires – rather than rely on field staff knocking on the door of every household and talking to people. The 2011 Census marketing communications campaign was critical to the whole campaign.

Not an easy challenge – over the past ten years there have been further societal changes including an increasingly diverse population with a particular increase in migrant communities, an ageing population, changing lifestyles and a hardening of attitudes towards government. Finally, the general public has become much more worried about the confidentiality of personal data.

The success of the census depended on achieving an overall response rate of 94 per cent nationally. However, as a low response rate from a particular population group would adversely affect the quality of census data for that group or local area, there was an additional target for no local authority area or key population group to be below 80 per cent.

### The creative strategy

The creative strategy was built on a simple and enabling thought – that each individual could participate to help shape their own local community. As befitted a campaign requiring a response, the thought was turned into a call-to-action – 'Help tomorrow take shape'.

The brand identity was created using the concept of origami to suggest a direct relationship between completing a census (traditionally a paper questionnaire) and the end 'benefits' of the census (i.e. public services) and this resonated with the research groups. The advertising campaign amplified this by creating a world made of the collective efforts of individuals and communities engaging with the census.

The purple origami objects were rendered life-size and set in the 'real' world, lending the campaign relevance to the England and Wales of today and creating impact and a strong visual mnemonic.

This purple origami would echo throughout the campaign, even the questionnaire itself, traditionally printed in blue, became a shade of purple to reinforce the idea.

### A 3-phase campaign

Making use of consumer insights from extensive research with families and communities in England and Wales, it was determined that response levels will be influenced by three key factors:

- *Education* – awareness and understanding of the census benefits;
- *Call-to-action* – clear direction of what they need to do and when;
- *Follow-up* – reminder for those people who had still not responded.

The three phases of the communications campaign – education, call-to-action and follow-up – would clearly need to correspond with key dates of census operational activity, such as the distribution of questionnaires on census day (27 March) and the door-to-door follow-up. These are set out at Figure 17.1, which shows the media used across the campaign dates.

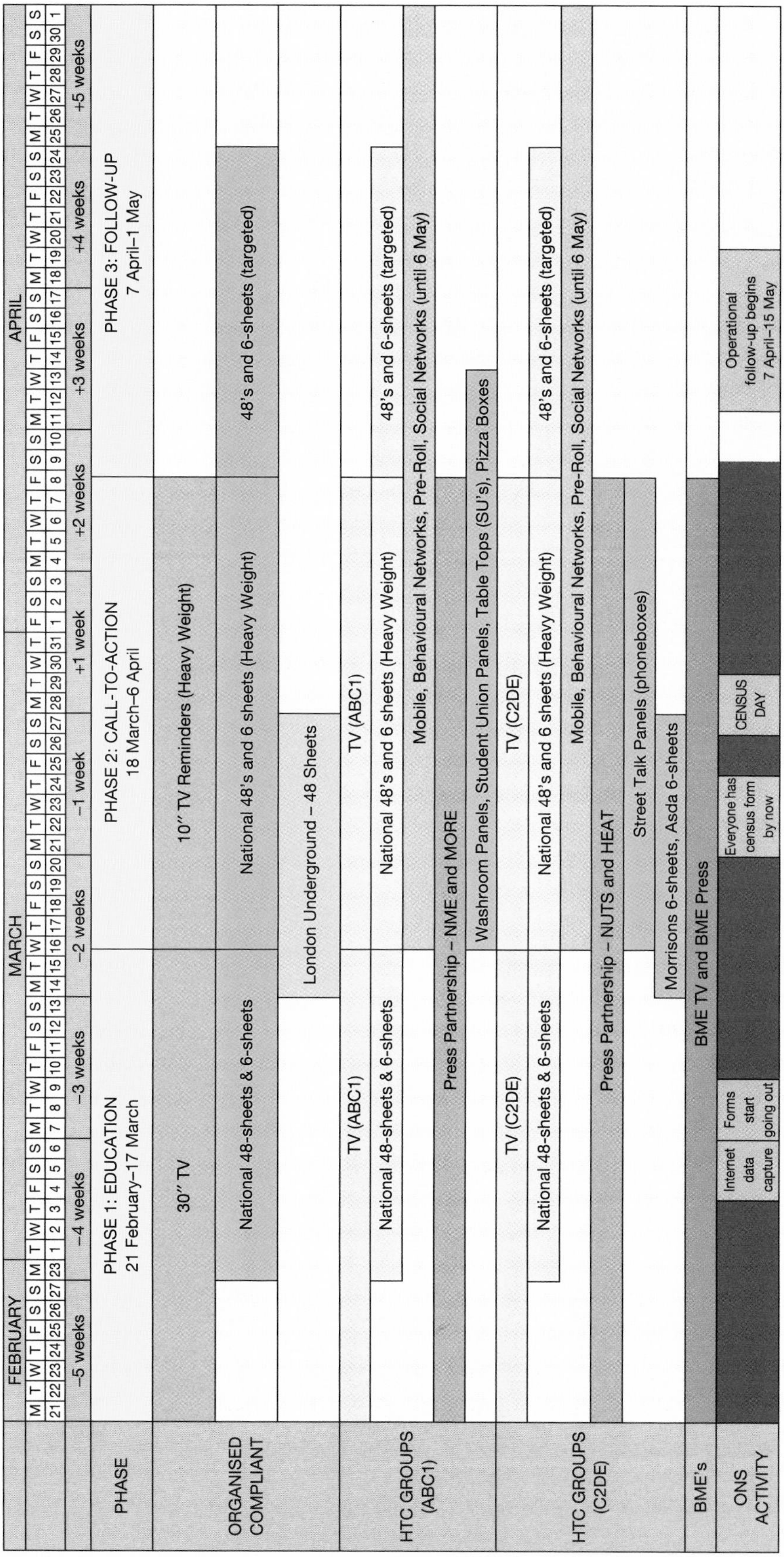

**Figure 17.1**　Broadcast and narrowcast media across the census phases

## Broadcast and narrowcast channels

The challenge was that, while cost-effective broadcast media, TV and outdoor, could reach the bulk of the population, many key audiences were notoriously hard to reach and engage in these channels. For example, young people and people from black and minority ethnic (BME) backgrounds were known to be less inclined to take part in the census. Therefore, in addition to the backbone of 'top-down' broadcast national channels, 'bottom-up' narrowcast channels were also required to help reach these audiences and add the frequency necessary to convince them the census was 'for them'. The narrowcast channels also provided tailoring of the messaging, to increase the sense of 'this is for me'.

It was clear that this campaign would need to work hard to overcome the apathy and disengagement of many audiences, so some targeted channels were deployed:

1. *Origami bus tour* – working in partnership with various local authorities, a census-branded, purple double-decker bus toured major towns and cities around England and Wales to consolidate awareness in advance of census day and provide a mobile questionnaire completion facility in key areas.

2. *Magazine partnerships* – working in partnership with IPC and Bauer to deliver credible engagement with young adults.

3. *Local authority toolkits* – to amplify the message in 'free' media channels (GP surgeries, schools, community centres, libraries, leisure centres).

4. *Black, minority and ethnic* ambassadors and community outreach activity.

5. *Student channels* – Student channels such as advertising in student unions, bars and cafés and washrooms, as well as ambient and take-away media, all using proximity targeting.

Campaign materials were also translated into nine languages to assist with inclusivity and overall comprehension. See Exhibit 17.1.

It was important to mitigate the risk of questionnaire responses dropping below target later in the campaign. Thanks to the unique code on every questionnaire, it was possible to track return rates by post code and audience on a daily basis. This created a unique opportunity for the campaign to be adjusted in 'real-time' and deploy additional activity, supporting the work of the door-to-door follow-up.

The task of Phase 1 was to create awareness and understanding and so develop the motivation to complete the census prior to distribution of the questionnaires themselves. The advertising campaign focused on the five key 'benefits' of the census for people in their local environments – health, education, transport, emergency services and facilities like parks. These five services were split across TV and outdoor:

Exhibit 17.1    **Targeted 'family' benefit messages for BME audiences**
*Source*: Bray Leino Ltd

- TV (transport, emergency services, facilities and health)
- Outdoor (transport, health, education and facilities).

TV was chosen as the lead medium for communicating the 'census story', it being the medium that could best communicate why the census is important (what it is) and why people should participate (the benefits/positive outcome to their local community and the country as a whole) and how to take part (paper or online). Like no other medium, it also has the benefit of reaching huge numbers of people very quickly and delivering a powerful and motivating message. The 30-second TV spot encompassed four benefits (transport, emergency services, facilities and health) and ways to complete the census (paper and online).

Outdoor was chosen because of presence and stature on the street. It also gave the opportunity to focus in on certain benefits and make the message more local: that is, personal to me and my family and local community. The campaign was split into 48-sheets which delivered scale and authority and the six-sheets which lent the campaign ubiquity and presence on the high street and other areas of high footfall.

The campaign exceeded all targets set by the ONS, and achieved a national response rate of over 94 per cent, with no local authority or key population group below 80 per cent.

*This case was written by Oliver Doerle at the Office for National Statistics and James Robertson at Bray Leino. Permission to use the material was kindly given by the Office for National Statistics.*

Exhibit 17.2    **High-impact 6-sheets and 48-sheets focused on the benefits**
Source: Bray Leino Ltd

Exhibit 17.3    **ONS and Bray Leino logos**
Source: Bray Leino Ltd

# Introduction

The Census minicase illustrates how important the creative strategy and channel planning are if direct marketing is to be effective. This chapter explores both direct marketing and personal selling. In many ways these topics complement each other in that they are both characterised by their personal and relatively transparent direct nature. 'Direct marketing' is a term used to refer to all media activities that generate a series of communications and responses with an existing or potential customer, just as experienced in the 2011 Census. Direct marketing is mainly concerned with the management of customer behaviour, and is used to complement the strengths and weaknesses of the other communication disciplines. To put this another way, advertising and public relations provide information and develop brand values but sales promotion, direct marketing and personal selling drive response, most notably behaviour. Both direct marketing and personal selling have the potential to engage customers directly and explicitly, and can provide both an intellectual as well as emotional basis upon which interaction and dialogue can be developed.

# The role of direct marketing

Direct marketing is a tool of marketing communications used to create and sustain a personal and intermediary-free communication with customers, potential customers and other significant stakeholders. In most cases this is a media-based activity and offers great scope for the collection and utilisation of pertinent and measurable data. There are a number of important issues associated with this definition. The first is that the activity should be measurable: that is, any response(s) must be associated with a particular individual, a particular media activity and a particular outcome, such as a sale or enquiry for further information. The second issue concerns the rewards that each party perceives through participation in the relationship. The customer receives a variety of tangible and intangible satisfactions. These include shopping convenience, time utility and the satisfaction and trust that can develop between customers and a provider of quality products and services when the customers realise and appreciate the personal attention they appear to be receiving.

The direct marketer derives benefits associated with precision target marketing and minimised waste, increased profits and the opportunities to provide established customers with other related products, without the huge costs of continually having to find new customers. In addition, direct marketing represents a strategic approach to the market. It actively seeks to remove channel intermediaries (at least from the initial communication), reduce costs, and improve the quality and speed of service for customers, and through this bundle of attributes presents a new offering for the market, which in itself may provide competitive advantage. First Direct, Churchill and the pioneer, Direct Line, all provide these advantages, which have enabled them to secure strong positions in the UK market.

Underpinning the direct marketing approach are the principles of trust and commitment, just as they support the validity of the other communication mix tools. If a meaningful relationship is to be developed over the long term and direct marketing is an instrumental part of the interaction, then the promises that the parties make to develop commitment and stability are of immense importance (Ganesan, 1994).

> ### Viewpoint 17.1   Everyone likes the direct approach
>
> Direct marketing, in all of its different formats, is used by a great many organisations, some to a greater extent than others. In the autumn of 2010 the prestige car brand Lexus launched its hybrid range and used direct marketing as the principal tool to deliver the communication strategy. Using the concept of evolution and natural selection, the direct and digital campaign was built around email and a direct mail pack. The goals were to generate awareness and interest among current Lexus customers and 'warm' prospects, with a view of stimulating brochure requests and test drives.
>
> In contrast, the National Trust launched a direct marketing campaign to help secure funding for the acquisition of a stretch of coast on the Llŷn Peninsula in North West Wales. Using direct mail, the campaign directed people to a bespoke microsite which contained information about the ecological importance, the threats facing the peninsula and an opportunity to make donations.
>
> President Obama's 2008 election campaign was rooted in the use of direct and digital marketing, as he targeted swing voters, non voters and others. Using database and email communications, Obama generated so much in donations online that he was able to outspend the Republicans by 4:1 in TV advertising, and spend millions on a 30-minute ad that was then dissected by the media for 24 hours, dominating the media in the last days of the campaign.
>
> Financial services companies such as Santander, Axa, Aviva, Barclays, Direct Line all use direct marking as a core element of their communications programmes. LoveFilm, the video rental company, charities such as Barnardos and Oxfam, and numerous B2B companies all invest heavily in direct marketing.
>
> *Source*:   Fernandez (2010a); Fernandez (2010b); Cooke (2008).
>
> **Question:**   If an organisation does not want to compete using advertising or direct marketing, what other methods could they use?
>
> **Task:**       Find two examples of companies using direct marketing and list the tools and media used.

# Types of direct brand

Direct marketing is assumed to refer to direct communication mix activity, but this is only part of the marketing picture. Using direct response media in this way is an increasingly common activity used to augment the communication activities surrounding a brand and to provide a new dimension to the context in which brands are perceived. However, direct marketing can be used by organisations in a number of different ways, very often reflecting the business strategy of the organisation. Four types can be identified and they should not be regarded as hierarchical, in the sense that there has to be progression from one type to another. They are reflections of the way different organisations use direct marketing and the degree to which the tool is used strategically.

## Type 1: complementary tool

At this level, direct response media are used to complement the other communication mix activities used to support a brand. Their main use is to generate leads and to some extent awareness, information and reinforcement. For example, financial services companies, tour operators and travel agents use DRTV to stimulate enquiries, loans and bookings, respectively.

## Type 2: primary differentiator

Rather than be one of a number of communication mix tools, at this level direct response media are the primary form of communication. They are used to provide a distinct point of differentiation from competitor offerings. They are the principal form of communication. In addition to the Type 1 advantages they are used to cut costs, avoid the use of intermediaries and reach finely targeted audiences (for example, book, music and wine clubs).

## Type 3: sales channel

A third use for direct marketing, and telemarketing in particular, concerns its use as a means of developing greater efficiency and as a means of augmenting current services. By utilising direct marketing as a sales tool, multiple sales channels can be used to meet the needs of different customer segments and so release resources to be deployed elsewhere and more effectively.

## Type 4: brand vehicle

At this final level, brands are developed to exploit market space opportunities. The strategic element is most clearly evident at this level. Indeed, the entire organisation and its culture are normally oriented to the development of customer relationships through direct marketing activities. Prime examples are Lastminute.com and Amazon.

# The growth of direct marketing

There can be little doubt that, of all the tools in the marketing communications mix, direct marketing has experienced the most growth in the past 15 years. The reasons for this growth are many and varied, but there have been three essential drivers behind the surge in direct marketing: technological advances; changing buyer lifestyles and expectations; and organisational expectations (see Figure 17.2). These forces for change demonstrate quite dramatically how a change in the context can impact on marketing communications.

## Growth driver 1: technology

Rapid advances in technology have heralded the arrival of new sources and forms of information. Technology has enabled the collection, storage and analysis of customer data to become relatively simple, cost-effective and straightforward. Furthermore, the management of this information is increasingly available to small businesses as well as the major blue chip multinational organisations. Computing costs have plummeted, while there has been a correspondingly enormous increase in the power that technology can deliver.

The technological surge has in turn stimulated three major developments. The first concerns the ability to capture information, the second to process and analyse it and the third to represent part or all of the information as a form of communication to stimulate interaction and perhaps dialogue to collect further information. For example, some organisations are incorporating quick response (QR) codes and image recognition technologies which tie in print with email. More Th>n, the insurance provider, has merged its email and direct mail services into a single department (Derrick, 2011).

## Growth driver 2: changing market context

The lifestyles of people in industrialised economies in particular, have evolved and will continue to do so. Generally, the brash phase of *selfishness* in the 1980s gave way to a more caring, society-oriented *selflessness* in the 1990s. The first decade of the twenty-first century suggests that a *self-oriented* lifestyle was prominent, reflected in short-term brand purchase behaviour and self-centred brand values and society behaviour. Perhaps the second decade will see further

**Figure 17.2**   Three forces for direct marketing

change as the global economy and forces for environmental adaptation bring about change to the way societies interact and individuals perceive their role within any one society. However, it seems as if there will be continued fragmentation of the media and finely tuned segmentation and communication devices will be necessary to communicate with discrete audiences.

Direct marketing offers a solution to this splintering and micro-market scenario and addresses some of the changing needs of customers, such as personalised, permission-based and informed communications. Management also benefit as direct marketing enables improved speed of response, lower waste, and justification for the use and allocation of resources.

## Growth driver 3: changing organisational expectations

Organisations can expect to continue experiencing performance pressures. These vary from the expectations of shareholders as they demand short-term returns on their investments to the impact this can have on managers. They are having to cope with an increasing cost base caused by demands on fuel and other resources by developing economies and a downward pressure on prices due to intense competition. This pressure on margins requires new routes to markets to reduce costs. Direct marketing addresses some of these changing management needs as there are no intermediary costs, there is fast access to markets (and withdrawal), plus opportunities to respond quickly to market developments and also justify their use and allocation of resources.

The impact of these drivers can be seen within the emergence of ideas about integrated marketing communications and an overall emphasis on relationship marketing principles. The enhanced ability of organisations to collect, store and manage customer lifestyle and transactional data, to generate personalised communications and their general enthusiasm for retention and loyalty schemes have combined to provide a huge movement towards an increased use of direct and interactive marketing initiatives.

---

**Scholars' paper 17.1**     **The evolution of direct marketing**

**Scovotti, C. and Spiller, L.D. (2006) Revisiting the conceptual definition of direct marketing: perspectives from practitioners and scholars, *The Marketing Management Journal*, 16(2), 188–202.**

Readers wishing to know more about the development of direct marketing will find this paper interesting. The authors review the literature, albeit up to 2005, and point out the contradictions, issues and anomalies.

---

# The role of the database

At the hub of successful direct marketing and CRM activities is the database. A database is a collection of files held on a computer that contain data that can be related to one another and which can reproduce information in a variety of formats. Normally the data consist of information collected about prospects and customers that are used to determine appropriate segments and target markets and to record responses to communications conveyed by the organisation. A database, therefore, plays a role as a storage, sorting and administrative device to assist direct and personalised communications.

Age and lifestyle data are important signals of product usage. However, there will be attitudinal variances between people in similar groups, demanding further analysis. This can, according to Reed (2000), uncover clues concerning what a direct mail piece should look like. So, older customers do not like soft colours and small type and sentences should not begin with 'and' or 'but'.

Increasingly, the information stored is gathered from transactions undertaken with customers, but on its own this information is not enough and further layering of data is required. The recency/frequency/monetary (RFM) model provides a base upon which life-style data, often bought in from a list agency, can be used to further refine the information held. Response analysis requires the identification of an organisation's best customers, and then another layer of data can be introduced which points to those that are particu-larly responsive to direct-response marketing activity (Fletcher, 1997). It is the increasing sophistication of the information held in databases that is enabling more effective targeting and communications.

Databases provide the means by which organisations, large and small, can monitor changes in customer lifestyles and attitudes or, in the business-to-business sector, the changing form of the interorganisational relationships and their impact on other members in the network as well as the market structure and level of competitive activity (Gundlach and Murphy, 1993). It is through the use of the database that relationships with participants can be tracked, analysed and developed. Crucially, database systems can be used, not only to identify strategically important customers and segments, but also to ascertain opportunities to cross-sell products (Kamakura et al., 2003).

However, the merging of data generated through transactions with attitudinal and lifestyle data poses a further problem. In essence, this paints a picture of what has been achieved, it describes behaviour. What it does not do is explain why the behaviour occurred. It may be possible to track back through a campaign to examine the inputs, isolate variables and make a judgement, but the problem remains that the information itself, what has been collected, does not provide insight into what underpins the behaviour. Pearson (2003) suggests that direct marketing and market research data sets should be brought together into what has been referred to as 'consilience' (Wilson, 1998) or a unity of knowledge. This data-rich information should then be capable of providing organisations with data intelligence and an opportunity to predict behaviour and offer a new form of data value.

# Permission marketing

There are a number of tensions associated with the use of the database. These tensions can be related to concerns about privacy and the need to communicate sensitively with audiences who experience varying needs for privacy (Dolnicar and Jordaan, 2007). For example, customers have varying tolerances regarding the level of privacy that a database can exploit. These tolerances or thresholds (Goodwin, 1991) vary according to the nature of the information itself, how it was collected and even who collected it.

The information on a database very often exists simply because a customer entered into a transaction. The business entity that received the information as part of a transaction has a duty to acknowledge the confidential nature of the information and the context in which it was collected before selling the details to a third party or exploiting the information to the detriment of the individual who provided it in the first place. Breaking privacy codes and making unauthorised disclosures of personal details lay open the tenuous relationship an organisation thinks it has with its 'loyal' customers. These tensions have given rise to regula-tions requiring customers to provide organisations with their formal, express permission to use their personal data in particular ways.

It is commonly agreed that Godin (1999) is the pioneer of permission marketing (PM) (Krishnamurthy, 2001; Gomez and Hlavinka, 2007) and that the aim of PM is to 'initiate, sustain and develop a dialogue with customers, building trust and over time lifting the levels of permission, making it a more valuable asset' (Kent and Brandal, 2003: 491). To put it another way, PM is about 'getting the okay from individuals to market to them' (Smith, 2004: 52).

PM occurs when consumers give their explicit permission for marketers to send them various types of promotional messages (Krishnamurthy, 2001). Essentially customers authorise a marketer to transmit promotional messages in certain 'interest' categories. This is usually obtained when a customer registers to enter a website or completes a survey indicating their interests when registering for a service. Marketers are then able to target advertising messages more closely with the interests and needs of their registered customers. Definitions of PM vary according to the focus of the researchers, but they range from education, trust and share of wallet, to enticement and clutter.

Customers benefit from using PM through:

- a reduction in search costs and clutter;
- better organisation of the information search processes;
- improved message relevance through personalisation, customisation and recognition.

For organisations the benefits of using PM are related to:

- improved segmentation and targeting precision in the acquisition of new customers, an increase in sales and the development of long-term, loyal customers;
- flexibility, resulting in: improved interactivity, lower sales costs, enhanced direct communication with customers and increased profitability.

# Direct response media

The choice of media for direct marketing can be very different from those selected for general advertising purposes. The main reason for using direct response media is that direct contact is made with prospects and customers in order that a direct response is solicited and a dialogue stimulated or maintained. In reality, a wide variety of media can be used, simply by attaching a telephone number, website address or response card.

Previously, broadcast media such as television and radio were the champions of the general advertiser. Now their adoption by direct marketers in the UK has changed the way these media operate. In terms of engagement (explored in Chapter 1), the broadcast format generated engagement through thinking and feeling. Its use as a direct response implement changes the engagement to a behavioural orientation.

Direct mail, telemarketing and door-to-door activities are the main offline forms of direct response media, as they allow more personal, direct and evaluative means of reaching precisely targeted customers. Internet-based direct work encompasses email, mobile and affiliate marketing as forms of direct linking.

## Direct mail

Direct mail refers to personally addressed advertising that is delivered through the postal system. It can be personalised and targeted with great accuracy, and its results are capable of precise measurement.

The generation of enquiries and leads, together with the intention of building a personal relationship with customers, are the most important factors contributing to the growth of direct mail. Management should decide whether to target direct mail at current customers with the intention of building loyalty and retention rates, or whether they should chase new customers. The decision, acquisition or retention, should be part of the marketing plan, but often this aspect of direct marketing lacks clarity, resulting in wastage and inefficiency. Direct mail can be expensive, at anything between £250 and £500 per 1,000 items dispatched. It should, therefore, be used selectively and for purposes other than creating awareness.

Organisations in the financial services sector have been heavy users of this medium and the financial health of the sector is dependent to a large extent on some of the major financial services companies maintaining their spend on direct mail. However, an increasing number of other organisations are experimenting with this approach, as they try to improve the effectiveness of their investment in the communication mix and seek to reduce television advertising costs. For example, Avaya sent USB sticks through direct mail to difficult to reach high-value influencers. Containing rich information, the USB sticks enabled visits for 12 per cent of those in the mailing group, compared to a norm of 6 per cent (McLuhan 2011). The growth in consumer-based direct mail activities has outstripped that of the business-to-business sector. The number of direct mail items sent to consumers has increased considerably in comparison with the B2B sector.

## Viewpoint 17.2    Saucy direct mail

Direct mail has been a core part of a large number of campaigns for many organisations. However, in most of these campaigns, although the copy is personalised, the actual process through which it is produced at the local printers, is mass production.

When 'The Campaign Company' (TCC) launched a demand-generation programme, at a time when the market was about the contract, they embarked on a different approach. First, they decided to use postcards as these had a strong personal feel. The style of the postcard was the typical British risqué seaside saucy humour, a style popularised by Donald McGill. The Sheffield artist Cecily Chua painted the five selected designs featuring bikini-clad women and muscle-bound lifeguards. The designs were selected to raise awareness of TCC services: social marketing, foundation trust recruitment, patient choice, public engagement, community cohesion and audience insight.

In addition, not only were the straplines tailored with a humorous comment relevant to the business in which the potential client operated, but the copy highlighted the bespoke, personalised nature of the work that TCC deliver.

However, perhaps the key point here is that all the cards were handwritten by the staff and directors of the Campaign Company. The handwritten element was important as it served to emphasise the importance of personal client relationships, not just holistic relationships based around an organisation. It also helped staff become engaged in the communication process and become actively involved in generating new business.

1250 cards were mailed to directors and chief executives only in the UK, due to the very culturally orientated messages. The postcards arrived on clients' desks just after the end of the summer holiday period, adding authenticity to the holiday postcard strategy.

*Source*:   Barda (2010); www.thecampaigncompany.co.uk/.

Question:   Why are postcards used so infrequently in business communications?

Task:        Find two other campaigns in which postcards were a core element.

| Exhibit 17.5 | **A postcard from The Campaign Company's direct mail programme** |
|---|---|
| | *Source*: The Campaign Company |

## Telemarketing

The prime qualities of the telephone are that it provides for interaction, is flexible and permits immediate feedback and the opportunity to overcome objections, all within the same communication event. Other dimensions of telemarketing include the development and maintenance of customer goodwill, allied to which is the increasing need to provide high levels of customer service. Telemarketing also allows organisations to undertake marketing research which is both highly measurable and accountable in that the effectiveness can be verified continuously and call rates, contacts reached and the number and quality of positive and negative responses are easily recorded and monitored.

Growth in telemarketing activity in the business-to-business sector has been largely at the expense of personal selling. The objectives have been to reduce costs and to utilise the expensive sales force and their skills to build on the openings and leads created by telemarketing and other lead generation activities. Some of the advantages of using the telephone as part of the media mix are that it allows for interaction between participants, it enables immediate feedback and sets up opportunities to overcome objections, all within the same communication event when both the sender and the receiver are geographically distant.

All of these activities can be executed by personal selling, but the speed, cost, accuracy and consistency of the information solicited through personal visits can often be improved upon by telemarketing. The complexity of the product will influence the degree to which this medium can be used successfully. However, if properly trained professional telemarketers are used, the sales results, if measured on a call basis, can outperform those produced by personal selling.

Contact centres use a variety of digital applications with the prime goals of reducing costs, improving efficiency and improving the client's reputation through quality of customer interaction. Automatic call distribution systems, call recording systems, computer–telephone integration, customer interaction management, predictive diallers and interactive voice response systems are just some of the ways in which technology is used in these environments.

Operator contact with customers can be also be supported by technology. Computer-assisted telephone interviewing (CATI) can provide varying degrees of technical support. The degree to which this is used depends on the task, the product and the nature of the target audience. The behaviour of call centre employees, however much they are regulated or controlled by various software applications, is a function of service quality, as perceived by callers. Referred to as *customer-orientation behaviours*, Rafaeli et al. (2008) identify five COBs that are related to service quality. These are:

- anticipating customer requests;
- offering explanations and justifications;
- educating customers;
- providing emotional support;
- offering personalised information.

When these five COBs are used by call centre employees, customers perceive a high level of service quality. The implication of this, as pointed out by the researchers, is that as call centre managers invariably seek to minimise call length in order to reduce costs and increase the number of transactions, their actions appear to endanger service quality.

The costs of telemarketing are high. It is estimated for example, that is costs £15–£20 to reach a decision-maker in an organisation. When this is compared with £5 for a piece of direct mail or £150+ for a personal sales call to the same individual, it is the effectiveness of the call and the return on the investment that determines whether the costs are really high.

---

### Scholars' paper 17.2    Call or go online?

Rhee, E. (2010) Multi-channel management in direct marketing retailing: Traditional call center versus Internet channel, *Database Marketing & Customer Strategy Management*, 17(2), 70–77.

This paper addresses issues associated with the impact on telemarketing following the rise of the Internet channel. The author looks at the benefits consumers perceive in using different channels. The research suggests that the Internet channel is helpful for purchases when there is low perceived risk and high experience and familiarity with the purchase. However, the call centre channel is helpful when there is high perceived risk and low experience and familiarity with the purchase.

---

## Carelines

Another reason to use telemarketing concerns the role which carelines can play within consumer/brand relationships. Manufacturers use contact centres to enable customers to:

- complain about a product performance and related experiences;
- seek product-related advice;
- make suggestions regarding product or packaging development;
- comment about an action or development concerning the brand as a whole.

What binds these together is the potential all of these people have for repurchasing the brand, even those who complain bitterly about product performance and experience. If these people have their complaints dealt with properly then there is a reasonable probability that they will repurchase.

The majority of careline calls are not about complaints but seek advice or help about products. Food manufacturers can provide cooking and recipe advice, cosmetic and toiletries companies can provide healthcare advice and application guidelines, while white goods and service-based organisations can provide technical and operational support.

Carelines are essentially a post-purchase support mechanism that facilities market feedback and intelligence gathering. They can warn of imminent problems (product defects), provide ideas for new products or variants and of course provide a valuable method to reassure customers and improve customer retention levels. Call operators, or *agents* as many of them are now being called, have to handle calls from a variety of new sources – web, social media, email, interactive TV and mobile devices – and it is appreciated that many are more effective if they have direct product experience. Instant messaging channels enable online shoppers to ask questions that are routed to a call centre for response.

While the Internet has provided further growth opportunities, it will also take on a number of the tasks currently the preserve of telemarketing bureaux. Websites enable product information and certain support advice to be accessed without the call centre costs, and focus attention on other matters that are of concern to the customer. Chat room discussions, collaborative browsing and real-time text conversations are options to help care for customers in the future. However, it is probably the one-to-one telephone dialogue between customer and agent that will continue to provide satisfaction and benefits for both parties.

## Inserts

Inserts are media materials that are placed in magazines or direct mail letters. These not only provide factual information about the product or service but also enable the recipient to respond to the request of the direct marketer. This request might be to place an order or post back a card for more information, such as a brochure.

Inserts have become more popular, but their cost is substantially higher than a four-colour advertisement in the magazine in which the insert is carried. Their popularity is based on their effectiveness as a lead generator, and new methods of delivering inserts to the home will become important to direct mailing houses in the future. Other vehicles, such as packages rather than letter mail, will become important.

## Print

There are two main forms of direct response advertising through the printed media: first, catalogues and, secondly, magazines and newspapers.

Catalogues mailed direct to consumers have been an established method of selling products for a long time. Mail order organisations for a range of products from clothing and music to gardening and cosmetics continue to exploit this form of direct marketing. The size of each catalogue, and the range of products included have been slimmed down so that mini-catalogues are popular.

Business-to-business marketers also use this medium, and organisations such as Dell and IBM now use online and offline catalogues, partly to save costs and partly to free valuable sales personnel so that they can concentrate their time selling into larger accounts. Direct response advertising through the press is similar to general press advertising except that the advertiser provides a mechanism for the reader to take further action. The mechanism may be a telephone number (call free) or a coupon or cut-out reply slip requesting further information. Dell has transformed its marketing strategy to one that is based around building customised products for both consumers and business customers. Consumer direct print ads which offer an incentive are designed explicitly to drive customers to the Dell website, where transactions are completed without reference to retailers, dealers or other intermediaries.

## Door-to-door

This delivery method can be much cheaper than direct mail as there are no postage charges to be accounted for. However, if the costs are much lower, so are the response rates. Responses are lower because door-to-door drops cannot be personally addressed, as can direct mail, even though the content and quality can be controlled in the same way.

---

**Viewpoint 17.3** **Onwards and upwards, direct to the Sky**

In the grip of the recession, Sky television made substantial use of direct marketing. In the year to June 2009 Sky invested £31.8 million in direct mail, a substantial 80 per cent increase on the previous year. Press advertising, media inserts and door-drop work account for the majority of its direct work. The result of this activity was that direct marketing accounted for 40 per cent of Sky's new customers in the period.

Plans to continue this level of direct marketing are limited as the marketing strategy refocuses on the system's capabilities and facilities and in particular, subscriptions to Sky+ boxes and high definition (HD) pictures. These benefits are not easily communicated through direct response and standard media. The need for face-to-face communication in order to demonstrate the benefits becomes more acute. As a result, resources were reallocated to experiential marketing, such as shopping centre stands, consumer exhibitions and events, the field sales force and relationships with major high street retailers such as Dixons, Tesco and Comet.

*Source*: Murphy (2009).

**Question:** Why might you recommend Sky to use direct marketing to launch an extension into radio?

**Task:** Buy a daily tabloid newspaper, cut out the direct response ads and consider what is similar about them.

**Exhibit 17.6** **Advertisement booth for Sky television**
*Source*: Keith Dannemiller/Corbis

Avon (Cosmetics) and Betterware are traditionally recognised as professional practitioners of door-to-door direct marketing. Other organisations, such as the utility companies (gas, electricity and water) and the domestic cleaning company, Molly Maid, are using door-to-door to create higher levels of market penetration.

### Radio and television

Of the two main forms discussed earlier, radio and television, the former is used as a support medium for other advertising, often by providing enquiry numbers. Television has greater potential because it can provide the important visual dimension, but its use in the UK for direct marketing purposes has been limited. One of the main reasons for this has been the television contractors' attitude to pricing. However, the industry has experienced a period of great change and has introduced greater pricing flexibility, and a small but increasing number of direct marketers have used the small screen successfully, mainly by providing freephone numbers for customers. Direct Line, originally a motor insurance organisation, has been outstanding in its use of television not only to launch but also to help propel the phenomenal growth of a range of related products.

### The Internet and digital media

The explosion of activity around digital media, the Internet, social media and email communications has been quite astonishing in recent years and now represents a major new form of interactive marketing communications. The establishment of digital television services, and the withdrawal of analogue services, have driven a new forms of interactivity. Initially home shopping and banking facilities were attractive to those whose lifestyles complement the benefits offered by the new technology, but fully interactive services now bring increased leisure and entertainment opportunities. (For more information on interactive marketing communications see Chapter 23.)

# Personal selling

In an era where relationship marketing has become increasingly understood and accepted as the contemporary approach to marketing theory and practice, so personal selling characterises the importance of strong relationships between vendor and buyer. The traditional image of personal selling is one that embraces the hard sell, with a brash and persistent salesperson delivering a volley of unrelenting, persuasive messages at a confused and reluctant consumer. Fortunately this image has receded as the professionalism and breadth of personal selling become more widely recognised and as the role of personal selling becomes even more important in the communications mix.

Personal selling activities can be observed at various stages in the buying process of both the consumer and business-to-business markets. This is because the potency of personal communications is very high, and messages can be adapted on the spot to meet the requirements of both parties. This flexibility, as we shall see later, enables objections to be overcome, information to be provided in the context of the buyer's environment and the conviction and power of demonstration to be brought to the buyer when the buyer requests it.

Personal selling is different from other forms of communication in that the transmitted messages represent, mainly, dyadic communications. This means that there are two persons involved in the communication process. Feedback and evaluation of transmitted messages are possible, more or less instantaneously, so that these personal selling messages can be tailored and be made much more personal than any of the other methods of communication.

Using the spectrum of activities identified by the hierarchy of effects, we can see that personal selling is close enough to the prospective buyer to induce a change in behaviour: that is, it is close enough to overcome objections, to provide information quickly and to respond to the prospects' overall needs, all in the context of the transaction, and to encourage them directly to place orders.

# The tasks of personal selling

The generic tasks to be undertaken by the sales force have been changing because the environment in which organisations operate is shifting dramatically. These changes, in particular those associated with the development and implementation of new technologies, have had repercussions on the activities of the sales force and are discussed later in this chapter.

The tasks of those who undertake personal selling vary from organisation to organisation and in accord with the type of selling activities on which they focus. It is normally assumed that they collect and bring into the organisation orders from customers wishing to purchase products and services. In this sense the order aspect of the personal selling tool can be seen as one of four order-related tasks:

1. *Order takers* are salespersons to whom customers are drawn at the place of supply. Reception clerks at hotels and ticket desk personnel at theatres and cinemas typify this role.

2. *Order getters* are sales personnel who operate away from the organisation and who attempt to gain orders, largely through the provision of information, the use of demonstration techniques and services and the art of persuasion.

3. *Order collectors* are those who attempt to gather orders without physically meeting their customers. This is completed electronically or over the telephone. The growth of telemarketing operations was discussed earlier, but the time saved by both the buyer and the seller using the telephone to gather repeat and low-value orders frees valuable sales personnel to seek new customers and build relationships with current customers.

4. *Order supporters* are all those people who are secondary salespersons in that they are involved with the order once it has been secured, or are involved with the act of ordering, usually by supplying information. Order processing or financial advice services typify this role. In truly customer-oriented organisations all customer-facing employees will be an order supporter.

| Table 17.1 | Tasks of personal selling |
| --- | --- |
| **Prospecting** | **Finding new customers** |
| Communicating | Informing various stakeholders and feeding back information about the market |
| Selling | The art of leading a prospect to a successful close |
| Information gathering | Reporting information about the market and reporting on individual activities |
| Servicing | Consulting, arranging, counselling, fixing and solving a multitude of customer 'problems' |
| Allocating | Placing scarce products and resources at times of shortage |
| Shaping | Building and sustaining relationships with customers and other stakeholders |

However, this perspective on personal selling is narrow because it fails to set out the broader range of activities that a sales force can be required to undertake. Salespeople do more than get or take orders. The tasks listed in Table 17.1 provide direction and purpose, and also help to establish the criteria by which the performance of members of the personal selling unit can be evaluated. The organisation should decide which tasks it expects its representatives to undertake.

Personal selling is the most expensive element of the communications mix. The average cost per contact can easily exceed £250 when all markets and types of businesses are considered. It is generally agreed that personal selling is most effective at the later stages of the hierarchy of effects or buying process, rather than at the earlier stage of awareness building. Therefore, each organisation should determine the precise role the sales force is to play within the communication mix.

# The role of personal selling

Personal selling is often referred to as *interpersonal communication*, and from this perspective Reid et al. (2002) determined three major sales behaviours: namely, getting, giving and using information:

- *Getting information* refers to sales behaviours aimed at information acquisition – for example, gathering information about customers, markets and competitors.
- *Giving information* refers to the dissemination of information to customers and other stakeholders – for example, sales presentations and seminar meetings designed to provide information about products and an organisation's capabilities and reputation.
- *Using information* refers to the salesperson's use of information to help solve a customer's problem. Associated with this is the process of gaining buyer commitment through the generation of information (Thayer, 1968, cited by Reid et al., 2002).

These last authors suggest that the using information dynamic appears to be constant across all types of purchase situations. However, as the complexity of a purchase situation increases, so the amount of giving information behaviours declines and getting information behaviours increase. This finding supports the need for a salesperson to be able to recognise particular situations in the buying process and then to adapt their behaviour to meet buyers' contextual needs.

However, salespeople undertake numerous tasks in association with communication activities. Guenzi (2002) determined that some sales activities are generic simply because they are performed by most salespeople across a large number of industries. These generic activities are selling, customer relationship management and communicating to customers. Other activities such as market analysis, pre-sales services and the transfer of information about competitors to the organisation are industry-specific. Interestingly he found that information-gathering activities are more likely to be undertaken by organisations operating in consumer markets than in b2b, possibly a reflection of the strength of the market orientation in both arenas.

The role of personal selling is largely one of representation. In business-to-business markets sales personnel operate at the boundary of the organisation. They provide the link between the needs of their own organisation and the needs of their customers. This linkage, or boundary spanning role, is absolutely vital, for a number of reasons that will be discussed shortly, but without personal selling, communication with other organisations would occur through electronic or print media and would foster discrete closed systems. Representation in this sense therefore refers to face-to-face encounters between people from different organisations.

Many authors consider the development, organisation and completion of a sale in a market exchange-based transaction to be the key part of the role of personal selling. Sales personnel provide a source of information for buyers so that they can make the right purchase decisions. In that sense they provide a good level of credibility, but they are also perceived, understandably, as biased. The degree of expertise held by the salesperson may be high, but the degree of perceived trustworthiness will vary, especially during the formative period of the relationship, unless other transactions with the selling organisation have been satisfactory. Once a number of transactions have been completed and product quality established, trustworthiness may improve.

As the costs associated with personal selling are high, it is vital that sales personnel are used effectively. To that end, some organisations are employing other methods to decrease the time that the sales force spends on administration, travel and office work and to maximise the time spent in front of customers, where they can use their specific selling skills.

The amount of control that can be exercised over the delivery of the messages through the sales force depends upon a number of factors. Essentially, the level of control must be regarded as low, because each salesperson has the freedom to adapt messages to meet changing circumstances as negotiations proceed. In practice, however, the professionalism and training that many members of the sales force receive and the increasing accent on measuring levels of customer satisfaction mean that the degree of control over the message can be regarded, in most circumstances, as very good, although it can never, for example, be as high as that of advertising.

This flexibility is framed within the context of the product strategy. Decisions that impact upon strategy are not allowed. There is freedom to adapt the manner in which products are presented, but there is no freedom for the sales representatives to decide the priority of the products to be detailed.

---

### Viewpoint 17.4    Flexible sales teams

Personal selling can take many forms, but the face-to-face form of communication can be a strong force for engagement and behaviour change. Emerging brands benefit when brand owners and entrepreneurs visit retailers in person, and start to establish a relationship. For example, when Sam Galsworthy launched Sipsmith, an alcohol-based brand, he used his motorbike to visit high-end style bars in and around London to ensure that bottles of his brands were given a prominent position at the bar, and to persuade bar managers to promote and recommend the brand to customers. As a result, the barmen got to know the face behind the brand, something that wholesalers are not able to do.

Many large organisations, especially those in the b2b sector, employ their own sales teams to visit customers to provide advice, technical support for the product line and to resolve any problems and difficulties. Grocery and FMCG producers use their sales force teams to develop sales with the multiple supermarkets and independent grocers. Providing adequate coverage can be difficult and expensive, so temporary sales force teams are often used for product launches and periods of high demand. Field marketing agencies can provide these facilities. When Kellogg's launched Rice Krispies Totally Chocolatey, a field sales team was used to visit hundreds of outlets in the London area, to get the brand established.

*Source*:   Benady (2009).

|  |  |
|---|---|
| **Question:** | Why should organisations maintain an employed, and expensive sales force when they can rent a sales force at any time? |
| **Task:** | Choose a brand that you would like to make, then consider the role a sales team might play in your communication strategy. |

> ### Scholars' paper 17.3    Tracking the use of technology
>
> **Christ, P. and Anderson, R. (2011) The impact of technology on evolving roles of salespeople,** *Journal of Historical Research in Marketing,* 3(2), 173–93.
>
> The role and adoption of technology within the sales force is an often neglected area. When attention is given to this subject the primary focus is inevitably on recent digital developments. This paper tracks the use of technology through the literature and goes back 130 years.

# Strengths and weaknesses of personal selling

There are a number of strengths and weaknesses associated with personal selling. It is interesting to note that some of the strengths can in turn be seen as weaknesses, particularly when management control over the communication process is not as attentive or as rigorous as it might be.

## Strengths

Dyadic communications allow for interaction that, unlike the other communication mix tools, provides for fast, direct feedback. In comparison with the mass media, personal selling allows for the receiver to focus attention on the salesperson, with a reduced likelihood of distraction or noise.

There is a greater level of participation in the decision process by the vendor than in the other tools. When this is combined with the power to tailor messages in response to the feedback provided by the buyer, the sales process has a huge potential to solve customer problems.

## Weaknesses

One of the major disadvantages of personal selling is the cost. Costs per contact are extremely high, and this means that management must find alternative means of communicating particular messages and improve the amount of time that sales personnel spend with prospects and customers. Reach and frequency through personal selling are always going to be low, regardless of the size of funds available.

Control over message delivery is very often low and, while the flexibility is an advantage, there is also the disadvantage of message inconsistency. This in turn can lead to confusion (a misunderstanding, perhaps, with regard to a product specification), the ramifications of which can be enormous in terms of cost and time spent by a variety of individuals from both parties to the contract.

The quality of the relationship can, therefore, be jeopardised through poor and inconsistent communications.

# When personal selling should be a major part of the communication mix

In view of the role and the advantages and disadvantages of personal selling, when should it be a major part of the communications mix? Table 17.2 indicates some key factors, using advertising as a comparison.

The following is not an exhaustive list, but is presented as a means of considering some of the important issues: complexity, network factors, buyer significance and communication effectiveness.

## Complexity

Personal selling is very important when there is a medium to high level of relationship complexity. Such complexity may be associated either with the physical characteristics of the product, such as computer software design, or with the environment in which the negotiations are taking place. For example, decisions related to the installation of products designed to automate an assembly line may well be a sensitive issue. This may be due to management's attitude towards the operators currently undertaking the work that the automation is expected to replace.

When the complexity of the offering is high, advertising and public relations cannot always convey benefits in the same way as personal selling. Personal selling allows the product to be demonstrated so that buyers can see and, if necessary, touch and taste it for themselves. Personal selling also allows explanations to be made about particular points that are of concern to the buyer or about the environment in which the buyer wishes to use the product.

## Buyer significance

The significance of the product to the buyers in the target market is a very important factor in the decision on whether to use personal selling. Significance can be measured as a form of risk, and risk is associated with benefits and costs.

**Table 17.2** When personal selling is a major element of the communications mix

|  | Advertising relatively important | Personal selling relatively important |
| --- | --- | --- |
| Number of customers | Large | Small |
| Buyers' information needs | Low | High |
| Size and importance of purchase | Small | Large |
| Post-purchase service required | Little | A lot |
| Product complexity | Low | High |
| Distribution strategy | Pull | Push |
| Pricing policy | Set | Negotiate |
| Web-enabled communications and exchanges | High | Low |
| Resources available for promotion | Many | Few |

*Source:* Adapted from Cravens (1987).

The absolute cost to the buyer will vary from organisation to organisation and from consumer to consumer. The significance of the purchase of an extra photocopier for a major multinational organisation may be low, but for a new start-up organisation or for an established organisation experiencing a dramatic turnaround, an extra photocopying machine may be highly significant and subject to high levels of resistance by a number of different internal stakeholders.

## Communication effectiveness

There may be a number of ways to satisfy the communication objectives of a campaign, other than by using personal selling. Each of the other communication tools has strengths and weaknesses; consequently differing mixes provide different benefits. Have they all been considered?

One of the main reasons for using personal selling occurs when advertising alone, or any other medium, provides insufficient communications. The main reason for this inadequacy surfaces when advertising media cannot provide buyers with the information they require to make their decision. For example, someone buying a new car may well observe and read various magazine and newspaper advertisements through which an emotional disposition towards a brand might be created. Then people go online and look at detailed information and comparison tests. The decision to buy, however, requires information and data upon which a balanced decision can be made. The rationality and emotional elements are brought together through experience of the car, through a test drive perhaps.

The decision to buy a car normally evokes high involvement, therefore car manufacturers try to provide a rich balance of emotional and factual information in their literature. From this perspective, buyers seek further information from the website and seek experience and reassurance from a dealership. Car buyers sign orders with the presence and encouragement of salespersons. Very few cars are bought on a mail order basis, although some, mainly used cars, are bought online.

Personal selling provides a number of characteristics that make it more effective than the other elements of the mix. As discussed, in business-to-business marketing the complexity of many products requires salespeople to be able to discuss with clients their specific needs; in other words, to be able to talk in the customer's own language, to build source credibility through expertise and hopefully trustworthiness, and build a relationship that corresponds with the psychographic profile of each member of the DMU. In this case, mass communications would be inappropriate.

## Channel network factors

When the number of members in a network is limited, the use of a sales force is advisable, as advertising is inefficient. Furthermore, the opportunity to build a close collaborative relationship with members may enable the development of a sustainable competitive advantage.

There are two further factors that influence the decision to use personal selling as part of the communications mix. When the customer base is small and dispersed across a wide geographic area it makes economic sense to use salespersons, as advertising in this situation is inadequate and ineffective.

Personal selling is the most expensive element of the communications mix. It may be that other elements of the mix may provide a more cost-effective way of delivering the message.

# Integration and supporting the sales force

In an effort to increase the productivity of the sales force and to use their expensive skills more effectively, direct marketing has provided organisations with an opportunity to improve levels of performance and customer satisfaction. In particular, the use of an inside telemarketing department is seen as a compatible sales channel to the field sales force. The telemarketing team can accomplish the following tasks: they can search for and qualify new customers, so saving the field force from cold calling; they can service existing customer accounts and prepare the field force should they be required to attend to the client personally; they can seek repeat orders from marginal or geographically remote customers, particularly if they are low-unit-value consumable items; finally, they can provide a link between network members that serves to maintain the relationship, especially through periods of difficulty and instability. Many organisations prefer to place orders online or through telesales teams, as it does not involve the time costs associated with personal sales calls. The routine of such orders gives greater efficiency for all concerned with the relational exchange and reduces costs.

Direct mail activities are also becoming more important in areas where personal contact is seen as unnecessary or where limited field sales resources are deployed to key accounts. As with telesales, direct mail is often used to supplement the activities of the field force. Catalogue and electronic communications such as fax can be used for accounts which may be regarded as relatively unattractive.

In addition to this, use of the Internet and mobile-based communications have provided new opportunities to reach customers. The website itself symbolises the changing orientation of marketing communications. Whereas once the brochure, mass media advertising and perhaps a communication mix incentive represented the central channel of communication, now the website and the database serve to integrate directed, sometimes interactive, one-to-one communications. These are supported in many cases by more call-to-action messages channelled through a variety of coordinated offline and digital media.

All of these activities free the field sales force to increase their productivity and to spend more time with established customers, key accounts or those with high profit potential.

# Strategic account management

One of the major issues concerning the development and maintenance of interorganisational relationships is the method by which very important and/or valuable customers are managed. Two main forms are considered here in turn: key account management and the emerging global account management disciplines.

# Key account management

The increasing complexity of both markets and products, combined with the trends towards purchasing centralisation and industrial concentration, mean that a small number of significant accounts have become essential for the survival of many organisations. The growth in the significance of key account management (KAM) is expected to continue, and one of the results will be the change in expectations of buyers and sellers, especially the demand for higher levels of expertise, integration and professionalism of sales forces.

It has long been recognised that particular customer accounts represent an important, often large, proportion of turnover. Such accounts have been referred to variously as national accounts, house accounts, major accounts and key accounts. Millman and Wilson (1995) argue that the first three are sales-oriented, tend to the short term and are often only driven by sales management needs. However, Ojasalo (2001) sees little difference in the terminology KAM, national account marketing (NAM) and strategic account management (SAM).

Key accounts may be of different sizes in comparison to the focus organisation, but what distinguishes them from other types of 'account' is that they are strategically important. Key accounts are customers who, in a business-to-business market, are willing to enter into collaborative exchanges and who are strategically important to the focus organisation.

There are two primary issues that arise. The first is that both parties perceive relational exchanges as a necessary component and that the relationship is long-term. The second aspect refers to the strategic issue. The key account is strategically important because it might offer opportunities for entry to new markets, represent access to other key organisations or resources, or provide symbolic value in terms of influence, power and stature.

The importance of the long-term relationship as a prime element of key account identification raises questions about how they are developed, what resources are required to manage and sustain them, and what long-term success and effectiveness results from identifying them.

In many ways KAM programmes are a means to reduce the various complexities and uncertainties that arise from the external and internal forces acting on both the selling and buying organisations. Brehmer and Rehme (2009) deduce that KAM-orientated complexity can be considered across two dimensions. The first is structural complexity, which is concerned with the number, location and geographical dispersion of a customer's units. The second is about operational complexity, and concern here is focused on the variety of product lines, services, systems, fulfilment facilities and commercial solutions.

There are three forms of uncertainty experienced by buyers according to Håkansson et al. (1977). These are *need uncertainty*, which concerns levels of demand, and whether increased interaction might increase or decrease the level of uncertainty. *Market uncertainty* concerns suppliers and perceptions of instability and the assumptions upon which decisions are made. The third element is *transaction uncertainty*, which is related to the physical transfer of products from supplier to buyer.

A primary goal of KAM programmes should therefore be one of reducing a buyer's uncertainties by coordinating an offer according to the prevailing complexities. To do this Brehmer and Rehme (2009) formulate a grid which they refer to as the 'Sales complexity management matrix'. This is reproduced at Figure 17.3.

By focusing on the operational and structural complexities experienced by organisations, KAM programmes can be formulated to meet the coordination needs of buyers. To see an example of KAM coordination, see Viewpoint 17.5.

| | Low Operational complexity | High Operational complexity |
|---|---|---|
| **High** Structural complexity | **Goal:** Reduce structural uncertainty **Focus on:** Coordination of functional units and/or geographical dispersed operations | **Goal:** Reduce strategic uncertainty **Focus on:** Coordination of operational *and* structural issues |
| **Low** Structural complexity | **Goal:** Reduce market uncertainty **Focus on:** Maintaining or strengthening market position | **Goal:** Reduce operational uncertainty **Focus on:** Coordination of operational aspects products, commercial agreements etc. |

**Figure 17.3** The sales complexity management matrix

*Source*: Brehmer and Rehme (2009). © Emerald Group Publishing Limited. All rights reserved.

## Viewpoint 17.5 | Typically Swedish coordination

Before the giant Swedish industrial company ABB embarked on a massive structural realignment, they determined that their customers were experiencing several negative issues when working with the company. Customer purchases were fragmented across ABB; there was an increasing demand to buy more complete systems, rather than mere products; and far too many sales calls were being made by sales engineers from different ABB companies. At one point, customer analysis revealed that ABB had approximately 40,000 customers, yet just 100 of these customers accounted for 60 per cent of total sales.

This sales fragmentation was far from cost-effective, the poor quality of service experienced by customers was threatening ABB's reputation and there was huge risk associated with so few customers responsible for such a high proportion of revenue. The solution was to move toward a more coordinated, networked company, whose primary task was to simplify things for the customers and help the customers with total solutions. This involved the creation of a new structure with four application-oriented industrial segments: manufacturing and consumer industry, process industry, oil, gas and petrochemicals and utilities, plus two product segments. The ABB global KAM programme established 30 global customers as key accounts. Each was assigned a top ABB executive to be responsible for the account, sending a clear signal that each of these customers was of strategic importance for the ABB group. In each of these industry segments, several KAM teams were formed, each built on sales personnel from relevant ABB companies that covered a particular customer.

In an attempt to reduce complexity and uncertainty, each of the KAM teams implemented a series of activities. In the Swedish market, for example, it was important to reduce operational complexity, and part of the solution was to improve the delivery service through coordination. Another was to improve the coordination of ABB's products and systems and so offer a complete overall offer to these key customers.

At an international level, the main need was to reduce structural complexity, achieved by a new international sales interface and the coordination of the international and national sales processes. Internationally the challenge was to coordinate a large range of products, commercial agreements and fulfilment systems, across national borders and different units. To achieve this, it was necessary for ABB to accept responsibility for their customers' final products, all of which were manufactured at different locations.

*Source*:   Based on Brehmer and Rehme (2009).

| | |
|---|---|
| **Question:** | Discuss the view that KAM is just a high-level service provision. |
| **Task:** | Make a list of the different ways a supplier might coordinate activities for a customer. |

| Exhibit 17.7 | **ABB Group headquarters** |
|---|---|
| | *Source*: ABB |

| Table 17.3 | Three ways of managing key accounts |
|---|---|

| KAM approach | Explanation |
|---|---|
| **Assigning sales executives** | Common in smaller organisations that do not have large resources. Normally undertaken by senior executives who have the flexibility and can provide the responsive service often required. They can make decisions about stock, price, distribution and levels of customisation. There is a tendency for key accounts to receive a disproportionate level of attention, as the executives responsible for these major customers lose sight of their own organisation's marketing strategy. |
| **Creating a key account division** | The main advantage of this approach is that it offers close integration of production, finance, marketing and sales. The main disadvantage is that resources are duplicated and the organisation can become very inefficient. It is also a high-risk strategy, as the entire division is dependent upon a few customers. |
| **Creating a key account sales force** | This is adopted by organisations that want to differentiate through service and they use their most experienced and able salespersons and provide them with a career channel.<br>Administratively, this structure is inefficient, as there is a level of duplication similar to that found in the customer-type structure discussed earlier. Furthermore, commission payable on these accounts is often a source of discontent, both for those within the key account sales force and those aspiring to join the select group. |

In order for these coordination activities to be designed and implemented a decision needs to be made about who in the organisation should be responsible for these key accounts. Generally speaking, there are three main responses: to assign sales executives, to create a key account division or to create a key account sales force (see Table 17.3).

The assignment of sales executives to these important accounts is common in smaller organisations. Those organisations that have the resources are able to incorporate the services of senior executives, who assume this role and bring to it the flexibility and responsive service that are required as the account grows in stature. They can make decisions about stock, price, distribution and levels of customisation.

These accounts may be major or national accounts, as very often their strategic significance is not recognised. There is a tendency for these accounts to receive a disproportionate level of attention, as the executives responsible for these major customers lose sight of their own organisation's marketing strategy.

A further way of managing these accounts is to create a key account division. The main advantage of this approach is that it offers close integration of production, finance, marketing and sales. The main disadvantage is that resources are duplicated and the organisation can become very inefficient. It is also a high-risk strategy as the entire division is dependent upon a few customers.

Should a key account sales force be preferred then issues concerning the management of this resource arise. Key account managers require particular skills, as, indeed, do the executives themselves.

## Key account managers

Abratt and Kelly (2002) report Napolitano's (1997) work that found that, to be successful, a KAM programme requires the selection of the right key account manager. This person should possess particularly strong interpersonal and relationship skills and be capable of managing larger, significant and often complex customers. Key account managers act as a conduit between organisations, through which high-value information flows in both directions. They must be prepared and able to deal with organisations where buying decisions can be protracted and delayed (Sharma, 1997).

Benedapudi and Leone (2002) agree that the key account manager is vitally important to the success of a KAM relationship, but they also view the relationship differences between the organisations as distinct from the interpersonal relationships between the customer firm's contact person and the supply-side firm's key account manager, or contact employee as they refer to them. These relationships will vary in strength, and there are differing consequences for the KAM relationship should the contact person leave the supply-side organisation.

Among the key success factors Abratt and Kelly report that, in addition to selecting the right key account manager, the selection of the right key account customers is also important for establishing KAM programmes. Not all large and high-volume customers are suitable for KAM programmes. Segmentation and customer prioritisation according to needs and an organisation's ability to provide consistent value should be used to highlight those for whom KAM would not be helpful.

In addition, particular sales behaviours are required at this level of operation. As the majority of key account managers are drawn internally from the sales force (Hannah, 1998, cited by Abratt and Kelly, 2002) it is necessary to ensure that they have the correct skills mix. It is also important to take a customer's perspective on what makes a successful KAM programme. Pardo (1997) is cited as claiming that the degree of impact a product has on the customer's business activity will determine the level of attention offered to the supplier's programme. Also, the level of buying decision centralisation will impact on the effectiveness of the KAM programme.

Abratt and Kelly found six factors were of particular importance when establishing a KAM programme: the 'suitability of the key account manager, knowledge and understanding of the key account customer's business, commitment to the KAM partnership, delivering value, the importance of trust and the proper implementation and understanding of the KAM concept' (p. 474).

One final point can be made concerning key account managers. The inference is that one, multitalented individual is the sole point of contact between the supplier and customer. This is not the case as there are usually a number of levels of interaction between the two organisations. Indeed, there could be 'an entire team dedicated to providing services and support to the key account' (Ojasalo, 2001: 210). Therefore, it is more appropriate to suggest that the key account manager should assume responsibility for all points of contact within the customer organisation.

Having established a KAM programme, one of the tasks that key account managers need to implement is to ensure the relationship benefits from a planned approach. The need for planning within key account relationships is argued by Ryals and Rogers (2007). They find that key account planning is not widely used and certainly fails to have a strategic focus. As if to try and remedy this situation, they also demonstrate the impact that key account planning can have on managers and their subsequent performance.

## Key account relationship cycles

A number of researchers have attempted to gain a greater understanding of KAM by considering the development cycles through which relationships move. Millman and Wilson offer the work of Ford (1980), Dwyer et al. (1987) and Wotruba (1991) as examples of such development cycles (see Table 17.4).

Millman and Wilson have attempted to build on the work of the others (included in Table 17.4) and have formulated a model that incorporates their own research as well as that established in the literature. McDonald (2000) has since elaborated on their framework, providing further insight and explanation.

The cycle develops with the *exploratory* KAM level, where the main task is to identify those accounts that have key account potential, and those that do not, in order that resources can be

**Table 17.4**    Comparison of relational models

| Ford (1980), Dwyer et al. (1987) | Wotruba (1991) | Millman and Wilson (1995) | McDonald (2000) |
|---|---|---|---|
| Pre-relationship awareness | Provider | Pre-KAM | Exploratory |
| Early stage exploration | Persuader | Early KAM | Basic |
| Development stage expansion | Prospector | Mid-KAM | Cooperative |
| Long-term stage commitment | Problem solver | Partnership KAM | Interdependent |
| Final stage institutionalisation | Procreator | Synergistic KAM | Integrated |
| | | Uncoupling KAM | Disintegrated |

*Source*: Updated from Millman and Wilson (1995). © Emerald Group Publishing Limited. All rights reserved.

allocated efficiently. Both organisations are considering each other: the buyer in terms of the supplier's offer in terms of its ability to match their own requirements; and the seller in terms of the buyer providing sufficient volumes, value and financial suitability.

The next level is *basic KAM*, where both organisations enter into a transactional period, essentially testing each other as potential long-term partners. Some relationships may stabilise at this level while others may develop as a result of the seller seeking and gaining tentative agreement with prospective accounts about whether they would become 'preferred accounts'.

At the *cooperative* KAM level, more people from both organisations are involved in communications. At the basic KAM level, both parties understand each other and, through experience, the selling company has established its credentials with the buying organisation. At this next level, opportunities to add value to the relationship are considered. This could be encouraged by increasing the range of products and services transacted, thereby involving more people in the relationship.

At the *interdependent* KAM level of a relationship, both organisations recognise the importance of the other to their operations, with the supplier either first choice, or only, supplier. Retraction from the relationship is now problematic as 'inertia and strategic suitability', as McDonald phrases it, hold the partners together.

*Integrated* KAM is achieved when the two organisations view the relationship as consisting of one entity where they create synergistic value in the marketplace. Joint problem solving and the sharing of sensitive information are strong characteristics of the relationship and withdrawal by either party can be traumatic at a personal level for the participants involved, let alone at the organisational level.

The final level is *disintegrating* KAM. This can occur at any time for a variety of reasons, ranging from company takeover to the introduction of new technology. The relationship may return to another, lower level and new terms of business are established. The termination, or readjustment, of the relationship need not be seen as a negative factor as both parties may decide that the relationship holds no further value.

McDonald develops Millman and Wilson's model by moving away from a purely sequential framework. He suggests that organisations may stabilise or enter the model at any level, indeed, he states that organisations might readjust to a lower level. The time between phases will vary according to the nature and circumstances of the parties involved. The labels provided by McDonald reflect the relationship status of both parties rather than of the selling company (e.g. prospective) or buying company (e.g. preferred supplier). While the Millman and Wilson and McDonald interpretations of the KAM relationship cycle provide insight, they are both primarily dyadic perspectives. They neglect to consider the influence of significant others, especially those other network member organisations that provide context and interaction in particular networks and that do influence the actions of organisations and those key individuals who are strategic decision-makers.

## Some final aspects of KAM

In mature and competitive markets, where there is little differentiation between the products, service may be the only source of sustainable competitive advantage. Key account management allows senior sales executives to build a strong relationship with each of their customers, thereby providing a very high level of service and strong point of differentiation.

This approach enables an organisation to select its most experienced and able salespersons and, in doing so, provide a career channel for those executives who prefer to stay in sales rather than move into management. Administratively, this structure is inefficient as there is a level of duplication similar to that found in the customer-type structure discussed earlier. Furthermore, commission payable on these accounts is often a source of discontent, both for those within the key account sales force and those aspiring to join the select group.

The development and management of key accounts is complex and evolving. Key account relationships are rarely static and should be rooted within corporate strategy, if only because of the implications for resources, which customers seek as a result of partnering in this way (Spencer, 1999). Key account relationships can generate positive financial value but not without considerable management effort (Kalwani and Narayanas, 1995; Ryals and Holt, 2007). Consideration of customer profitability appears to be the foundation for successful key account relationships.

# Global account management

The development of key account management approaches highlighted the strategic importance that some customers represent to organisations. KAM represents an attempt to meet the needs of these customers in a customised and personal way. However, there are many organisations whose customers are located in many different countries, regions and even on different continents, and the management of their needs demands different skills and resources from those adopted for KAM. The management of these customers is referred to as global account management (GAM) and in many ways is evidence of a new strategic approach to business development and marketing management in b2b organisations.

Understanding the nature of GAM is helped by Hennessey and Jeannet, who provide a useful definition:

> Global accounts are large companies that operate in multiple countries, often on two or more continents, are strategically important to the supplier and have some form of coordinated purchasing across different countries. (2003: 1)

As if to reinforce the nature of GAM, Birkinshaw (2003) refers to Hewlett-Packard, which regards Boeing as a national (key) and not a global account, as its decision-making is all US-centred. One of the characteristics of global accounts is that their decision-making units are influenced through inputs from various geographical locations. Wilson et al. (2000) highlight the important characteristic associated with the strategic coordination required by GAM. To them, a strategic global account is characterised as representing a major part of a supplier's corporate objectives and where the account expects the supplier to offer an integrated global product service offering.

---

### Scholars' paper 17.4 | Looking after the global accounts

**Capon, N. and Senn, C. (2010) Global Customer Management Programs: how to make them really work,** *California Management Review,* **52(2), Winter, 32–55.**

This paper considers the issues and characteristics associated with successful global account management programmes. The authors track the transformation from what was regarded as low-level purchasing, and is now high-status procurement. This involves the use of greater intellectual capital and sophisticated systems and processes that are designed to improve performance. They model the process and advise on the best approach from a managerial perspective.

---

It would therefore be a mistake to think that KAM and GAM are the same. Indeed, Birkinshaw (2003) makes the point that global and key accounts are not identical. He argues that the roots of global account management are to be found in supply chain management, unlike KAM, which has been influenced by the sales management perspective. Hennessey and Jeannet (2003) believe that national account managers are relationship managers, whereas global account managers have a greater focus on strategic issues and coordination of personnel in different countries. Millman and Wilson (1998) refer to the importance and significance of cultural diversity and organisational issues when adopting a global account management programme.

Wilson et al. (2000) consider how global account programmes can be delivered. They identified the need for three main global competences:

- a coordinated, globally competent supply chain;
- management of the interaction process *within* the supplying company, particularly the information and communication flows;
- the establishment of a forum, with the customer, of a collaborative design process.

This suggests that relationship management skills, in particular the use of interaction and collaboration to develop dialogue, are critical factors associated with GAM. Wilson et al. (2000) identify many competences that are necessary for GAM to be successful, ranging from strong communications and relationship management skills through cultural empathy and business and financial acumen. However, they make the point that global account managers need strong political skills, especially in view of the fact that they often operate without direct authority, particularly with regard to resources and processes. They refer to this role as 'political entrepreneur'.

Understanding the nature of GAM, its management and indeed associated research are at an early stage as the discipline is very young. Early work in the area suggests that there is no fixed strategic model that represents GAM, if only because GAM needs to be flexible and dynamic as engagement with key global customers evolves.

# Key points

- Direct marketing is a tool of marketing communications used to create and sustain a personal and intermediary-free communication with customers, potential customers and other significant stakeholders.

- It is concerned with the management of customer behaviour and is used to complement the strengths and weaknesses of the other communication disciplines.

- Four main forms of direct marketing can be identified: as a complementary tool, as a primary differentiator, as a sales channel and as a brand vehicle.

- There have been three essential drivers behind the surge in direct marketing: technological advances; changing buyer lifestyles and expectations; and organisational expectations.

- A database plays a central role as a storage, sorting and administrative device to assist strategy formulation, cross-selling, plus direct and personalised communications.

- PM occurs when consumers give their explicit permission for marketers to send them various types of promotional messages.

- Direct mail, telemarketing and door-to-door activities are the main offline forms of direct response media, as they allow more personal, direct and evaluative means of reaching precisely targeted customers. Internet-based direct work encompasses email, mobile and affiliate marketing as forms of direct linking.

- Personal selling activities can be observed at various stages in the buying process of both the consumer and business-to-business markets.

- Personal selling can be considered in terms of four different tasks; order takers, order getters, order collectors, and order supporters.

- Some of the issues associated with the deployment of personal selling include: complexity, network factors, buyer significance and communication effectiveness.

- The development of multichannel selling enables customers increased opportunities and touchpoints to access brands. For organisations such restructuring can lead to reduced channel costs, and more effective communications.

- KAM programmes are a means of reducing the various complexities and uncertainties that arise from the external and internal forces that act on both selling and buying organisations.

- The key account relationship cycle encompasses; exploratory KAM, basic KAM, cooperative KAM, interdependent KAM and integrated KAM.

# Review questions

1. Identify the key success factors underpinning the 2011 Census campaign featured in the minicase opening this chapter.

2. Explain the different levels of direct marketing, highlighting the key differences.

3. Write brief notes explaining the reasons why usage of direct marketing has grown in recent years.

4. Why does direct mail continue to have a strong role to play in the direct marketing activities for many organisations?

5. Why might permission marketing be seen as an unnecessary cost and an infringement of civil liberties?

6. Which industries might use personal selling as a primary element of their marketing communication mix?

7. What are the different types of personal selling and what are the tasks that salespeople are normally expected to accomplish?

8. Describe the role of personal selling and highlight its main strengths and weaknesses.

9. Identify the main difference between house or major accounts, key accounts and global account management.

10. Explain the concept of key account relationship cycles using the McDonald (2000) framework.

# References

Abratt, R. and Kelly, P.M. (2002) Perceptions of a successful key account management program, *Industrial Marketing Management*, 31, 5 (August), 467–76.

Barda, T. (2010) Wish you were here, *The Marketer*, February, 20–22.

Benady, D. (2009) Field marketing comes into its own in the recession, *Marketing*, retrieved 10 July 2010 from www.brandrepublic.com/features/.

Benedapudi, N. and Leone, R.P. (2002) Managing business-to-business customer relationships following key contact employee turnover in a vendor firm, *Journal of Marketing*, 66 (April), 83–101.

Birkinshaw, J.M. (2003) *The Blackwell Handbook of Global Management*, Boston, MA: Blackwell.

Brehmer, P.-O. and Rehme, J. (2009) Proactive and reactive: drivers for key account management programmes, *European Journal of Marketing*, 43, 7/8, 961–84.

Capon, N. and Senn, C. (2010) Global Customer Management Programs: how to make them really work, *California Management Review*, 52(2), Winter, 32–55.

Christ, P. and Anderson, R. (2011) The impact of technology on evolving roles of salespeople, *Journal of Historical Research in Marketing*, 3(2), 173–93.

Cooke, C. (2008) Obama's Digital Campaign, *WPP*, retrieved 12 August 2010 from www.wpp.com/wpp/marketing/digital/obamas-digital-campaign.htm.

Cravens, D.W. (1987) *Strategic Marketing*, Homewood, IL: Irwin.

Derrick, S. (2011) Top 100 Mailers: Best of both worlds, *Marketing*, 26 October, 11–12.

Dolnicar, S. and Jordaan, Y. (2007) A market-orientated approach to responsibly managing information privacy concerns in direct marketing, *Journal of Advertising*, 36, 2 (Summer), 123–49.

Dwyer, F.R., Shurr, P.H. and Oh, S. (1987) Developing buyer–seller relationships. *Journal of Marketing*, 51(2), 11–28.

Fernandez, J. (2010a) Lexus unveils DM push for its hybrid range, *Marketing Week*, 10 August 2010, retrieved 12 August 2010 from www.marketingweek.co.uk/disciplines/direct-marketing/lexus-unveils-dm-push-for-its-hybrid-range/3016840.article.

Fernandez, J. (2010b) National Trust uses DM for Welsh coastline appeal, *Marketing Week*, 10 August, retrieved 12 August 2010 from www.marketingweek.co.uk/sectors/not-for-profit/national-trust-uses-dm-for-welsh-coastline-appeal/3016859.article.

Fletcher, K. (1997) External drive, *Marketing*, 30 October, 39–42.

Ford, I.D. (1980) The development of buyer–seller relationships in industrial markets. *European Journal of Marketing*, 14(5/6), 339–53.

Ganesan, S. (1994) Determinants of long-term orientation in buyer–seller relationships, *Journal of Marketing*, 58 (April), 1–19.

Godin, S. (1999) *Permission Marketing: Turning Strangers into Friends, and Friends into Customers*, New York: Simon & Schuster.

Gomez, L. and Hlavinka, K. (2007) The total package: loyalty marketing in the world of consumer packaged goods (CPG), *Journal of Consumer Marketing*, 24, 1, 48–56.

Goodwin, C. (1991) Privacy: recognition of a consumer right, *Journal of Public Policy and Marketing*, 10, 1, 149–66.

Guenzi, P. (2002) Sales force activities and customer trust, *Journal of Marketing Management*, 18, 749–78.

Gundlach, G.T. and Murphy, P.E. (1993) Ethical and legal foundations of relational marketing exchanges, *Journal of Marketing*, 57 (October), 35–46.

Håkansson, H., Johansson, J. and Wootz, B. (1977) Influence tactics in buyer–seller processes, *Journal of Marketing Management*, 5, 6, 319–32.

Hannah, G. (1998) From transactions to relationships: challenges for the national account manager, *Journal of Marketing and Sales* (SA), 4(1), 30–3.

Hennessey, D.H. and Jeannet, J.-P. (2003) *Global Account Management: Creating Value*, Chichester: Wiley.

Kalwani, M.U. and Narayanas, N. (1995) Long-term manufacturer–supplier relationships: do they pay off supplier firms? *Journal of Marketing*, 59(1), 1–16.

Kamakura, W.A., Wedel, M., de Rosa, F. and Mazzon, J.A. (2003) Cross-selling through database marketing: a mixed factor analyzer for data augmentation and prediction, *International Journal of Research in Marketing*, 20, 1 (March), 45–65.

Kent, R. and Brandal, H. (2003) Improving email response in a permission marketing context, *International Journal of Market Research*, 45, 4, 489–503.

Krishnamurthy, S. (2001) A comprehensive analysis of permission marketing, *Journal of Computer-Mediated Communication*, 6, 2, (January), retrieved 8 March 2008 from www.jcmc.indiana.edu/vol6/issue2/krishnamurthy.html.

McDonald, M. (2000) Key account management: a domain review, *Marketing Review*, 1, 15–34.

McLuhan, R. (2011) Top 100 Mailers: How innovation is helping direct mail, *Marketing*, 26 October, 17–18.

Millman, T. and Wilson, K. (1995) From key account selling to key account management, *Journal of Marketing Practice: Applied Marketing Science*, 1(1), 9–21.

Millman, T. and Wilson, K. (1998) Global account management reconciling organisational complexity and cultural diversity, *The 14th Annual Industrial Marketing and Purchasing (IMP) Group Conference*, Turku School of Economics and Business Administration.

Murphy, D. (2009) Direct mail: finding its place in the mix, *Marketing: Top 100 Mailers*, 4 October, 4–9.

Napolitano, L. (1997) Customer–supplier partnering: a strategy whose time has come, *Journal of Selling and Sales Management*, 17(4), 1–8.

Ojasalo, J. (2001) Key account management at company and individual levels in business-to-business relationships, *Journal of Business and Industrial Marketing*, 16(3), 199–220.

Pardo, C. (1997) Key account management in the business-to-business field: the key accounts point-of-view, *Journal of Selling and Sales Management*, 17(4), 17–26.

Pearson, S. (2003) Data takes centre stage. Data 2003, *Marketing Direct*, Sponsored Supplement.

Rafaeli, A., Ziklik, L. and Doucet, L. (2008) The impact of call center employees' customer orientation behaviors on service quality, *Journal of Service Research*, 10, 3 (February), 239–55.

Reed, D. (2000) Too much, too often, *Marketing Week*, 12 October, 59–62.

Reid, A., Pullins, E.B. and Plank, R.E. (2002) The impact of purchase situation on sales-person communication behaviors in business markets, *Industrial Marketing Management*, 31, 3, 205–13.

Rhee, E. (2010) Multi-channel management in direct marketing retailing: Traditional call center versus Internet channel, *Database Marketing & Customer Strategy Management*, 17(2), 70–77.

Ryals, L.J. and Holt, S. (2007) Creating and capturing value in KAM relationships, *Journal of Strategic Marketing*, 15 (December), 403–20.

Ryals, L.J. and Rogers, B. (2007) Key account planning: benefits, barriers and best practice, *Journal of Strategic Marketing*, 15 (May–July), 209–22.

Scovotti, C. and Spiller, L.D. (2006) Revisiting the conceptual definition of direct marketing: perspectives from practitioners and scholars, *The Marketing Management Journal*, 16(2), 188–202.

Sharma, A. (1997) Who prefers key account management programs? An investigation of business buying behaviour and buying firm characteristics, *Journal of Personal Selling and Sales Management*, 17(4), 27–39.

Smith, J.W. (2004) Permission is not enough: empowerment and reciprocity must be included, too, *Marketing Management*, 13(3), 52.

Spencer, R. (1999) Key accounts: effectively managing strategic complexity, *Journal of Business and Industrial Marketing*, 14(4), 291–310.

Thayer, L. (1968) *Communication and Communication Systems*, Homewood, IL: Irwin.

Wilson, E.O. (1998) *Consilience: The Unity of Knowledge*, New York: Random House.

Wilson, K., Croom, S., Millman, T. and Weilbaker, D.C. (2000) *Global Account Management Study Report*, Southampton: The Sales Research Trust.

Wotruba, T.R. (1991) The evolution of personal selling, *Journal of Personal Selling and Sales Management*, 11(3), 1–12.

# Chapter 18

# Sales promotion, field marketing and brand experiences

In order to stand out or reduce customer decision-making time, organisations often encourage customers to make a purchase now, rather than at some point in the future. This can be achieved through the use of sales promotions. By adding value to the offer and hoping to bring forward future sales, these techniques can be a source of advantage, one that has a short- rather than long-run orientation.

The way brands are presented and displayed, and that includes packaging and shelf management in-store, can also be very influential in terms of customer perception, sales volumes, and market share. Therefore, a key aspect of marketing communications, especially in grocery markets, is field marketing. This consists of a range of merchandising and brand experience opportunities often necessary to support sales promotions, as well as to help a brand cut through the clutter of competitive and distracting messages.

## Aims and learning objectives

The aims of this chapter are to consider the role and techniques of sales promotion and field marketing and to appraise their contributions to the marketing communications mix.

The learning objectives of this chapter are to:

1. understand the value and the role of sales promotions;
2. discuss the objectives associated with using sales promotion;
3. explain the ways in which sales promotion is thought to work;
4. evaluate the merits of loyalty and retention programmes;
5. explain the different sales promotion methods and techniques;
6. explore ideas associated with field marketing and related activities;
7. describe ideas associated with brand experiences and events.

# Minicase

## Orange at the Glastonbury Festival

Retaining customers and cutting through the communications clutter is a challenge for many companies, especially when there are few functional differences between the different competitors. The mobile phone market, with standardised tariffs and pricing, faces this loyalty issue on a regular basis. One company, Orange, has addressed this issue in a variety of ways, including the use of sponsorship and the creation of customer brand experiences.

A key audience for Orange is 16–30-year-olds, as they are big phone and broadband users and future business purchasers. In the past, cinema and music has worked well for Orange. Sponsorship of Orange Wednesdays at cinemas has developed the brand profile and reputation, while Orange Play, an ad-funded music programme with ITV, is the most-watched music-TV show. The metrics show, unsurprisingly, that people who watch the show have a higher awareness of Orange than those who don't, as well as a higher intent to purchase.

The Glastonbury Festival is a three-day weekend for rock music enthusiasts. It is the largest green-field music and performing arts festival in the world and is normally held annually. Each festival now attracts over 180,000 people, and drives £22 million in revenue for the organisers. Each visitor is estimated to spend an average of £300, whilst the festivals are important for many local businesses. Glastonbury is partly funded through sponsorship and has deals established with the *Guardian* newspaper, Carlsberg who provide 22 bars and are the 'official' beer of the festival, and cidermaker Brothers Drinks. There is also a branded festival guide. In addition to these is Orange, who is the Official Communications Partner for the Glastonbury Festival.

Orange has sponsored a number of Glastonbury Festivals with the aim of offering visitors something that will enhance their festival experience. Orange invest in creating awareness outside the festival. In 2007, for example, Orange created an online and WAP competition for festival tickets. This was called 'Spot the bull' and involved people visiting the website, looking at live webcam pictures of a bull in a field, and then picking the spot they thought the bull would be at a certain time. There were over 250,000 entries, with those closest winning festival tickets.

However, the primary concern for Orange has been the visitor experience and it has used the festival to develop closer bonds with people, without any blatant promotional activity. When it first became involved with the festival it considered the issues visitors face when attending the festival, and it became apparent that Orange had an excellent opportunity to add value to the visitors' festival experience. Visitors are camping at the festival for three days, often in adverse weather conditions, and a major problem is that their phones quickly run out of charge as batteries do not last more than 24 hours. The answer for Orange, of course, was to provide phone-recharging facilities, and at the same time demonstrate its sustainability ethos, by providing eco-energy solutions.

So, in 2003 Orange trialled a truck for phone-charging at the event, and the response was unexpectedly strong. In 2005, the Orange 'chill 'n' charge' tent was created. This was an orange-coloured festival tent with both phone-charging and Internet facilities.

At the 2007 festival, the 'chill 'n' charge' tent carried no branding, it was simply a large tent, coloured orange. Research indicated that the tent was easily recognised as an 'Orange experience', and did not therefore need to be branded. Not using the logo was also compatible with the festival spirit and the need to play down obvious corporate and commercial initiatives. Over 50,000 people now use the 'chill 'n' charge' tent.

Orange also provided broadband 'pods'. These enabled people to check their emails, log on to their social networking site and upload pictures of what they had seen or tell their friends what they were up to, from the 'chill 'n' charge' tent.

Festivals can also be used to test new ideas. For example, Orange launched a 'pic stick' for the Glastonbury event. By attaching a mobile to a simple stick, visitors can take pictures over the heads of the crowd, of the performers on stage. Another idea involved wind chargers for mobile phones. The branded wind chargers were easily attached to a tent, but at the time they for demonstration rather than for sale. Despite that, the wind chargers generated a great deal of publicity, to the extent that people are still making enquiries about how to get them.

At the 2008 festival Orange introduced the 'Dance Charger'. This used kinetic energy to create power for mobile technology. In 2009 it was the Power Pump, which generated electricity using the energy created from a traditional foot pump, and in 2010 Orange introduced their Power Wellies. These converted heat into current and the product won *Time Magazine*'s '50 best inventions of 2010'.

In 2011 Orange continued their eco-energy developments. This time it was the Orange 'Sound Charge'. This device, developed in collaboration with GotWind who work in renewable energy, uses a twist on existing technology. This technique works by reversing the use of a product called Piezoelectric Film. The modified film can absorb invisible sound pressure waves. When placed inside a T-shirt, surrounding sound can be converted into energy. In addition, the Piezoelectric Film panel and electronics can be removed easily, in order that the shirt can be washed.

It is estimated that the device, when exposed to sound levels of around 80dB, approximately those experienced in a busy street, will generate up to 6 watt hours (W/h) of power over the course of the weekend festival. This is sufficient to charge two standard mobile phones or one Smartphone. What this means is that people can charge their mobile phones while listening to bands.

Orange has worked with the Glastonbury Festival over many years now and has become an integral part of the event. Orange has tried to provide eco-friendly solutions to enhance the festival-goer's experience. Their presence and branding activities are subtle and low-key, in keeping with the festival experience and ethos.

*This minicase was written by Chris Fill using a variety of sources including Knoepke (2011); Prince (2009); Bartlett (2007); Orange (2011); www.orange.co.uk/glastonbury; www.glastonburyfestivals.co.uk/history/2011/.*

| Exhibit 18.1 | **Orange 'chill 'n' charge' tent at Glastonbury Festival** |
|---|---|
| | *Source*: Press Association Images |

# Introduction

Orange's involvement with the Glastonbury Festival, described in the minicase, shows how the brand has immersed itself in its target audience. This has been achieved without overt advertising or blatant offers, but through an enhancement of the visitors' experience at the Glastonbury Festival. This brand experience approach has become a popular way of developing brands, and their relationships with customers, and is explored further in this chapter.

Orange also use sales promotion in particular circumstances, but not at the festival. The main task of sales promotion is to encourage the target audience to behave in a particular way, often to buy a product. Advertising, on the other hand, is usually geared towards developing market awareness. These two tools set out to accomplish tasks at each end of the attitudinal spectrum: the conative and cognitive elements respectively. Just as advertising is used to work over the long term, sales promotion can achieve upward shifts in sales in the short term.

Sales promotion offers buyers additional value, as an inducement to generate an immediate sale. These inducements can be targeted at consumers, distributors, agents and members of the sales force. A whole range of network members can benefit from the use of sales promotion.

This promotional tool is traditionally referred to as a form of *below-the-line communication* because, unlike advertising, there are no commission payments from media owners with this form of communication. The costs are borne directly by the organisation initiating the activity, which in most cases is a manufacturer, producer or service provider.

The second part of this chapter deals with another below-the-line approach: field marketing. Field marketing has emerged out of what was formally referred to as *merchandising* but now encompasses a wider range of activities, one of which is experiential marketing, again a growing and important aspect of marketing communications for several product categories.

# Understanding the value of sales promotions

There are many sales promotion techniques, but they all offer a direct inducement or an incentive to encourage receivers of these promotional messages to buy a product/service sooner rather than later. The inducement (for example, price deals, coupons, premiums) is presented as an added value to the basic product, one that is intended to encourage buyers to act 'now' rather than later. Sales promotion is used, therefore, principally as a means to accelerate sales. The acceleration represents the shortened period of time in which the transaction is completed relative to the time that would have elapsed had there not been a promotion. This action does not mean that an extra sale has been achieved, just that a potential future exchange is confirmed and transacted now.

Sales promotions consist of a wide range of tools and methods. These instruments are considered in more detail later in this chapter, but consideration of what constitutes sales promotion methods is important. In many cases, price is the determinant variable and can be used to distinguish between instruments. Sales promotions are often perceived purely as a price-discounting mechanism through price deals and the use of coupons. This, however, is not the whole picture, as there are many other ways in which incentives can be offered to buyers.

Reference has already been made to the idea that sales promotions are a way of providing value, and it is this value orientation that should be used when considering the nature and essential characteristics of sales promotions. Peattie and Peattie (1994) established a useful

| Table 18.1 | A value orientation of sales promotions |
| --- | --- |

| Value element | Explanation |
| --- | --- |
| Value-increasing | Value is increased by offering changes to the product quantity/quality or by lowering the price. Generally used and perceived as effective over the short term. |
| Value-adding | Value is added by offering something to augment the fundamental product/price offering. Premiums (gifts), information or opportunities can be offered as extras and the benefits realised over different periods of time: delayed (postal premiums), accumulated (loyalty programmes) or instant (scratch and win competitions). These have the potential to add value over the longer term. |

*Source*: Peattie and Peattie (1994).

way of discriminating between price and non-price sales promotion instruments. These are set out in Table 18.1 where reference is made to sales promotions that are value-increasing and sales promotions that are value-adding.

This demarcation is important because a large amount of research into sales promotion has been based on value-increasing approaches, most notably price deals and coupons (Gupta, 1988; Blattberg and Neslin, 1990; Krishna and Zhang, 1999). This tends to distort the way sales promotions are perceived and has led to some generalisations about the overall impact of this promotional discipline. There is a large range of other sales promotion instruments which add value, enhance the offering and provide opportunities to drive longer-term benefits (see Table 18.2). However, according to Gilbert and Jackaria (2002) research into these was limited, and it appears that little has changed in the past ten years.

As a result of this diversity of sales promotion instruments, it should be no surprise to learn that they are used for a wide range of reasons. Sales promotions can be targeted, with considerable precision, at particular audiences, and there are three broad audiences at whom sales promotions can be targeted: consumers, members of the distribution or channel network, and the sales forces of both manufacturers and resellers. It should be remembered that the

| Table 18.2 | A typology of sales promotion |
| --- | --- |

| Value-increasing (alters price/quantity or price/quality equation) | Value-adding (offers 'something extra' while leaving core product and price unchanged) |
| --- | --- |
| Discount pricing | Samples |
| Money-off coupons | Special features (limited editions) |
| Payment terms (e.g. interest-free credit) | Valued packaging |
| Refunds | Product trial |
| Guarantees | In-pack gifts |
| Multipack or multi-buys | In-mail gifts |
| Quantity increases | Piggy back gifts |
| Group buying | Gift coupons |
| Buybacks | Information (e.g. brochure, catalogue) |
|  | Clubs or loyalty programmes |
|  | Competitions/prize draws |

accuracy of these promotional tools means that many sub-groups within these broad groups can be reached quickly and accurately. However, sales promotions campaigns can backfire. When KFC offered a downloadable coupon that was endorsed by Oprah Winfrey, franchises could not keep pace with demand, especially as KFC had not placed any control or limit on the number of coupons that could be downloaded. The reasons why organisations use sales promotions are set out at Table 18.3.

As if in an attempt to categorise and manage this list, Lee (2002) suggests that the main reasons for the use of sales promotions can be reduced to four:

- as a reaction to competitor activities;
- as a form of inertia – this is what we have always done;
- as a way of meeting short-term sales objectives;
- as a way of meeting long-term objectives.

The first three are used widely, and Lee comments that many brand owners use sales promotion as a panic measure when competitors threaten to lure customers away. Cutting prices is undoubtedly a way of prompting a short-term sales response but it can also undermine a longer-term brand strategy.

| Table 18.3 | Reasons for the use of sales promotions |
| --- | --- |

| Reason | Explanation |
| --- | --- |
| Reach new customers | They are useful in securing trials for new products and in defending shelf space against anticipated and existing competition. |
| Reduce distributor risk | The funds that manufacturers dedicate to them lower the distributor's risk in stocking new brands. |
| Reward behaviour | They can provide rewards for previous purchase behaviour. |
| Retention | They can provide interest and attract potential customers and, in doing so, encourage them to provide personal details for further communications activity. |
| Add value | They can encourage sampling and repeat purchase behaviour by providing extra value (superior to competitors' brands) and a reason to purchase. |
| Induce action | They can instil a sense of urgency among consumers to buy while a deal is available. They add excitement and interest at the point of purchase to the merchandising of mature and mundane products. |
| Preserve cash flow | Since sales promotion costs are incurred on a pay-as-you-go basis, they can spell survival for smaller, regional brands that cannot afford big advertising programmes. |
| Improve efficiency | Sales promotions allow manufacturers to use idle capacity and to adjust to demand and supply imbalances or softness in raw material prices and other input costs, while maintaining the same list prices. |
| Integration | They can provide a means of linking together other tools of the promotional mix. |
| Assist segmentation | They allow manufacturers to price discriminate among consumer segments that vary in price sensitivity. Most manufacturers believe that a high-list, high-deal policy is more profitable than offering a single price to all consumers. A portion of sales promotion expenditures, therefore, consists of reductions in list prices that are set for the least price-sensitive segment of the market. |

## Viewpoint 18.1    Trident uses Beyoncé

For the price of a tube of chewing gum, Trident offered music fans an opportunity to see Beyoncé at the O2Arena. In order to promote awareness of the sales promotion event various stunts were staged. The first was in Piccadilly Circus, London, where 100 lookalike Beyoncés performed a flashdance, and in doing so attracted extensive media coverage and over a million views of YouTube. Tickets were given to people donating to buskers who were hired to cover various Beyoncé tracks, to people who sang Beyoncé numbers in the Lucky Voice karaoke bar and to the winners in a an enormous game of musical chairs held in a shopping centre. As a result of this activity over 67,000 visited the Trident Unwrapped website.

Downloading discount vouchers is now commonplace for many people. To capitalise on this, the convenience store Spar ran an online game called Shelf Sniper. This involved shooting products on a moving conveyor using the mouse to control a barcode scanner. By reaching level two of the game, individuals won a £1 voucher redeemable against £10 worth of shopping.

*Source*:   Based on Wallace (2010); Benady (2009).

**Question:**    Why have these brands used games and events to run the promotion?

**Task:**        What game might you use to support a sales promotion for a travel company?

Not too many years ago sales promotions were regarded as a key way of developing sales, particularly in the grocery market. However, the use of sales promotions has stagnated and in particular the use of on-pack promotions, bonus packs, competitions and price deals have failed to maintain the growth of previous years. Reasons for the decline include changing consumer behaviour, the rise of new interactive media and a distinct lack of innovation in the industry. Another important factor has been the expectations and drive of resellers, and the main supermarket chains in particular. They desire sales promotion programmes that are exclusive to them as this is seen as a major way of developing their retail brands. Supermarkets have effectively become media owners as their store space represents an opportunity for brand owners to promote their brands. On-pack promotions for individual stores are often too expensive and uneconomic so this form of promotion has suffered a great deal. Therefore, any form of sales promotion activity within their environments should be exclusive and tied into their brand.

New solutions have had to be found, and as Barrand (2004) suggests, the use of digital media and the integration of sales promotion within other campaigns has been successful. SMS, email, viral campaigns and the Internet are being used increasingly to drive sales by providing the veritable 'call-to-action', for a long time the province of sales promotion activities.

In the 1990s sales promotions were a potent part of the marketing communications mix. Their use fell but the recession revived them as consumers look for deals and means of saving money. However, the overall trend is to reduce the number of sales promotion events. This is because most major supermarkets try to control their in-store environments, reduce the amount of clutter and run their own promotions, designed to generate store traffic. As a result there has been an increase in what is referred to as *in-store* marketing, a small increase in the number of joint promotions between marketers and retailers, and huge interest in group-based discounts.

# The role of sales promotion

The role of sales promotion has changed significantly over recent years. At one time, when the largest proportion of communications budgets was normally allocated to advertising, the role of sales promotion was essentially behavioural – that is, selling. Now, at a time when advertising is not always the dominant discipline, the role of sales promotion might be engagement. This can be achieved through adding value to a brand as well as still selling product. In situations where sales promotion has assumed the focus of the communications spend, for reasons that are set out below, the role is also to help integrate aspects of the campaign. This is particularly evident in consumer markets that are mature, have reached a level of stagnation, and where price and promotion work are the few ways of inducing brand-switching behaviour.

## Short termism

The short-term financial focus of many developed economies has created a managerial climate, one that is geared to short-term performance and evaluation, over periods as short as 12 weeks. To accomplish this, communications tools are required that work quickly and impact directly upon sales. Many see this as leading to an erosion of the brand franchise.

## Managerial accountability

Following on from the previous reason is the increased pressure on marketing managers to be accountable for their communications expenditure. The results of sales promotion activities are more easily justified and understood than those associated with advertising. The number of coupons returned for redemption and the number of bonus packs purchased can be calculated quickly and easily, with little room for error or misjudgment. Advertising, however, cannot be so easily measured in either the short or the long term. The impact of this is that managers can relate the promotional expenditure to the bottom line much more comfortably with sales promotion than with advertising.

## Brand performance

Technological advances have enabled retailers to track brand performance more effectively. This in turn means that manufacturers can be drawn into agreements that promulgate in-store promotional activity at the expense of other more traditional forms of mass media promotion. Barcode scanners, hand-held, electronic shelf-checking equipment and computerised stock systems facilitate the tracking of merchandise, meaning that brand managers can be held responsible much more quickly for below-par performance.

## Brand expansion

As brand quality continues to improve and as brands proliferate on the shelves of increasingly large supermarkets, so the number of decisions that a consumer has to make also increases. As a result of multiple-brand decisions and a reduced amount of time to complete the shopping expedition, the tension associated with the shopping experience has increased considerably over the last decade.

Promotions make decision-making easier for consumers: they simplify a potentially difficult process. Thus, as brand choice increases, so the level of shopping convenience falls. The conflict this causes can be resolved by the astute use of sales promotions. Some feel that the cognitive shopper selects brands that offer increased value, which makes decision-making easier and improves the level of convenience associated with the shopping experience. However, should there be promotions on two offerings from an individual's repertoire then the decision-making is not necessarily made easier.

## Competition for shelf space

The continuing growth in the number of brands launched and the fragmentation of consumer markets mean that retailers have to be encouraged to make shelf space available. Sales promotions have helped manufacturers win valuable shelf space and assist retailers to attract increased levels of store traffic and higher utilisation of limited resources, but this approach is not always viable today.

The credibility of this promotional tool is low, as it is obvious to the receiver what the intention is of using sales promotion messages. However, because of the prominent and pervasive nature of the tool, consumers and members of the trade understand and largely accept the direct sales approach. Sales promotion is not a tool that hides its intentions, nor does it attempt to be devious (which is not allowed, by regulation).

The absolute costs of sales promotion are low, but the real costs need to be evaluated once a campaign has finished and all redemptions received and satisfied. The relative costs can be high, as not only do the costs of the premium or price discount need to be determined, but also the associated costs of additional transportation, lost profit, storage and additional time spent organising and administering a sales promotion campaign need to be accounted for.

In its favour, sales promotion allows for a high degree of control. Management is able to decide just when and where a sales promotion will occur and also estimate the sales effect. Sales promotions can be turned on and off quickly and adjusted to changed market conditions.

The intended message is invariably the one that is received, as there is relatively little scope for it to be corrupted or damaged in transmission. However, this view needs to be tempered by some of the problems companies have experienced by not thinking through the sales promotion exercise in the first place, only to find themselves exposed to exploitation and financial embarrassment.

***

| Scholars' paper 18.1 | Making mental adjustments to spend on promotions |
| --- | --- |

**Stilley, K.M. Inman, J.J., Wakefield, K.L. (2010) Spending on the Fly: Mental Budgets, Promotions, and Spending Behavior, *Journal of Marketing*, May, 74(3), 34–47.**

The authors develop ideas about how shoppers leave room in their mental budgets when in-store, to make unplanned purchases. They explore how the impact of promotions depends on whether a person in-store considers using any slack remaining in their mental budget. The results indicate that promotions on unplanned grocery items generate incremental spending, which increases with income but only when the item is purchased after the in-store slack is exceeded.

# Sales promotion plans: the objectives

The objectives of using this tool are sales-oriented and geared to stimulating buyers either to use a product for the first time or to use it on a routine basis.

One objective of sales promotion activity is to prompt buyers into action, to initiate a series of behaviours that result in long-run purchase activity. These actions can be seen to occur in the conative stage of the attitudinal set. They reflect high or low involvement, and indicate

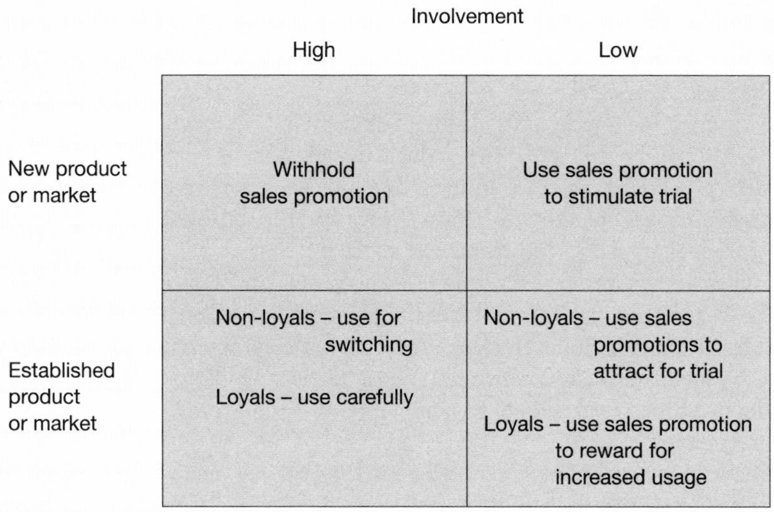

**Figure 18.1**   A sales promotion objectives grid

whether cognitive processing and persuasion occur via the central or peripheral routes of the ELM (Chapter 4). If the marketing objectives include the introduction of a new product or intention to enter a new market, then the key objective associated with low-involvement decisions and peripheral route processing is to stimulate trial use as soon as possible. When high-involvement decisions and central route processing are present, then sales promotions need to be withheld until a suitable level of attitudinal development has been undertaken by public relations and advertising activities.

If a product is established in a market, then a key objective should be to use sales promotions to stimulate an increase in the number of purchases made by current customers and to attract users from competing products (see Figure 18.1). The objectives, therefore, are either to increase consumption for established products or to stimulate trial by encouraging new buyers to use a product. Once this has been agreed, the desired trial and usage levels need to be determined for each of the target audiences. Before discussing these aspects, it is necessary first to review the manner in which sales promotions are thought to influence the behaviour of individuals.

# An overview of how sales promotions work

If the overriding objectives of sales promotions are to accelerate or bring forward future sales, the implication is that a behavioural change is required by the receiver for the sales promotion to be effective. The establishment of new behaviour patterns is the preferred outcome. If sales promotions are to work over the longer term, that is, to bring about repeat purchase behaviour, then the new behaviour patterns need to be learned and adopted on a permanent basis.

This is a complex task, and is referred to by behaviourists as *shaping*. The behaviourists' view is advocated by Rothschild and Gaidis (1981). They suggest that, by breaking the overall task into its constituent parts, a series of smaller sequential tasks can be learned. When the successive actions are aggregated the new desired pattern of behaviour emerges. This view emphasises the impact of external stimuli in changing people's behaviour.

The cognitive view of the way sales promotions operate is based on the belief that consumers internally process relevant information about a sales promotion, including information about past experiences, and make a reasoned decision in the light of the goals and objectives that individuals set for themselves.

The ELM suggests that individuals using the peripheral route will only consider simplistic cues, such as display boards and price reduction signs. Individuals using the central route of the ELM have a higher need for information and will develop the promotional signal to evaluate the value represented by the relative price and the salient attributes of the promoted product, before making a decision (Inman et al., 1990).

An alternative view considers the role of information processing and the mental budgets people make when shopping. This involves the psychological allocation of money to different account categories, such as food, clothing, drink and entertainment, in a person's mind. Once each mental budget is exhausted, consumers resist further spending in that category. However, there are opportunities to trade off an under-spend in one category to support additional purchases in another.

Research also shows that consumers use mental budgeting processes for grocery shopping trips. These are expectations based on experiences developed through previous shopping excursions. From these experiences Stilley et al. (2010a) suggest that consumers allocate an itemised portion of their mental budget for planned, anticipated brand or category purchases. Consumers also allocate a proportion of their mental budget for in-store, unplanned decisions, as if they are preparing to take advantage of store suggestions and promotional offers. Of the many issues that arise, one concerns what shoppers do with what might be saved from both the planned and unplanned mental budgets and whether this influences their purchasing activities and willingness to take advantage of sales promotions.

Reinforcing work by Heilman, Nakamoto, and Rao (2002), Stilley et al. (2010b) agree that savings derived from the planned mental list 'only increase[s] spending on unplanned items after in-store slack is depleted'. Another finding is that some promotions can encourage unplanned purchases, savings from other promotions are just taken into the in-store slack. Stilley et al. (2010b) suggest that there are benefits for retailers arising from an understanding of mental budgets. For example, store layout should incorporate the placement of displays of full-price, high-margin unplanned items early in the path a customer takes around a store. Other low-margin, unplanned promotional items should be placed later in the store path.

The main difference between the views of the behaviourists and those of the cognitive school of thought is that the former stress the impact of externally generated stimuli, whereas the latter emphasise the complexity of internal information processing.

The increasing proportion of budgets being allocated to sales promotions, and temporary price reductions (TPRs) in particular, has prompted concern about the costs and overall impact of these activities. It might be reasonable to expect that the sales curve following a price-based promotion would look like that depicted in Figure 18.2. There is plenty of evidence that sales

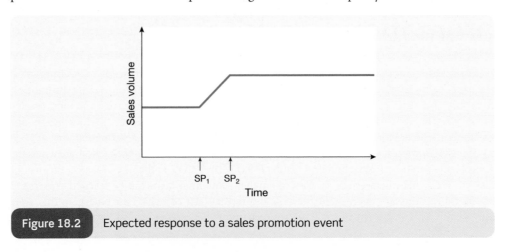

**Figure 18.2**　Expected response to a sales promotion event

volumes can be increased following use of a TPR (Ehrenberg, 2000). However, a long-term upward shift in demand is unrealistic, particularly in mature markets. Extra stock is being transferred to consumers, and therefore they have more than they require for a normal purchase cycle. Ehrenberg suggests that most people who use TPRs are actually infrequent purchasers of a given category. Research suggests that these types of promotion do not attract new buyers.

The graph shown in Figure 18.3 is more likely to occur, with sales volume falling in the period when buyers are loaded with stock and temporarily removed from the market. However, Dawes (2004) found that there were as many buyers in a market in the period following a promotion as there were when the TPR was running.

Promotional activity does not take place in a vacuum with new products: competitors will be attracted and some customers lost to competitive offerings; in mature markets, non-loyals will take advantage of a sales promotion and then revert to competitors' sales promotions when they re-enter the market. So, the third scenario is shown in Figure 18.4. The result is that overall demand for a brand *may* be reduced owing to the combined effects of competitive promotional activity. However, Dawes found that price promotions have a neutral impact on a brand, with the benefits of volume increases being countered by the consequent fall in profitability. It may be, therefore, that the second scenario is the more accurate interpretation.

Sales promotions incur a large number of hidden costs. It was stated earlier that the cost of a sales promotion is thought to be relatively low but, as Buzzell et al. (1990) and others have demonstrated, there are a host of other indirect costs that must be considered. Manufacturers, for example, use promotional deals to induce resellers to buy stock at a promotional price, in addition to their normal buying requirements. The additional stock is then held for resale at a later date, at regular retail prices. The effect of this forward buying

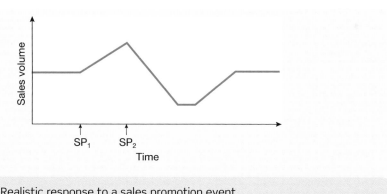

**Figure 18.3**   Realistic response to a sales promotion event

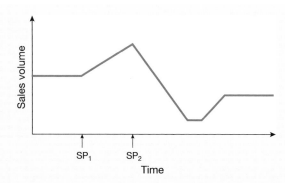

**Figure 18.4**   The destructive effect of competitive sales promotions

on the costs of the reseller can be enormous. Buzzell et al. point out that the promotional stock attracts higher interest charges, storage costs, expenses associated with the transfer of stock to different geographical areas of the organisation and the costs associated with keeping normal and promotional stock separate. When these are added to the manufacturer's forward buying costs, it is probable, they conclude, that the costs outweigh the benefits of the sales promotion exercise.

As if to demonstrate this point, of sales promotions, and BOGOFS in particular, are used by supermarkets and brand owners because they can change consumer purchasing patterns and can get consumers to try a new product. Indeed, Simms (2007) reports that they are just as effective as television advertising in encouraging trial. There are, however, several problems with BOGOFS. According to Binet, cited by Simms, 84 per cent of trade promotions are unprofitable. This year's volumes get added into next year's targets, so manufacturers chase increased volumes as average prices fall, with the net effect of diluting profits.

Promotions give a brand presence through extra facings, but they also incur difficulties for retailers. This is because of the impact promotions can have on the relatively stable logistics associated with normal trading patterns. The capacity that stores and lorries have is finite and known. Goods are moved by lorry from warehouses to stores whose sales performance is known. If a promotion is added to this mix, these logistics patterns are thrown into temporary chaos as both the stores and the transportation create room for the promotion at the expense of other items and higher margins.

These activities suggest that the relationship between the members of the network is market-oriented rather than relational. However, many of these extra costs are unknown, and the resellers are unaware of the costs they are absorbing as a result of the deal. In the future, resellers and manufacturers should work together on such promotions and attempt to uncover all the costs involved to ensure that the exercise is successful for both parties.

Not only the short-term costs associated with a sales promotion but also the long-term costs must be evaluated. Jones (1990) refers to this as the *double jeopardy of sales promotions*. He argues that manufacturers who participate extensively in short-term sales promotions, mainly for defensive reasons, do so at the expense of profit. The generation of sales volume and market share is at the expense of profit. The long-term effects are equally revealing. As the vast majority of sales promotions are TPRs, the opportunity to build a consumer franchise, where the objective is the development of brand identity and loyalty, is negated. Evidence shows that as soon as a sales promotion is switched off, so any increased sales are also terminated until the next promotion. The retaliatory effect that TPRs have on competitors does nothing to stabilise what Jones calls 'volatile demand', where the only outcome, for some products, is decline and obscurity.

Sales promotions can lead consumers to depend on the presence of a promotion before committing to a purchase. If the preferred product does not carry a coupon, premium or TPR, then they may switch to a competitor's product that does offer some element of increased value. A related issue concerns the speed at which sales promotions are reduced following the introduction of a new product. If the incentives are removed too quickly, it is probable that consumers will have been unable to build a relationship with the product. If the incentives are sustained for too long, then it is possible that consumers have only identified a product by the value of the incentive, not the value of the product itself. The process by which a sales promotion is removed from a product is referred to as fading, and its rate can be crucial to the successful outcome of a product launch and a sales promotion activity.

> ### Scholars' paper 18.2     Promotions and the double jeopardy
>
> Ehrenberg, A.S.C., Goodhardt, G.J. and Barwise, T.P. (1990) Double Jeopardy Revisited, *Journal of Marketing*, 54 (July), 82–91.
>
> The double jeopardy phenomenon is well established and understood. This paper, written by a distinguished array of authors, is used to explain and describe the wide range of empirical evidence for the existence of double jeopardy, the various theories that account for its occurrence, the issues and practical implications. Once they have read this, readers might be interested to read the following paper by Jones in the same year:
>
>     Jones, P.J. (1990) The double jeopardy of sales promotions, *Harvard Business Review*, (September/October), 145–52.

# Retention programmes

Despite questions about the use of sales promotions to build loyalty, the growth of retention programmes has been a significant promotional development in recent years, as demonstrated by the Tesco and Nectar programmes. The growth of retention, or loyalty, schemes has been encouraged by the widespread use of swipe cards. Users are rewarded with points each time a purchase is made. This is referred to as a 'points accrual programme', whereby loyal users are able to build up the necessary points, which are stored (often) on a card, and 'cashed in' at a later date for gifts or merchandise. The benefit for the company supporting the scheme is that the promised rewards motivate customers to accrue more points and, in doing so, increase their switching costs, effectively locking them into the loyalty programme and preventing them from moving to a competitor brand. Smart cards, which have a small microprocessor embedded, can record enormous amounts of information, which is updated each time a purchase is made. However, people have so many cards that a large number of loyalty cards are never used, or even scrapped.

Not only have loyalty schemes for frequent flyers been very successful, but the cards are also used to track individual travellers. Airlines are able to offer cardholders particular services, such as special airport lounges and magazines. Through its links to a database, the card also enables a traveller's favourite seat and dietary requirements to be offered. In addition, the regular accumulation of air miles fosters continuity and, hence, loyalty, through which business travellers can reward themselves with leisure travel. However, the airlines' desire to develop relationships with their customers might not be fully reciprocated, as many customers seek only convenience.

Perhaps the attention given to loyalty and retention issues is misplaced, because marketing is concerned with customer management, and that involves the identification, anticipation and satisfaction of customer needs. If these needs are being met properly, it might be reasonable to expect that customers would return anyway, reducing the need for overt 'loyalty' programmes. The withdrawal by Debenhams from the Nectar scheme in 2008 was made in order to better reward store-card holders, at a time when the trading environment was getting tighter. There is an argument that these schemes are important not because of the loyalty aspect but because the programme allows for the collection of up-to-date customer information and then the use of the data to make savings in the supply chain.

There has been a proliferation of loyalty cards, reflecting the increased emphasis on keeping customers rather than constantly finding new ones, and there is evidence that sales lift by about 2 or 3 per cent when a loyalty scheme is launched. However, there is little evidence to support the notion that sales promotions, and in particular the use of premiums, are capable of encouraging loyalty, whether that be defined as behavioural and/or attitudinal. Loyalty schemes do enable organisations to monitor and manage stock, use direct marketing to cross- and up-sell customers, and manage their portfolio in order to consolidate (increase?) customers' spending in a store. Whether loyalty is being developed by encouraging buyers to make repeat purchases, or whether the schemes are merely sales promotion techniques that encourage extended and consistent purchasing patterns is debatable. Customer retention is a major issue and a lot of emphasis, possibly misplaced, has been given to loyalty schemes as a means of achieving retention targets.

There are views that loyalty schemes are not only misguided but have cost industry a huge amount of money. Hastings and Price (2004), for example, have expressed strong views about the notion and viability of so-called 'loyalty' and points-based schemes. They claim that loyalty schemes are misunderstood for two main reasons. First, is the assumption that loyalty can be bought when, like love, true loyalty can only be given. Second, there is an assumption that points-based schemes can be profit centres.

## Viewpoint 18.2    Barclaycard score with loyalty pounds

Barclaycard Freedom is a card-based loyalty scheme and to be successful needs to engage two different audiences. One of these is Barclay's bank customers and the other is local retail businesses who provide the range of benefits arising from the scheme.

Knowing that a new card scheme had to be simple to use or risk being rejected, it was decided not to issue a new card but enable customers to use their current Barclaycard. Also, rather than award points it was decided to reward users with currency, pounds and pence which could be redeemed at the local businesses participating in the scheme.

To reach customers, the campaign featured a welcome pack that was mailed to each customer. Not only did this list the participating retailers but also provided directions on how to reach them. The next part of the campaign featured the use of television and national press advertising. The TV ad used music, 'Green Onions' by Booker T & The MGs, synchronised to someone shown using their Barclaycard. This was used to associate the simplicity and ease of use for people to do their shopping with Barclaycard Freedom. This music was also used within a virtual game called High Street Beats. This involved customers creating the 'Green Onions' track by hitting certain shopping items.

To reach and attract new businesses, the system was enabled through each retailer's point of sale system. However, it was the opportunity to reach a much wider audience, to attract more customers and the overall scale of the loyalty scheme that was the main selling point. Direct mail and telemarketing were used, and for large retailers, the Barclays sales force provided face-to-face contact to gain participation.

The scheme attracted 20,000 retail outlets and 13 per cent of Barclaycard's customers were participating on a regular basis. Spend at partner businesses rose by 14 per cent in the year after the launch and an average of £4.56 is deducted by each customer from their monthly bill.

*Source*:   Based on Bolger (2011); Jones (2010).

**Question:**   Are loyalty schemes overrated by marketers or are there real benefits for customers?

**Task:**   Make notes outlining about what you feel should be the next campaign to support Barclaycard Freedom. What would be your objectives and how would you formulate your mix?

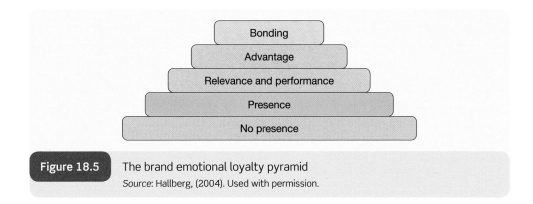

**Figure 18.5** The brand emotional loyalty pyramid
*Source*: Hallberg, (2004). Used with permission.

Hallberg (2004) reports a major study involving in excess of 600,000 in-depth consumer interviews. The study identifies different levels of loyalty and concludes that significant financial returns are gained only when the highest level of loyalty is achieved. These levels of loyalty are set out in Figure 18.5. Hallberg refers to the impact of emotional loyalty, a non-purchase measurement of attachment to a brand:

- At the 'no presence' level consumers are unaware of a brand and so there is no emotional loyalty.
- At the 'presence' level there is awareness but emotional loyalty is minimal.
- At the 'relevance and performance' level the consumer begins to feel that the brand is acceptable in terms of meeting their needs.
- At the 'advantage' level consumers should feel that the brand is superior with regard to a particular attribute.
- At the 'bonding' level emotional loyalty is at its highest because consumers feel the brand has several unique properties. They love the brand.

Loyalty schemes are exponentially effective when consumers reach the bonding stage. Although sales generally increase the further up the pyramid consumers move, it is only at the 'bonding' stage that sales start to reflect the emotional attachment people feel towards the brand. Hallberg refers to the success and market leadership that Tesco has achieved, but the principles established through this study should apply to loyalty programmes regardless of category or sector.

There is a proliferation of loyalty programmes to the extent that Capizzi et al. (2004) suggest that the market is mature. They also argue that five clear trends within the loyalty market can be identified (see Table 18.4).

These trends suggest that successful sales promotions schemes will be those that enable members to perceive significant value associated with their continued association with a scheme. That value will be driven by schemes run by groups of complementary brands, which use technology to understand customer dynamics and communications that complement their preferred values. The medium-term goal might be that these schemes should reflect customers' different relationship needs and recognise the different loyalty levels desired by different people.

| Table 18.4 | Five loyalty trends |
| --- | --- |
| **Trend** | **Explanation** |
| Ubiquity | Loyalty programmes have proliferated in most mature markets and many members have little interest in them other than the functionality of points collection. Managers are trying to reduce communication costs by moving the scheme online but also need to be innovative. |
| Coalition | Schemes run by a number of different organisations in order to share costs, information and branding (e.g. Nectar) appear to be the dominant structure industry model. |
| Imagination | Opportunities to exploit technologies and niche markets will depend on creativity and imagination in order to get customer data to feed into the loyalty system. Employ IST imaginatively. |
| Wow | To overcome consumer lethargy and boredom with loyalty schemes, many rewards in future will be experiential, emotional, unique in an attempt to appeal to life stage and aspirational lifestyle goals – to wow them. Differentiate to stand out. |
| Analysis | To be competitive the use of customer data analytics and business intelligence is becoming critical, if only to feed CRM programmes. Collect and analyse customer information effectively. |

*Source*: Adapted from Capizzi et al. (2004).

# Sales promotions: methods and techniques

As established earlier, sales promotions seek to offer buyers additional value, as an inducement to generate an immediate sale. These inducements can be targeted at consumers, distributors, agents and members of the sales force. A whole range of network members can benefit from the use of sales promotion.

The techniques considered in this section attempt to reflect the range and variety of techniques that are used to add value and induce a sale sooner rather than later. The nature and characteristics of the target audiences mean that different techniques work in different ways to achieve varying objectives. Consideration is given to the range of tasks that need to be accomplished among two key audiences: resellers and consumers.

The range of techniques and methods used to add value to offerings is enormous but there are growing doubts about the effectiveness and profitability associated with some sales promotions. Sales promotions used by manufacturers to communicate with resellers are aimed at encouraging resellers to either try new products or purchase more of the ones they currently stock. To do this, trade allowances, in various guises, are the principal means.

The majority of sales promotions are those used by manufacturers to influence consumers. Again, the main tasks are to encourage trial or increase product purchase. A range of techniques, from sampling and coupons to premiums, contests and sweepstakes, are all used with varying levels of success, but there has been a distinct shift away from traditional promotional instruments to the use of digital media in order to reflect consumers' preferences and media behaviour.

| Table 18.5 | Principal audiences and sales promotion goals | | |
|---|---|---|---|
| **Audience** | **Objectives** | **Explanation** | **Methods** |
| **Manufacturers to resellers** | For new products: *Sampling and trial* | For new products it is important to create adequate channels of distribution in anticipation of consumer demand. | Allowances: *Buying Count and recount Buy-back Advertising* |
| | | The task of marketing communications is to encourage resellers to distribute a new product and to establish trial behaviour. | |
| | For established products: *Usage* | One of the key objectives of manufacturers is to motivate distributors to allocate increased shelf space to a product thereby (possibly) reducing the amount of shelf space allocated to competitors. | Dealer contests Dealer conventions and meetings Training and support |
| | | The task of marketing communications, therefore, is to encourage resellers to buy and display increased amounts of the manufacturer's products and establish greater usage. | |
| **Manufacturers to consumers** | For new users: *Stimulate trial* | Before a customer buys a product they need to test or trial the product. Through the use of coupons, sampling and other techniques (see below), sales promotions have become an important element in the new product launch and introduction processes. | Sampling Coupons Price offs Bonus packs Refunds and rebates |
| | For established customers: *Increase product usage* | In mature markets customers need to be encouraged to keep buying a product. This can be achieved by attracting users from competitive brands, by converting non-users and by developing new uses. | Premiums Contests and sweepstakes |

The following two tables set out information about key sales promotions techniques used between manufacturers and their intermediary partners, and with consumers. It should also be appreciated that sales promotions are used by retailers to influence consumers and between manufacturers and dealer sales force teams, although these are not itemised here. Table 18.5 depicts information about the audiences and reasons for using sales promotions. Table 18.6 provides information about the various sales promotion methods and techniques.

Group buying agents such as Groupon, Wahanda, and LivingSocial have spearheaded the rise of this form of discounting. Clark (2010) refers to Groupon as the leading provider, which originated in Chicago, where coupon use is a natural part of everyday buying, unlike the UK and Europe, where coupon usage is a minority activity and often favoured by deal chasers. Groupon has over 50 million people subscribing to daily email updates (Birchall, 2011).

| Table 18.6 | Principal audiences and sales promotion methods |
| --- | --- |

| Audience | Method | Explanation |
| --- | --- | --- |
| **Manufacturers to resellers** | **Advertising allowance** | A percentage allowance is given against a reseller's purchases during a specified campaign period. Instead of providing an allowance against product purchases, an allowance can be provided against the cost of an advertisement or campaign. |
| | **Buying allowance** | In return for specific orders between certain dates, a reseller will be entitled to a refund or allowance of x per cent off the regular case or carton price. |
| | **Count and recount** | Manufacturers may require resellers to clear old stock before a new or modified product is introduced. One way this can be achieved is to encourage resellers to move stock out of storage and into the store. The count and recount method provides an allowance for each case shifted into the store during a specified period of time. |
| | **Buy-back** | Purchases made after the count and recount scheme (up to a maximum of the count and recount) are entitled to an allowance to encourage stores to replenish their stocks (with the manufacturer's product and not that of a competitor). |
| | **Dealer contests** | Used to hold a reseller's attention by focusing them on a manufacturer's products, not a competitor's. |
| | **Dealer conventions and meetings** | These enable informal interaction between a manufacturer and its resellers and can aid the development and continuance of good relations between the two parties. |
| | **Training and support** | This is an important communications function, especially when products are complex or subject to rapid change, as in IT markets. This can build stronger relationships and manufacturers have greater control over the messages that the resellers transmit. |
| **Manufacturers to consumers** | **Sampling** | Although very expensive, sampling is an effective way of getting people to try a product. Trial-size versions of the actual product are given away free. Sampling can also take the form of demonstrations, trial-size packs that have to be purchased or free use for a certain period of time. |
| | **Coupons** | These are vouchers or certificates that entitle consumers to a price reduction on a particular product. The value of the reduction or discount is set and the coupon must be presented at purchase. |
| | **Price offs** | These are a direct reduction in the purchase price, with the offer clearly labelled on the package or point of purchase display. |
| | **Bonus packs** | These offer more product for the regular pack price, typically a 2 for 1 offer. They provide direct impact at the point of purchase and represent extra value. |
| | **Refunds and rebates** | Used to invite consumers to send in a proof of purchase and in return receive a cash refund. |
| | **Premiums** | Items of merchandise that are offered free or at a low cost in return for product purchase. |
| | **Contests and sweepstakes** | A contest is a customer competition based on skill or ability. Entry requires a proof of purchase and winners are judged against a set of predetermined criteria. A sweepstake determines winners by chance and proof of purchase is not required. There is no judging and winners are drawn at random. |

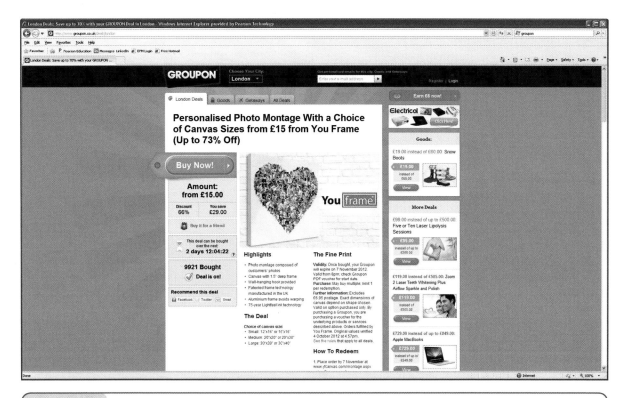

---

**Exhibit 18.2**   **Groupon**

The Groupon programme involves local businesses agreeing to offer a 50 to 70 per cent discount based on a minimum number of people taking up the offer. A further substantial share of the profit is then shared with the agent, if the deal attracts the required minimum number of participants. Each day, an email is sent to subscribers offering a range of discounts on local businesses.

Manning (2011) indicates that service providers such as restaurants and spas appear to be the most popular. Credit card details are taken from those opting to participate, and once the minimum number is reached, cards are debited and vouchers issued to be redeemed at the chosen business. This business model is both personalised and interactive and has proved to be attractive judging by the large number of organisations entering the market. For local businesses, group buying programmes force a compromise between poor financial return and the opportunity to attract large numbers of new customers and the potential repeat business. (See also Chapter 23.)

*Source*: Groupon.co.uk

---

**Viewpoint 18.3**   **A Blackberry is the prize**

Not all sales promotions are consumer-orientated. Trade promotions are used extensively within the b2b sector. For example, Research in Motion (RIM), owners of Blackberry, used an incentive-based programme as part of a campaign to establish RIM within the German market.

For RIM, Germany is a relatively small yet an emerging market. In order to capitalise on the opportunities, they needed a campaign that increased knowledge about RIM, and which drove sales. A campaign was developed for Mobilcom, a leading German network, in a call-centre environment. The plan was to increase product knowledge among Mobilcom's call-centre staff and to increase their sales by over 240 per cent.

With a budget of just £30,000, the six-week campaign called 'Wake up to Blackberry' had three core objectives. These were to:

- Increase knowledge via training held prior to the road show;
- Change perceptions through product demonstrations/road show: Blackberry isn't a stuffy, corporate brand but more an entertaining consumer brand that is approachable and easy to use;
- Increase sales from 480 over a six-week period to 1160.

The audience for the 'Wake up' campaign were 70 call-centre staff, each of whom was required to attend the road show and take part in training and the incentive.

At the start of the campaign emails were sent to all staff alerting them to the campaign and to generate interest and curiosity. When they arrived at their desks, they found a breakfast pack containing edible goodies in addition to details about the road show and the incentive scheme.

Training, in teams of 10, focused on Blackberry basics and was the first stage in trying to reposition the brand as a consumer smartphone. In essence this was about removing the barriers to selling Blackberry.

Next came the road show and product demonstrations. In the lobby staff received a product demonstration and literature about the product benefits and specifications. They also met with a Kylie Minogue look-alike, with whom they had their photo taken. A branded photo was printed out for the attendees to keep on their desk, in a branded frame, all designed to generate interest and word of mouth beyond the call centre.

There was also information about the incentive programme and prizes to be won. This involved a quiz based on the knowledge gained in their training session. For each Blackberry connection made, the salesperson was awarded €5. At the end of each week the person who achieved the greatest number of sales won a Blackberry smartphone. The incentive was run entirely online via a dedicated microsite which communicated weekly results, winners and regular message updates. An online gallery enabled attendees to view their photos with 'Kylie' and check the weekly winners.

All the objectives were met and the campaign was later rolled out to other call centres.

*Source*:   Ambition Communications (2011).

**Question:**   What do you believe might have been a core factor in this campaign? The incentive or the picture taken with the look-alike Kylie? Why?

**Task:**   If not Kylie, who would you choose to be associated with this type of campaign?

Whatever the promotion used, measurement and evaluation should be an integral part of the campaign. Measurement can be undertaken through a registration process, perhaps to claim a free gift. This approach enabled Orange to determine that its customers had 14 million free cinema trips over the five years their promotion had been running. It also helped to reveal that 3 million additional cinema visits had been stimulated and that Wednesday had become the most popular day to visit the cinema (Murphy, 2009).

# Other sales promotion devices

Table 18.6 provides a list of the main sales promotion devices used by organisations. In addition to these are various other sales promotion approaches, used either for particular audiences or situations.

The good old-fashioned 'brochure' is a sales promotion device that can be used to assist consumers, resellers and sales forces. Apart from the ability of the brochure to impart factual information about a product or service, brochures and sales literature stimulate purchase and serve to guide decisions. For service-based organisations, the brochure represents a temporary tangible element of the product. Inclusive tour operators, for example, might entice someone to book a holiday, but consumption may take place several months in the future. The brochure acts as a temporary product substitute and can be used to refresh expectations during the gestation period and remind significant other people of the forthcoming event (Middleton, 1989). Just as holiday photographs provide opportunities to relive and share past experiences, so holiday brochures help people to share and enjoy pre-holiday experiences and expectations. Consumption of inclusive tours, therefore, can be said to occur at the booking point, and the brochure extends or adds value to the holiday experience.

Sales literature can trigger awareness of potential needs. As well as this, it can be useful in explaining technical and complex products. For example, leaflets distributed personally at DIY stores can draw attention to a double-glazing manufacturer's products. Some prospective customers may develop an initial impression about the manufacturer, based on past experiences triggered by the literature, the quality of the leaflet and the way it was presented. The leaflet acts as a cue for the receiver to review whether there is a current need and, if there is, then the leaflet may be kept longer, especially where high involvement is present; value is thus added to the purchase experience.

Financial services companies use sales literature at various stages in the sales process. Mailers are used to contact prospective customers, corporate brochures are used to provide source credibility, booklets about the overall marketplace are left with clients after an initial discussion and product guides and brochures are given to customers after a transaction has been agreed. To help prevent the onset of cognitive dissonance, a company magazine is sent soon after the sale and at intermediate points throughout the year to cement the relationship between client and company.

An increasingly important and expensive approach is to license a TV cartoon character from *The Simpsons*, *Rugrats* or *South Park* or a cyber person such as Lara Croft who was used by Lucozade. These characters are used strategically to build brands, and part of the approach is to attract the attention of children and provide the parental agreement necessary for a purchase to be made.

Inevitably, there are issues concerning consistency of brand values and the need to prevent competitors using the same or similar characters to support their brands. It is also argued that in addition to a short-term sales increase there is a residual sales increase following promotions utilising these prime characters, especially if the promotion is based on a free gift or the chance to win an instant gift.

# Field marketing

Field marketing is a relatively new sector of the industry, one which seeks to provide support for the sales force and merchandising personnel, together with data collection and research facilities for clients. The sector started as a way of ensuring that products were accessible in retail outlets (McLuhan, 2007). The core function is merchandising and shelf-positioning skills, and as McLuhan reports 'at least 4 per cent of an fmcg product's sales depend on getting this right; the rate is higher for other product types' (p. 9).

Although this element remains important, field marketing has evolved so that it now encompasses ways in which people can experience a brand. This reflects an overall shift in marketing communications from one based largely on developing brand values through an emotional proposition, to one that emphasises changes in behaviour and calls-to-action.

The Field Marketing Council (FMC) states that the sector is about the use of people to communicate sales and marketing messages. This is quite an open remit and reflects the wide range of activities that practitioners within the area have recently encompassed. At a basic level, field marketing is concerned with getting free samples of a product into the hands of potential customers. At another level, field marketing is about creating an interaction between the brand and a new customer. At yet another level, it is about creating a personal and memorable brand experience for potential customers. The key to field marketing is the flexibility of services provided to clients. Sales forces can be hired on short-term contracts and promotional teams can be contracted to launch new products, provide samples (both in-store and door-to-door) and undertake a range of other activities that are not part of an organisation's normal promotion activities.

The decision about whether to own or to hire a sales force has to be based on a variety of criteria, such as the degree of control required over not only the salesperson, but also the message to be transmitted. A further criterion is flexibility. Ruckert et al. (1985) identified that in environments subject to rapid change, which brings uncertainty (for example because of shortening product lifecycles or major technological developments), the ability to adjust quickly the number of representatives in the distribution channel can be of considerable strategic importance. A further criterion is cost; for some the large fixed costs associated with a sales force can be avoided by using a commission-only team of representatives.

A large number of organisations choose to have their own sales force, but of these many use the services of a manufacturer's agent to supplement their activities. A number of pharmaceutical manufacturers use independent sales forces to supplement the activities of their own sales teams.

# Range of FM activities

Table 18.7 sets out the range of activities undertaken in the name of field marketing. To some extent it consists of tasks pulled from some of the five main promotional tools, repackaged and presented under a more contemporary title; for example, door-to-door and sales activities from personal selling, merchandising from both personal selling and sales promotion, sampling

| Table 18.7 | Essential features of field marketing activities |
| --- | --- |
| **Core activities** | **Essential features** |
| Sales | Provides sales force personnel on either a temporary or a permanent basis. This is for business-to-business and direct to the public. |
| Merchandising | Generates awareness and brand visibility through point-of-purchase placement, in-store staff training, product displays and leaflets. |
| Sampling | Mainly to the public at shopping centres and station concourses but also for business-to-business purposes. |
| Auditing | Used for checking stock availability, pricing and positioning. |
| Mystery shopping | Provides feedback on the level and quality of service offered by retail- and services-based staff. |
| Event marketing | Used to create drama and to focus attention at sports events, open-air concerts and festivals. Essentially theatrical or entertainment-based. |
| Door-to-door (home calls) | A form of selling where relatively uncomplex products and services can be sold through home visits. |

*Source*: Adapted from McLuhan (2000). Reproduced from *Marketing* magazine with the permission of the copyright owner, Haymarket Business Publications Limited.

(which is a straight sales promotions task) and event marketing from public relations. Field marketing is a response to market needs and is a development practitioners have pioneered to fulfil a range of customer needs that presumably had not been adequately satisfied.

Perhaps merchandising lies at the root of field marketing. This is concerned with the presentation and display of products in-store, in order to maximise impact, attention and 'pick-up' opportunities. Referred to as *point-of-sale (POS)*, these activities occur where a decision to purchase is made; normally this will be in the aisles.

POS is essentially about persuasion. This might be about using sampling to encourage customers to switch brands, or as Hilpern (2011) suggests, it can be concerned with convincing customers that they should buy the brand they were originally intending to purchase, a defensive orientation. Apart from aligning product labels, maximising shelf space usage for a brand and using shelf signage (barkers) effectively, a variety of new techniques are either being tested or are in use. For example, Lynx Excite have used a push button on the barker that releases a spray; Tesco use iPhone applications to allow shoppers to add to their virtual baskets by using a handset barcode scanner, and many retailers are experimenting with 3D signage (Hilpern, 2011).

Of central interest in merchandising is how and where products should be allocated within a scarce resource – namely, the capacity and location of shelf space. Academics are attracted by the theoretical, problem-solving and statistical issues, while practitioners, retailers, seek increased efficiency and profitability.

There has been extensive research, most of which concludes that the location of a product on a shelf has no major effect on the sales of a product (Russell and Urban, 2010). However, research by Drèze et al. (1994) cited by Russell and Urban, found that the 'vertical and horizontal positioning on the shelves for a number of (product) categories, led to an average difference in sales of 59 percent from the worst to the best position on the shelves. They also found that half of the categories had increased sales on the end of the display, while the other half favored the center.'

Field marketing can take place virtually anywhere, but common locations are in shopping centres and supermarkets where footfall is greatest. Typically these events require agency staff to dress up in an eye-catching way in order to form associations between the clothing and the brand (e.g. dressed in Mexican ponchos and sombreros to give out free samples of Pot Noodle in a supermarket). It is regarded as a cost-effective way of demonstrating a product, getting stand-out and creating opportunities for customers to trial a product with minimum risk. Field marketing is also used to sell relatively complex products where a degree of explanation is required (e.g. computers, broadband, TV and related products, or mobile phones).

---

## Viewpoint 18.4    Gillette cut it with field marketing

Gillette holds a dominant position in the razor market, with a reported 85 per cent of market share. This dominance is in part maintained by product innovations supported by communications designed to improve category usage.

The introduction of the Gillette Fusion Power 'Phenom' razor led to a campaign not only to introduce the razor and the supporting merchandise, but to also overcome the reluctance of many men to practise any form of skincare routine. The audience for the communication programme was aspirational males between the ages of 18 and 35. This is a difficult group to reach through conventional channels, especially as shops and stores are essentially a female-orientated environment.

The core activity for the campaign was to be based on a male-orientated introductory promotional discount. Product purchase then enabled entry into a competition.

Out-of-home media became the primary media channel. Sites associated with commuting in central London were selected. Digital six-sheet-poster sized advertising at all London rail terminals was used during the busiest parts of the day. Eye-catching moving imagery was used to introduced the Gillette

Series products, the 33 per cent price promotion, and an invitation to enter the competition. Using the tagline 'Live like a Champion – Experience the Best', the competition offered a choice of 'aspirational' man-based prizes. These included a tailor-made Savile Row suit, a supercar for the weekend, and a chauffeured speedboat trip to a show at the O2 arena.

Entry to the competition could only be made on a particular day, in a Superdrug store, through product purchase. Participation was assisted by GPS-based messaging to enable participants to text for the location of their nearest store.

On competition day, street teams toured the areas around the 50 busiest Superdrug stores, with the aim of grabbing the attention of consumers and to drive more shoppers into outlets. In addition to distributing conventional leaflets, the teams used 'bluecasting' pods, housed in branded Gillette rucksacks to communicate the competition and price promotion by broadcasting Bluetooth advertising to mobiles.

Inside the stores members of the field marketing teams attempted to engage potential customers by announcing the 33 per cent offer, explaining the benefits of Gillette's three-step grooming process, and of course handing out competition entry leaflets. They were supported by a 30-second in-store radio commercial, advertising the Gillette range and competition.

The campaign flowed into the following day where the same process was followed but this time the focus was on the Phenom razor, and the competition was replaced with the offer of a free skincare kit for those who purchased the Phenom razor.

PR support was provided by a £146,000 Lamborghini Gallardo car, strategically placed in the centre of London's Victoria station. This served to attract attention but also enabled the field marketing team to direct potential customers into Superdrug's store at the station.

The results and analysis of the campaign were extremely positive following the 10,622 Bluetooth mobile messages, 20,000 leaflets and 12,000 product samples. Eighty per cent of those who recalled the campaign rated it positively overall; they enjoyed the campaign and preferred it to conventional razor advertising. On the two in-store event days, sales of Gillette Fusion Power Phenom razors were six times greater in the 50 trial stores than in non-supported Superdrug control stores. In the same way, overall sales of Gillette Series products were three times greater than in the non-supported Superdrug control stores.

*Source*: Based on Barda (2009); Quilter (2009).

---

**Question:** Consider the view that launching new products into the grocery and fmcg markets can only be achieved through the use of field marketing.

**Task:** Make a list of the five critical activities a field marketing campaign must accomplish.

---

One of the reasons field marketing can take place at any location is thanks to digital technology. The use of apps and cloud technology in particular is helping to change the way in which the business works. Originally field marketing was about stock control and shelf positioning. These are essentially low-level jobs. The use of technology now allows field force agents to engage with in-store employees and this is enabled by real-time data and analysis. Through cloud technologies data can be accessed on demand. Without the need to manage hardware and software, field agents can present training materials, Web-based instruction tools, the latest product information, and even use tablets to present data about sales of brands in similar stores (Ryan, 2012). The use of real-time sales data allows for the identification of stores that show stock irregularities. Staff can then be sent out to the stores and locations where a problem needs to be fixed.

The second development, the use of apps (with tablets and smartphones), helps agents check that stores are stocking and presenting brands in the right way. Now they are able to photograph merchandising on shelves and record data. So, although field marketing is a more sophisticated business than it was originally, the operating margins have become much tighter, in turn generating a need to find alternative high-margin activities.

One way around this margin issue is to reduce costs, and the use of apps is a route forward some agencies are pursuing. So, rather than give a smartphone and an app to a paid agent, the new approach is to encourage the public to go into stores and get them to take pictures of stock and record simple information about the way products are displayed. They then upload the data for analysis by brand-owners, and get paid a small fee for their time and contribution. In a sense this is a variant on crowdsourcing and has raised alarm bells within the industry. Issues about consistency, coverage and ethics are voiced by those against this development. For field marketing agencies and their clients costs are halved.

So far the Field Agent app has been downloaded to over 10,000 smartphones in the UK, and according to Benady (2011) has approximately 1000 regular users. The app enables brands to upload tasks, for example, to check 100 Waitrose stores to see whether a particular item is being displayed correctly or that a promotion is well positioned. The task is then distributed to all users of the app who are near the target stores. This is based on information provided by the iPhones' geolocation technology. The offer could be £4–£6 to anyone who goes to the store, takes a picture of the promotional display and answers a few simple questions, such as how many products are on the shelf. Feedback can be received within minutes of a job being sent out (Benady, 2011).

---

### Scholars' paper 18.3    Give me the right space, please

**Russell, R.A. and Urban, T.L. (2010) The location and allocation of products and product families on retail shelves, *Annals of Operations Research*, 179(1), 131–47.**

As the title of the publication suggests, there is some complex maths in this paper. However, do not be put off by this as the paper provides some interesting insights into the shelf space allocation issue, and a rare literature review on the subject.

---

# Brand experience and events

A key aspect of field marketing concerns the growing interest in what is referred to as *experiential marketing* or *brand experience*. Many in the industry see their role as delivering brand-experience opportunities for their clients' customers. Others argue that brand experience occurs through various interactions with a brand: namely, purchasing, consumption and consideration. However, the term 'brand experience' appears to be owned by those in the field marketing industry and has evolved through the development of both sampling and event/roadshow activities. Unsurprisingly, therefore, mystery shopping has developed as an important aspect of field marketing. It is used increasingly by service-based operations, such as airlines, travel agents, restaurants and hotels, the intention being to understand how a customer experiences the service or purchase encounter and then feed the information into training and service improvements.

Exhibit 18.3    **Sampling and events associated with the WIRSPA campaign (see Chapter 10)**

*Source*: Bray Leino Ltd

Whether the brand experience industry lies inside or outside of field marketing is not particularly critical. However, what differentiates the experiential aspect from other FM activities is that it requires more precise targeting (not mass market) and it is more emotionally and physically engaging than sampling and many events or roadshows, which, in turn, Bashford (2004) claims can lead to stronger (positive) memories. She quotes Paul Ephremsen, a leading industry practitioner who says that field marketing is 'all about the numbers and not the interaction, and is driven by cost per sample', whereas brand experience is about 'creating an emotional bond between the brand and the consumer'.

The debate about what constitutes field marketing and experiential marketing is explored by Bashford (2007). She provides two definitions, set out in Table 18.8.

One of the essential tasks of field marketing is to continue to make brand signals available to consumers so that they can make the necessary brand associations that they have developed through advertising, brand and category experience. It is a matter of keeping brand values

| Table 18.8 | Two aspects of field marketing |
| --- | --- |

| Element | Explanation |
| --- | --- |
| Field marketing | The use of promotional staff in a marketing campaign to boost sales of a brand. Typically the field force will distribute product samples and carry out non-brand-related tasks that must be in place to maximise sales, such as compliance, auditing and merchandising. |
| Experiential marketing | The creation of a campaign delivered face-to-face, that engages the target audience in the brand through stimulation of some or all of the senses. This technique strives to forge a deeper connection with individuals and convey a sense of the brand's values. |

*Source*: Bashford (2007). Reproduced from *Marketing* magazine with the permission of the copyright owner, Haymarket Business Publications Limited.

alive at the point of purchase (Kemp, 2000). Field marketing has undoubtedly expanded its role in recent years and in doing so has begun to establish itself as a core marketing support activity. Indeed, Moyies (2000) claims that field marketing should be cross-fertilised with direct marketing and sales promotion, and in doing so would not only benefit clients but also enhance the credibility of the industry.

### Scholars' paper 18.4  Never mind the product, feel the experience

**Chang, T.-Y. and Horng, S.-C. (2010) Conceptualizing and measuring experience quality: the customer's perspective, *The Service Industries Journal*, 30(14) (December), 2401–19.**

More people are becoming aware of the importance and significance of experiences within marketing. These are characterised as satisfying customers' psychic or personal needs. These authors propose that experiences are considered as distinct economic offerings that are different from goods and services, to the extent that the focus of the economy has been transferred to experience. The number of papers on 'experience quality' is small, so this research paper makes an important contribution to this growing field. This paper provides an insight into the literature and the authors also provide a definition of experience quality.

Associated with this experience element is the growing use of events as a form of marketing communications. Events are a part of several aspects of marketing communications, including brand experience considered here but also product and corporate branding (Chapters 11 and 12) and sponsorship (Chapter 16). However, a deeper insight into the nature and characteristics of events can be found in the section about exhibitions and trade shows (Chapter 19).

Finally, some consumers experience brands in unexpected ways. Through increasingly open communications, typically Twitter and social networks, some companies can sense moods, intentions, desires and consumer frustrations and intervene to help people with personalised gifts or solutions. These activities are known as 'random acts of kindness' and can result in positive word of mouth and improvements to brand image. For example, when the owner of a toy company saw on Facebook that a child's birthday present had been lost in the post, he sent a toy bunny, free of charge, and a note that said 'Sorry Royal Mail let you down, hopefully this will put a smile on your little girl's face' (Behrman, 2012). Other examples include sending restaurant vouchers to customers picked at random, upgrading to next-day free delivery, sending out personalised keyrings and including free gifts with an order. A Scottish brewery might give away a box of beer one day, and then give someone £200-worth of shares in the company through its fan investor scheme. For a few months, staff at airline KLM selected eight Twitter followers who were feeling low or in need of a break, and gave them a free return flight to Amsterdam. The campaign resulted in an increase of 784 followers for KLM's UK Twitter feed.

# Key points

- Sales promotions offer a direct inducement or an incentive to encourage audiences to buy a product/service sooner rather than later. The inducement (for example, price deals, coupons, premiums) is presented as an added value to the basic product, one that is intended to encourage buyers to act 'now' rather than later.

- The role of sales promotion is to engage audiences and to motivate them so that they are persuaded to act now rather than at a later stage.

- The objective of sales promotion is to stimulate action. This can be to initiate a series of behaviours that result in long-run purchase activity, but the goal of sales promotion is to drive short-term shifts in sales. These actions can be seen to occur in the conative stage of the attitudinal set.

- The cognitive view of the way sales promotions operate is based on the belief that consumers internally process relevant information about a sales promotion, including memories of past experiences, and make a reasoned decision in the light of the goals and objectives that individuals set for themselves. The behaviourists' view is that when the various actions that are embedded within a sales promotion activity are aggregated, a new desired pattern of behaviour emerges.

- Many organisations have developed schemes designed to retain customers based on the notion that they, the customers, are loyal. This brings into debate the notion of what is loyalty. In many ways these schemes are a function of customer convenience and all that they achieve is sufficient leverage to hold on to a customer a fraction longer than might have been possible in the absence of the scheme.

- The range of techniques and methods used to add value to offerings is enormous and ranges from sampling and coupons to premiums, contests and sweepstakes, all used with varying levels of success. However, there has been a distinct shift away from traditional promotional instruments to the use of digital media in order to reflect consumers' preferences and media behaviour.

- Field marketing is a relatively new sector and seeks to provide support for the sales force and merchandising personnel along with data collection and research facilities. A key aspect of field marketing concerns the growing interest in what is referred to as experiential marketing or brand experience.

- What differentiates the experiential aspect from other FM activities is that it requires more precise targeting (not mass-market) and it is more emotionally and physically engaging than sampling and many events or roadshows.

# Review questions

1. What are the purposes of using sales promotion and why does it consume such a large share of promotional expenditure?

2. Write a brief note explaining how shaping works.

3. Identify the major differences between the behavioural and the cognitive explanations of how sales promotions work.

4. Write brief notes outlining some of the issues associated with loyalty programmes and customer retention initiatives.

5. How would you advise a newly appointed assistant brand manager on the expected outcomes of a sales promotion programme? (Choose any sector/industry of your choice.)

6. List the main sales promotion methods used by manufacturers and targeted at consumers.

7. Name five core activities associated with field marketing and explain their essential features.

8. To what extent should sales promotion, and field marketing be managed as an integrated unit?

9. Find three brand experience events and make notes of the main points of similarity.

10. Explain the term 'random acts of kindness' and suggest ways in which Orange might use this approach.

# References

Ambition Communications (2011) Wake up to Blackberry for Blackberry/RIM, *B2B Marketing*, retrieved 24 April 2012 from http://www.b2bmarketing.net/knowledgebank/branding/case-studies/case-study-wake-blackberry-blackberryrim-ambition-communications.

Barda, T. (2009) Case Study – Gillette, *The Marketer*, September.

Barrand, D. (2004) Promoting change, *Marketing*, 6 October, 43–5.

Bartlett, M. (2007) Glowing at Glastonbury, *The Marketer*, retrieved 7 July 2012 from www.themarketer.co.uk/articles/case-studies/glowing-at-glastonbury/.

Bashford, S. (2004) Field marketing: The great divide? *Event*, 8 September. Retrieved 14 October from www.brandrepublic.com/news.

Bashford, S. (2007) Which way forward? *Marketing*, 13 December, 12.

Behrman, D. (2012) Work: Better Business: acts of kindness, The *Guardian*, Friday 13 April, p. 2.

Benady, D. (2009) Brands struggle to kick the sales promotion habit, *Marketing*, 11 December, retrieved 13 July 2010 from www.brandrepublic.com/news.

Benady, D. (2011) Field marketing: Your brand in their hands, *Marketing*, 09 November 2011, retrieved 17 February 2012 from http://www.brandrepublic.com/features/1102824/Field-marketing-brand-hands/?DCMP=ILC-SEARCH.

Birchall, J. (2011) Best deal on the block, *Boldness in Business – FT*, 17 March, 36–9.

Blattberg, R.C. and Neslin, S.A. (1990) *Sales Promotion: Concepts, Methods and Strategies*, Englewood Cliffs, NJ: Prentice-Hall.

Bolger, M. (2011) Scoring Points, *The Marketer*, July/August, 20–2.

Buzzell, R.D., Quelch, J.A. and Salmon, W.J. (1990) The costly bargain of trade promotion, *Harvard Business Review* (March/April), 141–9.

Capizzi, M., Ferguson, R. and Cuthbertson, R. (2004) Loyalty trends for the 21st century, *Journal of Targeting Measurement and Analysis for Marketing*, 12(3), 199–212.

Clark, N. (2010) The power of the crowd, *Marketing Magazine*, 24 August 2010, retrieved 18 October 2011 from www.brandrepublic.com/features/1023618/power-crowd/?DCMP=ILC-SEARCH.

Dawes, J. (2004) Assessing the impact of a very successful price promotion on brand, category and competitor sales, *Journal of Product and Brand Management*, 13(5), 303–14.

Drèze, X., Hoch, S.J. and Purk, M.E. (1994) Shelf management and space elasticity, *Journal of Retailing*, 70(4), 301–26.

Ehrenberg, A.S.C. (2000) Repeat buying: facts, theory and applications, *Journal of Empirical Generalizations in Marketing Science*, 5, 392–770.

Ehrenberg, A.S.C., Goodhardt, G.J. and Barwise, T.P. (1990) Double Jeopardy Revisited, *Journal of Marketing*, 54 (July), 82–91.

Gilbert, D.C. and Jackaria, N. (2002) The efficacy of sales promotions in UK supermarkets: a consumer view, *International Journal of Retail and Distribution Management*, 30(6), 325–32.

Gupta, S. (1998) Impact of sales promotions on when, what and how much we buy, *Journal of Marketing Research*, 25(4), 342–55.

Hallberg, G. (2004) Is your loyalty programme really building loyalty? Why increasing emotional attachment, not just repeat buying, is key to maximizing programme success, *Journal of Targeting Measurement and Analysis for Marketing*, 12(3), 231–41.

Hastings, S. and Price, M. (2004) Money can't buy me loyalty, *Admap*, 39(2) (February), 29–31.

Heilman, M.C., Nakamoto, K. and Rao, A.G. (2002) Pleasant Surprises: Consumer Response to Unexpected In-Store Coupons, *Journal of Marketing Research*, 34 (May), 242–52.

Hilpern, K. (2011) Persuasion, *The Marketer*, May, 28–32.

Inman, J., McAlister, L. and Hoyer, D.W. (1990) Promotion signal: proxy for a price cut? *Journal of Consumer Research*, 17 (June), 74–81.

Jones, P.J. (1990) The double jeopardy of sales promotions, *Harvard Business Review*, (September/October), 145–52.

Jones, R. (2010) Barclaycard launches Freedom rewards scheme, The *Guardian*, Wednesday 17 March, retrieved 18 October 2011 from www.guardian.co.uk/money/2010/mar/17/barclaycard-launches-freedom-rewards-scheme.

Kemp, G. (2000) Elastic brands, *Marketing Business*, (October), 40–1.

Knoepke, D. (2011) Orange You Glad It's Glastonbury Sponsorship Time? 23 June, retrieved 7 July 2012 from www.sponsorship.com/About-IEG/Sponsorship-Blogs/Diane-Knoepke/June-2011/Orange-You-Glad-It-s-Glastonbury-Sponsorship-Time-.aspx.

Krishna, A. and Zhang, Z.J. (1999) Short or long duration coupons: the effect of the expiration date on the probability of coupon promotions, *Management Science*, 45(8), 1041–57.

Lee, C.H. (2002) Sales promotions as strategic communication: the case of Singapore. *Journal of Product and Brand Management*, 11(2), 103–14.

Manning, J. (2011) 5 reasons to go with the crowd, *The Marketer*, May, 42–3.

McLuhan, R. (2000) Fighting for a new view of field work, *Marketing*, 9 March, 29–30.

McLuhan, R. (2007) Face value, *Marketing*, 13 December, 9–10.

Middleton, V.T.C. (1989) *Marketing in Travel and Tourism*, Oxford: Heinemann.

Moyies, J. (2000) A healthier specimen, *Admap* (June), 39–42.

Murphy, C. (2009) How to use Promotional Merchandise, *The Marketer*, October, 33–6.

Orange (2011) Turn it up to 11 . . . Orange unveils the 'Sound Charge' retrieved 7 July 2012 from http://newsroom.orange.co.uk/2011/06/20/turn-it-up-to-11-orange-unveils-the-sound-charge-2011/.

Peattie, S. and Peattie, K.J. (1994) Sales promotion, in *The Marketing Book* (ed. M.J. Baker), 3rd edn., London: Butterworth-Heinemann.

Prince, D. (2009) Glastonbury Festival is not just a beanfeast – it's a £70 million business, too, The *London Evening Standard*, 19 June, retrieved 7 July 2012 from www.standard.co.uk/business/glastonbury-festival-is-not-just-a-beanfeast--its-a-70-million-business-too-6712875.html.

Quilter, J. (2009) Gillette launches experiential campaign around Superdrug stores, *Promotions & Incentives*, 23 February 2009, retrieved 17 June 2012 from http://www.brandrepublic.com/news/883496/Gillette-launches-experiential-campaign-around-Superdrug-stores/?DCMP=ILC-SEARCH.

Rothschild, M.L. and Gaidis, W.C. (1981) Behavioural learning theory: its relevance to marketing and promotions, *Journal of Marketing Research*, 45(2), 70–8.

Ruckert, R.W., Walker, O.C. and Roering, K.J. (1985) The organisation of marketing activities: a contingency theory of structure and performance, *Journal of Marketing* (Winter), 13–25.

Russell, R.A. and Urban, T.L. (2010) The location and allocation of products and product families on retail shelves, *Annals of Operations Research*, 179(1), 131–147.

Ryan, M. (2012) Forward Thinking Essays 2012: Access all areas, *Marketing*, retrieved 17 February 2012 from http://www.brandrepublic.com/promotional_feature/1112655/Forward-Thinking-Essays-2012-Access-areas-Martin-Ryan-CPM-UK/?DCMP=ILC-SEARCH.

Simms, J. (2007) Scant value in BOGOFS, *Marketing*, 7 November, 18.

Stilley, K.M., Inman, J.J. and Wakefield, K.L. (2010a) Planning to Make Unplanned Purchases? The Role of In-Store Slack in Budget Deviation, *Journal of Consumer Research*, 37(2), (August), 264–78.

Stilley, K.M., Inman, J.J. and Wakefield, K.L. (2010b) Spending on the Fly: Mental Budgets, Promotions, and Spending Behavior, *Journal of Marketing*, May, 74(3), 34–47.

Wallace, C. (2010) Trident has Beyoncé fans chewing up, *PR Week* 15 April 2010, retrieved 13 July 2010 from www.brandrepublic.com/news.

# Chapter 19

# Brand placement, exhibitions, packaging and licensing

The five primary tools of the communications mix work better if supported by other secondary or support tools and media. Of the growing number of approaches, several stand out. Product placement enables brands to be seen in the correct context and used by appropriate role models in order to help form effective brand associations. Exhibitions can be a significant part of a consumer marketing communications mix, while trade shows are a major part of the way B2B marketing is conducted. Packaging is always an important factor in the way consumer goods, which evoke low involvement, are presented. Licensing, in order to use another party's assets, has become more prevalent activity in the twenty-first century.

## Aims and learning objectives

The aims of this chapter are to consider a range of marketing communications activities that have no specific designation, yet which can make a major contribution to a marketing communication campaign. These activities are applied to both the b2b and b2c markets.

The learning objectives of this chapter are to:

1. understand the concept and issues associated with brand placement;
2. explain the differences and significance of exhibitions and trade shows;
3. consider the main advantages and disadvantages of using exhibitions as part of the communications mix;
4. examine the role and key characteristics of packaging as a form of marketing communications;
5. describe the principles and issues associated with licensing.

# Minicase

## Beyoncé – how brand licensing influences popular music acts

The rise in popularity of popular music in the post-Second World War era led to a demand to discover a stream of music acts. Rock 'n' roll, rhythm & blues, soul and country were among some of the popular genres that were arguably at the vanguard of this revolution. They were the result of a fusion of previously separate music cultures. This phenomenon of popular genres created a pool of popular music stars, including Elvis Presley, Chuck Berry and The Beatles. The music artist or pop star was born.

Just as most products at the time were developed, produced and distributed by a company that managed and controlled the majority of the value chain activities, so the popular music industry grew through a similar managerial approach. Organisations called 'record labels' controlled the manufacture and delivery of music products to the marketplace. Music acts did not possess music recording facilities, nor could they could manufacture or distribute music products. As a result they had no option other than to sign with a record company.

Record labels identified creative ideas and artists, bought the rights to fund, record, manufacture and promote popular music products, in return for a financial return. Marketing communications, such as live music, radio, TV promotion, plus public relations were used to create demand. During the pre-millennial period (1950 to 1999) record labels manufactured and distributed the physical recorded music, first through vinyl and later through cassette tapes and CD formats. Record labels dominated this period and music acts such as The Beatles, The Rolling Stones and Diana Ross were dependent upon their contracted record labels – Parlophone Records, Decca, and Motown respectively.

Record labels would use their research and development facilities to identify commercially viable music acts. The department responsible for this activity was known as 'Artist and repertoire' (A&R), and became the priority of record labels seeking to produce and market the most profitable roster of music acts.

Record labels were authorised to record, manufacture and distribute physical music products related to a music act's brand. Income came from the copyright ownership of the song and income from the manufacturing margins accrued through music product sales. Not surprisingly, some music acts broke away from their contracted record labels and formed their own companies. For example, The Beatles formed Apple Corps in an attempt to secure a greater influence over their work, and used Capital Records to undertake the distribution element, whilst EMI retained copyrights. The Rolling Stones also undertook a similar move.

Historically, the song was often owned or partially owned by the record label because it financed music act recording. A music act would normally receive an advance payment when signing with a record label. This would be recouped by the label upon successful promotion of a music act's brand through music product sales. This meant that the 'productising' of music acts often enabled record labels to control the promotion and own the major part of income generation of a music act. Such relationships meant that music acts could find themselves with limited control of their brand. Good examples of this can be seen with both Prince and George Michael, who both challenged their record label's control and ownership of their commercial brand identity.

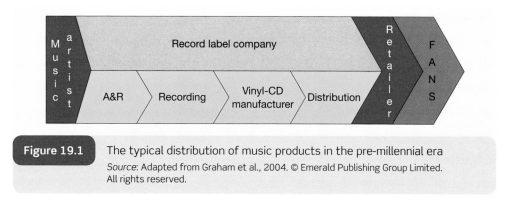

| **Figure 19.1** | The typical distribution of music products in the pre-millennial era |

*Source*: Adapted from Graham et al., 2004. © Emerald Publishing Group Limited.

Therefore, throughout the pre-millennial period music acts were very much dependent upon record labels to record, market, and distribute their music if they wanted to reach a global audience and sell millions of albums.

### The changing value of the music act and the nature of the music product

The turn of the century has seen the erosion of the record labels' dominant position. It has been challenged by technology and the subsequent digitalisation of recorded music. The nature of the music product has been extended and changed to encompass digital (non-physical) music products.

Now it is possible for music acts to control the production of their music and to distribute their products directly to consumers, independently. In addition, many consumers have changed their purchasing behaviour by preferring digital (streaming/downloading) rather than owning a physical music product. Music fans can now acquire music more cheaply through digital music product and streaming sites such as iTunes and Spotify. As a result, the recorded music industry has seen significant reductions in profit margins.

The digital revolution has seen major changes in the way a music act can develop creativity and share their brand value. Record labels, now commonly known as 'entertainment companies', have sought new ways to generate income. What is commonly referred to as the '360-degree deal' is an attempt by the entertainment (record) companies to develop an extended portfolio of income opportunities from the whole realm of commercial music brand activities. Accordingly, they have moved from their traditional pre-millennial business of control of singular rights (recorded music) to the management and control of multiple (music brand) rights.

These multiple rights deals seek to obtain a significant interest and income from a music act's concerts, merchandising, TV licensing, films, games and direct sales from an artist's websites. These multiple rights deals can provide immediate returns for an entertainment/record label to offset the lucrative advance established artists can command. As the value of 'physical product' recordings has declined so much, entertainment/record labels must seek new forms of income.

Today's increasing social media network, particularly among the young, has created a global audience obsessed not only with the music of music stars, but also with a seemingly insatiable appetite for all sorts of information about their private lives and lifestyles. Subsequently, the social media-literate fan base has created a new demand for an act's music brand beyond the traditional recorded music product. Paradoxically, while the commercial value of the physical music product has gone down, the commercial value of the music act's brand has gone up.

A music act's brand is a strategic combination of cultural messages that provide meaning and connection for and among an audience. In today's social media age a music brand cannot hide from an increasingly inquisitive public. Consistent messages (good or bad) will largely represent the expectations people have when engaging with an act. Reputation is one of the most important elements in building and developing a music brand, as it represents the relationship and current market value of a music act.

Because of the change in the traditional distribution of income, the evolution of the music brand is now pivotal to an act's commercial success. The focus

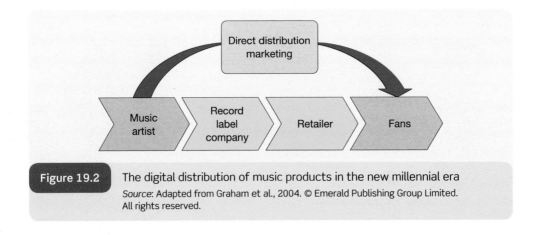

**Figure 19.2** The digital distribution of music products in the new millennial era
*Source*: Adapted from Graham et al., 2004. © Emerald Publishing Group Limited.
All rights reserved.

| Table 19.1 | The Beyoncé Knowles brand | |
|---|---|---|
| **The Music Act: Beyoncé Giselle Knowles** | | |
| **Private self** | **Physical self** | **Professional self** |
| Born Houston, Texas, USA | 30 years old | Since 1997: singer, songwriter, |
| Child prodigy | Female | dancer, actress, choreographer, |
| Married to Jay-Z | African American | fashion designer and model |
| Daughter: Blue Ivy Carter | Voluptuous (Bootylicious) | |
| **Music brand portfolio** | | |
| **The music brand** | **The extended brand** | **The brand partnership** |
| 4 Destiny's Child albums: *Destiny's Child, Destiny's Child Fulfilled, The Writing's on the Wall, Survivor* | 10 TV/films: *Carmen, Goldmember, The Fighting Temptations, The Pink Panther, Dreamgirls, Cadillac Records, Obsessed & A Star is Born* | Pepsi L'Oréal Tommy Hilfiger |
| 4 Solo albums: *Dangerously in Love, B'Day, I am Sash Fierce, 4* | Fashion: House of Dereon | Nintendo DS Vizio |
| Numerous duets: Lady Gaga, Shakira, Jay Z | Fragrance: Heat, Heat Rush, Pulse | |
| 16 Grammy awards | | |

© Ray Sylvester (2012)

upon a multiple income profile that is generated from the music brand can be seen throughout the music industry today. An act can now be seen as possessing a portfolio of music brand products and/or services. This portfolio is normally made possible through several levels of brand licensing:

- The music brand (live and recorded)
- The extended brand licensing (i.e. fashion)
- The brand partnership (i.e. endorsements).

Several high-profile, 360-degree deals have been brokered between music acts and music entertainment companies. Robbie Williams signed a deal with EMI in 2002 for a reputed £80 million, while Madonna received £120 million for a deal with Live Nation in 2007. A year later Jay-Z was said to have received a deal that would see him accrue up to £150 million over ten years. Beyoncé's portfolio provides an interesting example of how brand licensing is fundamental to both her income stream and that of her entertainment company.

## Summary

The music artist of the pre-millennial period (1950–99) had a predominant reliance upon income accrued from the record company which controlled manufacturing, distribution, retail placement and sale of physical music recording formats (vinyl, tape, CD).

The digital revolution of the new millennium (2000+) has, however, changed the nature and realm of music consumption. In 2012 the record industry body, the

| Exhibit 19.1 | **Beyoncé** |
|---|---|
| | *Source*: Rune Hellestad/Corbis |

British Phonographic Industry (BPI), announced that income from UK digital music sales overtook that of physical music recordings for the first time. The growth is welcome but digital music income is proportionately much less than physical formats. However, technology has also greatly extended the placement and value of the music act into multiple (potential income-generating) channels. The music act is now a music brand portfolio, redefining the way in which fans can engage with the multiple representations of a music act.

*This minicase was written by Ray Sylvester at Buckinghamshire New University, using a variety of resources including Graham et al. (2004) and Leeds (2007).*

# Introduction

Most of the tools of marketing communications presented so far focus on those regarded as the primary ones. However, in order to provide a difference and to cut through the noise of competing brands, it is necessary to provide additional resources and, preferably, integrated communications, right up to the point when customers make decisions. This chapter considers several other important means of communicating with both customers and distributors: brand placement, exhibitions and trade shows, packaging and licensing.

'Product placement', as it was originally termed, enables a brand to be observed in a more natural environment than if viewed on a shelf, online or in a shop window. Unsurprisingly, this part of marketing communications is growing and provides income for film producers, authenticity for brand managers and relief from advertising for consumers.

Exhibitions fulfil a role for customers in enabling them to become familiar with new developments, new products and leading-edge brands. Very often these customers will be opinion leaders and will use word-of-mouth communications to convey their feelings and product experiences to others. In the b2b market, exhibitions and trade shows are very often an integral and important component in the communications mix. Meeting friends, customers, suppliers, competitors and prospective customers is an important sociological and ritualistic event in the communication calendar for many companies. In the consumer sector, and in particular the FMCG market, it is important to provide a point of difference and offer continuity for those people who make the brand choice decisions at the point of purchase.

In addition, the way products are packaged not only influences brand perception but can also be an integral part of the customer purchasing process. Packaging moves with a brand back into the home and can be present while a brand is consumed. This provides a constant visibility and reinforcement of the brand, something other forms of communications cannot do.

As can be seen in the Beyoncé minicase, brand licensing has become an important element in the way the music industry markets and communicates with stakeholders. Licensing is a commercial arrangement whereby one party, who holds certain property rights or a trademark, grants permission to particular others – a manufacturing company, for example – to allow them the right to carry the designated logo or trademark. Some might see this as a variant of brand extension, but licensing has become a significant communications activity in its own right.

# Brand placement

One way of overcoming the irritation factor associated with advertisements screened in cinemas prior to a film showing is to incorporate the brand in the film that is shown. This practice, referred to as *product*, or more accurately, *brand placement*, is the inclusion of products and services in films (or media) for deliberate promotional exposure, often, but not always, in return for an agreed financial sum. It is regarded by some as a form of sales promotion, by others as sponsorship. In addition, placements can also carry social information. Homer (2009: 22) for example, claims that 'brand placements have been shown to be more effective when the featured brand is paired with a character who displays one or more desirable traits' (Karrh, 1998b).

For the purposes of this text, brand placement is regarded as a form of advertising, because the 'advertiser' pays a third party for the opportunity to present the product in their channel.

A wide variety of brands can be placed in this way, including drinks (both soft and alcoholic), confectionery, newspapers, cars, airlines, perfume and even holiday destinations and sports equipment. However, the development of brand placement has inevitably led to new formats and fresh approaches, some of which only serve to muddy the waters.

Hudson and Hudson (2006) set out the development of brand placement. Early forms of brand placement concerned brand owners making deals with film producers and film stars to openly endorse the brand. The brand owner would fund props and facilities for the film in return for spoken and visual endorsement. Some of the first television programmes were named after the brands that sponsored them, for example, *The Colgate Comedy Hour* and the *Kraft Television Theatre* (Hudson and Hudson, 2006).

The establishment of brand placement agencies in the 1980s helped formalise the process and removed much of the barter and haggling that had typified arrangements. The turning point occurred when the film *ET* depicted an alien being lured by Reese's Pieces. Hershey, the manufacturer, saw sales rise 65 per cent following the release of the film, and since then brand placement has grown year on year.

Two distinct forms of brand placement-related activity have emerged, partly as a result of the proliferation of the media, the consequential surge in the production of entertainment programmes and the media industries' need to generate income streams. Rather than place a brand within a film, television or radio programme where it assumes a passive role, hoping to get noticed, a new approach sees whole entertainment programmes built around a single brand. In contrast to the passivity of brand placement, here a brand is actively woven into the theme or the plot of the programme. This latter approach has been labelled 'branded entertainment'. Hudson and Hudson (2006) depict this as a continuum, represented at Figure 19.3.

Hackley and Tiwsakul (2006) suggest the term 'Entertainment Marketing'. They believe the term reflects the diversity of ways in which brands are inserted into entertainment vehicles. This perspective subsumes brand placement and incorporates celebrity endorsement and sponsorship – elements discussed elsewhere in this book.

## Characteristics of brand placement

### Strengths

By presenting the brand as part of the film, not only is it possible to build awareness, but source credibility can be improved significantly and brand images reinforced. The audience is assisted to identify and associate itself with the environment depicted in the film or with the celebrity who is using the brand. Brand placements can carry social information.

Levels of impact can be very high, as cinema audiences are very attentive to large-screen presentations. Rates of exposure can be high, particularly now that cinema films are being released through video outlets, satellite and various new regional cable and television organisations. Brand placement is often used as an integral part of an international marketing strategy. This is because, as McKechnie and Zhou (2003) observe, films are often produced for and play to audiences across cultures. However, it should be recognised that this approach constitutes a standardised marketing strategy, since it is difficult to customise across cultures because media content and placed brands are identical (Nelson and Devanathan, 2006).

Perhaps the major advantage is that the majority of audiences, worldwide, appear to approve of this form of marketing communications, if only because it is unobtrusive and integral to the

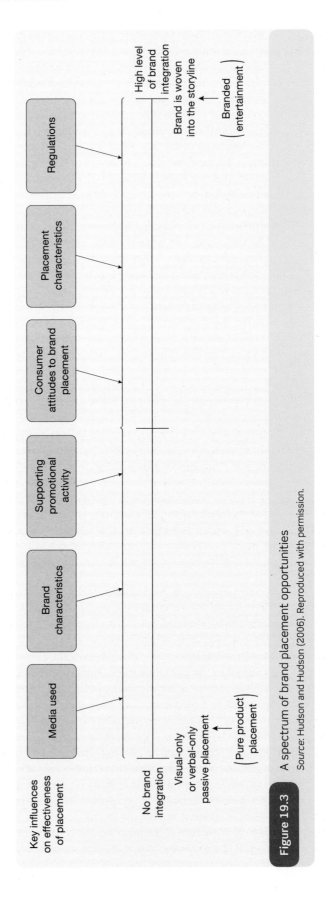

**Figure 19.3**    A spectrum of brand placement opportunities

*Source:* Hudson and Hudson (2006). Reproduced with permission.

film (Nebenzahl and Secunda, 1993). Audiences appear to have a positive attitude towards brand placement when they believe that media content is made more realistic. In addition, audiences believe that the naturalistic representation of brands serves to reinforce the integrity of fictionalised storylines and reflects the 'real life' experiences of the audience in the entertainment media setting (Lee et al. 2011).

## Weaknesses

Having achieved a placement in a film, there is still a risk that the brand will run unnoticed, especially if the placements coincide with distracting or action-oriented parts of the film. Associated with this is the lack of control the advertiser has over when, where and how the brand will be presented. If the brand is noticed, a small minority of audiences claim that this form of communication is unethical; it is even suggested that it is subliminal advertising, which is, of course, illegal. Gould et al. (2000) suggest that placements involving ethically charged brands, those that might be deceptive, that encroach upon artistic licence, are subliminal or excessively commercial are perceived negatively.

The absolute costs of brand placement in films can be extremely high, counteracting the low relative costs or cost per contact. The final major drawback of this form of communication concerns its inability to provide explanation, detail, or indeed any substantive information about the brand. The brand is seen in use and, it is hoped associated with an event, person(s) or objects that provide a source of pleasure, inspiration or aspiration for the individual viewer.

---

**Scholars' paper 19.1**     **Cross-cultural product placement**

**Lee, T., Sung, Y. and Choi, S.M. (2011) Young adults' responses to product placement in movies and television shows: A comparative study of the United States and South Korea, *International Journal of Advertising*, 30(3), 479–507.**

There are several papers about product placement. This particular one embraces cultural dimensions and attitudes towards product placement in films and television shows from two countries: the USA and Korea. Cross-cultural differences are observed for TV product placement.

---

Brand placement is not confined to cinema films. Music videos, television plays, dramas and soap operas can also use this method to present advertisers' brands. The novel *The Sweetest Taboo*, written by novelist Carole Matthews, includes frequent references to various Ford cars, which is not surprising as Ford paid her to mention their cars in her work (Plaut, 2004). Pervan and Martin (2002) found that brand placement in television soaps was an effective communications activity. They also concluded that the way a brand is used in the soap (i.e. positive and negative outcomes) may well have important implications for the attitudes held towards these brands. In addition, they suggested that organisations should study the consumption imagery associated with placed brands as this might yield significant information about the way in which these brands are actually consumed.

Brand placement is also used in radio. Van Reijmersdal (2011) found that placements on radio are perceived not only to be liked more than ads, but also as more credible than ads. This, in turn, affects brand recall positively. Thanks to the credibility issue, it is contended that brand placement receives more attention from listeners and so has a higher chance of being processed and recalled than commercials.

Brand placement is not confined to offline communications. For example, the toothpaste brand Pearl Drops was written into the plotline and integrated into the social network Bebo's interactive drama called *Sofia's Diary*, a teen-targeted programme.

## Viewpoint 19.1    Placed by Volvo

An excellent example of the use of brand placement by Volvo demonstrates the way in which contemporary marketing communications can be used by organisations.

The vampire-passion film series, *Twilight*, which features five films, was originally targeted at 16–24-year-old women. By including more action elements in the third film, *Eclipse*, it was hoped to attract more young men to the film series.

In the original novels the lead character drove a Volvo XC60, and sales of the S30 model rose following the release of the first *Twilight* film. Volvo saw the logic and credibility of the Swedish author and reference to Volvo in the novels, as an opportunity to develop their involvement in the films. Volvo developed an integrated, digital-based communication strategy, with brand placement as a pivotal element in the communication mix. The XC60 model was used in the second film as the car driven by the lead character, Edward.

For the film *New Moon*, a website was developed that offered fans an opportunity to attend the premiere, meet the cast and win the car. Following the film's release, many parents took their children to Volvo car showrooms to have their photographs taken next to the *Twilight* car.

In addition to media relations activities, Volvo then released TV and cinema ads which featured clips from the *Eclipse* film as well as flashes of the XC60. Viewers were driven to the website to play a game using the XC60 to navigate around the town of Forks, featured in the film.

*Source*:   Based on Fry (2010).

**Question:**   Consider the view that, if brand placement is a natural extension of conventional advertising campaigns, then it is a sensible, ethical and effective approach to marketing communications.

**Task:**   Choose two films and count the number of brand placements.

| Exhibit 19.2 | **Volvo placement in the film *The Twilight Saga: New Moon*** |
| :--- | :--- |
| | *Source*: Volvo Car UK Limited |

## Placement issues

The nature of a placement and the impact it has on the audience appear to be affected by a number of variables. Important issues concern: the nature of the placement (Sung et al., 2009) and its association with the storyline; whether the actors use the brand or if it remains a background object; whether the brand fits the plot; the degree to which the brand is prominently displayed; the medium used (de Gregorio and Sung, 2010), and the amount of time that the brand is actually exposed.

Research into brand placement appears to have focused on three main issues concerning consumer opinion. Lee et al. (2011b) refer to the perceived realism, ethicality, and influence of a brand placement. There is strong agreement that brand placements:

- can enhance the realism of film and TV content (Nebenzahl and Secunda, 1993; Gupta et al., 2000);
- have the potential to reinforce the integrity of a film and help viewers to become absorbed within the storyline (DeLorme and Reid, 1999);
- are perceived to be ethical, even if they are considered to be advertisements in disguise (Sung and de Gregorio, 2008).

Karrh et al. (2003) refer to the relative lack of control that marketers have over brand placement activities, but confirm that in comparison to advertising equivalents, brand placement can have a far greater impact on audiences and in most cases at a fraction of the cost of a 30-second advertisement.

Cultural background and ethical disposition can influence an audience's perception of brand placements (Nelson and Devanathan, 2006) whilst Russell and Belch (2005) refer to difficulties relating to the way the value of brand placement is perceived. There is a view, held by creative and media agencies, that the 'number of seconds on screen' is a valid measurement of effectiveness. Many do not agree and prefer to consider the context of the placement and the level of continuity within a defined communications strategy as more meaningful measures.

Brand placement can take varying forms but two main forms are considered in the literature: subtle versus prominent type of placements, or *implicit* and *explicit* brand placements (D'Astous and Séguin, 1999). The premise is that prominent/explicit placements are more persuasive (in terms of attitude change) than subtle/implicit placements, owing to their attention-getting power. However, prominence raises issues about distraction, irritation, and perceptions about self-serving that can inhibit persuasion. Research indicates that brand placement can impact attitudes through mere exposure (Hang, 2012). Homer (2009) found that attitudes decrease with prominent/explicit placements and are maintained where the placement is subtle/implicit.

Following research by Smit et al. (2009) into how brand placement is used in the Netherlands, their results revealed that a quarter of Dutch television contained a mixture of brand sponsorship announcements, commercials and brand placement programmes. They also found that approximately 10 per cent of programmes, excluding sports, news, foreign movies and foreign soap operas, included brand placements. They also found that 'of these the most popular genres for brand placement were human interest programmes, soap operas, games and quiz shows'. The researchers report that 'brands were portrayed visually and prominently, were visible for a relatively long period of time and were often connected to the plot'.

Practitioners perceive brand placement and brand-integrated programmes as the future of television advertising. Sponsors are enthusiastic about brand-integrating programmes simply because they see this format as more effective than a traditional 30-second commercial.

Brand placement is normally undertaken through specialised agencies and by dedicated professionals. Some practitioners believe that the emergence of these brand placement agencies might eventually weaken the position of advertising agencies.

The use of brand placement as a part of an international marketing strategy has several advantages. However, as Lee et al. (2011) suggest, local contextual elements such as the cultural environment, legal conditions, media infrastructure, plus public sentiment, all need to be considered when using brand placement on a global basis. They also warn that technologically sophisticated audiences are increasingly watching a range of content (soap operas, sitcoms and news programmes) via podcasts, mobile television (i.e. digital multimedia broadcasting) and interactive television (i.e. Internet protocol television) (Kwak et al. 2009). It is therefore important to understand the way consumers use television (active, passive and multi-tasking behaviours) and the impact this might have on the effectiveness of brand placement in different cultural contexts.

# Trade shows and exhibitions

Trade shows and exhibitions fulfil a role for customers by enabling them to become familiar with new developments, new products and leading-edge brands. Very often these customers will be opinion leaders and will use word-of-mouth communications to convey their feelings and both product and exhibition experiences to others. The role of trade fairs is to enable manufacturers, suppliers, and distributors to meet at a designated location. As these are drawn from a particular industry or related industries, the purpose is to exchange information about products and services and to build relationships. These events normally exclude consumers. Exhibitions are attended by consumers.

In the b2b market, trade shows are very often an integral and important component in the communications mix. Meeting friends, customers, suppliers, competitors and prospective customers is an important sociological and ritualistic event in the communication calendar for many companies. In the consumer sector, exhibitions provide a point of difference and offer continuity for those people who make the brand choice decisions at the point of purchase.

The idea of many suppliers joining together at a particular location to set out their products and services so that customers may meet, make comparisons and place orders is far from new. Indeed, not only does this form of promotional activity stretch back many centuries, it has also been used to explain the way the Internet works (Bertheron et al., 1996).

At a basic level, trade shows can be oriented for industrial users and exhibitions for consumers and the content or purpose might be to consider general or specialised products/ markets. According to Boukersi (2000), consumer-oriented general exhibitions tend to be larger and last longer than the more specialised industrial shows, and it is clear that this more highly segmented and focused approach is proving more successful, as evidenced by the increasing number of these types of exhibitions.

# Reasons to use exhibitions

There are many reasons to use exhibitions, but the primary ones appear not to be 'to make sales' or 'because the competition is there' but because these events provide opportunities to meet potential and established customers and to create and sustain a series of relational exchanges. Li (2007), cited by Geigenmüller (2010), stresses that the impact of trade shows on the development of valuable, long-term buyer–seller relationships is important.

The main aims are, therefore, to develop long-term partnerships with customers, to build upon or develop the corporate identity and to gather up-to-date market intelligence (Shipley and Wong, 1993) and to exchange information about products, services and corporate developments. This implies that exhibitions should not be used as isolated events, but that they should be integrated into a series of activities, which serve to develop and sustain buyer relationships.

After a tentative start to the 1990s, the exhibition industry in this century has grown considerably. With managers increasingly accountable for their promotional spend, a greater number of budgets are now channelled into exhibitions and related events. In 1995 visitors attended 773 exhibitions in the United Kingdom, where venues exceeded 2,000 square feet. By 2005, the number had risen to 944 exhibitions (Advertising Association, 2008).

Costs can be reduced by using private exhibitions. The increased flexibility allows organisations to produce mini or private exhibitions for their clients at local venues (e.g. hotels). This can mean lower costs for the exhibitor and reduced time away from their businesses for those attending. The communication 'noise' and distraction associated with the larger public events can also be avoided by these private showings.

---

### Viewpoint 19.2    Making an exhibit of cars in Beijing

The Beijing car show is a major event in a country where car sales increased 45 per cent in 2009. This rate growth should be considered against a background where only 50 out of 1000 people own a car. In Germany this figure is 500 in every 1000. So, the potential for car manufacturers is huge and this is why the Beijing car show is well attended.

Of the 1000 cars on show 80 per cent are made locally and compete with American, European and Japanese brands. Car shows in Europe are largely about dealers and dealerships, the media and specialist journalists, and suppliers and parts equipment manufacturers. The emphasis is on relationships, news, and profiling each firm's developments. Very few orders are agreed at the shows, although many pre-show agreements are ceremoniously signed for photographers and the crowds.

The Chinese show is a sales extravaganza. The country's car network is relatively young and there is an insufficient number of dealerships. As a result, consumers, having completed their Internet-based searches, arrive at the show armed with bags of cash, ready to secure their chosen vehicle.

*Source*:   Madden (2010); Bristow (2010).

**Question:**   How would you use marketing communications to attract visitors to a car show?

**Task:**   Make a list of the 10 critical activities associated with organising a trade show.

**Exhibit 19.3**    **Scene from the Beijing Car Show . . . it's official**

A security guard takes pictures of a Lamborghini Murciélago LP 670-4 Super Veloce China Limited Edition

*Source*: Feng Li/Getty Images

# Characteristics of exhibitions and trade fairs

The main reasons for attending exhibitions and trade fairs are that they enable organisations to meet customers (and potential customers) in an agreeable environment – one where both have independently volunteered their time to attend in order to place/take orders, to generate leads and to gather market information. The reasons for attending exhibitions are set out in Table 19.2.

---

**Scholars' paper 19.2** | **What is it with trade fairs?**

**Yuksel, U. and Voola, R. (2010) Travel trade shows: exploratory study of exhibitors' perceptions, *Journal of Business & Industrial Marketing*, 25(4), 293–300.**

This paper provides an insight into the motivations people and organisations have for participating in international trade shows. It also considers perceptions of effectiveness and the challenges faced by exhibiting firms. For exhibitors attendance is an effective and efficient way of presenting products/services a good way of improving relationships with customers.

---

From this it is possible to distinguish the following strengths and weaknesses of using exhibitions as part of the marketing communications programme.

## Strengths

The costs associated with exhibitions, if controlled properly, can mean that this is an effective and efficient means of communicating with customers. The costs per inquiry need to be calculated, but care needs to be taken over who is classified as an inquirer, as the quality of the audience varies considerably. Costs per order taken are usually the prime means of evaluating the success of an exhibition. This can paint a false picture, as the true success can never really be determined in terms of orders because of the variety of other factors that impinge upon the placement and timing of orders.

Products can be launched at exhibitions and, when integrated with a good PR campaign, a powerful impact can be made. This can also be used to reinforce corporate identity. Exhibitions are an important means of gaining information about competitors, buyers and technical and

---

**Table 19.2** Reasons exhibitors choose to attend exhibitions

To meet existing customers

To take orders/make sales

To get leads and meet prospective new customers

To meet lapsed customers

To meet prospective members of the existing or new marketing channels

To provide market research opportunities and to collect marketing data.

political developments in the market, and they often serve to facilitate the recruitment process. Above all else, exhibitions provide an opportunity to meet customers on relatively neutral ground and, through personal interaction, develop relationships. Products can be demonstrated, prices agreed, technical problems discussed and trust and credibility enhanced.

## Weaknesses

One of the main drawbacks associated with exhibition work is the vast and disproportionate amount of management time that can be tied up with the planning and implementation of exhibitions. However, good planning is essential if the full potential benefits of exhibition work are to be realised.

Taking members of the sales force 'off the road' can also incur large costs. Depending on the nature of the business, these opportunity costs can soar. Some pharmaceutical organisations estimate that it can cost approximately £5,000 per person per week to divert salespeople in this way.

The expected visitor profile must be analysed in order that the number of quality buyers visiting an exhibition can be determined. The variety of visitors attending an exhibition can be misleading, as the vast majority may not be serious buyers or, indeed, may not be directly related to the industry or the market in question. Research by Gopalakrishna et al. (2010) has found that approximately 40 per cent of first-time exhibitors, spanning a range of industries, do not return to the same show the following year. As Gopalakrishna et al. (2010) point out, a growing concern for managers is the ability to reach relevant decision-makers. The researchers' response was to attempt an understanding of attendee behaviour, as this would help trade show organisers segment their audiences. From their research data they determined a typology of business show visitors. These are depicted at Table 19.3.

| Table 19.3 | A typology of trade show visitors |
| --- | --- |
| **Segment name** | **Key characteristics** |
| **The basic shopper (40%)** | Basic shoppers make about 7 'serious' visits to booths, 75% are planned, and 70% of visits are made to standalone booths which are accessible on all four sides. |
| **The enthusiast (17%)** | Enthusiasts make an average of 24 visits while at the trade show, more than three times that of the basic shopper. 80% of their visits are planned and they prefer to be 'where the action is'. |
| **The niche shopper (17%)** | The niche shopper makes an average of 9.2 visits, which is greater than the basic shopper but lower than the enthusiast. The key characteristic of this type of shopper is that 40% of their serious visits are made to small-sized booths. The niche shopper prefers to work with specialty exhibitors who do not have a big presence at the show. |
| **The brand shopper (17%)** | Brand shoppers make about 10 serious visits and show the highest preference for large booths. They are the most thorough in planning which booths to attend, reflecting their need to plan and make their visit to the show as efficient as possible. |
| **The apathetic shopper (11%)** | Only 33% of the apathetic shoppers' booth visits are planned. They also prefer booths that are open on three sides, and which have a wide selection of products. The suggestion is that apathetic shoppers might represent 'newcomers' or attendees who are unfamiliar with the trade show. |

*Source*: Based on Gopalakrishna et al. (2010). © Emerald Group Publishing Limited. All rights reserved.

# Exhibitions as a form of marketing communications

As a form of marketing communications, exhibitions enable products to be promoted, they can build brands and they can be an effective means of demonstrating products and building industry-wide credibility in a relatively short period of time. Attendance at exhibitions may also be regarded from a political standpoint, in that non-attendance by competitors may be taken as an opportunity by attendees to suggest weaknesses.

In the B2B sector new products and services are often introduced at trade shows, especially if there are to be public relations activities and events that can be spun off the launch. In other words, exhibitions are not activities independent of the other communication tools. Exhibitions, if used effectively, can be part of an integrated communications campaign.

Advertising prior to, during and after a trade show can be dovetailed with public relations, sponsorship and personal selling. Sales promotions can also be incorporated through competitions among customers prior to the show to raise awareness, generate interest and to suggest customer involvement. Competitions during a show can be focused on the sales force to motivate and stimulate commercial activity and among visitors to generate interest in the stand, raise brand name awareness, encourage focus on particular products (new, revised or revolutionary) and generate sales leads and enquiries.

Perhaps above all else, trades shows and exhibitions play a major role in the development of relationships.

# Digital media and trade shows

In many ways the use of a website as brochureware represented a first attempt at an online exhibition. In these situations, commercial organisations provided opportunities for people who physically could not get to see a product to gain some appreciation of its size, configuration and capability (through text).

Online trade shows are Web-based platforms giving manufacturers, suppliers and distributors an opportunity to exchange information, virtually. This facilitates speed, convenience and control of cost factors that influence small and medium-sized organisations. As noted by Geigenmüller (2010), online show visitors can call on virtual halls and booths to obtain information about a firm's products and its services. Interaction between buyers and sellers occurs through chat rooms or video conferences, and forums. Online diaries or blogs are also used to discuss issues or leave messages for other participants.

However, the development of multimedia technologies has given not only commercial but also not-for-profit organisations the opportunity to showcase their wares on a global basis. One type of organisation to explore the use of this technology has been museums and art collections (static exhibits). Khoon et al. (2003) refer to the American History Documents (at www.indiana.edu/liblilly/histy/), Exploring Africa (at www.sc.edu/library/spcoll/sccoll/africa) and SCRAN (at www.scran.ac.uk) (which is a multimedia resource for Scottish history and culture) as examples of previous work and facilities in this area.

The use of multimedia technologies enables audiences across the world to access these collections and with the use of audio, video clips and streaming video, in addition to pictures and extensive text, these exhibitions can be brought to life, visited repeatedly, focus given to particular exhibits, materials updated quickly and unobtrusively and links made to other similar facilities. The key difference between this development and previous brochureware-type facilities is the feeling of virtual reality, the sense that a digital visitor is actually in the exhibition, even though seated several thousand miles away.

The use of ecommerce and digital media in the management and presentation of exhibitions is increasing. It is unlikely that online exhibitions will ever replace the offline, real-world version, if only because of the need to form relationships and to network with industry members, to touch and feel products and to sense the atmosphere and vitality that exhibitions generate. However, there is huge scope to develop specialised exhibitions, to develop online showcases that incorporate exhibits (products and services) from a variety of geographically dispersed locations.

# Marketing management of exhibitions

Good management of exhibitions represents some key aspects of marketing communications in general. Successful events are driven by planning that takes place prior to the exhibition, with communications inviting a range of stakeholders, not just customers, in advance of the exhibition event. Stands should be designed to deliver key messages and press releases and press information packs should be prepared and distributed appropriately.

During the event itself staff should be well briefed, trained and knowledgeable about their role in terms of the brand and in the exhibition process. After the exhibition it is vital to follow up on contacts made and discussions or negotiations that have been held. In other words, the exhibition itself is a planned marketing communications activity, one where activities need to be planned prior to, during and after the event. What is key is that these activities are coordinated, themed and supported by brand-oriented staff.

Above all else, exhibitions are an important way of building relationships and signalling corporate identity. Trade shows are an important means of providing corporate hospitality and showing gratitude to all an organisation's customers, but in particular to its key account customers and others of strategic interest. Positive relationships with customers, competitors and suppliers are often reinforced through face-to-face dialogue that happens both formally in the exhibition hall and informally through the variety of social activities that surround and support these events.

# Hospitality and events

As mentioned in the previous chapter, event management is closely connected with brand experience, public relations, sponsorship and branding. It is considered here as an adjunct to the experiences associated with attending exhibitions or trade shows. Prospective purchasers visit a designated area or location where, unlike an exhibition, a single brand is available to be tried, sampled and experienced or just enjoyed as an unobtrusive support. One example is Virgin Media's V-Festival of music.

### Product events

Product-oriented events are normally focused on increasing sales. Cookery demonstrations, celebrities autographing their books and the opening of a new store by the CEO or local MP are events aimed at generating attention, interest and sales of a particular product.

| Exhibit 19.4 | **Paddy Power give the Uffington White Horse a jockey** |

The public's attention was drawn to the annual Cheltenham Festival, a major horse racing event, by a 200ft wide and 110ft-tall jockey, depicted riding the 3,000-year-old chalk hillside engraving of a horse, known as the Uffington White Horse, in Oxfordshire. Sponsored by the betting firm Paddy Power, the temporary jockey was created out of lightweight canvas, took six hours at night to be pinned to the ground with tent pegs, five feet from the famous chalk stallion. News coverage of the stunt was extensive.

McGrath (2012); The *Sun* (2012); www.youtube.com/watch?v=b8p4HQGXgak.

*Source*: Paddy Power

Alternatively, events are designed to attract the attention of the media and, through stories and articles presented in the news, are able to reach a wide audience. See Exhibit 19.4 as an eye-catching example.

## Corporate events

Events designed to develop the corporate body are often held by an organisation with a view to providing some entertainment. These can generate considerable local media coverage, which in turn facilitates awareness, goodwill and interest. For example, events such as open days, factory visits and donations of products to local events can be very beneficial.

## Community events

These are activities that contribute to the life of the local community. Sponsoring local fun runs and children's play areas, making contributions to local community centres and the disabled are typical activities. The organisation attempts to become more involved with the local community as a good employer and good member of the community. This helps to develop goodwill and awareness in the community.

The choice of events an organisation becomes involved with is critical. The events should have a theme and be chosen to satisfy objectives established earlier in the communications plan. (See Chapter 16 for an example of sponsorship of local community events.)

# Packaging

Packaging has long been considered a means of protecting and preserving products during transit and while they remain in store or on the shelf prior to purchase and consumption. As Stewart (1995) aptly suggests, the function of packaging is to 'preserve product integrity'. In this sense, packaging can be regarded as an element of product strategy. To a certain extent this is still true; however, technology has progressed considerably and, with consumer choice continually widening, packaging has become a means by which buyers, particularly in consumer markets, can make significant brand choice decisions. Indeed, recent research by Silayoi and Speece (2007) has found that the way Asian consumers perceive the convenience of a package can be the most important factor in the decision-making process for some segments. To that extent, because packaging can be used to convey persuasive information and be part of the decision-making process, yet still protect the contents, it is an important means of marketing communications in particular markets, such as FMCG.

Low-involvement decision-making often requires peripheral cues to stimulate buyers into action. It has already been noted that decisions made at the point of purchase, especially those in the FMCG sector, often require buyers to build awareness through recognition. The design of packages and wrappers is important, as continuity of design, combined with the power to attract and hold the attention of prospective buyers, is a vital part of point-of-purchase activity. The degree of importance that manufacturers place upon packaging and design was seen in 1994, when Sainsbury's introduced its own cola. The reaction of the Coca-Cola company to the lookalike design of the own-label product is testimony to the value placed on this aspect of brand personality. There should be no doubt that packaging can provide a strong point of differentiation, one that is increasingly recognised by food manufacturers and producers (Wells et al. 2007).

# The communication dimensions of packaging

There are a number of dimensions that can affect the power and utility of a package. Colour is influential, as the context of the product class can frame the purchase situation for a buyer. This means that colours should be appropriate to the product class, to the brand and to the prevailing culture if marketing overseas. For example, red is used to stimulate the appetite, white to symbolise purity and cleanliness, blue to signal freshness, and green is increasingly being used to denote an environmental orientation and natural ingredients. From a cultural aspect, colours can be a problem. In China red is used to depict happiness, in Germany bright bold colours are regarded as appropriate for baby products, whereas in the United Kingdom pastel shades are more acceptable.

The shape of the packaging can be a strong form of persuasion. Verebelyi (2000) suggests that this influence may be due to the decorative impact of some brands. Various domestic cleaning products have packages with a twist in the neck, or a trigger action, facilitating directable and easier application.

The shape may also provide information about how to open and use the product, while some packages can be used for other purposes after the product has been consumed. For example, some jars can be reused as food containers, thereby providing a means of continual communication for the original brand in the home. Packaging can also be used as a means of brand identification, as a cue by which buyers recognise and differentiate a brand. The supreme example of this is the Coca-Cola contour bottle, with its unique shape and immediate power for brand recognition at the point of purchase.

---

**Scholars' paper 19.3** **Does packaging go with sponsorship?**

**Woodside, F. and Summers, J. (2011) Sponsorship leveraged packaging: An exploratory study in FMCG,** *Journal of Marketing Communications*, **17(2), April, 87–105.**

Integrated marketing communications often refers to the impact of a range of tools or media. Within the mix there are a number of pairs of tools that can work as primary/secondary drivers. This paper considers how consumers respond to sponsorship-leveraged packaging (SLP). This involves depicting the sponsored property's image, logos or symbols on the sponsoring brand's packaging (e.g. Weetbix sponsorship of Kids Triathlon). The paper contains useful insights into the relevant literature and associated theory.

---

Package size is important, as different target markets may consume varying amounts of product. Toothpaste is available in large-size family tubes and in smaller containers for those households that do not use so much. However, the size of a package can also be an important perceptual stimulus. Research by Raghubir and Krishna (1999) found that the height of a container was an important variable that consumers used to make judgements about the volume of the container.

However, Folkes and Matta (2004) counter this by referring to *Gestalt* theory, which is concerned with holistic perspectives. They say that consumers use multiple dimensions to make judgements about objects (packages). Their research suggests that there is a relationship between the attractiveness of a package and the volume of the package. As a broad generalisation, the greater the attractiveness, the greater is the perceived volume. The implications of this insight have been implicitly known by marketing management for years, judging by the effort that is given to create attractive packaging and shelf stand-out.

In certain markets packaging can be strategically important as it can affect positioning. Ampuero and Vial (2006) identify colour, typography, graphical forms and images as the key packaging variables from a design perspective. They then consider how these combine to produce optimum positioning conditions. They conclude that cold, dark-coloured packaging, which shows the product, is perceived to be associated with products that are elegant and expensive. The packaging for products targeted at customers for whom a low price is important should be light-coloured and show illustrations of people.

Washing and dishwasher powder manufacturers now provide plastic refill packs that are designed to provoke brand loyalty. These packs are cheaper than the original pack, partly because some of the packaging expense has been reduced as the customer has been introduced to the product at an earlier time. Purchase of the refill pack is dependent on product quality and customer satisfaction and, as long as the brand name is prominent for identification and reminder purposes, the decision to select the refill is quicker, as most of the risk (financial, physical and social) has been removed through previous satisfactory usage.

All packages have to carry information concerning the ingredients, nutritional values and safety requirements, including sell-by and use-by dates. Non-food packages must also attempt to be sales agents and provide all the information that a prospective buyer might need, while at the same time providing conviction that this product is the correct one to purchase. Labelling of products offers opportunities to manufacturers to harmonise the in-store presentation of their products in such a way that buyers from different countries can still identify the brand and remain brand loyal.

## Viewpoint 19.3    Positioning, packaging and presenting pasties perfectly

Ginsters make Cornish pasties and pies and had become an established brand in the impulse-buy, eat-now, out-of-home snacking market. The Ginsters brand had a rugged masculine persona, built partly on the humour used to build the brand and also because of the nature of the product and their main type of consumer.

Although successful, the marketing strategy had to change in order to develop the Ginsters brand. It was decided to enter the take-home, eat-later, comfort-food market. However, to achieve this, the brand had to have a wider appeal and this meant repositioning Ginsters so that it appealed to women, and housewives in particular.

To accomplish this strategy, a new range of multipack products were developed in order to make the offering relevant to families. Then, marketing communications messages were refocused on 'freshness and food quality', rather than humour. This was reinforced by emphasising the local sourcing and daily delivery of its ingredients. The quality message was reinforced by reference to Cornwall and the association people are known to make with the region as a source of traditional, good-value food.

Research revealed that the established logo, a red oval on a black background, and the product photography used on the packaging, were extremely important. However, the wording was changed to a simple 'Ginsters of Cornwall', a Cornish flag was introduced and a new Celtic-style font was incorporated. Great care was taken over the product photography, not only to capture detail about the fillings, but to also suggest a domestic environment, achieved by using a wood-effect background.

Investment in new packaging equipment and processes was necessary, as Ginsters now make over 3 million individual products every week. The revised pack design had a new matt-black finish, to replace the previous glossy sheen that research had found was perceived to be artificial and processed-food-orientated. Instore promotions and end-of-aisle locations in supermarkets were used to give the brand increased presence. Print ads in women's weekly magazines, coupled with a billboard campaign in major cities were used to provide awareness of Ginsters' repositioning.

Market share increased from 8.6 to 9.6 per cent, and year on growth exceeded 24 per cent.

*Source*:    Barda (2009); www.ipaeffectivenessawards.co.uk; www.spidexsoftware.co.uk.

**Question:**    To what extent is packaging an important element in the positioning process?

**Task:**    Find a product positioned for the take-home market and make notes about the marketing communications used. Are the communications effective?

Packages carry tangible and intangible messages. The psychological impact that packages can have should not be underestimated. They convey information about the product, but they also say something about its quality (Hall, 1991) and how it differs from competitive offerings. In some cases, where there is little to differentiate products, buyers may use the packaging on its own for decision-making purposes.

Gordon and Valentine (1996) argue that the market, competitive and associated products, provide a context within which a brand's packaging communicates. This is achieved by using packaging that conforms to a design code that has been established for the category, and permits consumers to identify quickly the range of brands in the product field. However, it does not necessarily allow for the identification of individual brands. They make the important point that it is this process that allows own-label brands to become part of a category without the support of advertising to establish credibility.

Packaging has been termed passive and active (Southgate, 1994). Passive packaging relies on vast amounts of advertising to infuse the design to create interest (e.g. Heinz). This is similar to the above-the-line approach to branding. Active packaging is more demonstrative and tends to work with the other marketing and communication elements. Connolly and Davison (1996) cite Tango as an example of this type of packaging.

# Licensing

This chapter signifies the end of the part of this book that has considered the tools and disciplines of marketing communications. It is fitting, therefore, to finish with a consideration of one of the least visible but most potent forms of contemporary marketing communications: licensing.

Licensing is not an option open to all organisations, yet of many of those who are able to utilise it, an increasing number are integrating this approach into their communication activities. Spurred by the surge in the numbers of digital characters and digital games, online and mobile games such as Angry Birds, Talking Friends, Moshi Monsters and MovieStarPlanet have, according to Macintosh (2012), not only attracted millions of players worldwide, in just a few years, but have also expanded into toys, clothing, TV shows, magazines and computer games.

According to Kwon et al. (2008), licensing is a commercial arrangement whereby a licensor, the party that holds the property rights or trademark, grants permission to others, called licensees, such as manufacturing companies, permitting them to manufacture products carrying the licensor's logo or trademark. Another simpler view is that a brand owner (licensor), grants a brand user (licensee), the right to use the brand in association with a defined product or service, for a specific period of time, and within defined terms, areas and territories, in return for the payment of a specific licence fee, royalty, or some such combination of financial rewards (Keller, 2003). Both interpretations are essentially the same, although the second might be closer to considering licensing as a form of brand extension (Weidmann and Ludwig, 2008). This is because the process of extension shifts the brand into a new, albeit slightly dissimilar, marketing context.

This practitioners' interpretation from Brand Licensing Europe (2012) states that

> it is the process of leasing a legally protected (that is, trademarked or copyrighted) entity – a name, likeness, logo, trademark, graphic design, slogan, signature, character, or a combination of several of these elements. The entity, known as the property or intellectual property, is then used in conjunction with a product. Many major companies and the media consider licensing a significant marketing tool.

Licensing is a form of brand alliance, of which there are many types. These are presented at Figure 19.4. Readers interested in brand alliances should read the paper by Ervelles, Horton and Fukawa (2008).

A licensed product carries two different brand names or logos simultaneously. These are the brands of the licensor and the licensee. Park, Jun, and Shocker (1996) refer to these as a *modifier*, such as a manufacturer's brand, and a *header*, the licensee's brand, such as the name or logo of a sports team. Kwon et al. (2008) cite as an example the licensing agreement between Ohio State University (OSU) and Nike over the OSU's Buckeyes' sweatshirt. Here Nike is the modifier and the header is OSU Buckeyes.

Licensing can benefit business in a number of ways. According to Weidmann and Ludwig (2008), licensing can:

● Expand a product portfolio;
● Increase the number of revenue streams;

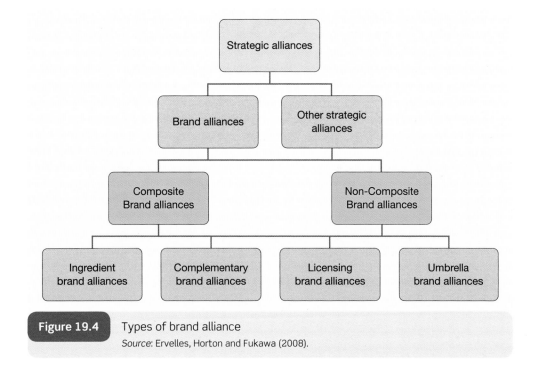

**Figure 19.4**    Types of brand alliance
*Source*: Ervelles, Horton and Fukawa (2008).

- Increase awareness, especially important when incorporated within an international marketing strategy;
- Build brand equity;
- Stimulate customer brand loyalty;
- Develop partnerships with retailers;
- Develop brand positioning.

Licensing enables brands to move into new businesses and markets without the major investment necessary for new manufacturing processes, machinery or facilities. Well-run licensing programmes are characterised by licensor's control over the brand image and how it is portrayed. This is achieved through an effective approvals process and other contractual obligations. The rewards of additional revenue (royalties) and profit are also accompanied by exposure in fresh media channels or even supermarket aisles (www.brandlicensing.eu).

---

**Viewpoint 19.4**    **Wensleydale please for Wallace & Gromit**

For small dairy producers such as Wensleydale Dairy Products (WDP), getting retail space and consumers to try their brands is extremely difficult, as dairy counters are dominated by the big-brand cheddar cheeses.

With a marketing strategy based on first broadening the product range and second improving the presentation and positioning of its flagship Wensleydale product, WDP teamed up with Aardman Animations, the creators of the animated characters Wallace & Gromit. The connection between the brands is rooted in Wallace's passion for Wensleydale cheese, a feature of all the Wallace & Gromit films. However, WDP had not yet capitalised on this opportunity.

In order to engage customers, a cookery book was developed, one that was anchored around a licensing agreement. This enabled WDP to use Wallace & Gromit for two months as part of an on-pack promotion. The cookery book itself featured different ways of using Wensleydale cheese. Cheesy recipes such as Gromit's Ginger Cheesecake, Wallace's Cheesy Fruit Bake and Yorkshire Rarebit were reproduced in 30,000 copies, which were given away free, with each purchase of a special promotional pack of cheese.

Retailers were very interested in this on-pack promotion and branches of the Co-op, Morrisons and Waitrose helped additional distribution through over 430 UK stores.

Working on a redemption rate of 5 per cent, the Wallace & Gromit's Cheesy Cook Book was offered on 600,000 packs. WDP could not afford to buy the end gondolas or aisle-end displays charged by the large grocery retailers, so the promotion was supported in-store by point of sale images, PR and several ads in selected trade magazines.

At the time of writing the outcome of this promotion was not available, although the indications were that performance was twice that expected.

*Source*:   Carter (2011); www.wensleydale.co.uk/; www.thedrum.co.uk/news/.

**Question:**   How might brand licensing work against the best interests of a brand?

**Task:**        Make a note of the markets in which you believe the use of licensing is not appropriate.

| Exhibit 19.5 | **Wallace and Gromit with Wensleydale cheese** |
| --- | --- |
| | *Source*: Christopher Furlong/Getty Images |

Weidmann and Ludwig (2008) make the point that licensed products offer opportunities for improved differentiation and standout. Breakfast cereals have used licensed character promotions for several decades, while cartoon and animated characters have been used in the fashion industry, and fashion chains offer licensed homeware and stationery. Not necessarily the first, but Bass (2004) indicates that the actor Jack Nicholson had a clause in his contract which rewarded him with a percentage of the licensing revenue generated by the film *Batman*. For licensors a common strategy is to license into 'accessory categories'. This occurs when the extension is something that accompanies consumption of the core product. Bass suggests that the strong emotional loyalty or bonding generated by a confectionery brand such as Kit Kat could lead into a Kit Kat mug, teaspoon, kettle and teapot.

---

### Scholars' paper 19.3    OK, so what exactly is a brand alliance?

**Ervelles, S., Horton, V. and Fukawa, N. (2008) Understanding B2C Brand Alliances between Manufacturers and Suppliers, *Marketing Management Journal*, 18(2), 32–46.**

The reason for singling out this paper is that the term 'brand alliance' has become increasing prevalent in the literature yet it remains fluid, loose and, at times, unclear. When trying to understand brand licensing it is helpful if the broader context of 'brand alliance' is clarified. This paper by Ervelles, Horton and Fukawa provides useful clarification of this term and they present a typology of the common types of brand alliances in b2c markets. They distinguish between strategic alliances and brand alliances, and between brand alliances and co-branding before evaluating composite brand alliances, including ingredient, umbrella, licensing and complementary brand alliances.

---

However, although brand licensing appears to be well established and accepted, there are certain risks associated with this marketing communications activity. For example, product failure, poor quality or just a failure to reach expectations can reflect poorly on the licensor and their brand as a whole. In an age where conversations are a potent form of communication, product reviews, customer feedback as well as media comment and word-of-mouth communication can all have a negative impact on a brand. Mattell's experience of poor product quality, and associated health risks when some of its Fisher-Price toys were discovered to be coated with a potentially toxic, lead-based paint, led to a massive product recall and consequential negative conversations (Edwards, 2010). These products, made under licence in China, serve to warn of the issues at stake.

# Key points

- Brand placement is the inclusion of products and services in films (or media) for deliberate promotional exposure, often, but not always, in return for an agreed financial sum.

- It is regarded by some as a form of sales promotion, by others as sponsorship, but the most common linkage is with advertising, because the 'advertiser' pays a third party for the opportunity to present the product in their channel.

- There are distinct forms of brand placement. One involves the passive placement of a brand within the media; the other sees whole entertainment programmes built around a single brand, one where it is actively woven into the theme or the plot of the programme. This is known as 'branded entertainment'.

- The main reasons for attending exhibitions (consumer shows) and trade fairs (b2b shows) are that: it enables organisations to meet customers (and potential customers) in an agreeable environment, one where both have independently volunteered their time to attend; to place/take orders; to generate leads; and to gather market information.

- As a form of marketing communications, exhibitions enable products to be promoted, they can build brands and they can be an effective means of demonstrating products and building industry-wide credibility in a relatively short period of time.

- Positive relationships with customers, competitors and suppliers are often reinforced through face-to-face dialogue that happens both formally in the exhibition hall and informally through the variety of social activities that surround and support these events.

- Packages carry tangible and intangible messages and packaging has become a means by which buyers, particularly in consumer markets, can make significant brand-choice decisions. Packaging conveys information about the product, but it also makes a statement about the quality of the product and how it differs from competitive offerings.

- Packaging has become a means by which buyers, particularly in consumer markets, can make significant brand-choice decisions and constitutes more than a means of preserving product integrity.

- Licensing is a commercial arrangement where a brand owner (licensor), grants a brand user (licensee), the right to use the brand in association with a defined product or service, for a specific period of time, and within defined terms, areas and territories, in return for the payment of a specific licence fee, royalty, or some such combination of financial rewards.

- A licensed product carries two different brand names or logos simultaneously. These are the brands of the licensor and the licensee.

- Licensing enables brands to move into new businesses and markets without the major investment necessary for new manufacturing processes, machinery or facilities.

- Well-run licensing programmes are characterised by the licensor's control over the brand image and how it is portrayed. This is achieved through an effective approvals process and other contractual obligations. The rewards of additional revenue (royalties) and profit are also accompanied by exposure in fresh media channels or even supermarket aisles.

# Review questions

1. Name two strengths and two weaknesses of brand placement.

2. Identify four examples of brand placement. Evaluate their effectiveness.

3. Evaluate the differences between consumer- and business-oriented trade shows.

4. As sales manager for a company making plastic mouldings for use in the manufacture of consumer durables, set out the reasons for and against attendance at trade shows and exhibitions.

5. Write brief notes explaining the role exhibitions might play in a company's integrated marketing communications strategy.

6. The development of inter-organisational relationships is best undertaken through personal selling rather than through exhibitions and trade shows. Discuss.

7. Find three brands where the shape of a package is an integral part of the product.

8. What is the difference between active and passive packaging?

9. Find three examples of brand licensing. What do you believe might be the goals associated with each of the licensing arrangements?

10. Make notes about the ideal context for the use of licensing.

# References

Advertising Association (2008) *Advertising Statistics YearBook 2008*, Henley on Thames: Advertising Association.

Ampuero, O. and Vial, N. (2006) Consumer perceptions of product packaging, *Journal of Consumer Marketing*, 23(2), 100–12.

Barda, T. (2009) Pies with Puff, *The Marketer*, February, 20–3.

Bass, A. (2004) Licensed extensions – Stretching to communicate, *Brand Management*, 12(1), September, 31–38.

Bertheron, P., Pitt, L.F. and Watson, R.T. (1996) The World Wide Web as an advertising medium, *Journal of Advertising Research*, 6(1) (January/February), 43–54.

Boukersi, L. (2000) The role of trade fairs and exhibitions in international marketing communications, in *The Handbook of International Marketing Communications* (ed. S. Moyne), London: Blackwell, 117–35.

Brand Licensing Europe (2012) What is Licensing? Retrieved 9 September 2012 from http://www.brandlicensing.eu/licensees-and-manufacturers-2/.

Bristow, M. (2010) Grand ambitions at Beijing car show, BBC News, 27 April 2010, retrieved 14 July 2010 from www.news.bbc.co.uk/1/hi/8644730.stm.

Carter, M. (2011) Wensleydale Dairy Products, *The Marketer*, 17 May.

Connolly, A. and Davison, L. (1996) How does design affect decisions at point of sale? *Journal of Brand Management*, 4(2), 100–7.

D'Astous, A. and Séguin, N. (1999) Consumer Reactions to Product Placement Strategies in Television Sponsorship, *European Journal of Marketing*, 33(9/10), 896–910.

DeLorme, D.E. and Reid, L.N. (1999) Moviegoers' experiences and interpretation of brands in films revisited, *Journal of Advertising*, 28(2), 71–95.

Edwards, H. (2010) The supply-chain reaction, *Marketing*, 19 May, retrieved 1 March 2012 from http://www.brandrepublic.com/opinion/1003783/Helen-Edwards-Branding-supply-chain-reaction/?DCMP=ILC-SEARCH.

Ervelles, S., Horton, V. and Fukawa, N. (2008) Understanding B2C Brand Alliances between Manufacturers and Suppliers, *Marketing Management Journal*, 18(2), 32–46.

Folkes, V. and Matta, S. (2004) The effect of package shape on consumers' judgments of product volume: attention as a mental contaminant, *Journal of Consumer Research*, 31(2), September, 390–402.

Fry, A. (2010) Cashing in on the Twilight phenomenon, *Marketing*, 21 July, 30–31.

Geigenmüller, A. (2010) The role of virtual trade fairs in relationship value creation, *Journal of Business and Industrial Marketing*, 25, 4, 284–92.

Gopalakrishna, S., Roster, C.A. and Sridhar, S. (2010) An exploratory study of attendee activities at a business trade show, *Journal of Business & Industrial Marketing*, 25, 4, 241–48.

Gordon, W. and Valentine, V. (1996) Buying the brand at point of choice, *Journal of Brand Management*, 4(1), 35–44.

Gould, S.J., Gupta, P.B. and Grabner-Kräuter, S. (2000) Product placements in movies: a cross-cultural analysis of Austrian, French, and American consumers' attitudes toward this emerging international promotional medium, *Journal of Advertising*, 29(4), 41–58.

Graham, G., Burnes, B., Lewis, J.G. and Langer, J. (2004) The transformation of the music industry supply chain, *International Journal of Operations & Production Management*, 24(11), 1087–1103.

Gregorio de, F. and Sung, Y.J. (2010) The influence of consumer socialization variables on attitude toward product placement, *Journal of Advertising*, 39(1), 85–99.

Gupta, P.B., Balasubramanian, S.K. and Klassen, M.L. (2000) Viewers' evaluations of product placements in movies: policy issues and managerial implications, *Journal of Current Issues and Research in Advertising*, 22(2), 41–52.

Hang, H. (2012) The implicit influence of bimodal brand placement on children, *International Journal of Advertising*, 31(3), 465–84.

Hackley, C. and Tiwsakul, R. (2006) Entertainment marketing and experiential consumption, *Journal of Marketing Communications*, 12(1), 63–75.

Hall, J. (1991) Packaged good, *Campaign*, 18 October, 21–3.

Homer, P. (2009) Product Placements: The Impact of Placement Type and Repetition on Attitude, *Journal of Advertising*, 38(3) (Fall), 21–31.

Hudson, S. and Hudson, D. (2006) Branded entertainment: a new advertising technique or product placement in disguise? *Journal of Marketing Management*, 22(5–6), 489–504.

Karrh, J.A. (1998b) Brand Placement: Impression Management Predictions of Audience Impact, Ph.D. dissertation, College of Journalism and Communications, University of Florida, Gainesville.

Karrh, J.A., McKee, K.B., Britain, K. and Pardun, C.J. (2003) Practitioners' evolving views of product placement effectiveness, *Journal of Advertising Research*, 43(2) (June), 138–50.

Keller, K.L. (2003) *Strategic Brand Management: Building, measuring and managing brand equity*, 2e, Upper Saddle River: Pearson Education.

Khoon, L.C., Ramaiah, C. and Foo, S. (2003) The design and development of an online exhibition for heritage information awareness in Singapore, *Program: Electronic Library and Information Systems*, 37(2), 85–93.

Kwak, H., Andras, T.L. and Zinkhan, G.M. (2009) Advertising to active viewers: consumer attitudes in the US and South Korea, *International Journal of Advertising*, 28(1), 49–75.

Kwon, H.H., Kim, H. and Mondello, M. (2008) Does a Manufacturer Matter in Cobranding? The Influence of a Manufacturer Brand on Sport Team Licensed Apparel, *Sport Marketing Quarterly*, 17, 163–72.

Lee, T., Sung, Y. and Choi, S.M. (2011) Young adults' responses to product placement in movies and television shows A comparative study of the United States and South Korea, *International Journal of Advertising*, 30(3), 479–507.

Lee, T., Sung, Y. and de Gregorio, F. (2011b) Cross-cultural challenges in product placement, *Marketing Intelligence & Planning*, 29(4), 366–84.

Leeds, J. (2007) The New Deal: Band as Brand, *New York Times*, 11 November, retrieved 14 July 2012 from www.nytimes.com/2007/11/11/arts/music/11leed.html?pagewanted=all (accessed in July 2012).

Li, L.Y. (2007) Marketing resources and performance of exhibitor firms in trade shows: a contingent resource perspective, *Industrial Marketing Management*, 36, 360–70.

MacIntosh, E. (2012) Exploring licensing's new gaming frontier, *Marketing*, 10 February.

Madden, N. (2010) Taking a spin around the China auto show, *Advertising Age*, 81, 18, p. 17.

McGrath, C. (2012) Accidental jumps trainer prepares for great leap forward at Festival, The *Independent*, p. 54.

McKechnie, S.A. and Zhou, J. (2003) Product placement in movies: a comparison of Chinese and American consumers' attitudes, *International Journal of Advertising*, 22(3), 349–74.

Nebenzahl, I.D. and Secunda, E. (1993) Consumer attitudes toward product placement in movies, *International Journal of Advertising*, 12, 1–11.

Nelson, M.R. and Devanathan, N. (2006) Brand placements Bollywood style, *Journal of Consumer Behaviour*, 5(3), 211–21.

Park, C., Jun, W.S.Y. and Shocker, A.D. (1996) Composite Branding Alliances: An Investigation of Extension and Feedback Effects, *Journal of Marketing Research*, 33(4), 453–66.

Pervan, S.J. and Martin, B.A.S. (2002) Product placement in US and New Zealand television soap operas: an exploratory study, *Journal of Marketing Communications*, 8, 101–13.

Plaut, M. (2004) Ford advertises the literary way, *BBC News/Business*, retrieved 20 March 2008 from http://news.bbc.co.uk/1/hi/business/3522635.stm.

Raghubir, P. and Krishna, A. (1999) Vital dimensions in volume perception: can the eye fool the stomach? *Journal of Marketing Research*, 36 (August), 313–26.

Reijmersdal van, E.A. (2011) Mixing advertising and editorial content in radio programmes: appreciation and recall of brand placements versus commercials, *International Journal of Advertising*, 30(3), 425–46.

Russell, C.A. and Belch, M. (2005) A managerial investigation into the product placement industry, *Journal of Advertising Research*, 45(1) (March), 73–92.

Shipley, D. and Wong, K.S. (1993) Exhibiting strategy and implementation, *International Journal of Advertising*, 12(2), 117–30.

Silayoi, P. and Speece, M. (2007) The importance of packaging attributes: a conjoint analysis approach, *European Journal of Marketing*, 41(11/12), 1495–517.

Smit, E., Reijmersdal van, E. and Neijens, P. (2009) Today's practice of brand placement and the industry behind it, *International Journal of Advertising*, 28(5), 761–82.

Southgate, P. (1994) *Total Branding by Design*, London: Kogan Page.

Stewart, B. (1995) *Packaging as an Effective Marketing Tool*, Surrey: Pira International.

*Sun* (The) (2012) Bookies causes a flutter with White Horse jockey stunt, 9 March, retrieved 12 April 2012 from http://www.thesun.co.uk/sol/homepage/news/4180538/Paddy-Power-puts-a-jockey-on-the-Uffington-White-Horse-to-promote-Cheltenham-Festival.html.

Sung, Y., Gregorio de, F. and Jung, J. (2009) Non-student consumer attitudes towards product placement: implications for public policy and advertisers, *International Journal of Advertising*, 28(2), 257–85.

Sung, Y. and de Gregorio, F. (2008) Brand new world: a comparison of consumers' attitudes toward brand placement in film, television shows, songs and video games, *Journal of Promotion Management*, 14(1/2), 85–101.

Verebelyi, N. (2000) The power of the pack, *Marketing*, 27 April, 37.

Weidmann, K.-P. and Ludwig, D. (2008) How risky are brand licensing strategies in view of customer perceptions and reactions? *Journal of General Management*, 33(3) (Spring), 31–52.

Wells, L.E., Farley, H. and Armstrong, G.A. (2007) The importance of packaging design for own-label food brands, *International Journal of Retail and Distribution Management*, 36(9), 677–90.

Woodside, F. and Summers, J. (2011) Sponsorship leveraged packaging: An exploratory study in FMCG, *Journal of Marketing Communications*, 17(2), April, 87–105.

Yuksel, U. and Voola, R. (2010) Travel trade shows: exploratory study of exhibitors' perceptions, *Journal of Business & Industrial Marketing*, 25(4), 293–300.

# Chapter 20
# Traditional media

Today the selection and use of particular media is necessary in order to enable conversations with and among audiences. The array of available media is continually growing but each has strengths and weaknesses that impact on the quality, effectiveness and the meaning attributed to a message by an audience.

This is the first of five chapters about the media and focuses on the nature and characteristics of conventional, or traditional, offline media.

## Aims and learning objectives

The aim of this chapter is to establish the principal characteristics of each main type of offline media. This will assist understanding of the management processes by which media are selected and scheduled to deliver advertisers' messages.

The learning objectives of this chapter are to:

1. determine the variety and types of traditional media;
2. explain the main criteria used to evaluate media and their use;
3. establish the primary characteristics of each type of medium;
4. examine the strengths and weaknesses of each type of medium;
5. provide a brief summary of the main UK trends in advertising expenditure on each type of medium;
6. consider the dynamics associated with direct response media;
7. explore ways in which media can be integrated.

# Minicase

## Smokefree South West – 'Wise-up to Roll-ups'

Smokefree South West launched a major campaign to target the 33 per cent of hand-rolling-tobacco (HRT) smokers in the South West, the highest percentage in the country. The first ever campaign of its kind targeting HRT or 'roll-ups', the objective was to highlight the inherent health risks of HRT and debunk the myths that have built up around smoking roll-ups, such as:

- Smokers thought hand rolling tobacco was more natural, with fewer additives.
- Many believed it allowed them greater control over their smoking.
- Many smokers believed that smoking hand rolling tobacco represented a more 'organic' and healthier option.
- Smokers enjoyed 'rolling up' and saw it as a real art form and skill.

In addition to busting the deeply entrenched myths regarding smoking hand-rolling tobacco, there was an additional challenge, since HRT smokers were immune to traditional anti-smoking campaigns and didn't think of themselves as 'normal' smokers. Finally, an additional requirement was to ensure that all claims made could be substantiated and were fully compliant with IPA, Clearcast and the RACC codes of practice on this sensitive subject.

### The 'Wise-up to Roll-ups' campaign

An integrated behaviour change campaign, 'Wise-up to Roll-ups' was developed and ran across the South West, including a hard-hitting TV and radio campaign, an eye-catching outdoor and press campaign and a campaign support website.

Proximity media – including washroom panels and beer mats in pubs and bars, together with sandwich bags and coffee cups, as well as waiting-room posters and leaflets in doctors' surgeries and clinics – were used to 'disrupt' roll-up smokers when they were most engaged in their habit.

The outdoor and proximity campaign featured a series of posters designed to look like hand-rolling tobacco pouches, but with the brand name replaced with an attention-grabbing word such as 'Stroke', 'Infertility' or 'Amputation' which highlighted the real health risks that roll-up smokers were taking.

The TV commercial featured a man who (the viewing audience first assume) is an ex-cigarette manufacturer, confessing to putting all the nasty chemicals into cigarettes. We later realise he's talking about when he used to smoke roll-ups. Like the outdoor, the aim is to really hit home the message that smoking roll-ups is just as bad for you as smoking cigarettes.

| Exhibit 20.1 | **High-impact outdoor advertising** |
|---|---|
| | *Source*: Bray Leino Ltd |

---

| Exhibit 20.2 | **Wise-up quit support pouch** |
| | *Source*: Bray Leino Ltd |

In addition to providing the motivation to quit by dispelling the myths about HRT, support was also provided to help HRT smokers to quit in the form of a 'Wise-up pouch'. Created in the style of a hand-rolling tobacco pouch, the pack contained information about the dangers of hand-rolling tobacco and quitting tools to aid smokers to quit. Smokers ordered a pouch by texting WISE to a unique text number, 0800 028 0553, or by going online to the dedicated website www.wiseupandquit.co.uk.

### A rolling success

The campaign, which was backed by Cancer Research UK and the Faculty of Public Health, has been an incredible success. Gabriel Scally, Regional Director of Public Health and Smokefree South West spokesperson said: 'Hand-rolled cigarettes present the same kinds of health risks to smokers as manufactured cigarettes, such as cancer, impotence, stroke and lung disease.'

Jean King, Cancer Research UK's director of tobacco control, said: 'This campaign dispels the dangerous myth, believed by many smokers, that hand-rolled cigarettes are more "natural" and so less harmful than manufactured ones. Smoking hand-rolling tobacco is just as harmful as cigarettes bought in packets.'

Professor Lindsey Davies, President of the Faculty of Public Health said: 'This is a ground-breaking campaign highlighting the dangers that hand rolling tobacco can cause. We fully endorse this campaign. Rolling your own presents as many risks as do normal cigarettes.'

Smokefree South West has already fulfilled over 5,000 Wise-up pouches across the South West and demand has been so high that more pouches have had to be printed.

*This case study was written by Kate Knight, Head of Social Marketing and Communications, Smokefree South West and James Robertson of Bray Leino. Permission to use the material was kindly given by Smokefree South West.*

---

| Exhibit 20.3 | **Smokefree South West and Bray Leino logos** |
| | *Source*: Bray Leino Ltd |

# Introduction

Organisations use a wide variety of media. These can be classified simply as *traditional* and *new*, or *conventional* and *digital*. However, these terms are too broad and misleading as to what constitutes new and old and, in any case, digital media are used within traditional media. A more meaningful classification is to consider the media in terms of their physicality or location. Here 'out-of-home' and 'broadcast' describes what these media are and how they work.

An alternative approach is to consider the media in terms of their source or ownership. Here media owned by others are segregated from media that the clients own themselves.

In this chapter consideration is given to what is referred to as 'conventional media' using the physicality classification as the main structure. Each is introduced here and their characteristics and market trends are examined, although the following four chapters provide greater depth and insight into each one. Subsequent chapters examine other more contemporary issues associated with the use of the media.

# Media classification by form

When classifying media in terms of their form, six main *classes* can be identified. These are broadcast, print, outdoor, digital, in-store and other media classes. Within each of these classes there are particular *types* of media. For example, within the broadcast class there are television and radio, and within the print class there are newspapers and magazines.

Within each type of medium there are a huge number of different media *vehicles* that can be selected to carry an advertiser's message. For example, within UK television there are the terrestrial networks (Independent Television Network, Channel 4 and Channel 5) and the satellite (BSkyB) and cable (e.g. Virgin Media) networks. In print, there are consumer and business-oriented magazines, and the number of specialist magazines is expanding rapidly. These specialist magazines are targeted at particular activity and interest groups, such as *Amateur Photographer*, *Golf World* and the infamous *Plumbing Monthly*! This provides opportunities for advertisers to send messages to well-defined homogeneous groups, which improves effectiveness and reduces wastage in the communication spend. Table 20.1 sets out the three forms of media – classes, types and vehicles – with a few examples.

# Media classification by source

The traditional demarcation regards media in terms of purely paid-for channels, used to support conventional advertising. The second classification of the media, by source, was presented earlier in the text (Chapter 1). Popularly known as POEM, which stands for paid-for, owned, and earned media, this classification reflects a practitioners' interpretation of the media. POEM assumes that media is not just about paid-for media but one that embraces all items that can be used to convey brand-orientated messages, regardless of whether a payment is necessary. With the digital explosion, reconfiguration of the media landscape and changing consumer behaviours, POEM reflects the increasing scope of contemporary media and the range of media opportunities to engage audiences.

In broad terms, much of this chapter is concerned with paid-for media; the following two chapters consider owned and earned media. (Chapters 23 and 24 are principally concerned with a mix of all media.)

| Table 20.1 | Summary chart of the main forms of media by form | |
|---|---|---|
| **Class** | **Type** | **Vehicles** |
| Broadcast | Television | *Coronation Street, X Factor*, Classic FM |
| | Radio | |
| Print | Newspapers | *The Sunday Times, The Mirror*, The *Daily* |
| | Magazines: consumer business | *Telegraph, Cosmopolitan, Woman, The Grocer, Plumbing News* |
| Out-of-Home | Billboards | 96-, 48- and 6-sheet |
| | Street furniture | Adshel |
| | Transit | Underground stations, airport buildings, taxis, hot-air balloons |
| Digital media | Internet | Websites, email, intranets, Facebook |
| | Digital television CD-ROM | Teletext, SkyText, Various including music, educational, entertainment |
| In-store | Point-of-purchase | Bins, signs and displays |
| | Packaging | The Coca-Cola contour bottle |
| Other | Cinema | Pearl & Dean, Orange Wednesdays |
| | Exhibitions and events | Ideal Home, The Motor Show |
| | Product placement | Films, TV, books |
| | Ambient | Litter bins, golf tees, petrol pumps, washrooms |
| | Guerrilla | Flyposting |

| Table 20.2 | POEM – A classification of the media by source | |
|---|---|---|
| **Type of Media** | | **Explanation** |
| P | Paid for | Advertising traditionally requires that media time and space are rented from a media owner, in order to convey messages and reach target audiences. The selection of the media mix is planned, predetermined and measured in terms of probable size of audience, costs and scheduling. |
| O | Owned | Organisations have a range of assets that they can use to convey messages to audiences, and through which they can develop conversations. Ownership means that there are no rental costs as with paid-for media. For example, a brand name or product display on a building, a telephone number or URL on a vehicle, or the use of the company website and its links to other sites, do not incur usage fees. |
| E | Earned | Earned media refers to comments and conversations, both offline and online, in social media, in the news, or through face-to-face communications, about a brand or organisation. These comments can be negative or positive but the media carrying them are diverse and can be referred to as 'unplanned', although many campaigns seek to stimulate strong word-of-mouth communications through earned media. |

| Viewpoint 20.1 | Lego use their own media |
| --- | --- |

Increasingly, organisations are exploiting the use of their own media and developing channel networks designed to enable customers to have positive experiences of their brands. For example, Lego have used their own digital media in a variety of ways to provide consumer experiences.

Lego have used their own media to build a fan club, develop social networks, and provide online games, message boards, online movies, as well as support a multiplayer game.

Through the use of a particular Lego website, audiences are invited to submit ideas and even design products. Over 120,000 networked brand ambassadors, mainly self-identified volunteer designers, many of whom are just 6–11-year-old boys, interact to promote ideas and share information, and through word-of-mouth pass on ideas and news about Lego-related events, products, and issues.

The Lego Friends range is aimed at girls aged between five and eight, and incorporates five mini-figure dolls, coloured bricks, animals and accessories. Lego also created a fictional Heartlake City world to accompany the range. This forms a backdrop for the Lego Friends range and includes a variety of sets including a tree house, beauty salon and veterinary clinic. This is because role play and themes are a key to success in the girls market. Some paid-for media (television, print) were used to launch the range, but crucially it is owned media that have been a crucial part of the success of the range. A dedicated microsite allows audiences to explore the Heartlake City world online, to interact with characters, and download additional themed materials that form the core of the media.

The Lego revival and very strong brand US strength has been attributed to their use of owned media.

*Source*:   Chapman (2011); Egol, Moeller, and Vollmer (2009).

Question:   How might companies balance the impact of a POEM-based media mix, when measurement of some media performance is so imprecise?

Task:       Find three organisations that have used earned media. How have they measured performance?

# Evaluative criteria

One of the key marketing tasks is to decide which combination of media vehicles should be selected to carry a message to an audience. The means by which this decision is reached is dealt with later (Chapter 24). First, however, it is necessary to consider the main characteristics of each type of paid-for media in order that media-planning decisions can be based on some logic and rationale. The fundamental characteristics concern the costs, the richness of the communication, the interactive properties and audience profile associated with a communication event.

## Costs

One of the important characteristics that need to be considered is the costs that are incurred using each type of medium. There are two types of cost: absolute and relative. Absolute costs are the costs of the time or space bought in a particular media vehicle. These costs have to be paid for and directly impact upon an organisation's cash flow. Relative costs are the costs of contacting each member of the target audience.

Television, as will be seen later, has a high absolute cost but, because messages are delivered to a mass audience, when the absolute cost is divided by the total number of people receiving the message, the relative cost is very low.

## Communication richness

The way in which a message is delivered and understood by a target audience varies across types of media. Certain media, such as television, are able to use many communication dimensions, and through the use of sight, sound and movement can generate great impact with a message. Other types of media have only one dimension, such as the audio capacity of radio or the written word on a page of text. The number of communication dimensions that a media type has will influence the choice of media mix. This is because certain products, at particular points in their development, require the use of different media in order that the right message be conveyed and understood. A new product, for example, may require demonstration in order that the audience understands the product concept. The use of television may be a good way of achieving this. Once it is understood, the audience does not need to be educated in this way again and future messages need to convey different types of information that may not require demonstration, so radio or magazine advertising may suffice (see Chapter 24, where media richness theory is explored).

## Interactive properties

Following on from the previous element is the important issue of interactive communications. The development of digital media has enabled interaction, which we know can lead to dialogue, and this in turn enables relationship development (Ballantyne, 2004). However, there are some circumstances in which interaction is not required due to the nature of the market, the product or the objectives of the campaign. In these circumstances the mix will need to consist of media that primarily deliver messages through a one-way, or monologic, communication format.

Marketing communications that seek to engage audiences through interaction, in particular those that deliver a call-to-action, will need to use media that enable interaction and to be used where support facilities are in place to facilitate interactive communications.

## Audience profile

The profile of the target audience (male, female, young or old) and the number of people within each audience that a medium can reach are also significant factors in media decisions. Based around demographics, attitudes, and psychographics, a profile of a typical user and their media habits can be developed. It is important that advertisers use media vehicles that convey planned messages to and between their audiences with as little waste as possible. Newspapers enable geographically dispersed audiences to be reached. The tone of their content can be controlled, but the cost per target reached is often high. Each issue has a short lifespan, so for positive learning to occur, a number of insertions may be required.

A large number of magazines contain specialised material that appeals to particular groups. These special-interest magazines (SIMs) enable certain sponsors to reach interested audiences with reduced wastage. General-interest magazines (GIMs) appeal to a much wider cross-section of society, to larger generalised target groups. The life of these media vehicles is generally long and their 'pass along' readership high. It should not be forgotten, however, that noise levels can also be high owing to the intermittent manner in which magazines are often read and the number of competing messages from rival organisations.

Television reaches the greatest number of people, but although advertisers can reach general groups, such as men aged 16–24, or housewives, it is not capable of reaching specific interest groups and it incurs high levels of wastage. This blanket coverage offers opportunities for cable and satellite operators to offer more precise targeting, but for now television is a tool for those who wish to talk to large, once mass, audiences. Television is expensive from a cash-flow perspective but not in terms of the costs per person reached.

Radio offers a more reasonable costing structure than television and can be utilised to reach particular geographic audiences. For a long time, however, this was seen as its only real strength, particularly when its poor attention span and non-visual dimensions are considered. Although radio will never overtake television in terms of usage and overall popularity, radio has been shown to be capable of generating a much closer personal relationship with listeners, witnessed partly by the success of Classic FM and local radio stations, than is possible through posters, television or print.

The interesting point about advertising through out-of-home media is that exposure is only made by the interception of passing traffic. Govoni et al. (1986) make the point that such interception represents opportunistic coverage. Consequently the costs are low, at both investment and per contact levels.

The use of direct marketing is well established, so the precise targeting potential of direct mail and its ability to communicate personally with target audiences is impressive. In addition, the control over the total process, including the costs, remains firmly with the sponsor.

---

**Scholars' paper 20.1**    **Engaging television**

**Heath, R. (2009) Emotional Engagement: How Television Builds Big Brands At Low Attention,** *Journal of Advertising Research*, **29(1) March, 62–73.**

This paper is principally concerned with engagement and the way in which television can build brands through low attention. An interesting and thought-provoking article and one which those interested in advertising and media should read.

---

# Print media

Newspapers and magazines are the two main types of media in this class. They attract advertisers for a variety of reasons, but the most important is that print media are very effective at delivering a message to a target audience.

Most people have access to either a newspaper or a magazine and they read in order to keep up to date with news and events or to provide themselves with a source of entertainment. However, increasing numbers of people are not taking the opportunity to read newspapers and advertising spend in press is declining and shifting to other media, most notably the Internet.

Of those people who do use printed media, most tend to have consistent reading habits and buy or borrow the same media vehicles regularly. For example, most people read the same type of newspaper(s) each day and their regular choice of magazine reflects either their business or leisure interests, which are normally quite stable. This means that advertisers, through marketing research, are able to build a database of the main characteristics (a profile) of their readers. This in turn allows advertisers to buy space in those media vehicles that will be read by the sort of people they think will benefit from their product or service.

The printed word provides advertisers with the opportunity to explain their message in a way that most other media cannot. Such explanations can be in the form of either a picture or a photograph, perhaps demonstrating how a product is to be used. Alternatively, the written word can be used to argue why a product should be used and detail the advantages and benefits that consumption will provide the user. In reality, advertisers use a combination of these two forms of communication.

Print media are most suitable for messages designed when high involvement is present in the target market. These readers not only control the pace at which they read a magazine or newspaper, but also expend effort to read advertisements because they care about particular issues. Where elaboration is high and the central processing route is preferred, messages that provide a large amount of information are best presented in the printed form.

Print media is often regarded as a secondary medium to television. There are several reasons for this, but one of them is linked to the perceived 'emotional power' of television. However, Heath and McDonald (2007) report research by OTX using the CEP*Test. This demonstrates that the emotive power of both print and television ads is basically the same. Their research suggests strongly that press is just as effective as television in building brands and is, in fact, superior with regard to attention-getting and communicating information. What this means is that advertisers can seriously reduce their media costs simply by switching some of their budget out of television and into print and still achieve the same impact.

## Newspapers

As indicated previously, newspaper readership is in decline and has been falling since the mid 1980s. This is most starkly visible among the young as they gather their news from other sources, most notably the Internet. The biggest shift has been away from the popular press, with some movement towards the quality press. The number of adults reading a paid-for national daily newspaper has fallen by 15 per cent and those reading any regional newspaper by 30 per cent (IPA, 2011). As a result advertising expenditure has not grown in this medium.

Faced with a declining market, newspapers are repositioning themselves as multi-platform publishing entities. In addition to the change from broadsheet to compact formats and the provision of online papers, innovation in the newspaper sector is critical. News International who own *The Times*, now charge for access to the online version of the newspaper. Their closure of the *News of the World* in 2011, following the investigation into phone-hacking allegations, and the subsequent launch of the *Sunday Sun* suggest there is some market resilience and opportunities for advertisers who wish to use the tabloid press. Innovation can also be seen in the growth of free papers, the increasing interest in local news and a cross-media orientation (WARC, 2007). This requires major structural change and some risk in anticipating consumer needs.

### Strengths

Readers are in control when reading a newspaper and as a result newspaper advertisements are seen positively. This means that readers choose which advertisements are read, how long they consider them (dwell time) and how often they are read. This facilitates 'comparison shopping' and is useful when readers experience high involvement. Newspapers provide wide exposure for advertisements, and market coverage in local, regional or national papers can be extensive. These media vehicles are extremely flexible as they present opportunities for the use of colour and allow advertisements of variable sizes, insertions and coupons.

### Weaknesses

The combination of a high number of advertisements and the small amount of genuine reading time that many readers give to newspapers means that most newspaper advertisements receive little exposure. Statistics show that newspaper circulation has fallen behind population growth; furthermore, teenagers and young adults generally do not read newspapers.

Advertising costs have risen very quickly and the competition to provide news, not just from other newspapers, but also from other sources such as cable, satellite and terrestrial television, means that newspapers are no longer one of the main providers of news. Printing technologies advanced considerably during the 1980s and 1990s, but the relatively poor quality of reproduction means that the impact of advertisements can often be lost.

## Magazines

Magazines can be considered in terms of their intended markets, for example, consumer and business magazines. These can be refined to reach quite specialised audiences and tend to be selective in terms of the messages they carry. In contrast, newspapers reach a relatively high percentage of the population and can be referred to as a mass medium. The messages that newspapers carry are usually for products and services that have a general appeal.

Customer magazines differ from consumer magazines because they are sent to customers direct, often without charge, and contain highly targeted and significant branded content material. These have made a big impact in recent years and, partly because of high production values, have become a significant aspect of many direct marketing activities. This medium is very popular with the retail sector, with most of the supermarkets offering their own magazine and brands such as John Lewis and Harrods plus Virgin Media (Electric!) all investing despite rising production and distribution costs. Durrani (2011) believes this is due to the deep levels of engagement associated with the medium.

Sales of magazines in pure hardcopy print format are falling. The magazine sector is in transition as digital formats are evolving. Publishers are having to innovate and develop their titles as media brands and extend reader relationships across mobile, tablet and the Web. Customer magazines, such as Google's own print b2b magazine, *Think Quarterly*, and campaigns that integrate print and digital communications with QR codes and augmented reality (see Chapters 21 and 22), are just some of the ways publishers are changing their approach to reaching and engaging their audiences (May, 2011).

### Strengths

The visual quality of magazines is normally very high, a result of using top-class materials and technologies. This provides advertisers with great flexibility with the visual dimension of their messages. The visual element of magazines is a real strength as it can be used to create impact and demand the attention of readers.

The large number and wide range of specialised titles means that narrow, specific target audiences can be reached much more successfully than with other media vehicles. For example, messages concerning ski equipment, clothing and resorts will be best presented in specialist ski magazines on the basis that they will be read by those who have an interest in skiing, rather than, for example, knitting, snooker or fishing. Magazines can provide a prestigious and high-quality environment, with the editorial providing authority, reassurance and credibility to the advertising that they contain.

Magazines are portable, can be read nearly anywhere and some have the potential to bestow status on the reader. Magazines are often passed along to others to read once the original user has finished reading them. This longevity issue highlights the difference between circulation (the number of people who buy or subscribe to a magazine) and readership (the number of people who actually read the vehicle, perhaps as a friend or partner at home, in a doctor's waiting room or at the instigation of a department head or workplace superior).

### Weaknesses

Magazine audience growth rates have fallen behind the growth in advertising rates. Therefore the value of advertising in magazines has declined relative to some other types of media. The long period of time necessary to book space in advance of publication dates and to provide suitable artwork means that management has little flexibility once it has agreed to use magazines as part of the media schedule. Apart from specialist magazines, a single magazine rarely reaches the majority of a market segment.

Several magazines must be used to reach potential users. Having reached the target, impact often builds slowly, as some readers do not read their magazine until some days after they have received it. The absolute and relative costs associated with magazines are fairly high, particularly costs associated with general-interest magazines. Special-interest magazines, however, allow advertisers to reach their target audiences with little waste and hence high levels of efficiency.

---

### Viewpoint 20.2　　The next magazine will be on a digital platform

The demise of the physical newsstand is not news, but the development of the digital newsstand represents the new approach publishers are adopting to reach their markets. For example, the launch of Apple's Newsstand platform in 2011, and Yahoo's Livestand app for iPad reflects changes in consumer behaviour, in magazine usage and how they engage with magazine brands.

IPC's *Marie Claire* is now available on 11 different platforms and is a significant consumer influencer. 35 per cent of Mac User's overall circulation is distributed via iPad users, and Evo has 6,000 iPad subscriptions, and downloads in the region of 300,000 for its enhanced digital edition.

The fashion magazine *Grazia* launched its 2012 spring collections edition at the same time as the London Fashion Week, and was sponsored by LG Mobile. The magazine provided support with an online behind-the-scenes documentary TV series. Through user-generated content it allowed readers to comment, influence and vote on both the front cover and editorial material. The entire 'print' product was accessible across all *Grazia* platforms, including graziadaily.co.uk, YouTube and Facebook.

Morrisons became the first bricks-and mortar-supermarket to launch a magazine as a free iPad app, downloaded from the App Store and Newsstand. Launched at the same time as the in-store magazine was redesigned, the app featured 38 pages, with some exclusive content. The iPad magazine recipes are presented as interactive cards, which not only showcase products and methods, but also allow readers to cook along in real time. Users can create shopping lists through the recipe cards and draw attention to wines that would complement the recipes. A new Twitter account was created enabling readers to interact with the magazine team.

*Source*: Fletcher (2012); Chapman (2012).

**Question:**　Why do you think magazines are so effective in a digital context?

**Task:**　Get a copy of any magazine and compare the content with a consumer magazine bought off the shelf of a retail store.

| Exhibit 20.4 | **Many of the growing number of digital magazines are designed to be accessed through tablets and mobiles** |
|---|---|

*Source*: Bertrand Guay/AFP/Getty Images

One final form of print media yet to be discussed is directories. Advertising expenditure on directories has continued to increase. One of the largest consumer directories is Yellow Pages, or Yell as they are now called, as they have diversified across new media (e.g. Yell.com).

---

### Scholars' paper 20.2 | Newspaper as media efficacy

**Danaher, P. and Rossiter, J. (2011) Comparing Perceptions of Marketing Communication Channels, *European Journal of Marketing*, 45(1/2), 6–42.**

Danaher and Rossiter's research demonstrates that clutter in newspapers is less bothersome to newspaper readers than clutter in other media. Their research concluded that print ads in newspapers are less intrusive than other forms of media (such as the 'interruptive' quality of radio and TV) and that consumers who read newspapers feel that engagement with the traditional print medium is a good use of the their time.

---

# Broadcast media

Fundamentally, there are two main forms of broadcast media: television and radio. Advertisers use this class of media because this class of media can reach mass audiences with their messages at a relatively low cost per target reached.

Approximately 99 per cent of the population in the United Kingdom, and most developed economies, have access to a television set and a similar number have a radio. The majority of viewers use television passively, as a form of entertainment. However, new technological applications have the potential to change this, so that television could be used proactively for a range of services, such as banking and shopping. Radio demands active participation, and can reach people who are out of the home environment.

Broadcast media allow advertisers to add visual and/or sound dimensions to their messages. The opportunity to demonstrate or to show the benefits or results that a particular product can bring gives life and energy to an advertiser's message. Television uses image, sound and movement, whereas radio can only use its audio capacity to convey meaning, but it does stimulate a listener's imagination and thus can involve audiences in a message. Both media have the potential to tell stories and to appeal to people's emotions. These are dimensions that print media find difficulty in achieving effectively within the time allocations that advertisers can afford.

Advertising messages transmitted through the broadcast media use a small period of time, called 'spots', normally 60, 30, 20 or 10 seconds, that are bought from the owners of the medium. The cost of the different time spots varies throughout a single transmission day and with the popularity of individual programmes. The more listeners or viewers that a programme attracts, the greater the price charged for a slice of time to transmit an advertising message. The time-based costs for television can be extremely large. For example, as at June 2012, the rate card cost of a nationwide 30-second spot in the middle of *Coronation Street* was £59,549 (www.itvsales.com).

However, this large cost needs to be put in perspective. The actual cost of reaching individual members of the target audience is quite low, simply because all the costs associated with the production of the message and the purchase of time to transmit the message can be spread across a mass of individuals, as discussed earlier.

The costs associated with radio transmissions are relatively low when compared with television. This reflects the lack of prestige that radio has and the pervasiveness of television. People are normally unable, and usually unwilling, to become actively involved with broadcast advertising messages. They cannot control the pace at which they consume such advertising and as time is expensive and short, so advertisers do not have the opportunity to present detailed information. The result is that this medium is most suitable for low-involvement messages. Where the need for elaboration is low and the peripheral processing route is preferred, messages transmitted through electronic media should seek to draw attention, create awareness and improve levels of interest.

As the television and radio industries become increasingly fragmented, so reaching particular market segments has become more difficult, as the target audience is often dispersed across other media. This means that the potential effectiveness of advertising through these media decreases. These media are used a great deal in consumer markets, mainly because of their ability to reach large audiences, but there is often considerable wastage and inefficiency. The result is that advertisers are moving their advertising spend to other media, most notably to the Internet for both online and mobile markets.

## Television

For a number of years there was above inflation growth in television advertising investment. However, annual growth since 2003 has been moderate and the recession in 2008 and 2009 saw television ad investment slashed by nearly 20 per cent. Growth has since returned with a 12 per cent + surge in 2011. Spot prices have been falling in tune with the market, making television far more cost-effective and efficient today than it was in the mid 1980s. The cost of reaching an audience through television has fallen by 32 per cent in this period. According to the IPA dataBANK, television viewing figures have remained constant for the past 30 years, when recorded viewing and new digital multi-channel viewing formats are included

(Binet and Field, 2007). TV remains the most effective medium in terms of accomplishing campaign objectives, especially hard business measures such as profit and return on investment (IPA, 2011).

## Strengths

From a creative point of view, this medium is very flexible and the impact generated by the combination of image and sound should not be underestimated. Consumer involvement and likeability of an advertisement is dependent upon the skill of the creative team. The prestige and status associated with television advertising is higher than that of other media: in some cases, the credibility and status of a product or organisation can be enhanced significantly just by being seen to be advertising on television.

The prestige and status associated with television advertising is higher than that of other media. The costs of reaching members of large target segments are relatively low, so the medium is capable of a high level of cost efficiency.

## Weaknesses

Because the length of any single exposure is short, messages have to be repeated on television in order to enhance learning and memory. This increases the absolute costs of producing and transmitting television commercials, which can be large, making this medium the most expensive form of advertising.

Television audiences are increasingly fragmented as the number of entertainment and leisure opportunities expands. For example, terrestrial television networks have experienced declining audiences as new channels and competitors (cable and satellite broadcasters) have entered the market, and as new sources of entertainment have emerged. This proliferation of suppliers has led to television clutter. In order to keep viewers, programmes are now promoted vigorously by television companies and a variety of techniques are being used to prevent viewers from channel grazing (switching).

The trend towards shorter messages has also led to increased clutter. Management flexibility over the message is frustrated, as last-minute changes to schedules are expensive and difficult to implement. The only choices open to decision-makers are either to proceed with an advertisement or to 'pull' it, should circumstances change in such a way that it would be inappropriate to proceed.

The adoption of some technological developments, most notably the development of interactive television (iTV), have been slow. However, this is changing as iTV (interactive) is increasingly recognised as the way forward (see Chapter 25 for more on iTV). However, as technology advances to create better, more commercially viable interactive opportunities so it also develops disruptive potential to benefit viewers who dislike their leisure time interrupted for ads. First, there was TiVo, a device to blank out ads when recording programmes, which was slow to catch on but is now gathering momentum. Now there are personal video recorders (PVRs) that enable viewers to pause live programmes, 'time-shift' programming to suit their own lifestyles and convenience and to fast forward through commercial breaks in a few seconds.

## Radio

There has been a rapid increase in the number of commercial radio services offered in the United Kingdom since 1973. In the period 2004–2010 the number of commercial radio stations in the UK rose 29 per cent to 387. This interest in radio is possibly due to a recognition of the versatility of what is often regarded as a secondary medium. However, advertising expenditure on radio reached a peak of £582 million in 2003, but has since fallen back to £436 million in 2011.

### Strengths

Radio enables specialised programming, which in turn attracts selective, narrow audiences. Radio is a mobile medium, in the sense that it can travel with audiences. This means that messages can be relayed to them, for example, even when shoppers are parking their cars near a shopping precinct, or whilst attending a sports or entertainment event. The production costs are low and radio has great flexibility, which management can use to meet changing environmental and customer needs. If it is raining in the morning, an advertiser can implement a promotional campaign for umbrellas in the afternoon.

Radio can complement other media like television, through 'visual transfer', and from a creative point of view, the medium needs the active imagination of the listener. It is referred to as a 'theatre of the mind'; listeners can build their own visual images as they listen. Radio also enables interactivity, as listeners can talk back via letter/telephone/email/text (www.rab.co.uk).

Radio has a high level of passive acceptance and the messages that are received are more likely to be retained than if they were delivered via a different medium. This combination of features makes radio an excellent support medium.

### Weaknesses

Because there is an absence of visual stimuli, the medium lacks impact and the ability to hold and enthuse an audience. Levels of inattentiveness can be high, which means that a high number of messages are invariably ignored or missed. When this is combined with low average audiences, high levels of frequency are required to achieve acceptable levels of reach.

# Outdoor media

The term 'outdoor media' has been replaced by many who refer to 'out-of-home' media. However, it is interesting to note that the industry association has recently been rebranded as the Outdoor Media Centre. Reference will therefore be made to outdoor media in this chapter.

Outdoor media consist of three main formats: street furniture (such as bus shelters); billboards (consisting primarily of 96-, 48- and 6-sheet poster sites); and transit (which covers the underground/metro, lorries, buses and taxis). The range of outdoor media encompasses a large number of different formats, each characterised by two elements. First, they can be observed at locations away from home. Second, they are normally used to support messages that are transmitted through primary media: broadcast and print. Outdoor can therefore, be seen to be a secondary but important support media for a complementary and effective communications mix. Other reasons for the use of outdoor expenditure are that it can reinforce messages transmitted through primary media, act as a substitute medium when primary media are unavailable (e.g. tobacco organisations deprived of access to television and radio) and provide novelty and interest (electronic, inflatable and three-dimensional billboards), which can help avoid the clutter caused by the volume of advertising activity.

One of the common strands that bind these diverse media together is that they are all used to reach consumers who are themselves in transit, moving from one place to another, even if this is a shopping trip, going to/from work or taking a holiday. Fitch (2007) comments that this class of media is not associated with any particular content. Advertising in television, radio, magazines, newspapers, cinema and the Internet media involves interrupting or accompanying editorial, informational or entertainment material. This is not the case with outdoor media.

There is a balance to be achieved between reaching people and enriching their landscape and annoying those who do not like to see commercial messages on every available space.

In Fitch's view, the use of outdoor media must take into account the following variables: 'the length of the ad exposure (viewer "dwell time" in relation to the ad), the ad's intrusiveness on the surrounding environment, and the likely mood and mindset of the consumers who will encounter the ad'. It is the interaction of these variables that shapes each individual's experience of outdoor media and hence the effectiveness of each communication.

Media spend on outdoor advertising reached a peak of £976m in 2007 and fell in 2008 and 2009 with the recession but has started to recover and reached £886m in 2011 (Outdoor Media Centre, 2011). Outdoor media accounted for approximately 5.6 per cent of total advertising expenditure in 2011.

## Billboards and street furniture

These are static displays and, as with out-of-home media generally, are unable to convey a great deal of information in the short period of time available in which people can attend to the messages. However, advances in technology permit precise targeting of poster campaigns on a national, regional or individual audience basis, or by their proximity to specific outlets, such as banks, CTNs (confectioner, tobacconist and newsagent) and off-licences. There are two key developments in the industry that concern the replacement of the traditional bucket-and-paste production process. The first is the use of biodegradable one-sheet posters. The second concerns the use of high-definition (HD) billboards, which are glue-less vinyl posters that can be clipped in and out of a frame, reused and eventually recycled (Gray, 2008). Evaluation using the POSTAR system allows for measurement of not only the size and type of audience but also the traffic flows, travel patterns and even how people read posters.

### Strengths

One of the main advantages of this medium is its ability to reach a large audience. This means that most members of a target audience are likely to have an opportunity to see the message, so the cost per contact is very low. It is generally recognised that outdoor media can provide tremendous support to other tools in the media mix, particularly at product launch, as back-up and when attempting to build brand name recognition.

| Exhibit 20.5 | **Bus shelter advertising for the WIRSPA campaign (see Chapter 10)** |
| --- | --- |
| | *Source*: Bray Leino Ltd |

The medium is characterised by its strong placement flexibility. Messages can be placed geographically, demographically or by activity, such as on the main routes to work or shopping. The potential impact is high, as good sites can draw the eye and make an impression. Gross rating points (GRPs) (see Chapter 24) can be developed quickly by reaching a large percentage of the target audience many times in a short period.

### Weaknesses

Messages transmitted by this medium do not allow for the provision of detailed information. Posters are passed very quickly and the potential attention span is therefore brief. This means that the message must be short, have a high visual impact and be capable of selling an idea or concept very quickly. Printing and production lead times are long; therefore, while control over message content is high, the flexibility in delivery once showings are agreed can be a limiting factor. The final disadvantage of out-of-home media to be mentioned is that the effectiveness of message delivery is very difficult to measure, and in an age when accountability is becoming an increasingly important factor, this drawback does not help to promote the usage of this medium.

## Transit

The names, signs and symbols that are painted on the sides of lorries and taxis can best represent transit or transport advertising. These moving posters, which travel around the country, serve to communicate names of organisations and products to all those who are in the vicinity of the vehicle. Indeed, transport advertising includes all those vehicles that are used for commercial purposes. In addition to lorries and taxis, transit media include buses, the Underground and Metro (trains, escalators and walkways), airplanes, blimps and balloons, ferries and trains, plus the terminals and buildings associated with the means of transport, such as airports and railway stations. For example, Terminal 5 at London's Heathrow airport incorporates a digital ad network, called The Runway. This was designed following eye-tracker research, and is for brands targeting shoppers in the luxury area of the building (McCabe, 2009).

Research has shown that transit and, in particular, taxi advertising has very good reach and that its main role should be as a support medium (Veloutsou and O'Donnell, 2005). Messages can be presented as inside cards, where the messages are exposed to those using the vehicle. An example of this would be the small advertising messages displayed on the curvature of the roof of London Underground trains. Outside cards are those that are displayed on the exterior of taxis, buses and other commercial vehicles.

The difference between outdoor and transport media is arbitrary, although the former are media static and the latter are media mobile.

### Strengths

The exposure time given to messages delivered via transport media can be high, but is dependent upon the journey time of the reader. The high readership scores that are recorded are due, possibly, to the boredom levels of travellers. The cost is relatively low, mainly because no extra equipment is necessary to transmit the message. Local advertisers tend to benefit most from transport advertising, as it can remind buyers of particular restaurants, theatres and shops.

### Weaknesses

The medium fails to cover all market segments, as only particular groups use transportation systems. In comparison with other media it lacks status, is difficult to read (particularly in the rush hour) and suffers from the high level of clutter associated with inside cards.

## Scholars' paper 20.3     Outdoor in perspective

**Meurs, van, L. and Aristoff, M. (2009) Split-Second Recognition: What Makes Outdoor Advertising Work?** *Journal of Advertising Research*, 49(1) March, 82–92.

There are few papers on outdoor advertising so this one is recommended not only for its content but also for its scarcity. The paper considers the format and content of outdoor advertising and how the format affects the speed of brand recognition, and how it enhances appeal of the product. The research indicates how consumers process outdoor advertising posters in real life within a split second, and how content and format are variables in this process.

See also: Taylor, C.R., Franke, G.R. and Bang, H.-K. (2006) Use and Effectiveness of Billboards: Perspectives from Selective-Perception Theory and Retail-Gravity Models, *Journal of Advertising*, 35(4), Winter, 21–34.

## Viewpoint 20.3     Escaping to the high seas

Some media mixes do not need to contain a variety of media to be effective. Sometimes a concentration of one particular type of media can be penetrative. Take for example the campaign run by Clipper Ventures to attract potential new sailors to the 'Clipper Round the World Yacht Race'. Here the company uses its own fleet of 68-foot racing yachts, crewed by members of the public, 40 per cent of whom had never set foot on a yacht before.

Clipper had previously used *The Sunday Times* and broadsheet newspapers and, while they were able to recruit the 'sailors' they needed, it was always a worry that they would not get enough of them. For the 2010–11 race Clipper wanted their new campaign to capture people's imagination as they went about their daily lives and to fill up the race spaces more comfortably. The appeal was based on people breaking free, escaping from their routine jobs, office routines and endless meetings.

Clipper realised that their potential audience was vast as there is no single type of person who might sign up. So the campaign needed to appeal to all ages and demographics, and to chief executives, taxi drivers, nurses and university students. However, there was one thing that was common to all of them: their spirit of adventure.

Rather than continue with print, the 2010–11 campaign was switched to outdoor media. In order to reach potential sailors, a poster campaign, using over 600 national railway and underground station sites around the country, was implemented.

The creative was an aerial shot of one of the yachts ploughing through the sea with several people on board. The slogan read 'Challenging week ahead?' and beside each figure in the boat was a job title, such as city trader, mechanic, housewife, with one final figure next to the question 'you?'.

The campaign generated over 3,000 website enquiries; more than 2,700 people heard about the race through word of mouth and the Clipper website had 80 per cent growth in traffic compared to a similar period in previous campaigns. The number of people signing up in August 2010 was double the largest number that Clipper had received in the same time period with previous campaigns. With two of the legs sold out, the campaign had put the process eight months ahead of where they had ever been before at that stage.

*Source*:   Barda (2010).

**Question:**   Why did Clipper use the slogan 'Challenging week ahead?'

**Task:**   Find another example where the media used were concentrated in a narrow field.

| Exhibit 20.6 | **An ad from the Clipper Ventures campaign (up to November 2011)** |
| --- | --- |
| | *Source*: Clipper Ventures |

# In-store media

As an increasing number of brand choice decisions are made during the shopping experience, advertisers have become aware of the need to provide suitable in-store communications. The primary objective of using in-store media is to direct the attention of shoppers and to stimulate them to make purchases. The content of messages can be easily controlled by either the retailer or the manufacturer. In addition, the timing and the exact placement of in-store messages can be equally well controlled.

As mentioned previously, both retailers and manufacturers make use of in-store media although, of the two main forms (point-of-purchase displays and packaging), retailers control the point-of-purchase displays and manufacturers the packaging. Increasingly, there is recognition of the huge potential of retail stores becoming an integrated media centre, with retailers selling and managing media space and time. Attention is given here to in-store media and the retail media format, while a consideration of packaging issues can be found earlier (Chapter 19).

## Point-of-purchase (POP)

There are a number of POP techniques, but the most used are window displays, floor and wall racks to display merchandise, posters and information cards, plus counter and checkout displays. The most obvious display a manufacturer has at the point of purchase is the packaging used to wrap and protect the product until it is ready for consumption.

Supermarket trolleys with a video screen attached have been trialled by a number of stores. As soon as the trolley passes a particular infrared beam a short video is activated, promoting brands available in the immediate vicinity of the shopper. Other advances include electronic overhead signs, in-store videos at selected sites around the store and coupons for certain competitive products dispensed at the checkout once the purchased items have been scanned. Indirect messages can also play a role in in-store communications: for example, fresh bread smells can be circulated from the supermarket bakery at the furthest side of the store to the entrance area, enticing customers further into the supermarket. Some aroma systems allow for the smell to be restricted to just 45 cm (18 inches) of the display.

End-of-row bins and cards displaying special offers are POP media that aim to stimulate impulse buying. With over 75 per cent of supermarket buying decisions made in store, a greater percentage of communication budgets will be allocated to POP items.

### Strengths

Point-of-purchase media are good at attracting attention and providing information. Their ability to persuade is potentially strong, as these displays can highlight particular product attributes at a time when shoppers have devoted their attention to the purchase decision process. Any prior awareness a shopper might have can be reinforced.

From management's point of view, the absolute and relative costs of POP advertisements are low. Furthermore, management can easily fine-tune a POP ad to reflect changing conditions. For example, should stock levels be high and a promotion necessary to move stock out, POP displays can be introduced quickly.

### Weaknesses

These messages are usually directed at customers who are already committed, at least partly, to purchasing the product or one from their evoked set. POP messages certainly fail to reach those not actively engaged in the shopping activity.

There can be difficulties maintaining message continuity across a large number of outlets. Signs and displays can also be damaged by customers, which can impact upon the status of a product. Shoppers can therefore be negatively influenced by the temporary inconvenience of damaged and confusing displays. Unless rigorously controlled by store management, the large amount of POP materials can lead to clutter and a deterioration in the perception shoppers have of a retail outlet.

## Retail media centres

Traditionally, retailers allow their stores to be used in a variety of ways by a variety of organisations to communicate messages to their audiences. These audiences are jointly owned, not necessarily in equal proportion, by the branded food manufacturers that use stores for distribution purposes, and the retailers that try to build footfall or store traffic through retail branding approaches. As a result, the management of the media opportunities and the messages that are communicated are uncoordinated, inconsistent and the media potential, to a large extent, ignored. In the past, retailers will have argued that their core business rests with retailing, not selling and managing media. However, the media world has developed considerably in recent years, often in tandem with developments in technology. For a long time, retailers have built databases using customer information and developed sales promotion-based loyalty programmes as a result.

# Cinema

The growth in cinema attendances in 2007 and 2009 has been linked to the increase in multi-plex cinemas (multiple screens at each site) and, as Esposito reports, the appalling summer weather that drove many people into the cinema for their entertainment. Advertisers have followed the crowds but have also listened to the research that shows that cinema audiences remember more detail than television audiences and, since they are a captive audience, there are no distractions.

The Cinema Advertising Association claims that cinema users are light TV viewers so this enables brands to reach a unique audience. With an average of ten new films being released each week, a broad swath of the population become potential cinema visitors.

Advertising messages transmitted in a cinema have all the advantages of television-based messages. Audio and visual dimensions combine to provide high impact. However, the audience is more attentive because the main film has yet to be shown and there are fewer distractions or noise in the communication system. The implication is that cinema advertising has greater power than television advertisements. This power can be used to heighten levels of attention and, as the screen images are larger than life and because they appear in a darkened room that is largely unfamiliar to the audience, the potential to communicate effectively with the target audience is strong.

With customer satisfaction levels improving, advertisers have consistently increased the adspend in this medium.

## Strengths

The mood of the audience is generally positive, particularly at the start of a show. This mood can be carried over into the commercials. Furthermore, the production quality of cinema messages is usually very high and transmission is often assisted by high-quality audio (digital surround-sound systems) that is being installed in the new multiplex arenas.

The production and transmission costs are quite low, which makes this an attractive media vehicle. The attention-getting ability and the power of this medium contribute to the high recall scores that this medium constantly records, often four times higher than the average recall scores for television commercials.

## Weaknesses

The costs associated with reaching local audiences are low; however, if an advertiser wishes to reach a national audience, the costs can be much higher than those for television. The audience profile for UK cinema admissions indicates that approximately 80 per cent of visitors are aged 15 to 34. With an increasing proportion of the population aged over 55 (the grey market), cinema advertising is limited by the audience profile and the type of products and services that can be realistically promoted.

The third and final weakness is, to some, the most important. The irritation factor associated with viewing advertising messages when customers have paid to see a film has been found to be very high. Some respondents, in a number of studies, have expressed such an intensity of feeling that they actively considered boycotting the featured products. So despite the acclaim and positive reasons for using cinema advertising, advertisers are advised to be careful about the films they select to run their commercials against (audience profile will also be affected) and whether they should use this medium.

## Viewpoint 20.4 — First aid goes interactive in cinema

The potential for interactive cinema advertising was demonstrated by St John Ambulance with an ad called 'Popcorn'. The aim was to highlight the everyday importance of first aid as nearly 150,000 people die each year when, if there had been first aid available, they might have survived.

The film was set in a packed cinema, and starts with a fictional advert featuring a happy family enjoying popcorn. A child then starts to choke and the mother, not knowing what to do, turns to the real cinema audience for help. A member of the audience suddenly stands up and shouts that she knows what to do and runs to the front of the cinema. She disappears behind the screen before reappearing within the advert itself, and then uses first aid to save the child.

Not finished with this, she then reappears in the real cinema while the advert finishes with a message explaining how viewers can receive a free pocket first aid guide. The film is a part of the charity's brand strategy called the 'The difference', designed to remind the public about the importance of first aid, and to encourage people to equip themselves with life-saving skills. The film was seeded with news, parenting and health online media and bloggers, and was uploaded to the charity's YouTube channel, and its Facebook page which has over 18,000 fans, and was linked from the charity's Twitter feed.

*Source*:  Anon (2010); www.sja.org.uk/sja/about-us/latest-news/popcorn.aspx.

**Question:**  How might the interactivity in the film influence people?

**Task:**  Think of a name to describe this type of interactive advertising.

**Exhibit 20.7**  **A scene from the St John Ambulance interactive film**
*Source*: St John Ambulance

# Ambient media

Ambient media are a fairly recent innovation and represent a non-traditional alternative to outdoor media. Ambient media are regarded as out-of-home media that fail to fit any of the established categories. Ambient media can be classified according to a variety of factors (see Table 20.3). Of these, standard posters account for the vast majority of ambient activity (59 per cent) with distribution accounting for 24 per cent and the four remaining categories just 17 per cent.

## Guerrilla tactics

Guerrilla media tactics are an attempt to gain short-term visibility and impact in markets where the conventional media are cluttered and the life of the offering is very short.

Traditionally, flyposting was the main method, practised most often by the music business. Now the term refers to a range of activities that derive their power and visibility from being outside the jurisdiction of the paid-for media. Sabotage is a stronger interpretation, as the tactics require the hijacking of conventional media events. Lanigan (1996) reports on the use of spray paint to sabotage other advertisers' posters, while the launch of the *Blah Blah Blah* music magazine involved sticking speech bubbles over posters carrying messages for other advertisers.

| Table 20.3 | Ambient media categories |
|---|---|
| **Ambient category** | **Explanation** |
| Standard posters | Washrooms, shopping trolleys, phone boxes |
| Distribution | Tickets, receipts, carrier bags |
| Digital | Video screens, projections, LED screens |
| Sponsorships | Playgrounds, golf holes, petrol pump nozzles |
| Mobile posters | Lorries, barges, sandwich boards |
| Aerials | Balloons, blimps, towed banners |

*Source*: Advertising Association (2003) *Advertising Statistics Yearbook*. Used by permission of WARC.

# Direct response media

This chapter on the media would not be complete without reference to direct response media. The principal use of the media is to convey one of two types of message: one is oriented towards the development of brands and attitudes; the other is aimed at provoking a physical (and mental) response. It follows that attitude and response-based communications require different media.

Conventional media (television, print or radio) once used just to develop brands and attitudes are now used as a mechanism or device to provoke a response, through which consumers/buyers can follow up a message, enter into an immediate dialogue and either request further information or purchase goods. The main difference with new media is the time delay or response pause between receiving a message and acting on it. Through direct response mechanisms, the response may be delayed for as long as it takes to make a telephone call, press a button or fill out a reply coupon. However, the response pause and the use of a separate form of communication highlight the essential differences.

Estimates vary, but somewhere between 30 per cent and 40 per cent of all television advertisements now carry a telephone number or web address. Direct response television (DRTV) is attractive to those promoting service-based offerings and increasingly travel brands and some FMCG brands are using it. Reid (1996) argues that DRTV can be likened to a video game. Level 1 is viewing the commercial, level 2 requires the respondent to act in order to receive more information and derive greater entertainment value. At level 3 there is an attempt to sell directly to the respondent. The main purpose for advertisers using this route is to extract personal information for the database and subsequent sales promotion and mailing purposes.

One aspect that is crucial to the success of a direct response campaign is not the number of responses but the conversion of leads into sales. This means that the infrastructure to support these promotional activities must be thought through and put in place, otherwise the work and resources put into the visible level will be wasted if customers are unable to get the information they require. The provision of the infrastructure alone is not sufficient – the totality of the campaign should support the brand. Indeed, this is a chance to extend brand opportunities and provide increased brand experiences.

# Key points

- Two classifications of the media are possible; one based on form and the other the source of the media vehicle. Using the form approach, media are classified according to six main classes, (broadcast, print, outdoor, new, in-store and other media classes), types and individual vehicles. The second classification considers media a function of its origin or source. This is popularised in terms of POEM.

- Understanding of the key characteristics of each type of media assists media selection and planning. The fundamental characteristics concern the costs, the richness of the communication, the interactive properties and audience profile associated with a communication event.

- The rich array of characteristics that each type of media possesses serve to engage audiences in different ways. These represent opportunities for organisations to make sure they use the right media to deliver against different goals.

- The overall trend in media spend is that organisations are increasingly moving funds from offline to online media. Digital media spend is increasing and at a rate far faster than any other type or class of media.

- The principal use of the media is to convey one of two types of message: one is oriented towards the development of brands and attitudes; the other is aimed at provoking a physical (and mental) response. It follows that attitude- and response-based communications require different media. One aspect that is crucial to the success of a direct response campaign is not the number of responses but the conversion of leads into sales.

- There is a growing body of evidence that shows that the effectiveness of the media increases considerably when media are used in combination. The use of multichannel campaigns has been spurred by digital media, and research which indicates that adults consume a portfolio of media that embraces 10–15 television channels, 10–15 websites and a similar number of magazines. This does not account for a wealth of other media such as radio and cinema. In addition, people are consuming media through time and place shifting and using their portfolio of media in an integrated format.

# Review questions

1. Explain the differences between media classes, types and vehicles. Give two examples of each to support your answer.

2. What does POEM stand for and how might it be used to develop a brand's communications?

3. Describe the main characteristics of the print media. Find examples to illustrate your points.

4. Compare and contrast newspapers and magazines as advertising media.

5. What do you think will be the impact on broadcast television of the growth in penetration by cable television? How will this affect advertisers?

6. If radio is unobtrusive, why should advertisers use it?

7. What are the strengths and weaknesses of outdoor advertising media? Why is this means of advertising sometimes referred to as the last true broadcast medium?

8. Why are the relative costs of each medium different?

9. Under what conditions should cinema be used as the primary medium?

10. What is a multichannel campaign and what is the optimal number of channels?

# References

Advertising Association (2003) *Advertising Statistics Year Book*, Henley: NTC. Also at www.adassoc.org.uk/inform/.

Anon (2010) St John Ambulance interactive ad shows future of cinema, *Utalk Marketing*, 3 November, retrieved 23 April 2012 from www.utalkmarketing.com/pages/article.aspx?articleid=19443&title=st_john_ambulance_interactive_ad_shows_future_of_cinema.

Ballantyne, D. (2004) Dialogue and its role in the development of relationship specific knowledge, *Journal of Business and Industrial Marketing*, 19(2), 114–23.

Barda, T. (2010) Clipper Ventures, *The Marketer*, October.

Binet, L. and Field, P. (2007) *Marketing in an era of accountability*, Henley: IPA-WARC.

Chapman, M. (2011) Lego launches first girls' range for 10 years, *Marketing*, 19 December, retrieved 18 March 2012 from http://www.brandrepublic.com/news/1109818/Lego-launches-first-girls-range-10-years/?DCMP=ILC-SEARCH.

Chapman, M. (2012) Morrisons to launch first supermarket magazine iPad app, *Marketing*, 9 March 2012, retrieved 16 March 2012 from http://www.brandrepublic.com/news/1121531/Morrisons-launch-first-supermarket-magazine-iPad-app/?DCMP=ILC-SEARCH.

Danaher, P. and Rossiter, J. (2011) Comparing Perceptions of Marketing Communication Channels, *European Journal of Marketing*, 45(1/2), 6–42.

Durrani, A. (2011) MAGAZINE ABCs: Brands continue to invest in print despite Sky retreat, *Marketing*, 19 August, retrieved 19 March 2012 from http://www.brandrepublic.com/news/1085654/MAGAZINE-ABCs-Brands-continue-invest-print-despite-Sky-retreat/?DCMP=ILC-SEARCH.

Egol, M., Moeller, L.H. and Vollmer, C. (2009) The promise of private-label media, *Strategy and Business*, 55, 26 May, (Summer).

Fitch, D. (2007) Outdoor advertising, retrieved 20 January 2008 from www.millwardbrown.com/Sites/MillwardBrown/Content/News/EPerspectiveArticles.aspx?id=%2f200711010001.

Fletcher, M. (2012) Sector Analysis: Magazines, *Media Week*, retrieved 16 March 2012 from http://www.brandrepublic.com/news/1119858/Sector-Analysis-Magazines/?DCMP=ILC-SEARCH.

Govoni, N., Eng, R. and Galper, M. (1986) *Promotional Management*, Englewood Cliffs, NJ: Prentice-Hall.

Gray, R. (2008) Green credentials on display, *Marketing*, 9 April, 33–4.

Heath, R. and McDonald, S. (2007) Press advertising: equal to TV in building brands. *Admap*, (April) 482, 34–6.

Heath, R. (2009) Emotional Engagement: How Television Builds Big Brands At Low Attention, *Journal of Advertising Research*, March, 62–73.

IPA (2011) *New models of marketing effectiveness*, London: IPA.

Lanigan, D. (1996) Guerrilla Media, *Campaign*, 5 April, 26–7.

May, M. (2011) Brands still on the paper trail, *Marketing*, 23 June, retrieved 16 March 2012 from http://www.brandrepublic.com/features/1075882/Brands-paper-trail/?DCMP=ILC-SEARCH.

McCabe, M. (2009) JCDecaux launches new digital offering for Heathrow Terminal 5, *Campaign*, 27 July 2009, retrieved 3 May 2011 from www.campaignlive.co.uk/news/.

Meurs, van, L. and Aristoff, M. (2009) Split-Second Recognition: What Makes Outdoor Advertising Work? *Journal of Advertising Research*, March, 82–92.

Outdoor Media Centre (2011) UK Outdoor Advertising Revenue, retrieved 19 March 2012 from http://www.outdoormediacentre.org.uk/outdoor_facts/factsAndFigures/UK_Outdoor_Revenue.

Reid, A. (1996) FMCG advertisers are starting to wise up to DRTV, *Campaign*, 26 April, 15.

Veloutsou, C. and O'Donnell, C. (2005) Exploring the effectiveness of taxis as an advertising medium, *International Journal of Advertising*, 24(2), 217–39.

WARC (2007) WARC Media report the newspaper market in 2007, retrieved 21 January 2008 from www.warc.com.

# Chapter 21
## Digital media

The development of digital-based technologies and Web-enabled communications has had a profound effect on the way marketing communications is used. However, the full potential of these new technologies has yet to be realised as customer behaviour adapts and new ways of incorporating these facilities successfully have to be found.

Interactivity and rapid two-way communications enabled by technology require the development of new communication strategies and a fresh understanding of how best to communicate with target audiences.

## Aims and learning objectives

The aim of this chapter is to consider the nature and characteristics of digital media and its contribution to marketing communications.

The learning objectives of this chapter are to:

1. explain the key forms of digital media;
2. understand what digital media enables users to do;
3. examine some of the issues arising from the design and use of websites;
4. explore the key differences between traditional and digital media;
5. explain what convergence means and how it influences marketing communications.

# Minicase

## Hiscox

Hiscox is an international specialist insurer, underwriting a diverse range of personal and commercial insurance risks. Established over 111 years ago, Hiscox provides specialist high and mid net worth insurance cover for homes, buildings and their contents, valuables and collections. They also provide extensive business insurance, finely tailored to the needs of over 100,000 small and medium-sized businesses, professionals and consultants in the UK. In addition to designing profession-specific policies, tailored to suit individual business needs, Hiscox London Market underwrites international businesses, via the Lloyd's insurance market, and specialist retail business from around the world.

The company principles are founded on challenging many of the conventions in the insurance industry. Hiscox focus on delivering very high-quality operations and superior customer service in particular. Indeed, one of their stated values is 'courage', in the sense that

they 'dare to be different'. This ethos of challenging, doing things differently where appropriate, is continued into their marketing communications. Their UK advertising strapline reads 'As good as our word' and this underpins their belief and desire that Hiscox is no ordinary insurer. Their UK advertising and their claims handling are based on the premise that their promises are genuine, not empty, and their operations are timely and not riddled with delays over the small print. They claim that integrity, trustworthiness and honour underpin everything they do.

In 2010 and 2011 Hiscox was the exclusive sponsor of a bespoke series of programmes on Channel 4, collectively known as *Intelligent Thinking on 4*. The series linked together some of the greatest thinkers, leaders, inventors, artists and civilisations in British science, history and art and began with the *Genius of Britain* programme. The series was the company's first broadcast sponsorship and provided a distinctive

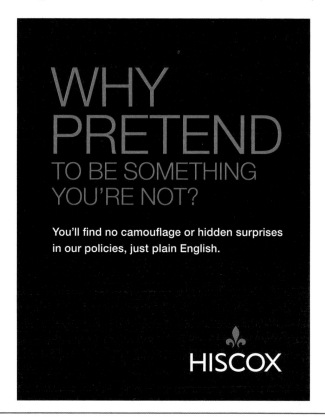

| Exhibit 21.1 | **A typical Hiscox ad** |
| --- | --- |
| | *Source*: Hiscox Insurance Company Ltd |

way of reaching their audiences through a collection of bold, thought-provoking idents. The creative message reinforced Hiscox's strong desire to be perceived as a brand people can trust.

Innovation is key within any organisation that seeks to challenge convention and with Hiscox it is key within their marketing communications. Many of their business and home insurance customers lead busy and complex lives, so communicating with them has become increasingly difficult.

To address this challenge, Hiscox ran a location-based UK marketing campaign, integrating with its outdoor advertising activity to tap into the power of on-the-move marketing. The campaign was run by Hiscox's media agency collaborating with location-based mobile media channel JiWire. JiWire works with BT Openzone to deliver targeted third-party ads in 205,000 public wifi areas throughout the UK in locations such as cafés, hotels, airports and railway stations. The media agency mapped the locations of Hiscox's outdoor ads to JiWire's wifi hotspots. This meant that people who logged on to public wifi close to one of Hiscox's outdoor posters were shown a relevant Hiscox digital ad encouraging them to get an insurance quote. This meant that someone near an outdoor ad in Manchester Piccadilly who then sat down for a break would automatically engage with the Hiscox brand when they opened their laptop (mobile phone, tablet, or other such device).

At one level the results of this campaign demonstrate the effectiveness of an integrated and targeted approach. The click-through rate, an awareness measure, was five times higher than that experienced by an average Hiscox online display campaign. At another level however, it is not yet clear how effective the campaign was at driving the follow through behaviour and the number of policies generated.  These results have yet to be published.

In 2012 Hiscox was the first UK brand to use Klaustech's new engaging ad format, AdCastPlus. The new technology allows online ads to stay visible on the side of a web page, even when a user scrolls down. This new technology enabled Hiscox to use existing video assets to create an integrated campaign, across key media touchpoints of print, outdoor, digital and TV sponsorship. It also allows ads to be booked into time slots, which can be planned to coincide with TV campaigns.

Hiscox position itself as a different kind of insurance company, compared with their competitors. The company's willingness to adopt digital, and often specialist technologies to help improve the way they engage customers, how they interact and develop dialogue with them, and do it cost-effectively, is an integral part of their of their strategic approach to marketing communications living the brand and company values.

*This minicase was written by Chris Fill using a variety of sources, including Eleftheriou-Smith (2012) and Haill (2011).*

# Introduction

Digitisation has enabled marketers and consumers to develop new forms of communication. The dramatic impact that these technologies have had on people does not need any amplification. The Hiscox minicase provides a glimpse into the way one organisation tries to adopt digital innovation to improve their marketing communications. This chapter starts by setting out the main types of digital media. It then proceeds to explain briefly what they are and examines the generic benefits that each of these types of digital media can bring – that is, what it enables users to do. This involves the creation, design, development and marketing functionality of websites. We then compare some of the key characteristics of traditional and digital media. The chapter concludes with a consideration of convergence issues and how these might impact on marketing communications in the future.

The following chapter builds on this one and explores social media, search, and various other forms of digitally driven interactive communications.

# Key forms of digital media

As already indicated, the range of digital media is vast and is growing rapidly. However, the following section considers some of the key types or forms of digital media and should not be considered to represent comprehensive coverage.

## The Internet

The Internet provides a wide variety of activities, including electronic mail, global information access and retrieval systems, discussion groups, multiplayer games and file transfer facilities, all of which not only help to transform the way we think about marketing communications, but also impact on business strategy, marketing channel structures, interorganisational relationships and the configuration of the marketing communications mix.

The Internet impacts upon marketing in two main ways: distribution and communication. The first concerns distribution and marketing channels. The Internet offers a new, direct route to customers, which can either replace or supplement current distribution/channel arrangements. The second element concerns the Internet as a communication medium. It provides a means of reaching huge new audiences and enabling the provision of vast amounts of information. These two elements, distribution and communication, combine under various titles such as ebusiness, ecommerce, and mcommerce to offer benefits for both buyers and sellers.

The Internet is an important way of providing product and service information and can enable organisations to provide frequent and intensive levels of customer support. With it come doubts about its ability to deliver competitive advantage and whether it could offer suitable levels of privacy, security and measures of advertising effectiveness.

The Internet is not a universal remedy for a manager's marketing communications problems, but is one that must be integrated into the marketing communications mix. Offline communications can be used to raise site awareness and interest among a wide audience and to provide them with the site address. Once at the website, in-depth product information can be exchanged for customer-specific details to refresh the database and fuel future communication activities. It is this holistic perspective of digital media that should be developed.

Traditional marketing communications strategies employ a mix of tools, media and messages, and often involve an emphasis on one type of communication device, depending on the context. Broadly speaking, it has been the norm to weight advertising over the other tools when dealing with consumer markets, and to weight personal selling when operating in the b2b sector. This reflects advertising's ability to raise awareness and develop brands, and personal selling's prime skill at provoking behavioural action and closing orders. These general approaches have been relaxed as audience and media fragmentation continues and new ways of doing business (e.g. mcommerce) gather impetus.

The Internet is the fastest-growing advertising medium, attracting revenues from a range of sources, some of which are investments previously devoted to television. Online advertising now equates to 29 per cent of total adspend. To demonstrate this extraordinary growth, online advertising attracted £153 million in 2000, £2,016 million by 2006 and £4,531 million by 2011 (Advertising Association, 2012).

Advertising online takes one of two main forms; display advertising and classified advertising. Display includes, banners, interruptive, sponsorships, tenancies and display on email. Classified advertising is principally concerned with paid-for search (see later in this chapter), but also includes recruitment and classifieds (including b2b).

The development of Web 2.0 had a major impact and added a new and critical dimension to the Internet. Constantinides and Fountain (2008) argue that there are three main principles associated with Web 2.0:

1. There is a focus on service-based, simple, open-source solutions as online applications.

2. It represents continual and incremental application development which requires users to participate and interact in new ways. So, from a position of consuming media, users are now contributors, reviewers and content editors.

3. Web 2.0 also represents a new service business model that has created new opportunities to reach small, individual business customers with low-volume products.

Many of the applications associated with Web 2.0 (social networks, RSS (really simple syndication), viral marketing, etc.) are explored later (Chapter 22).

The prime benefit of the Internet, as a hybrid medium, is that it is good at all of these activities, but it is not as good for any one task as a single communication tool might be. Interestingly, it excels at a part of the communication and decision-making process that the established communication tools fail to properly address – namely, the search for, and retrieval of, information pertinent to purchase behaviour. It might be said, therefore, that the Internet provides a complementary facility to the marketing communication tools and, as such, should be used with, and not instead of, the established means of marketing communications. Above all else, the Internet is a medium, not a tool.

## Database technologies

A marketing database is a collection of records that can be related to one another in multiple ways and from which information, usually customer-related, can be obtained in a variety of formats. This can be analysed to determine appropriate segments and target markets and used to stimulate and record individual responses to marketing communications. It, therefore, plays a role as a storage, sorting and administrative device to assist direct, personalised communications.

When customer-related transactional and response data are combined with additional information from external sources, such as a list broker, the database can become a potent source for marketing communication activities. Indeed, the increasing sophistication of information retrieval from databases enables much more effective targeting and communications.

Databases provide a means of monitoring changes in customer behaviour, identifying new target markets, and cross-selling products and services. The purpose of cross-selling is to reduce customer churn and increase switching costs (Kamakura et al., 2003). While increasing a customer's potential switching costs may not be compatible with relationship marketing principles, the result of successful implementation may be improved levels of customer retention and satisfaction where relationships are more discrete and transactional rather than collaborative in nature.

### Viewpoint 21.1　Encouraging people to register as organ donors

At the beginning of 2010 almost 1.76 million people were registered as organ donors (OD) in Scotland. Although this is a strong testament to the success of past campaigns, it still represented less than a third of the potential number of donors.

Analysis of the OD register revealed that past campaigns had not been effective at attracting older recruits. It was clear that marketing-driven recruitment, as measured by sign-up via Web or telephone, was delivering a relatively young profile. It was necessary, therefore, to develop a DM strategy that would deliver large numbers of recruits in a cost-effective way, and across all ages, but particularly an older audience.

However, as DM was a new channel for OD, and did not have a bank of past DM results, it made sense to test and learn. This involved two test mailings. The first was an initial small-scale exploratory mailing of 35,000 individuals. This was designed to provide insight, conserve resources and set a benchmark for the next phase. Phase 1 included a creative and format test;

- A letter pack versus a simple postcard
- A creative outer versus an official NHS-branded outer.

Results showed the postcard format generated a 5.7 per cent response, but was too short and too easy to ignore. The creative outer and letter drew a 13.4 per cent response, but the letter with an official NHS outer generated a huge 14.8 per cent response.

Phase 2 involved a bigger mailing, 100,000 individuals, with the goal of finding the 'best performer' that could be taken forward into the next major recruitment programme. This involved using a letter and envelope outer. By far the best performer of the variants used was an official NHS direct mailer which was timed to land whilst the above-the-line advertising and field marketing campaign were active. This generated a 14.5 per cent response rate almost exactly in line with phase 1. This is a phenomenally high response rate.

The official campaign rolled out in September 2010 using the 'the official NHS' direct mail format. Between September and December 2010 there were 19,308 recruits to the OD register. This was a huge number for this scale of campaign – given that marketing-driven recruitment to web or telephone in the previous years of 2008 and 2009 was approximately 11,000.

Demographic analysis showed that 77 per cent of direct mail recruits were over 40, including 34 per cent over 60. This was more than twice the proportion of over-40s that were being recruited through other marketing-driven channels.

The average cost-per-response was £3.59, an exceptionally low figure when compared with direct mail in charities, where they are typically many times higher.

Database analysis had helped identify that one of the biggest challenges to the ODR was attracting the older, harder-to-reach recruits who provide the majority of donations. By developing a creative to dispel myths, tackle barriers to action and exploit opportunities like family sign-up and the power of 'official' mail, the Scottish Government was able to spend its budget prudently and drive a really cost-effective test mailing strategy to provide a basis for better value to the taxpayer.

*Source*:   Ireland and Neill (2011).

**Question:**   What are the key difficulties faced by those attempting to use databases to drive efficient marketing communications?

**Task:**   List four other ways in which databases can be used to assist marketing communications.

There are many potential operational problems associated with interrogating and processing information within live databases. Ryals and Payne (2001) point out that the transaction processing performance may be slowed down when interrogating customer information and the structure of the database itself is constantly changing in response to the large volume of transactions. Many organisations use data warehouses (and smaller data marts). These are integrated stores of data collected from a variety of sources (e.g. customer contact centres, the sales force and market research) and are updated at intervals, making them non-volatile and easier for interrogating customer information.

## Multimedia

There is little agreement about what the term 'multimedia' means. Strictly speaking, the term refers to any presentation of information or material that uses two or more media. However, the term 'multimedia' has only gained prominence since the advent of digital technologies. So, multimedia is generally assumed to refer to the integration of text, audio and images in order to enhance the user interface with computer-based applications. As a result the 'streaming' of video and 'audio over the Internet' typify multimedia applications. As hardware and communications technology evolve, so new systems and applications develop to provide delivery of personalised email and marketing communication messages.

## Mobile technologies

Mobile phone technologies have advanced considerably and have enjoyed huge commercial success. Wireless application protocol, or WAP phones possess the usual email and text information services, but they also have an Internet browser facility. As a result, messages can not only be location-, but also time-specific. For example, a message can be sent when someone is in a town centre at lunch time, promoting a cafe, restaurant or shop. Mobile or proximity marketing is now a major industry as smartphone technology has established itself. The delivery of direct marketing messages to mobile devices using wireless technologies and the emerging near field communications technology is predicted to have a profound impact on marketing communications.

The Mobile Marketing Association (MMA) is a global community comprising over 40 countries and 700 member organisations. MMA believe that mobile marketing is a set of practices that enables organisations to communicate and engage with their audience in an interactive and relevant manner through any mobile device or network. They argue that the 'set of practices' includes 'activities, institutions, processes, industry players, standards, advertising and media, direct response, promotions, relationship management, CRM, customer services, loyalty, social marketing, and all the many faces and facets of marketing'.

Mobile marketing communications, to give it its full title, involves the delivery of direct marketing messages to mobile devices using wireless technologies. The prevailing usage is built around short message services (SMS), multimedia messaging services (MMS – which combines text with simple graphics and sound), wireless application protocol (WAP), mobile Internet and WAP push services and full multimedia, third-generation (3G) services for both product promotion and entertainment purposes.

The more common title for this activity is *mobile marketing*, while some in the industry refer to it as *proximity marketing*. These titles are misleading, because marketing is more than just communications, even if this is primarily a communications medium, nothing more. In view of this discrepancy and to avoid misunderstanding, the phrase *mobile communications* is used here.

Apart from the sheer volume of users, there are several reasons why the use of mobile communications has grown in recent years:

- *Interactivity*: the use of SMS provides recipients with the opportunity to respond directly to incoming requests. Simple yes/no answers are quick and easy to execute while opportunities to encourage interaction with brands exist 24/7, whether that be in- or out-of-home.

- *Smartphone technologies*: the recent developments in smartphone technologies have spurred a huge growth in usage. Among these are downloadable apps, which provide particular functionality or entertainment.

- *Personalisation*: mobile communications can enable messages that are customised to the personal needs of users. This means information can be highly targeted and contain relevant information.

- *Ubiquity*: the portability of mobiles means that it is possible to reach users at virtually any location, at any time and send them location-specific information.

- *Integration*: the effectiveness of mobile communications is optimised when it is used as a part of an integrated communications campaign.

- *Accountability*: the volume and nature of SMS responses can be measured, which is important from an investment perspective. In addition, it is possible to measure the contribution that different media make to drive responses. This in turn helps organisations to optimise their offline media spend and pursue integrated communications.

- *Cultural expectations*: as the number of mobile phones in circulation reaches saturation point, and as technology develops, enabling more efficient communication, so peer-group pressure and the entertainment industry encourage use of mobile phones. For example, presenters of television and radio programmes encourage their audiences to engage with them through text and mobile facilities in response to news items, quizzes and general topics of current interest. For many this form of communication and involvement has become a normal element of their leisure and entertainment expectations.

---

### Scholars' paper 21.1 — Centralised mobile coupon delivery

**Wray, J. and Plante, D. (2011) Mobile advertising engine for centralized mobile coupon delivery, *International Journal of Management and Marketing Research*, 4(1), 75–85.**

These authors refer to the changing balance of spend on traditional and digital media. They also observe that the majority of mobile and Internet campaign management platforms are developed on an individual seller basis, requiring customers to download or register at a range of websites in order to collect coupons. To help overcome this, the authors offer a more centralised coupon distribution approach using a mobile advertising engine that aggregates coupons from multiple corporations, tracks point of sales redemption, and reports campaign effectiveness using a mobile marketing and reporting platform.

---

The key attributes of mobile communications are that it is a personal channel, one which enables direct, targeted and interactive communications which can occur at any time and any place. SMS communications have underpinned its growth and are used not just for brand awareness-based advertising, but also as an effective way of delivering sales promotions, such as announcing special offers and 'text and win' events. However, as with email, it is also important to consider the potential privacy concerns of customers, especially as the receipt of unwanted messages (i.e. spam) may well increase.

One of the difficulties facing the mobile communications industry has been how to provide a direct link between the offline and online environments. One possible solution is to use quick response or QR codes. These are two-dimensional barcodes as represented at Exhibit 21.2.

By taking a picture of a QR code with a camera phone with a built-in QR code reader, consumers can access further brand-related material that is linked to the code. Used with great success in Japan, some believe the use of QR codes will transform mobile marketing in Europe. Murphy (2008) reports that others are not so positive, citing differences in the Japanese technology infrastructure, which serves to facilitate this type of use and Britain's less-than-favourable disposition towards the use of Java software. May (2011) reports that Land Rover include QR codes throughout their *Onelife* print magazine, while VW have promoted their Golf Match model using augmented reality and direct mail.

The potential to develop mobile communications is enormous, simply because the channel can deliver direct marketing messages related to advertising, sales promotion and public relations to individuals, regardless of location. These messages can be used to develop brand awareness,

| Exhibit 21.2 | **A QR code** |
|---|---|
| | *Source*: Colin Underhill/Alamy Images |

support product launches, incentivise customers through competitions and promotions and promote trade and distributor involvement, as well as provide branded entertainment. Although associated with consumer markets, their use within a business marketing context is highlighted by Barwick (2012). He makes the point that the surge in QR code popularity presents exciting opportunities for B2B marketers as well as those in consumer markets, since the codes are dynamic and a flexible resource.

Associated with QR codes is near field communications (NFC). Mobile phones equipped with an in-built NFC chip work when the device is held close to a NFC reader. This is expected to help make cashless purchases or for the phone to be used as a virtual 'mobile wallet'. NFC can also be used in conjunction with marketing communications. For example, it can enable people to access rich information from holding a device near a billboard or ad within a building or store. This emerging technology has the potential to fuse the contactless smartcard and the mobile phone (Ondrus and Pigneur, 2009). There is more on NFC later.

## Business applications

The phrase 'information systems and technology' (IST) is used to embrace the wide variety of new technologies that have been developed to improve the quality of life for the people who use IST and for those who benefit from their deployment. Ryssel et al. (2004: 197) refer to information technology as a term that embraces 'all forms of technology utilized to create, capture, manipulate, communicate, exchange, present and use information in its various forms (business data, voice conversations, still images, motion pictures, multimedia presentations and other forms, including those not yet conceived)'. They conceptualise the range of IST in terms of where the IST are used (internal or external) and across which broad functions (information, communication and decision support).

However, it is not the intention to provide a detailed examination of each of these systems or of the various technologies, as that is beyond the scope of this book. Readers interested in this aspect of technology are referred to Chaffey et al. (2008) or Rayport and Jaworski (2004).

A raft of increasingly sophisticated application programmes have evolved to meet the market needs. Initially electronic data interchange (EDI) via public networks, and now the Internet, managed the direct transmission between different companies' computer systems of data, relating to business transactions. The applications tended to focus on systems designed by suppliers to assist customers in their purchasing procedures, processes and overall decision-making. The level of sophistication and scope of these applications now embrace a network of transactions and flow of information between a number of organisations. Radjou (2003: 25) refers to 'supply network processes', which encompass the following categories:

- product lifecycle management;
- supply chain management;
- enterprise asset management;
- production network management;
- continuous demand management;
- order fulfilment and distribution management;
- aftermarket service management.

These applications serve to reduce costs, speed up processes, improve accuracy and provide added value for end-user customers. In terms of the relationships between organisations and their customers, these applications can serve to improve collaboration, both internally and externally. For example, enterprise-wide solutions such as complete enterprise resource planning (ERP) systems attempt to integrate all business processes across an organisation's accounting, manufacturing, sales and human resource departments. Further downstream, electronic point of sale (EPOS), which involves computerised tills linked back to a company's central computer(s), enables the data of every retail sale to be transmitted back to the organisation to facilitate sales and inventory management and, in a marketing context, can be used to better understand customer demand and buying behaviour. As networks, including the Internet, have extended to connect multiple businesses in the supply chain, sophisticated point-of-sale data have enabled collaborative marketing. This can assist suppliers by providing data about repeat purchase rates, customer profiles related to specific products, and the most effective ways of reaching and interacting with customers.

Interorganisational use of network technologies to share business information and coordinate supply chain activities has been termed 'eCollaboration' and is well established, particularly for high-technology-based companies.

## Interactive television

Another important technological development is digital broadcasting and the opportunities for interactive television. Digital television and interactive services are two related but different facilities. Digital television is well established, but full interactivity has yet to be delivered to the majority of the population. Potential advantages are consumer familiarity, the full-screen, high-quality sound and picture formats, fast channel and picture/text 'hopping', combining entertainment and shopping. The main disadvantage concerns its inability to deal with individual customers – that is, until TV-based email is widely established.

Digital services provide many benefits for consumers, one of which will be the opportunity to screen out intrusive advertising. Interactive or red button advertising has to be driven by consumers who decide which advertisements they want to watch, when, and how long they will stay involved. The creative possibilities are far ranging, but in order to retain audiences it will become increasingly important to develop creative ideas based on a sound understanding of the target audience and their interactive and buying patterns. In January 2008 Andy Duncan, Channel 4's CEO, is reported to have claimed that red button technology is 'slow', 'basic' and 'clunky' (Jones, 2008). Their exit was followed in April 2008 by Channel 5. They announced they were abandoning their interactive red button advertising facility, citing that it was too costly (the return was poor) and that it did not fit the organisation's strategy.

Currently on UK teletext there are pages about holiday bargains that direct potential users to the Internet (www.teletext.co.uk/holidays) where they will find a searchable database, plus weather reports, resort reviews and advice. This service claims a choice of preferred operators, competitive pricing, confidence – full financial protection, up-to-date offers and human interaction at the point of sale. It states that, in the future, customers will be able to access the full functionality of the website via digital television and/or mobile phone. The point is that digital television and interactive marketing communications are unlikely to thrive in isolation from other methods of communication. Just as online facilities need offline drivers, and just as bricks and clicks appear to be a more profitable format than clicks only, so an integrated perspective is required if digital television and interactive advertising are to be successful.

The BBC iPlayer and 4 on Demand are hybrid applications (databases, television content, interactivity and broadband) that have quickly become popular forms of access to entertainment content. These facilities enable people to watch recently transmitted television programmes (usually up to a week old) on their computers or television.

Recent developments and interest in 3D television have not been entirely successful. Of greater potential, especially to marketers, are the investments currently being made in Internet-based television by companies such as Apple, Samsung and Sony.

---

**Scholars' paper 21.2**  **Digital advertising compared**

**Cheng, J.S.-S., Blankson, C., Wang, E.S.-T., Chen, L.S.-L. (2009) Consumer attitudes and interactive digital advertising, *International Journal of Advertising*, 28(3), 501–25.**

This paper considers consumer attitudes towards four sub-types of interactive digital advertising. The authors identify advertising that is delivered via the Internet, email, mobile-phone-based texting or SMS, and MMS-type advertising. The differences in attitudes among these four sub-types of interactive are determined and compared using three attitudinal factors towards interactive digital advertising. These are 'informative', 'entertaining' and 'irritating'.

---

## Video conferencing

There are two main types of video conferencing systems: PC-based and room-based. PC-based, or desktop, systems are suitable for a small number of people, for short time periods. The cameras are usually fixed focus, with small field capability, and viewing screens are also small.

Transmission speeds are limited by modem and telephone line capabilities. An advantage is that software applications and files can be shared and viewed jointly.

Room-based systems use large, sophisticated (pan–tilt–zoom) cameras and wide television screens, which means that more people can participate. Transmission via ISDN (integrated services digital network), including satellite links, facilitates better picture/sound quality. Video conferencing can be used in marketing communications for research (audience polling), product promotion/launch, training, employee and/or channel member briefings and sales negotiations. The advantages of video conferencing include speed and convenience as travel costs, carbon footprints and time away from core tasks are minimised; there is potential to reduce message ambiguity as there is joint and simultaneous viewing of materials and instant feedback; and relationships with customers and stakeholders can be improved through increased personal communication.

One of the disadvantages is that all participants have to be available at the same time, which can be difficult across time zones. The connections are not always reliable and room time-slots often cannot be extended beyond the original booking. Some people are uneasy in front of cameras, which may impair effectiveness.

The use of video conferencing has increased, because the cost of the equipment has plummeted and there have been major technical advances, which have improved the clarity and reliability of many commercial systems. In addition, there have been periods of major global crisis, and an increasing number of messages about global warming, all of which have led some organisations to reduce their volume of air travel, and spurred the use of video conferencing.

### Kiosks

Electronic kiosks are terminals that can be accessed by the public for information and services. Very often, kiosks are operated via touch-screens and video displays and incorporate card readers, coupon printers and other devices specific to their application. Increasingly, electronic kiosks provide not only multimedia facilities but also enable access to the Internet (www.scala.com).

# What digital media enable users to do

The various technologically driven facilities referred to above can influence an organisation's marketing communications in many different ways. The implementation and benefits derived from technology will vary across organisations. This is because the level of strategic significance afforded to these investments, the culture, managerial skills, resources and degree to which the organisation has a true customer orientation, differ widely. This section considers some of the generic ways in which digital media can influence marketing communications. However, readers should be aware that the intensity of the influence is variable and far from uniform.

## Interactivity

Digital technology allows for true interactively based communications, where messages can be responded to more or less instantly. Although there has been considerable media attention given to the development and potential of interactive services, the reality is that only a relatively small proportion of the public has become immersed in interactive environments, as measured in terms of advertising space sold, usage and attitude research, and the number of transactions undertaken interactively.

The development of interactive services may well be best served by the identification of those most likely to adopt such services, who will encourage others in their social orbits to follow their actions. This strategy requires communication with innovators and early adopters to speed the process of adoption (Rogers, 1983). This is quite crucial, as the infrastructure and associated costs require an early stream of cash flows (Kangis and Rankin, 1996). The resources necessary to instal, develop and utilise interactive services once represented a barrier to adoption. However, costs have fallen, technology has developed and knowledge and understanding have increased. This reinvention process can take individuals varying amounts of time to accomplish and, hence, can impact on the speed of adoption, but the barrier to setting up and using interactive services has diminished.

In addition to the Internet, technological advances have enabled a range of other interactive communication opportunities. One area where interactivity has been subject to experimentation is television, and some organisations have experimented with interactive messages, most notably the very first interactive advertisement for Chicken Tonight, followed by Dove, Mazda, Tango and others. However, this feature has yet to be fully developed and some have backed away from this area to concentrate resources elsewhere.

One of the biggest factors accelerating the use of digital television is the variety of entertainment possibilities that the Internet can provide. The development of the BBC iPlayer and time-shifted recording facilities have helped change consumer behaviour and the consumption of television programmes. So, despite the rise of the Internet and growth of online behaviours, total television viewing in the UK has not changed over the past twenty years (Binet and Field, 2007). This impacts on advertisers and their use of television as a primary medium for campaigns.

Home shopping represents a significant change in buyer behaviour that may affect a range of ancillary activities. Several UK supermarket operators have invested heavily in shopping channels and they have had to learn new fulfilment operations and new processes and procedures to meet customer expectations. Although Tesco appears to have been particularly successful, there is little evidence to suggest that retailers will give up their high street presence, as predicted in the late 1990s. The physical shopping experience provides many consumers with significant entertainment and social interaction satisfactions and these are unlikely to be discarded for total virtual shopping.

The financial services sector can be expected to undergo further change as home banking in particular becomes a secure and more convenient transaction context. Entertainment possibilities will be even more attractive, as interactive games and interactive viewing through pay-per-view, video on demand and time shifting (which is, as Rosen pointed out as long ago as 1997, the option to view yesterday's programmes today) become easily accessible.

The use of mobile marketing, discussed later, represents a huge opportunity for the retail sector. The ability to reach individuals with personalised messages when they are in the proximity of a store, or when passing an outdoor poster site, can only help improvement engagement figures and the use of targeted communications.

The new technology and the new communication infrastructure offer increasing numbers of people the opportunity to experience interactive marketing communications. This may impact on their expectations and bring changes to the way in which people lead their lives.

However, the profit and performance outcomes of organisations involved in these developments indicate that these technological advances and changes in buyer behaviour are often lagged. While some consumers are ready and eager to take advantage of the new opportunities, many are not, and the process of diffusion needs to move forward in order that an increasing proportion of customers have the means and motivation to participate in the interactive environments.

## Viewpoint 21.2    Game, set and hopefully, a match

One of the most visible aspects of interactivity is the explosion of game-based entertainments. Some of the main in-game advertising opportunities concern perimeter advertising opportunities in virtual stadiums and billboards in virtual cityscapes. However, games can also be used to recruit staff. For example, Marriott International have developed a gamification strategy designed not only to develop the brand but also to recruit employees in the 18 to 27 year-old age group. The game is on Marriott's jobs and careers Facebook page, which has over 12,000 global active users, and is called 'My Marriott Hotel'. Players are required to manage a virtual hotel kitchen, restaurant and other areas. They buy equipment, manage resources within a budget, hire and train employees as well as serving guests. They earn points based on happy customers and lose them when there is poor service.

Interactive gaming is also used by the Royal Navy to recruit undergraduates. Again it is accessible through Facebook and iPhone/iPad apps, and users have their decision-making skills tested under various types of pressure. It is set onboard a Royal Navy Type 45 Destroyer and one of its nuclear submarines, and users need to complete five missions and then share their scores with others on the social network.

IBM use gaming as a demand generator, to the extent that 'CityOne' is claimed to be their best means of getting sales leads. This game aims to educate people, essentially prospects, about how to run a city in a more environmentally friendly and sustainable way, using technology and data to aid decision making. Strategically the game is linked to the organisation's reputational platform, 'Smarter planet' and in that sense provides continuity and logical linkages to other IBM initiatives.

*Source*:   Based on Weekes (2011); Shearman (2011).

> **Question:**   What other reasons might explain why organisations should consider using games as part of their marketing communication activities?
>
> **Task:**   Prepare a short presentation which demonstrates the potential of gaming to influence audiences.

## Multichannel marketing

Although not entirely responsible, new technology has enabled organisations to reach new markets and different segments using more than a single marketing channel. Database-generated telemarketing, direct mail, email and Internet channels now complement field sales, retail and catalogue selling and have allowed organisations to determine which customers prefer which channels, and which are the most profitable.

This in turn enables organisations to allocate resources far more effectively and to spread the customer base upon which profits are developed. A multichannel strategy should accommodate customers' channel preferences, their usage patterns, needs, price sensitivities and preferred point of product and service access. So, as Stone and Shan (2002) put it, the goal is to manage each channel profitably while optimising the attributes of each channel so that they deliver value for each type of customer.

Multichannel strategies have added new marketing opportunities, and enabled audiences to access products and services in ways that best meet their own lifestyle and behavioural needs. For organisations this has reduced message wastage, used media more efficiently and, in doing so, reduced costs and improved communication effectiveness.

Retailers are faced with particular problems that concern the amount of property/freehold they possess and the, as yet, unknown pattern of consumer shopping behaviour in the light of multichannel opportunities. The Arcadia Group (which owns Dorothy Perkins, Miss Selfridge,

Wallis, Topshop, etc.) made a significant attempt to make its own name synonymous with online shopping through the development of Zoom, an online shopping mall. Some people might think that retailers should dispose of their fixed assets and move into the Internet or perhaps reconfigure their store layouts. In most cases, the optimum solution is to develop a multichannel solution whereby a range of media and experiences is offered to consumers. So, some prefer online, some the high street, others will use interactive television, and some will prefer catalogue shopping. Most use a mix of these, dependent on category and need. This approach puts customers' needs first by determining their preferred marketing channels.

What may happen is that shopping activities become divided into categories that reflect particular channel options. Routine, unexciting purchases may be consigned to online and interactive channels, and the more explorative, stimulating and perhaps socially important purchases are prioritised for physical shopping expeditions. Many stores have recognised the need to adapt and provide more value (than a current product focus). Related benefits and enhanced services are important as they help differentiation and attract customers. For example, the bookstore Waterstones provides coffee bars and comfortable seating, an environment in which customers are encouraged to relax and consider their possible purchases. Larger stores and mainstream brands may need to establish themselves as 'destination' stores where the attraction for consumers is bounded by excitement, entertainment and a brand experience. In some destination stores it is possible to test products in simulated but related environments. For example, people can attend cookery classes in supermarkets or test drive a range of cars in the countryside.

In the United States these types of store are now relatively common, and experience shows that high street shopping is not about to die, but take a revised shape, form and role. Mercedes has a cafe on the Champs-Elysées in Paris, but its role is to remind, differentiate and bring the brand into people's consciousness away from the traditional frame of reference. There is no persuasion, as cars cannot be bought, or sold, but the brand is reinforced. Multichannel campaigns are examined in detail later (Chapter 23).

## Personalisation

For the first time, digital media have empowered organisations to personalise messages and communicate with stakeholders on a one-to-one basis, and on a scale that is commercially viable. This has driven the dramatic development of direct marketing, reshaped the basis on which organisations target and segment markets, stimulated interaction and dialogue, brought about a raft of new strategies and challenged the conventional approach to mass marketing and branding techniques.

The use of email communications is now extensive and viral marketing campaigns are quite common. As with all forms of communication, the successful use of email requires an understanding of the recipient's behaviour. Email communication enables a high degree of personalisation, and in order to personalise messages it is necessary to understand the attitudinal and behavioural characteristics of each email audience (Chaffey, 2003). Chaffey suggests that the following need to be considered:

● How many recipients read their emails from home and at work?

● Which times of the day and days of the week do they read their email?

● How soon after receipt is email opened and read?

● How do recipients configure their email readers?

It is important to understand the email behaviour of different audiences. This is because this knowledge can influence the degree of personalisation that is given to email communications, and website welcome messages. However, email communication that is based on an understanding of an audience's email behaviour should influence message content, the time when it should be sent and, most important, the keys to encouraging recipients to open the email and

| Table 21.1 | Types of personalisation (based on Vesanen, 2007) |
| --- | --- |

| Type of Personalisation | Segment marketing | Adaptive | Cosmetic | Transparent | Collaborative |
| --- | --- | --- | --- | --- | --- |
| Typical actor | Reader's Digest | Yahoo.com | Google.com | Amazon.com | Hairdresser |
| Approach | To match customer preferences better than with mass-marketing | To let customers choose from different options | The organisation changes the package of standard good | The organisation changes the content of a good with a standard look | The organisation and customer are together building the product |
| Occasion | Little customer knowledge, cheap | A lot of choices to choose from | Customer sacrifice is due to presentation | Customer contacts are repetitive | Determining either/or choices |
| Source of information | Purchase-/demographic information | Direct choice by customer | Purchase-/demographic-/behavioural information | Purchase-/demographic-/behavioural information | Direct interaction |
| Level of interaction | None | High | Low | Low | High |
| Variation of product | Possibly | No | No | Yes | Likely |

not delete it. These keys are the 'header' of the email, which contains the subject matter, and the 'from' address, which signifies whether the sender is known and, hence, strongly determines whether the email is perceived positively at the outset. If it is, then there is a stronger chance that the email will be opened and, therefore, a greater opportunity for response and interactivity.

However, many people now expect a high level of personalisation and virtual recognition as opportunities arising through 'personalisation' reach beyond email communication. Personalisation is a sensitive area, often twinned with privacy issues. Indeed there appears to be little agreement about what constitutes personalisation and to that end Vesanen (2007) identifies five types of personalisation. These are shown at Table 21.1.

Personalisation should be an integral aspect of relationship marketing, especially in b2b markets. The degree of personalisation will inevitably vary over the customer lifecycle and become more intimate as a relationship matures.

---

### Scholars' paper 21.3    Strategic issues arising from intrusion

**Truong, Y. and Simmons, G. (2010) Perceived intrusiveness in digital advertising: strategic marketing implications, *Journal of Strategic Marketing*, 18(3), June, 239–56.**

Following the increasing amount of advertising on digital media, concern has started to be expressed about negative consumer perceptions concerning its intrusiveness. This may be a challenge to the claimed added-value of this medium over traditional media. From this the authors explore the little strategic marketing issues that have arisen and, among other things, confirm previous findings that pushed Internet and mobile digital advertisements are seen as intrusive.

## Mobility

Digital technologies now support a range of devices (smartphones, pads, readers and tablets) and applications that enable mobile communications. 'Mobile commerce' refers to the use of wireless devices such as mobile phones for transactional activities; and because the wireless facility enables transactions to be undertaken in real time and at any location, a feature referred to as 'ubiquity', the impact on marketing communications has huge potential. Because of the ability to reach individuals, the opportunity to keep in touch, the increased convenience, localisation and personalisation opportunities offered by this new technology, it is possible to track people to particular locations. Then the delivery of personalised and pertinent information plus inducements and promotional offers in order to encourage specific purchase behaviour can have greater impact. Truong and Simmons (2010) refer to studies that have shown that mobile advertising can improve attitudes and recall; result in higher levels of consumer acceptance and responsiveness (Barwise and Strong, 2002); and increase purchase intentions for mobile services (Nysveen, Pedersen and Thorbjørnsen, 2005).

SMS communications are used increasingly not just for brand-awareness-based advertising but also as an effective way of delivering sales promotions, such as announcing special offers. However, as with email, it is also important to consider the potential privacy concerns of customers, especially as the receipt of unwanted messages (i.e. spam) may well increase.

An emerging technology, likely to change a raft of behaviours is called near field communications (NFC). NFC is a small chip that can be embedded in smartphones, and is already in most new credit cards. By presenting a phone to an advert, or signage that has a NFC symbol, information is automatically transferred to the phone. The applications are numerous, including access facilities (turnstiles at stations, offices and stadia), paying for car parking, getting information through ads (events, hotels, taxis), making credit card payments for store purchases, logging into computers and security systems, travel ticket payments, and even the exchange of business cards by touching phones. See Viewpoint 21.3 for an example of the uses to which this technology can be used.

---

### Viewpoint 21.3    Super-intelligent phones

This example is used by NFC Forum to demonstrate how NFC can be used.

7:30 – Eric gets on a train to go to his office, using his NFC-enabled phone to tap a reader and easily open the turnstile.

7:32 – He sees a poster announcing a free concert that evening. He touches his NFC-enabled phone to the N-Mark on the poster, which transfers the detailed information onto his phone. He reserves seats for the concert with his mobile phone, using mobile communications (e.g. SMS, Internet, packet-based connections), and the complimentary tickets are sent to his mobile phone. He sends a text message to his wife to invite her to the concert and dinner.

8:15 – When he arrives at his office, Eric touches his NFC-enabled phone to the office gate to unlock the security mechanism.

Noon – At lunch time, he pays for his meal using one of the credit cards stored in his phone.

13:00 – After lunch, Eric visits the office of his new business partner for a meeting. Those attending the meeting exchange electronic business cards, stored in their NFC-enabled phones, by touching their phones together.

18:00 – Eric meets his wife and they go to the concert venue. He touches his NFC-enabled phone to a turnstile at the entrance to the venue, their reservations are confirmed, and they are admitted.

20:00 – After the concert, they visit a shopping centre, where they make a few purchases and have dinner, using their NFC-enabled phones to pay for everything.

22:00 – When they arrive home, Eric realises that he left his NFC-enabled phone on the train. He immediately calls the mobile network operator and makes a request to disable all active NFC services in the phone. If his phone is later found and returned to him, he will be able to reactivate these services.

*Source*:   www.nfc-forum.org/aboutnfc/nfc_in_action/.

**Question:**   To what extent can NFC really assist marketing communications?

**Task:**   Make list of the ways NFC technology might assist promotional applications.

## Speed

Digital media enable marketing communications to be conducted at much faster – indeed, electronic speeds. This impact is manifest in direct communications with end-users and in the production process itself. Draft documents, film and video clips, contracts, address lists and research and feedback reports, to name but a few, can all now be transmitted and shared electronically, saving processing time and reducing the elapsed production time necessary to create and implement marketing communication activities and events.

## Efficiency

Efficiency is a broad term used to encompass a wide array of issues. New technology helps organisations to target their messages accurately to discrete groups or audiences. Indeed, one-to-one marketing is possible and, when compared with mass communications and broad audiences, it is clear that IST offers huge opportunities for narrowcasting and reduced communication waste. Rather than shower audiences with messages that some of them do not wish to receive, direct marketing should, theoretically, enable each message to be received by all who are favourably disposed to the communication.

This principle of narrowcasting applies equally well to communication costs. Moving away from mass media to direct marketing and one-to-one communications reduces the absolute costs associated with campaigns. The relative costs may be higher, but these richer communications facilitate interactive opportunities with a greater percentage of the target audience than previously experienced in the mass broadcast era.

A further type of efficiency can be seen in terms of the accuracy and precision of the messages that are delivered. Marketing communications delivers product information, specifications and service details, contracts, designs, drawings and development briefs when customising to meet customer needs. The use of IST can help organisations provide customers with precise information and reduce opportunities for information deviance.

## Enhanced relationships

Digital technology is used by organisations to gather and use information about customers in order to better meet their needs. Through the use of a database, organisations now seek to develop longer-term relationships with customers, with programmes and strategies that are dubiously termed 'customer loyalty schemes'. While there may be doubt about the term 'loyalty', and the effectiveness of campaigns designed to increase loyalty (Binet and Field, 2007), there can be no doubt that digital media have helped develop new forms of sales promotion and have influenced customer relationships. What should also be clear is that the existence of IST in an organisation or relationship is no guarantee that additional value will be created (Ryssel et al., 2004).

Some customer-service interface functions have been replaced with technology in the name of greater efficiency, cost savings and improved service. Financial services organisations are able to inform customers of their bank balances automatically without human intervention. Meyronin (2004: 222) refers to this as an 'infomediation' strategy and suggests that this neglect of the human interaction in the creation of joint value in service environments may be detrimental.

The rapid development of social media and social networks in particular, has added a new dimension to the way brands and their customers interact and the way in which brand-based relationships are fashioned. Indeed Fournier and Avery (2011: 194) refer to open-source branding which involves 'participatory, collaborative, and socially-linked behaviors whereby consumers serve as creators and disseminators of branded content'.

Relationships with intermediaries have also been affected by new technology. The development of ecommerce has given rise to channel strategies that either result in channel functions and, hence, members being discarded, or give rise to opportunities for new functions and members. These processes, disintermediation and reintermediation respectively, are both dynamic and potentially destabilising for organisations and their channel partners.

# Websites

Websites are the cornerstone of Internet activity for organisations, regardless of whether they are operating in the b2b, b2c, not-for-profit, or third sectors. The design characteristics of a website can be crucial in determining the length of stay, activities undertaken and the propensity for a visitor to return to the site at a later time. When the experience is satisfactory, then both the visitor and the website owner might begin to take on some of the characteristics associated with relationship marketing.

To understand a website's interactive capabilities, consideration will first be given to its strengths and weaknesses, then the issues associated with the development of a website will be identified, and finally the processes involved in attracting and managing website activity will be examined.

Websites can be used for a variety of purposes but essentially they are either product-oriented or corporate-oriented. Product-oriented websites aim to provide product-based information such as brochureware, sales-based enquiries, demonstrations and endorsements through to online transactions and ongoing technical support as the main activities.

Corporate-oriented websites aim to provide information about the performance, size, prospects, financial data and job opportunities relating to the organisation. They also need to relate to issues concerning the ethical expectations and degree of social responsibility accepted by the company, if only to meet the needs of prospective investors and employees. The demarcation is not necessarily as clear-cut as this might suggest, but the essence of a site's orientation is largely derived from the organisation's approach to branding.

The strengths and weaknesses of website facilities are set out in Table 21.2. However, it should be remembered that these are generalised comments and that some organisations have attended to these issues and have been able to develop the strengths and negate some of the weaknesses to such a degree that their websites are particularly attractive and user friendly and encourage repeat visits.

## Strengths

Any www user can create a website, consisting of a home page and a number of linked pages. Business pages can carry advertising, product catalogues, descriptions, pricing, special offers,

| Table 21.2 | Strengths and weaknesses of website-based communications |
|---|---|

| Strengths | Weaknesses |
|---|---|
| Quick to set up and easy to maintain | Access and page downloading speeds can be slow but increasing broadband access has reduced this type of problem. |
| Flexibility | Huge variability in website design and user friendliness |
| Variety of information | Attract large amounts of unsolicited email |
| High level of user involvement | Security and transaction privacy issues |
| Potentially high level of user convenience (and satisfaction) | Variable levels of Internet penetration across UK households |
| Range of service facilities | Inconsistent fulfilment standards (online transactions only) |
| Global reach and equal access opportunities | Variability and speed of technology provision |
| Open all hours – reduced employment costs | Lack of regulation concerning content and distribution |
| Very low relative costs (per person reached) | Online search time costs prohibitive for many users |
| Can provide cost efficiencies in terms of marketing research | |

press releases – all forms of promotional material. They can link to online order pages, so that potential customers can order directly, or to email facilities for requesting further information or providing feedback. Consumer interest and activity can be monitored easily, allowing for timely market research, rapid feedback and strategy adaptation.

Barriers to entry are low, it is relatively inexpensive to create/maintain a site and share of voice is theoretically equal for all participants, although in practice this is clearly not the case. Large organisations can buy banner ads and have a better chance of appearing in the first few results presented by search engines (see eChapter 34 for more detail on Search). Good design can add to brand appeal and recognition.

Potential customers actively seek products and services, which is both time- and cost-effective from a company's point of view, and indicative of positive attitudes, perception and involvement. Channel communications can also be swift and supportive. Coverage is global, without the need for huge investment or expensive staff to be employed around the clock. Savings can be made in advertising budgets, travel, and postage and telephone costs. Different time zones no longer matter in the virtual environment, and language barriers are less of an issue.

## Weaknesses

The disadvantages are that the speed of access, page location and loading can still be too slow for many users, especially for users in rural locations where there is no broadband or wi-fi strength is weak. However, as broadband penetration accelarates, so these problems disappear. Perversely however, even broadband and the extra bandwidth bring other difficulties. The launch of the BBC iPlayer in 2008 generated over 17 million users in the first seven weeks (BBC Radio). Even then the infrastructure was starting to creak and people are downloading greater and greater volumes of material.

Potential customers are easily put off by slow or unreliable connections and this frustration can result in negative images of the company or product. Poorly designed websites, which confuse rather than clarify, also create a poor impression, one that can deter a return visit.

Unsolicited email is extremely annoying to many users and may be counterproductive. Worries over the security of financial details and transactions online, while not discouraging some people from seeking information, may still be a barrier to full ecommerce. Fulfilment issues, principally delivery problems (such as long delays), wrong items, incorrect billing, plus the associated inconvenience of returning products or otherwise seeking resolution, may deter repeat purchase.

Some regard ecommerce as transactional websites or extended enterprises, but it is more to do with information/communication management and the impact on relationships. Ecommerce should be aimed at building new relationships with established customers and providing potential customers with a reason to change. The idea that ecommerce provides process efficiencies is correct, but these features need to be transformed into benefits for customers.

## Website design

The design and functionality of a website is now recognised as an important integral aspect of an organisation's communication strategy. Indeed, many organisations now update their sites on a regular basis. For example, $O_2$ recognised that their website was confusing and frustrating (Shearman, 2012), witnessed by the number of people having to phone the organisation on its customer service line. A revised strategy incorporating a website that encouraged exploration and experience was planned. What constitutes a suitable website has also been the subject of much debate and speculation, marked by a lack of substantial empirical work to determine a common framework. Of the many ideas available two are featured here, if only because of their currency at the time of writing and the background of the researchers involved.

Karayanni and Baltas (2003) suggest that websites have four main characteristics. These are set out in Table 21.3 and were presented in the context of b2b markets.

This breakdown is useful because it indicates the main facilities that a successful site should provide. However, what it does not provide is a depth of insight and balance that would help organisations design their sites more appropriately. Rayport and Jaworski (2004) offer a 7Cs framework, which they subsequently develop into a map that can be used to analyse sites and to design sites more effectively.

| Table 21.3 | Four aspects of website design |
| --- | --- |
| **Website characteristic** | **Explanation** |
| Interactivity | The provision of solutions in response to the provision of personal information and the ability of users to customise preferences. This can be delivered through memory storage/organisation and response to individual needs. |
| Navigability | The structure and organisation of the site combined with the ease with which information can be retrieved. |
| Multimedia design | The Internet offers all the facilities that each of the other media provide individually. This provides opportunities for stimulation as well as flexibility and visitor involvement with a site. |
| Content  Company content | Information relating to the organisation, its markets, culture and values are important to establish credibility and reduce risk. |
| Customer content | This concerns both the provision of information, for example a *frequently asked questions* facility, and the collection of information about customers and the market. |

| Table 21.4 | The 7Cs of the customer interface |

| Type of community | Explanation |
| --- | --- |
| Context | Layout and design of website |
| Content | Text, sound, pictures and video material |
| Community | Site-enabled, user-to-user communication |
| Customisation | Site facilities to tailor itself to user needs |
| Communication | The ways in which two-way communication is enabled |
| Commerce | Ability to enable commercial transactions |
| Connection | The number of other linked sites |

Rayport and Jaworski (2004).

The 7Cs of the customer interface design are intended to cover the range of elements necessary for good website design. These are set out in Table 21.4.

---

**Scholars' paper 21.4**    **Perceptions of online purchasing risk**

**Boshoff, C., Schlechter, C. and Ward, S.-J. (2011) Consumers' perceived risks associated with purchasing on a branded website: The mediating effect of brand knowledge, *South African Journal of Business Management*, 42(1), 45–54.**

This paper reports a study into the impact of the perceived risks associated with purchasing online from a well-established, branded website. It also assessed whether a consumer's brand knowledge (brand awareness and brand image) mediates the impact of risk perceptions on the intention to purchase from the website.

---

## Context

The context of a site is concerned with the balance between the functional and aesthetic look and feel. The functionality of some sites can dominate the aesthetic and will try to provide text-based information rather than emphasising the visual elements of the site. Conversely other sites attempt to provide warm feelings for visitors and use multimedia facilities and Flash technologies to create an emotional engagement with the site.

Where there is a balance between the functional and emotional content, visitors experience a site that provides a suitable level of information, is easy to navigate and yet is interesting and stimulating in terms of the emotional satisfaction derived from using the site. This need not be the optimal site design for all organisations, as the context should reflect the values and purpose of the organisation itself. At one extreme, high fashion and luxury brands will focus on aesthetically styled sites while the Driver and Vehicle Licensing Agency, for example, would be expected to be predominately functional.

## Content

This refers to what is presented on the site in terms of audio, text, graphics, images and video. The content can be considered in terms of the following:

- *offering mix* – the balance between information, products and services;
- *appeal mix* – the balance between functional (attribute and benefits) and emotional (feelings and brand engagement) appeals;
- *multimedia mix* – the selected combination of audio, text, graphics, images and video;
- *timeliness mix* – the time sensitivity of the information determines how often a site needs to be updated. For example, www.BBC.co.uk/news has to be updated on a frequent and regular basis, whereas a site dealing with largely historical or archive data (e.g. family trees) needs less regular attention.

---

### Viewpoint 21.4    ASOS websites are tops

ASOS.com, a global online fashion and beauty retailer, have won a number of awards for their website. They offer over 50,000 branded and own-label product lines and have websites targeting the UK, USA, France, Germany, Spain, Italy and Australia. The company deliver to over 190 other countries from their central distribution centre in the UK.

ASOS attract 17.5 million unique visitors a month and had 8 million registered users and 4.4 million active customers from 160 countries (at 31 March 2012). With this amount of activity it is critical that their website delivers a high-quality browsing and shopping experience. This is reflected in the way the

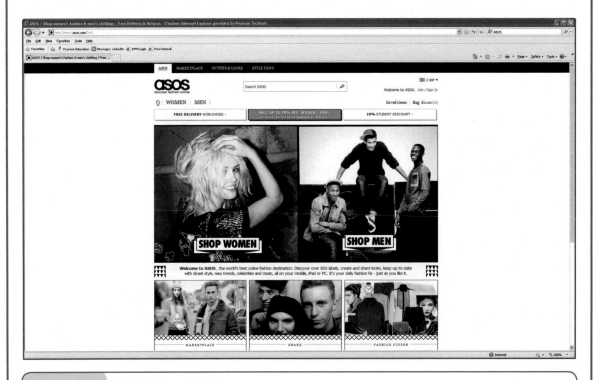

Exhibit 21.3    **The ASOS website**

*Source*: prshots.com/ASOS

website manages stock availability/reservation periods, delivery options, the delivery features, returns processes, security, payment options, all of which visitors can access immediately from their shopping bag. So good is the ASOS site that it has won many awards.

One of the key features of retail-orientated sites is the way in which they encourage multiple purchases. When a product is put into the shopping basket, the system should not assume the shop browsing event is over. So, rather than take the shopper to their basket or even checkout, they should be informed that the product is safely in the basket, but product viewing should be allowed to continue. This can be achieved through the use of a clear and transparent mini-bag facility. Visitors have to make a decision to visit their shopping basket rather than be directed by the software. Both ASOS and Top Shop employ these techniques.

The ASOS website has also been designed to encourage open communication by involving users through the marketplace blog, and social tools so that visitors can 'love' products and boutiques, and create fashion feeds. Even the tone of voice is uniform which, with the simple style guide, provides users with a consistent experience.

ASOS have also won awards for their mobile site. eDigital Research's latest mCommerce Benchmark study was based on an assessment of the customer experience for websites viewed on smartphones. It did well because the site design and its navigation is simple. It is compatible with the main site and the product and price information is clear, while it offers multiple images of clothes. The mobile site uses tabs to present brief yet critical product, delivery, and returns information.

*Source*: Revolution Awards, (2012); Charlton (2011); Rouke, P. (2011) www.Asos.com.

**Question:** How might the design of a website provide competitive advantage?

**Task:** Visit ASOS.com and list three features that you feel enhance your visitor experience.

## Community

The increasing role and significance of online communities indicate that site design should reflect the needs and significance of these communities to organisations. Online communities are about the interaction between the users of a site, not between the site and users. These interactions may be one-to-one (email) or among many (chat rooms) but are significant to organisations as they can be a source of information about customer feelings and attitudes that may be strong or weak.

## Customisation

This refers to the extent to which a site is capable of being adapted to the individual needs of visitors. When customisation is initiated by customers it is referred to as 'personalisation', but when driven and managed by the organisation it is called 'tailoring'. Obviously, different sites will provide varying levels of customisation, from low through medium to high levels, and this will be reflected in the users' site experience.

## Communication

The type of communication provided by a site is, to some extent, a reflection of the type of relationship offered by the organisation. The communication may be broadcast (content update reminders or mass mailings), in which case one-way communication prevents user response and with it opportunities for dialogue. Alternatively, interactive communication (user ratings or feedback) enables user response that can lead to dialogue.

### Connection

Connection is concerned with the degree to which a site is linked or connected to other sites. These links may be located on other web pages and, when clicked, take the user to another site. If a transaction then occurs, a commission is payable to the affiliate site. Outside links make it difficult for the user to return to the original page and are therefore not used a great deal. Framed links attempt to overcome this problem. Pop-up windows present a new site within the original site but can be annoying to users.

### Commerce

The ability of a site to support financial transactions is an important feature of product-dominated websites. Apart from the need to provide a secure and risk-free trading environment, the key activities associated with these sites are: registration, shopping carts, credit card approval, one-click shopping, orders through affiliate sites, configuration facilities (different combinations of products and services), and order tracking and delivery options. All of the 7Cs can be mapped and a site analysed against these criteria. Use of this mapping approach (that is, the identification of which element applies to a website) can enable website designers to better understand how their site appears to visitors and enables sites to be developed according to the planned needs of organisations.

To conclude this section, it should be noted that there is little empirical research that shows how different website design features impact on visitor responsiveness. Indeed Kent et al. (2003) make the point that there is a gulf between what many organisations expect of a website capability to foster relationships and the actual websites that are designed to facilitate these relationships. They argue that there is an inconsistency in what is thought to be possible through a website and the practice, that it is generally recognised that websites are all too often poorly used dialogic tools, and that the actual design of a website can have a strong impact on the way in which visitors perceive the organisation and hence can influence its relationship-building potential.

## Websites – visitor behaviour

It is possible to deconstruct users' website behaviour into a number of discrete activities, but the resultant list would be far too complex to be of any practical assistance. However, several authors have tried to discriminate among Internet users and segment the market accordingly. For example, Lewis and Lewis (1997) were among the first and they segmented the Internet on the basis of people who use the Internet. Later Forsyth et al. (2000) grouped users on the basis of those who are active online consumers, a behavioural approach to segmentation.

The design of websites should take into account the needs of these different types of user and also the different stages each has reached in terms of their experience in using the Internet, their stage in the adoption process and the different stages users have reached in the buying process. For the purposes of the rest of this text, reference is made to two broad categories: active (goal-directed) and passive (experiential) information seekers.

The initial goal is to generate awareness of the website, and this needs to be understood in the knowledge that there are many Web users who have no interest in a particular (your) website and those who are said to have a potential interest. The task is therefore to drive awareness levels among those who might find the site useful.

The second phase is to encourage the potential segment to actually visit the site. The problem is that there are two types of information seeker, passive and active. Passive seekers have no intention of hitting any particular site, whereas active seekers do have the express intention

| Exhibit 21.4 | **The website for authentic Caribbean rum (see Chapter 10)** |
|---|---|
| | *Source*: Bray Leino Ltd |

of visiting a particular site. Part of the communication strategy must therefore be geared to facilitating active seekers and attracting passive information seekers.

The next phase is to ensure that active seekers, once on the website, are able to find the information they need quickly and efficiently so that they are inclined to revisit. This entails good site access and, once the site is found, good site design so that navigation is easy, simple and fast. This normally means that the design of the site is simple and is user-, rather than technology-oriented. Passive information seekers, on the other hand, need to be made curious and stimulated to want to know more about the site and the products and services available. Here the objective is to convert hitters into visitors. A site registration book, supported perhaps with sales promotion devices, or a site design that is sufficiently intriguing, may allow these goals to be met. Research suggests that there are three main elements that strongly influence the perceived quality of a website visit (Oxley and Miller, 2000):

● all are content-oriented and refer to whether the site material is relevant to the needs of the visitor;

● the degree to which the content (and design) encourages curiosity to explore the site;

● whether the content is presented in an interesting way.

These three points correlate strongly with the idea of 'likeability', that advertising effectiveness improves when an individual assigns significant value, represented by relevance, curiosity and interest, to any particular form of marketing communication discipline, and advertising in particular in this case. Therefore, the main factors that might influence the way an individual perceives a website may be similar to the way they process and evaluate other marketing communications and, especially, advertising messages. Goldsmith and Lafferty (2002) have made similar observations and consider theories concerning attitudes towards the ad as developed by Lutz et al. (1983) and Bruner and Kumar (2000).

Attitudes developed towards advertisements can also impact on attitudes towards the brand and hence are better indicators of purchase intentions. Goldsmith and Lafferty also refer to ad brand recall and the fact that consumers who have strong emotional feelings towards a brand, a positive attitude, are more likely to be able to recall it. Therefore, investment in marketing communications that seeks to establish top-of-mind awareness of a brand, and also creates positive attitudes, is more likely to be successful.

# Key differences between traditional and digital media

Having considered the characteristics of traditional media in the previous chapter, this appears to be the right point at which to bring traditional and digital media together. The Internet and digital media facilities provide an interesting contrast with traditional media (see Table 21.5). Space (or time) within traditional media is limited and costs rise as demand for the limited space/time increases. On the Internet space is unlimited, so absolute costs remain very low and static, while relative costs plummet as more visitors are recorded as having been to a site. Another aspect concerns the focus of the advertising message. Traditionally, advertisers tend to emphasise the emotional rather than information aspect, particularly within low-involvement categories. Digital media allow focus on the provision of information, so the emotional aspect of advertising messages tends to have a lower significance. As branding becomes a more important aspect of Internet activity, it is probable that there will be a greater use of emotions, especially when the goal is to keep people at a website, rather than driving them to it.

Apart from the obvious factor that digital media, and the Internet in particular, provide interactive opportunities that traditional media cannot provide, it is important to remember that opportunities-to-see are generally driven by customers rather than by the advertiser that interrupts viewing or reading activities. People drive the interaction at a speed that is convenient to them; they are not driven by others.

**Table 21.5**    Comparison of new and traditional media

| Traditional media | New media |
| --- | --- |
| One-to-many | One-to-one and many-to-many |
| Greater monologue | Greater dialogue |
| Active provision | Passive provision |
| Mass marketing | Individualised marketing |
| General need | Personalised |
| Branding | Information |
| Segmentation | Communities |

| Table 21.6 | Comparison of information content |
| --- | --- |

| Websites/Internet | Traditional media |
| --- | --- |
| Good at providing rational, product-based information | Better at conveying emotional brand values |
| More efficient as costs do not increase in proportion to the size of the target audience | Costs are related to usage |
| Better at prompting customer action | Less effective for calling to action except point-of-purchase and telemarketing |
| Effective for short-term, product-oriented brand action goals and long-term corporate identity objectives | Normally associated with building long-term values |
| Poor at generating awareness and attention | Strong builders of awareness |
| Poor at managing attitudes | Capable of changing and monitoring attitudes |
| Measures of effectiveness weak and/or in the process of development | Established methodologies, if misleading or superficial (mass media); direct marketing techniques are superior |
| Dominant orientation – cognition | Dominant orientation – emotion |

Management control over Internet-based marketing communications is relatively high, as not only are there greater opportunities to control the position and placement of advertisements, promotions and press releases, but it is also possible to change the content of these activities much more quickly than is possible with traditional media. The goals outlined above indicate the framework within which advertising needs to be managed.

In addition to considering the attributes of the two different forms of media, it is also worth considering the content of the information that each is capable of delivering. These are set out in Table 21.6.

As mentioned earlier, digital media are superior at providing rational, product-based information, whereas traditional media are much better at conveying emotional brand values. The former have a dominant cognition orientation and the latter an emotional one. There are other differences, but the predominant message is that these types of media are, to a large extent, complementary, suggesting that they should be used together, not one independently of the other.

# Convergence in marketing communications

Ideas concerning the nature and characteristics of the concept of integrated marketing communications (previously explored in Chapter 9) continue to be discussed. There can be little doubt that there are genuine benefits for organisations and their stakeholders by striving to achieve the principles of IMC. More recently, however, there is a growing body of thought concerning media convergence. At one level, convergence refers to a technological 'bringing together' of digital devices. Thus, information in different formats – audio, text, search, still and moving pictures, which previously required multiple devices to receive, such

| Table 21.7 | Dimensions of media convergence |
|------------|--------------------------------|
| **Convergence dimension** | **Explanation** |
| Media technology | Digitalisation and a reduction in number of technological devices necessary to send and receive a variety of streams of information |
| Media content | Almost all media content can now be produced, edited, distributed and stored digitally. This negates any need to keep media (and devices) separate |
| Media economics | The increasing horizontal concentration of media ownership, typified by the mergers of different media companies across different sectors, plus the re-organisations experienced by several media organisations. |

as an individual computer, television, radio or newspaper – can be accessed through a single (converged) device. However, at another level, convergence refers to what Murdock (2000), cited by Herkman (2007), sees as three different dimensions, or what Murdock refers to as *levels*. These are media technology, media forms (and contents) and media economics. They are explained in Table 21.7.

New technology has driven the IMC concept not only through the development of direct marketing opportunities but also through ecommerce. Guens argues that IMC provides the *opportunity* for organisations to integrate their communications and that ecommerce has provided the *ability* for organisations to integrate their communications (2005). The proposition is that these two streams converge at the organisation's website. The website has become a central point for an organisation's digital communications. It is a point at which the complexity of messages that arise from different functional areas and departments can be integrated and managed, together with the array of messages emanating from a variety of external stakeholders.

It may be that centralising marketing communications in this way has not helped to draw the offline and online communications into an integrated whole. Indeed, it appears that, if marketing communications is to be audience-centred, it is crucial that the apparent focus on the technology and digitisation gives way to a more considered understanding of the meaning and interpretation that audiences give to the array of branded messages they receive, whether they be channelled through offline or online media.

At a macro level, media convergence and integrated marketing communications present an interesting context. Convergence should propel integration, but evidence suggests that truly integrated marketing communications is not taking place at a level or consistency that some popular commentators suggest is happening or is necessary. Apart from the technological, content and economic convergence, integrated marketing communications needs to adopt an audience-centred approach, one that accounts for the meaning different audiences bestow on the messages they receive.

# Key points

- The range of digital media is vast and is growing rapidly but consideration has been given to some of the key types or forms of digital media. The Internet, databases, multimedia, mobile phone technologies, business applications (software), interactive television, video conferencing and electronic kiosks have been examined.

- The benefits arising from using digital media are many, but consideration has been given to interactivity, multichannel marketing, personalisation, speed, mobility, efficiency, enhanced relationships and issues relating to strategy.

- The website has become the fulcrum for many organisations and their marketing communications. The design characteristics of a website can therefore be crucial in determining the length of stay, activities undertaken and the propensity for a visitor to return to the site at a later time. The 7Cs framework by Rayport and Jaworski provides a useful design checklist. When the experience is satisfactory, then both the visitor and the website owner might begin to take on some of the characteristics associated with relationship marketing.

- Space is unlimited on the Internet, so absolute costs remain very low and static, while relative costs plummet as more visitors are recorded as having been to a site. Digital media are superior at providing rational, product-based information, whereas traditional media are much better at conveying emotional brand values. The former have a dominant cognition orientation and the latter an emotional one. There are other differences, but the predominant message is that these types of media are, to a large extent, complementary, suggesting that they should be used together, rather than independently of each other.

- At one level convergence refers to a technological 'bringing together' of digital devices. This means that information in different formats, such as audio, text, search, still and moving pictures, which previously required multiple devices, such as an individual computer, television, radio or newspaper, is accessed through a single (converged) device. At another level, convergence refers to media technology, media forms (and content) and media economics.

- It is also argued that IMC provides the *opportunity* for organisations to integrate their communications and that digital media, albeit in the form of ecommerce or emarketing, provides the *ability* for organisations to integrate their communications and, in doing so, converge systems, processes, structures and messages.

# Review questions

1. Prepare brief notes explaining how the database has influenced marketing communications.

2. Discuss ways in which use of the Internet has assisted organisations to develop their marketing communications.

3. Identify different ways in which multimedia applications might be configured.

4. Why has the use of mobile communications been slow but is now about to increase rapidly?

5. Why is interactivity so important in contemporary marketing communications?

6. How would you advise a website be designed from a marketing perspective?

7. To what extent can digital marketing assist marketing?

8. Prepare notes identifying how digital media have affected the structure of the marketing communications industry.

9. List four differences between digital and conventional media.

10. What is convergence and how might this affect marketing communications?

# References

Advertising Association (2012) The Expenditure Report, *WARC*, retrieved 8 June 2012 from www.expenditurereport.warc.com/.

Barwick, R. (2012) HOW TO: Use QR codes as part of your marketing mix, *B2B Marketing*, retrieved 4 January 22012 from http://www.b2bmarketing.net/knowledgebank/integrated-marketing/best-practice/how-use-qr-codes-part-your-marketing-mix.

Barwise, P. and Strong, C. (2002) Permission-based mobile advertising, *Journal of Interactive Marketing*, 16(1), Winter, 14–24.

Binet, L. and Field, P. (2007) *Marketing in the era of accountability*, Institute of Practitioners in Advertising, Henley-on-Thames: WARC.

Boshoff, C., Schlechter, C. and Ward, S.-J. (2011) Consumers' perceived risks associated with purchasing on a branded website: The mediating effect of brand knowledge, *South African Journal of Business Management*, 42(1), 45–54.

Bruner, G.C. and Kumar, A. (2000) Web commercials and advertising hierarchy of effects, *Journal of Advertising Research*, January/April, 35–42.

Chaffey, D., Mayer, R., Johnston, K. and Ellis-Chadwick, F. (2003) *Internet Marketing*, 2nd edn., Harlow: Pearson.

Chaffey, D., Mayer, R., Johnston, K. and Ellis-Chadwick, F. (2008) *Internet Marketing Strategy, Implementation and Practice*, 4th edn., Harlow: Pearson Education.

Charlton, G. (2011) ASOS has the best mobile commerce site: study, 31 May retrieved 11 June 2012 from http://econsultancy.com/uk/blog/7588-asos-has-the-best-mobile-commerce-site-study.

Cheng, J.S.-S., Blankson, C., Wang, E.S.-T., Chen, L.S.-L. (2009) Consumer attitudes and interactive digital advertising, *International Journal of Advertising*, 28(3), 501–525.

Constantinides, E. and Fountain, S.J. (2008) Web 2.0: Conceptual foundations and marketing issues, *Journal of Direct, Data and Digital Marketing Practice*, 9, 231–44.

Eleftheriou-Smith, L.-M. (2012) Hiscox becomes first UK brand to use AdCastPlus platform, *Mediaweek*, 20 April 2012, retrieved 8 June 2012 from http://www.brandrepublic.com/news/1128090/Hiscox-becomes-first-UK-brand-use-AdCastPlus-platform/?DCMP=ILC-SEARCH.

Forsyth, J.E., Lavoie, J. and McGuire, T. (2000) Segmenting the e-market, *The McKinsey Quarterly*, 4, retrieved 10 November 2004 from www.mckinseyquarterly.com/article.

Fournier, S. and Avery, J. (2011) The Uninvited Brand, *Business Horizons*, 54(3), May, 193–207.

Goldsmith, R.E. and Lafferty, B.A. (2002) Consumer response to websites and their influence on advertising effectiveness, *Internet Research: Electronic Networking Applications and Policy*, 12(4), 318–28.

Guens, T.W. (2005) Current and future developments in electronic commerce, in *Marketing Communication: Emerging Trends and Developments* (ed. A. Kimmel), Oxford: Oxford University Press.

Haill, O. (2011) Case Study: Hiscox, *The Marketer*, May, pp. 20–22.

Herkman, J. (2007) Current Trends in Media Research, retrieved 18 January 2008 from www.nordicom.gu.se/common/pub1_pdf/261.

Ireland, N. and Neill, J. (2011) *Capturing an older generation for the Organ Donation Register*, Case study submission, Tangible Communications.

Jones, G. (2008) iTV returns will be worth the wait, *Marketing*, 9 April, p. 21.

Kamakura, W.A., Wedel, M., de Rosa, F. and Marzon, J.A. (2003) Cross-selling through database marketing: a mixed factor analyzer for data augmentation and prediction, *International Journal of Research in Marketing*, 20(1) (March), 45–65.

Kangis, P. and Rankin, K. (1996) Interactive services: how to identify and target the new markets, *Journal of Marketing Practice: Applied Marketing Science*, 2(3), 44–67.

Karayanni, D.A. and Baltas, G.A. (2003) Website characteristics and business performance: some evidence from international business-to-business organizations, *Marketing Intelligence and Planning*, 21(2), 105–14.

Kent, M.L., Taylor, M. and White, W.J. (2003) The relationship between website design and organisational responsiveness to stakeholders, *Public Relations Review*, 29(1) (March), 63–77.

Lewis, H. and Lewis, R. (1997) Give your customers what they want. Cited in Chaffey et al. (2003).

Lutz, J., Mackensie, S.B. and Belch, G.E. (1983) Attitude toward the ad as a mediator of advertising effectiveness, *Advances in Consumer Research*, 10, Ann Arbor, MI: Association for Consumer Research.

May, M. (2011) Brands still on the paper trail, *Marketing*, 23 June, retrieved 16 March 2012 from http://www.brandrepublic.com/features/1075882/Brands-paper-trail/?DCMP=ILC-SEARCH.

McCormick, A. (2011) Online Influence, *Revolution*, September, 32–3.

Meyronin, B. (2004) ICT: the creation of value and differentiation in services, *Managing Service Quality*, 14(2/3), 216–25.

Murdock, G. (2000) Digital Futures: European Television in the Age of Convergence, in *Television Across Europe: A Comparative Introduction* (eds J. Wieten, G. Murdock and P. Dahlgren), London: Sage, 35–8.

Murphy, D. (2008) Crack the code, *Marketing*, 6 February, 30–1.

Nysveen, H., Pedersen, P.E. and Thorbjørnsen, H. (2005) Intentions to use mobile services: Antecedents and cross-service comparisons, *Journal of the Academy of Marketing Science*, 33, 330–46.

Ondrus, J. and Pigneur, E.Y. (2009) Near field communication: an assessment for future payment systems, *Information Systems E-Business Management*, 7, 347–61.

Oxley, M. and Miller, J. (2000) Capturing the consumer: ensuring website stickiness, *Admap* (July/August), 21–4.

Radjou, N. (2003) Supply chain processes replace applications: 2003 to 2008, in *Achieving Supply Chain Excellence through Technology* (ed. N. Mulani), San Francisco, CA: Montgomery Research, 24–8.

Rayport, J.F. and Jaworski, B.J. (2004) *Introduction to E-Commerce*, Boston, MA: McGraw-Hill/Irwin.

Revolution Awards (2012) Best Website 2012, *Revolution Awards*, p. 39.

Rogers, E.M. (1983) *Diffusion of Innovations*, 3rd edn., New York: Free Press.

Rosen, E.M. (1997) Digital TV will soon overtake the Internet, *Revolution* (July), 6–7.

Rouke, P. (2011) Persuasive checkout best practice from ASOS, *EConsultancy.com*, 30 November, retrieved 12 June 2012 from http://econsultancy.com/uk/blog/8391-persuasive-checkout-best-practice-from-asos.

Ryals, L. and Payne, A. (2001) Customer relationship management in financial services: towards information-enabled relationship marketing, *Journal of Strategic Marketing*, 9, 3–27.

Ryssel, R., Ritter, T. and Gemunden, H.G. (2004) The impact of information technology deployment on trust, commitment and value creation in business relationships, *Journal of Business and Industrial Marketing*, 19(3), 197–207.

Shearman, S. (2011) Navy looks to social gaming to drive recruitment, *marketingmagazine.co.uk*, 11 April retrieved 7 October 2011 from http://www.brandrepublic.com/news/1064861/Navy-looks-social-gaming-drive-recruitment/?DCMP=ILC-SEARCH.

Shearman, S. (2012) O$_2$ plans radical revamp of confusing brand site, *Marketing*, 7, March, p. 5.

Stone, M. and Shan, P. (2002) Transforming the bank branch experience for customers, *What's New in Marketing*, 10 (September), retrieved 23 August 2004 from http://www.wnim.com/archive/.

Truong, Y. and Simmons, G. (2010) Perceived intrusiveness in digital advertising: strategic marketing implications, *Journal of Strategic Marketing*, 18(3), June, 239–56.

Turner, C. (2008) How NME achieved multi-platform success, *Utalk Case Studies*, retrieved 28 February 2008 from www.utalkmarketing.com/pages/.

Vesanen, J. (2007) What is personalization? A conceptual framework, *European Journal of Marketing*, 41(5/6), 409–18.

Weekes, C. (2011) Game on, *B2B Marketing*, September, 23–4.

Wray, J. and Plante, D. (2011) Mobile advertising engine for centralized mobile coupon delivery, *International Journal of Management and Marketing Research*, 4(1), 75–85.

# Chapter 22
# Social, search and interactivity

The development of social media, and social networks in particular, represents a democratisation of the media landscape as new forms of interactive communications, relationships and behaviour emerge. The use of social media within a marketing communications context has in many ways so far been experimental.

The significant changes in consumer behaviour, technology, media usage and digital formats experienced in recent years require organisations to find and adopt very different marketing (communications) strategies from the tried and trusted formulas used previously. The search continues.

## Aims and learning objectives

The aims of this chapter are to explore ways in which organisations and individuals can use social media, search, and other forms of interactivity to communicate effectively.

The learning objectives are to enable readers to:

1. consider the characteristics of social media;
2. explore the issues associated with social media and marketing;
3. explain how social networks can be used in marketing communications;
4. understand and identify the characteristics associated with viral marketing, web logs and microblogging, podcasting, RSS, and online communities;
5. evaluate search engine marketing and distinguish the main features of both pay-per click and search engine optimisation;
6. discuss the features of email marketing communications for both customer acquisition and retention;
7. understand how the use of SMS, apps, widgets, affiliate marketing and augmented reality can enhance marketing communications.

# Minicase

## Inspired by Iceland

Three hours' flight time from London and five from New York is Iceland, a small island in the North Atlantic. At one time, Iceland, with just 318,000 people, was one of Europe's poorest countries, but it transformed itself into a financial hub, and one of the wealthiest European countries.

Iceland's strength was built first on finance and then tourism and, as part of the country's investment plan, 'Promote Iceland' was created. This is a public–private partnership designed to improve the competitiveness of Icelandic industries in foreign markets, and to stimulate economic growth through increased exports. The website states that the aims of Promote Iceland are to:

- Enhance Iceland's good image and increase awareness of the country abroad. Assist Icelandic companies in marketing their goods and services abroad. Promote Iceland as a tourist destination and help promote Icelandic culture abroad.

- Offer training and consultancy services to companies, associations and individuals in Iceland, to help them reach success in the international marketplace.

- Promote investment opportunities and attract foreign direct investment to Iceland in line with the current policies of the government.

Promote Iceland assists Icelandic companies seeking to grow internationally, by developing networks and connections through trade associations, chambers of commerce, embassies and consulates around the world. It provides opportunities through professional connections, as well as arranging bilateral events, such as seminars, trade fairs, press trips, and trade delegations.

In addition, Promote Iceland is responsible for managing Iceland's identity and associated communications. The goal is to ensure that tourists form images that Iceland is an exciting destination. This involves promoting Icelandic culture abroad, as well as strengthening the image of Iceland as an attractive option for direct foreign investment.

The banking debacle which preceded the financial crisis in 2008 dealt Iceland several severe blows. Its three banks were bankrupted and nationalised, the economy spiralled into chaos, and various international governments froze any Icelandic assets within their control. In addition to this, in 2010 the volcano Eyjafjallajokull unexpectedly erupted, and sent plumes of ash into the Icelandic and surrounding airspace. This grounded many airlines for days throughout Northern Europe, and the net effect was to further isolate the island, and cause tourism numbers to plummet. All of these events led to considerable negative media comment about Iceland, all of which not only turned off the financial community and investors, but also drove potential tourists elsewhere. Tourism numbers fell by 30 per cent in the two remaining weeks of April 2010 alone, and was projected to decline over the summer. Off-peak season tourism had always been flat so the prospects looked grim.

Something had to be done.

A campaign was developed, 'Inspired by Iceland'. The goal was to reposition Iceland as an all-year-round destination and so increase visitor numbers during the off-peak months. Rather than create a conventional tourism marketing campaign targeting overseas tourists, a different, participative approach was adopted. The 'Inspired by Iceland' campaign strategy involved the island's population, who would be the media. Thousands of Icelanders were encouraged to open their doors to welcome visitors and invite them into their homes and lives in order that they experience something unique. By showing how they live and the hidden beauty of Iceland, Icelanders were made a central part of the campaign and renewal of the country. The target was the 'enlightened tourist', people sceptical of traditional tourism promises, people who would respond positively to claims that this is an experience 'not for everyone'. As 'honorary Icelanders' these winter visitors had access to special experiences, ones that offered them a unique look into the life of Iceland, experiences that they would talk about and share with their friends and communities.

The campaign started with 'Iceland hour' when the entire country stopped and an address by the President of Iceland was made to the nation. In this he urged his fellow citizens to open their doors to visitors from around the world, and let people experience the real Iceland. He pledged to do this and he urged all Icelanders to share their stories and feelings about their country. The speech was webcast live online and covered by almost every global news media.

The response of the nation was immediate, as thousands of Icelanders went online and uploaded their invitations to the Inspired by Iceland website and Facebook pages, and told the world how much they love their country.

Carefully targeted digital, press and outdoor channels were used to spread the individual invites internationally and drive 'enlightened tourists' to take up the unique invitations on the website and social pages. To promote the stories, viral ads, live webcam feeds, Facebook pages and films were created, featuring celebrities including Bjork, Damon Albarn and Stephen Fry.

The event made news in 57 countries. The idea generated 1.18 billion global media impressions. Consideration of Iceland as a winter holiday destination more than doubled (an increase of 124 per cent) amongst 'enlightened tourists' exposed to the campaign. Within two weeks of the launch, over 85 per cent of Icelanders were aware of the campaign. After six weeks, over half of the Icelandic public had contributed stories. On Facebook alone over 45,000 fans were recruited and over 2 million stories were seen and sent out by fans. Between June and August the live webcams were viewed 60 million times.

The country was perceived as a safe place to visit within just 10 weeks of the campaign launching. The most successful winter in Iceland's history then unfolded, with visitor numbers up 27 per cent against forecasts. With an additional 73,000 tourists, an additional £127.4 million was generated for Iceland's economy. Tourism increased by 16.85 per cent in winter 2011, compared with winter 2010.

Through 'Inspired by Iceland', a budget of just £2 million, and a small but involved population, a new type of tourism campaign was created. Using people as media, global perceptions of Iceland were changed in a short period of time. The success of the social participation campaign 'Inspired by Iceland' led to a further campaign being launched in February 2012. In this development Promote Island partnered with AOL for the launch of its first branded blog, in a cross-platform involving the *Huffington Post, MyDaily, AOL Travel* plus AOL advertising platforms, Advertising.com and goviral, designed once again to raise awareness of Iceland as a year-round holiday destination.

The aim was to offer *deeper social integration* with the target audience, affluent consumers, through video, blogs and social media. The campaign features a 12-minute documentary on Iceland, called *Islander*, which was run on *Huffington Post UK's* Inspiration page. Also involved is a trailer for the documentary, distributed across goviral, the first live camera feed on display advertising format Project Devil, and sponsored content.

*This minicase was written by Chris Fill using a variety of sources, including Eleftheriou-Smith (2012); Owens (2012); Puri (2011) plus*

*http://www.advertolog.com/promote-iceland/print-outdoor/iceland-14757905/*

*http://www.canneslions.com/work/2012/integrated/entry.cfm?entryid=6857&award=101&order=0&direction=1*

*http://fanfest.eveonline.com/en/sponsors/promote iceland*

*http://www.islandsstofa.is/en.*

| Exhibit 22.1 | **Inspirational image of Iceland** |

*Source*: Brynjar Ágústsson, brynjar photoshelter.com/Promote Iceland

# Introduction

Interaction is a key feature of digital media and is one of the main ways that they differ from traditional media. It was through interaction that the Iceland campaign, featured in the minicase, broke with convention and became so successful. Interaction is key because it denotes the critical functionality that enables participants in communication networks to receive and respond to messages, to share knowledge and create content.

The communication landscape today is more open and democratic than it used to be. Democratisation is enabled through interactivity, and the inherent transparency (Fournier and Avery, 2011) as a wide spectrum of electronic facilities enables all parties to a communication event to participate.

Perhaps the strongest characteristic of interactivity is that it enables communications to move from one-way and simple two-way models to one that is literally 'interactive'. Interactivity normally precedes the establishment of dialogue between participants in the communication process. This in turn enables all participants to contribute to the content that is used in the communication process. This is referred to as *user-generated-content*, as demonstrated by people uploading videos to YouTube or even emailing comments to radio and television programmes. This symbolises a shift in the way in which marketing communications has developed. If the maintenance of 'relationships' is a central marketing activity, then interactive marketing communications has an important role to play in these relationships.

This chapter starts with a consideration of social media which includes social networks, viral, blogging, including microblogging (Twitter), RSS, and online communities. It then considers search engine marketing, before examining email, SMS, apps, widgets, affiliates, and augmented reality.

# Social media

Social media embrace a range of applications, all of which incorporate a form of word-of-mouth communication. Kietzmann et al. (2011: 1) state that 'Social media employ mobile and Web-based technologies to create highly interactive platforms via which individuals and communities share, co-create, discuss, and modify user-generated content.'

The impact of personal influences on the offline communication process can often be important if communication is to be successful. Online personal influencers such as opinion leaders and opinion formers, often bloggers, are equally important. Organisations target these individuals with messages, knowing that they will be disseminated to a wider audience. Recommendations to provide information and to support and reinforce purchasing decisions are an integral part of this word-of-mouth process.

The role of opinion formers is much diminished in the online world, especially with the predominant 18–25-year-old user group. For them expert opinion, as represented by opinion formers, is rejected in favour of peer-group recommendation (opinion leaders). For example, www.last.fm, a social music platform, tracks individual music preferences based on what people play on their computers or iPods, locates individuals into neighbourhoods who share similar tastes and then waits for them to interact. People share views, interests and favourite music and then make recommendations to others in their neighbourhood, based on shared preferences (Crow, 2007). Although there is a hint of social engineering, the power of peer group and opinion leader recommendation has seen this model copied by others, including book libraries.

The terms 'social media' and 'social networks' have become increasingly prevalent. Although similar, they do not mean the same, yet are often used interchangeably, and mistakenly. Kaplan

| Table 22.1 | A classification of social media | | |
| --- | --- | --- | --- |

| | | Social presence/Media richness | | |
| --- | --- | --- | --- | --- |
| | | Low | Medium | High |
| **Self-presentation/ Self-disclosure** | **High** | Blogs | Social networking sites (e.g., Facebook) | Virtual social worlds (e.g., Second Life) |
| | **Low** | Collaborative projects (e.g., Wikipedia) | Content communities (e.g., YouTube) | Virtual game worlds (e.g., World of Warcraft) |

Kaplan and Haenlein (2010) Used with permission

and Haenlein (2010: 61) define social media as 'a group of Internet based applications that build on the ideological and technological foundations of Web 2.0 and that allow the creation and exchange of User Generated Content'. In order to understand the range of social media, they develop a classification scheme. To do this, they identify two key elements of social media: first, social presence/media richness and, second, social processes in the form of self-presentation/self-disclosure. Within these parameters they classify core aspects of social media. Table 22.1 shows this classification.

In other words, *social media* refers to a broad range of Web-based applications, and social networking sites are one of the many applications that are available. Others include weblogs, content communities (e.g. YouTube), collaborative projects (e.g. Wikipedia), virtual game worlds (e.g. World of Warcraft) and virtual social worlds (e.g. Second Life).

Seven main aspects of social media are considered here: social networks, viral marketing, podcasts, web logs (or blogs), microblogging, RSS and online communities.

---

### Scholars' paper 22.1    So what are social media?

**Kaplan, A.M. and Haelein, M. (2010) Users of the world unite! The challenges and opportunities of social media, *Business Horizons*, 53(1), 59–68.**

This paper is important because it attempts to clarify what social media might be. The authors describe the concept of social media, and then present a classification of social media which groups applications as collaborative projects, blogs, content communities, social networking sites, virtual game worlds, and virtual social worlds. They conclude with ten pieces of advice for companies wishing to utilise social media.

---

The role and presence that an organisation seeks to adopt in social media is critical, as experience suggests brands have settled well into this environment. Kietzmann et al. (2011: 242) refer to a 'rich and diverse ecology of social media sites, which vary in terms of their scope and functionality'. This diversity has posed problems for organisations as they attempt to adapt and implement digital strategies, in an environment where their level of control and influence is much reduced. They develop a framework consisting of seven building blocks. These refer to identity, conversations, sharing, presence, relationships, reputation, and groups. These blocks are constructs designed to enable insight into the different levels of social media functionality which in turn, they argue, can help organisations develop more effective configurations and use of social media. See Table 22.2.

| Table 22.2 | The building blocks of social media |
| --- | --- |

| Building blocks | Explanation |
| --- | --- |
| Identity | The extent to which users reveal their identities in a social media setting. This can include disclosing information such as name, age, gender, profession, location, and also information that portrays users in certain ways. |
| Conversations | The enormous number and diversity of social media conversations leads to format and protocol implications for firms that seek to host or track these conversations. Differences in the frequency and content of a conversation can have major implications for how firms monitor and make sense of the 'conversation velocity' – that is, the rate and direction of change in a conversation. |
| Sharing | Social media users exchange, distribute, and receive content. Firms wishing to engage with social media need to evaluate what objects of sociality their users have in common as, without these objects, a sharing network will be primarily about connections between people but without anything connecting them together. |
| Presence | The extent to which users can know if other users are accessible. It includes knowing where others are, in the virtual world and/or in the real world, and whether they are available. If users prefer to engage in real time, the social media platform should offer a presence or status line indicator, along with a suitable mechanism through which these users can contact each other and interact. |
| Relationships | This about the associations users have that lead them to converse, share objects of sociality, meet up, or simply just list each other as a friend or fan. The way users are connected can determine the characteristics of information exchange. Some relationships are fairly formal, regulated, and structured (LinkedIn), while others can be informal, unregulated and without structure (Skype). |
| Reputation | The extent to which users are able to identify the status of others, and themselves, in a social media context. Reputation can be a matter of trust, but this can be based on the number of endorsements from others (LinkedIn), content voting (YouTube) or aggregators (Twitter). |
| Groups | Users can form communities and sub-communities and so the more 'social' a network becomes, so the larger the potential groups (of friends, followers, and contacts) become. Organisations should be prepared to help users manage their groups. |

Based on Kietzmann et al. (2011).

Having identified the building blocks, Kietzmann et al. (2011) recommend that organisations develop strategies to monitor, understand, and respond to different social media activities. They suggest a framework, called the '4Cs'.

1. *Cognise.*   Each organisation should try to recognise and understand its social media landscape.

2. *Congruity.*   Each organisation should develop strategies that match the different social media functionalities and their goals.

3. *Curate.*   Each organisation should develop a policy about who should listen to conversations on a social media platform and when.

4. *Chase.*   Each organisation should undertake environmental scanning to understand the speed of conversations and the information flows that could affect the organisation and the market.

As if to confirm the importance of a well-considered digital strategy, Truong and Simmons (2010: 250) report research that finds that the use of inappropriate and intrusive pushed Web-based advertising and mobile digital formats 'can lead to a negative impact upon brand equity'.

# Social networks

One particular interpretation of online communities is the rapid development of social networks. Social networks are about people using the Internet to share lifestyle and experiences. The participants in these networks not only share information and experiences, but they can also use the interactive capacity to build new relationships. The critical aspect of social networks is that the content is user-generated and this means users own, control and develop content according to their needs, not those of a third party.

Social networks enable people to share experiences. Typical sites include MySpace, Bebo, YouTube and, of course, Facebook, which has experienced rapid growth and market dominance in recent years. These sites provide certain segments of the population, mainly the 16–25-year-old group, with an opportunity to use online networks to reach their friends, generate new ones and share experiences, information and insights. The activity might also be regarded as a supplement to their offline social networks. Some sites encourage ranking and rating of content that has been added to the site by others – for example Digg and Flickr. What is happening is that social networks are helping to re-engineer the way in which parts of society link together and share information (Walmsley, 2007).

The results of a European-wide study undertaken by Forrester Research reveal that there are six key characteristics that typify the dominant usage by online consumers of social media (Pinkerfield, 2007). There are those whose core activity on these sites is to publish content (9 per cent); those who prefer to comment (18 per cent); networkers (1 per cent); those who gather information (12 per cent); people who prefer to listen and observe interaction (49 per cent); and finally a large group who ignore all these activities (41 per cent).

When these data are aggregated on a country-by-country basis, it is revealed that the Dutch are the most active users, publishing the most blogs and Web pages. The Spanish prefer to comment, while the Italians actively gather information. French users are most likely to read blogs and reviews (are listeners), while UK users prefer to visit social media sites and make comments – typical of networkers. The study found that the Germans tend to ignore most social media.

The growth of Facebook and other networks is partly a reflection of the relative investment made in them. MySpace has seen little investment and has attracted widespread criticism, whereas Facebook is perceived to be innovative and eager to meet the needs of its target audience. For example, as part of its strategic development in 2007, Facebook allowed its users to build and instal applications within the social network. The more obvious marketing strategy would have been to charge developers the opportunity to access Facebook's users. However, as a result of opening the site up in this way, and free of charge, huge numbers of people switched to the site and within a couple of months over 1,700 new applications, such as SuperPoke, which encourages users to 'slap, chest-bump or headbutt', photo slideshows and online data storage, had been developed, integrated and accessed by site visitors.

With 85 per cent of Facebook's revenue driven from advertising, the relaunch of its ad platform early in 2012, partly in response to Google+, and advertiser disenchantment, was a major move. The new offering included mobile ads and revised/updated brand pages offering improved opportunities for interaction with consumers. However, concern was expressed at the time about whether the revised facilities represented too much of an intrusion. Twitter introduced a 'Quick bar' for mobile advertising, but they were forced to withdraw it following negative consumer response (Shearman, 2012).

The relative immaturity of the social networking arena and the way in which content is developed raises challenges about how organisations can best use social networks as part of their marketing communications to reach their target audiences. Creating fan pages and groups are established approaches. Unlike groups, fan pages are visible to unregistered people and are indexed, which helps improve reputation. Groups, on the other hand, facilitate viral marketing and are better at involving people and stimulating behaviour.

However, questions arise about the effectiveness of online ads in a social networking environment. Many users do not like brand advertising and prefer to take advice from their online peers in these communities when deciding what to buy, rather than listen to advertisers. Social networking is becoming a media channel in its own right and it is one that is reflecting the voice of consumers instead of those of brand owners.

An understanding of social media reveals that brand communications should not be invasive, intrusive or interruptive. In order to work, marketing communications need to become part of the context in which site users interact. Online advertising will continue to form a major revenue stream for the owners of these social networking sites and online communities, but increasingly this needs to be supplemented with the use of a mixture of sponsorship, brand placement and public relations. Asda approached Mumsnet.com, a parenting online community, for advice about the extent to which its clothing products encouraged the sexualisation of children. This followed the well-publicised outcry concerning Primark's sales of padded bikini tops for young children (Charles, 2010).

---

### Viewpoint 22.1  Privacy issues challenge Facebook's advertising strategy

In 2009 Facebook started to accept advertising on its site and it is estimated that in the first two years revenues were in the region of £25 million. However, the basis on which this advertising success has been built is both morally and ethically questionable.

In 2011 an Austrian student, Max Schrems, enquired about the data held by Facebook about him. Facebook's response was to send him 1,222 pages of data, on a CD. However, he realised that the data was incomplete, that Facebook was withholding data collected from the social networking site.

Facebook enables advertisers to target specific types of people with specific messages. This is known as *behavioural advertising* and is achieved by gathering data from each user's likes and dislikes posted on their walls and from their personal details. In addition, they get data about their family, friends and contacts, their music preferences, their educational background, and they also are aware of changes in lifestyle, such as when someone is planning a holiday, a wedding or major purchase. Indeed, everything people share with their friends, including brand and advertising-related activities, is tracked, monitored and stored for future commercial use. This includes private online chats that users have deleted.

Facebook can also use keyword searches to find out about attitudes and positions regarding politics, sexual issues, nationalism and religion, among others. All of Facebook's 800+ Million users agree to allow the social network to use their personal information when they sign the 4,000-word contract.

The European Commission is concerned about these practices and has drawn up measures to prevent this 'eavesdropping' approach to behavioural targeting. A Directive launched in January 2012 prevents targeted advertising unless users specifically allow it.

In its defence, Facebook argues that advertisers only see aggregated and anonymous data and so no names or attached personal details are seen by them.

*Source*:  Lewis (2011); Wasserman (2011); Whittaker (2011).

**Question:**  To what extent should social networks be responsible for an individual's personal data in an age of sharing and connectivity?

**Task:**  Find five ads on your preferred social network. Make notes about how each of them might be relevant to you.

# Viral marketing

Viral marketing involves the use of email to convey messages to a small part of a target audience where the content is sufficiently humorous, interesting or persuasive that the receiver feels emotionally compelled to send it on to a friend or acquaintance. For example, football matches between teams from the same city are always full of tension, grit and passion, and that is just the fans. One such cup match was played between Everton and Liverpool in February 2009. The match was being screened live but there was a technical error with the automated advertising system, just as the match went into extra time. So, as fans watched a Tic Tac ad interrupt the match, unknown to them, the winning goal was scored by Everton.

Once the inevitable arguments died down, the agency WCRS, who developed the ad for Tic Tac, decided to use the event to make a 20-second viral for a little bit of fun. The aim was to re-create Dan Gosling's goal, but instead they used two teams dressed as orange and lime Tic Tac men. Filmed on a winter's day on the Hackney Marshes, the viral not only poked fun at the issue but also provided entertainment around the Tic Tac brand (Nettleton, 2009).

Viral can also be used to support product launches, as demonstrated by the launch of Google Wave. Since this is essentially a collaboration tool which allows users to swap messages, pictures, video, and gadgets and merges them into a single, user-friendly application, it was important to demonstrate the features of the new product. This was achieved using a viral based on a scene from the film *Pulp Fiction*. The visual effects are performed through a remote user clicking on Google Wave, and the audio was just the dialogue from the film. The viral was viewed 500,000 times in the first two weeks, posted on 335 blogs and featured in over 4,600 tweets (GoViral, 2009).

The term 'viral marketing' was developed by a venture capital company, Draper Fisher Juvertson (Juvertson and Draper, 1997). The term was used to describe the Hotmail email service, one of the first free email address services offered to the general public and one that has grown enormously. According to Juvertson (2000: 12), they defined the term simply as 'network-enhanced word-of-mouth'. However, although the literature contains a variety of terminology used to explain what viral marketing is, for example *stealth marketing* (Kaikati and Kaikati, 2004), *interactive marketing* (Blattberg and Deighton, 1991) and *referral marketing* (De Bruyn and Lilien, 2004), *viral marketing (communications)* is the term used here.

Porter and Golan (2006: 33) suggest that viral advertising is 'unpaid peer-to-peer communication of provocative content originating from an identified sponsor using the Internet to persuade or influence an audience to pass along the content to others'. They argue that these materials are usually seeded through the Internet, are often distributed through independent third-party sites, are usually personal, more credible than traditional advertising, and humour is almost invariably employed in executions. Kirby, a leading viral marketing consultant, agrees, indicating that there are three key elements associated with viral marketing (2003):

- *content*, which he refers to as the 'viral agent', is the quality of the creative material and whether it is communicated as text, image or video;
- *seeding*, which requires identifying websites or people to send email in order to kick start the virus;
- *tracking*, or monitoring, the impact of the virus and in doing so providing feedback and a means of assessing the return on the investment.

However, although these qualities might be present, it is necessary that receivers of viral messages are predisposed to open the message, derive value from the message and be sufficiently engaged to become a part of the virus campaign by sending it on to others.

There is no doubt that viral marketing is difficult to control and can be very unpredictable, yet despite these characteristics, organisations are incorporating this approach within their marketing communications in order to reach their target audiences. Increasingly organisations are using word-of-mouth communications to generate conversations before the official launch. Kellogg's used social media for six months before officially launching Special K Crackers with conventional media. Ford in America used social media to encourage word-of-mouth communication for a year before running TV ads for the latest edition Fiesta (Anon, 2010). The key reasons for this approach are that it helps identify interested communities and consumer groups and it also encourages feedback, in a similar way to test marketing.

# Web logs

Web logs, or *blogs* as they are commonly known, are personal online diaries. Although individual issues are recorded and shared, a large proportion of blogs concern organisations and public issues, and they are virtually free. As Wood et al. (2006) conclude, blogging represents a simple, straightforward way of creating a Web presence.

Even if the quality and content of blogs vary considerably, their popularity has grown enormously. The informality of blogs enables information to be communicated in a much more relaxed manner than most other forms of marketing communication. This is typified by the use of podcasting and the downloading of blogs to be 'consumed' at a later, more convenient time or while multi-tasking. Blogs represent user-generated content and are often a key indicator of the presence of an opinion leader or former.

Blogs can be understood using a number of criteria, other than the basic consumer or corporate demarcation. Typically, the content and the type of media are the main criteria. A blog can be categorised by its content or the general material with which it is concerned. The breadth of content is only limited by the imagination, but some of the more mainstream blogs tend to cover topics such as sport, travel, music, film, fashion and politics. Blogs can also be categorised according to the type of media. For example, 'vlogs' contain video collections, whereas a 'photoblog' is a collection of photos and a 'sketchblog' contains sketches.

Nardi et al. (2004), as cited by Jansen et al. (2009), found five reasons why people choose to blog:

- documenting their lives,
- providing commentary and opinions,
- expressing deeply held emotions,
- articulating ideas through writing,
- forming and maintaining communities.

These appear to be a list of outward-facing reasons. What is not mentioned here are inner-directed reasons, such as the need for feedback, or psychological issues relating to the need for self-esteem, reassurance and reinforcement of an individual's identity.

Business-related or corporate blogs represent huge potential as a form of marketing communications for organisations. This is because blogs reflect the attitudes of the author, and these attitudes can influence others. As consumers write about their experiences with brands, opportunities exist for organisations to identify emerging trends, needs and preferences, and to also understand how brands are perceived. Sony used blogging as an integral part of its campaign to establish the Handycam and Cybershot brands. When shooting the ad in Miami, dubbed as 'Sony Foam City', Sony invited 200 visitors, mainly bloggers. Each was equipped with a Sony camera and encouraged to capture the soapy event, which involved covering parts of Miami with foam. Clips of the ad and the making of the ad were then leaked onto the Internet in advance of the launch of the ad being released and created a buzz around the brands.

Organisations can set up *external* corporate blogs to communicate with customers, channel partners and other stakeholders. Many major organisations use external blogs to provide information about company issues and other organisations use blogs to launch brands or attend to customer issues. The other form of corporate blog is the *internal* blog. Here the focus is on enabling employees to write about and discuss corporate policies, issues and developments. Some organisations encourage interaction between their employees and customers and the general public. Although problems can arise through inappropriate comments and observations, blogging is an informal communication device that can serve to counter the formality often associated with planned marketing communications.

---

### Scholars' paper 22.2 | Magazines or blogs to build a brand?

**Colliander, J. and Dahlén, M. (2011) Following the Fashionable Friend: The Power of Social Media,** *Journal of Advertising Research,* **51(1), 313–20.**

Social media and blogs in particular have become extremely fashionable, especially among writers, readers and, increasingly, marketers. Colliander and Dahlén demonstrate the importance of social media and of building brand relationships. They achieve this by showing how the writer–brand relationship and the credibility a writer is perceived to have affect readers' perceptions of brand publicity on blogs. The research is anchored in measuring brand publicity through blogs and online magazines. They find that blogs generate higher brand attitudes and purchase intentions.

---

Therefore, enabling people to blog, perhaps by creating dedicated Web space, facilitates interaction and communication through people with similar interests. There is also an added attraction in that communities of bloggers can attract advertisers and form valuable revenue streams. Blogs can be used by organisations as a form of public relations in order to communicate with a range of stakeholders. For example, a blog on an intranet can be used to support internal communications, on an extranet to support distributors and on the Internet to reach and influence consumers.

# Microblogging

Microblogging or *nanoblogging*, as it is sometimes referred to, is a short-format version of blogging. It is a form of eWoM and uses web social communication services (Jansen et al., 2009) of which Twitter is probably the best known. A microblog, or tweet, consists of a short comment, a post of 140 characters, which is shared with a network of followers. This makes production and consumption relatively easy in comparison to blogs.

These posts can be distributed though instant messages, email, mobile phones or the Web. Therefore, as Jansen et al. put it, people can share brand-related thoughts at any time, and more or less anywhere, with people who are connected via Web, cellphone or IM and email, on an unprecedented scale.

We know that WoM has a particularly significant impact on purchasing decisions, but eWoM can take place close to or even during a purchase process. Although eWoM may be less personal than face2face WoM, it has substantially greater reach and has greater credibility because it is in print and accessible by others (Hennig-Thurau et al., 2004). The implication of this is that microblogging offers huge potential to marketers. Twitter recognises this potential, and in April 2010 announced that it was to allow advertising on its site. However, these are not conventional adverts. These ads are tweets, and be an integral part of the conversations, referred to as 'Promoted tweets'. These messages, limited to 140 characters, appear at the top of the page when a user has searched for that word, and will only show up in search results (Steele, 2010).

---

### Viewpoint 22.2    In a tailspin with Twitter

The use of Twitter as a form of conversation and brand development has increased enormously in recent years. However, its use comes with a health warning, as illustrated by Qantas, the Australian airline. Early in November 2011 the entire fleet of Qantas aircraft was grounded following a dispute with staff. Three weeks after that was resolved, or at least the planes were flying again, Qantas decided to launch an engagement programme with its customers, using Twitter. Based on a competition to win a holiday, the key tweet asked customers to name their 'dream luxury flight experience'.

Bang, that was it as tweeters responded with a hail of messages abusing the airline about the shutdown and the apparent intransigence with unions. Some called for improved punctuality, and planes that arrive intact, while others pointed a finger at their lack of a digital strategy and incompetence. The stream of anger, bile and sarcasm manifested itself in a number of ways, including the 'obligatory "*Hitler downfall*" video to illustrate the absurdity of the situation'. See creamglobal.com.

It seems as if Qantas not only mistimed the competition but also underestimated Twitter's propensity to be used to inflame, rather than to conform to positive brand-building initiatives.

*Source*:   Barnett (2011); Christensen (2011); http://blog.creamglobal.com/right_brain_left_brain/2011/11/qantas-competition-twisted-by-twitter.html.

**Question:**   Why might have Qantas misjudged the use of Twitter on this occasion?

**Task:**        Find three other Twitter-enabled catastrophes.

### Exhibit 22.2    Qantas and Twitter logos

*Source*: Mick Tsikas/Press Association Images; Twitter

Jansen et al. explore the commercial potential and find that of all microblogs (in their sample), 19 per cent mention an organisation, product or service. Of these, '20% express a sentiment or opinion concerning that company, product or service' (2009: 2184). They also find that the ratio of positive to negative tweets is approximately 50 to 35 per cent. This last point is interesting as it is generally accepted that in offline WoM a positive brand experience is likely to be shared with three people, whereas a negative experience is usually shared with nine others.

In 2012 brands such as Nokia, British Airways, Disney and Walkers were among the first to establish branded pages when they were first launched by Twitter. The feature at the time was that these pages enabled brands to have more control and branded content than they had on their Facebook pages (Shearman, 2012).

# Podcasting

Podcasting emerged as a major new form of communication in 2005 and has grown significantly since then. This is mainly because of the huge growth in the adoption of MP3 players and the desire for fresh, up-to-date or different content.

Podcasting is a process whereby audio and video content is delivered over the Internet to iPods, MP3 players and computers, on demand. A podcast is a collection of files located at a feed address, which people can subscribe to by submitting the address to an aggregator. When new content becomes available it is automatically downloaded using an aggregator or feed reader which recognises feed formats such as RSS (see below).

In many ways podcasting is similar to radio broadcasts, yet there are a couple of major differences. First, podcast material is pre-recorded and time-shifted so that material can be listened to at a user's convenience, that is, on demand. The second difference is that listeners can take the material they have chosen to listen to, and play it at times and locations that are convenient to them. They can listen to the content as many times as they wish simply because the audio files can be retained.

Podcasting is relatively inexpensive and simple to execute. It opens up publishing to a host of new people, organisations as well as individuals, and it represents a new media channel for audio content. Users have control over what they listen to, when they listen to it and how many times they listen to the content.

# RSS

RSS stands for 'really simple syndication' and refers to the distribution of news content on the Web. Rather than trawl all relevant Web pages to find new content and updates, RSS allows for specific content to be brought together and made available to an individual without their always having to return to numerous sites. Just checking the RSS feed to see whether something new has been posted online can save huge amounts of time.

Originally email was the preferred way of notifying people of breaking news and information updates. The problem with email is that, not only has the user to sort out and organise the separate strands of information, they also have to contend with the increasing amounts of spam and unwanted material that accompanies it. In addition, RSS feeds allow content updates to be read in a reader, not online.

From a publisher's point of view, RSS feeds enable information to reach a wide audience. This is because of syndication. Once content has been created, RSS feeds allow the content to be grouped (syndicated) with websites that publish similar content. These are referred to as *aggregator websites*. Each feed consists of brief information about headlines, a summary of the content and a link to the article on the requisite website.

From a marketing perspective, RSS feeds act as a media channel, delivering a variety of information about news stories, events, headlines, project updates and even corporate information, often as press releases. This information is delivered quickly and efficiently to audiences who have signed up and effectively given express permission to be sent the information.

# Interactive online communities

Armstrong and Hagel (1996) were two of the first researchers to propose the benefits of virtual communities. They also saw that the development of these communities is one of the key elements that differentiate interactive from traditional media. Communities of people who share a common interest(s), who interact, share information, develop understanding and build relationships all add value, in varying degrees, through their contribution to others involved with the website. In a sense, user groups and special interest groups are similar facilities, but the key with all these variations is the opportunity to share information electronically, often in real time.

Chaffey et al. (2006) refer to Durlacher (1999), who argues that there are four main types of community, defined by their purpose, position, interest and profession, as set out in Table 22.3.

Communities can be characterised by several determining elements. Muniz and O'Guinn (2001) identify three core components:

● consciousness of kind: an intrinsic connection that members feel towards one another;

● the presence of shared rituals and traditions that perpetuate the community's history, culture and consciousness;

● a sense of moral responsibility, duty or obligation to the community as a whole and its individual members.

Within these online or virtual communities five particular characteristics can be identified. The first concerns the model of communication, which is essentially visitor-to-visitor and in some cases customer-to-customer. Second, communities create an identity that arises from each individual's involvement and sense of membership and belonging. The more frequent and intense the interaction, the stronger the identity the participants feel with the community.

| Table 22.3 | Four Types of virtual community |
| --- | --- |
| **Type of community** | **Explanation** |
| **Purpose** | People who are attempting to achieve the same goal or who are experiencing a similar process. |
| **Position** | People who are experiencing particular circumstances. These might be associated with life-stage issues (the elderly, the young), health issues or perhaps career development opportunities. |
| **Interest** | People who share a hobby, pastime or who are passionately involved with, for example, sport, music, dance, family ancestry, jigsaws, wine, gardening, film, etc. |
| **Profession** | People involved with the provision of b2b services. Often created by publishers, these portals provide information about jobs, company news, industry issues and trading facilities, for example, auctions. |

Third, relationships, even close friendships develop among members, which in turn can facilitate mutual help and support. The fourth characteristic concerns the language that the community adopts. Very often specialised languages or codes of (electronic) behaviour emerge that have particular meaning to members. The fifth and final characteristic refers to the methods used to regulate and control the behaviour and operations of the community. Self-regulation is important in order to establish acceptable modes of conduct and interaction among the membership.

The role that members assume within these communities and the degree to which they participate also varies. There are members who attend but contribute little, those who create topics, lead discussions, those who summarise and those who perform brokerage or intermediary roles among other members. Edwards (2011) refers to the 1,9,90 rule. This suggests that 1 per cent of any community are drivers, those who create large amounts of activity. 9 per cent are influencers. These are people who either formally or informally, edit shape, modify and fashion content. The remaining 90 per cent read, observe and consider the community's content, they lurk around the community rather than participate in it. The implication for marketers is that key messages need to reach the drivers and influencers: 10 per cent of the audience.

According to Jepsen (2006) the number of consumers undertaking product information search within virtual communities can be expected to develop simply because the number of experienced Internet users will grow. The provision and form of online communities will inevitably develop and frameworks will emerge in order that understanding about the way they operate (effectively) is disseminated. Szmigin and Reppel (2004) have offered their customer bonding triangle framework, which is built on interactivity, technical infrastructure and service value elements. It is argued by the authors of this framework that it is the fit between the elements that determines the level of bonding between community members. Further work is required in this area, but this framework provides an interesting conceptualisation of the elements that characterise this approach.

The knowledge held in virtual communities can be expected to be of significant value when searching for product information. In 1999 Kozinets presented four segments related to virtual communities, based around two dimensions. These are presented in Table 22.4.

Jepsen speculates that information provided by the virtual community may be sufficiently strong for insiders that it replaces information from offline sources. This is probably not the case for any of the other three segments.

As a final comment, how should marketers manage all of this activity? Well, apart from developing an integrated approach to marketing communications, strategy and tactics, organisations should learn to listen to social media rather than invade and interrupt it. Coca-Cola have developed a 4Rs model to assist their approach to this important issue. The 4Rs are regarded as pillars of their social media strategy; reviewing, responding, recording and redirecting.

| Table 22.4 | Segments in virtual communities |
| --- | --- |
| **Community segment** | **Explanation** |
| **Insiders** | Insiders have strong social ties to other members of the community and consumption and participation is central to their self-image. |
| **Devotees** | Devotees participate because of their strong ties and identification with the product. |
| **Minglers** | Minglers are tied to some other members but do not have strong associations with the community as a whole or the product. |
| **Tourists** | Tourists do not have ties to the product or other members and are transient through the community. |

Based on Kozinets 1999.

Fawkes (2010) explains that conversations around the various Coke brands are tracked by specialist service companies. This review provides insight into the nature of the conversations and the overall sentiment being expressed about the brands. The response is enabled in two ways. Subject matter experts from a variety of departments inside the organisation respond to the specific or unusual queries and questions. A 'blog squad' of social media power users deal with the more general and orthodox questions posed by individuals.

The recording element refers to the development of blogs, podcasts and video material designed to entertain their audiences with compelling content. The redirecting pillar concerns the way Coca-Cola enables people to find and connect with the content that they create. This is achieved by interconnecting links through Google, Facebook and other major interfaces and search engines, through to MyCokeRewards. See also www.coca-cola.com.

Any discussion of social media and branding should consider the important point made by Fournier and Avery (2011: 193), namely that 'the Web was created not to sell branded products, but to link people together in collective conversational webs'.

At a time when interruptive offline advertising was increasingly more expensive and evaded by consumers at every reasonable opportunity, social media represented an opportunity to lower costs and improve returns. It was first thought that by simply switching budget from offline to online all would be fine. Unfortunately fine it was not, and it is now recognised that brands have struggled to make a significant and harmonious presence in social media. The reality is that the 'technology that was supposed to empower marketers has empowered consumers instead' (p. 193). Those interested in how the media landscape has changed and the impact social media have on brands, readers are directed to Scholars' Paper 22.3.

---

**Scholars' paper 22.3     Social media reject brands**

**Fournier, S. and Avery, J. (2011) The uninvited brand,** *Business Horizons,* **54(3), 193–207.**

This paper challenges readers to consider the issues facing brands and brand management in an age of social media. The authors explore many concerns, including the impact of open source branding within an emerging cultural landscape and marketing strategies within an environment where brands have to abandon control, where brand building gives way to brand protection, and where once brand differentiation was an imperative, but now slides into brand resonance and need to be invited into consumers' lives.

---

# Search engine marketing

Websites need visitors and the higher the number of visitors, the more effective the website is likely to be. Many people know of a particular site and simply type in the address or use a bookmark to access it. However, the majority of people arrive at sites following a search using particular keywords and phrases to locate products, services, news, entertainment and the information they need. They do this through search engines, and the results of each search are displayed in rank order. It is understandable, therefore, that those ranked highest in the results lists are visited more often than those in lower positions.

Consequently, from a marketing perspective it is important to undertake marketing activities to attain the highest possible ranking position, and this is referred to as *search engine marketing (SEM)*. There are two main search engine marketing techniques; search engine optimisation (SEO) and pay-per-click (PPC), with the latter outweighing the former quite substantially (Jarboe, 2005).

# Search engine optimisation

Search engine optimisation (SEO), or as it used to be referred to, *organic search*, is a process used to win a high-ranking position on major search engines and directories. To achieve top-ranking positions, or least a first page listing, it is necessary to design Web pages and create links with other quality websites, so that search engines can match closely a searcher's key words/phrases with the content of registered Web pages.

Each search engine, such as Google, MSN Search and Yahoo, uses an algorithm to compare the content of relevant site pages with the key words/phrases used to initiate the search. Search engines use robotic electronic spiders to crawl around registered sites and from this to compile an index of the words they find, placed there by the designer of each website. When a search is activated, it is the database housing these keyword/phrases that is searched, not the millions of World Wide Web pages.

In order to get a high ranking, it is important for a site to be registered, which is normally achieved by adding the URL of a site directly into a search engine. Some sites are automatically registered if there are links with another company that is already registered. Once registered, a high ranking is best achieved by attaining a match between the search words/phrases entered by the searcher and the words/phrases on the pages stored in the index. Achieving a good match can be helped by understanding, if not anticipating, the words and phrases that are likely to be used by individual searchers. Through Web analytics, the study of website visitors' behaviour, it is possible to analyse the search terms used by current visitors. This can also help improve the matching process; however, there are some fundamental activities that can influence ranking positions.

Some designers believe that 'key-phrase density' is important. This refers to the number of times a key phrase is repeated in the text of a Web page. Others believe that it is not density or frequency that matters but the quality of the tags that is paramount.

Another factor concerns the number of inbound links from what are regarded as good-quality sites. The greater the number of quality links, the higher the ranking is likely to be. Two further factors that affect a page's ranking concern the use of tags. The use of keywords in the *title tag* of a Web page and the *meta tags*, which signify the content and describe what searchers will find when they click on the site, are embedded by Web page designers and read by some search engine spiders. When key words and phrases used by searchers match those in these tags, it is likely that the site will have a higher ranking.

For example, the airline easyJet, which sells more than 98 per cent of its seats via the www.easyjet.com website, uses search engine optimisation to drive traffic to its websites across Europe. It is vital that 'easyJet' appears when the search phrases associated with the discount airlines business are used.

| Viewpoint 22.3 | Searching the market for meerkats |
| --- | --- |

Comparethe market.com, a price comparison site for car insurance, were ranked fourth in the market and lacked the resources their main competitors could being, especially in terms of advertising budgets, necessary to drive awareness, Web visits and click through. Their name was instantly forgettable, their identity and name were very similar to their nearest competitor (gocompare), they had no single point of differentiation and they were last to the market. The task was to find a strong point of differentiation.

In this market it is easy to get people to remember 'compare' led brand names but very difficult to get them to remember how one is different from the other. Fortunately the one element that distinguished this brand from the competition was the word 'market' in their name. It was reasoned that rather than use a rational attribute-based positioning like their competitors, who were perceived to be irritating and disliked, the key was to differentiate through entertainment.

In search terms the word 'market' was expensive. At the time it was worth £5 per click so the task was to find a cheaper term or phrase that could be used by people as a substitute for 'market'.

The word 'meerkat' costs only 5p and so a campaign was built around a Russian meerkat called Aleksandr Orlov. He was portrayed as founder of www.comparethemeerkat.com, a site for comparing meerkats, and as someone who is frustrated by the confusion between Comparethemarket.com and Comparethemeerkat.com. The joke caught the imagination of the target audience and the site quickly assumed number one position. Orlov was an instant success, and quickly spawned tens of thousands of Facebook followers and instant recognition.

*Source*:   Jukes (2009); VCCP (2009); Ramsay (2009).

**Question:**   To what extent is the success of SEO just a function of second-guessing the keywords people are likely to use?

**Task:**   Identify two words that could be confused when used for search purposes.

# Pay-per-click searches

Pay-per-click (PPC) is similar to display advertising found in offline print formats. Ads are displayed when particular search terms are entered into the search engine. These ads appear on the right-hand side of the results page and are often referred to as sponsored links. However, unlike offline display ads, where a fee is payable in order for the ad to be printed, here a fee is only payable once the display ad is clicked, and the searcher is taken through to the company's Web page. As Clarke (2008) suggests, this action affirms that an individual finds the ad to be relevant and not intrusive.

It is important for organisations to maintain high visibility, especially in competitive markets, and they cannot rely on their search engine optimisation skills alone. PPC is a paid search list and once again, position in the listings (on the right-hand side of the page) is important. The position in the list is determined mainly through a bidding process. Each organisation bids an amount they are willing to pay for each searcher's click, against a particular key word or phrase. Unsurprisingly, the higher the bid, the higher the position where a search result appears on a page. To place these bids, brokers (or PPC ad networks) are used and their role is to determine what a competitive cost per click should be for their client. They achieve this through market research to determine probable conversion rates, and from this deduce what the purchase and lifetime value of customers are likely to be. Consideration needs to be given to the quality of the landing page to which searchers are taken (not the home page), and whether the call-to-action is sufficiently strong.

Search engine marketing is important if only because of the relative ineffectiveness of other online marketing activities. The goal of SEM is to drive traffic to websites, and ranking on the search-results page is achieved in two fundamentally different ways. In SEO ranking searches are based on content while the PPC approach relies entirely on price as a ranking mechanism. Of these two main approaches, research indicates that the PPC model attracts far more investment (by advertisers) than the SEO model. This indicates that paid ads or sponsored links have low credibility and do not carry high levels of trust. Added to this is the overwhelming research that shows that SEO is more effective in terms of recall and driving site traffic (Jansen and Molina, 2006). However, Kimberley (2010) reports that research undertaken by IAB has found that brands are failing to exploit the potential offered by search engine marketing.

# Email marketing

There are two key characteristics associated with email communications. First, they can be directed at clearly defined target groups and individuals. Second, email messages can be personalised and refined to meet the needs of individuals. In this sense email is the antithesis of broadcast communications, which are scattered among a mass audience and lack any sense of individualisation, let alone providing an opportunity for recipients to respond. In addition, email can be used with varying levels of frequency and intensity, which is important when building awareness, reinforcing messages or when attempting to persuade someone into a trial or purchase.

Organisations need to manage two key dimensions of email communications: outbound and inbound email. Outbound email concerns messages sent by a company, often as a part of a direct marketing campaign, designed to persuade recipients to visit a website, to take a trial or make a purchase. The inbound dimension concerns the management of email communications received from customers and other stakeholders. These may have been stimulated either by an individual's use of the website, exposure to a news item about the product or organisation, or through product experience, which often entails a complaint.

Managing inbound email represents a huge opportunity not only to build email lists for use in outbound campaigns, but also to provide high levels of customer service interaction and satisfaction. If undertaken properly and promptly, this can help to build trust and reputation, which in turn can stimulate word-of-mouth communication – all essential aspects of marketing communication. Activity-triggered emails that incorporate the interests of the target audience and which follow up on audience behaviour are deemed to be more successful and good practice, if only because of the higher conversion rates and return on investment.

The use of email to attract and retain customers is still a main feature of many marketing communications campaigns. Using appropriate email lists is a fast, efficient and effective way to communicate regularly with a market. Email-based marketing communication enables organisations to send a variety of messages concerning public relations-based announcements, newsletters and sales promotions, to distribute online catalogues and to start and manage permission-based contact lists. Many organisations build their own lists using data collected from their CRM system. By acquiring email responses and other contact mechanisms, addresses and contact details can be captured for the database and then accessed by all customer support staff. The use of email to attract and retain customers has become a main feature of many organisations' marketing communications campaigns. Indeed, email can be used to deliver messages at all points in the customer relationship lifecycle.

# Short message services (SMS)

Although different in format, short message services (SMS), or 'texting', can be regarded as an extension of email communication. SMS is a non-intrusive but timely way of delivering information and as Doyle (2003) points out, the global system for mobile communication (GSM) has become a standard protocol, so that users can send and receive information across geographic boundaries. Apart from pure text, other simple applications consist of games, email notifications, and information-delivery services such as sports and stock market updates.

Yaobin et al. (2010) undertook a study into the reasons why consumers use SMS. The research was based in China, where SMS is used extensively and the results highlighted three main reasons for use. These concern the perceived utilitarian value of SMS, the level of intrinsic enjoyment and the satisfaction derived from the involvement in communication. The third reason was the relatively low costs of use.

For some time organisations were relatively slow at adopting SMS despite the low costs and high level of user control (target, content and time). However, as organisations recognise these benefits, so SMS has become an integral part of the media mix for many organisations.

However, marketers also need to consider the potential concerns of consumers, most notably security and privacy. Just as with email, there is the potential for unwanted messages (i.e. spam) and Internet service providers (ISP) need to manage the increasing numbers of unsolicited messages through improved security systems as SMS becomes more widespread. Given that most consumers pay for SMS functionality, marketers should realise that invading personal privacy greatly reduces the potential value and effectiveness of SMS.

---

### Scholars' paper 22.4    Thriving networks and tribal identities

**Hamilton, K. and Hewer, P. (2010) Tribal mattering spaces: Social-networking sites, celebrity affiliations, and tribal innovations, *Journal of Marketing Management*, 26(3–4), March, 271–89.**

Further to the exploration of tribes (Chapter 3) in consumer behaviour, these authors use ideas about tribal identities and fandom to explore Web 2.0. They argue that social networks which focus on iconic celebrities provide a rich context to consider the interaction, connectivity, and creativity of the fans that populate them.

---

# Apps

An app is a mobile application, a piece of software that is downloaded and runs on mobile devices such as smartphones and tablets. Apps enable users to do things such as find a cinema, restaurant, bank or other destination, read news, update a grocery list, track a team's score, play games, remember where the car is parked, all on a mobile phone (Sullivan, 2010). Procter & Gamble launched an app to support its Pampers brand, called *Hello Baby*, which allows pregnant women to track the development of their baby.

From a marketing communication perspective, apps enable a brand to be connected with a user as they move around. Some apps can become an integral part of a user's life, some can strengthen brand awareness, and others offer opportunities for more frequent interaction and brand engagement.

| Exhibit 22.3 | **A range of apps on a smartphone** |
|---|---|
| | *Source*: Tony French/Alamy Images |

It is estimated that over 200,000 apps are available for Apple's iPhone and iPod Touch. Unsurprisingly, people prefer free apps, which is significant in terms of the limited opportunities brands have to recover the $100,000+ necessary to develop a mainstream app.

Goddard (2010) suggests that apps can be categorised into four types. These are campaign-based, popular gimmick, straight utility, and branded utility. See Table 23.5.

Apps enable brands such as Chanel, Ford, Pepsi, Visa, Lynx and many others, to provide users with branded content, as Yuill (2010) suggests, anywhere, at anytime, to suit the user.

| Table 22.5 | Categories of apps |
|---|---|
| **Type of community** | **Explanation** |
| **Campaign-based** | Apps which have high brand-value content but little everyday utility. This means they will attract attention in the short term but will not serve to retain users. |
| **Popular gimmick** | Apps characterised by low brand value, which are not very useful. Their value lies in supporting short-term campaigns or events, but they can become obsolete when the campaign finishes. Often good for entertainment purposes, but once seen there is little value in repeating. |
| **Straight utilities** | Apps that serve as everyday tools. For example, location finders, currency converters, and recipe and menu directories can be useful but competition is high and standout opportunities are rare. |
| **Branded utilities** | Apps which are both useful and develop the brand promise. These are considered to be the most powerful types of mobile apps, simply because engagement occurs through the functionality which is tied to the essential value of the brand. |

Based on Goddard (2010).

# Widgets

Widgets are standalone applications that enable users to interact with the owner of the widget. As Chaffey (2008) suggests, the applications can provide functionality such as a calculator or real-time information, as in travel updates or weather forecasts. Widgets sit on a desktop, are relatively cheap to develop, easy to manage and ideally are distributed virally.

The real benefit of widgets is that they provide a way of advertising a brand, delivering online public relations or even driving direct response sales via affiliate marketing.

To date, attempts by brands to derive commercial benefit from social networking sites have been thwarted by the prevailing network culture that is essentially one that rejects advertising and outright commercialism. Sponsored widgets might provide a means of overcoming these difficulties as they offer benefits that might appeal to social network users. For example, Jamiroquai use a widget that allows their fans to keep up-to-date on video releases, tour dates and tracks. Cadbury have created a game called 'Room with a Goo'. In it players are required to stop crème eggs being smashed, blended and splattered. A widget on the Bebo site enables users to destroy or rebuild others Cadbury's Crème Eggs by either hugging or karate-chopping the eggs, virtually. A whole range of widget applications can be seen at www.directory.snipperoo.com.

# Affiliate marketing

Associated with the concepts of communities and networks, affiliate marketing has become an essential aspect of online marketing communications and ecommerce. It is estimated by Walmsley (2010) that the UK affiliate marketing market was worth £4 billion in 2009. Since then various commentators have referred to the increasing use of affiliate marketing and how instrumental it is to a range of brands. Affiliate schemes are based on a network of websites on which advertisements or text links are placed. Those who click on them are taken directly to the host site. If this results in a sale, only then will the affiliate receive a commission, or payment for the ad.

Cookies contain information generated by a Web server and stored in a user's computer. These provide fast access to a site and are used to track, monitor and record transactions and pay commission plus any agreed charges. As with many online marketing schemes, management can be undertaken in-house or outsourced. If the latter approach is adopted then many of the relationship issues discussed earlier need to be considered and managed.

Amazon is probably one of the best examples of affiliate marketing schemes. Amazon has thousands of affiliates who all drive visitors to the Amazon website. If a product is sold to the visitor as a result of the click-through, then the affiliate is rewarded with a commission payment. Affiliate schemes are popular because they are low-cost operations, paid on a results-only basis and generating very favourable returns on investment.

McCormick (2010) reports on the use of affiliate marketing by Lastminute.com. This organisation considers its affiliate network as a team and an integral part of its marketing programme. Affiliates receive emails twice a week advising about key-performing products and offers in their key sales areas. Blogs are used to provide up-to-date information. Lastminute.com also provides its affiliates with advice and facilities to generate increased income. For example, these include bespoke banners for placement by the key affiliate partners and templates and designs for email newsletters. Even quiet or underperforming affiliates are reached with communications that flag relevant offers to get them operating once again.

Review sites constitute a large proportion of affiliate activity, so these are targeted with specific offers to be run against each relevant review. Feedback is encouraged and analysis shows that clicks through from affiliates rose in 2009 by 22.4 per cent.

# Augmented reality

Glasses Direct enable customers to see, online, how they look with different frames. The 'online mirror' technologies behind this facility are referred to as augmented reality (AR). By mixing the real world with digitally generated information or images, AR opens opportunities for both business- and consumer-orientated interactive marketing communications (Clewson, 2009). So, augmented reality allows people to see what they look like in different clothes, without having to get changed into them and, with developments in mobile technology, without a change of location.

At the time of writing AR-based technologies are developing, but they are increasingly used in mobile applications in connection with location facilities. For example, they can be used as virtual wardrobes, shop fronts, store layouts and as a means of locating shops, tube stations, restaurants, pubs and theatres with a mobile phone (Benady 2009).

---

### Viewpoint 22.4    E.ON augment the FA Cup

E.ON's sponsorship of the FA Cup involved two trophy tours. One was the conventional nationwide tour enabling fans to physically get close to the famous cup. The other was a virtual tour enabled through augmented reality (AR). Fans of the two finalists were able to go online and, using a webcam, capture an image of themselves lifting the FA Cup.

Marketing communications used to support the activities involved a national print campaign and viral video seeded across a range of targeted websites. Both were intended to raise awareness, and the former to drive traffic to the website where there were instructions on how to use the AR facility and, of course, register with E.ON.

The press work included an augmented reality marker, so that people with enabled phones could access the virtual FA Cup online, straightaway.

The digital campaign lasted just one week and over 90,000 users visited the site in that period, while the seeded content prompted three times the normal click-throughs.

*Source*:   Dundas (2010).

> **Question:**   How might augmented reality assist marketing communications?
>
> **Task:**       Identify three markets (eg fashion) where augmented reality might be applicable.

| Exhibit 22.4 | **Augmented reality in action** |
| --- | --- |
| | *Source*: Geoff Caddick/PA Wire |

# Key points

- Social media embrace a range of Internet based applications, all of which are characterised by two key elements. These are social presence/media richness, and secondly, social processes in the form of self-presentation/self-disclosure.

- Social networks are about people using the Internet to share lifestyle and experiences. Participants in these networks also use the interactive capacity to build new relationships. The critical aspect of social networks is that the content is user-generated and this means users own, control and develop content according to their needs, not those of a third party.

- The relative immaturity of the social networking arena and the way in which content is developed raise challenges about how organisations can best use social networks as part of their marketing communications to reach their target audiences. Questions arise about the effectiveness of online ads in a social networking environment. Many users do not like brand advertising and prefer to take advice from their online peers in these communities when deciding what to buy, rather than listen to advertisers. Social networking is becoming a media channel in its own right and it is one that is reflecting the voices of consumers instead of those of brand owners.

- Viral marketing involves the use of email to convey messages to a small part of a target audience where the content is sufficiently humorous, interesting or persuasive that the receiver feels emotionally compelled to send it on to a friend or acquaintance.

- Blogs are personal online diaries. Business-related or corporate blogs represent huge potential as a form of marketing communications for organisations. This is because blogs reflect the attitudes of the author, and these attitudes can influence others. Microblogging is a short format version of blogging and Twitter is probably the best known. A microblog, or tweet, consists of a short comment, a post of 140 characters, which is shared with a network of followers. This makes production and consumption relatively easy in comparison to blogs.

- Podcasting is a process whereby audio and video content is delivered over the Internet to iPods, MP3 players and computers, on demand. A podcast is a collection of files located at a feed address, which people can subscribe to by submitting the address to an aggregator.

- RSS (really simple syndication) refers to the distribution of news content on the web. Rather than trawl all relevant Web pages to find new content and updates, RSS allows for specific content to be brought together and made available to an individual without their always having to return to numerous sites. RSS feeds act as a media channel delivering a variety of information about news stories, events, headlines, project updates and even corporate information, often as press releases. This information is delivered quickly and efficiently to audiences who have signed up and effectively given express permission to be sent the information.

- Online communities are people who share a common interest(s), who interact, share information, develop understanding and build relationships. Coca-Cola have developed a useful model to assist their approach to using communities. Their 4Rs are regarded as pillars of their social media strategy: reviewing, responding, recording and redirecting.

- The goal of search engine marketing (SEM) is to drive traffic to websites, and ranking on the search-results page is achieved in two fundamentally different ways. In SEO ranking, searches are based on content, while the PPC approach relies entirely on price as a ranking mechanism.

- Email-based marketing communication enables organisations to send a variety of messages concerning public relations-based announcements, newsletters and sales promotions, to distribute online catalogues and to start and manage permission-based contact lists.

- An app is a mobile application, a piece of software that is downloaded and runs on mobile devices such as smartphones and tablets. Apps enable a brand to be connected with a user as they move around. Some apps can become an integral part of a user's life, some can strengthen brand awareness, and others offer opportunities for more frequent interaction and brand engagement.

- Affiliate marketing schemes are based on a network of websites on which advertisements or text links are placed. People who click on them are taken directly to the host site. If this results in a sale, only then will the affiliate receive a commission, or payment for the ad.

- Affiliate marketing has become an essential aspect of online marketing communications and ecommerce.

# Review questions

1. How might brands imitate Iceland's use of social media to engage their target audiences?

2. Appraise the concept of word-of-mouth communication and consider its use within social networks.

3. Make brief notes concerning the ways in which marketing communications should be used within online communities.

4. Explain the basic principles of search engine marketing.

5. Describe the way in which both search engine optimisation and pay-per-click systems operate.

6. Write a report examining the use of email as a form of marketing communications. Find examples to support the points you make.

7. What are the advantages and disadvantages of using SMS as a primary form of communication?

8. Discuss the three key elements that Kirby associates with successful viral marketing.

9. Goddard (2010) suggests that apps can be categorised into four types. What are they and how are they different?

10. What is a cookie and why are they important to affiliate marketing?

# References

Anon (2010) Brands use social media to drive pre-launch buzz, *Brand Week*, retrieved 25 May 2010 from www.warc.com/news/.

Armstrong, A. and Hagel III, J. (1996) The real value of on-line communities, *Harvard Business Review*, 74, 3 (May/June), 134–41.

Barnett, E. (2011) Hard lessons from blunders in social media marketing, The *Sunday Telegraph*, 27 November 2011, p. 8.

Benady, D. (2009) The future of shopping, *Revolution*, December, 48–51.

Blattberg, R.C. and Deighton, J. (1991) Interactive marketing: exploiting the age of addressability, *Sloan Management Review*, 33, 1, 5–14.

Chaffey, D. (2008) Using branded widgets, gadgets and buttons for web marketing, retrieved 8 April 2008 from www.davechaffey.com/Internet-Marketing/C8-Communications/E-tools/Online-PR/Using-Widgets-Marketing.

Chaffey, D., Ellis-Chadwick, F., Johnston, K. and Meyer, R. (2006) *Internet Marketing*, 3rd edn, Harlow: Pearson.

Charles, G. (2010) Asda calls in Mumsnet to approve kids' clothes, *Marketing*, 21 April, p. 1.

Christensen, N. (2011) Qantas competition hashtag hijacked, *The Australian*, November 22, retrieved 13 January 2012 from http://www.theaustralian.com.au/business/in-depth/qantas-competition-hashtag-hijacked/story-fnaskcqt-1226202578451.

Clarke, I., III. (2008) Emerging value propositions for m-commerce, *Journal of Business Strategies*, 25, 2, 41–58.

Clewson, T. (2009) Don't believe the hype, *Revolution*, December, 44–7.

Colliander, J. and Dahlén, M. (2011) Following the Fashionable Friend: The Power of Social Media, *Journal of Advertising Research*, 51(1), 313–20.

Crow, D. (2007) Talking about my generation, *The Business*, 28 July, 18–20.

De Bruyn, A. and Lilien, G.L. (2004) A multi-stage model of word-of-mouth through electronic referrals, *eBusiness Research Centre Working Paper*, February.

Doyle, S. (2003) The big advantage of short messaging, retrieved 16 May from www.sas.com/news.

Dundas, C. (2010) Digital makes the brand connection, *Admap* (April), retrieved 2 June 2010 from www.warc.com/ArticleCenter.

Durlacher (1999) UK on-line community, *Durlacher Quarterly Internet Report*, Q3, 7–11, London.

Edwards, J. (2011) Influencer metrics are getting a Klout, *B2B Marketing*, November/December, p. 14.

Eleftheriou-Smith, L.-M. (2012) AOL partners Promote Iceland for pan-Euro campaign, *Marketing*, 23 February 2012, retrieved 3 July 2012 from http://www.brandrepublic.com/news/1118846/AOL-partners-Promote-Iceland-pan-Euro-campaign/?DCMP=ILC-SEARCH.

Fawkes, F. (2010) Coca-Cola's Approach To Social Media, *FSFK*, May 17, retrieved 9 June 2010 from http://www.psfk.com/2010/05/brand-news-coca-cola%E2%80%99s-approach-to-social-media.html.

Fournier, S. and Avery, J. (2011) The uninvited brand, *Business Horizons*, 54, 193–207.

Goddard, M. (2010) Sizing up a proposed app, *ABA Bank Marketing*, 42, 4 (May), 20–23.

GoViral (2009) Viral View: Social Technographics: Are you keeping up with your online audience? *Campaignlive*, 6 Nov 2009, retrieved 14 June 2010 from http://www.brandrepublic.com/News/964382/Viral-View-Social-Technographics-keeping-online-audience/?DCMP=ILC-SEARCH.

Hennig-Thurau, T., Gwinner, K.P., Walsh, G. and Gremler, D.D. (2004) Electronic word-of-mouth via consumer-opinion platforms: what motivates consumers to articulate themselves on the internet? *Journal of Interactive Marketing*, 18(1), (Winter) 38–52.

Jansen, B.J. and Molina, P.R. (2006) The effectiveness of web search engines for retrieving relevant e-commerce links, *Information Processing and Management*, 42, 4 (July), 1075–98.

Jansen, B.J., Zhang, M., Sobel, K. and Chowdury, A. (2009) Twitter Power: Tweets as Electronic Word of Mouth, *Journal of the American Society for Information Science and Technology*, 60, 11, 2169–88.

Jarboe, G. (2005) Why does search engine marketing look like a penny-farthing bicycle? *Internet Search Engine Database*, 11 January, retrieved 27 July 2007, from www.isedb.com/news/article/1086/.

Jepsen, A.L. (2006) Information search in virtual communities: is it replacing use of offline communication? *Journal of Marketing Communications*, 12, 4 (December), 247–61.

Jukes, M (2009) Creative review: Comparethemarket.com, 26 February, retrieved 20 September from www.brandrepublic.com/InDepth/Features/930643/APG-Creative-Strategy-Awards---Comparethemarketcom-meerkat-campaign-VCCP.

Juvertson, S. (2000) *What is Viral Marketing?* Draper Fisher Juvertson website, retrieved March 12 2006 from http://www.dfj.com/cgi-bin/artman/publish/printer_steve_may00.shtml.

Juvertson, S. and Draper, T. (1997) *Viral marketing*, Draper Fisher Juvertson website, Retrieved 12 March 2006 from http://www.dfj.com/cgi-bin/artman/publish/printer_steve_tim_may97.html.

Kaikati, A.M. and Kaikati, J.G. (2004) Stealth marketing: how to reach consumers surreptitiously, *California Management Review*, 46, 4, 6–22.

Kaplan, A.M. and Haelein, M. (2010) Users of the world unite! The challenges and opportunities of social media, *Business Horizons*, 53, 59–68.

Kietzmann, J.H., Hermkens, K., McCarthy, I.P. and Silvestre, B.S. (2011) Social media? Get serious! Understanding the functional building blocks of social media, *Business Horizons*, 54, 3 (May–June), 241–51.

Kimberley, S. (2010) Search marketing fails to deliver full potential, *Marketing*, 30 June, p. 7.

Kirby, J. (2003) The message should be used as a means to an end, rather than just an end in itself, *VM-People*, 16 October, retrieved 31 August 2007 from www.vm-people.de/en/vmknowledge/interviews/interviews_detail.php?id=15.

Kozinets, R.V. (1999) E-tribalized marketing: the strategic implications of virtual communities on consumption, *European Management Journal*, 17, 3, 252–64.

Lewis, J. (2011) Think you control your Facebook data? Think again, The *Sunday Telegraph*, 27 November 2011, p. 6.

McCormick, A. (2010) Digital Report: Keep your affiliates onside, *Marketing*, 28 April, 41–3.

Muniz Jr, A.M. and O'Guinn, T.C. (2001) Brand community, *Journal of Consumer Research*, 27, 4, 412–32.

Nardi, B.A., Schiano, D.J., Gumbrecht, M. and Swartz, L. (2004) Why we blog, *Communications of the ACM*, 47, 12, 41–46.

Nettleton, K. (2009) Men dressed as Tic Tacs re-enact missed Everton goal, *Campaign*, 11 February, retrieved 14 June 2010 from www.campaignlive.co.uk/news/880522/Men-dressed-Tic-Tacs-re-enact-missed-Everton-goal/?DCMP=ILC-SEARCH.

Owens, J. (2012) Tourism: Iceland opens doors to the 'enlightened', *PR Week*, 3 May, retrieved 3 July 2012 from http://www.brandrepublic.com/features/1129887/Tourism-Iceland-opens-doors-enlightened/?DCMP=ILC-SEARCH.

Pinkerfield, H. (2007) New social media user types unveiled, *Revolution*, 28 June 2007, retrieved 13 August 2007 from http://www.brandrepublic.com/News/667634/New-social-media-user-types-unveiled/.

Porter, L. and Golan, G.J. (2006) From subservient chickens to brawny men: a comparison of viral advertising to television advertising, *Journal of Interactive Advertising*, 6, 2, 30–8.

Puri, G. (2011) Effies show how adland is adapting to straitened times *Campaign*, 15 September, retrieved 3 July 2012 from http://www.brandrepublic.com/analysis/1091895/Effies-show-adland-adapting-straitened-times/?DCMP=ILC-SEARCH.

Ramsay, F. (2009) Building on Animal Magic, *Marketing*, 19 August, 20–21.

Shearman, S. (2011) Emirates targets rivals with Facebook strategy, *Marketing*, 23 November, p. 3.

Shearman, S. (2012) Twitter's branded venture, *Marketing*, 15 February, 10–11.

Shearman, S. (2012) Facebook's new brand offensive, *Marketing*, 7 March, 12–13.

Steele, F. (2010) Twitter unveils advert Tweets in bid for profits, *Times Online*, 13 April, retrieved 13 April from http://business.timesonline.co.uk/tol/business/industry_sectors/media/article7095914.ece.

Sullivan, E.A. (2010) Marketing App-titude, *Marketing News*, 43, 3, 15 March, p. 6.

Szmigin, I. and Reppel, A.E. (2004) Internet community bonding: the case of macnews.de, *European Journal of Marketing*, 38, 5/6, 626–40.

Truong, Y. and Simmons, G. (2010) Perceived intrusiveness in digital advertising: strategic marketing implications, *Journal of Strategic Marketing*, 18, 3, 239–56.

VCCP (2009) Comparethemarket.com 'meerkat campaign', *campaignlive.co.uk*, retrieved 17 September 2009 from http://www.brandrepublic.com/InDepth/Features/930643/APG-Creative-Strategy-Awards---Comparethemarketcom-meerkat-campaign-VCCP.

Walmsley, A. (2007) Social networks are here to stay, *Marketing*, 27 June, 15.

Walmsley, A. (2010) Make your affiliations pay, *Marketing*, 5 May, 13.

Wasserman, T. (2011) Facebook's New Advertising Strategy Is Brilliant and Unexpected, 3 October 2011 retrieved 14 January 2012 from http://mashable.com/2011/10/03/facebook-ad-strategy/.

Whittaker, Z. (2011) Facebook faces European crackdown on targeted advertising, 27 November 2011, retrieved 14 January 2012 from http://www.zdnet.com/blog/london/facebook-faces-european-crackdown-on-targeted-advertising/1138.

Wood, W., Behling, R. and Haugen, S. (2006) Blogs and business: opportunities and headaches, *Issues in Information Systems*, V11, 2, 312–16.

Yaobin, L., Deng, Z. and Bin, W. (2010) Exploring factors affecting Chinese consumers' usage of short message service for personal communication, *Information Systems Journal*, 20, 2, 183–208.

Yuill, M. (2009) Smartphones and app stores driving mobile media, *Admap*, 503, (March) retrieved 2 June 2010 from www.warc.com/articlecenter/.

# Chapter 23

# Multichannel campaigns: media and tools

For many organisations the use of digital, interactive-based marketing communications has become an important channel to reach and communicate effectively with specific audiences.

However, using individual digital media in isolation or other media and tools has been shown to be less effective than developing campaigns in which a variety of channels (tools and media) are integrated. Multichannel marketing programmes are now an important aspect of marketing strategy.

## Aims and learning objectives

The aims of this chapter are to explore the characteristics of multichannel marketing and to consider the ways in which digital media influence each of the communication tools online, and shape multichannel campaigns.

The learning objectives are to enable readers to:

1. appraise the nature and characteristics of interactivity as a form of communication;
2. describe multichannel marketing and some of the inherent issues;
3. explain the primary techniques and issues relating to online advertising;
4. explore ways in which online and interactivity can assist sales promotions;
5. discuss developments in public relations which have resulted from digital technology;
6. examine how the potency of personal selling can be improved through online and digital media;
7. consider any issues arising through the use of online direct marketing;
8. evaluate ways in which multichannel communications can improve campaign effectiveness.

# Minicase

## The Salvation Army

The Salvation Army is the seventh-largest UK charity ranked by fundraising income, and the largest provider of social services in the UK after the government. It is equally good at raising money. Large-scale donor recruitment campaigns have historically recruited donors at an immediate ROI of more than 1.0.

In 2007, the year before we received our campaign brief, 99,737 donors responded to cold appeals. Few other charities would expect to recruit donors at an ROI of more than 1.0. Yet, despite this performance we accepted the challenge to accelerate the growth and maintain returns. This required finding significant numbers of new donors, with the same profile and behaviour as current donors, for the same return on media investment.

We did three very simple things. Asked what they were doing, what they weren't doing, and discovered the gaps we could fill.

### What they were doing?

The Salvation Army focuses the bulk of its fundraising activities on Christmas, with almost all of the donors recruited each year recruited in the six weeks running up to Christmas Day.

In 2007 the campaign consisted of cold and warm direct mail, door drops, inserts, product despatch, and press activity. Six media channels, but all print-based.

Creative messages revolved around the social services that the Salvation Army provided to the community, with a strong grounding in Christian values.

Donors mostly responded via post. Telephone response accounted for under 15 per cent of all donations, and the Internet for less than 2 per cent, while 90 per cent of donations came as cheques. The answer to the question, 'What weren't they doing?' was simply, 'They were not using any form of broadcast or digital activity.'

### Discovering gaps

Using the Touchpoints media diary, five key insights were revealed. First, the potential donor audience are heavy TV viewers; second, messages on TV will prompt them to donate; third, they spend very little time online, are not motivated to give by messages they see online, *but*, crucially, will nonetheless actually give via a charity website.

Our most significant insight came when we compared the relative reach of media channels. The

### Life will be hard for many people this Christmas without The Salvation Army

Homeless and ill, Steve might have died alone on the streets if we had not offered him a place at one of our centres and the chance to get off the streets for good. And there will be many other desperate people who need us this Christmas, including lonely older people, children who have been neglected or abused, and families facing hardship. **Please help us give them the love and help they need, by sending your Christmas donation today.**

**£19** will provide a Christmas box to a family in need, filled with food and a gift for each child.

**£28** will pay for five lonely older people to enjoy a proper Christmas lunch and friendship at a Salvation Army community centre.

**£47** will help pay for a 'meal run' to reach out to people sleeping rough to give them a hot meal and some practical support to start sorting out their problems.

**£63** will provide a homeless person with three weeks in a Salvation Army centre and support and advice to help them get off the streets for good.

**£250** will help keep a Salvation Army drop-in centre open for anyone in need this Christmas.

DM15322

### Yes, here is my Christmas gift for people in need.

In order for us to process your donation efficiently please complete your details below.

Title (Mr, Mrs, Miss, Ms) [ ]    Name [ ]
Address [ ]
                                         Postcode [ ]
Here is my gift of:   £19 [ ]   £28 [ ]   £47 [ ]   £63 [ ]   £250 [ ]
I prefer to give: £ [ ]    *Thank you*
Please make your cheque/postal order payable to The Salvation Army or fill in your credit/debit card details below.
Credit/Debit/CAF Card No.  (We are unable to accept AmEx or Diners Club cards.)
[ ][ ][ ][ ][ ][ ][ ][ ][ ][ ][ ][ ][ ][ ][ ][ ][ ][ ][ ]
Start date [ ] / [ ]    Expiry date [ ] / [ ]    Maestro Issue No. [ ]

You could make your gift worth 25% more by making a Gift Aid declaration. Please tick the box below.
☐ I am a UK taxpayer and I want The Salvation Army to claim back the tax on all donations I have made in the past four years, and all future donations.    *giftaid it*
NB You must pay an amount of income tax or capital gains tax at least equal to the tax we (and other charities you donate to) reclaim on your donations in the tax year.

Please return this form with your donation to: Lieut-Colonel Marion Drew,
The Salvation Army 202, Freepost SN1457, MELKSHAM SN12 7BR.

**You can make your credit card gift by calling:**
☎ **0800 298 2877**
or give online at salvationarmyappeals.org.uk

Funds will be used to help vulnerable people and support many other areas of The Salvation Army's vital work.
The Salvation Army will not share your details with any other organisation. If you don't want to hear from us again, please tick this box. ☐

The Salvation Army is a registered charity no. 214779, and in Scotland SC009359.

---

| Exhibit 23.1 | **A typical creative used by the Salvation Army** |
|---|---|
| | *Source*: The Salvation Army |

Touchpoints planning tool enabled us to ascertain the combined reach of the current schedule, and to model the addition of other media.

The print media schedule (a combination of warm mail, cold mail, door drops, inserts and press) had been carefully honed over years. It was at its limit for efficient volume – no more could be added without impacting cost per new donor and immediate return on investment. However, the key finding was that it only reached 64 per cent of potential donors.

Our internal planning tools allow us to model the impact of adding new media channels. Within the budgets available, if we added television to the media mix, our reach of the core potential donor audience jumped from 64 per cent to 90 per cent. In other words, we could increase the potential donor pool by 41 per cent.

### Year one

In the first year we used the targeting, messaging, the call-to-action, and the bulk of the communications schedule that had been used in the previous year. To reach incremental new donors we added a DRTV campaign as a standalone, non-integrated media channel. In addition, we also added paid search as a standalone media channel, designed to act as a giant fax machine, enabling those donors who did want to give online to do so more easily and efficiently.

TV channels and programmes were selected using our audiences' viewing preferences, overlaid with bespoke response data from MC&C databases. To reach the required audience, we ended up with an unusual mix of channels – much more airtime from traditional terrestrial channels, and much less from satellite and cable channels than the norm.

We also ended up with an equally unusual pattern of investment. TV campaigns typically start with a bang, building coverage quickly, and then continue at lower weights. We reversed this norm, starting at low weights, and building to a peak on Christmas Eve.

We also invested in paid search. Investment was restricted to brand-related and creative-related terms only. No generic charity or Christmas messages were used. We created copy to reflect the messages that searchers would have seen in the media that drove them to the search engine. All of this reflected our desire to facilitate a journey online, and not to initiate one.

The results for year one were 116,000 new donors, a maintained ROI, a new source of new donors and an additional £500,000 income, representing 20 per cent growth year on year. The return on investment online doubled.

### Year two

We repeated this formula in year two but doubled the TV budget, and added radio to the media mix. The aim was to increase donor reach again, and up-weighting even more during our key days running up to Christmas Eve. The result was yet again more donors, more income, and better ROI. And a real jump in online income of 94 per cent up year on year.

However, this online income posed us an issue: what was generating it? Clearly an element of it can be

**Figure 23.1** Salvation Army donor demographic

attributed to the very efficient paid-search activity, our online fax machine. But a much larger element, in fact the vast majority, just turned up on the website and gave. They did so out of the goodness of their hearts, but what prompted such goodness?

To answer this question we turned to our in-house statisticians. We created a data set of all media events that would cause a response (every individual TV and radio spot, press ad, insert, door drop, piece of cold mail and piece of warm mail). From this we were able to quantify the value of any one media channel on response attributed not just to online, but to any other media channel. Guess what? Inter-connectivity. No surprises, TV and direct mail drive online response. TV drives response to all other media channels. But equally, direct mail, inserts and press advertising drive response recorded to TV commercials.

### Creating an integrated planning tool

Armed with a lot more information, we were able change the investment levels across the media channels as well as the timing of activities. We stopped thinking just about the results to cold mail or radio, and started thinking about results to the campaign as a whole. And not just about a donor seeing one piece of communication, but their journey from the first mail piece in November right up to the Google search on Christmas Eve.

The results? We have seen two more years of incremental growth. As I write this in spring 2012, we have just finished a campaign that generated 80 per cent more response than the 2007 campaign did, at a 14 per cent higher ROI on recruitment, and with 22 per cent higher proportion of donors who have never given before. That translates into another record year of income for the Salvation Army – their second in a row.

*This minicase was written by Mike Colling of Mike Colling and Company Ltd. Permission to use the material was kindly given by the Salvation Army.*

*A longer more detailed version can be found at the website supporting this book at www.pearson.com/ and at www.Fillassociates.co.uk/*

| Exhibit 23.2 | **Logos for MC&C and Salvation Army** |
|---|---|
| | *Source*: Mike Colling and Company Ltd and The Salvation Army |

# Introduction

The Salvation Army minicase serves to show how understanding the channel's customers, or donors in this case, can impact on marketing performance. It also reveals how certain combinations of channels can generate disproportionate outcomes. This chapter considers this important development in marketing: namely, the role and nature of multichannel marketing and its influence on multichannel campaigns. The Salvation Army minicase demonstrates vividly the impact of testing, and adding relevant tools and media to a channel strategy. The case also highlights the importance of the interlinking or mutual reinforcement of the different instruments, and that impact is created by using combinations of media. The result is that new donors, or customers, can be reached and overall campaign performance increased, cost-effectively.

It is apparent that interactivity underpins much of multichannel marketing and contemporary media and customer communication. This chapter commences with a consideration of interactivity, moves on to examine multichannel selling, and explores the way in which each of the communication tools can be used online and interactively. The chapter concludes with a consideration of ways and issues associated with merging the tools and media into multichannel campaigns.

# Interactivity

Interactivity is a key characteristic of contemporary marketing communications. It is crucial because it signifies the available functionality, the ability of all participants in a communication network to respond to messages, often in real time. This is not a feature of most offline marketing communications such as radio or billboards and posters. It is also key because it indicates that this type of communication environment is open – that is, more democratic than conventional marketing communications. The latter tend to be one-sided and driven primarily by organisations and the satisfaction of their more overt needs. The word 'interactivity' suggests that all parties to a communication event are legitimately enabled to communicate. Finally, the word 'interactive' is used to cover a wide spectrum of electronic environments, one that is not limited or defined by the Internet. For example, mobile communications do not operate online, yet can be used to reach people digitally wherever they are, and have the potential to engage them interactively. Personal selling incorporates interactive behaviours.

Back in 1995 Deighton and Grayson speculated correctly about the impact of the move towards digital-based marketing communications and how electronic dialogue would make marketing communications more conversational. Well, the conversational movement has gained considerable impetus and it is now a central marketing communications activity for many organisations. What enables these conversations is the interactive capacity within digital media.

Two researchers based in Zagreb, Vlasic and Kesic (2007) reviewed the literature to consider the various interpretations offered by others working in the field. At a simple level they found that it is about the interchanging roles of senders and receivers within a communication event. However, this view casts little light on the depth and significance of the topic. They cite Hoey (1998) who, among others, sees it as direct communication without time–space constraints.

Some authors stress the measurability element (Morowitz and Schmittlein, 1998), while others focus on the communication and information control perspective (Liu and Shrum, 2005; Lockenby, 2005) and the influence the communication bestows on parties to the communication process. Vlasic and Kesic (2007: 111) deduce that interactivity brings benefits concerning 'convenience, diversity, relationship and intellectual challenges alongside the very important aspect of control of communication and relationships'.

Considering these perspectives, it can be concluded that interactive marketing communications concern processes through which individuals and organisations attempt to engage others with messages that are delivered primarily, but not exclusively, through electronic channels, and which offer all parties an opportunity to respond. Interaction can occur through the same or a different channel from that used to convey the previous message. However, the purpose is to build and sustain relationships that are based on mutual satisfaction, achieved through the exchange of information, goods or services that are of value to those involved.

Perhaps the strongest characteristic of interactive marketing communications is that it enables communications to move from one-way and two-way models to one where communication flows in real time. Interactivity normally precedes the establishment of dialogue between participants in the communication process. This, in turn, enables all participants to contribute to the content that is used in the communication process. This is referred to as *user-generated content*, as demonstrated by people uploading videos to YouTube, contributing to blogs, tweeting or even emailing comments to presenters of television news programmes. This form of interactivity symbolises a shift in the way in which marketing communications have developed, especially in an online environment. So, when the maintenance of 'relationships' is a central marketing activity it is possible to conclude that interactive marketing communications have an important role to play.

When the Internet began to be developed commercially in the early 1990s, organisations attempted to use the traditional offline promotional tools and processes in the new online context. This was understandable, as it was all that was known at the time. However, lessons were learned quickly, as it soon became apparent that marketing communications worked differently in an electronic environment. It was also realised that it was necessary to integrate offline communications with the online version in order to maximise returns. Some call the outcome of this confluence *inline communication*.

# Multichannel marketing

The idea that brands can reach their target market through a single channel has long been rejected. With markets and audiences fragmenting, it is necessary to utilise a number of channels and so optimise the number of opportunities for customers to be touched by a brand.

As a result, organisations have restructured their operations, developed and then reconfigured a number of different channels in their search to reduce costs, and attempt to better meet the preferred 'touchpoints' of their different customers.

Restructuring has often taken the form of introducing multiple sales channels with the simple objective of using less expensive channels to complete selling tasks that do not require personal, face-to-face contact. Technology-enhanced channels, mainly in the form of Web-based and email communications, have grown considerably, often at the expense of telephone and mail facilities. Payne and Frow (2004) have developed a categorisation of sales channels and these are depicted in the vertical column of Table 23.1.

In order to better meet the needs of customers, organisations need to evolve their mix of channels. Customers will then be able to interact with their supplying organisations, using the mix of channels that they prefer to use. Therefore, marketing communications needs to be used in order to best complement the different audiences, channel facilities and characteristics. Through mixing channels and communications in a complementary way, higher levels of customer service can be achieved. The proliferation of channels may, however, lead organisations to believe that the greater the number of channels, the greater the chances of commercial success. In addition to the fact that multichannel customers are known to spend up to 30 per cent more than single-channel customers, the Internet and overseas call centres also offer substantial (short-term) cost savings (Myers et al., 2004).

| Table 23.1 | Comparison of channel characteristics | | |
|---|---|---|---|
| **Channel** | **Breadth** | **Dominant form of communication** | **Cost/contact** |
| Field sales | Key account, service and personal representation | Dialogue | High |
| Outlets | Retail branches, stores, depots and kiosks | Interactive | Medium |
| Telephony | Traditional telephone, facsimile, telex and contact centres | One-way and two-way | Low to medium |
| Direct marketing | Direct mail, radio and traditional television | One-way and two-way | Low |
| ecommerce | Email, Internet, interactive television | Interactive | Very low |
| mcommerce | Mobile telephony, SMS, WAP and 3G | Interactive | Very low |

The development of multichannel marketing can be considered as two main phases. The first concerns developments in the way the sales force operates, and the second the development of digital technologies. This is not to suggest that these are independent, discrete activities, just that multichannel selling initiatives commenced first.

## Categorising customers

One of the first, simple approaches to managing channels is to categorise accounts (customers) according to their potential attractiveness and the current strength of the relationship between supplier and buyer (see Figure 23.2). A strong relationship, for example, is indicative of two organisations engaged in mutually satisfying relational exchanges. A weak relationship suggests that the two parties have no experience of each other or, if they have, that it is not particularly satisfying. If there have been transactions, it may be that these can be classified as market exchange experiences. Attractiveness refers to the opportunities a buying organisation represents to the vendor: how large or small the potential business is in an organisation.

For reasons of clarity, these scales are presented as either high or low, strong or weak. However, they should be considered as a continuum and, with the use of some relatively simple evaluative criteria, accounts can be positioned on the matrix and strategies formulated to move accounts to different positions, which in turn necessitate the use of different sales channel mixes.

| | High    Strength of relationship    Low | |
|---|---|---|
| High | Section 1<br>Strategic investment | Section 2<br>Select and build |
| Low | Section 3<br>Adjust and maintain | Section 4<br>Reduce all support |

Account potential

| Figure 23.2 | Account investment grid |
|---|---|

| | High ← Strength of relationship → Low | |
|---|---|---|
| High ↑ Account potential ↓ Low | Key account management Field force selling | Field force selling Telemarketing/call centre Website Email |
| | Directed field force selling Telemarketing/call centre Website Email | Direct mail Telemarketing Email |

**Figure 23.3**    Multichannel mix allocation

*Source*: After Cravens et al. (1991). © Emerald Group Publishing Limited. All rights reserved.

Based on the original approach developed by Cravens et al. (1991), appropriate sales channels are superimposed on the grid so that optimum efficiency in selling effort and costs can be managed (Figure 23.3). Accounts in Section 1 vary in attractiveness, as some will be assigned key account status. The others will be very important and will require a high level of selling effort (investment), which has to be delivered by the field sales force. Accounts in Section 2 are essentially prospects because of their weak relationship but high attractiveness. Selling effort should be proportional to the value of the prospects: high effort for good prospects and low for the others. Care should be given to allocating a time by which accounts in this section are moved to other parts of the grid, thereby saving resources and maximising opportunities for growth. All the main sales channels should be used, commencing with direct and email to identify prospects, telesales for qualification purposes, field sales force selling directed at the strong prospects and telesales and website for the others. Website details provide support and information for those accounts that wish to remain distant. As the relationship becomes stronger, so field selling takes over from telemarketing and the coordinating activities of the contact or call centre. If the relationship weakens, then the account may be discontinued and selling redirected to other prospects.

Accounts in Section 3 do not offer strong potential and, although the relationship is strong, there are opportunities to switch the sales channel mix by reducing, but not eliminating, the level of field force activity and to give consideration to the introduction of telemarketing for particular accounts. Significant cost reductions can be achieved with these types of accounts by simply reviewing the means and reasoning behind the personal selling effort. Accounts in Section 4 should receive no field force calls, the prime sales channels being telesales, email, the website and perhaps catalogue selling, depending upon the nature of the website.

Establishing a multiple sales-channel strategy based on the grid suggested above may not be appropriate to all organisations. For example, the current level of performance may be considered as exceeding expectations, in which case there is no point in introducing change. It may be that the costs and revenues associated with redeployment are unfavourable and that the implications for the rest of the organisation of implementing the new sales channel approach are such that the transition should be either postponed or rejected. Payne and Frow (2004) suggest a range of channel options or strategies can be identified that relate to the channel needs of target segments. These range from a single dominant channel such as those used by Amazon and Egg, a customer segment approach designed for use with different channel types such as intermediaries, B2B end-user customers and consumers, one based on the different activity channels that customers prefer to use, such as a mix of online and offline resources to identify, see, demonstrate, select and pay for a computer and, finally, a truly integrated multichannel strategy utilising CRM systems to integrate all customer information at whichever contact point the customer chooses to use.

These strategies reflect some of the approaches that can be used and indeed various combinations can be used to meet customers' channel needs. However, experience has shown that costs can be reduced through the introduction of a multiple sales channel approach, and that levels of customer satisfaction and the strength of the relationship between members of the network can be improved considerably. In addition, it is vital to remember that customers will move into and use new channel mixes over the customer life cycle and that channel decisions should be regarded as fluid and developmental.

---

**Scholars' paper 23.1**  **Multichannel marketing**

Valos, M.J. (2009) Structure, people and process challenges of multichannel marketing: Insights from marketers, *Journal of Database Marketing & Customer Strategy Management*, 16(3), 197–206.

This article explores the utility of strategic implementation theory and the issues faced when marketers attempt to implement multichannel marketing. Implementation is proving difficult, mainly because of the complexities involved. The paper provides some interesting background material and is written in an accessible way.

---

# Online advertising

Online advertising expenditure is growing. It is growing faster than any other sector in the marketing communications industry. It was worth about £2 billion in 2006 and rose to £4.5 billion in 2011. By way of contrast, in 2011 television advertising revenue was worth £4.2 billion (Advertising Association, 2012). However, there are issues concerning what is included in each element, some arguing that the two groups do not contain directly comparable advertising elements.

Advertising, and indeed all digital promotional activity, needs to be planned and managed in just the same way as traditional media. Setting suitable goals is part of this process and Cartellieri et al. (1997), consultants with McKinsey, provide a useful set of objectives in this context:

- delivering content: click-through to a corporate site that provides more detailed information (e.g. health advice at www.nhsdirect.co.uk/);
- enabling transactions: a direct response that leads to a sale (e.g. air travel at www.easyjet.com/);
- shaping attitudes: development of brand awareness such as product launches (e.g. http://www.hillaryclinton.com/?splash=1);
- soliciting response: encouraging interaction with new visitors (e.g. www.towards-sustainability.co.uk/);
- improving retention: reminding visitors and seekers of the organisation and developing reputation and loyalty (e.g. www.ferrymiles.com/).

First, it is necessary to consider the scope of online advertising, or what Goldsmith and Lafferty (2002) refer to as 'Internet advertising'. Two different issues can be identified. One concerns all offline media that are used to drive traffic to an interactive site. The second concerns advertising material that only appears in an online environment. Both need to be used together in an integrated manner if a website is to be successful, as they are complementary forms of advertising.

Online advertising is not confined to an organisation's website. Traffic needs to be directed from other sites (where target customers are thought to visit), to the destination or advertiser's home page. To achieve this, these advertisements need to be placed on other suitable websites where it is thought the target audience is most likely (or known) to visit – for example, links from Harry Potter pages to Warner Bros. Therefore, advertisements are bought and placed on other websites and, through careful analysis, it is possible to place the ads on sites where it is thought that members of the target market will pass and be prompted to click the banner and be taken to the advertiser's own corporate or microsite.

Just like offline ads, interactive online ads are used to achieve one of two main tasks:

- to create brand awareness and make a favourable impression such that the reader develops a positive image of the brand;
- to provoke the reader to behave in particular ways. This is direct-response advertising, and it is used to provide readers with a call-to-action. This may be in the form of a click-through to the advertiser's destination site or to a purchase or phone call.

The vast majority of interactive online ads are direct-response, making use of the interactive capacity to provide immediate measurement of the success or otherwise of each campaign. For many brands, offline communications are used to create brand images while online ads are used to generate the call-to-action.

The most common form of ads are referred to as 'banner ads' (see below), but as technology and marketing knowledge have improved, so more sophisticated versions of the banner ad have evolved. Some of these are outlined below.

## Banner ads

Referred to generically as *display advertising*, these are the dominant form of paid-for online advertising. Fifty-five per cent of all online ads are banner ads, which are responsible for 96 per cent of all Internet ad awareness. Although effective as a standalone ad, banner ads are linked through to an advertiser's chosen destination and therefore can act as a gateway to other websites. Banner ads are linked to keywords submitted by a searcher into a search engine. The ad should therefore be strategically positioned to catch the optimum, or even greatest, traffic flow.

Certain product groups, such as computer-related products, represent a large proportion of all banner ads, whereas financial products account for a small amount. Therefore, banners are said to signpost, whereas media-rich content provides action. These allow for a depth of material and online transactions. Increasing numbers of these ads incorporate Flash, rich media, multipurpose units and sky-scrapers (very tall banner ads) as these formats generate better recall scores than the standard banner.

Instead of transferring visitors to an orthodox website, banner ads can also be used to transfer visitors to a games or a competition site. These games provide entertainment, seek to develop user involvement and can act as an incentive to return to the site at a later date. In addition, data about the user can be captured in order to refine future marketing offers. These ads can be saved for later use and are, therefore, more adaptable and convenient than interstitial ads (ones that pop up as users move between websites) and cannot be controlled by the user. Banner ads can also be used to transfer users to an interactive microsite.

The aim of banner ads is to attract attention and stimulate interest, but the problem is that click-through rates are very low, and have fallen to 0.19 per cent (McCormick 2011, reporting Forrester). This leads to the question of whether banner ads are worthwhile. Briggs and Hollis (1997) wrote a seminal paper on the topic in which they reported their finding that click-through rates are determined by five main factors. To these five a sixth can be been added.

| Table 23.2 | Determinants for click-through |
|---|---|

| Source of motivation to click through | Factor |
|---|---|
| Audience | Innate disposition to click through |
| Audience | Immediate relevance or need of product or service |
| Audience | Pre-existing source appeal (product or organisation) |
| Advertising | Immediate relevance of the message |
| Advertising | Curiosity generated by the banner |
| Advertising | The execution or attractiveness of the message (ad) |

Based on Briggs and Hollis (1997). Used with permission from WARC.

Action, that is click-through, might be driven by the way an ad has been designed and executed (see Table 23.2). This addition is based on the work of Lutz et al. (1983) who investigated attitude change and the way people engage cognitively with ads. Dichter (1966) also found that people's predisposition to engage with word-of-mouth communication could be stimulated by the executional qualities of an ad.

An interesting outcome from Briggs' and Hollis' work was that banner ads were regarded as an important and effective form of online communication. Making allowances for the scope of their research, click-through was seen as unnecessary for the development of brand awareness and even the development of brand attitudes. Click-through rates can be improved when online ads are integrated with a sales promotion device that is designed to reward the behaviour. Special offers, competitions and other incentives can increase rates by as much as 10 per cent. However, it should always be remembered that incentives cost money, and these costs should be considered when analysing the overall return from a banner-based campaign. Another way of improving click-through is to consider not only the design and attractiveness of the ad, but also its placement and timing. This is because audience volumes and composition vary throughout any month or day period (Chaffey et al., 2006).

Since the leading work of Briggs and Hollis, banners have declined in importance to the extent that they are not well regarded, either by customers or clients, and many commentators regard online display to be dead. However, what is interesting is that UK spend on online display rose by 27.5 per cent (IAB PwC, 2011). The resolution of this apparent contradiction appears to rest with two main developments. The first concerns retargeting which occurs when ads are placed within the browsing patterns of target audiences. Banners are thought to be more effective when used within a retargeting programme.

The second development concerns integration. According to Warner (2011), by integrating banners into social and mobile strategies and by rewarding customers through loyalty programmes when they engage with these richer ads, banners have a renewed role to play within digital marketing strategies.

Research into online ads, and based on dwell-time analysis, demonstrates that it is the creative that has four times the impact on ad performance as the media plan. Going by the dwell times, the ad formats shown in Figure 23.4 proved the most popular.

## Pop-ups

Also known as *transitional online ads*, pop-ups appear in separate browser windows, when Web pages are being loaded or closed. Technically, interstitials appear during Web page loading and superstitials appear during closing (Gay et al., 2007). Originally they were intended to appear as a relief to the boredom that can set in when downloading files took a long time.

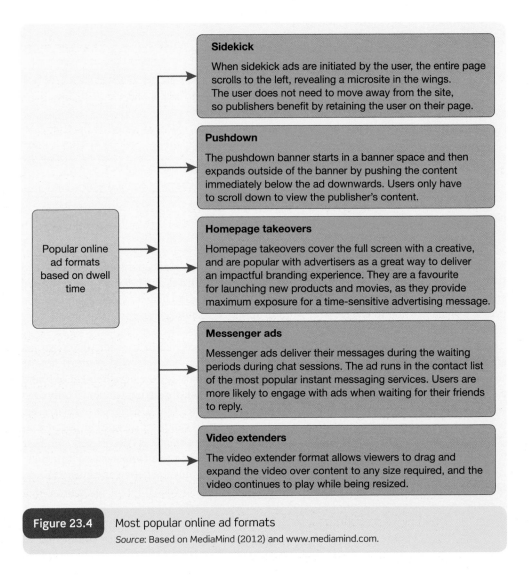

**Figure 23.4**    Most popular online ad formats

*Source*: Based on MediaMind (2012) and www.mediamind.com.

In that sense, they were regarded as supportive communications. However, as broadband speeds and computer technology have accelerated, so the 'waiting' times experienced by users have been minimised, to the extent that pop-ups are now generally regarded as an intrusive pain.

Research by McCoy, Everard and Galletta (2007) was aimed at understanding the impact and intrusiveness of online ads. The results showed that these types of ads, especially pop-ups, are perceived to be annoying and more intrusive than display ads. What is more, they impeded recall of both the website and the ad.

## Microsites

This type of site is normally product- or promotion-specific, and is often run as a joint promotion with other advertisers. Creating a separate site avoids the difficulty of directing traffic to either of the joint partners' sites. Microsites are much less expensive to set up than traditional sites and are particularly adept at building awareness, as click-throughs to microsites are higher than through just banners.

## Viewpoint 23.1    Emotional use of microsites impacts behaviour

This campaign had the overall objective of reducing the number of people killed in transport accidents in the State of Victoria in Australia. To achieve this goal, a new and insightful approach was required to deal with the speeding problem.

The insight revolved around the idea that it is not just the death of a person that is of concern, serious as it is, but it is also about the many other people whose lives are affected by one single act of speeding.

The new approach was based on the death of Luke Robinson. He was 19, when as a result of driving too fast, he died in March 2010. Luke's family and friends agreed to participate in a campaign designed to influence young drivers to cut their speed once they realised how many people are affected by a fatal road accident. The campaign was launched four months after his death, and was designed to support the government's Arrive Alive road safety policy objective of reducing injury and death from road trauma by 30 per cent by 2017.

The 'Everybody hurts when you speed' campaign kicked off with 26 testimonial commercials, over a two-week period, each aired on television and simultaneously online. Each testimonial suggested a personal perspective on the Luke Robinson road tragedy but the full story was not revealed at this stage. The goal was to create expectation and curiosity about what these ads were and how they were tied together.

As they were rolled out, viewers started to piece the stories together but it was only at the end on the night of the highest-rating TV reality show finale, they came together to form a three-minute mega-commercial. The raw emotion of the testimonials generated extensive commentary on TV, radio talkback and in newspaper editorials and online forums.

At the heart of the campaign, which used a variety of media to reach different drivers, was a microsite (everybodyhurts.com.au). This was designed to influence the core audience, males aged 18 to 45. Once at the microsite, and once they had seen two stories, visitors were given a link to a Facebook application. When clicked, it captured the names of the individual's own friends at random from their Facebook account and spread them around the 'ripple effect page' in the same way as the initial landing page featured Luke's family and friends.

Visitors could then forward relevant videos, together with their own comments, to others who they thought would benefit from receiving them. Email was used for friends not on Facebook.

The success of the campaign can be measured in the number of fatalities, and for a third year in a row, the number of casualties fell (287). In addition, the number of people caught speeding fell by 25 per cent in 2010 compared to 2008, and spontaneous recall of the campaign rose to 82 per cent by week 4 of the campaign, one of the highest figures ever recorded.

*Source*:  Grey Group (2011) Turnbull (2010); www.3aw.com; www.3aw.com.au/blogs/3aw-generic-blog/luke-robinson-the-ripple-effect/20100712-105t4.html
www.campaignbrief.com/2010/07/grey-melbourne-and-tac-extends.html

**Question:**  To what extent is this emotional approach likely to reduce speeding in the long term?

**Task:**  Find three similar social marketing programmes and determine what made them successful, or not.

# Everybody hurts when you speed.

TAC

**Exhibit 23.3    The TAC – Everybody Hurts campaign**
*Source*: Transport Accident Commission, Victoria

## Rich media ads

The essential difference between regular and rich media banner ads is that the latter allow for significantly more detailed and enhanced messages to be accessed by the target audience. Rich media ads closely resemble offline ads and this helps to move online ads from a largely informational perspective to one that is much more emotional. This suggests that rich media are more likely to deliver stronger branding messages than in the past, which of course would negate the behavioural advantage inherent in this interactive environment.

Streaming video and other more visitor-engaging material, such as Flash and Shockwave, provide depth and interest for users. It is accepted that media-rich banner ads are highly effective, if only because the medium is said to be the message.

## Online video

One area that is growing quickly is online video advertising. For a time there were a number of technical issues that impeded its use, but the growth in broadband connections enabling users to download the data required to view online video, the increasing use of TiVo and devices that let users fast-forward through television commercials, plus of course the huge impact of YouTube and Flikr, are encouraging the development of online video advertising.

Online video ads can be used in a number of different ways apart from simply showing ads at the beginning or end of programmes. Online video content normally plays in an unstoppable loop, so the ads are unavoidable. In addition, advertisers will be able to place ads within video streams, another reason preventing users from avoiding them. Also, video ads can be embedded within Web pages and online articles, relating closely to the site content. To date, many online ads are directly derived from television ads, but the 30-second format is not appropriate for the online environment. This means specific content for online ads needs to be developed. See the *Guardian* film site for some examples of this (www.http://film.guardian.co.uk/Featurepages/).

It was mentioned earlier that there have been some difficulties associated with the development of online video advertising. One of these concerns the difficulties controlling online content. There is a risk that ads can show up on pages that include content with which they may not want to be associated. For example, in August 2007 some major brands, including Virgin Media, AA, Vodafone and Direct Line, all withdrew their advertising from Facebook. Their actions were a response to their ads being positioned next to communications for the British National Party (BNP), the controversial, far-right political party. Their withdrawal represented a response to the lack of control that brands have in certain online environments when buying space through media-buying agencies. In this particular instance, Facebook reacted swiftly by introducing a blocking process that enables advertisers to opt out of different parts of the site (Davidson, 2007). In much the same way, advertisers do not want to be associated with illegally uploaded, copyrighted content, often a problem on some user-generated-content sites.

The development of video advertising has also been frustrated by the difficulties associated with searching online video. Video-search engines currently index content through the use of 'tags', which are supplied by content producers or users. However, this tagging process is not always used properly and some tags are too general to attach appropriate advertising (Holahan, 2006). One further and important difficulty rests with online ad effectiveness. The statistics, according to Warner, cited by McCormick (2011), indicate that this format is not as effective, or as popular, as other formats.

One technical development reported by a commercial journalist concerns a video-search feature that allows advertisers to append messages to particular points within videos (Holahan, 2007). So, as an example, users on a La Liga football website will, at some point in the future, be able to search for videos of particular players performing certain shots, tricks, celebrations, tackles or scoring goals. Advertisers could pay to be linked with particular players, teams or actions, and their ads would play at certain points when the video is requested.

# Online gaming

The development of game technology has prompted enormous growth in the numbers of consumers who play online games. This in turn has attracted advertisers. According to Chang et al. (2010), the advergaming industry appears to have started in the late 1980s, when Sega Games put up Marlboro billboards in its racing games (Chambers, 2006). From this start, IGA has gained huge popularity with advertisers, such that the global industry was predicted to be worth US $1 billion by the end of 2011 (Goodman, 2007). Whether these figures are realised is not the real issue. It is the growth of and interest in this advertising variant that contribute to the growing diversity of the advertising arena.

It should be noted that there are two forms of game-based advertising.

## 1 In-game advertising (IGA)

Yang et al. (2006: 63) refer to in-game advertising (IGA) as 'the placement of brands in games (usually in the form of billboards, posters, or sponsor signage in sports and racing games (Schwarz 2005)'.

In many ways this resembles the model through which product placement is considered to work. However, as Cauberghe and de Pelsmacker (2010) point out, the interactive context of in-game brand placements can evoke cognitively involving experiences for players. This is something which the static nature of traditional product placements in television programmes and films cannot achieve.

Chang et al. (2010) conclude that the effectiveness of in-game advertising is improved when two main elements are attended to. First the advertising needs to be integrated into the game. They found that the sense of realism felt by players is not disturbed or can even be improved when the advertising is an integral part the game. The second element concerns the selection of an appropriate game in which the advertising is to be placed. By selecting a game with attributes that are similar to those of the advertised brand, such as sports brands with sports-based games, the media vehicle, the game, can enhance advertising effects.

## 2 Advergaming

Cauberghe and de Pelsmacker (2010: 5) distinguish advergaming on the basis that 'the game is specially made to promote the brand'. These games tend to be relatively simple in design, with few rules and are easy to play. This is mainly because advergames are distributed across different platforms, such as websites, viral marketing, mobiles and commercials on interactive digital television.

Mainstream advertising works partly on the principle of association, and IGA works on there being a positive association between an advertiser and the game. Lewis and Porter (2010) report that when there is a large incompatibility between the advertising and a game, perceptions of the realism of the game are reduced and the level of annoyance felt by players increases.

Chang et al. (2010) conclude that to be successful it is important to integrate the advertising closely into a game. This means embedding it as an integral part of the game, not at the periphery or as an add-on. This helps to enhance the sense of realism for players.

They also recommend that it is important to select an appropriate game as the advertising vehicle. Player annoyance can be reduced if there is a close alignment between the game's attributes and those of the brand being advertised.

In much the same way, each player has a psychological profile. So those playing sports games are more predisposed to sports brands being integrated into the game.

Cauberghe and de Pelsmacker's (2010) research results are interesting because they find that brand prominence affects recall. Prominence in an advergame refers to the extent to which a brand is an integral and dynamic part of the game. Brands that are placed prominently in a game are likely to benefit from a player's focus on the interactive content and consequent intensive processing of ads. The result is higher brand recall (Schneider and Cornwell, 2005; Chaney et al., 2004). This works for products that evoke both high and low involvement.

Various theories have been put forward concerning the number of times an offline or traditional ad should be repeated in order for learning to occur. Cauberghe and de Pelsmacker found repetition not to be a recall factor in an advergaming environment. Their research found that 'playing the game several times had no positive influence on brand recall, but impacted the development of brand attitudes negatively'. Again this is a function of the intensity of cognitive processing associated with gaming. The researchers' recommendation is that advertisers should work with more complex advergames.

---

### Scholars' paper 23.2    A gale of creative destruction

**Evans, D.S. (2009) The Online Advertising Industry: Economics, Evolution, and Privacy, *Journal of Economic Perspectives*, 23(3), Summer, 37–60.**

Although the online advertising business appears to be moving forward at a breathtaking speed, this paper provides an interesting view of some of the essential properties of the market. The author considers the development of online advertising and explains some of the basic concepts. He refers to online advertising as 'one of those "gales of creative destruction" that will reshape several industries and radically change traditional ways of delivering advertising messages from sellers to prospective buyers'.

---

# Online sales promotions

Sales promotions play a similar role online as they do offline: namely, to provoke a behavioural response. Indeed, sales promotions are so good at provoking responses they can be up to five times more effective than direct mail. Using sales promotions online enables the interactive functionality of the web to be developed and this is important when attempting to engage customers with a brand for the first time. Some would argue that a more appropriate term for this activity is 'interactive sales promotions'. This is because this tool can be used in a mobile arena and is not restricted to an online context.

The main aims of using online sales promotions are, first, that they can either attract or retain customers, and second, that they provide interest and involvement with the brand by encouraging interaction and return visits. In reality, sampling, free gifts, ecoupons, price deals and competitions are the main incentives used interactively.

Organisations use incentive-based online promotions because they are capable of delivering two main sources of value. First, they engage customers, providing them with a reason to stay on a site or return to it more frequently than they might otherwise have done. Second, because interactive promotions require customers to opt-in and give permission, they deliver huge amounts of pertinent data about customers, potential customers and the market, without too much effort on the the part of the customer or the organisation.

Online sales promotions are generally less expensive than hard-copy versions, but to date Web-based sales promotions have not been used extensively to develop brand differentiation or add value. The issue here is that sales promotions are normally used to bring forward future sales, to provide a reason to buy now. On the Internet this motivation does not exist in the same way, and for many people the only reason to use the Internet is to find information and to compare prices. However, digital media are being used increasingly to deliver sales promotion activities. Indeed, there has been a decline in the use of traditional, on-pack promotions (Barrand, 2004) and a significant growth in the use of SMS, email and the Internet as means of delivering interactive sales promotions.

If traditional forms of sales promotion might be in need of innovation, the use of the Internet to deliver risk-free sampling and trial opportunities, involving trivia games, interactive loyalty programmes, instant-win gratification experiences, plus other opportunities to earn points and prizes, reflects an industry determined to adapt and reinvent itself.

---

### Viewpoint 23.2    Groupies drive the discounts

Groupon is a new collective-based sales promotion scheme. The power of group buying is used to secure large daily discounts on a variety of events, products, shops and restaurants usually. The discounts are substantial, over 50 per cent, and sometimes as much as 90 per cent. These enable retailers to attract customers and move unwanted stock. If a predetermined number of subscribers click on the deal, they are issued with a coupon which they present to the retailer, either offline or online. If an insufficient number of subscribers respond, the deal is withdrawn and no one is entitled to it.

The first Groupon deal was made in Chicago in October 2008, and was based on a half-price offer for pizzas. They have over 5 million registered subscribers and can reach 140 cities in 18 countries.

Considerable research is undertaken prior to entering new markets and certain businesses are not invited to be part of the scheme. These include abortion clinics, plastic surgeons, shooting ranges, and strip clubs. Merchants who sign up to participate in the Groupon programme are not required to pay any front-loaded costs, which is different from display advertising and many other media-based activities. However, due to the size of the discount, and Groupon's fee on each deal, the return for each merchant is low.

Groupon gathers personal details from registered consumers and then uses email and social networking sites to contact those who might be interested in particular products or services. The copy used to promote Groupon deals is considered to be a major factor in the success of the programme.

There have been complaints about the programme concerning alleged problems some consumers had about realising deals. Negative publicity arose about an ad transmitted during the Super Bowl. This ad was withdrawn. In the UK the OFT (Office of Fair Trading) ruled that Groupon had to improve its website, so that Groupon should:

- provide accurate, honest and transparent reference prices on deals where ads compare an original 'reference' price against the sale price;
- make realistic assessments of a supplier's abilities to provide goods or services offered in the deal in the quantity or timeframe suggested;
- clearly and prominently display limitations applying to the deals;
- take reasonable steps to back up claims related to any beauty or health products offered;
- ensure information regarding refunds and cancellation policies are in accordance with current regulations;
- deliver and operate fair terms and conditions.

*Source*:    various including Tovey (2012); www.en.wikipedia.org/wiki/Groupon; www.bbc.co.uk; www.groupon.com.

| | |
|---|---|
| **Question:** | Why might a merchant be attracted to a Groupon-type scheme when they could be overwhelmed by demand and unable to satisfy their new customers? |
| **Task:** | Find the current Groupon discount offers being made in your area. Do any of these look attractive? |
| | (See also Chapter 18.) |

Sampling can be an important stage in customer relationship development and in certain markets the Internet enables this admirably. For example, music and software can be downloaded for trial purposes, while services such as photo processing can be tested risk-free through introductory offers. Another area experiencing growth is the rather oddly termed 'ecoupons'. Downloaded ecoupons can be redeemed online using a code at checkout, or printed off and used offline in-store, as the Groupon insight demonstrates.

# Online public relations

The use of online public relations is an increasingly important part of an organisation's marketing communications. Online public relations is concerned with maximising opportunities to present the organisation (and its products and services) in a positive manner. The goal, as with traditional media relations work, is to create 'mentions' in a variety of targeted media, including other websites. This is important for establishing links and achieving higher search engine rankings. It is also important to build relationships, both with the target stakeholder groups and with journalists and others in the media.

Developments in digital media have been instrumental in assisting public relations move from a predominantly one-way model of communication to an interactive model. In 2001 Hurme suggested that public relations practitioners can be divided into two broad groups: those that predominantly use traditional media and those that adopt online communications. Since that article was written, an increasing number of practitioners have moved over to online communications, but the realisation of the potential to develop true dialogue with stakeholders remains unfulfilled in many cases. Therefore, opportunities for interactivity and dialogue have increased even if websites are not being designed to fulfil this requirement completely.

Website hosts are able to sell advertising space and they also have opportunities to engage with public relations activities. This might lead to the conclusion that owners of websites have evolved into surrogate media owners, in the sense that they are free to publish content without recourse to the origin of the material. The problem is that the content they present (on their own behalf) has not been influenced by an independent third party, such as an opinion former, and may be no more than brochureware. However, the role is more complex than this, because websites can now fulfil the role of fax machines. Previously, press releases were faxed to designated journalists. Now press releases are posted on the website and emailed as attached files to specified individuals on mailing lists. All those interested can view the files at their discretion and initiative, and then choose to enter into an interaction or even dialogue, in order to expand on the information provided. Email is regarded as essential by journalists, broadcasters and bloggers. However, the key difference is that, unlike the first two groups, bloggers prefer to receive attachments with full details and supplemental information (Burns, 2008).

In many ways e-newsletters and white papers are a natural extension of email communications. The differences concern content and goals. Email communications are sales-driven with product-related content. Newsletters and white papers are reputation-driven, with a diverse range of content concerning organisational and/or technical-related material. These communications can be an essential part of the 'stickiness' that good websites seek to develop. Recipients who find these communications of value either anticipate their release or return to the host's website to search in archived files for past copies and items of interest.

Most large organisations provide online newsroom facilities but the quality of information provided has been found to be less than satisfactory. Callison (2003), cited by Waters et al. (2010), found that the average number of items available through these newsrooms was 6.5. These covered press releases, executive biographies, and executive photographs. Other items found in online newsrooms included annual reports and financial data, audio and video archives, downloadable graphics, copies of executive speeches and organisational histories. What is also interesting is that only 60 per cent of organisations in a survey undertaken by Esrock and Leichty (1999) provided the names of a media contact person for follow-up questions to the news release they had made available.

Social media news releases allow photos, audio, and video to be embedded and linked to blogs without virus concerns. These types of releases not only increase the possible number of people discovering the release via search engines, but also enable interaction and consumer comment.

Other forms of public relations are more easily observable. Statements concerning an organisation's position on an issue of public interest, corporate social responsibility or environmental matters can be published, while investor relations and public affairs issues are easily accommodated. Sponsorship activities are an important part of interactive online marketing communications, whether they be in the form a partnership deal or direct sponsorship of a social networking site. Websites can also play an important role in terms of crisis management. In the event of an organisational crisis or disaster, up-to-date information can be posted quickly, either providing pertinent information or directing visitors to offline information and associated facilities.

A large number of the activities undertaken in the name of public relations follow the established pattern of organisations using public relations to contact journalists, broadcasters, and bloggers in hopes of gaining media placements to disseminate news content. While assisting this process, digital media have, however, played a role in a new trend called 'media catching'. This involves reversing this established process. Now practitioners are being contacted by journalists and others seeking specific material for stories, articles, blogs, and websites where there are pressing deadlines. Rather than 'Here is a story please run it', media catching is about 'Do you have a story please?' See also Chapter 15 for more on media catching.

---

### Viewpoint 23.3  China presents a core issue for Apple

In January 2012 The *Telegraph* ran a headline stating that Apple was 'attacking problems at its factories in China'. The report claimed that Tim Cook, Apple's chief executive, had sent an email to all 60,000 staff stating that Apple 'cares about every worker in its supply chain'. He referred to measures the company was taking and had been taking over several years, to eradicate these unacceptable practices. It would 'continue to dig deeper' into problems in China. Cook claimed that: 'Any accident is deeply troubling, and any issue with working conditions is cause for concern. Any suggestion that we don't care is patently false and offensive to us. As you know better than anyone, accusations like these are contrary to our values. It's not who we are.' There are interesting references here to Apple's corporate personality and its identity (see Chapter 15).

So, why write the email? Well, Apple was responding to a number of articles in the *New York Times (NYT)* which documented the company's problems in China. It also claimed that there were divisions within Apple about how the issues should be managed. The paper said more than half of the suppliers audited by Apple had broken at least one part of its conduct code for the past four or five years and had even broken the law in some cases. 'Most people would still be really disturbed if they saw where their iPhone comes from,' one unnamed former Apple executive told the newspaper.

It is clear that Apple has been treating this issue seriously. Since 2007 it has extended its monitoring, and its annual reports have exposed several problems. The latest report found that at least 90 factories required workers to work for more than 60 hours a week, in a country where the law sets a maximum of 40 hours. There were also five cases of child labour at factories.

Despite the mounting criticism which has threatened to taint the company's brand, its shares have risen to record levels. Christmas sales have been high and contributed to the timely announcement that the company had doubled its profits in the first three months to $13.1 billion (£8.35 billion) in 2012. So, at a time when Apple has been monitoring its Chinese factories, sales have continued to soar. This in turn has put pressure on the company's supply chain to increase production and maintain quality. However, a sinister adjunct to this is that the *NYT* reports that there has been a wave of suicides, explosions and poisonings.

Apple's use of public relations and its online communications have been tested by these issues. The need for a fast response and to be seen to act decisively has been critical in attempting to control the China problem and attendant allegations. If not, online media interest in particular will increase and the issue could spiral into a crisis.

*Source*:   Based on Moore (2012); www.apple.com/supplierresponsibility/.

**Question:**   To what extent is multichannel marketing likely to generate ethical issues?
**Task:**         Visit the Apple website (www.apple.com), read the latest reports on these and similar issues.

| Exhibit 23.4 | **Apple logo** |
| --- | --- |
| | *Source*: Imagine China |

# Online personal selling

Face-to-face personal communications are, by definition, always interactive. However, the online application for the purposes of buying and selling remains the one part of the mix that cannot be addressed. However, indirectly digital technology has been of great importance to the way organisations manage their sales force and their digital marketing programmes.

Remembering the high costs associated with maintaining a sales team, digital technology has enabled some sales activities to be realigned. Contact centres and telesales teams can now undertake some of the more low-value activities that the sales force used to undertake. This frees them up to find new business and build relationships. On the other hand, the technology has also enabled management to reduce the size of the sales force and with it the amount of face-to-face selling.

Video conferencing does provide this facility, but costs and logistics limit the practical application of this tool to conferencing and non-sales meetings. Although the Skype telephone software enables people to talk over the Internet using their PCs free of charge, using next-generation peer-to-peer software, the online environment is an impersonal medium and, as such, does not allow for direct personal communication.

The recognition of this limitation should direct management attention to the use of the Internet as a complementary role within the communications mix. However, it has been determined that the Internet can impact upon sales performance indirectly through sales management activities (Avlonitis and Karayanni, 2000). They demonstrate how managing and analysing data can refine segmentation and customer classification schemes, allowing sales people to spend more time on core activities.

Sales force automation (SFA) is a growing and significant area for organisations to invest in. SFA involves the application of information technology to support the sales function. According to Boujena et al. (2009: 138) these technologies seek to improve 'performance by increasing the efficiency and productivity of salespeople and improving both the quality and quantity of communications among salespersons, the buying organization, and the selling firm'. They identify the most often-cited benefits of SFA/IT on five main levels. These are set out in Table 23.3.

| Table 23.3 | Benefits of sales force automation |
| --- | --- |

| SFA benefit | Explanation |
| --- | --- |
| Productivity | SFA can lead to a reduction of errors, reduced support costs, improved closing rates, faster responses and better customer prospecting, development, and account profiling. |
| | SFA reduces the time spent on administrative tasks and provides faster access to timely information. This may enable better territory management by increasing salespersons' availability to customers and more relevant information delivery. |
| Information processing | Through CRM databases, SFA applications improve a salesperson's ability to gather, analyse, and share product, customer, and competitor information. This helps salespeople to better inform customers about product specifications and usage situations and more accurately fulfil customer needs. |
| Communication effectiveness | SFA can enhance a salesperson's ability to communicate clearly and rapidly with customers and contacts, which improves their responsiveness and capacity to fit customer needs. Easier information exchange helps maintain customer relationships. Organisations can share contact information and improve coordination across the company's various customer service functions. |
| Perceived competence | Competence refers to a customer's perception that a salesperson is knowledgeable in areas related to products, customer needs, and market intelligence. By increasing both the volume and the quality of market intelligence and the speed of access, SFA increases the perceived competence of salespersons. |
| Customer relationship quality | Customer relationship quality refers to the bundle of intangible value related to the interchange between buyers and sellers. It is defined as a buyer's trust in a salesperson and satisfaction with the relationship. SFA may help salespersons in developing customer trust by influencing trust-driving behaviours: namely, customer orientation, competency, honesty, dependability, and likability. |

Based on Boujena, Johnston, and Merunka (2009).

In much the same way, customer relationship management systems (CRM) have experienced real growth, even if the outcomes have not always reached customer expectations. CRM incorporates technologies and systems that enable all employees who have an interface with customers, to have real-time, up-to-date information in order to deliver high levels of customer service.

Establishing what constitutes CRM is far from easy based on the various interpretations that have been placed on the term. Ang and Buttle (2003) suggest that there are three main approaches: *strategic*, where CRM is seen as a core business strategy; *operational*, where CRM is about automating different aspects of an organisation's selling, marketing and service functions; and, finally, *analytical*, where CRM is about manipulating data to improve the efficiency and effectiveness of each phase of the customer relationship lifecycle. To these should be added social CRM, the incorporation of social media as the primary means of communication, for CRM, rather than email.

It might therefore be possible to suggest that CRM is the delivery of customer value through the strategic integration of business functions and processes, using customer data and information systems and technology.

# Online direct marketing

Direct marketing is a primary online communications tool because it can be used interactively to generate both transactional- and relational-based responses within a target audience. Direct marketing activities are often used to integrate a range of activities, but when used to lead campaigns, either offline or online, they should be based on database technologies that target the right audience, shape the creative, are deliverable through appropriate channels and can measure responses.

Interactive direct marketing underpins the majority of communication activities in the online environment. There are some branding-based communications, but the majority of activity is wrapped up as direct marketing, whether that be in the form of direct response advertising (e.g. banners or rich media), sales promotion (e-coupons or sampling) or public relations (e.g. sponsorship, blogs and podcasts).

Offline direct marketing is used to drive traffic to a website. This might be undertaken by branding or by providing incentives. For example, many insurance companies use direct response television ads to inform consumers of their low-cost/high-value insurance deals to be found at their website. Originally, advertising was the primary offline tool used to drive traffic. Following the reassessment and consolidation of dot-com growth at the beginning of 2000, direct marketing (and direct mail in particular) became the key primary traffic generator. It

---

### Scholars' paper 23.3     These are their preferred channels

**Thomas, J.S. and Sullivan, U.Y. (2005) Managing Marketing Communications with Multichannel Customers, *Journal of Marketing*, 69 (October), 239–51.**

This paper considers ways in which customers' multichannel choices or preferences can be determined through database management. It then considers the general process for managing marketing communications with multichannel retail customers. From this the authors demonstrate the application of the prediction process using a multichannel retailer.

does this in one of two main ways: the first is to launch a teaser campaign appealing to people's innate curiosity or, second, the direct mail piece is part of a sales promotion campaign in which the promise of a reward lures people to a website.

The most obvious form of online direct marketing is email and a close application, viral marketing, both of which have been discussed earlier (Chapter 22). Direct marketing once revolved around direct mail and telemarketing with a view to acquiring new, 'cold' customers. Now direct marketing is used to converge different media in order to convert warm prospects.

# Multichannel campaigns

This consideration of interactivity and the tools and media of marketing communications has assumed that each discipline is an individual, standalone element, and that they operate in environments unaffected by each other, or indeed any other influence. Obviously, this is far from reality, and as demonstrated in the Salvation Army minicase, in a world of integrated marketing communications, media neutral planning and open planning approaches, each needs to be considered in the light of its effectiveness when deployed with other elements of the mix. These may involve online, offline or increasingly as inline formats; cross-channel campaigns that use tools and media in various combinations provide superior levels of customer service.

The reason for this move is that there is a growing body of evidence that shows that the effectiveness of the media increases considerably when they are used in combination. Just as it was shown earlier (Chapter 16) that the impact of sponsorship improves when advertising is used before, during and after the sponsored event, so the impact of particular media can improve when they are used collectively within a campaign. Snoddy (2007) reports on research referred to as 'brain fingerprinting'. This technical study claims to have scientifically proven that when newspaper advertising is used with television ads, the brand impact scores rise by 72 per cent. As a result, the Newspaper Marketing Agency claims that newspapers provide a complement for, and improve, the impact and response to television ads.

Catalogues, once a popular way of buying clothes and household items, are no longer a fashionable marketing channel and have faded with the development of the Internet and online shopping. While the huge bulky catalogues have all but disappeared, they have been replaced with newer, slimmer and highly targeted catalogues. The product scope is narrow and the aim is to drive people to the brand's website. The new slim-line catalogues contain a fraction of the products available, but provide a preview and an incentive to visit the website. Referred to as 'flick-to-click', this approach reflects changing consumer behaviour. Research reported by Murphy (2007) found that 66 per cent of consumers prefer the combination of catalogue to view and online to buy. The most popular categories were clothing, travel, cosmetics and gardening. It is suggested that this behaviour is a function of time-poor customers who prefer to read something offline, at a time convenient to them, perhaps late at night when relaxing (not in front of a computer screen).

Outdoor has long been seen as an important support for television and print media, often used to reinforce brand messages or to create attention.

What is key of course is to understand which media people use and how and when. Before the arrival of digital media, individuals used a limited media mix. This was often based around a few television channels, a Sunday and a weekday paper, maybe a couple of magazines and perhaps cinema. This mix has been transformed, so that today research indicates that adults consume a portfolio of media that embraces 10–15 television channels, 10–15 websites and a similar number of magazines. This does not account for a wealth of other media such as radio and cinema. In addition, people are consuming media through time and place shifting and using their portfolio of media in an integrated format (Binet and Field, 2007).

## Viewpoint 23.4    Multichannel painting

Multichannel campaigns are used in both consumer and business marketing contexts. This example from the b2b sector is typical of the approach taken to reach customers through a particular mix of tools and media channels.

Dulux Decorator Centres (DDC) are part of AkzoNobel, the world's largest paint and coatings company and a world-leading chemicals producer. When DDC launched a new brand identity, the aim of the rebrand was to provide a stronger point of differentiation, and to stand out against their competitors. The market is characterised by price-based activity and trade promotions. In turn, this affects margins and reduces customer loyalty as they seek out bargains.

A campaign anchored around a new positioning of 'We know decorating' sought to convey friendliness and an approachable tone which reflects in-store conversations and relationships between staff and trade customers. This is because a large number of customers are sole traders, and for some the DDC stores become a meeting point where they discuss projects and share advice. As a result, staff and customers build up good relationships.

The campaign was targeted at a range of audiences, including employees, suppliers and DDC's key customer groups comprising decorating contractors from both SMEs and larger contracting organisations, as well as professional decorators.

The campaign was presented first internally to head office, store staff, regional managers and other AkzoNobel-related businesses, and then at a supplier conference. This was followed by direct mail activity. This used two key strands. The first was to communicate various brand features, such as online ordering, and the second was to augment the regular 'Decorator Deals' mailer, which was split between Nectar and non-Nectar card holders. This direct mail activity contained a trade promotion involving targeted vouchers. A new website featuring the new branding was established as part of the campaign and the organisation's social media activity on Facebook and Twitter was also incorporated.

DDC are a founder member of Nectar Business, a b2b loyalty programme. This is designed specifically for SMEs. DDC reward their customers with Nectar points which they can collect and spend with a number of b2b partners.

So successful is the loyalty programme that in 2010 10 per cent of DDC's new customers came from the Nectar Business base. Furthermore, the scheme aids customer retention as DDC's best-performing Nectar customers have a significantly higher retention rate over a 12-month period than non-Nectar customers. To DDC, a Nectar customer is worth nearly six times that of a non-Nectar customer per annum.

*Source*:   Clarke (2012); Anon (2011).

**Question:**   How might the loyalty scheme be a central element of a multichannel campaign?

**Task:**    Make a list of the various tools and media used in the DDC campaign. What would you add, budget permitting?

The IPA analysis also found that, when advertising is coupled with sponsorship or public relations, the strongest measures of effectiveness in terms of communication goals were achieved. What is also clear is that multichannel campaigns are more effective than single-channel activity.

Of course, the possible number of channel combinations is huge and too numerous for each to be considered here. However, the IPA found that the use of three advertising media is optimal, although for large brands this might need to be increased. Integrated multimedia

---

**Exhibit 23.5**    **Snickers into the long game**

Snickers has a long association with football but at the time of the South African World Cup it did not have a sponsorship deal. To overcome this it decided to stage the longest-ever football game.

To achieve this it needed players, so a multimedia campaign using traditional, online, and social channels was used to invite men to try and win a place. 130,000 participants went to a microsite where they played an online game of football in attempt to get selected. The lucky 36 then spent 42 hours playing football, breaking the Guinness World Record, with the match streamed to a 9.7 million audience.

---

campaigns have been shown by the IPA to be more effective and efficient than single-channel campaigns (Binet and Field, 2007).

Wakolbinger et al. (2009) observe that it is the impact of the Internet that has motivated many marketers to pursue integrated, multichannel communication strategies. The belief is that cross-channel campaigns are more effective than single channel programmes. Briggs et al. (2005) suggest that TV advertising has a greater absolute reach than print and online advertising, but acknowledge that it incurs higher costs. Their conclusion is that cross-media advertising may maximise productivity of advertising expenditures.

It is also commonly accepted that online advertising, in general, works best with offline media. The main reason for this is that it is necessary to drive people to a particular website. To date, there is no firm evidence to show that any one type of offline media is best suited to this task and a great deal depends on the nature of the product or service, as well as the audience's involvement in the category.

Wakolbinger et al. (2009) sought to find whether the use of print (newspaper) and online advertising together is more effective than using these media independently of each other. They found no statistically significant evidence to suggest that either newspaper or online advertising when used independently was more effective than the other. They also found nothing to verify that a cross-media campaign was any more effective. However, their results did confirm a trend towards the use of integrated cross-media campaigns, and they recommended that organisations should supplement traditional print advertising with new media channels.

In 2011 the IPA's analysis of the most successful campaigns during the period 2004 to 2010 supports the findings of Binet and Field (2007), referred to earlier, concerning the optimum number of channels. When it comes to achieving business goals (profit, market share, etc.), diminishing returns set in once the number of advertising media used reaches three (IPA, 2011). When interactive and Web channels, plus direct marketing, sales promotion and public relations are included in the mix, there does not appear to be a limit, apart from budget, to achieve both business and communication effects.

Broadbent (2011) considered these outcomes and suggests two reasons to explain why campaigns using many channels are less likely to be effective. The first is that the evidence indicates that brands that underspend in a channel, relative to their market share, struggle to grow. The second concerns the extent to which multichannel campaigns have integrated content. Broadbent explains that many campaigns run with seven channels and each requires content. The way each is produced, who produces it and under what brief and guidance varies considerably and it is really hard to integrate the content of a three-channel campaign, let alone seven.

| Scholars' paper 23.4 | Multichannel communications |
| --- | --- |

Godfrey, A., Seiders, K. and Voss, G.B. (2011) Enough Is Enough! The Fine Line in Executing Multichannel Relational Communication, *Journal of Marketing*, 75 (July), 94–109.

Increasingly organisations are developing their relationships with customers across a range of channels. This involves the use of personalised messages and constitutes multichannel relational communications. These authors provide some interesting insights into this strategy, and consider three key drivers of relational communication effectiveness: volume of communication, mix of communication channels, and alignment of those channels with customers' preferences. From their research they argue that reciprocity explains response to lower levels of communication, and reactance explains response to higher levels of communication.

# Key points

- Interactivity is a key characteristic of contemporary marketing communications. It used to cover a wide spectrum of mainly electronic environments, not limited or defined by the Internet.

- Interactivity normally precedes the establishment of dialogue between participants in the communication process. This in turn enables all participants to contribute to the content that is used in the communication event.

- Interactive marketing communications concerns processes through which individuals and organisations attempt to engage others with messages that are delivered primarily, but not exclusively, through electronic channels, and which offer all parties an opportunity to respond. Interaction can occur through the same channel as that used to convey the previous message, or a different channel.

- As a result of market and audience fragmentation, organisations have restructured their operations, developed and then reconfigured a number of different channels in their search to reduce costs, and attempt to better meet the preferred 'touchpoints' of their different customers.

- Restructuring has often taken the form of introducing multiple sales channels with the simple objective of using less expensive channels to complete selling tasks that do not require personal, face-to-face contact. Technology-enhanced channels, mainly in the form of Web-based, text and email and increasingly mobile communications, have grown considerably, often at the expense of telephone and mail facilities.

- Online advertising expenditure is growing faster than any other sector in the marketing communications industry. Interactive online ads are used to create brand awareness and brand values, and to provoke particular behaviours. This is essentially direct response advertising. Banners, pop-ups, microsites, rich media ads, online video, and gaming are some of the more mainstream forms of online advertising.

- Organisations use incentive-based online promotions because they are capable of delivering two main sources of value. First, they engage customers, providing them with a reason to stay on a site or return to it more frequently than they might otherwise have done. Second, because interactive promotions require customers to opt-in and give permission, they deliver huge amounts of pertinent data about customers, potential customers and the market, without too much effort on the part of the customer or the organisation.

- Group-based discount schemes have become popular in recent years, typified by the rise of Groupon.

- Developments in digital media have been instrumental in assisting public relations move from a predominantly one-way model of communication to an interactive model.

- Public relations practice involves contacting journalists, broadcasters, and bloggers in the hope of gaining media placements to disseminate news content. 'Media catching' reverses this so that now some journalists contact practitioners seeking specific material for stories, articles, blogs, and websites where there are pressing deadlines.

- Indirectly digital technology has been of great importance to the way organisations manage their sales force and their digital marketing programmes. Sales force automation involves the application of information technology to support the sales function.

- Customer relationship management systems (CRM) incorporate technologies and systems that enable all employees who have an interface with customers to have real-time, up-to-date information in order to deliver high levels of customer service.

- Interactive direct marketing underpins the majority of communication activities in the online environment. Direct marketing is a primary online communications tool because it can be used interactively to generate both transactional- and relational-based responses within a target audience.

- Direct marketing activities should be based on database technologies that target the right audience, shape the creative, are deliverable through appropriate channels and can measure responses. Email and viral marketing are primary elements used as part of direct marketing.

- Multichannel or cross-channel campaigns use tools and media in various combinations in order to provide superior levels of customer service. This is partly a result of research that shows that the effectiveness of the media increase considerably when they are used in combination.

- The IPA's analysis finds that in attempting to achieve business goals (profit, market share etc), diminishing returns set in once the number of advertising media used reaches three. When interactive and Web channels, plus direct marketing, sales promotion and public relations are included in the mix, there does not appear to be a limit, apart from budget, to achieve both business and communication effects.

# Review questions

1. Define interactive marketing communications and explain its key characteristics.
2. What might go wrong with the use of interactive marketing communications?
3. Identify reasons why organisations use online advertising. How did the Salvation Army use online advertising?
4. Describe three types of online ad formats.
5. What are the differences between in-game advertising and advergame advertising?
6. How do group discount schemes, such as Groupon, work?
7. Identify the two main types of value derived by organisations when using sales promotions online.
8. To what extent is online public relations just online advertising?
9. Explain the concept 'media catching'.
10. According to the IPA, multichannel advertising campaigns are most effective when there are 3, 4 or 5 media. Why is this?

# References

Advertising Association (2012) Advertising: Expenditure Report 2011, retrieved 24 April 2012 from http://expenditurereport.warc.com/.

Ang, L. and Buttle, F.A. (2003) ROI on CRM: a customer journey approach, *CRM Today*, retrieved 16 May 2011 from www.crm2day.com/library/EpFlupuEZVRmkpZCHM.php.

Anon (2011) Case Study: DDC sees significant ROI after investment in Nectar Business loyalty scheme, retrieved 2 May 2012 from http://www.b2bmarketing.net/knowledgebank/crm-marketing/case-studies/case-study-ddc-sees-significant-roi-after-investment-nectar.

Avlonitis, G.J. and Karayanni, D. (2000) The impact of Internet use on business-to-business marketing, *Industrial Marketing Management*, 29, 441–59.

Barrand, D. (2004) Promoting change, *Marketing*, 6 October, 43–5.

Binet, L. and Field, P. (2007) *Marketing in an era of accountability*, Henley: IPA-WARC.

Boujena, O., Johnston, W.J., and Merunka, D.R. (2009) The benefits of sales force automation: a customer's perspective, *Journal of Personal Selling & Sales Management*, XXIX, 2 (Spring), 137–50.

Briggs, R. and Hollis, N. (1997) Advertising on the web: is there response before click-through? *Journal of Advertising Research*, (March/April), 33–45.

Briggs, R., Krishnan, R. and Borin, N. (2005) Integrated Multichannel Communication Strategies: Evaluating the Return on Marketing Objectives – The Case of the 2004 Ford F-150 Launch, *Journal of Interactive Marketing* 19, 3, 81–90.

Broadbent, T. (2011) Channel Planning: effectiveness lies in channel integration, *Admap* (January), retrieved 17 May from www.warc.com/Content/ContentViewer.aspx?MasterContentRef=fbf731f8-4087-449f-a232-0f69f2863b17&q=direct+marketing.

Burns, K.S. (2008) A historical examination of the development of social media and its application to the public relations industry. Paper presented the International Communication Association conference, Montreal (May).

Callison, C. (2003) Media relations and the Internet: How Fortune 500 company websites assist journalists in news gathering, *Public Relations Review*, 29, 29–41.

Cartellieri, C., Parsons, A., Rao, V. and Zeisser, M. (1997) The real impact of Internet advertising, *McKinsey Quarterly*, 3, 44–63.

Cauberghe, V. and de Pelsmacker, P. (2010) Advergames: The Impact of Brand Prominence and Game Repetition on Brand Responses, *Journal of Advertising*, 39, 1 (Spring), 5–18.

Chaffey, D., Ellis-Chadwick, F., Johnston, K. and Meyer, R. (2006) *Internet Marketing*, 3rd edn, Harlow: Pearson.

Chambers, J. (2006) The Sponsored Avatar: Examining the Present Reality and Future Possibilities of Advertising in Digital Games, retrieved 16 May 2011 from http://ir.lib.sfu.ca/retrieve/1630/8878e0c3d9c0a0bc67670b8d9a0f.doc.

Chaney, I.M., Lin, K.H. and Chaney, J. (2004) The Effects of Billboards Within the Gaming Environment, *Journal of Interactive Advertising*, 5 (Fall).

Chang, Y., Yan, J., Zhang, J. and Luo, J. (2010) Online in-game advertising effect: examining the influence of a match between games and advertising, *Journal of Interactive Advertising*, 11, 1 (Fall), 63–73.

Clarke, V. (2012) Campaign of the Month: Modern makeover for Dulux Decorator Centres, *B2B Marketing*, April, p. 10.

Cravens, D.W., Ingram, T.N. and LaForge, R.W. (1991) Evaluating multiple channel strategies, *Journal of Business and Industrial Marketing*, 6, 3/4, 37–48.

Davidson, D. (2007) Advertisers back Facebook move, *Brand Republic*, 9 August 2007, retrieved 13 August 2007 from http://www.brandrepublic.com/News/730452/Advertisers-back-Facebook-move/.

Deighton, J. and Grayson, K. (1995) Marketing and seduction: building exchange relationships by managing social consensus, *Journal of Consumer Research*, 21(4), 660–76.

Dichter, E. (1966) How word-of-mouth advertising works, *Harvard Business Review*, 44 (November/December), 147–66.

Esrock, S.L. and Leichty, G.B. (1999) Corporate World Wide Web pages: Serving the news media and other publics, *Journalism & Mass Communication Quarterly*, 76, 456–67.

Evans, D.S. (2009) The Online Advertising Industry: Economics, Evolution, and Privacy, *Journal of Economic Perspectives*, 23(3) Summer, 37–60.

Gay, R., Charlesworth, A. and Esen, R. (2007) *Online Marketing: A Customer-Led Approach*. Oxford: Oxford University Press.

Godfrey, A., Seiders, K. and Voss, G.B. (2011) Enough Is Enough! The Fine Line in Executing Multichannel Relational Communication, *Journal of Marketing*, 75 (July), 94–109.

Goldsmith, R.E. and Lafferty, B.A. (2002) Consumer response to web-sites and their influence on advertising effectiveness, *Internet Research: Electronic Networking Applications and Policy*, 12, 4, 318–28.

Goodman, M. (2007) Advertising and Games: 2007 In-Game Advertising Forecast, Yankee Group, 6 July, retrieved 2 May 2012 from http://www.yankeegroup.com/ResearchDocument.do?id=16395#_Toc171417702.

Grey Group (2011) Everybody hurts when you speed, *Case Studies on Warc*, retrieved 18 May 2011 from www.warc.com/Content/ContentViewer.aspx?MasterContentRef=1092174d-9e64-495d-862b-cf5726923dc2&q=microsites.

Hoey, C. (1998) Maximizing the effectiveness of web based marketing communications, *Marketing Intelligence and Planning*, 16, 1, 31–7.

Holahan, C. (2006) Up next: online video ad boom? *Business Week*, 7 November, retrieved 26 October 2007 from www.businessweek.com/technology/content/nov2006/tc20061106_523381.htm.

IAB PwC (2011) Adspend Study 2010, Internet Advertising Bureau, retrieved 18 May 2011 from www.iabuk.net/en/1/home.

Lewis, B. and Porter, L. (2010) In-Game Advertising Effects: Examining Player Perceptions of Advertising Schema Congruity in a Massively Multiplayer Online Role-Playing Game, *Journal of Interactive Advertising*, 10, 2, 46–60.

Liu, Y. and Shrum, L.J. (2005) Rethinking interactivity, in *Advertising, Promotion and New Media* (eds M.R. Stafford and R.J. Faber), New York: M.E. Sharpe, 103–24.

Lockenby, J.D. (2005) The interaction of traditional and new media, in *Advertising, Promotion and New Media* (eds M.R. Stafford and R.J. Faber), New York: M.E. Sharpe, 13.

Lutz, J., Mackensie, S.B. and Belch, G.E. (1983) Attitude toward the ad as a mediator of advertising effectiveness, *Advances in Consumer Research*, X. Ann Arbor, MI: Association for Consumer Research.

McCormick, A. (2011) Display is dead, *Revolution*, May, 20–25.

McCoy, S., Everard, A., Polak, P. and Galletta, D.F. (2007) The effects of online advertising, *Communications of the ACM*, 50, 3 (May), 84–8.

MediaMind (2012) Five digital ad formats that make a difference for your brand, brandrepublic.com, 2 March, retrieved 3 May 2012 from http://www.brandrepublic.com/research/1119390/Five-digital-ad-formats-difference-brand/?DCMP=ILC-SEARCH.

Moore, M. (2012) Apple 'attacking problems' at its factories in China, The *Telegraph*, 27 January 2012, retrieved 3 February 2012 from www.telegraph.co.uk/technology/apple/9043924/Apple-attacking-problems-at-its-factories-in-China.html.

Morowitz, V.G. and Schmittlein, D.C. (1998) Testing new direct marketing offerings: the interplay of management judgement and statistical models, *Management Science*, 44(5), 610–28.

Murphy, D. (2007) Off the page, on to the web, *The Marketer*, (October), 31–3.

Myers, J.B., Pickersgill, A.D. and Metre van, E.S. (2004) Steering customers to the right channels, *McKinsey Quarterly*, 4, 16 November. Retrieved 5 September 2012 from www.mckinsey.com/practices/marketing/ourknowledge/pdf/Steering_customers_to_the_right_channel.pdf.

Payne, A. and Frow, P. (2004) The role of multichannel integration in customer relationship management, *Industrial Marketing Management*, 33, 6 (August), 527–38.

Schneider, L.-P. and Cornwell, B.B. (2005) Cashing in Crashes via Brand Placement in Computer Games, *International Journal of Advertising*, 24, 3, 321–43.

Schwarz, J. (2005) R-U-GAME? *iMedia Connection*, retrieved 16 May 2011 from www.imediaconnection.com/content/5354.asp.

Snoddy, R. (2007) A potent brain wave for newspapers, *Marketing*, 2 May, 18.

Thomas, J.S. and Sullivan, U.Y. (2005) Managing Marketing Communications with Multichannel Customers, *Journal of Marketing*, 69 (October), 239–51.

Tovey, A. (2012) Groupon ordered to clean up practices by OFT, The *Telegraph*, 16 March 2012, retrieved 19 March 2012 from http://www.telegraph.co.uk/finance/newsbysector/retailandconsumer/9148108/Groupon-ordered-to-clean-up-practices-by-OFT.html.

Turnbull, J. (2010) Family plea for drivers to slow down, *Herald Sun*, 11 July retrieved 18 May 2011 from http://www.heraldsun.com.au/news/family-plea-for-drivers-to-slow-down/story-e6frf7jo-1225890374628.

Valos, M.J. (2009) Structure, people and process challenges of multichannel marketing: Insights from marketers, *Journal of Database Marketing & Customer Strategy Management*, 16, 197–206.

Vlasic, G. and Kesic, T. (2007) Analysis of customers' attitudes toward interactivity and relationship personalization as contemporary developments in interactive marketing communications, *Journal of Marketing Communications*, 13, 2 (June), 109–29.

Wakolbinger, L.M., Denk, M. and Oberecker, K. (2009) Effectiveness of combining online and print advertising, *Journal of Advertising Research*, 49(3) (September), 360–72.

Warner (2011) Display is dead, *Revolution*, May, 20–25.

Waters, R.D., Tindall, N.T.J. and Morton, T.S. (2010) Media Catching and the Journalist–Public Relations Practitioner Relationship: How Social Media are Changing the Practice of Media Relations, *Journal of Public Relations Research*, 22, 3, 241–64.

Yang, M., Roskos-Ewoldsen, D.R., Dinu, L. and Arpen, L.M. (2006) The Effectiveness of In-Game Advertising: Comparing College Students' Explicit and Implicit Memory for Brand Names, *Journal of Advertising*, 35, 4, 143–52.

# Chapter 24

# Media planning: delivering the message

Media planning is essentially a selection and scheduling exercise. The selection concerns the choice of media vehicles to carry messages on behalf of the advertiser. With media fragmentation, audiences are switching between media with greater regularity, which impacts on media scheduling. Decisions regarding the number of occasions, timing and duration that a message is exposed, in the selected vehicles, to the target audience have become increasingly critical.

In addition, ideas about owned and earned media, and social media and search in particular, have changed the way media are understood by marketers and used by consumers. This impacts on the way in which media selection has changed and how it should be managed.

## Aims and learning objectives

The aims of this chapter are to introduce the fundamental elements of media planning, and to set out some of the issues facing media planners.

The learning objectives of this chapter are to:

1. explain the role of the media planner and highlight the impact of media and audience fragmentation;

2. consider various theories concerning the content of different media and related media switching behaviours;

3. examine the key concepts used in media selection: reach and cover, frequency, duplication, rating points and CPT;

4. appreciate the concept of repetition and the debate concerning effective frequency and recency planning;

5. understand the concepts of effectiveness and efficiency when applied to media selection decisions;

6. introduce media source effects as an important factor in the selection and timing of advertising in magazines and television programmes;

7. explore the different ways in which advertisements can be managed and scheduled.

# Minicase

## Which?

Which? is the UK's leading consumer organisation, funded entirely by its members' subscriptions. The organisation offers reviews of product and service sectors, providing advice on how consumers can obtain best value. This advice is truly independent and impartial and is provided in a straightforward and easy to understand way. All product reviews are based on rigorous and completely independent research. Advice and reviews are available via magazines, websites, and advice lines.

Up until 2005 subscribers were recruited only via a prize draw mechanic, based on 5 million direct mailings sent each year. However, response rates, ROIs and subscriber numbers had been falling steadily. Reliance on direct mail to a small group of prospects had caused the brand to disappear from public view.

Research highlighted that the magazine was not seen as contemporary and was thought to review mostly white goods. Potential subscribers thought they could either live without the information or find it elsewhere.

In order to reverse the long-term decline in new members a new strategy was required. Three core tasks were established.

- Get consumers who knew the Which? brand but thought it wasn't relevant to them to reappraise it.

- Replace the prize draw message with brand-led messages.
- Maintain marketing returns on investment.

To achieve these outcomes research was undertaken. This found that the two key variables concerning potential Which? subscribers were:

- a tendency to research a product/service before making a purchase
- a lack of confidence in one's own research abilities.

The next stage involved developing a new consumer proposition. At the heart of Which?'s offer are the 'best buy' guides, listing the product/service that offers best value for the consumer. But this was our crown jewel and we didn't want to give it away. So we created a new set of information – 'How to get the most out of products and services guides' – a series of free guides providing independent and impartial advice in areas of mass consumer confusion – e.g. changes in technology. See Exhibit 24.1 for some of the other titles.

Which? had been a heavy user of direct mail but the new strategy needed a new media mix. The new mix needed to reach our new target audience when they were considering purchasing a new product/service.

| Exhibit 24.1 | **Some of the new product offerings from Which?** |
| | *Source*: Which? |

In addition, it needed to reach more people than direct mail was able to do and so put Which? back in the public eye.

In order to catch prospects when they were in consideration mode, 'broadcast' media, DRTV, newspaper and inserts, were essential. Each media vehicle was chosen on its efficiency at reaching our target audiences, its efficiency in generating response, and its cost per contact and thus resultant cost per subscriber.

Television formed a vital role within this new media mix. Our key objective at this stage was to maximise reach against an audience of researchers, who were in the initial stages of a research project at the time. This direct response activity essentially harvested those consumers who were already in the market, and for whom a simple reminder of the Which? offering was sufficient.

Television has a unique advantage over press and inserts. That advantage derives from its high reach, and high dwell time. Even relatively heavy weights of DRTV activity are still effective, as the schedule is still building cover and reaching new people. Weights of press and insert activity are quickly limited as frequency rather than cover builds.

While this initial activity recruited many new researchers/subscribers, there remained a hard core rump of our audience whose needs were not met by our current messaging. It was necessary therefore to dispel the perception that Which? was an old-fashioned brand, and to overcome the rational objection that Which? just tests washing machines.

To help change the image a new message was required. This centred on the range and modernity of the products and services tested, and that the tests are unrivalled in terms of thoroughness. However, the media planning had to change as well. For DRTV the goal was to maximise cover, and limit frequency. We ran lowish-weight, continual drip activity, with programming selected for lower attention to view, so as to maximise immediate response.

For TV-based brand image work we maximised cover again, but we also focused on frequency. Our initial objective was to maximise 4+ frequency, but this evolved as our understanding of the campaign dynamics built. We selected very different airtime, seeking high attention to view and dwell time programming for our core audiences. We were seeking to impart a long-term attitudinal change, and not maximise immediate behaviour change.

Further research uncovered the journey that consumers experience from first contemplating the need to purchase goods or services, through active research at category and product level, to finally arriving at price and supplier choices. We used this journey to evolve our media planning, with very significant results. This is set out at Figure 24.1.

They described a journey that begins with large numbers of consumers contemplating a purchase.

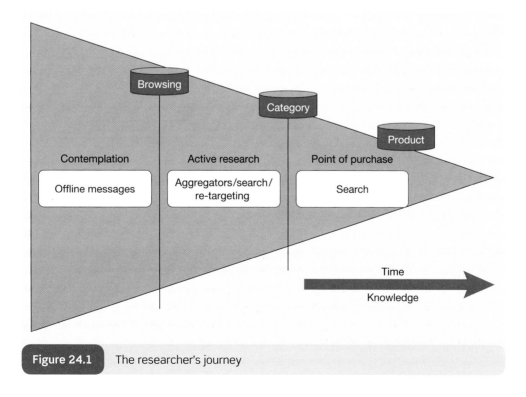

**Figure 24.1**   The researcher's journey

They haven't taken any research action at this stage, and this is when an emotional DRTV message is potentially most effective, nudging them into the start of their research. From contemplation our target consumers move to active research: investigating at the product or service sector level.

This is now where rational messaging is more important. Historically this would have been the sole domain of print media, newspapers and magazines, but online research is increasingly important for the population as a whole, and the sole channel for many groups. Press and insert advertising are effective here, but especially so search, affiliates and display activity on aggregator sites.

We then experienced another breakthrough. Historically we had optimised each media channel on a standalone basis, typically maximising one plus cover for each channel on a monthly basis. In any one month around 60 per cent of our target audience saw our TV, our print media and our search and 84 per cent saw at least one of our messages. But only a very small number saw at least one TV, print and search message. Given that consumers use all three channels, it made sense to expose them to messages from all

of them during their journey. So, we re-planned our media schedules to maximise the number of our target audience seeing at least one TV, print and search message within a month. The results were dramatic – 44 per cent more response, and a 51 per cent improvement to our five-year ROI.

In six years Which? completely transformed its marketing activity, its media planning and business results. The move from direct mail, to a mixed brand uplift and direct response strategy, and then to one which required maximising the number of our target audience who see a message in each of our major channels: TV, print and search complemented our research activities. Each stage of media planning had a significant impact on results. Subscription numbers rose from 831,000 to more than 1,330,000 in June 2011. Our cost of acquiring a new subscriber fell by 44 per cent and our true return on investment rose from 8 per cent to an eye-watering 176 per cent.

*This case was written by Mike Colling of Mike Colling & Company Limited. Permission to use the material was kindly given by Which?*

| Exhibit 24.2 | **Mike Colling & Company and Which? logos** |
| --- | --- |
| | *Source*: Mike Colling & Company Limited and Which? |

# Introduction

Once a message has been created and agreed, a media plan should be determined. The Which? minicase demonstrates how devising an optimum route for the delivery of a message to the target audience is an integral part of effective marketing communications. Media planning is normally undertaken by specialists, either as part of a full-service advertising agency or as a media independent whose primary function is to buy air time or space from media owners (e.g. television contractors or magazine publishers) on behalf of their clients, the advertisers. This traditional role has changed since the mid 1990s, and many media independents now provide consultancy services, particularly at the strategic level, plus planning and media research and auditing services.

Media departments are responsible for two main functions. These are to 'plan' and to 'buy' time and space in appropriate media vehicles. There is a third task – to monitor a media schedule once it has been bought – but this is a function of buying. Planners define the target audience and choose the type of medium. Buyers choose programmes, frequencies, spots and distribution and assemble a multichannel schedule (Armstrong, 1993). In the past the media planner has been pre-eminent, but the role of the buyer is changing. Some feel the role of the buyer is in the ascendancy, but there are others who feel that the role is capable of increased automation and that many software packages already fulfil many functions of the media buyer. Such a move has implications for the type of person recruited. In the United States, for example, many semi-skilled people have been recruited on a part-time basis to do many parts of the traditional media planner's job.

This chapter is concerned with the various issues associated with the selection, optimisation and scheduling of media. However, ideas about what constitutes media have changed considerably in recent years (see Chapter 20) and the emergence of POEM reflects the increasing prevalence of owned and earned media, in addition to paid-for media. Much of the first part of this chapter is concerned with the management of paid media. Issues relating to the incorporation and management of owned and earned media are considered later in the chapter.

# Media planning and the media mix

As mentioned earlier, media planning is essentially a selection and scheduling exercise. The selection refers to the choice of paid media vehicles to carry the message on behalf of the advertiser. Scheduling refers to the number of occasions, timing and duration that a message is exposed, in the selected vehicles, to the target audience. However, there are several factors that complicate these seemingly straightforward tasks. First, the variety of available media is huge and increasing rapidly. This is referred to as *media fragmentation*. Second, the characteristics of the target audience are changing equally quickly. This is referred to as *audience fragmentation*. Both these fragmentation issues are discussed later in this chapter. The job of the media planner is complicated by one further element: money. Clients have restricted financial resources and require the media planner to create a schedule that delivers their messages not only effectively but also efficiently, which means within the parameters of the available budget.

The task of the media planner, therefore, is to deliver advertising messages through a selection of media that match the viewing, reading or search habits of the target audience at the lowest possible cost. In order for these tasks to be accomplished, three sets of decisions need to be made about the choice of media, vehicles and schedules.

Decisions about the choice of media are complex. While choosing a single one is reasonably straightforward, choosing media in combination and attempting to generate synergistic effects is far from easy. Advances in technology have made media planning a much faster, more accurate process, one that is now more flexible and capable of adjusting to fast-changing market conditions.

One of the key tasks of the media planner is to decide which combination of vehicles should be selected to carry the message to the target audience. In addition, McLuhan (1966) said that the medium is the message: that is, the choice of medium (or vehicle) says something about

**Table 24.1**    A summary of media characteristics

| Type of paid media | Strengths | Weaknesses |
|---|---|---|
| **Print** | | |
| **Newspapers** | Wide reach<br>High coverage<br>Low costs<br>Very flexible<br>Short lead times<br>Speed of consumption controlled by reader | Short lifespan<br>Advertisements get little exposure<br>Relatively poor reproduction, gives poor impact<br>Low attention-getting properties |
| **Magazines** | High-quality reproduction that allows high impact<br>Specific and specialised target audiences<br>High readership levels<br>Longevity<br>High levels of information can be delivered | Long lead times<br>Visual dimension only<br>Slow build-up of impact<br>Moderate costs |
| **Television** | Flexible format, uses sight, movement and sound<br>High prestige<br>High reach<br>Mass coverage<br>Low relative cost, so very efficient | High level of repetition necessary<br>Short message life<br>High absolute costs<br>Clutter<br>Increasing level of fragmentation (potentially) |
| **Radio** | Selective audience, e.g. local<br>Low costs (absolute, relative and production)<br>Flexible<br>Can involve listeners | Lacks impact<br>Audio dimension only<br>Difficult to get audience attention<br>Low prestige |
| **Outdoor** | High reach<br>High frequency<br>Low relative costs<br>Good coverage as a support medium<br>Location-oriented | Poor image (but improving)<br>Long production time<br>Difficult to measure |
| **Digital media** | High level of interaction<br>Immediate response possible<br>Tight targeting<br>Low absolute and relative costs<br>Flexible and easy to update<br>Measurable | Segment-specific<br>Slow development of infrastructure<br>High user set-up costs<br>Transaction security issues |
| **Transport** | High length of exposure<br>Low costs<br>Local orientation | Poor coverage<br>Segment specific (travellers)<br>Clutter |
| **In-store POP** | High attention-getting properties<br>Persuasive<br>Low costs<br>Flexible | Segment-specific (shoppers)<br>Prone to damage and confusion<br>Clutter |

the brand and the message itself. He went on to say that the medium is the *massage*, as each medium massages the recipient in different ways and so contributes to learning in different ways. For example, Krugman (1965) hypothesised that television advertising washes over individuals. He said that viewers, rather than participate actively with television advertisements, allow learning to occur passively. In contrast, magazine advertising requires active participation if learning is to occur. Today, online and interactive advertising actively promotes involvement and participation.

The various media depicted in Table 24.1 have wide-ranging characteristics. These, and the characteristics of the target audience, should be considered when deciding on the optimal media mix. It should be clear that simply deciding on which media to use is fraught with difficulties, let alone deciding on the optimal combination – how much of each media should be used – before even considering the cost implications.

# Media switching behaviour

The range of media has grown dramatically in the past 30 years and is continuing to grow as technology, in particular, advances. However, even before digital media started to change the media landscape, researchers had recognised that different media have different capabilities and that media were not completely interchangeable. In other words, different tasks can be accomplished more effectively using particular media. This implies that there is a spectrum of media depending on the content they carry.

Daft and Lengel (1984) were the first to propose that this content issue concerned the richness of the information conveyed through each medium. As a result, the tasks facing managers should be considered according to the degree of fit with the most appropriate media based on the richness of the information. Communication media help resolve ambiguity and facilitate understanding in different ways and to different degrees. They established that there were four main criteria that determined what level of richness a medium possessed:

- the availability of instant feedback;
- the capacity to transmit multiple cues;
- the use of natural language;
- the degree of personal focus.

Media richness theory (MRT) holds that there is a hierarchy or spectrum of media ranging from personal or face-to-face encounters as the richest media through to single sheets of text-based information as lean media at the other end. Rich media facilitate feedback, dialogue iteration and an expression of personal cues such as tone of voice, body language and eye contact that, in turn, help establish a personal connection. In descending order of richness the other media are telephone, email, letter, note, memo, special report, fliers and bulletins. At this end of the richness scale numeric and formal written communication is slow, often visually limited and impersonal.

MRT suggests that rich media reduce ambiguity more effectively than others, but are more resource-intensive than lean media. If rich media allow for more complex and difficult communications, then lean media are more cost-effective for simple or routine communications. McGrath and Hollingshead (1993) developed a matrix showing the levels of richness required to perform certain tasks successfully and efficiently. Their media richness grid identifies the level of fit between the information richness requirements of the tasks and the information richness capacity of the media (see Table 24.2).

Social influence theory (SIT) was developed by Fulk et al. (1990). This is intended to complement MRT as it also assumes that the relatively objective features of media do influence

**Table 24.2**    A media richness grid

| | Computer text systems | Audio systems | Video systems | Face-to-face communication |
|---|---|---|---|---|
| Generating ideas and plans | Good fit | Marginal fit: medium too resource-intense | Poor fit: medium too resource-intense | Poor fit: medium too resource-intense |
| Choosing correct answer: intellective tasks | Marginal fit: medium too constrained | Good fit | Good fit | Poor fit: medium too resource-intense |
| Choosing preferred answer: judgement tasks | Poor fit: medium too constrained | Good fit | Good fit | Marginal fit: medium too resource-intense |
| Negotiating conflicts of interest | Poor fit: medium too constrained | Poor fit: medium too constrained | Marginal fit: medium too constrained | Good fit |

*Source*: Adapted from McGrath and Hollingshead (1993).

**Table 24.3**    Factors influencing the choice of technology

| Factor | Explanation |
|---|---|
| Experience and familiarity | With virtual operations, the amount of experience using a particular interactive medium |
| Permanence | The degree to which users need an historical record of team interactions or decisions |
| Symbolic meaning | The subjective meanings attached to the use of a particular medium |
| Time constraints | The amount of time available to the user to use a medium in order to execute their tasks |
| Access to technology and/or support | The number of and access to available media influences media choice |

*Source*: Duarte and Snyder (2001).

how individuals perceive and use media. However, these researchers argue that SIT has a strong social orientation because different media properties (such as ability to transmit richness) are subjective and are influenced by attitudes, statements and the behaviour of others. This approach recognises that members of groups influence other people in terms of their perceptions of different media. The main difference between MRT and SIT is that MRT identifies rich media as inefficient for simple or routine communication whereas SIT suggests rich media can be just as appropriate for simple messages as it is for ambiguous communication.

A third approach, the technology acceptance model (TAM) relates to the utility and convenience a medium offers. The perceived usefulness and perceived ease of use are regarded as the main issues that are considered when selecting media (King and Xia, 1997). Perceived usefulness refers to the user's subjective assessment that using a specific computer application will improve their job performance. Perceived ease of use addresses the degree to which a user expects the identified application to be free of effort.

## Influential factors for media selection

In addition to these richness, social and utility issues of media selection, other factors are also important. Duarte and Snyder (2001) propose a list of factors influencing technology selection (see Table 24.3).

## Switching behaviour

It is clear that different media have different properties and that people switch between media according to their tasks, social environment, familiarity and access to different media. What is important, therefore, is to understand switching behaviour and the decision-making process that people use. Decisions are made through *rational* and *systematic* processes or alternatively there are unaccountable factors that 'bound' decision-making. The classic, eight-stage rational–linear decision-making model (situation analysis, objectives setting, through to choosing and evaluating alternatives, making the decisions, evaluation and consequences) is well known and its criticisms well documented. Simon (1972, 1987) showed that people make decisions within 'bounded rationality', performing limited searches and accepting the first acceptable alternative, what is regarded as 'satisficing behaviour'.

Srinavasan (1996) developed a satisfaction–loyalty curve whereby an individual's level of satisfaction is the biggest determinant of their switching behaviour. As their satisfaction increases, so does loyalty, and the reverse is equally true. For each person there is a point at which decreasing satisfaction intersects with the decreasing loyalty levels. This is the point at which switching occurs and the current brand is abandoned in favour of another.

Keaveney (1995) distinguishes between involuntary, simple and complex switching behaviours. Involuntary switching may be due to factors beyond an individual consumer's control (e.g. business liquidated), whereas simple switching is characterised by individual events where consumers can identify a single incident or factor causing the switch: for example, a price change. Complex switching behaviour occurs when a customer's loyalty has decreased due to a variety of factors, which might include core product failure, price changes and poor service. It should be noted that switching is very often a routine behaviour influenced by the expectations of the context in which the media decision is made. For example, when sending text-based documents to team members, most people would select email and use file attachments.

As a final comment on media switching behaviour, it is useful to return to MRT and to consider the reasons why individuals move towards rich or lean media. These are set out in Table 24.4. Therefore, movement between media is based on a range of criteria and will vary according to the context and individual skills and preferences.

**Table 24.4** Reasons for moving to richer or leaner media

| Movement | Reasons |
|---|---|
| Towards a richer medium | Message complexity |
| | Increased comfort |
| | Time pressure |
| | Timely discussion required |
| | Need to rest from computer-based medium |
| Towards a leaner medium | Desire for written record |
| | Reducing cost |
| | Convenience (of being asynchronous or distant) |
| | Share individual written work (attachment) |
| | External pressure or requirement |

# Vehicle selection

The discussion so far has explored unpaid media, and increasingly the Internet and the use of email communications fit this range. However, organisations need to use media that are owned by others in order to convey their messages. These paid-for media have particular characteristics and ability to deliver rich or lean content. The discussion now moves on to consider different paid-for media and the ways in which organisations develop a media mix to meet their communications needs.

Increasingly, organisations are required to prove how advertising adds value to the bottom line. While this is not a new question, it is one that is being asked more often and in such a way that answers are required. As advertisers attempt to demonstrate effectiveness, contribution and return on investment, senior managers are increasingly haunted by questions concerning the choice of media, how much should be spent on message delivery and how financial resources are to be allocated in a multichannel environment.

---

### Viewpoint 24.1    Media vehicles for 'You & Us'

When UBS launched their 'You & Us' global campaign, advertising played an important role in communicating what UBS stand for to their clients. The aim was to help support their efforts to build stronger client relationships, and help them to make more confident financial decisions, hence the phrase 'You & Us'. With television and print their aim was to increase relevance in specific markets. Regional variations are also being created.

The television spot, titled 'Everywhere', emphasises the global/personal dimension and follows meetings between two people that occur in interesting, unusual locations around the world. This speaks of the benefits that accrue from being able to access the resources of a global financial firm through a strong, personal relationship.

The advertising focuses on two key themes: globality and understanding. Both strands of communication support the core message of proactively finding solutions to our customers' needs, but each does so in a slightly different way that makes the overall message accessible.

The print advertising reflects the visual tones and style used in the television work, and places an increased graphic emphasis on 'You & Us'. Critically, the new press ads were designed to enable the reader to project themselves into the situation depicted, thus fostering empathy.

In order to deliver these messages a media plan was established. This set out the specific types of media the campaign was to use and where possible certain types of media and specific vehicles. One of the first decisions was whether television, a class of media, had a role to play. Once the answer was yes, particular television channels in the target countries, such as the USA, UK, Germany, France, Italy and in Asia were selected. This was then followed by the selection of print and outdoor media and particular vehicles were then determined.

**Question:**   Why do you believe UBS used television in order to reach high net worth individuals and businesses?

**Task:**       Visit the site www.ubs.com and follow the links through 'About Us' and then 'You & Us'. View the campaign detail and see the television and print ads. Make notes on what impresses you and what you might have done differently.

---

Management's attention towards media decision-making has increased as the media have become more visible and significantly more important. For example, Brech (1999) reports that companies need to make choices about the split between the Internet, mass media, digital TV, outdoor and print media. Companies such as BT, IKEA and ScottishPower need to use media strategically in order that they reach the right audience, in the right context, at the right time and at an acceptable cost. To help organisations achieve these goals a variety of approaches have been adopted. For example, New PHD is an agency retained by BT to advise about strategic (media) planning and budget allocation. However, ZenithOptimedia implements decisions for press and radio and the Allmond Partnership manages television and cinema, while Outdoor Connections handles poster-buying. This division provides objectivity, reduces partisan approaches and can deliver more effective media plans. Cost per response is certainly one way of measuring effectiveness, but the communication impact, or share of mind, is also important. There has also been a move away from volume of media to one where media decisions are made by looking at media in the context of the brand's total communications.

A further problem facing clients and media agencies concerns the quality of the integrated media experience. For a long time, some organisations have used above-the-line media to reach audiences of 20 million people. With fragmented media it is difficult to generate consistent levels and types of impact. Increasingly, media management is being outsourced so there are fewer in-house areas of expertise. All this means that, to forge appropriate solutions, advertisers and media agencies need to work closely together so that the relationship becomes so close that it acts more as an extension to the marketing department. Decisions regarding which vehicles are to carry an advertiser's message depend on an understanding of a number of concepts: reach and coverage, frequency, gross rating points, effective frequency, efficiency and media source effects.

# Media planning concepts

There are several fundamental concepts that underpin the way in which traditional media should be selected and included in the media plan. These are reach, frequency, gross rating points, duplication and effective frequency.

## Reach and coverage

Reach refers to the percentage of the target audience exposed to a message at least once during the relevant time period. Where 80 per cent of the target audience has been exposed to a message, the figure is expressed as an '80 reach'.

*Coverage*, a term often used for reach, should not be confused or used in place of reach. Coverage refers to the size of a potential audience that might be exposed to a particular media vehicle. For media planners, therefore, coverage (the size of the target audience) is very important. Reach will always be lower than coverage, as it is impossible to reach 100 per cent of a target population (the universe).

Building reach within a target audience is relatively easy, as the planner needs to select a range of different media vehicles. This will enable different people in the target audience to have an opportunity to see the media vehicle. However, there will come a point when it becomes more difficult to reach people who have not been exposed. As more vehicles are added, so repetition levels (the number of people who have seen the advertisement more than once) also increase.

## Frequency

Frequency refers to the number of times a member of the target audience is exposed to a media vehicle (not the advertisement) during the relevant time period. It has been stated that targets must be exposed to the media vehicle, but to say that a target has seen an advertisement simply because they have been exposed to the vehicle is incorrect. For example, certain viewers hop around the channels as a commercial break starts. This has been referred to as 'channel grazing' by Lloyd and Clancy (1991). Individuals have different capacities to learn and to forget, and how much of a magazine does a reader have to consume to be counted as having read an advertisement? These questions are still largely unanswered, so media planners have adopted an easier and more consistent measure – opportunities to see (OTS).

This is an important point. The stated frequency level in any media plan will always be greater than the advertisement exposure rate. The term 'OTS' is used to express the reach of a media vehicle rather than the actual exposure of an advertisement. However, a high OTS could be generated by one of two different events. First, a large number of the target audience are exposed once (high reach) or second, a small number are exposed several times (high frequency).

This then raises the first major issue. As all campaigns are restricted by time and budget limitations, advertisers have to trade off reach against frequency. It is impossible to maximise both elements within a fixed budget and set period of time.

To launch a new product, it has been established that a wide number of people within the target audience need to become aware of the product's existence and its salient attributes or benefits. This means that reach is important but, as an increasing number of people become aware, so more of them become exposed a second, third or fourth time, perhaps to different vehicles. At the outset, frequency is low and reach high, but as a campaign progresses so reach slows and frequency develops. Reach and frequency are inversely related within any period of time, and media planners must know the objective of a campaign: is it to build reach or develop frequency?

---

### Scholars' paper 24.1 — Digital says no to reach and frequency

**Cheong, Y., De Gregorio, F., and Kim, K. (2011) The Power of Reach and Frequency In the Age of Digital Advertising: Offline and Online Media Demand Different Metrics,** *Journal of Advertising Research*, 50(4), December, 403–15.

This empirical paper explored the use of reach and frequency concepts. The findings are that the concepts are still used to evaluate offline media schedules. However the use and practicality in online contexts is more limited, with agencies using qualitative and cost-based measures.

---

## Gross rating point

To decide whether reach or frequency is the focus of the campaign objective, a more precise understanding of the levels of reach and frequency is required. The term *gross rating point* is used to express the relationship between these two concepts. GRPs are a measure of the total number of exposures (OTS) generated within a particular period of time. The calculation itself is simply reach × frequency:

*reach × frequency = gross rating point*

Media plans are often determined on the number of GRPs generated during a certain time period. For example, the objective for a media plan could be to achieve 450 GRPs in a burst (usually four or five weeks). However, as suggested earlier, caution is required when interpreting a GRP, because 450 GRPs may be the result of 18 message exposures to just 25 per cent of the target market. It could also be an average of nine exposures to 50 per cent of the target market.

Rating points are used by all media as a measurement tool, although they were originally devised for use with broadcast audiences. GRPs are based on the total target audience (e.g. all women aged 18–34, or all adults) that might be reached, but a media planner needs to know, quite rightly, how many GRPs are required to achieve a particular level of effective reach and what levels of frequency are really required to develop effective learning or awareness in the target audience. In other words, how can the effectiveness of a media plan be improved?

---

### Viewpoint 24.2    Media mix transparency at Anglian

The formulation and delivery of the right media mix has been a challenge for many organisations. Anglian, the home improvement company, experimented with various combinations of media to determine which configuration of the media mix works best for them.

Anglian's traditional mix includes press, radio, DRTV, direct mail and door drops. With a campaign to promote their replacement windows, the company experimented with different combinations of three of these media.

Unsurprisingly, they found that direct mail works best when implemented at the end of a television campaign, as awareness levels have been raised. Television worked best when used with press and door drops and direct mail worked best with current customers. As a result of the experiments, radio was removed from Anglian's media mix.

The company also reviewed the effectiveness of their website. One of their goals was to increase the number of leads generated from their paid search activities. Analysis found that there was an unusually high bounce rate (66 per cent) from the page visitors first encounter when clicking through from another site or sponsored link. This page is known as the 'landing page' and 'bounce' refers to a failure to click through the site from the landing page. It was found that the page did not contain the information or even products that visitors were looking for, despite clicking on a link that suggested a match.

Changes were made to the information provided about the products; prices and images were included, and they tested changes to the title to the form used by prospects when responding to see whether 'Get a free quote' or 'Get a call back' worked best. Online price discounts, price matching promises and pick & mix sale offers were all incorporated.

One of the results of this landing page work was that the 'Get a call back' invitation generated a 108 per cent increase in conversions.

*Source*:   Anon (2009); Benjamin (2009).

Question:   Why do you think Anglian did not incorporate the website in their experiment to determine the optimum media mix?

Task:   Go to the Anglian website www.anglianhome.co.uk and make a list of the ways they prompt people into further action.

---

Homer (2009) reports that media and audience fragmentation has resulted in lower ratings across media. Referring to Ephron (2003), to achieve the same impact as in 1980 it now requires 100 spots instead of 10 to drive 100 ratings. This has led advertisers to increase their frequency of advertising, which effectively is an increase in repetition. However, although research shows that a low to moderate increase in repetition does enhance persuasion, at high levels, wear-out and tedium occur, which leads to a decline in a liking of that particular stimulus (Batra and Ray 1986).

## Effective frequency

There are a number of reasons why considering the effectiveness of a media plan has become more important in recent years. First, there is the combination of media and audience fragmentation plus increasing media costs. Second, there is short-termism, increased managerial accountability and intensifying competition. This last point about competition refers to the media planning industry itself and the restructuring and concentration of media buying points (centralisation) in response to clients' globalisation strategies and their need for more cost-effective ways of buying media.

Frequency refers to the number of times members of the target audience are exposed to the vehicle. It says nothing about the quality of the exposures and whether any impact was made. Effective frequency refers to the number of times an individual needs to be exposed to an advertisement before the communication is effective. Being exposed once or possibly twice is unlikely to affect the disposition of the receiver. But the big question facing media planners is: how many times should a message be repeated for effective learning to occur? The level of effective frequency is generally unknown, but there has been some general agreement following work by Krugman (1972) that, for an advertisement to be effective (to make an impact), a target should have at least three OTS, the three-hit theory. The first exposure provokes a 'What is this?' reaction, the second reaction is 'What does this mean to me?' The reaction to the third is 'Oh, I remember' (du Plessis, 1998). The three-exposure theory is based on messages that first provide understanding, second, provide recognition and third, actually stimulate action. More than 10 exposures is regarded as an ineffective plan and hence a waste of resources.

Determining the average frequency partially solves the problem. This is the number of times a target reached by the schedule is exposed to the vehicle over a particular period of time. For example, a schedule may generate the following:

*10 per cent of the audience is reached ten times ($10 \times 10 = 100$)*
*25 per cent of the audience is reached seven times ($25 \times 7 = 175$)*
*65 per cent of the audience is reached once ($65 \times 1 = 65$)*
*Total = 340 exposures*

*Average frequency = 340/100 = 3.4*

This figure of average frequency is misleading because different groups of people have been reached with varying levels of frequency. In the example above, an average frequency of 3.4 is achieved but 65 per cent of the audience is reached only once. This means that the average frequency, in this example, may lead to an audience being underexposed.

Members of the target audience do not buy and read just one magazine or watch a single television programme. Consumer media habits are complex, although distinct patterns can be observed, but it is likely that a certain percentage of the target audience will be exposed to an advertisement if it is placed in two or more media vehicles. Those who are exposed once constitute unduplicated reach. Those who are exposed to two or more of the advertisements are said to have been duplicated. Such overlapping of exposure, shown in Figure 24.2, is referred to as duplicated reach.

Duplication provides an indication of the levels of frequency likely in a particular media schedule. Duplication also increases costs, so if the objective of the plan is unduplicated reach, duplication brings waste and inefficiency. So media plans need to specify levels of duplicated and unduplicated reach.

Nevertheless, it is generally agreed that a certain level of GRPs is necessary for awareness to be achieved. It is also accepted that increased GRPs are necessary for other communication effects to be achieved. These levels of GRPs are referred to as *weights*, and the weight of a campaign reflects the objectives of the campaign. For example, a burst designed to achieve 85 per cent coverage with eight OTS would make a 680 rating, which is considered to be

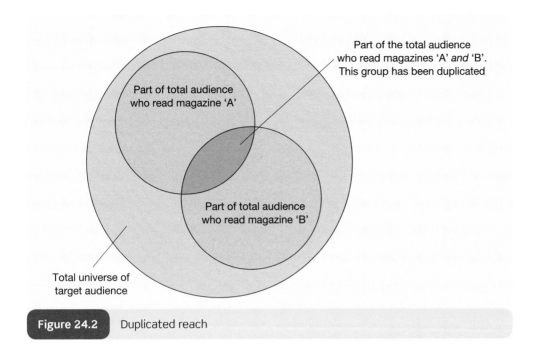

Part of the total audience who read magazines 'A' *and* 'B'. This group has been duplicated

Part of total audience who read magazine 'A'

Part of total audience who read magazine 'B'

Total universe of target audience

**Figure 24.2**    Duplicated reach

heavy. Such high ratings are often associated with car launches and, for example, products that are market leaders in their class, such as Nescafé or Pantene. An average rating would be one set to achieve a 400 rating, through 80 per cent coverage and five OTS over the length of a five-week period.

Our understanding about how learning works can assist the quest for effective frequency levels. The amount of learning in individuals increases up to a certain point, after which further exposure to material adds little to our overall level of knowledge. The same applies to the frequency level and the weightings applied to exposures.

Coverage and reach figures only show the numbers of people who are exposed to the vehicle. Effective reach measures those that are aware of the message. This ties in with the previous discussion on effective frequency levels. Essentially, media planners recognise that effective advertising requires that, in addition to the other aspects of advertising planning, a single transmission (reach) of an advertisement will be unproductive (Krugman, 1975; Naples, 1979). A minimum of two exposures and a reach threshold of 45 per cent of the target audience are required for reach to be regarded as effective (Murray and Jenkins, 1992).

## Recency planning

A relatively new perspective to counter the effective frequency model has emerged from the United States. This is known as *recency planning*, and developed at a time when the weak theory of advertising started to gain greater acknowledgement as the most acceptable general interpretation of how advertising works. There is also a growing general acceptance that advertising is not the all-powerful communication tool it was once thought to be, and that the timing and presentation of advertising messages need to be reconsidered in the light of the way advertising is currently thought to work.

If it is accepted that consumer decision-making is more heavily influenced by 'running out' of particular products (opening empty fridges and store cupboards), than by exposure to advertising messages that are repeated remorselessly, then it follows that advertising needs to be directed at those people who are actually in the market and prepared to buy (Ephron, 1997).

| Table 24.5 | The differences between effective frequency and recency planning |
| --- | --- |

| Recency planning model | Effective frequency model |
| --- | --- |
| Reach goal | Frequency goal |
| Continuity | Burst |
| One-week planning cycle | Four-week planning cycle |
| Lowest cost per reach point | Lowest cost per thousand |
| Low ratings | High ratings |

*Source*: Adapted from Ephron (1997). Used by permission of WARC.

As many fast-moving consumer goods products are purchased each week, Jones (1995) argues that a single exposure to an advertising message in the week before a purchase is to be made is more important than adding further messages, thereby increasing frequency. Recency planning considers reach to be more important than frequency.

The goal of this new approach is to reach those few consumers who are ready to buy (in the market). To do this the strategy requires reaching as many consumers as possible in as many weeks as possible (as far as the budget will extend). This requires a lower weekly weight and an extended number of weeks for a campaign. Advertising budgets are not cut; the fund is simply spread over a greater period of time. According to Ephron, this approach is quite different from effective frequency models and quite revolutionary (see Table 24.5).

This approach has been greeted with a number of objections. It has not been universally accepted, nor has it been widely implemented in the UK market. Gallucci (1997), among others, rejected the notion of recency planning because effectiveness will vary by brand, category and campaign. He claims that reaching 35 per cent of the Indonesian cola market once a week will not bring about the same result as reaching 65 per cent four times a week.

The development of banner advertising on the Internet raises interesting questions concerning effective frequency in new media. Is the frequency rate different and, if so, how many times is exposure required in order to be effective? Research into this area is in its infancy and no single, accepted body of knowledge exists. Broussard (2000) reports that, in a limited study concerning the comparison of a direct-response and a branding-based campaign on the Internet, the lowest cost per lead in the direct-response campaign was achieved with low frequency levels. Results from the branding campaign suggest that up to seven exposures were necessary to improve brand awareness and knowledge of product attributes.

The debate concerning the development of recency planning and effective frequency will continue. What might be instrumental to the outcome of the debate will be a better understanding of how advertising works and the way buyers use advertising messages that are relevant to them.

# Media usage and attitudes

A large number of people have a negative attitude towards advertising, and TV ads in particular. Advertising is regarded as both intrusive and pervasive. Beale (1997) developed a four-part typology of personality types based upon respondents' overall attitudes towards advertising (see Table 24.6). Through an understanding of the different characteristics, it is possible to make better (more informed) decisions about the most appropriate media channels to reach target audiences.

| Table 24.6 | Advertising attitudes for media determination |
| --- | --- |

**Cynics (22 per cent)**
This group perceives advertising as a crude sales tool. They are resentful and hostile to advertisements, although they are more likely to respond to advertisements placed in relevant media.

**Enthusiasts (35 per cent)**
Enthusiasts like to get involved with advertising and creativity is perceived as an important part of the process. Apart from newspapers, which are regarded as boring, most types of media are acceptable.

**Ambivalents (22 per cent)**
While creativity is seen as superfluous and irrelevant, ambivalents are more disposed to information-based messages or those that promise cost savings. The best advertisements are those that use media that reinforce the message.

**Acquiescents (21 per cent)**
As the name suggests, this group of people has a reluctant approach to advertising. This means that they see advertising as unavoidable and an inevitable part of their world. Therefore, they are open to influence through a variety of media.

*Source*: Adapted from Beale (1997). Used with kind permission.

It is common for advertisers and media planners to discuss target markets in the context of heavy, medium, light and non-users of a product. It is only now that consideration is being given to the usage levels of viewers and readers. ZenithOptimedia has determined that television audiences can be categorised as heavy, medium and light users based on the amount of time they spend watching television. One of the implications of this approach is that if light users consume so little television, then perhaps it is not worthwhile trying to communicate with them and resources should be directed to the medium and heavy user groups. The other side of the argument is that light users are very specific in the programmes that they watch, therefore it should be possible to target messages at them and a heavy number of GRPs should be used. However, questions still remain about the number of ratings necessary for effective reach in each of these categories.

A more contemporary study by Schultz et al. (2006) sought to discover how media consumption is determined by an individual's need to access media. Using criteria based on the amount of time spent with all forms of media, the amount of simultaneous media usage, the need to provide or receive information and the speed at which a medium delivers the information, four clusters were identified. These were:

- Zeros – this group consists of people who are not active media consumers.
- Traditionals – this group use media sequentially, one form of media at a time.
- Information hounds – this group are heavy media users and information providers.
- Network creators – this group are heavy users but primarily use slow media and use the information largely for their own purposes.

The researchers believe this media consumption model should be used to enhance the media planning process by being used in addition to the general demographic-, geographic- and psychographic-based approaches. Further research was based around three key dimensions: media usage, media influence and simultaneous media usage (see Table 24.7).

Ostrow (1981) was the first to question how many rating points should be purchased. He said that, rather than use average frequency, a decision should be made about the minimum level of frequency necessary to achieve the objectives and then maximise reach at that level. Ostrow (1984) suggested that consideration of the issues set out in Table 24.8 would also assist.

The traditional approach of using television to reach target audiences to build awareness is still strong. For example, Procter & Gamble, Unilever, Nestlé, Kellogg's and BT all spend in excess of 70 per cent of their budgets on television advertising. However, many major advertisers have moved from a dominant above-the-line approach to a more integrated and

| Table 24.7 | The SIMM database – media usage dimensions |
| --- | --- |

| Media dimension | Explanation |
| --- | --- |
| Media usage | Average usage of media, based on minutes, for both weekday and weekend consumption. Includes newspaper, direct mail, magazines, radio, television and the Internet. |
| Media influence | The self-reported average for each media category across eight product groups: electronics, apparel, groceries, home improvement, cars, medicines, telecom services and eating out. |
| Simultaneous media usage | This is an average of all pairs of media that were reported as 'used simultaneously'. If a pair is reported as regularly consumed then it was assumed to be 70 per cent of the time. If reported as occasional, then it was defined as 30 per cent of the time. |

*Source*: Schultz et al. (2006).

| Table 24.8 | Issues to be considered when setting frequency levels |
| --- | --- |

| Issues | Low frequency | High frequency |
| --- | --- | --- |
| **Marketing issues** | | |
| Newness of the brand | Established | New |
| Market share | High | Low |
| Brand loyalty | Higher | Lower |
| Purchase and usage cycle times | Long | Short |
| **Message issues** | | |
| Complexity | Simple | Complex |
| Uniqueness | More | Less |
| Image versus product sell | Product sell | Image |
| Message variation | Single message | Multiple messages |
| **Media plan issues** | | |
| Clutter | Less | More |
| Editorial atmosphere | Appropriate | Not appropriate |
| Attentiveness of the media in the plan | Holds | Fails to hold |
| Number of media in the plan | Less | More |

*Source*: Adapted from Ostrow (1984).

through-the-line approach as a more effective way of delivering messages to target audiences. Nescafé now uses 48-sheet posters and Unilever, traditionally a heavy user of television, has begun to use radio and posters as support for its television work.

## Efficiency

All promotional campaigns are constrained by a budget. Therefore a trade-off is required between the need to reach as many members of the target audience as possible (create awareness) and the need to repeat the message to achieve effective learning in the target audience. The decision about whether to emphasise reach or frequency is assisted by a consideration of the costs involved in each proposed schedule or media plan.

There are two main types of cost. The first of these is the *absolute cost*. This is the cost of the space or time required for the message to be transmitted. For example, the cost of a full-page, single-insertion, black-and-white advertisement, booked for a firm date in the *Sunday Times*, is £16,645 (June 2012). Cash flow is affected by absolute costs.

In order that an effective comparison be made between media plans the *relative costs* of the schedules need to be understood. Relative costs are the costs incurred in making contact with each member of the target audience.

Traditionally, the magazine industry has based its calculations on the cost per thousand people reached (CPT). The original term derived from the print industry is CPM, where the 'M' refers to the Roman symbol for thousand. This term still has limited use but the more common term is CPT: CPT = space costs (absolute) × 1,000/circulation. The newspaper industry has used the milline rate, which is the cost per line of space per million circulation.

Broadcast audiences are measured by programme ratings (United States), and television audiences in Britain are measured by television ratings or TVRs. They are essentially the same in that they represent the percentage of television households that are tuned to a specific programme. The TVR is determined as follows:

*TVR = number of target TV households tuned into a programme*
*× 100/total number of target TV households*

A single TVR, therefore, represents 1 per cent of all the television households in a particular area that are tuned into a specific programme.

A further approach to measuring broadcast audiences uses the share of televisions that are tuned into a specific programme. This is compared with the total number of televisions that are actually switched on at that moment. This is expressed as a percentage and should be greater than the TVR. Share, therefore, reveals how well a programme is perceived by the available audience, not the potential audience. The question of how to measure relative costs in the broadcast industry has been answered by the use of the rating point or TVR. Cost per TVR is determined as follows:

*Cost per TVR = time costs (absolute costs)/TVR*

Intra-industry comparison of relative costs is made possible by using these formulae. Media plans that only involve broadcast or only use magazine vehicles can be evaluated to determine levels of efficiency. However, members of the target audience do not have discrete viewing habits; they have, as we saw earlier, complex media consumption patterns that involve exposure to a mix of media classes and vehicles. Advertisers respond to this mixture by placing advertisements in a variety of media, but have no way of comparing the relative costs on an inter-industry basis. In other words, the efficiency of using a *News at Ten* television slot cannot be compared with an insertion in *The Economist*. Attempts are being made to provide cross-industry media comparisons, but as yet no one formula has yet been provided that satisfies all demands. The television and newspaper industries, by using CPT in combination with costs per unit of time and space respectively, have attempted to forge a bridge that may be of use to their customers.

Finally, some comment on the concept of CPT is necessary, as there has been speculation about its validity as a comparative tool. There are a number of shortcomings associated with the use of CPT. For example, because each media class possesses particular characteristics, direct comparisons based on CPT alone are dangerous. The levels of wastage incurred in a plan, such as reaching people who are not targets or by measuring OTS for the vehicle and not the advertisement, may lead to an overestimate of the efficiency that a plan offers.

Similarly, the circulation of a magazine is not a true representation of the number of people who read or have an opportunity to see. Therefore, CPT may underestimate the efficiency unless the calculation can be adjusted to account for the extra or pass-along readership that occurs in reality. Having made these points, media buyers in the United Kingdom continue to use CPT and cost per rating point (CPRP) as a means of planning and buying time and space.

Target audiences and television programmes are priced according to the ratings they individually generate. The ratings affect the cost of buying a spot. The higher the rating, so the higher the price will be to place advertisements in the magazine or television programme.

---

**Scholars' paper 24.2**    **Media planning for radio**

**Pelsmacker, de, P., Geuens, M. and Vermeir, I. (2004) The importance of media planning, ad likeability and brand position for ad and brand recognition in radio spots,** *International Journal of Market Research,* **46, Quarter 4, 465–78.**

These authors consider a range of issues associated with radio advertising in Belgium. The paper is welcome not only because it considers radio, which is often overlooked, but also because it explores media planning issues in the light of ad likeability. Among other things, they find that radio campaigns are more effective if the other instruments of the marketing mix are used to build a strong position for the brand and that likeable ads enhance the effectiveness of radio advertising.

---

# Planning, placing and measuring ads online

The decision to place online ads is complicated not just by deciding which of the various formats discussed previously should be used, but also by where and when the ads need to be placed. Table 24.9 sets out the various options available for placing online ads.

Longhurst (2006) argues that much of the online media planning work is based on dividing the expenditure (investment) by the anticipated response (click-throughs) to determine a cost per response. This figure is then used to compare with other media combinations. The problem is that this approach is not market-oriented and the investment sum is all too often simply determined by taking a preset percentage of the main budget. It also fails to take into account the increasing variety of social media opportunities.

The media planning concepts referred to in this chapter (reach, frequency, etc.) evolved to help manage traditional media. The interruption model has been the main way traditional media has been used. This is predicated on the idea that the media manages audiences, influences what they see, when they see it and shapes the pattern of their media behaviour. Advertisers therefore, interrupted an audience's viewing or reading to deliver product messages, for which, according to the advertiser's segmentation analysis, they were suitable recipients.

The planning approach for conventional media has been based on the development of what is known as the 'block plan'. In this approach the goal was to place messages in locations where the 'target' audience was most likely to notice and be receptive to them. This required the construction of a complex, coloured spreadsheet containing the detail of reach, frequency, costs and timing (Morris, 2011). The block plan accounted for the use of paid media, that is, space and time rented from media owners.

However, technological advances have brought about huge changes in the types of available media and the way in which people now use media. As Moore (2007) rightly points out, people use conventional media for information and entertainment. Now they can be active participants as opportunities to be interactive enables user-generated-content (Chapter 25) through search,

| Table 24.9 | Online ad placement opportunities |
| --- | --- |

| Location for ad placement | Explanation |
| --- | --- |
| Portals | Major portals such as Google, Yahoo and MSN attract the majority of online ads. Smaller portals enable more specific targeting of messages to reach defined target audiences – for example, airlines or ferries on a travel portal. |
| Community websites | Social networking sites consist of communities of people who share common pastimes, health, geographic or other interests. These represent ideal opportunities to reach specific target audiences. |
| Search engines | Pay-per-click ads based on users searching on particular key words constitute a major source of revenue for each search engine. |
| Shopping comparison sites | Ads placed on sites where a comparison of shopping products has been requested are going to reach a high proportion of a target audience. |
| Chat rooms | In return for providing software and hosting, companies can place ads on relevant pages. |
| Online forums | Ads can be targeted to meet the needs and interests of the topics and subjects being discussed. |
| Blogs | Blog sites are provided for bloggers to write, but in order to sustain the site ads need to be placed, again targeted to the principal subjects under discussion. |
| Podcasts | Opportunities to place ads around specific podcasts are currently limited but will increase as podcasting becomes more mainstream. |
| RSS aggregators | These enable subscribers to receive specific information and short news updates from organisations that bring information together (aggregators) and feed it out. Some RSS aggregators are beginning to sell ad space on the various news feeds. |
| Mobile devices | Opportunities to reach audiences on the move increase as technology improves. |
| Newsletters | The content or theme of a newsletter will attract appropriate advertisers. |
| Online magazines | Whether a manufacturer or an association produces these, they still provide good opportunities to reach audiences with specific interests. |

*Source*: Based on Gay et al. (2007).

downloading, sharing, publication and involvement in virtual communities. Advertisers should not try to interrupt participants but facilitate interaction. Moore (2007), media manager for the drinks-based group, Diageo, in the United Kingdom, suggests that, in addition to the need for information and entertainment, media now need to satisfy four new consumer motivations: to discover, participate, share and express (themselves). What he does not say is that these do not apply to all consumers in the same way. Most people consume a mixture of conventional and new media, with particular audiences skewed more to one rather than the other. The argument that mass media advertising is in permanent decline is a fallacy, proved by the continuing investment by a range of brands in television advertising. There has certainly been a readjustment of media budgets to reflect contemporary media usage, but the new is not going to wipe out the old.

The early years of digital and online media saw attempts to use the established methods of measurement and evaluation. However, it became clear that these methods were not entirely suitable, simply because digital media are used differently. Instead of measuring how often a message is delivered or the share of audience reached with a message, it becomes more important to measure a consumer's expectations of a brand and their interaction with brands. Put another way, these might be considered as dwell time (the amount of time consumers spend with a brand), dwell quality (a consumer's perceived richness resulting from brand interaction) and dwell insight (what motivates a consumer to spend time with a brand).

What does this mean for the block plan? It means that paid media now needs to be augmented with earned and owned media. This means using media that works continually, not just at particular campaign points or bursts of six weeks. With communications continually switched 'on', all the paid, owned and earned media need to be linked. It is often the case that the role of paid media changes from one of leading communications activities to one that supplements the entire media activity designed to reflect an audience's relationship, levels of advocacy and journey with a brand. A block plan cannot reflect this and so although it continues to have a presence within agencies as a support for paid media activities, it is not the core of media planning as it used to be.

# Media source effects

CPT is a quantitative measure, and one of its major shortcomings is that it fails to account for the qualitative aspects associated with media vehicles. Before vehicles are selected, their qualitative aspects need to be considered on the basis that a vehicle's environment may affect the way in which a message is perceived and decoded.

An advertisement placed in one vehicle, such as *Cosmopolitan*, may have a different impact on an identical audience to that obtained if the same advertisement were placed in *Options*. This differential level of 'power of impact' is caused by a number of source factors, of which the following are regarded as the most influential:

- *vehicle atmosphere* – editorial tone, vehicle expertise, vehicle prestige;
- *technical and reproduction characteristics* – technical factors, exposure opportunities, perception opportunities;
- *audience and product characteristics* – audience/vehicle fit, nature of the product.

## Vehicle atmosphere

### Editorial tone

This refers to the editorial views presented by the vehicle and the overall tone of the material contained. Understandably, some clients do not want to be associated with particular television shows or certain specialist magazines that are characterised by sex or violence.

### Vehicle expertise

Magazines and journals can reflect a level of expertise and represent source credibility. Readers who regard particular magazines, especially some of the consumer SIMs (e.g. *Golf Monthly*), business-to-business magazines (e.g. *Fire & Rescue*) and academic journals (e.g. *Journal of Marketing*), as important sources of credible information are more relaxed and open to persuasion.

## Vehicle prestige

The message strategy adopted for each advertisement should be appreciated, as this can have a strong effect upon the scheduling. The prestige of a vehicle is important to some products, especially when targeted at audiences where vehicle status is important: for example, *Country Life*. Transformational advertisements have been shown to be more effective in prestige-based vehicles than in expertise-based vehicles (and vice versa for information-based advertisements).

# Technical and reproduction characteristics of a vehicle

## Technical factors

The technical characteristics of the vehicle, such as its visual capability, may influence the impact of the message. The use of colour, movement and sound may be necessary for the full effectiveness of a message to be realised. Other messages may need only a more limited range of characteristics, such as sound. For example, the promotion of inclusive tour holidays benefits from the communication of an impression (photograph/drawing) of the destination resort. This is important, as each destination needs to be differentiated, in the minds of the target audience, from competing destinations.

## Exposure opportunities

The possibility that an advertisement will be successfully exposed to the target increases as more consideration is given to the likelihood of successful communication. Each vehicle has a number of time slots or spaces that provide opportunities for increased exposure. The back pages of magazines or facing matter often command premium advertising rates, just as prime-time spots or film premieres on television always generate extra revenue for the television contractors.

## Perception opportunities

Being exposed to the message does not mean that the message is perceived. A reader may not perceive an advertisement when searching for the next page of an article. Similarly, a car driver may not 'hear' a radio message because their attention may be on a passing car or a strange engine noise. The solution is to use strong attention-grabbing materials, such as loud or distinctive music or controversial headlines. In addition, new, imaginative ways of attracting attention are being developed. Car dealers have used incentives to attract audiences to test drive a car and receive vouchers for a free video film or have free subscriptions to particular magazines.

---

### Viewpoint 24.3    Digital perception at Terminal 5

When Heathrow airport opened Terminal 5, a raft of new advertising technology was released. Over 200 digital screens have been built into the infrastructure of the airport, all with strategic placement. Here the advertising panels have been sited alongside the path that passengers take from check-in to their flight. Some giant displays are referred to as 'global gateways', with some dominating the security area. Some digital ads are incorporated into the flight-information screens.

The digital screens enable ad continuity so that a passenger may see a seemingly endless line of the same ads. This opportunity to reach a mass of people in this way is a first for this part of the advertising industry. Now the industry has the opportunity to use digital technology to deliver moving, interactive, responsive and time-specific advertising. This means that interactive ads can be changed for morning, noon and afternoon customers, unlike the traditional outdoor poster sites that need two weeks, several rolls of paper and a bucket of paste. Visa have taken four giant lightboxes that measure 29m × 36m and should be seen by all passengers as they move through to the departure areas.

Digital and interactive screens have been installed at other airports following the T5 launch, in the London Underground, in and around various new shopping centres and maybe even a bus shelter near you.

*Sources:* Bainbridge (2008); Bokaie (2008).

**Question:** To what extent are these digital screens and their location likely to aid the exposure and perception opportunities (to reach travellers with effective messaging)?

**Task:** Next time you visit an air or rail terminal, look out for digital screens and make a note of which brands are using them.

| Exhibit 24.3 | **London Heathrow – an electronic billboard in Terminal 5** |
|---|---|
| | *Source*: JCDecaux Airport/Peter Winterbottom |

# Audience/product characteristics

## Audience/vehicle fit

The media plan should provide the best match between the target market and the audience reached by the vehicles in the media schedule. The more complex the target market description or consumer profile, the greater the difficulty of matching it with appropriate vehicles. Weilbacher (1984) argues that media evaluation based on product usage may be better than using demographics and psychographics. These may be inappropriate and inefficient when matching markets with audiences. As advertising is directed at influencing consumer behaviour, product usage is a more logical measure of media evaluation. This view is supported by media planners targeting heavy, medium and light users.

This perspective contrasts with the view of Rothschild (1987). He regards demographic and psychographic factors as relatively stable and enduring factors, and thus suitable influences on the media selection decision. By contrast, the dynamic factors (those that vary within an individual with respect to brand choice, purchase behaviour and time of adoption between products) are seen as being more suitable for influencing media strategy.

## Nature of the product

In addition to this, consideration needs to be given to the nature of the product itself. Audiences have particular viewing patterns, therefore it does not make sense to advertise when it is known that the target audience is not watching (for example, promoting children's sweets late at night or photocopiers in consumer-interest magazines).

Prime television spots such as *Coronation Street* or major sporting occasions such as the Olympic Games attract many major competitive brands. It may be wise to avoid competing for time and look for other suitable programmes.

## Vehicle mood effects

The mood that a vehicle creates can also be an important factor. Aaker et al. (1992) report on the work of a number of studies in this area. These suggest that food advertisements using transformational appeals are more effective when placed in situation comedies than in thrillers and mystery programmes. Advertisements for analgesics work better in both adult westerns and situation comedies (Crane, 1964).

These qualitative, vehicle-related source effects need to be considered as support for the quantitative work undertaken initially. They should not be used as the sole reason for the selection of particular media vehicles, if only because they are largely subjective.

# Scheduling

This seeks to establish when the messages are transmitted in order that the media objectives be achieved at the lowest possible cost. The first considerations are the objectives themselves. If the advertising objectives are basically short-term, then the placements should be concentrated over a short period of time. Conversely, if awareness is to be built over a longer term, perhaps building a new brand, then the frequency of the placements need not be so intensive and can be spread over a period so that learning can occur incrementally.

The second consideration is the purchasing cycle. It has been noted before that the optimum number of exposures is thought to be between three and ten, and this should occur within each purchasing cycle. Obviously, this is only really applicable to packaged goods, and is not as applicable to white or brown goods or, indeed, the business-to-business sector. However, the longer the cycle, the less frequency is required.

The third consideration is the level of involvement. If the objective of the plan is to create awareness, then when there is high involvement few repetitions will be required compared with low-involvement decisions. This is because people who are highly involved actively seek information and need little assistance to digest relevant information. Likewise, where there is low involvement, attitudes develop from use of the product, so frequency is important to maintain awareness and to prompt trial.

Finally, the placement of an advertisement is influenced by the characteristics of the target audience and their preferred programmes. Selecting compatible 'spots' is likely to improve message delivery considerably.

## Timing of advertisement placements

The timing of placements is dependent on a number of factors. One of the overriding constraints is the size of the media budget and the impact that certain placement patterns can bring to an organisation's cash flow. Putting cost to one side, many researchers have identified and labelled different scheduling patterns. There are many approaches to scheduling. Figure 24.3 and the following are presented as a synthesis of the more common scheduling options.

## Continuity patterns

Continuous patterns involve regular and uniform presentation of the message to the target audience. Over the long term, a continuous pattern is more appropriate for products and services where demand is crisis-led – e.g. plumbing, or where there is a long purchase cycle. These continuous patterns are often used for mature products, where reminder advertising is appropriate. A rising pattern is used when activity centres around a particular event, such as the World Cup Final, the Olympic Games or a general election. A fading pattern may follow an initial burst to launch a new product or to inform of a product modification.

## Flighting patterns

Flighting allows advertisers the opportunity to spread their resources across a longer period of time. This may improve the effectiveness of their messages. A flighting pattern may be appropriate in situations where messages need to reflect varying demand, such as that experienced by the retail sector throughout the year. Flighting is also adopted as a competitive response to varying advertising weights applied by rivals. These schedules are used for specific events, such as support for major sales promotions and responses to adverse publicity or one-off market opportunities.

Flighting patterns, as set out in Figure 24.3, can also be used in short and often heavy periods of investment activity. Because of the seasonality of the product (e.g. for inclusive tour operators), advertising at other times is inappropriate and a waste of resources. This approach can also be used to respond quickly to a competitor's potentially damaging actions, to launch new products or to provide unique information, such as the announcement of a new organisation as a result of merger activity, or to promote information about a particular event such as an impending share offer.

## Pulsing patterns

Pulsing seeks to combine the advantages of both the previous patterns. As a result, it is the safest of all the options, but potentially the most expensive. It allows advertisers to increase levels of message activity at certain times of the year, which is important for times when sales traditionally increase, as with fragrance sales in December and ice-cream in June.

Whereas flighting presents an opportunity for individuals to forget messages during periods of no advertising, pulsing helps to prevent the onset of forgetting, to build high levels of awareness and to provide a barrier that holds back competitor attack.

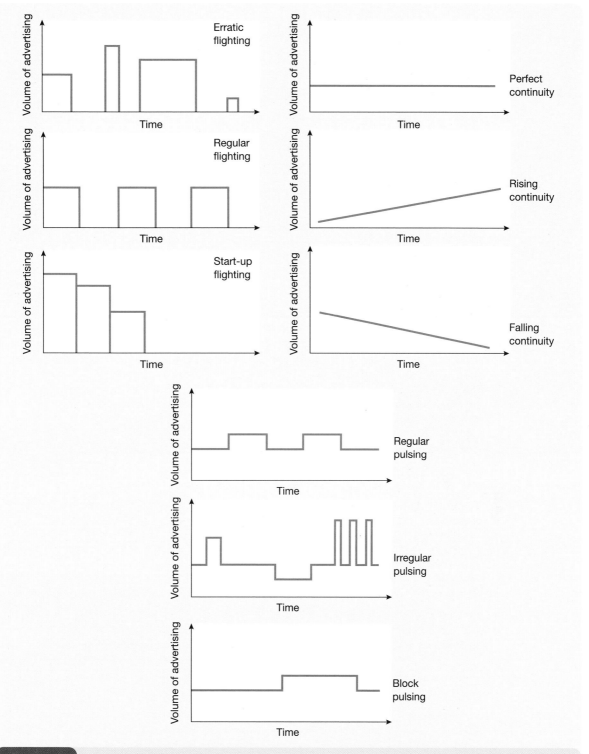

**Figure 24.3**  Flighting patterns

# Key points

- Media planning is concerned with the selection and scheduling of media vehicles designed to carry an advertiser's message.

- The variety of media is rapidly increasing and is referred to as 'media fragmentation'. This makes the media planner's task increasingly complicated because the size of audience available to each media reduces, making the number of media required to reach a target market increasingly large.

- Media richness theory (MRT) holds that there is a hierarchy of media ranging from the richest media such as personal or face-to-face encounters through to lean media typified by single sheets of text-based information.

- Social influence theory (SIT) complements MRT as it also assumes that the relatively objective features of media do influence how individuals perceive and use them. The technology acceptance model (TAM) relates to the perceived usefulness and perceived ease of use as the main issues that are considered when selecting media.

- There are several fundamental concepts that underpin the way in which media should be selected and included in a media plan. These concepts refer to the percentage of the target audience reached, the number of times they receive a message, the number of media they are exposed to and various measures associated with the efficiency with which media deliver messages.

- The greater the number of exposures, the more likely an individual is to learn about the message content. The question is how many times should a message be repeated for effective learning to occur: i.e. what is the effective frequency?

- Recency planning is a reach-based model and argues that a single exposure to an advertising message in the week before a purchase is more important than adding further messages, thus increasing frequency. Recency planning considers reach to be more important than frequency.

- The efficiency of a schedule refers to the costs involved in delivering messages. There are two main types of cost. The first of these is the *absolute cost*, which is the cost of the space or time required for the message to be transmitted. The second concerns the costs incurred in making contact with each member of the target audience. These are referred to as the *relative costs* and are used to compare different media schedules.

- The magazine industry uses calculations based on the cost per thousand people reached (CPT). Broadcast audiences are measured by television ratings or TVRs. These represent the percentage of television households that are tuned to a specific programme.

- Different media impact on audiences in different ways because of three main factors. These are the *vehicle atmosphere* – editorial tone, vehicle expertise, vehicle prestige; their *technical and reproduction characteristics* – technical factors, exposure opportunities, perception opportunities; and finally their *audience and product characteristics* – audience/vehicle fit, nature of the product.

- The scheduling of a media plan seeks to establish when the messages are transmitted in order that the media objectives be achieved at the lowest possible cost. Various factors affect the schedule: the campaign objectives; the purchasing cycle; the level of involvement; and the characteristics of the target audience and their preferred programmes. The selection of compatible 'spots' is likely to improve message delivery considerably.

- Developing a block plan to manage the media mix is only applicable to managing paid media. The incorporation of social media and search render the block plan redundant.

# Review questions

1. Compare media richness theory, social influence theory and the technology adoption model.

2. What are the main tasks facing media planners and how did Which? overcome them?

3. If the rate at which information decays within individuals is known, then the task of the media planner is simply to place messages at suitable intervals in the path of decay. Discuss.

4. Why is it important that a media planner knows whether reach or frequency is the main objective of a media plan?

5. Why are frequency levels so important? Explain the concept of effective frequency.

6. How does recency planning differ from effective frequency?

7. Why might reach and frequency be inappropriate when developing media plans today?

8. How does planning for digital media differ from that for conventional media?

9. Write a brief report outlining the principal characteristics of media source effects.

10. What is the block plan and why is it of less use today than it used to be?

# References

Aaker, D., Batra, R. and Myers, J.G. (1992) *Advertising Management*, 4th edn, Englewood Cliffs, NJ: Prentice-Hall.

Anon (2009) Latitude; Anglian, *Revolution; Success Stories 2009*, December 4–5.

Armstrong, S. (1993) The business of buying: time, lads, please, *Media Week*, 3 September, 26–7.

Batra, R. and Ray, M.L. (1986) Affective Responses Mediating Acceptance of Advertising, *Journal of Consumer Research*, 13 (September), 234–49.

Bainbridge, J. (2008) Now ad campaigns can take off, The *Independent*, 17 March 2008, p. 10.

Beale, C. (1997) Study reveals negativity towards ads, *Campaign*, 28 November, p. 8.

Benjamin, K. (2009) Harmonising mail with other media, *Marketing*, 14 October, 15–17.

Bokaie, J. (2008) Gateway to Britain, *Marketing*, 19 March, 16.

Brech, P. (1999) When the media luck stops with you, *Media Week*, 19 November, 22–3.

Broussard, G. (2000) How advertising frequency can work to build online effectiveness, *International Journal of Market Research*, 42(4), 439–57.

Cheong, Y., De Gregorio, F. and Kim, K. (2011) The Power of Reach and Frequency In the Age of Digital Advertising: Offline and Online Media Demand Different Metrics, *Journal of Advertising Research*, December, 403–15.

Crane, L.E. (1964) How product, appeal, and program affect attitudes towards commercials, *Journal of Advertising Research*, 4 (March), 15.

Daft, R.L. and Lengel, R.H. (1984) Information richness: a new approach to managerial behavior and organizational design, in *Research in Organizational Behavior*, 6 (eds L.L. Cummings and B.M. Straw), Homewood, IL: JAI Press, 191–233.

Duarte, D.L. and Snyder, N.T. (2001) *Mastering Virtual Team*, 2nd edn, San Francisco, CA: Jossey-Bass.

Ephron, E. (1997) Recency planning, *Admap* (February), 32–4.

Ephron, Erwin (2003), The Paradox of Product Placement, *Mediaweek* (June 2), 20.

Fulk, J., Schmitz, J.A. and Steinfield, C.W. (1990) A social influence model of technology use, in *Organizations and Communication Technology* (eds J. Fulk and C. Steinfield), Newbury Park, CA: Sage.

Gallucci, P. (1997) There are no absolutes in media planning, *Admap* (July/August), 39–43.

Gay, R., Charlesworth, A. and Esen, R. (2007) *Online Marketing: A Customer-Led Approach*, Oxford: Oxford University Press.

Homer, P. (2009) Product Placements: The Impact of Placement Type and Repetition on Attitude, *Journal of Advertising*, 38(3), (Fall), 21–31.

Jones, P. (1995) *When Ads Work: New Proof that Advertising Triggers Sales*, New York: Simon & Schuster, Free Press/Lexington Books.

Keaveney, S.M. (1995) Consumer switching behavior in service industries: an exploratory study, *Journal of Marketing*, 59(2), 71–82.

King, R.C. and Xia, W. (1997) Media appropriateness: effects of experience on communication media choice, *Decision Sciences*, 28(4), 877–909.

Krugman, H.E. (1965) The impact of television advertising: learning without involvement, *Public Opinion Quarterly*, 29 (Fall), 349–56.

Krugman, H.E. (1972) How potent is TV advertising? Cited in du Plessis (1998).

Krugman, H.E. (1975) What makes advertising effective? *Harvard Business Review*, 53(2) (March/April), 96–103.

Lloyd, D.W. and Clancy, K.J. (1991) CPMs versus CPMis: implications for media planning, *Journal of Advertising Research*, 31(4) (August/September), 34–44.

Longhurst, P. (2006) Budgeting for online: is it any different? *Admap*, November, 36–7.

McGrath, J.E. and Hollingshead, A.B. (1993) Putting the 'group' back into group support systems: some theoretical issues about dynamic processes in groups with technological enhancements, in *Group Support Systems: New Perspectives* (eds L.M. Jessup and J.S. Valacich, 78–9). New York: Macmillan.

McLuhan, M. (1966) *Understanding Media: The Extensions of Man*, New York: McGraw-Hill.

Moore, L. (2007) 21st century media: let your brand lose control, *Marketing*, 5 December, 10–11.

Morris, R. (2011) The Modern Media Mix, *Campaignlive*, 8 July 2011, retrieved 23 April 2012 from http://www.brandrepublic.com/features/1079039/Modern-Media-mix/?DCMP=ILC-SEARCH.

Murray, G.B. and Jenkins, J.R.G. (1992) The concept of effective reach in advertising. *Journal of Advertising Research*, 32(3) (May/June), 34–42.

Naples, M.J. (1979) *Effective Frequency: The Relationship Between Frequency and Advertising Effectiveness*, New York: Association of National Advertisers.

Ostrow, J.W. (1981) What level of frequency? *Advertising Age* (November), 13–18.

Ostrow, J.W. (1984) Setting frequency levels: an art or a science? *Marketing and Media Decisions*, 24(4), 9–11.

Pelsmacker, de, P., Geuens, M. and Vermeir, I. (2004) The importance of media planning, ad likeability and brand position for ad and brand recognition in radio spots, *International Journal of Market Research*, 46, Quarter 4, 465–78.

Plessis, E. du (1998) Memory and likeability: keys to understanding ad effects, *Admap* (July/August), 42–6.

Rothschild, M.L. (1987) *Marketing Communications*, Lexington, MA: D.C. Heath.

Shultz, D.E., Pilotta, J.P. and Block, M.P. (2006) Media consumption and consumer purchasing, *ESOMAR, Worldwide Multi-media Measurement*, Shanghai, Retrieved 12 March 2008 from http://www.bigresearch.com/esomar2006.pdf.

Simon, H. (1972) Theories of bounded rationality, in *Decision and Organisation* (eds C.B. McGuire and R. Radner), London: North-Holland, 161–76.

Simon, H. (1987) Bounded rationality, in *The New Palgrave* (eds J. Eatwell, M. Milgate and P. Newman), London: Macmillan.

Srinivasan, M. (1996) New insights into switching behaviour: marketers can now put a numerical value on loyalty, *Marketing Research*, 8(3), 26–34.

Weilbacher, W. (1984) *Advertising*, New York: Macmillan.

# Chapter 25
# Creativity

Marketing communications, and advertising in particular, is used primarily to convey meaning *between* organisations and their audiences, and increasingly *among* audiences. In order that the intended meaning is the one that is ascribed during a communication event, it is generally considered important to be 'creative'. Today as content and associated connections are a central element in the marketing communications mix, it is important to understand what creativity might mean and what are the processes used to generate creative communications.

## Aims and learning objectives

The aim of this chapter is to consider creativity and the processes used to develop marketing communication messages.

The learning objectives of this chapter are to:

1. explore ideas concerning what creativity might be and its impact on effective communications;
2. describe the issues associated with creativity and its impact on attention;
3. consider the processes used in organisations to stimulate and manage creativity;
4. examine ideas concerning message framing;
5. review the role of and characteristics associated with storytelling;
6. appreciate the elements and issues associated with user-generated content.

# Minicase

## Johnnie Walker – 'Keep Walking'

Johnnie Walker is a premier whisky brand, whose roots in Kilmarnock, Scotland, can be traced to the early 1800s. Since then successive generations of the Walkers have developed the brand, preserving the quality blend, introducing square bottles to get more in a box and to protect them in transit, using ships' captains to act as brand ambassadors, and a unique diagonal label in order to use bigger print for the name to stand out. The Johnnie Walker brand became recognised internationally and in the early 1900s registered the JOHNNIE WALKER®RED LABEL and JOHNNIE WALKER®BLACK LABEL, which have been preserved and added to with GREEN, GOLD and the premier BLUE LABELs.

In 1908, while at lunch with the Walker brothers, Tom Browne a renowned cartoonist, made a sketch of a striding man on the back of a menu. This was later adopted as the iconic signifier for the Johnnie Walker brand and was used in its advertising for many years before being replaced.

In the 1990s the brand experienced declining sales during difficult trading conditions, mainly due to the market entry of cheaper blends. A campaign was developed to restablish the brand's credentials and to reverse the commercial performance of the Johnnie Walker whisky brand.

Research undertaken by the agency found that people viewed masculine success best demonstrated, not through material wealth, but a person's desire for self-improvement. So, when the 'Striding Man' image was resurrected from the brand's history, an association with progress, forward thinking and development was established. The campaign idea 'Keep Walking' emerged naturally with the 'Striding Man' representing the association with the human need for progress. The emotional tie to the brand appealed at a deep level to consumers and represented a means by which people could both recognise and become involved with the brand and its communications. Technically the 'Keep Walking' principle represented a unique creative platform from which a raft of advertising and brand communications could be developed with an inherent consistency, coherence and integration potential.

The ad campaign used TV and print with the TV campaign based on individual 'walks'. These are stories of personal progress experienced by celebrities and notable people whilst the print work used inspiring quotes about journeys of progress.

Once the 'personal walks' campaign had become established and understood, the campaign evolved to accommodate various expressions of progress, as

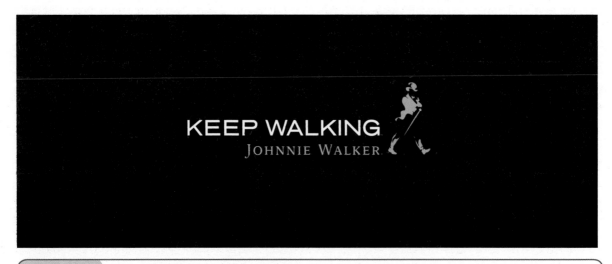

| Exhibit 25.1 | **The Johnnie Walker 'Striding Man'** |
| --- | --- |
| | *Source*: John Walker/Bartle Bogle Hegarty |

this enabled the needs of different Johnnie Walker brands to be addressed. It was at this point that the brand was placed in a wider range of media channels including websites, sports sponsorship via Formula 1, internal and consumer awards and a charitable fund.

The 'Keep Walking' global campaign ran in more than 120 markets, using over 50 TV ads and more than 150 print ads. In eight years the campaign generated incremental sales of $2.21bn (£1.4bn), or a sales growth of 48 per cent. The brand was also recognised professionally, picking up numerous awards, including the grand prix, a gold award and a special prize of best international multimarket campaign.

Since then a more recent campaign extended the walking theme. Called 'Walk With Giants' the campaign shared the stories of some of the world's most inspirational men, including Sir Richard Branson, Sir Ranulph Fiennes, Lewis Hamilton, Jenson Button and Ozwald Boateng.

The question then became how should the Johnnie Walker brand be developed? How should the 'Keep Walking' creative platform evolve?

The answer lay within a participative, global arena. In September 2011 a new campaign was announced, this one incorporating paid, owned and earned media. Using the 'Keep Walking' creative platform, this campaign sought to inspire consumers to participate in order to encourage progress. They used conventional and social media to stimulate support for initiatives in the fields of the arts, technology and business.

Consumers in each participating market were urged to debate and ultimately decide which initiative they think has the most potential to shape the future in their country.

The campaign culminated the following Spring when Johnnie Walker activated the preferred initiatives in each participating market – Bulgaria, Brazil, Greece, Lebanon, Spain, Thailand and Vietnam, and so demonstrated their untapped potential.

The 'Keep Walking' project was run from central Facebook hubs and featured extensive TV, outdoor and digital activity as well as a dedicated free iPhone app. TV spots of 60 and 30 seconds were aired globally and run throughout the course of the campaign. Called 'Step Together', the advert featured a young man who encourages members of his local community to work together to discover a better environment to live in. The emotive advert communicated the benefits of people participating for the greater good,

which was the ethos of the 'Keep Walking' project. Consumers were able to help shape the outcome of the campaign by earning 'steps' – a virtual currency that could be attributed to each initiative, by participating in a series of challenges on official Johnnie Walker Facebook pages or via a free iPhone pedometer app, with all brand communications driving people to these destinations.

At the launch of the campaign, Gavin Pike, Global Brand Director for Johnnie Walker, said the aims were 'to build affinity with inventive, open-minded consumers who want to progress in life, never standing still . . . to encourage like-minded consumers to connect, collaborate and champion causes that inspire them'. Through this it was hoped to build engagement and showcase some of the pioneering thinking that could lead towards a better future.

Each of the three initiatives chosen for year one embodied the Johnnie Walker notion of progress:

### Pavegen: Powering urban areas using only footsteps

Pavegen's pioneering paving slabs convert kinetic energy from footsteps into renewable electricity, so everyday walking can be harnessed to power applications such as street lightning. An interactive, people-powered light installation would appear in the markets where Pavegen earned the most steps.

### Ze Frank: Giving cities a voice

In markets where Ze Frank earned the most steps, the innovative artist would unveil a 'pop up' public artwork which revealed the local community's collective vision for their country or city. Ze Frank would use the submissions of individuals – their photos and statements of hope – as part of the inspiring piece.

### Hub Culture: Encouraging and enabling enterprise

In markets where Hub Culture gained the most support, this private network of doers and thinkers would create a pop-up space in a major city where people could develop their business ideas through one-on-one advice sessions or a series of talks led by inspiring entrepreneurs and business leaders.

*This case was written by Chris Fill using material from various sources including IPA (2011); Brook (2008); www.diageo.com.*

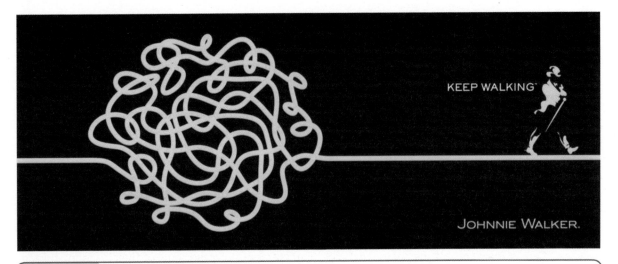

| Exhibit 25.2 | **Walk with giants** |
| --- | --- |
| | *Source*: Johnnie Walker/Bartle Bogle Hegarty |

# Introduction

Whether advertising converts people into becoming brand-loyal customers or acts as a defensive shield to reassure current buyers, and whether central or peripheral cues are required, there still remains the decision about the nature and form of the message to be conveyed: the creative strategy.

The Johnnie Walker minicase presents the different campaigns the brand has used around a simple and single idea of 'keep walking'. Tied into the underlying strategy, the creative output has consistency and imagination. These can be considered as we move through this chapter.

Ideas about the role and nature of creativity have been recognised as an important element not only within marketing communications, but also within other disciplines and the arts. Both academics and practitioners have much to gain through further insight into what constitutes the right creative process. However, there are many varying views and, as with most social sciences, there is no one right way that organisations should manage creativity. In this chapter consideration is given to exploring what creativity might be, the processes organisations use to manage the creative process and consider ways in which the creative process can be harnessed. Here message framing and storytelling are developed before concluding with a review of a more contemporary perspective of content generation and creativity: namely, user-generated content.

# What is creativity?

Whatever it is, creativity matters, and is generally agreed to be a central element of effective advertising (Kim et al. 2010; El-Murad and West 2004).

Early holistic ideas about creativity considered it to be about a violation of expectations, often expressed through contradictory ideas (Blasko and Mokwa 1986; Reid and Rotfield 1976). These views have given way to a general agreement that creativity in advertising has two main characteristics. The first is that creative ads are divergent, or highly unique or novel, and second, relevant or meaningful (Smith et al. 2007).

A recent contribution by Ang, et al. (2007) conceptualises advertising creativity in three dimensions: novelty, meaningfulness, and connectedness. They concluded that many ads that scored high on recall and attitude toward the advertisement had also recorded high scores on each of these three dimensions of creativity.

Heath et al. (2009) believe that creativity in contemporary branded advertising involves a variety of elements. These include characters (who express mild emotion: e.g. love, irritation, excitement, boredom, curiosity, amusement), situations (that are considered humorous, poignant, or dramatic), and visuals (that are elegant or attractive, beautifully shot footage with high production values), and background music (that is pleasant, uplifting or evocative).

Smith and Yang (2004) refer to two key components of advertising creativity; divergence and relevance. They contest that a creative ad uses a divergent appeal (unexpected and unusual, such as fear or humour), to deliver a relevant core message about the brand (such as an attribute or benefit), yet still allow the audience to interpret and assign meaning to the message within the linkage between the fear or humour and the product. Ideas about divergence and relevance have several interpretations and these are represented in Table 25.1, drawn from Smith et al. (2008).

| Table 25.1 | Interpretations of the dimensions of creativity |
|---|---|
| **Dimension** | **Explanation** |
| *Divergence* | |
| **Originality** | Ads that contain elements that are rare, surprising, or move away from the obvious and commonplace. |
| **Flexibility** | Ads that contain different ideas or switch from one perspective to another. |
| **Elaboration** | Ads that contain unexpected details or finish and extend basic ideas so they become more intricate, complicated, or sophisticated. |
| **Synthesis** | Ads that combine, connect, or blend normally unrelated objects or ideas. |
| **Artistic value** | Ads that contain artistic verbal impressions or attractive colours or shapes. |
| *Relevance* | |
| **Ad-to-consumer relevance:** | Refers to situations where the ad contains execution elements that are meaningful to consumers. For example, using Beatles music in an ad could create a meaningful link to baby boomers, thereby making the ad relevant to them. |
| **Brand-to-consumer relevance** | Refers to situations where the advertised brand (or product category) is relevant to potential buyers. For example, the advertisement could show the brand being used in circumstances familiar to the consumer. |

*Source*: Derived from Smith et al. (2008).

# Creativity and attention

Creativity in advertising is considered to be important because of the common belief that creativity is an effective way of getting people to attend to an ad (Rossiter and Percy, 1998; Yang and Smith, 2009). Kover's (1995) research around the impact of emotive content and attention led to the identification of two attention-getting strategies; forcing and subversion. Forcing strategies involve the use of surprising, irrelevant or perhaps mildly shocking content. He gives as an example the famous Apple ad shown during the 1984 Super Bowl. This strategy is not used so much today.

Subversion strategies require an ad to seduce an audience, to slip by them as if unnoticed. Kover uses the words *charming* and *seductive* to describe this sort of creativity and refers to ads by O2, Honda, and M&S Food campaigns as examples of this approach.

Much research into creativity in advertising is concerned with what is referred to as 'attention effects'. This is related to the links between increased attention to an ad, heightened motivation to process the message, and the depth of processing that follows (Smith and Yang 2004). Here, as Baack et al. (2008) comment, the amount of attention paid to advertisements is a function of the amount of cognitive capacity allocated to a task. Only when consumers focus more attention on the advertisement itself, rather than divide their attention among multiple tasks, do higher levels of processing occur. The greater the originality or divergence and personal relevance a creative ad displays, the greater the attention it attracts, which leads to a greater depth of message processing. What follows from this are higher recall and recognition scores.

---

### Scholars' paper 25.1   Is it art or advertising?

**Hetsroni, A. and Tukachinsky, R.H. (2005) The Use of Fine Art in Advertising: A Survey of Creatives and Content Analysis of Advertisements,** *Journal of Current Issues and Research in Advertising,* **27(1) (Spring), 93–107.**

A slightly different paper, in that the managerial thrust is avoided. Here the authors examine the use of fine art (paintings and sculptures) in advertising, using content analysis of print advertisements, and a survey of advertising creatives. The findings are that ads which show art tend to use a soft-sell approach and promote prestigious goods with some over-representation of cultural establishments, cosmetics, fashion apparel and furniture. The predominant artistic style in these ads is Renaissance. The representation of modern art is significantly lower, and non-Western art is largely absent.

---

However, Yang and Smith (2009) and Heath et al. (2009) question the proposition that creativity works by increasing attention. They all agree that some attention is necessary, but it is not the direction of attention, but the level of attention that is important. Yang and Smith had inconclusive results from their research, yet Heath (2010) found that creativity does not increase attention; if anything, it decreases it. This might raise an argument that it would be better to use force-based strategies. However, as Binet and Field (2007) found, emotion-based ads are more successful than information-led campaigns. The conclusion, therefore, is that creative ads enable open-minded message processing, which in turn can increase a willingness to view an ad again.

West et al. (2008) considered the ways practitioners and consumers perceive creativity in advertising. They found that practitioners tend to consider creativity on the basis of an ad's relevance, its originality, and the degree to which an ad is goal-directed. Here creativity is related to the achievement of their client's marketing goals. Consumers, on the other hand, consider the execution used in an ad as the primary means of determining its creativity. For the public, creativity is essentially about whether an advertisement is relevant to their needs.

# The importance of context

According to Kim et al. (2010), it is crucial that creative advertising has a product-, or audience-relevant context if it is to be effective. This contrasts with fine art where creativity is not bounded by this type of contextual constraint or the setting of objectives by one party, as its goal is to please or stimulate the viewer's senses.

Kim et al. (2010) argue that it is the surrounding culture that influences advertisers, ad creators, and consumers when determining what constitutes the contextual component of advertising creativity. They offer the research findings of Koslow, Sasser, and Riordan (2003: 94) who found that 'creatives perceive advertisements to be more appropriate if the ads are artistic, whereas account executives perceive advertisements to be more appropriate if the ads are strategic'.

Interpretations of what constitutes advertising creativity, therefore, varies depending on the viewer's context. This may be relative to their role (a client striving to meet market share targets), culture (the societal values and norms of behaviour) or perspective (media commentator or blogger).

Culture is a critical component of international advertising effectiveness as it influences how consumers in different countries and regions perceive advertising. In Asian countries, for example, collectivistic values such as sharing, trustworthiness and sincerity are a key aspect of their advertising. In contrast, American and European cultures are more individual and the advertising stresses individualistic appeals, such as 'the one for you', and 'you have the right to be you'. This can lead to different interpretations or forms of originality in advertising. For example, in Asian advertising there is an absence of what Westerners refer to as the 'big idea', when referring to creativity, and a much stronger focus on making the brand and the message socially appropriate (Han and Shavitt, 1994).

---

### Viewpoint 25.1    Knighted creativity

Sir John Hegarty has been a leading light in the advertising industry for over 45 years. He was fired from Benton and Bowles in 1967 as a junior art director for insubordination! This was not to hinder his career and in 1970 became a founding partner of Saatchi and Saatchi. In 1973 he co-founded TBWA before forming his current agency BBH with John Bartle and Nigel Bogle in 1982. In 1990 he was voted Advertising Man of the Decade and was awarded a knighthood in 2007 for services to advertising. In 2011 he was given a special award at the Cannes Lions International Festival of Creativity. Not a bad track record for a youthful insubordinate!

In 2011 he published his views in book form *Hegarty on Advertising: Turning Intelligence into Magic*. He describes the fundamentals of a successful advertising campaign as being 'exactly what it was 50–100 years ago . . . It's vital to advertise something of value. Understand that value and find a way of expressing it in a way that captures people's imagination. And probably the most effective strategy you can use in advertising is to tell the truth. If you look back at many of the greatest campaigns, that's exactly what they did.'

One of Hegarty's most memorable campaigns was in the mid 1980s for Levi's. This involved the then unknown actor Nick Kamen, who stripped down to his boxer shorts in a laundrette to the soundtrack of Marvin Gaye's 'I Heard it on the Grapevine'. At the time the Levi's brand was declining in popularity but the campaign uplifted sales by some 800 per cent, put Marvin Gaye back in the charts and sent the sales of boxer shorts rocketing!

As BBH's Worldwide Creative Director, he has certainly been involved in many successful campaigns. Hegarty follows the emphasis on creativity laid down by Bill Bernbach of DDB in the late 1960s, proposing that 'creativity isn't an occupation, it's a pre-occupation'. Amongst BBH's current list of global clients are British Airways, Google, Burberry, Sprite and Baileys.

Hegarty identifies a number of key issues relating to creativity and those who are involved in it within the advertising industry:

● *'Don't chase the money, chase the opportunity.'* It is now much easier for those aspiring to get into the advertising business. Media developments now mean that an ad does not have to wait to get TV exposure, it can be aired quickly and easily via YouTube.

● *'Technology is a tool for creativity.'* Clearly advances in technology are influencing idea generation and creative outputs, but this also means that it is getting harder to keep advertising and ads fresh. Technology presents an opportunity to challenge and disrupt the status quo.

● *'Write from your own philosophy and beliefs.'* Telling the truth is a key element of advertising, telling it with wit and intelligence is an important factor in engaging with the target audience.

● *'Creativity is an expression of one's self.'* There is a need for those involved in creative advertising to be inquisitive and seek reference points from as wide a range of sources as possible. Advertising is about storytelling which requires crafting.

● *'80% idea, 20% execution.'* Given the volume of advertising production, Hegarty argues that a significant percentage of this is poor. Good is not good enough; creatives need to be prepared to throw away ideas that might be good and search for something great.

● *'Never be ordinary.'* Advertising is about making a difference and this requires those involved in producing it to be different.

*Source*:    Based on Hegarty (2011); www.bbh.co.uk; www.lcc.arts.ac.uk; www.ica.org.uk; www.hegartyonadvertising.com.

---

**Question:**    Explain what Hegarty means by storytelling in advertising.

**Task:**    Look at some examples of BBH's creative work on their website. Which ads do you like and why?

---

The idea that culture influences creativity can also be seen in terms of what people attend to when viewing ads. People in Asian cultures tend to practise holistic processing and prefer to consider the entire picture or field. Westerners practise analytic processing and attend to the primary object and its categories. To illustrate this, Kim et al. cite the work of Masuda and Nisbett (2001) who showed American and Japanese students images of a fish in the centre of an underwater scene, against a background of rocks and plants. When a new background was introduced, the Japanese participants had greater difficulty recognising the target fish than the Americans. So, removing an object from its context indicated an Asian preference for context rather than content-focused advertising.

Finally, advertisers in many Asian nations use emotional rather than cognitive or rational appeals. This is because they prefer to help consumers feel happy and relaxed. Mircale (1987: R75) suggests this is why advertisers in these cultures are prone to using 'famous talents, parodies, fantasies, classical music, melancholy, nostalgia, and humor'. He says this leads to advertising in Asian regions that is perceived to be pleasant, friendly, and understanding. This compares to American advertising which stresses product benefits, calls to action, and reasons to buy.

# Creativity as a signal

Marketing communications, and advertising in particular, can be interpreted as a signal of a client's belief in their offering and of the marketing effort they have made. The more that is spent on advertising, the greater the client's risk. From this observation, consumers experience reduced levels of uncertainty and have more confidence that the advertiser will keep their promise (Kirmani, 1997).

Ambler and Hollier (2004) argue that advertising expense may be a signal of wealth, that the advertiser can afford such wastefully expensive advertising, and is evidence of the brand's ability to serve the market and of previous success. Indeed, these authors refer to the interesting concept of perceived 'corporate ability'. This concerns consumers' beliefs that an organisation can generate new products and is capable of improving the quality of their existing products. This is a powerful concept, because research shows that, not only are new products introduced more successfully when perceived corporate ability is high, but the valuation of the company also increases (Luo and Bhattacharya, 2006).

From this Dahlen et al. (2008) argue that advertising creativity can also be considered to be a signal of 'brand ability', the equivalent of corporate ability. The generation of creative advertising concepts can be a signal of an ability to work and think in new and different ways, relative to the history of the brand and compared to category advertising standards. It might also say something about higher product quality, and how interesting a brand might be. This is because creative advertising says something about a client's perceived effort and confidence to convey the brand's offer, and to say something different to the competition.

Dahlen et al. (2008) find that the level of advertising creativity sends signals similar to those about advertising expense. More rather than less advertising creativity generates signals that the client is making a big(ger) marketing effort.

# The creative process

Academic interest and investigation into the processes associated with the development of creative advertising are thin. Na et al. (2009) and others have interpreted the process in terms of a linear sequence of activities. For example, Hill and Johnson (2004) developed a 13-point process which they refer to as the 'advertising problem delineation communication and response' process (APDCR). Na and colleagues (2009) offer a less detailed approach, highlighting four stages of decision making.

As with any collaborative-service-based project, the level of interaction between client and provider is crucial to the quality and success of outcome: in this case, creative advertising. Indeed, the relationship that develops or exists between these two parties is an important factor, although little research has been undertaken in this area.

There are many other possible influences on the creative process. One major factor concerns the prevailing regulations and industry standards about what is acceptable behaviour. Closely associated with this are client attitudes towards risk and the extent to which the organisation wants to push the boundaries of advertising outputs.

As mentioned earlier, one of the more interesting yet under-researched areas concerns the nature of the relationship between client and agency and the effect the interaction between these two parties can have on the development of creative advertising. Two main relationship styles have been observed: master–servant and partnership. With the former the agency experiences little involvement by the client and has a relatively free rein to develop work. The collaborative implication of the partnership approach can lead to conflict as well as mutually rewarding outputs. However, some organisations are known to require an excessive number of reviews and approval meetings in the process can dilute creativity (Holtz et al. 1982) just as excessive client involvement can impede and even frustrate the development of creative advertising (LaBahn and Kohli, 1997).

Another influential element concerns the need for the client and agency to not only share information but for the client to provide information that that can assist the development of creative advertising. For example, the information contained in the creative and client briefings should be as detailed as possible in order to shape quality creative outcomes (Hackley, 2000), but there is substantial anecdotal and some empirical evidence to indicate that as many as 40 per cent of clients fail to give agencies sufficient information (Helegsen, 1994) and that some clients do not provide a creative brief at all (Rossiter, 2008).

---

**Scholars' paper 25.2**   Practitioners' views on advertising

**Nyilasy, G. and Reid, L.N. (2009) Agency practitioners' meta-theories of advertising,** *International Journal of Advertising*, 28(4), 639–68.

This paper explores the academician–practitioner gap and finds that is far from easy to bridge the gaps found. The authors explore practitioners' ideas about how advertising works, and within this the belief that creativity must not be bounded by rules. This was found to be more important than any other guiding principle in advertising work. The primacy of creativity denies any chance that a set of rules could, or should, be created in order to guide advertising.

---

Edwards (2012) raises an interesting point when she suggests that 'many agency teams are not so much creatives as curators'. The issue is that some creative ideas are not new, merely recycled, adapted or, to put it more brutally, plagiarised, for new clients. She cites the Honda 'cog' ads where the agency apparently admitted giving copies of a 1987 film depicting a domino-style chain reaction to its scriptwriters. Other 'evidence' of curation includes Guinness, who were accused of using an idea for an ad presented by one director and having it made by another, Nike, who featured a montage of 40 clips from popular culture, while an ad for confectionery brand Aero was said to bear a strong similarity to a YouTube skateboarder video.

# The creative code

We have seen that there are many internal and external influences on the creative process and, indeed, individual stakeholders can have varying levels of impact on the development of creative advertising. Stuhlfaut (2011) refers to clients, agency managers, media specialists, and account planners, as well as market conditions, which have all been shown to have varying levels of influence on the creative process and its outputs.

However, the development of advertising materials and associated processes occurs within organisations and is therefore embedded within the prevailing organisational context and culture. This embraces the organisational climate, leadership style, the available mix of skills/resources, and structure and systems.

Stuhlfaut (2011) refers to organisational culture as a learned system of meaning, which is shared among participants. People use an implicit framework of language, behaviour and symbols to communicate these meanings and provide a common bond within their community. Organisations such as advertising agencies, and all those working within creative departments, work within, and are constrained by, this framework of organisational culture.

We know that individuals tend to identify with their (employer's) organisation and to a greater or lesser extent, align themselves with the organisation's values. It is not unrealistic to expect that creatives would choose to use methods, styles, techniques and strategies that fit with the perceived values, and which serve to constrain the range of creative outcomes and outputs. For new creatives, therefore, it is important to learn and understand the values, as this will influence what they do, how they do it, and how creative success is determined.

Another way of considering these issues is to ask: do the creatives have the right skills and an appropriate amount of development time, and is the budget sufficient? Although the larger advertising budgets might attract better agency service, the budget itself does not appear to be a significant factor in shaping creative advertising output (Koslow, Sasser and Riordan, 2006).

---

### Viewpoint 25.2    Dentsu's creative code

Dentsu was founded 110 years ago and is the largest single-brand agency in the world. The company occupies over 45 floors of the headquarters in Tokyo and has several domestic branches, plus offices all over the world. The HQ building is huge, has its own underground station and the vast reception area is always busy, with over 3,000 visitors each day.

Creativity is ingrained into the culture to the point that the company strives to ensure that everyone who works for Dentsu is inspired creatively every day. Dentsu believes that their inspiration comes from what's around them, so it ensures their 'creative environment' is always changing. From what's on the walls, desks and on show in reception, the creative feel all contributes to the general office ambience. Dentsu has a project called 'Our Good Entrance, Good Innovation' which incorporates 'change' as its theme, and each month features a different idea. One such event was the Dentsu Entrance Library. One hundred employees, drawn from senior management, and all grades and employee occupations, each selected five books to contribute to the library, which are on display in reception for everyone to see and use.

All staff work in close-knit teams and the creative culture is grounded in ideas that are down-to-earth, honest and tinged with a sense of humour. A phrase developed a long time ago has been passed down through successive generations. Translated as 'table talk', the term is used to describe the Dentsu creative process. In addition to a tea-ceremony room, all the offices have areas where there is time, space and peace for people to talk. The flooring in these creative spaces is made of tatami, a traditional Japanese flooring, which is instrumental in creating a relaxed atmosphere. All of this is deliberately designed to create uncluttered spaces for 'table talk'.

Staff are located in open-plan seating areas but are encouraged to surround themselves with whatever stimulates their minds. Examples of their creative work and new innovations are stuck on the walls, cabinets, desks and in the surrounding corridors, all designed to trigger creative conversations.

The working environment, the easy-to-talk atmosphere and team spirit are all important parts of Dentsu's corporate personality, and are regarded as key to the production of award-winning and commercially successful work.

*Source*: Campaignlive (2011); www.dentsu.com.

**Question:**   To what extent does the creative environment at Dentsu represent a creative code?

**Task:**      Find two ads that appeal to you. Make notes about what it is in these ads that resonates with you.

---

Another way of reviewing creativity is to consider how all of these influences compete and result in considerations of power over a campaign. As Hackley and Kover (2007: 65) observe, this usually means that creatives 'operate in a climate of latent or actual conflict'. With political power resting with clients and account managers, creatives, Hackley and Kover report, have to use cunning strategies to get their work accepted.

It is against this background that Stuhlfaut (2011) offers an interesting concept which he refers to as the 'creative code'. Citing Goodenough (1981: 52), the code shapes the development of advertisements which are regarded as cultural artefacts or 'material manifestations of what is learned'. Through this process a sub-cultural creative code is understood and made available to others. Just as organisation theory suggests that people make mental maps of their experiences in order to help them behave appropriately (Weick 1979), so a creative code serves to direct or limit what internal and external stakeholders believe an acceptable creative might be. However, this raises questions about whether a weak culture and code serves to encourage greater creativity because there are fewer constraints. To what extent does a creative code influence the creative process, and how might an agency or client influence the creative code, in order to achieve particular types of output?

# Message framing

The principle of building a border around an idea or story and then presenting a contained and managed view of an issue, is well known and practised regularly by politicians, and advertising and public relations professionals. Known as *framing*, the concept has roots in communication studies, psychology and sociology. As with a number of concepts, there is little agreement on framing and, as Tsai (2007) indicates, it is controversial and empirically unproven. However, of the many definitions Dan and Ihlen (2011) cite Entman's (1993: 52) as one definition quoted more often than others. To frame is to:

> *select some aspects of a perceived reality and make them more salient in a communicating context, in such a way as to promote a particular problem definition, causal interpretation, moral evaluation, and/or treatment recommendation.*

By cropping and framing an item any distracting or contradictory elements are removed and focus can be given to the interpretation intended by the source. Gamson and Modigliani (1989) indicate that those who use framing to influence public opinion often compete with each other to frame the issues of interest. The goal of these *framing contests* (Pan and Kosicki, 2001) is to get, first, the media to adopt that particular frame and then the audience.

The framing principle is used in advertising to present predetermined brand elements. Competitors frame their messages and stories in order that their brands stand out, have clarity and focus and be positioned distinctly and clearly.

Message framing works on the hedonic principles of our motivation to seek happiness and to avoid pain. So, messages can be framed to either focus a recipient's attention on positive outcomes (happiness) or take them away from the possible negative outcomes (pain). For example, a positively framed message might be a yoghurt that is presented as 'contains real fruit' or a car as 'a stylish design'. Conversely messages could be presented as 'contains only 5 per cent fat' and 'low carbon emissions'; these are regarded as negatively framed. According to Buda (2003), negative framing gets more attention and information is processed more intensely than positively framed messages.

Many practitioners work on the basis that positive are better than negative messages, whereas others believe negative framing promotes deeper thinking and consideration. However, there is little empirical evidence to support any of these views. Therefore, in an attempt to understand when it is better to use positive or negative framing, Tsai argues that it is necessary to develop a holistic understanding of the target audience. This involves considering three factors: self-construal; consumer involvement; and product knowledge. These are explained at Table 25.2.

| Table 25.2 | Factors associated with message framing | | |
|---|---|---|---|

| Factor | Explanation | | |
|---|---|---|---|
| Self-construal | Independent | | Individuals (the self) seek to distinguish themselves from others. These individuals respond best to positive framing. |
| | Interdependent | | Individuals (the self) try not to distinguish themselves from others. These individuals respond best to negative framing. |
| Consumer involvement | High involvement Low involvement | | Refers to the extent to which personal relevance and perceived risk influence decision-making within a product category. When high, negative framing is preferred; when low, positive framing is preferred. |
| Product knowledge | High Low | | Product knowledge consists of two elements: behavioural (usage) experience and mental (search, exposure and information). Message framing is more suitable where product knowledge is low. |

*Source*: Based on Tsai (2007).

Tsai believes that these three factors moderate an individual's response when they are exposed to positively or negatively framed brand messages. In turn, these influence the three main dimensions of a brand's communication. These are generally accepted by researchers such as Mackenzie and Lutz (1989) and Lafferty et al. (2002) to be attitude to the ad, attitude to the brand and purchase intention. Tsai develops a conceptual model to demonstrate this, through which he argues brand communication persuasiveness is moderated by these three factors.

His research concludes that positive message framing should be used when the following exist:

*Independent self-construal × low consumer involvement × low product knowledge*

Negative framing should be used in the case of:

*Interdependent self-construal × high consumer involvement × low product knowledge*

While message framing may provide a strategic approach to the way in which messages should be presented, it is also necessary to consider how the detail of a message should be included in order to maximise effectiveness. Consideration is now given to the balance of information and emotion in a message, the structure in terms of how an argument should be presented and the actual appeal, whether it be based on information or emotion.

---

**Scholars' paper 25.3    Can creativity be defined?**

**El-Murad, J. and West, D. (2004) The Definition and Measurement of Creativity: What Do We Know?** *Journal of Advertising Research*, 44(2), June, 188–201.

The paper looks at creativity as arguably the most important element in achieving advertising success. It reviews trends in creativity research in order to establish what is known about advertising creativity, how it can be measured and how it can be enhanced and encouraged. Theories underpinning creativity are examined in order to establish a definition. Issues including the marketing environment and management practice are discussed as well as assessing 'myths' surrounding creative enhancement. They identify a management need to address obstacles, including self doubt, fear of risk taking, opposition and criticism and provides a good basis for understanding key principles in understanding what creativity is and the barriers to successful development.

# Storytelling

Stories are considered to be an integral part of the way we lead our lives as they enable us to make sense of our perceived world and our role within it. Stories are embedded in music, novels, fairytales, films, news, religion, politics and plays. They are the foundation of word-of-mouth communication and a significant dimension of brands and the advertising used to support them, yet they are often an understated aspect of marketing communications.

The versatility of storytelling is recalled by Barker and Gower (2010). They believe that in addition to helping to sell products (Wylie, 1998), storytelling is used by organisations for communication (Jones and LeBaron, 2002), to introduce and manage change (Boje, 1991), for leadership (Marshall and Adamic, 2010), organisational learning (Lämsä and Sintonen, 2006), and even design management (DeLarge, 2004). Woodside et al. (2008) refer to the use of storytelling through blogs, suggesting it may be a more effective way of driving purchase intentions than traditional websites.

People use storytelling to help make sense of their lives and the events that they encounter and to derive meaning from their relationships and social activities (Merchant et al. 2010). Stories work because they fit or match the way people think and retrieve information from memory (McKee, 2003; Weick, 1995). McKee (2003) argues that stories are effective at persuasion because they involve people emotionally.

Stories consist of a theme and a plot, the latter conveying the former. Papadatos (2006) refers to themes within stories, and identifies three main elements; hardship, reciprocity and a defining moment. Each story has a sequence of events, or plot. The normal sequence starts with anticipation, and then progresses through a crisis, getting help, and then achieving a goal. See Table 25.3 for more information about these elements.

| Table 25.3 | Elements of storytelling | |
| --- | --- | --- |
| | **Element** | **Explanation** |
| **Theme** | Hardship | In order to overcome obstacles perseverance and determination in the face of these difficulties and hardship are critical so that the end product has a sense of being earned. |
| | Reciprocity | An appreciation that there is a fair or equal exchange, that the give and take of life is present. |
| | Defining moments | Human experience is punctuated with moments that stand out, or even change lives, and these are the moments that are remembered and treasured. |
| | Anticipation | Stories begin with a sense of hope for the future – a new job, home, baby, activity, all of which represent anticipation about the future. |
| **Plot** | Crisis | The feeling of anticipation is often followed by a negative, an unanticipated event or crisis that disrupts the path to the future. |
| | Help along the way | The crisis is mediated by the arrival of unexpected help. This might be in the form of advice from a new person or organisation, a tip from a friend or information from a specialist such as a mentor, an experienced teacher, protector, or trusty sage. As a result, there is a period of hard work and endurance. |
| | The goal is achieved | Following much discomfort and many obstacles, stories conclude with the goal accomplished and for many, muted celebration. |

Stories are used to frame our understanding and to encourage individuals to want to become a part of the story itself and to identify with a brand and/or its characters. Strong brands are built around a core theme or platform from which a series of linked stories can be developed. Cordiner (2009) refers to brands having a moral premise (platform): Honda's power of dreams, and Starbucks' 'third space' about having somewhere for each of us between work and home. He suggests that the television programme *The Wire* has a platform based on broken America. The platform for Harley Davidson is to empower individuals to be free from the 'prison of suburban life'. Virgin's platform is to challenge the establishment, and Google's is to set information free and connect people.

Nike's platform is a will to win and from this stories about winning can be developed. One such story concerns an athletics coach who was annoyed about the quality of sports equipment, and running shoes in particular. Inspiration arrived whilst eating his breakfast waffles. He then spent several months in the garage with a waffle iron and some rubber. What emerged was a new running shoe and a new company, Nike (Cordiner, 2009).

Stories can be understood in terms of four main categories. These are:

1. *Myths and origins* can be used to recall how a company started and what its principles are, but very often the focus is on how it overcame early difficulties and achieved success. The current values can often be seen embedded in these stories. For example, the founders of HP started the company in a garage. As the company grew, so a stream of stories centred on the garage developed. These referred to the roots of the company, and became a central and controlling element in the culture of the company.

2. *Corporate prophecies* are predictions about an organisation's future, which are often based on past stories or stories about other organisations.

3. *Hero stories* recall people from the organisation who confronted and overcame a dilemma. The story provides a set of behaviours and values to be copied by others, especially during periods of crisis. These stories help people establish priorities and make decisions. This is a common approach as used by US Airways, with respect to their pilot C.B. Sullenberger, who landed his plane safely on the Hudson river in January 2009. He became the hero of 'the miracle on the Hudson'.

4. *Archived narratives are an organisation's collection* of stories which trace its history and development. With organisations changing names, being merged, bought out and reconstituted, there is an increasing need to access key stories from the past in order to provide a sense of history.

McLellan (2006) identifies four main aspects associated with storytelling in organisations: story gathering, sharing, making, and storytelling.

1. *Story gathering* refers to the processes and activities associated with the collection of information and stories. These include research and getting feedback from customers, undertaking focus groups to understand user behaviour, analysing data and determining patterns of behaviour. As Watchman and Johnson (2009) observe, whether customers, prospects, employees or the general public are the audience, they all have stories about a brand. These stories are rich with clues and insights about what is meaningful and emotionally compelling about the category, the brand or a company. Developing a persuasive story begins with understanding our audience, not merely what they want, but what they feel and why.

2. *Story sharing* is about enabling the transfer of knowledge and engineering situations in order to encourage people at work to share stories. This might be accomplished online, through communities and social networks, or by submissions to magazines, video sites or even work-based meetings and discussions. LEGO and other companies encourage employees to share experiences by posting events and stories on the intranet. (See below.)

3. *Story making* is concerned with creating a story that delivers a truth or core message, in a simple and straightforward, uncomplicated way.

4. *Storytelling* concerns the way in which a story is presented and this involves framing it so that is focused, easy to understand, relevant and memorable.

Microsoft developed a 'storytelling framework' to generate focused relevant communications. The framework acts as a filter so that key messages are constantly reinforced. Using a 'master narrative' which sets out the three key elements that all Microsoft stories must contain, the framework provides a means of simplifying stories and communications emerging from a complex environment. Rather than promote this approach as a communication device, Microsoft stressed the business significance of the storytelling framework (Love, 2006).

---

### Viewpoint 25.3    Using chiefs to tell stories

Halo is a hugely successful series of videogames about how the human race resists alien forces. The Xbox game from Microsoft has a strong and loyal fan base. However, in order to grow it was necessary to reach a mainstream audience. The problem was, depicting scenes of violence and aggression in the promotional material would only reinforce the mainstream audience's preconceptions.

The Master Chief is the central figure and lead character in the videogame series. Research found that Halo fans believed the Master Chief to be an heroic figure and it was his story that motivated them to play this game. The character Master Chief represents the classic heroic qualities: bravery, sacrifice, duty and selflessness.

Traditionally these games are promoted by featuring the continuous action, thrills, spills, violence and endeavour of the good overcoming the bad that is to be experienced playing the game. The goal for the launch of Halo3 was to engage audiences emotionally so that they perceived the Master Chief as a hero and would be motivated to take part in the story itself.

A campaign called 'Believe' was created. This was based on drawing people into stories about the Master Chief. To do this a history of the Master Chief's feats, achievements and heroic deeds was created, and anchored in a virtual Museum of Humanity. A year before launch a teaser ad ('Starry Night') ran just once on TV, throughout the region Europe, Middle East and Africa (EMEA). This was preceded by promotion on the web, designed to make the ad an appointment to view.

The TV ad, which featured artifacts and a monument from an historic battle in which Master Chief heroically led his troops to victory, was used to introduce the museum and the whole campaign leading up to the launch. Further TV and viral films were used to depict different aspects of the Master Chief's past, supported by fictitious war veteran testimonials, which all served to develop folk lore and establish the concept of the museum.

All around Europe, statues were erected in honour of the hero Master Chief, murals were painted and street plaques created, all commemorating various fictional battleground sites. A war photography exhibition was held in UK cinemas, showing the work of fictional war photographer Jake Courage. A huge PR and events programme throughout mainstream and specialist press, ensured maximum exposure and excitement about the launch of Halo 3. On the day before launch, celebrity film premiere-style parties, linked over Xbox LIVE and streamed on xbox.com, were held.

The results of this integrated campaign broke all expectations. With a target of an additional 375,000 users, 600,000 were recruited. Opening day sales were £84 million, smashing the Spiderman 3 record.

The 'Starry Night' pre-launch campaign ad has been viewed over 10 million times at sites such as YouTube. The war veteran testimonial viral films were viewed over 7 million times in their first 24 hours of release. The Museum of Humanity centrepiece television spot has been viewed over 2 million times online. Such is the power of storytelling.

*Source:*   Gallery et al. (2009); Cowen (2007).

**Question:**   How might a campaign be considered to be patronising?

**Task:**        Using Google, find out about the marketing communications used to launch a film of your choice. How might it have been improved?

The following comment by Warlick (2009) was posted at the foot of the account of this tale about Halo 3. 'The "Believe" campaign catapulted Halo 3 from an ordinary video game into a worldwide cultural phenomenon due to its ability to build an emotional rapport with the audience. The innovative stream of interactive TV, Web and cinema advertisements was an inspired approach that successfully attracted an audience beyond the typical gamer.'

Storytelling is effective at reaching a range of audiences, not just customers. One important audience is employees, as demonstrated at LEGO, where storytelling has become a central form of communication. At the turn of the century, the company was struggling and even making losses. As part of the change programme it was decided to improve the competences of managers and employees. This was accomplished by identifying exemplary employees and telling stories about them. A series of short videos were made, each explaining the difficulties and challenges they had faced and how these were resolved using the 'LEGO spirit' or new approach. These were distributed internally and employees were also encouraged to contribute their own material.

In much the same way, storytelling was used to launch a new brand, Bionicle, part of the LEGO revival programme. This new range of toys was effectively a new category of toys which brought together construction sets and action figures, both rolled into one. To position Bionicle, an ongoing epic story was used, based around the action figures. Each year new activities, characters and products were introduced, using the same intellectual property and always under the same brand/story umbrella (Fonnesbaek and Andersen, 2005).

# User-generated content (UGC)

So far in this chapter attention has been given to the issues associated with organisation-driven creativity. However, it is important to consider the increasing numbers of messages that are developed and communicated by ordinary individuals, just like you and me. Not only are these used to communicate with organisations of all types and sizes but they are also shared with peers, family, friends and others in communities such as social networks and specialist interest online communities (e.g. reunion and family history sites). This is referred to as *user-generated content* (UGC) and can be seen in action at YouTube, Flickr, Twitter and DIGG.

UGC can be considered to be all of the ways in which people make use of social media (Kaplan and Haenlein, 2010) and describes the various forms of media content that are publicly available and created by end-users. According to Christodoulides et al. (2011), one interpretation of UGC requires that three core conditions need to be met. First, the content needs to be published either on a publicly accessible website or on a social networking site accessible to a selected group of people. Second, the material needs to show some creative effort and, finally, it has to have been created outside of professional routines and practices.

In December 2006 *Time* named 'you' (the consumer) as its Person of the Year and in January 2007 *Advertising Age* followed suit when it named 'the consumer' as its Advertising Agency of the Year. Simms (2007) reports that both awards were made on the basis that consumers were regarded as responsible for making and generating more engaging brand communications than any one agency, during the previous year. It has to be said that most of this content was online but this is changing as the offline world becomes a target for content generation. See Viewpoint 25.4 for an example of how brands are trying to generate UGC offline. UGC can appear in many ways and in a variety of formats. The original format for UGC can be seen in letters to newspapers. The letter becomes part of the content of the newspaper and sits alongside the editorial and journalist-written copy. More recently however, digitisation has enabled faster, more immediate posting opportunities for UGC.

---

### Viewpoint 25.4    UGC gets competitive

Traditionally, the Oxo brand has been positioned around families. For years the TV ad formula was to show a family eating a meal where the OXO gravy featured as part of the storyline. That model no longer works, and to help the brand become more contemporary a new approach was adopted. This involved inviting families to develop and submit a script for their next TV campaign. The script had to be uploaded to the OXO Factor channel on YouTube. Five were selected by a panel of judges and shown on broadcast TV prime time slots. The public then voted for their favourite, which won £10K and was broadcast during the final of The X Factor.

Doritos sourced a user-generated ad using a competition supported by D&AD and Channel 4. Using an on-pack promotion and an online campaign, the public were invited to develop and shoot a 29-second TV ad., using a competition tool kit to be found on the Doritos website. Doritos ran a weekly TV show on its website, which screened a variety of content, including industry tips and judges' comments.

The 'directors' of the top 15 spots were then invited to pitch their ad to a panel of judges, who chose the three best ads. These were then voted for by the public. The winner received £100,000, plus £1 for every vote cast for them.

*Source*:   Benady (2009); Williams, (2010).

| Question: | Are there areas or subjects where user-generated content might not be helpful? |
|---|---|
| Task: | If some of your friends offered to create online content for you, which three topics would you request? |

---

Email enables viewers to interact with television and radio programmes, with presenters encouraging audiences to write and tell them 'what you think' about a topic. Discussion boards and online forums can only work through consumer participation and user-generated-content. One of the more common forms of UGC is blogging. This involves individuals, sometimes in the name of organisations, but more often as independent consumers, posting information about topics of personal interest. Sometimes these people develop opinion leader status and organisations feed them information about the launch of new brands, so that they pass on the information to opinion followers.

Social networks thrive on the shared views, opinions and beliefs, often brand-related, of networked friends. YouTube and Flickr provide opportunities for consumers to share video and photos respectively, with all material posted by users. Users post their content and respond to the work of others, often by rating the quality or entertainment value of content posted by others.

What is interesting is that, although people understand the rules and norms associated with communicating across peer groups and social networks, organisations have yet to master these new environments. Firms are not able to use traditional forms of free communication with as much credibility and authority as individuals regularly do within these contexts. One of the reasons for this is the democratisation of the media and the language codes that have emerged. A simple example is SMS texting. Although used by millions everyday to great effect, mobile communications and text messaging are only now becoming commercially prominent, mainly as a result of smartphone technology.

Muñiz and Schau (2007) refer to what they call 'vigilante marketing'. In these circumstances, consumers create self-generated advertising content to promote brands with which they have a strong affiliation. They refer to a brand community site based on the Apple Newton. This was an early PDA launched in 1993 and discontinued by Apple in 1998 as Palm Pilot undercut the Newton on price and exceeded it on quality, size and overall value. Many users at the time blamed Apple for poor communications and not explaining the Newton accurately enough to attract more customers. Roughly 3–4,000 Newton users still participate in online forums. They create what the authors label as *brand artefacts*, some of which closely resemble ads, all for a brand that ceased production nearly a decade earlier. Their actions serve to maintain a brand that has a special meaning for them.

---

**Scholars' paper 25.4**    **Can we get creative attention?**

**Heath, R.G., Nairn, A.C. and Bottomley, P.A. (2009) How Effective is Creativity? Emotive Content in TV Advertising Does Not Increase Attention,** *Journal of Advertising Research*, **49(4) (December), 450–63.**

This is one of a series of papers published by Heath about the role and nature of attention in advertising and the creative process. Here he and his colleagues consider emotive creativity and whether it can increase attention as per the conventional wisdom. All readers interested in this subject should be familiar with this paper and the attendant arguments.

---

# Sourcing content

UGC can be derived through one of three main processes:

1. *Crowdsourcing* – Organisations can prompt the public into action, via the Web community, to develop specific types of content and materials. Where organisations deliberately invite the entire web community to suggest material that can be used commercially, in return for a reward, the term *crowdsourcing* is used. In this circumstance the crowd may consist of amateurs or businesses. The difference between crowdsourcing and outsourcing is that the latter is directed at a predetermined, specific organisation.

2. *Open-source materials* – The public may take the initiative themselves and communicate with a specific organisation or industry. Where a group of people voluntarily offer ideas and materials, without invitation, prompting or seeking a reward from an organisation, the term *open-source materials* is used.

3. *Friendsourcing* – the public may exchange information and ideas amongst themselves, without any direct communication with an organisation or brand owner. This occurs when friends and families communicate and share ideas and materials among themselves, for their own enjoyment, bonding and enrichment.

Some marketers are using the increasing occurrence of UGC as an opportunity to listen to and observe consumers and to find out what meanings they attribute to products, brands and company actions. Some companies invite consumers to offer content (ads): crowdsourcing. Unilever dissolved their 16-year-old relationship with their ad agency Lowe London, in order to embark on a crowdsourcing strategy. Focusing on their Peperami brand, they searched for material to support a TV and print campaign. The result was 1185 ideas, and the winner won £6,000 (Charles, 2009).

Ideas about co-creation and collaboration now pervade marketing communications. As noted in reference to communication (Chapter 2), there is an increasing role for messages to be shared with audiences, not sent to or at them (Earls, 2010). Understanding the relationships audiences prefer with product categories and brands enables the identification of opportunities to share and collaborate.

# Key points

- Creativity in advertising is considered to be important because of the belief that creativity is an effective way of getting people to attend to an ad. This can lead to improved motivation to process the message, and from this higher recall and recognition scores can develop.

- Creativity in advertising has two main characteristics. The first is that creative ads are divergent, or highly unique or novel, and second, they are relevant or meaningful to the audience. The higher the originality or divergence and the more personally relevant, the greater the attention the ad attracts.

- Some researchers (e.g. Heath, 2009) believe that creativity does not generate increased attention; if anything, it decreases it.

- Kover (1995) identified two attention-getting strategies; forcing and subversion. Forcing strategies involve the use of surprising, irrelevant or perhaps mildly shocking content. Subversion strategies require an ad to seduce an audience, to slip by them as if unnoticed.

- What is understood to be creativity varies according to culture and context.

- Creativity in advertising can be interpreted by consumers as a signal of marketing effort by the brand owner.

- Advertising agencies, and all those working within creative departments, work within and are constrained by the prevailing organisational culture.

- The creative code refers to the framework within each agency shapes the development of advertisements.

- Framing is concerned with the selection of particular elements in order to restrict and focus the way people perceive a problem, brand, issue or communication event.

- People use storytelling to help make sense of their lives and the events that they encounter and to derive meaning from their relationships and social activities (Merchant et al. 2010).

- Stories consist of themes (hardship, reciprocity and a defining moment) and plots (a sequence of events; anticipation, crisis, getting help, and achieving a goal).

- User-generated content (UGC) is about the ways in which people make use of social media (Kaplan and Haenlein, 2010) and the various forms of media content that are publicly available and created by end-users.

- UGC has three primary characteristics: the content needs to be published either on a publicly accessible website or on a social networking site accessible to a selected group of people. The material needs to demonstrate some creative effort, and it has to have been created outside of professional routines and practices.

# Review questions

1. Write brief notes describing early ideas about creativity and explain the terms 'divergence' and 'relevance'.

2. What do forcing and subversion mean in the context of creativity?

3. Explain the arguments concerning creativity and attention. How can these be related to the Johnnie Walker minicase?

4. Identify the core issues associated with the view that creativity does not generate increased attention.

5. Draw the outline of a short presentation designed to explain and give examples of the creative code.

6. Outline the principles associated with framing. How does this concept assist those responsible for marketing communications?

7. Make notes explaining the elements of storytelling.

8. What are the four main categories that constitute stories?

9. Using different media, find three examples of user-generated content.

10. Explain the terms 'crowdsourcing', 'open-source' and 'friendsourcing'.

# References

Ambler, T. and Hollier, E.A. (2004) The Waste in Advertising Is the Part That Works, *Journal of Advertising Research*, 44, 4, 375–89.

Ang, S.H., Lee, Y.H. and Leong, S.M. (2007) The Ad Creativity Cube: Conceptualization and Initial Validation, *Journal of the Academy of Marketing Science*, 35, 2, 220–32.

Baack, D.W., Wilson, R.T. and Till, B.D. (2008) Creativity and Memory Effects: Recall, Recognition, and an Exploration of Nontraditional Media, *Journal of Advertising*, 37, 4 (Winter), 85–94.

Barker, R.T. and Gower, K. (2010) Strategic application of storytelling in organizations, *Journal of Business Communication*, 45, 3 (July), 295–312.

Benady, D. (2009) Advertising to the YouTube generation, *Marketing*, 25 November, 34–5.

Binet, L. and Field, P. (2007) *Marketing in the era of accountability*, Institute of Practitioners in Advertising, Henley-on-Thames: WARC.

Blasko, V.J. and Mokwa, M.P. (1986) Creativity in Advertising: A Janusian Perspective, *Journal of Advertising*, 15, 4, 43–50.

Boje, D.M. (1991) The storytelling organization: A study of story performance, *Administrative Science Quarterly*, 36, 106–26.

Brook, S. (2008) Johnnie Walker strolls off with three IPA awards, the *Guardian*, 4 November 2008, retrieved 18 January 2012 from http://www.guardian.co.uk/media/2008/nov/04/advertising-marketingandpr1.

Buda, R. (2003) The interactive effect of message framing, presentation order, and source credibility on recruitment practices, *International Journal of Management*, 20(2), 156–63.

Campaignlive (2011) On the Creative Floor: Dentsu – Interview with Tatsuya Tsujinaka, Dentsu's senior creative director, retrieved 1 May 2012 from http://www.brandrepublic.com/features/1104624/Creative-Floor-Dentsu/?DCMP=ILC-SEARCH.

Charles, G. (2009) Peperami ad will be test case for crowd-sourcing, *Marketing*, 4 November, p. 2.

Christodoulides, G., Jevons, C. and Blackshaw, P. (2011) The Voice of the Consumer Speaks Forcefully in Brand Identity: User-Generated Content Forces Smart Marketers to Listen, *Journal of Advertising Research*, Supplement, March, 101–8.

Cordiner, R. (2009) Set free your core narrative: the brand as storyteller, *Admap*, October, retrieved 8 July 2010 from www.warc.com.

Cowen, N. (2007) Halo 3 review: Third time's the charm, the *Telegraph*, 26 September, Retrieved 6 November 2010 from www.telegraph.co.uk/technology/3354551/Halo-3-review-Third-times-the-charm.html.

Dahlen, M., Rosengren, S. and Torn, F. (2008) Advertising Creativity Matters, *Journal of Advertising Research*, September, 392–403.

Dan, V. and Ihlen, Ø. (2011) Framing Expertise: A Cross-Cultural Analysis of Success in Framing Contests, *Journal of Communication Management*, 15, 4, 368–88.

DeLarge, C.A. (2004) Storytelling as a critical success factor in design processes and outcomes, *Design Management Review*, 15, 76–81.

Earls, M. (2010) The wisdom of crowds, *Admap*, (May) retrieved 10 May 2010 from www.warc.com/.

Edwards, H. (2012) Opinion: Helen Edwards, *Marketing*, 15 February, p. 18.

El-Murad, J. and West, D.C. (2004) The Definition and Measurement of Creativity: What Do We Know? *Journal of Advertising Research*, 44, 2, 188–201.

Entman, R.M. (1993) Framing: Toward Clarification of a Fractured Paradigm, *Journal of Communication*, 43, 4, 51–8.

Fonnesbaek, J. and Andersen, M.M. (2005) Story selling: how LEGO told a story and sold a toy, *Young Consumers*, Quarter 2, 31–9.

Fryer, B. (2003) Storytelling that moves people: A conversation with screenwriting coach Robert McKee, *Harvard Business Review*, 6, 51–55.

Gallery, C., Rothenberg, T., Cohen, N. and Courage, J. (2009) Xbox Halo 3 – heroic storytelling, Account Planning Group – (UK), Gold & Grand Prix, Creative Strategy Awards, retrieved 8 July 2010 from www.warc.com/.

Gamson, W.A. and Modigliani, A. (1989) Media Discourse and Public Opinion on Nuclear Power: a constructionist approach, *American Journal of Sociology*, 95, 1–37.

Goodenough, W.H. (1981) *Culture, Language, and Society*, Menlo Park, CA: Benjamin/Cummings.

Hackley, C. (2000) Silent running: tacit discursive and psychological aspects of management in a top UK advertising agency, *British Journal of Management*, 11, 239–54.

Hackley, C. and Kover, A.J. (2007) The trouble with creatives: negotiating creative identity in advertising agencies, *International Journal of Advertising*, 26, 1, 63–78.

Han, S.P. and Shavitt, S. (1994) Persuasion and Culture: Advertising Appeals in Individualistic and Collectivistic Societies, *Journal of Experimental Social Psychology*, 30, 4, 326–50.

Heath, R.G. (2010) Creativity in TV ads does not increase attention, *Admap*, (January) retrieved 23 October 2011 from www.warc.com.

Heath, R.G., Nairn, A.C. and Bottomley, P.A. (2009) How Effective is Creativity? Emotive Content in TV Advertising Does Not Increase Attention, *Journal of Advertising Research*, (September), 450–63.

Hegarty, J. (2011) *Hegarty on Advertising: Turning Intelligence into Magic*, London: Thames & Hudson.

Helegsen, T. (1994) Advertising Awards and Advertising Agency Performance Criteria, *Journal of Advertising Research*, 34 (July/August), 43–53.

Hetsroni, A. and Tukachinsky, R.H. (2005) The Use of Fine Art in Advertising: A Survey of Creatives and Content Analysis of Advertisements, *Journal of Current Issues and Research in Advertising*, 27(1) (Spring), 93–107.

Hill, R. and Johnson, L.W. (2004) Understanding creative service: a qualitative study of the advertising problem delineation, communication and response (APDCR) process, *International Journal of Advertising*, 23, 3, 285–307.

Holtz, M.R., Ryans, J.K. and Shanklin, W.L. (1982) Agency/client relationships as seen by influentials on both sides, *Journal of Advertising*, 11, 1, 37–44.

IPA (2011) *New Models of Marketing Effectiveness From Integration to Orchestration*, WARC.

Jones, S.E. and LeBaron, C.D. (2002) Research on the relationship between verbal and nonverbal communication: Emerging integrations, *Journal of Communication*, 52, 3, 499–521.

Kaplan, A.M. and Haenlein, M. (2010) Users of the world, unite! The challenges and opportunities of Social Media, *Business Horizons*, 53, 1 (January–February), 59–68.

Kim, B.H., Han, S. and Yoon, S. (2010) Advertising Creativity in Korea: Scale Development and Validation, *Journal of Advertising*, 39, 2 (Summer), 93–108.

Kirmani, A. (1997) Advertising Repetition as a Signal of Quality: If It's Advertised So Much, Something Must Be Wrong, *Journal of Advertising*, 26(3), 77–86.

Koslow, S., Sasser, S.L. and Riordan, E.A. (2003) What Is Creative to Whom and Why? Perceptions in Advertising Agencies, *Journal of Advertising Research*, 43 (March), 96–110.

Koslow, S., Sasser, S.L. and Riordan, E.A. (2006) Do marketers get the advertising they need or the advertising they deserve? *Journal of Advertising*, 35, 3, 81–101.

Kover, A.J. (1995) Copywriters' implicit theories of communication: An exploration, *Journal of Consumer Research*, 21, 4, 596–611.

LaBahn, D.W. and Kohli, C. (1997) Maintaining client commitment in advertising agency/client relationships, *Industrial Marketing Management*, 26, 6, 497–508.

Lafferty, B.A., Goldsmith, R.E. and Newell, S.J. (2002) The dual credibility model: the influence of corporate and endorser credibility on attitudes and purchase intentions, *Journal of Marketing Theory and Practice*, 10, 3, 1–12.

Lämsä, A.-M. and Sintonen, T. (2006) A narrative approach for organizational learning in a diverse organisation, *Journal of Workplace Learning*, 18, 106–20.

Love, M. (2006) Cutting through the clutter at Microsoft, *Strategic Communication Management*, Retrieved 24 August 2009 from www.melcrum.com/articles/clutter_at_microsoft.shtml.

Luo, X. and Bhattacharya, C.B. (2006) Corporate Social Responsibility, Customer Satisfaction, and Market Value, *Journal of Marketing*, 70(4), 1–18.

MacKenzie, S.B. and Lutz, R.L. (1989) An empirical examination of the structural antecedents of attitude toward the ad in an advertising pretesting context, *Journal of Marketing*, 53, 48–65.

Marshall, J. and Adamic, M. (2010) The story is the message: shaping corporate culture, *Journal of Business Strategy*, 31, 2, 18–23.

Masuda, T. and Nisbett, R.E. (2001) *Attending Holistically Vs. Analytically: Comparing the Context Sensitivity of Japanese and Americans*, Ann Arbor: University of Michigan Press.

McLellan, H. (2006) Corporate Storytelling Perspectives, *The Journal for Quality & Participation*, 26(1) (Spring), 17–20.

Merchant, A., Ford, J.B. and Sargeant, A. (2010) Charitable organizations' storytelling influence on donors' emotions and intentions, *Journal of Business Research*, 63, 7 (July), 754–62.

Mircale, G.E. (1987) Feel-Do-Learn: An Alternative Sequence Underlying Japanese Consumer Response to Television Commercials, in *Proceedings of the 1987 Conference of the American Academy of Advertising*, Columbia: University of South Carolina, R73–R78.

Muniz, A.M. and Schau, H.J. (2007) Vigilante marketing and consumer-created content communications, *Journal of Advertising*, 36(3) (Autumn), 35–50.

Na, W., Marshall, R. and Woodside, A.G. (2009) Decision system analysis of advertising agency decisions, *Qualitative Market Research: An International Journal*, 12, 2, 153–70.

Nyilasy, G. and Reid, L.N. (2009) Agency practitioners' meta-theories of advertising, *International Journal of Advertising*, 28(4), 639–68.

Pan, Z. and Kosicki, G. (2001) Framing as a Strategic Action in Public Deliberation, in S.D. Reese, O.H. Gandy and A.E. Grant (eds), *Framing Public Life: Perspectives on Media and Our Understanding of the Social World*, Mahwah, NJ: Lawrence Erlbaum, pp. 35–65.

Papadatos. C. (2006) The art of storytelling: how loyalty marketers can build emotional connections to their brands, *Journal of Consumer Marketing*, 23, 7, 382–4.

Reid, L.N. and Rotfield, H.J. (1976) Toward an Associative Model of Advertising Creativity, *Journal of Advertising*, 5, 4, 24–9.

Rossiter, J. and Percy, L. (1998) *Advertising, Communications, and Promotion Management*, Singapore: McGraw Hill, International Editions.

Rossiter, J.R. (2008) Envisioning the future of advertising creativity research: alternative perspectives, Defining the necessary components of creative, effective ads, *Journal of Advertising*, 37, 4, 139–44.

Simms, J. (2007) Advertising: and now a word from our customers, *Marketing*, 31 January. Retrieved 16 September 2007 from http://www.brandrepublic.com/News/629458/Advertising-word-customers/.

Smith, R.E. and Yang, X. (2004) Toward a General Theory of Creativity in Advertising: The Role of Divergence, *Marketing Theory*, 4(1/2), 31–58.

Smith, R.E., Chen, J. and Yang, X. (2008) The impact of advertising creativity on the hierarchy of effects, *Journal of Advertising*, 37, 4 (Winter), 47–61.

Smith, R.E., MacKenzie, S.B., Yang, X., Buchholz, L.M. and Darley, W.K. (2007) Modelling the Determinants and Effects of Creativity in Advertising, *Marketing Science*, 26, 6, 819–833.

Stuhlfaut, M. (2011) The creative code: an organisational influence on the creative process in advertising, *International Journal of Advertising*, 30, 2, 283–304.

Tsai, S.-P. (2007) Message framing strategy for brand communication, *Journal of Advertising Research*, 47, 3 (September), 364–77.

Warlick, M. (2009) Xbox Halo 3 – heroic storytelling, *Creative Strategy Awards*, retrieved 8 July 2010 from www.warc.com/.

Watchman, E. and Johnson, S. (2009) Discover Your Persuasive Story, *Marketing Management*, 18, 2, 22–7.

Weick, K.E. (1979) *The Social Psychology of Organizing*, Reading, MA: Addison-Wesley.

Weick, K.E. (1995) *Sensemaking in organizations*, Thousand Oaks, CA: Sage.

West, D.C., Kover, A.J. and Caruana, A. (2008) Practitioner and customer views of advertising creativity, *Journal of Advertising*, 37, 4, 35–45.

Williams, M. (2010) Doritos ramps up prize fund for latest ad competition, *Campaignlive.co.uk*, 16 February, retrieved 6 April 2010 from www.campaignlive.co.uk/news/984073/Doritos-ramps-prize-fund-latest-ad-competition/.

Woodside, A., Sood, S. and Miller, K. (2008) When consumers and brands talk: storytelling theory and research in psychology and marketing, *Psychology & Marketing*, 25, 2, 97–145.

Wylie, A. (1998) Story telling: A powerful form of communication, *Communication World*, 15, 30–33.

Yang, X. and Smith, R.E. (2009) Beyond Attention Effects: Modelling the Persuasive and Emotional Effects of Advertising Creativity, *Marketing Science*, 28, 935–49.

# Chapter 26
## Messages and appeals

The message an organisation conveys is a critical aspect of marketing communications. This means consideration must be given to what organisations say, how they say it and the meaning people are expected to ascribe to these messages. Ensuring that the right balance of information and emotion is achieved and that the presentation of the message is appropriate for the target audience represents an important, yet immensely interesting part of the creative process.

## Aims and learning objectives

The aim of this chapter is to consider some of the ways in which marketing communication messages can be presented.

The learning objectives of this chapter are to:

1. consider the importance and characteristics of source credibility;
2. explore the advantages and disadvantages of using spokespersons;
3. explain the different ways messages can be constructed;
4. discuss the use of information and emotions in advertising messages;
5. examine the various ways in which advertising appeals can be presented;
6. describe how informational and transformational motives can be used as tactical tools in a communications plan.

# Minicase

## Lynx Jet – fantasy appeals

Lynx is a male grooming product from Unilever, primarily targeted at 15 to 25-year-old males, and is sold in Ireland, UK and Australia. Throughout the rest of the world it is known as Axe. Lynx is strongly differentiated as an unpretentious, fun brand.

Lynx advertising uses a consistent appeal based upon sexual attraction and humour. Each ad is based on the story that a young aspirational man uses Lynx deodorant spray, which then inexplicably draws young women to him. At another level, the Lynx Effect, as it is known, boosts confidence and association with the brand can serve to boost the ego. So successful and popular has been the Lynx Effect advertising format that competitors have copied it, with limited success, and brands such as Specsavers, in an entirely different category, have developed spoofs.

In Australia in 2005 Lynx sales had been falling as perceptions of the brand failed to lift or differentiate it from competitors. A campaign was required that could draw attention back to the brand and re-establish it as the fun brand for young men.

The root of the campaign emerged with the insight that young Australian 18- to 25-year-old men traditionally take an international trip to see the world. This is seen as a first trip abroad without parents, and is considered to be a rite of passage into manhood. This led to the creation of an imaginary airline, called Lynx Jet, which would carry these young men on fantasy flights. It was staffed by sexy airline cabin crew called 'mostesses' pictured striding across the tamac. The underlining campaign strategy was to parody traditional airline advertising and marketing, particularly that used by Virgin Atlantic.

The creative idea was to mimick airline advertising and marketing strategies through the creation of a virtual airline and to use communications that included content about key destinations, pricing, services and loyalty programmes, such as a frequent flyer programme, which was called the Lynx Jet Mile High club.

To add authenticity, the original brief required that the airline be seen to fly, that there be a tangible

**LYNXjet Direct Response Campaign.**

| Exhibit 26.1 | **Lynx Jet 'mostesses' in a parody of airline advertising** |

*Source*: Unilever, Australasia

aircraft. As a result it was negotiated that Jetstar would allow one of their planes to be painted in the colour yellow of the Lynx campaign. The Boeing 717 would fly routes along Australia's eastern seaboard and would be competitively priced against local carriers such as Jetstar and Virgin Blue. However, although the in-flight attendants on the designated flights were not expected to dress or behave like the 'mostesses' in the Lynx TV ads, there were complaints from airline staff, the general public, and Jetstar marketing consultants. As a result Jetstar withdrew the plane and ceased all involvement with the deal.

When the television ads were first broadcast, a special edition Lynx deodorant, called Lynx Jet, was launched. The website 'lynxjet.com' encouraged visitors to sign up to the Mile High club and they could try to book trips online, although all flights were already fully booked.

A series of ads were developed, each depicting a different airline service, such as in-flight pillow fights, body massages and a spacious bar. To deliver these messages a wide range of media were used. Paid media included television, radio, outdoor and newspapers, with the very first ad aired during an Australian World Cup qualifying match, reaching a large proportion of the target audience.

Owned media included a full replication of an airline website, as depicted at Exhibit 26.2. This was an important support element as it enabled young males to interact with the brand.

In addition to this, field marketing activity was also used to bring the brand to the audience. A branded mobile Mile High club travelled around cities in the south-east, offering body massages. Mostesses appeared at a variety of events and gave out business cards with their phone numbers and access details to the airline. Direct mail was used to send welcome letters to people registering online for the Mile High club. Lynx Jet was also seen to be sponsoring online travel sites. The net effect of all of this activity was to drive earned media. This could be seen in terms of the high level of word of mouth comment, evidenced by the amount of blogs and blogging activity, and the intensity of media and public debate about the campaign's appropriateness, motives, and morals.

WEBSITE

| Exhibit 26.2 | **The Lynx Jet website** |
|---|---|
| | *Source*: Unilever, Australasia |

In addition to the controversy and extensive public relations activity, the commercial outcomes of the Lynx Jet campaign were better than planned. Sales rose by 20 per cent in the first four weeks, and a temporary market share of 84 per cent was recorded. The number of page views exceeded 650,000 during the campaign and perceptions about how sexy the brand is rose 10 per cent among the target audience.

The campaign also won a raft of prizes including the Grand Prix and two Gold Lions at the Cannes Lions Festival in 2006.

*This minicase was written by Chris Fill using a variety of sources including: Anon (2011); Wentz (2006); Adforum (2006); Duncan (2005)*

# Introduction

Having considered what creativity might be and some of the issues associated with developing the right messages for the right audience, attention now falls on the form of the message itself. This is referred to as the message appeal and the bulk of this chapter is given to considering the variety and forms of the different appeals.

The Lynx Jet campaign described in the minicase sets out an extreme example of an emotional appeal using sex and fantasy to change perceptions of a brand. In terms of the goals set and the target audience the campaign appears to have been successful. However, the intensity and controversial nature of the campaign material probably changed the perception of various non-target audiences in a way that may not have been in the long-term interests of the brand.

This chapter builds on ideas considered in the previous chapter about creativity and associated processes, and explores four broad elements. First, attention is given to the source of a message and issues relating to source credibility. Second, the role and issues associated with using spokespersons, to either be the face of a brand or to endorse it, is explored. Third, the need to balance the use of information and emotion in messages and the way messages are constructed is reviewed before finally exploring the various appeals and ways in which messages can be presented.

# Message source

Messages are perceived in many different ways and are influenced by a variety of factors. However, a critical determinant concerns the credibility that is attributed to the source of the message itself. Kelman (1961) believed that the source of a message has three particular characteristics. These are: the level of perceived credibility as seen in terms of perceived objectivity and expertise; the degree to which the source is regarded as attractive and message recipients are motivated to develop a similar association or position; and the degree of power that the source is believed to possess. This is manifested in the ability of the source to reward or punish message receivers. The two former characteristics are evident in various forms of marketing communications, but the latter is directly observable in personal selling situations, and perhaps in the use of sales promotions.

Following this work on source characteristics, three key components of source credibility can be distinguished:

- What is the level of perceived expertise (how much relevant knowledge is the source thought to hold)?
- What are the personal motives the source is believed to possess (what is the reason for the source to be involved)?
- What degree of trust can be placed in what the source says or does on behalf of the endorsement?

No matter what the level of expertise, if the level of trust is questionable, credibility will be adversely affected.

---

**Scholars' paper 26.1**    **A very credible credibility concept**

**Kelman, H.C. (1961), Process of Opinion Change, *Public Opinion Quarterly*, 25 (Spring), 57–78.**

This is a seminal paper in this subject and all students of marketing communications should be familiar with it. Kelman suggested that successful communications emanate from sources that are credible, attractive and powerful. Subsequently, there has been much research into the impact and effect of source credibility in different situations and on different subjects. The prevailing view remains that people think more about messages from sources that they consider to be highly credible, than those from low-credibility sources.

---

# Establishing credibility

Credibility can be established in a number of ways. One simple approach is to list or display the key attributes of the organisation or the product and then signal trustworthiness through the use of third-party endorsements and the comments of satisfied users.

A more complex approach is to use referrals, suggestions and association. Trustworthiness and expertise are the two principal elements of source credibility. One way of developing trust is to use spokespersons to speak on behalf of the sponsor of an advertisement and, in effect, provide a testimonial for the product in question. Credibility, therefore, can be established by the initiator of the advertisement or by a spokesperson used by the initiator to convey the message.

Effectively, consumers trade off the validity of claims made by brands against the perceived trustworthiness (and expertise) of the individuals or organisations who deliver the message. The result is that a claim may have reduced impact if either of these two components is doubtful or not capable of verification but, if repeated enough times, will enable audiences to accept that the products are very effective and of sufficiently high performance for them to try.

## Credibility established by the initiator

The credibility of the organisation initiating the communication process is important. An organisation should seek to enhance its reputation with its various stakeholders at every opportunity.

However, organisational credibility is derived from the image, which in turn is a composite of many perceptions. Past decisions, current strategy and performance indicators, the level of perceived service and the type of performance of network members (e.g. high-quality retail outlets) all influence the perception of an organisation and the level of credibility that follows.

One very important factor that influences credibility is branding. Private and family brands in particular allow initiators to develop and launch new products more easily than those who do not have such brand strength. Brand extensions (such as Stella Artois cidre) have been launched with the credibility of the product firmly grounded in the strength of the parent brand name (Stella Artois). Consumers recognise the name and make associations that enable them to lower the perceived risk and in doing so provide a platform to try the new product.

The need to establish high levels of credibility allows organisations to divert advertising spend away from a focus on brands to one that focuses on the organisation. Corporate advertising seeks to adjust organisation image and to build reputation.

---

### Viewpoint 26.1    Max Factor uses a source of credibility

Max Factor claims that its products are so good that they are used by the experts in their industry: 'The make-up of make-up artists'. Many of its recent campaigns feature expert make-up artists who work on blockbuster Hollywood movies. However, many of these experts are not known by the general public. The development of 'trustworthiness' therefore relies on the film credential.

As with all use of spokespersons, Max Factor needs to ensure that when using experts its target audiences perceive the messages to be genuinely believable. In this case, Max Factor uses these experts because they are perceived to be objective and independent simply because their job gives them freedom of choice with regard to the products they use.

Potential new customers seeing these advertisements are challenged on the grounds that, if the brand is good enough for these experts, then it should be good enough for them. If a viewer is already a Max Factor customer, then product experience will contribute to a support argument and these advertising messages are used to reinforce previous brand choice decisions. Either way, these Max Factor advertisements are extremely powerful.

**Question:**  To what extent does the use of experts evade focus on product attributes and quality?

**Task:**  Using various magazine ads for fragrances and cosmetics, make a list of the different ways source credibility is established.

# Credibility established by a spokesperson

People who deliver the message are often regarded as the source, when in reality they are only the messenger. These people carry the message and represent the true source or initiator of the message (e.g. manufacturer or retailer). Consequently, the testimonial they transmit must be credible. There are four main types of spokesperson: the expert, the celebrity, the chief executive officer and the consumer.

*The expert* has been used many times and was particularly popular when television advertising first established itself in the 1950s and 1960s. Experts are quickly recognisable because they either wear white coats and round glasses or dress and act like 'mad professors'. Through the use of symbolism, stereotypes and identification, these characters (and indeed others) can be established very quickly in the minds of receivers and a frame of reference generated that does not question the authenticity of the message being transmitted by such a person. Experts can also be users of products – for example, professional photographers endorsing cameras, secretaries endorsing word processors and professional golfers endorsing golf equipment.

*Entertainment and sporting celebrities* are being used increasingly, not only to provide credibility for a range (e.g. Jenson Button for Vodafone, Keira Knightly for Chanel), but also to grab the attention of people in markets where motivation to decide between competitive products may be low. The celebrity enables the message to stand out among the clutter and noise that typify many markets. It is also hoped that the celebrity and/or the voice-over will become a peripheral cue in the decision-making process: Joanna Lumley for Privilege car insurance, Chris Addison and Alexander Armstrong for Direct Line, and Kevin Spacey for American Airlines.

There are some potential problems that advertisers need to be aware of when considering the use of celebrities. First, does the celebrity fit the image of the brand and will the celebrity be acceptable to the target audience? Consideration also needs to be given to the longer-term relationship between the celebrity and the brand. Should the lifestyle of the celebrity change, what impact will this change have on the target audience and their attitude towards the brand?

---

**Scholars' paper 26.2**    **Cooking up celebrity appeal**

**Halonen-Knight, E. and Hurmerinta, L. (2010) Who endorses whom? Meanings transfer in celebrity endorsement, *Journal of Product & Brand Management*, 19(6), 452–460.**

This paper explores how meaning is transferred in celebrity endorsement within a study of the partnership between celebrity chef Jamie Oliver and Sainsbury's, a leading UK supermarket chain. The authors conclude that celebrity endorsement can be perceived as a brand alliance, so they stress that the importance of selection and management of brand alliance partners should be extended to celebrity endorsements.

---

The second problem concerns the impact that the celebrity makes relative to the brand. There is a danger that those receiving the message remember the celebrity but not the brand that is the focus of the advertising spend. The *celebrity* becomes the hero, rather than the product being advertised. Loveless (2007) reports on the financial services company First Plus who used celebrity mathematician Carol Vorderman to endorse their loan products. Some saw a mismatch between this celebrity's values and those of the brand, and the possibility that the company she was endorsing might make some people worse off was highlighted. In these situations the endorser can overshadow the product to the extent that consumers might have trouble recalling the brand.

| Exhibit 26.3 | Speedy broadband, superfast Usain Bolt and Richard Branson |
|---|---|

In order to convey the message that Virgin Media has the fastest broadband speeds, the world's fastest man over 100 metres, Usain Bolt, was used to provide speed-related associations, in the 2012 'Keep Up' campaign. Through the use of gentle visual humour, Bolt was shown impersonating CEO Branson, taking over his office and sporting his trademark blonde goatee. Richard Branson played himself with a significant 'background' role, trying to get into his own office. The TV ad, supported by print and digital, balanced an informational strategy with attention-getting emotional content.

*Source*: Tom Oldham/Virgin Media

Some CEOs have relished the chance to sell their own products and there have been some notable business people who have 'fronted' their organisation. One of the more prominent CEOs in the UK is Ryanair's Michael O'Leary. Outspoken and controversial on many airline-related issues, he is reported to have stated that the firm does not need a marketing director, as he can do the job. Furthermore, he refers to the British Airway's 'To fly. To serve' campaign as nonsense (Eleftheriou-Smith, 2012). Ryanair do no advertising and their marketing strategy is rooted firmly in being the lowest-cost provider in Europe. Richard Branson is used selectively within the Virgin portfolio but has fronted campaigns for Virgin Financial products and the group as a whole. See Exhibit 26.3.

When using consumers as the spokesperson to endorse products, the audience is being asked to identify with a 'typical consumer'. The identification of similar lifestyles, interests and opinions allows for better reception and understanding of the message. Consumers are often depicted testing similar products, such as margarine and butter. The Pepsi Challenge required consumers to select Pepsi from Coca-Cola through blind taste tests. Showing someone using the product, someone who is similar to the receiver, means that the source is perceived as credible and the potential for successful persuasion is considerably enhanced.

## Sleeper effects

The assumption so far has been that high credibility enhances the probability of persuasion and successful communication. This is true when the receiver's initial position is opposite to that contained in the message. When the receiver's position is favourable to the message, a moderate level of credibility may be more appropriate.

Whether source credibility is high, medium or low is of little consequence, according to some researchers (Hannah and Sternthal, 1984). The impact of the source is believed to dissipate after approximately six weeks and only the content of the message is thought to dominate the receiver's attention. This sleeper effect (Hovland et al., 1949) has not been proved empirically, but the implication is that the persuasiveness of a message can increase over time. Furthermore, advertisers using highly credible sources need to repeat the message on a regular basis, in order that the required level of effectiveness and persuasion be maintained (Schiffman and Kanuk, 1991).

# Structural elements in a message

An important part of any message strategy is a consideration of the best way of communicating the key points or core message. This needs to be accomplished by structuring messages carefully to avoid encouraging objections and opposing points of view. The following are regarded as some of the important structural features that can shape the pattern of a message.

## Message balance

It is evident from previous discussions that the effectiveness of any single message is dependent on a variety of factors. From a receiver's perspective, two elements appear to be significant: first, the amount and quality of the information that is communicated and, second, the overall judgement that each individual makes about the way a message is communicated.

This suggests that the style of a message should reflect a balance between the need for information and the need for pleasure or enjoyment in consuming the message. Figure 26.1 describes the two main forms of appeal. Messages can be product-oriented and rational or customer-oriented and based on feelings and emotions.

It is clear that when dealing with high-involvement decisions, where persuasion occurs through a central processing route, the emphasis of the message should be on the information content, in particular the key attributes and the associated benefits. This style is often factual and product-oriented. If the product evokes low-involvement decision-making, then the message should concentrate on the images that are created within the mind of the message

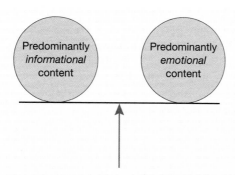

**Figure 26.1**    The balance of emotions and information in messages

recipient. This style seeks to elicit an emotional response from receivers. Obviously, there are many situations where both rational and emotional messages are needed by buyers in order to make purchasing decisions.

## Conclusion drawing

Should the message draw a firm conclusion for the audience or should people be allowed to draw their own conclusions from the content? Explicit conclusions are more easily understood and stand a better chance of being effective (Kardes, 1988). However, it is the nature of the issue, the particular situation and the composition of the target audience that influence the effectiveness of conclusion drawing (Hovland and Mandell, 1952). Whether or not a conclusion should be drawn for the receiver depends upon the following:

1. *The complexity of the issue*
   Healthcare products, central heating systems and personal finance services, for example, can be complex, and in the case of some members of the target audience their cognitive ability, experience and motivation may not be sufficient for them to draw their own conclusions. The complexity of the product requires that messages must draw conclusions for them. It should also be remembered that even highly informed and motivated audiences may require assistance if the product or issue is relatively new.

2. *The level of education possessed by the receiver*
   Better-educated audiences prefer to draw their own conclusions, whereas less-well-educated audiences may need the conclusion drawn for them because they may not be able to make the inference from the message.

3. *Whether immediate action is required*
   If urgent action is required by the receiver, then a conclusion should be drawn very clearly. Political parties can be observed to use this strategy immediately before an election.

4. *The level of involvement*
   High involvement usually means that receivers prefer to make up their own minds and may reject or resent any attempt to have the conclusion drawn for them (Arora, 1985).

## One- and two-sided messages

This concerns how the case for an issue is presented. One approach is to present the case for and against an issue – a two-sided message. Alternatively just the case in favour of an issue can be presented – a one-sided message. Research indicates that one-sided messages are more effective when receivers favour the opinion offered in the message and when the receivers are less well-educated.

Two-sided messages, where both the good and the bad points of an issue are presented, are more effective when the receiver's initial opinion is opposite to that presented in the message and when they are well-educated. Credibility is improved by understanding the audience's position and then fashioning the presentation of the message. Faison (1961) found that two-sided messages tend to produce more positive perceptions of a source than one-sided messages.

## Order of presentation

Further questions regarding the development of message strategy concern the order in which important points are presented. Messages that present the strongest points at the beginning use what is referred to as the *primacy* effect. The decision to place the main points at the beginning depends on whether the audience has a low or high level of involvement. A low level may require an attention-getting message component at the beginning. Similarly, if the target has an opinion opposite to that contained in the message, a weak point may lead to a high level of counter-argument.

A decision to place the strongest points at the end of the message assumes that the *recency* effect will bring about greater levels of persuasion. This is appropriate when the receiver agrees with the position adopted by the source or has a high positive level of involvement.

The order of argument presentation is more relevant in personal selling than in television advertisements. However, as learning through television is largely passive, because involvement is low and interest minimal, the presentation of key selling points at the beginning and at the end of the message will enhance message reception and recall.

# Message appeal

The presentation of a message requires that an appeal be made to the target audience. The appeal is important, because unless the execution of the message appeal (the creative) is appropriate to the target audience's perception and expectations, the chances of successful communication are reduced.

There are two main factors associated with the presentation. Is the message to be dominated by the need to transmit product-oriented information or is there a need to transmit a message that appeals predominantly to the emotional senses of the receiver? The main choice of presentation style, therefore, concerns the degree of factual information transmitted in a message against the level of imagery thought necessary to make sufficient impact for the message to command attention and then be processed. There are numerous presentational or executional techniques, but the following are some of the more commonly used appeals.

## Information-based appeals

Information or rational appeals can be presented through four main types of appeal. These are factual, slice-of-life, demonstration and comparative appeals.

### Factual

Sometimes referred to as the 'hard sell', the dominant objective of these appeals is to provide, often detailed, information. This type of appeal is commonly associated with high-involvement decisions where receivers are sufficiently motivated and able to process information. Persuasion, according to the ELM, is undertaken through the central processing route. This means that ads should be rational and contain logically reasoned arguments and information in order that receivers are able to complete their decision-making processes.

### Slice of life

As noted earlier, the establishment of credibility is vital if any message is to be accepted and processed. One of the ways in which this can be achieved is to present the message in such a way that the receiver can identify immediately with the scenario being presented. This process of creating similarity is used a great deal in advertising and is referred to as slice-of-life advertising. For example, many washing powder advertisers use a routine that depicts two ordinary women (assumed to be similar to the target receiver), invariably in a kitchen or garden, discussing the poor results achieved by one of their washing powders. Following the advice of one of the women, the stubborn stains are seen to be overcome by the focus brand.

On successful decoding of this message the overall effect of this appeal is for the receiver to conclude the following: that person is like me; I have had the same problem as that person; they are satisfied using brand X, therefore I, too, will use brand X. This technique is simple, well-tried, well-liked and successful, despite its sexist overtones. It is also interesting to note that a number of surveys have found that a majority of women feel that advertisers use inappropriate stereotyping to portray female roles, these being predominantly housewife and mother roles.

## Demonstration

A similar technique is to present the problem to the audience as a demonstration. The focus brand is depicted as instrumental in the resolution of a problem. Headache remedies, floor cleaners and tyre commercials have traditionally demonstrated the pain, the dirt and the danger respectively, and then shown how the focus brand relieves the pain (Panadol), removes the stubborn dirt (Flash or Cillit Bang) or stops in the wet on a coin (or the edge of a rooftop – Continental tyres). Whether the execution is believable is a function of the credibility and the degree of life-like dialogue or copy that is used.

## Comparative advertising

Comparative advertising is a popular means of positioning brands. Messages are based on the comparison of a brand with either a main competitor brand or all competing brands, with the aim of establishing and maintaining superiority. The comparison may centre on one or two key attributes and can be a good way of entering new markets. Entrants keen to establish a presence in a market have little to lose by comparing themselves with market leaders. However, market leaders have a great deal to lose and little to gain by comparing themselves with minor competitors.

---

### Viewpoint 26.2    Coffee wars

The use of comparative advertising, especially by coffee house brands, is particularly prominent during periods of economic downturn. The aim is to maintain the discretionary spend on out-of-home coffee and to ensure that competitors do not win it. Not surprising therefore that coffee wars have broken out, and many of the attacks have been aimed at Starbucks.

In the USA Dunkin' was the winner in a nationwide taste test. This result was subsequently used in Dunkins' comparative advertising. This featured a white-coated woman polling hard-working, blue-collar Americans who, it claims, are its most loyal customers. Starbucks, whose customer base is known to be much more more middle class, responded through print and outdoor ads warning customers to 'Beware of cheaper coffee. It comes with a price.' Starbucks has always claimed that it uses superior, better-quality beans, with better-trained staff, and, increasingly, more stringent environmental standards.

In the UK Costa coffee is using comparative advertising and has targeted market leader Starbucks. This time the press ads read 'Sorry, Starbucks the people have voted.' The ads explain how research has shown that seven out of 10 coffee-lovers prefer Costa's cappuccino to Starbucks'.

This is not the end of the Starbucks tale. Back in the USA ad-based attacks from competitors continue to rise. This time it was from the upmarket brand, Caribou Coffee whose ads were directed squarely at the Starbucks customer base. The first ad promoted mochas reformulated with 'real chocolate'. The ad starred two trendily attired plastic dolls one of whom asks, when a human-sized person sits down with a frothy Caribou beverage, 'Why don't we ever get Caribou coffee?' The boy doll replies, 'Because we're not real.' Starbucks refused to respond and focused its communications on raising money for AIDS relief in Africa, and continued support for Via, its instant-coffee product.

Away from coffee, Domino's and Subway have been having a spat following another taste test. Domino's won 2 to 1 and used this in its ads when they responded to Subway's runaway success with the $5 footlong. Subway responded with a solicitor's letter, which Domino's featured in their next phase of advertising. This time the CEO burnt the letter and a press release about the 'food fight' encouraged consumers to visit Domino's website, click an icon of the letter, and watch it burn.

*Source:*   Bainbridge (2009); York (2009).

**Question:**   How reasonable is it for Starbucks to respond with legal action in the light of these individual advertising attacks on its reputation?

**Task:**   Find another food brand and examine the way its competitors treat the market leader.

## Emotions- and feelings-based appeals

Appeals based on logic and reasons are necessary in particular situations, especially where there is high involvement. However, as products become similar and as consumers become more aware of what is available in the category, so the need to differentiate becomes more important. Increasing numbers of advertisers are using messages that seek to appeal to the target's emotions and feelings, a 'soft sell'. Cars, toothpaste, toilet tissue and mineral water often use emotion-based messages to differentiate their products' position.

There are a number of appeals that can be used to elicit an emotional response from an individual receiver. Of the many techniques available, the main ones that can be observed to be used most are fear, humour, animation, sex, music and fantasy and surrealism.

### Fear

Fear is used in one of two ways. The first type demonstrates the negative aspects or physical dangers associated with a particular behaviour or improper product usage. Drink driving, life assurance and toothpaste advertising typify this form of appeal. For example, Scottish Widows, a financial services brand owned by Lloyds TSB has used a lady dressed in a black cape to symbolise the 'Widow'. The 'Widow' has become synonymous with the brand, even taking on iconic status, especially as research shows that four out of five people can link the image with the company.

The second approach is the threat of social rejection or disapproval if the brand is not used. This type of fear is used frequently in advertisements for such products as anti-dandruff shampoos and deodorants and is used to support consumers' needs for social acceptance and approval.

Fear appeals need to be constrained, if only to avoid being categorised as outrageous and socially unacceptable. There is a great deal of evidence that fear can facilitate attention and interest in a message and even motivate an individual to take a particular course of action: for example to stop smoking. Fear appeals are persuasive, according to Schiffman and Kanuk (1991), when low to moderate levels of fear are induced. Ray and Wilkie (1970), however, show that should the level of fear rise too much, inhibiting effects may prevent the desired action occurring. This inhibition is caused by the individual choosing to screen out, through perceptive selection, messages that conflict with current behaviour. The outcome may be that individuals deny the existence of a problem, claim there is no proof or say that it will not happen to them.

## Humour

If receivers are in a positive mood they are more likely to process advertising messages with little cognitive elaboration (Batra and Stayman, 1990). The use of humour as an emotional appeal is attractive because it can attract attention, stimulate interest and foster a positive mood. This can occur because there is less effort involved with peripheral rather than central cognitive processing, and this helps to mood protect. In other words, the positive mood state is more likely to be maintained if cognitive effort is avoided. Both Yellow Pages and 118 118 have used humour to help convey the essence of their brand and to help differentiate it from the competition.

Zhang and Zinkhan (2006) found that humour is more effective when there is low rather than high involvement. They also consider whether the media used also influences the impact of humour. For example, television and radio demand less effort to process messages compared with print work. The choice of media used to deliver humorous content can therefore be critical.

It is also argued that humour is effective because argument quality is likely to be high – that is, the level of counter-argument can be substantially reduced. Arguments against the use of humour concern distraction from the focus brand, so that while attention is drawn, the message itself is lost. With the move to global branding and standardisation of advertising messages, humour does not travel well. While the level and type of humour are difficult to gauge in the context of the processing abilities of a domestic target audience, cultural differences seriously impede the transfer of jokes around the world.

Visual humour such as that generated by Catherine Tate, *Little Britain, Miranda* and the older lavatorial humour that made Benny Hill so popular, is according to Archer (1994), more universally acceptable than word-based humour. This is partly because word-based humour can get lost in translation, without local references to provide the clues in order to decipher the joke. Humour, therefore, is a potentially powerful yet dangerous form of appeal. Haas (1997) reports that UK advertising executives have significantly higher confidence in the use of humour than their US counterparts, but concludes that 'humour is a vague concept and [. . .] its perception is influenced by many factors' (p. 15). These factors shape the context in which messages are perceived and the humour conveyed.

---

### Scholars' paper 26.3    Does humour work for global brands?

**Laroche, M., Vinhal Nepomuceno, M., Huang, L. and Richard, M.-O. (2011) What's So Funny? The Use of Humor in Magazine Advertising in the United States, China and France, *Journal of Advertising Research*, 51(2), 404–16.**

Humour is a common basis for advertising message appeals and this is an interesting paper not least because of the countries included in the study. Does humour work differently across different continents and cultures? The authors use a content analysis method to examine how widely humour is used and its use in advertising different types of product. They compare its use in luxury goods and personal consumer products, including automobiles. Humour was found to be used most widely in general in the US and most commonly used in automobile advertising in China. They identify similar levels of the use of humour in advertising luxuries in China and France.

---

## Shock

Advertising strategy may also be considered in terms of the overall response a target audience might give on receipt of particular messages. Some organisations choose a consistent theme for their campaigns, one that is often unrelated to their products or services. One such strategy is the use of shock advertising. Shock advertising, according to Venkat and Abi-Hanna (1995), 'is generally regarded as one that deliberately, rather than inadvertently, startles and offends its audience'.

Dahl et al. (2003) suggest that shock advertising by definition is unexpected and audiences are surprised by the messages because they do not conform to social norms or their expectations. They argue that audiences are offended because there is 'norm violation, encompassing transgressions of law or custom (e.g. indecent sexual references, obscenity), breaches of a moral or social code (e.g. profanity, vulgarity), or things that outrage the moral or physical senses', for example gratuitous violence and disgusting images (p. 268). The clothing company French Connection's use of the FCUK slogan and the various Benetton campaigns depicting a variety of incongruous situations (for example a priest and a nun kissing and a man dying of AIDS) are examples of norm violation. Shock advertising is not only used by commercial organisations such as Diesel, Egg and Sony Entertainment but is also used by not-for-profit organisations such as the government (anti-smoking), charities (child abuse), climate change (Greenpeace) and human rights campaigners (Amnesty International). See Viewpoint 26.3 for ways in which shock tactics have been used to stop smoking.

---

### Viewpoint 26.3    Shocking tactics to stop smokers

The NHS launched a series of public service advertisements as part of an anti-smoking campaign using television, press, internet and posters to show smokers having a fish hook pulled through their cheek. This was intended to illustrate how they were 'hooked' on cigarettes, a representation of a smoker's craving for cigarettes. The campaign attracted a huge number of complaints, with many claiming the pictures would have negative effects on children and that the ads were offensive, frightening and distressing. Despite this, the Department of Health claimed that the 'Get Unhooked' campaign was 'highly effective'.

The Non-Smokers' Rights Association (NSR) in France also used shock advertising tactics in an attempt to deter teenagers from taking up the habit. The approach they used was to depict young people smoking as if they were performing oral sex. The assertion was that letting children smoke is tantamount to child abuse.

Cigarette companies have been required to display graphic images on packaging to shock people into giving up smoking. In April 2010, the Australian government introduced a 25 per cent increase in cigarette tax and then announced that all cigarette packaging would be in plain cartons. The packs are only allowed to depict the brand name and must include a 'graphic photo depicting the gruesome consequences of smoking'. All branding materials, such as logos, slogans, design features, and use of color have been banned.

*Source*:   Varley (2010); Kamenev (2010); Lichfield (2010).

Question:   Do you believe that the use of advertising to shock people into a change of behaviour is morally wrong?

Task:        Find an ad that uses shock techniques. What are the elements in the ad that generate the shock impact?

---

The main reason for using a shock advertising strategy is that it is a good way to secure an audience's attention and achieve a longer-lasting impact than through traditional messages and attention-getting devices. The surprise element of these advertisements secures attention,

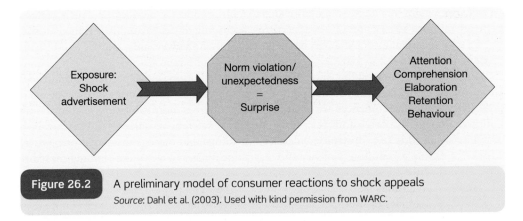

**Figure 26.2** A preliminary model of consumer reactions to shock appeals
*Source*: Dahl et al. (2003). Used with kind permission from WARC.

which is followed by an attempt to work out why an individual has been surprised. This usually takes the form of cognitive engagement and message elaboration in order that the message be understood. Through this process a shocking message can be retained and behaviour influenced. This process is depicted in Figure 26.2.

Shocking ads also benefit from word-of-mouth communication as these messages provoke advertisement-related conversations (Dichter, 1966). These can be distributed orally or digitally as virals. The credibility of word-of-mouth communication impacts on others who, if they have not been exposed to the original message, often seek out the message through curiosity. Associated with this pass-along impact is the generation of controversy, which can lead to additional publicity for an organisation and its advertisements. This 'free' publicity, although invariably negative, is considered to be desirable as it leads to increased brand awareness without further exposure and associated costs. This in turn can give the organisation further opportunities to provide more information about the advertising campaign and generate additional media comment.

The use of shock tactics has spread to viral marketing (a topic discussed in more detail in Chapter 23). Virals delivered through email communications have an advantage over paid-for advertising because consumers perceive advertising as an attempt to sell product, whereas virals are perceived as fun, can be opened and viewed (repeatedly) at consumer-determined times. Furthermore, virals are not subject to the same regulations that govern advertising, opening opportunities to convey controversial material. For example, a Volkswagon viral showed a suicide bomber exploding a device inside a car but the vehicle remained in one piece ('small but tough'). Another for Ford Ka showed a cat being decapitated by the sunroof. As Bewick (2006) suggests, joking about terrorism and pets is a sure-fire way of generating shock, and with that comes publicity.

---

**Scholars' paper 26.4** **Do humorous violent virals violate brands attitudes?**

**Brown, M.R., Bhadury, R.K. and Pope, N.K.L. (2010) The Impact of Comedic Violence on Viral Advertising Effectiveness, *Journal of Advertising*, 39(1), Spring, 49–65.**

Issues concerning violence in advertising have always raised questions about acceptability, morals and brand impact. Here the authors review violence when it has a comedic or an intended humorous slant. Their research indicates that humorous ads that combine higher levels of violence intensity with more severe consequences appear to elicit greater ad message involvement, improved retention of brand information, higher pass-along probabilities and greater ad likeability. Attitudes toward the brand remain unaffected. An interesting paper and well worth reading.

## Animation

Animation techniques have advanced considerably in recent years, with children as the prime target audience. However, animation has been successfully used in many adult-targeted advertisements, such as those by Schweppes, Compaq, Tetley Tea, Direct Line Insurance and British Gas. The main reason for using animation is that potentially boring and low-interest/involvement products can be made visually interesting and provide a means of gaining attention. A further reason for the use of animation is that it is easier to convey complex products in a way that does not patronise the viewer.

## Sex

Sexual innuendo and the use of sex as a means of promoting products and services are both common and controversial. Using sex as an appeal in messages is excellent for gaining the attention of buyers. Research shows, however, that it often achieves little else, particularly when the product is unrelated (Paek and Nelson 2007). Therefore, sex appeals normally work well for products such as perfume, clothing and jewellery but provide for poor effectiveness when the product is unrelated, such as cars, photocopiers and furniture. The degree to which sex-based advertising appeals work or are seen to be acceptable should also be considered a function of culture. For example, the use of sex appeals in Chinese society has increased in recent years as people have become more tolerant about the subject of sex. However, a study by Cui and Yang (2009) found that, despite this increasing openness, Chinese consumers remain 'cautious about embracing sex appeals in advertising' (p. 242).

The use of sex in advertising messages is mainly restricted to getting the attention of the audience and, in some circumstances, sustaining interest. It can be used openly, as in various lingerie, fragrance and perfume advertisements, such as WonderBra and Pretty Polly, and Gucci, raunchily as in King of Shaves and sensually as with Lexus, surprisingly. The Lynx Jet campaign set out at the beginning of this chapter demonstrates how sex and fantasy appeals were made to work together.

## Music

Music can provide continuity between a series of advertisements and can also be a good peripheral cue. A jingle, melody or tune, if repeated sufficiently, can become associated with the advertisement. Processing and attitudes towards the advertisement may be directly influenced by the music. Music has the potential to gain attention and assist product differentiation. Braithwaite and Ware (1997) found that music in advertising messages is used primarily either to create a mood or to send a branded message. In addition, music can also be used to signal a lifestyle and so communicate a brand identity through the style of music used.

Many advertisements for cars use music, partly because it is difficult to find a point of differentiation (*Independent*, 18 October 1996), and music is able to draw attention, generate mood and express brand personality (e.g. BMW, Nissan Micra, Peugeot, Renault).

Some luxury and executive cars are advertised using commanding background music to create an aura of power, prestige and affluence, which is combined with strong visual images in order that an association be made between the car and the environment in which it is positioned. There is a contextual juxtaposition between the car and the environment presented. Readers may notice a semblance of classical conditioning, where the music acts as an unconditioned stimulus. Foxall and Goldsmith (1994) suggest that the stimulus elicits the unconditioned emotional responses that may lead to the purchase of the advertised product.

## Fantasy and surrealism

The use of fantasy and surrealism in advertising has grown, partly as a result of the increased clutter and legal constraints imposed on some product classes. In fantasy appeals, associations with certain images and symbols allow the advertiser to focus attention on the product. The receiver can engage in the distraction offered and become involved with the execution of the advertisement. If this is a rewarding experience it may be possible to affect the receiver's attitudes peripherally. Readers may notice that this links to the earlier discussion on 'liking the advertisement'.

Finally, an interesting contribution to the discussion of message appeals has been made by Lannon (1992). She reports that consumers' expectations of advertisements can be interpreted on the one hand as either literal or stylish and on the other as serious or entertaining, according to the tone of voice. This approach vindicates the view that consumers are active problem-solvers and willing and able to decode increasingly complex messages. They can become involved with the execution of the advertisement and the product attributes. The degree of involvement (she argues implicitly) is a function of the motivation each individual has at any one moment when exposed to a particular message.

Advertisers can challenge individuals by presenting questions and visual stimuli that demand attention and cognitive response. Guinness challenged consumers to decode a series of advertisements that were unlike all previous Guinness advertisements and, indeed, all messages in the product class. The celebrity chosen was dressed completely in black, which contrasted with his blond hair, and he was shown in various time periods, past and future, and environments that receivers did not expect. He was intended to represent the personification of the drink and symbolised the individual nature of the product. Audiences were puzzled by the presentation and many rejected the challenge of interpretation. 'Surfer' and 'Bet on Black' are more recent Guinness campaigns that seek to convey the importance and necessity to wait (for the drink to be poured properly). To accomplish this, they portray a variety of situations in which patience results in achievement.

When individuals respond positively to a challenge, the advertiser can either provide closure (an answer) or, through surreal appeals, leave the receivers to answer the questions themselves in the context in which they perceive the message. One way of achieving this challenging position is to use an appeal that cognitively disorients the receiver (Parker and Churchill, 1986). If receivers are led to ask the question 'What is going on here?' their involvement in the message is likely to be very high. Benetton consistently raises questions through its advertising. By presenting a series of messages that are socially disorienting, and for many disconcerting, Benetton continually presents a challenge that moves away from involving individuals in an approach where salience and 'standing out' predominates. This high-risk strategy, with a risk of rejection, has prevailed for a number of years.

The surrealist approach does not provide or allow for closure. The conformist approach, by contrast, does require closure in order to avoid any possible counter-arguing and message rejection. Parker and Churchill argue that, when questions are left unanswered, receivers can become involved in both the product and the execution of the advertisement. Indeed, most advertisements contain a measure of rational and emotional elements. A blend of the two elements is necessary and the right mixture is dependent upon the perceived risk and motivation that the target audience has at any one particular moment.

The message appeal should be a balance of the informative and emotional dimensions. Furthermore, message quality is of paramount importance. Buzzell (1964) reported that, 'Advertising message quality is more important than the level of advertising expenditure' (p. 30). Adams and Henderson Blair (1992) confirm that the weight of advertising is relatively unimportant, and that the quality of the appeal is the dominant factor. However, the correct blend of informative and emotional elements in any appeal is paramount for persuasive effectiveness.

An alternative approach is to use the soft-sell, hard-sell demarcation, well established in the academic and practitioner worlds of advertising. A soft-sell appeal is designed to provoke an affective or feelings response from the receiver of the message, one in which human emotions are emphasised. These types of appeal tend to be subtle and indirect, and an image or atmosphere may be conveyed (Okazaki et al. (2010).

A hard-sell appeal is one in which the objective is to induce receivers to think in rational terms about the message. These appeals tend to be direct, emphasising a sales orientation, and often specify the brand name and product recommendations. Factual information, including numerous product (pack) shots, emphasises specific differentiating product features or some other dimension relevant to consumers. These two broad types of appeal are underpinned by three dimensions. These are feeling versus thinking, implicit versus explicit, and image versus fact.

Okazaki et al. (2010) believe that soft-sell appeals lead to more positive attitudes to the ad and to increased ad believability. This suggests that soft-sell appeals can strengthen purchase intentions. Hard-sell advertising appeals can also strengthen purchase intention. However, this is not accomplished directly through the creation of a favourable attitude, but through the formulation of convincing ad content.

# Copycat messaging

There are certain occasions where the appeal used by a follower brand can be judged to mimic that of the brand leader. The reasoning for adopting a copycat approach may be that the category has been revolutionised by the brand leader. For example, Magners revitalised the stagnant UK cider market by demonstrating its refreshment property through television and poster ads that showed the drink being poured over ice. Sales boomed to £17m in 2006 with the result that competitors are copycatting the approach. For example, Bulmers now claim their cider brand is 'born for ice' and a new brand, Maguires, has entered the market, also based on the over-ice proposition (Bowery, 2007).

A similar style of message can be used strategically to reduce the potency of the brand leader's marketing communications. Bowery refers to Matalan's use of four models that aped Marks & Spencer's iconic campaign based around Twiggy and three other models. Matalan did not reinforce their approach with a subsequent high-profile campaign, but M&S have continued the message strategy to great effect.

# Advertising tactics

The main creative elements of a message need to be brought together in order for an advertising plan to have substance. The processes used to develop message appeals need to be open but systematic.

The level of involvement and combination of the rational/emotional dimensions that receivers bring to their decision-making processes are the core concepts to be considered when creating an advertising message. Rossiter and Percy (1997) have devised a deductive framework that involves the disaggregation of the emotional (feel) dimension to a greater degree than that proposed by Vaughn (1980) (see Chapter 14 for details). They claim that there are two broad types of motive that drive attitudes towards purchase behaviour. These are informational and transformational motives and are now considered in turn.

## Informational motives

Individuals have a need for information to counter negative concerns about a purchase decision. These informational motives (see Table 26.1) are said to be negatively charged feelings. They can become positively charged, or the level of concern can be reduced considerably, by the acquisition of relevant information.

| Table 26.1 | Informational motives |
| --- | --- |
| **Motive** | **Possible emotional state** |
| Problem removal | Anger–relief |
| Problem avoidance | Fear–relaxation |
| Incomplete satisfaction | Disappointment–optimism |
| Mixed approach–avoidance | Guilt–peace of mind |
| Normal depletion | Mild annoyance–convenience |

## Transformational motives

Promises to enhance or to improve the user of a brand are referred to as transformational motives. These are related to the user's feelings and are capable of transforming a user's emotional state, hence they are positively charged. Three main transformational motives have been distinguished by Rossiter et al. (1991) (see Table 26.2). Various emotional states can be associated with each of these motives, and they should be used to portray an emotion that is appropriate to the needs of the target audience.

For example, Cancer Research UK changed the approach it used to communicate with donors. For a while, its campaigns used to convey messages about family loss and in that sense adopted a negative approach. The charity then adopted an 'All Clear' campaign. This conveyed messages about people diagnosed with cancer and their improved chances of recovery due to the benefits of the research. For many people this is low-involvement with transformational motives. This means that the use of an emotional-based claim in the message is important. The happy ending, based on people surviving, achieves this while the endline uses a voice-over that requests a donation so that the words 'all clear' can be heard by more people in the future.

One of the key communication objectives, identified earlier, is the need to create or improve levels of awareness regarding the product or organisation. This is achieved by determining whether awareness is required at the point of purchase or prior to purchase. Brand recognition (at the point of purchase) requires an emphasis upon visual stimuli, the package and the brand name, whereas brand recall (prior to purchase) requires an emphasis on a limited number of peripheral cues. These may be particular copy lines, the use of music or colours for continuity and attention-grabbing frequent use of the brand name in the context of the category need, or perhaps the use of strange or unexpected presentation formats.

| Table 26.2 | Transformational motives |
| --- | --- |
| **Motive** | **Possible emotional state** |
| Sensory gratification | Dull–elated |
| Intellectual stimulation | Bored–excited |
| Social approval | Apprehensive–flattered |

| Viewpoint 26.4 | Messaging functional foods |
| --- | --- |

A rapidly growing segment of the food industry aims to make it easier for consumers to improve health and reduce the risk of chronic disease by imbuing products with nutrients that promise benefits. Increasingly, food manufacturers are redeveloping foods so that they provide functional benefits. These products claim to improve a person's health, by lowering their cholesterol level, for example, or by improving their digestive systems, providing extra energy or even making people cleverer. Brands such as Tropicana juice drink contain extra calcium to build bone health and strength. Kingsmill make Head Start, a bread that contains Omega-3, designed to improve brain health. The success of Actimel yoghurt drinks is based on its probiotic content that provides immunity and eases the digestive tract. These and many other products are based on scientific developments and are proving to be popular.

One of the problems facing functional food manufacturers is how best to communicate the benefits. Providing too much scientific information makes audiences become confused and switch off. Providing too little information about the benefits can result in the message not getting through. When Kellogg's launched Rice Krispies Muddles, a prebiotic for children, the message failed to penetrate the market and the brand was altered to Rice Krispies Multigrain.

There is an argument that in the future, specialist functional foods need to be targeted at specific niche, lifestage segments, perhaps middle-agers with high cholesterol, and older women with brittle bones. These need to be coupled with simplified messages that convey particular health benefits.

*Sources*:   Based on Weeks (2010); Bashford (2007); Simms (2007).

**Question:**   Should functional foods provide transformational or informational messages?

**Task:**   Select a grocery product of your choice, visit the website and determine whether the overall message is informational or transformational. Justify your response.

Advertising tactics can be determined by the particular combination of involvement and motives that exist at a particular time within the target audience. If a high-involvement decision process is determined, with people using a central processing route, then the types of tactics shown in Figures 26.3 and 26.4 are recommended (Rossiter and Percy, 1997). If a low-involvement decision process is determined, with the target audience using a peripheral processing route, then the types of tactics shown in Figures 26.5 and 26.6 are recommended.

The Rossiter–Percy approach provides for a range of advertising tactics that are oriented to the conditions that are determined by the interplay of the level of involvement and the type of dominant motivation. These conditions may only exist within a member of the target audience for a certain period. Consequently, they may change and the advertising tactics may also have to change to meet the new conditions. There are two main points that emerge from the work of Rossiter and Percy. The first is that all messages should be designed to carry both rational, logical information and emotional stimuli, but in varying degrees and forms. Second, low-involvement conditions require the use of just one or two benefits in a message, whereas high-involvement conditions can sustain a number of different benefit claims. This is because persuasion through the central processing route is characterised by an evaluation of the alternatives within any one product category.

**Option 1:** An emotional claim

Correct emotional portrayal very important when brand is introduced

Getting the target to like the advertisement is not important

**Option 2:** A rational claim

If the target's initial attitude to the brand is favourable, then make benefit claims clear

If they are against the brand, use a refutational approach

If there is a clear brand leader, use a comparative approach

| Figure 26.3 | Message tactics where there is high involvement and informational motives |
| --- | --- |

*Source*: After Rossiter and Percy (1997). Used with kind permission.

**Option 1:** An emotional claim

Use emotion in the context of the prevailing lifestyle groups

Identification with the product is as important as liking the advertisement

**Option 2:** A rational claim

Include information as well

Overstate the benefits but do not understate them

Use repetition for reinforcement

| Figure 26.4 | Message tactics where there is high involvement and transformational motives |
| --- | --- |

*Source*: After Rossiter and Percy (1997). Used with kind permission.

**Option 1:** An emotional claim

Use a demonstration format to present the product

Liking the advertisement is not necessary

**Option 2:** A rational claim

Use the limited number of benefits

The benefits should be stated so that they can be learned easily and quickly

| Figure 26.5 | Message tactics where there is low involvement and informational motives |
|---|---|

*Source*: After Rossiter and Percy (1997). Used with kind permission.

**Option 1:** An emotional claim

Emotional authenticity is vital

The execution/display of the emotion should be unique

'Likeability' is very important

**Option 2:** A rational claim

Brand recognition is by association

Repetition is used for reinforcement

| Figure 26.6 | Message tactics where there is low involvement and transformational motives |
|---|---|

*Source*: After Rossiter and Percy (1997). Used with kind permission.

# Key points

- Source credibility consists of three key elements: the level of perceived expertise; the personal motives the source is believed to possess, and the degree of trust that can be placed in what the source says or does on behalf of the endorsement.

- Consumers trade off the validity of claims made by brands against the perceived trustworthiness (and expertise) of the individuals or organisations who deliver the message.

- The use of spokespersons can draw attention and publicity to a brand, but should they fail to provide credibility or contravene a society's norms then the brand may be harmed. There are four main types of spokesperson: the expert, the celebrity, the chief executive officer and the consumer.

- An important part of any message strategy is a consideration of the best way of communicating the key points or core message. This needs to be accomplished by structuring messages carefully to avoid encouraging objections and opposing points of view.

- Messages should reflect a balance between the need for information and the need for pleasure or enjoyment in consuming the message and should either draw a firm conclusion for the audience or allow people to draw their own conclusions from the content.

- The argument for the brand or issue can be presented for and against an issue – a two-sided message. Alternatively just the case in favour of an issue can be presented – a one-sided message. Credibility is improved by understanding the audience's position and then fashioning the presentation of the message.

- Messages that present the strongest points at the beginning use what is referred to as the *primacy* effect. A decision to place the strongest points at the end of the message assumes that the *recency* effect will bring about greater levels of persuasion. This is appropriate when the receiver agrees with the position adopted by the source or has a high positive level of involvement.

- The main choice of presentation style concerns the degree of factual information transmitted in a message against the level of imagery thought necessary to make sufficient impact for the message to command attention and then be processed.

- Increasing numbers of advertisers are using messages that seek to appeal to a target audience's emotions and feelings. This is necessary when products become similar and as consumers become more aware of what is available in the category. Of the many techniques available, the main ones used are fear, humour, animation, sex, music and fantasy and surrealism.

- Information or rational appeals can be presented through four main types of appeal. These are factual, slice-of-life, demonstration and comparative appeals.

- Emotional appeals seek to elicit an emotional response from an individual receiver. Of the many techniques available, the main ones that can be observed to be used most are fear, humour, animation, sex, music and fantasy and surrealism.

- It is claimed that there are two broad types of motive that drive attitudes towards purchase behaviour. These are informational and transformational motives. Individuals have a need for information to counter negative concerns about a purchase decision. These informational motives are said to be negatively charged feelings. They can become positively charged, or the level of concern can be reduced considerably, by the acquisition of relevant information.

- Promises to enhance or to improve a brand are referred to as transformational motives. These are related to the user's feelings and are capable of transforming a user's emotional state, hence they are positively charged.

# Review questions

1. Explain the concept of source credibility using the Lynx Jet minicase to illustrate your response.

2. Why do advertisers use spokespersons in their advertising? Find examples of each type of spokesperson.

3. Discuss what is meant by the term 'balance' when applied to an advertising message.

4. How might an understanding of conclusion drawing assist the development of an advertising message?

5. Select five print advertisements and comment on the nature and extent to which the order of presentation features in each of them.

6. Under what conditions would an informational appeal best be used?

7. Find examples of advertising messages that are predominantly information-based appeals.

8. Make notes concerning the issues that can arise from using a shock- or fear-based message appeal.

9. Why do you believe emotional appeals are more effective than information-based appeals?

10. Explain the difference between informational and transformational motivations.

# References

Abbot, L. (2009) 10 Guerrilla & Ambient Marketing Examples, retrieved 7 August 2010 from www.mrlukeabbot.com.

Adams, A.J. and Henderson Blair, M. (1992) Persuasive advertising and sales accountability, *Journal of Advertising Research*, 32(2) (March/April), 20–5.

AdForum (2006) LynxJet – 'LynxJet' – Universal McCann (Sydney), retrieved 25 May 2012 from http://uk.adforum.com/creative-work/ad/player/6686120/sxi:960940/__tstck__.

Anon (2011) Lowe Hunt for Lynx Body Spray: The Lynx Jet Project, retrieved 25 May 2012 from http://thisisnotadvertising.wordpress.com/tag/lynx-jet/.

Archer, B. (1994) Does humour cross borders? *Campaign*, 17 June, 32–3.

Arora, R. (1985) Consumer involvement: what it offers to advertising strategy, *International Journal of Advertising*, 4, 119–30.

Bainbridge, J. (2009) Sector Insight: Coffee shops, Marketing, 15 April, retrieved 28 May 2012 from http://www.brandrepublic.com/analysis/898657/Sector-Insight-Coffee-shops/?DCMP=ILC-SEARCH.

Bashford, S. (2007) Functional foods: Now with added . . . *Marketing*, 29 August, 26–9.

Batra, R. and Stayman, D.M. (1990) The role of mood in advertising effectiveness. *Journal of Consumer Research*, 17 (September), 203–14.

Bewick, M. (2006) Pushing the boundaries. *The Marketer*, September, 25.

Bowery, J. (2007) Haven't I seen you before? *Marketing*, 6 June, p. 17.

Braithwaite, A. and Ware, R. (1997) The role of music in advertising, *Admap*, (July/August), 44–7.

Brown, M.R., Bhadury, R.K. and Pope, N.K.L. (2010) The Impact of Comedic Violence on Viral Advertising Effectiveness, *Journal of Advertising*, 39(1), Spring, 49–65.

Buzzell, R. (1964) Predicting short-term changes in market share as a function of advertising strategy, *Journal of Marketing Research*, 1(3), 27–31.

Cui, G. and Yang, X. (2009) Responses of Chinese consumers to sex appeals in international advertising: a test of congruency theory, *Journal of Global Marketing*, 22, 229–45.

Dahl, D.W., Frankenberger, K.D. and Manchanda, R.V. (2003) Does it pay to shock? Reactions to shocking and nonshocking advertising content among university students, *Journal of Advertising Research*, 43, 3 (September), 268–81.

Dichter, E. (1966) How word-of-mouth advertising works, *Harvard Business Review*, 44 (November/December), 147–66.

Duncan (2005) Lynx Jet Airline Fantasy for Young Men, 17 November 2005, retrieved 25 May 2012 from http://theinspirationroom.com/daily/2005/lynx-jet-fantasy/.

Eleftheriou-Smith, L.-M. (2011) Targeting the High-Flyers, *Marketing*, 23 November, 22–3.

Eleftheriou-Smith, L.-M. (2012) Ryanair's O'Leary: I'm our marketing director, *Marketing*, 7 March, p. 6.

Faison, E.W. (1961) Effectiveness of one-sided and two-sided mass communications in advertising, *Public Opinion Quarterly*, 25 (Autumn), 468–9.

Foxall, G.R. and Goldsmith, R.E. (1994) *Consumer Psychology for Marketing*, London: Routledge.

Haas, O. (1997) Humour in advertising, *Admap*, (July/August), 14–15.

Halonen-Knight, E. and Hurmerinta, L. (2010) Who endorses whom? Meanings transfer in celebrity endorsement, *Journal of Product & Brand Management*, 19(6), 452–60.

Hannah, D.B. and Sternthal, B. (1984) Detecting and explaining the sleeper effect, *Journal of Consumer Research*, 11 September, 632–42.

Hovland, C.I. and Mandell, W. (1952) An experimental comparison of conclusion drawing by the communicator and by the audience, *Journal of Abnormal and Social Psychology*, 47 (July), 581–8.

Hovland, C.I., Lumsdaine, A. and Sheffield, F.D. (1949) *Experiments on Mass Communication*, New York: Wiley.

Kamenev, M. (2010) Australian smokers get a rude shock, *GlobalPost*, May 10, 2010, retrieved 10 August 2010 from www.globalpost.com/dispatch/asia/100508/smoking-australia-law-packaging-tobacco-tax.

Kardes, F.R. (1988) Spontaneous inference processes in advertising: the effects of conclusion omission and involvement on persuasion, *Journal of Consumer Research*, 15 (September), 225–33.

Kelman, H. (1961) Processes of opinion change, *Public Opinion Quarterly*, 25 (Spring), 57–78.

Lafferty, B.A., Goldsmith, R.E. and Newell, S.J. (2002) The dual credibility model: the influence of corporate and endorser credibility on attitudes and purchase intentions, *Journal of Marketing Theory and Practice*, 10(3), 1–12.

Lannon, J. (1992) Asking the right questions – what do people do with advertising? *Admap*, (March), 11–16.

Laroche, M., Vinhal Nepomuceno, M., Huang, L. and Richard, M.-O. (2011) What's So Funny? The Use of Humor in Magazine Advertising in the United States, China and France, *Journal of Advertising Research*, 51/2, 404–16.

Lichfield, J. (2010) French in uproar over oral sex anti-smoking posters, the *Independent*, 24 February 2010, retrieved 10 August 2010 from www.independent.co.uk/news/world/europe/french-in-uproar-over-oral-sex-antismoking-posters-1908559.html.

Loveless, H. (2007) Our Carol Vorderman loan nightmare, *Mail on Sunday*, 28 October, retrieved 26 March 2008 from www.thisismoney.co.uk/campaigns/loansinsu/article.

Okazaki, S., Mueller, B. and Taylor, C.R. (2010) Measuring soft-sell versus hard-sell advertising appeals, *Journal of Advertising*, 39(2), Summer, 5–20.

Paek, H.-J. and Nelson, M.R. (2007) A cross-cultural and cross media comparison of female nudity in advertising, *Journal of Promotion Management*, 13, 1/2, 145–67.

Parker, R. and Churchill, L. (1986) Positioning by opening the consumer's mind, *International Journal of Advertising*, 5, 1–13.

Ray, M.L. and Wilkie, W.L. (1970) Fear: the potential of an appeal neglected by marketing, *Journal of Marketing*, 34 (January), 54–62.

Rossiter, J.R. and Percy, L. (1997) *Advertising and Promotion Management*, 2nd edn, New York: McGraw-Hill.

Rossiter, J.R., Percy, L. and Donovan, R.J. (1991) A better advertising planning grid, *Journal of Advertising Research*, (October/November), 11–21.

Schiffman, L.G. and Kanuk, L. (1991) *Consumer Behavior*, 4th edn, Englewood Cliffs, NJ: Prentice-Hall.

Simms, J. (2007) Biggest brands, *Marketing*, 22 August 2007, retrieved 6 November 2007 from www.brandrepublic.com/InDepth/Features/734340/Functional-foods-added/.

Varley, M. (2010) When to use the 'shock' factor and why it works, *Utalk*, 2 March 2010, retrieved 10 August 2010 from www.utalkmarketing.com/pages/Article.aspx?ArticleID=16945.

Vaughn, R. (1980) How advertising works: a planning model, *Journal of Advertising Research*, 20(5), 27–33.

Venkat, R. and Abi-Hanna, N. (1995) *Effectiveness of Visually Shocking Advertisements: Is it Context Dependent?* Administrative Science Association of Canada Proceedings, 16, 3, 139–46.

Weeks, C. (2010) Battle over functional foods heats up, *Globe and Mail*, 11 October, retrieved 7 May 2012 from http://www.theglobeandmail.com/life/health/health-benefits-or-hype-battle-over-functional-foods-heats-up/article1752149/.

Wentz, L. (2006) Unilever's 'Lynx Jet' Wins Media Grand Prix, *Advertising Age*, 20 June, retrieved 25 May 2012 from http://adage.com/article/cannes06/unilever-s-lynx-jet-wins-media-grand-prix/110038/.

York, E.B. (2009) Nasty comparative campaigns, *Advertising Age*, 80(42), retrieved 28 May from http://web.ebscohost.com/ehost/detail?vid=18&hid=21&sid=d58cb5d7-c7b8-4385-aa9a-9760aee490ad%40sessionmgr14&bdata=JnNpdGU9ZWhvc3QtbGl2ZQ%3d%3d#db=bch&AN=47270410.

Zhang, Y. and Zinkhan, G.M. (2006) Responses to humorous ads: does audience involvement matter? *Journal of Advertising*, 35(4), Winter, 113–27.

# Author index

# Subject index

LIBRARY, UNIVERSITY OF CHESTER